SCHOLARLY MISCONDUCT

Law, Regulation, and Practice

Also by Ian Freckelton

The Law Reform Digest (et al.) vols 1 and 2 (1983, 1987)

The Trial of the Expert (1987)

Police in Our Society (with Hugh Selby) (1988)

Expert Evidence (7 vols, with Hugh Selby) (1993–current)

Controversies in Health Law (with Kerry Petersen) (1999)

Indictable Offences in Victoria (4th edn, 1999; 5th edn, 2010 with Danielle Andrewartha; 6th edn, with Kerryn Cockcroft, 2016)

Expert Evidence: Law, Practice, Procedure and Policy (with Hugh Selby) (1999, 2003, 2006, 2010, 2013, 2016)

Expert Evidence in Criminal Law (with Hugh Selby) (1999)

Expert Evidence in Family Law (1999)

Australian Judicial Attitudes toward Expert Evidence (with Prasuna Reddy and Hugh Selby) (1999)

Victorian Criminal Law, Investigation & Procedure (6 vols) (2000–current)

Australian Magistrates' Attitudes Toward Expert Evidence (with Prasuna Reddy and Hugh Selby) (2001)

Criminal Injuries Compensation: Law, Practice and Policy (2001)

Causation in Law and Medicine (with Danuta Mendelson) (2002)

Involuntary Detention and Therapeutic Jurisprudence: International Perspectives on Civil Commitment (with Kate Diesfeld) (2003)

Disputes and Dilemmas in Health Law (with Kerry Petersen) (2006)

Death Investigation and the Coroner's Inquest (with David Ranson) (2006, 2016)

Regulation of Health Practitioners (2006)

The COAT Practice Manual for Tribunals (with Pamela O'Connor and Peter Sallmann) (2006)

Appealing to the Future (with Hugh Selby) (2010)

Coercive Care: Rights, Law and Policy (with Bernadette McSherry) (2013)

Expert Evidence and Criminal Jury Trials (with Jane Goodman-Delahunty, Jacqueline Horan, and Blake McKimmie) (2016)

SCHOLARLY MISCONDUCT

Law, Regulation, and Practice

Ian Freckelton QC

OXFORD
UNIVERSITY PRESS

OXFORD
UNIVERSITY PRESS

Great Clarendon Street, Oxford, OX2 6DP,
United Kingdom

Oxford University Press is a department of the University of Oxford.
It furthers the University's objective of excellence in research, scholarship,
and education by publishing worldwide. Oxford is a registered trade mark of
Oxford University Press in the UK and in certain other countries

First Edition published in 2016
Impression: 2

Published in the United States of America by Oxford University Press
198 Madison Avenue, New York, NY 10016, United States of America

British Library Cataloguing in Publication Data
Data available

Library of Congress Control Number: 2015950681

ISBN 978–0–19–875540–1

Printed in Great Britain by
CPI Group (UK) Ltd, Croydon, CR0 4YY

For Julia

In Memory of Chris Holt

PREFACE

'Scholarly misconduct' presents as a relatively innocuous concept. Slightly problematic, perhaps, tending to the malign, but possibly a matter best left to the insular world of the academe.

However, as is revealed in comprehensive and forensic detail in this monumental book, this term hides a multitude of sins and involves sex, drugs, murder, corruption, fraud, nepotism, hoaxes, denigration, defamation and a host of other crimes and misdemeanours. It is a problem that is of long standing, widespread, pernicious, and dangerous. In some cases it has resulted in injury and deaths, the execution of innocent people, and the destruction of individual and institutional reputations.

In this path-breaking work, Ian Freckelton QC, one of Australia's most prolific and original scholars, editors, teachers, and advocates, documents the various forms of scholarly misconduct, their incidence in Australia and elsewhere, their consequences and the responses to them. The forms of misconduct are many: plagiarism (of which some twenty or so varieties are identified), conflicts of interest, forensic misconduct, sexual misconduct, and the activities that hide under the deceptively bland rubric of 'intemperate denigration and disputation'. It is an activity that is undertaken by undergraduate and graduate students, scientists, medical practitioners, researchers, politicians, and judicial officers.

There could be few scholars more suited for this task. With conscious or unconscious irony, Freckelton implicitly describes himself in the words of Ralph Waldo Emerson: a person who 'studies in his sleep, in his waking, in his meals, in his pleasures'. He is a perfect match of theory and practice, of scholar and practitioner, of originator and commentator. No task or combination of tasks appears to be too large or too hard and this book is another product of his prodigious energy and talents.

There is no lack of examples of scholarly misconduct in all its forms. Reaching back into history, Freckelton identifies Ptolemy of Alexandria, Newton, Pasteur, Burt, and others as possibly being guilty of this offence.

The book is replete with numerous case studies, from many disciplines and countries. They are described and discussed in considerable detail. Many have been subject of articles, books, documentaries, films, inquiries, and litigation, both criminal and civil. Their consequences range from the minor to the tragic. One case of forensic misconduct in Massachusetts may have affected 40,000 cases in which the scientist's evidence was relied upon. In other cases of scientific fraud, reliance on falsified results affected the treatment of thousands of patients. A number of examples are given from the United States where forensic misconduct resulted in the execution of accused persons who were subsequently exonerated. Many innocent accuseds have languished for decades on the basis of false scientific evidence. Increasingly, innocence projects are uncovering instances of long-term and systemic fabrications.

Merely to classify and catalogue the numerous instances of misconduct would be interesting enough in itself, but it would not be sufficient from a scholarly point of view. This book does far more. It aims to examine and understand the range of conduct, the types of people who engage in them, their motivations, the means by which they are detected and the institutional responses to them.

Importantly, it moves beyond seeking explanations in individual motivations or pathologies particularly as most forms of scholarly misconduct take place in institutional contexts. There is always a temptation when analysing such conduct to explain them as isolated instances, the perpetrator as a 'rotten apple' in an otherwise healthy organization. Characterizing offenders as having personality disorders, or as being greedy, selfish, weak, overly-ambitious, narcissistic, or acting out of character is often the quickest and most pragmatic response.

The reality is often otherwise and as Freckelton amply demonstrates, it is in the systemic forces that produce misconduct, such as commercialization, managerialism, and reward structures that the key to understanding the causes can be found. More relevantly, it is also in the institutional responses to such misconduct that the remedies lie. Too often institutions are reluctant to investigate or disclose misconduct because of the possible harm to their reputation and income. Often this reluctance is due to a misplaced trust in previously trusted individuals whose credentials and past conduct appeared impeccable.

Our understanding of scholarly misconduct has an analogue in the evolving understanding of institutional child sexual abuse: a protracted and contested process of identifying that the phenomenon exists at all; the documentation of its prevalence and consequences; the inclination to identify and blame individuals only and finally a recognition of the fact that the long term response is to ensure that the institutions in which the offenders worked take responsibility both for contributing to the offending behaviour and establishing mechanisms for preventing its reoccurrence.

Although this is a book about scholarly misconduct and the law, and as one would expect, it thoroughly canvasses the criminal, civil, and administrative responses to the various forms of misconduct, Freckelton recognizes that legal responses are a partial and inadequate response to what are often ethical and professional issues. To borrow from the criminological literature, a range of 'protective factors' are needed, none of them being perfect but all of which may contribute to reducing misconduct, detecting and responding to it. These include peer review, close supervision, research and ethical protocols and the like. Where the legal responses are too often highly adversarial, formal, expensive and protracted, responses that involve cultural change are more cooperative, collegial and likely to be more effective in the long term. There is, as this book argues, no simple solution but in the final chapter a well-considered range of suggestions to restore scholarly integrity is presented to deal with each of the various forms of misconduct.

As has been the case so often in the past, Ian Freckelton has done the scholarly and wider community a great service. This book adds to his impressive list of publications and to the growing literature on an old but increasingly significant problem. If there were an exemplar of good scholarly conduct, this is it. I am sure that both the author and publisher hope and expect that it will be widely, fairly, meticulously, and scrupulously cited in many publications in the future.

Arie Freiberg
Emeritus Professor
Monash University

ACKNOWLEDGEMENTS

Scholarly misconduct has two aspects to it: there are those who do not engage in it and who are persons of inspiring integrity and commitment to scholarly values, and there are the few who do engage in it and whose behaviour detracts from the regard in which scholars are held. I refer to the first category first because I believe them to be representative of the general body of scholars, in academia and elsewhere.

A book such as this risks tarring scholars with the bad brush of the misbehaviour, incompetence, and indifference to important values of a small number of persons whose behaviour is anathema and embarrassing to most of their colleagues.

However, it is my strong belief that telling the story and learning the lessons that are available to be learned, however confronting and uncomfortable the process, is an exercise worth undertaking.

Many whom I hold in the highest regard have contributed to a book which has had a lengthy and complex gestation. Its conception was with Professor Danuta Mendelson of Deakin University (who no longer remembers it) when she alerted me to the research fraud and criminal proceedings brought against Dr Scott Reuben in the United States (see Chapter 3). This occurred around the same time as Bruce Hall succeeded in his defamation action against Dr Norman Swan and the ABC in Australia after their coverage of allegations of research fraud against him (see Chapter 3).

At a similar time the practising certificate of William Keough,[1] a Melbourne solicitor, was cancelled by the Victorian Civil and Administrative Tribunal for his plagiarism in a postgraduate course at Melbourne University and in the *Journal of Law and Medicine*, leading in due course to an editorial on the subject in the same journal[2] (see Chapter 6).

Later the Philippines Supreme Court expressed itself completely ideologically divided about whether one of its number had engaged in problematic plagiarism in one of his judgments[3] (see Chapter 6). The dissenting judgment in the case by Justice Lourdes Sereno is an inspiring articulation of principle in a fraught judicial situation. Shortly afterwards she was appointed the 24th Chief Justice of the Supreme Court of The Philippines in an important affirmation of her stance on integrity.

Then Massachusetts drug tester, Annie Dookhan, was sentenced to jail for her faking of forensic test results (see Chapter 5). Also in the United States, none other than Harvard Medical School, and various high-profile researchers, were sued under the *False Claims Act* for research fraud.

I was assisted in the obtaining of some perspective by the landmark work over a significant period of time by Brian Martin at the University of Wollongong. In addition I was prompted to reflect upon attitudes over time to 'secondary usage', including particularly in classical literature on the subject when asked to speak at the Hellenic Museum in Melbourne about such

---

[1] See *Legal Services Commissioner v Keough* [2010] VCAT 108.

[2] Freckelton I, 'Plagiarism in Law and Medicine: Challenges for Scholarship, Academia, Publishers and Regulators' (2010) 17 *Journal of Law and Medicine* 645.

[3] *In the Matter of the Charges of Plagiarism, Etc., Against Associate Justice Mariano C. Del Castillo (Resolution)* 8 February 2011, AM No. 10-7-17—SC, *(Republic of the Philippines Supreme Court)*: <http://sc.judiciary.gov.ph/jurisprudence/2011/february2011/10-7-17-SC.htm#_ftn8> (unpaginated) [accessed 18 Dec 2015].

matters to the Greek–Australian Medico-Legal Association, and was assisted in that regard by the excellent book, *Plagiarism in Latin Literature* by Scott MacGill.[4] In the course of that I stumbled across the notion of 'plagiarism studies',[5] and the phenomenology of retractions sponsored by Retraction Watch[6] and websites dedicated to exposure of plagiarism such as the VroniPlag Wiki in Germany[7] and Dissernet in Russia.[8]

Attendance at the International Academy of Law and Mental Health Congress in Berlin, drew to my attention the potential for plagiarism to become a political issue with multiple German politicians by 2013 having been accused, and then found guilty, of plagiarism infractions in their theses (see Chapter 6). A little later an aspect of the scandal involving the federal politician Craig Thomson, in Australia, served to emphasize this phenomenon and remove it from a German context. And then the 'plagiarism disease' broke out in Hungary and brought down that country's President, raising consciousness globally of the potential repercussions of this form of intellectual dishonesty (see Chapter 6). It was not long before similar difficulties embroiled the Romanian Education Minister also costing him his role in public life, followed by bitterly contested accusations against the Romanian Prime Minister, Victor Ponta, who also ultimately handed in his doctorate because of impropriety in his research (see Chapter 6). In the meanwhile the Iranian Minister for Science and Transport survived plagiarism allegations. So too did the Russian President, Vladimír Putin (like Vice-President Joe Biden had in the United States in relation to his undergraduate legal work), experience claims that his thesis had been significantly plagiarized from the work of two United States academics two decades before his 1997 submission (see Chapter 6).

By 2014 though the fraudulent work of Dr Dong-Pyou Han in his HIV vaccine research had prompted criminal charges which were resolved by the imposition of a significant jail term in 2015, raising the role of the criminal law as a regulatory mechanism for such matters (see Chapter 3). Throughout 2014 Japan was transfixed by the bizarre saga of Dr Haruko Obokata's fraudulent research—a celebrity scholar was being brought crashing down with ripple effects tragically affecting all around her. My presentation on the subject at the Ninth International Symposium on Advances in Forensic Medicine in Fukuoka, Japan, yielded thought-provoking, albeit mixed responses. Later at Nusa Dua in Bali, Toronto in Canada, and Costa Navarino in Greece, I received further feedback from persons attending presentations I gave on related subjects at the 2014 meetings of the World Association of Medical Law, the International Association of Forensic Mental Health Services, and the Greek–Australian Medico-Legal Association, the 2014 Congress of the Australian and New Zealand Association of Psychiatry, Psychology and Law (ANZAPPL). And then in 2015 important discussions took place at the International Academy of Law and Mental Health Congress in its Vienna session on the ethics that should attach to the editing and publication of scholarly journals. Later in the same year I presented an account at the joint conference in Canberra of the Royal Australian and New Zealand College of Psychiatry Faculty of Forensic Psychiatry and ANZAPPL about self-revelations by those responsible for large-scale research fraud and plagiarism. Feedback from all of these presentations assisted in the evolution of the book.

---

[4] MacGill S, *Plagiarism in Latin Literature* (Cambridge: Cambridge University Press, 2012).

[5] See Terry R, 'Plagiarism and Plagiarism Studies': <http://www.english.heacademy.ac.uk/explore/publications/newsletters/newsissue13/terry.htm>, viewed 25 May 2014.

[6] Retraction Watch, 'Tracking Retractions as a Window into the Scientific Process': <http://retractionwatch.com>, viewed 25 May 2014.

[7] VroniPlag Wiki, 'Kollaborative Plagiatsdokumentation': <http://de.vroniplag.wikia.com/wiki/Home> [accessed 18 Dec 2015].

[8] See Serghei Golunov, *The Elephant in the Room: Corruption and Cheating in Russian Universities* (New York: Columbia University Press, 2014).

However, improprieties in scholarship have many other manifestations—from sexual harassment and exploitation to fraudulent use of the research of others and even the manipulation of research and the faking of data. The world of academia has spawned its fair share of homicides and attempted murders, and no shortage of intoxication-fuelled forms of unpleasant behaviour. Not all, however, are related to the scholarly endeavour—some are just the stuff of human unhappiness and desire for changed circumstances. In New Zealand, for instance, the nation was gripped by the trials of Vicky Calder for the attempted murder by what was asserted to be acrylamide poisoning of the eminent plant scientist, Professor David Lloyd in the early 1990s.[9] A decade later, in 2001, Professor Colin Bouwer, head of the Department of Psychiatry at the University of Otago in Dunedin, was found guilty of murdering his wife by insulin injections.[10] However, each of these cases took place in the private domain, rather than as part of scholarly interaction.

At Harvard in 2012 a cheating scandal profoundly embarrassed the university and resulted in procedural reforms.[11] Then, months later, a remarkable instance of cheating enveloped 162 students at the University of Tasmania Law School, some of whom were found to have shared information improperly while sitting an online assessment for the subject 'Civil and Criminal Law Procedure'.[12] The Vice-President of the Law Society of Tasmania, Anthony Mihal, said academic misconduct was viewed seriously by the Supreme Court before law students could be admitted to the bar to practise law. He said academic misconduct did not mean automatic exclusion, but would be considered by the court when deciding whether a person was a 'fit and proper person' to be practising, and it was important that students disclosed such conduct.[13]

It became apparent to me that dishonesty in multiple forms afflicts institutions of higher learning and research, incorporating misdemeanours by staff as well as students, thereby potentially eroding institutions' reputations for integrity. Of course, there are occasions when the loose ethics of staff members are a poor example indeed for students.

The allegedly opportunistic theft of research funds by Poul Thorsen of Denmark underlined the issue.[14] This means that processes for resolving suspicions and accusations must be such as to command all stakeholders' respect and confidence.

---

[9] 'Scientist in Poison Scandal Dies' (31 May 2006) *New Zealand Herald*: <http://www.nzherald.co.nz/nz/news/article.cfm?c_id=1&objectid=10384337> [accessed 18 Dec 2015].

[10] See Marks V, and Richmond C, 'Colin Bouwer: Professor of Psychiatry and Murder' (2008) 101(8) *Journal of the Royal Society of Medicine* 400; Marks V, and Richmond C, *Insulin Murders* (RSM Press, 2007).

[11] Perez-Pena R, 'Students Accused of Cheating Return Awkwardly to a Changed Harvard' (16 September 2013) *New York Times*: <http://www.nytimes.com/2013/09/17/education/students-accused-of-cheating-return-awkwardly-to-a-changed-harvard.html?_r=0> [accessed 18 Dec 2015].

[12] See Mather A, 'Law Students to Re-sit Exam Amid Fears Online Assessment was Compromised' (31 August 2013) *The Mercury*: <http://www.themercury.com.au/news/law-students-to-re-sit-exam-amid-fears-online-assessment-was-compromised/story-fnj4f7kx-1226707906897> [accessed 18 Dec 2015]; Whealing J, 'Law Students to Sit Exam Again after Cheating Scandal' (16 September 2013) *Lawyers Weekly*: <http://www.lawyersweekly.com.au/folklaw/law-students-to-sit-exam-again-after-cheating-scan> [accessed 18 Dec 2015].

[13] See Mather A, 'Law Students to Re-sit Exam Amid Fears Online Assessment was Compromised' (31 August 2013) *The Mercury*: <http://www.themercury.com.au/news/law-students-to-re-sit-exam-amid-fears-online-assessment-was-compromised/story-fnj4f7kx-1226707906897>, viewed 27 September 2013; Whealing J, 'Law Students to Sit Exam Again after Cheating Scandal' (16 September 2013) *Lawyers Weekly*: <http://www.lawyersweekly.com.au/folklaw/law-students-to-sit-exam-again-after-cheating-scan>, viewed 25 September 2013.

[14] See Robert F Kennedy Jr, 'Central Figure in CDC Vaccine Cover-Up Absconds with $2M' (5 November 2010) *Huffington Post*: <http://www.huffingtonpost.com/robert-f-kennedy-jr/central-figure-in-cdc-vac_b_494303.html> [accessed 18 Dec 2015].

During my career as a barrister I have appeared as counsel for students and staff at universities who have been accused of significant misconduct, been briefed on behalf of universities, been appointed to disciplinary panels and have prosecuted (including the former chiropractor, Malcolm Hooper, to whom reference is made in Chapter 2, and the fake psychologist, Dusan Milosevic, to whom reference is made in Chapter 4) and defended large numbers of health practitioners, lawyers, teachers, architects, and other professionals whose integrity, including their usage of scholarly material, has been impugned. In time past I sat on the Psychologists Registration Board, the Medical Practitioners Board, and the Disciplinary Appeals Board, all in Victoria, arriving at decisions in respect of professional propriety. Reference is made to decisions in which I participated in Chapter 4, in relation to Peter Noble and Timothy Watson-Munro.

During the writing of this book, I was briefed during 2014 for Robert Barnes in the Eastman judicial inquiry before Acting Justice Martin in the Australian Capital Territory which, amongst other things, scrutinized the scientific evidence given at trial and inquest by Mr Barnes in relation to gunshot residue analysis in the high profile trial of a man charged, and ultimately convicted, of murdering an Assistant Commissioner of the Australian Federal Police. These experiences too contributed to recommendations advanced within this modest book.

The journey into misconduct in the scholarly area inevitably has a forensic component when it takes place on the part of those undertaking expert work as a witness or report-writer for court proceedings. Reviewing developments in this regard took me back from a different perspective to issues arising in expert evidence and report-writing, the first area on which I wrote when employed at the Australian Law Reform Commission by Justice Kirby during the 1980s. In this context I acknowledge the intellectual debt I owe to the rigour of the Hon. Michael Kirby AC, CMG and the Hon. Tim Smith and also the work of William C Thompson, with whom I spent such interesting time at a forensic statistics conference in The Netherlands in 2014. At the time of writing this book I was completing another book for Oxford University Press on *Expert Evidence and Criminal Jury Trials* (2016, with Jane Goodman-Delahunty, Jacqueline Horan, and Blake McKimmie) and the 6th edition of my book on *Expert Evidence: Law, Practice, Procedure and Advocacy* for Thomson-Reuters. This created synergies.

Many have generously provided assistance and ideas to the evolution of this book: the Hon Philip Cummins AM; Professors Janice Reid OAM, Hilary Astor, Kate Diesfeld, Jenny Morgan, Bernadette McSherry, Jane Goodman-Delahunty, Patrick Keyzer, Eilis Magner, Mirko Bagaric, Peter Doherty AC, Danuta Mendelson, Bruce Winick, David Wexler, Ken Pope, John Dawson, and Warren Brookbanks; Associate Professors George Mendelson, Stefan Sjöström, Kerry Petersen, and Mark Nolan; Drs Patricia Molloy and Jacqueline Horan; and Paul Lawrie, Peter Molloy, Chris Holt, Bruce Mann, Richard Balfour, and Julia Freckelton all drew my attention to examples of scholarly misconduct and writing about the phenomenon of which I would otherwise have been unaware, or made suggestions for improvements to aspects of the text.

In Crockett Chambers, Simon McGregor, Peter Matthews, Nick Dubrow, and Sara Hinchey (now Judge Hinchey, the Victorian State Coroner) have all provided tolerant but generous-spirited support to my obsession with bringing this book to its happy conclusion. They have been good friends.

Dr Kerry Ferguson, previously the Pro Vice-Chancellor for Equity and Student Services, Professor Janice Reid, Dr David List, and Dr Patricia Molloy all gave generously of their time to read early drafts of chapters and made thoughtful and stimulating suggestions which assisted me to see issues in ways I would not previously have thought about. Vincent Jewell assisted with translations from the Italian and with research suggestions.

Scholars at Deakin University and the University of New England, the International Academy of Law and Psychiatry in Berlin and Vienna, the International Symposium on Legal Medicine in Fukuoka, the International Association of Forensic Mental Health Services in Toronto, and the Australian and New Zealand Association of Psychiatry, Psychology and Law in Adelaide and Canberra, where I presented aspects of the work, as it was evolving, have also added to the thought process of the book, as did the impetus to look at classical progenitors to modern plagiarism as a result of an invitation by Eugenia Mitrakas to address some of the issues at Melbourne's Hellenic Museum. Leo Freckelton too read through drafts and helped to update URL references.

Liz Richardson made contributions by way of research assistance on an early draft of the book in 2012. Without her assistance, the chapters of the book on intemperate denigration and whistleblowers, in particular, would be much the poorer. I am very grateful to her for her intellectual energy and enthusiasm.

In 2015 through the auspices of the Melbourne Law Research Service at the University of Melbourne, I was generously provided with extensive assistance to check citations and the accuracy of quotations, and to render the book into OUP referencing style. This painstaking work was undertaken over a prodigious number of hours by Cate Read and also by William Huntley. I am enormously grateful for the dedication shown by them, in particular Cate, over a period of months of punctilious work, which unearthed any number of infelicities which otherwise would have detracted from the quality of the final product.

However, to the extent that there are omissions and errors in the *Scholarly Misconduct* the responsibility is wholly mine. What can be said is that there would have been many more and worse were it not for the generous assistance given by those who read, commented upon, and corrected earlier drafts of this book.

Fittingly, the early work on this book was undertaken at Balliol College at Oxford University and the final touches were applied at the Schloss Dürnstein in Austria, overlooking the Danube, and then the Rabbit Hotel in Thailand and Tarraleah in central Tasmania. It is hard to contemplate more congenial locations for the pursuit of scholarship.

Professor Arie Freiberg AM was judiciously selected as the person asked to write a foreword to the book. His diverse career in academia (including as my dean in stints in Criminology at the University of Melbourne and then at the Faculty of Law at Monash University) has been one of inspiring, affirming, and often courageous support for scholarship and integrity. There is no more appropriate person to write in relation to the subject matter of this work. I am grateful to him for agreeing to undertake this role.

In some respects this is an unusual book. It takes courage to publish scholarly works about controversial matters. Not all publishers have the necessary fortitude and pedigree of independence.[15] Some become timorous and 'risk-averse'. Oxford University Press is a beacon of scholarly values and rigour. I could not be more delighted that it is OUP that is publishing this book and I am particularly grateful for the support from first Amy Jones and then Faye Mousley who have endured my anxieties and frustrations with great tolerance and forbearance. After them Emily Brand, Georgie Strachan, and Matthew Humphrys ushered *Scholarly Misconduct,* through the editorial process with dedication, professionalism, and good humour.

[15] The history of OUP is well worth reading: see Ian Gadd, Simon Eliot, and W Roger Louis, *The History of Oxford University Press*, 3 vols (Oxford: Oxford University Press, 2014).

Chapters 6 and 3 respectively draw upon and develop material published by me in I Freckelton, 'Plagiarism in Law and Medicine: Challenges for Scholarship, Academia, Publishers and Regulators' (2010) 17 *Journal of Law and Medicine* 645; and I Freckelton, 'Criminalising Research Fraud' (2014) 22 *Journal of Law and Medicine* 241. Permission from Thomson Reuters is respect of these articles is gratefully acknowledged.

Few people are genuinely excited by scholarly pursuits. I am most fortunate to have been nurtured, challenged and encouraged in my intellectual life by my extraordinary wife, Dr Patricia Molloy, and, in earlier times, by her inspiring mother, Dr Maureen Molloy, who spurred on this venture in its initial stages and whose discourse and intellectual enthusiasm I greatly miss. Their energy has sustained me when the burdens of workaday cases in the courts around Australia, articles submitted to journals, decisions needing to be made on tribunals, regular travel and speaking engagements, and the general vicissitudes of life have threatened to divert me from my commitment to this book and other scholarly pursuits.

I have been kept young(ish) by the tales of student challenges in law and medicine by my talented children Leo and Julia who, I am confident, are going to make fine (and ethical) contributions to those disciplines. And my youngest, Lloyd, has played a nurturing role in encouraging adventurous holidays and maintaining a modicum of equilibrium in me by regular distractions of football-kicking, bowling on our makeshift bush pitch near the beach, and chances to pound tennis balls at him on diverse courts. Towards the end of the editing of the book Serena Lloyd (formerly of Somerset, now of Lanzarote in the Canary Islands) lent a tolerant ear on Kangaroo Island, in Airey's Inlet, Byron Bay, and Wollomomby to tales of new discoveries and finessing of the manuscript.

And of course, the contributions of my four-footed companions, Zoot, Zac and then Otis and Penny, in insisting on walks, swims, and ball-throwing, as well as providing hours of company during the compositional and editing parts of *Scholarly Misconduct*, assisted in retaining the last vestiges of my authorial sanity.

Ian Freckelton
December 2015

TABLE OF CONTENTS

Table of Cases xvii
Table of Statutes xxiii
List of Abbreviations xxv

1. **Introduction** 1
2. **Research Misconduct: Profiles, Principles, and Problems** 19
3. **Research Misconduct: Examples and Solutions** 54
4. **Conflicts of Interest** 170
5. **Forensic Misconduct** 199
6. **Plagiarism** 254
7. **Dishonesty in Employment** 326
8. **Intemperate Denigration and Disputation** 345
9. **Sexual Misconduct** 394
10. **Substance-affected Misconduct** 439
11. **Whistleblowing** 455
12. **Reasserting Scholarly Integrity** 499

Appendices 521
Bibliography 565
Index 627

TABLE OF CASES

A and B v Hampshire Constabulary [2012] EWJC 1517 (QB) 245
A Local Authority v S [2009] EWHC 2115 (Fam) 236
Adamson v Kenworthy (1932) 49 RPC 57 338
AJG, Re [2004] QCA 88 ..... 277, 306–9
Ali, Re (unreported GMC Fitness to Practise Panel 16 December 2009) 304–5
Alsabti v Board of Registration in Medicine, 404 Mass 547 (1989) 301–3
Anderson v IMTT-Québec Inc [2013] FCA 90 469
Arthur JS Hall & Co v Simons [2002] 1 AC 615 243
Arthur v Offit (D Va Civ No 01:09-cv-1398, 10 March 2010); 2010 WL 883745; 2010 US Dist LEXIS 21946 ..... 365–6, 369
Baigent and Leigh v Random House Group Ltd [2006] EWHC 719 (Ch) 229
Barach v University of New South Wales [2010] FWA 1170; (2010) 62 AILR 101 ..... 62, 101–127, 489–90
Barach v University of New South Wales [2010] FWAFB 3307; (2010) IR 259 ..... 194, 490
Barach v University of New South Wales [2011] NSWSC 99 490
Barach v University of New South Wales [2011] NSWSC 431 490
Barach v University of New South Wales [2013] NSWSC 1054 490
Barefoot v Estelle 463 US 880 (1983) 217–18
Baxendale-Walker v Middleton [2011] EWHC 998 (QB) 245
Bennett v State 776 SW 2d 227 (Tex Crim App 1989) 217
Birtchnell v Equity Trustees [1929] HCA 24; (1929) 42 CLR 384 334
Board of Trustees of Leland Stanford Junior University v Roche Molecular Systems Inc 131 S Ct 2188 (2011) 332–3
Bridges v California 314 US 252 (1941) 367
Briscoe v LaHue 460 US 325 (1983) 222, 246
British Chiropractic Association v Singh [2009] EWHC 1101 (QB) 369–70
British Chiropractic Association v Singh [2010] EWCA Civ 350; [2011] WLR 133 370
British Reinforced Concrete Co v Lind (1917) 34 RPC 101 ..... 331, 338
Bruno Appliance and Furniture Inc v Hryniak [2014] 1 SCR 126 168
Burlington Industries Inc v Ellerth 524 US 742 (1998) 395
Cabassi v Vila (194) 64 CLR 130 222
Cala Homes (South) Ltd v Alfred McAlpine Homes East Ltd [1995] FSR 818 202
Carnahan v Coates (1990) 71 DLR (4th) 464 222
Catch the Fire Ministries Inc v Islamic Council of Victoria Inc [2006] VSCA 384; (2006) 15 VR 207 381
Chamberlain v The Queen (No 2) [1984] HCA 7; (1984) 153 CLR 521 203
Chambers v James Cook University of North Queensland (No 2) [1995] IRCA 48; (1995) 61 IR 145 ..... 403, 413, 433
Chan v Zacharia [1984] HCA 36; (1984) 154 CLR 178 334
Chapman v Luminis Pty Ltd (No 4) (2001) 123 FCR 62 202
Chiropractic Board of Australia v Hooper (Review and Regulation) [2013] VCAT 878 148
Chiropractic Board of Australia v Hooper (Review and Regulation) [2013] VCAT 1346 148
Chou v University of Chicago and ARCH Development Corporation 254 F 3d 1347 (Ct App, Fed Cir 2001) 332, 339–41
Cojocaru v British Columbia Women's Hospital and Health Center [2013] 2 SCR 357 318
Commercial Banking Co of Sydney Ltd v RH Brown & Co (1972) 126 CLR 337 168
Commonwealth v Griffiths [2007] NSWCA 370; (2007) 70 NSWLR 268 ..... 222, 246–7
Complaint of Doe, In Re 640 F 3d 869 (8th Cir 2011) 311
Consult Development Pty Ltd v DPC Estates Pty Ltd [1975] HCA 8; (1975) 132 CLR 373 334

Containment Technologies Group Inc v American Society of Health System Pharmacists (D Ind, No 1:07-cv-0997-DFH-TAB, 26 August 2009); 2009 WL 2750093; 2009 US Dist LEXIS 25421 .... 367, 369
Cooke v Plauen Holding [2001] FMCA 91 404–5
Council for the Regulation of Healthcare Professionals v General Medical Council [2005] EWHC 579 (Admin); [2005] All ER (D) 169 232
Crampton v Nugawela (1996) 41 NSWLR 176 348
Crawford v Jenkins [2014] EWCA Civ 1035 222
Dalton v Miller 984 P 2d 666 (Col App, 1999) 222
Darker v Chief Constable of the West Midlands Police [2001] 1 AC 435 222–3
Darwish v Deakin University [2002] VCAT 87 300
Daubert v Merrell Dow Pharmaceuticals 509 US 579 (1993) 4, 19, 200
Davie v Magistrates of Edinburgh 1953 SC 34 200
Dawkins v Lord Rokeby (1873) LR 8 QB 255 222
Derry v Peek (1889) 14 App Cas 337 168
Dilworth v Dudley 75 F 3d 307 (Ct App 7th Cir 1996) 365
Doheny & Adams v The Queen [1997] 1 Cr App R 369 209
D'Orta-Ekenaike v Victoria Legal Aid [2005] HCA 12; (2005) 223 CLR 1 .... 222, 243, 246
Doyle v Olby (Ironmongers) Ltd [1969] 2 QB 158 168
Doyle v Riley (1995) EOC 92-748 405
DPP v Gianello [2014] VCC 2015 327
Eco3 Capital Ltd & Ors v Ludsin Overseas Ltd [2013] EWCA Civ 413 168
Edisonia Ltd v Forse (1908) 25 RPC 546 338
El Naschie v MacMillan Publishers Ltd (trading as Nature Publishing Group) and Schiermeier [2011] EWHC 1468 (QB) 37, 363, 373–5
El Naschie v MacMillan Publishers Ltd (trading as Nature Publishing Group) and Schiermeier [2012] EWHC 1809 (QB) 37, 363, 373–5
Electrolux Ltd v Hudson [1977] FSR 312 338
English v Emery Reimbold & Strick Ltd [2002] 3 All ER 385 315
Estelle v Smith 451 US 454 (1981) 217–18
Evans v London Medical College (University of London) [1981] 1 WLR 184 223
Fabian v Margulies (1985) 53 OR (2d) 380 (Ont CA) 222
Fasold v Roberts [1997] FCA 439; (1997) 70 FCR 489 350–2
Flanagan v University College Dublin [1988] IR 724 269
Fletcher Construction Australia Ltd v Lines MacFarlane & Marshall Pty Ltd (No.2) [2002] VSCA 189; (2002) 6 VR 1 318
Fogarty v The United Kingdom [2001] ECHR 762; (2001) 34 EHRR 302 403
Formby v University of Wollongong [1999] AIRC 879 431
Formby v University of Wollongong [1999] AIRC 871 .... 425, 429–31
Freyd v Whitfield 972 F Supp 940 (D Md Civ No L-96-627, 18 July 1997) 367
Fuste v Riverside Healthcare Association 265 Va 127; 575 SE 2d 858 (Va Sup Ct 2003); 2003 Va LEXIS 13 366
Gauci v Kennedy [2007] FCA 1051 .... 405, 434
General Medical Council v Meadow [2006] EWCA Civ 1390; [2007] QB 462 .... 202–3, 222–31, 237–8, 240, 242–3, 507
Giannarelli v Wraith [1988] HCA 52; (1988) 165 CLR 543 .... 243, 246
Gibson v Cotter [2006] NZHC 592 222
GLS v PLP (Human Rights) [2013] VCAT 221 .... 404–5, 433
Greater Glasgow Health Board's Application [1996] RPC 207 348
Griffiths v Ballard [2005] NSWSC 1450 246
Hall v A & A Sheiban Pty Ltd [1989] FCA 72; (1989) 20 FCR 217 425
Hall v Swan [2009] NSWCA 371 .... 109, 112, 140, 142, 145
Hamod v New South Wales (No 10) [2008] NSWSC 611 222
Hinden, Re 654 A 2d 864 (1985) 303–5, 306
Holdfast NZ Ltd v Henkel KgaA [2007] 1 NZLR 336 270
Honeysett v The Queen [2014] HCA 29; (2014) 88 ALJR 786 4
Huang v Abayawickrama [2011] FMCA 235 426

Huang v Abayawickrama (No 2) [2012] FMCA 747 426
Huang v University of New South Wales [2008] FMCA 11 425
Hudspeth v Scholastic Cleaning (Ruling No 8) [2014] VSC 567 . . . . 248, 253
Humzy-Hancock, Re [2007] QSC 34 . . . . 270, 307–8, 323
IG Markets Ltd v Crinion [2013] EWCA Civ 587 315
In the Matter of an Investigation of the West Virginia State Police Crime Laboratory, Serological Division (1993) 438 SE 2d 501 (W Va Sup Ct App) 209
In the Matter of the Charges of Plagiarism, Etc., Against Associate Justice Mariano C. Del Castillo (Dissenting Opinion, Sereno J) 15 October 2010 AM No 10-7-17-SC (Republic of the Philippines Supreme Court) 312
In the Matter of the Charges of Plagiarism, Etc., Against Associate Justice Mariano C. Del Castillo (Resolution) 8 February 2011 AM No 10-7-17-SC (Republic of the Philippines Supreme Court) 312
In the Matter of Charles Selx Limited's Application to the Comptroller under Section 56 of the Patents Act 1949 (1953) 71 RPC 158 . . . . 331, 338
Iowa Supreme Court Attorney Disciplinary Board v Cannon 789 NW 2d 256 (Iowa 2010) 509
Irving v Penguin Books Ltd [2000] EWHC QB 115 381–2
Jaber v Wayne State University Board of Governors (Mich Ct App 6th Cir 9 July 2012) 300
James v Keogh [2008] SASC 156; (2008) 101 SASR 42 242
James v Medical Board of South Australia [2006] SASC 267; (2006) SASR 445 . . . . 95, 222
James v Surf Road Nominees Pty Ltd [2004] NSWCA 475 318
Jamieson v The Queen (1993) 117 CLR 574 222
Janssen-Ortho Inc v Apotex Inc [2009] FCA 212 315
Johnson v Gibson 169 F 3d 1239 (10th Cir 1999) 211
Jones v Kaney [2011] UKSC 13; [2011] 2 AC 398 . . . . 222, 242–6, 508
Journal-Gazette Co v Bandido's Inc 712 NE 2d 446 (Ind 1999) 367
Kaplan v Corcoran 545 F 2d 1073 (7th Cir 1976) 311
Kaplan v Johnson 409 F Supp 190 (ND Ill 1976) 311
Keith Henry & Co Pty Ltd v Stuart Walker & Co Pty Ltd [1958] HCA 33; (1958) 100 CLR 342 334
Kinge v New York (NY 79 AD 3d No 09426 23 December 2010) slip of 1473 208
Kracunas v Iona College 119 F 3d 80 (2nd Cir 1997) 405
Krakowski v Eurolynx Properties Ltd (1995) 183 CLR 563 168
Kraus v Menzie [2012] FCAFC 144 404
Kumar, Re (unreported GMC Fitness to Practice Panel 1 February 2011) 305
Kumar, Re (unreported GMC Fitness to Practice Panel 25 May 2011) 234
La Trobe University, Re ex p Wild [1987] VR 447 . . . . 9, 282
Lab Tests Auckland Ltd v Auckland District Health Board [2008] NZCA 385; [2009] 1 NZLR 776 355
Larrikin Music Publishing Pty Ltd v EMI Songs Australia Pty Ltd [2010] FCA 29; (2010) 263 ALR 155 299
Latcha v The Queen (1998) 104 A Crim R 390 209
Law Institute Journal: Re Pickering (unreported, Solicitors' Board, Vic 6 February 1992) 308
Law Society of Upper Canada v Burgess [2006] ONLSHP 66 305–6
Legal Services Commissioner v Keough [2010] VCAT 108 307–9
Lesapo v North West Agricultural Bank and Another [1999] ZACC 16; 2000 (1) SA 409 17
Leslie v Graham [2002] FCA 32 404
LIFFE Administration and Management v Pinkava [2007] EWCA Civ 217; [2007] 4 All ER 981 331
Liveri, Re [2006] QCA 152 . . . . 306, 308
Lott v Levitt 556 F 3d 564 (Ct App 7th Cir 2009) 365
M v Australian National University [1996] IRCA 411 433
McAleer v The University of Western Australia [2007] FCA 52; (2007) 159 IR 96 413–14
McAleer v The University of Western Australia (No 3) [2008] FCA 1490; (2008) 171 FCR 499 414
McBride, Re (unreported Medical Tribunal of New South Wales 29 April 1996) 142–5, 161

McBride v Walton [1994] NSWCA 199 (15 July 1994) 143–4
McGuirk v University of New South Wales [2010] NSWCA 104 346
McMillan v Togus Regional Office, Department of Veteran Affairs Fed Appx 849 (2nd Cir 2005) 120, 368
McMillan v Togus Regional Office, Department of Veteran Affairs F Supp 2d 305 (2003) 294, 368
Macquarie International Health Clinic Pty Ltd v Sydney Local Health District [2013] NSWSC 970 247
Magan Medical Clinic v California State Board of Medical Examiners 249 Cal App 2d 124 (1967) 181
Marrinan v Vibart [1963] 1 QB 234 223
Marrinan v Vibart [1963] 1 QB 528 223
Marroquin v Exxon Mobil Corporation (D Va Vic No 08-391 27 May 2009); 2009 WL 1529455; 2009 US Dist LEXIS 44834 366
Meadow v General Medical Council [2006] EWCA Civ 1390; [2007] 1 QB 462 . . . . 225–37, 240, 242–7
Meadow v General Medical Council [2006] EWHC 146 (Admin); [2006] 2All ER 329 . . . . 202–3, 222–3, 227–37
Mengiste v Endowment Fund for Rehabilitation of Tigray [2013] EWHC 1087 (Ch) 248
Mercury Energy Ltd v Electricity Corporation of New Zealand [1994] NZLR 385 . . . . 2, 354
Merk v International Association of Bridge, Structural, Ornamental and Reinforcing Iron Workers Local 771 [2005] 3 SCR 425 469
Metabolife International v Wornick 72 F Supp 2d 1160 (D Cal Civ No 99-1095-R 17 November 1999) 369
Mitchell v Forsyth 472 US 511 (1985) 222
Mitchell v Gibson 262 F 3d 1036 (10th Cir 2001) 211
Moore v Regents of University of California 51 Cal 3d 120 (1990) 181
Munster v Lamb (1883) 11 QBD 588 223
Murch, Re (unreported GMC Fitness to Practise Panel 24 May 2010) 146
Murphy v AA Matthews 841 SW 2d 671 (Mo 1992) 222
Mustac v Medical Board (WA) [2004] WASCA 156 241
Napolitano v Princeton University Trustees 453 A 2d 263 (NJ Super AD 1982) 270
National Association for the Advancement of Colored People v Button 371 US 415 (1963) 367
National Justice Compania Naviera SA v Prudential Assurance Co Ltd (Ikarian Reefer) [1993] 2 Lloyd's Rep 68 . . . . 202, 228–9
New York Time Co v Sullivan 376 US 254 (1964) 367–8
New Zealand Climate Science Education Trust v National Institute of Water and Atmospheric Research Ltd [2012] NZHC 2297; [2013] 1 NNZLR 75 354–5
New Zealand Public Service Association Inc v Hamilton City Council [1997] 1 NZLR 30 355
NHS Manchester v Fecitt [2011] EWCA Civ 1190 . . . . 458, 468
Noah v Shuba [1991] FSR 14 330
Noble, Re [2002] PRBD (Vic) 6 241
Noone, Director of Consumer Affairs Victoria v Operation Smile (Australia) (No 2) [2011] VSC 153 367
Noone v Operation Smile (Australia) Inc [2012] VSCA 91; (2012) 38 VR 569 353
Obieta v New South Wales Department of Education and Training [2007] FCA 86 404
Oelofse, Re (unreported GMC Fitness to Practise Panel 10 December 2010) 232
OG, Re [2007] VSC 520; (2007) 18 VR 164 306
Orr v The University of Tasmania [1956] 1 Tas SR 155 . . . . 414, 426–428
Orr v The University of Tasmania [1957] HCA 32; (1957) 100 CLR 526 427
Oshinyemi, Re (unreported GMC Fitness to Practise Panel 30 April 2012) 234
Owens v University of Melbourne [2008] VSC 174; (2008) 19 VR 449 478
Palmer v Durnford Ford [1992] QB 483 222
Patchett v Sterling Engineering Co Ltd (1955) 72 RPC 50 331
Patel, Re (unreported GMC Fitness to Practise Panel 31 March 2011) 233
Patel v General Medical Council [2003] UKPC 16 324

Peek v Gurney (1873) LR 6 HL 377 168
Persaud, Re (unreported GMC Fitness to Practise Panel 20 June 2008) 304
Phillips v Symes (No 2) [2004] EWHC 2330 (Ch); [2005] 1 WLR 2043 243
Pierce v State 786 P 2d 1255 (Okla Crim App 1990) 211
Plews v Pausch [2006] 11 WWR 513 256
Pool, Re (unreported GMC Fitness to Practise Panel 13 June 2014) 235
Preece v HM Advocate [1981] Crim LR 783 . . . . . 200, 205
Psychologists Registration Board of Victoria v Glamcevski [2010] VCAT 1927 309–10
Psychology Board of Australia v Milosevic [2013] VCAT 12 219
Public Prosecutor v Weiler Tribunal de Grand Instance de Paris 0718523043
3 March 2011 376–7
Queensland Nursing Council v Webb [2007] QNT 5 310
R v Bowman [2006] EWCA Crim 417 202
R v C(G) (1997) 110 CCC (3d) 233 (Newfoundland CA) 200–1
R v Clark [2000] EWCA Crim 54; [2000] All ER (D) 1219 227
R v Clark [2003] EWCA Crim 1020; [2003] All ER (D) 223 (Apr) 227
R v DD [2000] 2 SCR 275 201
R v Gaudet (1998) 40 OR (3rd) 1 (Ontario Court of Appeal) 314
R v Harris [2005] EWCA Crim 1980; [2006] 1 Cr App R 5 202
R v McIlkenney (1991) 93 Cr App R 287 208
R v Maguire [1992] 1 QB 936 208
R v Mohan [1994] 2 SCR 9 201
R v Piggott, Griffiths and Simeon [2002] NSWCCA 218 246
R v Richardson; R v Conlon; R v Armstrong; R v Hill Times 20 October 1989 (CA) 208
R v Ward (1993) 96 Cr App R 1 208
Ramanujam, Re (unreported GMC Fitness to Practise Panel 18 May 2011) 305
Rath v Guardian News and Media Ltd and Goldacre [2008] EWHC 398 (QB) 370
Reeves-Board v Queensland University of Technology [2002] 2 Qd R 85 478
Reynolds v Times Newspapers Ltd [2001] 2 AC 127 374
Rindos v Hardwick (unreported WASC 31 March 1994) 357–9
Roth v United States 354 US 476 (1957) 367
Roy v Prior [1971] AC 47nough 223
Roylance v General Medical Council (No 2) [2000] 1 AC 311 486
Salha v General Medical Council [2003] UKPC 80; (2004) 80 BMLR 169 303
Scopes v State 154 Tenn 105; 289 SW 363 (1927) 351
Shanahan v University of Western Sydney [2005] AIRC 473 428–9
Sheikholeslami v University of New South Wales (No 3) [2008] FMCA 35 425
Sheldon v Metro-Goldwyn Pictures Corporation 81 F 2d 49 (2nd Cir 1936) 266
Shephard, Re (unreported GMC Fitness to Practise Panel 27 May 2011) 305
Shin v Kung [2004] HKCA 205 317
Smart v Forensic Science Service Ltd [2013] EWCA Civ 783 246
SmithKline Beecham (New Zealand) Ltd v Minister of Health (unreported
HC Wellington CP49/02) 355
Sorger v Bank of Nova Scotia (1998) 30 OR (3rd) 1 (Ontario Court of Appeal) 314
South Australia v Johnson (1982) 42 ALR 161 168
Spencer Industries Pty Ltd v Collins [2003] FAC 542; (2003) 58 IPR 425 . . . . . 331, 338
Stanton v Callaghan [2000] QB 75 222–3
Stevenson Jordan & Harrison Ltd v MacDonald & Evans [1952] 1 TLR 101;
(1951) 69 RPC 10 330
Stevens Institute of Technology v Hine 2007 WL 2188200; 2007 NJ Super
Unpub LEXIS 1268 367
Sweezy v State of New Hampshire 354 US 234 (1957) 368, 472
Taco Company of Australia Inc v Taco Bell Pty Ltd [1982] FCA 136; (1982) 42 ALR 177 352
Taylor v Director of the Serious Fraud Office [1999] 2 AC 177 223
Taylor v Sciberras [2004] NSWADT 104 405
Thomson v University of London (1864) 33 LJ Ch 625 9
Toben v Jones [2003] FCAFC 137; (2003) 129 FCR 515 381

Triplex Safety Glass Co v Scorah [1937] 1 Ch 211; [1938] RPC 21 .... 331, 338
Underwager v Salter 22 F 3d 730 (Ct App 7th Cir 1994) 365
United States ex rel Jones v Brigham and Women's Hospital 678 F 3d 72 (1st Cir 2012) 13, 150–1
United States v Blech 550 Fed Appx 70 (2nd Cir 2014) 330
United States v Dubilier Condenser Corporation 289 US 178 (1933); amended 289 US 706 (1933) 331
United States v El Paso Natural Gas Co 376 US 651 (1964) 315
United States v Frazier 387 F 3d 1244 (11th Cir 2004) 200
United States v Hines 55 F Supp 2d 62 (D Mass 1999) 200
University of New South Wales v Huang [2012] FCA 308 426
University of Western Australia v Gray [2009] FCAFC 116; (2009) FCR 346 .... 179, 336
University of Western Australia v Gray (No 20) [2008] FCA 498; (2008) 246 ALR 603 337
Varghese v Landau (2004) CanLII 5084 (Ont SC) 222
Velevski v The Queen [2002] HCA 4; (2002) 187 ALR 233 200
Victoria University of Technology v Wilson [2004] VSC 33; (2004) 60 IPR 392 .... 331, 335
Vinuya v Rolulo (28 April 2010) GR No 162230 (Republic of the Philippines Supreme Court) 311–12
Wakefield, Re (unreported GMC Fitness to Practise Panel 24 May 2010) 146
Walker-Smith, Re (unreported GMC Fitness to Practise Panel 24 May 2010) 146
Walker-Smith v General Medical Council [2012] EWHC 503 (Admin) 137, 146, 148
Watson v M'Ewan; Watson v Jones [1905] AC 480 223
Watson-Munro, Re [2000] PRBD (Vic) 4 240
Watson-Munro, Re [2004] PRBD (Vic) 1 240
Watson-Munro, Re [2002] PRBD (Vic) 2 240
Whitney v California 274 US 357 (1927) 367
WIC Radio Ltd & Mair v Simpson [2008] 2 SCR 420 377
Worthington Pumping Engine Co v Moore (1902) 20 RPC 41 331
X (Minors) v Bedfordshire County Council [1985] 2 AC 633 223
Young v Hones (No 2) [2013] NSWSC 1429 246
Z v Dental Complaints Assessment Committee [2008] NZSC 55; [2009] 1 NZLR 1 355

TABLE OF STATUTES

Accident Compensation Act 1985 (Vic, Aust) 478
Act of 18 December 1998 on the Institute of National Remembrance (Commission for the Prosecution of Crimes Against the Polish Nation) (Poland) 381
Americans with Disabilities Act 1990, Pub L No 101-336, 104 Stat 327 (1990) (US) 452
An Act for the Encouragement of Learning, by Vesting the Copies of Printed Books in the Authors or Purchasers of Such Copies, During the Times Therein Mentioned 8 Anne c 19 (1710) (Statute of Anne) (UK) 255
Anti-Evolution Act of 1925, 49 Tenn Code Ann ch 27 § 1922 (US) 351
Arkansas Code Annotated (West)(US) 369
Australian Research Council Act 2001 (Cth Aust) 162
Baudžiamasis kodeksas [Criminal Code] (Lithuania) 381
California Code of Criminal Procedure (West) (US) 369
Civil Law (Wrongs) Act (ACT, Aus) 371–2
Civil Service Reform Act 1978, Pub L No 95-454, 92 Stat 1111 (1978) (US) 474
Código Penal [Penal Code] (Spain) 381
Code Penal [Criminal Code] (Luxembourg) 381
Comprehensive Drug Abuse Prevention and Control Act of 1970, Pub L No 91-513, 84 Stat 1236 (1970) 451
Criminal Code Act 1899 (Qld, Aust) 130, 185
Criminal Code, RSC 1985 c C-46 (Can) 469
Defamation Act 2005 (NSW. Aust) 371–3
Defamation Act 2005 (Qld, Aust) 371–3
Defamation Act 2005 (SA, Aust) 371–3
Defamation Act 2005 (Tas, Aust) 371–3
Defamation Act 2005 (Vic, Aust) 371–3
Defamation Act 2005 (WA, Aust) 371–3
Defamation Act 2006 (NT, Aust) 372
Defamation Act 2013 (UK) 371, 374
Denial of Holocaust (Prohibition) Law 5746-1986 (Israel) 381
Dodd-Frank Wall Street Reform and Consumer Protection Act 2010, Pub L No 111-203, 124 Stat 1376 (2010) (US) 479
Drug Abuse Control Amendments 1965, Pub L no 89-74, 79 Stat 226 (1965) (US) 451
Drug-Free Workplace Act 1988, 41 USC 81 (US) 452
Emergency Ordinance No 31 of March 2002 (Romania) 381
Employment Rights Act 1996 (UK) 467
Employment Standards Act, SNB 1982 c E-7.2 (Can) 469
Enterprise and Regulatory Reform Act 2013 (UK) 468
Evidence Act 1995 (Cth Aust) 200
False Claims Act, 31 USC §§ 3729-3733 (US) 118, 149
Federal Rules of Evidence (US) 149–52, 473–4, 479, 506, 515
Food, Drug and Cosmetic Act 1938, Pub L No 75-717, 52 Stat 1040 (1938) (US) 451
Forensic Sciences Act 2011 sec 2, NC Sess Laws 2011-19 (US) 222
Good Laboratory Practice (Codification Amendments Etc) Regulations 2004 (UK) SI 994/2004 167
Good Laboratory Practice Regulations 1999 (US) SI 1999/3106 . . . . . 126, 130, 167
Health Practitioner Regulation National Law Act 2009 (Qld, Aust) 306
Health Practitioner Regulation National Law (Victoria) Act 2009 (Vic, Aust) 306
Higher Education Support Act 2003 (Cth Aust) 162
Independent Broad-Based Anti-Corruption Commission Act 2011 (Vic, Aust) 477, 483
Independent Commission Against Corruption Act 1988 (NSW, Aust) 328, 475
Labour Standards Act 1978, RSS 1978 c L-1 (Sas, Can) 469
National Health and Medical Research Council Act 1992 (Cth Aust) 162
NC Gen Stat § 15A-1461 (Lexis 2014) (US) 221
No-FEAR Act (Notification and Federal Employee Antidiscrimination and Retaliation Act 2002), Pub L No 107-174, 116 Stat 566 (2002) (US) 474
NY CLS Exec § 995-b(1) (Lexis 2014) (US) 220
Ombudsman Act 1973 (Vic, Aust) 478, 483
Ombudsman Act 1974 (NSW, Aust) 475

Patents Act 1990 (Cth Aust) 338
Patient Protection and Affordable Care Act of 2010, Pub L No 111-148, 124 Stat 119 (2010) (US) 180, 507
Poisons and Therapeutic Goods Act 1966 (NSW, Aust) 246
Prevention of Corruption Act 1988 (India) 218
Protected Disclosure Act 2012 (Vic, Aust) 466–7, 477, 483
Protected Disclosures Act 1994 (NSW, NSW) 475, 493
Protected Disclosures Act 2000 (NZ)............................ 466
Protected Disclosures Amendment (Public Interest Disclosures) Act 2010 (NSW, Aust) 475
Public Finance and Audit Act 1983 (NSW, Aust)............................ 475
Public Health Service Act, Pub L No 78-410, 58 Stat 682 (1944) (US).................... 479–80
Public Interest Disclosure Act 1944 (ACT, Aust)....................... 475
Public Interest Disclosure Act 1998 (UK)..................466–7, 480
Public Interest Disclosure Act 2003 (WA, Aust).................... 466, 477
Public Interest Disclosure Act 2008 (NT, Aust) 466–7, 475
Public Interest Disclosure Act 2010 (Qld, Aust)................466, 475, 483
Public Interest Disclosure Act 2012 (ACT, Aust)................... 466, 475
Public Interest Disclosure Act 2013 (Cth Aust) 459, 466
Public Interest Disclosure Act, SNB 2012 c 112 (NB, Can).................. 471
Public Interest Disclosure Act, SS 2011 c P-38.1 (Sas, Can)................. 471
Public Interest Disclosure (Northern Ireland) Order 1998 (UK)........... 467
Public Interest Disclosure and Whistleblower Protection Act, SNL 2014 c P-37.2 (Newf, Can) 471
Public Interest Disclosure of Wrongdoing Act, SNS 2010 c 42 (NS, Can) 471
Public Interest Disclosure (Whistleblower Protection) Act, CCSM c P217 (Man, Can) 470
Public Interest Disclosure (Whistleblower Protection) Act, SA 2012 c P-39.5 (Alb, Can) 470
Public Interest Disclosures Act 1994 (NSW, Aust) 466, 475, 493
Public Interest Disclosures Act 2002 (Tas, Aust) 466, 476
Public Sector Management Act 1994 (WA, Aust)........................ 477
Public Servants Disclosure Protection Act, SC 2005 c 46 (Can) 469, 471
Public Service of Ontario Act 2006, SO 2006 c 35 Sch A (Ont, Can) 471
Racial Discrimination Act 1975 (Cth Aust) 381
Racial and Religious Tolerance Act 2002 (Vic, Aust) 381
Sarbanes-Oxley Act of 2002, Pub L No 107-204, 116 Stat 745 (2002) (US)...................... 472–4
Saskatchewan Employment Act, SS 2013 c S-15.1 (Sas, Can) 469
Securing the Protection of our Enduring and Established Constitutional Heritage (SPEECH) Act 2010, Pub L No 111-223................. 124
Stat 2480 (US)........................... 365
Sex Discrimination Act 1975 (UK)........ 403
Sex Discrimination Act 1984 (Cth Aust) 404, 406, 412, 425
Strafgesetzbuch [Criminal Code] (Germany)........................ 381
Tertiary Education Quality and Standards Agency Act 2011 (Cth Aust) 164
United Nations Convention against Corruption, opened for signature 31 October 2003, 2349 UNTS 41 (entered into force 14 December 2005)......468, 473
United States Constitution............... 367
University and Small Business Patent Procedures Act of 1980 (US).......... 333
University of Sydney (Intellectual Property) Rule 2002 343
University of Western Australia Act 1911 (WA, Aust)........................ 337
Verbotsgesetz [Prohibition Act] 1947 (Austria)........................... 381
Whistleblower Protection Act 1989, Pub L No 101-12, 103 Stat 16 (1989) (US)................... 472, 474
Whistleblowers Protection Act 1993 (SA, Aust).................466, 476, 482
Whistleblowers Protection Act 1994 (Qld, Aust)..................... 474–5
Whistleblowers Protection Act 2001 (Vic, Aust).......188, 467, 475, 478, 493, 495

LIST OF ABBREVIATIONS

11SS	Eleven Station Temperature Series
7SS	Seven Station Temperature Series
AAMC	Association of American Medical Colleges
AAU	Association of American Universities
ABC	Australian Broadcasting Corporation
ACT	Australian Capital Territory
ADHD	Attention Deficit Hyperactivity Disorder
AdW	Alliance of German Scientific Organizations
AFDL	Australian Forensic Drug Laboratory
AGAL	Australian Government Analytical Laboratories
AIDS	Acquired Immune Deficiency Syndrome
AJRCCM	American Journal of Respiratory and Clinical Care Medicine
AMBT	autologous bone marrow transplantation
ANU	Australian National University
ANZPAA	Australia and New Zealand Policing Advisory Agency
APA	American Psychiatric Association
APS	Australian Psychological Society
ARC	Australian Research Council
ARIC	Australian Research Integrity Committee
ASCLD/LAB	American Society of Crime Laboratory Directors/Laboratory Accreditation Board
ASIC	Australian Securities & Investment Commission
AUCC	Association of Universities and Colleges of Canada
AUS$	Australian dollars
AVCC	Australian Vice-Chancellors Committee
CA$	Canadian dollars
CAMH	Centre for Addiction and Mental Health
CEO	Chief Executive Officer
CFS	Chronic Fatigue Syndrome
CFSL	Central Forensic Science Laboratory
CGS	copper gallium selenide
CIA	Central Intelligence Agency
CIHR	Canadian Institutes of Health Research
CLIA	Clinical Laboratory Improvement Act
CMEC	Complementary Medicine Evidence Centre
CME	Continuing Medical Education
CMS	Centers for Medicare and Medicaid Services
CNATDCU	National Council for Certification of Titles, Diplomas and University Certificates
COI	Conflict of interest
COPE	Committee on Publication Ethics
CPE	Continuing Professional Education
CRFP	Council for the Registration of Forensic Practitioners
CRI	Cancer Research Institute
CSI	Crime Scene Investigation
Cth	Commomwealth
DAMP	Deficits in Attention, Motor Control and Perception

DECREASE III	Dutch Echographic Cardiac Risk Evaluation Applying Stress Echo III
DFG	Deutsche Forchungsgemeinschaft (Germany's main provider of research funds)
DIISR	Department of Innovation, Industry, Science and Research
DOX	doxorubicin
DSM-IV	Diagnostic and Statistical Manual of Mental Disorders, 4th edition (APA)
EJIL	European Journal of International Law
ESC	European Society of Cardiology
ETC	Educational Testing Centre
FCA	False Claims Act
FEB	Forensic Evidence Bureau
FDA	Food and Drug Administration (United States)
GMC	General Medical Council
HDC	high dose chemotherapy
HIV	Human Immunodeficiency Virus
IBAC	Independent Broad-based Anti-corruption Commission
ICAC	Independent Commission against Corruption
ICD-10	International Classification of Diseases, 10th edition (WHO)
ILAC	International Laboratory Accreditation Cooperation
IP	intellectual property
IRA	Irish Republican Army
JACS	Journal of the American Chemical Society
JAMA	Journal of the American Medical Association
JPY	Japanese Yen
LAK-RLP	Landesarztekammer Rheinland-Pfalz
LSE	London School of Economics
MIM model	misappropriation (incorporating plagiarism), interference and misrepresentation model
MIT	Massachusetts Institute of Technology
MPTS	Medical Practitioners Tribunal Service
NCI	National Cancer Institute
NEC	National Ethics Council
NHMRC	National Health and Medical Research Council
NIFS	National Institute of Forensic Science
NIH	National Institutes of Health
NIMH	National Institute of Mental Health
NIST	National Institute of Standards and Technology
NIWA	National Institute of Water and Atmospheric Research Ltd
No-FEAR Act	Notification and Federal Employee Antidiscrimination and Retaliation Act of 2002
NSABP	National Surgical Adjuvant Breast and Bowel Project
NSERC	Natural Sciences and Engineering Research Council
NSF	National Science Foundation
NSW	New South Wales (Australia)
NT	Northern Territory (Australia)
NTEU	National Tertiary Education Union
NZ	New Zealand
OeAWI	Austrian Agency for Research Integrity
OoSTP	Office of Science and Technology Policy
OPI	Office of Public Integrity
ORI	Office of Research Integrity
OSI	Office of Scientific Integrity

OTC	Ornithine Transcarbamylase
PAD	Peripheral Artery Disease
PBD	Paediatric Bipolar Disorder
PCaW	Public Concern at Work
PCL-R	Psychopathy Checklist Revised
PCR	Polymerase Chain Reaction
PD	Protected Disclosure
PID	Public Interest Disclosure
PTSD	Post-traumatic Stress Disorder
Qld	Queensland
RCR	Responsible Conduct of Research
RMIT	Royal Melbourne Institute of Technology
SA	South Australia
SEK	Swedish Krona
SFI	Significant Financial Interest
SIDS	Sudden Infant Death Syndrome
SIRT	Selective Internal Radiation Therapy
SLAPP	Strategic Lawsuit to Silence Public Participation
SSHRC	Social Sciences and Humanities Research Council
SSRI	Selective Serotonin Reuptake Inhibitor
STAP	Stimulus-triggered Acquisition of Pluripotency
Tas	Tasmania (Australia)
TEQSA	Tertiary Education Quality and Standards Agency
UCLA	Medical Center of the University of California
UKAS	United Kingdom Accreditation Service
UNE	University of New England
US$	US dollars
USDA	US Department of Agriculture
UWA	University of Western Australia
UWA Act	University of Western Australia Act 1911
UWS	University of Western Sydney
VCAT	Victorian Civil and Administrative Tribunal
Vic	Victoria (Australia)
VUT	Victoria University of Technology
WA	Western Australia
WAME	World Association of Medical Editors
WHO	World Health Organization
WISER	Witwatersrand Institute for Social and Economic Research
Wits	University of Witwatersrand

The only ethical principle which has made science possible is that the truth shall be told all the time. If we do not penalise false statements made in error, we open up the way for false statements by intention. And a false statement of fact, made deliberately, is the most serious crime a scientist can commit.

Dorothy L Sayers, *Gaudy Night (Lord Peter Wimsey)* (Hodder and Stoughton 1935)

1

INTRODUCTION

Scholars and Scholarship

The terms 'scholars' and 'scholarship' conjure up many images and associations, some of them vivid and evocative. Perhaps in part as a result of art relating to scholars (including alchemists[1]), in particular how and where they have been depicted, our notions of persons devoted disinterestedly to lives of learning and study have been formed with visual components.[2] Images abound of scholars distracted from the cares of the world, sometimes a little dishevelled, and given over to learning and study; in seventeenth century 'Golden Age' Dutch art they became a trope.[3]

In 1876 Ralph Waldo Emerson captured this idealized notion of a scholar memorably, if floridly:

> [A] mechanic, is driven by his work all day, but it ends at night; it has an end. But, as far as the mechanic or farmer is also a scholar or thinker, his work has no end. That which he has learned is that there is much more to be learned. The wiser he is, he feels only the more his incompetence...A thousand years,—tenfold, a hundred-fold his faculties, would not suffice. The demands of his task are such that it becomes omnipresent. He studies in his walking, at his meals, in his amusements, even in his sleep...He is but as a fly or a worm to this mountain, this continent, which his thoughts inhabit.[4]

More recently, Jacob Bronowski, the Polish-born English mathematician, biologist, and historian of science, extolled the ethics of scholars and scholarship:

> By the worldly standards of public life, all scholars in their work are of course oddly virtuous. They do not make wild claims, they do not cheat, they do not try to persuade at any cost, they appeal neither to prejudice nor to authority, they are often frank about their ignorance, their disputes are fairly decorous, they do not confuse what is being argued with

---

[1] See eg Sven Dupre, Dedo Von Kerssenbrock-Krosigk, and Beat Wismer (eds), *Art and Alchemy: The Mystery of Transformation* (Chicago: University of Chicago Press, 2014); Samuel Scarborough, 'Alchemical Art as a Method of Communication' (2005) 9(1) *Journal of the Western Mystery Tradition:* <http://www.jwmt.org/v1n9/imagery.html> [accessed 18 Dec 2015].

[2] See eg Tassos A. Kaplanis, 'The Scholar in His Study: Depictions of a Renaissance Tradition in Vitsentzos Kornaros's Erotokritos' in Efrosini Camatsos, Tassos A Kaplanis, and Jocelyn Pye (eds), *His Words Were Nourishment and his Counsel Food: A Festschrift for David W Holton* (Cambridge: Cambridge Scholars Publishing, 2014); Dora Thornton, *The Scholar in His Study: Ownership and Experience in Renaissance Italy* (New Haven: Yale University Press, 1998); John Walsh, *Jan Steen: The Drawing Lesson* (Los Angeles: Getty Publications, 1996), at p. 76.

[3] See eg Thomas Wyck (1616–1667), 'A Scholar in his Study'; Johannes Vermeer (1632–1675), 'The Geographer'; Gerbrand van den Eeckhout (1621–1674), 'Scholar with his Books'; Willem van Drielenberg (1632–1687), 'A Scholar in his Study Reading'; Cornelis Bisschop (1630–1674), 'A Scholar in his Study'; Karel van der Pluym (1625–1672), 'A Scholar in his Study'; Salomon Koninck (1609–1656), 'A Scholar in his Study'; Johan Michael Bretschneider (1656–1727), 'In the Scholar's Study'; Julius Fehr (1860–1900), 'A Rabbi Scholar in his Study'.

[4] Ralph Waldo Emerson, 'Immortality' in *Letters and Social Aims*, in Glen M Johnson and Joel Myerson, *Collected Works of Ralph Waldo Emerson*, vol. VIII (Cambridge, MA: Harvard University Press, 2010).

> race, politics, sex or age, they listen patiently to the young and to the old who both know everything. These are the general virtues of scholarship, and they are peculiarly the virtues of science.[5]

The pages that follow, document with sadness multiple examples of deficits in scholarly virtue, especially in recent times. An attempt is made in this book to identify and contextualize the important contemporary ethical, disciplinary, and legal issues arising from scholarly misconduct.

Lawyers and philosophers can seem to be obsessed by or enamoured of definitions.[6] Sometimes this is an arid exercise engaged in for its own sake and little else. However, sharpness in the use of terminology should conduce to clarity of thinking and rigour of analysis.[7] It is also fundamental to the fair resolution of allegations of any kind of impropriety; otherwise imprecision can result in unfairness to those against whom accusations are made, as well as those who make the accusations.

In the pages of this book a broad approach is adopted as to what constitutes scholarship—in other words, looking well beyond the traditional academy of the universities[8] and focusing on scholarly conduct in the contemporary environment wherever and however engaged in. The reason is that the forum and nature of scholarship has evolved considerably[9] and in the Internet Age much modern acquisition and ventilation of learning, as well as research and opinion leadership, take place outside the tertiary sector. Scholars move between universities, think tanks, government and private research establishments, and even the media. They publish in books and traditional scholarly journals but also in open access publications, blogs, reports for government and corporations, and in opinion pieces in the media. Submissions to courts and judgments are often learned, analysing both precedents and a range of other forms of publications from diverse sources of scholarship; like many other areas, law is properly to be viewed as an embedded discipline.[10] Scholarly discourse has become more diverse and the conceptualization of what constitutes scholarship needs to reflect such social changes, as well as how we now acquire knowledge.

Etymologically,[11] 'scholars' are pupils in a school but by extension they are also persons devoted to learning or 'learned persons', perhaps persons aspiring to be, or appearing to be, learned or knowledgeable.[12] While there was a longstanding tradition of respect for scholarship and scholars in ancient societies such as Greece and Rome,[13] many within contemporary life also identify benefit from being viewed as scholarly. There can be a caché for politicians, academics, journalists, institutions, professionals of all kinds, and many within the

---

[5] Jacob Bronowski, *Science and Human Values* (London: Faber & Faber, 1956), p. 75.

[6] Defined by Aristotle as 'a phrase signifying a thing's essence': *Topics* 1, 5.

[7] See Fabrizio Macagno, 'Definitions in Law' (2010) 2 *Bulletin Suisse de Linguistique Appliquée* 199.

[8] The term 'academy' (Greek ακαδημια) has its origin in Plato's school of philosophy, founded in approximately 385 BC at Akademia, a sanctuary of Athena, the goddess of wisdom and skill, north of Athens in Greece. Plato's immediate successors as 'scholarch' of *Akademia* were Speusippus (347–339 BC), Xenocrates (339–314 BC), Ptolemon (314–269 BC), Crates (c 269–266 BC), and Arcesilaus (c 266–240 BC).

[9] See Gill Nicholls, *The Challenge to Scholarship: Rethinking Learning, Teaching and Research* (New York: Routledge, 2005).

[10] See eg Mauro Zamboni, *Law and Politics: A Dilemma for Contemporary Legal Theory* (New York: Springer, 2007); Allen F Repko, *Interdisciplinary Research: Process and Theory* (New York: Sage Publications, 2011), ch. 2; Patricia Ewick, Robert A Kagan, and Austin Sarat (eds), *Social Science, Social Policy and the Law* (New York: Russell Sage Foundation, 1999).

[11] Latin: schola; LL scholaris: OF: escolier; OE: scolere.

[12] See Karl M Wiig, *Knowledge Management* (Arlington, Tx, Schema Press, 1993).

[13] See Robin Osborne (ed), *Studies in Ancient Greek and Roman Society* (Cambridge: Cambridge University Press, 2004).

general community, to be seen to possess information beyond that of the ordinary person, to be able to engage in discourse about it, and to be capable of applying it to needs, difficulties, and challenges. As Sir Francis Bacon identified in 1597, '*ipsa scientia potestas est*'—knowledge itself is power.[14] The advantages arising from being regarded as scholarly extend to prestige, popularity, and vocational, commercial, and social advancement. An example of questionable behaviour in this regard is the buying and selling of degrees at prestigious universities.[15]

In countries such as Australia—which has significant undercurrents of anti-intellectualism, at best a modest support for research and development, and a propensity to engage in schadenfreude[16] or cutting down of tall poppies[17]—scholarliness is less sought after as an accolade than in Europe, Middle Eastern, and North American cultures. However, the possession and wielding of scholarliness remain a competitive advantage in many contexts in all countries.

This fact creates the temptation to orchestrate the appearance of scholarship without the required investment of time, research, rigour, and originality to achieve the substance. Outside the tertiary sector, this can occur in the commercial environment, including in accounting firms that do forensic work or in institutes of forensic medicine or in scientific research establishments. For those aspiring to be successful politicians in Russia, the preparedness to engage in plagiarism has been asserted by Sergei Parkhomenko to be part of the quest for kudos: 'To them it is just part of the trappings of power: a Brioni suit, a BMW car, a state award, a Breguet watch, a beautiful blonde by his side, a PhD degree'.[18]

Importantly though, in the contemporary environment, factors are at play additional to those that previously existed. As Rehn has identified, cheating, the unwarranted taking advantage of others' work in one form or another, and the resort to short-cuts have become common in many theatres of scholarly endeavour:

> It isn't difficult to cheat in science. In the social sciences, it is exceptionally easy. If you want to, you can make up all your data, create a bogus organization, make up your informants, and invent all your interviews and field notes. You can tell stories and fantasize. It can be done.[19]

The propensity to engage in diverse forms of unethical conduct within the many areas of scholarship is the subject of this book which is about the scholars who are alleged not to have conformed to the somewhat idealized view of scholarliness promulgated by Bronowski. It deals with those who are asserted to have defiled the honourable traditions of the academy

---

14 See Francis Bacon, *Meditationes Sacrae* in James Speddin et al. (ed), *The Works of Francis Bacon*, 14.95; 79. For a discussion of this see Jose Maria Rodriguez Garcia, 'Scientia Potestas Est—Knowledge in Power: Francis Bacon to Michel Foucault' (2001) 28(1) *Neohelicon* 109.

15 See, for example, Iranian Interior Minister, Ali Kordan, who in due course admitted that an honorary degree he claimed to have received from Oxford University was not genuine: see 'Iran Minister Retracts Oxon Claim' (30 September 2008) *BBC News:* <http://news.bbc.co.uk/2/hi/middle_east/7644381.stm> [accessed 18 Dec 2015]; 'Iranian MPs Sack Ahmadinejad Ally Over Fake Oxford Degree' (5 November 2008) *The Guardian*: <http://www.theguardian.com/world/2008/nov/05/ali-kordan-fake-oxford-degree> [accessed 18 Dec 2015].

16 See Wilco W van Dijk and Jaap W Ouwerkerk, *Schadenfreude: Understanding Pleasure at the Misfortune of Others* (Cambridge: Cambridge University Press, 2013), 6.

17 A concept made popular by New South Wales Premier Jack Lang in 1931 who described his egalitarian policies as 'cutting the heads off tall poppies' but traceable back to Herodotus, *The Histories*, 5: [92]f; Aristotle, *Politics*, Bk 3: 1284a; Livy, *History of Rome*, Bk 1. See also Norman T Feather, 'Attitudes Towards the High Achiever: The Fall of the Tall Poppy' (1989) 41(3) *Australian Journal of Psychology* 239.

18 See Masha Lipman, 'Russia's Dissertation-Fraud Muckrakers' (9 March 2013) *The New Yorker*: <http://www.newyorker.com/news/news-desk/russias-dissertation-fraud-muckrakers> [accessed 18 Dec 2015].

19 Alf Rehn, *The Scholar's Progress: Essays on Academic Life and Survival* (iUniverse, 2006), 5.

and of scholarly endeavour and into whose behaviour it has become necessary to inquire and whose misconduct (if proved) it is important to discourage. This volume deals with notorious examples of such allegations but is important to observe that while mud can unfairly attach to those the subject of allegations, some against whom scholarly misconduct has been alleged are wholly innocent. Allegations against others have never been proved. Thus, care needs to be taken in the drawing of any adverse inferences merely because scholars figure in the pages within this book.

The following pages also wrestle with what constitutes ethical conduct amongst contemporary scholars, including academics employed within universities. It analyses the proliferation of research misconduct (Chapters 2 and 3), conflict of interest (Chapter 4), and plagiarism (Chapter 6). It also deals with the less commonly identified issue of scholarly misconduct engaged in by a small percentage of academics and others who provide forensic expertise for the courts (Chapter 5), and the continuing debates about when sexual relationships between staff and students or between senior staff and junior staff cross the line into constituting sexual misconduct (Chapter 9). It grapples with the contentious issue of dishonesty within scholarship, focusing upon ownership of work product (Chapter 7) and also reflects on the role that alcohol and other substances can have upon health and safety within the scholarly workplace, as well as the ethics of research into intoxicating substances (Chapter 10). It acknowledges limitations upon what is acceptable to the community in terms of disputation, denigration, and offensive utterances amongst scholars and explores the controversial issue of the location of lines of delineation in respect of such matters (Chapter 8). It also identifies the role of the internal informer, 'the whistleblower' or 'bell-ringer', as fundamental to ventilation about each of these matters and scrutinizes the need for judicious nurturing of such a role to promote effective investigation of scholarly misconduct (Chapter 11). Its final chapter argues for the creation of a new culture of honesty and openness within research institutions—both the academy and private enterprise research bodies. It contends that value needs to be accorded to publication of disproofs, as well as proofs, and urges the creation of adequately funded and supported disciplinary and regulatory oversight entities (Chapter 12).

Research Integrity

A broad approach is also taken in the following pages to the definition of 'research' which, in accordance with the December 2011 Tri-Agency Framework for the Responsible Conduct of Research in Canada, can be regarded straightforwardly as being '[a]n undertaking intended to extend knowledge through a disciplined inquiry or systematic investigation'.[20] This is consonant with the definition of 'knowledge' employed by the United States Supreme Court in *Daubert v Merrell Dow Pharmaceuticals Inc*—connoting 'more than subjective belief or unsupported speculation... [It] applies to any body of known facts or to any body of ideas inferred from such facts or accepted as truths on good grounds'.[21]

The focus in this work is not on cheating by undergraduate students, although it is apparent that such dishonesty can be tracked in retrospect to transition seamlessly into comparable conduct as a postgraduate and later into research activities conducted in other parts of a career. It also does not deal with allegations of watering down of scholastic standards in

[20] Government of Canada, Panel on Responsible Conduct of Research, *The Tri-Agency Framework: Responsible Conduct of Research* (2011) 16, available at: <http://www.rcr.ethics.gc.ca/eng/policy-politique/framework-cadre/#1> [accessed 18 Dec 2015].

[21] 509 US 579 at 590 (1993); see also *Honeysett v The Queen* (2014) HCA 29 at [23].

contexts such as the excessive nurturing of overseas students.[22] Nor does it concentrate upon recruitment and retention issues in respect of full fee-paying students, although these can incorporate corrupt practices.[23] Rather, it deals with issues that arise in the work undertaken and the transaction of relationships that are part and parcel of scholarly life.

A review of scholarly misconduct suggests that it is comparatively rare for a scholar to engage in just the one form of lack of scholarly integrity (eg, only plagiarism, rather than also misrepresentation of qualifications, or conflict of interest, or research fraud) or to initiate a one-off intellectually deceptive enterprise. This should not be regarded as unduly surprising—traits of personality,[24] such as disingenuousness, narcissism, irresponsibility, and grandiosity, are relatively stable and tend to exist across different contexts at a similar stage in a person's life; such patterns cannot usually be compartmentalized. Research fraud, insensitivity to conflicts of interest, and plagiarism frequently co-exist and can be part of a general lack of respect for others' entitlements—a preparedness to place an individual's own interests selfishly ahead of those of others. A contribution of this book is the demonstration that scholarly misconduct can be extraordinary, far-reaching in its consequences, and deeply ethically offensive; it is not a quaint or eccentric phenomenon. Rather, it has become a widespread, recidivist manifestation of intellectual dishonesty, often hard both to detect and to regulate effectively. Scholarly misconduct has been quietly tolerated for a long while (and sometimes still) but has now become so damaging a phenomenon that confidence in scholarship requires urgent remedial responses, not just corralling and management.

The aetiologies for lack of scholarly integrity in respect of the selected topics are explored within this book. It is essential to understand reasons and motivations if we are to take effective steps to reduce the incidence of scholarly misconduct. It is apparent that they are diverse and often complex. Some are personal to the scholar, in terms of the individual's personality, or their drive to be or be seen to be successful. There are external pressures too. Some arise from imperatives for the outputs of scholarliness. These can come in many forms—commercial, promotional, psychological, to name but some.[25] The need for students to satisfy assessment requirements is obvious and part of their responsibilities, but less well-appreciated is the contemporary requirement for maintenance of position in most universities that employees publish a designated number of fruits of their scholarly endeavour. This is often described in terms of the requirement to publish or lose one's employment.[26] The

---

22 Linton Besser and Peter Cronau, 'Degrees of Deception' (21 April 2015) *Four Corners*: <http://www.abc.net.au/4corners/stories/2015/04/20/4217741.htm> [accessed 18 Dec 2015]; Australian Government Productivity Commission, International Education Services (Canberra: AGPS, April 2015), <http://www.pc.gov.au/research/completed/international-education/international-education.pdf> [accessed 18 Dec 2015].

23 Independent Commission against Corruption, 'Learning the Hard Way: Managing Corruption Risks Associated with International Students at Universities in NSW' (Sydney: ICAC, April 2015), <http://www.icac.nsw.gov.au/media-centre/media-releases/article/4781> [accessed 18 Dec 2015].

24 See in respect of certain traits of personality Brent W Roberts, Kate E Walton, and Wolfgang Viechtbauer, 'Patters of Mean-Level Change in Personality Traits Across the Life Course: A Meta-Analysis of Longitudinal Studies' (2006) 132(1) *Psychological Bulletin* 1.

25 See eg Tracey Bretag, 'Publish or Perish: Ramifications for Online Academic Publishing' in Laura A Wankel, and Charles Wankel (eds), *Misbehavior Online in Higher Education* (Bradford: Emerald Publishing, 2012).

26 The phrase 'publish or perish' appeared in a non-academic context in a 1932 book: Harold J Coolidge and Robert H Lord, *Archibald Cary Coolidge: Life and Letters* (New York: Houghton Mifflin Company, 1932) 308. In 1938, the phrase appeared in a college-related publication: *Association of American Colleges Bulletin*, vol 24 (1938) 465. The expression also appears in Logan Wilson, *The Academic Man: A Study in the Sociology of a Profession* (Oxford: Oxford University Press, 1942) 63, 197. See also Eugene Garfield, 'What is the Primordial Reference for the Phrase "Publish or Perish"?' (1996) 10(12) *The Scientist* 11; S Rajaesekaran, 'Publish to Flourish: Is it Corrupting Science?' (August 2012) (1) *Bone & Joint* 360 5.

impetus for expert witnesses to take a particular position under cover of learnedness and scholarly authority in forensic matters—for instance, to assist the prosecution—can also be intense, and short-cuts and rationalizations, abandonment of neutrality, and fabrication of results can be an outcome.

Disciplinary repercussions and a variety of forms of litigation in recent years have highlighted the risks posed to scholarly integrity when academic proprieties are breached, when research methodologies are seriously defective or rationalizations permitted, and when probity is not accorded high standing. This book characterizes such conduct as 'scholarly deviance' and endeavours to place it in a workplace, psychological, and historical perspective. It does so through tales of misconduct from a variety of jurisdictions and sometimes in bizarre scenarios—painting of mice, colouring in of toad members, and planting of lichens on an obscure island off the Scottish coast. In doing so it highlights a serious and troubling propensity on the part of significant numbers of scholars to attempt in brazen and indefensible ways to mislead others in order to make their theories plausible, accepted and influential, to ignore conflicts of interest, or to take advantage illicitly of others' work.

The Scholarly Environment

Universities,[27] research institutions, forensic laboratories, and even professions, have not enjoyed an unsullied history in dealing robustly with frauds, distortions, dishonesty, plagiarism, conflicts of interest, and sexual predation. Generally, they have attempted to do so internally until malcontent and internal or external aggrievement have required them to do otherwise.

Many high-profile examples of allegations of scholarly misconduct will be adverted to in the succeeding pages, some well-known, some less so, some modern, some in the past, some proven, some not. One of the focuses of the book's analysis of such instances is upon how institutions have responded to such behaviour. The walls of the academy have been high in many senses and universities have traditionally expressed an assertive preference for informal self-regulation. Often this has been for self-serving and self-protective reasons. Too often both universities and research institutions have attempted to address threats to their reputation behind the scenes, in a collegiate or avuncular way, so as not to impair perceptions of the stature of the institution and so as to allow the perpetrator a dignified outcome or, in some instances, a respectful and mutually comfortable exit. A comparable fraternalist phenomenon has been especially pronounced, and exposed as such in latter times, in relation to misconduct by health practitioners and to abuses committed by the clergy—it has existed in many vocations, including within the academy.

Recent years have seen the reduction in the significance of traditional forms of teaching within university culture and have prioritized the publishing of research that has been funded by external sources. As was observed in a report in relation to the tragic events surrounding the homicidal conduct of Dr Valery Fabrikant at Concordia University:

> [T]here is a risk that a production-driven research culture will tempt people to engage not only in undesirable modalities of research but in actual falsification and fraud. Several recent and highly publicized instances of scientific fraud have attracted the attention of the

[27] See the useful discussion of the evolution of universities, their mission statements and their involvement in research in Chapter 2 of Ann Monotti and Sam Ricketson, *Universities and Intellectual Property: Ownership and Exploitation* (Oxford: Oxford University Press, 2003). See also Walter Rüegg, 4 vols, *A History of the University in Europe* (Cambridge: Cambridge University Press, 1992).

scholarly community, and measures to prevent it are now under discussion within universities, granting agencies, and the editorial boards of scientific journals... [28]

The milieu of academia is no longer as removed from the ordinary world as it once was and some would still prefer it to be. It intersects with the spheres of politics, business, the media, and the professions in multiple ways. All are affected by commercial, regulatory, and legal interests which constitute a major source of funding and thereby commercial viability.[29] Each of these intersections has the potential to provide an opportunity or even a fillip for scholarly misconduct.

There is also the phenomenon of private universities that are profit-oriented. The Dawkins reforms in Australia flowing from the report of 1987 not only proposed amalgamation of the then 19 universities[30] with 51 advanced education institutions; they initiated a new era of increased executive control over academic freedom and a new level of scrutiny and imposition of accountability over the quality of the academic work product.[31] Astor has described these phenomena as 'transformative cultural changes'.[32] Thornton[33] has been more negative, arguing that international reforms to universities, including corporatization of the academy, have led to corrosive management practices that have alienated academics from one another and led to bullying and harassment of staff, as well as other forms of misconduct perpetrated against academics, sometimes by their colleagues, albeit under pressures from government. It is also clear that pressures to publish and to continue to publish have contributed to some researchers perceiving themselves to be under unwarranted workplace pressures; they have played a role in the compromising of scholarly values (including plagiarism of others' work, vanity publishing, ghost-writing, gift-authorship, and self-plagiarism) and on occasion falsification of data.[34] As Dr Tracey Bretag, an academic at the University of South Australia and editor of the *International Journal for Educational Integrity*, put it in relation to the University of Queensland research controversies involving Professor Murdoch and Dr Barwood:[35]

> The intense pressure on academics to continue to publish in ridiculous timeframes often under-resourced while having heavy teaching loads, I think when you create that environment when there is so much pressure I guess that's when maybe people might be tempted to take shortcuts even when they know it's the wrong thing to do... I think these sorts of breaches we might see more and more of because there is so much pressure on researchers to publish in quality journals.[36]

[28] Harry W Arthurs, Roger Blais, and Jon Thompson, *Integrity in Scholarship: A Report to Concordia University* (April 1994) 7: <https://schoolshooters.info/sites/default/files/Arthurs_report%20on%20%20Fabrikant.pdf> [accessed 18 Dec 2015].

[29] See Ronald Bailey, *Scrutinizing Industry-Funded Science: The Crusade Against Conflicts of Interest* (New York: American Council on Science and Health, 2008); Marc A Rodwin, *Medicine, Money and Morals: Physicians' Conflicts of Interest* (New York: Oxford University Press, 1993)

[30] There are now 40 universities in Australia: <http://www.australianuniversities.com.au/list/> [accessed 18 Dec 2015].

[31] See Simon Marginson, *Educating Australia: Government, Economy and Citizen Since 1960* (Melbourne: Cambridge University Press, 1997).

[32] Hilary Astor, 'Australian Universities in Court: Causes, Costs and Consequences of Increasing Litigation' (2008) 19(3) *Australasian Dispute Resolution Journal* 158.

[33] Margaret Thornton, 'Corrosive Leadership (Or Bullying by Another Name): A Corollary of the Corporatised Academy?' (2004) 17(2) *Australian Journal of Labour Law* 161.

[34] See Sandeep B Bavdekar, 'Authorship Issues' (2012) 29(1) *Lung India* 76.

[35] Who are subject to criminal charges which have not yet been determined—see Chapter 3.

[36] Elise Worthington, 'University of Queensland Investigates Fresh Claims of Research Misconduct by Former Academics', *ABC News*, 8 November 2013: <http://www.abc.net.au/news/2013-11-07/uq-investigates-fresh-claims-of-research-misconduct/5077276> [accessed 18 Dec 2015].

In addition, new factors are at play in the tertiary environment. Some of these have the potential to erode the efficacy of checks and balances, such as the rigour of peer reviewing and of editorial oversight in scholarly journals. For instance, the temptations are substantial for journals that compete for primacy in the intellectual marketplace to publish articles that contain what appear to be research breakthroughs. The impact factor, which is determined by citation rates, is a yardstick for the success of scholarly journals which has the potential to compromise the rigour of reviewing processes.[37] In part it was this, together with concerns about pressures exerted by the commercial realities, which led Marcia Angell famously to assert in 2009:

> [I]t is no longer possible to believe much of the clinical research that is published, or to rely on the judgment of trusted physicians or authoritative medical guidelines. I take no pleasure in this conclusion, which I reached slowly and reluctantly over my two decades as an editor of *The New England Journal of Medicine.*[38]

Temptations and Compromises

The mixing of business with academia runs the risk of compromising the integrity and independence of universities by reason of conflicts of interest at both a personal and an institutional level. A consequence can be an adverse impact on the integrity of scholarly research. The controversies in relation to the conduct of experiments by a team led by Gilles-Eric Séralini, a Professor of Molecular Biology at the University of Caen in France, in relation to Monsanto's NK603 maize (a form of rootworm resistant maize/corn) and a herbicide given to rats, suggesting that it may be carcinogenic, are exemplary. The team did not have a financial conflict of interest in respect of the outcomes from their research, but the research occurred in a context with major commercial repercussions and it was highly publicized and contested. A documentary film was created by the research team to promote the research, a book was written, and extensive media coverage solicited—all of them taking place in the sensitive political context of the ongoing debates about the safety of the genetic modification of crops.

Afterwards the work was enveloped in controversy with over 700 scientists signing a petition calling on Séralini to release all the data from his research and questioning the study's integrity. Russia and Kazakhstan halted imports of the maize.[39] In due course the key paper was repudiated by food standards agencies (including the European Food Safety Authority, which identified serious design and methodology defects in the study) and in November 2013 *Food and Chemical Toxicology* retracted the paper that was the focus of the research after the authors declined to withdraw it.[40] Séralini and his colleagues retaliated to the impugning of

---

[37] See Harvey Marcovitch, 'Editors, Publishers, Impact Factors, and Reprint Income' (2010) 7(1) *PLoS Med:* e1000364; Andreas Lundh, Marija Barbateskovic, Asbjorn Hróbjartsson, and Peter C Gøtzsche, 'Conflicts of Interest at Medical Journals: The Influence of Industry-Supported Randomised Trials on the Journal Impact Factor' (2010) 7 *PLoS Med:* e354.

[38] Marcia Angell, 'Drug Companies and Doctors: A Story of Corruption' (15 January 2009) *The New York Review of Books* 56: <http://www.nybooks.com/articles/archives/2009/jan/15/drug-companies-doctorsa-story-of-corruption/> [accessed 18 Dec 2015].

[39] Deniza Gertsberg, 'Séralini's GMO Study Ignites a War', *GMO Journal*, 14 November 2012: <http://gmo-journal.com/2012/11/14/seralinis-gmo-study-ignites-a-war/> [accessed 18 Dec 2015].

[40] Barbara Casassus, 'Study Linking GM Maize to Rat Tumours is Retracted', *Nature*, 28 November 2013: <http://www.nature.com/news/study-linking-gm-maize-to-rat-tumours-is-retracted-1.14268> [accessed 18 Dec 2015]; Kate Kelland (Reuters), 'Controversial GMO Study by Gilles-Eric Seralini Retracted', *Huffington Post*, 28 November 2013: <http://www.huffingtonpost.com/2013/12/02/gmo-study-seralini-retracted_n_4357450.html> [accessed 18 Dec 2015].

their work by suing Marc Fellous, President of the French Association of Plant Biotechnology, for defamation. They succeeded in their quest for vindication, but only a symbolic one euro in damages was awarded, as sought by Séralini, together with a fine on probation of €1000 and €4000 in court fees.[41] Regardless of whether the scholarly work was seriously flawed, as Fellous alleged, and Séralini et al denied, there can be no doubt that the political disputation, and major financial interests, in relation to genetic modification of crops constituted a backdrop to what became an unedifying scholarly dispute (in part played out in the courts) that was highly influenced by collateral factors.[42]

The collision of business and academia can also result in compromises (or the appearance of compromises) to integrity and research independence. An example of this risk became apparent during 2011 concerning the London School of Economics (LSE), which had accepted a large donation from a charity run by Saif al-Islam Gaddafi (who was sentenced to death in Libya in July 2015), the son of the former Libyan President, Muammar al-Gaddafi.[43] (see Chapter 4, p 193) The origin of the money paid to the LSE may have been money paid to the dictator's son as bribes, according to an inquiry conducted by Lord Woolf, the former Lord Chief Justice of England and Wales. Saif al-Islam was allowed to lay out 'objectives and expectations' for the research programme funded by the charity, according to leaked LSE documents. Lord Woolf expressed himself carefully, refraining from drawing conclusions as to whether there was or would have been excessive influence by the donor over the use of the funds from Saif's foundation. He acknowledged that universities in the modern environment have to compete internationally for students, funding, and academics. However, and importantly, he observed that this poses ethical and reputational challenges, requiring infrastructures to 'protect the core principles of any university which is operating on a more expansive and international market'.[44] He analogized the role of the modern university to that of a global company and concluded that proper structures of governance are needed to protect academic integrity against influence from the interests of private donors.[45]

It is apparent that the once hidden world of the academy which used to be exposed to oversight only at the behest of the university concerned[46] is now both more public than it used to be and more subject to criticism and evaluation by the media, corruption investigators, ombudsmen, and the courts.[47] For instance, available data show that there were four reported cases of litigation in Australia involving universities during the 1960s. During the 1970s there were nine such cases. In the years immediately after 1985 such litigation took place between three and five times per year. The rate of litigation increased dramatically during the 1990s, and in 2005 alone there were 92 court hearings during the calendar year. This

---

41 Mae-Wan Ho, 'Victory for Independent Science' (26 January 2011) Institute of Science in Society: <http://www.i-sis.org.uk/victoryForIndependentScience.php> [accessed 18 Dec 2015].

42 See below at 183, for issues relating to the decision of La Trobe University in Melbourne, Australia, to take sponsorship from Swisse Vitamins.

43 See Jeevan Vasagar, 'Gaddafi donation to LSE may have come from bribes, inquiry finds', *The Guardian*, 30 November 2011: <http://www.theguardian.com/education/2011/nov/30/gaddafi-donation-lse-bribes-inquiry> [accessed 18 Dec 2015].

44 Lord Justice Woolf, *An Inquiry into the LSE's Links with Libya and Lessons to be Learned* (October 2011) 1.25: <http://www.lse.ac.uk/newsAndMedia/woolf/pdf/woolfReport.pdf> [accessed 18 Dec 2015].

45 Ibid, 1.25–1.26.

46 See Patty Kamvounias and Sally Varnham, 'Legal Challenges to University Decisions Affecting Students in Australian Courts and Tribunals' (2010) 34(1) *Melbourne University Law Review* 140; Patty Kamvounias and Sally Varnham, 'In-House or In Court? Legal Challenges to University Decisions' (2006) 18(1) *Education and the Law* 1; cp Gail Mason, 'Harm, Harassment and Sexuality' (2002) 26(3) *Melbourne University Law Review* 596.

47 See Astor, above n 32. For an example of the role of the University Visitor, see *Re La Trobe University; Ex parte Wild* [1987] VR 447; *Thomson v University of London* (1864) 33 LJ Ch 625.

phenomenon is mirrored in many countries. Astor has commented that the changes '[mirror] the increase in complaints received by ombuds and confirms their concerns, and the concerns of academics and other observers, that university disputing is increasing markedly'.[48]

A percentage of the increased incidence of litigation involving the tertiary sector is attributable to scholars' malcontent with, and difficulty in adjusting to, the managerial demands for output and efficiencies in the 'new academy'. Other social changes are playing a role too. The levels of deference previously characteristic of the attitudes of students towards academics, especially senior academics, are nowhere near as pronounced. Conduct perceived or experienced as harassing or improper, whether sexually, racially, or otherwise exploitative or offensive, is tending to result in the preferring of complaints and demands for action by university authorities. In turn this has fed into an increasing incidence of formal investigation and litigation in relation to academic misconduct. Arguably, the combination of these phenomena is leading to a reduced level of respect for and trust in scholars and their work product.

The Social Context for Scholarly Misconduct

This is not to say though that the general community is indifferent to accuracy and honesty as valued ethical qualities. The public and somewhat moralistic expostulations that erupted in the United Kingdom in 2014 after Shia LaBoeuf was revealed not only to have plagiarized graphic novelist Daniel Clowes's work in a short film but then as a result of the terms of his apology for plagiarizing, give an indication of the public's view of the unacceptability of plagiarism.[49] Similar reactions are evident in Australia over a period of time arising from the Ern Malley affair, the Helen Demidenko scandal, and the Andrew Slattery controversy. Each provides a perspective on how our community views the perpetrating of dishonesty, whether outright fraud or a more innocent hoax—they show us that authenticity is a quality we continue to value and whose transgression we continue to find offensive.

The Ern Malley affair was a literary hoax directed towards ridiculing modernist poetry and, although the quality of the poetry of James McAuley and Harold Stewart was acclaimed by some, the deception in their methods was castigated by others.[50] It was emulated by the United States physicist, Alan Sokal, who in 1996 succeeded in having published a spoof article in the postmodern journal, *Social Science*.[51] His purpose was later described by him to be to demonstrate that 'a leading North American journal of cultural studies...would publish an article liberally salted with nonsense if (a) it contained the right buzzwords and (b) flattered the editors' ideological preconceptions'.[52] While his hoax was equally successful as the Ern Malley affair, it did not prompt as much criticism.

---

[48] Astor, above n 32, 160.

[49] See Jenn Selby, 'Shia LaBoeuf retires from public life after plagiarism scandal sparks bizarre (also plagiarised) apology spree' (10 January 2014) *The Independent*: <http://www.independent.co.uk/news/people/news/shia-labeouf-announces-retirement-from-public-life-after-plagiarism-scandal-sparks-bizarre-apology-spree-9051553.html> [accessed 19 Dec 2015].

[50] See eg Robert Hughes in his foreword to Michael Heyward, *The Ern Malley Affair* (St Lucia: University of Queensland Press, 1993). See also Christine Wertheim, 'The Fall and Rise of Ernest Lalor Malley' (Spring 2009), Issue 33, *Cabinet Magazine*: <http://cabinetmagazine.org/issues/33/wertheim.php> [accessed 19 Dec 2015].

[51] Alan Sokal, 'Transgressing the Boundaries: Toward a Transformative Hermeneutics of Quantum Gravity' (Spring/Summer 1996) 46/47 *Social Science* 217.

[52] See Alan Sokal, *Beyond the Hoax: Science, Philosophy and Culture* (Oxford: Oxford University Press, 2008).

The situation with the Australian lawyer, Helen Demidenko/Darville/Dale, who pretended in *The Hand That Signed the Paper*[53] not just to be of Ukrainian background (to the extent of dressing up in Ukrainian national costume for publicity purposes) but to be providing a factual account of events in the Ukraine based on the experiences of authentic survivors, was regarded as offensive by reason of the misimpressions deliberately orchestrated by the author about herself, the issues involved, and the literary product itself.[54] The author was later sacked from the *Courier Mail* for plagiarism.[55]

In relation to the 2013 Slattery controversy, where a poet utilized the work of several others, passing it off as his own, general opinion was close to uniform—a series of the writer's prizes were taken away in spite of his defence that his poetry had deliberately incorporated others' work and phraseology. The difficulty was that he had given no signal that he was using the wording of Seamus Heaney, Charles Bukowski, Emily Dickinson, and Sylvia Plath as a literary device. His rationalizations—that he had written in the Ern Malley tradition and then that his poems were in the 'cento format', which is a collage of lines from other poems—were transparently an *ex post facto* confabulation. The result was disqualification from the Josephine Ulrick Prize and the Cardiff International Poetry Competition Prize, general condemnation, and, no doubt, grave difficulties in attracting future literary grants (he had received Australia Council grants of $15,000 each in 2008 and 2010). Poets Anthony Lawrence, Margie Cronin, and David Musgrave commented:

> Serial plagiarism seems to imply a lack of empathy and, in extreme cases, something like sociopathy. When exposed, some plagiarists say they are simply paying homage to other writers or use words like 'collage', 'cento' or 'sampling'. It seems that, even when the game is up and the evidence is irrefutable, the word 'plagiarism' just can't be uttered.[56]

Ultimately, what has been found offensive and socially unacceptable in artistic, as well as in scholarly, frauds is the deception inherent in them which makes us feel tricked and demeaned after the truth has emerged. Intellectually, there has been unfairness in the usage of others' work. Sometimes there has been abuse of public moneys, as, for instance, when the

[53] Helen Demidenko, *The Hand That Signed the Paper* (St Leonards, NSW: Allen & Unwin, 1995). The book won the Miles Franklin Award and the Australian Literary Society Gold Medal. It was lauded for its literary qualities by Andrew Riemer, *The Demidenko Debate* (St Leonards, NSW: Allen and Unwin, 1996). The Demidenko scandal bore features in common with the earlier Marlo Morgan controversy in which Morgan (Marlo Morgan, *Mutant Message Down Under: A Woman's Journey into Dreamtime Australia*, New York: HarperCollins, 1994) purported to tell an autobiographical tale of being kidnapped by a lost Aboriginal tribe. See Melissa Katsoulis, *Telling Tales: A History of Literary Hoaxes* (London: Hachette, 2013); Cath Ellis, 'Helping Yourself: Marlo Morgan and the Fabrication of Indigenous Wisdom' in Maggie Nolan and Carrie Dawson (eds), *Who's Who?: Hoaxes, Imposture and Identity Crises in Australian Literature* (Brisbane: University of Queensland Press, 2004); Larissa Behrendt, 'In Your Dreams: Cultural Appropriation, *Popular Culture and Colonialism*' (1998) 4 *Law, Text and Culture* 256.

[54] See Matthew Rimmer, 'The Demidenko Affair: Copyright Law, Plagiarism and Ridicule' (2000) 5(3) *Media and Arts Law Review* 159; Sue Vice, *Holocaust Fiction* (New York: Routledge, 2003), 143; Robert Manne, *The Culture of Forgetting: Helen Demidenko and the Holocaust* (Melbourne: Text Publishing, 1996); Michael Heyward, 'The Demidenko Scandal' (1996), Issue 1, *Australian Humanities Review*: <http://www.australianhumanitiesreview.org/archive/demidenko/heyward.1.html>; [accessed 19 Dec 2015]; Jeff Sparrow, 'The return of Helen Demidenko: from literary hoaxer to political operator' (8 July 2015) *The Guardian*: <http://www.theguardian.com/commentisfree/2015/jul/08/the-return-of-helen-demidenko-on-culture-war-and-the-value-of-truth> [accessed 19 Dec 2015].

[55] See Editorial, 'Imitators and Fabricators' (1996) 20(50–51) *Journal of Australian Studies* 1; Therese-Marie Meyer, *Where Fiction Ends: Four Scandals of Literary Identity Construction* (Würzburg: Königshausen & Neumann, 2006), 137.

[56] See Susan Wyndham, 'Plagiarism the word that can't be uttered', *The Sydney Morning Herald*, 13 September 2013: <http://www.smh.com.au/entertainment/books/plagiarism-the-word-that-cant-be-uttered-20130913-2tpha.html> [accessed 19 Dec 2015].

individual has contrived to be the beneficiary of awards, prizes, or grants. But it is the lack of authenticity, an attribute which, for good reason, we continue to value highly,[57] that is most repugnant when fraudsters and plagiarists pretend and deceive. Essentially it is our trust that has been breached and we have been duped. This is, and should be, difficult to forgive.

Understanding Scholarly Impropriety

One reason for trying to gain a more sophisticated understanding about the misconduct of scholars is to learn who is responsible for it and why they engage in it. Another is to appreciate its impact and thus what can be done to investigate whether it has occurred and to take effective prophylactic steps.

Prevalence studies have suggested that research fraud may be a relatively common phenomenon. A 1993 study claimed that 75 per cent of university students engage in some form of research misconduct.[58] If this were generalizable, it would establish a troubling base from which widespread later impropriety could emerge. In a meta-analysis of survey data about the phenomenon of falsification and fabrication of research, only 1.97 per cent of scientists admitted to having fabricated, falsified, or modified data or results at least once, but up to 33.7 per cent admitted to having engaged in a variety of dubious research practices. In a survey asking about the behaviour of colleagues, admission rates were 14.12 per cent (N = 12, 95 per cent CI: 9.91–19.72) for falsification, and up to 72 per cent for other questionable research practices.[59] In a sample of postdoctoral fellows at the University of California, San Francisco, 3.4 per cent admitted they had modified data in the past and 17 per cent were willing to select or omit data to improve their results.[60] However, 81 per cent of biomedical trainees stated that they were willing to select, omit, or fabricate data to win a grant or publish a paper.[61] This suggests a cultural problem of troubling proportions, although it needs to be acknowledged that the relevant definitions for the various forms of conduct examined differed significantly.

In addition, since the turn of the millennium the activist investigations of Vroniplag in Germany and Dissernet in Russia have unearthed multiple examples of plagiarism amongst politicians holding postgraduate degrees. This has come at a cost for many senior political figures in both countries, as well as in others.

The more we can understand the psychological factors that generate or predispose to scholarly misconduct, the better the chances we will be able to devise strategies to reduce its incidence. As Ramamoorti and Olson observed in a cognate context: 'Fraud is a human endeavor, involving deception, purposeful intent, intensity of desire, risk of apprehension, violation of trust, rationalization etc. So it is important to understand the psychological factors that might influence the behavior of fraud perpetrators.'[62] In Chapter 2 a case study

57 See Charles B Guignon, *On Being Authentic* (New York: Psychology Press, 2004).

58 Donald L McCabe and Linda K Trevino, 'Academic Dishonesty: Honor Codes and Other Contextual Influences' (1993) 64(5) *Journal of Higher Education* 522.

59 Daniele Fanelli, 'How Many Scientists Fabricate and Falsify Research? A Systematic Review and Meta-Analysis of Survey Data' (2009) 4(5) *PLoS ONE* e5738.

60 Susan Eastwood, Pamela Derish, Evangeline Leash, and Stephen Ordway, 'Ethical Issues in Biomedical Research: Perceptions and Practices of Postdoctoral Research Fellows Responding to a Survey' (1996) 2(1) *Science and Engineering Ethics* 89.

61 Michael W Kalichman and Paul J Friedman, 'A Pilot Study of Biomedical Trainees' Perceptions Concerning Research Ethics' (1992) 67(11) *Academic Medicine* 769.

62 Sri Ramamoorti and William Olsen, 'Fraud: The Human Factor' (July 2007) 23(6) *Financial Executive*, Retrieved from <http://international.westlaw.com> on 7 January 2015.

of research fraud is presented, utilizing the autobiographical account of the social scientist, Diederik Stapel. It is followed by reference to the self-serving accounts of their conduct in books written by the discredited researchers William McBride and Andrew Wakefield, while in Chapter 6 the self-disclosures of Jayson Blair and his explanations for his conduct are reviewed. Each account constitutes a remarkable opportunity provided by the perpetrator's own words for gaining insight into the motives and rationalizations of persons who have been found to have engaged in significant intellectual dishonesty.

Difficulties have also emerged in relation to fraud and serious misconduct in the forensic areas. The jailing of Annie Dookhan (see Chapter 5) for manufacturing test results (apparently to impress her employers and to enhance her reputation for achieving in her scientific work for the prosecution, what others could not) has had major ramifications for drug convictions over a lengthy period in Massachusetts. Before that, forensic pathologist Dr Ralph Erdmann[63] also ultimately served jail time as a result of manufacturing significant numbers of fake autopsy results to assist the prosecution. These, and other cases of forensic misconduct suggest that a lack of integrity in the forensic context may, at least in part, also be generated by the desires for preferment or the obtaining of kudos within the workplace.

Responses to Scholarly Misconduct

In an important development in 2012 the United States First Circuit Court of Appeals in *United States ex rel Jones v Brigham and Women's Hospital*[64] overturned a first instance decision and permitted a potentially landmark case to be brought for research misconduct against not only high-profile senior academics in the Alzheimer's research area but also Harvard Medical School. The significance of the decision is that it enabled recourse to be had against not only the individual miscreant but also their employer. In turn, such exposure has the constructive potential to galvanize employers, such as universities and research institutions, to exercise closer supervision over the conduct of their employees.

In Australia investigations by New South Wales, Western Australian, and Queensland anti-corruption commissions have been initiated to evaluate claims of scholarly misconduct—including the turning of a blind eye to student plagiarism,[65] allegations of an academic offering marks for sex,[66] concerns arising from claims of conflict of interest and nepotism,[67] and later an allegation of faked research.[68] This constitutes a new form of quasi-legal accountability

[63] Roberto Suro, 'Ripples of a Pathologist's Misconduct in Graves and Courts of West Texas', *The New York Times*, 22 November 1992: <http://www.nytimes.com/1992/11/22/us/ripples-of-a-pathologist-s-misconduct-in-graves-and-courts-of-west-texas.html> [accessed 19 Dec 2015].

[64] 678 F 3d 72 (1st Cir, Mass, 2012) (No 10-2301).

[65] Independent Commission Against Corruption (NSW), *Report on Investigation into the University of Newcastle's Handling of Plagiarism Allegations* (Sydney, June 2005), available at: <http://www.icac.nsw.gov.au/investigations/past-investigations/investigationdetail/61> [accessed 19 Dec 2015].

[66] Corruption and Crime Commission (Western Australia), *Report on the Investigation of Alleged Public Sector Misconduct of Dr Nasrul Ameer Ali as a Sessional Academic Employed by Curtin University of Technology* (Perth, 2 September 2010) (Commissioner Len Roberts-Smith QC) ('the Ali Report'), <https://www.ccc.wa.gov.au/Publications/Reports/Published%20Reports%202010/Misconduct%20by%20Sessional%20Academic%20at%20Curtin%20University%20of%20Technology.pdf> [accessed 19 Dec 2015].

[67] Crime and Misconduct Commission (Queensland), *An Examination of Suspected Official Misconduct at the University of Queensland* (Brisbane, September 2013), available at: <http://www.ccc.qld.gov.au/research-and-publications/publications/misconduct/uq/an-examination-of-suspected-official-misconduct-at-the-university-of-queensland> [accessed 19 Dec 2015].

[68] See Rob Kidd, 'University of Queensland Scientists Accused of Falsifying Research', *Courier Mail*, 4 September 2013: <http://www.couriermail.com.au/news/queensland/university-of-queensland-scientists-

for the conduct of academics employed by tertiary institutions, as well as for the institutions themselves. It can result in devastatingly adverse publicity and, on occasions, be a precursor to the preferring of criminal charges.

Forensic misconduct too can have many manifestations, even as the basis for inquiries into convictions for criminal offences. In Canada the misconduct of the forensic pathologist Charles Smith[69] was ultimately accounted by the Goudge Inquiry as a product of a failure to appreciate that his role was not to support the prosecution in criminal cases, as well as a preparedness to give inappropriately unscientific evidence. It came at a serious cost in terms of the many cases in which evidence was found to have been unreliable.

In Australia, Robert Barnes, an expert in gunshot residue and explosives at the Victorian Forensic Science Centre, was investigated in 1993 for 'scientific misconduct', 'after serious concerns were raised about evidence he had given in a number of cases, and after an internal review of his cases had shown a persistent failure to follow established procedures for examining and recording evidence'.[70] No finding of such misconduct was ever made. However, subsequently in 2013–2014 the quality of his scientific work in the analysis of gunshot residue in a high-profile investigation into the assassination of a senior police officer, constituted important aspects of the terms of reference of the judicial inquiry into the conviction of the accused man many years previously.[71] In turn this resulted in a scathing report by Acting Justice Martin to the Full Court of the Australian Capital Territory (ACT) Supreme Court which critiqued the preparedness of the forensic scientist uncritically to assist the prosecution and recommended that the trial verdict 19 years before should be overturned.[72] The verdict in due course was quashed and a retrial ordered. The damage done to the reputation of forensic science for scholarly integrity and impartiality was serious.

Moves Towards Protecting Scholarly Integrity

Change is in the wind. There are many indications that there is decreasing contemporary tolerance for scholarly misconduct, whether it be the product of serious incompetence or bias, or whether dishonesty is unequivocally involved. Multiple politicians in a number of diverse parts of the world have lost their jobs when their plagiarism has been exposed. When scientists, doctors, and others are revealed to have engaged in research fraud, discussion is increasingly turning towards their being criminally prosecuted. Most prominently, this occurred in 2015 when in the United States Dong-Pyou Han was found guilty of misuse of $US19 million of research funds when he fabricated AIDS research with the proceeds. He was sentenced to 57 months' imprisonment.

accused-of-falsifying-research/story-fnihsrf2-1226709953275?nk=d0c34e45a0e29d2dad3689e68b232ce1> (viewed 7 January 2015).

[69] Stephen Goudge, *Inquiry into Pediatric Forensic Pathology in Ontario*, vol 1 (Ontario: Queen's Printer for Ontario, 2008) 14: <http://www.attorneygeneral.jus.gov.on.ca/inquiries/goudge/report/v1_en_pdf/Vol_1_Eng.pdf> [accessed 19 Dec 2015].

[70] Jack Waterford, 'Crucial Evidence Used in Eastman Trial Came from Expert Sacked in Victoria', *Canberra Times*, 7 November 2012: <http://www.canberratimes.com.au/act-news/crucial-evidence-used-in-eastman-trial-came-from-expert-sacked-in-victoria-20121106-28wod.html> [accessed 19 Dec 2015].

[71] Inquiry into the Conviction of David Harold Eastman for the Murder of Colin Stanley Winchester, 'Terms of Reference', available at: <http://www.justice.act.gov.au/publication/view/2031/title/eastman-inquiry-terms-of-reference> [accessed 19 Dec 2015].

[72] Inquiry into the Conviction of David Harold Eastman for the Murder of Colin Stanley Winchester, *Report of the Board of Inquiry* (2014) (Acting Justice Brian Martin), available at: <http://www.eastmaninquiry.org.au/report-and-annexures/> (viewed 7 January 2015).

There is an increasing acceptance of the importance in its own right of integrity in the conduct of scholarship, both in terms of reducing fraud and plagiarism and compelling suitable disclosures when there are conflicts of interest. This has had a political outcome. A core element of the Obama campaign in 2009 was a commitment to enhance scientific integrity within all aspects of government in the United States. On election, President Obama signed a landmark Presidential Memorandum on the subject with a view to restoring 'scientific integrity in government decision making'. His administration proclaimed that:

> - Science and technology are essential to achieving a broad range of national goals: driving economic growth and job creation; allowing Americans to live longer, healthier lives; developing clean sources of energy that reduce our dependence on foreign oil; protecting our environment for future generations of Americans; strengthening national and homeland security; and more.
> - Realizing the potential of science and technology to help achieve all of these goals requires that the Administration's decisions about public policy be guided by the most accurate and objective scientific advice available. The public must be able to trust that advice, as well, and to be confident that public officials will not conceal or distort the scientific findings that are relevant to policy choices.
> - Accordingly, the President is assigning to the Director of the Office of Science and Technology Policy (OSTP) the responsibility of ensuring the highest level of integrity in all aspects of the executive branch's involvement with scientific and technological issues.
> - Within 120 days, the Director of OSTP must develop a strategy for ensuring that:
>   - The selection of scientists and technology professionals for science and technology positions in the executive branch is based on those individuals' scientific and technological knowledge, credentials, and experience;
>   - Agencies make available to the public the scientific or technological findings or conclusions considered or relied upon in policy decisions;
>   - Agencies use scientific and technological information that has been subject to well-established scientific processes such as peer review; and
>   - Agencies have appropriate rules and procedures to ensure the integrity of the scientific process within the agency, including whistleblower protection.[73]

On 17 December 2010 John Holdren, Assistant to the President for Science and Technology and Director of the Office of Science and Technology Policy, issued a Memorandum on Scientific Integrity. Amongst other things, it required that federal agencies 'develop policies that ensure a culture of scientific integrity. Scientific progress depends upon investigation, open discussion, refined understanding, and a firm commitment to evidence. Science, and public trust in science, thrives in an environment that shields scientific data and analyses from inappropriate influence'.[74]

The American Chemical Society observed that:

> The hallmarks of scientific integrity include incorporation of all relevant scientific information; succinct and understandable presentation; and thorough identification, quantification, and explanation of uncertainties. Attempts to alter or selectively use data or to bias analysis are unethical and do not serve the national interest.[75]

---

[73] The White House, 'Fact Sheet on Presidential Memorandum on Scientific Integrity' (Briefing Room, Statements and Releases, 9 March 2009), <http://www.whitehouse.gov/the-press-office/fact-sheet-presidential-memorandum-scientific-integrity> (original formatting altered) [accessed 19 Dec 2015].

[74] John P Holdren, 'Memorandum for the Heads of Executive Departments and Agencies: Scientific Integrity' (Office of Science and Technology Policy, 17 December 2010), <http://www.whitehouse.gov/sites/default/files/microsites/ostp/scientific-integrity-memo-12172010.pdf> [accessed 19 Dec 2015].

[75] American Chemical Society, 'Scientific Insight and Integrity in Public Policy' (Public Policy Statement 2011–2014) 2: <http://www.acs.org/content/dam/acsorg/policy/publicpolicies/promote/scientificintegrity/2011-09-scientific-insight-and-integrity-in-public-policy.pdf> [accessed 19 Dec 2015]. An outcome, as of

In addition, reforms to the investigation of scientific misconduct have been championed and in some instances implemented over recent years in a number of countries in an effort to reclaim integrity in scholarship and to rehabilitate confidence in the processes of investigation into complaints of misconduct.

Aspirations of the Book

When a conversation about research fraud, plagiarism, conflict of interest, bitter internal disputation, alcohol-fuelled misconduct on campus, or sexual impropriety in the workplace occurs in the company of almost any scholar, whether employed within academia or in a research institution, a personal tale emerges of how they have been a victim of such conduct or how someone close to them has been wronged or exploited. Feelings run hot about such subjects among scholars, almost higher than in respect of any other topic. Probity is an emotive issue because it goes to trustworthiness and authenticity of both scholars and their work.

This book is not specifically about the subject of research integrity; there are many works on that issue.[76] Rather, it seeks to understand more about the phenomenon of scholarly misconduct so that suitable prophylactic measures can be taken before too much further harm is done to the fabric of scholarly integrity. This book aspires to do more than chronicle and catalogue the many stories about the misconduct of scholars, entertaining and sensational though many of them are. By assembling allegations about such matters, collating them, analysing them, and attempting to identify patterns, it aims to arrive at better awareness and knowledge as to the kinds of scholar who engages in such conduct, where it is established; the motivations for such behaviour; the profiles of persons who act as whistleblowers in such matters; the causes and effects of proven conduct; and the success and fairness, or otherwise, of the investigative and adjudicative mechanisms that have been employed to probe allegations of scholarly misconduct.

The approach adopted in the following pages is to identify important instances of alleged and proven misconduct by scholars occurring for the most part within recent years, although placing them in an historical perspective. Use is made too of scholars' accounts, sometimes self-serving and rationalizing, of their own conduct. The focus is not so much on recording the technicalities of the scientific or medical deceit, as it is upon the individuals and institutions responsible, the circumstances of detection, and the measures taken to determine whether the conduct constituted a breach of integrity. Such an exercise is important, partly because these instances tend to be recorded only within the discipline concerned and to become briefly a scandal or a *cause célèbre*. Sometimes they are documented more broadly by a learned or populist book or by a small number of articles within the relevant discipline and by the publication of expostulations in the media or on blogs. Memories endure in the area for a short time, but not far beyond. Generally such scandals are consigned quite quickly to the dustbin of history after a resolution is obtained (often pragmatically) to the specific issue, the problem only to be repeated in a cognate domain not long afterwards. Too frequently

28 January 2011, was the United States Department of the Interior's policy initiative on the *Integrity of Scientific and Scholarly Activities*: <http://www.doi.gov/scientificintegrity/index.cfm> [accessed 19 Dec 2015].

[76] See eg Francis L Macrina, *Scientific Integrity: Text and Cases in Responsible Conduct of Research* (4th edn, Washington DC: ASM Press, Washington DC, 3rd edn, 20052014); Adil E Shamoo and David B Resnik, *Responsible Conduct of Research* (2nd edn, New York: Oxford University Press, New York, 2nd edn, 2009); Committee on Science, Engineering, and Public Policy, National Academy of Sciences, National Academy of Engineering, and Institute of Medicine of the National Academies, *On Being a Scientist: A Guide to Responsible Conduct in Research* (3rd edn, Washington DC: National Academies Press, Washington DC, 3rd edn, 2009).

ad hoc responses principally directed towards damage control within the institution fail to address the fundamental causes of the problem.

By viewing the scandals, affairs, and crises en masse, from an international perspective and across disciplines, including those that are forensic and within private enterprise, it becomes possible to understand the phenomenon of scholarly misconduct from a more informed perspective and to identify features in common and aspects of the problem which are often ignored because of outrage and distress about particular instances and particular individuals.

The book also reflects on specific and broad-based means of reducing the incidence of scholarly misconduct. It takes the unapologetic stance that proven intellectual dishonesty, manifested in research fraud, covert conflicts of interest, and plagiarism, as well as sexual harassment and exploitation, are grossly unacceptable forms of scholarly misconduct, requiring robust investigation and the adoption of stern punitive and deterrent measures against persons and institutions. However, rigorous investigations and imposition of deterrent sanctions can only go so far. There is a broader cultural context within scholarly endeavour that also needs to be addressed if the values of integrity within the scholarly workplace are to be reasserted. It reflects upon what these are and how cultural change can start to be effected.

One of the distinctive focuses of the book is an evaluation of the means of resolving allegations of impropriety by scholars, in particular the resort to law and legal processes. What becomes apparent from a review of large numbers of cases, including those that have become notorious, is that too often internal processes within universities and institutions have been procedurally flawed, requiring revision and further or overlapping inquiries, too slow, and impugned (sometimes with good reason) as to the quality of their findings. Surprisingly often the law has become involved by the institution of litigation in one form or another. This focus on process and the involvement of the law is a lens through which misconduct by scholars, and within academia, has not previously been viewed.

Such a perspective is important given what seems to be an increasing tendency for such matters to be taken before the courts by one party or another. Recourse to the law in respect of scholarly misconduct arises by way of criminal prosecutions, civil actions for damages, defamation actions, litigation for wrongful dismissal and discrimination, and via appellate actions against internal decisions within universities. It also occurs through the involvement of anti-corruption commissions and parliamentary and ombudsman inquiries to which members of the public, colleagues, rivals, and others can make complaint, sometimes very publicly. The following pages argue that, while the courts constitute a fundamental bulwark against procedural and substantive unfairness,[77] there are limits to the utility of the law in resolving issues related to the functioning of the academy and the conduct of research. In a more and more litigation-conscious society[78] there is an inevitability about formalization and 'lawyerization' of processes involving allegations of misconduct. However, there are also advantages in such matters being transacted without at least initial recourse to the courts but openly, formally, and attended by proper process and in conformity with the basic precepts of procedural fairness. Such procedures go to integrity and reliability amongst persons, institutions, and processes on which we need to repose intellectual confidence and trust.

[77] See Jerome Frank, *Courts on Trial: Myth and Reality in American Justice* (Princeton, NJ: Princeton University Press, 1973), at p 132, referring to the check and balance of the courts against 'an arbitrary tyrannical executive'. See too *Chief Lesapo v North West Agricultural Bank and Another* [1999] ZACC 16; 2000 (1) SA 409 (CC) at [22].

[78] See Jethro Koller Lieberman, *The Litigious Society* (New York: Basic Books, 1983); Thomas Frederick Burke, *Lawyers, Lawsuits and Legal Rights: The Battle over Litigation in American Society* (Berkeley: University of California Press, 2002).

Accordingly, the pages that follow review different areas in which scholarly misconduct has taken place, often successfully and for a lengthy period. They do so, on occasion using as a significant source for such information articles in newspapers, popular magazines, and industry journals. This is because, somewhat surprisingly, there is comparatively little written on the subject matter in peer-reviewed scholarly journals or in book chapters or learned tomes.

The book then reflects on measures to enhance accountability, regulatory, disciplinary, and associated responses to scholarly misconduct. It reviews many statements of values, by universities and others. It does not suggest that there is a simple solution. Rather, it argues that cultural change is necessary, reinforced by clear articulations of principle, buttressed by firm and unapologetic imposition of sanctions against persons whose lack of integrity has brought disrepute upon scholarship, scholarly institutions, and perceptions of the trustworthiness of scholarly work. Its argument is that this reassertion of values in relation to scholarliness is required, not just because of the importance of respect for qualities such as integrity, but because there is the likelihood of seriously adverse consequences when research is faked, when people retail scholarship deceptively, when unacknowledged copying of others' work takes place, when fabrication or bias infects forensic work, when gratuitous offence is given or uncollegiate behaviour indulged in, and when predation and harassment take place within the scholarly workplace.

It is hoped that the numbers, nature, and repetition of instances of unequivocal breach of scholarly values documented in this book will be found confronting and disturbing. It is a very different picture that emerges of a small cross-section of scholars from that depicted in the idealized Golden Age Dutch portraits. An aspiration of *Scholarly Misconduct: Law, Regulation, and Practice* is that these pages will play a role in galvanizing preparedness to articulate values and relevant protocols and to constitute and support independent offices of scholarly integrity that have the resources, powers, and authority to conduct independent and rigorous merits and process review investigations into misconduct by scholars.

2

RESEARCH MISCONDUCT
Profiles, Principles, and Problems

Introduction

Integrity[1] or probity[2] in the conduct of research lies at the heart of its reliability and therefore its potential to make an authentic contribution to knowledge, acquisition of credentials, and the development of new scholarly insights. There are a number of checks and balances to the absence of integrity and probity in scholarly research, ranging from peer review, supervision, ethics committee procedures, colleagues' critiques and re-analyses, further experimentation, and responses elicited within the academic marketplace, a marketplace that is intensely competitive and which rejoices (sometimes maliciously) in the exposure of error and infelicity in methodology. However, an important question is whether, rhetoric aside, these measures are in fact achieving the objectives of eliminating, minimizing or at least substantially guarding against research fraud.

Awareness of the need for scholarly transparency in the interest of promoting integrity is far from new. As long ago as 1661, for instance, Robert Boyle argued that scientific accounts of experiments should be candid, honest, and precise, allowing for scrutiny outside 'dark and smoakie laboratories' by a community of judicious experts who understand the importance of separating speculation from fact.[3] This gave rise to the notion of reproducibility, and in due course falsifiability, highlighted as one of the indicia for reliability in the leading United States Supreme Court decision on expert evidence in *Daubert v Merrell Dow Pharmaceuticals*[4] as an underpinning of scientific method.[5]

However, opportunities and temptations exist for scholars across a wide range of domains to take research short-cuts, to manipulate sources unrepresentatively and selectively, to fabricate results, and to distort data in order to reach predetermined outcomes which are personally advantageous. Events of recent years, as seen below, demonstrate unequivocally that the mechanisms which we have constructed thus far to guard against research fraud can be subverted effectively by the unscrupulous. Such measures on their own have proved to be inadequate to curtail scholarly fraud.

---

[1] A notion derived from the Latin (*integer*, or whole), referring to wholeness deriving from qualities such as honesty and consistency of character. Law academic Stephen Carter has argued that integrity is conceptually distinguishable from honesty and has three components: '*discerning* what is right and what is wrong; *acting* on what you have discerned, even at personal cost; and *saying openly* that you are acting on your understanding of right from wrong': Stephen L Carter, *Integrity* (New York: Basic Books, 1996) 7 (original formatting altered), 10.

[2] A notion derived from the Latin (*probus*: good, upright; *probitas*, goodness, uprightness).

[3] See 'A Præface Introductory' in Robert Boyle, *The Sceptical Chymist or Chymico-Physical Doubts and Paradoxes* (London: J Crooke, 1661), available at: <http://www.gutenberg.org/files/22914/22914-h/22914-h.htm> [accessed 19 Dec 2015].

[4] 509 US 579 (1993). See further Ian Freckelton and Hugh Selby, *Expert Evidence: Law, Practice, Procedure and Advocacy* (6th edn, Pyrmont, NSW: Lawbook Co/Thomson Reuters, 2016).

[5] See also in Canada *R v Trochym* [2007] 1 SCR 239.

There are plausible reasons to postulate that, while the actual incidence of such fraud is not known, it is increasing significantly.[6] There is likely to be a much higher incidence of subtle forms of research misconduct than the more extreme and better-known.[7] There can be no denying that retractions of articles for fraud in scholarly journals have reached unprecedented levels.[8] However, retractions only achieve so much as a scholarly response to breach of research trust: Steen[9] in 2011 endeavoured to assess the impact of retracted studies. He analysed 180 retracted articles that involved human subjects or 'freshly derived human material', along with 851 published studies citing that research. He found that the retracted papers were cited over 5,000 times and that 6,573 patients received treatment in studies eventually retracted because of fraud. One study alone, published in 2001, included 2,161 women being treated for postpartum bleeding and the downstream studies included more than 400,000 subjects, with 70,501 receiving treatment. In short the formal retraction seemed to play little role in curtailing reference to, and application of, the principles within the problematic article.

In addition, the financial costs of retractions occasioned by fraud are significant. A 2014 study, for instance, found retractions to have accounted for US$58 million in direct funding by the National Institutes of Health in the United States, with each retracted article accounting for a mean of US$392,582 in direct costs.[10] It has also been observed that there is a significant incidence of dishonest duplication in applications for research funding, this too resulting in substantial financial losses.

What can be said with confidence is that the consequences of fraud in research are very serious both in principle and in very practical respects. The outcomes can be wide-ranging—from damage done reputationally to the institution within which the conduct was perpetrated, to harm to persons unwittingly associated with it. Most importantly, there can be adverse effects for subjects and patients,[11] as well as for the status and even viability of whole areas of research which can be tarnished by the opprobrium attaching to them by virtue of the fraud.[12] Put another way, the damage to the evidence base of medical and scientific research and its reputation can be far-reaching.[13]

Finally, at a broader level, as Sledge has asserted: 'Unethical and dishonest clinical experiments have long-standing and disastrous effects on ethical and honest clinical experiments, a Gresham's law of science.'[14]

---

[6] Harold R Garner, Lauren J McKiver, and Michael B Waitkin, 'Research Funding: Same Work, Twice the Money?' (2013) 493 *Nature* 599.

[7] See LK John, G Loewenstein, and D Prelec, 'Measuring the Prevalence of Questionable Research Practices' (2012) 23(5) *Psychological Science* 524.

[8] See Michael Royston, 'Retracted Scientific Studies: A Growing List' (28 May 2015) *The New York Times*: <http://www.nytimes.com/interactive/2015/05/28/science/retractions-scientific-studies.html?_r=0> [accessed 19 Dec 2015].

[9] R Grant Steen, 'Retractions in the Medical Literature: How Many Patients are Put at Risk by Flawed Research?' (2011) 37(11) *Journal of Medical Ethics* 688, 688–9.

[10] Andrew M Stern, Arturo Casadevall, R Grant Steen, and Ferric C Fang, 'Research: Financial Costs and Personal Consequences of Research Misconduct Resulting in Retracted Publications' (2014) 3 *eLife* e02956: <http://dx.doi.org/10.7554/eLife.02956> [accessed 19 Dec 2015].

[11] See Steen, above n 9.

[12] See Sandra L Titus, James A Wells, and Lawrence J Rhoades, 'Repairing Research Integrity' (2008) 453(7198) *Nature* 980; Paolo A Nussenzveig, and Renata Zukanovich Funchal, 'Integrity: Misconduct by a Few Damages Credibility for Many' (2008) 454(7204) *Nature* 574.

[13] See Prathap Tharyan, 'Criminals in the Citadel and Deceit All Along the Watchtower: Irresponsibility, Fraud and Complicity in the Search for Scientific Truth' (2012) 10(1) *Mens Sana Monographs* 158.

[14] George W Sledge Jr, 'Why Big Lies Matter: Lessons from the Bezwoda Affair', *Medscape*: <http://www.medscape.com/viewarticle/408908> [accessed 19 Dec 2015]. Also available at (2000) 5(1) *Medscape Women's Health* 4.

As analysed in Chapter 3, one response to the problem is to invoke the sanctions and the potential for deterrence of the criminal law. There has now been a sequence of decisions in which fraudulent research conduct has been visited by significant criminal sanctions, including, in 2015, the imposition of 57 months' imprisonment on Dr Dong Pyou-Han, together with a court order that he repay US$7.2 million in research funds that he had improperly obtained.

This chapter reviews the phenomenology of research fraud, instancing and classifying various forms, identifying patterns, and reviewing the profiles of those who tend to be its perpetrators. It discusses the attempts made by tertiary institutions to enunciate ethical principles that should guide research and which bind university employees. It is intended to be read in conjunction with Chapter 3 which provides extensive examples of research misconduct and argues for a new culture of integrity and for the creation of effective mechanisms for investigation and response to such misconduct.

Definitions of Research Misconduct

A major contribution to the identification and construction of criteria for classifying scientific misconduct was published in 1830 by Charles Babbage (1791–1871),[15] who held Newton's chair at Cambridge University and undertook research in relation to astronomy, mathematics, and the development of computers. It retains contemporary relevance the better part of two centuries later. In *Reflections on the Decline of Science in England and on Some of Its Causes*,[16] Babbage distinguished various forms of impositions that have been practised in science, including what he termed:

- hoaxing,
- forging,
- trimming, and
- cooking.

His notion was that the difference between a forgery and a hoax is that, while a hoaxer wants his or her deception to be uncovered (at some stage);[17] sometimes to make a particular point about science or about the human condition; sometimes to achieve retribution against a particular individual;[18] a forger wants their fraudulent work to be successful in the long term: '[T]he deceit is intended to last for a time, and then be discovered, to the ridicule of those who have credited it; whereas the forger is one who, wishing to acquire a reputation for science, records observations which he has never made.'[19]

Babbage gave as an example of hoaxing the assertion in 1788 by Cavaliere Giuseppe Gioeni, a knight of Malta, published in Naples, of an account of a new family of Testacea, consisting of two valves united by the body of the animal, 'of which he described, with great minuteness, one species, the specific name of which has been taken from its habitat, and the generic he took

[15] See Maboth Moseley, *Irascible Genius: a Life of Charles Babbage Inventor* (London: Hutchinson, 1964).

[16] Charles Babbage, *Reflections on the Decline of Science in England and on Some of its Causes* (London: B Fellowes, 1830), available at: <http://www.gutenberg.org/files/1216/1216-h/1216-h.htm> [accessed 20 Dec 2015].

[17] See eg, the notorious teaching hoax by Dr Myron L Fox organized by three psychology professors: Donald H Naftulin, John E Ware Jr, and Frank A Donnelly, 'The Doctor Fox Lecture: A Paradigm of Educational Seduction' (1973) 48(7) *Journal of Medical Education* 630, available at: <http://www.er.uqam.ca/nobel/r30034/PSY4180/Pages/Naftulin.html> [accessed 20 Dec 2015].

[18] See Ian Haywood, *Faking It: Art and the Politics of Forgery* (Brighton: Harvester Press, 1987).

[19] Babbage above n 16, Chapter V: 'Of Observations, Section 3: On the Frauds of Observers'.

from his own family, calling it Gioenia Sicula'.[20] However, hoaxes can be pranks, attempts to swindle and malicious attempts to make other legitimate scholars look foolish. Occasionally, hoaxers delude themselves and genuinely believe in their spurious findings.

A more modern but comparable example of 'hoaxing' is 'the Piltdown man', discovered in 1911 and discredited in 1953 where parts of an ape and a human skull were combined, supposedly to represent a 'missing link' in human evolution (see p 58). Hoaxes can be intended to expose naïveté and credulousness and to mock pseudo-wisdom.

'Forging', which Babbage thought rare, is the counterfeiting of results, today more often called fabrication of research outcomes.[21]

'Trimming' consists of manipulation of data by eliminating outliers to make results look more accurate, while keeping the average the same: it 'consists in clipping off little bits here and there from those observations which differ most in excess from the mean, and in sticking them on to those which are too small; a species of "equitable adjustment", as a radical would term it, which cannot be admitted in science'.[22]

'Cooking' under Babbage's classificatory scheme is the unjustifiable selection of data:

> the object of which is to give to ordinary observations the appearance and character of those of the highest degree of accuracy. One of its numerous processes is to make multitudes of observations, and out of these to select those only which agree, or very nearly agree. If a hundred observations are made, the cook must be very unlucky if he cannot pick out fifteen or twenty which will do for serving up. Another approved receipt, when the observations to be used will not come within the limit of accuracy, which it has been resolved they shall possess, is to calculate them by two different formulae. The difference in the constants employed in those formulae has sometimes a most happy effect in promoting unanimity amongst discordant measures. If still greater accuracy is required, three or more formulae can be used.[23]

Babbage incorporated within his analysis of forging, scenarios that could have outcomes in litigation. In particular he instanced a legal action in which a question arose in a case in Tuscany as to whether a word had been erased from a deed. The party asserting fraud summoned in aid the views of Professor Gazzeri, the Professor of Chemistry in Florence:

> who, concluding that those who committed the fraud would be satisfied by the disappearance of the colouring matter of the ink, suspected (either from some colourless matter remaining in the letters, or perhaps from the agency of the solvent having weakened the fabric of the paper itself beneath the supposed letters) that the effect of the slow application of heat would be to render some difference of texture or of applied substance evident, by some variety in the shade of colour which heat in such circumstances might be expected to produce. Permission having been given to try the experiment, on the application of heat the important word reappeared, to the great satisfaction of the court.[24]

Babbage's trimming and cooking fall under the modern rubric of 'falsifying' of scholarly research. Scholarly conventions and standards of scientific probity were to a degree different in the era of Babbage, yet the feuds, priority disputes and porous notions of scientific truthfulness from previous centuries remain contemporary—what is at their heart is the transducing of basic conventions of scholarly probity. Not surprisingly, then, reference continues to be made in many analyses of research fraud to the Babbage taxonomy.

[20] Ibid.
[21] Ibid.
[22] Ibid.
[23] Ibid.
[24] Ibid.

In 1993, the United States Congress created the Commission on Research Integrity in response to continuing controversy concerning problems experienced in relation to the capacity of both the scientific community and government in dealing with misconduct in research. Its role was to advise the Secretary of Health and Human Services and Congress about ways to improve the public health service response to misconduct in biomedical and behavioural research that received government funding. Aside from recommending the development and dissemination of clear standards of research behaviour, it emphasized the need for a consistent and contemporary definition of research misconduct:

> Significant misbehavior that improperly appropriates the intellectual property or contributions of others, that intentionally impedes the progress of research, or that risks corrupting the scientific record or compromising the integrity of scientific practices. Such behaviors are unethical and unacceptable in proposing, conducting, or reporting research, or in reviewing the proposals or research reports of others.[25]

It instanced as examples of such conduct the 'MIM model': misappropriation (incorporating plagiarism), interference and misrepresentation.[26]

The Office of Research Integrity of the United States Department of Health and Human Services[27] provides the following straightforward modern definition of research misconduct' which is derivative of Babbage's taxonomy:

> Research misconduct means fabrication, falsification, or plagiarism in proposing, performing, or reviewing research, or in reporting research results.
> (a) *Fabrication* is making up data or results and recording or reporting them.
> (b) *Falsification* is manipulating research materials, equipment, or processes, or changing or omitting data or results such that the research is not accurately represented in the research record.
> (c) *Plagiarism* is the appropriation of another person's ideas, processes, results, or words without giving appropriate credit.
> (d) Research misconduct does not include honest error or differences of opinion.[28]

In 2007 the Australian Code for the Responsible Conduct of Research (which in 2015–2016 was being revised) provided that:

> Research misconduct includes fabrication, falsification, plagiarism or deception in proposing, carrying out or reporting the results of research, and failure to declare or manage a serious conflict of interest. It includes avoidable failure to follow research proposals as approved by a research ethics committee, particularly where this failure may result in unreasonable risk

---

25 Commission on Research Integrity, *Integrity and Misconduct in Research*, Report to the Secretary of Health and Human Services, the House Committee on Commerce, and the Senate Committee on Labor and Human Resources (Washington, DC: United States Department of Health and Human Services, Public Health Service, 1995) 15: <http://ori.hhs.gov/images/ddblock/report_commission.pdf> (viewed 8 January 2015).

26 Ibid 15–16.

27 United States Department of Health and Human Services, The Office of Research Integrity, 'Definition of Research Misconduct': <http://ori.hhs.gov/definition-misconduct> (viewed 8 January 2015).

28 Imperial College London has adopted the Royal College of Physicians' definitions of research misconduct as including piracy, plagiarism and fraud: 'These descriptions are neither exclusive nor exhaustive: (a) Piracy is the deliberate exploitation of ideas and concepts from others without acknowledgement. (b) Plagiarism is the copying of ideas, data or text (or a combination of these) without permission or acknowledgement. (c) Fraud involves deception—usually, but not exclusively, the invention of data. This could also include the omission from analysis and publication of inconvenient components of a data set. (d) Gift authorship is the practice of arranging to credit someone with authorship or co-authorship in such a way that deliberately exaggerates or gives a misleading impression of their actual contribution': Imperial College London, *Investigation of Allegations of Research Misconduct* (Ordinance D17, revised 7 February 2014): <http://www.imperial.ac.uk/admin-services/secretariat/college-governance/charters-statutes-ordinances-and-regulations/ordinances/staff/> [accessed 20 Dec 2015].

or harm to humans, animals or the environment. It also includes the wilful concealment or facilitation of research misconduct by others.[29]

The Council of Canadian Academies in 2010 provided a more broad-based definition:

> Research misconduct is the failure to apply, in a coherent and consistent manner, the values and principles essential to encouraging and achieving excellence in the search for knowledge. These values include *honesty*, *fairness*, *trust*, *accountability*, and *openness*.[30]

The approach in Scandinavia too has been less specific with a tendency to avoid prescriptive definitions:

> In the Nordic countries, formal definitions have never been considered critical or even feasible, since dishonesty is regarded as ranging from minor deviations from good scientific practice to obvious misconduct. Scientific dishonesty has therefore been broadly characterised, and the establishment of a verdict relies on sound judgment rather than rigorous definitions.[31]

The 'Singapore Statement on Research Integrity' was formulated and released in 2010 on the initiative of the Second World Conference on Research Integrity. The Singapore Statement defined academic research integrity as requiring:

- honesty in all aspects of research,
- accountability in the conduct of research,
- professional courtesy and fairness in working with others, and
- good stewardship of research on behalf of others.[32]

It identified an important set of responsibilities for those undertaking scientific research:

1. **Integrity**: Researchers should take responsibility for the trustworthiness of their research.
2. **Adherence to Regulations**: Researchers should be aware of and adhere to regulations and policies related to research.
3. **Research Methods**: Researchers should employ appropriate research methods, base conclusions on critical analysis of the evidence and report findings and interpretations fully and objectively.
4. **Research Records**: Researchers should keep clear, accurate records of all research in ways that will allow verification and replication of their work by others.
5. **Research Findings**: Researchers should share data and findings openly and promptly, as soon as they have had an opportunity to establish priority and ownership claims.
6. **Authorship**: Researchers should take responsibility for their contributions to all publications, funding applications, reports and other representations of their research. Lists of authors should include all those and only those who meet applicable authorship criteria.
7. **Publication Acknowledgement**: Researchers should acknowledge in publications the names and roles of those who made significant contributions to the research, including writers, funders, sponsors, and others, but do not meet authorship criteria.
8. **Peer Review**: Researchers should provide fair, prompt and rigorous evaluations and respect confidentiality when reviewing others' work.

---

29 National Health and Medical Research Council, Australian Research Council, *Australian Code for the Responsible Conduct of Research* (Australian Government, 2007) 10.1, available at: <https://www.nhmrc.gov.au/guidelines-publications/r39> [accessed 20 Dec 2015].

30 The Expert Panel on Research Integrity, *Honesty, Accountability and Trust: Fostering Research Integrity in Canada* (Ottawa: Council of Canadian Academies, 2010) 5, 41, available at: <http://www.scienceadvice.ca/en/assessments/completed/research-integrity.aspx> [accessed 20 Dec 2015].

31 Magne Nylenna, Daniel Andersen, Gisela Dahlquist, Matti Sarvas et al. (National Committees on Scientific Dishonesty in the Nordic Countries), 'Handling of Scientific Dishonesty in the Nordic Countries' (1999) 354(9172) *Lancet* 57, 58.

32 Singapore Statement on Research Integrity, 'Principles': <http://www.singaporestatement.org/statement.html> (viewed 8 January 2015) (original formatting altered).

9. **Conflict of Interest:** Researchers should disclose financial and other conflicts of interest that could compromise the trustworthiness of their work in research proposals, publications and public communications as well as in all review activities.
10. **Public Communication:** Researchers should limit professional comments to their recognized expertise when engaged in public discussions about the application and importance of research findings and clearly distinguish professional comments from opinions based on personal views.
11. **Reporting Irresponsible Research Practices:** Researchers should report to the appropriate authorities any suspected research misconduct, including fabrication, falsification or plagiarism, and other irresponsible research practices that undermine the trustworthiness of research, such as carelessness, improperly listing authors, failing to report conflicting data, or the use of misleading analytical methods.
12. **Responding to Irresponsible Research Practices:** Research institutions, as well as journals, professional organizations and agencies that have commitments to research, should have procedures for responding to allegations of misconduct and other irresponsible research practices and for protecting those who report such behavior in good faith. When misconduct or other irresponsible research practice is confirmed, appropriate actions should be taken promptly, including correcting the research record.
13. **Research Environments:** Research institutions should create and sustain environments that encourage integrity through education, clear policies, and reasonable standards for advancement, while fostering work environments that support research integrity.
14. **Societal Considerations:** Researchers and research institutions should recognize that they have an ethical obligation to weigh societal benefits against risks inherent in their work.[33]

At the Second World Conference on Research Integrity the European Code of Conduct for Research Integrity, adopted by the European Science Foundation and the All European Academies,[34] was launched. Its intent was to address the 'proper conduct and principled practice of systematic research in the medical, natural and social sciences and the humanities'.[35] It stands as a canon for self-regulation and advances a set of recommendations. It adopted the Singapore taxonomy of research fraud and observed that '[t]he two most serious violations of the ethos of science are fabrication and falsification'.[36] It advanced a set of principles for investigating research misconduct:

Integrity of the process

- Investigations into research misconduct allegations must be fair, comprehensive and conducted expediently but without compromising accuracy, objectivity, and thoroughness.
- Those parties involved in the procedure must ensure that any interests they have which might constitute a conflict of interest are disclosed and managed.
- Detailed and confidential records will be maintained on all aspects of the procedure.

Uniformity

- Procedures for dealing with misconduct should be spelled out in sufficient detail so that the transparency of the process and uniformity within one domain of jurisdiction from one case to another is ensured.

---

[33] Singapore Statement on Research Integrity, 'Responsibilities': <http://www.singaporestatement.org/statement.html> [accessed 20 Dec 2015] (original formatting altered).

[34] ALLEA is the European Federation of Academies of Sciences and Humanities. As of 2015 it incorporated 58 member academies in over 40 countries: see ALLEA | ALL European Academies, <http://www.allea.org/Pages/ALL/4/731.bGFuZz1FTkc.html> [accessed 20 Dec 2015].

[35] European Science Foundation and All European Academies, *The European Code of Conduct for Research Integrity* (March 2011) 3: <http://www.esf.org/fileadmin/Public_documents/Publications/Code_Conduct_ResearchIntegrity.pdf> [accessed 20 Dec 2015].

[36] Ibid [2.2.4].

Fairness

- Investigation of research misconduct allegations should be conducted in a manner that is fair to all parties and in accordance with relevant laws.
- Persons accused of research misconduct must be given full details of the allegation(s) in writing and allowed a fair process for responding to allegations, asking questions, presenting evidence, calling witnesses, and providing responses to information presented.
- Allow witnesses to be accompanied by or seek advice and assistance from anyone of their choosing.
- Proportionate action should be taken against persons found to have committed research misconduct.
- Any action(s) taken should be subject to appeal. Of course, there should be an authority issuing the final decision.

Confidentiality

- The procedure should be conducted as confidentially as possible, in order to protect those involved in the investigation. Such confidentiality should be maintained provided this does not compromise the investigation of the allegation, health and safety, or the safety of participants in research.
- Where possible any disclosure to third parties should be made on a confidential basis.
- If the organisation and/or its staff have legal obligations to inform third parties of research misconduct allegations, those obligations must be fulfilled at the appropriate time through the correct mechanisms.

No detriment

- Anyone accused of research misconduct is presumed innocent.
- No person should suffer any unnecessary penalty when accused of research misconduct before the allegation is proven.
- No person should suffer any penalty for making an allegation of research misconduct *in good faith*, but action should be taken against persons found to have made allegations in bad faith.[37]

The Singapore Statement influenced the United Kingdom Research Integrity Office's *Code of Practice for Research: Promoting Good Practice and Preventing Misconduct*, published in September 2009[38] and the UK Universities' 'Concordat to Support Research Integrity'[39] of 2012, which committed its signatories to:

- maintaining the highest standards of rigour and integrity in all aspects of research;
- ensuring that research is conducted according to appropriate ethical, legal and professional frameworks, obligations and standards;
- supporting a research environment that is underpinned by a culture of integrity and based on good governance, best practice and support for the development of researchers;
- using transparent, robust and fair processes to deal with allegations of research misconduct should they arise;

---

[37] Ibid [2.5] (Annex I).

[38] United Kingdom Research Integrity Office, *Code of Practice for Research: Promoting Good Practice and Preventing Misconduct* (September 2009), available at: <http://www.ukrio.org/publications/code-of-practice-for-research/> [accessed 20 Dec 2015].

[39] Universities UK, *The Concordat to Support Research Integrity* (July 2012): <http://www.universitiesuk.ac.uk/highereducation/Documents/2012/TheConcordatToSupportResearchIntegrity.pdf> [accessed 20 Dec 2015]. The signatories to the Concordat were the UK Department for Employment and Learning, the Higher Education Funding Council for England, the Higher Education Funding Council for Wales, the National Institute for Health Research, the Research Council UK, the Scottish Funding Council, Universities UK, and the Wellcome Trust.

- working together to strengthen the integrity of research and to reviewing progress regularly and openly.[40]

Underlying the Concordat was commitment in research to:

- **Honesty** in all aspects of research, including in the presentation of research goals, intentions and findings; in reporting on research methods and procedures; in gathering data; in using and acknowledging the work of other researchers; and in conveying valid interpretations and making justifiable claims based on research findings.
- **Rigour**, in line with prevailing disciplinary norms and standards: in performing research and using appropriate methods; in adhering to an agreed protocol where appropriate; in drawing interpretations and conclusions from the research; and in communicating the results.
- **Transparency and open communication** in declaring conflicts of interest; in the reporting of research data collection methods; in the analysis and interpretation of data; in making research findings widely available, which includes sharing negative results as appropriate; and in presenting the work to other researchers and to the general public.
- **Care and respect** for all participants in and subjects of research, including humans, animals, the environment and cultural objects. Those engaged with research must also show care and respect for the stewardship of research and scholarship for future generations.[41]

The Concordat classified research misconduct as 'behaviour or actions that fall short of the standards of ethics, research, and scholarship required to ensure that the integrity of research is upheld. It is a problem because it can cause harm (for example to patients, the public and the environment), damages the credibility of research, undermines the research record, and wastes resources'.[42] It noted that it can take many forms:

- **Fabrication**: making up results or other outputs (eg, artefacts) and presenting them as if they were real;
- **Falsification**: manipulating research processes or changing or omitting data without good cause;
- **Plagiarism**: using other people's material without giving proper credit;
- **Failing to meet ethical, legal and professional obligations**: for example failure to declare competing interests; misrepresentation of involvement or authorship; misrepresentation of interests; breach of confidentiality; lack of informed consent; misuse of personal data; and abuse of research subjects or materials;
- **Improper dealing with allegations of misconduct**: failing to address possible infringements such as attempts to cover up misconduct and reprisals against whistleblowers.[43]

In 2013 the 'Montreal Statement on Research Integrity in Cross-Boundary Research Collaborations', a product of the Third World Congress on Research Integrity, elaborated on the Singapore Statement:

> Responsibilities of Individual and Institutional Partners in Cross-Boundary Research Collaborations
>
> ***General Collaborative Responsibilities***
>
> 1. ***Integrity***: Collaborating partners should take collective responsibility for the trustworthiness of the overall collaborative research and individual responsibility for the trustworthiness of their own contributions.

---

40 Ibid 4.
41 Ibid 11.
42 Ibid 17.
43 Ibid.

2. ***Trust***: The behavior of each collaborating partner should be worthy of the trust of all other partners. Responsibility for establishing and maintaining this level of trust lies with all collaborating partners.
3. ***Purpose***: Collaborative research should be initiated and conducted for purposes that advance knowledge to the benefit of humankind.
4. ***Goals***: Collaborating partners should agree at the outset on the goals of the research. Changes in goals should be negotiated and agreed to by all partners.

Responsibilities in Managing the Collaboration

5. ***Communication***: Collaborating partners should communicate with each other as frequently and openly as necessary to foster full, mutual understanding of the research.
6. ***Agreements***: Agreements that govern collaborative research should be understood and ratified by all collaborating partners. Agreements that unduly or unnecessarily restrict dissemination of data, findings or other research products should be avoided.
7. ***Compliance with Laws, Policies and Regulations***: The collaboration as a whole should be in compliance with all laws, policies and regulations to which it is subject. Collaborating partners should promptly determine how to address conflicting laws, policies or regulations that apply to the research.
8. ***Costs and Rewards***: The costs and rewards of collaborative research should be distributed fairly among collaborating partners.
9. ***Transparency***: Collaborative research should be conducted and its results disseminated transparently and honestly, with as much openness as possible under existing agreements. Sources of funding should be fully and openly declared.
10. ***Resource Management***: Collaborating partners should use human, animal, financial and other resources appropriately.
11. ***Monitoring***: Collaborating partners should monitor the progress of research projects to foster the integrity and the timely completion and dissemination of the work.

Responsibilities in Collaborative Relationships

12. ***Roles and Responsibilities***: Collaborating partners should come to mutual understandings about their roles and responsibilities in the planning, conduct and dissemination of research. Such understandings should be renegotiated when roles or responsibilities change.
13. ***Customary Practices and Assumptions***: Collaborating partners should openly discuss their customary practices and assumptions related to the research. Diversity of perspectives, expertise and methods, and differences in customary practices, standards and assumptions that could compromise the integrity of the research should be addressed openly.
14. ***Conflict***: Collaborating partners should seek prompt resolution of conflicts, disagreements and misunderstandings at the individual or institutional level.
15. ***Authority of Representation***: Collaborating partners should come to agreement on who has authority to speak on behalf of the collaboration.

Responsibilities for Outcomes of Research

16. ***Data, Intellectual Property and Research Records***: Collaborating partners should come to agreement, at the outset and later as needed, on the use, management, sharing and ownership of data, intellectual property, and research records.
17. ***Publication***: Collaborating partners should come to agreement, at the outset and later as needed, on how publication and other dissemination decisions will be made.
18. ***Authorship and Acknowledgement***: Collaborating partners should come to agreement, at the outset and later as needed, on standards for authorship and acknowledgement of joint research products. The contributions of all partners, especially junior partners, should receive full and appropriate recognition. Publications and other products should state the contributions of all contributing parties.

19. ***Responding to Irresponsible Research Practices***: The collaboration as a whole should have procedures in place for responding to allegations of misconduct or other irresponsible research practice by any of its members. Collaborating partners should promptly take appropriate action when misconduct or other irresponsible research practice by any partner is suspected or confirmed.
20. ***Accountability***: Collaborating partners should be accountable to each other, to funders and to other stakeholders in the accomplishment of the research.[44]

The committees that investigated the conduct of the social psychologist Diederik Stapel in The Netherlands[45] (see p 37) were called upon to investigate fraud in his research work. In 2012 they defined research misconduct as:

> the fabrication, falsification or unjustified replenishment of data, as well as the whole or partial fabrication of analysis results. It also includes the misleading presentation of crucial points as far as the organization or nature of the experiment are concerned.

The committees classified a publication as fraudulent if in at least one of the experimental studies in the publication fraud had been proved beyond reasonable doubt.

St Vincent's Hospital in Victoria, Australia, links its definition with the relevant Australian Code (see Appendix 1) and makes clear an important exclusion:

> **Research misconduct** is defined as the deviation from standards and provisions of the Australian Code for the Responsible Conduct of Research 2007, and includes fabrication, falsification, plagiarism or deception in proposing, carrying out or reporting the results of research, and failure to declare or manage a serious conflict of interest. It includes avoidable failure to follow research proposals as approved by a research ethics committee, particularly where this failure may result in unreasonable risk or harm to humans, animals or the environment. It also includes the wilful concealment or facilitation of research misconduct by others.
>
> Research misconduct does not include differences in interpretation of, or judgments about, data.[46]

What can be seen from the various definitions, therefore, is that there is considerable divergence. All draw upon the legacy of Babbage, incorporating fabrication, falsification, and manipulation of data. Most include plagiarism. Some incorporate breaches of protocols from a research integrity framework or instructions or limitations imposed by an ethics committee. Some extend to conflict of interest and obstructing or impeding others' research work. Some even incorporate failure to report others' misconduct. The level of definitional variation is undesirable and there is much to be said for moving towards a single agreed approach to what is designated a serious lack of integrity in respect of research, so that there is a consistency of approach, and a reduction in any ambiguity that can be pleaded by way of excuse or mitigation by those whose conduct would generally be regarded by colleagues or the general public as falling significantly below acceptable standards.

---

[44] 'Montreal Statement on Research Integrity in Cross-Boundary Research Collaborations': <http://www.researchintegrity.org/Statements/Montreal%20Statement%20English.pdf> [accessed 20 Dec 2015].

[45] Levelt Committee (Tilburg University), Noort Committee (Groningen University), and Drenth University (University of Amsterdam), *Flawed Science: The Fraudulent Research Practices of Social Psychologist Diederik Stapel* (28 November 2012) [2.4.1], available at: <https://www.commissielevelt.nl/> [accessed 20 Dec 2015].

[46] St Vincent's Hospital, Research Governance Unit, *Complaints Handling and Research Misconduct* (Procedure 3.2) 1, available at: <http://www.svhm.org.au/research/governance/Pages/IBC-Operatingprocedures.aspx> [accessed 20 Dec 2015].

Lack of Research Integrity in Historical Perspective

Lack of research integrity is not a new phenomenon. This book concentrates on events of relatively recent years but it is important to contextualize the phenomenon historically so as to view it in a proper perspective. Reconsideration of earlier experimentation has shed light on many pieces of research which, today, we suspect or know to have been affected by fraud. It also provides examples of flawed methodology that may or may not have been engaged in with a sinister purpose.

The work of Gregor Mendel, for instance, who excluded data that he regarded as the result of experimental error or otherwise anomalous, is arguably not to be regarded as fraudulent but as the product of inadequate adherence to statistical proprieties to which we subscribe today.[47] A similar claim has been made in relation to the work of Sir Cyril Burt (see below p 72), whose experiments were later substantially independently replicated, although it is strongly arguable that many of his data were fabricated.

However, different issues arose in respect of the work of Robert Millikan, the United States physicist, who, when he described the charge of an electron, pointedly 'neglected' to mention that he eliminated various data points and then used work done with a colleague, publishing it in his own name.[48] René Blondlot's work on X-rays that he described as N-rays (after the University of Nancy where he was a Professor of Physics) is an example of a cognate phenomenon—self-deception by a scientist who became too absorbed by what he was hoping would be the outcomes of his research. In due course his rays were shown to be experimental artefacts or the result of observer effects but significantly, and illustratively of the triumph of aspiration over objectivity, he (and his supporters) continued to believe in them and to evangelize them until the time of his death.[49]

Louis Pasteur's transgressions were different again.[50] To his discredit, in 1881 he omitted to refer to the fact that he used a vaccine against anthrax made by a competitor, instead emphasizing the use of a vaccine to inactivate bacilli by oxygen. Pasteur's notebooks show that he was seriously disingenuous when he suggested publicly that his dramatically successful vaccine had been developed by exposing anthrax bacteria to oxygen. The truth was that he never disclosed that he made his vaccine by secretly relying on a technique used by

---

[47] See though Ronald Fisher, 'Has Mendel's Work Been Rediscovered?' (1936) 1(2) *Annals of Science* 115, 132: '[T]he data of most, if not all, of the experiments have been falsified so as to agree closely with Mendel's expectations'. See also, Daniel L Hartl and Daniel J Fairbanks, 'Mud Sticks: On the Alleged Falsification of Mendel's Data' (2007) 175(3) *Genetics* 975.

[48] See John Grant, *Corrupted Science: Fraud, Ideology and Politics in Science* (Wisely, Surrey: Facts, Figures & Fun, 2007) 26; Committee on the Conduct of Science, National Academy of Sciences, 'On Being a Scientist' (1989) 86(23) *Proceedings of the National Academy of Sciences of the United States of America* 9053; David L Goodstein, *On Fact and Fraud: Cautionary Tales from the Front Lines of Science* (Princeton: Princeton University Press, 2010). See also, Edward Jenner who claimed credit for an experiment that involved inoculating an eight-year-old boy with cowpox, and then with smallpox; a Dorset farmer, Benjamin Jersey, having successfully performed the same action on his family 22 years earlier.

[49] See Irving M Klotz, 'The N-Ray Affair' (1980) 242(5) *Scientific American* 168; Mary Jo Nye, *Science in the Provinces: Scientific Communities and Provincial Leadership in France, 1860–1930* (Berkeley: University of California Press, 1986). It has been argued plausibly that this kind of 'wishful thinking' was responsible for the deficits in scientific method involved in Stanley Pons and Martin Fleischmann's now debunked theories of cold fusion, the notion that sustained nuclear fusion reactions can be created at room temperature in a chemistry laboratory, thereby offering an almost inexhaustible source of energy: see Thomas F Gieryn, *Cultural Boundaries of Science: Credibility on the Line* (Chicago: University of Chicago Press, 1999) 187; Gary Taubes, *Bad Science: The Short Life and Weird Times of Cold Fusion* (New York: Random House, 1993).

[50] See Grant, above n 48, 22; Gerald L Geison, *The Private Science of Louis Pasteur* (Princeton, NJ: Princeton University Press, 1995), based on an analysis of Pasteur's 102 laboratory notebooks.

a rival, Jean-Joseph Toussaint, a veterinarian, that involved a chemical, potassium bichromate.[51] In addition, his most famous experiment—on a boy, Joseph Mesiter, who had been bitten by a rabid dog and seemed to be facing certain death—was not what it seemed. Pasteur claimed that he had previously trialled his rabies vaccine on 50 dogs without a failure. However, his laboratory notebooks tell another story. He had tested a vaccine on dogs but it was prepared by a quite different method than the one he used on Joseph. At the time he injected Joseph with the vaccine there were no conclusive results as to its efficacy from previous trials. He just guessed correctly and the results were positive.

These are but a few historical examples of the phenomenon of fraudulent conduct of research in medicine and science. They are illustrative of the fact that short-cuts, reconstruction, misuse of the work of others, manipulation of data and even outright falsification of results have taken place occasionally throughout the evolution of knowledge. The more contemporary questions are whether the incidence of this phenomenon has changed, what forms it is now taking, who is responsible for it, why it occurs, and what steps can be taken to address the problem.

Perspectives on Research Fraud

Fraud in research is growing in public exposure. It has well and truly entered community consciousness. It is even the subject of popular novels.[52] As will be seen in Chapter 3, some of the perpetrators have repeatedly occupied the front pages of newspapers. A significant number have been the subject of in depth feature stories in *The New York Times*, *The Guardian* and *Time*. An aspect of this increasing profile is that we are becoming more attuned to the phenomenon and ready to 'uncover scandals' and unmask research charlatans. This is so both in respect of research fraud and plagiarism. It is impossible to identify with any accuracy the incidence of research fraud, although it appears it is not insignificant (see Chapter 1). As Malcolm Green, the former Vice-Principal of the Faculty of Medicine at Imperial College London, has observed: 'It is highly likely that for every case of fraud that is detected there are a dozen or more cases that go undetected.'[53]

Plausible claims have been made that research fraud is becoming more common. A 2012 survey of more than 2,700 researchers conducted by the *British Medical Journal* (*BMJ*) found that one in seven United Kingdom-based scientists or doctors had witnessed colleagues intentionally altering or fabricating data during their research or for the purposes of publication. The survey, which was emailed to 9,036 academics and clinicians who had submitted articles to the *BMJ* or acted as peer reviewers for the journal (response rate 31 per cent), found that 13 per cent of these researchers admitted knowledge of colleagues 'inappropriately adjusting, excluding, altering, or fabricating data for the purpose of publication'.[54]

---

[51] See Lawrence K Altman, 'The Doctor's World: Revisionist History Sees Pasteur as Liar Who Stole Rival's Ideas', *The New York Times*, 16 May 1995: <http://www.nytimes.com/1995/05/16/science/doctor-s-world-revisionist-history-sees-pasteur-liar-who-stole-rival-s-ideas.html> [accessed 20 Dec 2015].

[52] See eg Carl Djerassi, *Cantor's Dilemma* (Penguin Books, New York, 1989).

[53] Cited in Aniket Tavare, 'Managing Research Misconduct: Is Anyone Getting it Right?' (2011) 343 *BMJ* d8212: <http://www.bmj.com/content/343/bmj.d8212?ijkey=3HOrgPYu.IS/M&keytype=ref&siteid=bmjjournals> [accessed 20 Dec 2015].

[54] See Anika Tavare, 'Scientific Misconduct is Worryingly Prevalent in the UK, Shows BMJ Survey' (2012) 344 *BMJ* e377.

In 1976, fewer than ten fraud retractions for every one million studies published were recorded, compared with 96 retractions per million in 2007.[55] A detailed review of all 2,047 biomedical and life-science research articles indexed by PubMed as retracted on 3 May 2012 revealed that only 21.3 per cent of retractions were attributable to error. By contrast, 67.4 per cent of retractions were found to be attributable to misconduct, including fraud or suspected fraud (43.4 per cent), duplicate publication (14.2 per cent), and plagiarism (9.8 per cent). The authors of the review argued that incomplete, uninformative, or misleading retraction announcements have led to a previous underestimation of the role of fraud in the ongoing retraction epidemic. Retractions can exhibit distinctive temporal and geographic patterns that may reveal underlying causes and patterns of conduct. What such data require is reflection on whether there are factors within the contemporary scholarly workplace which are conducing to unethical behaviour, rather simply than a focus on the prevalence of the phenomenon, the harm that it is causing, and the incidence of retractions.

However, the evidence about the growth in detection of scientific misconduct, in part evidenced by the incidence of retractions, should not necessarily be interpreted as an increase in the incidence of scientific misconduct. What can be said is that the numbers of articles being published has increased dramatically and that researchers and journal editors are becoming more aware of the phenomenon of scientific misconduct.[56] However, the reasons for retraction of articles are diverse and subject to a host of influences and considerations.[57] There are many pressures upon journal editors to take action falling short of retracting an article. Fanelli pointed out in 2013 that significant stigma currently surrounds retractions, and that the opaqueness of many retraction notices betrays 'feelings of embarrassment. Nearly 60 per cent of retraction notices linked to misconduct only mention error, loss of data or replication failure, and less than one-third point to a specific ethical problem. Editors writing these notices often use ambiguous euphemisms in place of technical definitions of misconduct, perhaps to prevent legal actions. Although retraction notices are becoming more transparent, many journals still lack clear policies for misconduct and retraction, fail to distinguish between misconduct and error, and existing policies are applied inconsistently.'[58] Her persuasive argument was that we should work towards encouraging editors and authors who proactively removed flawed publications from the literature as exemplars of integrity.

For research fraud to accomplish its objective, so far as the perpetrator is concerned, at least some of the time it must achieve an objective that is predetermined—for instance, a position that a funder hopes will be demonstrated through experimentation. Generally, there is an imperative for research outcomes to be published in apparently plausible and respected forums. While journals' ethical policies, especially those on conflicts of interest, have tended to become more sophisticated since the turn of the millennium, with some adopting a uniform approach, only around half of biomedical journals, principally those with higher impact factors, have been identified to have formal misconduct policies, mainly for handling

[55] Ferric C Fang, R Grant Steen, and Arturo Casadevall, 'Misconduct Accounts for the Majority of Retracted Scientific Publications' (2012) 109(42) *Proceedings of the National Academy of Sciences of the United States of America* 17028.

[56] See Daniele Fanelli, 'Why Growing Retractions are (Mostly) A Good Sign' (2013) 10(12) *Plos Med* 1001563.

[57] See Peter Williams and Elizabeth Wager, 'Why and How do Journal Editors Retract Articles: Findings from a Qualitative Study' (2013) 19 *Science and Engineering Ethics* 1.

[58] See Daniele Fanelli, 'Why Growing Retractions are (Mostly) A Good Sign' (2013) 10(12) *Plos Med* 1001563; Elizabeth Wager and Peter Williams, 'Why and How Do Journals Retract Articles? An Analysis of Medline Retractions 1988–2008' (2011) 37 *Journal of Medical Ethics* 567.

allegations.[59] Worryingly, since a response to allegations would reasonably require an *a priori* definition, relatively few journals have publicly available definitions of misconduct. While some journals and editors' associations have taken significant steps to prevent and detect misconduct and respond to allegations, the content, visibility of, and access to these policies vary considerably. Research misconduct can be viewed as a subset of research error—what distinguishes it is its intentionality. Research error in published scholarly literature is significant in dimensions. For instance, Bakker and Wicherts[60] in 2011 reviewed 281 psychological research articles for statistical error. They found that approximately 18 per cent of statistical results in the psychological literature were incorrectly reported. Not surprisingly, inconsistencies were more common in low-impact journals than in high-impact journals where reviewing tends to be more rigorous. Moreover, around 15 per cent of the articles contained at least one statistical conclusion that proved, on recalculation, to be incorrect; that is, recalculation rendered the previously significant result insignificant, or vice versa.

Similarly, in 2004 García-Berthou and Alcaraz[61] reviewed the congruence in 44 articles published in *Nature* and the *BMJ* by comparing the reported test statistics and *df* with the reported *p* value. They found that 11.6 per cent of the statistical results reported in *Nature* and 11.1 per cent of the statistical results reported in the *BMJ* were incongruent. At least one such error appeared in 38 per cent and 25 per cent of the articles of *Nature* and the *BMJ* respectively.

In short, then, it is necessary to locate research misconduct within the fabric of mistake, error, and poor scholarship but also to separate it out by reference to its key element of what motivates it—the deliberate engagement, for the range of reasons discussed above, in dishonest construction and presentation of the fruits of scholarly labour. That said, pragmatically, destigmatizing removal of articles from published literature via retractions needs to take place more frankly, quicker and with less hesitation so as to preserve the integrity of the scholarly corpus of work available for other scholars to incorporate into their research, treatment, analysis, and application.

Learning from Scandal

Richard Smith, a former editor of the *BMJ*, has observed that '[r]esponses to fraud are driven by scandals. They accumulate to a point where the scientific community can no longer ignore them and "something has to be done"'.[62] A significant number of frauds have periodically distressed and embarrassed the scientific and medical research establishment. Their pathogenesis has been complex and relatively little studied in a generic way.[63] Almost all have had

[59] See Xavier Bosch, 'Improving Biomedical Journals' Ethical Policies: The Case of Research Misconduct' (2014) 40(9) *Journal of Medical Ethics* 644; see too, Elizabeth Wager and Peter Williams, 'Hardly Worth the Effort? Medical Journals' Policies and their Editors' and Publishers' Views on Trial Registration and Publication Bias: Quantitative and Qualitative Study' (2013) 347 *BMJ* f5248: <http://www.bmj.com/content/bmj/347/bmj.f5248.full.pdf> (viewed 13 January 2015).

[60] Marjan Bakker and Jelte M Wicherts, 'The (Mis)reporting of Statistical Results in Psychology Journals' (2011) 43(3) *Behavior Research Methods* 666.

[61] Emili García-Berthou and Carles Alcaraz, 'Incongruence between Test Statistics and *P* Values in Medical Papers' (2004) 4 *BMC Medical Research Methodology* 13.

[62] Richard Smith, 'Research Misconduct: The Poisoning of the Well' (2006) 99(5) *Journal of the Royal Society of Medicine* 232–7.

[63] See though Royal College of Physicians of London, 'Fraud and Misconduct in Medical Research: Causes, Investigation and Prevention: A Report of the Royal College of Physicians' (1991) 25(2) *Journal of the Royal College of Physicians of London* 89; Robert G Petersdorf, 'The Pathogenesis of Fraud in Medical Science' (1986) 104(2) *Annals of Internal Medicine* 252.

an instructive attribute from which there was the potential for lessons to be learned to reduce the potential for further fraud. Sometimes such matters have been attended to and been the subject of considered response, but all too often reactions have taken place only within the discipline or sub-discipline concerned, rather than being extrapolated more broadly and seen within the bigger context of abuse of research proprieties. What has occurred has been a short-lived scandal with the outlawing of an individual from the relevant intellectual community without the systemic and much more confronting questions being asked about how the deception took place without early effective detection and in spite of the checks and balances set in place in an attempt to guard against such deception. Instead, the individual has been pilloried and demonized and the employing institution and the discipline have proceeded, a little chastened, but much as before, with science and medicine paying little heed to the fact that the barriers against research misconduct have again been exposed as inadequate.

Too frequently, the institutional approach to allegations of research fraud has consisted of either a 'civilized resolution' of allegations behind the scenes (prioritizing the reputation of the university or research body) or, paradoxically, when this has proved not to be possible, haranguing of the accuser or, less often, the person the subject of the allegations. It is rare for the notifier or whistleblower to receive much by way of gratitude or recognition for their intellectual integrity or courage (see Chapter 10). Frequently, revelation of improper conduct by a colleague has wrought savage personal consequences for those who have been the source of initial expressions of concern or who have 'blown the whistle' from inside.[64] What has tended not to be prompted by identified instances of research misconduct, is a reflective and measured response directed towards changing the culture that allowed or encouraged the conduct.

Motives for Research Fraud

There are many reasons it is important to understand why it is and how it could be that highly educated, often otherwise decent and law-abiding scholars, engage in research misconduct. It is only by such appreciation that we have the potential to respond adequately and to devise both investigative and deterrent strategies.

Misconduct has been said to represent 'the dark side of the hypercompetitive environment of contemporary science', with its emphasis on funding, numbers of publications, and impact factors.[65] It has been said to be 'like doping: [i]t is about gaining an unfair advantage in a competition'.[66] As such it tends to evolve in a hidden place without the light that accountability and transparency usually bring being shone on the phenomenon. Sometimes it is put in terms of 'bad apples' in a barrel. However, there are good reasons to view the barrel itself as playing a role in facilitating and enabling the state of the apples that it holds.[67] This is not to justify in any way the relinquishment of ethical responsibility by scholars who 'go bad' but to recognize that their conduct does not take place in a vacuum and that there is a range of situational, personality, and institutional issues that play a contextual role in particular conduct engaged in by particular scholars whose research becomes seriously unacceptable.

---

[64] Thomas Faunce, Stephen Bolsin, and Wei-Ping Chan, 'Supporting Whistleblowers in Academic Medicine: Training and Respecting the Courage of Professional Conscience' (2004) 30(1) *Journal of Medical Ethics* 40.

[65] Ferric C Fang, Arturo Casadevall, and RP Morrison, 'Retracted Science and the Retraction Index' (2011) 79(10) *Infection and Immunity* 3855, 3857.

[66] Victoria Stern, 'Research Misconduct on the Rise' (2012) 7(12) *Clinical Oncology News* 24, 26, available at: <http://media.wix.com/ugd/53772d_6766ad47dab4f030daaf64d9bebfe6a7.pdf> [accessed 20 Dec 2015].

[67] See Barbara K Redman, *Research Misconduct Policy in Biomedicine: Beyond the Bad-Apple Approach* (Cambridge, Mass: The MIT Press, 2013).

Inevitably fraudulent research behaviour involves a high level of rationalization and an element of moral disengagement on the part of perpetrators. This is a phenomenon well recognized in many other forms of social deviance.[68] There are a number of psychological devices that tend to be adopted to reduce the operation of the inhibitions that otherwise regulate ethical conduct and discourage unethical conduct—including minimization of what is done, cognitive restructuring or distortion of behaviour, disputing the harm that may flow, minimizing the human aspects of the injurious effects of conduct, justification by reference to the advantages flowing from the conduct (ie the end justifying the means), investing conduct with a high (albeit spurious) moral purpose, redefining actions as honourable or necessary or socially acceptable, sanitizing the behaviour by the deployment of euphemisms, and blaming others by displacing personal responsibility for what is being done.[69] When conduct is engaged in to some degree with others, this too can facilitate a reduction in a person's perception of personal responsibility—the fact that conduct is engaged in company or across institutions can weaken moral controls and regulatory responsiveness.[70] The pages that follow in this book eloquently give voice to the employment of each of these psychological devices on the part of scholars who have engaged in one form or another of misconduct.

David Wright, a Michigan State University Professor, and later Director of the United States Office of Research Integrity, has researched why scientists engage in deception. He has argued that there are four basic reasons: some form of mental disorder, foreign nationals who learned somewhat different scientific standards, inadequate mentoring, and, most commonly, tremendous and increasing professional pressure to publish studies.[71]

However, this fails to have regard to the psychological mechanisms referred to above and also to the ambition of some scholars to obtain a competitive advantage over their rivals, obsessive perfectionism, a fear of failure or perceived failure,[72] preparedness to take short-cuts to accelerate career opportunities, and the inclination by some to fabricate research in order to achieve kudos, opportunity, or research grants that would not otherwise be available.[73] Lawson has argued in relation to medical practitioners who engage in fraudulent practices that:

> The usual motivation appears to be a mixture of intense career and peer pressure to produce significant results and publications, financial incentives to obtain funding grants, and personality disorders or weaknesses, especially vanity and arrogance—the messiah complex.
>
> There appear to be two main groups of fraudsters. The first group is the overly ambitious young researcher, determined to climb rapidly up the career ladder. The second group is more perplexing—senior doctors, often at the height of their careers, and often occupying prestigious positions.[74]

---

[68] See eg, James R Detert, Linda K Trevino, and Vicki L Sweitzer, 'Moral Disengagement in Ethical Decision-making: A Study of Antecedents and Outcomes' (2008) 93(2) *Journal of Applied Psychology* 374.

[69] See eg, Albert Bandura, *Self-Efficacy: The Exercise of Control* (New York: WH Freeman, 1997); Albert Bandura, 'Selective Moral Disengagement in the Exercise of Moral Agency' (2002) 31(2) *Journal of Moral Education* 101; Albert Bandura, 'Moral Disengagement in the Perpetration of Inhumanities' (1999) 3(3) *Personality and Social Psychology Review* 193.

[70] See Philip G Zimbardo, 'The Psychology of Evil: A Situationist Perspective on Recruiting Good People to Engage in Anti-Social Acts' (1995) 11(2) *Research in Social Psychology* 125.

[71] See Martha Mendoza (Associated Press), 'Allegations of Fake Medical Research Hit New High', Rense.com, 12 July 2005: <http://rense.com/general66/newhigh.htm> [accessed 20 Dec 2015]. See also, Goodstein, above n 48, 3.

[72] Donald S Kornfeld, 'Research Misconduct: The Search for a Remedy' (2012) 87(7) *Academic Medicine* 877.

[73] See Gerhard Falk, *Fraud: Deceit Among Scientists, Academics, Writers and Philanthropists* (Lanham, Md: University Press of America, 2007).

[74] Gerald Lawson, 'Painting the Mice' (2012) 14(2) *O&G Magazine* 45, 48, available at: <http://www.ranzcog.edu.au/editions/doc_view/1016-45-painting-the-mice.html> [accessed 20 Dec 2015].

A combination of ordinary unadulterated laziness, unregulated ambition, and a sense of being beyond administrative rules often facilitates research misconduct. On occasion the mania that can drive excessive production of publications can play a role—including in the context of a bipolar illness or a cyclothymic disorder. Sometimes personality disorders, including outright psychopathy, can be involved.

The extent of pecuniary benefits available for successful fraud and the pressures on those within the academic and research communities have produced new incentives to depart from accepted standards of propriety in the research area. These are not always inhibited and responded to by institutions in the way that one might expect or wish. Redman has observed: 'Research institutions at universities can be particularly dysfunctional environments. Dramatic reductions in state and federal funding for research have produced highly competitive workplaces with fewer checks on research misconduct than those in business settings.'[75] In addition, workplace dissatisfaction, a known risk factor for deviance in the workplace, is growing, especially in the tertiary sector with graduates carrying heavy loans, lay-offs of academics as part of cost-cutting, and both postgraduates and many staff feeling inadequately supported in their research endeavours.

Profiles of the Fraudulent

Fraudulent (and plagiarist) activity is rarely engaged in as a one-off. It is seductive when it goes undetected and such conduct tends to be a highly recidivist form of behaviour. However, and this needs to be emphasized, most scholars are persons of integrity who subscribe and adhere to principles of scientific propriety. It is a small, but significant, proportion of scholars that is engaging serially in this form of professionally deviant behaviour and bringing the rigorous research of others into undeserved disrepute.

In order to understand such activity and those who engage in it, endeavours that are fundamental to reducing the incidence of research fraud (and plagiarism), it is useful to plot what kinds of people commence such conduct, what gains they obtain from it, what motivations drive them to persist in it, and how they respond to those who raise queries about their methodologies and publications. Such information is potentially useful for regulators.

Certain kinds of personalities have figured prominently among those who have been discovered to have engaged in fraudulent conduct—those with a pathological need for affirmation, the grandiose, the narcissistic, those with an overly robust sense of entitlement, and, at times, those with a loosened grip on reality and propriety.[76] Thus, there can be elements of both personality disorder and pathology among perpetrators of significant research fraud. Often they are charismatic, powerful figures whose industry and ambition lead them to assume an influential role in their discipline at a precocious age and which drive them to ever more determined efforts to achieve prominence and leadership in their field.

Anecdotal experience suggests that persons with either manic/cyclothymic elements to their personality or a formal diagnosis of bipolar disorder appear to be over-represented. However, more commonly, it is simply a decision on the part of some to take anti-social advantage of the opportunities that exist in the vast maelstrom of globalized research endeavour and

75 Redman, above n 67, 29.

76 See James M DuBois, Emily E Anderson, John Chibnall, Kelly Carroll et al. 'Understanding Research Misconduct: A Comparative Analysis of 120 Cases of Professional Wrongdoing' (2013) 20(5–6) *Accountability in Research: Policies and Quality Assurance* 320.

scholarly output to portray results in ways that do not wholly conform to the truth, and that are consistent with the preconceived aims of the research, the actual results notwithstanding. Thereby, they advantage themselves and seek to promote their reputation. Psychologically there is often a deep wellspring of inadequacy and low self-esteem in such persons and a craving for constant attention and ego-gratification or reinforcement through the medium of high-profile publications in their name.[77]

Another characteristic of those who engage in such conduct is that they tend to respond combatively to allegations of scholarly impropriety with aggressive denial and strategically intimidating responses. Their reputations and their often fragile egos are threatened, never mind everything that their hard work, including their dishonesty, has sought to accomplish, so such a reaction should not be surprising. They can be obsessive and remarkably persistent in their defence, availing themselves at considerable expense of multiple tactics, including those in the legal domain, to dispute the accusations against them. Commonly, the nature of their responses and the tactics they employ are not related to the objective strength or accuracy of the allegations they are facing. Thus they may sue their accusers, maintain a campaign for years against those who accuse them or find against them, or write self-serving accounts of how they have been victimized and misunderstood. Sometimes this even occurs when the allegations made are not overly serious.

A Self-Portrait of Research Fraud: Diederik Stapel

A remarkable and in some respects chilling opportunity for better understanding of the aetiology of extensive research fraud, the attraction of it, and the processes by which it can be accomplished, was provided by the disgraced Dutch social psychologist, Diederik Stapel. In 2012 Stapel published his autobiography, *Ontsporing*, in English *The Derailment*.[78] It constitutes one of the most articulate and riveting descriptions of deviant professional conduct ever written. It is perhaps not constructive to engage in speculation as to whether the author has a form of a personality disorder or psychopathy. What is helpful is the capacity it provides for the reader to identify cognitive distortions that can facilitate an abrogation of professional integrity. In Stapel's case there remain such distortions but what he does do in *The Derailment* is to provide to the reader an opportunity to learn through his *ex post facto* accounts about his mindset when he engaged in the relevant conduct.

---

[77] See, for instance, the fabricated research of John Darsee, a clinical investigator at the Brigham and Women's Hospital, a teaching affiliate of Harvard University, which resulted in the retraction of multiple journal articles and more than 45 abstracts: Carol Ann Cochan and John M Budd, 'The Persistence of Fraud in the Literature: The Darsee Case' (1992) 43(7) *Journal of the American Society for Information Science* 488, available at: <http://www.h2mw.eu/redactionmedicale/2012/02/Darsee%20J%20Am%20Soc%20Information%20Science.pdf> [accessed 20 Dec 2015]. See also the absurdly high output of Robert Slutsky, a cardiologic radiologist at the University of California, San Diego, which in due course was found to have generated 48 questionable and 12 fraudulent publications: William P Whitely, Drummond Rennie, and Arthur W Hafner, 'The Scientific Community's Response to Evidence of Fraudulent Publication: The Robert Slutsky Case' (1994) 272(2) *Journal of the American Medical Association* 170; Horace Freeland Judson, *The Great Betrayal: Fraud in Science* (Orlando: Harcourt, 2004); 'The Morality of Scientists: II Report of the Faculty Ad Hoc Committee to Investigate Research Fraud, 30 September 1986' (1987) 25(4) *Minerva* 504. See also, the case of Mohammed El Naschie discussed in Chapter 7 who, as the editor-in-chief of the journal *Chaos, Solitons and Fractals*, reportedly misused his editorial privilege as editor-in-chief in order to self-publish.

[78] *Faking Science: A True Story of Academic Fraud* ©2014 by Diederik Stapel, translated by Nicholas JL Brown, available at <http://nick.brown.free.fr/stapel/> [accessed 20 Dec 2015]. Extracts used with permission. The opinions expressed in the present work do not necessarily reflect the opinions of Diederik Stapel. (Viewed 19 May 2015; translations slightly revised by Nicholas JL Brown, June 2015).

As is outlined in Chapter 3, Stapel was responsible for premeditated and thoroughgoing scholarly fraud in psychological research for one-and-a-half decades—between 1996 and 2011.[79] His modus operandi, to use Babbage terminology, commenced with trimming and evolved into outright forging. Stapel's fraud incorporated no fewer than 55 publications, many of them co-authored, but for which he was principally responsible. He ascribes an altruistic purpose for *Ontsporing*: 'an attempt to reconstruct my spin-off and the inevitable crash into a very solid wall that followed it. Hopefully, this reconstruction will allow for a better understanding of what happened, for me but also for others who want to know.'[80]

Stapel outlines the frustration he experienced when his experiments did not yield the desired results and thereby the temptation he felt to manipulate his data so that the outcomes would conform to experimental anticipation. His attitudes towards science are revealing. He describes it as having become 'about convincing people'[81]: journals to publish articles, superiors to promote researchers, funding bodies to make grants, award-distributing bodies to make awards. To Stapel all of such 'success' was about producing approbation which he found to be seductive: 'Applause is nice. Success feels good'.[82] Tellingly, he also characterizes modern science as 'about marketing. As a scientist, if you can't get enough people interested in your ideas and discoveries, the value of your career stock drops substantially. In contemporary science the message is not just "publish or perish"... but also increasingly "sell or sink". Science is a business... [the] constant shortage of resources means that scientists spend a great deal of their time chasing after subsidies, grants, and lucrative gigs in the private sector... They have to bring both their work and themselves in to the spotlight... '[83] Thus he depicts a scholarly marketplace dominated by commerciality and ambition, with many features in common with share-dealing on the stock market—the most notable stock is the breakthrough form, perhaps biotech. The notion of commodified scholarship is a telling and revealing analogy.

He describes today's scientists as not just 'treasure hunters looking for hidden jewels; they're also sales managers with objective publication targets to meet'.[84] He chronicles his experience of the dynamics within academia too, conceding that 'over time, my need to score and my quest for applause came to dominate. Scoring gets you applause, and an objective high score gets you loud applause. And loud applause is great, because it drowns out some of the doubts you're having about whether what you're doing and who you are is really worth anything'.[85]

The picture he paints is one where the aspiration of at least a proportion of scholars is to be a 'celebrity intellect', the focus of attention and adulation in an environment where this constitutes the apogee of the profession of scholar, bringing an array of benefits that transcend kudos and include significant financial advantage. The fallacy in Stapel's view of science is that he generalizes from his own needs and aspirations—he appears to believe that he is representative of the community of scholars. However, his neediness to address deep-seated feelings of inadequacy and insecurity is illustrative—it provides something of a psychological

---

Martin Enserink has noted that the title is 'apparent reference to *Ontspoorde Wetenschap* (*Derailed Science*), a recent book by Dutch journalist Frank van Kolfschooten in which Stapel features prominently': Martin Enserink, 'Final Report: Stapel Affair Points to Bigger Problems in Social Psychology' (28 November 2012) *Science*: <http://news.sciencemag.org/people-events/2012/11/final-report-stapel-affair-points-bigger-problems-social-psychology> [accessed 20 Dec 2015].

79 See also John M Budd, 'The Stapel Case: An Object Lesson in Research Integrity and its Lapses' (2013) *Synesis* G47: <http://www.synesisjournal.com/vol4_g/Budd_2013_G47-53.pdf> [accessed 20 Dec 2015].

80 Stapel, n 78, iii.

81 Stapel, n 78, 86.

82 Stapel, n 78, 89.

83 Stapel, n 78, 92–3.

84 Stapel, n 78, 97.

85 Stapel, n 78, 97.

explanation for his preparedness first to test ethical limits and then to breach them egregiously and persistently.

In the broader context, Stapel makes the interesting point that today's enhanced access to information has brought its own new dynamics, with the internet seeming 'to increase the demand for simple, elegant analyses that depicted social reality with couple of swift brush strokes'. He identifies an impetus not to publish grand theoretical pieces but 'short, hard-hitting research reports'.[86]

He concedes that he adapted readily to this 'market opportunity'. Stapel describes learning early in his career the technique of developing a series of experiments, when the first had succeeded, that contained 'just a few small variations in the topic and questions. That allowed me to write three or four articles: lots of thin slices of salami, earning me lots more applause'.[87] From there, he developed techniques that:

> could put a healthy-looking shine on otherwise mediocre results. If I didn't get the effect I wanted across all the different measures I'd used or the questions I'd asked, I would use the ones that did show that effect. If an effect was present in an experiment, but not strongly enough to be tapped by all the types of measurements I'd used, I would make it stronger by combining the measures where the effect seemed to be only partly working. If I'd designed a study for six groups of participants who'd all been given slightly different tasks or shown different things and one group gave a strange result that I couldn't explain, I would change the design so that the strange result disappeared, but the overall setup still appeared coherent. Then it became a three- or four- or five-group design, instead of six. The inexplicable results went into the trash. If an experiment didn't work, I would go hunting in the dataset for outliers (strange cases where individual participants have unexpected answers or measurements that are wildly different from the average), and look for reasons why it was OK to throw them out. If they were a little older, or younger, or slower, or faster, or in whichever way not quite 'normal', then maybe it was OK to eliminate them, to bring the results more in line with what I'd been expecting.
>
> I knew that this was at the outer limits of what was acceptable, or even beyond those limits in some cases, but...I wanted the results so badly. Plus, it worked in an earlier study, and the results were really almost, *almost* right, and it must be true because it's so logical, and it was such a great idea, and I surely wasn't the only person doing this sort of thing. What I did wasn't whiter than white, but it wasn't completely black either. It was grey, and it was what everyone did. How else did all those other researchers get all those great results?

What is particularly pronounced in this respect is his resort to moral relativism[88] as a form of minimization of the wrongfulness of his behaviour, his amoral methodologies. He relates spending years precariously balancing on 'the outer limits' until 'the grey became darker and darker until it was black, and I fell off the edge into the abyss'.[89] Thus the picture that he paints is one of unclear ethical boundaries which he navigated for a long while until some kind of almost involuntary event occurred in which he found himself behaving unmistakably unethically. The rationalization and minimization of his own culpability is evident—an abrogation of his professional responsibility to conduct himself properly and do the hard work, rather than have resort to intellectual 'short-cuts' and excuses to generate results which he wanted.

---

[86] Stapel, n 78, 110.

[87] Stapel, n 78, 101.

[88] See Samuel Fleischacker, *Integrity and Moral Relativism* (Leiden: Brill, 1992); J David Velleman, *Foundations for Moral Relativism* (Cambridge: Open Book Publishers, 2013); Jeffrey Beatty and Susan Samuelson, *Business Law and the Legal Environment* (Melbourne, Cengage Learning, 2015), 32.

[89] Stapel, n 78, 102.

Stapel describes having had trouble with his results for some time and finding that his 'grey techniques' for 'improving' his results were still not accomplishing the objectives that he wanted:

> I couldn't resist the temptation to go a step further. I wanted it so badly. I wanted to belong, to be part of the action, to score. I really, really wanted to be really, really good. I wanted to be published in the best journals and speak in the largest room at conferences. I wanted people to hang on my every word as I headed for coffee or lunch after delivering a lecture. I felt very alone.[90]

Thus, his explanation is that he yielded to a temptation whereby his desire to be outstanding brought him undone. He makes himself appear a tragic and honourable victim. The cognitive distortions are apparent. To Stapel he is a hero with a tragic flaw:

> My desire for answers became bigger than the wonder that I was able to experience when I looked the messy truth square in the face. My desire for clear, simple solutions became stronger than the deep emotions that I felt when I was confronted with the ragged edges of reality. It had to be simple, clear, beautiful, and elegant. It had to be too good to be true.[91]

However, he goes a step further, almost pathologizing his conduct, apparently thereby in his mind mitigating his culpability. He describes reality as becoming 'fickle' for him and to be exhausting.[92] His ambitions were for different and more adulatory approbation by reason of his capacity to make remarkable and memorable contributions to scholarship:

> I started to be unhappy with my complicated and not particularly elegant message. I was bored with the unimpressive assortment of tiny effects and barely significant results that I'd assembled over time. My work received plaudits, but always in terms such as 'professional,' 'conscientious,' 'interesting.' What I produced was never described as 'beautiful,' 'brilliant,' 'elegant,' 'powerful,' or 'fascinating.' I built on what others had discovered, but I was never at the start of the chain of research; I was always at the end. . . . I published all kinds of things, but for whom? My minor artisanal discoveries were too trivial to make it into textbooks, and my theories were too dry for anyone to want a chapter on them in the handbook they were editing. At conferences I was still in the small-to-medium rooms off to one side. I'd never been invited to be the keynote speaker. I was bored. I wanted to come up with a line of research that everyone would want to follow.[93]

Later in the book he uses another analogy, painting himself as a kind of Jekyll and Hyde scholar:

> Six days a week I'm a solid, normal professor, and on the seventh day I turn into a kind of guerrilla scientist, a research hustler. Two identities in one person. I'm like an onion: peel off another layer and there's something else weird underneath, every time. I'm disgusted with myself. It's good that this [discovery] has happened because I want it to stop.[94]

Whether this goes beyond a rather hackneyed attempt to absolve himself of responsibility is highly questionable.

Then he provides an almost cinematic description of how he unequivocally crossed the line into outright falsification:

> I was alone in my tastefully furnished office at the University of Groningen. I'd taken extra care when closing the door, and made my desk extra tidy. Everything had to be neat and

[90] Stapel, n 78, 102–3.
[91] Stapel, n 78, 207.
[92] Stapel, n 78, 108.
[93] Stapel, n 78, 111.
[94] Stapel, n 78, 138.

> orderly. No mess. I opened the computer file with the data that I had entered and changed an unexpected 2 into a 4; then, a little further along, I changed a 3 into a 5. It didn't feel right.
>
> I looked around me nervously. The data danced in front of my eyes. When the results are just not quite what you'd so badly hoped for; when you know that that hope is based on a thorough analysis of the literature; when this is your third experiment on this topic and the first two worked great; when you know that there are other people doing similar research elsewhere who are getting good results; then, surely, you're entitled to adjust the results just a little?
>
> No. I clicked on 'Undo Typing.' And again. I felt very alone. I didn't want this. I'd worked so hard. I'd done everything I could and it just hadn't quite worked the way I'd expected. It just wasn't quite how everyone could see that it logically had to be.
>
> I looked at the door of my office. It was still closed. I looked out the window. It was dark outside. 'Redo Typing.' And again. For a moment I had the feeling that someone was standing behind me. I turned round slowly, fearfully. There was nobody there. I looked at the array of data and made a few mouse clicks.[95]

He discovered that the process of fraud was remarkably straightforward, an important revelation in itself. Again he implicitly suggests that in some way the ease of transgression and the absence of effective checks and balances together constitute a feature of his conduct that makes it, and him, less ethically culpable:

> when I started to fake my studies, it was very, very easy. I was always alone. Nobody checked my work; everyone trusted me. I did everything myself. Everything. I thought up the idea, I did the experiment, and I evaluated the results. I was judge, jury, and executioner. I did everything myself because I wanted to be one of the elite, to create great things and score lots of major publications. I did it all myself, with a big cookie jar right next to me. No mom, no lock, not even a lid. And full. I worked day after day, with the cookie jar full of goodies sitting, open, right there with me—and nobody watching. I could take whatever I wanted. One cookie. Nobody noticed. One piece of candy. Mmm, nice. Another one. That's enough for now. Another one. I should stop, but I can't. Just one more. And all this time, the serpent of temptation, of desire for fame and success and applause, was whispering, hissing softly in my ear…[96]

As he put it though: 'I didn't feel anything: no disgust, no shame, no regrets';[97] feelings were sacrificed to accomplishment, guilt gave way to ambition. In Stapel's words, his fraud arose as a noxious interaction of person and scholarly workplace: 'being driven by success, the fear of failure, an insatiable desire for elegant solutions to complex problems, the inevitable wish to make the world a better place for oneself and others and to create meaning where it seemed to be missing, and a toxic environment that allowed all this to happen.'[98]

He reiterates the theme of the almost complete absence of scientific control structures in social psychology, which he says made it too hard for him to resist temptation.

Stapel likens his fraud to an addiction, another exercise in trying to reduce his blameworthiness, although he admits that it was probably a combination of different factors, including:

> You could come up with a whole list of possible explanations: a desire to achieve something, naked ambition, laziness, nihilism, a lust for power, status anxiety, the urge to find solutions, the need to feel whole, pressure to 'publish or perish,' arrogance, emotional flakiness, loneliness, disappointment, low attention span, addiction to answers, etc, but none of these constructs had sufficient *explanatory power* to reveal why I'd done what I had. You'd need the

95 Stapel, n 78, 103.
96 Stapel, n 69, 78, 115–16.
97 Stapel, n 78, 118.
98 Stapel, n 78, 191.

whole set, and then a whole lot more. I'd spent years trying to find simpler and more concise explanations and theories to describe human behavior, but all the time that I'd been looking for order, structure, and simplicity I'd been keeping my eyes more and more tightly shut to reality until the inevitable happened, and I'd crashed and burned.[99]

This illustrates another theme of *The Derailment* that what happened was something that was fore-ordained—it was not all the fault of Stapel.

Once he started faking his data, he portrays himself as being in a cycle from which he could not extricate himself. He describes various unsuccessful attempts he made to quit what he described as his 'drug'. He outlines candidly the straightforward modus operandi that he utilized:

I preferred to do it at home, late in the evening, in fact at the beginning of the night, when everyone was asleep. I would make myself some tea, put my laptop on the kitchen table, get my notebook from my backpack, take out my fountain pen, and make a careful list of all the results and effects I needed to create for the study I was doing. Neat tables with the results I expected based on extensive reading, theorizing, and thinking. Simple, elegant, comprehensible. Next I started to enter the data, column by column, row by row. I tried to imagine how the participants' answers to my questionnaire would look. What were some reasonable answers that might be expected? 3, 4, 6, 7, 8, 4, 5, 3, 5, 6, 7, 8, 5, 4, 3, 3, 2. When I'd input all the data, I ran some quick preliminary analyses. Often these didn't show what I was expecting, so I went back to the matrix of data to change a few things. 4, 6, 7, 5, 4, 7, 8, 2, 4, 4, 6, 5, 6, 7, 8, 5, 4. And so on, until the analyses provided the results I was looking for. That is, until the data showed what was logical, and therefore true. I always worked as fast as possible. It was a terrible, nauseating experience that I wanted to be over quickly. I wanted to stop, but I couldn't. I could have stopped, but I didn't want to. Quickly, panting for breath, stumbling as I approached the finishing line, I typed in the last of the data, hoping I wouldn't have to stop and throw up into the bushes by the side of the road.[100]

He describes feelings of grandiosity and a sense that he became an illusionist, perhaps again seeking refuge in a quasi-mental illness excuse:

I was a magician. I created my own reality, and everyone thought it was real. Magic is a combination of technical ability and distraction. I was pretty good at the technical aspects of my work, which made it easy to hide what I was doing with smoke and mirrors. The research I did was never too extreme, too weird, or too flashy. It was usually completely logical; sometimes even a bit dull.[101]

He highlights a cumulative toll of what he was doing, though:

[becoming] more and more isolated, more and more detached from reality, because I couldn't be myself. I was accumulating secrets and had more and more to hide. I talked less and less, partly because I didn't want to let anything slip out in conversation, but also because I didn't think that I had anything to say. What I thought and felt was based on lies and fantasy, on nothing. I wanted to put everything behind me and blot out the memories. Sweep it all away and carry on as if nothing had happened. I'd stopped enjoying my work.[102]

A theme of Stapel's autobiography is his expression of contrition for his conduct. There can be no doubt that he does express regret in his accounts of his professional life but in doing so he portrays himself as a victim to others' schadenfreude. His distress is mostly for his own plight. To be fair, there is acknowledgment (for which he deserves credit) of the consequences

99 Stapel, n 78, at 162.
100 Stapel, n 78, at 119.
101 Stapel, n 78, 128.
102 Stapel, n 78, 128.

of the disrepute into which his actions have brought social psychology,[103] and the impact of his behaviour on his co-researchers and students:

> ...all the way down the hierarchy—science, academia, psychology, social psychology, the University of Tilburg, my close colleagues, co-authors, students, and supervisees—all have taken a substantial hit. Colleagues, students, and supervisees have worked for years on experiments and studies whose empirical basis now turns out to be nothing more than dust. Dozens of published articles are going to have to be retracted, removed from their CVs, and apologized for. Some of their best insights and discoveries are revealed to be no more than mirages. The pride with which they defended their theses has gone, shriveled, replaced in many cases with feelings of guilt and shame. 'It's unfair!' I want to shout. 'I did it. They didn't do anything wrong. They couldn't have known. They worked really hard, in good faith. I'm the only one you should blame.'[104]

Mostly, though, it is all about Stapel and his family. His focus is dominated by self-pity and distress about the consequences of the exposure of his conduct. It is on portraying himself in a sympathetic human light and to emphasize the dreadful consequences which discovery of his misconduct have had for him—to avoid criminal prosecution and perhaps to lay the groundwork for an attempt to make a 'comeback' to some form of professional life. Borsboom and Wagenmakers, reviewing his book, identify a related issue. They have expressed reservations about the authenticity of Stapel's apparent contrition, noting his propensity for poetic descriptions of his wife which they assert are plagiarized from the fiction writers Raymond Carvers and James Joyce whose work he only acknowledges in appendices: 'This odd path to attribution is telling; the reader cannot help but wonder whether there may be yet another literary layer of deceit under the apparently candid book.'[105]

Stapel's autobiography has been very controversial. It is self-serving and repeatedly self-justifying. It is permeated by narcissism and minimization of his conduct. It is attention-seeking, and displays at best modest insight into the ramifications of his behaviour. It craves forgiveness and rehabilitation.[106] However, at times it is also searing in its attempts at honesty and self-revelation; for this there is reason to be appreciative. Perhaps what is so confronting about it is that to anyone who has worked in a scholarly environment the flamboyant portrayal by Stapel of himself is of a person that we can all recognize. It is not of the 'Bernard Madoff of social psychology', or a 'monster', as he bitterly designates himself,[107] but of a familiar, self-absorbed, fallible, and ambitious scholar who has been exposed for temptations to which he has succumbed. Uncomfortably, it makes one wonder how many other Stapels there are (perhaps whom we have encountered) who have not yet been exposed or whose misconduct has been less extreme, but similarly sociopathic and unethical.

What *The Derailment* does in a way that no other professional responsible for large-scale research fraud has done before is to enable us to understand better the process of rationalization

---

103 For instance: 'Day after day, week after week, I'm getting spat on, insulted, and tarred and feathered in news reports, feature columns, background stories, human interest pieces, editorial comments, and readers' letters. I've sullied the name of science, sinned against the holiest of holies, and now my name is being dragged through the mud of the mass media...' Stapel, n 78, (167).

104 Stapel, n 78, 171–2.

105 Denny Borsboom and Eric-Jan Wagenmakers, '*Derailed: The Rise and Fall of Diederik Stapel*' (book review): (2013) 26(1) *Observer*: <http://www.psychologicalscience.org/index.php/publications/observer/2013/january-13/derailed-the-rise-and-fall-of-diederik-stapel.html> [accessed 20 Dec 2015].

106 Yudhijit Bhattacharjee, 'The Mind of a Con-Man' (26 April 2013) *The New York Times*: <http://www.nytimes.com/2013/04/28/magazine/diederik-stapels-audacious-academic-fraud.html?pagewanted=all&_r=0> [accessed 20 Dec 2015].

107 Stapel, n 78, 182.

that can lead a professional to betray the values of their profession. Stapel has inadvertently provided us with a means of appreciating better than we would otherwise have done, the archetypal mindset of a person who engages in a systematic course of research fraud. We need to harness his account to enhance processes for detection of research misconduct and, at the broader level, to reframe research culture so as to reduce the incentives for Stapel-like conduct.

Motives for Unfounded Allegations of Research Fraud

Allegations of research misconduct can be a made for a number of collateral motives, including professional rivalry, turf protection (for instance against an iconoclast), personal malice, or political correctness prevailing at a given time. The allegations may or may not be justified or ultimately proven. Personal attacks, especially those brought by resentful competitors of the subject of the allegations, aspirants to research ascendancy, or when a scholar has died or is no longer able effectively to defend him or herself, need to be viewed with considerable circumspection in spite of the fact that they may be mounted from what appears to be the moral high ground. There is also the potential for unfair allegations to be raised out of no more than professional jealousy, because of some real or imagined slight that is less than rational, or because of the intellectual correctness of the time. Once such allegations are raised, it is not easy for those who have made them to qualify or abandon their position—their credibility is then also on trial. Controversies persist, for instance, about the motives, as well as the justification for, Derek Freeman's withering critiques in 1983[108] of Margaret Mead's legendary anthropological research in Samoa.[109] What can be said with confidence is that although Freeman succeeded in identifying flaws in Mead's idealized portrayal of the idyllic life of Samoa, and that there are real question marks over her account of Samoan sexual permissiveness, Freeman's alternative hypothesis of a male-oriented culture addicted to rape and disrupted by ruthless competition appears to have been heavily influenced by personal antipathy towards Mead's iconic status.[110]

Sometimes retractions of scholars' publications are lobbied for by those who simply disagree with their views or approaches. The extraordinary campaign, successful in 2013, to have Stephan Lewandowsky's critiques of climate scepticism retracted from the journal which had published them is an example of what can be the politicization of campaigns aimed at securing retractions.[111] This does not mean necessarily that such campaigns are disingenuous or without warrant, but it does introduce an extra element to the dynamic of accusation and defence.

Peer Reviewing

Peer reviewing in scholarly journals is generally regarded as the most important protection against research fraud. However, it has become apparent that it constitutes only a limited

[108] Derek Freeman, *Margaret Mead and Samoa: The Making and Unmaking of an Anthropological Myth* (Cambridge: Harvard University Press, 1983).

[109] See Margaret Mead, *Coming of Age in Samoa* (William Morrow and Company, 1928).

[110] See the analysis in Ron Robin, *Scandals and Scoundrels: Seven Cases that Shook the Academy* (Berkeley: University of California Press, 2004).

[111] S Lewandosky, J Cook, K Oberauer, and M Marriott, 'Recursive Fury: Conspiracist Ideation in the Blogosphere in Response to Research on Conspiracist Ideation' (2013) 4 *Frontiers of Psychology* 73. The article was retracted by the journal (after it was viewed more than 65,000 times), according to the author, on the basis of legal concerns, not academic or legal reasons. It was then posted on a site by the University of Western Australia for over a year and, finally, republished by the *Journal of Social and Political Psychology* in 2015. An account of the saga was written by Stephan Lewandowsky, 'Restoring Recurrent Fury' (8 July 2015): <http://www.shapingtomorrowsworld.org/rf2015.html> [accessed 20 Dec 2015].

protection against both research misconduct and plagiarism.[112] A systematic review of the available evidence on peer review concluded that 'the practice of peer review is based on faith in its effects, rather than on facts'.[113] In addition, Richard Smith, a former editor of the *BMJ*, has contended that 'we have little evidence on the effectiveness of peer review, but we have considerable evidence on its defects. In addition to being poor at detecting gross defects and almost useless for detecting fraud it is slow, expensive, profligate of academic time, highly subjective, something of a lottery, prone to bias, and easily abused'.[114]

In the aftermath of the scandal involving Jon Sudbø (see below, p 82), Barnett Kramer, editor-in-chief of the *Journal of the National Cancer Institute*, observed that: 'We know only about the cases where someone blows the whistle. We have no idea what the true numerator is... [W]hen it comes to outright fabrication, editors remain, to a large extent, at the mercy of the investigators who submit the final products of their research.'[115]

The all too frequent failure of peer review to guard effectively against both error and fraud has been highlighted by the need for 89 retractions of the work of Dr Joachim Boldt (see below p 90), over 60 retractions of the work of Dr Peter Chen (see below, p 47), 55 retractions of the work of Professor Stapel (see below p 75), and 179 retractions of the work over 19 years of the work of Dr Yoshitaka Fujii (see below p 91), to name just four of those responsible for research fraud to whom reference is made in Chapter 3.

Some of the difficulty lies in co-authors taking no or very limited responsibility for publications in which they are named as collaborators. This has prompted journals such as the *Journal of the American Medical Association* to require one author to take sole responsibility for the integrity of each submitted manuscript and for each author to provide details of their respective contributions. It has also resulted in well-founded calls for journals to have clearer online instructions and protocols.[116]

Many of the articles that have needed to be retracted during the past decade have been in prestigious publications. Reviewers had not picked up the faking of data in the research studies. However, this is not surprising. Dr Joachim Boldt (see p 90), Dr Haruko Obokata (see p 98), Professor Diederik Stapel (see p 75), and Dr Yoshitaka Fujii (see p 91), for instance, wrote well and they fabricated data in a plausible way. Their frauds were sophisticated and sustained.

Reviewers are not paid. Peer reviewing tends to be low on the scale of scholars' work priorities, not assisting in productivity evaluations or promotion applications, leading many to undertake the task in a perfunctory or self-serving way. Reviewers cast a critical eye over manuscripts

---

112 See Tom Jefferson, Melanie Rudin, Suzanne Brodney Folse, and Frank Davidoff, 'Editorial Peer Review for Improving the Quality of Reports of Biomedical Studies' (2007) 18(2) *Cochrane Database of Systematic Reviews*, doi: 10.1002/14651858.MR000016.pub3.

113 Tom Jefferson, Philip Alderson, Elizabeth Wager, and Frank Davidoff, 'Effects of Editorial Peer Review: A Systematic Review' (2002) 287(21) *Journal of the American Medical Association* 2784; see also, Joanne Travaglia and Deborah Debono, *Peer Review in Medicine: A Comprehensive Review of The Literature* (Centre for Clinical Governance Research in Health, University of New South Wales, Sydney, 2009): <http://www.health.vic.gov.au/clinicalengagement/downloads/pasp/literature_review_peer_review.pdf> [accessed 20 Dec 2015].

114 Richard Smith, 'Peer Review: A Flawed Process at the Heart of Science and Journals' (2006) 99(4) *Journal of the Royal Society of Medicine* 178, 179. He refers to the tendency for 'negative studies' not to be peer reviewed as worthy of publication and to the 'Mathew effect' whereby well-known researchers tend much more readily to make their way through peer review: 'To those who have, shall be given; to those who have not shall be taken away even the little that they have': 180.

115 See Brian Vastag, 'Cancer Fraud Case Stuns Research Community, Prompts Reflection on Peer Review Process' (2006) 98(6) *Journal of the National Cancer Institute* 374, 376.

116 Armen Y Gasparyan, Lilit Ayvazyan, Sergey V Gorin, and George D Kitas, 'Upgrading Instructions for Authors of Scholarly Journals' (2014) 55(3) *Croatian Medical Journal* 271.

submitted for publication and utilize their knowledge of the specialist area to identify if the position taken by the author(s) is plausible, whether the author displays a knowledge of the relevant literature, and whether the data are internally consistent, properly statistically interpreted and support the conclusions drawn. Reviewers do not call (save in extraordinary circumstances) for laboratory notes or original data. This leaves open the very real possibility for fabricated studies to make their way through peer review, even when reviewers are properly critical and sceptical.

In addition, the selection of a peer reviewer by the editor can go a long way in itself to determining whether an article will be accepted or rejected. It remains the situation that many journals ask authors which peer reviewers they prefer and which ones they do not want. Further, peer reviewers usually are not provided with primary data (such as from the laboratory), meaning that their reviews have inherent and important limitations in terms of being an effective check and balance on the commission of fraud.

Another phenomenon that has eroded the value of peer reviewing as an effective check and balance against research misconduct that has taken place, has been manipulation of the refereeing system within scholarly journals by which persons who have written articles have themselves written reviews of their own articles or influenced those who have done so.[117] An aspect of this takes place in certain open access journals and books, or so-called 'vanity publishing' where scholarly standards are often very low,[118] and the checks and balances against research fraud and plagiarism are close to non-existent.[119]

In addition, a number of researchers have been exposed as having orchestrated fake reviewing of the manuscripts they have submitted to scholarly journals.[120] This constitutes another aspect of vulnerability in the peer-reviewing process which unscrupulous scholars have taken advantage of on an as yet unknown number of occasions.[121] A prominent example was the conduct of Professor Hyung-In Moon, a South Korean plant compound researcher. When his misconduct was detected, *Pharmaceutical Biology* published the following retraction notice:

> The peer-review process for the above article was found to have been compromised and inappropriately influenced by the corresponding author, Professor HI Moon. As a result the findings and conclusions of these articles cannot be relied upon. The corresponding author and the publisher wish to retract these papers to preserve the integrity of material published in the journal. The publisher acknowledges that the integrity of the peer review process should have been subject to more rigorous verification to ensure the reviews provided were genuine and impartial. The publisher apologises for any inconvenience rendered to the readers of the journal and wishes to assure the reader [sic] that measures have been taken to ensure that the peer review process is comprehensively checked to avoid a similar error occurring.[122]

---

[117] See Josh Fischman, 'Fake Peer Reviews, the Latest Form of Scientific Fraud, Fool Journals' (2012) 59(7) *The Chronicle of Higher Education* A18.

[118] See Claire Shaw, 'Hundreds of Open Access Journals Accept Fake Science Paper', *The Guardian,* 4 October 2013: <http://www.theguardian.com/higher-education-network/2013/oct/04/open-access-journals-fake-paper> [accessed 20 Dec 2015].

[119] See Martin Eve, 'Flawed Sting Operation Singles Out Open Access Journals', *The Conversation,* 4 October 2013: <https://theconversation.com/flawed-sting-operation-singles-out-open-access-journals-18846> [accessed 20 Dec 2015].

[120] See Fischman, above n 117; Henry Fountain, 'Science Journal Pulls 60 Papers in Peer-Review Fraud' (10 July 2014) *The New York Times*: <http://www.nytimes.com/2014/07/11/science/science-journal-pulls-60-papers-in-peer-review-fraud.html?_r=0> [accessed 20 Dec 2015].

[121] See Brian Stallard, 'Science Fraud! Peer Review IS Vulnerable', *Nature World News,* 11 July 2014: <http://www.natureworldnews.com/articles/8022/20140711/science-fraud-peer-review-vulnerable.htm> (viewed 26 January 2015).

[122] Jae-Chul Jung and Hyung-In Moon, 'Statement of Retraction: Larvicidal Activity of 4-Hydroxycoumarin Derivatives Against *Aedes Aegypti*, (2011) 49 *Pharmaceutical Biology* 190–3' (2012) 50(9) *Pharmaceutical*

Three further retractions in the same terms followed in the *International Journal of Food Sciences and Nutrition*. Professor Moon's modus operandi was to suggest preferred reviewers who were actually himself or colleagues, sheltering under bogus identities and accounts. Sometimes the names of real people were provided (whose credentials could be confirmed by a Google check) but he created email accounts attributed to them which he or associates could use to impersonate the individuals. On other occasions the proposed reviewers did not exist at all—they were simply proxies for the authors. The reviews provided were always favourable, although they would tend to provide suggestions for improvement to the manuscripts—no doubt for camouflage purpose.[123]

Similarly, *Optics and Laser Technology* in 2012 retracted an article where the submitted manuscript was subverted in the reviewing process by others, resulting in the following notice:

> The Publisher hereby confirms that the retraction of this article was in no way due to any wrong-doing by the authors. On the contrary, the authors were the victims of a third party who invalidated the editorial process of this article by faking reviewer reports.[124]

More common, though, is the orchestrated subverting of the review process as a deliberate strategy by authors. The most notorious example of this is the conduct of Chen-yuan (Peter) Chen, formerly of Taiwan's National Pingtung University of Education. It has emerged that Chen utilized at least 130 email accounts, a large number of which were falsified, to secure fake reviews of his manuscripts. A bogus 'peer review and citation ring' of approximately 100 bogus scholars was engineered. The *Journal of Vibration and Control*, a leading journal in acoustics, has withdrawn 60 papers it had published under Chen's name.[125]

The repercussions have been extensive. Sage has published a statement that Chen provided an 'unsatisfactory response' when confronted by the accusations and as a publisher has expressed:

> regret that individual authors have compromised the academic record by perverting the peer review process and apologise to readers. On uncovering problems with peer review and citation SAGE immediately put steps in place to avoid similar vulnerability of the Journal to exploitation in the future.[126]

Biology 1199: <http://informahealthcare.com/doi/pdfplus/10.3109/13880209.2012.712023> [accessed 20 Dec 2015].

123 See also, Guang-Zhi He, 'Retracted: *Entamoeba Histolytica*: Cloning, Expression and Evaluation of the Efficacy of a Recombinant Amebiasis Cysteine Proteinase Gene (ACP1) Antigen in Minipig' (2012) 130(2) *Experimental Parasitology* 126: <http://www.sciencedirect.com/science/article/pii/S001448941100347X> [accessed 21 Dec 2015]—'This article has been retracted as the author fabricated information during the review process to obtain a favourable review. As such this article represents a severe abuse of the scientific publishing system. The scientific community takes a very strong view on this matter and apologies are offered to readers of the journal that this was not detected during the submission process.'

124 Dahai Han, Haoran Chen, and Lixia Xi, 'Retraction Notice to 'PMD Mitigation Through Interleaving LDPC Codes with Polarization Scramblers, (2012) 44(8), *Optics & Laser Technology* 2327–2331' (2013) 48 *Optics & Laser Technology* 612: <http://www.sciencedirect.com/science/article/pii/S0030399212001922> [accessed 21 Dec 2015].

125 Fred Barbash, 'Scholarly Journal Retracts 60 Articles, Smashes 'Peer Review Ring', *The Washington Post*, 10 July 2014: <http://www.washingtonpost.com/news/morning-mix/wp/2014/07/10/scholarly-journal-retracts-60-articles-smashes-peer-review-ring/> [accessed 21 Dec 2015]; see too Cat Ferguson, Adam Marcus, and Ivan Oransky, 'Publishing: The Peer-Review Scam' (26 November 2014) 515 *Nature*: <http://www.nature.com/news/publishing-the-peer-review-scam-1.16400> [accessed 21 Dec 2015].

126 Rung-Fang Chang, CY Chen, Fang-Pei Su, and Hsin-Chang Lin, 'Retraction Notice: A Two-Step Approach for Broadband Digital Signal Processing Technique' (26 April 2013) *Journal of Vibration and Control* (July 2014) 20 *Journal of Vibration and Control*: <http://jvc.sagepub.com/content/20/10/NP5> [accessed 21 Dec 2015]. See also, 'SAGE Statement on Journal of Vibration and Control' (Press Release, London, 8 July 2014): <http://www.uk.sagepub.com/aboutus/press/2014/jul/7.htm> [accessed 21 Dec 2015].

Chen has since resigned his university position. However, the scandal assumed wider dimensions with the resignation also of the Education Minister for Taiwan, Chiang Wei-ling.[127] He was named as a co-author of several of Chen's retracted papers but claimed to have had no knowledge of Chen's frauds, saying that he was resigning to 'safeguard [his] reputation'.[128] The Ministry of Science and Technology has acknowledged that it funded the research for approximately 40 of Chen's dubious publications and stated that, if Chen were proven to have breached research ethics, the Ministry would demand a return of research funds and impose a lifetime ban on his access to such funding. Prosecutors also announced that they were undertaking an investigation into Chen's conduct with a view to the potential preferring of charges against him.

The Committee on Publication Ethics (COPE) was so troubled by the phenomenon of peer review fraud that it issued a statement on the issue:

> The Committee on Publication Ethics (COPE) has become aware of systematic, inappropriate attempts to manipulate the peer review processes of several journals across different publishers. These manipulations appear to have been orchestrated by a number of third party agencies offering services to authors. This statement is issued on behalf of COPE after consultation with a variety of publishers to underscore the seriousness with which we take these issues and our determination to address them.
>
> While there are a number of well-established reputable agencies offering manuscript-preparation services to authors, investigations at several journals suggests that some agencies are selling services, ranging from authorship of pre-written manuscripts to providing fabricated contact details for peer reviewers during the submission process and then supplying reviews from these fabricated addresses. Some of these peer reviewer accounts have the names of seemingly real researchers but with email addresses that differ from those from their institutions or associated with their previous publications, others appear to be completely fictitious
>
> We are unclear how far authors of the submitted manuscripts are aware that the reviewer names and email addresses provided by these agencies are fraudulent. However, given the seriousness and potential scale of the investigation findings, we believe that the scientific integrity of manuscripts submitted via these agencies is significantly undermined.[129]

The World Association of Medical Editors (WAME) has joined the call for greater vigilance:

> Editors should remain alert to the possibility of peer review manipulation, especially if reviewer comments are submitted extremely rapidly or the review is extremely positive and superficial. In such cases, it may be helpful to invite an additional, independent review, or to redouble efforts to check the identity and contact details of the suggested reviewer.
>
> While these recommendations are intended to help prevent the problem of fraudulent peer review, other methods to subvert peer review undoubtedly will be developed. Editors should be appropriately skeptical of potential new sources of reviewer names and contact information.[130]

---

[127] See Mimi Leung and Yojana Sharma, 'Education Minister Resigns over Research Fraud Scandal' (14 July 2014) Issue No. 329, *University World News:* <http://www.universityworldnews.com/article.php?story=20140714143140161> [accessed 21 Dec 2015].

[128] Agence France-Presse, 'Taiwanese Education Minister Chiang Wei-ling Resigns Over Academic Publishing Scandal', *South China Morning Post,* 15 July 2014: <http://www.scmp.com/news/china/article/1554344/taiwanese-education-minister-chiang-wei-ling-resigns-over-amid-academic> [accessed 21 Dec 2015].

[129] Committee on Publication Ethics, 'COPE Statement on Manipulation of Peer Review Processes': <http://publicationethics.org/news/cope-statement-inappropriate-manipulation-peer-review-processes> [accessed 21 Dec 2015]. See too Elizabeth Moylan, 'Inappropriate Manipulation of Peer Review' (26 March 2015) BioMed Central Blog: <http://blogs.biomedcentral.com/bmcblog/2015/03/26/manipulation-peer-review/> [accessed 21 Dec 2015].

[130] World Association of Medical Editors, Policy Statements: <http://www.wame.org/policy-statements#Best%20Practices%20for%20Peer%20Reviewer%20Selection> (viewed 22 December 2015).

It is to be hoped that the position adopted by COPE constitutes the start of a concerted effort to regulate and improve the system of peer reviewing so that the prospects of its achieving its objectives are considerably enhanced.

Retractions

Even when scientific misconduct has been found to attend published research, too often retractions have not followed or have been very slow to follow.[131] Many journals also do not have clear retraction policies.[132] Some editors are fearful of retracting articles when authors vehemently deny fraud and threaten legal action because of the asserted damage to their reputation if such a step is taken.

It appears that the likelihood that an article published in a higher impact journal will be retracted is higher than that for an article published in a lower impact journal.[133] Retraction notices are posted in PubMed and are available free of charge. The PDF versions of retracted articles often carry a watermark to inform readers that the article has been retracted. Authors are generally consulted regarding the wording of a retraction, but final decisions are at the discretion of the journal. A problem for journals arises (commonly), however, when information emerges about research fraud committed some time previously in respect of other pieces of published work. Editors are often ill-equipped to investigate the legitimacy of manuscripts published in their own journal, especially in the absence of availability of the primary data underpinning a manuscript. The result is that articles, whose authors have been demonstrated to have falsified data in other contexts, and may well have falsified other data, can remain on the public record and continue to be influential on practice and continuing research.

A controversial example of the slowness of retractions and the limited capacity of journals to retract articles they have published arose in respect of the notorious case of Professor Ranjit Chandra, holder of the Order of Canada and five honorary doctorates for his nutritional research, and a visiting professor at universities on four continents. Chandra is the author of over 200 published articles. In 2001 Chandra published an article in *Nutrition* claiming that his multivitamin formula could reverse memory problems in persons over the age of 65, postulating that the supplement might delay the onset of Alzheimer's disease.[134] The article had previously been rejected by the *BMJ* after a review by a statistician stated that the study had 'all the hallmarks of being completely invented'.[135] The journal followed up on a trial which had been published in *The Lancet* in 1992.[136] At the *BMJ*'s request, his employer, Memorial University in Newfoundland, investigated and concluded that the study could not have been completed as Chandra claimed but, under pressure from a threat of litigation from Chandra, took no further action against him.[137] When asked to produce his data, Chandra declined and resigned from the university. In 2005 *Nutrition* retracted the

---

[131] See Jennifer Couzin and Katherine Unger, 'Cleaning Up the Paper Trail' (2006) 312(5770) *Science* 38.

[132] Michel C Atlas, 'Retraction Policies of High-Impact Biomedical Journals' (2004) 92(2) *Journal of the Medical Library Association* 242.

[133] Fang, Casadevall, and Morrison, above n 65, 3856.

[134] Ranjit K Chandra, 'Can Nutrient Supplements Improve Functional Outcome in the Elderly' (2003) 19(11–12) *Nutrition* 978. See Doug Payne, 'Nutrition Retracts 2001 Paper', *The Scientist,* 3 March 2005: <http://www.the-scientist.com/?articles.view/articleNo/23286/title/Nutrition-retracts-2001-paper/> [accessed 21 Dec 2015].

[135] Payne, above n 134.

[136] Ranjit K Chandra, 'Effect of Vitamin and Trace-element Supplementation on Immune Responses and Infection in Elderly Subjects' (1992) 340(8828) *The Lancet* 1124.

[137] See Terry Hamblin, 'The Secret Life of Dr Chandra' (2006) 332(7537) *BMJ* 369; see also Richard Smith, 'Investigating the Previous Studies of a Fraudulent Author' (2005) 331(7511) *BMJ* 288.

paper.[138] However, Professor Chandra's research has ranged over many areas, and been very influential, including in relation to the claim that certain types of baby formula protect against allergy in babies and young children.[139] In spite of a wide array of concerns about Chandra's data over a lengthy period of time, in the two years after the retraction of the *Nutrition* article, other journals did not retract his articles or issue warnings about them, leading to criticism of journals' hesitancy to take robust action in respect of authors whose data have been shown to be falsified.[140]

Another control against research fraud is supervision. However, once again the likelihood of senior academics intruding sufficiently into others' research, especially if the perpetrators of fraud are senior themselves, is very small. Time and a variety of logistics militate against the rigour of such oversight in practice.

A further check and balance against scholarly fraud is the potential for co-authors, co-workers, or members of ethics committees to identify short-cuts, emergence of 'odd' data, and failures to obtain proper consent, conform to ethical protocols, and to engage properly with institutional ethics committees. However, this requires active involvement by such persons and not preparedness in a supine way to take the accolades and advantages of co-authorship (including gift authorship) without meaningful involvement. Researchers such as Fujii traded on the preparedness of some of his colleagues to take something for nothing in return for putting their name on publications to which they made no or no substantial contribution. In turn this enabled greater plausibility for the studies. Such difficulties highlight the need for significant changes to the culture of both the conduct of research and collaboration among scholarly colleagues.

University and Institutional Policies

Most tertiary institutions have developed policies directed towards the conduct of research. An example is that of the University of Melbourne which defines 'research misconduct' as:

> constituted by a failure to comply with the principles or specific provisions of the code and includes but is not limited to conduct in, or in connection with, research that is (a) dishonest, reckless or negligent and (b) seriously deviates from accepted standards within the scientific and scholarly community for proposing, conducting or reporting research, such as following, includes—
> (a) the fabrication or falsification of data or results,
> (b) the use of another person's ideas, work or data without appropriate acknowledgement,
> (c) misleading ascription of authorship to a publication including the listing of authors without their permission, attributing work to people who have not in fact contributed to the publication, the lack of appropriate acknowledgement of work primarily produced by a research student/trainee or associate, and
> (d) failure to disclose conflicts of interest or cases where a conflict of interest might reasonably be perceived to exist.

It articulates guiding principles for the conduct of research:

> This Code of Conduct ('the code') prescribes standards of responsible and ethical conduct expected of all persons (academic staff, students, technical and other support staff) engaged

---

[138] See Joseph Schwarcz, *Science, Sense and Nonsense: 61 Nourishing, Healthy, Bunk-free Commentaries on the Chemistry that Affects Us All* (Doubleday Canada, 2009) 152.

[139] See Elisabeth Sterken, 'Letter to the Editor: The Impact of Scientific Misconduct on Child Health' (2006) 9(2) *Public Health Nutrition* 273.

[140] See Andrea Gawrylewski, 'Under Suspicion, But Not Retracted', *The Scientist*, 1 March 2007: <http://www.the-scientist.com/?articles.view/articleNo/24822/title/Under-suspicion--but-not-retracted/> [accessed 21 Dec 2015].

in research ('research workers') in The University of Melbourne based upon the following guiding principles:

(a) Research is original investigation undertaken in order to gain knowledge and understanding and make this widely available
(b) Research workers should, in all aspects of their research—
    (i) demonstrate integrity and professionalism;
    (ii) observe fairness and equity;
    (iii) demonstrate intellectual honesty;
    (iv) effectively and transparently manage conflicts of interest or potential conflicts of interest; and
    (v) ensure the safety and well being of those associated with the research
(c) Research methods and results should be open to scrutiny and debate.[141]

Similarly, the National Health and Medical Research Council (the NHMRC) in Australia provides guidelines in relation to research integrity. It has observed that:

> The [Australian Code for the Responsible Conduct of Research] outlines that the responsible conduct of research is a shared responsibility. NHMRC publishes guidelines to support integrity in research. It is the responsibility of researchers to design and conduct research and organisations which employ researchers and/or fund research to ensure that research is conducted with integrity.[142]

Oxford University defines 'misconduct' similarly (but subtly differently) in respect of research as:

> Misconduct in Research for the purpose of this Code of Practice and Procedure means actual or attempted acts of fabrication, falsification, plagiarism or deception when proposing, conducting or reporting results of research, or deliberate, dangerous, reckless or negligent deviations from accepted practice in carrying out research. It includes failure to follow established protocols if this failure results in unreasonable risk or harm to humans, other vertebrates or the environment, and facilitating of Misconduct in Research by collusion in, or concealment of, such actions by others. It also includes the intentional or reckless unauthorised use, disclosure or removal of, or damage to, research-related property of another, including apparatus, materials, writings, data, hardware or software or any other substances or devices used in or produced by the conduct of research. It does not include honest error or honest differences in the design, execution, interpretation or judgement in evaluating research methods or results, or misconduct unrelated to the research process. It does not include poor research.[143]

It requires all members of the university, as well as all individuals permitted to work in university institutions, to report any incident of misconduct, whether they have witnessed it or suspected it.[144] Oxford University provides protection from disciplinary proceedings for all such reports made in good faith. It sets up a panel to inquire into allegations, usually consisting of two members, normally with a member of the department or faculty with relevant expertise, and another person from within the university, but outside the department or

---

[141] University of Melbourne, Regulation 17.1.R8, Code of Conduct for Research, University Secretary's Department: Statutes and Regulation: <http://www.unimelb.edu.au/ExecServ/Statutes/r171r8.html> (viewed 16 January 2015).

[142] Australian Government, National Health and Medical Research Council, *Research Integrity*: <http://www.nhmrc.gov.au/research/responsible-conduct-research-0> [accessed 21 Dec 2015]. See also, Australian Government, National Health and Medical Research Council, and Australian Research Council, *Australian Code for the Responsible Conduct of Research* (Australian Government, 2007), available at: <http://www.nhmrc.gov.au/guidelines-publications/r39> [accessed 21 Dec 2015].

[143] University of Oxford, Personnel Services, 'Academic Integrity in Research: Code of Practice and Procedure': <http://www.admin.ox.ac.uk/personnel/cops/researchintegrity/> [accessed 21 Dec 2015].

[144] Cambridge University too stipulates that: 'All members of the University, and individuals permitted to work in University institutions, have a responsibility to report to the Head of the relevant institution any incident of misconduct, whether this has been witnessed, or is suspected': University of Cambridge,

faculty, with relevant expertise, or from outside the university. The purpose of the preliminary investigation is to evaluate the facts of the allegations in order to ascertain whether there is sufficient evidence to amount to a prima facie case of misconduct. The panel may interview anyone relevant, including the person the subject of the complaint and must prepare a report, setting out the evidence which has been evaluated, accounts of interviews, if any, and its conclusions. If it finds no evidence of misconduct, the panel must dismiss the complaint but, if it concludes that prima facie evidence of misconduct exists, the report must be referred to the appropriate person for action under the University's relevant disciplinary procedure.

Particular tertiary institutions define what is expected of those undertaking research. For instance the Massachusetts Institute of Technology (MIT) observes that:

> Unethical behavior in research and scholarship strikes at the heart of the scholarly and educational enterprise. A shared understanding of expectations and responsibilities is, therefore, critical—not only to the quality of the research enterprise but also to the collegial life of this community. Academic misconduct can take many forms, including fabrication or falsification of data, theft of ideas or direct plagiarism, and deliberate interference with the integrity of the work of others. Whatever the form, academic misconduct is behavior that may lead to a variety of disciplinary actions, including, in severe cases, expulsion of a student, dismissal of an employee, or termination of tenure.
>
> Misconduct arises most readily in an environment in which supervision at each relevant level is not reasonably exercised. Laboratory and center directors and department heads must make clear the standards and protocols for research, scholarship, and creative work in their organizations and must set a tone (by example, through discussion and review of research, and, when possible, with written guidelines) that will make adherence to those standards a matter of course.[145]

It provides that those who believe in good faith that an act of academic misconduct is taking place or has taken place should in most circumstances present their concerns to the person's supervisor and in some circumstances communicate with the suspected person. Supervisors who become aware of situations of possible academic misconduct are obliged to report them to the Vice President for Research for investigation.

Other universities link their requirements in relation to scholarly integrity to the principles espoused in national schemes. An example is Yale University which states that it is committed to 'ethically responsible research', and 'subscribes to the Department of Health and Human Services' Office of Research Integrity (ORI) guidance on what are considered to be essential elements of an appropriate Responsible Conduct of Research (RCR) Program.'[146]

Another phenomenon is that some universities, such as Harvard, require scholars to undertake courses in the responsible conduct of research. In addition, organizations such as the National Institutes of Health (NIH) in the United States impose requirements for the funding of research. The NIH has published the following 'basic principles':

> 1. Responsible conduct of research is an essential component of research training. Therefore, instruction in responsible conduct of research is an integral part of all research training programs, and its evaluation will impact funding decisions.

Human Resources Division, Policies and Procedures, 'Misconduct in Research': <http://www.admin.cam.ac.uk/offices/hr/policy/misconduct.html> [accessed 21 Dec 2015].

[145] Massachusetts Institute of Technology, Policies and Procedures, 10.0 Academic Misconduct and Dishonesty—10.1 Procedures for Dealing with Academic Misconduct in Research and Scholarship: <http://web.mit.edu/policies/10/10.1.html> [accessed 21 Dec 2015].

[146] Yale University, Office of Research Administration, *Responsible Conduct of Research*: <http://researchadministration.yale.edu/responsible-conduct-research#academicintegrity> (viewed 17 January 2015).

2. Active involvement in the issues of responsible conduct of research should occur throughout a scientist's career. Instruction in responsible conduct of research should therefore be appropriate to the career stage of the individuals receiving training.
3. Individuals supported by individual funding opportunities such as fellowships and career development awards are encouraged to assume individual and personal responsibility for their instruction in responsible conduct of research.
4. Research faculty of the institution should participate in instruction in responsible conduct of research in ways that allow them to serve as effective role models for their trainees, fellows, and scholars.
5. Instruction should include face-to-face discussions by course participants and faculty; ie, on-line instruction may be a component of instruction in responsible conduct of research but is not sufficient to meet the NIH requirement for such instruction, except in special or unusual circumstances.[147]

Conclusions

Definitions of scholarly misconduct in research continue to vary somewhat, making evaluations of prevalence highly problematic, although there are many indications that its incidence is rising concerningly. Motives for engagement in such conduct can be identified, as can the profiles of persons who succumb to the temptation to behave unethically. Personality characteristics of those who engage in research misconduct have common features but are not uniform. These forms of insight are fundamental pieces of intelligence for the generation of prophylactic, as well as investigative, strategies. For this reason the revelations of Diederik Stapel in his autobiography, *The Derailment,* are particularly valuable in giving a human face to research fraud and depicting how such conduct can develop, self-sustain, and be rationalized. It is notable that institutions such as major universities are endeavouring to articulate expectations and requirements as to how research will be conducted. This constitutes a constructive commencement in the educational domain of reasserting and reframing a culture of integrity in face of modern temptations for engagement in scholarly misconduct. Chapter 3 will argue that these measures need to be matched by effective investigative, disciplinary, criminal, and potentially civil law processes to respond to the multi-faceted reality of research misconduct.

The further component of the response to publications which are defective by reason of error or fraud (or plagiarism) is their expeditious removal from access by way of journal retractions. Coordination of responses to effect this by publishers/editors needs attention so that there are consensus protocols to which there is consistent adherence. As in comparable contexts, processes need to be established to extend fairness to authors who are the subject of allegations but also to ensure that there is decisiveness when clear evidence shows a lack of a reliability or integrity in a publication.

[147] National Institutes of Health, 'Update on the Requirement for Instruction in the Responsible Conduct of Research', 24 November 2009: <http://grants1.nih.gov/grants/guide/notice-files/NOT-OD-10-019.html> [accessed 21 Dec 2015].

3

RESEARCH MISCONDUCT

Examples and Solutions

Introduction

As identified in Chapter 2, fraud within research has been an issue which has contaminated the integrity of science and medicine in more ways and in more respects than has been appreciated until recently. It has had many adverse repercussions for the regard in which scholarly research is held. This chapter builds upon Chapter 2 by exploring the contexts within which research misconduct has arisen. It does so, utilizing historical examples to give perspective to the modern phenomenon and then outlines the circumstances surrounding a significant number of contemporary instances of serious fraud within published research. Its aim is to identify patterns which can be utilized to enhance investigative processes and the construction of prophylactic and deterrent responses. It reviews the emerging resort to the criminal law in an attempt to inhibit dishonest conduct of research, in particular fabrication of research results. It concludes by proposing changes which should be implemented to reduce the incidence of the problems identified.

Hoaxes

Hoaxes in the sense that they were defined by Babbage take many forms. They are sometimes directed towards an individual; more often they are at large. On occasions they are constructed to provide career advantage to the hoaxster. Sometimes they are designed to be damaging to a rival. Sometimes they are simply mischievous and their purpose is obfusc.[1] They can be highly damaging and contain elements of dishonesty, which raise the issue of when and how they should be responded to by the criminal law.

As identified above in Chapter 2, the following forms of hoaxes can be identified:

- pranksterism or trickery,
- swindlery or extortion, and
- attempts to make legitimate scholars look foolish.

The following part of this chapter reviews a number of notorious examples of hoaxes in research, reviewing how they were executed and the apparent purposes in why they were set in motion.

The Lying Stones Hoax

An example of a scientific hoax directed maliciously towards a specific individual was the set of 'tricks' played upon Dr Johann Bartholomew Adam Beringer, the chief physician to the

---

[1] See Curtis D MacDougall, *Hoaxes* (New York: Macmillan, 1940).

prince bishop and a scholar at the University of Würzburg in the early 18th century. He was known to be pretentious and arrogant, a virtuoso savant. Beringer developed a particular interest in oryctics—things dug from the earth—and collected natural rarities such as fossils, then called 'natural stones'.

At the instigation of one of his rivals, J Ignatz Roderick, a professor of geography, algebra, and analysis also at the University of Würzburg, and also of the Honourable Georg von Eckhart, a privy councillor and a librarian to the court and the university, an elaborate hoax was constructed to destroy Beringer's scholarly reputation. Its motive was to prick his arrogance and make him a laughing stock. Later the perpetrators were to claim that they devised the scheme because Beringer was so interpersonally obnoxious and despised them.

The two rivals employed three young men from the local area to provide Beringer with a series of stones that they said that they had dug up from nearby Mount Eivelstad. They were in the shape of insects, frogs, toads, birds, scorpions, snails, slugs, and other creatures. Beringer became more and more excited by the finds which he duly added to his collection and announced his intention to write a book about his discoveries.[2] The conspirators panicked and spread rumours about the stones' lack of authenticity in order to discourage him from proceeding to publication. However, this did not succeed as Beringer formed the view that they were trying to rob him of the kudos that would ensue from his great discovery: 'I caught the rumor circulating throughout the city... that every one of these stones... [was] 'recently sculpted by hand, made to look as though at different periods they had been resurrected from a very old burial, and sold to me as to one indifferent to fraud and caught up in the blind greed of curiosity; further, that I, once deceived, in my wretched turn, was deluding the world, and trying to sell new hoaxes as genuine antiques, to the silent laughter of prudent souls'.[3]

The fossils supplied by the employees of his rivals at this stage became more and more unlikely—leaves, flowers, plants, and whole herbs, and then 'depictions of the sun and the moon, of stars, and of comets with their fiery tails. And lastly, as the supreme prodigy commanding the reverent admiration of myself and of my fellow examiners, were magnificent tablets engraved in Latin, Arabic and Hebrew characters with the ineffable name of Jehovah.'[4] Beringer was able to rationalize the legitimacy of even these: 'For whatever power has fashioned [them] the agent... has surpassed his limits by employing the art of writing, and has traced the characters of several languages, but especially those of the sacred tongue, so exactly in accordance with the rules of Hebrew orthography that they were adjudged in the opinion of experts to extol in eloquent titles the most holy name, power and wisdom of God, and thus perhaps manifest the one and only author of these wondrous stones.'[5] His obsessionality and desire for fame rendered him absurdly gullible. As Gould has put it: 'Beringer, in his overweening and stubborn arrogance, simply could not quench his ambition once a clever and plausible hoax had unleashed his ardor and vanity.'[6] Finally, he was supplied with a fossil with his own name on it!

---

[2] Johann Bartholomäus Adam Beringer, *The Lying Stones of Dr Johann Bartholomew Adam Beringer, being his Lithographiæ Wirceburgensis* (originally published in 1726 with 50 medical corollaries as the inaugural dissertation of GL Hueber, translated and annotated by Melvin E Jahn and Daniel J Woolf, Berkeley, University of California Press, 1963).

[3] Ibid, 94.

[4] Ibid, 21.

[5] Ibid, 23.

[6] See Stephen Jay Gould, *The Lying Stones of Marrakesh: Penultimate Reflections in Natural History* (New York: Three Rivers Press, 2000), 23.

At this stage Beringer realized he had been the victim of an elaborate hoax. He attempted to buy back all copies of his recently published 1726 book. This ruined him financially. However, in the years before he died Beringer took the matter to law and exposed the plot engaged in by Roderick and Eckhart. Both were disgraced.

A series of hoaxes were perpetrated in archaeology in the 19th and early 20th centuries.[7] They have sounded a warning for claims made of remarkable discoveries of antiquities, the possibility needing to be considered that for a variety of motives such claims may not be well-founded and may be made for a collateral commercial or other motive.[8]

The Inhabitants of the Moon Hoax

In 1835 a series of articles were published in the new 'penny newspaper', the *New York Sun*, by its editor (a former court reporter), Richard Adams Locke. They reported on the remarkable astronomical observations of the Moon allegedly made by the eminent astronomer Sir John Herschel.[9] The descriptions in the newspaper were said to be reprinted from the (non-existent) *Edinburgh Journal of Science*. Detailed descriptions were given of winged beings, plants, animals, and a sapphire temple. Sales and subscriptions to the newspaper soared. In one of the articles the following claims were made:

> We counted three parties of these creatures, of twelve, nine and fifteen in each, walking erect towards a small wood... Certainly they were like human beings, for their wings had now disappeared and their attitude in walking was both erect and dignified... About half of the first party had passed beyond our canvas; but of all the others we had perfectly distinct and deliberate view. They averaged four feet in height, were covered, except on the face, with short and glossy copper-colored hair, and had wings composed of a thin membrane, without hair, lying snugly upon their backs from the top of the shoulders to the calves of their legs.[10]

The reports enhanced the credibility of the story with attribution of detailed information about the creatures said to have been observed and quoted experts who commentated on the significance of the discovery and similarities of some of the birds to those on the Earth. The rival of the *New York Sun*, the *New York Herald*, immediately disputed the scholarly authenticity of the discovery, and attacked it as a hoax. Circulation numbers of both papers climbed

---

[7] See Nathan Beal, 'Five of the Most Famous Scientific Hoaxes' (2 March 2015) *Washington Post*: <http://www.washingtonpost.com/national/health-science/five-of-the-most-famous-scientific-hoaxes/2015/03/02/a0b64f9e-b6cd-11e4-9423-f3d0a1ec335c_story.html> [accessed 21 Dec 2015].

[8] A hoax not otherwise referred to in these pages (because of its lack of any semblance of scholarliness) is the hoax relating to the 'Hitler diaries' announced to have been discovered on 22 April 1983 by *Stern* magazine. Within two weeks, the West German *Bundesarchiv* revealed that the diaries were 'grotesquely superficial fakes' made on modern paper using modern ink and characterized by multiple historical inaccuracies. The editors of *Stern*, Peter Koch and Felix Schmidt, were obliged to resign, while Frank Giles stood down as editor of *The Sunday Times*, and William Broyles left *Newsweek*. The diaries were actually written by Konrad Kujau, a notorious Stuttgart forger; both he and a co-conspirator, Gwerd Heidemann, were convicted at trial in 1984 and each sentenced to 42 months' imprisonment for forgery and embezzlement. See Robert Harris, *Selling Hitler* (London: Arrow/Random House, 1996); Sally McGrane, 'Diary of the Hitler Diary Hoax', *The New Yorker*, 25 April 2013: <http://www.newyorker.com/books/page-turner/diary-of-the-hitler-diary-hoax> [accessed 21 Dec 2015].

[9] Son of William Herschel, discoverer of Uranus. For an extensive account of the hoax, see Matthew Goodman, *The Sun and the Moon: The Remarkable True Account of Hoaxers, Showmen, Dueling Journalists, and Lunar Man-Bats in Nineteenth Century New York* (New York: Basic Books, 2008).

[10] Nancy Atkinson, 'The Great Moon Hoax of 1835', *Universe Today*, 1 April 2011: <http://www.universetoday.com/84577/the-great-moon-hoax-of-1835/> (viewed 18 January 2015). See also, David B Sachsman and David W Bulla (eds), *Sensationalism: Murder, Mayhem, Mudslinging, Scandals, and Disasters in 19th-Century Reporting* (New Brunswick: Transaction Publishers, 2013) 243; Rob Knop, 'April 1st: The Great Moon Hoax', 365 *Days of Astronomy*, 1 April 2011: <http://cosmoquest.org/x/365daysofastronomy/2011/04/01/april-1st-the-great-moon-hoax/> [accessed 21 Dec 2015].

as they disputed the likelihood of the existence of bat-like men on the Moon being accurate. In due course Locke confessed when two professors at Yale University commenced to scrutinize his claims.[11]

The Cardiff Giant Hoax

The 'Cardiff Giant' hoax in 1869, when Gideon Emmons and Henry Nichols purported to discover a ten-foot-long petrified giant in a small hamlet in Cambridge, New York, became highly controversial until belief in it petered out by the beginning of the 20th century.[12] At first, diverse views held by scholars on the statue's legitimacy were touted. Dr John Boynton, a science lecturer, declared that the giant was a statue created by a Jesuit priest during the early 17th century to place local Indian tribes in a state of awe, while New York State geologist James Hall was convinced that the giant was an ancient statue. The motivation for the hoax appears to have been mixed—a desire on the part of the perpetrator, George Hull, a cigar-maker, get-rich-quick entrepreneur, and religious sceptic, to show that people could be made to believe anything, and a collateral commercial aspiration to make a handsome profit from people's gullibility.[13]

The Atlantis Hoax

On 20 October 1912 Paul Schliemann, grandson of the legendary archaeologist Heinrich Schliemann, discoverer of Troy, announced that he had discovered definite proof that the lost continent of Atlantis[14] existed. He published in William Randolph Hearst's *American* the claim[15] that he had located a 4000-year-old Babylonian manuscript that chronicled the violent end of the Atlanteans, as well as a hoard of Atlantean coins. He maintained that the Tihuanaco relics discovered by his grandfather were identical in every respect to what he had discovered, save that his carried non-Peruvian inscriptions. What he was postulating was that some Atlanteans had made their way to Egypt, while others had gone to Peru. He asserted that he had gained access to a Chaldean manuscript which shed light on the dispersal of the Atlanteans. He let it be known that he would soon publish a book on the subject. Implausibilities in his account were identified by many archaeologists and others, while calls were made for access to the coins and manuscripts. However, he maintained his silence:

---

[11] See too Edgar Allan Poe who asserted that Locke's hoax was plagiarized from his own 'The Adventure of One Hans Pfaall' (1835) in JH Ingram (ed) *Works of Edgar A. Poe* (London: Chandos Books, 1878), vol 1, pp 39–93. Poe later also wrote 'The Balloon-Hoax', which was first printed as an article in *The Sun* newspaper in New York. It gave a detailed and plausible account of a lighter-than-air, 75-hour balloon trip by famous European balloonist Monck Mason across the Atlantic Ocean along with a diagram and specifications of the craft. Poe's editor at the time 'The Balloon-Hoax' was published was John Locke.

[12] Mark Rose, 'When Giants Roamed the Earth' (2005) 58(6) *Archaeology* 30, available at: <http://archive.archaeology.org/0511/etc/giants.html> [accessed 21 Dec 2015]; Robert McNamara, 'The Cardiff Giant', *About Education*: <http://history1800s.about.com/od/popularentertainment/ss/Cardiff-Giant.htm> (viewed 18 January 2015).

[13] Compare also the 1866 Calaveras Skull Hoax where a native American skull was planted in a Californian mineshaft (probably by malevolent miners) and Josiah Whitney, head of California's geological survey, and Professor of Geology at Harvard University, was convinced that it was the oldest known human being: see William H Dall, 'The Calaveras Skull' (1899) 51(1) *Proceedings of the Academy of Natural Sciences of Philadelphia* 2; Ralph W Dexter, 'Historical Aspects of the Calaveras Skull Controversy' (1986) 51(2) *American Antiquity* 365.

[14] Utilized by Plato in the *Timaeus* and the *Criteas* (c360BC) as a fictitious device to present the idea of a hubris-filled people (the Atlanteans) who received condemnation from the gods.

[15] Paul Schliemann, 'How I Discovered Atlantis, the Source of All Civilization' (1912) *New York American*. See also, Frank Joseph, *The Atlantis Encylopedia* (Franklin Lakes, NJ: New Page Books/The Career Press, 2005): <http://conspiration.ca/e_book/the_atlantis_encyclopedia.pdf> [accessed 21 Dec 2015]; Robert Silverberg, *Scientists and Scoundrels: A Book of Hoaxes* (New York: Crowell, 1965) ch 8, 143ff.

> He had nothing at all to say. The game was up. Goaded by his need to seem important, he had invented the whole story out of thin air. He had no proof. His book never appeared. This pathetic little man had his moment of public attention, and for a brief while his name was on people's lips, as once his grandfather's had been. Then he vanished back into the obscurity from which he had come.[16]

The Piltdown Man Hoax

Probably the most notorious scientific hoax of the 20th century, and one with a legal connection, was the anthropological hoax of the Piltdown Man, believed by most to have been perpetrated by Sussex solicitor, Charles Dawson (1864–1916), who had a longstanding interest in anthropology and geology.[17] On 18 December 1912, along with geologist Edward Woodward and seminarian Teilhard de Chardin, Dawson claimed to have made a remarkable discovery[18] which was officially announced as the discovery of 'Piltdown Man' at a meeting of the Geological Society of London.[19] Within several months, the British Museum made casts of the finds available for study. At first the scientific community was accepting of Piltdown Man, there being considerable enthusiasm for the theory that human beings had originated from Europe,[20] although a level of disputation erupted early as to whether the jaw and the skull of the discovery were congruent—whether they belonged together.

From the start there were multiple internal inconsistencies in Piltdown Man. However, at first they tended to generate controversies about interpretation rather than questions about whether the discovery was genuine. In 1953 matters came to the fore, though, at a London conference on human origins convened by the Wenner-Gren Foundation. The conference included Kenneth Oakley, a geologist from the British Museum who had been using various novel chemical analyses to test the age of fossil remains including Piltdown Man, and Joseph Weiner, a South-African-born anthropologist from Oxford University. They shared a scepticism about the age of the Piltdown remains, the association of the jaw and the skull, and the circumstances in which the fossils were collected.

Thomson summarized their discoveries as follows:

> Oakley's chemical analyses exposed the whole fraud. Not a single bone or artifact from Piltdown was authentic. Many had been stained with potassium dichromate to make them look older, but also so that they might resemble remains from another Pleistocene site, Red Crag in Sussex. As it happens, some of the animal remains were from Red Crag! The jaw

---

[16] Silverberg, above n 15, 158.

[17] The hoax had many features in common with the earlier 'Waterton Ape Man Hoax' perpetrated by the English naturalist Charles Waterton (1782–1865) who claimed to have encountered and killed an ape man in 1825 in South America. He maintained that because of its humanlike face and apelike head he retained only its head and shoulders which he preserved using his own methods of taxidermy and brought back to England. In fact the head and shoulders were from a red howler monkey which he had reshaped in what was later described as a 'taxidermic frolic'. See Charles Waterton, *Wanderings in South America* (New York: Cosimo Inc, 2005, originally EP Dutton & Co, 1825); Richard Hobson, *Charles Waterton: His Home, Habits and Handiwork* (London: Whittaker & Co, 1867); Richard Aldington, *The Strange Life of Charles Waterton* (London: Evans Brothers, 1949); Peter Dance, *Animal Fakes and Frauds* (Sampson Low, 1976).

[18] See Keith Thomson, 'Piltdown Man: The Great English Mystery Story' (1991) *American Scientist* 194, available at: <http://www.clarku.edu/~piltdown/map_prim_suspects/abbott/abbot_defense/piltman_englishmystery.html> (viewed 19 January 2015).

[19] See Charles Dawson, 'The Piltdown Skull' (1913) 2 *The Hastings and East Sussex Naturalist* 73, available at: <http://www.clarku.edu/~piltdown/map_report_finds/Pilt_skull.html> [accessed 21 Dec 2015]; Frank Spencer, *Piltdown: A Scientific Forgery* (New York: Oxford University Press, 1990); Joseph S Weiner, *The Piltdown Forgery* (Oxford: Oxford University Press, [1955] 2003).

[20] Jonathan Maxwell, *Piltdown Man and Other Hoaxes: A Book About Lies, Legends, and the Search for the Missing Link* (Salt Lake City: American University & Colleges Press, 2012) 17, 20.

> was actually from a sub-fossil orangutan (Oakley thought it might have been stolen from the Museum); the cranium was modern, if unusually thick (perhaps that of an Australian aborigine), whereas the canine discovered by Teilhard came from a modern ape.
>
> The faking of the other items also became apparent. Some of the bone elements had also been treated chemically to change the calcium phosphate to gypsum, or calcium sulphate. The Piltdown II material turned out to be from the same individual as Piltdown I. The Barcombe Mills material was also modern and chemically treated. The bone implement was from a fossil elephant femur that had been cut with a steel knife. The molar teeth on the jaw had all been shaped with a steel file. The canine that Teilhard had discovered was unusual because it had not been stained with potassium dichromate. It had merely been colored with artist's Vandyke brown oil paint. One of the elephant molars was particularly interesting because it had almost certainly come from a site in Tunisia.[21]

Carbon dating in 1959 showed the cranium to be about 620 years old, the jaw about 500 years old and the jaw from an orangutan.[22] By the time of the revelations, though, the principal players were deceased. Theories have proliferated as to the identity of the perpetrator and whether others played a significant role. The conventional view is that Dawson harboured aspirations of election to the Royal Society as a result of the kudos that would come with such an honour.[23] This theory is bolstered by the fact that Dawson has been shown to be responsible for a number of other archaeological frauds.[24] That leaves the most likely explanation for the hoax being straightforward self-promotion.[25] However, a range of others have been suspected of being responsible for the fraud or at least of being implicated in it, Teilhard de Chardin included.[26]

The Piltdown Man hoax remains substantially a mystery, both in terms of a definitive identification of all those responsible for it, and in terms of their motives.

Criminalization of Hoaxing

Pellegrini[27] has argued that we are vulnerable to hoaxing because many of us are suggestible and gullible, and we are glad to believe the surprising and the thrilling since it entertains more as apparent fact than it does as fiction. This leads her to advocate the use of criminal sanctions to protect against foreseeably damaging hoaxing:

> Laws should provide for a charge of perpetrating a hoax in addition to making a false statement or whatever other options might exist. This will give the prosecutor more sanctions, and provide a fuller range of penalties appropriate to the offense. Also, to best serve the

---

[21] Thomson, above n 18, 198 (footnotes omitted).

[22] Maxwell, above n 20, 112.

[23] Compare the archaeological frauds over a period of 20 years by Fujimura Shinichi: see Shoh Yamada, 'Politics and Personality: The Anatomy of Japan's Worst Archaeology Scandal' (2002) 6(3) *Harvard Asia Quarterly* 48; Michele A Miller, 'A Hoax in Japan' (2002) 3(2) *Athena Review*: <http://www.athenapub.com/japhoax.htm> [accessed 21 Dec 2015].

[24] See Miles Russell, *Piltdown Man: The Secret Life of Charles Dawson and The World's Greatest Archaeological Hoax* (Stroud, Gloucestershire: Tempus, 2003). Compare too the purported discovery of the lost Philippines tribe, the Tasaday: Robin Hemley, *Invented Eden: The Elusive, Disputed History of the Tasaday* (Lincoln: Bison Books, Uni of Nebraska Press, 2007), exposing the hoax in John Nance, *The Gentle Tasaday: A Stone Age People in the Philippine Rain Forest* (New York: Harcourt Brace Jovanovich, 1975).

[25] See also the 'Piltdown Chicken Affair', arising from the publicizing of a fossil in China in 1999: see Willie Maartens, *Mapping Reality: A Critical Perspective on Science and Religion* (Bloomington: iUniverse, 2006), 275.

[26] See eg Stephen J Gould, 'Piltdown Revisited' (March 1979) 88 *Natural History* 86; Stephen J Gould, 'The Piltdown Conspiracy' (August 1980) 89 *Natural History* 8; Stephen J Gould, 'Piltdown in Letters' (June 1981) 90 *Natural History* 12.

[27] Laura A Pellegrini, *An Argument for the Criminal Hoax* (Ann Arbor, Mich: ProQuest, 2008).

> taxpaying public, full restitution must be not only allowable under the law but a requirement for anyone convicted of perpetrating a hoax, no exceptions.... For all hoax categories, there is a need for legislative response regarding punishment of hoaxes.[28]

While such a response can be criticized as harsh and retributive, the advantage of the Pellegrini argument is that it identifies that the motives of hoaxing in the research context are frequently malign, self-serving, or indifferent as to the legitimacy of their results and that the consequences should be very adverse, meaning that punitive and deterrent measures should be important aspects of providing protection to a vulnerable public, as can the capacity for courts to mandate the hoaxer to compensate the hoaxed so as to reduce the extent of the deleterious outcome.

Concluding Observations

Hoaxes are often bizarre phenomena. They rely upon credulity and sometimes upon inflated egos and passing fashions.[29] While they can be entertaining, and on occasion are directed towards making a collateral point, they can have a serious aspect because of their resort to orchestrated deceit and the malicious use which they make of apparent scholarship. To the extent that they constitute an abuse of medical or scientific knowledge, they constitute a form of scholarly misconduct and need to be responded to robustly by measures likely to deter the individuals involved from repeating their conduct and others from emulating them.

Forging, Trimming, and Cooking

For those minded to be fraudulent,[30] practicalities are important if they are to succeed in their enterprise—the fraud must be able to be executed effectively and plausibly and it must be difficult for supervisors, reviewers (eg of scholarly journals) or members of institutional ethics committees to identify. While fraudsters are generally prepared to run surprisingly high levels of risk of detection, fuelled by overconfidence and narcissism, they tend to make decisions on the basis of confidence that the odds of non-discovery are in their favour.

What is also apparent is that while there are the conceptual distinctions described (for instance, by Babbage), those who engage in research fraud often utilize more than one modality. An example in this regard was Dr Andrew Friedman, a brilliant surgeon and Associate Professor of Obstetrics, Gynecology and Reproductive Biology at Brigham and Women's Hospital and Harvard Medical School, who both manipulated data and fabricated outcomes in order to perpetrate his frauds. Later he was to describe his panic and a series of cognitive distortions in which he indulged to effect his frauds for a period of over three years.[31] Ultimately, he admitted both to altering and fabricating information in permanent patient medical records by changing dates, amending and adding text, and fabricating notes for clinical visits that did not occur. After being identified, he entered into a voluntary exclusion agreement with the Office of Research Integrity in which he agreed:

(1) to exclude himself from any contracting or subcontracting with any agency of the United States Government and from eligibility for, or involvement in,

---

[28] Pellegrini, at 84–5.

[29] See Lucy Goodchild van Hilten, 'Science Hoaxes: Why Do We Fall for Them—and Who Benefits?' (1 April 2015): <http://www.elsevier.com/connect/science-oaxes-why-do-we-fall-for-them-and-who-benefits> [accessed 21 Dec 2015]; Roger Pielke Jr, 'Fooling Ourselves with Science: Hoaxes, Retractions and the Public' (3 June 2015), *The Guardian*: <http://www.theguardian.com/science/political-science/2015/jun/02/fooling-ourselves-with-science> [accessed 21 Dec 2015].

[30] See eg the self-revelations of Dr Stapel, above, at p 42.

[31] See Associated Press, 'Charges of Fake Research Hit New High', *NBC News*, 10 July 2005: <http://www.nbcnews.com/id/8474936/#.VLzIAEeUd8F> [accessed 21 Dec 2015].

nonprocurement transactions (eg, grants and cooperative agreements) of the United States Government... for a period of three years beginning April 19, 1996;

(2) that for a period of two years immediately following the three year voluntary exclusion above, any institution that submits an application for PHS support for a research project on which Dr Friedman's participation is proposed or that uses him in any capacity on PHS supported research must concurrently submit a plan for supervision of his duties; the supervisory plan must be designed to ensure the scientific integrity of Dr Friedman's research contribution, and the institution must submit a copy of the plan to ORI; and

(3) to exclude himself from serving in any advisory capacity to PHS, including but not limited to service on any PHS advisory committee, board, and/or peer review committee, or as a consultant for a period of three years beginning April 19, 1996.[32]

Outright fabrication, known as forging in the Babbage taxonomy of fraud, has proven to be the most successful form of misconduct for researchers because it provides a carte blanche of opportunities for complete faking of outcomes. This avoids the risk that others might detect research flaws such as inappropriate sampling, problematic methodologies or unjustifiable misinterpretation of data. A number of examples of 'forging' are provided later in this chapter.

Multi-faceted Breaches of Research Integrity

Just as it is rare for researchers to engage in a one-off example of fraud or plagiarism, provided they are not detected early, so also is it uncommon for their modus operandi to be one-dimensional; often they formulate a number of dishonest strategies both to accomplish their object and to reduce the prospects of being detected. Frequently the dishonesty encompasses multiple components, comprehending deficits in proper data selection, research methodology, often including fabrication of data, and finally, misinterpretation of test results. And because professional life is not wholly compartmentalized from personal life,[33] there are occasions when the dishonesty spills over into the non-work life of the practitioner. An extreme example of this is the case of Dr Edward Erin in the United Kingdom, while a more conventional example of multi-factorial professional fraud is the nanotechnology research undertaken by Jan Schön.

Edward Erin: The Tangled Web of Deceit

In 2003 a team of researchers at Imperial College London commenced to trial a drug for asthma on patients at St Mary's Hospital. The trial was headed by Professor Peter Barnes from the National Heart and Lung Institute and included a highly regarded United States physician, Dr Sally Wenzel, Professor of Medicine and Director of the Asthma Institute at Pittsburgh's Montefiore Hospital; Professor Andrew Bush, Imperial College's Professor of Paediatrics, and Professor of Paediatric Respirology; Dr Trevor Hansel, Medical Director of the Imperial Clinical Respiratory Research Unit; and Dr Onn Min Kon, consultant respiratory physician and lead clinician for tuberculosis services at St Mary's and Hammersmith Hospitals. Dr Edward Erin, an experienced consultant, was part of the trial.[34]

[32] National Institutes of Health, Department of Health and Human Services, 'Andrew Friedman, MD, Harvard Medical School' (1996) 25(15) *Findings of Scientific Misconduct*: <http://grants.nih.gov/grants/guide/notice-files/not96-125.html> [accessed 21 Dec 2015].

[33] Arguably because it is indicative of a trait of character that applies across different domains of life: see Ian Freckelton, '"Good Character" and the Regulation of Medical Practitioners' (2008) 16(3) *Journal of Law and Medicine* 488.

[34] See John Lawless, 'Exposed: The Asthma Drug Trials That Led to Cancer and Death', *The Independent*, 18 June 2013: <http://www.independent.co.uk/news/uk/home-news/exposed-the-asthma-drug-trials-that-led-to-cancer-and-death-8662548.html> [accessed 21 Dec 2015].

The costs of the trial were partly funded by the pharmaceutical manufacturer of Golimumab, the drug being tested. The United Kingdom team's clinical study utilized 38 modestly ill persons with asthma. The results were promising—no doubt in a way that was encouraging to the manufacturer. In parallel an international experiment almost eight times as large, and using severely ill patients, was also undertaken contemporaneously. Dr Erin's role was in relation to the larger study and included analysing the sputum from patients' lungs to enable evaluation of the potential effects of the drug. From 2004 to 2006, three-quarters of 309 patients with severe and uncontrolled asthma who had volunteered to take part in the international trial were given Golimumab, in three different strengths; the remainder were given placebos.

The trials were subject to rigorous controls with the result that those running the study did not see the ongoing results. This was to try to avoid compromising the trial until all the data had been collated up to the 24th week. However, by 25 February 2007, when the data were unlocked, the effects of Golimumab were discovered. They included pneumonia and cancer. The *American Journal of Respiratory and Clinical Care Medicine* (AJRCCM) reported:

> One death occurred in the 200mg group. This patient was hospitalised in an unresponsive state one week after receiving the fourth Golimumab dose. The patient's respiratory status declined, requiring ventilatory support, and the patient died from septic shock following diagnosis of small-bowel pneumatosis. Eight malignancies were reported in Golimumab-treated patients: breast cancer in the 50mg group; B-cell lymphoma and malignant melanoma in the 100mg group; and cervical carcinoma, renal cell carcinoma, colon cancer (stage 0), and two basal cell carcinomas in the 200mg group.[35]

One test subject had to have her breast removed; another was discovered with fast-growing polyps. This was disastrous for the trial which, of course, was abruptly terminated.

However, another aspect to the trial was the discovery that Dr Erin had been fabricating data from the sputum results—in favour of positive outcomes for the drug. He changed one figure from 3.81 to 23.81. In September 2010 a letter, signed by Professor Barnes, Professor Andrew Bush, Dr Trevor Hansel, and Dr Onn Min Kon, was sent retracting the published research. It cited, among other things, an example of the way Erin had altered his data.

An article in which Erin was lead author[36] was cited by other writers in the field over 70 times until it was retracted.[37] Since then citations continued with the number more than doubling. Three further retractions followed. Professor Barnes was later to postulate that Erin may have been driven by a desire to enhance his career: 'It is very difficult to see why he would do it. It is as if he had a compulsion to change things. These people lie about things they don't need to lie about. We have never had anything like it in my 30 years.'[38]

Extraordinarily, shortly after the first signs of Erin's fraudulent conduct were discovered, he was arrested and charged, in February 2008. However, it was not his research work that generated the criminal proceedings. He was found guilty of two counts of attempting to administer poison, in a coffee and an orange juice, with intent to induce a miscarriage in his secretary who had become pregnant in the course of an affair with Erin that began at a

[35] Ibid.

[36] Edward M Erin, Brian R Leaker, Grant C Nicholson, Andrew J Tan et al. 'The Effects of a Monoclonal Antibody Directed Against Tumor Necrosis Factor-α in Asthma' (2006) 174(7) *American Journal of Respiratory and Critical Care Medicine* 753.

[37] From the Editor, 'Retraction of Four Articles and Abstracts' (2011) 183(3) *American Journal of Respiratory and Critical Care Medicine* 418.

[38] Lawless, above n 34.

Christmas party.[39] He was sentenced to six years' imprisonment and ordered to pay a fine of £30,000. Old Bailey judge Richard Hone QC described Erin as 'a liar, a cheat and a predator' who exploited his position and his wealth to seduce women.[40]

Erin's dishonest behaviour did not even end at this point. He convinced a fellow inmate to steal his victim's telephone and to send a text from it 'confessing' that she had made up her allegations against Erin. However, instead (there being little honour among fraudsters), the inmate took his story to a reporter from *The Sun* who then secretly filmed Erin reviewing the plot with the inmate. The video was used as evidence against the disgraced doctor at his next trial in which he was found guilty of attempting to pervert the course of justice. Erin's sentence of imprisonment was extended by a further two years. It is quite apparent that Erin's propensity to dishonesty comprehended both his professional life and his personal life, raising the issue of the extent to which it should be viewed as a character trait not readily amenable to remediation.

Jan Hendrik Schön: Nanotechnology Frauds

Jan Hendrik Schön was a researcher in condensed matter physics and nanotechnology.[41] He received his PhD from the University of Konstanz in 1997 and in the same year was employed by Bell Labs, the institution that had done much of the work towards the invention of the first laser and been the first to use radio telescopes to detect the echo of the Big Bang.[42] Schön's research at Bell Labs was into the transformation of the properties of materials by the application of an electric field. He built high-performance transistors made not from the usual silicon but from the semiconductor copper gallium selenide (CGS). He worked with CGS crystals creating what he asserted were means of conducting electricity without resistance. He described what he maintained was the world's first organic electrical laser, and the first ever light-emitting transistor. In 2001 he claimed to have built the world's smallest transistor by wiring up a single molecule and having used a thin layer of organic dye molecules to assemble an electric circuit that functioned as a transistor when acted on by an electric current. This placed him at the forefront of international nanotechnology research.[43] The potential of his work was enormous as it raised the possibility of a movement away from silicon-based electronics to organic electronics, allowing reduction in the size of chips well beyond what was possible with silicon.

Underlying Schön's work was the observation of a variety of phenomena in the set-up of the organic transistor, in turn depending on the effective preparation of aluminium oxide layers. By 2001 Schön was listed as a scientist responsible for publishing a new research paper every

---

[39] See Rebecca Evans and Emily Nash, 'Doctor Edward Erin Guilty of Attempting Poison Abortion', *The Mirror*, 19 October 2009: <http://www.mirror.co.uk/news/uk-news/doctor-edward-erin-guilty-of-attempting-425897> [accessed 21 Dec 2015]. The article entertainingly summarized Erin's psychopathic personal life: 'To the outside world, Dr Edward Erin seemed a model of professionalism and well-heeled respectability. A wealthy hospital consultant, seemingly devoted to his doctor wife and their two children, his only passions appeared to be skiing and rock-climbing. In the medical world, he was lauded for his pioneering research into nasal allergies. But behind this veneer of virtuousness there was a seedier figure—a serial adulterer who revelled in the sexual freedom of the 'open relationship' his wife allowed him. He had affairs with at least two medical colleagues and is thought to have had a string of other lovers.'

[40] Lawless, above n 34.

[41] See Leonard Cassuto, 'Big Trouble in the World of "Big Physics"', *Salon*, 17 September 2002: <http://www.salon.com/2002/09/16/physics/> [accessed 21 Dec 2015].

[42] See Alcatel-Lucent, 'Bell Labs': <https://www.alcatel-lucent.com/bell-labs> [accessed 21 Dec 2015].

[43] See Hank Campbell, 'Jan Hendrik Schön: World Class Physics Fraud Gets Last Laugh—A Whole Book About Himself', *Science2.0*, 5 May 2009: <http://www.science20.com/science_20/jan_hendrik_sch%C3%B6n_world_class_physics_fraud_gets_last_laugh_whole_book_about_himself> [accessed 21 Dec 2015].

eight days, including a series of papers in both *Nature* and *Science* that promised a transformation in nanotechnology. However, Professor Lydia Sohn of Princeton University and Professor Paul McEuen of Cornell University expressed concern about anomalies in Schön's methodology, including the use of duplicate data. This prompted Lucent Technologies, which ran Bell Labs, to conduct a formal investigation into his work by a committee chaired by Professor Malcolm Beasley of Stanford University. When the committee requested copies of raw data, it was informed somewhat lamely by Schön that he had not kept laboratory notebooks and that his data files had been deleted from his computer because of limited space on the hard drive. He also informed the committee that all of his experimental samples had been discarded or were not available for examination because of damage to them.[44]

The Committee's explosive report was released in September 2002, exonerating all of Schön's co-workers but finding him to have engaged in no fewer than 16 instances of scientific misconduct. The Committee found Schön's misconduct to fall into three categories: 'substitution of data', 'unrealistic precision of data' and 'results that contradict known physics'.[45] The 'substitution' category was that Schön had recycled graphs representing data from one type of material, changed labels, and passed them off as coming from different materials. The second category of misconduct involved manipulation of data—such as replacing raw data with averaged, filtered, or smoothed curves—or the fabrication of entire data sets. Some of his graphs, for example, appeared to have been generated by matching a known equation, with no experimental input whatsoever.[46]

After the Committee's report, Schön was fired by Bell Labs which, along with Lucent Technologies, its owner, was adversely affected by the negative publicity arising from the scandal. It emphasized that Schön's case was 'an individual case performed by an individual. In this case, we had an individual who didn't live up to the scientific requirement for integrity.'[47] In written comments on the report, Schön admitted to having made mistakes and apologized, but insisted his findings were all based on experimental observation: 'I am convinced that they are real, although I could not prove this to the investigation committee.'[48]

He returned to Germany to work as a process engineer but in June 2004 the University of Konstanz announced that it had revoked his doctoral degree as a result of Schön's 'dishonourable conduct'. Schön was not intimidated by his alma mater. He took legal action against the University and was successful at first instance, but failed on appeal to the Administrative Court of Baden-Württemberg in Mannheim which ruled that the University was entitled to rescind the degree:

> The awarding of a doctorate is a confirmation of the recipient's ability to conduct independent scientific research, Judge Reinhard Schwan said in his oral explanation of the verdict…A Ph.D. brings with it the public perception of being a member of the scientific community and a presumed high level of trustworthiness, the judge said. When a recipient

---

[44] Eugenie Samuel Reich, *Plastic Fantastic: How the Biggest Fraud in Physics Shook the Scientific World* (New York: Palgrave Macmillan, 2009) 99f.

[45] Malcolm R Beasley, Supriyo Datta, Herwig Kogelnik, Herbert Kroemer, and V Don Monroe, *Report of the Investigation Committee on the Possibility of Scientific Misconduct in the Work of Hendrik Schön and Co-Authors* (September 2002) 2: <http://www.alcatel-lucent.com/wps/DocumentStreamerServlet?LMSG_CABINET=Docs_and_Resource_Ctr&LMSG_CONTENT_FILE=Corp_Governance_Docs/researchreview.pdf> [accessed 21 Dec 2015].

[46] Ibid, 3.

[47] See Kenneth Chang, 'Panel Says Bell Labs Scientist Faked Discoveries in Physics', *The New York Times*, 26 September 2002: <http://www.nytimes.com/2002/09/26/us/panel-says-bell-labs-scientist-faked-discoveries-in-physics.html> [accessed 21 Dec 2015].

[48] Ibid.

has violated basic principles of good scientific practice, the title is no longer applicable and should be corrected, he said.[49]

Schön's frauds were brazen and always liable to be exposed giving how cutting edge his nanotechnology work was. What ultimately brought him undone was questionable generation of records and an inability to produce any of his primary data for independent evaluation when required. His deficits in research integrity were various and incorporated his earlier doctoral research.

Victor Ninov: The Heavy Elements Fraud

On occasion, it is determination that in one way or another experimentation will establish a particular outcome that is responsible for fraud in research. An example in this regard is the work of Dr Victor Ninov, an investigator at Lawrence Berkeley National Laboratory (named in honour of the Nobel Prize-winning physicist, Ernest Lawrence) who claimed to have discovered two new elements: unonoctium, a 'super-heavy' element, called '118', by reference to its supposed atomic number, and its decay product, livermorium, called '116'.[50] The research was done using the laboratory's 88-inch cyclotron, a particle accelerator, to fire a beam of krypton atoms onto lead. In 1999 the discovery was announced in *Physical Review Letters*,[51] the most prestigious journal in the field. However, in a short time the deceit unravelled and the paper was retracted.[52] The fraud was perpetrated in the midst of rivalry between the Lawrence Berkeley National Laboratory, a German team at the Laboratory for Heavy Ion Research (GSI), and a Russian team at Dubna.[53]

Ninov came to Berkeley from GSI where he had played a role in the discovery of elements 110, 111, and 112. The laboratory undertook its own review after follow-up experiments in other laboratories (including at GSI and the Riken Institute which was later to experience its own infamy because of the fraud of Dr Obokata) were unable to replicate Ninov's results. Ultimately Ninov's employers concluded that 'after starting with small instances of data fabrication that did not change an experiment's main conclusions, Ninov based his discovery of elements 116 and 118 on a web of falsified data.'[54] Analysis of his earlier work showed a pattern of spuriously created data. The announcement of the retraction of the

[49] Gretchen Vogel, 'Jan Hendrik Schön Loses his Ph.D.', *Science Insider*, 19 September 2011: <http://news.sciencemag.org/education/2011/09/jan-hendrik-sch%C3%B6n-loses-his-ph.d> (viewed 21 January 2015).

[50] Ninov's 'discovery' was one of several bogus discoveries of what have been asserted to be elements: Sir John Herschel purported to discover 'junonium' in 1858; Sir William Crookes claimed to have discovered 'victorium' in 1898 (although it was later shown to be a mixture of gadolinium and terbium); Dmitri Mendeleev purported to have 'discovered' newtonium and coronium in 1903, elements asserted (wrongly) to be lighter than air; clairvoyants Besant and Leadbeater claimed to have discovered occultum in 1909; Joly claimed to have discovered hibernium in 1922; Rolla maintained he had discovered florentium in 1927, and Allison purported to have discovered virginium and alabamine in 1931–1932 by magneto-optic methods; see Marco Fontani, Mariagrazia Costa, and Mary Virginia Orna, *The Lost Elements: The Periodic Table's Shadow Side* (Oxford: Oxford University Press, 2014).

[51] Victor Ninov, KE Grigorich, W Loveland et al. 'Observation of Superheavy Nuclei Produced in the Reaction of 86Kr with 208Pb' (1999) 83 *Physical Review Letters* 1104.

[52] See George Johnson, 'At Lawrence Berkeley, Physicists Say a Colleague Took Them for a Ride' (15 October 2002) *The New York Times*: <http://www.nytimes.com/2002/10/15/science/at-lawrence-berkeley-physicists-say-a-colleague-took-them-for-a-ride.html?scp=2&sq=victor%20ninov&st=cse&pagewanted=1> [accessed 21 Dec 2015].

[53] It was the Russian team, working with a group from the Lawrence Livermore National Laboratory in California, that discovered the 'heaviest element' once again, in 2006: Katharine Sanderson, 'Heaviest Element Made—Again' (17 October 2006) *Nature*: <http://www.nature.com/news/2006/061016/full/news061016-4.html> [accessed 21 Dec 2015].

[54] Rex Dalton, 'The Stars Who Fell to Earth' (December 2002) 420 *Nature* 728: <http://research.ncsu.edu/sparcs-docs/integrity/Nature_misconduct.pdf> [accessed 21 Dec 2015].

article communicating the discovery was very circumspect: 'Science is self-correcting. If you get the facts wrong, your experiment is not reproducible. There are many lessons here, and the lab will extract all the value it can from this event. The path forward is to learn from the mistakes and strengthen the resolve to find the answers that nature still hides from us'.[55] The laboratory's director, Charles V Shank, has been reported as having been more candid at an internal meeting, conceding that the retraction was 'a result of fabricated research data and scientific misconduct by one individual'.[56]

Ninov responded by filing a formal grievance with the Lawrence Berkeley National Laboratory, after its finding that he had engaged in research fraud. However, his standing to pursue such a position was weakened by revelations by GSI which undertook reanalyses of his work that Ninov's data in that institution had been 'spuriously created'.

Ultimately, Ninov's fraudulent conduct, as so often, when scrutinized, was revealed to be part of a pattern of cognate behaviour. It may be that he genuinely believed that the outcome of his experimentation would be established by further work, but was prepared to take a short-cut by faking his research. Alternatively, it is possible that his dishonest conduct was entrenched and constituted simple succumbing to ambition over integrity. Again, as is common, his initial reaction was to commence legal action against the employer which exposed him and took proper remedial action.

Unsophisticated Research Fraud

Some research fraud is sophisticated, convoluted, and relatively well camouflaged. However, other research deceptions have been executed at a remarkably primitive level, although the motivation behind the fraud has been unequivocally dishonest. The 'Charlton Brimstone butterfly', the 'patchwork mouse', 'midwife toad', and 'unlikely lichen' fabrications, for instance, were undertaken audaciously, albeit at a ridiculously low level of sophistication—each involved nothing more than the drawing of deceptive marks onto the research subjects and the faking of plant location. They are examples of undeniably deliberate fraud but utilizing a form of brazen deception that was inevitably going to be identified at some stage. The conduct was both outrageous and desperately and absurdly self-harming, raising the issue of whether at some level the perpetrators wanted to be detected.

William Charlton: The Brimstone Butterfly Fraud

In 1702 a butterfly collector by the name of William Charlton (1642–1702) sent a new butterfly for examination to the esteemed London entomologist James Petiver.[57] It resembled the English Brimstone Butterfly save for its black spots and apparent blue moons on the lower wings. However, a few years later another entomologist, Carl Linnaeus, classified Charlton's butterfly to be a new species, naming it the Papilio Eclipsis and included it in the 12th edition of his *Systema Naturae* that was published in 1767.

---

[55] 'Element 118 Disappears Two Years After it was Discovered' (2 August 2001) *physics-world.com*: <http://physicsworld.com/cws/article/news/2001/aug/02/element-118-disappears-two-years-after-it-was-discovered> [accessed 21 Dec 2015].

[56] See Elizabeth Wilson, 'Superheavy Furor' (22 July 2002) 80(2) *Chemical and Engineering News*: <http://pubs.acs.org/cen/topstory/8029/8029notw6.html> [accessed 21 Dec 2015].

[57] Michael A Salmon, Peter Marren, and Basil Harley, *The Aurelian Legacy: British Butterflies and Their Collectors* (Berkeley: University of California Press, 2000) 66; see too, David KC Cooper (ed), *Doctors of Another Calling: Physicians Who are Known Best in Fields Other Than Medicine* (Maryland: Rowman & Littlefield, 2014) 53.

It was 30 years later that the Danish entomologist, John Christian Fabricius, utilized new technology and discovered that the butterfly was a fraud. The spots had been painted on the wings of a Brimstone Butterfly. The keeper of national curiosities at the British Museum, Dr EW Gray, is said to have been so enraged by the deception that he indignantly stamped the specimen to pieces.[58] The reason for Charlton's conduct remains unknown although it continues to be the subject of speculation.

Paul Kammerer: The Case of the Midwife Toad

One of the more entertaining and absurd examples of research fraud (albeit with a tragic ending) was the notorious 'case of the midwife toad'.[59] An Austrian scientist, Paul Kammerer, was at the heart of experiments that promised remarkable insights into the mechanisms of evolution. For his work he was hailed as 'a second Darwin'.[60] He was also a remarkable polymath: a 'prodigy, musician, mountaineer, research zoologist, popular lecturer, lover of beautiful women. After a day in the laboratory, he would go home to compose symphonies; he named his daughter Lacerta after a genus of small lizards. By any standards, Kammerer seems to have possessed extraordinary personal charm, a brilliant if unorthodox scientific imagination and unexcelled experimental skill: the failure of other scientists to duplicate his experiments was often due merely to their lack of his technical virtuosity'.[61]

Kammerer designed a series of experiments on salamanders, sea squirts, and sea toads to investigate whether injuries or other adverse events could be passed on by inheritance and thereby play an important role in evolution—the theory of Lamarckianism. He first worked on the sea squirt (*Ciona intestinalis*), and purported to show that, when the two siphon ends were amputated, the new siphon tubes became longer upon regeneration than the original tubes, and that the complete elongation was inherited by the next generation. However, he did not publish this work in peer-reviewed form, simply referring to it in his books and short papers.

He then worked on the midwife toad (*Alytes Obstetricans*). Most toads mate in water and, as a result, have black, scaly bumps (also known as nuptial pads) on their hind limbs that assist adherence while they are mating. By contrast, though, the midwife toad mates on land and does not have such bumps. Kammerer's theory was that if midwife toads were forced to mate in water they would evolve by developing such bumps and their offspring would inherit them in accordance with Lamarckian theory. He filled a fishtank with water, placed midwife toads in it and in 1909 announced the birth of midwife toads with black, scaly marks on their hind limbs.[62] The announcement of his results was groundbreaking in terms of evolutionary theory and attracted enormous scientific interest. He was hailed as a successor to Charles Darwin and his work was described as revolutionary.[63]

---

[58] See Jeannie Swales, 'Common Brimstone Butterfly', *The Scarborough News*, 30 March 2014: <http://www.thescarboroughnews.co.uk/news/common-brimstone-butterfly-1-6524802> [accessed 21 Dec 2015].

[59] See Arthur Koestler, *The Case of the Midwife Toad* (New York: Random House, 1971); Lester R Aronson, *The Case of the Midwife Toad* (1975) 5(2) *Behavior Genetics* 115; Sander Gliboff, 'The Case of Paul Kammerer: Evolution and Experimentation in the Early 20th Century' (2006) 39(3) *Journal of the History of Biology* 525; E Lachman, 'Famous Scientific Hoaxes' (1976) 69(3) *The Journal of the Oklahoma State Medical Association* 87.

[60] Koestler, above n 59, 93. See generally, 91–3.

[61] Robert Clairborne, 'Can Genes Learn? Arthur Koestler Thinks So', *The New York Times*, 2 April 1972: <http://www.nytimes.com/books/00/01/02/specials/koestler-toad.html> [accessed 21 Dec 2015].

[62] Paul Kammerer, 'Verebung Erzwungener Fortpflanzungsanpassungen. III. Mitteilung: Die Nachkommen der Nicht Brutpflegenden Alytes Obstetricians' (1909) 28 *Archiv für Entwicklungsmechanik der Organismen* 447; Paul Kammerer, *The Inheritance of Acquired Characteristics* (New York: Boni and Liveright Publishers, 1924).

[63] Randy Moore, 'People and Places: Paul Kammerer: 1880–1926' (2011) 31(3) *Reports of the National Center for Science Education* 2.1: <http://reports.ncse.com/index.php/rncse/article/viewFile/42/31> [accessed 21 Dec 2015].

However, matters took a different turn when in 1926 Professor GK Noble, Curator of Reptiles at the American Museum of Natural History, examined Kammerer's toads and discovered that, instead of the asserted bumps, they displayed subcutaneous inkspots where black ink had been injected under their skin.[64] Kammerer responded by implausibly claiming that the toads had died and he had highlighted the areas where the pads had formed by ink.[65]

Goldschmidt rationalized Kammerer's conduct as misguided enthusiasm, contending that:

> [He] became so obsessed with [his] idea that he 'improved' upon his records. I have reason to believe, from what I have seen in his laboratory, that he continued his experiments, which ended by the death of the specimens, by starting again with similar looking animals. His 'Aquarianer' mind did not consider this wrong. He simply did not know what an experiment amounted to. In later years he probably became so absorbed with the necessity for proving his claims that he started inventing results or 'doctoring' them. Though the actual results of all this amounted to falsification, I am not certain that he realized it and intended it.[66]

Alma Mahler-Werfel, who worked for a short time as laboratory assistant to Kammerer, expressed similar views in her memoirs, reporting that:

> I kept records, and did so very exactly. But this did not please Kammerer: an inexact record with a positive result would have pleased him more. I do not say that there was something fraudulent in him: no, he desired the results of his research so ardently [to be in his favour] that he could unconsciously depart from the truth. This also explains to me his later procedure and the charge of the English research institutes that 'the results of his experiments proved invalid upon being examined further.' On that occasion the mimicry of salamanders was the subject. This experiment, too, which I helped test was published too quickly and not sufficiently observed.[67]

There are many reasons for suspecting that Kammerer suffered from a bipolar illness,[68] with rapidly cycling manic and depressive symptoms, unaddressed by remedial medication.[69]

At the time of his death in the Theresien hills of Austria by self-inflicted gunshot, Kammerer had accepted the prestigious position of Professor of Biology at Moscow University. His final word was published in a somewhat attention-seeking way in *Science*:

> The principal matter of importance in this is an artificial coloring, probably with India ink, through which the black coloring of the skin in the region carrying the stripes is said to have been faked. Therefore it would be a matter of deception that presumably will be laid to me only.
>
> [...]
>
> Who besides myself had any interest in perpetrating such falsifications can only be very dimly suspected.... I hope that I shall gather together enough courage and strength to put an end of my wretched life tomorrow.[70]

64 Gladwyn K Noble, 'Kammerer's Alytes' (1926) 118(2962) *Nature* 209.

65 Brunella Antomarini, *Thinking Through Error: The Moving Target of Knowledge* (Lanham, Md: Lexington Books, 2012) 9.

66 Richard B Goldschmidt, 'Research and Politics' (1949) 109(2827) *Science* 219, 221.

67 Alma Mahler-Werfel, *Mein Leben* (Frankfurt am Main: Fischer, 1960) 54.

68 See Koestler, above n 59, 95.

69 While Carl Lange in Denmark and William Hammond in New York used lithium to treat mania from the 1970s, its routine use for treating the condition only dated from the work of Australian psychiatrist, John Cade, in 1949.

70 Paul Kammerer, 'Paul Kammerer's Letter to the Moscow Academy' (1926) 64(1664) *Science* 493, 494. See also, John R Whittaker, 'Paul Kammerer and the Suspect Siphons', *MBL Science* (1985): <http://hermes.mbl.edu/publications/pub_archive/Ciona/Kammerer/index.html> [accessed 21 Dec 2015].

William Summerlin: The Patchwork Mouse Affair

In the 1970s history repeated itself eerily. Stephen Lock in his 'imperfect history' of 'research misconduct' dates the modern story of research fraud to this time and to the conduct of William Summerlin.[71] In 1974 Summerlin was a dermatologist working at Memorial Sloan-Kettering Center in New York City, undertaking immunological research into rejection of organ transplants in humans and animals.[72] His theory was that the placement of donor organs in tissue culture for a time before transplantation could avoid the immune reaction that causes transplant rejection. He transplanted black melanocyte pigment cells into white mice which lacked melanocytes, and also undertook corneal transplants into rabbits from human cadavers. His results appeared to corroborate his theory. However, other immunologists were unable to replicate his work—always a warning sign and, indeed, a sign that has often set in train suspicion and scepticism that has led to the uncovering of research fraud.

The tendency identified by Summerlin was for the dark cells to move out of the mouse's transplanted tissue, producing a grey patch.[73] However, on an occasion that became infamous Summerlin took with him to a senior colleague one of the white mice on which he had been working and darkened some of the skin grafts with a felt-tipped pen. His downfall came about in the context of care of the mouse—a laboratory assistant observed that alcohol was able to wash away the dark colour and so informed the laboratory director.

Summerlin was promptly suspended from duties and a six-person committee was appointed to review the scientific reliability of his work. In the process, the committee members discovered anomalies in a series of experiments that he had done into both human corneal transplants into rabbits and the mouse transplant work, concluding that he had falsely reported his outcomes. Infamy followed, with Summerlin being dismissed, albeit with the payment of a year's salary and some words from the head of Sloan-Kettering directed to providing a reassuring and humane explanation for Summerlin's conduct: '[A]fter discussion with Dr Summerlin, his wife, and his personal psychiatrist, I have concluded that the most rational explanation for Dr Summerlin's recent performance is that he has been suffering from an emotional disturbance of such a nature that he has not been fully responsible for the actions he has taken or the presentations he has made.'[74] Summerlin himself later attributed his deceptive behaviour to a combination of mental and physical exhaustion, a heavy clinical and experimental workload, and pressure to publicize positive results.[75] He moved to rural Louisiana and then Arkansas to practise as a dermatologist.

Thus, the damage control explanation advanced that was mutually satisfactory to Sloan-Kettering and Summerlin was that it was work pressure that had resulted in an 'emotional disturbance', a temporary psychiatric condition that had relieved him of the capacity to make ethical decisions. In such circumstances, Summerlin's conduct was portrayed as not overly culpable, being the product of pathology, and not to be attributed institutionally at the feet of either the organization or Summerlin's supervisor who, the head of Sloan-Kettering was

---

[71] Stephen Lock, 'Research Misconduct 1974–1990: An Imperfect History' in Stephen Lock, Frank Wells, and Michael Farthing (eds), *Fraud and Misconduct in Biomedical Research* (3rd edn, London: BMJ Books, 2001).

[72] See Joseph R Hixson, *The Patchwork Mouse* (Garden City, NY: Anchor Press, 1976).

[73] William T Summerlin, 'Allogenic Transplantation of Organ Cultures of Adult Human Skin' (1973) 1(3) *Clinical Immunology and Immunopathology* 372; William T Summerlin, GE Miller, and RA Good, 'Successful Tissue and Organ Transplantation Without Immunosuppression' (1973) 52 *The Journal of Clinical Investigation* 34a.

[74] Hixson, above n 72, 91.

[75] Marcel C La Follette, 'The Evolution of the 'Scientific Misconduct' Issue: An Historical Overview' (2000) 224(4) *Proceedings of the Society for Experimental Biology and Medicine* 211.

at pains to emphasize, had been placed 'in an extremely difficult situation, and it is understandable, and indeed inevitable, that during this time it may have been impossible for him to maintain the close, day-to-day supervision which, viewed now in retrospect, might have prevented or terminated more quickly this regrettable affair'.[76]

Reflections on how Summerlin could have been allowed to become so prominent and to have been nurtured for so long ensued. One of the best-known was an article by Barbara Culliton who observed:

> There is no sin in science more grievous than falsifying data. There is no accusation that can be made against a man more serious than that he is guilty of such a sin. The very thought of fakery threatens the powerful mystique of the purity of science. It stirs deep and contradictory feelings of incredulity, outrage, and remorse among the entire scientific community.[77]

She made the point that, beyond the mouse-painting behaviour, the controversies about Summerlin brought into question all of his scholarly work and the reputation of Summerlin's supervisor, Professor Robert Good, who had lent the prestige of his stature to Summerlin's work, as well as the reputation and internal stability of Sloan-Kettering itself. Hixson, author of *The Patchwork Mouse* in 1976,[78] expressed the view that what gave rise systemically to the Summerlin phenomenon was the combination of major financial inducements for medical breakthroughs and the temptation on the part of those supervising and employing him not to place anything in his path which might inhibit potential breakthroughs in research understanding.

John Heslop Harrison: The Unlikely Lichen Fraud

Another example of unsophisticated fraud emerged many years after his conduct in relation to the introduction by Professor John Heslop Harrison (1881–1967) of the Royal Society and Newcastle University of alien sedges onto the inner Hebridean island of Rum to advance one of his botanical hypotheses—that the Hebrides had escaped the Ice Age. Professor Harrison had claimed to discover on Rum a number of species of lichens and other plants that were non-existent on the mainland, indicating that the ice sheets that had destroyed plants elsewhere had spared Rum.[79] He proclaimed:

> Thus on scattered nunataks, and on cliff ledges, it is pictured that most of the Alpine plants, exemplified by the sedge *Carex capitata, C. bicolor,* and *C. glacialis,* the wood-rush *Luzula spicata,* the grass *Poa alpina,* the Arctic Scurvy Grass (*Cochlearia arctica*), the Fleabane (*Erigeron uniflorus*), the Alpine Saw-wort (*Saussurea alpina*) and the Norwegian sandwort (*Arenaria norvegica*) amongst the flowering plants, and *Andreaea blytii, A. hartmani* and *Ditrichum vaginans* amongst the mosses, survived the rigours of the Ice Age.[80]

In the 1940s, however, John Raven, a classics scholar from Cambridge University with a passionate interest in botany, discovered nine or ten specimens of the *Carex bicolor* growing neatly in a cleared spot (one wilted, as if badly planted) on Rum, but nowhere else on the island.[81] When specimens of the relevant plants were located, they were only in curiously isolated clumps. And the soil in which one of them was growing was different from that

---

[76] Hixson, above 72, 93.

[77] Barbara J Culliton, 'The Sloan-Kettering Affair: A Story Without a Hero' (1974) 184(4137) *Science* 644, 644.

[78] Hixson, above n 72, 182.

[79] See Karl Sabbagh, *A Rum Affair: A True Story of Botanical Fraud* (New York: Farrar, Strauss, and Giroux, 2000) 23f.

[80] Ibid, 25–26.

[81] Ibid, 117.

existing anywhere on the island.[82] Raven wrote to Harrison alerting him: 'I am very sorry to say that I was gravely perturbed by a certain amount that I saw in Rum.'[83] Raven published some of his findings in *Nature* in 1949 without making any direct accusation. This led to some delisting of Professor Harrison's discoveries.[84] It also prompted Harrison to write to Raven in bitter terms, accusing him of betrayal and conspiracy, and then commenting: 'In my opinion your exaltation of trifles, capable of simple explanation by any ordinary person, indicates that consciously or unconsciously you are influenced by something quite unknown to me'.[85] Harrison was allowed to retain his professorial position and much of his reputation as a doyen of modern botany. He never forgave Raven, at first accusing him of verging on 'impertinence',[86] and continued to engage in acrimonious disputation with him, for instance writing to him after his wife's death in 1952 and accusing him of 'the pain and unnecessary suffering your lust for notoriety caused her'.[87]

Raven did not hold back in the 12,000-word report that he penned, concluding that:

> The Professor is deliberately indulging in the most culpable dishonesty in order to secure for himself an immediate reputation and an immortal place in the annals of British botany... The Professor is clearly a man of very humble origin: he is in fact, I have been told credibly enough, the son of a miner.[88] He is obviously able and almost equally obviously ambitious.[89]

However, for reasons that never became clear, he sealed his report in the library of Trinity College, until both he and Harrison 'are safely in our graves'.[90] In 1955 the botanist RB Cooke, who accompanied Professor Harrison on a number of his expeditions, wrote to Dr George Taylor, Keeper of Botany at the Natural History Museum: 'You may say what fools Harrison must have thought us to be, or rather I should say I was. It was a very sad chapter in my life to be so taken in'. Sabbagh has argued that other discoveries by Professor Harrison, including that the melanism of moths was due to some kind of pollution and his studies into sawflies and his discovery of the *Maculinea arion* (large blue) butterfly on Rum may also have been afflicted by fraud.

The 'Unlikely Lichen Fraud' is a further example of a primitively executed and brazen deception perpetrated by a doyen in his scholarly area. The motive appears to have been to provide further evidence for a particular evolutionary theory to which he had become overly

82 Raven's account was corroborated by that of his friend, Tom Creighton, who accompanied him on the expedition, in an interview he gave to Raven's widow: see Sabbagh, above n 79,126.

83 Ibid, 134.

84 Other discoveries of Professor Harrison have also come into doubt. Writing of his insect discoveries, Magnus Magnusson, in his *Rum: Nature's Island* (Edinburgh: Luath Press, 1997), noted: '[M]any of the insects he found were subsequently confirmed from the localities in which he found them, but the problem... was that a few spectacular rarities have never been seen on Rum again... particularly the large blue butterfly, which is now extinct in Britain, and the slender Scotch Burnet Moth. Some of these more unusual records, it is suspected, may have been mischievously introduced': as cited in the 1999 review by Edward Teague, 'A Rum Affair: How Botany's 'Piltdown Man' was Unmasked', *natural SCIENCE*, available at: <http://web.archive.org/web/20131103154825/<http://naturalscience.com/ns/books/book08.html> (snapshot dated 3 November 2013 [accessed 21 Dec 2015]

85 Sabbagh, above n 79, 143.

86 Ibid, 259.

87 Ibid, 221.

88 In fact he was the son of an ironmonger.

89 Richard Eder, 'Up the Garden Path', 13 August 2000, *The New York Times* (online): <https://www.nytimes.com/books/00/08/13/reviews/000813.13ederlt.html> [accessed 21 Dec 2015].

90 Sabbagh, above n 79, 7. His son, John Heslop-Harrison (1920–1998), followed in his father's footsteps, becoming Director of the Royal Botanic Gardens in Kew and a Fellow of the Royal Society: see <http://www.royalsoced.org.uk/cms/files/fellows/obits_alpha/heslop-harrison_john.pdf> [accessed 21 Dec 2015].

attached. It, together with the Charlton Brimstone butterfly case, the midwife toad case, and the patchwork mouse case, is one of a sequence of straightforward (albeit methodologically impoverished) attempts to make false claims when the evidence for the theory underlying them had not been forthcoming by orthodox scientific experimentation.

Premeditated Fabrications

As identified above, the most difficult form of research fraud to detect is wholesale forgery, fabrication of data—either where experiments were never undertaken, or where the outcomes were not to the liking of the experimenter, namely they did not accord with the results to which the researcher aspired. There have been many notorious examples of this phenomenon leading to considerable numbers of retractions of published articles. The following section identifies some of these instances, identifying a readily discernible pattern in this form of research misconduct.

Sir Cyril Burt: Inherited Intelligence

One of the most apparently premeditated research frauds perpetrated in the 20th century was the fabrication of research by Sir Cyril Burt into IQ testing.[91] Burt's position was that heredity plays a much greater factor in inheritance of intelligence than environment. A major source of evidence for this contention lay in experiments he conducted over nearly two and a half decades into twins. In each study Burt reported cumulative results for the twins studied up to that point, starting in 1943 (15 pairs) and continuing until 1966. In 1955 he added six pairs of twins, resulting in 21 sets and by 1966 his studies had reached 53 sets of twins. In each study Burt reported correlation coefficients indicating the similarity of intelligence scores for monozygotic twins who were reared apart. A high coefficient was indicative of similar intelligence scores, thereby supporting his arguments in favour of the significance of heredity. He reported the following, remarkably uniform but implausible coefficients:

1943: r = .770;
1955: r = .771;
1966: r = .771.

On the face of it, the results were devastatingly supportive of inheritance being the dominating factor for intelligence. However, the study was the largest twin study up to that time and the likelihood of his having been able to access so many twins came into question. Clouds gathered after his death in 1971, Gillie in 1976 publishing in *The Sunday Times* an article proclaiming:

> The most sensational charge of scientific fraud this century is being levelled against the late Sir Cyril Burt, father of British educational psychology. Leading scientists are convinced that Burt published false data and invented crucial facts to support his controversial theory that intelligence is largely inherited.[92]

He argued that two of Burt's alleged collaborators did not exist.

Burt's biographer and great supporter, who spoke at his funeral, Leslie Hearnshaw, urged giving Burt the benefit of the doubt until he had examined all of Burt's private papers in

[91] See Leon J Kamin, *The Science and Politics of IQ* (Potomac, Md: Lawrence Erlbaum Associates, 1974); Leslie S Hearnshaw, *Cyril Burt, Psychologist* (Ithaca, NY: Cornell University Press, 1979). See also, Arthur R Jensen, 'IQ and Science: The Mysterious Burt Affair' (1991) Issue 105, *Public Interest* 93; Raymond E Fancher, 'The Burt Case: Another Foray' (1991) 253(5027) *Science* 1565.

[92] Oliver Gillie, 'Pioneer of IQ Faked his Research Findings', *The Sunday Times*, 24 October 1976, 1.

preparation for his biography. However, by the time of the biography he was satisfied that the accusations of fraud against Burt were most likely correct.

While controversies continue, with some attempting to rehabilitate Burt's reputation,[93] the general consensus is that his research was both flawed and probably, at least, partly fabricated.[94] Goodhart[95] has drawn attention to the fact that, although Mackintosh has confirmed that Burt was at times prepared to manipulate his data and to make some false claims about them, particularly in his old age. Burt was far from alone in this regard and key parts of his twin work were later largely replicated.[96] Nonetheless, the Sir Cyril Burt saga highlights the fact that wholesale fabrication of data by a well-known person in the field can be difficult to detect and can result for a considerable while in the duping of other researchers and experts. Such a technique is particularly available where the perpetrator is renowned and likely to be deferred to by others in the discipline.

John Darsee: Cardiology

In May 1981 colleagues identified concerns about Dr John Darsee's labelling of samples in his cardiology research at the Brigham and Women's Hospital in Boston and the Harvard Medical School Hospital. Darsee was a notoriously hard worker and had been responsible for more than 100 publications over 14 years. His supervisor set in train an investigation straightaway.[97] At the time Darsee was involved in a multi-institutional project funded by the National Institutes of Health (NIH).[98] The warning sign about the integrity of his research was that Darsee's data were significantly different from those being gathered at Duke University, Johns Hopkins University and the VA Medical Center. He was unable to account for the discrepancies. The Dean of the Harvard Medical School and the NIH convened separate committees to investigate the situation. The Harvard committee identified substantial evidence that Darsee had been fabricating data in the course of the study, while the NIH committee[99] discovered systematic falsification of data in five other studies in which Darsee had been involved.

Ultimately, 52 of Darsee's publications were retracted from between 1982 and 1989[100] and he was barred from receiving NIH funding for ten years.[101] As was the way in the 1980s, he was not charged with any criminal offences, including as to his misuse of research funds.

---

93 See eg, Robert B Joynson, *The Burt Affair* (New York: Routledge, 1989); Nicholas J Mackintosh (ed), *Cyril Burt: Fraud or Framed?* (Oxford: Oxford University Press, 1995).

94 See eg, Alan Poling, 'The Consequences of Fraud' in David J Miller and Michel Hersen (eds), *Research Fraud in the Behavioral and Biomedical Sciences* (New York: Wiley, 1992) 150.

95 CB Goodhart, 'Review: Cyril Burt, Fraud or Framed?' *Galton Institute Newsletter* (September 1996): <http://www.galtoninstitute.org.uk/Newsletters/GINL9609/Burt_review.htm> (viewed 26 January 2015).

96 See eg, Thomas J Bouchard Jr, David T Lykken, Matthew McGue, Nancy L Segal et al. 'Sources of Human Psychological Differences: The Minnesota Study of Twins Reared Apart' (1990) 250(4978) *Science* 223 who found a 70 per cent, as against 77 per cent, heritability of IQ scores amongst twins.

97 See Fox Butterfield, 'Harvard Suspends Doctor for Fraud', *The New York Times*, 16 December 1981: <http://www.nytimes.com/1981/12/16/us/harvard-suspends-doctor-for-fraud.html> [accessed 21 Dec 2015].

98 See Carol A Kochan and John M Budd, 'The Persistence of Fraud in the Literature: The Darsee Case' (1992) 43(7) *Journal of the American Society for Information Science* 488.

99 Neil C Moran, Elmer C Hall, Charles M Huguley Jr, and Panagiotis N Symbas, 'Report of *Ad Hoc* Committee to Evaluate Research of Dr John R Darsee at Emory University' (1985) 23(2) *Minerva* 276.

100 See Richard Smith, 'Investigating Previous Studies of a Fraudulent Author' (2005) 331 (7511) BMJ 288.

101 See William J Broad, 'Notorious Darsee Case Shakes Assumptions about Science', *The New York Times*, 14 June 1983: <http://www.nytimes.com/1983/06/14/science/notorious-darsee-case-shakes-assumptions-about-science.html> [accessed 21 Dec 2015].

The NIH identified a systemic issue in the lack of sufficient supervision from Darsee's superiors.[102] By 1992, in spite of the retractions, though, Kochan and Budd expressed the concern that: 'Despite the publicity his case received, and the extensive reviews to which his papers were subjected, his work remains alive in the research literature of cardiology. Several years after the reviews of his works, Darsee's articles are cited positively (even if the approval is implicit) in subsequent papers.'[103] The fact that so many of Darsee's papers were able to make their way through the checks and balances was described by his superior at Harvard, Dr Eugene Braunwald, as illustrative of 'the extraordinary difficulty of detecting fabrication by a clever individual'.[104] Broad observed that:

> [E]vents show that Dr Darsee easily got through the triple safety net that guards against chicanery. The first net is peer review, in which experts advise the Government about what scientific work should be funded. The second is the referee system, in which scientific journals send a manuscript out for review to judge whether it merits publication. The final defence is replication, in which scientists in distant labs repeat the work to see if it stands up.[105]

Robert Slutsky: Radiology

By 1985 Robert Slutsky was a dynamic young physician, a radiology consultant, and an Associate Clinical Professor in the Department of Radiology at the University of California, San Diego. His particular area of research interest was the study of ventricular capacity in patients with heart disease, using X-rays and other non-invasive mechanisms for assessing heart function. One of the attributes that distinguished him was that he had published a remarkable 137 papers and reviews in 34 journals within seven years. At one stage he was publishing a paper every ten days while he was simultaneously a resident and an Associate Clinical Professor. However, when he was being considered for promotion, a member of the committee evaluating his application observed duplication of data between two of his published works. This prompted the establishment of ad hoc committee to investigate the integrity of his work. The committee found that three of Slutsky's most recent manuscripts described experiments that had never been performed. It called for further investigations. Slutsky resigned and his lawyer asked that 15 papers published by Slutsky in eight journals be retracted on the basis that 'information had recently come to Dr Slutsky's attention which cast some doubt on the results'.[106]

In due course further investigations by a committee at the University of California, San Diego, concluded that 79 of Slutsky's publications were valid, 55 were questionable, and 13 were outright fraudulent.[107] It emerged that Slutsky forged signatures on copyright forms and multiple publications included 'gift co-authorship' which blurred the capacity to detect error. It may well be that in some cases these authors were flattered or perceived themselves to be advantaged by the favour of incorporation in authorship of his publications, but by their conduct they facilitated his fraud by the camouflage they inadvertently provided. The committee suggested that the peer review system might be overloaded and that problems with the numbers of submitted manuscripts, as well as with the provision of training to referees for journals, needed to be addressed.[108]

---

[102] See Barbara J Culliton, 'Emory Reports on Darsee's Fraud' (1983) 220(4600) *Science* 936. See also, Moran et al. above n 99.

[103] See Kochan and Budd, above n 98, 491.

[104] Broad, above n 101.

[105] Ibid.

[106] Horace Freeland Judson, *The Great Betrayal: Fraud in Science* (New York: Harcourt, 2004) 129.

[107] See Robert L Engler, James W Covell, Paul J Friedman, Philip S Kitcher, and Richard M Peters, 'Misrepresentation and Responsibility in Medical Research' (1987) 317(22) *The New England Journal of Medicine* 1383; Janny Scott, 'At UC San Diego: Unraveling a Research Fraud Case', *Los Angeles Times*, 30 April 1987: <http://articles.latimes.com/1987-04-30/news/mn-2837_1_uc-san-diego> [accessed 21 Dec 2015].

[108] Janny Scott, 'Professors Urge Closer Guard Against Research Fraud', *Los Angeles Times*, 26 November 1987: <http://articles.latimes.com/1987-11-26/news/mn-24804_1_research-fraud> [accessed 21 Dec

Diederik Stapel: Social Psychology

By 2010 Professor Diederik Stapel from The Netherlands was the Dean of Tilburg University's School of Social and Behavioral Sciences. Previously, he had been employed at the University of Amsterdam, where he studied between 1993 and 1999 and from which he obtained his doctorate in 1997, and by the University of Groningen, where he held the position of full professor from 2000 to 2006. Stapel published a series of well-regarded studies on human attitudes and behaviour—he was 'an academic star in the Netherlands and abroad'.[109] His publications were lively and tendentious.[110] They were often on diverse modern subjects, including arguing that a rubbish-filled environment tended to bring out people's racist tendencies and that eating meat made people selfish and less social. He received multiple grants and prestigious awards for his research on social cognition and stereotyping but like a cross-section of psychologists, especially in The Netherlands, he did not make his raw data readily available for others' scrutiny.

However, in 2011 three young researchers reported their suspicions of data falsification by Stapel. Later investigation found that they were not the first to air such concerns about him, two professors, for instance, having previously observed his research results to have been 'too good to be true'.[111]

Impressively, on the complaints being made, committees were promptly formed by each of the universities with which Stapel had been associated to investigate whether he had engaged in research fraud. Given that many of his publications were co-authored with young researchers, an interim investigation was conducted to evaluate whether others had been accessories in Stapel's frauds. The interim report found that he had acted alone and that the problems with Stapel's publications included research fraud, but also 'sloppy science', or a 'failure to meet normal standards of methodology'. This highlighted a research culture in which such deficits remained undetected for a lengthy period of time.[112]

The preliminary findings which extended to a large volume of publications stimulated the analysis of the whole volume of Stapel's research work. The Committees expressed the view that this constituted the first instance of a fraudster's whole body of scientific work being scrutinized in depth and that it was vital for such an exercise to be undertaken in relation to Stapel so as to reassert the discipline's critical functions and to correct the frauds that he had perpetrated—to cleanse the scientific record.

After an exhaustive investigation the three Committees published a joint report, determining that Stapel's fraud was 'very substantial'[113] and that it included no fewer than 55 publications which bore his name in the 15 years between 1996 and 2011, most of them co-authored and many of them published in prestigious, peer-reviewed journals. The Drenth Committee

2015]. See also WP Whitley, D Rennie, and AW Hafner, 'The Scientific Community's Response to Evidence of Fraudulent publication: The Robert Slutsky Case' (1994) 272(2) *Journal of the American Medical Association* 170.

109 Yudhijit Bhattacharjee, 'The Mind of a Con Man', *The New York Times*, 26 April 2013: <http://www.nytimes.com/2013/04/28/magazine/diederik-stapels-audacious-academic-fraud.html?partner=rss&emc=rss&_r=0> [accessed 21 Dec 2015].

110 See John M Budd, 'The Stapel Case: An Object Lesson in Research Integrity and its Lapses' (2013) *Synesis* G47: <http://www.synesisjournal.com/vol4_g/Budd_2013_G47-53.pdf> [accessed 21 Dec 2015].

111 Levelt Committee (Tilburg University), Noort Committee (Groningen University), and Drenth University (University of Amsterdam), *Flawed Science: The Fraudulent Research Practices of Social Psychologist Diederik Stapel* (28 November 2012) [2.4.1], available at: <https://www.commissielevelt.nl/> [accessed 21 Dec 2015].

112 Ibid, Foreword, at p 5.

113 Ibid, [3.1].

from the University of Amsterdam also found strong indications of fraud in two chapters of Stapel's doctoral dissertation. In due course Stapel surrendered his doctoral degree certificate to the Rector Magnificus of the University of Amsterdam. The Committees observed that the young researchers who gathered data to show that something was amiss with Stapel's work deserved praise for reporting what they had identified. Their contribution was courageous—as the Committees noted, 'they were in a dependent position and had much to lose'.[114] More dryly, they noted with regret that previous communications expressing concern about Stapel's work had not been acted upon.

In their joint report in November 2012, the three Committees found that Stapel had manipulated existing datasets or fabricated his own. They provided the following analysis of his modus operandi:

> In a first variant the research preparation would proceed normally. Stimuli and questionnaires were developed, and the number of subjects and the procedure to be followed were determined after extensive discussions with the co-authors. In the end, however, the questionnaires were not administered. In these cases Mr Stapel created his own datasets, which largely confirmed the prior expectations.
>
> In a second variant Mr Stapel altered data in existing datasets. These data actually were collected and were usually entered by a student assistant, who then forwarded the dataset to Mr Stapel. After manipulating the data Mr Stapel passed the dataset to the PhD student, who had been required to set down his or her expectations about the outcomes in advance. The Committees are in possession of datasets entered by student assistants and the datasets ultimately given to the PhD student. The differences between the datasets clearly show the changes made.
>
> In a third variant Mr Stapel had contacts with fellow researchers and then sent them datasets that he claimed to have had in his possession for some considerable time, asking them to analyse and write up the study. In this variant too, Mr Stapel supplied fabricated datasets of obscure origin.[115]

The Committees found that great harm had been occasioned by Stapel's fraud with individuals being demoralized and stigmatized by their association with him, and the faculties and universities where he worked also having their international reputations harmed. But also, and more importantly, 'the standing of science, and of social psychology in particular, has been badly dented by Mr Stapel's actions'.[116] They found it to be particularly disturbing that, while Stapel's co-authors were not complicit in his misconduct, his misrepresentations, his flagrantly fraudulent data, and his findings were 'invariably accepted without criticism, even when doubt would have been reasonable'.[117]

The Committees' findings in this respect are confronting. They concluded that Stapel abused the trust that is the basis of all scientific collaboration, using his position of prestige and power to commit fraud and also to stifle doubt about his methods. He was seen as a charismatic intellectual leader—'people who are admired are not readily suspected of fraud, and there will be a tendency to put forward "alternative explanations" rather than to suspect fraud'.[118]

In another important observation, the Committees noted that a technique employed by Stapel with his PhD students was for relationships between him and them to become

[114] Ibid.
[115] Ibid, [3.2].
[116] Ibid, [3.7].
[117] Ibid, [4.1].
[118] Ibid, [4.2].

'extremely friendly'.[119] He blurred the usual boundaries. Many students viewed Stapel as a personal friend—they socialized with him, ate with him, and visited his home. This was another impediment to the adoption of a critical attitude on the part of PhD students regarding their supervisor's possibly fraudulent actions.[120]

The outcome of these dynamics was that Stapel's power, charisma, and prestige combined to manipulate those best positioned to evaluate his work critically to be deferential and uncritical. He was intimidating and did not refrain from communicating that questioning his proposed research methodologies constituted a betrayal of trust in him. In addition, the Committees noted that Stapel's research was conducted both inside and outside his working environment, this also reducing the level of scrutiny apt to be employed in reviewing his work critically.

Another frank and significant contribution made by the Committees' analysis was the admission that, during the relevant period in The Netherlands, no explicit attention was paid to combatting or preventing scientific misconduct within the research environment. There was no formal code of ethics relating to research integrity until the end of the 20th century—'[w]hatever measures existed were more implicit, and any action was at the discretion of individual researchers'.[121] They commented that in the Faculty of Psychology at the University of Amsterdam there was no formal structure directed at enforcing standards of scientific integrity and no culture of transparency, information-sharing, peer review, or joint responsibility:

> It was easy for researchers to go their own way. Nobody looked over their shoulder, they did not share their data with other members of the various research groups, and there was no peer review. This rather naïve delegation of trust and the absence of detailed checks of raw and coded data, in particular on the part of supervisors and co-supervisors, members of doctoral examination committees, tutorial leaders and co-authors, created a working environment and work culture in which any individual researcher who ever would attempt to transgress the boundaries of integrity was very likely to have gone unnoticed. People trusted each other's scientific integrity: no feedback, no warnings, no correction.[122]

This complacency meant that scientific integrity was not given a high priority in the sense of explicit attention and detailed monitoring being given to such matters, although it can fairly be said that these are an implicit responsibility of senior staff and a collective responsibility within research groups.

At Tilburg University the Committees observed that Stapel's powerful position, especially after he became Dean, was characterized by signals from the university administration that Stapel held a special and trusted position. The Committees found that the culture that evolved was one that facilitated and sustained Stapel's fraudulent conduct. They commented that, typically, a person who suspects fraud will approach a close colleague in the hope they will be able to obtain advice as to what they should do by way of response or reporting. Even this step can be very difficult: 'It makes it much easier for whistleblowers if there is an independent university confidential counsellor for scientific integrity, who is not part of the management line.'[123]

---

[119] Ibid.
[120] Ibid.
[121] Ibid, [4.3].
[122] Ibid.
[123] Ibid, [4.5].

The Committees found that at Groningen University the 'Stapel group' had no protocols for fundamental matters such as the collection of data or research reports. This did not conduce towards vigilance.

The Committees also scrutinized the research culture of the three universities and found a pattern of violations of basic rules of sound research. They concluded:

> [T]here was a general culture of careless, selective and uncritical handling of research and data. The observed flaws were not minor 'normal' imperfections in statistical processing, or experimental design and execution, but violations of fundamental rules of proper scientific research with a possibly severe impact on the research conclusions. The Committees are of the opinion that this culture partly explains why the fraud was not detected earlier.[124]

In this regard, they particularly highlighted the need for investigations to be designed in such a way that facts that might refute the research hypotheses are given at least an equal chance of emerging as are facts that confirm the research hypotheses. This form of bias, generally described as 'verification bias',[125] which repressed unwelcome outcomes, was found in most of Stapel's publications. In addition, the Committees noted a pattern in Stapel's publications of unduly broad descriptions of research subjects, and use of non-standard variants of conventional measuring instruments, without acknowledgment. Assessments were on occasion self-assessments, and experimental conditions were manipulated without regard to the fact they may have influenced each other. Put another way, much of the research was fundamentally unscientific in its methodology, an attribute that was not identified or at least effectively addressed by co-researchers or supervisors. Further, there was frequently a failure by Stapel and his co-researchers to adhere to elementary statistical obligations.

The Committees noted that the fraud of Stapel exposed a bigger issue—there had repeatedly been an abrogation of the critical function, not just by Stapel's co-researchers and colleagues but also by members of doctoral boards and reviewers of prestigious journals. They commented that they could reach no conclusion other than that 'from the bottom to the top there was a general neglect of fundamental scientific standards and methodological requirements. This certainly also applies to the editors and reviewers of international journals'.[126] The Committees observed that reviewers failed to identify basic statistical flaws, encouraged irregular practices and reviews were frequently expressed so as to tell an interesting, elegant, concise and compelling story rather than insisting on scientific diligence—their priorities were misconceived. Depressingly, they commented:

> In the case of the fraud committed by Mr Stapel, the critical function of science has failed on all levels. Fundamental principles of scientific method have been ignored, or set aside as irrelevant. In the opinion of the Committees this has contributed significantly to the delayed discovery of the fraud.... However, the discussion of factors that facilitated Mr Stapel's fraud, the power derived from his celebrity-like status and the failure of the critical function of his scientific world do not alter the Committees' conclusion that the fraud committed by Mr Stapel was such that these factors and circumstances do not excuse his actions in any way whatsoever.[127]

The Committees advanced a series of recommendations to decrease the potential for repetition of the kind of misconduct engaged in by Stapel. Stapel himself accepted a portion of

---

[124] Ibid, [5.1].
[125] Ibid.
[126] Ibid, [5.6], [5.3].
[127] Ibid.

the critiques but adhered to implausible rationalizations. Responding to the interim report, Stapel stated:

> I have failed as a scientist, as a researcher. I have adjusted research data and faked research. Not just once, but many several times, and not just briefly, but over a long period of time. I am ashamed of this and I am deeply sorry…I was not able to withstand the pressure to score points, to publish, to always have to be better. I wanted too much, too fast. And in a system where there is little control, where people often work alone, I took the wrong path.[128]

In a statement posted on Tilburg University's website in November 2011, Stapel apologized to his colleagues, stating: 'I have failed as a scientist and researcher…I feel ashamed for it and have great regret.'[129] By 9 November 2011 he had renounced a doctorate awarded to him by the University of Amsterdam. However, by 2012, as outlined in Chapter 2, Stapel had published a book giving his account of the steps leading to his conduct, and at a level accepting responsibility for and reflecting on what he had done.[130] Interestingly, he pointedly commented too:

> I made up research, and wrote papers about it. My peers and the journal editors cast a critical eye over it, and it was published. I would often discover, a few months or years later, that another team of researchers, in another city or another country, had done more or less the same experiment, and found the same effects. My fantasy research had been replicated. What seemed logical was true, once I'd faked it.

In June 2013, shortly after the publication of *The Derailment*, prosecutors reached a settlement with Stapel by which he agreed to undertake 120 hours of community service work and forfeit welfare benefits equivalent to 18 months' salary in exchange for not being prosecuted for research fraud. Controversially, and high questionably, they described it as 'a fitting conclusion' to the scandal that has been so confronting for academia in The Netherlands.[131]

Reflecting on the fallout from the scandal, Carey has observed that:

> In recent years, psychologists have reported a raft of findings on race biases, brain imaging and even extrasensory perception that have not stood up to scrutiny. Outright fraud may be rare, these experts say, but they contend that Dr Stapel took advantage of a system that allows researchers to operate in near secrecy and massage data to find what they want to find, without much fear of being challenged.[132]

The Stapel research frauds were scrutinized in a rigorous and highly reflective way by the three committees convened to evaluate Stapel's work longitudinally. Their review demonstrates the extent of Stapel's fraud but much more. It plots the way in which a charismatic and high-profile researcher was able to neutralize each one of the checks and balances that are designed to safeguard the integrity of research. There is a great deal to be learned from the strategies

---

[128] Kate Kelland, 'Dutch Psychologist Admits He Made Up Research Data', *Reuters*, 2 November 2011: <http://www.reuters.com/article/2011/11/02/us-dutch-scientist-fraud-idUSTRE7A12PL20111102> [accessed 21 Dec 2015].

[129] Benedict Carey, 'Fraud Case Seen as a Red Flag for Psychology Research', *The New York Times*, 2 November 2011: <http://www.nytimes.com/2011/11/03/health/research/noted-dutch-psychologist-stapel-accused-of-research-fraud.html> [accessed 21 Dec 2015]. See also, Martin Enserink, 'Dutch University Sacks Social Psychologist Over Faked Data', *Science Insider*, 7 September 2011: <http://news.sciencemag.org/education/2011/09/dutch-university-sacks-social-psychologist-over-faked-data> [accessed 21 Dec 2015].

[130] Diederik Stapel, *Ontsporing* (2012): *Faking Science: A True Story of Academic Fraud* (2014) trans. Nicholas JL Brown: <http://nick.brown.free.fr/stapel/FakingScience-20141214.pdf> [accessed 21 Dec 2015].

[131] 'Diederik Stapel, Disgraced Dutch Psychologist Accepts Punishment' (26 June 2013) *Huffington Post*, <http://www.huffingtonpost.com/2013/06/29/diederik-stapel-dutch-psychologist-punishment_n_3516104.html> [accessed 21 Dec 2015].

[132] Carey, above n 129.

successfully employed by Stapel to orchestrate and succeed for many years in forged and multifariously unethical research. His case is an exemplar of most of the systemic deficits that can enable an unscrupulous researcher to succeed for a lengthy period with research fraud.

Failures of Peer Reviewing and the Need for Retractions

The proliferation of research frauds exposed in recent years has raised grave questions about the functioning of peer-reviewing in relation to the discipline of anaesthetics and more broadly within medicine and science. They have also required a troubling incidence of retractions in a wide variety of high-profile scholarly journals. Inevitably too they have involved the wasting of large sums of money in research grants. Some have emanated from the area of cancer research, others in relation to peri-operative employment of fluids (see Boldt, Fujii), some in relation to immunology (see Melendez, Das), some in relation to the diagnosis and treatment of controversial medical conditions such as chronic fatigue syndrome (see Mikovits), and stem cell research (see Obokata). In short, within medicine the areas afflicted by research fraud have covered a wide range of disciplines. All have in common that the prophylactic mechanism of peer review was manipulated by the researcher and, on any objective analysis, found seriously wanting.

The following section of this chapter identifies a sequence of deeply troubling frauds within medical science that resulted in publication of grossly flawed alleged breakthroughs in knowledge and technique. The cases raise confronting questions about peer review and journal publication processes.

Roger Poisson: Cancer Research

Professor Roger Poisson was the head of cancer research at the Saint-Luc Hospital, a teaching hospital at the University of Montreal. His hospital, along with Saint Mary's Hospital and the Jewish General Hospital, all in Montreal, were part of a Canadian–United States multi-site National Surgical Adjuvant Breast and Bowel Project (NSABP) study, which began in 1958. It was sponsored, among others, by the National Cancer Institute of Canada. Between 1977 and 1991 Poisson oversaw investigators who enrolled 1,511 patients into 22 NSABP trials. His orientation in published research was to identify advantages in lumpectomies, rather than full mastectomies.

In 1991 a protocol statistician, Teresa Wright, examined a file and observed virtually identical records for the same patient but with different dates for the patient's surgery. One date would have made the patient ineligible for the trial the subject of the research. When Wright reported the anomaly, it triggered an evaluation of data and consent forms showing that 13 of 20 out of Poisson's consent documents had been signed after the relevant randomization date. In addition, investigators found reports labelled '*vrai*' (true) and '*faux*' (false), suggesting that Poisson had premeditatedly been running two tracks of files.[133]

In February 1991 Poisson admitted having falsified data and the Office of Scientific Integrity was notified. His 16-year affiliation with the NSABP was terminated and he was barred from research at Saint-Luc's Hospital and from receiving United States federal funding for eight years. The Food and Drug Administration banned him for life from testing experimental drugs.[134] What had occurred became public knowledge in 1994 and Poisson, his attorney,

[133] Mackenzie Carpenter and Steve Twedt, 'Discovering Fraud in Breast Cancer Research A Gradual Process', *Pittsburgh Post-Gazette*, 26 December 1994, A-1, A-6.

[134] See Bernard Fisher and Carol K Redmond, 'Fraud in Breast-Cancer Trials' (1994) 330(20) *The New England Journal of Medicine* 1458.

and various loyal patients mounted a strenuous defence of his professional conduct. He wrote to *La Presse* maintaining, in essence, that his deceptions were justified—'a patient admitted to the protocol would be better treated, get the best possible care'.[135] He argued that he had learned lessons the hard way but insisted that, although 'I should have been more rigorous', the flaws in his research were 'in my mind small things that did not have any impact on the treatment of the cancer'.[136]

Keranen has identified four strands to the public defence mounted by and on behalf of the researcher: 'Poisson's devotion to his patients and career, his concern for patient rights, the technical insignificance of his actions, and his status as international scapegoat. The central message uniting all four themes was Poisson's enduring commitment to patient care'.[137] However, he was unsuccessful in assuming the moral high ground and Poisson was the subject of consistent and devastating condemnation from most professional quarters.[138] Although he likened himself to a Rudyard Kipling hero—'Man is great once he has lost everything and is capable of rising again'—he did not rise again.[139]

Werner Bezwoda: High Dose Chemotherapy

During the late 1980s autologous bone marrow transplantation (ABMT) with high dose chemotherapy (HDC) was regarded as a promising treatment combination for metastatic breast cancer and for high-risk breast cancer.[140] During the 1990s it was adopted in some sectors of the oncology community and not only influenced clinical decision-making for many patients but also generated fraught and contested health insurance coverage decisions and court challenges in the United States.

Randomized clinical trials began in 1990–1991 to evaluate how the combination of treatments compared with more conventional treatments. However, recruitment to such trials did not prove easy and modest numbers of women participated. The availability and access to ABMT and HDC became a 'feminist issue' with complaints that managed care discriminated against women's opportunity to avail themselves of these life-saving treatments because of women's needs being accorded second class status.

Werner Bezwoda, a leading South African oncologist from the University of Witwatersrand in Johannesburg, published an article in the 1995 *Journal of Clinical Oncology*[141] purporting to be the report of a randomized trial comparing HDC and autologous stem cell transplantation with standard dose chemotherapy for patients with breast cancer. It publicized positive results.

Bezwoda presented his research in May 1999 at the conference of the American Society of Clinical Oncology, maintaining that: 'High-dose chemotherapy using the CMVP combination

---

[135] See Arthur Schafer, 'The Moral Anatomy and Ethical Pathology of the Randomized Clinical Trial' in Peter P De Deyn (ed), *The Ethics of Animal and Human Experimentation* (London: John Libbey, 1994) 272.

[136] See Fran Lowry, 'Dr Roger Poisson: "I have Learned My Lesson the Hard Way"' (1994) 151(6) *Canadian Medical Association Journal* 835, 836; Clyde H Farnsworth, 'Doctor Says He Falsified Cancer Data to Help Patients', *The New York Times*, 1 April 1994: <http://www.nytimes.com/1994/04/01/us/doctor-says-he-falsified-cancer-data-to-help-patients.html> (2 February 2015) [accessed 21 Dec 2015].

[137] Lisa Keränen, *Scientific Characters: Rhetoric, Politics and Trust in Breast Cancer Research* (Tuscaloosa: University of Alabama Press, 2010) 52.

[138] See the summary by Christine Gorman, 'Breast Cancer: A Diagnosis of Deceit', *Time*, 24 June 2001: <http://content.time.com/time/magazine/article/0,9171,164051,00.html> [accessed 21 Dec 2015].

[139] See James S Olson, *Bathsheba's Breast: Women, Cancer and History* (Baltimore: Johns Hopkins University Press, 2002) 219.

[140] See Siddhartha Mukherjee, *The Emperor of All Maladies: A Biography of Cancer* (New York: Scribner, 2010).

[141] Werner R Bezwoda, Leslie Seymour and Roger D Dansey, 'High-dose Chemotherapy with Hematopoietic Rescue As Primary Treatment for Metastatic Breast Cancer: A Randomized Trial' (1995) 13(10) *Journal of Clinical Oncology* 2483.

was found to be able to be given safely to younger patients with high-risk breast cancer. The high-dose chemotherapy resulted in a significantly low relapse rate, and high-dose chemotherapy was associated with significantly longer disease-free and overall survival in this patient population'.[142] However, of the five studies discussed at the meeting, his was the only one with such results, the others showing no result from HDC. This led to significant scepticism in many parts of the oncology community and when a group of United States cancer experts examined some of Bezwoda's data they found problems, including that Bezwoda had not obtained ethics committee clearance for his work, as was his obligation. They reported their concerns to the University of Witwatersrand.[143] The University convened an inquiry which found that the data claimed by Bezwoda for the control group were inaccurate, members of that group in fact being given a quite different treatment than that identified in Dr Bezwoda's research.

In due course Dr Bezwoda admitted that he had 'committed a serious breach of scientific honesty and integrity' and had misrepresented his results.[144] He was removed from his university position.[145] However, the fraud came at a greater cost. Aside from the reputational harm that he did to his university and to the area of science, it is likely that numbers of medical practitioners prescribed HDC on the basis of Dr Bezwoda's data and that patients gave informed consent to what was a toxic treatment on the basis of his research. In addition, his fraud tarnished HDC for breast cancer. As Sledge[146] put it: 'Transplant physicians have made Dr Bezwoda's data a centerpiece of their public presentations in recent years. Some have used it as a club to beat down skeptics. By doing so, transplanters unwittingly tied the reputation of their discipline in the breast cancer arena to his results. High-dose chemotherapy will be injured in Dr Bezwoda's fall from grace.'

Jon Sudbø: Oral Cancer

Dr Jon Sudbø was a Norwegian dentist, physician and oral cancer researcher. He was employed as consultant oncologist at the Radium Hospital and an Associate Professor at the University of Oslo. In 2005 he published an article in *The Lancet* which purported to be an analysis of several Norwegian health surveys and registries suggesting that the use from non-steroidal anti-inflammatory drugs, such as ibuprofen and naproxen, could reduce the incidence of oral cancer in smokers, although long-term use could increase the risk of dying of heart disease.[147] The article was fast-tracked into the journal because of its results being striking. It, and other work undertaken by Sudbø, attracted considerable approbation, among other things being hailed as an important step in preventing oral cancer.

---

[142] 'Is More Better? ASCO Plenary Session Opens Debate on High-Dose Chemotherapy' (1999) 4(3) *The Oncologist* 269, 271.

[143] Peter Cleaton-Jones, 'Scientific Misconduct in a Breast-Cancer Chemotherapy Trial: Response of University of the Witwatersrand' (2000) 355(9208) *The Lancet* 1011; Raymond B Weiss, Robert M Rifkin, F Marc Stewart, Richard L Theriault, Lori A Williams, Allen A Herman, and Roy A Beveridge, 'High Dose Chemotherapy for High-Risk Primary Breast Cancer: An On-Site Review of the Bezwoda Study' (2000) 355(9208) *The Lancet* 999.

[144] Denise Grady, 'Breast Cancer Researcher Admits Falsifying Data', *The New York Times*, 5 February 2000: <http://www.nytimes.com/2000/02/05/us/breast-cancer-researcher-admits-falsifying-data.html> [accessed 21 Dec 2015].

[145] Henri E Cauvin, 'Cancer Researcher in South Africa Who Falsified Data is Fired', *The New York Times*, 11 March 2000: <http://www.nytimes.com/2000/03/11/us/cancer-researcher-in-south-africa-who-falsified-data-is-fired.html> [accessed 21 Dec 2015].

[146] George W Sledge Jr, 'Why Big Lies Matter: Lessons from the Bezwoda Affair', Medscape: <http://www.medscape.com/viewarticle/408908> [accessed 21 Dec 2015]. Also available at (2000) 5(1) *Medscape Women's Health* 4.

[147] Jon Sudbø, J Jack Lee, Scott M Lippman, J Mork, Smione Sagen, N Flatner, Ari Ristimäki, Asle Sudbø, Li Mao, X Zhou, Wanja Kildal, Jan F Evensen, Albrecht Reith, and AJ Dannenberg, 'Non-Steroidal Anti-Inflammatory Drugs and the Risk of Oral Cancer: A Nested Case-Control Study' (2005) 366(9494) *The Lancet* 1359.

About a year later the Director of the Division of Epidemiology at the Norwegian Institute of Public Health, Camilla Stoltenberg, queried the use that Sudbø had made of data from her institute. A feature which suggested that something was grossly wrong was that in the analysis of the data 250 of the sample of 908 were reported to have the same birthday. An investigation led by Professor Anders Ekbom from the GS Institute in Stockholm determined that Sudbø fabricated data in his PhD research project and that many of his subsequent publications were contaminated by these false data. It recommended that the articles be retracted.

Investigations showed evidence of the same phenomenon in respect of papers, including those published by him in the *New England Journal of Medicine*[148] and in the *Journal of Clinical Oncology*,[149] where Sudbø lied about having taken blood samples from all the smokers in a survey, when in fact he had not done so at all. The former reported that patients with an abnormal number of chromosomes in cells taken from pre-cancerous mouth lesions (leukoplakia) were at high risk for developing cancer whereas, conversely, those with a normal number of such chromosomes were at a low risk. This prompted the cancellation in the United States of a National Cancer Institute grant.[150]

The embarrassment resulted in a report that Norway was considering passing a law making the kind of fraud in which Sudbø was implicated a criminal offence for which a jail sentence could be imposed.[151] The Norwegian Board of Health revoked Sudbø's licence to practise as a dentist and a physician, commenting that:

> [A]ll medical research can have significance in terms of diagnosing and treating patients. This connection is obvious in cases where research is performed on patient samples. The aim of research will often be to improve diagnosis and treatment. Verifiability and accuracy are absolutely necessary and completely fundamental to all research. To a significant extent, all modern medicine is based on research. The health services and the general public must be able to trust the research results published in internationally renowned journals. According to the assessment of the Norwegian Board of Health, strict requirements must therefore be placed on the conduct of health care personnel in connection with research.
>
> [...]
>
> The Norwegian Board of Health is of the opinion that you have behaved dishonestly in connection with this article. By adhering to improper research practices you have lost trust. Improper research practices will furthermore weaken trust in practice of your profession in general. We find that your actions were a wilful breach of proper research practices, and that you acted in a manner that was scientifically dishonest.
>
> The Norwegian Board of Health notes that basing research published in a scientific article in an internationally respected journal on fabricated data is such a severe breach of what is expected of the conduct of a physician/dentist that the Norwegian Board of Health finds that general trust in you as a physician and a dentist has been seriously impaired. This is the

---

148 Jon Sudbø, Wanja Kildal, Björn Risberg, Hanna S Koppang, Håvard E Danielsen, and Albrecht Reith, 'DNA Content as a Prognostic Marker in Patients with Oral Leukoplakia' (2001) 344(17) *The New England Journal of Medicine* 1270; Jon Sudbø, Scott M Lippman, J Jack Lee, Li Mao, Wanja Kildal, Asle Sudbø et al. 'The Influence of Resection and Aneuploidy on Mortality in Oral Leukoplakia' (2004) 350(14) *The New England Journal of Medicine* 1405.

149 Jon Sudbø, Roy Samuelsson, Björn Risberg, Stig Heistein, Christian Nyhus, Margaretha Samuelsson et al. 'Risk Markers of Oral Cancer in Clinically Normal Mucosa as an Aid in Smoking Cessation Counseling' (2005) 23(9) *Journal of Clinical Oncology* 1927.

150 See Brian Vastag, 'Cancer Fraud Case Stuns Research Community, Prompts Reflection on Peer Review Process' (2006) 98(6) *Journal of the National Cancer Institute* 374.

151 'Doctor Who Faked Cancer Study Admits More Fraud', *Parker Waichmann LLP*, 23 January 2006: <http://www.yourlawyer.com/articles/title/doctor-who-faked-cancer-study-admits-more-fraud> [accessed 21 Dec 2015].

case even though it cannot be documented that patients have suffered as a consequence of the *Lancet* article. In the assessment of the Norwegian Board of Health, such conduct is incompatible with the practice of your profession both as a physician and a dentist.[152]

The fraud of Dr Sudbø lacked subtlety and was characterized by multiple aspects of dishonesty. Again, the author was able to subvert review processes, in part because of the fact that his research results offered such promise and even the highest profile journals were prepared to raise few questions before publishing his analyses because of the kudos that might attach to publication of his apparent breakthroughs.

Anil Potti: Chemotherapy

In 2006 Associate Professor Anil Potti, Joseph Nevins (his supervisor), and others from Duke University were undertaking landmark work in cancer treatment.[153] They reported in the *New England Journal of Medicine* that they could predict the course of patients' cancer utilizing 'expression arrays', which log the pattern of thousands of genes.[154] A little later in *Nature Medicine* they announced that they had developed a technique utilizing gene expression in cell lines, developed from individual tumours, to predict which chemotherapy would be most effective for a patient suffering particular forms of lung, breast, or ovarian cancer.[155] The work in developing individualized treatments for cancer was described by Duke University's Chancellor of Clinical Research as 'the holy grail of cancer'.[156]

However, other researchers who had been unable to replicate Potti's findings began to ask to see his data and to be given more information on his methodologies. Their pressure intensified after the publication of a paper in the *Journal of Clinical Oncology*.

Drs Baggerly and Coombes from the MD Anderson Cancer Center in Houston identified significant errors in Potti's work. They concluded that in one of their papers Dr Potti and his colleagues had mislabelled the cell lines they used to derive their chemotherapy prediction model, describing those that were sensitive as resistant, and vice versa.[157] This meant that even if the predictive method described by the Potti team at Duke actually worked, which Dr Baggerly and Dr Coombes seriously doubted, patients whose doctors relied on this paper would end up being given a drug they were less likely to benefit from instead of more likely.

Within a few months of the papers' publication (and at the time questions were being raised about the quality of the data) Potti and colleagues planned to launch three clinical trials based on their work. They also intended to use their gene-expression data to guide therapeutic

---

[152] Letter from Norwegian Board of Health to Jon Sudbø, 'Revocation of Authorization as Physician and Dentist: Jon Sudbø', 21 November 2006: <https://www.helsetilsynet.no/no/Norwegian-Board-of-Health-Supervision/Decisions-in-individual-cases/Revocation-Authorization-Physician-Dentist/> [accessed 21 December 2015].

[153] For the sequence of developments see Gina Kolata, 'How Bright Promise in Cancer Testing Fell Apart' (7 July 2011) *The New York Times*: <http://www.nytimes.com/2011/07/08/health/research/08genes.html?_r=0> [accessed 21 Dec 2015]; 'An Array of Errors', *The Economist*, 10 September 2011: <http://www.economist.com/node/21528593> [accessed 21 Dec 2015].

[154] Anil Potti, Sayan Mukherjee, Rebecca Petersen et al. 'A Genomic Strategy to Refine Prognosis in Early Stage Non-Small-Cell Lung Cancer' (2006) 355 *New England Journal of Medicine* 570.

[155] Anil Potti, Holly K Dressman, and Andrea Bild, 'Genomic Signatures to Guide the Use of Chemotherapies' (2006) 12 *Nature Medicine* 1294.

[156] 'Did Anil Potti, Former Duke Cancer Researcher, Conduct Research Fraud?' (14 February 2012) *Huffington Post*: <http://www.huffingtonpost.com/2012/02/13/anil-potti-duke-cancer-fraud-university-research_n_1273264.html> [accessed 21 Dec 2015].

[157] Keith A Baggerly and Kevin R Coombes, 'Deriving Chemosensitivity from Cell Lines: Forensic Bioinformatics and Reproducible Research in High-Throughput Biology' (2009) 3(4) *Annals of Applied Statistics* 1309.

choices in a lung-cancer trial paid for by America's National Cancer Institute (NCI). That led Lisa McShane, a biostatistician at the NCI who was already concerned about Dr Potti's results, to try to replicate the work. She was no more successful in this regard than Dr Baggerly and Dr Coombes. The more questions she asked, the more problems emerged.

In light of these matters, the NCI expressed its concern about what had taken place to Duke University's administrators. It was only at this stage that Duke University suspended the trials. In October 2009, the pressures led officials from the university to arrange for an external review of the work of Dr Potti and Dr Nevins, and to halt the three trials for the time being. The review committee, however, had access only to material supplied by the researchers themselves, and was not presented with either the NCI's specific concerns or the problems discovered by the team at the Anderson centre. When it failed to identify problems, the three trials began enrolling patients again in February 2010.

In July 2010, matters came to a head when the *Cancer Letter* reported that Dr Potti had submitted a variety of documents, including grant applications, which contained false statements.[158] Professor Nevins reviewed the original data and found major discrepancies between Potti's published results and the original. He concluded that there was no legitimate reason for such a differential.[159] Then 15 more scientists from Europe communicated their concerns regarding the validity and reliability of the report to the National Cancer Institute. A consequence was that a five-year grant worth US$729,000 from the American Cancer Society was suspended during the probe. Nine papers had been retracted by early 2012,[160] Dr Potti concluded his association (with encouragement) with Duke University and the trials stopped.

During 2010 Duke University announced the resignation of Dr Anil Potti. In 2011 the *New England Journal of Medicine* retracted the 2006 paper by Potti and colleagues. Ultimately 18 of Potti's papers were retracted or corrected. It emerged too that Dr Potti had falsely claimed to be a Rhodes Scholar from Australia,[161] although he claimed that the issue arose from an unintentional misunderstanding.[162] More importantly, the scandal that enveloped Dr Potti resulted in the discrediting of an approach which promised to match chemotherapy in a personalized way to patients' own genetic make-up—promoted as a crucial breakthrough in of cancer care.[163] It also resulted in the betrayal of trust of 112 patients with cancer who had committed themselves to Dr Potti's revolutionary therapy. Although criticism was made of

158 See John D'Angelo, *Ethics in Science: Ethical Misconduct in Scientific Research* (Boca Raton, FL: CRC Press, 2012) 38.

159 See Bhavin Patel, Anahita Dua, Tom Koenigsberger, and Sapan S Desai, 'Combatting Fraud in Medical Research: Research Validation Standards Utilized by the Journal of Surgical Radiology' (2013) 1 *Publications* 140.

160 'Dr Anil Potti Resigns from Duke University Amid Study Reliability Concerns', *Medical News Today*, 20 November 2010: <http://www.medicalnewstoday.com/articles/208795.php> [accessed 21 Dec 2015]; 'Did Anil Potti, Former Duke Cancer Researcher, Conduct Research Fraud?' *Huffington Post*, 13 February 2012: <http://www.huffingtonpost.com/2012/02/13/anil-potti-duke-cancer-fraud-university-research_n_1273264.html> [accessed 21 Dec 2015].

161 Natasha Singer, 'Duke Scientist Suspended Over Rhodes Scholar Claims', *The New York Times*, 20 July 2010: <http://www.nytimes.com/2010/07/21/health/research/21cancer.html?_r=0> [accessed 21 Dec 2015].

162 See Taylor Doherty, 'Potti Letter Addresses Scandal: Former Researcher Calls Rhodes Controversy a Misunderstanding' (11 January 12012) *The Chronicle*: <http://www.dukechronicle.com/articles/2012/01/11/potti-letter-addresses-scandal-former-researcher-calls-rhodes-controversy-misunderstanding#.VbQ3S0vy_7I> [accessed 21 Dec 2015]. See letter of Anil Potti (20 January 2011): <http://archive.dukechronicle.com/potti_south_carolina_letter.pdf> [accessed 21 Dec 2015].

163 Scott Pelley, 'Deception at Duke: Fraud in Cancer Care?' *CBS News*, 5 March 2012: <http://www.cbsnews.com/news/deception-at-duke-fraud-in-cancer-care/> [accessed 21 Dec 2015].

Professor Nevins' supervision, no adverse finding was made against him. The misconduct was regarded as that of the researcher whom he supervised.

In September 2015 the Office of Research Integrity formally confirmed that Dr Potti had been found to have engaged in misconduct in research supported by funding from the National Heart, Lung and Blood Institute (NHLBI), the National Institutes of Health (NIH), and the National Cancer Institute by including false research data in published papers, a submitted manuscript, a grant application, and the research record. It noted that he had neither admitted nor denied the ORI's findings but had entered into a voluntary settlement agreement whereby he had refrained from applying from federal funding since 2010 and that if he applied for any Public Health Service (PHS)-supported research funding over the succeeding five years, he would have his research supervised. In addition, and importantly, he agreed that 'any institution employing him shall submit, in conjunction with each application for PHS funds, or report, manuscript, or abstract involving PHS-supported research in which the Respondent is involved, a certification to ORI that the data provided by the Respondent are based on actual experiments or are otherwise legitimately derived and that the data, procedures, and methodology are accurately reported in the application, report, manuscript, or abstract'.[164]

The fallout from Dr Potti's conduct was wide-ranging, and took place over an extensive period of time. In January 2015 Goldberg[165] argued in the *Cancer Letter* that the scandal involving Potti could have been avoided if officials at Duke had listened properly and responded appropriately to the concerns expressed by a third-year medical student, Bradford Perez, who wrote a three-page document to Duke Medical School deans warning of Potti's misconduct in April 2008, when the clinical trials were getting started. Goldberg asserted that Potti's collaborators and deans at the school pressured Perez into not taking the matter further and denied that there had been any whistleblower at all. Instead of heeding the warnings, Duke used Potti's research in advertising for its cancer center, and a Duke physician featured on '60 Minutes' hailing his findings as the 'holy grail' of cancer research. Goldberg revealed that the student had suffered a range of repercussions and had to repeat a portion of his studies. Arthur Caplan, director of the Division of Medical Ethics at the NYU Langone Medical Center who reviewed the material in Goldberg's article, observed that: 'The medical student was very brave... That was quite an act of courage.'

Responding to that report, Duke officials said it had 'acknowledged years ago there are many aspects of this situation that would have been handled differently had there been more complete information at the time decisions were made'.[166]

Potti was made the subject of reprimand by both the North Carolina and Missouri licensing boards.[167]

[164] Federal Register of the United States Government, *Notice in relation to Office of Research Integrity Action in Respect of Dr Anil Potti* (11 September 2015), available at: <https://www.federalregister.gov/articles/2015/11/09/2015-28437/findings-of-research-misconduct> [accessed 21 Dec 2015].

[165] Paul Goldberg, 'Duke Officials Silenced Med Student Who Reported Trouble in Anil Potti's Lab' (9 January 2015), *Cancer Letter*: <http://www.cancerletter.com/articles/20150109_1> [accessed 21 Dec 2015].

[166] See Fred Barbash, 'Scientist Falsified Data for Cancer Research Once Described as "Holy Grail," Feds Say' (9 November 2015) *The Washington Post*: <https://www.washingtonpost.com/news/morning-mix/wp/2015/11/09/scientist-falsified-data-for-cancer-research-once-described-as-holy-grail-feds-say/> [accessed 21 Dec 2015].

[167] Missouri State Board of Registration for the Healing Arts, 'Settlement Agreement in relation to Dr Anil Potti' (6 March 2012): < https://renew.pr.mo.gov/secured%20data/healingarts/orders/MED-2011002469.pdf> [accessed 21 Dec 2015].

Lawsuits on behalf of patients proliferated but by mid-2012 a number of such actions had been settled (without findings because of the litigation not having gone to trial), his medical licence remained intact, and he was practising as a medical oncologist in a cancer centre in North Dakota.[168] The lawsuits continued until May 2015 when a final announcement by Duke was made that all had been settled. Potti's case is one of a series that may well provide considerable financial inducement to institutions to monitor the research and publications of their employees more closely than previously occurred because of the potential for them otherwise to become co-defendants in multiple legal actions.

Judy Mikovits: Chronic Fatigue

In 2009 Judy Mikovits, a former scientist at the National Cancer Institute, and others associated with the Whittemore-Peterson Institute for Neuro-Immune Disease (the Institute) published in *Science* an article[169] which suggested a potential aetiology for the controversial disorder, Chronic Fatigue Syndrome (CFS). Dr Mikovits's research found that 67 per cent of patients sampled were infected with a virus called XMRV, compared with 4 per cent of the controls:

> Chronic fatigue syndrome (CFS) is a debilitating disease of unknown etiology that is estimated to affect 17 million people worldwide. Studying peripheral blood mononuclear cells (PBMCs) from CFS patients, we identified DNA from a human gammaretrovirus, xenotropic murine leukemia virus–related virus (XMRV), in 68 of 101 patients (67%) as compared to 8 of 218 (3.7%) healthy controls. Cell culture experiments revealed that patient-derived XMRV is infectious and that both cell-associated and cell-free transmission of the virus are possible. Secondary viral infections were established in uninfected primary lymphocytes and indicator cell lines after their exposure to activated PBMCs, B cells, T cells, or plasma derived from CFS patients. These findings raise the possibility that XMRV may be a contributing factor in the pathogenesis of CFS.[170]

Patients showered praise on the lead researcher, Dr Judy Mikovits, and on the Institute, which had been founded by Harvey and Annette Whittemore, a wealthy and politically well-connected Nevada couple seeking to help their daughter, who had been diagnosed with CFS. The Institute was also the beneficiary of donations from many quarters and optimism was high about vital breakthroughs in relation to CFS.[171]

However, doubts proliferated about the legitimacy of the research underpinning the article.[172] This led to an editorial 'Expression of Concern' published in *Science*.[173] A September

---

[168] Stephen J Lee, 'Controversial Cancer Scientists Now Works in Grand Forks Cancer Center', *Bakken Today*, 20 August 2012: <http://www.bakkentoday.com/event/article/id/243218/publisher_ID/40/> [accessed 21 Dec 2015].

[169] Vincent C Lombardi, Francis W Ruscetti, Jaydip Das Gupta, Max A Pfost et al. 'Detection of an Infectious Retrovirus, XMRV, in Blood Cells of Patients with Chronic Fatigue Syndrome' (2009) 326(5952) *Science* 585.

[170] Ibid, 585.

[171] See David Tuller, 'Fallout From Fatigue Syndrome Retraction is Wide' (6 February 2012) *The New York Times*: <http://www.nytimes.com/2012/02/07/health/fallout-from-fatigue-syndrome-retraction-is-far-and-wide.html> [accessed 21 Dec 2015].

[172] See eg, Clifford H Shin, Lucinda Bateman, Robert Schlaberg, Ashley M Bunker et al. 'Absence of XMRV Retrovirus and Other Murine Leukemia Virus-Related Viruses in Patients with Chronic Fatigue Syndrome' (2011) 85(14) *Journal of Virology* 7195; Konstance Knox, Donald Carrigan, Graham Simmons, Fernando Teque et al. 'No Evidence of Murine-Like Gammaretroviruses in CFS Patients Previously Identified as XMRV-Infected' (2011) 333(6038) *Science* 94; Tobias Paprotka, Krista A Delviks-Frankenberry, Oya Cingöz, Anthony Martinez et al. 'Recombinant Origin of the Retrovirus XMRV' (2011) 333(6038) *Science* 97.

[173] Bruce Alberts, 'Editorial Expression of Concern' (2011) 333(6038) *Science* 35.

2011 article,[174] also published in *Science*, added further weight to the suspicion that the research was at least seriously flawed. The researchers compiled coded replicate samples of blood from 15 subjects previously reported to be XMRV/MLV-positive (14 with CFS) and from 15 healthy donors previously determined to be negative for the viruses. The samples were distributed in a blinded fashion to nine laboratories which performed assays designed to detect XMRV/MLV nucleic acid, virus replication, and antibody. Only two laboratories reported evidence of XMRV/MLVs. However, replicate sample results showed disagreement, and reactivity was similar among CFS subjects and negative controls. The researchers concluded that the results indicated that the assays did not reproducibly detect XMRV/MLV in blood samples and that blood donor screening was not warranted.

Mikovits continued to decline to retract the article but, by November 2011, the XMRV retrovirus research had been discredited and was suspected of being fraudulent. Mikovits was fired by the Institute for refusing to share a cell line with another Institute researcher[175] and then accused in a civil suit by her former employer of misappropriating laboratory notebooks and computer data about her studies. In addition, Mikovits was subsequently arrested and jailed briefly in California on remand.[176] After four nights she was released but it was claimed that a number of the laboratory notebooks had still not been returned and that computer data had been deleted by her. In December 2011, a judge ruled against her in the civil case,[177] with the criminal case pending. Ultimately the criminal case did not proceed[178] and civil litigation between her and her former employer persisted unresolved into 2015.

The fallout from the scandal is substantial, although no finding of research fraud was ever made. While Mikovits has re-established herself doing further research in the area, patients desperate for research breakthroughs in relation to CFS (other than psychological explanations) have been deeply disillusioned by the discredited research from Mikovits and her colleagues.[179] As of 2014 Mikovits continued to deny wrongdoing of any kind and to assert the legitimacy of her research, and she had co-written a book with a lawyer justifying her conduct.[180] Her success in portraying herself as a martyr has prompted reflections within journalism about the ethics of coverage of what has been described as 'pseudoscience' and the risks that the media can raise high-profile scientists to positions that their achievements do not warrant and thereafter lend them unjustified legitimacy.[181]

---

[174] Graham Simmons, Simone A Glynn, Anthony L Komaroff, Judy A Mikovits et al. 'Failure to Confirm XMRV/MLVs in the Blood of Patients with Chronic Fatigue Syndrome: A Multi-Laboratory Study' (2011) 334(6057) *Science* 814.

[175] See Edyta Zielinska, 'Chronic Fatigue Researcher Fired' (4 October 2011) *The Scientist*: <http://www.the-scientist.com/?articles.view/articleNo/31280/title/Chronic-Fatigue-Researcher-Fired/> [accessed 21 Dec 2015].

[176] See Stephen H Jenkins, *Tools for Critical Thinking in Biology* (Oxford: Oxford University Press, 2015), 223.

[177] See Ewen Callaway, 'Institute Claims Victory in Civil Suit Against Judy Mikovits' *Nature.com* (20 November 2011): <http://blogs.nature.com/news/2011/12/institute-claims-victory-in-civil-suit-against-judy-mikovits.html> [accessed 21 Dec 2015].

[178] See Joe Cohen, 'Criminal Charges Dropped Against Chronic Fatigue Syndrome Researcher Judy Mikovits' (13 June 2012) *Science*: <http://news.sciencemag.org/2012/06/criminal-charges-dropped-against-chronic-fatigue-syndrome-researcher-judy-mikovits> [accessed 21 Dec 2015].

[179] See David Tuller, 'Fallout from Fatigue Syndrome Retraction is Wide', *The New York Times*, 6 February 2012: <http://www.nytimes.com/2012/02/07/health/fallout-from-fatigue-syndrome-retraction-is-far-and-wide.html?pagewanted=all> [accessed 21 Dec 2015].

[180] Kent Heckenlively and Judy Mikovits, *Plague: One Scientist's Intrepid Search for the Truth about Human Retroviruses and Chronic Fatigue Syndrome (ME/CFS), Autism, and Other Diseases* (New York: Skyhorse Publishing, 2014).

[181] See Julia Belluz, 'How Should Journalists Cover Quacks like Oz or the Food Babe?' (13 April 2015) *Vox*: <http://www.vox.com/2015/4/13/8385295/science-reporting-ethics> [accessed 21 Dec 2015].

Alirio Melendez: Immunopharmacology

Professor Alirio Melendez was a high-profile immunopharmacologist whose principal work at the National University of Singapore was on the treatment of sepsis. He also worked on the issue of whether resveratrol controls inflammation and argued that it could be used to reduce the impact of anaphylactic shock and treat appendicitis, peritonitis, and systemic sepsis.

However, an anonymous whistleblower prompted investigations first into a paper Professor Melendez published in *Nature* and then into another in *Science*. That led the University to convene an investigative committee. However, Professor Melendez declined to provide information to the investigation, even though members of the committee travelled to England to speak with him. He did no more than protest his innocence. He was also accorded the opportunity (pursuant to the National University of Singapore Code on Research Integrity) to respond to the committee's findings but declined to do so.

The committee ultimately identified evidence of fabrication, falsification and plagiarism associated with 21 papers, including the two in the original allegation. The University declined to release its report. However, it confirmed that Professor Melendez engaged in 'serious scientific misconduct' during his employment in Singapore.[182] It also stated publicly that, in 21 of the 70 papers he authored or co-authored while at the University, it found evidence of plagiarism from others' work, plagiarism from his own work, making up data for an experiment (usually by manipulating images from another experiment), alteration of data (such as by manipulating images of gels and micrographs), and mismanagement, which included failure to keep or safeguard records.

Professor Melendez left Singapore in 2009 for professorial positions at the universities of Glasgow and Liverpool. In November 2011 Professor Melendez resigned his position at Liverpool University after having been suspended. He issued a statement accepting that someone in his university committed scientific fraud but denying it was he. He took responsibility for overseeing the impugned project and trusting his co-workers which he said 'may have been a mistake in hindsight, but one has to trust all team members'.[183] He asserted that there were multiple errors in the committee report and proclaimed that 'I will keep fighting for my right to be heard and to clear my name of the allegations of which I am accused, for which I maintain my complete innocence'.[184] In 2012 Glasgow University reported on its own investigation of research conducted by and in association with Professor Melendez. It declined to publish its findings and stated that it was not the university policy to comment on individual cases, saying only that there was 'no evidence that our current staff contributed, falsified or duplicated data to any publications co-authored with Melendez.'[185] However, after pressure about its secretive response, by May 2013 the university confirmed that its investigation had 'found evidence that data had been fabricated or otherwise falsified for five publications.'[186]

[182] Adele Yung and Yojana Sharma, 'Academic Found Guilty of Fraud on 'Unprecedented' Scale' (11 January 2013) Issue 254, *University World News*: <http://www.universityworldnews.com/article.php?story=20130110821066> [accessed 21 Dec 2015].

[183] 'Alirio Melendez Categorically Denies Data Falsification, Alleges Cover-up', *Retraction Watch*, 17 October 2013: <http://retractionwatch.com/2013/10/17/alirio-melendez-categorically-denies-data-falsification-alleges-cover-up/> [accessed 21 Dec 2015].

[184] Alirio J Melendez, 'Paper-by-Paper Review' on Prof AJ Melendez, *Public Denial of Allegations* (24 October 2013): <http://www.ajmelendez.co.uk/?page_id=21> [accessed 21 Dec 2015].

[185] See Paul Jump, 'University of Glasgow Tight-Lipped over Ethics Inquiry' (30 August 2012) *Times Higher Education*: <http://www.timeshighereducation.co.uk/news/university-of-glasgow-tight-lipped-over-ethics-inquiry/420998.article> [accessed 21 Dec 2015].

[186] Paul Jump, 'Glasgow Confirms Academic's Papers were "Falsified"' (20 May 2013) *Times Higher Education*: <http://www.timeshighereducation.co.uk/news/glasgow-confirms-academics-papers-were-falsified/2003958.article> [accessed 21 Dec 2015].

Even by 2015 there was much that was not publicly known about the specific conduct engaged in by Professor Melendez owing to the fact that the reports into his conduct had not been publicly released in Singapore or in Scotland in spite of the fact that over 20 of his published articles had been determined by the National University of Singapore to have been affected by intellectual dishonesty. At no time had he ever admitted any form of impropriety save a failure to oversee the work of his co-authors adequately.[187]

Joachim Boldt: Anaesthetics

Professor Extraordinary Joachim Boldt of the University of Giessen built up a formidable reputation during his tenure at the Klinikum Ludwigshafen from the 1990s in relation to the perioperative use of intravenous fluids. He was an advocate for the use of colloids, in particular hydroxyethyl starch solutions, to boost blood volume during surgery.

In November 2010 he was suspended from the Klinikum Ludwigshafen for a scientific publication in *Anesthesia and Analgesia* in 2009 that had been discovered to lack sufficient background research. The investigation was prompted by an email sent to the journal's editor-in-chief, observing that: '[t]he results are all very consistent, all very much statistically significant with very small standard deviation'.[188] The writer commented that the results were 'extraordinary given the small number of included patients' and that 'the reported effect on coagulation tests and bleeding is particularly "magic"'.[189] When another email arrived shortly afterwards, also questioning the results, the editor-in-chief wrote repeatedly to Boldt asking him to respond to the issues of concern. However, Boldt obdurately did not reply and the editor-in-chief's concerns were ultimately placed before the State Medical Association of the Rhineland-Palatinate, the Landesarztekammer Rheinland-Pfalz (LAK-RLP). It only had the authority to look into whether Boldt had complied with the applicable ethical code. It found that the article in question had not been approved, as it should have been, by a properly constituted ethics committee. The LAK-RLP and the Klinikum Ludwigshafen then formed a committee to investigate the integrity of Boldt's research.

The head of the perfusion team at the hospital informed the committee that albumin, the subject of what Boldt had alleged was his research, had not been used as a priming solution at the hospital since 1999 and had not been delivered to operating theatres for many years. The committee concluded that there was no convincing evidence that the study the subject of purported research by Boldt had been undertaken at all. In response to questions posed to him, Boldt admitted forging the signatures of co-authors on the copyright transfer form submitted to *Anesthesia and Analgesia*.

By February 2011 he had been stripped of his professorial title and the Klinikum Ludwigshafen released the results into the investigation it had conducted into Boldt's publications. It concluded that, in most of the studies investigated, the conduct of research failed to meet required standards. In none of the publications had ethical approval been granted by the relevant committee. The necessary explanations for study participants and the existence of the provision of consent often could not be established.

False data were identified in at least ten of the 91 articles examined, which had been published between 1999 and 2011. The incorrect data included data on patient numbers/study groups as well as data on the timing of measurements. The Hospital reported that since

---

187 See Retraction Watch, 'Alirio Melendez Categorically Denies Data Falsification, Alleges Cover-Up': <http://retractionwatch.com/2013/10/17/alirio-melendez-categorically-denies-data-falsification-alleges-cover-up/> [accessed 21 Dec 2015].

188 See Jacqui Wise, 'Boldt: The Great Pretender' (2013) 346 *British Medical Journal* 1738.

189 Ibid.

learning of Boldt's conduct it had intensified its requirements for study conduct and created a 'Scientific Steering Committee'.[190]

In 2011 the LAK-RLP reviewed the status of ethics approval for 101 articles published by Boldt. Tellingly, and showing a pattern of circumvention of this important check and balance by Boldt, but raising the issue of how this could have occurred so often for so long, it could not verify such approval for 89 articles, including 22 published in *Anesthesia and Analgesia*. As a result, the editors of *Acta Anaesthesiologica Scandinavica, Anaesthesia, Anastheesiolgie Intensivmedizin Notfallmedizin Schmerstherapie, Anesthesia and Analgesia, Anesthesiology, British Journal of Anaesthesia, Critical Care Medicine*, and *Canadian Journal of Anesthesia*, all of which had published articles by Boldt, retracted them.[191] For a short period, this constituted a record for retractions.

As Wise has observed, the fraud of Boldt was more than an effective duping of journals, journal editors, and peer reviewers. It had significant clinical ramifications and put patients' lives at risk. The use of hydroxyethyl starch, a synthetic colloid, compared with intravenous fluids such as crystalloids has been controversial for many years. There was a difference of approach between Europe, where hydroxyethyl starch was more commonly used than in the United States. This was in spite of a 1998 Cochrane review published in the *British Medical Journal* that found 4 per cent more deaths when colloids were used. In this context, the studies of Boldt which were favourable to the use of colloids were influential in both the provision of treatment and in the formulation of pro-colloid clinical guidelines. Notably, after Boldt's various publications were retracted, six medical groups, including the Association of Surgeons and the Intensive Care Society, announced that they would withdraw the United Kingdom consensus guidelines on intravenous fluid therapy. A meta-analysis published in the *Journal of the American Medical Association* in February 2013 found that excluding Boldt's studies affected the balance of published research and suggested that hydroxyethyl starch was associated with a significantly increased risk of death and acute kidney injury.[192] Another meta-analysis published in the *British Medical Journal* after exclusion of the Boldt articles found an increase in adverse events with colloids in patients with sepsis.[193] In short, it is likely that Boldt's fraudulent research caused many unnecessary deaths.

Yoshitaka Fujii: Anaesthetics

The Boldt scandal occurred contemporaneously with the exposure of an anaesthetic research and publication scandal of unprecedented proportions by the Japanese scholar, Associate Professor Yoshitaka Fujii.[194] Fujii had a highly distinguished and remarkably prolific publication record

---

[190] 'Hospital Presents Results of Final Report: Committee Completes Investigations in the Case of Dr Boldt', *KliLu*, 9 August 2012: <http://www.klilu.de/content/veranstaltungen___presse/pressearchiv/2012/hospital_presents_results_of_final_report_committee_completes_investigation_in_the_case_of_dr_boldt/index_ger.html> (viewed 26 January 2015).

[191] See, eg, 'Editors-in-Chief Statement Regarding Published Clinical Trials Conducted Without IRB Approval by Joachim Boldt' (EIC Joint Statement, 12 March 2011): <http://www.aaeditor.org/EIC.Joint.Statement.on.Retractions.pdf> (viewed 26 January 2015).

[192] Ryan Zarychanski, Ahmed M Abou-Setta, Alexis F Turgeon, Brett L Houston et al. 'Association of Hydroxyethyl Starch Administration with Mortality and Acute Kidney Injury in Critically Ill Patients Requiring Volume Resuscitation: A Systematic Review and Meta-Analysis' (2013) 309(7) *The Journal of the American Medical Association* 678.

[193] Nicolai Haase, Anders Perner, Louise Inkeri Hennings, Martin Siegemund et al. 'Hydroxyethyl Starch 130/0.38-0.45 Versus Crystalloid or Albumin in Patients with Sepsis: Systematic Review with Meta-Analysis and Trial Sequential Analysis' (2013) 346 *BMJ* 839.

[194] See Adam Marcus and Ivan Oransky, 'How the Biggest Fabricator in Science Got Caught' (21 May 2015) *Nautilus*: <http://nautil.us/issue/24/error/how-the-biggest-fabricator-in-science-got-caught> (viewed 23 May 2015); Australian anaesthetist Daniel Jolley has described the conduct of Fujii as the

of 20 years in a broad cross-section of highly regarded anaesthetic journals. In some years he published more than a dozen articles that purported to emanate from multiple randomized clinical trials that tested the efficacy and side-effects of drugs given to reduce nausea and vomiting after surgery. His problematic publications commenced in 1993. Fujii had something of a peripatetic career[195] which 'may have also provided a smokescreen for his fraudulent behaviour. Over two decades, he held posts at five institutions, and adjunct positions at two more, making it easy for him to claim that data had been generated or ethics approval had been granted while he was in a previous post'.[196]

Suspicions about the legitimacy of Fujii's many studies dated back to 2000 when Peter Kranke, an anaesthesiologist at University Hospital Wurzburg in Germany, and others began to question Fujii's publication rate, describing Fujii's data in a letter published in *Anesthesia and Analgesia* as 'incredibly nice'.[197] One of the co-authors of the letter, Christian Apfel, then of the University of Würzburg, in Germany, approached the United States Food and Drug Administration to alert them to the issues he and his colleagues had raised. However, he did not receive a response. Doubts ensued about Fujii's studies of other drugs, such as the anti-emetic ramosetron.

Matters came to a head in September 2011 when Fujii's employer, Toho University, was persuaded to begin an investigation after Fujii submitted an article to the *Canadian Journal of Anesthesia* in which the editor found indicia of plagiarism.[198] The focus shifted to Fujii's failure to obtain institutional ethics approval for various of his clinical trials.[199] On 8 March 2012 the Toho University Faculty of Medicine announced that eight of Fujii's manuscripts had been retracted because of the fact they had proceeded without proper ethics approval. It dismissed him.[200] In April 2012 Carlisle, an English anaesthetist, published an analysis of 169 allegedly randomized controlled trials undertaken by Fujii and concluded, tactfully, that 'the distributions of continuous and categorical variables reported in Fujii's papers, both human and animal, are extremely unlikely to have arisen by chance and if so, in many cases with likelihoods that are infinitesimally small.... Until such time that these results can be explained, it is essential that all Fujii et al's data are excluded from meta-analyses or reviews of the relevant fields'.[201] This led the Japanese Society of Anaesthesiologists to set up a Special Investigation Committee to look further into the matter in March 2012. It interviewed Fujii and his co-authors and investigated his original research data, his laboratory notebooks, and the records that the relevant institutions held.

'biggest academic fraud in the history of medicine': Daniel Jolley, 'Fujii, Anesthesia & Research Fraud', *Gas Exchange*, 15 November 2012: <http://gasexchange.com/articles/fujii-anesthesia-research-fraud/> [accessed 21 Dec 2015].

195 See Hindawi Publishing Corporation, 'Yoshitaka Fujii', *Hindawi*, 11 March 2010: <http://www.hindawi.com/96130824//> [accessed 22 Dec 2015]. It included time at the Royal Victoria Hospital at McGill University in Canada.

196 David Cyranoski, 'Retraction Record Rocks Community: Anaesthesiology Tries to Move on After Fraud Investigations' (2012) 489(7416) *Nature* 346: <http://www.nature.com/news/retraction-record-rocks-community-1.11434> [accessed 22 Dec 2015].

197 Peter Kranke, Christian C Apfel, and Norbert Roewer, 'Reported Data on Granisetron and Postoperative Nausea and Vomiting by Fujii et al. Are Incredibly Nice!' (2000) 90(4) *Anesthesia and Analgesia* 1004.

198 See Kas Muijres, 'Fraud; Comparison Among Different Fraudsters and their Techniques' (2013) *Social Cosmos* 64.

199 Cyranoski, above n 196.

200 Masaru Kuroda, 'Disciplinary Decision Concerning Dr Yoshitaka Fujii', *Toho University*, 6 March 2012: <http://www.toho-u.ac.jp/english/information/march_6_2012.html> [accessed 22 Dec 2015].

201 John B Carlisle, 'The Analysis of 168 Randomised Controlled Trials to Test Data Integrity' (2012) 67(5) *Anaesthesia* 521, 536.

The Society[202] concluded that three of Fujii's papers had not been fabricated, that there was no evidence to determine whether 37 papers had been fabricated but that no fewer than 172 papers were fabrications: 'Both the number of animals and patients are totally different from the institutional records, although some of his early studies might have been done properly.' It found that he fabricated the contention that his studies were double-blind randomized controlled trials. It observed that Fujii deliberately refrained from identifying the institution and the period of study in his papers so that he could proffer the excuse that the data he presented were obtained from a previous hospital or workplace where he had been employed. Like Boldt, he took active measures to avoid external oversight of his work and would avoid identifying any research ethics committee that had given authorization for his work. He presented his papers as though they were multi-hospital studies so as to make persons from any other institution his co-authors and blur the tracks of his research and lack of real collaboration. The Society found that all the fabrications were done by Fujii alone—none of his co-authors was involved; the reason for putting co-authors on his papers was to escape from suspicions of fraudulent activity. Many co-authors were at the extreme end of being 'gift authors'; they provided no approval to Fujii's submission of papers in their names and did not even receive reprints of accepted papers. However, from this exculpation the Society excepted Fujii's supervisor, Professor Hidenori Toyooka, who published dozens of papers with Fujii and, although he was aware of the issues raised by Kranke in 2000, took no action.[203]

Fortunately, most of Fujii's research was of low impact and posed relatively few risks to patients. Ironically, it appears that the relatively obscure nature of many of his publications meant that many of his co-authors were not even aware of having been named by Fujii as co-authors.

Multiple formal retractions have followed, including by the *Canadian Journal of Anesthesia* which has retracted 33 articles written by Fujii. After his dismissal, Fujii found work at Fukushima University, near the nuclear disaster zone, but when news of the adverse findings reached the university the job offer was withdrawn. He has disappeared from sight and is believed to be working part-time as an anaesthesiologist in hospitals in Tokyo, where there is an acute shortage of such practitioners.[204]

There is relatively little indication of what motivated Fujii's extraordinary sequence of pre-meditated and carefully concealed frauds. He did not receive prizes for any of his studies, although he applied unsuccessfully for them, and he received little by way of honoraria or direct financial rewards. However, he did obtain an amount of public research funding and garnered fees for speaking at industry seminars.[205] He secured and maintained the position of associate professor at a well-regarded teaching hospital.

It has been observed that 13 per cent of retracted articles since 2000 have been in the field of anaesthetics, possibly a product of the high levels of publication in the area, the mobility of anaesthetists, and certainly an inadequate level of effective peer-reviewing and supervision of

---

[202] Koji Sumikawa, 'The Results of Investigation into Dr Yoshitaka Fujii's Papers' (2012) 2, available at: <http://www.anesth.or.jp/english/pdf/news20120629.pdf> [accessed 22 Dec 2015].

[203] When Professor Toyooka was approached by Science Insider to respond, he declined to do so: see Dennis Normile, 'A New Record for Retractions? (Pt 2)' (2 July 2012) *ScienceInsider*: <http://news.sciencemag.org/education/2012/07/new-record-retractions-part-2> (viewed 20 July 2015).

[204] David McNeill, 'Japanese Fraud Case Highlights Weaknesses in Scientific Publishing', *The Chronicle of Higher Education*, 8 October 2012, available at: <http://www.ruppweb.org/CHE_The-Great-Pretender_Oct_8_2012.pdf> [accessed 22 Dec 2015].

[205] Normile, 148.

academic practitioners. Miller has commented: 'While an experienced fraudster will always be difficult to detect, we can only hope that greater oversight from all universities, adherence to the requirements of validated reporting guidelines, and greater rigour in editorial peer review will minimize or eliminate the likelihood of such extensive and serial fraud from reoccurring.'[206] This seems somewhat optimistic in the circumstances.

Marc Hauser: Psychology

In the summer of 2007, while eminent Harvard psychologist Professor Marc Hauser was in Australia, academic authorities entered his laboratory and seized computers, videotapes, unpublished manuscripts, and notes. In 2010 a committee found Hauser guilty of multiple counts of research fraud.[207] Professor Hauser was a leader in the field of animal and human cognition, Harvard's leading primate psychologist and, ironically, an expert on the evolution of morality.

In 2006 Hauser had written a well-received book, *Moral Minds: How Nature Designed Our Universal Sense of Right and Wrong*.[208] His work probed the evolutionary roots of moral behaviour in the responses of cotton-top tamarins to teasing by researchers. However, a former laboratory assistant alleged that when Hauser viewed videotapes of rhesus monkeys, in an experiment on their capacity to learn sound patterns, he recorded behaviour that other people in the laboratory could not see, in a way that consistently favoured his hypothesis. When confronted with these discrepancies, the assistant alleged that Hauser asserted imperiously that his interpretation was right and the others wrong.[209] Ultimately, he admitted to making 'significant mistakes', suggesting that his errors may have been the product of confirmation bias.

Harvard Dean of Arts and Sciences Michael Smith accepted that, '[w]hile different issues were detected for the studies reviewed, overall, the experiments reported were designed and conducted, but there were problems involving data acquisition, data analysis, data retention, and the reporting of research methodologies and results'.[210] The immediate consequence was that certain of Hauser's papers were retracted because the data produced in the published experiments did not support the published findings, and in respect of another a correction was published.

'Dishonesty in cognitive science is somehow more disturbing than dishonesty in biology or physical science', said psychologist David Premack, an Emeritus Professor of the University of Pennsylvania, in an email to *USA Today*: 'The latter threatens the lives of people, producing a kind of harm we readily comprehend. The former puzzles us: it produces no physical harm, but threatens our standards, a kind of harm we do not readily understand. Because he caused no physical harm, we see him as discrediting everything he touched, including science itself. Hauser, a gifted writer, had no need for shortcuts.'[211]

---

206 Donald R Miller, 'Retraction of Articles Written by Dr Yoshitaka Fujii' (2012) 59(12) *Canadian Journal of Anaesthesia* 1081, 1084.

207 Nicholas Wade, 'Harvard Finds Scientist Guilty of Misconduct', *The New York Times*, 20 August 2010: <http://www.nytimes.com/2010/08/21/education/21harvard.html> [accessed 22 Dec 2015].

208 Marc D Hauser, *Moral Minds: How Nature Designed Our Universal Sense of Right and Wrong* (New York: Ecco, 2006).

209 Scott O Lilienfeld, 'Fudge Factor: A Look at a Harvard Science Fraud Case', *Scientific American*, 1 October 2010: <http://www.scientificamerican.com/article/fudge-factor/> (viewed 2 February 2015).

210 'FAS Dean Smith Confirms Scientific Misconduct by Marc Hauser', *Harvard Magazine*, 20 August 2010: <http://harvardmagazine.com/2010/08/harvard-dean-details-hauser-scientific-misconduct> [accessed 22 Dec 2015].

211 Dan Vergano, 'Updated: Harvard Says Marc Hauser Guilty of Scientific Misconduct', *USA Today*, 20 August 2010: <http://content.usatoday.com/communities/sciencefair/post/2010/08/marc-hauser-harvard-science-misconduct-/1#.VM7hFmiUd8F> [accessed 22 Dec 2015].

The United States Department of Health and Human Services Office of Research Integrity announced an investigation into the conduct of Hauser. His Dean stated that Harvard was also cooperating with the National Science Foundation and the United States Attorney's Office in light of the fact that Hauser had received federal grants. For a time Professor Hauser remained employed by Harvard but was suspended from teaching courses on 'Origins of Evil' and 'Hot Topics in Cognitive Science and Neuroscience'.[212] However, in due course he resigned in disgrace.

Professor Gross commented of the scandal: '[T]here seems to me to be little doubt that Hauser is guilty of scientific misconduct, though to what extent and severity remains to be revealed…irreversible damage has been done to the field of animal cognition, to Harvard University and most of all to Marc Hauser'.[213]

By 2012 the Office of Research Integrity concluded that in six cases Hauser engaged in research misconduct in work supported by the National Institutes of Health. One paper was retracted and two were corrected. It identified other problems in his unpublished work. In 2014 Harvard's 85-page internal report was released under freedom of information entitlements. It showed that on multiple occasions Hauser rebuffed the expression of concerns by persons within his laboratory about how his data were obtained. It described a 'disturbing pattern of misrepresentation of results and shading of the truth… [and a] reckless disregard for basic scientific standards'.[214] After leaving Harvard he published a high-profile book on the nature of evil[215] but showed no insight or remorse into the deficits in research conduct. The Hauser case is one of many that illustrates the collateral forms of damage occasioned by obdurate engagement in research misconduct and refusal to acknowledge fault in respect of manifest fraud. It is an example of the belief on the part of a number of persons who have engaged in research fraud that they can 'ride out' the adverse publicity and re-establish their scholarly authority.

Don Poldermans: Cardiology

Prior to 2011 Dr Don Poldermans was a highly respected cardiovascular medicine researcher who was head of perioperative care at the Erasmus Medical Centre in Rotterdam, associated with Erasmus University. He was the author of over 500 peer-reviewed articles. He was a member of the European Society of Cardiology Committee for Practice Guidelines and also acted as the Chairperson of the Task Force for the European Society of Cardiology (ESC) which published the 'Guidelines for Preoperative Cardiac Risk Assessment and Preoperative Cardiac Management in Non-Cardian Surgery'.[216] Dr Poldermans was the lead investigator of the Dutch Echographic Cardiac Risk Evaluation Applying Stress Echo III (DECREASE III), a study on the perioperative use of extended-release fluvastatin (Lescol XL, Novartis) in patients undergoing vascular surgery. That study showed in 2008 that patients treated with fluvastatin who were not already taking a statin had nearly a 50

[212] 'Marc Hauser's Return', *Harvard Magazine* (July–August 2011): <http://harvardmagazine.com/2011/07/marc-hausers-return> [accessed 22 Dec 2015].

[213] Charles Gross, 'Disgrace: On Marc Hauser', *The Nation*, 21 December 2011: <http://www.thenation.com/article/165313/disgrace-marc-hauser?page=full#> [accessed 22 Dec 2015].

[214] See Carolyn Y Johnson, 'Harvard Report Shines Light on Ex-Researcher's Conduct', *The Boston Globe*, 30 May 2014: <http://www.bostonglobe.com/metro/2014/05/29/internal-harvard-report-shines-light-misconduct-star-psychology-researcher-marc-hauser/maSUowPqL4clXrOgj44aKP/story.html#comments> [accessed 22 Dec 2015].

[215] Marc Hauser, *Evilicious: Cruelty = Desire + Denial* (Create Space, 2013).

[216] See Vineet Chopra and Kim A Eagle, 'Perioperative Mischief: The Price of Academic Misconduct' (2012) 125(10) *American Journal of Medicine* 953.

per cent reduction in myocardial ischemia as well as reductions in cardiovascular death/non-fatal myocardial infarction.

The study that gave rise to the inquiry into Dr Poldermans's conduct aimed to identify the factors with the potential to contribute to improved estimates of the risks of complications. After concerns were raised about Dr Poldermans's use of data by a colleague who became a whistleblower, a series of papers principally authored by Dr Poldermans of Erasmus University was retracted.

An investigative committee established by Erasmus University in 2011–2012 found that Dr Poldermans did not follow study protocols, did not collect data properly, failed on occasions to obtain patients' informed consent, and in a number of cases, fabricated data.[217] It found Dr Poldermans to be personally responsible for the use of the problematic data, having performed the relevant analyses himself and then having made findings and conclusions on the basis of them. It concluded that the errors could not have escaped his attention and observed that he consistently declined invitations for an interview with the committee.[218]

Dr Poldermans's work suggested that beta blockers had a neutral effect on mortality and encouraged researchers to focus on reduction of non-fatal myocardial infarction. The adverse effect of Dr Poldermans's work was exposed when a team of United Kingdom researchers conducted a meta-analysis of beta blocker trials for those at risk of cardiac events undergoing high or immediate risk surgery or vascular surgery without Dr Poldermans's (false) data and found that the use of perioperative beta blockers was associated with a 27 per cent increase in 30-day mortality.[219] Their immediate and very pointed recommendation was that: 'Guideline bodies should retract their recommendations based on fictitious data without further delay. This should not be blocked by dispute over allocation of blame... Any remaining enthusiasts might best channel their energy into a further randomized trial which should be designed carefully and conducted honestly.'[220] However, as late as 2014 the *New England Journal of Medicine* had not retracted key articles by the Poldermans group and, troublingly, had not even published an expression of concern in relation to them.[221]

As a result of the inquiry Erasmus University dismissed Dr Poldermans for violating academic integrity[222] and Dr Poldermans resigned from the European Society for Cardiology Committee for Practice Guidelines. Subsequently, Dr Poldermans took responsibility for the less serious charges against him but continued to deny the fabrication of data.[223] He

---

[217] Erasmus MC Follow-Up Investigation Committee, *Report on the 2012 Follow-Up Investigation of Possible Breaches of Academic Integrity*, 30 September 2012: <https://cardiobrief.files.wordpress.com/2012/10/integrity-report-2012-10-english-translation.pdf> [accessed 22 Dec 2015].

[218] Ibid, 24.

[219] Sonia Bouri, Matthew James Shun-Shin, Graham D Cole, Jamil Mayet, and Darrel P Francis, 'Meta-Analysis of Secure Randomised Controlled Trials of ß-Blockade to Prevent Perioperative Death in Non-Cardiac Surgery' (2014) 100(6) *Heart* 456.

[220] Ibid, 456.

[221] See Zosia Kmietowicz, 'Researchers "Disappointed" that Influential Study Was Not Retracted' (2014) 349 *British Medical Journal* g6063, referring to the views of Graham Cole and Darrel Francis, of Imperial College London; Larry Husten, 'New England Journal of Medicine Declines to Retract Articles from Disgraced Research Group' (26 September 2014) *Forbes*: <http://www.forbes.com/sites/larryhusten/2014/09/26/new-england-journal-of-medicine-declines-to-retract-papers-from-disgraced-research-group/> [accessed 22 Dec 2015]; see too Lilian Anekwe, 'New Guideline on Beta Blockers Challenges ESC Advice' (22 February 2014) 383 *The Lancet* 682.

[222] Erasmus University, 'Erasmus MC Dismisses Professor', *Erasmus MC*, 17 November 2011: <http://www.erasmusmc.nl/corp_home/corp_news-center/2011/2011-11/ontslag.hoogleraar/?lang=en> [accessed 22 Dec 2015].

[223] See Don Poldermans, 'Scientific Fraud or a Rush to Judgment?' (2013) 126(4) *American Journal of Medicine* e5.

described problems with a whistleblower who worked with him, accusing him of misconduct, but accepting overall responsibility for errors and acknowledging that he should have been suspicious when there were numerous warning signs about his work.[224]

Dipak Das: Cardiology

Professor Dipak K Das was an Indian-born cardiovascular researcher. He earned his PhD from New York University and spent most of his tenured career at the University of Connecticut. He was a prodigious publisher with 588 publications listed to his name by Google Scholar. A particular area of his research interest was the benefits of resveratrol,[225] an anti-oxidant found in grape skin, which he argued had the potential for promoting health by preventing coronary heart disease or killing cancer cells.[226]

Much of his work involved cutting and pasting photographic images from a form of research record known as a 'western blot'.[227] Because western blots have often been subject to manipulations in the past, many journals require that the images not be altered in any way without an explicit description of the procedure. However, concerns emerged via anonymous accusations in 2008 that he was 'Photoshopping' his images and also engaging in a variety of forms of fraudulent research.

The University of Connecticut, working with the Office of Research Integrity, conducted a three-year investigation into Das's work and generated a 60,000-page report which found 145 counts of fabrication and falsification of data in his research. The five-person investigation committee singled out 26 of what it identified were the most questionable publications. Das was listed as an author on all of them. Topics of the studies ranged from how broccoli protects mammalian hearts to the superiority of crushed garlic over processed garlic. Nine of the papers dealt with Das's special area of interest in resveratrol. The committee's report stated that several of the images were changed—some were duplicated, others were spliced together or simply erased, a task readily done with Photoshop software.

The University returned two grants to the National Heart, Blood and Lung Institute (worth US$890,000) and alerted 11 journals that had published articles that the university concluded were fraudulent. It sacked Das from his position of Director of the University of Connecticut's Cardiovascular Research Center. He disputed the findings and criticized the investigation, maintaining that he had been the victim of discrimination by reason of his Indian background. He then filed a US$35 million lawsuit against the University alleging discrimination and libel.[228] He passed away before the matter came to trial.

As a result of the investigation's findings, all externally funded research was frozen in Das's laboratory and close to US$1 million in federal research grants awarded to Das were returned

224 See Larry Husten, 'Don Poldermans and the Dutch Research Scandal', *Forbes*, 15 October 2012: <http://www.forbes.com/sites/larryhusten/2012/10/15/don-poldermans-and-the-dutch-research-scandal/> [accessed 22 Dec 2015].

225 See Ole Vang and Dipak K Das (eds), 'Resveratrol and Health' (Special Issue) (2011) 1215 *Annals of the New York Academy of Sciences* 1–170.

226 See Nicholas Wade, 'University Suspects Fraud by a Researcher Who Studied Red Wine', *The New York Times*, 11 January 2012: <http://www.nytimes.com/2012/01/12/science/fraud-charges-for-dipak-k-das-a-university-of-connecticut-researcher.html?_r=0> [accessed 22 Dec 2015].

227 Ibid.

228 Christine Stuart, 'Fired Scientist Sues University of Connecticut', *Courthouse News Service*, 7 March 2013: <http://www.courthousenews.com/2013/03/07/55507.htm> [accessed 22 Dec 2015]; William Weir, 'Discredited Scientist Plans to Sue UConn for Libel', *The Hartford Courant*, 25 January 2013: <http://articles.courant.com/2013-01-25/health/hc-uconn-lawsuit-20130125_1_uconn-health-center-research-misconduct-uconn-officials> [accessed 22 Dec 2015].

to funders, including the National Heart, Lung and Blood Institute. The university took the initiative of notifying 11 scientific journals of the potential research implications of Das's conduct. It has been observed that:

> The significance of the case seems more to reflect on the general system of apportioning research money. Researchers complain that federal grants are increasingly hard to get, even for high-quality research, yet money seemed to have flowed freely to Dr Das, who was generating research of low visibility and apparently low quality.[229]

However, there have been other perspectives with some reflecting that the need for research results to be presented in a way that highlights their potential significance can lead to problematic temptations for misrepresentation of outcomes: 'If you are blatantly honest about your failures, you will get nowhere', David Rowe, Director of the Center for Regenerative Medicine and Skeletal Development at the University of Connecticut's Health Center, told the *Boston Herald*. 'The fact is that reviewing agencies want success. Therefore you spin your data in the most favorable way. That's where the dangers begin to come–that you spin it a little more than you can justify and then one thing leads to another. It's a very mushy, very fuzzy line.'[230]

Haruko Obokata: Stem Cell Research

The scandal surrounding Dr Haruko Obokata is the most extraordinary example of research fraud in the modern era. She led a research unit for cellular programming at the Kiken Center for Developmental Biology on Kobe, Japan. Obokata was a former researcher at Harvard Medical School, young (31), female, glamorous, dynamic, and quirky. She became a 'celebrity scientist', a darling of the media, known for decorating her office with 'Moomin' cartoons, painting it pink and yellow, wearing a sleeved Japanese cooking garment, the 'kappogi', given to her by her grandmother, during experiments rather than the orthodox laboratory coat, and posing for photographs festooned with long, false eyelashes.[231]

In January 2014 *Nature* published two papers of which she was the lead author, suggesting a breakthrough in regenerative medicine whereby pluripotent stem cells known as STAP (stimulus-triggered acquisition of pluripotency) cells could be created by the application of external stressors, such as a bacterial toxin or a weak acid bath.[232] The research was described as a potential 'game changer'[233] and raised hopes of a relatively easy means of creating stem cells—highly versatile cells which could be used to heal damaged organs, repair spinal cords

---

229 Wade, above n 226.

230 See Amina Khan, 'Resveratrol Researcher Faked Data, Report Says; What Drives Academic Fraud?' *Los Angeles Times*, 12 January 2012: <http://articles.latimes.com/2012/jan/12/news/la-dipak-das-resveratrol-diederik-stapel-20120112> [accessed 22 Dec 2015].

231 See, for example, Rowan Hooper, 'Stem-Cell Leap Defied Japanese Norms', *The Japan Times*, 15 February 2014: <http://www.japantimes.co.jp/news/2014/02/15/national/science-health/stem-cell-leap-defied-japanese-norms/#.VM7muWiUd8E> [accessed 22 Dec 2015]; Kirk Spitzer, 'Science Scandal Triggers Suicide, Soul-Searching in Japan', *Time*, 8 August 2014: <http://time.com/3091584/japan-yoshiki-sasai-stem-cells-suicide-haruko-obokata/> [accessed 22 Dec 2015].

232 Haruko Obokata, Teruhiko Wakayama, Yoshiki Sasai, Koji Kojima, Martin P Vacanti, Hitoshi Niwa, Masayuki Yamato, and Charles A Vacanti, 'Stimulus-triggered Fate Conversion of Somatic Cells into Pluripotency' (2014) 505(7) *Nature* 641; Haruko Obokata, Yoshiki Sasai, Hitoshi Niwa, Mitsutaka Kadota, Munazah Andrabi, Nozomu Takata, Mikiko Tokoro, Yukari Terashita, Shigenobu Yonemura, Charles A Vacanti, and Teruhiko Wakayama, 'Bidirectional Developmental Potential in Reprogrammed Cells with Acquired Pluripotency' (2014) 505(7485) *Nature* 676.

233 Maan Pamintuan-Lamorena, 'New Advances in Stem Cell Research Could Become a Game Changer', *Japan Daily Press*, 30 January 2014: <http://japandailypress.com/new-advances-in-stem-cell-research-could-become-a-game-changer-3043305/> [accessed 22 Dec 2015].

or treat diseases such as Parkinson's disease, Alzheimer's disease, and diabetes. The study was even hailed as a potential Nobel prize-winner, heralding the next pillar of development in medicine.[234]

Dr Obokata was held up, too, as paving the way for young female scientists in Japan.[235] Her findings were described as 'remarkable' by Professor Robin Lovell-Smith of the Medical Research Council and 'a major scientific discovery' by Dr Dusko Ilic, a reader in stem cell science at King's College London, who added: 'The approach is indeed revolutionary. It will make a fundamental change in how scientists perceive the interplay of environment and genome.'[236]

However, Dr Obokata's fall from grace arrived quickly—those whom the media promote they can also destroy. At the start of 2014 she was described by colleagues to the media as original, tenacious, and having a 'never-give-up attitude',[237] but it emerged that her lifestyle had started to become too close to that of a rock star. It was alleged that during part of her research Obokata resided in a luxury hotel and took over 50 business trips. Suspicions were voiced that she had engaged in defective methodologies: an image showing a genome analysis in one of her studies published in *Nature* appeared to have been spliced together, images from two placentas from two different experiments looked almost the same, and images in the articles seemed to have been duplicated from her 2011 thesis even though they related to different experiments.[238]

By February, Rikagaku Kenkyujo (Institute of Physical and Chemical Research, better known as Riken, a network of research institutions established in 1917 and which received over US$ 1 billion a year in government research funds) had set up an investigative panel to look into Dr Obokata's research after the airing of concerns about its legitimacy. With almost unparalleled speed, by the end of March Dr Obokata was denounced by the investigation and her reputation irretrievably destroyed. In a report made available to the media Dr Obokata was exposed as having fabricated data, doctored images and engaged in plagiarism, a devastating combination of unscholarly activities. The committee stated:

> [T]here was research misconduct by Dr Obokata on two points. Research misconduct warps the essence of science and significantly undermines credibility, not only within the science community, but also with the general public. Research misconduct is prohibited precisely because of the need to ensure robust, healthy exchange of information among scientists in their search for truth, and to promote the advancement of science. In manipulating the image data of two different gels and using data from two different experiments, Dr Obokata acted in a manner that can by no means be permitted. This cannot solely be explained by her immaturity as a researcher. Given the poor quality of her laboratory notes it has become clearly evident that it will be extremely difficult for anyone else to accurately trace or understand her experiments, and this, too, is considered a serious obstacle to health information exchange. Dr Obokata's actions and sloppy data management lead us to the conclusion that

234 See John Ross, 'Science Can Keep its House in Order', *The Australian*, 19 August 2014: <http://www.theaustralian.com.au/higher-education/science-can-keep-its-house-in-order/story-e6frgcjx-1227028449507?nk=3a30c91a692d5b5c522e0f8e2030b375> [accessed 22 Dec 2015].

235 Ida Torres, 'Stem Cell Researcher Paves the Way for Young, Female Japanese Scientists', *Japan Daily Press*, 4 February 2014: <http://japandailypress.com/stem-cell-researcher-paves-the-way-for-young-female-japanese-scientists-0443567/> [accessed 22 Dec 2015].

236 James Gallagher, 'Stem Cell "Major Discovery" Claimed', *BBC News*, 29 January 2014: <http://www.bbc.com/news/health-25917270> [accessed 22 Dec 2015].

237 Ryosuke Nonaka, 'STAP Cell Pioneer Nearly Gave Up on Her Research', *The Asahi Shimbun*, 30 January 2014: <http://ajw.asahi.com/article/behind_news/AJ201401300073> [accessed 22 Dec 2015].

238 Junko Yoshida, 'Obokata Scandal Puts Research in Peril', *EE Times*, 12 April 2014: <http://www.eetimes.com/author.asp?section_id=36&doc_id=1321893> [accessed 22 Dec 2015].

> she sorely lacks, not only a sense of research ethics, but also integrity and humility as a scientific researcher.[239]

The committee stated that Obokata's 'manipulation was used to improve the appearance of the results'. It concluded that, although Obokata was principally responsible, the other authors of one of the papers had not falsified data but still bore a 'heavy responsibility' for failing to verify the accuracy of the research findings.[240] Shortly afterwards Dr Obokata was admitted to hospital because her 'mental and physical condition is unstable', according to her lawyers.[241]

However, Dr Obokata galvanized her resolve, issued a defiant statement saying that she would appeal the 'one-sided conclusion' of the committee, and proclaimed that she rejected the findings of tampering, fabrication, and plagiarism.[242] Her lawyer made the limited concession that Dr Obokata had been 'anxious to complete the [two papers for *Nature*] due to concern that someone could overtake her and make a new discovery unless she publishes it quickly'.[243] The position being asserted, therefore, seemed to be that she may have made some modest errors due to the pressure to publish ahead of professional rivals.

Dr Obokata's appeal proved unsuccessful, this step in the process also being dealt with remarkably quickly;[244] the train journey towards Dr Obokata's sacrificial reputational destruction seemed unstoppable. By June she agreed to retract first one of the articles[245] and then both.[246] By July 2014 there was speculation that Obokata might be charged with criminal fraud (which in Japan carries a penalty of imprisonment of up to ten years, together with obligations of restitution) or use of deception to obstruct business (which carries a penalty of imprisonment of up three years).[247] This persisted into 2015 when a former Riken researcher

---

[239] Research Paper Investigative Committee, 'Report on STAP Cell Research Paper Investigation', 31 March 2014: <http://www3.riken.jp/stap/e/f1document1.pdf> [accessed 22 Dec 2015], 9. The next day, on 1 April 2014, Riken announced 'Measures to Prevent Further Instances of Research Misconduct': <http://www3.riken.jp/stap/e/r15document6.pdf> [accessed 22 Dec 2015].

[240] Monte Morin, 'Scientist Accused of Manipulating Data in STAP Stem Cell Study' (1 April 2014) *Los Angeles Times*: <http://articles.latimes.com/2014/apr/01/science/la-sci-sn-japanese-lab-cites-misconduct-in-stap-cell-controversy-20140331> [accessed 22 Dec 2015].

[241] Karen Kaplan, 'Haruko Obokata Says She Created STAP Stem Cells "More than 200 Times"', *Los Angeles Times*, 9 April 2014: <http://articles.latimes.com/2014/apr/09/science/la-sci-sn-stap-stem-cell-haruko-obokata-responds-20140409> [accessed 22 Dec 2015]; John Hofilena, 'Embattled Stem Cell Researcher Obokata Hospitalized for "Mental Condition"', *Japan Daily Press*, 8 April 2014: <http://japandailypress.com/embattled-stem-cell-researcher-obokata-hospitalized-for-mental-condition-0846936/> [accessed 22 Dec 2015].

[242] John Hofilena, 'Lead Scientist in Research Cell Scandal to Fight Riken's Findings', *Japan Daily Press*, 2 April 2014: <http://japandailypress.com/lead-scientist-in-stem-cell-research-scandal-to-fight-rikens-findings-0246717/> [accessed 22 Dec 2015].

[243] Maan Pamintuan-Lamorena, 'Riken Will Not Reinvestigate STAP Study, Says Scientist Committed Research Misconduct', *Japan Daily Press*, 9 May 2014: <http://japandailypress.com/riken-will-not-reinvestigate-stap-study-says-scientist-committed-research-misconduct-0948288/> [accessed 22 Dec 2015].

[244] Alexander Martin, 'Riken Rejects Obokata Appeal Over Stem-Cell Study', *The Wall Street Journal*, 8 May 2014: <http://blogs.wsj.com/japanrealtime/2014/05/08/riken-rejects-obokata-appeal-over-stem-cell-study/> [accessed 22 Dec 2015].

[245] John Hofilena, 'Riken Researcher Obokata Agrees to Retract 1 Out of 2 STAP Cell Papers', *Japan Daily Press*, 29 May 2014: <http://japandailypress.com/riken-researcher-obokata-agrees-to-retract-1-out-of-2-stap-cell-papers-2948845/> [accessed 22 Dec 2015].

[246] John Hofilena, 'Japanese Stem Cell Scientist Finally Agrees to Retract Papers on STAP Cells', *Japan Daily Press*, 4 June 2014: <http://japandailypress.com/japanese-stem-cell-scientist-obokata-finally-agrees-to-retract-papers-on-stap-cells-0449037/> [accessed 22 Dec 2015].

[247] Mark Schreiber, 'Ongoing Obokata Story Seeks Out Scandal', *The Japan Times*, 5 July 2014: <http://www.japantimes.co.jp/news/2014/07/05/national/media-national/ongoing-obokata-story-seeks-scandal/#.VM8NtGiUd8F> [accessed 22 Dec 2015].

filed a criminal complaint against Obokata alleging she stole samples of embryonic stem cells before reporting that she had created her version of stem cells with a novel technique.[248]

As of the end of July 2014 the playing out of Dr Obokata's extraordinary life in the media continued with reports that she had been physically injured when being harassed by journalists trying to solicit her reactions to her fall from grace.[249]

By August matters took a darker turn with her co-author and supervisor, Yoshiki Sasai, a well-regarded Japanese scientist, hanging himself in his office. In a suicide note he said he had grown weary of the media coverage of the scandal and apologized for the turmoil, but urged Obokata to continue her work and prove her detractors wrong.[250] Two weeks later, another collaborator, Dr Vacanti, announced his retirement.

Issues relating to Dr Obokata and those associated with her radiated out from her own work, raising escalating doubts about the integrity of Riken research and the rigour of some Japanese science. The head of the committee investigating Dr Obokata's work, Dr Shunkuke Ishii, resigned from the committee over anonymous allegations that at least one of his own papers contained problematic data. He said that the step he was taking was out of concern that the incident could complicate the committee's investigation.[251] By May 2014 four of the members of the committee were facing allegations of irregularities in their published work. The problems even extended to work done by one of Dr Obokata's co-authors, Nobel laureate Shinya Yamanaka, a stem-cell scientist at Kyoto University, who defended accusations that one of his papers from 2000 contained manipulated images but apologized for not having laboratory notes to back up the experiment on which he had reported.[252] Thomas Knöpfel, a founder of Riken's Brain Science Institute and then a leading neuroscientist at Imperial College London, expressed concern about the investigative processes which so readily laid blame at the feet of a young researcher—'It appears to me that Riken is more concerned about damage control and blame shifting' than about clarification. In part he blamed the Obokata affair on a prioritization by Riken on publishing in high-impact journals rather than a focus on generating good science: 'My observation was that Riken is driven by individual egos and interests beyond the healthy competition required for attaining a high scientific and ethical standard.'[253] There can be no doubt that the exposure of Obokata's failings, and the concerns expressed about those of others associated with her engendered both national and international shaming. Significant damage was done to Riken's reputation for scientific integrity. These are likely to be powerful deterrents for such conduct in Japan. In June 2014 a committee investigating Riken went so far as to call for its biological research centre to be disbanded immediately to prevent conduct comparable to that of the by then

---

248 See 'Obokata May Face Criminal Charges as Former Colleague Alleges She Stole Stem Cells' (27 January 2015) *The Japan Times*: <http://www.japantimes.co.jp/news/2015/01/27/national/science-health/obokata-may-face-criminal-charges-former-colleague-alleges-stole-stem-c> [accessed 22 Dec 2015].

249 'Obokata Injured While Fleeing Pack of NHK Reporters, Lawyer Says', *The Japan Times*, 24 July 2014: <http://www.japantimes.co.jp/news/2014/07/24/national/obokata-injured-fleeing-pack-nhk-reporters-lawyer-says/#.VM8OPWiUd8E> [accessed 22 Dec 2015].

250 See Spitzer, above n 231.

251 David Cyranoski, 'Investigator of Controversial Stem-Cell Study Resigns', *Nature*, 25 April 2014: <http://blogs.nature.com/news/2014/04/investigator-of-controversial-stem-cell-study-resigns.html> [accessed 22 Dec 2015].

252 David Cyranoski, 'Accusations Pile Up Amid Japan's Stem-Cell Controversy', *Nature*, 7 May 2014: <http://www.nature.com/news/accusations-pile-up-amid-japan-s-stem-cell-controversy-1.15163> [accessed 22 Dec 2015].

253 David McNeill, 'Academic Scandal Shakes Japan', *The New York Times*, 6 July 2014: <http://www.nytimes.com/2014/07/07/world/asia/academic-scandal-shakes-japan.html?_r=2> [accessed 22 Dec 2015].

disgraced scientist Dr Obokata.[254] At the end of August the laboratory issued a statement that, although attempts to replicate STAP cells in accordance with what Obokata claimed to be her experiments had failed, it would continue with the attempt.[255]

Another outcome of the investigations was that suspicion fell on the legitimacy of Obokata's 2011 doctoral dissertation which involved research into pluripotent stem cells taken from the marrow and lungs of mice. Waseda University found that she engaged in 11 instances of copyright violations in her dissertation and had plagiarised some 4000 words (20 pages) from a United States National Institutes of Health website on stem cells. It commented, devastatingly, that: 'The reliability and appropriateness of the dissertation is extremely low. Without a defect in the screening process it is difficult to believe that a doctoral degree would have been granted.'[256] It observed that the Professor of Medical Bioscience at Waseda University in charge of the dissertation committee also bore a very heavy responsibility for what had occurred. As the committee could not identify plagiarism in the part of the thesis relating to the results of Obokata's experiments, it did not at that stage recommend that her thesis be retracted. The focus was on the standards of Waseda University that enabled the doctorate to be awarded, Eisuke Enoki of the Faculty of Medicine at Kinki University expressing the concern that the fact that such an impoverished piece of work had passed the doctoral screening system risked reducing the trust reposed in Japan's degree system.[257] Allegedly, 'The shockwaves from Ms Obokata's rise and vertiginous fall continue to reverberate. Japan's top universities are rushing to install anti-plagiarism software and are combing through old doctoral theses amid allegations that they are honeycombed with similar problems'.[258] Dr Obokata's supervisor was suspended from work for a month and the executive allowance of the president of the University was reduced as further fall-out on the issue.[259]

However, matters did not end at this point in relation to the status of Dr Obokata's doctorate. In October 2014 Waseda University announced that it proposed to strip the researcher of her doctorate unless she corrected flaws in her dissertation. The President of the University stated by way of reasons that: 'We decided to revoke the degree in light of the detrimental effect on society this could have.'[260] In a response issued by her lawyer Dr Obokata apologized to the University for the trouble she had caused and stated that she would comply with its decision.[261] By October 2015 Waseda University announced that it had decided to strip Obokata of her doctorate as she had not remedied its flaws.[262]

254 'Committee Urges Research Center to be Disbanded After STAP Controversy', *GlobalPost*, 12 June 2014: <http://www.globalpost.com/dispatch/news/kyodo-news-international/140612/committee-urges-research-center-be-disbanded-after-sta> [accessed 22 Dec 2015].

255 'Riken: No Confirmation of STAP Cells, But Verification Tests Will Continue', *The Asahi Shimbun*, 27 August 2014: <http://ajw.asahi.com/article/behind_news/social_affairs/AJ201408270074> [accessed 22 Dec 2015].

256 'Waseda: Obokata Committed Plagiarism but Can Keep Doctorate', *The Asahi Shimbun*, 18 July 2014: <http://ajw.asahi.com/article/behind_news/social_affairs/AJ201407180049> [accessed 22 Dec 2015]; 'Waseda Rapped on Dissertation Scrutiny', *The Japan Times*, 18 July 2014: <http://www.japantimes.co.jp/news/2014/07/18/national/science-health/waseda-panel-says-obokatas-doctorate-stay-despite-scandal/#.VM8UhmiUd8F> [accessed 22 Dec 2015].

257 Ibid.

258 McNeill, above n 253.

259 'Waseda to Strip Obokata of Doctorate Unless She Corrects Her Dissertation', *The Japan Times*, 7 October 2014: <http://www.japantimes.co.jp/news/2014/10/07/national/science-health/waseda-strip-obokata-doctorate-unless-corrects-dissertation/#.VM8VzmiUd8F> [accessed 22 Dec 2015].

260 Alexander Martin, 'Japanese University May Strip Stem-Cell Scientist of Doctorate', *The Wall Street Journal*, 7 October 2014: <http://www.wsj.com/articles/japanese-university-may-strip-stem-cell-scientist-of-doctorate-1412683955> [accessed 22 Dec 2015].

261 Ibid.

262 'Waseda to Strip Biologist Obokata of Doctorate' (30 October 2015) *The Japan Times*: <http://www.japantimes.co.jp/news/2015/10/30/national/waseda-strip-biologist-obokata-doctorate/#.VjU7WmAxE6h> [accessed 22 Dec 2015].

After months of undertaking what she claimed were 'verification experiments', in December 2014 Obokata resigned from Riken, admitting that there were no significant results from her work. She maintained that she was 'exhausted now and extremely puzzled. I am keenly aware of my responsibility for troubling a number of people because of my inexperience. I can't even find the words for an apology.'[263] Her apology was accepted. Ultimately she returned the fees she had received for the publication of her papers in *Nature*.[264] The Science and Technology Minister told a news conference: 'Wrongness based on inexperience cannot be accepted in science. It has been confirmed that STAP cells do not exist.'[265] His contention in this regard was confirmed by an independent committee which concluded that the cells in question were probably mixed with embryonic stem cells created using well-established methods. The committee's chairman, Dr Isao Katsura, the Director of the National Institute of Genomics, commented that lack of proper oversight was the biggest reason for the scandal: 'The rush for patents and funding can cause researchers to forget the basics of science. There are social responsibilities. If we look away from that, terrible things can happen.'[266]

The saga relating to Dr Obokata had a number of unusual elements. The private organization, Riken, responded very promptly and efficiently to expressions of concern about the work of Dr Obokata. That was to its credit, although some reservations must be entertained about the inquiry having been conducted so quickly and a question remains about whether a longer investigation would have been preferable.

The committee of inquiry made its emphatic decision very quickly and an appeals committee was convened almost straightaway, at Dr Obokata's request. It affirmed the first instance decision. The perceived dynamics and speed of the research fraud investigation have elicited expressions of muted concern, both within Japan and internationally, the director of the Centre for Stem Cells and Regenerative Medicine at King's College London, Professor Fiona Watt, for instance, saying: 'I'm outside this field but the whole process of the investigation and the conclusions have come out very quickly. I don't condone fraudulent research in any way, but I do think that senior scientists have a duty of care to their younger colleagues, and I hope that Dr Obokata will not be treated as a scapegoat.'[267] It is arguable that issues of hubris, gender, youth, and institutional protection contributed to the plummet from grace of Dr Obokata.

The fact that once again a leading journal had been duped by scholarly fraud was the subject of an editorial by *Nature* itself in July 2014 in the aftermath of the Obokata scandal. It lamented that conclusions in submitted papers can seem 'misleadingly robust'.[268] It noted that the problems can lie in sloppiness in the handling of data, the analysis of data, and inadequate keeping of laboratory notes, as well as in selection bias in the data presented. It acknowledged the escalation in the incidence of retractions in recent years and expressed

---

263 James Gallagher, 'Stem Cell Scandal Scientist Haruko Obokata Resigns', *BBC News*, 19 December 2014: <http://www.bbc.com/news/health-30534674> [accessed 22 Dec 2015].

264 'Obokata Returns STAP Cell Paper Publication Fees to Riken' (7 July 2015) *The Japan Times*: <http://www.japantimes.co.jp/news/2015/07/07/national/science-health/obokata-returns-stap-cell-paper-publication-fees-riken/#.Vbf7iUvy_7I> [accessed 22 Dec 2015].

265 Agence France-Presse, 'Embattled Japanese Researcher Haruko Obokata Says She Will Resign', *South China Morning Post*, 19 December 2014: <http://www.scmp.com/news/asia/article/1666498/embattled-japanese-researcher-haruko-obokata-says-she-will-resign> [accessed 22 Dec 2015].

266 Toko Sekigucki, 'STAP Cells "Likely Never Existed"', *The Wall Street Journal*, 26 December 2014: <http://www.wsj.com/articles/stap-cells-likely-never-existed-1419581151> [accessed 22 Dec 2015].

267 Ian Sample, 'Stem Cell Scientist Haruko Obokata Found Guilty of Misconduct', *The Guardian*, 2 April 2014: <http://www.theguardian.com/science/2014/apr/01/stem-cell-scientist-haruko-obokata-guilty-misconduct-committee> [accessed 22 Dec 2015].

268 Editorial, 'STAP Retracted' (2014) 511(7507) *Nature* 5, 6.

the somewhat forlorn aspiration that its 'addition of a checklist intended to improve the standards of reporting, and our use of statistical advisers' would reduce the problem in its journal.[269] Candidly, it commented:

> Although editors and referees could not have detected the fatal faults in this work, the episode has further highlighted flaws in *Nature*'s procedures and in the procedures of institutions that publish with us. We—research funders, research practitioners, institutions and journals—need to put quality assurance and laboratory professionalism ever higher on our agendas, to ensure that the money entrusted by governments is not squandered, and citizens' trust in science is not betrayed.[270]

The Obokata scandal saw the award, and then removal, of doctoral qualifications in questionable circumstances, and the collision of celebrity science, the potential for a highly lucrative research development, poor supervision, and over-ready assumption of collaborative kudos by co-authors, the failure once again of peer-review processes, and the retributive response of the scientific establishment against a young scientist guilty of both hubris and scholarly misconduct. The reputations of tertiary science in Japan, the scientist, her colleagues, the institution,[271] the oversighting mechanisms, the publishing journal and science itself were all seriously and tragically damaged. By 2015 Obokata's employer had turned on her irretrievably: it was seeking from her JPY600,000 in compensation for fees associated with the publication of her discredited research.[272]

Anna Ahimastos: Vascular Medicine

Until 2015 Dr Anna Ahimastos was a highly regarded post-doctoral Australian researcher who was employed by the Baker IDI Heart and Diabetes Institute in Melbourne, an independent 90-year-old medical research body focused on cardiovascular disease (including stroke and hypertension), diabetes, obesity, and their complications, such as kidney disease. In 2010, ironically, Ahimastos was named a 'Tall Poppy' as part of an Australian Institute of Policy and Science campaign to recognize scientific excellence. She was soon to be cut down. Her area of particular research interest was the potential for blood pressure medications, such as ramipril, an ACE inhibitor, to assist the ambulation without pain of patients with peripheral artery disease. A 2013 study published in the *Journal of the American Medical Association* (*JAMA*)[273] in which she was the lead author purported to be a randomized, double-blind, placebo-controlled trial conducted among 212 patients with peripheral artery disease between 2008 and 2011 in three Australian hospitals. The study noted that approximately 27 million people in Europe and North America have peripheral artery disease (PAD) and that intermittent claudication occurs in approximately one-third of such patients, typically presenting as pain within leg muscle groups that occurs during walking but relieved by rest. Patients with such claudication have significant impairment in ambulatory function, resulting in functional disability and important lifestyle limitation.

---

[269] Ibid.

[270] Ibid.

[271] Riken has announced that it proposes to 'change the center's name and cut its size in half': Martin, above n 262.

[272] See Mami Maruko, 'Riken to Ask Obokata for Y600,000 in Publishing Fees for Debunked Paper' (20 March 2015) *The Japan Times*: <http://www.japantimes.co.jp/news/2015/03/20/national/science-health/riken-to-ask-obokata-for-¥600000-in-publishing-fees-for-debunked-paper/#.VUdvtEvy_7I> [accessed 22 Dec 2015].

[273] Anna A Ahimastos, Philip J Walker, Christopher Askew et al. 'Effect of Ramipril on Walking Times and Quality of Life Among Patients With Peripheral Artery Disease and Intermittent Claudication: A Randomized Controlled Trial' (2015) 309(5) *Journal of the American Medical Association* 453; National Institute for Health and Care Excellence, 'Symptoms of Peripheral Arterial Disease: Ramipril' (June 2015): <https://www.nice.org.uk/advice/esuom45/chapter/full-evidence-summary> [accessed 22 Dec 2015].

The study purported to establish that for patients with intermittent claudication, 24-week treatment with ramipril resulted in significant increases in pain-free and maximum treadmill walking times compared with placebo. An outcome of the work by Ahimastos and her colleagues was change in management of PAD so that influential recommendations proposed prescription of ramipril for patients with PAD.[274]

However, in due course anomalies in Ahimastos' work were identified internally within the Institute. They resulted in the discovery that Ahimastos had fabricated data; this invalidated the results of the study. In September 2015 the *JAMA* retracted the 2013 article,[275] with the authors stating:

> A system of good clinical practice was in place; however, clinical governance and audit procedures will be reviewed and strengthened to minimize the chance of possible recurrence of such behavior. We are also in the process of examining other studies for which Dr Ahimastos had oversight of data collection and integrity.
>
> We sincerely regret that this study has been compromised. We feel deeply disappointed and let down by this situation and are committed to rapidly correcting the public record and implementing practices to prevent recurrence.[276]

The repercussions for other publications by the group and, more importantly, for patient treatment, remain to be evaluated.

Dr Virginia Barbour, the Chair of the Committee on Publication Ethics (COPE) and a Director of the World Association of Medical Editors (WAME), in the context of revelations about the Ahimastos fraud, was quoted by popular media as expressing concern about the pressures upon researchers to publish.[277] However, the Ahimastos case is more than a researcher succumbing to publication pressures. It is a further and troubling example of a researcher working on an important clinical area, which impacts on the well-being of very large numbers of patients, successfully duping a high-profile publisher. While it may be to the credit of Ahimastos' private sector (albeit government-funded) employer that it identified the error and took suitable remedial action, Australia's ramipril research fraud is another example of the potential for data falsification and manipulation to deceive and manipulate scholarly colleagues, as well as the peer-reviewing process, raising real risks for the evidence-based treatment of patients.

Flawed Research Fraud Investigations

In a number of cases research fraud inquiries have miscarried with confusion, multiplicity and unfair delay. In the United States the notorious Imanishi-Kari saga proved to be a catalyst for the institution of significant reform to investigative and oversight mechanisms. A similar impetus to reform occurred as a result of the unsatisfactory resolution to the investigations

274 See, eg, Thuy Bich Au, Jonathan Golledge, Philip J Walker, Kate Haigh, and Mark Nelson, 'Peripheral Arterial Disease: Diagnosis and Management in General Practice' (2013) 42(6) *Australian Family Physician* 397.

275 As did *Circulation Research* in relation to a further article: <http://circres.ahajournals.org/content/117/7/e64> [accessed 22 Dec 2015].

276 <http://jama.jamanetwork.com/article.aspx?articleid=2442406> [accessed 22 Dec 2015].

277 See Virginia Barbour, 'Publish or Perish Culture Encourages Scientists to Cut Corners' (12 October 2015) *Asian Scientist Magazine*: <http://www.asianscientist.com/2015/10/features/conversation-publish-perish-research-ethics/> [accessed 22 Dec 2015]; Sophie Scott and Alison Branley, 'High-profile Researcher Admits Fabricating Scientific Results Published in Major Journals' (17 September 2015) *ABC News*: <http://www.abc.net.au/news/2015-09-17/high-profile-researcher-admits-to-fabricating-scientific-results/6781958> [accessed 22 Dec 2015].

into the research conduct of Michael Briggs and Bruce Hall in Australia, while in the United Kingdom the problems with the Banerjee investigations also provided a fillip for institutional change.

The Imanishi-Kari Saga

One of the most troubling of sagas relating to concerns of suspected research fraud arose when Dr Margot O'Toole, a postdoctoral fellow, reviewed the laboratory notebook of Dr Thereza Imanishi-Kari, a researcher trained in Kyoto and an Assistant Professor at MIT's Centre for Cancer Research. Dr O'Toole formed the view that data on 17 of the notebook pages were inconsistent with data in a key paper published in *Cell* in 1986 by Dr Imanishi-Kari and five others about genes that regulate immune responses in mice.[278] The researchers had injected a mouse with a gene that altered its immune system so that it could produce antibodies against a given bacterium or virus, raising the possibility that the human immune system could similarly be modified to transform our capacity to fight off infections. The results challenged orthodox understanding of the operation of the immune system and included proposals for new approaches to the development of treatment diseases, such as immunodeficiency virus (HIV) and acquired immune deficiency syndrome (AIDS).

There was involvement for others who had been co-authors in the publication. In particular, David Baltimore, who had won the Nobel Prize for Medicine in 1975 and who was one of the most influential biomedical scientists in the United States, was promptly implicated. He suggested at a meeting with Dr O'Toole that she write to *Cell* outlining her different interpretation with his having a right of reply.[279] However, matters were not resolved[280] and Professor Baltimore felt obliged to resign as President of Rockefeller University in New York.

The allegations by Dr O'Toole led to hearings at both MIT and Tufts University, the institution to which Dr Imanishi-Kari had moved, after learning she would not be granted tenure at MIT. Each investigation found errors in the research methodology of Dr Imanishi-Kari, but not research misconduct.

In due course NIH constituted an investigative panel that exonerated Dr Imanishi-Kari of wrongdoing, concluding that the issues related to legitimate differences in research approach and data interpretation. It found some of her language misleading but that this was attributable to her non-English speaking background, and that she had not intended to deceive. Professor Baltimore asked NIH officials what they advised and was recommended to write to *Cell* to detail the infelicities in the paper. The authors did so, correcting the errors.[281]

However, two scientists at the NIH drew issues that troubled them to the attention of the chair of the Energy and Commerce Committee, the body that oversaw the budget for the NIH, headed by Democratic Congressman John Dingell. At this point the inquisitorial aspect of the political process intruded.

In the course of the hearings before Congressman Dingell, Baltimore lost his composure and somewhat petulantly alleged that the investigation represented a threat to scientific freedom.

---

[278] David Weaver, Moema H Reis, Christopher Albanese, Frank Constantini, David Baltimore, and Thereza Imanishi-Kari, 'Altered Repertoire of Endogenous Immunoglobulin Gene Expression in Transgenic Mice Containing a Rearranged Mu Heavy Chain Gene' (1986) 45(2) *Cell* 247, retracted by David Weaver, Christopher Albanese, Frank Constantini, and David Baltimore (1991) 65(4) *Cell* 536.

[279] See Daniel J Kevles, *The Baltimore Case: A Trial of Politics, Science and Character* (New York: WW Norton & Co, 1998).

[280] Ibid, 239.

[281] Ibid, 163.

He implied that scientists had the right to monitor themselves, because it was only they who were able to understand how science works.[282]

A consequence of the hearing was that Congressman Dingell formed the view that the various investigations to that point had been inadequate and brought in the Secret Service to examine the notebooks of Dr Imanishi-Kari. It concluded that she had tampered with data that she had submitted in support of her defence. This in turn resulted in involvement by the Office of Scientific Integrity (OSI), the fraud unit of the NIH, which accused Dr Imanishi-Kari of falsifying data and proposed that she be precluded from receiving research grants for ten years. In the midst of controversy about its processes, the OSI was reconstituted in 1992 into the Office of Research Integrity (ORI). In 1994 (more than eight years after Dr O'Toole had first raised her concerns) the ORI issued a report upholding the OSI's findings. This propelled Professor Baltimore and colleagues into a withdrawal of their article.

However, an appeals board in 1996 (consisting of two experienced lawyers) found Dr Imanishi-Kari not guilty of all matters that the ORI had found against her. It found much of the ORI's case irrelevant, adding that it was 'internally inconsistent, lacked reliability or foundation, was not credible or corroborated, or was based on unwarranted assumptions'.[283] It broadcast a warning about the way in which the allegations of whistleblowers should be used:

> While we share others' concern that a 'whistleblower' be protected from adverse consequences, we are also concerned about the implications of involving a whistleblower too heavily in an investigation. Such involvement can compromise both the ability of the investigators to maintain objectivity and the ability of the whistleblower to avoid becoming too invested in the outcome. We think that happened here.[284]

Baltimore pronounced the decision 'a victory for science and rational analysis' and commented that the 'sad thing is that it took two judges and a retired scientist to undo the work of a 'scientific' office', referring to the findings against Imanishi-Kari by the ORI, which the federal ruling panel rejected.[285]

In turn this had ramifications for David Baltimore who was seen by himself and many others as having been vindicated. He was elected President of the California Institute of Technology in Pasadena and then in 2006 President of the American Association for the Advancement of Science. Dr Imanishi-Kari was reinstated as a staff member at Tufts University and the National Institutes of Health awarded her a grant to assist women who were re-entering science after having taken time off. In 1997 she was promoted to Associate Professor.

As Reich[286] put it: 'The message that many scientists took away from this case is that it is risky and unethical to go public with a fraud allegation because of the possibility of smearing an innocent person and of provoking a political backlash against science.' The case and its significance remain controversial.[287] Historian Roy Porter summed up one view by asking: 'We all wish to avoid a science police, but can we really rely on the internal dynamics of science to root out frauds and fakes? In our culture of suspicion and complaint, that is a question

[282] Roy Porter, 'The Science Police', *The New York Times*, 20 September 1998: <http://www.nytimes.com/books/98/09/20/reviews/980920.20portert.html> [accessed 22 Dec 2015].

[283] Shane Crotty, *Ahead of the Curve: David Baltimore's Life in Science* (Berkeley: University of California Press, 2001), 201. See Kathleen Fackelmann, 'Appeals Panel Reverses Fraud Ruling' (1996) 150(1) *Science News* 4; Judson, above n 106, 191–243; Kevles, above n 279, ch 17.

[284] Appeal Panel Decision, 21 June 1996, 168, quoted in Kevles, above n 279, 375.

[285] Stacey E Blau, 'Panel Clears MIT Scientist of Fraud: Imanishi-Kari, Baltimore Vindicated', *The Tech*, 116(28), 26 June 1996: <http://tech.mit.edu/V116/N28/baltimore.28n.html> [accessed 22 Dec 2015].

[286] Reich, above n 44, 188.

[287] See eg, Kevles, above n 279; Judson, above n 106.

that cannot be ducked.'[288] On any view of the lengthy matter, though, the Imanishi-Kari saga constitutes a warning for how a resolution to allegations of research fraud needs to be arrived at authoritatively and promptly without the contamination and unfairness occasioned by a multiplicity of inquiries and the complexities introduced by the intrusion of the political process, as well as where whistleblowers play too great a role in driving an outcome.

The Michael Briggs Fraud

In the 1980s the side-effects of the new generation of contraceptive pills were controversial and contested. A British scientist who had been the Professor of Human Biology and Head of the Sciences School at Victoria's Deakin University, Michael Briggs, 'purported to assess possible risks of heart and arterial disease in women after prolonged use of the pill',[289] focusing on changes in fats in the blood-lipids. His research gave rise to the most important review of such risks published to that time. It was extensively relied on by pharmaceutical companies which marketed contraceptive pills. Schering AG of West Germany and Wyeth from the United States financed much of Professor Briggs's research. A number of products, such as Logynon and Trinordial in Britain and TriLevlen and Priphasil in the United States, were granted licences on the basis of Briggs's work over more than a decade.

On the basis of rumours about the integrity of Professor Briggs's research, the chairperson of the Ethics Committee of Deakin University in Victoria, Australia, Dr Jim Rossiter, wrote to him in 1983, raising issues about his methodology and research practices. He was not satisfied with Briggs's response and made a formal complaint to Deakin University's Vice-Chancellor who set up a preliminary committee to assess whether charges should be laid. Professor Briggs opposed this and sought an injunction from the Victorian Supreme Court to prevent the committee undertaking the task. Ultimately, the inquiry was halted on the instruction of the University Visitor, Sir Brian Murray, Governor of Victoria, who ruled that the Vice-Chancellor had failed to establish that there was a prima facie case before initiating an inquiry. The decision was not readily amenable to appeal.[290]

However, matters did not conclude at this point. As is often the case with allegations of scholarly fraud and misconduct, too much momentum had been built up. In 1985, a new inquiry was instituted on receipt of a further formal complaint by Rossiter and two other scientists. It included new material.

Shortly afterwards, Briggs resigned and the university inquiry was thereupon terminated. He retired to Marbella in the Costa del Sol. When very unwell, he was interviewed by *The Sunday Times* and admitted that he had:

- pretended to have organized studies of the effects of oral contraceptives which he had not done. He said the studies had been organized by someone else, but declined to name this person.
- produced a study on animals which he had never done. This study, on beagle bitches, later helped persuade the British government that arrangements which previously delayed the granting of licenses were no longer necessary.
- included in scientific papers complex biochemical test results, the origins of which he could not name. In relation to one paper, he said, he was unaware even of the country in which the analyses were purported to have been done.[291]

---

288 Porter, above n 282.

289 See Brian Deer, 'The Pill: Professor's Safety Tests Were Faked', *The Sunday Times*, 28 September 1986, available at: <http://briandeer.com/social/medical-fraud.htm> [accessed 22 Dec 2015].

290 Brian Martin, 'Fraud and Australian Academics' (1989) 5(2) *Thought and Action* 95, available at: <http://www.bmartin.cc/pubs/89ta.html> [accessed 22 Dec 2015].

291 Deer, above n 289.

Shortly afterwards, in 1986 he died of natural causes.

Just before Briggs died, though, Deakin University set up yet another inquiry into all aspects of Briggs's conduct, designed to establish whether the researcher's co-workers had been implicated and potentially to rehabilitate Deakin University's research reputation which by that time had been seriously damaged. In 1987 the committee reported that data in some of Briggs's publications had been fabricated. As was later to occur with the Stapel Committees, it exonerated the perpetrator's collaborators at Deakin University.[292] The Briggs saga constitutes a serious indictment of Australia's investigative processes when serious allegations of research misconduct are raised within universities.

The Bruce Hall Saga

One of Australia's most notorious instances of the making of allegations of scientific fraud concerned Professor Bruce Hall. Its troubled history, the multiplicity of inquiries which it generated (18 in all, as well as multiple court hearings), and its cost (estimated in 2006 as possibly AUS$10 million[293]), like the Imanishi-Kara saga, played a significant role in promoting important reform in the mechanisms for investigation of allegations of research fraud in Australia.

Hall was a nephrologist. His area of research involved suppressor cells in the immunology of rejection and tolerance in transplanted organs. Over his career he contested a series of accepted immunological dogmas, variously attracting the ridicule and antagonism of many traditional immunologists.

In 2001 whistleblowers from within Professor Hall's laboratory raised more than 450 separate allegations against Hall, including complaints of scientific fraud, financial fraud, workplace bullying, and incorrect attribution of articles.[294]

In April 2002 Dr Norman Swan on the Australian Broadcasting Commission (ABC) Radio National's *Science Show* revealed details of the complaints against Professor Hall, and discussed them with the complainants.[295] In due course Swan's broadcasts became the subject of successful actions by Hall and his wife for defamation.

Inquiries were constituted by the University of New South Wales. In 2003 it released the outcomes of two parallel internal inquiries by Professor Bruce Dowton, Dean of the Faculty of Medicine, who carried out an initial investigation of the complaints, and another by Professor Elspeth McLachlan, the Pro-Vice-Chancellor (Research), whose focus of inquiry was on complaints made to the National Health and Medical Research Council (NHMRC). The outcomes were broadly similar in that unsatisfactory conditions and relationships were identified at Professor Hall's laboratory but no conclusive evidence of scientific misconduct or fraud.

The inconclusive aspect of these outcomes led to the establishment of an external inquiry to address the allegations of scientific misconduct and fraud as defined by the NHMRC and the Australian Vice-Chancellors Committee (AVCC). It was constituted by Sir Gerard Brennan, previously a Chief Justice of the High Court of Australia (chair); Professor John Chalmers of

292 Martin, above n 290.

293 Margaret Rice, 'A Call for Integrity in the Fish Bowl', *The Sydney Morning Herald*, 22 December 2006: <http://www.smh.com.au/news/national/a-call-for-integrity-in-the-goldfish-bowl/2006/12/21/1166290677344.html> [accessed 22 Dec 2015].

294 The following summary draws upon Rice, above n 293.

295 For a transcript of the broadcasts, see *Hall v Swan* [2009] NSWCA 371.

the University of Sydney; Sir David Weatherall of Oxford University; and Professor Judith Whitworth of the Australian National University.

In January 2003 the report of what became known as the Brennan Inquiry was received by the University. Thereafter Hall argued that, without powers to cross-examine, the Brennan report could not find out whether the allegations made by the whistleblowers were mischievous or based on false information. He asserted that the Brennan report incorrectly quoted him and was precious in its description of written reports, poor management in the laboratory, and poor communication between workers.

The University Council decided at first not to release the report and then reversed its decision and then determined to order release of a redacted version. That prompted an application by lawyers acting on behalf of Professor Hall for an injunction.[296] They were unsuccessful.

Pursuant to the University's Enterprise Agreement it was then necessary for it to consider whether the Brennan report gave rise to allegations of misconduct or serious misconduct as defined by the Agreement and, if so, whether such allegations could be 'resolved through guidance, counselling, conciliation or other appropriate action'. A report on the subject was provided to the Vice-Chancellor and on the basis of that, and the Brennan Report, 23 matters relevant to the determination were identified. Professor Hall was given an opportunity to respond. At the conclusion of that process, a decision was made that in relation to six matters there had been no misconduct or serious misconduct, and with respect to the remaining six the evidence was inconclusive. Professor Hall elected to have the remaining six matters referred directly to the Vice-Chancellor, Rory Hume, who investigated them and concluded that:

> *Allegation 1:* A paper that was submitted or authorised to be submitted contained data and statements for which there were no supporting experiments.
>
> *Finding:* Professor Hall was not guilty under the Enterprise Agreement. Rather he had committed an error of omission reflecting the pressure of mitigating circumstances.
>
> *Allegation 2:* A grant application by Professor Hall contained a figure with a conclusion 'all differences are significant at $P < 0.05$', but omitted relevant facts.
>
> *Finding:* Guilty of misconduct, but, given the mitigating circumstances and the Vice-Chancellor's belief that grant proposals are preliminary data yet to be validated and that there was no intention to deliberately deceive, he deemed the transgression to be minor and warranting no further action.
>
> *Allegation 3:* A grant application by Professor Hall contained a statement when no experiments to support the statement were ever done in Hall's laboratory or in the laboratory of any other author of the grant application. *Finding:* Guilty of misconduct despite the mitigating circumstances. Hall was censured.
>
> *Allegation 4:* Failure to notify the granting body of the details once the absence of the experiments outlined in Allegation 3 became apparent. *Finding:* Guilty of misconduct warranting censure. However, Professor Hall's lack of action did not demonstrate an intention to deceive.
>
> *Allegation 5:* The publication of an abstract which contained a statement for which no experiments were performed in Hall's laboratory.
>
> *Finding:* Guilty of misconduct in failing to take reasonable steps to ensure that the abstract was accurate, but, in view of mitigating circumstances, including the Vice-Chancellor's view

[296] In *Hall v University of New South Wales*, unreported, Supreme Court of New South Wales 25 February 2003 Levine J issued an interim injunction. However, in *Hall v University of New South Wales* [2003] NSWSC 669 McClellan J declined to issue a final injunction.

that 'abstracts have very little potential to damage the fabric of science,' along with the premise that individuals' interpretations of the abstracts differ, no further action was taken.

Allegation 6: That Professor Hall must accept the main responsibility for allowing a substantial degree of procedural laxity in his laboratory at Liverpool Hospital. Here, there were mitigating circumstances against a background of a complex research laboratory and Hall's need to supervise a busy clinical service and a teaching program.

Finding: Guilty of misconduct. Hall was advised of his error of judgement, but, given the circumstances, no further action was taken.[297]

The Vice-Chancellor concluded that Professor Hall was not guilty of scientific misconduct, but rather of having committed errors of judgment that were deserving of censure but not dismissal. Upon the release of the Vice-Chancellor's findings, a noted immunologist referred to the allegations against Hall as 'much ado about nothing'.[298]

In September 2006 the Australian Communications and Media Authority concluded an investigation into Swan's 2005 *Science Show*, finding that the ABC had failed to comply with three of the ABC's codes of conduct because it did not make every reasonable effort to ensure that the factual content of the programme was accurate and balanced (as well as that it had not responded within 60 days of receiving a complaint about the report).

Suzanne Hodgkinson, Director of Neurology at Liverpool Hospital and a medical scientist and also a researcher in her own right, as well as Professor Hall's wife, sued for defamation in relation to statements made by Norman Swan's 2002 programmes. She was successful.

Professor Hall also sued in defamation, alleging that Swan's programme involved 12 defamatory imputations that Hall:

(a) exploited Ms Hong Ha, a PHD (*sic*) student, for free labour;
(b) in April 2001 fraudulently presented two experiments which were never done to the Transplantation Society of Australia and New Zealand's Annual Conference;
(c) gave an opinion on the actual treatment of transplant patients at the Transplantation Society of Australia and New Zealand's Annual Conference which he knew was based on fraudulently misrepresented animal data;
(d) committed scientific fraud by intentionally submitting a paper containing fabricated experiments to the Journal of Experimental Medicine;
(e) committed scientific fraud by intentionally submitting papers to two journals, which passed off as new findings, findings that Hall had already published;
(f) fraudulently misrepresented data from an experiment in a grant application to the National Health and Medical Research Council by not disclosing that two repeat experiments failed to replicate the original findings;
(g) committed scientific misconduct by deliberately misrepresenting in his CV annexed to a National Health and Medical Research Council grant application that he had a significant role in the authorship of two papers when he had the least significant role;
(h) dishonestly removed Hong Ha's name from two scientific papers when she was entitled to authorship of those papers;
(i) committed scientific fraud by including his wife's name as an author on scientific papers when his wife had no involvement in the preparation of the papers;
(j) fraudulently claimed in a letter written in relation to a patent dispute that his wife deserved credit for transplantation immunology work that was actually done by Dr Clara He;

---

[297] Martin B Van Der Weyden, 'Managing Allegations of Scientific Misconduct and Fraud: Lessons from the "Hall Affair"' (2004) 180(4) *Medical Journal of Australia* 149, 150 (Footnotes omitted).

[298] Ibid.

(k) fraudulently subsidised his wife's laboratory out of his National Health and Medical Research Council grant; [and]
(l) fraudulently transferred $46,000 from Dr Clara He's National Health and Medical Research Council research grant to cover his own research assistant.[299]

After a deliberation of less than three and a half hours the Supreme Court jury made findings against Professor Hall. However, this was not the end of the legal disputation.

Hall appealed to the New South Wales Court of Appeal[300] where he was successful. The Court concluded that: '[I]t was not rational for the jury to conclude, if that is what it did, that the broadcast conveyed only a call for an investigation. It would have been rational to conclude that the broadcast included a call that 'at the very minimum' there should be an independent inquiry, but not to the exclusion of conveying any of the imputations.'[301] It found that:

> The appellant was working as a scientist and was a Professor of Medicine at the University of New South Wales and at the Liverpool Hospital. It is difficult to comprehend more serious claims against a scientist, in a professional sense, than the claims of scientific fraud, scientific misconduct and fraudulent use of scientific grants. The only rational answer to the questions as to whether these imputations are defamatory is 'yes'. No reasonable jury, properly directed, could answer these questions in the negative.[302]

After the case was returned to the Supreme Court, it was settled, with the ABC paying all costs including more than AUS$1 million in Hall's legal fees.[303] In a statement read to the court in 2014, the ABC stated that it 'regreted' any overshadowing of Professor Hall's major research achievements on immune tolerance and the effects of the broadcast on his ongoing research.'[304] As of the second half of 2015 Professor Hall continued to work at the South Western Sydney Clinical School of the University of New South Wales and continued to undertake research into the cellular mechanisms of the immune response to transplanted tissues.

Martin Van Der Weyden, editor of the *Medical Journal of Australia*, has argued that multiple lessons should be learned from the Hall saga, including that:

> allegations of serious scientific misconduct should be dealt with from the start by an external and independent inquiry; the inquiry should have statutory power to investigate and inquire; the inquiry should have sufficient scientific expertise to ensure credibility; to preserve public confidence, the inquiry should aim for the highest degree of transparency and accessibility of the final report; there is a need for uniform processes and procedures for dealing with and adjudicating on scientific research; [and] fraud and there is a need to shift the emphasis from managing misconduct and fraud to preventing them.[305]

---

[299] *Hall v Swan* [2009] NSWCA 371, [6] ('the plaintiff' omitted from the start of each listed claim).
[300] Ibid.
[301] Ibid, [49].
[302] Ibid, [100].
[303] See Paul Sheehan, 'ABC Management Finds Sorry is the Hardest Word' (6 March 2014) *The Age*: <http://www.theage.com.au/comment/abc-management-finds-sorry-is-the-hardest-word-20140305-347fc.html> [accessed 22 Dec 2015].
[304] Sally Jackson, 'ABC Settles Science Show Defamation Suit Brought by Bruce Hall', *The Australian*, 4 March 2014: <http://www.theaustralian.com.au/business/media/abc-settles-science-show-defamation-suit-brought-by-bruce-hall/story-e6frg996-1226844862688?nk=ccceefd37d166846fd531480b86526eb> [accessed 22 Dec 2015]. See too, Jeremy R Chapman, Geoffrey W McCaughan, and Philip O'Connell, 'Professor Bruce Hall and the ABC' (2014) 201(6) *Medical Journal of Australia* 322.
[305] Martin Van Der Weyden, 'Preventing and Processing Research Misconduct: A New Australian Code for Responsible Research' (2006) 184(9) *Medical Journal of Australia* 430, 430 (formatting altered).

He contended that a national body should be established to oversee and evaluate the handling of research misconduct. Hall himself agreed.[306] Whether the involvement of the courts in the Hall saga was constructive is open to real doubt. An outcome of the Hall matter was an impetus towards establishing the Australian Research Integrity Committee to oversee universities' investigations into research misconduct (see below, p 162). It should also be consciousness that processes which depend upon resolution of allegations of research fraud which are not independent of the institution in respect of which allegations are made run the risk of failing to command the respect which is necessary for confidence in the integrity of the investigative process.

The Banerjee Frauds

The difficulties with the multiple investigations into the fraudulent conduct of Mr Anjan Banerjee are described below in the section dealing with disciplinary sanction (see below, p 139).

Criminal Prosecutions

Concerns about the extent and ramifications of research fraud have been building for some years. Redman and Merz,[307] for instance, identified from public records all investigators holding degrees which they had completed who had been found guilty of research misconduct by the United States Office of Research Integrity between 1994 and December 2001. Thirty six had been found guilty of falsification or fabrication, 10 plagiarism and 12 of misrepresentation. Seventeen scientists had committed only the one infraction while 26 had committed multiple breaches. All 43 had been excluded from Public Health Service advisory boards (for a mean of 3.5 years), 30 had been debarred from Public Health Service grants and contracts (for a mean of 3.4 years), 230 had been subjected to institutional oversight (for a mean of 3.2 years), and 14 were required to retract or correct papers. The study found a significant reduction in publication by the persons concerned with 12 individuals publishing nothing after the finding of misconduct. Nonetheless most reported that they had recovered or maintained useful scientific lives after the initial damage to their reputations. Forty-three percent of academic scientists whom they could trace remained employed in academia after being found guilty of misconduct and 19 of the 37 continued to publish at least one scholarly paper per year. Redman and Merz observed that the picture of the consequences painted by their investigations was that 'both the hardship of punishment and the chance for redemption, is perhaps more positive than it should be.'

An outcome of the concern about the incidence and recidivism of scientific fraud had been the giving of serious consideration to invocation of the criminal law to act as a deterrent. In 1991 in the aftermath of the Breuning case (p 115), Susan Kuzma of the United States Department of Justice, for instance, argued that '[u]npleasant and unsettling as it is to contemplate, criminal prosecution can serve a valuable role in deterring and condemning some forms of scientific misconduct and therefore should not be rejected in favour of internal controls'.[308]

[306] Bruce M Hall, 'Australia Needs an Office of Academic Integrity' (2006) 185 (11–12) *Medical Journal of Australia* 619; Rice, above n 293.

[307] Barbara K Redman and Jon F Merz, 'Scientific Misconduct: Do the Punishments Fit the Crime?' (2008) 321(5890) *Science* 775, 775.

[308] Susan M Kuzma, 'Criminal Liability for Misconduct in Scientific Research' (1991–1992) 25(2) *University of Michigan Journal of Law Reform* 357, 357. See too Benjamin K Sovakool, 'Using Criminalization and Due Process to Reduce Scientific Misconduct' (2005) 5(5) *American Journal of Bioethics* W1.

In 2000 Professor Alexander McCall Smith, then a Professor of Law and Medical Ethics at the University of Edinburgh, addressed a summit on research misconduct and argued that such conduct should be criminalized. By 2013 an editorial in *Nature* argued in favour of the relevance of the criminal law for research fraud:

> Science likes to shelter its crooks with euphemisms. The prefix 'research' softens fraud, and to deliberately obtain public money through deception gets labelled misconduct, among other things. This reflects the fact that the crime is viewed as being against professional standards rather than against the laws of wider society... At the very least, academic investigators could learn from police methods for dealing with allegations of serious misconduct... And researchers might be less tempted to be cavalier with the truth—and with our money—if they knew who else could knock on their door.[309]

Richard Smith, a former editor of the *British Medical Journal*, has argued that the incidence of scientific fraud has reached a point where it is failing the public and it is time to criminalize research fraud.[310] In 2014 the *Medical Journal of Australia* polled its readers, asking: 'Should medical research fraud be treated as a criminal offence?' Seventy three percent of respondents replied in the affirmative, with 23 per cent saying 'Maybe' and just 4 per cent asserting that it should not be treated as criminal conduct.[311] The *Wall Street Journal* did the same (also in 2014) with even more emphatic results: 92.6 per cent of the votes (n=258) were in favour of use of criminal charges.[312]

In Canada Professor Zulfiquar Bhutta, Co-Director of the Centre for Global Child Health at Toronto's Hospital for Sick Children maintained in 2014 that: '[W]hen somebody is determined to commit something like this and does, and if it is brought to light, then I think the full weight of law needs to come on that person... Individuals generally get off with just a slap on the wrist at the time and at the most a dismissal from service.'[313] However, the issue remains controversial and Professor Julian Crane, the Director of the Wellington Asthma Research Group at the Wellington School of Medicine at the University of Otago in New Zealand, has contended that the research system should place its emphasis on a collaborative approach rather than criminalization: 'Criminalizing research misconduct is a sad, bad, even mad idea that will only undermine the trust that is an essential component of research and requires good governance not criminal investigators'.[314]

In a series of high-profile cases, in the United States, the United Kingdom, Korea, and Australia, research scholars who have been alleged to have engaged in fraud have been criminally prosecuted in recent years. As set out in Chapter 6, a high-profile French researcher

---

309 Editorial, 'Call the Cops' (2013) 504(7478) *Nature*: <http://www.nature.com/news/call-the-cops-1.14288> [accessed 22 Dec 2015].

310 Richard Smith, 'Should Scientific Fraud Be a Criminal Offence?' on *The BMJ* (BMJ Blogs) (9 December 2013): <http://blogs.bmj.com/bmj/2013/12/09/richard-smith-should-scientific-fraud-be-a-criminal-offence/> [accessed 22 Dec 2015]. See also, Adam Marcus and Ivan Oransky, 'Commit Fraud, Go to Jail?' (2014) *Labtimes*: <http://labtimes.org/labtimes/ranking/dont/2014_01.lasso> [accessed 22 Dec 2015]; see also, L Song Richardson, 'When Human Experimentation is Criminal' (2009) 99(1) *The Journal of Criminal Law and Criminology* 89; Ian Freckelton, 'Criminalising Research Fraud' (2014) 22(2) *Journal of Law and Medicine* 241.

311 'In Brief—MJA Insight Poll' (2014) 201(7) *Medical Journal of Australia* 373.

312 See Ed Silverman, 'Should Research Fraud be a Crime? A Reader Poll', *The Wall Street Journal*, 16 July 2014: <http://blogs.wsj.com/pharmalot/2014/07/16/should-research-fraud-be-a-crime-a-reader-poll/> [accessed 22 Dec 2015].

313 See Helen Branswell, 'Should Research Fraud be Treated as a Crime? Toronto Expert Says Yes', *The Hamilton Spectator*, 15 July 2014: <http://www.thespec.com/news-story/4633340-should-research-fraud-be-treated-as-a-crime-toronto-expert-says-yes/> [accessed 22 Dec 2015].

314 Ibid. See also, Zulfiqar A Bhutta and Julian Crane, 'Should Research Fraud be a Crime?' (2014) 349(7969) *The BMJ* g4532.

(Professor Michel Sixou) who engaged in plagiarism has also found himself subject to the criminal process.[315]

Stephen Breuning

During the 1980s the psychologist, Dr Stephen Breuning, was one of the United States' most prominent researchers in the field of treatment of mental retardation.[316] He was employed by the University of Pittsburgh. He was particularly known for his work in relation to the use of Ritalin and Dexadrine for treating Attention Deficit Hyperactivity Disorder (ADHD).[317] In 1983 Professor Robert L Sprague, a Professor of Psychology at the University of Illinois, was informed by a young colleague that Dr Breuning was obtaining perfect agreement among nurses in their independent ratings of tardive dyskinesia movements of patients being prescribed medication when this was highly unlikely.[318] Professor Sprague undertook his own investigations and found that an abstract that Dr Breuning had submitted for a symposium on tardive dyskinesia, claiming to have examined 45 patients, was almost certainly faked. He identified that a number of aspects of Dr Breuning's research in relation to tranquilliser medication for intellectually disabled children had been falsified. This led him to report his concerns to the National Institute of Mental Health (NIMH), which referred the issues to the University of Pittsburgh.

When confronted with the concerns of Professor Sprague, Dr Breuning made some admissions to falsification of a report, and resigned from the faculty. As the conduct in respect of the study related to work done before Dr Breuning had joined the university, the University investigative committee that had been convened concluded that it did not have jurisdiction over the matter.[319]

However, Professor Sprague declined to let the matter rest and agitated with the NIMH itself to investigate the conduct of Dr Breuning on the basis that it was the body that had funded much of Dr Breuning's research. In February 1985 the NIMH agreed and appointed an expert review panel.[320] In 1986 the panel concluded that Dr Breuning engaged in 'serious scientific misconduct' in that he 'knowingly, willfully, and repeatedly engaged in misleading and deceptive practices in reporting results of research'. Although his studies were supposedly based on research involving thousands of subjects, it concluded that 'only a few of the experimental subjects described in publications and progress reports were ever studied'.[321] The

---

315 See Frédéric Dessort, 'Plagiat: Une Universitaire Toulousaine Condamnée au Pénal', *EducPros.fr*, 7 January 2014: <http://www.letudiant.fr/educpros/actualite/universite-plagiat-christine-marchal-sixou-une-universitaire-toulousaine-condamnee-au-penal.html> [accessed 22 Dec 2015].

316 See Philip M Boffey, 'US Study Finds Fraud in Top Researcher's Work on Mentally Retarded', *The New York Times*, 24 May 1987: <http://www.nytimes.com/1987/05/24/us/us-study-finds-fraud-in-top-researcher-s-work-onmentally-retarded.html> [accessed 22 Dec 2015].

317 See Janny Scott, 'Researcher Admits Faking Data to Get $160,000 in Funds', *Los Angeles Times*, 20 September 1988: <http://articles.latimes.com/1988-09-20/news/mn-2318_1_research-fraud> [accessed 22 Dec 2015].

318 See Allan J Kimmel, *Ethical Issues in Behavioral Research: Basic and Applied Perspectives* (2nd edn, Oxford: Blackwell Publishing, 2007) 303.

319 See Michael Lewis, *Poisoning the Ivy: The Seven Deadly Sins and Other Vices of Higher Education in America* (New York: ME Sharpe, 1997), 132.

320 Consisting of Dr Arnold Friedhof, Professor of Psychiatry at the New York University School of Medicine; Dr C Keith Conners, Director of Psychiatric Research at the Children's Hospital National Medical Center in Washington; Dr Richard Shader, Chairman of Psychiatry at Tufts University School of Medicine; Dr Herbery Vaughan Jr, Professor of Neuroscience at the Albert Einstein College of Medicine; and Dr Edward Zigler, Professor of Psychology at Yale University.

321 Boffey, above n 316.

panel commented that its work was 'complicated by Dr. Breuning's shifting and often contradictory explanations' of where various studies were said to have been carried out.[322]

As a result of the panel report, the Federal Alcohol, Drug Abuse and Mental Health Administration recommended that Dr Breuning be banned from receiving grants or contracts from funders for ten years. It also recommended that the Justice Department prosecute Dr Breuning. Dr Breuning's response was to denounce the panel review as no more than a 'shoddy investigation' and to maintain that the findings on which he had reported had not been disproved and that other scientists had reproduced some of them.[323]

However, matters went further and Dr Breuning was charged with two counts of filing false information on a research grant application. He pleaded guilty before the District Court of Maryland and was sentenced to 60 days in a halfway house, five years of probation, 250 hours of community service, repayment of US$11,352, and to abstain from psychological research for the period of his probation.[324] He agreed not to undertake any work as a psychologist for at least ten years. However, for a concerning period of time fear of legal action inhibited efforts to record retractions of Dr Breuning's fraudulent research in prominent journals and thereby to curtail the influence of his spurious research.[325]

A co-author of Dr Breuning, Dr Alan Poling, reflected later on the ramifications of the Breuning frauds (of which he had been unaware at the time of their commission).[326] He started from the proposition that '[f]raud compromises science in every regard'[327] and mused: 'I wonder what the outcome would have been in the absence of a Robert Sprague.'[328] He expressed concern that clinical decisions about the pharmacological treatment of retarded children may have been based on Dr Breuning's fraudulent data[329] and declaimed:

> A scientist who engages in fraudulent practices is not guilty of petty mischief that results in personal gain but harms no one. Fraud destroys the very fabric of science, and its consequences are as egregious as enduring. For these reasons, legitimate scientists must recognise fraud for the serious problem that it is. They must also be willing to confront it at the level of specific cases and general issues.[330]

Eric Poehlman

A United States researcher who was sentenced to actual jail time for research fraud was Eric Poehlman, a physiologist from the University of Vermont, who published prolifically for two decades in the fields of human obesity and ageing. His sentencing by Judge William Sessions III in 2006[331] constituted a landmark in the regulation of research fraud by the law.

---

322 Ibid.

323 Ibid.

324 See Gregory Byrne, 'Breuning Sentenced' (1988) 242(4881) *Science* 1004; Mohammad Salhab, 'A History of Fraud and Deceit in Medical Research' (2010) 5(1) *Surgery Journal* 1; Daniel S Greenberg, 'Issue of Scientific Fraud Not Easily Faced' (16 August 1989) *Chicago Tribune*: <http://articles.chicagotribune.com/1989-08-16/news/8901050101_1_stephen-e-breuning-federal-charges-nimh> [accessed 22 Dec 2015].

325 See AJ Hostetler, 'Fear of Suits Blocks Retractions', *The Scientist*, 19 October 1987: <http://www.the-scientist.com/?articles.view/articleNo/9012/title/Fear-of-Suits-Blocks-Retractions/> [accessed 22 Dec 2015].

326 Poling, above n 94, 140–57.

327 Ibid, 141.

328 Ibid, 142.

329 See also, Eugene Garfield and Alfred Welljams-Dorof, 'The Impact of Fraudulent Research on the Scientific Literature: The Stephen E Breuning Case' (1990) 263(10) *The Journal of the American Medical Association* 1424; Salhab, above n 324.

330 Poling, above n 94, 154.

331 See Rex Dalton, 'Obesity Expert Owns Up to Million-Dollar Crime' (2005) 434(7032) *Nature* 424.

Poehlman's exposure began in the autumn of 2000 when a 24-year-old research technician, Walter DeNino, who had graduated with a double major in nutritional sciences and dietetics, was comparing measurements in patient data taken several years apart and provided to him by Poehlman in relation to how fat lipids in the blood change with age. Poehlman anticipated that the data would show an increase in low density lipoprotein which deposits cholesterol in arteries, and show a decrease in high density lipoprotein which carries it to the liver for breakdown. However, a first run through of the data by Poehlman did not support the research hypothesis.[332]

Poehlman took the electronic data home and returned them to DeNino the next week explaining that he had corrected some mistaken entries and asked DeNino to run another statistical analysis. The trend reversed but when DeNino compared the two sets of data the changes in patient data all supported Poehlman's hypothesis for no apparent reason. When DeNino confronted Poehlman about the discrepancies and asked to see the patient files to check the integrity of the results, Poehlman dismissed his concerns.

DeNino contacted a postdoctoral fellow who had also worked for Poehlman and had had similar experiences and been implicitly threatened with the loss of his job if he continued to raise the issues. After further investigations confirmed his concerns, DeNino approached the University of Vermont's general counsel and lodged a formal allegation of scientific misconduct. Unfortunately for all concerned, it took six years to resolve, with Poehlman in his first written response suggesting that there were difficulties with his data but that these were attributable to errors brought about by handling by multiple technicians and postdoctoral students over the years. When he appeared before an investigative panel, he claimed to be inept with Excel files, accused persons such as DeNino of plotting against him and maintained that DeNino had examined data that were merely imputed and not the actual data. When the university proceeded from an investigative panel to a formal investigation, Poehlman sought an injunction from the courts to stop it, attempting to impugn the credibility of DeNino by suggesting that DeNino was homophobic and anti-gay.[333]

The formal investigation by the University of Vermont in 2001,[334] oversighted by the Office of Research Integrity of the United States Department of Health and Human Services,[335] established that the concerns raised by DeNino were justified. It found that Dr Poehlman fabricated data as part of a longitudinal study of ageing and projects in respect of transitions to menopause, hormone replacement therapy, and weight loss. It concluded that, in each instance, 'Poehlman has committed scientific misconduct for the purpose of placing into the scientific literature results that, although unsupported by research, would be consistent with his theories of age-related deterioration, likely to enhance his reputation, and likely to yield him further opportunities for publication and grant funding'.[336] Ultimately, Dr Poehlman admitted falsifying 17 federal grant applications, in relation to which the NIH and the US Department of Agriculture (USDA) expended nearly US$3 million in research funding. He conceded 'falsifying and fabricating' data in ten journal articles published between 1992 and

332 Jeneen Interlandi, 'An Unwelcome Discovery', *The New York Times*, 22 October 2006: <http://www.nytimes.com/2006/10/22/magazine/22sciencefraud.html?pagewanted=all&_r=0> [accessed 22 Dec 2015].

333 Ibid.

334 The University of Vermont College of Medicine, Office of the Dean, 'Investigation Report: In the Matter of Eric T Poehlman', 18 April 2002, available at: <http://www.ori.dhhs.gov/sites/default/files/uvm_report.pdf> [accessed 22 Dec 2015].

335 John E Dahlberg and Christian C Mahler, 'The Poehlman Case: Running Away from the Truth' (2006) 12(1) *Science and Engineering Ethics* 157.

336 University of Vermont College of Medicine, above n 334, 39.

2001, and agreed to seek their retraction.[337] He also entered into a voluntary exclusion agreement in which he agreed:

(1) to exclude himself permanently from serving in any advisory capacity to PHS including but not limited to service on any PHS advisory committee, board, and/or peer review committee, or as a consultant;
(2) to exclude himself permanently from any contracting or subcontracting with any agency of the United States Government and from eligibility or involvement in nonprocurement programs of the United States Government referred to as 'covered transactions'...; the respondent agrees that he will not petition HHS to reverse or reduce the scope of the permanent voluntary exclusion or administrative actions that are the subject of this Agreement; and
(3) to execute and deliver letters requesting retraction or correction to the editors of the journals that published the ten papers named in the Agreement and cited above, and to sign the letters requesting the retraction or correction prepared for his signature by ORI without alteration or modification in any way.[338]

Poehlman was also criminally charged. At his sentencing hearing, he started by expressing contrition:

> Speaking quickly and stammering occasionally, he apologized to friends and former colleagues, some of whom were listening in the back of the courtroom. He apologized to his mother, who sat in the front row, crying. And he apologized to Walter DeNino, the former protégé who turned him in, who was also sitting in the courtroom, several rows back on the prosecution's side. 'I have wanted to say I'm sorry for five years,' Poehlman said, without turning around to face DeNino. 'I want to make it very clear I am remorseful. I accept the responsibility. There's no way that I can turn back the clock. And I'm not that individual that I was years ago.'[339]

In a letter to the judge he explained that he was 'motivated by my own desire to advance as a respected scientist' and added that he was ashamed of himself 'for falsifying and fabricating data.... I believed that because the research questions I had framed were legitimate and worthy of study, it was okay to misrepresent "minor" pieces of data to increase the odds that the grant would be awarded'.[340]

Poehlman was sentenced to one year and a day in federal prison, followed by two years of probation. In delivering sentence Judge Session observed that: 'When scientists use their skill and their intelligence and their sophistication and their position of trust to do something which puts people at risk, that is extraordinarily serious. In one way, this is a final lesson that you are offering.'[341]

An action was also brought against Poehlman, among other things, under the False Claims Act[342] (also known as 'the Lincoln Law').[343] It was settled in 2005 with Poehlman agreeing to

---

[337] US Department of Health and Human Services, The Office of Research Integrity, 'Press Release—Dr Eric T Poehlman' (17 March 2005): <http://www.ori.dhhs.gov/press-release-poehlman> [accessed 22 Dec 2015].

[338] US Department of Health and Human Services, The Office of Research Integrity, 'Case Summary—Eric T Poehlman' (last updated 25 November 2013): <http://www.ori.dhhs.gov/poehlman_notice> [accessed 22 Dec 2015].

[339] Interlandi, above n 332.

[340] Eli Kintisch, 'Poehlman Sentenced to 1 year of Prison' (2006) Issue 238 *Science* 5, available at: <http://news.sciencemag.org/2006/06/poehlman-sentenced-1-year-prison> (viewed 10 March 2015).

[341] Interlandi, above n 332.

[342] 31 USC §§ 3729–3733.

[343] 31 USC §3729(a), as well as under the provisions of permissive exclusion under the Medicare, Medicaid, and other federal health care programmes. See p 149 of this chapter.

pay US$180,000 to the United States government over a three-year period, with DeNino (the relator) receiving a 12 per cent share of that sum, and Poehlman paying DeNino's legal costs.[344]

The Poehlman case generated considerable reflection within the United States medical community. Poehlman succeeded by producing results that confirmed pre-existing research hypotheses. This conduced against critical evaluation. He was popular and charismatic. He was also very successful, which meant that many researchers were financially dependent on him and his continuing grant successes. Poehlman, perhaps in later self-justification, maintained that he felt highly responsible for other researchers who were financially reliant on him. He became 'grant-dependent. But it created a maladaptive behavior pattern. I was on a treadmill, and I couldn't get off'.[345] A more critical perspective has been provided by Sox and Rennie who have argued that five lessons need to be learned from the Poehlman frauds:

> First, the scientific community must assume that every article written by an author who has committed scientific fraud is unreliable until someone close to the work has explained the specific reasons why he or she can vouch for its integrity. Second, the guilty scientist's coauthors bear primary responsibility for publicly validating or retracting their joint publications. Third, journal readers cannot necessarily count on journal editors to retract tainted articles. Fourth, in the interests of transparency, editors should use the word 'retraction' only in cases of fraud. Finally, even when a journal has published a retraction, authors continue to cite a fraudulent article, often for years.[346]

Luk Van Parijs

In 2004 Luk Van Parijs was an Associate Professor of Biology at the Massachusetts Institute of Technology (MIT). He was confronted by members of his laboratory with allegations that he had engaged in data falsification. He made immediate admissions and was sacked from MIT after an investigation that took the better part of a year. He was also subject to investigations by Harvard Medical School where he had been a graduate student and by the California Institute of Technology at Pasadena where he had been a postdoctoral student, as well as by the ORI of the United States Department of Health and Human Services.

It became apparent that Van Parijs had engaged between 1997 and 2004 in a pattern of research fraud in research funding applications into the shutting down of genes via virus-based techniques, including via the mechanism of ribonucleic acid (RNA) interference. In 1997 David Baker, a neuroimmunologist at the University of London expressed concerns about a paper co-authored by Van Parijs published in the same year by the *Journal of Experimental Medicine*. The view of the whistleblower was that a series of cytometry plots purportedly from different samples appeared to have been partly duplicated. At the time Van Parijs was a graduate student. It was not until 2009, though, that Baker received a letter of apology from the editor of the journal, expressing regret for its lack of response to the 1997 communication. The editor declined to comment on the suggestion that action by the journal in a timely way might have averted the later scandal which involved years of research conducted by Van Parijs.[347] Baker observed that the case was an illustration of the importance of addressing

---

[344] Settlement Agreement and Stipulation for Entry of Judgment, *United States of America v Eric T Poehlman* (United States District Court for the District of Vermont, Case No. 2:05.cv.66, 11 March 2005), available at: <http://www.ori.dhhs.gov/sites/default/files/poehlman_settlement_agreement_final.pdf> [accessed 22 Dec 2015]. See also, Patricia M Tereskerz, *Clinical Research and the Law* (Chichester, West Sussex: John Wiley & Sons, 2012) 130f.

[345] Interlandi, above n 332.

[346] Harold C Sox and Drummond Rennie, 'Research Misconduct, Retraction, and Cleansing the Medical Literature: Lessons from the Poehlman Case' (2006) 144(8) *Annals of Internal Medicine* 609, 612–3.

[347] See Eugenie Samuel Reich, 'Fraud Case We Might Have Seen Coming', *Nature*, 28 July 2011: <http://www.nature.com/news/2011/110728/full/news.2011.437.html> [accessed 22 Dec 2015].

scientific fraud early. He commented that others may well have noticed the anomalies in Van Parijs' work but not spoken up: 'People are afraid to stick their head above the parapet because the whistleblower never comes off well.'[348]

In February 2011 Van Parijs was charged in the District Court of Boston on the basis of a 2003 grant application to the NIH for which he was responsible. He entered a plea of guilty. The government sought a six-month jail term to deter others minded to behave similarly, but Judge Denise Casper opted instead to impose a sentence of six months of home detention with electronic monitoring, 400 hours of community service and a payment of US$61,117 to MIT for money that had to be returned to the NIH. She accepted that Van Parijs was genuinely remorseful. A whistleblower in his case who spoke to *Nature* had a different perspective: 'Luk's actions resulted in many wasted years as people struggled to regain their career paths. How do you measure the cost to the trainees when their careers have been derailed and their reputations brought into question?'[349] The observation of Professor Peter Doherty, a Nobel prize winner, acknowledged both positions: 'Driven by ambition and, perhaps, insecurity, a genuinely bright guy who could easily have made it as a legitimate scientist essentially destroyed his career. At least some of the results that he faked later turned out to be true, establishing that he had real scientific insight and explaining how it was he got away with it for so long.'[350] However, as Doherty acknowledged, the collateral damage to Parijs' fraud was 'enormous. Apart from what happened to Luk and his family, the postdocs and students named on any one of the retracted papers lost credit for the enormous effort they would have put into generating the legitimate data that no doubt formed the backbone of the publications in question. Then there was the waste of time and both human and financial resources as others tried unsuccessfully to repeat the work. It would be impossible to calculate the cost'.[351]

Woo-Suk Hwang

One of the most notorious scientific frauds of recent times has been that generated by Professor Woo-Suk Hwang,[352] a high-profile South Korean veterinarian and an academic at Seoul National University, who claimed in 2004[353] to have been the first person to have created human stem-cell lines using cloned embryos derived from patients suffering from spinal cord injury and other disorders. In an article announcing the breakthrough, Hwang and colleagues maintained that they had used 242 eggs derived from 16 volunteers. However, question marks emerged at an early juncture about the team's adherence to ethical proprieties with claims that junior members of the research team had donated their eggs.[354] Hwang and colleagues played a key role in creating an Afghan hound, Snuppy, the world's first cloned dog.[355]

348 Ibid.

349 Eugenie Samuel Reich, 'Biologist Spared Jail for Grant Fraud' (2011) 474(7353) *Nature* 552, available at: <http://www.nature.com/news/2011/110628/full/474552a.html> [accessed 22 Dec 2015].

350 Peter Doherty, *The Knowledge Wars* (Melbourne: Melbourne University Press, 2015), 95.

351 Ibid.

352 See Apoorva Mandevilli, 'Profile: Woo-Suk Hwang' (2005) 11(5) *Nature Medicine* 464; David Cyranoski, 'Verdict: Hwang's Human Stem Cells Were All Fakes' (2006) 439(7073) *Nature* 122; Rhodri Saunders and Julian Savulescu, 'Research Ethics and Lessons from Hwanggate: What Can We Learn from the Korean Cloning Fraud?' (2008) 34(3) *Journal of Medical Ethics* 214.

353 See Woo Suk Hwang, Young June Ryu, Jong Hyuk Park, Eul Soon Park et al. 'Evidence of a Pluripotent Human Embryonic Stem Cell Line Derived from a Cloned Blastocyst' (2004) 303(5664) *Science* 1669, since retracted: <http://www.sciencemag.org/content/303/5664/1669.full> [accessed 22 Dec 2015]; Woo Suk Hwang, Sung Il Roh, Byeong Chun Lee, Sung Keun Kang et al. 'Patient-Specific Embryonic Stem Cells Derived from Human SCNT Blastocysts' (2005) 308(5729) *Science* 1777, since retracted: <http://www.sciencemag.org/content/308/5729/1777> [accessed 22 Dec 2015].

354 See David Cyranoski, 'Korea's Stem-Cell Stars Dogged by Suspicion of Ethical Breach' (2004) 429(6987) *Nature* 3.

355 See Byeong Chun Lee, Min Kyu Kim, Goo Jang, Hyun Ju Oh et al. 'Dogs Cloned From Adult Somatic Cells' (2005) 436(7051) *Nature* 641.

In January 2006 Hwang admitted to falsifying data, although he persisted in the assertion that he had the ability to do what he had claimed. Hwang had been the only scientist in South Korea licensed to undertake human stem cell research but in 2006 the government revoked his licence. In South Korea, scientific fraud was illegal only if a person used fraudulent data to gain grants.[356] Prosecutors argued that he duped two companies, SK Group and NongHyup, into supplying research funds but the court rejected the allegations on the ground that the firms provided money without expecting to benefit.[357] However, Hwang was found guilty of buying human eggs in violation of Korea's bioethics law and of embezzling 830 million won *c.*£UK470,000 of government money.

The scientific community was divided about how the court should deal with Hwang. Alan Colman, a stem cell scientist at the Institute of Medical Biology in Singapore, expressed the view that Hwang was a talented experimentalist and that he should be excluded from eligibility for research funding for a stipulated period of time.[358] In June 2009, Hwang received an award from the Jang Yeong-sil Memorial Foundation for scientific excellence. Two months later the South Korean province of Gyeonggi announced that it planned a collaboration with Hwang to develop transgenic animals able to grow organs for transplantation to humans. In October 2009, 33 parliamentarians submitted a petition to the Seoul Central District Court Criminal Division pleading for leniency in sentencing Hwang so that he could continue his research without impediment.[359]

Seoul District Court Judge Bae Ki-ryul imposed a two-year jail sentence, suspended for three years, although the prosecution had sought a four-year jail term to be actually served. The lesser sentence was imposed on the basis of what the sentencing judge classified as Hwang's dedication to the development of Korea's biotechnology, his lack of a criminal record and his deep remorse. Both the prosecution and Hwang appealed to the Seoul High Court against the convictions. On 16 December 2010, the High Court reduced Hwang's sentence to an 18-month jail term wholly suspended for two years. Hwang then appealed to the Supreme Court but was unsuccessful in early 2014.[360] The court also sent Hwang's plea to overturn his dismissal from Seoul National University back to a lower court for review and upheld previous rulings acquitting him of fraud charges. The ruling came two weeks after Hwang obtained a United States patent for a purportedly cloned human embryonic stem cell line.

Controversies in relation to Hwang persist. Dr Kim of the Center for Democracy in Science and Technology in South Korea has argued that: 'If we let someone like him [get away with it], whose scandal will remain in the history of science, what would the world think of our country's scientific system?'[361] However, Hwang showed himself increasingly determined to re-enter the research arena. In an interview in *The Dong-A Ilbo* newspaper on 24 February 2014, Hwang said he wanted to resume work on human stem cells, telling

356 David Cyranoski, 'Woo Suk Hwang Convicted, But Not of Fraud' (2009) 461(7268) *Nature* 1181.

357 Park Si-soo, 'Hwang Convicted of Embezzlement, Cleared of Fraud', *The Korea Times*, 26 October 2009: <http://www.koreatimes.co.kr/www/news/nation/2009/10/117_54275.html> [accessed 22 Dec 2015].

358 Cyranoski, above n 356.

359 David Cyranoski, 'Hwang Verdict Imminent' (2009) 461(7267) *Nature* 1035.

360 See Mi-Young Ahn and Dennis Normile, 'Korean Supreme Court Upholds Disgraced Cloner's Criminal Sentence', *Science*, 27 February 2014: <http://news.sciencemag.org/asiapacific/2014/02/korean-supreme-court-upholds-disgraced-cloners-criminal-sentence> [accessed 22 Dec 2015].

361 Choe Sang-Hun, 'Korean Scientist's New Project: Rebuild After Cloning Disgrace', *The New York Times*, 28 February 2014: <http://www.nytimes.com/2014/03/01/world/asia/scientists-new-project-rebuild-after-cloning-disgrace.html> [accessed 22 Dec 2015].

the paper: 'I ask the Seoul government and the Korean people to give me just one more chance.'[362]

He said in an interview that: 'I created an illusion and made it look as if it were real.... I was drunk in the bubble I created.'[363] Shortly afterwards it was revealed that Britain's first cloned dog was created by a firm headed by Hwang.[364] By the end of 2014 a film about Hwang was topping Korea's box office.[365]

Scott Reuben

Scott Reuben was the Professor of Anesthesiology and Pain Management at Baystate Medical Center in Springfield, Massachusetts. Having been educated at Columbia University and the State University of New York at Buffalo in 1985, he undertook his anaesthesiology residency at Mount Sinai Medical Center in New York. In 1991 he joined Bayside which serves as the western campus for Tufts University School of Medicine. Over a period of some 12 years Reuben worked and published on the way in which pain relief is provided to patients undergoing orthopaedic surgery. His work sought to encourage surgeons to move away from the first generation of nonsteroidal anti-inflammatories (NSAIDs) to multimodal analgesia therapy utilizing the newer COX-2 inhibitors,[366] such as Merck's Vioxx, and Pfizer's Celebrex and Bextra. He claimed that using such drugs in combination with Pfizer's anticonvulsant Neurontin and later Lyrica before and during surgery decreased postoperative pain and the use of addictive opiate painkillers such as morphine. In a 2007 editorial published in *Anesthesia and Analgesia*, Reuben was described as having been at the 'forefront of redesigning pain management protocols' through studies characterized as 'carefully planned' and 'meticulously documented'.[367]

The drugs the subject of Reuben's published research were highly controversial, Vioxx and Bextra being withdrawn from sale in 2004 because of what by then had emerged as an elevated risk of heart attacks, thrombosis and strokes for their users. This left Pfizer's Celebrex as the only available COX-2 inhibitor but with a major cloud over its safety.

Reuben was a member of Pfizer's speaker's bureau and received five independent research grants from Pfizer. His studies consistently were supportive of Pfizer's claims as to the efficacy and safety of Celebrex.

Starting in 2000 Reuben entered into contracts with Pfizer, Merck, and Wyeth to perform research funded by the companies and to publish the results of his research, as shown in Table 3.1:

---

362 Ahn and Normile, above n 360.

363 Sang-Hun, above n 361.

364 See Sam Webb and Vincent Graff, 'Korean Scientist Behind Britain's First Cloned Dog is a Convicted Fraudster Who Was Forced to Quit University for Making Up Results', *Daily Mail*, 10 April 2014: <http://www.dailymail.co.uk/news/article-2601265/Korean-scientist-Britains-cloned-dog-convicted-fraudster-forced-quit-university-making-results.html> [accessed 22 Dec 2015].

365 See Bob Grant, 'Korean Stem Cell Film Tops Box Office', *The Scientist*, 9 October 2014: <http://www.the-scientist.com/?articles.view/articleNo/41184/title/Korean-Stem-Cell-Film-Tops-Box-Office/> [accessed 22 Dec 2015].

366 COX-2 inhibitors are a form of NSAID which directly targets COX-2, an enzyme responsible for inflammation and pain. Selectivity for COX-2 has the potential to reduce adverse effects of other NSAIDs, including renal failure.

367 Brendan Borrell, 'A Medical Madoff: Anesthesiologist Faked Data in 21 Studies', *Scientific American*, 10 March 2010: <http://www.scientificamerican.com/article/a-medical-madoff-anesthestesiologist-faked-data/> [accessed 22 Dec 2015].

Table 3.1 False Articles and Pharmaceutical Funding of Professor Reuben's Research

False Articles	Funding Pharmaceutical Company	Amount of Funding
'The Effect of Cyclooxygenase-2 Inhibition on Analgesia and Spinal Fusion' (2005) 87 *Journal of Bone and Joint Surgery* 536	Pfizer	$63,425
'The Effect of Cyclooxygenase-2 Inhibition on Acute and Chronic Donor-Site Pain After Spinal Fusion Surgery' (2006) 31 *Register of Anesthesia and Pain Medicine* 6		
'Evaluating the Analgesic Efficacy of Administering Celecoxib as a Component of Multimodal Analgesia for Outpatient Anterior Cruciate Ligament Reconstruction Surgery' (2007) 105 *Anesthesia and Analgesia* 222	Pfizer	$73,512
'The Effect of Initiating a Preventive Multimodal Analgesic Regimen on Long-Term Patient Outcomes for Outpatient Anterior Cruciate Ligament Reconstruction Surgery' (2007) 105 *Anesthesia and Analgesia* 228		
'A Prospective Randomized Trial on the Role of Perioperative Celecoxib Administration for Total Knee Arthoplasty: Improving Clinical Outcomes' (2008) 106 *Anesthesia and Analgesia* 1258	Pfizer	$118,200
'The Effect of Intraoperative Valdecoxib Administration on PGE2 Levels in the CSF' (2005) 1 (Supp) *Journal of Pain* 21 (Abstract 649)	Pfizer	$41,420
'Evaluation of the Safety and Efficacy of the Perioperative Administration of Rofecoxib for Total Knee Arthoplasty' (2002) 17(1) *Journal of Arthroplasty* 26	Merck	$49,375
'Evaluation of Efficacy of the Perioperative Administration of Venlaxifine XR in the Prevention of Post-Mastectomy Pain Syndrome' (2004) 27 *Journal of Pain and Symptom Management* 133	Wyeth	$16,000

In his 2002 article for the *Journal of Arthroplasty* Reuben claimed to have enrolled 100 patients. However, he later admitted to having only collected data on 26 patients. For a 2008 article in *Anesthesia and Analgesia* he claimed to have collected data on 200 patients; in fact he had no data at all.[368] In at least one instance Reuben forged the name of a co-author on a manuscript—an incident of fraud that came to light when the alleged author was informed of the situation after inquiries made by *Anesthesiology News*.[369]

Ultimately, Reuben was charged with criminal fraud. In submissions to the United States District Court (District of Massachusetts)[370] Reuben contended that he had not been

[368] Adam Marcus, 'Reuben Sentenced in Fraud Case', *Anesthesiology News*, 25 June 2010: <http://anesthesiologynews.com/ViewArticle.aspx?d=Web%2BExclusives&d_id=175&i=June%2B2010&i_id=637&a_id=15399> [accessed 22 Dec 2015].

[369] Ibid.

[370] Government's Sentencing Memorandum, *United States v Reuben* (United States District Court, District of Massachusetts, Case No. 10-CR-30002-MAP, 22 June 2010), available at: <http://i.bnet.com/blogs/uas-reuben-sentencing-memo.pdf> [accessed 22 Dec 2015] at 7.

motivated by greed and that the funds which he received from pharmaceutical companies went to his employer. It was urged on his behalf that Reuben did not need the publications to further his career. He contended that, if not for his bipolar 'disorder', he 'would not have had the stamina to maintain all of this activity'; namely, the wrongful acts committed between 2000 and 2008.[371] It was argued on his behalf that he had not engaged in any form of inadequate patient care, his wife had left him, he had attempted suicide, he had liquidated almost all his savings to repay the pharmaceutical companies, and his professional reputation had been devastated. The court received submissions from the prosecution urging imposition of a jail sentence of 14 months and from the defence urging the imposition of home detention. It determined to impose a six-month sentence of imprisonment.

The 2010 prosecution of Scott Reuben sent tidal waves of warning throughout the international research community. Reuben was described in 2010 by Brendan Borrell in *Scientific American* as 'a medical Madoff'.[372] By 2015, 25 of Reuben's publications had been retracted. However, what is most significant about the Reuben saga is the involvement of the criminal law. The government prosecution signalled preparedness by regulatory authorities (at least in the United States) to initiate not just disciplinary proceedings, but also criminal proceedings, against those suspected of having misused research funding for career or pecuniary advantage. The essence of the prosecution consisted in Professor Reuben being charged with, and pleading guilty to, having obtained financial advantage by research deception.[373] The criminal conduct involved 'defrauding pharmaceutical companies, falsifying clinical research results, sending false articles based on false clinical research results to a number of scholarly medical journals, which published these false articles, which in turn led members of the pain management medical community to read these false articles and in some instances base their treatment protocols for their patients on the false article they read'.[374] The prosecution tendered a victim impact letter by the editor of the *Journal of Bone and Joint Surgery* which attested to having published an article by Reuben that 'purported to define a new method of [pain] management following spinal fusion, a procedure which is performed more than 250,000 times a year in the United States alone' and explained the measures taken by the journal after the fraudulent nature of Reuben's publication was identified.[375] The letter concluded that the 'reputation of the *Journal of Bone and Joint Surgery* as an absolutely reliable source of quality patient care information has been permanently damaged, and we will never fully recover. Most importantly, while it is impossible to measure, many patients have been adversely affected by his [Reuben's] actions'.[376] Similarly, in a further exhibit tendered by the prosecution, Dr Jacques Chelly, Director of the Division of Regional Anesthesia and Acute Interventional Pain at the University of Pittsburgh Medical Center, said that a consequence of Reuben's fraud was that multimodal analgesia had been left 'in shambles concerning many of the drugs we use. The big chunk of what people had based their protocol on is gone'.[377]

The wisdom of hindsight suggests that conduct by persons such as Reuben is very difficult for journal editors and reviewers to detect.[378] However, the case highlights the harm that can be done by research fraud that fabricates results to achieve predetermined objectives, whether

371 Ibid, 10.
372 Borrell, above n 367.
373 The charge was health care fraud in violation of 18 USC §1347.
374 Government's Sentencing Memorandum, above n 370, 7.
375 Ibid, 8.
376 Ibid.
377 Ibid.
378 See Heike L Rittner, Peter Kranke, Michael Schäfer, Norbert Roewer, and Alexander Brack, 'What Can We Learn from the Scott Reuben Case? Scientific Misconduct in Anaesthesiology' (2009) 58(12) *Anaesthetist* 1199.

those are of direct pecuniary advantage to the perpetrator or generated by other motivations. Victims include journal reputations and, in the medical arena, patients whose treaters are persuaded on the basis of unmeritorious research to use treatment modalities they would not otherwise have adopted.

Craig Grimes

In 2012, a Pennsylvania State University Professor of Material Sciences and Engineering, Craig Grimes, was charged with US$3 million of research frauds between 2005 and 2011 arising from research into the potential to convert carbon dioxide into energy.[379] His victims included Pennsylvania State University, the NIH, and the National Science Foundation (NSF).

Grimes sought a US$1,196,000 grant from the NIH to perform research related to the measurement of gases in a patient's blood. The trial was funded on the basis of the importance of the measurement of such gases in detecting the presence of a disease in newborn babies with necrotizing enterocolitis. He represented in the application that he would direct US$509,274 to the Hershey Medical Center to conduct clinical research on adult and infant subjects. However, the money was never paid, instead being misappropriated in part for his own use. The clinical studies were never performed.[380]

Part of his misrepresentations included a US$1.9 million grant application to the Department of Energy in 2009. As part of the application Grimes represented he had not received other funding for the project when in fact he had received a grant of funding for the same research from the NSF. University administrators queried him about having two grants that sounded very similar but he assured them there was no overlap, although he openly acknowledged both sources of funding in a 2010 publication. The Department of Energy Inspector-General identified the similarity in the two grants and the NSF began its investigation into whether there had been precluded duplication.[381] Grimes resigned his position at Pennsylvania State University.

After leaving Pennsylvania State University, Grimes was employed as a full-time Professor of Material Science and Engineering at Nanjing Industry University, but suspended in 2012 as the criminal proceedings became imminent.[382]

On 30 November 2012 United States Middle District Chief Judge Kane sentenced Grimes to 41 months' imprisonment and ordered him to repay more than US $640,000 in restitution to his university and the NIH and NSF. Grimes maintained that he had been overtaken with research zeal and ignored grant rules and regulations, while the prosecutor, Assistant Attorney Joseph Terx, summarized his position, contending that Grimes 'is not a mad scientist. He's a dishonest scientist'.[383]

---

379 Dan Miller, 'Former Penn State Professor Pleads Guilty to Defrauding Government of $3 Million in Grants', *Penn Live*, 21 February 2012: <http://www.pennlive.com/midstate/index.ssf/2012/02/former_penn_state_professor_cr.html> [accessed 22 Dec 2015].

380 The United States Attorney's Office, Middle District of Pennsylvania, 'Former Penn State Professor Who Plead Guilty in $3 Million Federal Research Grant Fraud Sentenced in Federal Court' (Press Release, 30 November 2012): <http://www.justice.gov/usao/pam/news/2012/Grimes_11_30_2012.htm> [accessed 22 Dec 2015].

381 Eugenie Samuel Reich, 'Duplicate-Grant Case Puts Funders Under Pressure' (2012) 482(7384) *Nature* 146, available at: <http://www.nature.com/news/duplicate-grant-case-puts-funders-under-pressure-1.9984> [accessed 22 Dec 2015].

382 Li Qian, 'US Professor Hired in Nanjing Charged with Crimes', *Shanghai Daily*, 12 February 2012: <http://en.people.cn/90882/7726577.html> (viewed 3 February 2015).

383 'Craig Grimes, Ex-Penn State Professor, Sentenced for More than $3 Million in Research Grant Fraud', *Huffington Post*, 30 December 2012: <http://www.huffingtonpost.com/2012/12/03/craig-grimes-sentenced_n_2232658.html> [accessed 22 Dec 2015].

Steven Eaton

In 2013 Steven Eaton became the first person in the United Kingdom to receive a jail sentence for falsifying clinical test results. Eaton had been employed by the Edinburgh branch of the United States pharmaceutical firm, Aptuit, to conduct preclinical trials on animals to assess the efficacy of new treatments on behalf of several drug companies. The Edinburgh Sheriff Court was informed that between 2003 and 2009 Eaton manipulated results of experiments to make it appear that they had been successful when in fact they had failed.[384] He selectively reported analytical data used to assess whether analytical methods were working effectively to assess the concentration of a drug in the blood.[385]

When his superiors identified Eaton's fraud, they reported him to the Medicines and Healthcare Products Regulatory Agency which prosecuted him under the *Good Laboratory Practice Regulations* 1999 (UK).

Jim Stephenson, the defence solicitor advocate representing Eaton, submitted that his client had been under pressure during the period of his offending and had been having trouble with his personal life. He asserted that Eaton had not gained financially from his conduct but the court was offered no motive for why Eaton had manipulated the data.[386]

In sentencing Eaton to the maximum term of imprisonment available (three months), Sheriff O'Grady was less than sympathetic:

> I feel that my sentencing powers in this are wholly inadequate. You failed to test the drugs properly — you could have caused cancer patients unquestionable harm. Why someone who is as highly educated and as experienced as you would embark on such a course of conduct is inexplicable.[387]

Dong-Pyou Han

In 2008 Dr Dong-Pyou Han worked in a team led by Professor Michael Cho at Case Western Reserve University in Cleveland testing an experimental HIV vaccine on rabbits with assistance from substantial funding from the National Institutes of Health.[388] In 2009 Han and his team were recruited to Iowa State University. Han was an assistant professor. Ultimately, the research team of which Han was a member received at least US$19 million in funding from the United States government.[389]

---

[384] See Richard Gray, 'Scientist Jailed for Faking Medicine Test Results', *The Telegraph*, 17 April 2013: <http://www.telegraph.co.uk/news/uknews/crime/10001149/Scientist-jailed-for-faking-medicine-test-results.html> [accessed 22 Dec 2015].

[385] Medicines and Healthcare Products Regulatory Agency, UK Government, 'Pre-Clinical Trial Data Scam—First Ever Successful Prosecution under Good Laboratory Practice Regulations' (Press release, 12 March 2013): <http://web.archive.org/web/20130320011717/<http://www.mhra.gov.uk/NewsCentre/Pressreleases/CON249630> [accessed 22 Dec 2015].

[386] See Gray, above n 384.

[387] 'Scientist Steven Eaton Jailed for Falsifying Drug Test Results', *BBC News*, 17 April 2013: <http://www.bbc.com/news/uk-scotland-edinburgh-east-fife-22186220> [accessed 22 Dec 2015].

[388] 'Scientist Behind Fake HIV Breakthrough Sentenced to Prison after Spiking Results' (1 July 2015) *The Guardian*: <http://www.theguardian.com/society/2015/jul/01/iowa-scientist-hiv-breakthrough-dong-pyou-han> [accessed 22 Dec 2015].

[389] 'ISU Researcher Dr Dong-Pyou Han Resigns for Faking AIDS Research Worth Millions', *Huffington Post*, 25 December 2013: <http://www.huffingtonpost.com/2013/12/25/isu-researcher-aids-faking-han_n_4500383.html> [accessed 22 Dec 2015]; Andy Soltis, 'Professor Admits Faking AIDS Vaccine to get $19M in Grants', *New York Post*, 26 December 2013: <http://nypost.com/2013/12/26/professor-admits-faking-aids-vaccine-to-get-19m-in-grants/> [accessed 22 Dec 2015].

Han's research fraud, which started while he was at Case Western, was uncovered by scientists at Harvard University.[390] It consisted of adding human blood components to rabbit blood to make it appear that a vaccine on which he was working was effective in neutralizing or controlling the HIV virus.[391] NIH officials were later to state that they were flabbergasted with the results and the success led Dr Cho, Dr Han's superior, to work on a particular region of the HIV virus which responded to the vaccine. The falsified assay results were widely reported at national and international scholarly gatherings between 2010 and 2012, giving false hope for this direction in research.[392]

Once Dr Cho became aware that a person in his laboratory had committed research misconduct, he and an Iowa State University integrity officer devised a 'sting operation' to try to determine who was responsible. In addition to Dr Han, who it turned out was solely responsible, suspicion fell on three other laboratory researchers until they were eliminated from suspicion.

The nature and the seriousness of Dr Han's conduct became apparent after an extensive investigation conducted by the Iowa State University of Science and Technology and the ORI. They jointly concluded that Dr Han had falsified research materials by providing collaborators with spiked serum results, having faked the relevant data files. Dr Han made extensive admissions about his misconduct and entered into a voluntary exclusion agreement for three years to exclude himself from eligibility for any federal research grants and eligibility for service on any advisory committee to the United States Public Health Service. He also resigned from the university.

Before his resignation, Dr Han wrote to the university, confessing to his misconduct in 2009, explaining that he had engaged in it because he wanted the results to look better and saying, 'I was foolish, coward, and not frank'.[393]

Iowa State University agreed to reimburse the NIH US$496,000 for salary and other costs paid to Dr Han. In addition, the NIH decided not to make the final US$1.38 million payment on a grant to the research team as a result of the conduct of Dr Han.

James Bradac, who was responsible for overseeing AIDS vaccine results for the NIH, stated that Dr Han's conduct was the worst case of research fraud he had encountered in two decades at the agency.[394] There were many repercussions to the discovery of Dr Han's misconduct. United States Senator Chuck Grassley questioned whether the NIH had responded strongly enough to what he asserted was 'brazen fraud'.[395] Arthur Caplan, a Professor of Medical Ethics

---

390 David Pitt, 'AIDS Scientist Dong-Pyou Han Pleads Not Guilty to Faking Study', *Huffington Post*, 2 July 2014: <http://www.huffingtonpost.com/2014/07/02/aids-scientist-not-guilty_n_5551007.html> [accessed 22 Dec 2015].

391 Adam Marcus and Ivan Oransky, 'Crack Down on Scientific Fraudsters', *The New York Times*, 10 July 2014: <http://www.nytimes.com/2014/07/11/opinion/crack-down-on-scientific-fraudsters.html?_r=0> [accessed 22 Dec 2015].

392 Health and Human Services Department, 'Findings of Research Misconduct—Dong-Pyou Han', *Office of the Federal Register*, 23 December 2013: <https://www.federalregister.gov/articles/2013/12/23/2013-30424/findings-of-research-misconduct> [accessed 22 Dec 2015]; US Department of Health and Human Services, The Office of Research Integrity, 'Case Summary—Han, Dong-Pyou' (last updated 23 December 2013): <http://ori.hhs.gov/content/case-summary-han-dong-pyou> [accessed 22 Dec 2015].

393 Pitt, above n 390.

394 Corinne Lestch, 'Iowa Professor Cops to Faking Results of Big-Bucks AIDS Vaccine Research', *New York Daily News*, 27 December 2013: <http://www.nydailynews.com/news/national/professor-cops-faking-aids-vaccine-research-data-article-1.1559245> [accessed 22 Dec 2015].

395 Tony Leys, 'ISU Loses $1.4 million in Fraud Case', *Iowa City Press-Citizen*, 8 July 2014: <http://www.press-citizen.com/story/news/2014/07/08/iowa-state-loses-14-million-in-fraud-case/12351289/> [accessed 22 Dec 2015].

at New York University, called for Dr Han to be prosecuted in order to send a message to university officials and researchers that fraud in such activities can be a criminal offence.[396]

By June 2014, Dr Han had been arrested and charged on a four-count grand jury felony indictment of making false statements. He initially pleaded not guilty to the charges but by February 2015 entered into a plea agreement. This involved his admitting that he 'knowingly and wilfully caused Iowa State University professor Dr Michael Cho, to make materially false, fictitious, and fraudulent statements and representations' in an NIH grant application and then in a progress report. The falsity of the representations arose from data that had been fabricated by Dr Han. The prosecution and Dr Han stipulated as a recommendation to the court that the loss involved was between US$7 and $20 million.[397]

The prosecution argued that: 'Dr Han's conduct was egregious, long-running and manipulated the grant funding process and Dr Cho's laboratory.' It drew to the court's attention the fact that: 'accurate facts and data are essential in research, and the data must be unbiased and truthful, or the entire system is compromised.' It argued for the imposition of a prison sentence on the basis of Dr Han being highly educated, a trusted employee who knew what he was doing was wrong and who did not abstain from the conduct until it was exposed—he did not stop of his own accord: 'while this crime allegedly started with a simple mistake, Dr Han chose to, and went to considerable effort, to manipulate scientific data for a significant period of time.' It emphasized the need to deter others minded to behave similarly.[398]

On behalf of Dr Han it was argued that: 'This case is about human failings', Dr Han having realized the cross-contamination after his findings had generated considerable excitement: 'He could not bring himself to dash the hopes of the research team, and all the others interested in the perceived potential and progress of their efforts.' He hoped and expected that the neutralizing effects would be generated by another mechanism but 'made the foolish decision to spike subsequent samples so it would appear that neutralizing activity was still occurring in subsequent samples. He then continued to present the resulting false data to Dr Cho'.

Thus on behalf of Dr Han it was put that he had allowed an accident to turn into a lie and lacked the fortitude to confront colleagues and friends and dash their hopes. It was argued that it was not necessary for the court to impose a sentence of imprisonment, given Dr Han's acceptance of his errors, his shame, his contrition, his age (58), and the price that he had already paid for his conduct. It was argued that: 'Dr Han knew it would inevitably be discovered, and that its harm could only be mitigated if the research produced legitimate results as efforts continued, but still could not bring himself to reveal the truth to Dr Cho, the research team, and his colleagues in the scientific community. This is not a fraud case where Dr Han received extra benefits or money, as he only received his salary while the research continued, along with the prestige accompanying the potential of the false data. And even that prestige was inevitably going to be lost when the truth was discovered, which Dr Han knew would occur at some point in the future.'[399]

---

[396] Grant Rodgers, 'Former Iowa State Researcher Indicted', *Des Moines Register*, 20 June 2014: <http://www.desmoinesregister.com/story/news/crime-and-courts/2014/06/20/former-iowa-state-researcher-indicted/11033633/> [accessed 22 Dec 2015].

[397] See Dong-Pyou-Han Plea Agreement, attached to Tony Leys, 'Ex-ISU Scientist Pleads Guilty of AIDS Vaccine Fraud' (25 February 2015) *Des Moines Register*: <http://www.desmoinesregister.com/story/news/2015/02/25/dong-pyou-han-iowa-state-university-guilty-plea/23996449/> [accessed 22 Dec 2015].

[398] United States District Attorney Rachel Scherle Sentencing Memorandum, 29 June 2015, attached to Tony Leys, 'Ex-ISU Scientist Seeks Mercy in AIDS-Vaccine Fraud Case' (20 June 2015) *Des Moines Register*: <http://www.desmoinesregister.com/story/news/2015/06/29/ex-iowa-state-university-scientist-seeks-mercy-aids-vaccine-fraud-case/29474519/> [accessed 22 Dec 2015].

[399] United States Public Defender Joseph Herrold's Sentencing Memorandum, 29 June 2015, attached to Tony Leys, 'Ex-ISU Scientist Seeks Mercy in AIDS-Vaccine Fraud Case' (20 June 2015) *Des Moines Register*:

On 1 July 2015 Judge Gritzner sentenced Dr Han to 57 months' imprisonment and three years of supervision upon release. He also ordered him to repay US$7.2 million to the NIH. Judge Gritzner accepted that Dr Han was a good man who 'made a terribly tragic decision over and over again'. He said that he did not fear that Han would commit more crimes but concluded that 'the court cannot get beyond the breach of the sacred trust in this kind of research... The seriousness of this offense is just stunning.' He noted that it was likely that Han would be deported back to his native Korea after serving his term of imprisonment.[400]

Professor Caplan's observation about the case was that, too often, serious ethical and legal violations by researchers can end up being settled privately without the public's knowledge: 'I think it sends an appropriate message about research misconduct and misuse of taxpayer funds and the dangers that misconduct can cause to vulnerable patients. If you lie about research, you can wind up really harming people, because other people rely on your claims.'[401]

However, other issues about the capacity of funders to investigate and identify research fraud were raised controversially by the case. While United States funding agencies, such as the National Science Foundation, have an Inspector-General able to investigate concerns about misconduct, including fraud, the agencies which are part of the Department of Health and Human Services, such as the NIH and the ORI, do not have much by way of powers. The ORI, for instance, is not able itself to investigate suspected fraud or misconduct; it oversees probes by employing institutions and when misconduct or fraud are found, it can impose funding preclusions and refer matters for prosecution (to the Department of Justice) or to the Inspector-General of the Department of Health and Human Services.[402]

Caroline Barwood and Bruce Murdoch

Professor Bruce Murdoch, a neuroscientist at the University of Queensland's Centre for Neurogenic Communication Disorders Research, and Dr Caroline Barwood, a speech pathologist, were two of the authors of a landmark study on Parkinson's disease published in the *European Journal of Neurology* in 2011. A whistleblower alleged that there was no evidence that their research into Parkinson's disease was carried out.[403]

The University of Queensland's Vice-Chancellor asked the journal to retract the article and ordered an internal misconduct investigation by the university. The university was unable to identify any data to prove that the study was conducted and both academics resigned their positions at the university. The university returned the first two instalments of a AUS$300,000 bursary awarded to Barwood and the conduct of the two scholars was referred to the Crime and Misconduct Commission of Queensland (as it then was).[404] The university then began to examine more than 100 published papers associated with the two academics. Media reported that concerns existed in relation to 11 papers published in seven journals, as well as one paper that had been wholly republished. The university referred its concerns to the editors of the

<http://www.desmoinesregister.com/story/news/2015/06/29/ex-iowa-state-university-scientist-seeks-mercy-aids-vaccine-fraud-case/29474519/> [accessed 22 Dec 2015].

400 Tony Leys, 'Ex-ISU Scientist Sentenced to 57 Months in Prison' (1 July 2015) *Des Moines Register*: <http://www.desmoinesregister.com/story/news/crime-and-courts/2015/07/01/dong-pyou-han-sentencing-iowa-state-scientist-aids-vaccine-fraud-case/29560297/> [accessed 22 Dec 2015].

401 Ibid.

402 See Sara Reardon, 'US Vaccine Researcher Sentenced to Prison for Fraud' (1 July 2015) 523 *Nature*: <http://www.nature.com/news/us-vaccine-researcher-sentenced-to-prison-for-fraud-1.17660> [accessed 22 Dec 2015].

403 Sarah Elks, 'Probe on Academics Uncovers New Concerns', *The Australian*, 21 January 2014, 5.

404 ABC Radio National, 'CMC Confirms Misconduct by Queensland Academics', *PM*, 7 November 2013 (Elise Worthington): <http://www.abc.net.au/pm/content/2013/s3886274.htm> [accessed 22 Dec 2015].

various journals, resulting in early 2014 in the retraction of a study that had been published in *Aphasiology*. A retraction notice on the publisher's website states the study claimed to have a control group of 15, but only seven participants were documented and control data were re-used to enlarge the group—'lack of independence within control data is not acknowledged in the manuscript'.[405]

By 2014 Murdoch had published more than 13 books and 380 peer-reviewed articles. He was an editorial board member of ten international journals and an editorial consultant to 20 other international journals. He was the founder of the Centre for Neurogenic Communication Disorders Research at the University of Queensland. The Centre has since been shut down.

In October 2014, Barwood was charged in the Magistrates' Court of Queensland with two counts of fraud, and two counts of attempted fraud contrary to s 408C of the Queensland Criminal Code and two counts of general dishonesty contrary to s 135.1 of the *Criminal Code Act* 1995 (Cth). In December 2014 Murdoch was charged with three counts of fraud, seven counts of fraudulent falsification or records and five counts of general dishonesty.[406] At the time of writing, neither researcher had participated in a committal hearing, and no adverse finding had been made against either of them in respect of the criminal charges which had been preferred.

Evolving Approaches to the Preferring of Charges

For the most part the criminal charges brought against researchers have been in the nature of fraud or obtaining financial advantage by deception. Such charges are well-recognized and of long standing on the statute books. Their essence is that the researcher has derived some form of benefit by virtue of their dishonesty—generally in respect of not undertaking bona fide research when they have obtained funding to do so. At the heart of such conduct lies the making of profit of one kind or another and a serious breach of trust in the conduct of research.

The exception in this regard was the charge brought in Scotland against Steve Eaton under the *Good Laboratory Practice Regulations* 1999 (UK). This was a somewhat obscure source of prosecutorial power that had the potential of only a minor criminal count. It was less than desirable.

For the most part, the exercise of prosecutorial power in the cases that have proceeded to adverse findings has appeared straightforward. In each of the cases, the conduct was serious and the discretion to charge was exercised in a way that was unsurprising given the nature of the conduct and its foreseeable consequences to a variety of stakeholders.

The penalties in such cases (mostly in the United States) have varied significantly:

- **Breuning** (plea of guilty: 2003): 60 days in a halfway house, five years of probation, 250 hours of community service, repayment of US$11,352, and to abstain from psychological research for the period of his probation;
- **Poehlman** (plea of guilty: 2006): one year and a day in federal prison, followed by two years of probation;
- **Van Parijs** (plea of guilty: 2011): six months of home detention with electronic monitoring, 400 hours of community service and a payment of US$61,117 to MIT for money that had to be returned to the NIH;

[405] Caroline H S Barwood and Bruce E Murdoch, 'Cognitive Linguistic Deficits in Relapsing-Remitting Multiple Sclerosis' (2013) 27(12) *Aphasiology* 1459, retracted by 'Statement of Retraction' (2014) 28(6) *Aphasiology* 770: <http://www.tandfonline.com/doi/pdf/10.1080/02687038.2014.908038> [accessed 22 Dec 2015].

[406] See Elise Worthington, 'Former University of Queensland Professor Bruce Murdoch Charged Over Fake Parkinson's Research', *ABC News*, 12 December 2014: <http://www.abc.net.au/news/2014-12-12/university-of-queensland-professor-on-fraud-charges/5964476> [accessed 22 Dec 2015].

- **Hwang** (largely a contested hearing: 2014): 24 months' imprisonment, suspended for three years;
- **Reuben** (plea of guilty: 2010): 6 months' imprisonment;
- **Grimes** (plea of guilty: 2012): 41 months' imprisonment and repayment of more than US$640,000 in restitution;
- **Eaton** (plea of guilty: 2013): 3 months' imprisonment;
- **Han** (plea of guilty: 2015): 57 months' imprisonment and repayment of $7.2 million in restitution.

For the most part, those charged, after negotiations, have pleaded guilty and have been sentenced to a period of imprisonment, varying from a period of time in a halfway house (jail in the community) to 57 months' imprisonment. The period of incarceration has varied and will continue to vary depending on factors such as the extent of the period of offending, the sum involved, the harm caused by the fraud the offender's obtaining of advantage from their conduct, and the degree to which the accused person concedes culpability for their breach of trust and cooperates in the criminal investigation into their conduct. Mental illness and expression of genuine contrition may mitigate sentences. However, as yet it must be conceded that the number of cases available for analysis is very modest indeed and it is important to be cautious in extrapolating from their outcomes.

However, an evolution in responses from misconduct regulators (associated with prosecutors) is identifiable in recent years. Criminal charges are starting to be brought in a number of countries against those identified as responsible for egregious research fraud. While the amount of grant money which has been wasted by such fraud, can usually be calculated with some precision, the damage done to patients who receive treatment when otherwise they might have received a better intervention or whose hopes are manipulated by deceit are not so easily identified. In addition, co-authors, supervisors and whole areas of research can fall into undeserved disrepute as a result of the research fraud, and the reputations of departments, journals and publishing houses can also be adversely affected. While biomedical research, like much of professional practice, functions on the basis of trust and integrity, the commission of research fraud constitutes a gross abuse of such trust.

Given that such conduct is engaged in by professionals who are well positioned to make considered choices about what they are doing, and to be cognizant of its consequences, there is much to be said for the criminal law being utilized, at least in serious matters. While there are limits to the efficacy of the criminal law as a deterrent, and it is not yet possible to measure whether the invocation of the criminal law is being efficacious in deterring such conduct,[407] the imposition of clear findings of guilt, the recording of convictions, and the utilization of stern sentencing outcomes, in combination have the potential to recognize the seriousness of research fraud and to go some distance towards dissuading others from the temptation of engaging in it.

Destruction of Research Data

The way in which a researcher responds to allegations of research misconduct can itself give rise to criminal liability. This can be the product of a cynical attempt to hide engagement in fraudulent conduct, or obduracy on the part of the person the subject of allegations, or as a result of the complex dynamics that can evolve between whistleblowers and those against whom they make allegations. However, whatever the cause of unpreparedness to make data available for inspection, this constitutes a fundamental impediment to the imposition of

[407] See Reardon, n 402.

accountability for the quality of research and constitutes a potential licence for unchecked commission of fraud.

The Gillberg Controversy

The divisive saga involving Christopher Gillberg, professor of child and adolescent psychiatry at Gothenburg University, which spanned the years 2002 to 2012, raises such issues confrontingly. The events involving Professor Gillberg have been described as 'perhaps the greatest research scandal in Sweden'.[408] In addition, they had an extraordinary legal outcome which made its way to the Grand Chamber of the European Court of Human Rights. The case arose in respect of the imposition of criminal penalties upon, amongst others Professor Gillberg, for the destruction of extensive quantities of research data.

The origins of what became a bitter dispute lay in a meeting on the Swedish island of Resö between Professor Gillberg and Dr Leif Elinder, a paediatrician. Professor Gillberg was a world expert on autism spectrum disorders, attention deficit hyperactivity disorder (ADHD), and a concept developed in the 1970s known as DAMP—deficits in attention, motor control and perception. He was the author of more than 500 peer-reviewed articles, many in prominent scholarly journals. At the meeting a conversation took place about Professor Gillberg's work. Dr Elinder had developed strong reservations about Professor Gillberg's approach to the diagnosis and treatment of children with behavioural problems. After the meeting, Dr Elinder's concerns about Professor Gillberg's preparedness to diagnose up to 10 per cent of Sweden's children with a variety of neuropsychiatric disorders and to treat them with pharmacotherapies grew. He was joined in his concerns by Eva Kärfve, an associate professor of sociology at Lund University who edited a book, to which Dr Elinder contributed, attacking Professor Gillberg's work.[409]

Professor Gillberg's response was to accuse Associate Professor Kärfve of having been manipulated by association with Scientology. Shortly after the publication of the Elinder book, a follow-up of work undertaken by Professor Gillberg was published by the *Journal of the American Academy of Child and Adolescent Psychiatry*.[410] Professor Gillberg discussed the findings at the annual meeting of the Royal College of Psychiatrists in London in 2001. However, by 2002 Associate Professor Kärfve and Dr Elinder went to the stage of accusing Professor Gillberg of research fraud. They launched a series of actions to attempt to obtain access to the raw data of Professor Gillberg's Gothenburg study. When Professor Gillberg declined to provide the data, maintaining that he had guaranteed confidentiality to all of the participants, Associate Professor Kärfve took action in Sweden's Administrative Court of Appeal (*Kammarrätten i Göteborg*) to obtain them and also demanded that an inquiry be undertaken by Gothenburg University. The parents of the children who had participated in the Gothenburg study opposed the application.

In multiple judgments at trial level and on appeal Sweden's administrative courts held against Professor Gillberg. However, the ethics committee of the Gothenburg University declined to convene an inquiry; it supported Professor Gillberg and asserted that Professor Kärfve and Dr Elinder lacked bona fides in their application as they were not acting as true researchers. However, the University and Professor Gillberg failed to provide the data as ordered. Shortly after the final court orders his three research colleagues informed

---

[408] Thomas Brante, 'More on Data Destruction and Research Misconduct in Sweden' (2004) 329 *British Medical Journal* 72.

[409] See Jonathan Gornall, 'Hyperactivity in Children: The Gillberg Affair' (2007) 335 *British Medical Journal* 370.

[410] Peder Rasmussen and Christopher Gillberg, 'Natural Outcome of ADHD with Developmental Coordination Disorder at Age 22 Years' (2000) 39 *American Academy of Child and Adolescent Psychiatry* 1424.

the Vice-Chancellor of the University that they had shredded all the data. This resulted in Professor Gillberg being charged with and convicted in 2005 of misuse of office (*tjänstefel*).[411] Professor Gillberg was given a conditional sentence and ordered to pay fines and costs. He was fined SEK37,500 (approximately €4,000). He applied for leave to appeal but was refused. The Vice-Chancellor of the university, Professor Gunnar Svedberg, was also convicted of misuse of office for having disregarded, through negligence, his obligations as Vice-Chancellor by failing to ensure that the documents were available for release as ordered in accordance with the judgments of the Administrative Court of Appeal. He was sentenced to fines of SEK32,000 (approximately €3,400) and resigned his position.

The Parliamentary Ombudsman also decided to initiate criminal proceedings against the Chair of the Board of Gothenburg University, but the charges were later dismissed. Finally, by a judgment issued on 17 March 2006, the three officials who had destroyed the research material were convicted of the offence of suppression of documents and were sentenced to a conditional sentence and fines.[412]

Professor Gillberg unsuccessfully appealed his conviction and sentence to the Swedish Court of Appeal (*Hovrätten för Västra Sverige*). It rejected Professor Gillberg's assertion that he had been precluded from complying with the order to make the data available by provisions in the World Medical Association Declaration of Helsinki—Ethical Principles for Medical Research Involving Human Subjects, which provides (as amended in October 2008) that:

> Authors, editors and publishers all have ethical obligations with regard to the publication of the results of research. Authors have a duty to make publicly available the results of their research on human subjects and are accountable for the completeness and accuracy of their reports. They should adhere to accepted guidelines for ethical reporting. Negative and inconclusive as well as positive results should be published or otherwise made publicly available. Sources of funding, institutional affiliations and conflicts of interest should be declared in the publication. Reports of research not in accordance with the principles of this Declaration should not be accepted for publication.

The Court of Appeal concluded that it was not open to Professor Gillberg to provide greater provision for secrecy to participants in the trials than was provided under Swedish law and thus that his promises of confidentiality did not take precedence over the law. Professor Gillberg was refused leave to appeal to the Supreme Court of Sweden in 2006.

The next step in the unfortunate and bitterly divisive saga was transacted before the European Court of Human Rights (third Section) in 2010 in *Gillberg v Sweden*.[413] It was argued on behalf of Professor Gillberg that the Swedish courts' decisions were in legal error on the ground that they breached Articles 8[414] and 10[415] of the European Convention on Human Rights

---

[411] See Caroline White, 'Clash Over Public Access Rights and Patient Confidentiality Sparks Trial' (2005) 330 *British Medical Journal* 273.

[412] See Swedish Parliamentary Ombudsman, *Report for the Period 1 July 2005 to 30 June 2006*: <http://www.informath.org/apprise/a6400/b2060.pdf> [accessed 22 Dec 2015].

[413] [2010] ECHR 1676.

[414] '1. Everyone has the right to respect for his private and family life, his home and his correspondence.
2. There shall be no interference by a public authority with the exercise of this right except such as is in accordance with the law and is necessary in a democratic society in the interests of national security, public safety or the economic well-being of the country, for the prevention of disorder or crime, for the protection of health or morals, or for the protection of the rights and freedoms of others.'

[415] '1. Everyone has the right to freedom of expression. This right shall include freedom to hold opinions and to receive and impart information and ideas without interference by public authority and regardless of frontiers. This Article shall not prevent States from requiring the licensing of broadcasting, television or cinema enterprises.

(ECHR). However, he did not succeed. The Court reiterated (by 5 votes to 2) that the declarations of the World Medical Association could not take precedence over Swedish Law[416] and concluded that Professor Gillberg in his capacity as head of the Department of Child and Adolescent Psychiatry at the University (a State institution) 'intentionally failed to comply with his obligations as a public official from the judgments of the Administrative Court of Appeal'.[417] It found unanimously that Professor Gillberg had not had his right to freedom of expression violated by his conviction for misuse of his office. Judge Power observed that:

> The public has an obvious interest in the findings and implications of research. Progress in scientific knowledge would be hampered unduly if the methods and evidence used in research were not open to scrutiny, discussion and debate. Thus, the requests for access, in my view, represented important matters of public interest....
>
> Confidentiality in medical research relationships, although an important matter of public interest and meriting the law's protection, cannot be said to be absolute. There may be times when a person owing a duty of confidence is obliged to disclose information that was given 'in confidence' as, for example, where disclosure is necessary to prevent a risk of foreseeable harm to a patient or to a third party or where it is made on foot of a court order. Thus, at the outset of any clinical research project or other 'confidential' therapeutic relationship, the legal boundaries within which the duty of confidence arises ought to be clearly established.
>
> If what appears to be the applicant's perception of the binding nature of his promise of confidentiality were correct, then courts could rarely, if ever, order disclosure of 'confidential' records even where the protection of other important interests were in issue. Yet case law from various jurisdictions indicates that applications for disclosure of 'confidential' records are frequently brought before the courts and it is not unusual for courts to engage in a balancing exercise of the competing interests involved.
>
> No medical practitioner or academic researcher, no matter how committed to the principle of confidentiality, is permitted to act outside the law. Respect for the rule of law upon which the foundations of democracy rest requires respect for lawful Court orders. The applicant was not entitled to do what he did and his conviction with a suspended sentence was not, in my view, disproportionate having regard to all the circumstances of the case.

However, Judges Gyulumyan and Ziemele dissented, finding that Professor Gillberg's Article 8 rights had been violated. They observed that the reasons for the destruction of the data 'concerned the best interests of the children and the protection of the families involved in... research at the University of Gothenburg. The researchers had promised confidentiality of the information collected about the individuals concerned. There is no question that the promise of confidentiality is essential for the purposes of medical, social, and behavioural studies. It is only with this guarantee that researchers can expect research subjects to submit the most accurate data. In other words, if science is to make progress in areas that are important for human beings, the confidentiality and protection of research data is of key importance.' They observed that Article 8 refers not only to the protection of the privacy of third persons but also refers to the notion of privacy in the context of work by a 'researcher in a sensitive medical sphere and his authority as a professional medical researcher.' Thus, they found that the arguments on behalf of Professor Gillberg in respect of his ethical obligations should have

---

2. The exercise of these freedoms, since it carries with it duties and responsibilities, may be subject to such formalities, conditions, restrictions or penalties as are prescribed by law and are necessary in a democratic society, in the interests of national security, territorial integrity or public safety, for the prevention of disorder or crime, for the protection of health or morals, for the protection of the reputation or rights of others, for preventing the disclosure of information received in confidence, or for maintaining the authority and impartiality of the judiciary.'

[416] At [115].

[417] At [116].

been examined more carefully by the Swedish courts. The dissenting judges found that the Swedish courts had been too 'formalistic' and 'in a sense self-righteous'[418] in their analysis of the issues. They concluded that the courts should have had regard to:

> the major chilling effect that an imposition of a criminal sentence on a researcher and the subsequent criminal record will have. A criminal sentence is clearly disproportionate in view of the important interests involved, even if balanced against the fundamental principle of access to information as regulated in Sweden. Surely, the State would want to promote medical science both in the interests of the population and also for reasons of competition and economic development. Surely, Sweden would want to be among those States which promote medical research in compliance with the human rights of those individuals who agree to participate in such research and with respect for the researchers. It is therefore desirable that a more nuanced approach to the principle governing access to information be called for today.
>
> It may very well be that the applicant was liable to disciplinary punishment for his behaviour, but criminal responsibility for protecting at least equally important public and State interests seems to be an exaggerated reaction.[419]

Professor Gillberg then appealed the decision of the Third Section of the Court to the Grand Chamber of the European Court of Human Rights. He argued that he had a right under Article 8 of the ECHR not to impart confidential information and that this right had been breached by his criminal conviction. He also contended that his moral integrity, his reputation and his honour had been adversely affected by the conviction to a degree falling within the scope of Article 8, and that he had suffered personally, socially, psychologically, and economically; he asserted he had lost income because he had been dismissed by the Norwegian Institute of Public Health and because he could have written at least five books during the time that had been taken up by the case. He argued that the Swedish authorities had put him in the impossible dilemma of having either to breach his promise of secrecy to the participants in the study by complying with the Administrative Court of Appeal's judgments, which in his opinion were wrong, or to refuse to comply with the judgments and run the risk of being convicted for misuse of office. He chose to keep his promise of secrecy and received support for that decision from numerous renowned and highly respected scientists.

Again Professor Gillberg lost, this time unanimously.[420] In 2012 the Grand Chamber observed that he had been convicted of misuse of office in his capacity as a public official: 'His conviction was not the result of an unforeseeable application of that provision and the offence in question has no obvious bearing on the right to respect for 'private life'. On the contrary, it concerns professional acts and omissions by public officials in the exercise of their duties. Nor has the applicant pointed to any concrete repercussions on his private life which were directly and causally linked to his conviction for that specific offence'.[421] It held that none of Professor Gillberg's rights to expression had been affected and, as he was not the doctor of the research participants, he had no duty of professional secrecy towards them.

The capacity for others to scrutinize researcher's data so as to evaluate the integrity of research is a check and balance that is particularly important in an environment in which significant numbers of researchers have falsified their data. This is not to say that this had been what Professor Gillberg did but it is to observe that the issues that arose in the Gillberg case were genuinely important for an important area of intellectual disputation, and that his

418 At [5].
419 At [5]–[6].
420 *Gillberg v Sweden* [2012] ECHR 569.
421 *Gillberg v Sweden* [2012] ECHR 569 at [70].

destruction of his records meant that the legitimacy of his work could not be established. The destruction of records involved 25 years of work from a highly recognized researcher. As Brante observed, 'this situation creates problems: we have several books, accepted PhD-theses and articles in scientific journals that are based on Gillberg's data, and there are numerous DAMP-centres all over the country treating children guided by these findings which cannot be verified being based on now non-existent data spanning such a long time.'[422] A dilemma arose as to what should be done with the fruits of research whose status is now that it is based upon data that cannot be reviewed and verified. Brante, for instance, drew inspiration from the maxim '*contra spoliatorem omnia praesumuntur*'[423] and argued for the need for researchers generally to adhere to the sentiments expressed in the American Psychological Association's Ethical Rule 8:14: 'After research results are published, psychologists do not withhold the data on which their conclusions are based from other competent professionals who seek to verify the substantive claims through reanalysis and who intend to use such data only for that purpose, provided the confidentiality of the participants can be protected and unless legal rights concerning proprietary data preclude their release.' This led him to the extreme position that all of the Gillberg research should be withdrawn.[424] He was not successful in this respect—journals did not retract Professor Gillberg's publications and Professor Gillberg went on to develop his theories further, including from his position at the University of Gothenburg.

However, against the issue of the status of Professor Gillberg's research must be balanced the need to ensure the privacy of the subjects of research. It is important in the context of the Gillberg saga to recall that his accusers were making very serious allegations (which were never proved) of research impropriety against Professor Gillberg. It is most unfortunate, and arguably a systemic failing, that no middle path was able to be found which was mutually satisfactory in a protracted and bitter saga of disputation by which his data could not have been provided in an anonymized form which would have been sufficient to enable objective assessment of the legitimacy of his methodology and data interpretation. This was attempted but by the stage of the attempt the adversarialism of the parties (for a complex variety of reasons) had become intractably entrenched; as Judge Power noted at first instance in the European Court of Human Rights, 'Notwithstanding the existence of such safeguards, the applicant nevertheless persisted in his opposition to the release of the documentation insisting upon the binding nature of his promise of confidentiality to the research participants.'

---

422 Thomas Brante, 'More on Data Destruction and Research Misconduct in Sweden' (2004) 329 *British Medical Journal* 72, 75.

423 See generally *Armory v Delamirie* (1722) 93 ER 664 where a chimney thief found a ring with jewels in it and took it for appraisal of its worth. When the jeweller returned the ring without the jewel, the chimney sweep took action to recover the ring and the judge instructed the jury to presume the strongest case against him, and make the value of the best jewels the measure of their damages. See also *R v Arundel* (1617) 1 Hob 109, 80 ER 258; *Sullivan v General Motors Corp*, 772 F Supp 358, 360 (ND Ohio 1991); *Welsh v United States*, 844 F 2d 1239, 1246 (6th Cir 1988); *Saloustis v Nikic* [1961] Law Society Judgment Scheme 11; Craig Jones, 'The Spoliation Doctrine and Expert Evidence in Civil Trials' (1998) 32 *University of British Columbia Law Review* 293; British Columbia Law Institute, *Report on Spoliation of Evidence, Report No* 34, (Vancouver, British Columbia Law Institute, 2004), 3–10; Margaret M Koesel, Tracey L Turnbull, and Daniel F Gourash, *Spoliation of Evidence: Sanctions and Remedies for Destruction of Evidence in Civil Litigation* (Chicago, Il: American Bar Association, 2006), ix; Jamie S Gorelick, Stephen Marzen, and Lawrence B Solum, *Destruction of Evidence* (Wolters Kluwer, updated as of 20 April 2015); 'Omnia Praesumuntur Contra Spoliatorem' (1962) *Adelaide Law Review* 344.

424 See also Aubrey Blumsohn, 'Ghost-Statistics, Raw Data and the Meaning of Authorship. Are We Learning Any Lessons from Scandals in Pharmaceutical Research?' (2007) 94 *Radical Statistics*: <http://www.fraudinscience.org/PG/blumsohn07radstats.pdf> [accessed 22 Dec 2015]; Sven Ove Hansson and Barbro Bjorkman, 'Bioethics in Sweden' (2006) 15(3) *Cambridge Quarterly of Healthcare Ethics* 285.

Confidentiality of data within research cannot be absolute. Researchers are obliged to act within the law, and thus to comply with court orders, but at a broader level should regard themselves as subject to the ethical obligation of transparency in respect of their data selection, retention, and interpretation. Otherwise, to use lawyers' language, their work descends into being a mere 'ipse dixit'—an assertion that cannot be evaluated. The Gillberg saga was no doubt contaminated by concerns arising from the perceived association of those who raised concerns about Professor Gillbergs's research with particular stances in relation to medication for children and adolescents whose behaviour is unorthodox and with the Church of Scientology that has an extreme position in respect of such matters.[425] The events surrounding Professor Gillberg provided a fillip for the creation of an independent agency in Sweden to investigate allegations of research misconduct.[426] However, the conviction of Professor Gillberg for the criminal offence of misuse of his office ultimately stands as strong legal authority about the ethical and legal obligation of researchers to accord primacy to their obligations to obey the law, at pain of criminal penalties, regardless of guarantees of absolute protection that they may have given to research participants. Non-compliance with transparency obligations, especially in face of allegations of research impropriety, will rarely be able to be rationalized on the basis of the need to guarantee complete anonymity for research participants.

Disciplinary Proceedings

An important forum for the resolution of research fraud allegations for practitioners subject to formal registration and regulation is that of the disciplinary hearing. A number of cases have been particularly prominent in this regard in the modern era:[427] in relation to a Scottish nephrologist, Dr Anderton, British psychiatrist, Dr Uzair Siddiqui; the British surgeon, Anjan Banerjee; the British obstetrician, Dr Malcolm Pearce; the prominent Australian researcher, Dr William McBride, discoverer of Thalidomide deformities; and the English scholars, Professor Walker-Smith, Professor Murch, and Dr Wakefield, who identified spurious links between MMR vaccine and autism.[428]

The following section of the chapter identifies a sequence of notorious disciplinary cases brought against health practitioners for research fraud. Then it draws conclusions about the role of disciplinary hearings as a means of imposing accountability for this form of professional misconduct.

Dr Anderton

In July 1977 Dr John Anderton, a kidney specialist and former Secretary of the Royal College of Physicians in Edinburgh, was struck off the medical register for conducting a sham drug trial into the efficacy of Amlodipine, made by Pfizer.[429] The trial extended over 15 months and provided Dr Anderton with over £40,000. He forged consent forms for 17 patients, obliged his assistant to attest falsely that she had witnessed the signatures and then invented a

[425] See Matthew Smith, *Hyperactive: The Controversial History of ADHD* (London: Reaktion Books, 2013), 175.

[426] See Caroline White, 'Destruction of Data Prompts Calls for Swedish Agency to Investigate Research Misconduct' (2004) 329 *British Medical Journal* 72.

[427] A little earlier, in 1975, Dr JP Sedgwick, a High Wycombe family doctor, had his name removed from the medical register after participating in a clinical trial and returning 101 completed clinical trial forms, with an assortment of forged signatures from the seven other participating doctors.

[428] The adverse findings against Professor Walker-Smith were overturned on appeal: *Walker-Smith v General Medical Council* [2012] EWHC 503 (Admin).

[429] See Peter Mitchell, 'Edinburgh Doctor Struck Off Because of Clinical-Trial Fraud' (1997) 350(9073) *Lancet* 273; Clare Dyer, 'Consultant Struck Off Over Research Fraud' (1997) 315(7102) *BMJ* 205.

series of results for tests that had never been conducted on patients. A Pfizer monitor identified the forged signatures, after it was noticed that the name of Dr Anderton's assistant was wrongly spelt on the consent forms. The GMC found that Dr Anderton had 'repeatedly behaved dishonestly' and had abused the trust of his administrative staff.[430] It found him guilty of serious professional misconduct and cancelled his registration. He claimed to have been suffering from a breakdown at the time of his forgeries.[431]

Two years later he applied again for registration but the GMC was informed that Dr Anderton's conduct had put '[e]xtremely sick people... at unnecessary risk and Pfizer had to discard all the data at a cost of nearly £250,000'.[432] He was unsuccessful in his application.

Dr Siddiqui

In 1988 a clinical monitor from a pharmaceutical company identified that a psychiatrist, Dr Uzair Siddiqui, had fabricated data in relation to a clinical trial and invented the identity of one patient completely.[433] When he was challenged about the anomalies, Dr Siddiqui somewhat implausibly maintained that he had not performed the study himself but had delegated it to a registrar whose name he could not remember and whose current whereabouts he did not know. Her identity was discovered and she denied any involvement in the study. The pharmaceutical company reported the matter to the General Medical Council (GMC). A Professional Conduct Committee found Dr Siddiqui guilty of serious professional misconduct and his name was erased from the medical register.

Dr Pearce

In 1995 a prominent British obstetrician and a Senior Lecturer at St George's Hospital Medical Centre, Dr Malcolm Pearce, was found guilty of serious professional misconduct and struck off the medical register by the GMC after claiming to have performed a pioneering operation. He had claimed in the *British Journal of Obstetrics and Gynaecology* (of which he was an assistant editor) that a 29-year-old African woman had given birth to a healthy baby girl after he had successfully relocated a five-week-old ectopic embryo into her womb. However, this account was entirely false. Dr Pearce had tampered with his records, the patient could not be identified, and none of his colleagues knew anything of his alleged research. In the same issue of the journal Dr Pearce published the results of a three-year, purportedly double-blind randomized control trial involving 191 women who were prone to miscarriage and who had been treated with either the hormone, human chorionic gonadotropin, or a placebo.[434] Sir Robert Kilpatrick, chairman of the GMC Disciplinary Committee, observed that this 'web of deceit has had incalculable consequences for public confidence in the integrity of research'.[435]

---

430 'Disgraced Doctor Seeks Reinstatement', *BBC News*, 17 August 1999: <http://news.bbc.co.uk/2/hi/uk_news/scotland/422288.stm> [accessed 23 Dec 2015].

431 Ibid.

432 Tom Kelly, 'Struck Off Doctor Loses Appeal Over Bogus tests', *The Birmingham Post*, 18 August 1999, 8, available at: <http://www.thefreelibrary.com/Struck-off+doctor_loses+appeal+over+bogus+tests.-a060491198> [accessed 23 Dec 2015].

433 See Frank Wells, 'Historical Aspects of Research Misconduct: Europe' in Frank Wells and Michael Farthing (eds), *Fraud and Misconduct in Biomedical Research* (4th edn, London: Royal Society of Medicine Press Press, 2008) 74–5; see also, 'GMC Professional Conduct Committee' (1988) 296(6617) *British Medical Journal* 306.

434 See Robert K Kamei, 'Professionalism: Looking for Your Blind Spots' (2006) 35(12) *Annals Academy of Medicine* 848: <http://www.annals.edu.sg/pdf/35VolNo12Dec2006/V35N12p848.pdf> [accessed 23 Dec 2015].

435 See Roger Dobson, 'Science: Doctoring the Evidence', *The Independent*, 9 August 1998: <http://www.independent.co.uk/arts-entertainment/science-doctoring-the-evidence-1170688.html> [accessed 23 Dec 2015].

The scandal that ensued also led to the resignation of Pearce's immediate superior and co-author, Professor Geoffrey Chamberlain, as President of the Royal College of Obstetricians and Gynaecologists and as editor of the College's journal. Professor Chamberlain claimed that his involvement in the article had been a 'gift authorship' by Pearce and that he had no idea that the work was fraudulent.[436]

Dr Williams

Dr Mark Williams, a senior lecturer at Bristol, was the author of a pioneering study into anti-angina medication which purported to be the product of interviews with 181 severely disabled adults who were also physically examined, and then allegedly followed up by telephone.[437] Inquiries later made into his research, after it had emerged that he had lied about his qualifications in order to secure the post of Senior Lecturer in Public Health Medicine at Bristol University, exposed that only about a third of the 181 subjects of the research could recall the original visit and none confirmed a telephone follow-up. The GMC erased his name from the medical register.

Mr Banerjee

Mr Anjan Banerjee had authored 49 publications within 18 months of his graduation as a medical practitioner.[438] In 2000, by which time he had become a consultant surgeon, Mr Banerjee was suspended for 12 months by the GMC for publishing fraudulent articles ten years previously. The first article (in *Gut*) was found to contain information that was deliberately falsified, while the second was an abstract that he submitted around the same time to the British Society of Gastroenterology, claiming that the results were based on urine samples from 12 healthy adults, whereas in fact they were exclusively from his own urine. King's College Hospital, where Mr Banerjee was employed at the relevant time, undertook an inquiry shortly afterwards, which made adverse findings about Mr Banerjee's conduct, but took no further action.[439]

Mr Yates, who chaired the Professional Conduct Committee of the GMC in relation to Mr Bannerjee, observed:

> Medical research is central to the advance of medical practice and must always be conducted with scrupulous honesty and integrity. It is highly irresponsible, and potentially dangerous for patients, for a doctor to falsify research. The committee consider that these events illustrate seriously irresponsible and dishonest behaviour on your part.[440]

The whistleblower to the GMC was the consultant cardiologist, Dr Peter Wilmshurst of the Royal Shrewsbury Hospital, who had campaigned for several years in relation to the phenomenon of research fraud. The case took a surprisingly long time to reach the GMC and evidentiary difficulties emerged because the authorities at King's College Hospital in London, where Mr Banerjee had been employed at the time of the incidents, had shredded the laboratory books that had existed when Mr Banerjee was undertaking his research. The matter was further complicated by the fact that evidence emerged that the research in Mr Banerjee's Master of Surgery degree, which included the article submitted to *Gut*, was also fraudulent.[441]

---

436 See Salhab, above n 324, 1.

437 See Clare Dyer, 'Doctor Admits Research Fraud' (1998) 316(7132) *BMJ* 647.

438 Peter Wilmshurst, 'Dishonesty in Medical Research' (Address to the Medico-Legal Society, 9 December 2004) 75(1) *Medico-Legal Journal* 3, available at: <http://www.medico-legalsociety.org.uk/articles/dishonesty_in_medical_research.pdf> (viewed 4 February 2015).

439 Peter Wilmshurst, 'The Code of Silence' (1997) 349(9051) *Lancet* 567.

440 See Annabel Ferriman, 'Consultant Suspended for Research Fraud' (2000) 321(7274) *BMJ* 1429.

441 Ibid.

The editor of *Gut*, Michael Farthing,[442] made telling points in an editorial which formalized the retraction of Banerjee's article:

> The Banerjee case illustrates a number of important deficiencies in the way in which we handle alleged cases of research misconduct in the UK. Firstly, it is evident that it is relatively simple to fabricate data and get it published in a reputable medical journal. In the majority of cases it will be virtually impossible for reviewers and editors to identify fraudulent material. Detection in this case, and in many others will almost always depend on the willingness of a vigilant whistleblower to speak out. There is little to gain for whistleblowers, particularly when their comments fall on deaf ears, or they are threatened with professional extinction. Secondly, the case demonstrates the potential weakness of the *internal inquiry*. Although it is unclear as to the location of the final resting place of the King's Banerjee Report, it is alleged that its findings were not in Banerjee's favour. It then took almost a decade and the persistent efforts of an external whistle blower, who had no conflicting interests, to bring the case to the GMC.... The case also shows the importance of the role of the research supervisor as a custodian of research quality.

There was an important disciplinary footnote to the Banerjee case. Timothy Peters, Professor of Clinical Biochemistry at King's College School of Medicine and Dentistry, London, was found guilty of serious professional misconduct and given a severe reprimand by a Professional Conduct Committee of the GMC for failing to take action over falsified research published by Mr Banerjee. The chair of the Committee, Mrs Clark-Glass, found that from 1988 colleagues had raised doubts about Mr Banerjee's research and eventually he had admitted falsifying his results: 'Thereafter you took insufficient steps either to prevent Dr Banerjee from further falsifying his research or to ensure that, where such research had been published, timely retractions of it were made... these events amount to a series of culpable omissions on your part, representing highly irresponsible behaviour. This conduct fell seriously short of the standards expected of a person in your position.'[443]

Dr Prasad

One of the more bizarre cases of alleged research fraud involved Dr Ashok Prasad, an Indian psychiatrist who worked in the United Kingdom and then in Australia from 1987, until he left while a hearing by Victoria's Medical Practitioners Board was pending. He claimed to be the great-grandson of India's first President.

Professor David Copolov, Director of the Mental Health Research Institute of Victoria, identified anomalies in research that Dr Prasad was undertaking into whether being born in winter was a risk factor for developing schizophrenia.[444] Professor Copolov identified that data that Prasad claimed to have obtained about the hemisphere in which subjects were born could not have been obtained from where he claimed—the Medical Records Office. It became apparent to him that the data on which Dr Prasad relied were fabricated. Dr Prasad maintained that he had a collaborator who wished to remain anonymous who had obtained the data. He then claimed to be unwell. When he was stood down, he claimed to have been awarded the Anna-Monika Medal for research into depression. However, it turned out that this too was false.

---

[442] Michael J G Farthing, 'Retractions in *Gut* 10 Years After Publication' (2001) 48(3) *Gut* 285 at 286 (footnote omitted).

[443] Clare Dyer, 'Professor Reprimanded for Failing to Act Over Fraud' (2001) 322(7286) *BMJ* 573, 573; Sarah Boseley, 'Medical Establishment "Covered Up" for Fraudulent Consultant', *The Guardian*, 22 November 2002: <http://www.theguardian.com/news/2002/nov/22/medicineandhealth.lifeandhealth> [accessed 23 Dec 2015].

[444] This account derives from the interview given by Professor Copolov and Dr Kerry Breen with Norman Swan on ABC Radio National's *Health Report*: ABC Radio National, 'Scientific Fraud and Defamation', *Health Report*, 17 August 1998 (Norman Swan): <http://www.abc.net.au/radionational/programs/healthreport/scientific-fraud-and-defamation/3552080#transcript> [accessed 23 Dec 2015].

An inquiry was established, chaired by Professor John Funder, to report to the Minister for Health. The report which was laid before the Victorian Parliament concluded in March 1988 that 'the figures produced by Dr Prasad on the monthly distribution of birth dates of schizophrenic patients, and on the monthly ratios of Australian-born to non-Australian-born schizophrenic patients, are clearly false'.[445] It also found that 'Dr Prasad's claim that his PhD was passed in 1987... [has] been rejected as false by his PhD supervisor'.[446] It recommended that his resignation should be accepted.[447]

In 1988 the Medical Practitioners Board of Victoria cancelled Dr Prasad's temporary registration, although lawyers on his behalf sought injunctions twice in the Supreme Court of Victoria, claiming the Board did not have jurisdiction. According to the later President of the Board, Dr Kerry Breen, once the hearing was able to proceed, the outcome was in little doubt 'because the evidence against him was really quite powerful'.[448]

The Board concluded that the figures produced by Dr Prasad in his research on the monthly distribution of birth dates of patients with schizophrenia and the monthly ratios of Australian-born to non-Australian-born patients with schizophrenia were 'clearly false'.[449] Likewise it found that his claim that he had collected data on 8,000 patients with schizophrenia from Royal Park Hospital records was false.[450] It observed that '[t]here is no evidence to support Dr Prasad's claim that he was assisted in collecting this data by an un-named associate' and concluded that responsibility for the false figures rested with Dr Prasad.[451] It found that a paper, entitled 'Post Partum Psychiatric Disorders in Aboriginal Women' which Dr Prasad presented to the Marcé Society in Stockholm in September 1987, was based on fabrication. It found that it was obvious that Dr Prasad was not awarded the Anna-Monika Medal and had not obtained a PhD in psychiatry, but rather that he had forged the signature of his PhD supervisor at the University of London.[452] It noted a suggestion by a psychiatrist that Dr Prasad may have been suffering from pseudologia fantastica[453] but, on the basis of the evidence before it, rejected the submission put on behalf of Dr Prasad that he was suffering from a significant mental illness or personality disorder. It reached 'a high degree of satisfaction' that the conduct of Dr Prasad had been dishonourable and disgraceful and amounted to infamous conduct in a professional respect.[454]

---

445 John Funder, *Report to the Minister Containing a Summary of the Resolutions of the Committee of Enquiry Examining Research Practices Employed by Dr Ashoka Prasad in relation to the Research Project Entitled 'Seasonality Study'* (Report No 92, 1987–1988) [1]: <http://www.parliament.vic.gov.au/papers/govpub/VPARL1987-88No92.pdf> [accessed 23 Dec 2015]. See also, Theodor J Strehlow, *Index to Victorian Parliamentary Papers 1950–1992* (Victorian Government Printer, Melbourne, 1995): <http://www.lib.unimelb.edu.au/collections/bibhome/vicind50.pdf> (viewed 4 February 2015).

446 Ibid, [6].

447 Ibid, [11].

448 'Scientific Fraud and Defamation', above n 444.

449 Medical Board of Victoria, 'Section 17 Inquiry—Dr Ashoka Prasad', 12 December 1988 (copy on file with author) 4.

450 Ibid, 4.

451 Ibid, 4.

452 Ibid, 4.

453 See Bryan H King and Charles V Ford, 'Pseudologia Fantastica' (1988) 77(1) *Acta Psychiatrica Scandinavica* 1, who concluded that the term 'pseudologia fantastica', which is present in the diagnostic criteria for conditions such as Munchausen syndrome, could be characterized by the following: '(1) the stories are not entirely improbable and are often built upon a matrix of truth; (2) the stories are enduring; (3) the stories are not told for personal profit *per se* and have a self-aggrandizing quality; and (4) they are distinct from delusions in that the person when confronted with facts can acknowledge these falsehoods' 1.

454 Medical Board of Victoria, n 449, 6.

By the time Prasad was deregistered he had left Australia for Canada where, after he was apparently nominated for the Nobel Peace Prize, he was struck off in British Columbia.[455] After this, according to Professor Copolov, he engaged in an ongoing retributive campaign against him. As of 2014 he was continuing to generate publicity against Professor Copolov, Dr Kerry Breen, by then a former President of the Victorian Medical Practitioners Board, and a member of the Australian Research Integrity Committee, and those who conducted the Health Department Inquiry into his conduct, claiming that he had been the victim of racism.[456]

Dr McBride

In a case which remains one of the most fraught and fiercely contested ever brought against a scholar and registered health practitioner, on 30 July 1993 the Medical Tribunal of New South Wales removed from the medical register the name of Dr William McBride, one of Australia's best-known medical practitioners and researchers. Dr McBride had achieved multiple accolades as the person who had discovered the link between the drug Thalidomide and birth deformities.[457] Dr McBride was awarded a medal and prize money by the prestigious L'Institut de la Vie of the French Government in connection with his discovery. Using the prize money, he established Foundation 41, a medical research foundation dedicated to investigating the causes of birth defects. He had been named Man of the Year in 1962, Australian of the Year in the same year, Commander of the Order of the British Empire in 1969, Father of the Year in 1972, and Officer of the Order of Australia in 1977.

In 1982 Dr McBride published a paper in the *Australian Journal of Biological Science* on experiments on rabbits with hyoscine (also known as scopolamine), a component of Debendox (another morning sickness drug),[458] which appeared to support the hypothesis that Debendox was teratogenic. After the publication, another scientist, Phillip Vardy, confronted with him in relation to the rabbits upon which experimentation had taken place, asserting that these had been fraudulently increased in number. When the confrontation between Vardy and McBride failed to resolve the matter, Vardy wrote to members of the Research Advisory Committee of Foundation 41. Considerable publicity followed, including assertions by Dr Norman Swan on the ABC's *Science Report* to the effect that Dr McBride had engaged in scientific fraud.

In due course, a hearing, consuming 180 sitting days (46 of which consisted of Dr McBride giving evidence[459]) and chaired by District Court Judge Wall, found that in an article published in the *Australian Journal of Biological Science* Dr McBride 'deliberately made false statements... in relation to the experimental data, deliberately misreported the method of the experiment and included spurious data'.[460] The Tribunal concluded that the explanation for this conduct was 'to strengthen the appearance of the experiment as a properly designed experiment in order to enhance the publishability of the Article and hence provide support for his hypothesis that hyoscine may be a teratogen'.[461] The Tribunal found that

---

455 'Scientific Fraud and Defamation', above n 444.

456 Ashok J Prasad, 'Racism in Medical Profession!' (10 March 2014) *India Medical Times*: <http://www.indiamedicaltimes.com/2014/03/10/guest-article-racism-in-medical-profession-dr-ashok-jahnavi-prasad/> [accessed 23 Dec 2015].

457 See Michael Magazanik, *Silent Shock* (Melbourne: Text Publishing, 2015).

458 Dr McBride's position is that 'it is however related in pharmacological action to two components of that drug': William McBride, *Killing the Messenger* (Cremorne, NSW: Eldorado, 1994). 220.

459 See Phillip Knightley, 'Foreword' in McBride, n 458.

460 Cited in *Re McBride* (unreported, Medical Tribunal of New South Wales, 29 April 1996), available at: <http://www.mcnsw.org.au/resources/378/McBride.pdf> 2 [accessed 23 Dec 2015].

461 Ibid.

Dr McBride did not simply alter the experimental data to fit the hypothesis but he 'invented material data to support his hypothesis that hyoscine was a possible teratogen. When he did this he crossed the line that separates error of judgement and moral turpitude'.[462]

Prior to the Medical Tribunal hearing, a research advisory committee at Foundation 41, chaired by a former Chief Justice of Australia, Sir Harry Gibbs,[463] had found Dr McBride guilty of 'deliberate falsification'. It concluded that the rabbit experiment published in the *Australian Journal of Biological Sciences* 'was not conducted in accordance with proper scientific method and was not honestly reported'. It found that the experiment 'and its published results does suggest that in relation to the publication of those results Dr McBride was lacking in scientific integrity'.[464] It concluded 'the motive underlying at least three of [these frauds] was a passionate belief in the truth and wider-than-scientific importance of a right-seeming doctrine that lay so far out of the accepted canon that it was felt to be the subject of unfair discrimination by orthodox scientists.'[465]It required him to arrange the publication of a Note in correction of the article. After a meeting with the Board of Foundation 41, Dr McBride resigned.

However, the action that Dr McBride took in purported compliance with the Committee's requirement was the subject of adverse finding by the Tribunal:

> In relation to the preparation and publication of the Note the Tribunal has found Dr McBride caused to be published in the Note statements which were misleading and which he knew were misleading. The Tribunal has found that the explanation for this conduct is that he did not wish to be made public that members of the Research Advisory Committee of Foundation 41 had considered a complaint by the co authors of the Article that the description of the rabbit experiments and experimental data published in the Article did not correspond with their recollection of the experiments nor with the contemporaneous records of the experiments and as a result the committee had directed that there be a retraction of the relevant published material.
>
> […]
>
> Dr McBride was responsible for the wording of the Note which was a deliberate distortion of the true situation and was the first step on a course of evasion and deception to avoid accountability for his fraudulent conduct which the Tribunal found has continued up to and during the course of the inquiry.[466]

The Tribunal concluded that:

> Dr McBride's conduct in causing the publication of the Article in its fraudulent form was not the honest mistake of a naïve man, ignorant in the ways of true science; it was not an error of judgment caused by an excess of zeal because of concern to get out an early warning to the public that hyoscine hydrobromide may be a teratogen. His acts were not made in haste; they were not made by a man in poor physical or mental health. His acts demonstrated a course of conduct of premeditated deception in the field of medical research and indicate a serious flaw or defect in his character, a trait of dishonesty.[467]

---

462 Ibid.

463 See George F Humphrey, 'Scientific Fraud: The McBride Case' (1992) 32(3) *Medicine, Science and Law* 199.

464 McBride, n 458, 181.

465 McBride, n 458, 179

466 Unreported, Medical Tribunal of New South Wales, 30 July 1993, vol 8, 9, as cited in *Re McBride* (Unreported, Medical Tribunal of New South Wales, 29 April 1996) 2–3.

467 Unreported, Medical Tribunal of New South Wales, 30 July 1993, as cited in *McBride v Walton* [1994] NSWCA 199 (15 July 1994) 76, available at: <http://caselawsearch.lawlink.nsw.gov.au/ccaarchivejudgments/1994/1994_199.pdf> [accessed 23 Dec 2015].

> The lack of all sense of intellectual and moral honesty which this episode reveals in the life of a man long trained in the academic and clinical disciplines of an honourable profession and charged with the destiny of a medical research institute depending on public support is most reprehensible and demonstrates a lack of good character in the context of fitness to practise medicine.[468]

The Tribunal was highly critical of the way in which Dr McBride responded to the expression of concern by his researcher, Vardy, and found this to be indicative of a flaw of character.

In analysing the appropriate protective orders that it could make, the Tribunal determined that the dishonesty of Dr McBride in relation to the original article continued to be demonstrated by his denials, evasions, attempted justifications, and lies told in response to questions and inquiries up to and including the hearing before that Tribunal itself. The Tribunal found that the history of this conduct included 'many opportunities for the practitioner to make an honest disclosure of what happened and to retrieve his good character'.[469]

The majority members of the Tribunal (Prof GD Tracey dissenting) were of the view that they were unable to repose in Dr McBride their trust and confidence to be scrupulously honest and straightforward in the event that some conflict should arise in the future between his duty to be honest and self-interest. The likelihood of such an occurrence was thought to be 'not exceptionally remote'.[470] The majority members, having reviewed their determination, expressed their conclusions as follows:

> Dr McBride's conduct, his statements and his writings which have been reviewed by the Tribunal, indicate to the majority members of the Tribunal a serious degree of intellectual and moral dishonesty. He has exhibited and still exhibits a degree of casuistry which is incompatible with a real insight and understanding of the obligations required of a medical practitioner and incompatible with membership of an honourable and self respecting profession. The majority conclude that in the light of the findings and the conclusion reached in relation to Dr McBride's lack of good character public confidence in the integrity of the profession would be seriously undermined if he were to remain a member of the profession.[471]

The majority accordingly concluded that the appropriate order was for the removal of Dr McBride's name from the register.

Dr McBride appealed the decision to the Court of Appeal but met with no success, Handley JA observing: 'Far from subsequent events having established that the Appellant had reformed so that, at the time of the hearing by the Tribunal, he could then be regarded as being of good character, these events, in my view, would seem to indicate that, even now, the Appellant lacks any real insight into the gravity of what he has done.'[472]

He then embarked on a public relations campaign and a series of applications to the Medical Tribunal for restoration of his name on the medical register. Part of his strategy was the publication of an autobiography, *Killing the Messenger*, in which he described his views of the Gibbs Committee, including that it 'sought to undermine my reputation as the first doctor to

---

468 Ibid, 23.

469 Unreported, Medical Tribunal of New South Wales, 30 July 1993, vol 8, 18, as cited in *Re McBride* (unreported, Medical Tribunal of New South Wales, 29 April 1996) 3.

470 Unreported, Medical Tribunal of New South Wales, 30 July 1993, as cited in *Re McBride* (unreported, Medical Tribunal of New South Wales, 29 April 1996) 3.

471 Unreported, Medical Tribunal of New South Wales, 30 July 1993, vol 8, 23, as cited in *Re McBride* (unreported, Medical Tribunal of New South Wales, 29 April 1996) 4.

472 *McBride v Walton* [1994] NSWCA 199 (15 July 1994) 83 (Powell JA).

warn the world of the dangers of thalidomide'.[473] He also provided his view of the Tribunal's decision:

> One short paper I had written on the possible harmful effects of a drug which is a plant derivative of the deadly nightshade group, used both as a medicine and a poison since the time of the ancient Egyptians, that paper and its single claim, 'Results indicate interference by the drug with the function of the cholinergic nerves on the development of the chick and rabbit embryo', had destroyed my reputation and with it my authority to give evidence on behalf of children born deformed after their mothers had taken drugs produced by pharmaceutical-industrial-marketing complex.[474]

He denounced the decision of Medical Tribunal as having 'a puritanical aspect'[475] and argued that emerging evidence suggested that although 'I had perhaps acted in a non-orthodox manner',[476] his assertions in the impugned article may well have been correct. He also attacked the role of Dr Norman Swan, a medical journalist, for the publicity that he gave to the conduct of Dr McBride and proclaimed that he had been the victim of a miscarriage of justice. He contended that an aspect of the reasoning of the Tribunal amounted to a 'miscarriage of justice'[477] and argued that attachment to 'pure science' was 'sentimental, even quasi-religious, in the context of day-to-day research.'[478] He denied that dishonesty had been proven against him.[479]

In 1995 the Medical Tribunal (chaired by District Judge Freeman) heard an application by Dr McBride for re-registration on the basis that he had 'identified the defect in my character and realized the error of my ways'.[480] However, the Tribunal found a discrepancy between what Dr McBride asserted on the one hand and his evidence and conduct on the other. It emphasized that while it may have been pride that caused him to be dishonest, it was 'patent dishonesty' which was the flaw of character standing in the way of his being re-registered.[481] The Tribunal remarked on Dr McBride's preparedness to 'confuse the end with the means' and found that he was evasive when pressed about such matters. Taking into account Dr McBride's 'continuing absence of insight', it declined to re-register him.[482]

In 1998, however, the Tribunal (chaired by Judge Blanch) received another application from Dr McBride for him to resume registered status. On this occasion it was persuaded that it was in the public interest to allow Dr McBride to return to medicine, albeit in a limited capacity. He was significantly assisted by a character reference from the former Chief Justice of New South Wales, Sir Laurence Street, who informed the Tribunal that Dr McBride was a changed man, that Dr McBride admitted his dishonesty in his research, and that he was prepared to give an undertaking to refrain from medical research and to be supervised in his practice. Dr McBride informed the Tribunal that he no longer wished to practise in New South Wales but to work in American Samoa as a gynaecologist and obstetrician.[483] Thus concluded one of the mostly highly publicized impositions of disciplinary consequences on a medical

473 McBride, above n 458, 187.
474 McBride, above n 458, 217.
475 Ibid, 237.
476 McBride, above n 458, 240.
477 McBride, above n 458, 249.
478 McBride, above n 458, 254.
479 McBride, above n 458, 255.
480 *Re McBride* (unreported, Medical Tribunal of New South Wales, 29 April 1996) 1.
481 Ibid, 7.
482 Ibid, 7, 9, 11.
483 'McBride Cleared to Return to Work', *ABC Science*, 9 November 1998: <http://www.abc.net.au/science/articles/1998/11/09/14272.htm> (viewed 4 February 2015); Amanda Keenan, 'Shamed Medical Hero Back on the Good Books', *The Australian*, 10 November 1998, 1.

practitioner for research misconduct. Unfortunately, the effectiveness of the consequences as a deterrent to others minded to behave similarly is open to serious doubt.

Professor Walker-Smith, Professor Murch, and Dr Wakefield: The MMR Vaccination Case

The most extensive investigation ever conducted by Britain's regulator of doctors, the GMC, concluded in highly controversial circumstances in mid-2010 after a Fitness to Practise Panel heard evidence and submissions for 148 days over a period of two-and-a-half years. The panel deliberated in camera for 45 days before delivering a decision which was successfully appealed to the High Court.[484]

The three doctors the subject of investigation were:

- Professor John Walker-Smith, a Professor of Paediatric Gastroenterology at the Royal Free Hospital School of Medicine, who also held an honorary clinical contract with the Royal Free Hampstead NHS Trust;
- Professor Simon Murch, at the relevant time a Senior Lecturer in Paediatric Gastroenterology with the Royal Free Hospital School of Medicine, who also held an honorary consultant contract with the Royal Free Hampstead NHS Trust; and
- Dr Andrew Wakefield, a Senior Lecturer in the Departments of Medicine and Histopathology at the Royal Free Hospital, and after 1 May 1997 a Reader in Experimental Gastroenterology.

The case involved research ethics and research governance, particularly in relation to children. It has been asserted that: 'The alleged autism–vaccine connection is, perhaps, the most damaging medical hoax of the last 100 years.'[485]

The GMC made extensive findings of fact.[486] It concluded that in 1996 Dr Wakefield was involved with providing advice to a solicitor acting for persons who alleged they had suffered harm caused by the administration of the measles and measles/rubella (MMR) vaccine. It found that he provided the solicitor with costing proposals for a research study which was to involve selected vaccinated children, including five with an enteritis/disintegrative disorder. In due course the Legal Aid Board agreed to provide £55,000 towards the proposed study. However, the GMC found that the money provided was not needed because the study in relevant respects had already been funded by the NHS. It found that his conduct in attempting to 'double-dip' in relation to funding was dishonest and misleading. It was a misuse of public funds.

The GMC Committee found that Dr Wakefield and Professors Walker-Smith and Murch submitted an application to the Ethical Practices Sub-Committee of the Royal Free Hampstead NHS Trust, for a project entitled 'A new paediatric syndrome: enteritis and disintegrative disorder following measles/rubella vaccination', which sought approval for a study involving 25 children.[487] Its purpose was to assess whether a percentage of children after the vaccination experienced symptoms and signs of intestinal disease or dysfunction, namely pain, bloating, alternating constipation and diarrhoea, steatorrhoea (presence of excess fat in faeces), and failure to thrive. Dr Wakefield was to be responsible, it found, for arranging MRI and EEG

484 *Walker-Smith v General Medical Council* [2012] EWHC 503 (Admin).

485 Dennis K Flaherty, 'The Vaccine-Autism Connection: A Public Health Crisis Caused by Unethical Medical Practices and Fraudulent Science' (2011) 45(10) *Annals of Pharmacotherapy* 1302, 1302.

486 *Re Wakefield Walker-Smith and Murch* (unreported, Fitness to Practise Panel, 28 January 2010), available at: <http://www.casewatch.org/foreign/wakefield/gmc_findings.pdf> [accessed 23 Dec 2015]; see too *Re Wakefield* (unreported, GMC Fitness to Practise Panel, 24 May 2010); *Re Walker-Smith* (unreported, GMC Fitness to Practise Panel, 24 May 2010); *Re Murch* (unreported, GMC Fitness to Practise Panel, 24 May 2010) (copies on file with author).

487 *Re Wakefield* [5]; *Re Walker-Smith* [2]; *Re Murch* [2].

procedures. The Chairman of the Ethics Committee raised with Dr Wakefield and Professor Walker-Smith the intensive regime that would be required of the children. A response was provided that the children would have the investigations, including lumbar punctures, even if there were no clinical trial and that five had already been investigated on a clinical need basis. By reason of these reassurances, ethics approval was given.

The GMC found that as a responsible consultant each doctor had a responsibility to ensure that an application to an ethics committee was true and accurate and that only children who met the stated inclusion criteria were admitted to the study. It found in respect of Dr Wakefield that he should have declared to the Ethics Committee the funding from the Legal Aid Board.

It also made a series of detailed findings in respect of a number of children who underwent a programme of investigations as part of the study without ethics committee approval. It found that colonoscopies were carried out on a series of children when they were not clinically indicated. This led it to conclude in respect of Dr Wakefield and Dr Walker-Smith that they had engaged in professional misconduct. In relation to Dr Wakefield it found that:

> [S]hortcomings and the aggravating factors in this case including in broad terms the wide-ranging transgressions relating to every aspect of his research; his disregard for the clinical interests of vulnerable patients; his failure to heed the warnings he received in relation to the potential conflicts of interest associated with his Legal Aid Board funding; his failure to disclose the patent; his dishonesty and the compounding of that dishonesty in relation to the drafting of the Lancet paper; and his subsequent representations about it, all played out against a background of research involving such major public health implications, could not be addressed by any conditions on his registration. In addition, the Panel considered that his actions relating to the taking of blood [under informal circumstances] exemplifies a fundamental failure in the ethical standards expected of a medical practitioner.
>
> […]
>
> The Panel considers that Dr Wakefield's conduct in relation to the facts found falls seriously short of the relevant standards and that suspension would not be sufficient or appropriate against a background of several aggravating factors and in the absence of any mitigating submissions made on his behalf. Dr Wakefield's continued lack of insight as to his misconduct serve only to satisfy the Panel that suspension is not sufficient and that his actions are incompatible with his continued registration as a medical practitioner.[488]

Although it made various adverse findings against Professor Murch, who was a junior consultant in the department at the relevant time, the GMC did not find him to have engaged in serious professional misconduct, although it concluded he had committed 'errors of judgment' when acting in good faith.

The GMC Committee cancelled the registration of Dr Wakefield and Dr Walker-Smith. Both appealed although Dr Wakefield abandoned his appeal. However, he has continued to protest his innocence, including by a self-serving book,[489] albeit with little credibility.[490]

However, the decision of the GMC in respect of Dr Walker-Smith was reversed on appeal to the High Court, with Mitting J concluding:

> The panel had no alternative but to decide whether Professor Walker-Smith had told the truth to it and to his colleagues, contemporaneously. The GMC's approach to the fundamental

488 *Re Wakefield Walker-Smith and Murch* (unreported, Fitness to Practise Panel, 28 January 2010), 61–61.

489 Andrew J Wakefield, *Callous Disregard: Autism and Vaccines—The Truth Behind a Tragedy* (New York: Skyhorse Publishing, 2010).

490 See Susan Dominus, 'The Crash and Burn of an Autism Guru', *The New York Times*, 20 April 2011: <http://www.nytimes.com/2011/04/24/magazine/mag-24Autism-t.html?pagewanted=all&_r=3&> [accessed 23 Dec 2015].

> issues in the case led it to believe that that was not necessary-an error from which many of the subsequent weaknesses in the panel's determination flowed. It had to decide what Professor Walker-Smith thought he was doing: if he believed he was undertaking research in the guise of clinical investigation and treatment, he deserved the finding that he had been guilty of serious professional misconduct and the sanction of erasure; if not, he did not, unless, perhaps, his actions fell outside the spectrum of that which would have been considered reasonable medical practice by an academic clinician. Its failure to address and decide that question is an error which goes to the root of its determination.[491]

The reversal of the decision about Dr Walker-Smith dissipated the important and emphatic nature of the GMC's findings, following its extensive investigation, about the dishonesty and lack of integrity of Dr Wakefield.

Dr Hooper Hyperbaric Oxygen Therapy

Reliance on scholarly publications takes many forms in terms of professional misconduct. In 2013 the Victorian Civil and Administrative Tribunal (the Tribunal) in Australia made findings of professional misconduct and cancelled the registration of a chiropractor, Dr Malcolm Hooper, who made a variety of claims in advertising his practice on the internet about the efficacy of hyperbaric oxygenation treatment for a large number of medical conditions, including cerebral palsy, multiple sclerosis, Alzheimer's disease, autism, stroke, and dementia.[492]

The Tribunal accepted expert evidence that none of the various (30) conditions which Dr Hooper maintained could be treated effectively by hyperbaric oxygen therapy were so regarded by the peak bodies for such treatment in the United States, Australia, or Europe. The Tribunal had particular regard to a defence mounted by Dr Hooper that his website contained a great many scholarly articles (over 900) that enabled patients to make a balanced and informed choice about the treatments that he offered. It rejected this, instead accepting evidence from an expert that the large volume of material on the website did not assist potential patients to discern among the various technical articles or to appreciate the significance of them for their particular medical conditions.[493]

The Tribunal found that it was Dr Hooper's ethical responsibility to give a balanced perspective of the state of the medico-scientific literature as to the efficacy of hyperbaric oxygen treatment for the conditions that he maintained were treatable by hyperbaric oxygen and that he had failed to do so. This meant that his advertising was misleading and deceptive. It cancelled his registration, observing that:

> It is of fundamental importance, that patients be able to consent to treatment in an informed way, they should not be misrepresented as to the treatment, and the methods of surrounding the treatment, such as note taking and monitoring, be carried out in a proper fashion. Again, in our view, the only way that a proper message can be sent to deter this kind of behaviour by other members of the profession and give the public confidence that the profession is properly regulated, in this instance, is cancellation of registration.[494]

The decision of the Tribunal and the sanctions it imposed (as well as the fact that it required Dr Hooper to pay the costs of hearings that extended over many weeks of tribunal time) sent a powerful message that professionals must avoid false, misleading and deceptive promotion of their work to their patients or potential patients. They cannot simply rely on large tracts of professional literature that they place or summarize on their website—they are obliged to

---

491 *Walker-Smith v General Medical Council* [2012] EWHC 503 (Admin) [186].

492 *Chiropractic Board of Australia v Hooper (Review and Regulation)* [2013] VCAT 878.

493 Ibid, [44]–[45].

494 *Chiropractic Board of Australia v Hooper (Review and Regulation)* [2013] VCAT 1346 [26].

make such information comprehensible and accessible, and ensure that it provides a balanced account of the state of medico-scientific knowledge at the relevant time in respect of matters such as treatment efficacy and other options of treatment.

It is apparent, then, that disciplinary tribunals constitute a front-line response to complaints that registered practitioners have engaged in various forms of scholarly fraud, including in respect of their research or, as identified in respect of Hooper, in their inappropriate assumption of a scholarly appearance. Increasingly they tend to be constituted by members of the relevant profession but also by others, including lawyers, and sometimes lay members. Proceedings are formal and the stakes high in terms of continuing registration so legal representation tends to be experienced and assertive. Disciplinary hearings are required to comply with the rules of procedural fairness, although the rules of evidence and procedure utilized by the courts do not have to be followed. However, as the proceedings are quasi-criminal, generally the rules of evidence are applied to some degree to ensure that only reliable evidence is received and therefore can form the basis of decision-making. The general purpose of disciplinary hearings is to protect the community from risk and also to uphold the standing of the profession concerned. This means that when findings of seriously unprofessional conduct are made, there is the potential for registration to be made subject to conditions, to be suspended for a time or to be cancelled. Decisions of disciplinary tribunals are public and the results are usually placed on a publicly accessible register. The reasons for decisions in countries such as the United Kingdom, Canada, Australia, and New Zealand are generally available for members of the public and the media to read, at least for a time.

The yardsticks for findings tend to be a combination of codes of ethics and conduct, guidelines issued by professions, and expert opinion evidence given by experienced practitioners in the relevant profession in relation to its understood and shared values. The shame, notoriety, and financial and professional consequences that can accompany an adverse disciplinary decision in relation to research misconduct (amongst other forms of impropriety) constitute a significant deterrent for many practitioners. In addition, disciplinary hearings constitute an opportunity for professions to re-articulate their values and to communicate to the community and to the profession that compliance with standards, such as scholarly integrity, are a prerequisite to continuing membership of the profession.

However, not all scholars are members of a registered profession. Removal 'merely' from a professional association or society is not so significant a consideration for most scholars and for scholars, such as scientists, the registration issue tends not to be an important consideration.

United States False Claims Act Litigation

In the United States lawsuits can be brought for research fraud under the *False Claims Act*,[495] which imposes civil liability on any person who either 'knowingly presents, or causes to be presented, a false or fraudulent claim for payment or approval',[496] or 'knowingly makes, uses, or causes to be made or used, a false record or statement material to a false or fraudulent claim'.[497] A person acts 'knowingly' if he or she '(i) has actual knowledge of the information; (ii) acts in deliberate ignorance of the truth or falsity of the information; or (iii) acts in reckless disregard of the truth or falsity of the information'.[498] The legislation is unusual

[495] 31 USC §§ 3729–3733. Also known as 'Lincoln's Law', because it dates back to the *False Claims Act* of 2 March 1863, ch 67, 12 Stat 696 (1863).

[496] 31 USC §3729(a)(1)(A).

[497] 31 USC §3729(a)(1)(B).

[498] 31 USC §3729(b)(1).

(and mirrored in some 29 states and the District of Columbia) in that it can be brought into operation by whistleblowers (relators) through what are known as '*qui tam*' proceedings.[499]

In 2012 the best known litigation under the False Claims Act was concluded. It arose from a suit brought in 2006 by Kenneth Jones, a former statistician at the Massachusetts General Hospital, alleging that Professor Marilyn Albert submitted a grant application to the NIH based on manipulated data. Professor Albert was a former Professor of Psychiatry at Harvard Medical School, and by the time of trial Director of the Division of Cognitive Neuroscience at Johns Hopkins University School of Medicine, Massachusetts General Hospital, and Brigham and Women's Hospital. Jones maintained that the data in relation to an Alzheimer's trial were significant in appearing to suggest that Alzheimer's was associated with decreased flow of blood to the brain, when it fact the data did not establish this. The research by Albert and others was directed towards the potential to predict who might be likely to develop Alzheimer's disease based on measurements in various sectors of the brain. The results of the trial were published in the *Annals of Neurology* in April 2000.

When Jones identified what he regarded as anomalies in the research, he focused on data produced by one of the researchers, Ronald Killiany. The lawsuit alleged that Killiany (by the time of the litigation an Associate Professor at the Boston University School of Medicine) revised his initial MRI measurements to prove the hypothesis of the trial. Killiany had re-measured the scans of 30 participants—13 in the normal group, 12 in the questionable group, and five in the 'converter group'.[500] Jones had particular concerns about 23 of those re-measurements. He told Albert that the alterations were substantial and that, according to his analysis, the alterations were responsible for the apparent statistical significance. He asked Albert to look into the issue. She authorized an investigation into the matter by Killiany's superior, a well-regarded neuro-anatomist, Mark Moss. However, she declined to appoint an independent or external investigator. Moss found that Killiany's second set of measurements was more accurate than the first but did not find any form of fraud. Jones was dissatisfied with Moss's assessment and asked that the scans in question be re-measured. Albert refused. In her deposition, Albert stated that she believed that an additional set of measurements would confuse instead of answer the question as to which data set was more accurate, so she did not have the scans re-measured. Jones continued to work with data generated from Killiany's tracings until 30 July 2001, when he told Albert that he would no longer work with Killiany's data without 'neutralizing' it.[501] After that, Jones did not work with any MRI data generated from Killiany's work. When the team made an application for NIH funding in late 2001, Jones asserted that the evidence supported a conclusion that Albert and the other defendants violated the *False Claims Act* by '(1) "knowingly submitting an application for a grant to the [NIH] that was based on falsified and fraudulently manipulated study data and false statements of blinded, reliable methodologies", and (2) receiving NIH funds while knowingly in violation of regulations that require applicant institutions to investigate and report allegations of scientific misconduct'.[502]

At the heart of the lawsuit was the proposition that Killiany could have undertaken re-measurements provided that he remained blind to the clinical status of the participants.

[499] *qui tam pro domino rege quam pro se ipso in hac parte sequitur* ('he who brings a case on behalf of our lord the King, as well as for himself'): see Charles Doyle, 'Qui Tam: The False Claims Act and Related Federal Statutes', CRS Report for Congress—R40785, Congressional Research Service, 6 August 2009, 1, n 2: <https://www.fas.org/sgp/crs/misc/R40785.pdf> [accessed 23 Dec 2015].

[500] *United States ex rel Jones v Brigham and Women's Hospital*, 678 F 3d 72, 78 (1st Cir, 2012).

[501] Ibid.

[502] Ibid, 76.

This was accepted at first instance but characterized as a matter about which scientists could reasonably disagree—the court determined that the matter could not be litigated under the False Claims Act as it related to a scientific dispute rather than an issue of scientific fraud.[503]

The decision on appeal was significant in many respects. If the defendants were found guilty, they could have been ordered to pay as much as US$45 million to the government. By statutory provision, too, whistleblowers in such a matter can be ordered to receive 15 per cent to 30 per cent of funds recovered.[504]

At first instance the case was dismissed three days before it was due to go to trial. However, on appeal the United States Court of Appeals for the First Circuit[505] reversed the decision and concluded that the first instance court had abused its discretion by failing to receive relevant expert testimony on the subject. The First Circuit Court found that:

> However, we disagree that the creation of the data in question was necessarily a matter of scientific judgment. The district court relied on 'the undisputed fact that tracing the EC is highly subjective and thus two scientists who use the same protocol manually to trace the EC may nevertheless obtain different results.' This reliance, however, misses the point that the various results produced in this case were obtained by one scientist purportedly using the same protocol. Although the decision as to which measurement method to employ was a question of scientific judgment, that is not the issue here.
> [...]
> The revisions in question do not implicate questions of scientific judgment as the district court suggested, because all the measurements in question were purportedly generated by a single protocol...whether Killiany's measurements were more or less accurate than the initial measurements is not at issue. Even if Killiany's re-measurements fall within an accepted range of scientific accuracy, a question remains as to whether the data was falsified by intentionally exaggerating the EC boundaries of normal subjects to achieve a desired result. We conclude that the distribution of revisions presents a genuine issue of material fact as to whether...Killiany cherry-picked measurements to revise in a non-random fashion 'in order to produce data that would support his hypothesis on the role of EC volume and the prediction of prodromal AD'.[506]

The court found that: 'the dispute at the heart of this case is not about resolving which scientific protocol produces results that fall within an acceptable range of "accuracy". Nor about whether Killiany's re-measurements, the basis for the preliminary scientific conclusions reported in the [funding application], are "accurate" insofar as they fell within a range of results accepted by qualified experts'.[507] Rather, it concluded that:

> [T]he essential dispute is about whether Killiany falsified scientific data by intentionally exaggerating the re-measurements of the EC to cause proof of a particular scientific hypothesis to emerge from the data, and whether statements made in the Application about having used blinded, reliable methods to produce those results were true. If the jury should find that statements in the Application are false, they must also determine whether those statements were material and whether the Defendants acted knowingly in violating the FCA [False Claims Act]. Because we conclude that genuine issues of material fact remain on these

503 See Toni Clarke, 'Alzheimer's Research Fraud Case Set for Trial', *Chicago Tribune*, 11 May 2012: <http://articles.chicagotribune.com/2012-05-11/lifestyle/sns-rt-us-science-fraudbre84a0o8-20120511_1_research-fraud-case-new-trial-grant-application> [accessed 23 Dec 2015].

504 See Chapter 11 below.

505 *United States ex rel Jones v Brigham and Women's Hospital*, 678 F 3d 72 (1st Cir, 2012).

506 Ibid, 87–8 (emphasis from original omitted).

507 Ibid, 96.

central issues, we vacate the district court's order and remand for further proceedings consistent with this opinion.[508]

Ultimately, the matter was settled out of court but the First Circuit decision on appeal underlined the potential significance of the *False Claims Act* as a mechanism for resolving allegations of research misconduct in the traditional court environment of civil litigation.[509] It has been suggested that other jurisdictions should emulate the *qui tam* provisions of the False Claims Act.[510] However, this is not to suggest that the litigation has been uncontroversial. A question arises as to what is the best forum for aspects of scientific misconduct to be resolved. Susanne Hadley, a former Deputy Director of the Office of Scientific Integrity (the predecessor of the Office of Research Integrity), for instance, has commented in relation to a case where a former Cornell University epidemiologist won a *False Claims Act* plagiarism case that '[t]he plaintiff may do just fine, but that might just exacerbate the perception that these kinds of questions have gone beyond the ability of the scientific community to deal with'.[511]

Reforms to Procedures Relating to Scholarly Misconduct Allegations

The international impetus for reform of mechanisms and processes for investigating and adjudicating on allegations against scholars has built over the past two decades. In a number of countries there have been ongoing scandals involving prominent individuals and institutions accused of serious improprieties that have generated momentum for major reforms. Most recently, for instance, such pressures have engulfed scholarly institutions in Germany, The Netherlands, and Romania. In the United States the scandal over the treatment of Imanishi-Kari, in England the Banerjee affair, and in Australia the Michael Briggs and Barry Hall sagas have demonstrated the unsatisfactory nature of processes existing at the relevant times. In Norway the problems highlighted by the fraud of Jon Sudbø generated legislation on ethics and integrity in research, creating the National Commission for the Investigation of Research Misconduct (Granskingsutvalget) which oversees research across both the public and private sectors.[512] Although the primary responsibility for investigation of suspected research misconduct remains within institutions such as universities, the Norwegian National Commission can undertake an investigation if the institution is unable effectively to do so or if there are serious conflicts of interest. Similarly, Poland has established an independent commission which can investigate research misconduct at its own initiative.[513]

On a number of occasions, mechanisms and processes, especially those created by universities, have been exposed as self-serving for the institution which has not wanted or been able to come to terms with the seriousness of career-threatening allegations. Usually, the

---

508 Ibid (emphasis from original omitted).

509 See Janice Hopkins Tanne, 'Alzheimer's Researchers Face Trial for Scientific Fraud and Defrauding US Government' (2012) 344(5) *BMJ* e3608.

510 See Thomas A Faunce, Gregor Urbas, and Lesley Skillen, 'Implementing US-Style Anti-Fraud Laws in the Australian Pharmaceutical and Health Care Industries' (2011) 194(9) *Medical Journal of Australia* 474.

511 Gary Taubes, 'Plagiarism Suit Wins; Experts Hope It Won't Set a Trend' (1995) 268(5214) *Science* 1125, 1125.

512 By contrast, the Deutsche Foschungsgeneinschaft (DFG) requires universities to have an ombudsman with whom cases of suspected research misconduct should be discussed and a committee to investigate research misconduct. The DFG also has its own ombudsmen to whom scientists can turn for advice.

513 See Aniket Tavare, 'Managing Research Misconduct: Is Anyone Getting it Right?' (2011) 343 BMJ d8212: <http://www.bmj.com/content/343/bmj.d8212?ijkey=3HOrgPYu.IS/M&keytype=ref&siteid=bmjjournals> [accessed 23 Dec 2015].

reason has been the potential for adverse publicity reflecting on the university's own integrity and impacting on its reputation. On other occasions, the investigative and decision-making mechanisms and processes have been shown to be inadequately responsive, deficient in quality and lacking in fairness. Awareness of such inadequacies has often only been achieved because of divisive campaigns mounted on behalf of the persons concerned or because of a proliferation of inquiries or the intervention of the courts by way of appeals.

International Initiatives

Redman has accurately identified that there is a host of problems encountered by current regulatory regimes in respect of research misconduct, including resistance by those who are regulated, not surprisingly, but also what she calls 'ritualistic compliance', 'regulatory capture' (when those who regulate become too close to those whom they should regulate) and ambiguity in performance standards.[514] To this list can be added problematic and unclear regulatory procedures. However, there is a growing will to address these impediments to effective regulation. One option in this regard is the provision of rewards to institutions that foster ethical research and, concomitantly, penalizing institutions in which unethical conduct takes place as a lever for encouraging institutions to take more responsibility for what takes place within them.[515] There is much to be said for this.

As outlined above, the second, third, and fourth world congresses on research integrity have constituted a catalyst for considerable efforts towards formulating consistent approaches to the conduct of ethical research and towards regulation of unethical conduct. The 2010 European Code of Conduct for Research Integrity[516] was launched at the Singapore second conference and a product of the conference was the Singapore Statement on Research Integrity. This was advanced further in 2013 by the Montreal Statement on Research Integrity on Cross-Boundary Collaborations.[517] In the United Kingdom, Universities UK in 2012 promulgated 'The Concordat to Support Research Integrity'[518] to commit to consistent, fair and rigorous policies in relation to the quality of research. There is an increasing international consensus on the issue.

The following pages document the systems for investigating research misconduct as they exist across a number of different countries.

Europe

There is considerable diversity of approach to the procedures and oversight mechanisms in relation to research misconduct within the different countries of Europe.[519] Many leave

[514] Barbara K Redman, Research Misconduct Policy in Biomedicine: Beyond the Bad-Apple Approach (Cambridge, Mass: The MIT Press, 2013).

[515] See Sandra L Titus and Xavier Bosch, 'Tie Funding to Research Integrity' (2010) 466(7305) *Nature* 436; Sandra L Titus, James A Wells, and Lawrence J Rhoades, "Repairing Research Integrity" (2008) 453(7198) *Nature* 980.

[516] European Science Foundation and All European Academies, above n 35.

[517] 'Montreal Statement on Research Integrity in Cross-Boundary Research Collaborations': <http://www.wcri2013.org/doc-pdf/MontrealStatement.pdf> (viewed 20 November 2015).

[518] Universities UK, *The Concordat to Support Research Integrity* (July 2012): <http://www.universitiesuk.ac.uk/highereducation/Documents/2012/TheConcordatToSupportResearchIntegrity.pdf> [accessed 23 Dec 2015]. The signatories to the Concordat were the UK Department for Employment and Learning, the Higher Education Funding Council for England, the Higher Education Funding Council for Wales, the National Institute for Health Research, the Research Council UK, the Scottish Funding Council, Universities UK, and the Wellcome Trust.

[519] See Ian Halliday, 'European Science Foundation and Research Integrity' in Tony Mayer and Nicholas Steneck (eds), *Promoting Research Integrity in a Global Environment* (Singapore: World Scientific, 2012).

regulation to institutions such as universities. In countries such as France this is the situation,[520] prompting calls in some quarters for more attention from national authorities.[521] Some, like The Netherlands and the United Kingdom, have established oversight mechanisms. Some, like Ireland, Germany and Switzerland,[522] have devolved responsibility to agencies or professional bodies. And the position within countries is in flux. For instance, the *Croatian Medical Journal* worked with the United States Office of Research Integrity in 1999, among other things, establishing a research integrity editor.[523] However, by 2010 concerns were being expressed that Croatia's leadership position in relation to research integrity was being seriously eroded.[524]

However, since 1992 Denmark has constituted a Committee on Scientific Dishonesty, consisting of eight members, including a Supreme Court judge and seven senior researchers. In 1994, too, the Research Council of Norway established an eight-member national committee of persons, including a judge and leading researchers nominated by the scientific community, to oversee investigations into scientific misconduct. In the same year a similar system was created in Finland with a National Research Ethics Committee, constituted by a university chancellor, six professors, a theologian and four civil servants, functioning as an appellate body.[525] By 2009, 92 institutions had signed on to the Committee's 'Good Scientific Practice and Procedures for Handling Misconduct in Science'.

In 1997 Germany's main provider of research funds, the Deutsche Forchungsgemeinschaft (DFG), created a commission of seven to ten prominent scientists to discuss research standards and oversight procedures. In 2001 it alerted the research community that it proposed to withhold funding from institutions that did not comply with its research guidelines. It also appointed three ombudsmen to receive complaints. It has a standing Committee of Inquiry on Allegations of Scientific Misconduct. In 2013 it revised its guidelines for 'Safeguarding Good Scientific Practice'.[526] It obliges German universities and independent research institutes to formulate rules of good scientific practice in a discussion and decision-making process that involves their academic members. In addition, the Max Planck Society for the Advancement of the Sciences, Germany's principal such organization, has developed guidelines for detecting, assessing, and imposing sanctions for research fraud.

The United States

The involvement of the United States government in regulating scientific misconduct dates from 1981, when hearings were convened by Al Gore, then a Congressman and Chair of the Investigations and Oversight Subcommittee of the House Science and Technology Committee.

---

520 See *Comité d'éthique du CNRS*, 'Research Integrity in a Competitive Context': <http://www.cnrs.fr/comets/spip.php?article75> [accessed 23 Dec 2015].

521 See eg, Jean-Pierre Alix, 'France: How to Improve a Decentralized, Ambiguous National System' in Mayer and Steneck, above n 519.

522 See Emilio Bossi, 'Challenges Encountered by the Swiss Academies of Arts and Sciences When Introducing Concepts for Promoting Scientific Integrity' in Mayer and Steneck, above n 519.

523 Ned Stafford, 'Polish Academy is to Establish a National Commission on Research Ethics' (2011) 342(1) *BMJ* d511, available at: <http://www.english.pan.pl/index.php?option=com_content&view=article&id=335%253Apolish-academy-is-to-establish-a-national-commission-on-research-ethics&catid=15%253Anews&Itemid=1> [accessed 23 Dec 2015].

524 See Matko Marušić, 'Croatia Moves Away from Fostering Research Integrity' (2010) 376(9753) *The Lancet* 1627.

525 See Eero Vuorio, 'Finland: How to Revise National Research Integrity Guidelines in the Changing International Landscape?' in Mayer and Steneck, above n 519.

526 Deutsche Forchungsgemeinschaft, *Safeguarding Good Scientific Practice* (2013), available at: <http://www.dfg.de/en/research_funding/principles_dfg_funding/good_scientific_practice/index.html> [accessed 23 Dec 2015].

The President of the National Academy of Sciences maintained to the Subcommittee that the issue was not of major proportions and that it occurred so seldom as not to merit over-much concern: 'the matter of falsification of data, I contend, need not be a matter of social concern. If it were not for stories in the press, it wouldn't cross the conscience of science.' He argued that congressional hearings in relation to the phenomenon only 'give currency to concern over this remarkable infrequent' breach of scientists' ethical obligations.[527]

The trigger for the hearings was two scandals which had recently unfolded. The first involved John Long, an associate professor at Massachusetts General Hospital who was found to have faked cell lines in his research on Hodgkin's disease, and had the fruits of his research published in the *Journal of the National Cancer Institute* in 1979. At first he had denied the allegations against him, when confronted by them, but information from a whistleblower co-worker revealed that the cell lines that he had claimed were from patients with Hodgkin's disease were in fact from an owl monkey. Before the Subcommittee Long accepted responsibility for his conduct and denied that competition for federal funds, the pursuit of awards or 'publish-or-perish' pressures were responsible for his unethical conduct. However, he did concede that the falsification of his experimental results was likely to yield him funds additional to the US$3,000,000 in NIH funds that he had already received.

The other perpetrator of research fraud who was publicly excoriated at the Subcommittee hearings was Dr Vijay Soman, an Assistant Professor at Yale Medical School.[528] The vehicle for information about Dr Soman being placed before the Subcommittee was Dr Philip Felig of the School of Medicine at Yale University. He had been the Dean of the Columbia School of Medicine. In 1978 Dr Soman and Dr Felig reviewed and recommended rejection of a paper by Dr Helena Wachslicht-Rodbard about insulin receptors and anorexia nervosa that had been submitted to the *New England Journal of Medicine*. The following month they submitted a similar paper to for publication by the *American Journal of Medicine*, where Felig was an associate editor. By coincidence the paper came to the attention of Dr Wachslicht-Rodbard who had no difficulty in recognizing it. When she complained of the plagiarism to the *New England Journal of Medicine*, he responded that in his view it was 'trivial' and reflected the exercise of 'bad judgment', without more. He published it in revised form.[529]

However, an audit of Dr Soman's work disclosed that other work he had undertaken had been characterized by unethical conduct: blood tests, for example, which should have been done were never done and patients who were cited as being in the study had not participated. Soman resigned from Yale, at its request, claiming that his conduct was attributable to work pressures, and was believed to have left the United States. In due course Yale announced changes in relation to how it proposed to deal with allegations of fraud.[530]

Dr Felig lamented that his own reputation had been seriously tarnished by his association with Dr Soman, even though he, Dr Felig, had not been responsible for any improper conduct. He called for senior researchers, similar to himself, to be more attentive to their supervisory responsibilities and to monitor their junior colleagues better. Although he argued that the scientific community should be responsible for investigating complaints of scientific misconduct, he expressed the view that there should be an institutional review led by

[527] See 'When the Cheating Has to Stop' (9 April 1981) *New Scientist* 68.

[528] See Gordon Moran, *Silencing Scientists and Scholars in Other Fields: Power, Paradigm Controls, Peer Review and Scholarly Communication* (Greenwood, Conn: Ablex Publishing Corporation, 1998), 69.

[529] See William J Broad: 'Imbroglio at Yale (I): Emergence of a Fraud' (1980) *Science* 38; William J Broad, 'Imbroglio at Yale (II): A Top Job Lost' (10 October 1980) 210 *Science* 171.

[530] William J Broad, 'Yale Announces Plan to Handle Charges of Fraud' (1982) 218 *Science* 37.

independent third parties into the challenges to the authenticity of scientific data. A major issue of contention in the hearings before the Subcommittee was the speed and effectiveness of investigations into allegations of fraud by the NIH and the need for blacklisting of scientists found to have engaged in research misconduct.[531]

At the hearings multiple senior scientists and administrators sought to provide reassurance that the phenomenon of research misconduct was neither serious nor widespread, being confined to a few bad apples. An outcome of the hearings was the establishment of the federal Office of Scientific Integrity (later the Office of Research Integrity) to investigate allegations of scientific fraud in research supported by the NIH. The United States National Science Foundation established a similar office for its grantees.

Each organization requires institutions that apply for research support to have a set of procedures for addressing allegations of scientific misconduct. Gross usefully summarizes these:

> [T]he usual drill is that after an allegation is made to a department chair or dean, an inquiry is undertaken to determine if a formal investigation is warranted. If so, it is carried out by a small committee of faculty members from other departments. During both phases the accused scientist is given opportunities to respond, and the entire investigation is supposed to be confidential. The committee has full access to the accused scientist's computer files, unpublished data and notes from research supported by the government.
>
> If the investigation finds misconduct, the university can pursue a variety of actions, ranging from the removal of the scientist from the tarnished project to the withdrawal of the scientist's published papers to his firing. The ORI or an equivalent federal agency then conducts its own investigation. It has the power to deny future research funds to the disgraced scientist. Federal prosecution for misuse of research funds is also a possibility. Partial or total secrecy is often maintained until after the federal investigation is completed. Sometimes the process of resolving scientific conduct can be prolonged, as appeals of ORI decisions are possible.[532]

On a finding of scientific misconduct, the ORI will seek redress for any injury sustained. The available administrative remedies are remedial in orientation and designed to protect the integrity of the research programme that have been affected. By contrast, the statutory remedies include civil fines and even criminal penalties which are oriented towards punishment and deterrence.[533]

The ORI is the largest of its kind in the world. It promotes proper research conduct at more than 5,000 institutions. In 2010 it was notified of 288 allegations of research misconduct and opened 28 of its own investigations.[534] It has a staff of 25 (which has dropped from 50 in the early 2000s) and a budget in excess of US$9 million.

However, the extent of governmental support for the ORI is no longer unequivocal. For instance, in March 2014 the Director of the ORI, David Wright, who had taken over after the Office had had no Director for two years, resigned in frustration, maintaining that the level

---

531 Around the same time though Dr Stephen Arnold of Tulane University was found by investigations by Tulane University and additional analysis by the Office of Research Integrity to have engaged in scientific misconduct by intentionally falsifying research results published in Science and having given false information to investigating officials at Tulane University. His research had been supported by the National Institute of Diabetes and Digestive and Kidney Diseases and the National Institutes of Health. He admitted his misconduct and entered into a voluntary exclusion agreement for five years not to receive federal funding: National Institutes of Science, 'Findings of Scientific Misconduct: Dr Stephen Arnold' (15 October 1981): <http://grants.nih.gov/grants/guide/notice-files/NOT-OD-02-003.html> [accessed 23 Dec 2015].

532 Gross, above n 213.

533 See Samuel J Tilden, 'Incarceration, Restitution, and Lifetime Debarment: Legal Consequences of Scientific Misconduct in the Eric Poehlman Case' (2010) 16(4) *Science and Engineering Ethics* 737.

534 Colin Macilwain, 'Scientific Misconduct: More Cops, More Robbers?' (2012) 149(7) *Cell* 1417.

of bureaucracy in the Department of Health and Human Services was obstructing him doing his job to such a degree that he no longer wished to continue.[535]

Canada

In Canada the research integrity system is non-legislated and decentralized, depending on institutions such as universities to investigate and police the phenomenon of research fraud.[536] However, in 2008 the Minister of Industry called on the Natural Sciences and Engineering Research Council (NSERC), the Social Sciences and Humanities Research Council (SSHRC), and the Association of Universities and Colleges of Canada (AUCC) to review the then existing policy framework for scholarly research and financial misconduct. They found the integrity system for research in Canada to be essentially sound but argued that Canada's three federal agencies for giving grants—the NSERC, the SSHRC, and the Canadian Institutes of Health Research (known as the Tri-Council)—should review and strengthen their framework for research integrity and research misconduct.

In October 2010 the Expert Panel on Research Integrity of the Council of Canadian Academies produced a report on *Honesty, Accountability and Trust: Fostering Research Integrity in Canada.*[537] It defined 'research integrity' as 'the coherent and consistent application of values and principles essential to encouraging and achieving excellence in the search for, and dissemination of, knowledge. These values include honesty, fairness, trust, accountability, and openness'.[538] It identified four gaps in Canada's research integrity policy framework:

- the lack of a system-wide approach;
- the absence of a centralized function for information management and research;
- a shortage of education and training programmes and materials and absence of an independent source of advice; and
- the need for a centralized approach to dealing with issues related to conflict of interest, incentives and privacy/transparency.[539]

The Panel identified 11 fundamental principles, each relating to the core values of science:

1. Conduct research in an honest search for knowledge. (*Honesty; Fairness; Trust; Openness*);
2. Foster an environment of research integrity, accountability, and public trust. (*Trust; Accountability*);
3. Know your level of competence and your limitations; act accordingly. (*Honesty; Trust; Accountability*);
4. Avoid conflicts of interest, or if they cannot be avoided, address them in an ethical manner. (*Trust; Accountability, Openness*);
5. Use research funds responsibly. (*Honesty; Accountability*);
6. Review the work of others with integrity. (*Fairness; Trust*);
7. Report on research in a responsible and timely fashion. (*Trust; Openness*);
8. Treat data with scholarly rigour. (*Honesty; Accountability*);
9. Treat everyone involved with research fairly and with respect (*Fairness; Trust*);
10. Acknowledge all contributors and contributions in research (*Fairness; Accountability; Openness*);
11. Engage in the responsible training of researchers. (*Fairness; Trust*).[540]

---

535 See Jocelyn Kaiser, 'Top US Scientific Misconduct Official Quits in Frustration with Bureaucracy', *Science*, 12 March 2014: <http://news.sciencemag.org/people-events/2014/03/top-u.s.-scientific-misconduct-official-quits-frustration-bureaucracy> [accesed 24 Dec 2015].

536 See generally, Ronald Heslegrave, 'Research Integrity in the Canadian Contest' in Mayer and Steneck, above n 519.

537 Expert Panel on Research Integrity, *Honesty, Accountability and Trust*, above n 24.

538 Ibid, 3 (emphasis from original omitted).

539 Ibid, 2–3

540 Ibid, 4.

The Panel proposed a more comprehensive, multifaceted approach to research integrity with the following characteristics:

- a system-wide approach that encompasses all disciplines;
- a common set of definitions, values, and principles that are accepted and implemented by all actors in the research enterprise;
- a fair and timely process for managing allegations of misconduct;
- a centralized mechanism for information management and research on issues related to research integrity; and
- a strong focus on proactive and preventative measures by way of education, training, and advice.[541]

It proposed the creation of a legislated Canadian Council for Research Integrity to provide confidential advice, to gather information, to disseminate and report information about research integrity and infractions, and to develop and promote best practices and standards with respect to education, training and effective self-assessment policies and practices.

An outcome has been the creation of the 'Tri-Agency Framework: Responsible Conduct of Research',[542] which is a joint policy of the Canadian Institutes of Health Research (CIHR), the Natural Sciences and Engineering Research Council, and the Social Sciences and Humanities Research Council to promote and assist research, and to foster a positive research environment. The Framework requires compliance from all researchers applying for funds from the three agencies. Specifically, it mandates that researchers strive to follow the best research practices:

> honestly, accountably, openly and fairly in the search for and in the dissemination of knowledge. In addition, researchers shall follow the requirements of applicable institutional policies and professional or disciplinary standards and shall comply with applicable laws and regulations. At a minimum, researchers are responsible for the following:
> a. Using a high level of rigour in proposing and performing research; in recording, analyzing, and interpreting data; and in reporting and publishing data and findings.
> b. Keeping complete and accurate records of data, methodologies and findings, including graphs and images, in accordance with the applicable funding agreement, institutional policies and/or laws, regulations, and professional or disciplinary standards in a manner that will allow verification or replication of the work by others.
> c. Referencing and, where applicable, obtaining permission for the use of all published and unpublished work, including data, source material, methodologies, findings, graphs and images.
> d. Including as authors, with their consent, all those and only those who have materially or conceptually contributed to, and share responsibility for, the contents of the publication or document, in a manner consistent with their respective contributions, and authorship policies of relevant publications.
> e. Acknowledging, in addition to authors, all contributors and contributions to research, including writers, funders and sponsors.
> f. Appropriately managing any real, potential or perceived conflict of interest, in accordance with the institution's policy on conflict of interest in research, in order to ensure that the objectives of the Framework (Section 1.3) are met.[543]

---

541 Ibid, 3, 50.

542 Government of Canada, Panel on Responsible Conduct of Research, *The Tri-Agency Framework: Responsible Conduct of Research* (2011), available at: <http://www.rcr.ethics.gc.ca/eng/policy-politique/framework-cadre/#1> [accessed 24 Dec 2015]. See also Susan V Zimmerman and Karen Wallace, 'Promoting Responsible Conduct of Research: A Canadian Perspective' (2013) 20 *Accountability in Research* 395.

543 Ibid, [2.1.2] (footnote omitted).

Examples of breaches of policies of the agencies are provided:

a. *Fabrication*: Making up data, source material, methodologies or findings, including graphs and images.
b. *Falsification*: Manipulating, changing, or omitting data, source material, methodologies or findings, including graphs and images, without acknowledgment and which results in inaccurate findings or conclusions.
c. *Destruction of research records*: The destruction of one's own or another's research data or records to specifically avoid the detection of wrongdoing or in contravention of the applicable funding agreement, institutional policy and/or laws, regulations and professional or disciplinary standards.
d. *Plagiarism*: Presenting and using another's published or unpublished work, including theories, concepts, data, source material, methodologies or findings, including graphs and images, as one's own, without appropriate referencing and, if required, without permission.
e. *Redundant publications*: The re-publication of one's own previously published work or part there of, or data, in the same or another language, without adequate acknowledgment of the source, or justification.
f. *Invalid authorship*: Inaccurate attribution of authorship, including attribution of authorship to persons other than those who have contributed sufficiently to take responsibility for the intellectual content, or agreeing to be listed as author to a publication for which one made little or no material contribution.
g. *Inadequate acknowledgment*: Failure to appropriately recognize contributions of others in a manner consistent with their respective contributions and authorship policies of relevant publications.
h. *Mismanagement of conflict of interest*: Failure to appropriately manage any real, potential or perceived conflict of interest, in accordance with the Institution[']s policy on conflict of interest in research, preventing one or more of the objectives of the Framework (Section 1.3) from being met.[544]

Researchers in breach of such obligations are expected to be proactive in rectifying a breach, such as by correcting the research record, providing a letter of apology to those affected by the breach or by repaying funds.[545] The Framework articulates responsibilities for institutions, as well as for individuals. The Agencies have also established a Panel on Responsible Conduct of Research[546] in an attempt to ensure a coherent and uniform approach to promoting the responsible conduct of research and addressing allegations of breaches of Agency policies. Its role is to govern and implement the Framework, with support from the Secretariat on Responsible Conduct of Research.[547]

Japan

In 2005 the Science Council of Japan (which was established in 1949) published an influential report on *Scientific Misconduct and its Prevention*.[548] It emphasized that '[s]cientific misconduct may seriously harm human life and also violate human rights, as science and technology penetrate deeply into daily life with enormous influence. Furthermore, the misconduct damages the trust that society has in science and technology'.[549] It stressed the

544 Ibid, [3.1.1].

545 Ibid, [2.5].

546 Government of Canada, 'Panel on Responsible Conduct of Research': <http://www.rcr.ethics.gc.ca/eng/prcr-gcrr/tor-cdr/> [accessed 24 Dec 2015].

547 Government of Canada, 'Panel on Responsible Conduct of Research': <http://www.rcr.ethics.gc.ca/eng/srcr-scrr/tor-cdr/> [accessed 24 Dec 2015].

548 Science Council of Japan, *Scientific Misconduct and its Prevention* (May 2005): <http://www.scj.go.jp/ja/scj/print/pdf/taigai_reefe.pdf> [accessed 24 Dec 2015].

549 Ibid.

personal responsibility of scientists to refrain from and prevent scientific misconduct. It undertook to continue its efforts to provide guidelines for scientists and to establish 'a neutral organization for investigation and judgment of scientific misconduct'.[550] It followed this report by the promulgation of a 'Code of Conduct for Scientists'.[551]

However, Masui has observed that, '[e]specially in Japan, researchers are socialized into obedience and seem to like to do as they are asked.... The research communities seem to be afraid of the costs of being free, flexible and responsible'.[552]

China

Controversies have proliferated about the quality of modern Chinese scholarship.[553] In the decade between 2001 and 2011 its share of scientific papers included in the Scientific Citation Index (SCI), maintained by Thomson, grew from a negligible share to 9.5 per cent, taking it to the status of being the country second only behind the United States, although it still ranked sixth for the number of times papers were cited by others. In 2010, though, *Nature* noted rising concern about fraud in Chinese scholarship, reporting that in one Chinese government survey a third of more than 6,000 researchers at six leading institutions admitted to plagiarism, falsification, or fabrication of results.[554] In but one area, for instance, the United Kingdom journal, *Acta Crystallographica*, retracted 70 published articles on crystal structures that it found were fabrications by researchers at Jinggangshan University in Jiangxi province.

Clark has argued that:

> The whole affair is driven by a demand for quantity over quality—it's what drives promotions, appointments and research grants in China. This often depends on getting research papers published in Western journals because of the lack of notoriety of the homegrown variety.
>
> [...]
>
> [T]here needs to be action taken to curb the activity as its [sic] happening, in China. The fact that the black market seems to be operating so openly, suggests prosecutions are rare and it's perhaps a low priority for authorities. One thing institutions could do is release more data.[555]

Fallout was substantial after three professors at the prestigious Zhejiang University were found guilty of plagiarism in 2009. The Ministry of Education, among other things, committed itself to dealing with the incidence of cheating within academia.[556]

Another positive sign came in 2013 when, after an investigation, GlaxoSmithKline dismissed Jingwu Zang, head of its research and development operations in China, who denied being

550 Ibid.

551 Science Council of Japan, 'Statement: Code of Conduct for Scientists' (approved 3 October 2006): <http://www.scj.go.jp/en/report/code.html> [accessed 24 Dec 2015].

552 Tohru Masui, 'The Integrity of Researchers in Japan: Will Enforcement Replace Responsibility?' in Mayer and Steneck, above n 519, 53.

553 See eg, David Cyranoski, 'Named and Shamed' (2006) 441(7092) *Nature* 392.

554 Jane Qiu, 'Publish or Perish in China' (2010) 463(7278) *Nature* 142: <http://www.nature.com/news/2010/100112/full/463142a.html> [accessed 24 Dec 2015]. See also, Elizabeth Heitman and Sergio Litewka, 'International Perspectives on Plagiarism and Considerations for Teaching International Trainees' (2011) 29(1) *Urologic Oncology* 104.

555 Liat Clark, 'China's Academic Scandal: Call Toll-Free Hotlines to Get Your Name Published', *Wired*, 2 December 2013: <http://www.wired.co.uk/news/archive/2013-12/02/china-academic-scandal> [accessed 24 Dec 2015].

556 Kent Ewing, 'Betraying Confucius: Academic Fraud in China', *Asia Times*, 21 January 2010: <http://www.atimes.com/atimes/China/LA21Ad01.html> [accessed 24 Dec 2015].

personally responsible for fraud, and placed others on leave concerning allegations of misrepresentation of data in a research paper.[557]

In March 2012 China's Ministry of Education[558] issued a regulation to monitor academic integrity in relation to research in Chinese higher education institutions. The new regulation required universities to set up a system to supervise experimental data and an expert panel to investigate academic misconduct. It also required a set of protocols to be followed in all institutions including the giving of lectures on academic integrity, and training for academics and students alike in such matters. The edict from the Ministry warned that efforts must be made to prevent overemphasis on 'the link between academic achievement and material reward and promotion'.[559] It also stated that academic misconduct should be investigated by 'an expert panel of no less than five members formed by university authorities'.[560] By 2015 the China Association for Science and Technology (CAST) reported that it had investigated dozens of scientists who had been involved in peer review scams, many of which involved ghostwritten and fraudulent papers, some of them utilising fake peer reviewing mechanisms. Similarly the National Natural Science Foundation of China announced in November 2015 that it had investigated authors of 22 retracted papers whom it had supported by funding. It stated that it was taking steps to retrieve such funding. Finally, also in the second half of 2015, China's National Health and Family Planning Commission released regulations which required institutions to undertake investigations into allegations of scientific misconduct and forbade researchers to apply their names to papers they did not research or write.[561]

While there is a long way to go, and fundamental changes to be made, the signs are positive that key Chinese funding and health and scientific organizations are commencing to take serious steps to staunch the flow of fraudulent publications which had been the product of a corrupt and unscholarly culture.

Australia

In spite of controversies such as the very different sagas involving Dr William McBride and Professor Bruce Hall, as well as continuing consternation about research integrity, including serious accusations of impropriety, the consciousness of the need to develop independent and high quality investigative mechanisms to evaluate allegations of lack of research integrity has been slow to develop.[562] Neither Australia nor New Zealand had significant involvement in either the 2009 Singapore or the 2013 Montreal world congresses on research integrity and their universities, research institutions and their academies are not numbered among the supporters of the declarations. Their tertiary institutions have no equivalent to the 2012 United Kingdom Concordat and there is no comparable articulation of principle to that existing in Europe since 2011.

Some limited progress has been made. In 2009 the Australian Research Council, the National Health and Medical Research Council, and the Commonwealth Department of Innovation,

---

557 Kevin Grogan, 'GSK Sacks China R & D Chief over Data Fraud', *PharmaTimes*, 12 June 2013: <http://www.pharmatimes.com/article/13-06-12/GSK_sacks_China_R_D_chief_over_data_fraud.aspx> [accessed 24 Dec 2015].

558 'New Rules to Prevent Academic Misconduct', *China Daily*, 15 March 2012: <http://www.chinadaily.com.cn/china/2012-03/15/content_14836889.htm> [accessed 24 Dec 2015].

559 Ibid.

560 Ibid.

561 Mara Hvistendahl, 'China Pursues Fraudsters in Science Publishing' (20 November 2015)' *Science Insider*: <http://news.sciencemag.org/asiapacific/2015/11/china-pursues-fraudsters-science-publishing> [accessed 24 Dec 2015].

562 See Sylvia Rumball and John O'Neill J, 'Research Integrity in New Zealand' in Mayer and Steneck, above n 519.

Industry, Science and Research (DIISR) engaged with key stakeholders, including universities and the National Tertiary Education Union (NTEU), to develop a proposal to create an Australian Research Integrity Committee (ARIC). It was formally established in April 2010, although it does not have a statutory basis,[563] and is chaired by a former Acting Commonwealth Ombudsman, Ron Brent. Its four members were appointed for an initial three-year term and have been reappointed for a second.

Since February 2011 Australia has had a Research Integrity Framework.[564] It is a condition of funding from government that institutions ensure that research is conducted according to the Australian Code for the Responsible Conduct of Research[565] and that institutions have in place procedures for managing allegations of research misconduct.[566] The ARIC provides a review system to respond to allegations of research misconduct administered by the ARC and the NHMRC to:

- Review the process by which a nominated institution has managed an allegation of research misconduct;
- Provide findings and, where relevant, recommendations to the CEO of the ARC and/or the CEO of the NHMRC; and
- Publish de-identified information on its activities at least annually.[567]

The consequence of this is that the focus of ARIC review is not on the merits of allegations of research impropriety but on adherence to process by the initially investigating entity.

Applications for ARIC review may be made in relation to:

- Allegations of research misconduct involving any health or medical research conducted at or under the auspices of institutions in receipt of research funding under the National *Health and Medical Research Council Act* 1992 (Cth); or
- Allegations of research misconduct involving [any other form of research] conducted at or under the auspices of institutions in receipt of research funding under the Australian *Research Council Act 2001* (Cth) and/or funding [of a variety of] research grants.[568]

Like an ombudsman, the ARIC will also conduct an independent review of such matters, considering whether the institutional process followed by an institution in the relevant case of alleged research misconduct was undertaken in accordance with the processes outlined in the Code and with relevant institutional policy and procedures.

The existence of the potential for ARIC overview should enable better external response to allegations of research fraud. However, it has significant limitations and, in the absence of

---

563 It is set up as a 'working committee' pursuant to s 39 of the *National Health and Medical Research Council Act 1992* (Cth) and under the executive powers of the CEO of the ARC. This means that its reporting requirements are minimal, as illustrated by ARIC's contribution to the 2012–2103 NHMRC Annual Report, where it reported that it and its secretariat had 'continued to work on refining operational procedures and the ARIC 'request for review' form': Australian Government, National Health and Medical Research Council, *Annual Report 2012–2013* (Commonwealth of Australia, 2013) 87: <https://www.nhmrc.gov.au/_files_nhmrc/publications/attachments/nh162_nhmrc_annual_report_1213.pdf> [accessed 24 Dec 2015].

564 See Australian Research Council and National Health and Medical Research Council, *Australian Research Integrity Committee Framework* (February 2011): <http://www.arc.gov.au/pdf/ARIC_framework_feb_11.pdf> (viewed 11 March 2015).

565 Ibid, 81.

566 See Ren Yi, 'National, Institutional and International Approaches to Research Integrity: An Australian Perspective' in Mayer and Steneck, above n 519. 'The Group of Eight' Universities have established a 'Research Integrity and Ethics Group' with a focus on the practical implementation of the Code: <https://go8.edu.au/contact-listing/go8-research-integrity-and-ethics-group> [accessed 24 Dec 2015].

567 *Australian Research Integrity Committee Framework*, above n 564, 4.

568 *Australian Research Integrity Committee Framework*, above n 564, 6 (formatting altered). Specified in the table at s 41-10(1) of the *Higher Education Support Act* 2003 (Cth), items 7, 8, 10 and 11(b).

a regulatory regime for academics comparable to that which applies to health practitioners, continues to leave the ultimate sanctions to be imposed on academics for research misconduct to the institutions employing them. In addition, an ARIC panel will not inquire into:

1) Allegations of research misconduct (as distinct from allegations or complaints about institutions' processes in response to allegations of research misconduct).
2) The merits of any findings made by a research misconduct inquiry (whether internal or external) at the institutional level, except to the extent that a finding of an error or flaw in the institution's processes necessarily reflects on the merits of the finding of the inquiry conducted under those processes.
3) Institutional processes involving allegations of misconduct on the part of an employee other than research misconduct, and any sanctions applied to such a matter.
4) Institutional decisions regarding sanctions consequent upon a finding of research misconduct.
5) Funding agency decisions regarding sanctions consequent upon a finding of research misconduct.
6) Institutional processes still underway.[569]

The positive aspect of the ARIC regime is that it has the potential to some degree to curtail the multiplicity and longevity of inquiries such as those set in train in relation to the allegations against Professor Bruce Hall. In addition, it establishes a fair, independent and consistent suite of processes for investigation and determination of such matters. Its coverage is significant but it only applies to those institutions in receipt of ARC and NHMRC funding, meaning that many researchers and institutions, such as those in hospitals, may not be covered.

In addition, it does not extend beyond research misconduct. This may include plagiarism engaged in by academics but it does not extend to sexual misconduct, forensic misconduct, authorship disputation, intemperate denigration of other scholars, or many issues relating to contested issues relating to intellectual property. Such matters are dealt with by:

- universities, hospitals or research centres as employers;
- ombudsman institutions where they have jurisdiction to review processes utilized by employers;
- regulatory bodies for registered practitioners, such as medical practitioners, dentists, psychologists, nurses, pharmacists and occupational therapists; and
- professional associations, such as learned colleges for specialist medical practitioners, the Institute of Chartered Accountants, the Institute of Engineers and the Australian Psychological Society.

In far as research misconduct consists of misuse of funding from sources, such as pharmaceutical companies, ARIC does not have jurisdiction.

In addition, even in respect of research misconduct, the most important elements of the accountability process shown to be deficient continue to rely on the same institutions that have previously failed to deliver clear, expeditious, and fair outcomes—universities which can be subject to conflict of interest pressures in respect of allegations likely to reduce the regard in which they are held in an increasingly financially strained and competitive tertiary sector.

Finally, the ARIC framework provided that persons, groups, or organizations can only submit requests for ARIC review up to 60 working days following formal notification from an institution that it has finalized its investigation/inquiry into the allegation of research misconduct. Some flexibility in this regard is created by a statement that '[l]ater requests may be

[569] *Australian Research Integrity Committee Framework*, above n 564, 6.

assessed on a case by case basis taking exceptional circumstances into account'. No indication is given of what might constitute such 'exceptional circumstances'. This is problematic given that ARIC has no significant public presence. It has no website, produces no public annual reports, and has not made publicly accessible any report into any investigations (the number of which is not publicly known) it has undertaken.

The fact of ARIC's relative invisibility also goes to its efficacy because, regardless of the quality of those overviews it does undertake, there is no feedback loop—no means of institutions or researchers or the public learning from the insights, criticisms, or findings of ARIC.

More and better accountability is necessary if Australia is to stigmatize intellectual dishonesty and other forms of scholarly impropriety sufficiently to deter those tempted to engage in them. The start of increased regulation of the tertiary sector in Australia can be seen in the creation of the Tertiary Education Quality and Standards Agency (TEQSA) under the *Tertiary Education Quality and Standards Agency Act* 2011 (Cth) (the TEQSA Act) to regulate and assure the quality of the higher education sector,[570] and the creation of the Australian Research Integrity Committee.

These initiatives are federal, although technically universities are State entities. They are part of a move towards national reform of the tertiary sector and the creation of cross-State and Territory mechanisms for increased accountability.

However, in terms of a coordinated, independent capacity for high-level investigation of serious allegations of research misconduct, Australia's research integrity system has serious limitations. While the ARIC has the capacity to review whether processes engaged in by primary institutions have adhered adequately to Australia's research integrity framework, the principal role for investigating allegations of misconduct continues to lie with the institutions that have patently struggled in the past to manage the task effectively, fairly and in such a way as to command the confidence of the scholarly community and the general community.

It is because of the limitations of ARIC and the history of difficulties in conducting effective investigations into research misconduct that calls have been made for the establishment in Australia of a Research Ombudsman, an Office of Research Integrity or an Office of Academic Integrity, modelled on the entities in North America.[571] Such an entity would be significantly better positioned, provided it was adequately empowered and resourced, to undertake authoritative and high quality independent investigations into the merits (rather than just the investigative processes undertaken by others) of allegations of scholarly misconduct than the framework currently existing in Australia. Straightforward reference to the unfortunate processes and critiques of the Hall, McBride, and other sagas of investigations into allegations of lack of integrity calls out for the establishment of such a body.

A Comprehensive System for Regulation of Scholarly Misconduct

It is apparent that the international incidence of research fraud has assumed deeply concerning proportions. Fourteen per cent of scientists in a meta-analysis admitted to knowing

[570] The higher education sector in total employs over 107,000 people in Australia and in 2009 had close to $19.9 billion in total revenue: Australian Government, Tertiary Education Quality and Standards Agency, 'About TEQSA': <http://www.teqsa.gov.au/about> [accessed 24 Dec 2015].

[571] See, eg, *Hall*, above n 306; David Vaux, 'From Fraud to Fair Play: Australia Must Support Research Integrity', *The Conversation*, 25 July 2013: <http://theconversation.com/from-fraud-to-fair-play-australia-must-support-research-integrity-15733> [accessed 24 Dec 2015].

of a colleague's involvement in serious misconduct.[572] According to Nicholas Steneck, a consultant to the United States Office of Research Integrity, the numbers of cases of research misconduct may number in the tens of thousands: 'Studies suggest that as many as one in every 100 researchers engages in serious misconduct over the course of a three to five year period.'[573]

The numbers of identified false applications for funding, of funds diverted to personal use, of distorted data and falsified research findings, surprisingly often on the basis of completely fabricated research, are confronting. This is requiring an escalating rate of retractions of articles, including in prestigious journals.[574] The conduct involved has been exposed in multiple countries across the full gamut of medical and scientific disciplines.

The consequences of research misconduct can be wide-reaching, bringing disrepute not just on the perpetrator but on professional colleagues in any way associated with the flawed research, supervisors, departments, schools, institutions, areas of intellectual inquiry, and whole disciplines. As was observed by the European Science Foundation[575] in 2010: 'Scientific and scholarly research is a shared enterprise, aimed at discovery and dissemination of new knowledge. Any doubt or distrust about the ethical standards employed in this pursuit can materially put into question the basis of our scientific understanding.' Research misconduct of its essence is harmful for the development of knowledge—it can mislead other researchers, it can subvert public confidence and it can result in restrictions being imposed on lines of inquiry or avenues of research.

In addition, it is important to acknowledge that the personal toll for the innocent who are caught up in such matters, often junior researchers, and on those who bring issues to the attention of the authorities (the 'whistleblowers'), in face of intimidation, cover-up, and attempts at dissuasion, is not easily measured.

On occasion, too, substantial amounts of money are wasted which could have been expended much more productively. There is an opportunity cost in that the misused funds might have been awarded to a more deserving researcher.[576]

Most importantly, patients have been caught up in clinical trials and experiments that are characterized by fraud, having their hopes of breakthroughs for their own or others' treatment for serious conditions cruelly dashed. The consequences of the fraudulent research by persons such as Dr Darsee, Dr Slutsky, Dr Boldt, Dr Fujii, Dr Poldermans, Dr Berwoda, Dr Poisson, Dr Das, Dr Potti, Dr Erin, Dr Obokata, and Dr Ahimastos, to name but some, are serious indeed, and deserve to be marked by more than mere words.

---

572 Daniele Fanelli, 'How Many Scientists Fabricate and Falsify Research? A Systematic Review and Meta-Analysis of Survey Data' (2009) 4(5) *PLoS One* e5738: <http://journals.plos.org/plosone/article?id=10.1371/journal.pone.0005738> [accessed 24 Dec 2015].

573 Nicholas Steneck, 'Address at the First World Conference on Research Integrity', *Fostering Responsible Research*, Lisbon, 16–19 September 2007, as cited in European Science Foundation, *Fostering Research Integrity in Europe* (December 2010) [2.1]: <http://www.oeawi.at/downloads/ESF-research-integrity-report.pdf> [accessed 24 Dec 2015].

574 See R Grant Steen, 'Retractions in the Scientific Literature: Is the Incidence of Research Fraud Increasing?' (2011) 37(4) *Journal of Medical Ethics* 249; Fang, Steen, and Casadevall, above n 65; R Grant Steen, Arturo Casadevall, and Ferric C Fang, 'Why Has the Number of Retractions Increased?' (2013) 8(7) *PLoS ONE*: <http://journals.plos.org/plosone/article?id=10.1371/journal.pone.0068397> [accessed 24 Dec 2015].

575 European Science Foundation, *Fostering Research Integrity in Europe*, above n 573, [2.1].

576 See Jennifer Kulynych, 'Intent to Deceive: Mental State and Scienter in the New Uniform Federal Definition of Scientific Misconduct' (1998) *Stanford Technology Law Review* 2, [32].

Research misconduct is a serial activity whose psychological explanations are not uniform. It is perpetrated by junior and senior personnel alike. While of its very nature it is covert, it can be brazen and audacious. It tends to be repeated and reflective of a preparedness to indulge in dishonesty across multiple professional (and sometimes also personal) domains.

It is not easily discovered or investigated. The grant application system and the processes for publication in scholarly journals, reviewing processes notwithstanding, rely on trustworthiness. Not everything can be checked and effectively scrutinized. Too often the only opportunity to evaluate the integrity of research is by reference to the original documentation which is seldom externally reviewed. There is good reason to conclude that the pressures for high levels of publication by scholars are leading to a situation where quantity of research output can be an enemy of quality. The most problematic area of research fraud is where researchers simply invent or fabricate data to underpin a pre-organized position which they are wishing to advance. This, arguably the worst form of scholarly misconduct, as Diederik Stapel has highlighted, ironically can be the most difficult to detect.

There is significant facility for abuse of research processes. Trust is part and parcel of scholarly culture. There is much that we can learn from both the conduct of fraudsters as described in the preceding pages and through their own words of minimization and denial. Fraud is hard to expose. Its incidence is unknown but significant and the consequences for research dishonesty can be far-reaching in terms of the advance of knowledge, wastage of resources, and the effects on direct and indirect victims. The Obokata saga is particularly, and tragically, illustrative of this.

Each of these factors suggests that our response as a community needs to be one that enhances and facilitates the potential for research fraud to be discovered and it needs to be robust when such conduct comes to light. It is colleagues—other researchers, technicians, supervisors, and sometimes rivals—who are best placed to identify and draw attention to dubious methodologies. Systems must be in place which in a real sense provide whistleblowers with anonymity, security, and as much protection as possible against retribution on making their concerns known. The feasibility of such an aspiration is discussed further in Chapter 11 of this volume.

We also know now that one of the main checks and balances, peer review of scholarly articles submitted for publication, has major limitations. All too many articles with gross deficits, including in prestigious, high-impact journals, have made their way successfully through the process. In addition, too many supervisors and co-authors have been problematically lax in their involvement. Ethics committees have routinely been duped. Further work needs to be done by publishers, journal editors, and reviewers to optimize the potential efficacy of the reviewing process and to articulate a culture of intolerance towards scholarly misconduct.

Work continues on different methods to identify research misconduct. An innovative study has suggested that the very language used in fraudulent papers may be an indicator. Markovitz and Hancock[577] from Stanford University examined over 2,000,000 words published in 253 biomedical articles that were retracted in the four decades between 1973 and 2013 because they contained fraudulent data. They compared the articles to controls published in the same journals during the same time period: 253 articles that were not retracted and 62 publications that were retracted but for reasons such as ethics violations, not fraud. They used word analysis techniques and rated how abstract or concrete the text was and calculated the presence of certain kinds of terminology. Their conclusion was that the papers that were fraudulent tended to be vaguer, more difficult to read, and to have fewer quantifying words. They

[577] David M Markowitz and Jeffrey T Hancock, 'Linguistic Obfuscation in Fraudulent Science' (8 November 2015) *Journal of Language and Social Psychology* (published online).

would contain more jargon and more technical terms. They would have more references, and would be more convoluted and difficult to understand readily. They called this 'linguistic obfuscation'. The Markovitz and Hancock analysis provides to journal editors and reviewers a set of markers that should put them on notice that something sinister may lurk in manuscripts with the identified characteristics.

There are issues at a broad level within medicine and science whereby an inappropriate value is placed upon the publication of positive outcomes, as against negative studies that establish that theories or hypotheses have not been borne out by data. Removal of the 'positive publication bias' would be a constructive step in reconfiguring expectations and pressures to arrive at publishable outcomes.[578]

While fairness must be extended to persons and entities on whom suspicion falls, processes for investigation need to be independent, prompt, efficient, suitably resourced, informed, and authoritative. The processes need to be clearly designated so that all parties affected can know with confidence how the investigations and decision-making will take place and what the rights of all concerned are.

Then there need to be clear sanctions. Serious research fraud should generally be regarded as incompatible with ongoing entitlement to research funding, continued employment in a research position, or involvement in a responsible position within the academy. It is an egregious betrayal of trust and research integrity. For practitioners, such as doctors, who are registered or licensed, proven research misconduct may well render them no longer a fit and proper person, at least for a time, for the privileges of that status.

Until recent years, prosecutorial authorities in many countries have been diffident about preferring criminal charges against persons who have derived some form of benefit from research that has either not been carried out or that is characterized by serious and wilful misrepresentations as to its methodologies or outcomes. Such matters have been perceived to be a form of intra-disciplinary disputation, akin to workplace issues—best to be resolved without the intervention of the criminal law. However, given the substantial sums of money, as well as the consequences described above that can flow from applications for research grants and from the conduct of research which yields false outcomes, the time has come to recognize and categorise research fraud for what it is—a form of obtaining financial advantage by deception, or fraud. Most jurisdictions have statutory offences that adequately cover money being obtained from government or private or other entities for the conduct of research that is either not carried out at all or that is obtained by deception or that is not carried out in a bona fide way.

It should not be necessary to have resort to obscure provisions such as those found in the Good Laboratory Regulations (UK).[579] The provisions utilized should enable the imposition of significant penalties which provide for condign punishment, which effect suitable deterrence for the person in case they contemplate repeating their behaviour, and

[578] See Amy J Sutton, Susan J Duval, Richard L Tweedie, Keith R Adams et al., 'Empirical Assessment of Effect of Publication Bias on Meta-Analyses' (2000) 320(7249) *BMJ* 1574; Silvia Palma and Miguel Delgado-Rodriguez, 'Assessment of Publication Bias in Meta-Analyses of Cardiovascular Diseases' (2005) 59(10) *Journal of Epidemiology and Community Health* 864; David S Liebeskind, Chelsea S Kidwell, James W Sayre, and Jeffrey L Saver, 'Evidence of Publication Bias in Reporting Acute Stroke Clinical Trials' (2006) 67(6) *Neurology* 973; Kerry Dwan, Douglas G Altman, Juan A Arnaiz, Jill Bloom et al., 'Systematic Review of the Empirical Evidence of Study Publication Bias and Outcome Reporting Bias' (2008) 3(8) *PLoS One* 3081: <http://journals.plos.org/plosone/article?id=10.1371/journal.pone.0003081> [accessed 24 Dec 2015].

[579] The Good Laboratory Practice Regulations 1999 (UK) SI 1999/3106, as amended by The Good Laboratory Practice (Codification Amendments Etc) Regulations 2004 (UK) SI 994/2004.

which are such as to dissuade others from emulating the conduct concerned. The message given, for instance, by the failure to prosecute Diederik Stapel, is highly problematic in its ambiguity.

Penalties imposed by those sentencing for research fraud should be of real consequence so that they reflect that research fraud is generally effected over a significant period of time, with genuine premeditation, by persons who are educationally elite and seeking to advantage themselves further, and that perpetrators are taking advantage of a funding system that depends on trust and trustworthiness. However, penalties should not be so crushing, save in exceptional circumstances, as to preclude the person making a useful contribution within their vocation at some stage in the future.

An aspect of the imposition of criminal penalties should be orders for reparation so that funding bodies and employers are not financially disadvantaged by the criminal behaviour. It is also appropriate that non-criminal sanctions for research fraud should include financial restitution as generally it has been pecuniary and associated advantage that have contributed to malign motivations on the part of researchers.

A development in Australia has been the involvement of statutory anti-corruption commissions and ombudsmen in investigating allegations of research misconduct. Such bodies are high-profile and comparatively well-resourced. Their reports are public and have the potential to name and shame and thereby to deter. On occasions criminal prosecution ensues from their investigations. However, whether they are the optimal bodies to be conducting investigations into scholarly misconduct is debatable.

On occasion civil action has been taken against those responsible for research fraud. Once again longstanding legal doctrine enables action, including by virtue of the tort of deceit, an action that dates back to 1201.[580] An action for deceit requires proof on the balance of probabilities that the defendant made a false representation to the plaintiff; that it was done fraudulently, in the knowledge that it was false, or without belief it its truthfulness or being recklessly indifferent as to its truth or falsity; that the defendant intended the plaintiff to believe in and rely on the false representation, and that the plaintiff was induced to rely on the representation and thereby suffered loss.[581] The tort of deceit allows the plaintiff a remedy for all causally related losses.[582]

Depending on the terms on which funding is obtained, actions in contract or for a statutory form of misrepresentation (such as under consumer protection law) may also be possible.

[580] See Danuta Mendelson, *The New Law of Torts* (3rd edn, South Melbourne: Oxford University Press, 2014); Gregory Klass, 'Meaning, Purpose, and Cause in the Law of Deception' (2012) 100(2) *Georgetown Law Journal* 449. In Canada the Supreme Court has required proof that the defendant induced the plaintiff to act as an element of the tort: *Bruno Appliance and Furniture Inc v Hryniak* [2014] 1 SCR 126. In *Eco3 Capital Ltd & Ors v Ludsin Overseas Ltd* [2013] EWCA Civ 413, the Court of Appeal confirmed there to be no need for a separate, standalone requirement to prove an intention to deceive for the tort of deceit to be made out.

[581] See *Krakowski v Eurolynx Properties Ltd* (1995) 183 CLR 563; *Derry v Peek* (1889) 14 App Cas 337 at 374; *Peek v Gurney* (1873) LR 6 HL 377; *Commercial Banking Co of Sydney Ltd v RH Brown & Co* (1972) 126 CLR 337.

[582] See eg, *South Australia v Johnson* (1982) 42 ALR 161; *Doyle v Olby (Ironmongers) Ltd* [1969] 2 QB 158.

What is essential is that an independent investigative entity such as an Office of Scholarly Integrity be constituted in each country. It should be empowered itself to investigate allegations of research misconduct so that an authoritative, fair and prompt resolution is obtained to the raising of such serious allegations. The precedent from the United States of the involvement of the Office of Research Integrity has been constructive. However, it is important that the Office continue to be suitably resourced and institutionally supported. For countries such as Australia, New Zealand, France, and Canada, where no such entity exists, it is overdue to consider seriously the creation of such a body.

4

CONFLICTS OF INTEREST

Introduction

As already discussed in respect of research fraud, and as will become apparent in the chapters dealing with plagiarism (Chapter 6), and forensic misconduct (Chapter 5), the phenomenon of scholars engaging in disingenuous behaviour has had many manifestations. They have in common an absence of integrity. An aspect of such conduct is working, subject to a conflict of interest where the reality, appearance or potential for bias has intruded upon research propriety. As was observed in a report into the Concordia University tragedy, where an academic murdered a number of colleagues,[1] 'professors or administrators can materially damage their university's financial interests and reputation by allowing their desire for personal gain or prestige to outweigh their responsibilities to their institution, their colleagues, their students and, on occasion, their discipline'.[2]

Issues in respect of conflict of interest have figured prominently in accusations made in the political arena against persons in relation to their scholarly work and have also erupted in the debates and exposés of conduct by large multinational pharmaceutical companies and industry-funded scientific research.[3] Conflicts of interest can relate both to the scholar and to their employing institution. They have been the subject of important statements of principle in many contexts, including universities' and funders' articulation of policies.[4] However, translation of policies into action has been variable. For instance, while the Association of American Medical Colleges (AAMC) and the Association of American Universities (AAU) have developed recommendations and guidance on conflict of interest policies governing research with human participants, surveys indicate that research institutions have not fully implemented these recommendations.

'Conflict of interest' in the research context has been defined by the Canadian Tri-Agency Framework as having the potential to arise:

> when activities or situations place an individual in a real, potential or perceived conflict between the duties or responsibilities related to research, and personal, institutional or other interests. These interests include, but are not limited to, business, commercial or financial interests pertaining to the individual, their family members, friends, or their former, current or prospective professional associates.[5]

---

1 See Chapter 8.

2 Harry W Arthurs, Roger A Blais and Jon Thompson, *Integrity in Scholarship: A Report to Concordia University* (April 1994) 27: <https://schoolshooters.info/sites/default/files/Arthurs_report%20on%20%20 Fabrikant.pdf> [accessed 24 Dec 2015].

3 See eg Ronald Bailey, *Scrutinizing Industry-Funded Science: The Crusade against Conflicts of Interest* (New York: American Council on Science and Health, 2008).

4 See Bernard Lo and Marilyn J Field, *Conflict of Interest in Medical Research, Education, and Practice* (Washington DC: National Academies Press, 2009).

5 Government of Canada, Panel on Responsible Conduct of Research, *The Tri-Agency Framework: Responsible Conduct of Research* (2011) 15, available at: <http://www.rcr.ethics.gc.ca/eng/policy-politique/framework-cadre/#1> [accessed 24 Dec 2015].

The history of unethical human experimentation during the 20th century and evolving concerns about the conduct of pharmaceutical companies[6] have raised consciousness within the general community and among scholars, little by little, about the undesirability of conflicts of interest in research. Nonetheless, the temptations to undertake research that is financially enabled by companies that stand to profit from the outcome, and not to make full disclosure lest the research be regarded as contaminated by the source of enabling funding, have resulted in many instances of conflict of interest, some of which have generated disciplinary responses from professions, institutions, and universities.

This chapter reviews a selection of examples of conflict of interest and the guidance that tertiary institutions are increasingly (but non-uniformly) providing to reduce the incidence of undeclared conflicts of interest. It argues for clearer statements of principle, rigorous internal responses, and the creation of external mechanisms to investigate allegations of serious conflict of interest within the tertiary sector.

Taxonomies of Conflicts of Interest

Conflicts of interest arise from circumstances where a person has a real, apparent (or perceived), or potential opportunity to prioritize their own interests, or those of any other person or organization, over the interests of the institution that employs them.[7] A conflict of interest arises when personal, including financial, considerations have the potential to compromise or bias professional objectivity.[8] It is unhelpful to attempt to define conflicts of interest exhaustively as they can arise in so many, including indirect, circumstances.[9] An apparent or perceived conflict of interest occurs when a reasonable person might consider that a professional's objectivity is compromised. A potential conflict of interest occurs in a situation where an actual conflict of interest may at some point arise. The concern about conflict of interest arises because of the need to avoid self-interest being the sole or principal determinant of

[6] See Leonard J Weber, *Profits Before People? Ethical Standards and the Marketing of Prescription Drugs* (Bloomington: Indiana University Press, 2006); Michael A Santoro and Thomas M Gorrie (eds), *Ethics and the Pharmaceutical Industry* (Cambridge: Cambridge University Press, 2005); Howard Brody, *Hooked: Ethics, the Medical Profession and the Pharmaceutical Industry* (Lanham, Md: Rowman & Littlefield, 2007); David Healy, *Pharmageddon* (Berkeley: University of California Press, 2012).

[7] See Marc A Rodwin, *Medicine, Money and Morals: Physicians' Conflicts of Interest* (New York: Oxford University Press, 1993); Michael Davis and Andrew Stark (eds), *Conflict of Interest in the Professions* (New York: Oxford University Press, 2001).

[8] In his 1909 *The Doctor's Dilemma: Preface on Doctors*, George Bernard Shaw highlighted the conflict of interest in fee-for-service medicine: 'And what other men dare pretend to be impartial where they have a strong pecuniary interest on one side? Nobody supposes that doctors are less virtuous than judges; but a judge whose salary and reputation depended on whether the verdict was for plaintiff or defendant, prosecutor or prisoner, would be as little trusted as a general in the pay of the enemy. To offer me a doctor as my judge, and then weight his decision with a bribe of a large sum of money and a virtual guarantee that if he makes a mistake it can never be proved against him, is to go wildly beyond the ascertained strain which human nature will bear': George Bernard Shaw, *The Doctor's Dilemma: Preface on Doctors* (Project Gutenberg, first published 1909, 2004 edn), 'Doubtful Character Borne By the Medical Profession'; <http://www.gutenberg.org/files/5069/5069-h/5069-h.htm> [accessed 24 Dec 2015].

[9] As observed by La Trobe University: 'There is no single definition of a conflict of interest, but it usually includes situations where two or more competing interests arise, or could be perceived to arise. An example may be where a researcher, or their close friend or family member, has some financial interest in the funding body or research partner for a proposed project. A conflict can involve financial and non-financial interests, and may be direct or indirect. It might include the interests of the staff member themselves, or the interests of a business partner or associate, family member, friend or person with a close personal relationship with the staff member': La Trobe University, 'Conflicts of Interest': <http://www.latrobe.edu.au/legalservices/research-contracts/conflicts-of-interest> [accessed 24 Dec 2015].

decision-making and the aspiration for conduct to be 'impartial', 'independent', 'objective', and 'unbiased'.[10]

Conflicts of interest are often divided into two categories: intangible (such as involving academic activities and scholarship) and tangible, such as where financial benefit is obtained.[11]

Conflicts of interest result in bias which can have many manifestations in research methodology and outcomes:

- failure to start from a null hypothesis;
- a desire to validate a theory;
- exclusion of data that are unsupportive of a desired outcome;
- over-reliance on a particular perspective;
- internal or external pressures to reach a certain result (eg, a match or an association between a pharmacotherapy and an improved therapeutic outcome);
- indifference to the adverse outcomes for research participants.

In short, conflicts of interest can give rise to many aspects of research fraud and even plagiarism, as well as forensic misconduct.

Because of the fact that conflicts of interest have the potential to place co-workers 'in a difficult position', some institutions, such as the University of Western Australia, have implemented a mandatory notification system: 'All employees have a duty to report any concerns regarding a conflict of interest affecting another employee. Any concerns would ordinarily be

---

[10] See Davis and Stark, above n 7, 4. See also, Lo and Field, above n 4.

[11] See eg, University of Texas, Arlington, Regulatory Services, 'Conflict of Interest': <http://www.uta.edu/research/administration/departments/rs/conduct-of-research/Conflict_of_Interest.php> [accessed 24 Dec 2015], which provides the following examples of where potential conflicts of interest might arise:

> A researcher holds an executive position with a company that stands to benefit from the research being conducted at the institution. In this situation, it is very easy for the public to suspect that the researcher would not be objective in conducting or reporting the results of the research. Either positive or negative research results are likely to affect the company. If the researcher has an executive position in the company, he/she also has a fiduciary responsibility to that company. This places the researcher in conflict with his/her primary responsibility to the institution to conduct the research in an objective and ethical manner.
>
> An institution's researcher holds equity over a certain dollar amount or percentage of a company that stands to benefit from the research study at the institution. In this situation, the researcher does not have a fiduciary responsibility to the company. Instead, the conflict is purely financial. Good research results that benefit the company may also benefit the researcher financially. Research results that negatively impact the company would also reduce the value of the researcher's equity. This does not necessarily mean a researcher would conduct research unethically, however, the likelihood of that occurring and the public perception that the research is tainted are increased when researchers hold significant equity in a company that can benefit from his/her research.
>
> A researcher receives significant financial compensation in the form of consulting payments or payment for services on a company's advisory board from a company that will be affected by the research study. As in the previous example, this situation involves financial benefits to the researcher. He or she could easily feel pressured to report only positive results if his or her future income from the company might be affected.

An academic conflict of interest could occur if an individual interferes with the peer-review process for some type of intangible personal gain. Bias, for example, can cause a reviewer to respond positively to a manuscript because it presents results favouring a method or production in which the reviewer has a personal interest, or a reviewer may act to delay the publication of a competitor's manuscript in order to strengthen his or her own chances for publication or funding. These intangible academic interests are indigenous to every researcher. Indeed, the drive for recognition can be overwhelming, particularly when a future position or livelihood depends on public achievements. Sources of intellectual bias, such as these, have long been recognized by the research community, but they must also be recognized and addressed by the individual researcher.

raised with their supervisor or supervisor's manager or, when appropriate, Director Human Resources or directly with the Senior Deputy Vice Chancellor'.[12]

Conflicts of interest have the real and foreseeable potential to erode trust because they go to integrity, as well as the appearance of integrity in research. Historical examples of research where the well-being of subjects was irrelevant or inadequately taken into account include:

- The Nazi doctor experiments, principally in 1943 and 1944 under the direction of Dr Josef Mengele, utilizing twins, and involving hypothermia exposure, malaria experiments, mustard gas, incendiary bomb and high-altitude exposure, sulfonamide treatment, sea water experiments, sterilization procedures, and administration of poisons.[13]
- The Unit 731 biological and chemical experiments conducted by the development unit of the Imperial Japanese Army (under Commander Shiro Ishii) during the Second Sino-Japanese War between 1937 and 1945. They included vivisection of living persons and injection of prisoners with diseases, including venereal diseases.[14]
- The experiments conducted by the Soviet secret services (under Grigory Mairanovsky[15]) on prisoners within gulags to develop tasteless, odourless poisons. They included administration of mustard gas, ricin, digitoxin, and C-2.
- The Tuskegee study of syphilis in the Negro male between 1932 and 1972, conducted by the United States Public Health Service—whose object was to study the effects of the disease on untreated subjects. Men were deliberately infected with the disease and, even when there was knowledge that penicillin could treat the illness, it was withheld.[16]
- The Willowbrook hepatitis studies between the 1950s and 1970s, conducted by Dr Saul Krugman of New York University, at the Staten Island Willowbrook School for the Retarded. Intellectually disabled children were infected with hepatitis to document and assess its effects on the body and the responses to potential vaccines.[17]
- Project MKULTRA, part of the CIA mind-control programme run by the Office of Scientific Intelligence in the 1950s and 1960s, run by Dr Sidney Gottlieb, which involved administration of LSD to CIA employees, military personnel, prostitutes, mentally ill patients, and various members of the general public to evaluate reactions.[18]
- The Monster Study conducted on 22 stuttering orphan children in 1939 by Wendell Johnson at the University of Iowa, for which the university apologized in 2001. The

[12] University of Western Australia, Human Resources, 'University Policy On: Conflicts of Interest' (Policy No. UP12/32) [3.6.1]–[3.6.2]: <http://www.hr.uwa.edu.au/policies/policies/conduct/conflicts> [accessed 24 Dec 2015].

[13] See Robert J Lifton, *The Nazi Doctors: Medical Killing and the Psychology of Genocide* (New York: Basic Books, 1986); George J Annas and Michael A Grodin (eds), *The Nazi Doctors and the Nuremberg Code: Human Rights in Human Experimentation* (New York: Oxford University Press, 1992).

[14] See Hal Gold, *Unit 731 Testimony* (New York: Tuttle Publishing, 2011); William R La Fleur, Gernot Böhme and Susumu Shimazono (eds), *Dark Medicine: Rationalizing Unethical Medical Research* (Bloomington: Indiana University Press, 2008); Joshua A Perper and Stephen J Cina, *When Doctors Kill: Who, Why and How* (New York: Springer, 2010) 81ff.

[15] See Vadim J Birstein, *The Perversion of Knowledge: The True Story of Soviet Science* (New York: Perseus Books, 2013).

[16] See James H Jones, *Bad Blood: The Tuskegee Syphilis Experiment* (New York: Free Press, 1993); Fred D Gray, *The Tuskegee Syphilis Study: The Real Story and Beyond* (Montgomery: New South Books, 1998); Susan Reverby (ed), *Tuskegee's Truths: Rethinking the Tuskegee Syphilis Study* (Chapel Hill: University of North Carolina Press, 2000).

[17] Michael A Grodin and Leonard H Glantz (eds), *Children as Research Subjects: Science, Ethics, and Law* (New York: Oxford University Press, 1994) 17ff; Timothy F Murphy, *Case Studies in Biomedical Research Ethics* (Cambridge, Mass: MIT Press, 2004) 149ff.

[18] See Colin A Ross, *The CIA Doctors: Human Rights Violations by American Psychiatrists* (Austin, Texas: Greenleaf Book Group, 2006); Jim Keith, *Mind Control, World Control* (2nd edn, Kempton, Illinois: Adventures Unlimited Press, 1998).

children were divided into two cohorts, positive speech therapy being administered to half and negative, belittling (and likely counter-therapeutic) therapy to the other half.[19]

- The Stanford prison experiment conducted by psychologist Philip Zimbardo in which undergraduate volunteers played the role of guards and prisoners in a mock prison with the volunteers excessively adapting to their roles and a third of the guards exhibiting sadistic behaviours towards the prisoners, resulting in the experiment having to be terminated prematurely.[20]
- The Milgram obedience to authority figure experiments conducted by Yale University psychologist Stanley Milgram during the 1960s and 1970s in which subjects inflicted pain on subjects believed to have a heart condition in response to orders to do so.[21]

These experiments, many of them conducted within universities, but all of them with scholarly aspirations, had in common that the well-being of the participants was an insignificant consideration in how they were conducted. Today they are considered unethical and repugnant for this reason, the obligations of the researcher to do no harm (non-maleficence) and to communicate properly with research subjects being mandatory. Importantly this troubling sequence of examples of unethical research has played an influential role in the determination of many to formulate protocols and obligations for human subject researchers that will constitute an effective impediment to recurrence of such practices.

This is especially so in contexts that are, or in effect are, clinical trials. As observed in a State Government discussion paper from Victoria, Australia:

> Although [a conflict of interest] may arise in many forms, it will typically arise when the staff member has an interest in a company which has a commercial relationship with the employer, and the staff member is in a position to influence the outcome of research or other activities that will lead to financial gain or other advantage. For example, such potential conflicts would arise where the staff member has an equity interest or holds an executive position in a start up or other company that has contracted with the organisation to conduct further research.
>
> Clinical trials are a particular concern, given the use of human lives. It is therefore preferable that the researchers engaged in clinical trials do not have any financial interest in the outcome of the trials (for example a significant equity interest or an executive position in a company commissioning the research), so that they are not vulnerable to any allegation of lack of objectivity.[22]

University Conflict of Interest Policies and Procedures

Many university policies are predicated upon the famous dictum of United States Supreme Court Justice Louis Brandeis in 1913 that: 'Sunlight is said to be the best of disinfectants;

---

[19] See Marla R Patton, *The Monster Study Revisited* (University of Arkansas, 1992).

[20] See Philip G Zimbardo, *The Lucifer Effect: Understanding How Good People Turn Evil* (New York: Random House, 2008).

[21] See Stanley Milgram, *Obedience to Authority: An Experimental View* (London: Pinter & Martin, 2010); Blass T (ed), *Obedience to Authority: Current Perspectives on the Milgram Paradigm* (Psychology Press, 1999); Arthur G Miller, *The Obedience Experiments: A Case Study of Controversy in Social Science* (New York: Praeger, 1986). For the Australian application of the Milgram experiments, see Gina Perry, *Behind the Shock Machine: The Untold Story of the Notorious Milgram Psychology Experiments* (Brunswick: Scribe Publications, 2012).

[22] State Government of Victoria, Department of Innovation, Industry and Regional Development, *Managing and Commercialising Intellectual Property: A Guide for Victorian Universities and Research Institutes* (Melbourne, 2002) 24, as cited in University of Melbourne, Office for Research Ethics and Integrity, 'Conflict of Interest': <http://www.orei.unimelb.edu.au/content/conflict-interest> [accessed 24 Dec 2015].

electric light the most efficient policeman'.[23] Generally, however, it has been recognized that more than disclosure is necessary to address the actual or potential danger caused by a conflict of interest. It is common for universities to stipulate that conflicts of interest or external interests that are not appropriately declared and managed may constitute research misconduct.[24]

The University of Melbourne, for instance, has observed that:

> [A conflict of interest] may compromise, or have the appearance of compromising, an employee's professional judgment in conducting, evaluating, or reporting on research. It may affect, or be seen to affect, not only the collection, analysis, and interpretation of data, but also the hiring of staff, procurement of materials, sharing of results, choice of licensees, choice of protocol, involvement of human subjects, and the use of statistical methods.[25]

It has instanced the following examples:

- Where the research is sponsored by a related body.
- Where the researcher or a related body may benefit, directly or indirectly, from any inappropriate dissemination of research results (including any delay in or restriction upon publication of such results).
- Where the researcher or a related body may benefit, directly or indirectly, from the use of University resources.
- Where the researcher conducts a clinical trial which is sponsored by any person or organisation with a significant interest in the results of the trial.
- Where private benefits or significant personal or professional advantage are dependent on research outcomes.[26]

Like many universities, it has required the disclosure of such conflicts and identified strategies for managing them, including:

- Public disclosure of an investigator's financial interest in any research sponsor or the commercial success of any therapeutic strategy or product that is the subject of any research results being reported.
- Monitoring of any research project by independent reviewers.
- Modification of any research proposal or plan.
- Disqualification of any Investigator from participating in all or a portion of any sponsored research.
- Divestiture by an Investigator of any financial interest in any research sponsor.
- Severance of any relationship between an Investigator and a research sponsor which may create actual or potential conflicts of interest.[27]

Similarly, Oxford University requires its staff and students to recognize and disclose activities that might give rise to conflicts of interest or the perception of conflicts and to ensure

---

[23] Louis D Brandeis, 'What Publicity Can Do', *Harper's Weekly*, 20 December 1913, available at: <http://www.law.louisville.edu/library/collections/brandeis/node/196> [accessed 24 Dec 2015]. See also, letter from Louis Brandeis to his fiancée, Alice Goldmark, dated 26 February 1891, and quoted in Louis D Brandeis, ed., Melvin I Urofsky, and David W Levy, *Letters of Louis D Brandeis* (Albany: State University of New York Press, 1971–1978), volume 1 (1870–1917) 100: 'If the broad light of day could be let in upon men's actions, it would purify them as the sun disinfects.'

[24] See eg, The University of Sydney, 'Research Misconduct': <http://sydney.edu.au/research_support/integrity/misconduct.shtml> [accessed 24 Dec 2015]. See also, Sheldon Krimsky, 'When Conflict-of-Interest is a Factor in Scientific Misconduct' (2007) 26(3) *Medicine and Law* 447.

[25] University of Melbourne, Office for Research Ethics and Integrity, above n 22.

[26] Ibid.

[27] Ibid.

that such conflicts are seen to be properly managed or avoided. It notes that, if properly managed:

> [A]ctivities can usually proceed as normal whilst at the same time upholding the person's obligations to the University, meeting regulatory and other external requirements and protecting the integrity and reputation of the University and its members. By contrast, conflicts which are not managed effectively may jeopardise the University's public standing and may cause serious damage to the reputation of the University and of the individuals concerned.[28]

It records that a conflict of interest arises:

> where the commitments and obligations owed by an individual member of staff or student to the University or to other bodies, for example a funding body, are likely to be compromised, or may *appear* to be compromised, by:
> - that person's personal gain, or gain to immediate family (or a person with whom the person has a close personal relationship), whether financial or otherwise; or
> - the commitments and obligations that person owes to another person or body.[29]

Oxford University divides conflicts of interest into financial and non-financial, stipulating that the former arise 'where there is or appears to be opportunity for personal financial gain, financial gain to close relatives or close friends, or where it might be reasonable for another party to take the view that financial benefits might affect that person's actions'.[30] It defines 'financial' interest broadly to mean anything of monetary value, such as payments for services, equity interests, and intellectual property rights, observing that:

> The level of financial interest is not the determining factor as to whether a conflict should be disclosed. What might be 'not material' or 'not significant' for one person might be very significant for another. Good practice in many situations will mean the disclosure of 'any' financial interest, however small. A conflict will arise if the interest might provide, or be reasonably seen by others, to provide an incentive to the individual which affects their actions and where he or she has the opportunity to affect a University decision or other activity (because for example he or she is the decision-maker or the principal investigator on a research project).[31]

In respect of non-financial interests, it notes that they may come into conflict or be perceived to do so, with a person's obligations or commitments to the university or to other bodies, such as their college or body of which they are a trustee:

> Such non-financial interest may include any benefit or advantage, including, but not limited to, direct or indirect enhancement of an individual's career, education or gain to immediate family (or a person with whom the person has a close personal relationship).[32]

Oxford University notes that in many situations a declaration of conflict of interest and a brief written record to that effect are all that is necessary. However, on occasions more active management is required by a written plan:

> One or more of the following strategies may be appropriate to manage the conflict of interest:
> - not taking part in discussions of certain matters;
> - not taking part in decisions in relation to certain matters;
> - referring to others certain matters for decision;
> - resolving not to act as a particular person's supervisor;

---

28 University of Oxford, Research Support, 'Statement of Policy and Procedure on Conflict of Interest', 25 June 2012: <http://www.admin.ox.ac.uk/researchsupport/integrity/conflict/policy/> [accessed 24 Dec 2015] [5].

29 Ibid [10] (formatting altered; footnote omitted).

30 Ibid [14].

31 Ibid [16].

32 Ibid [17] (footnote omitted).

- divesting or placing in trust certain financial interests;
- publishing a notice of interest;
- standing aside from any involvement in a particular project; and/or
- declaring an interest to a particular sponsor or third party.[33]

Yale University defines 'conflict of interest' more narrowly than Oxford, stipulating it to exist:

> when an individual has a significant financial interest (SFI) that could directly and significantly affect his or her University activities. Generally, this will be when the external interest provides an incentive to affect the individual's conduct of his or her University activities and when the individual has the opportunity to affect the University decision or other activity (for example, because he or she is the decision-maker or the principal investigator for a research project). Conflicts of interest can arise naturally from an individual's engagement with the world outside the University, and the mere existence of a conflict of interest does not necessarily imply wrongdoing on anyone's part. When conflicts of interest do arise, however, they must be recognized, disclosed and either properly managed or eliminated.[34]

Boston University observes that: 'Conflicts of interest (COIs) arise where one could financially benefit from research, causing or appearing to cause potential bias in its design, conduct or reporting. COIs are not inherently bad, and often come as a result of successful business partnerships and hours of hard work, all of which uphold the highest standards of integrity.'[35]

Harvard Medical School has identified that in working 'in a global age of discovery', bridging disciplines and industries is key to being competitive, both financially and intellectually.[36] It endorses creative ways to foster collaboration, including with government and corporations that commercialize innovations and bring therapies to patients. However, it recognizes the risk of conflicts of interest, arising from competing Faculty commitments and financial interest that may impact upon financial endeavours. It is pointed in not denouncing such conflicts per se: 'Conflicts generally are positive indicators that our *Faculty* members are recognized thought-leaders who have professional opportunities, government funding and support from the companies working to translate *Research* to the bedside. Thus, a conflict does not equate to inappropriate activity. Rather it indicates a collaborative interaction between our *Faculty* and outside entities where additional institutional attention is needed to safeguard the integrity of our *Faculty* and their *Research*.'[37] Rather, it has fashioned an extensive policy on conflicts of interest and commitment to outline unacceptable practices and guide its scholars so as to identify and disclose certain relationships with outside entities.

It is apparent, therefore, that while it has become relatively standard in recent years for tertiary institutions to have policies in relation to conflict of interest, key definitions and even basic approaches to the issue differ significantly.

The next part of this chapter reviews important and illustrative instances of conflict of interest.

---

33 Ibid [22] (formatting altered).

34 Yale University, Office of Research Administration, *Yale University Policy on Conflict of Interest*, revised 29 November 2012, 2 (emphasis in original omitted), available at: <http://coioffice.yale.edu/yale-policies-procedures> [accessed 24 Dec 2015].

35 Boston University, 'Conflicts of Interest in Research': <http://www.bu.edu/orc/programs-committees/coi/> [accessed 24 Dec 2015].

36 Harvard Medical School, 'policy on Conflicts of Interest and Commitment': <http://hms.harvard.edu/about-hms/integrity-academic-medicine/hms-policy/faculty-policies-integrity-science/interim-policy-statement- conflicts-interest-and-commitment> [accessed 24 Dec 2015].

37 Ibid.

Financial Conflict of Interest

There is a clear conflict of interest when a scholar permits their own financial interests to conflict with those of either their institution or of a patient/client, although there is an important distinction to be drawn between conflicting interests and conflicts of interest. The extent of the connections between doctors and the pharmaceutical industry has raised confronting issues about the credibility of contemporary medical research and highlighted the need for adherence to suitable guidelines.[38]

Community and professional views in relation to conflicts of interest within medicine have shifted significantly over recent years.[39] Most prominently, major constraints have been imposed in many countries and within a number of professional organizations about the links permitted between 'Big Pharma' and researchers—called by some '[d]ancing with the porcupine'.[40] This has encompassed covert payment arrangements and sponsoring of research conferences and individual practitioners by purveyors of medication. Topol and Blumenthal[41] suggested in 2005 that one in ten United States physicians was engaged in a formal consultancy with investment industry. Too often continuing professional education (CPE) sponsored by Big Pharma has been a masquerade for promotion of specific products and has functioned by exploitation of conflicts of interest deliberately created to create a sense of obligation on the part of medical practitioners. The problem is exemplified by demonstrated correlations between attendance at sponsored CPE and doctors' increased prescription rates of the sponsor's medication.[42]

In a 2009 editorial in the *American Journal of Psychiatry* it was acknowledged that:

> [T]here are also unfortunate examples of prominent companies failing to report important information about drugs that is critical for their safe use. The problem for psychiatry and indeed for all of medicine is how clinicians can obtain unbiased, up-to-date information on newly approved drugs. The interacting system of industry-supported clinical trials, advisory boards, and speakers bureaus not always, but nonetheless too often, has resulted in conflicts of interest that have demeaned both psychiatry and the pharmaceutical industry.[43]

The authors accepted that:

> [E]ach of us has a personal stake and a professional role in the conflict of interest issue. Most of us may never receive a check from a pharmaceutical company. However, by

---

[38] See eg, John Abramson, *Overdo$ed America: The Broken Promise of American Medicine* (New York: Harper Collins, 2004) in Denis G Arnold, Tom L Beauchamp and Norman E Bowie (eds), *Ethical Theory and Business* 9th edn (Englewood Cliffs: Prentice-Hall, 2013); Jerome P Kassirer, *On the Take: How Medicine's Complicity with Big Business Can Endanger Your Health* (New York: Oxford University Press, 2004).

[39] Marc A Rodwin, *Conflicts of Interest and the Future of Medicine: The United States, France and Japan* (Oxford: Oxford University Press, 2011).

[40] See Steven Lewis, Patricia Baird, Robert G Evans, William A Ghali, Charles J Wright, Elaine Gibson, and Françoise Baylis, 'Dancing with the Porcupine: Rules for Governing the University-Industry Relationship' (2001) 165(6) *Canadian Medical Association Journal* 783.

[41] Eric J Topol and David Blumenthal, 'Physicians and the Investment Industry' (2005) 293(21) *The Journal of the American Medical Association* 2654.

[42] See eg, Ashley Wazana, 'Physicians and the Pharmaceutical Industry: Is a Gift Ever Just a Gift?' (2000) 283(3) *The Journal of the American Medical Association* 373.

[43] Robert Freedman, David A Lewis, Robert Michels, Daniel S Pine, Susan K Schultz, and Carol A Tamminga et al. (eds), 'Conflict of Interest—An Issue for Every Psychiatrist' (2009) 166(3) *American Journal of Psychiatry* 274, 274–5.

> allowing companies to pay for and thus dictate our continuing medical education (CME), we support the marketing context in which these acts occur. Our ethical principles as physicians are designed to protect our patients in many ways—*primum non nocere*, confidentiality, prohibitions of boundary violations. We now need to protect our patients from conflicts of interest in the selection of their treatment. The Food and Drug Administration (FDA) has already taken leadership in limiting gifts and other inducements that historically were part of drug marketing. Guidelines for the type of pharmaceutical industry support that we each accept for our professional activities, including CME, and how our receipt of this support is shared with our patients when we prescribe drugs need to be more precisely defined by APA and our other professional organizations.[44]

In 2009 the Institute of Medicine[45] developed extensive recommendations in relation to the avoidance of conflict of interest. These were operationalized by the American Psychiatric Association (APA) in 2010, which provided that:

> [M]embers should exercise vigilance, caution, and strive for the prevention of conflict whenever possible.
> A. Gifts and meals often accompanied by product endorsement and promotional literature may influence physicians' decisions about prescriptions, laboratory tests, or procedures.
> B. Contact with pharmaceutical representatives represents marketing and should be distinguished from balanced education and critical scientific information as a basis for prescribing. Samples and starter packets may influence decisions to prescribe products that have equivalent and less costly alternatives.
> C. Conflict of interest ethical principles and ongoing studies should be integrated parts of continuing medical education, including distinguishing marketing and promotion from balanced, scientific clinical evidence.
> D. Consulting arrangements with industry should be based on a substantive contribution and commensurate compensation.
> E. Constructive collaboration with industry for research of new products and public education for the benefit of the community should not be discouraged. However, funding should be commensurate to the research and reflect active participation and documented remuneration. The role of the member in a scientific publication or sponsored information document should be specifically and accurately acknowledged.
> F. Physicians have a continuing responsibility to review the scientific and clinical evidence base on newly developed treatment options and incorporate new options for the patient populations they treat.[46]

Whether such broadly expressed guidelines are sufficient is highly debatable, but at least the promulgation of such requirements formally requires compliance and thereby goes some way towards creating a culture that is intolerant of conflicts of interest.

In the United States a series of rules have been developed in relation to the reporting of income by researchers. However, a number of high-profile medical practitioners have already been found to have breached them with a considerable potential for deterrence of others. An example is the world-renowned Harvard child psychiatrist, specializing in the treatment of childhood bipolar disorder, Professor Joseph Biederman, who earned over US$1.6 million in consulting fees from pharmaceutical companies between 2000 and 2006 but failed to

---

44 Ibid 275–6.

45 Lo and Field, above n 4.

46 American Psychiatric Association, 'Policy on Conflicts of Interest Principles and Guidelines: With Special Interest for Clinical Practice and Research' (December 2010): <https://www.google.com.au/url?sa=t&rct=j&q=&esrc=s&source=web&cd=1&cad=rja&uact=8&ved=0CB0QFjAA&url=<http%3A%2F%2Fwww.psychiatry.org%2FFile%2520Library%2FLearn%2FArchives%2FPosition-2010-Conflicts-of-Interest-Guidelines.pdf&ei=2BLXVPmTHairmAXv2oGoDQ&usg=AFQjCNG8YYnR4rBKTzO2s9WErLN05zctNQ&bvm=bv.85464276,d.dGY> (viewed 8 February 2015).

report the payments in accordance with his obligations (see below p 186).[47] Part of Professor Biederman's failure to report funding, as part of his conflict of interest obligations, was in relation to the requirements of the National Institutes of Health that researchers report to universities earnings of US$10,000 from entities such as drug manufacturers.

In addition, many universities have caps on the sums that researchers can earn from the company whose product is being studied. Professor Biederman was in default also of this requirement.

In the United States, Minnesota, Vermont, West Virginia, Maine, and Massachusetts, and the District of Columbia, have legislated for mandatory physician payment disclosure.[48] California requires adherence to government guidance and industry codes of marketing, public disclosure, the establishment of compliance programmes for promotion, and limits of gifts and incentives to medical and health care professionals (requiring them to be less than US$100). There is good reason to conclude that these statutory reforms are constructive and constitute a sound first step in bringing greater transparency to doctor–industry relationships.[49]

In 2007 Senators Charles Grassley and Herb Kohl introduced proposed federal legislation, the *Physicians Payment Sunshine Bill*, which required public disclosure of payments to physicians from industry. It was not passed. However, under the Obama health reforms the Patient *Protection and Affordable Care Act* 2010 (US)[50] mandated disclosure by drug and device manufacturers and group-purchasing organizations of payments to physicians and teaching hospitals. It also created enforcement mechanisms through imposition of penalties for non-compliance. Required disclosure encompasses a number of categories including entertainment and gifts, food, travel, consulting fees, speaking fees, compensation for services (other than consulting fees), honoraria, certain research-related funding or grants, education or conference funding, physician ownership and investment interests, forms of equity, royalties or licences, and charitable contributions paid by the industry, which must be reported to the Department of Health and Human Services, which then will make the information public. Certain forms of payments are exempt, such as samples and small gifts, certain educational materials, certain indirect payments, short-term loans, rebates, and discounts.[51]

Comparable legislation does not exist in countries such as the United Kingdom, Australia, and New Zealand. There are good reasons for it to be considered.

Another development has been a militant reaction by students in some medical schools, including at Harvard, requiring disclosure of industry ties by professor and lecturers to their students.[52]

---

[47] Gardiner Harris and Benedict Carey, 'Researchers Fail to Reveal Full Drug Pay', *New York Times*, 8 June 2008: <http://www.nytimes.com/2008/06/08/us/08conflict.html?pagewanted=all&_r=1&> [accessed 24 Dec 2015].

[48] The first 30 months of data showed 32,227 reported payments to 11,734 Massachusetts physicians: a total of US$76.7 million: Aaron S Kesselheim, Christopher T Robertson, Kent Siri, Puneet Batra, and Jessica M Franklin, 'Distributions of Industry Payments to Massachusetts Physicians' (2013) 368(22) *The New England Journal of Medicine* 2049.

[49] See Susan Chimonas, Natassia M Rozartio, and David J Rothman, 'Show Us the Money: Lessons in Transparency from State Pharmaceutical Marketing Disclosure Laws' (2010) 45(1) *Health Services Research* 98.

[50] *Patient Protection and Affordable Care Act of 2010*, Pub L No 111–148, 124 Stat 119.

[51] See Tim K Mackey and Bryan A Liang, 'Physician Payment Disclosure Under Health Care Reform: Will the Sun Shine?' (2013) 26(3) *Journal of the American Board of Family Medicine* 327.

[52] See Duff Wilson, 'Harvard Medical School in Ethics Quandary', *New York Times*, 2 March 2009: <http://www.nytimes.com/2009/03/03/business/03medschool.html?pagewanted=all> [accessed 24 Dec 2015].

What is apparent from this very brief survey is that the mood within the general community and within medicine has changed in the United States in relation to the preparedness to tolerate actual or potential conflicts of interest. Some other countries, including the United Kingdom, New Zealand, and Australia, are lagging behind these changes, and need to catch up.

Moore v Regents of University of California

An archetypal scenario which is illustrative of an unethical conflict of interest is the case of *Moore v Regents of University of California*.[53] The plaintiff, John Moore, was a male who underwent treatment for hairy-cell leukaemia at the Medical Center of the University of California (the UCLA Medical Center). The defendants were Dr David Golde, a physician at the UCLA Medical Center, the Regents of the University who owned and operated it, a researcher, a genetics institute, and a pharmaceutical corporation (Sandoz). Moore attended the UCLA Medical Center after being diagnosed with leukaemia. Extensive amounts of blood, bone marrow aspirate, and other bodily substances were withdrawn from him for testing. This enabled his diagnosis to be confirmed. Dr Golde and the other defendants became aware that in principle certain blood products and blood components from patients with particular characteristics could be of considerable commercial and scientific value.

In 1976 Dr Golde recommended to Mr Moore that he consent to his spleen being removed 'to slow down the progress of his disease'.[54] Mr Moore signed a suitable consent form but before the operation it had been decided that portions of Mr Moore's spleen should be utilized for research activities which were not connected to Mr Moore's clinical care. He was not informed of this. In fact, Dr Golde established an extremely valuable cell line from Mr Moore's T-lymphocytes and the Regents applied for a patent on it. Mr Moore learned of what had taken place and took legal action, maintaining that a variety of forms of fiduciary duty had been breached by the defendants. The majority of the Supreme Court of California held that (1) a physician must disclose personal interests unrelated to the patient's health, whether research or economic, that may affect the physician's professional judgment; and (2) a physician's failure to disclose such interests may give rise to a cause of action for performing medical procedures without informed consent or breach of fiduciary duty. It affirmed a previous decision of the California Court of Appeal that '[c]ertainly a sick patient deserves to be free of any reasonable suspicion that his doctor's judgment is influenced by a profit motive'.[55] The majority determined that when a doctor seeks a patient's consent for a medical procedure, to comply with their fiduciary duty and obtain their patient's informed consent, they are obliged to disclose personal interests unrelated to the patient's health, whether research or economic, that may affect the doctor's judgment. It allowed an action for breach of fiduciary duty and of informed consent but not for conversion. While countries' law on fiduciary duties differs, the *Moore* decision has established an influential precedent by which exploitation of patients' tissues has the potential to be actionable by patients.

---

[53] 51 Cal 3d 120 (1990). See also, Jennifer Lavoie, 'Ownership of Human Tissue: Life after *Moore v. Regents of the University of California*' (1989) 75(7) *Virginia Law Review* 1363; Joseph M Healey Jnr and Kara L Dowling, 'Controlling Conflicts of Interest in the Doctor-Patient Relationship: Lessons from *Moore v. Regents of the University of California*' (1991) 42(3) *Mercer Law Review* 989; Helen R Bergman, 'Case Comment: *Moore v. Regents of the University of California*' (1992) 18(1-2) *American Journal of Law and Medicine* 127; Jeffrey A Potts, '*Moore v. Regents of the University of California*: Expanded Disclosure, Limited Property Rights' (1992) 86(2) *Northwestern University Law Review* 453.

[54] *Moore v Regents of University of California*, 51 Cal 3d 120, 126 (1990).

[55] *Magan Medical Clinic v California State Board of Medical Examiners*, 249 Cal App 2d 124, 132 (1967).

Investment in Research Outcomes

Jesse Gelsinger. The death of Jesse Gelsinger during a biotechnology clinical trial has prompted important reflection about a number of confronting issues, including the potential contamination of research decision-making when researchers hold financial interests in outcomes—a situation that is not uncommon. Jesse was an 18-year-old male with a mild form of ornithine transcarbamylase (OTC) deficiency, a disorder of nitrogen metabolism that could be controlled by diet and pharmacotherapy.[56] He was in good health. In 1999 a team of researchers led by James Wilson at the Institute for Human Gene Therapy at the University of Pennsylvania conducted a gene therapy trial in relation to the disease. Jesse was the 18th and last participant in the trial. It involved the injection into the liver of adenovirus vector particles containing a gene with a view to correcting the genetic defect that created the disease symptoms. Jesse died within four days from what was probably an immune reaction.[57] His death resulted in worldwide adverse publicity and the Food and Drug Administration (FDA) suspending all trials at the Institute. Multiple investigations were undertaken, including by a Senate subcommittee, the FDA, the National Institutes of Health, and internally.

The position of Wilson was that Jesse's death was the result of an idiopathic response and may have resulted from another genetic defect which had not previously been known about or a parvovirus infection.[58] However, some researchers claimed that the reaction was foreseeable by reason of the high dose of adenovirus that was administered to elicit an immune response.[59] In addition, Jesse was not told that during pre-clinical animal studies monkeys had died—that information appeared on the consent form submitted to the National Institutes of Health review board, but not on the documentation provided to Jesse.[60]

A wrongful death suit was instituted (and settled very quickly) which made a series of allegations, including negligence, failure to make proper disclosure about potentially lethal toxicities, and a conflict of interest in that researchers and members of the University of Pennsylvania held patents which covered several aspects of the technology employed, and held equity in a private sector biotechnology company, Genovo, which was a collaborator in the project.[61] These conflicts were not disclosed to participants, including Jesse. Jesse's father contended in the aftermath that:

---

[56] See Sheryl Gay Stolberg, 'The Biotech Death of Jesse Gelsinger', *New York Times*, 28 November 1999: <http://www.nytimes.com/1999/11/28/magazine/the-biotech-death-of-jesse-gelsinger.html> [accessed 24 Dec 2015].

[57] Compare the Northwick Park drug trial scandal run by Paraxel involving TGN1412 (which became known as the '*Elephant Man Trial*') where multiple participants had adverse reactions causing significantly adverse consequences, and the involvement of Scotland Yard, after safe doses on initial testing on humans were not used: see Husain Attarwala, 'TGN1412: From Discovery to Disaster' (2010) 2(3) *Journal of Young Pharmacists* 332; Michael Goodyear, 'Learning From the TGN1412 Trial' (2006) 332(7543) *BMJ* 677; Philippa Roxby, 'Northwick Park Drug Trial Disaster—Could It Happen Again?' *BBC News*, 24 May 2013: <http://www.bbc.com/news/health-22556736>; 'Drug Trial Four "Are Conscious"', *BBC News*, 17 March 2006: <http://news.bbc.co.uk/2/hi/health/4815780.stm> [accessed 24 Dec 2015].

[58] For a discussion of a number of the clinical issues, see Susan Jenks, 'Gene Therapy Death—"Everyone Has to Share in the Guilt"' (2000) 92(2) *Journal of the National Cancer Institute* 98.

[59] See Julian Savulescu, 'Harm, Ethics Committees and the Gene Therapy Death' (2001) 27(3) *Journal of Medical Ethics* 148.

[60] See Osagie Obasogie, 'Ten Years Later: Jesse Gelsinger's Death and Human Subjects Protection', *Bioethics Forum*, 22 October 2009: <http://www.thehastingscenter.org/Bioethicsforum/Post.aspx?id=4034> [accessed 24 Dec 2015]; Barbara Sibbald, 'Death But One Unintended Consequence of Gene-Therapy Trial' (2001) 164(11) *Canadian Medical Association Journal* 1612.

[61] See Patricia M Tereskerz, *Clinical Research and the Law* (Chichester, West Sussex: John Wiley & Sons, 2012) 126.

> The financial conflicts of interest for both the sponsor (James Wilson) and the University were basically ignored by the University's Conflict of Interest Committee. This led to a blindness on the part of all parties to the dangers they were seeing. These were not bad men doing evil. They were men blinded by ambition and greed. They have told me that they could not have foreseen Jesse's death, yet their data was screaming at them to stop. We trusted a system that was untrustworthy, one that didn't even pay attention to its own stops. So we sued and settled within 6 weeks.[62]

The University of Pennsylvania agreed to pay US$517,496 in fines, and Wilson and others agreed to restrictions on their clinical research activities which, among other things, precluded them from conducting human trials for five years.[63] The University of Pennsylvania submitted to a series of obligations in terms of enhanced oversight over human subject research, as well as mandatory training on conflict of interest and informed consent for all investigators and clinical coordinators participating in clinical research.[64]

It is far from straightforward to draw clear conclusions from the circumstances of Jesse Gelsinger's death.[65] However, it can fairly be said that the level of disclosure of risk to the participants in the trial, including Jesse, was inadequate and that the investment of those driving the trial in its conduct may have contributed to the failure to make proper communication about risks which, had the appropriate communication been made, may well have endangered the viability of the trial because it would have dissuaded many of the participants (perhaps including Jesse) from involvement.

When Disclosure May Not Be Enough

It is apparent that professional and community expectations about conflict of interest are becoming more stringent. In 2014 the resignation of Ken Harvey, an Adjunct Associate Professor in La Trobe University's School of Public Health, over the funding of the university by the vitamin manufacturer Swisse prompted an important debate.[66] Swisse signed a memorandum of understanding with La Trobe University to contribute AUS$15 million over six years towards a new complementary medicine evidence centre (CMEC) to be housed at the university. It was proposed that one of the centre's roles would be conducting Swisse-commissioned research to examine the quality and efficacy of Swisse products.

In a media release about the partnership, Deputy Vice-Chancellor (Research) Keith Nugent said that, although the university was still seeking other industry or government partners to fund the centre, it would undertake 'independent' research into the safety, efficacy, and cost-effectiveness of complementary medicines and nutraceuticals sold in Australia. He

[62] Paul Gelsinger quoted in 'A Comment from Paul Gelsinger on Gene Therapy and Informed Consent' on *Bioethics.net* (31 January 2008): <http://www.bioethics.net/2008/01/a-comment-from-paul-gelsinger-on-gene-therapy-and/> [accessed 24 Dec 2015].

[63] Melinda Wenner, 'Gene Therapy: An Interview with an Unfortunate Pioneer', *Scientific American*, 17 August 2009: <http://www.scientificamerican.com/article/gene-therapy-an-interview/> [accessed 24 Dec 2015].

[64] 'U.S. Settles Case of Gene Therapy Study That Ended With Teen's Death' (2005) 51(21) *University of Pennsylvania Almanac*: <http://www.upenn.edu/almanac/volumes/v51/n21/gts.html> [accessed 24 Dec 2015].

[65] See Robin Fretwell Wilson, 'The Death of Jesse Gelsinger: New Evidence of the Influence of Money and Prestige in Human Research' (2010) 36(2-3) *American Journal of Law & Medicine* 295.

[66] Letter of resignation from Adjunct Associate Professor Ken Harvey to Professor John Dewar, Vice-Chancellor of Monash University, 3 February 2014: <http://www.australiandoctor.com.au/getmedia/6c7bc42c-10ac-42f1-8830-270aad3ad99f/Harvey_Resignation_4Feb2014.aspx> [accessed 24 Dec 2015].

asserted that Swisse would 'have its products undergo rigorous and independent, scientific assessment'.[67]

In his letter of resignation, though, Dr Harvey, a vociferous critic of Swisse's claims about its products, said he was concerned about 'fundamental conflicts of interest both for the proposed CMEC and the staff involved'.[68] He said that industry-sponsored research was more likely to report positive outcomes than trials funded by other sources and that contract research for industry could also be specifically designed to provide a particular result: 'For example, performing a battery of 60 or more tests of mental functioning while administering a multi-vitamin preparation is likely to find that one or two tests will show statistical significance due to random chance'.[69] He argued that there are numerous ways in which sponsors can elicit the results they want from research, including:

- designing research in such a way that the product tested will look good (testing against placebo instead of current best practice, for example, or conducting so many tests that at least one will come out favourably simply by chance),
- distorting results to exaggerate positives and minimize negatives,
- manipulating data, and
- cherry-picking the best results (and putting negative findings in 'the bottom drawer').[70]

Harvey received support from a variety of sources in relation to his stand on the issue. Senior Research Fellow at the University of New South Wales, Dr Adam Dunn, observed: 'If your work is funded by the industry, you're more likely to produce results that are going to suit the industry's bottom line. Grant funding is one way that industry can influence what research gets done'.[71] Physician and ethicist Professor Paul Komesaroff argued that, while independent research into complementary medicines is critically important, it has to be of a high standard and quality so the community can have confidence in the results. Higher education researcher Tim Pittman said explicit agreement was needed on the extent to which industry partners would control the research agenda: 'Is the researcher saying this is what we need to look at, these are the important questions that we need answered, or is it the company saying no, we want you to look at this or that research, which allows it to close off potentially contentious issues'.[72] Dr Dunn said post-funding policy arrangements needed to address the criticisms of the deal adequately.

Swinburne University of Technology, which already collaborated with Swisse, also committed to be involved in the project. It was suggested that Swisse also approached Bond University and also Monash University's School of Public Health, both of which declined to participate.[73]

---

[67] Julia Medew, 'Academic Quits Over Swisse Deal With Uni', *The Age*, 5 February 2014: <http://www.theage.com.au/victoria/academic-quits-over-swisse-deal-with-uni-20140204-31zhl.html> [accessed 26 Dec 2015].

[68] Ibid.

[69] Ibid. See also, Sean Parnell, 'La Trobe University Insists on Conditions in Swisse Deal', *The Australian*, 5 February 2014: <http://www.theaustralian.com.au/higher-education/la-trobe-university-insists-on-conditions-in-swisse-deal/story-e6frgcjx-1226818554893?nk=9dd2e821661af573fb4f491515a2d639> [accessed 26 Dec 2015].

[70] Karina Bray, 'Returns on Influence' (April 2014) *Choice* 30, 31.

[71] Reema Rattan, 'Academics Back Professor Over Swisse Research Collaboration', *The Conversation*, 5 February 2014: <https://theconversation.com/academics-back-professor-over-swisse-research-collaboration-22815> [accessed 26 Dec 2015].

[72] Ibid.

[73] Karina Bray, 'Ken Harvey Quits Over Swisse Deal', *Choice*, 6 February 2014: <http://www.choice.com.au/media-and-news/consumer-news/news/harvey-quits-uni-over-swisse-deal.aspx> [accessed 26 Dec 2015].

The question is whether the independence of La Trobe University and its commissioned research are compromised or will inevitably be seen to be compromised in relation to its commercially advantageous arrangement with Swisse.[74] Certainly, the memorandum of understanding, while in principle leaving the university independent, would be seen by a reasonable person to impose significant pressures on any testing to take place in relation to Swisse products or those of its rivals. There was proper disclosure, about which there was little option in the circumstances, but the more difficult issue is whether the independence of the university is necessarily limited by the arrangement.

Nepotism

The temptation exists within the scholarly domain for favouritism to be extended to relatives and friends, not on the basis of merit but by reason of consanguinity or association from amity. This category of conflict of interest can take many forms. Australia's most notorious recent example of nepotism in the tertiary sector, which cost two very senior academics their positions arose in relation to the offer of a publicly funded place in the undergraduate medical programme to the daughter of Professor Paul Greenfield, the University of Queensland's Vice-Chancellor. The offer was made by his deputy and close colleague, Professor Michael Keniger, the University's Acting Vice-Chancellor. Ms Greenfield did not satisfy the entrance requirements for the course and 343 other applicants who were ranked above her on merit did not receive such an offer.

A scandal erupted in relation to the offer of the place, and an internal investigation was commissioned, the role being given to a Senior Counsel at the Queensland Bar. The investigation did not focus per se on whether misconduct had occurred and, on receipt of its report, a subcommittee of the University Senate approached both men to discuss whether they wished to resign. By the end of 2011 both the Vice-Chancellor and the Acting Vice-Chancellor had resigned. The matter was ultimately referred to the Crime and Misconduct Commission of Queensland which reported on the matter in September 2013[75] and forwarded a brief of evidence to the Director of Public Prosecutions to consider whether criminal proceedings should be brought against the two men for breach of s 92A (misconduct in public office) and s 408C(1)(d) (fraud) of the *Criminal Code* (Qld).

The Commission observed:

> Conflicts of interest can and will occur at all levels of the public sector. However, they may not always be immediately evident—they may arise out of a request for assistance, a casual conversation or an oblique suggestion, hence the difficulty in identifying them as a potentially improper exercise of influence. To ensure that conflicts of interest are dealt with transparently, important principles or practices should be accepted and adopted by all publicly funded entities. In particular, it is essential to:
>
> - have robust policies that help and encourage officers to identify, declare and report conflicts of interest
> - ensure merit and equity is the basis for selection in publicly funded organizations

[74] See Ranjana Srivistava, 'If Vitamins Don't Work, Will Industry-Sponsored Scientists Tell Us So?' *The Guardian*, 6 February 2014: <http://www.theguardian.com/commentisfree/2014/feb/07/if-vitamins-dont-work-will-sponsored-scientists-be-willing-to-tell-us> [accessed 26 Dec 2015].

[75] Crime and Misconduct Commission (Queensland), *An Examination of Suspected Official Misconduct at the University of Queensland* (Brisbane, September 2013), available at: <http://www.ccc.qld.gov.au/research-and-publications/publications/misconduct/uq/an-examination-of-suspected-official-misconduct-at-the-university-of-queensland> [accessed 26 Dec 2015].

- keep documentation that details the matters in conflict and the parties involved, the process followed by the decision makers, and the manner in which the conflict was resolved
- develop a culture in which integrity issues can be raised openly with senior managers
- instil an attitude in staff that a perceived conflict between integrity and personal loyalty to senior colleagues should not prevent the reporting of suspected misconduct.[76]

Acquiring Experience: The Albanian Immigrant Appendicitis Scandal

A series of rumours was circulating in 2001 about whether surgery residents in Greek hospitals were falsely diagnosing Albanian immigrants with appendicitis and undertaking laparotomy appendectomies in order to accumulate surgery time.[77] The issue was raised with Dr John Ioannidis, then at the University of Ioannina Medical School, later at Stanford, who designed a study to evaluate whether, mathematically, there was a differential between the incidence of appendectomies on Greek residents as against Albanian immigrants in Greece. The team[78] identified from 2,027 non-incidental appendectomies that the odds for a negative appendectomy were 3.4 times higher (with a 95 per cent confidence interval) for patients with Albanian names than for patients with Greek names. Their tactful conclusions were that 'Albanian immigrants in Greece are at high risk for negative appendectomies. Socioeconomic, cultural and language parameters underlying health care inequalities in highly mobile immigrant populations need better study'.[79] This tended to corroborate the hypothesis that procedures were taking place for collateral reasons arising out of a conflict of interest.

Non-Revelation of Conflicts of Interest

Professor Biederman. A prominent example of failure to disclose conflict of interest occurred in the lucrative and controversial area of research undertaken into medications for Paediatric Bipolar Disorder (PBD) and for Attention Deficit Hyperactivity Disorder (ADHD). An inquiry conducted by Senator Charles Grassley, Republican of Iowa, revealed in 2008 that Joseph Biederman, Professor of Psychiatry at Harvard University, who was also Director of Research at the Johnson and Johnson Center for Paediatric Psychopathology Research at the Massachusetts General Hospital, earned at least US$1.6 million in consulting fees from drug manufacturers between 2000 and 2007 but failed to report all but about US$200,000 of this income to university officials. At the same time he was receiving federal funds from the National Institutes of Health (NIH) in spite of the fact that NIH rules provided unequivocally that researchers could not receive more than US$20,000 from a drug company whose drug they are funded by the NIH to research. Researchers were also obliged to disclose to the NIH any payment from a drug company of US$10,000 or more.

Professor Biederman was not alone in his conduct. Two other scholars, Professors Thomas Spencer and Timothy Wilens, who undertook research into ADHD and PBD without

---

[76] Ibid 40.

[77] David H Freedman 'Lies, Damned Lies, and Medical Science', *The Atlantic*, 4 October 2010: <http://www.theatlantic.com/magazine/archive/2010/11/lies-damned-lies-and-medical-science/308269/> [accessed 26 Dec 2015].

[78] Athina Tatsioni, Antonia Charchanti, Evangelia Kitsiou, and John PA Ioannidis, 'Appendicectomies in Albanians in Greece: Outcomes in a Highly Mobile Immigrant Patient Population' (2001) 1(5) *BMC Health Services Research* (unpaginated).

[79] Ibid.

proper disclosure of receipt of drug company moneys, were also found to have engaged in misconduct.[80] The matter was 'resolved'. In July 2011 the practitioners issued a letter to their colleagues after reaching an 'arrangement' with Harvard University and the Massachusetts General Hospital. They conceded the conduct but maintained:

> We always believed that we were complying in good faith with the institutional policies and that our mistakes were honest ones. We now recognize that we should have devoted more time and attention to the detailed requirements of these policies and to their underlying objectives.
>
> We conclude this process with a heightened appreciation for the importance of compliance with institutional policy. We accept responsibility for our actions and the subsequent remedial actions imposed: refraining from all paid industry-sponsored activities for a period of one year, with an additional two year monitoring period during which we must obtain approval from institutional officials at HMS and MGII before engaging in any paid activities and then report upon our activities; additional training; and a delay of consideration for promotion or advancement.[81]

In 2010 Harvard University Medical School issued new conflict of interest rules, after an 18-month review. The rules prohibited staff from accepting personal gifts and giving industry-sponsored talks at events where the material was prepared in advance by the company. In addition, the cap on entitlement to receive funds from outside companies was halved to US$10,000 annually, when the staff member was conducting research on technology owned or licensed by a given company.[82]

Professor Nemeroff. The outcome of the concerns about Professors Biederman, Spencer and Wilens was very similar to the resolution of matters concerning Emory University Professor of Psychiatry and Chairman of the Department of Psychiatry and Behavioral Science, Charles Nemeroff.[83] Professor Nemeroff was also the subject of a Congressional inquiry into conflict of interest by federally supported researchers led by Senator Grassley.[84] Professor Nemeroff was a prominent researcher on pharmacotherapy for anti-depressants, particularly investigating the effects of five antidepressants manufactured by GlaxoSmithKline between 2000 and 2007.[85] He sat on a series of corporate advisory boards, including that of Smith-Kline Beecham Pharmaceuticals, which donated an endowed chair to the university.

---

[80] Xi Yu, 'Three Professors Face Sanctions Following Harvard Medical School Inquiry', *The Harvard Crimson*, 2 July 2011: <http://www.thecrimson.com/article/2011/7/2/school-medical-harvard-investigation/> [accessed 26 Dec 2015].

[81] Letter from Joseph Biederman, Thomas Spencer, and Timothy Wilens to their Colleagues in the Department of Psychiatry, Massachusetts General Hospital and Harvard Medical School, 1 July 2011: <http://www.thecrimson.com/flash-graphic/2011/7/2/medical-school-colleagues-letter/> [accessed 26 Dec 2015].

[82] Xi Yu, 'Harvard Medical School Restricts Ties to Industry', *The Harvard Crimson*, 21 July 2010: <http://www.thecrimson.com/article/2010/7/21/policy-medical-schools-harvard/> [accessed 26 Dec 2015].

[83] Scott Jaschik, 'More Scrutiny on Conflicts of Interest', *Inside Higher Ed*, 6 October 2008: <https://www.insidehighered.com/news/2008/10/06/emory> [accessed 26 Dec 2015]; Emory University, 'Emory Announces Actions Following Investigation', 22 December 2008: <http://shared.web.emory.edu/emory/news/releases/2008/12/conflict_of_interest_action.html#.VNdOYPmUeSq> [accessed 26 Dec 2015].

[84] He had previously had conflict with the whistleblower and activist, Professor David Healy: see Trudo Lemmens, 'Confronting the Conflict of Interest Crisis in Medical Interest' (2004) *Monash Bioethics Review* 19; Alison Bass, *Side-Effects: A Prosecutor, A Whistleblower and a Bestselling Antidepressant on Trial* (New York: Algonquin Books, 2008).

[85] Gardiner Harris, 'Top Psychiatrist Didn't Report Drug Makers' Pay', *New York Times*, 3 October 2008: <http://www.nytimes.com/2008/10/04/health/policy/04drug.html?pagewanted=all&_r=0> [accessed 26 Dec 2015]; Jane Akre, 'Million Dollar Conflict-of-Interest by Emory Psychiatrist Uncovered by Grassley', *Injury Board National News Desk*, 6 October 2008: <http://news.legalexaminer.com/

Emory University announced that its investigation found that, in violation of university rules, Professor Nemeroff had received more than US$800,000 he omitted to report to the University from GlaxoSmithKline for some 250 speaking engagements between 2000 and 2006: 'Though Dr Nemeroff viewed these talks as educational lectures not subject to disclosure, Emory policies required otherwise. The investigation determined that Dr Nemeroff should have abided by the policies and/or sought clarification if, as he later stated, he believed the policies and regulations were ambiguous.'[86] The University stated that its inquiry had found no evidence that Nemeroff's speaking engagements affected care for patients. In 2008, Professor Nemeroff issued a statement through Emory University: 'I regret the failure of full disclosure on my part that has led to the current situation. I believe that I was acting in good faith to comply with the rules as I understood them to be in effect at the time.'[87] He agreed to step down as Chair of Psychiatry. The University announced that he would remain as a professor, but would not submit grant applications in which he would play a role for at least two years. The next year Emory University announced new conflict of interest rules.[88]

Dr Thomas Kossmann. One of Australia's best-known adverse findings of conflict of interest against a scholar is the controversial case of Professor Thomas Kossmann, head trauma surgeon at the Alfred Hospital in Melbourne from 2001 to 2008. Professor Kossmann was subject to a conflict of interest obligation: 'You must not be engaged by, or concerned or interested, directly or indirectly in any other business or occupation without the prior written consent of the health service.'[89] Data later showed that nearly 80 per cent of Professor Kossmann's patients were compensable, despite only 50 per cent of patients at his hospital having that status.

Professor Kossmann resigned from his position in April 2008 after complaints about his clinical conduct and billing practices.[90] This occurred only a year after the hospital had offered Kossmann a five-year extension of his contract with a 40 per cent increase in remuneration and AUS$1.38 million in bonuses.[91] The Victorian Ombudsman, George Brouwer, reported to parliament about him and found that Professor Kossmann had 'acted inconsistently with his employment contract, codes of conduct and good medical practice guidelines. In my view, he failed to act with integrity and placed his private interests ahead of his public duty'.[92]

million-dollar-conflict-of-interest-by-emory-psychiatrist-uncovered-by-grassley.aspx?googleid=248920> [accessed 26 Dec 2015].

86 'Emory Announces Actions Following Investigation', 22 December 2008: <http://shared.web.emory.edu/emory/news/releases/2008/12/conflict_of_interest_action.html#.VNdOYPmUeSq> [accessed 26 Dec 2015].

87 Ibid.

88 Emory University, Conflict of Interest Office, Research Administration: <http://www.coi.emory.edu/> [accessed 26 Dec 2015].

89 Clause 4.1 of the Bayside Health contract quoted in Vanessa Taylor, 'Another Hospital Saga: The Chronicles of Professor Kossmann and Bayside Health' (2010) 18(1) *Journal of Law and Medicine* 76, 90.

90 Ibid.

91 Geoff Wilkinson, '$1.4m Lure for Trauma Surgeon Thomas Kossmann to Stay', *Herald Sun*, 10 June 2008: <http://www.heraldsun.com.au/news/victoria/m-lure-for-surgeon-to-stay/story-e6frf7kx-1111116586159?nk=9dd2e821661af573fb4f491515a2d639> [accessed 26 Dec 2015].

92 George E Brouwer, *Whistleblowers Protection Act 2001: Report of an Investigation into Issues at Bayside Health* (Ombudsman Victoria, October 2008) [18], available at: <https://www.ombudsman.vic.gov.au/Publications?page=11> [accessed 26 Dec 2015]. The Ombudsman also found that: 'Professor Kossmann's conduct was inconsistent with the terms and conditions of his employment and various professional standards, some of which I have referred to above. I consider that he exploited his position as the Professor/Director of Trauma and used his position as the Director of the National Trauma Research Institute to make himself more valuable and marketable to global medical suppliers. In my view, he failed to act with integrity and has placed his own private interests ahead of his public duty. Bayside Health has since expressed the view that Professor Kossmann's conduct in this regard was 'deceptive and in breach of his contract of employment': Ibid [150].

However, he found that the responsibility for how matters had evolved was not all that of the trauma surgeon. Professor Kossmann's 'appetite for undertaking surgical procedures' was highly remunerative for his hospital as well as for him: 'His position of power and influence, unchecked by what I consider should be normal administrative controls, enabled him to create a field of practice in which he benefited both professionally and financially.'[93] The Ombudsman report scrutinized Professor Kossmann's commercial arrangements with implant suppliers, credentialling and clinical privileges, employment contractual arrangements, bank accounts and taxation issues and relationships with colleagues.[94] The Ombudsman then published a further investigation which examined inadequate auditing for the billing by Kossmann and other medical practitioners to the Victorian WorkCover Authority and the Transport Accident Commission.[95] It found that Professor Kossmann had sought to maximize his personal income from medical supply companies, including using his position at the Alfred Hospital to do so.

Ombudsman Brouwer agreed with an earlier finding by the hospital's Peer Review Panel[96] that Professor Kossmann had billed the Transport Accident Commission, WorkSafe and Medicare for surgery that had not been performed, or performed by him, or was not necessary. However, the Ombudsman conceded that the conduct of Professor Kossmann took place within 'a dysfunctional hospital racked by back-biting and interpersonal conflicts over a number of years'.[97] He also criticized the Transport Accident Commission for failing to monitor and audit Professor Kossmann's bills, resulting in 'significant financial incentives for what in my opinion were inappropriate billing practices'.[98]

However, the Victoria Police, the Royal Australian College of Surgeons, Monash University and the Australian Taxation Office all declined to take action against Dr Kossmann. The circumstances surrounding Dr Kossmann became more complicated when Dr Kossmann sued the Alfred for AUS$30 million over claims he had been unlawfully dismissed and defamed. The matter was settled on terms that were not publicly disclosed and 'Alfred Health, the hospital's operator...apologized for the distress the peer review process and its aftermath had caused the surgeon and his family, friends and colleagues. It was sorry for the toll the affair had taken on the Kossmann family and wished them all the best for the future'.[99] It is clear that a difference of perspectives existed between the view of the Peer Review Panel and the Ombudsman, on the one hand, and other entities which also investigated Professor Kossmann's conduct. The multiplicity of investigations was unfortunate in terms of enabling a clear understanding as to whether or not Professor Kossmann had engaged in improper conduct of a serious kind. The saga highlights the escalating sensitivities that exist, though, in respect of conduct which might be perceived as constituting a conflict of interest, or an inappropriate garnering of benefits as a hospital and university employee.

---

93 Ibid [13].

94 Ibid.

95 George E Brouwer, *An Investigation into the Transport Accident Commission's and the Victorian WorkCover Authority's Administrative Processes for Medical Practitioner Billing* (Ombudsman Victoria, July 2009), available at: <https://www.ombudsman.vic.gov.au/Publications?page=11> [accessed 26 Dec 2015].

96 Ibid [11]. The panel found that Professor Kossmann misrepresented his surgical experience to the Alfred in his curriculum vitae, engaged in surgical practices and decision-making that were inappropriate, unnecessary and outside the accepted norm, and did not have the required expertise to practise or teach spinal and pelvic surgery: see Brouwer, above n 92, Recommendation 6.

97 Brouwer, above n 92, [32].

98 Ibid [14].

99 Geoff Wilkinson, 'Top Doctor Thomas Kossmann Wins Apology as The Alfred Settles $30m Lawsuit', *Herald Sun*, 22 January 2011: <http://www.heraldsun.com.au/news/victoria/top-doctor-thomas-kossmann-wins-apology-as-the-alfred-settles-30m-lawsuit/story-e6frf7kx-1225992594816> [accessed 26 Dec 2015].

Distortion of Priorities: The National Women's Hospital Scandal

One of the most notorious examples of conflict of interest in the medical/tertiary sectors occurred in the course of treatment that was not provided to women by reason of a research experiment conducted at the National Women's Hospital in New Zealand. Associate Professor Herbert Green and his research team from 1966 onwards identified women with a diagnosed cervical cancer precursor, for whom assertive treatment was the accepted clinical response.[100] However, the decision was made merely to monitor the women in an effort to show that they were no more likely to develop invasive or malignant cancer than other women. A significant number of the women died of cancer.

After an article in *Metro Magazine*,[101] District Court Judge Sylvia Cartwright was commissioned by the New Zealand government to undertake an inquiry into the events at the hospital. She concluded that the trial was fundamentally flawed in terms of not being scientifically valid, not being ethical and not having been assessed by persons independent of the investigators.[102] Thus, not only was the thesis of the trial conceptually defective but those who participated in it were not enabled to do so informedly by reason of the key elements of the trial being withheld from them, which, among other things, meant that they were deprived of potentially efficacious treatment for their condition. It was a case where research objectives were privileged over both patient health and ethical methodology. The research agenda was skewed by a conflict of interest in concluding the research, regardless of the human cost. Judge Cartwright observed that:

> [H]ad patients been informed of their inclusion in the trial, informed of the types of treatment available to them, informed of the risks of procedures which were not conventional, definitive treatment for carcinoma in situ, and given the opportunity freely to decide whether or not to be part of the trial, then the trial could not be so severely criticised.[103]

The Medical Council of New Zealand upheld allegations of professional misconduct against other persons involved in the experiment: Professor Bonham (Associate Professor Green's superior and head of the hospital), Professor Seddon, and Dr Bruce Faris. However, the allegations arising from research misconduct and conflict of interest against Associate Professor Green were never heard because his state of health did not permit them to proceed. An application for judicial review of the Cartwright Inquiry, brought by a friend and neighbour of Associate Professor Green and Dr Faris, was dismissed by the High Court. The Inquiry and its recommendations have continued to be the subject of debate in New Zealand.[104] However, it is uncontroversial that the Cartwright recommendations led to better awareness of conflict of interest issues, the establishment of the Office of Health and Disability Commissioner in New Zealand[105] and to the Code of Health Consumers'

---

[100] See William A McIndoe, Malcolm R McLean, Ronald W Jones, and Peter R Mullins, 'The Invasive Potential of Carcinoma In Situ of the Cervix' (1984) 64(4) *Obstetrics & Gynecology* 451.

[101] Sandra Coney and Phillida Bunkle, 'An 'Unfortunate Experiment' at National Women's' (1987) *Metro Magazine* 47, available at: <http://www.cartwrightinquiry.com/?page_id=131#respond> [accessed 26 Dec 2015].

[102] Silvia Cartwright, *The Report of the Committee of Inquiry into Allegations Concerning the Treatment of Cervical Cancer at National Women's Hospital and into Other Related Matters* (Auckland, NZ: Government Printing Office, July 1988) 139–40, available at: <https://www.nsu.govt.nz/health-professionals/national-cervical-screening-programme/legislation/cervical-screening-inquiry-0> [accessed 26 Dec 2015].

[103] Ibid 136.

[104] See eg, Linda Bryder, *A History of the 'Unfortunate Experiment' at National Women's Hospital* (Auckland, NZ: Auckland University Press, 2009); Joanna Manning (ed), *The Cartwright Papers: Essays on the Cervical Cancer Inquiry, 1987–88* (Wellington, NZ: Bridget Williams Books, 2009).

[105] Health and Disability Commissioner (New Zealand), 'History': <http://www.hdc.org.nz/about-us/history> [accessed 26 Dec 2015].

Rights.[106] In addition, in the aftermath of the inquiry new oversight of research was instituted[107] with health ethics committees being established throughout New Zealand, the National Cervical Screening Programme being set up and teaching practice fundamentally changing at the National Women's Hospital and Auckland Medical School.

Inappropriate Revelation of Patient Identity

In general it is incumbent upon health practitioners to keep details of their professional relationship with a patient confidential. On occasion, though, there can be temptations to disclose details about the patient to practitioners' scholarly advantage. An example of this arose in a case before Britain's General Medical Council in 1995 in respect of medical practitioners from the Royal Cornhill Hospital in Aberdeen who published a case report about a particularly vulnerable category of patients, persons with bulimia nervosa who had self-harmed. The report, published in the *British Journal of Psychiatry*,[108] contained identifying information. The medical practitioners did not secure the patient's agreement for this and a local Aberdeen paper published details that were in the report, including that one of the patients was a 26-year-old pre-registration doctor. A friend recognized her identity and informed the patient.

The patient complained to the General Medical Council, contending that, although she had consented to her case being used for teaching and research, she had not agreed to its publication in a journal. Somewhat surprisingly, the medical practitioners were found not guilty, but an outcome of the case was clearer instruction from the General Medical Council about the form of consent practitioners must obtain and the *British Medical Journal* thenceforth requiring written consent from patients when it was proposed that the journal publish any personal information about them.[109]

Whistleblowing about Conflict of Interest: The University of Toronto and Dr Olivieri

A high-profile example of conflict of interest issues arose in the now-notorious Canadian saga relating to Dr Nancy Olivieri, a haematologist at the Hospital for Sick Children ('the Hospital'), who was also employed by the University of Toronto. She formed the view that an experimental iron-chelating drug (deferiprone) that she was trialling in patients with thalassaemia major was losing efficacy and causing serious adverse effects, including liver fibrosis. The hope had been that the trials would yield results that would lead to the licensing of deferiprone for therapeutic use.

Not surprisingly, Apotex, the company that manufactured the drug and which was funding the trial, did not share the views of Dr Olivieri who communicated that she intended to inform the drug trial participants of her concerns. Thereupon Apotex terminated the trial and

[106] Health and Disability Commissioner (New Zealand), 'The HDC Code of Health and Disability Services Consumers' Rights Regulation 1996': <http://www.hdc.org.nz/the-act--code/the-code-of-rights/the-code-(full)>.

[107] See John Dawson and Nicola Peart (eds), *The Law of Research: A Guide* (Dunedin, NZ: University of Otago Press, 2003); Tereskerz, above n 61.

[108] Richard J Parkin and John M Eagles, 'Blood-Letting in Bulimia Nervosa' (1993) 162(2) *British Journal of Psychiatry* 246.

[109] See Richard Smith, 'Ethical Issues in the Publication Process' in Frank Wells and Michael Farthing (eds), *Fraud and Misconduct in Biomedical Research* (4th edn, London: Royal Society of Medicine Press Press, 2008), pp 14–28.

withdrew financial support. It invoked a confidentiality agreement in the research contract and threatened legal action if Dr Olivieri made her findings public. However, Dr Olivieri presented her results at a scientific meeting and submitted them for publication.[110] Litigation brought by Apotex and then also by her, as well as an extraordinary level of controversy, ensued.[111]

Since the early 1990s the University of Toronto and Apotex had been engaged in negotiations about a potential multimillion-dollar donation, intended to allow the construction of a new biomedical research centre to benefit the University and its affiliated health care institutions. In the spring of 1998, agreement in principle was reached on what at that time would have been the largest donation the University had ever received. It was to have been matched by other sources to provide the approximately CA$92 million needed for the new biomedical research centre. Later in 1998, after the controversy involving Dr Olivieri became public, the University and Apotex suspended discussions until the dispute involving Dr Olivieri and Apotex was resolved.

The University of Toronto and the Hospital did not support Dr Olivieri and referred her to the Canadian College of Physicians and Surgeons, alleging she had engaged in research misconduct. The Hospital unilaterally established a review of the controversy and appointed Dr Arnold Naimark of the University of Manitoba as the reviewer. Dr Olivieri elected not to participate in the review; Dr Naimark was critical of some respects of Dr Olivieri's conduct.

The consequences of the dispute included acrimonious and personalized disputation. One of Dr Olivieri's former collaborators, a clinical pharmacologist, Dr Koren, began to send anonymous letters to the media and colleagues disparaging Dr Olivieri and those who supported her. In due course this led to disciplinary action against Dr Koren for 'gross misconduct' after Dr Olivieri was able to establish the identity of the person who was the author of the letters.

The University and the Hospital attempted to dismiss Dr Olivieri from her position, but ultimately she was reinstated, in the shadow of law suits and counter-suits, after receiving substantial support from professional colleagues. She was vindicated by an independent 500-page report in 2001 commissioned by the Canadian Association of University Teachers,[112] which recommended that she receive redress[113] and by the College of Physicians and Surgeons of Ontario that made no adverse finding or criticism of her conduct, describing her disclosures as 'diligent'.[114] It was found that, contrary to allegations it made, Apotex had conducted itself

---

[110] Nancy F Olivieri, Gary M Brittenham, Doreen Matsui, Matitiahu Berkovitch et al., 'Iron-Chelation Therapy with Oral Deferiprone in Patients with Thalassemia Major' (1995) 332(14) *The New England Journal of Medicine* 918.

[111] See Kassirer, above n 38; Sheldon Krimsky, *Science in the Private Interest: Has the Lure of Profits Corrupted Biomedical Research?* (Lanham, Md: Rowman & Littlefield, 2004); Marcia Angell, *The Truth About the Drug Companies: How They Deceive Us and What to Do About It* (New York: Random House, 2005); Miriam Shuchman, *The Drug Trial: Nancy Olivieri and the Scandal that Rocked the Hospital for Sick Children* (Toronto: Random House, 2005).

[112] Jon Thompson, Patricia Baird, and Jocelyn Downie, *Report of the Committee of Inquiry on the Case Involving Dr Nancy Olivieri, the Hospital for Sick Children, the University of Toronto, and Apotex Inc*: <http://www.caut.ca/docs/af-reports-indepedent-committees-of-inquiry/the-olivieri-report.pdf> [accessed 26 Dec 2015]. See too Howard Brody, *Hooked: Ethics, the Medical Profession and the Pharmaceutical Industry* (Lanham, Md: Rowman & Littlefield, 2007), 99ff.

[113] The Report also commented that: 'The general features of this situation are not unique to the Hospital for Sick Children and the University of Toronto, and given the current absence of the necessary protections, it could occur at many institutions across Canada. As we specify in our sections on recommendations and lessons to be learned, it is essential to put in place measures to ensure that, in the conduct of clinical research trials, the public interest is protected from inappropriate actions by trial sponsors': Ibid 15.

[114] *Laurence Becker v Nancy F Olivieri*, 'Complaints Committee Decision and Reasons' (The College of Physicians and Surgeons of Ontario, November 2001), 17, 18: <http://www.caut.ca/docs/default-source/academic-freedom/olivieri_cpso.pdf?sfvrsn=2> [accessed 26 Dec 2015].

inappropriately and 'against the public interest'; Dr Olivieri had behaved honourably and should have been supported by the University and the Hospital.[115] It can safely be assumed that this was an unwelcome finding for Apotex; however, it was well received by Dr Olivieri and was accompanied by a series of further measures to recompense her.[116] The case is one of many instances of the travails experienced by ethical persons who 'blow the whistle' on research improprieties, including conflicts of interest. These matters are explored further below in Chapter 9. It also was a catalyst for important changes to disciplinary investigations in Canada.

Perceptions of Influence: The London School of Economics Scandal

In 2011 it became known that a £1.5m donation in tranches of £300,000 annually had been made to the London School of Economics (LSE) from a charity run by Saif al-Islam Gaddafi, the son of the former Libyan President, Muammar al-Gaddafi.[117] The origin of the money paid to the LSE may have been money paid to the dictator's son as bribes, according to an inquiry conducted by Lord Woolf, the former Chief Justice of England and Wales.[118] Lord Woolf found a 'disconcerting number of failures in communication and governance'[119] in the LSE's relations with the Libyan regime and commented: 'It is a matter of real regret that the question of the Libyan gift proceeded to Council [the LSE's governing body] when due diligence remained, at best, embryonic'.[120]

The inquiry report found that an LSE academic, David Held, a Professor of Political Science, first approached Saif about the possibility of funding his Centre for the Study of Global Governance in December 2008, shortly after the dictator's son had been awarded his PhD by the LSE but before the formal graduation ceremony. Professor Held was an academic adviser to Saif during his studies and was director of the research programme funded by Saif's charity.

The decision was made by the LSE that the gift would not only be accepted, in spite of protests, but would be depicted not as coming from Saif directly but from 'private sector sources'.[121] Lord Woolf observed that the 'private aspect of this gift was particularly troublesome', the hiding of its provenance being politically essential or it might have been regarded as 'unacceptable money from the Libyan state'.[122]

However, the situation was even worse than this. Saif al-Islam received unusual levels of support while undertaking his degree.[123] In addition, he was allowed to lay out 'objectives and

---

[115] Thompson, Baird and Downie, above n 112, 14. See too Howard Woodhouse, *Selling Out: Academic Freedom and the Corporate Market* (McGill-Queen's University Press, Quebec, 2009).

[116] See James Turk, 'The Greatest Academic Scandal of Our Era' (May 1999) *University of Calgary Faculty Association Newsletter* 'Interview', republished at: <http://www.mcmaster.ca/mufa/turk.htm> [accessed 26 Dec 2015].

[117] See Jeevan Vasagar, 'Gaddafi Donation to LSE May Have Come From Bribes, Inquiry Finds', *The Guardian*, 30 November 2011: <http://www.theguardian.com/education/2011/nov/30/gaddafi-donation-lse-bribes-inquiry> [accessed 26 Dec 2015].

[118] '[T]here is a risk that the money was to come from payments made by private companies operating in Libya to gain Saif's favour and influence the award of contracts in Libya': Lord Justice Woolf, *An Inquiry into the LSE's Links with Libya and Lessons to be Learned* (Woolf Report) (October 2011) [1.18]: <http://www.lse.ac.uk/newsAndMedia/woolf/pdf/woolfReport.pdf> [accessed 26 Dec 2015].

[119] Ibid [1.14].

[120] Ibid [3.24].

[121] Ibid [3.12].

[122] Ibid.

[123] Ibid [1.16].

expectations' for the research programme funded by the charity, according to leaked LSE documents. Lord Woolf expressed himself carefully but devastatingly: 'I come to no conclusions as to whether there was or would have been excessive influence by the donor over the use of the funds from Saif's foundation. However, what has been made plain is that proper structures of governance are needed to protect academic integrity against influence from the interests of private donors.'[124] He recommended the creation of an ethical code to provide guidance to universities in such situations and the creation of an ethics committee at LSE to deal with such matters. These issues are pertinent to the position in which Victoria's La Trobe University placed itself during 2014 in relation to the memorandum of understanding it entered into with Swisse.

Corruption

At the extreme edge of conflict of interest scenarios is outright corruption. On occasion, such matters within academia have been exposed in various countries, prompting concerns about the framework of integrity.[125]

In 2009 German prosecutors launched an investigation into around 100 academics at some of the country's top universities on the suspicion that they had granted doctorates to significant numbers of unqualified students after taking bribes from a consultancy firm. The investigation took place after a raid on an academic consultancy, the Institute for Scientific Counselling (Institut für Wissenschaftsberatung) in Bergisch Gladbach, in March 2008. Prosecutors in Cologne maintained that the institute helped doctoral candidates find a supervisor and paid lecturers to take on PhD students. The institute pledged to clients that it would assist them to find a suitable topic on which to write a dissertation and a professor well-suited for overseeing the dissertation. It charged as much as €20,000 for its services, with approximately €4,000 going to the professors. As this was already part of an academic's work, it meant that they were being doubly paid for this part of their work.[126]

A former director of the Bergisch Gladbach consultancy[127] was convicted on bribery charges in July 2008 and sentenced to imprisonment for three and a half years and a €75,000 fine for having paid a law professor in Hanover[128] up to €4,000 to accept PhD candidates, some of whom did not fulfil the prerequisites for studying towards a PhD. The law professor was also convicted of accepting bribes. In addition, the law professor at the University of Hanover who received money from the consultancy for accepting doctoral candidates was given a

[124] Ibid [6.44].

[125] For concerns about issues in Russia, see Elena Denisova-Schmidt, 'Justification of Academic Corruption at Russian Universities' (Edmond J Safra Working Papers, No. 30, 14 November 2013), available at: <http://ssrn.com/abstract=2353513> [accessed 26 Dec 2015]. See also, in relation to corruption in Chinese universities, Roger Y Chao Jr, 'China Needs a Comprehensive Anti-Corruption Strategy' (8 November 2013) Issue No. 295, *University World News*: <http://www.universityworldnews.com/article.php?story=20131105151800642>; Haohao Li, Xiaoqing He and Shuai Wang, 'Academic Anticorruption in China's Universities' (Keynote Address, International Conference on Higher Education (ICHE), Trier, 28 August 2010): <http://www.intconfhighered.org/Academic%20Anticorruption%20in%20China%27s%20universities-Haohao%20Li1.doc>.

[126] Jochen Leffers, 'Academic Corruption: Germany Rocked by Allegations of Ph.D. Bribes', *SpiegelOnline*, 24 August 2009: <http://www.spiegel.de/international/germany/academic-corruption-germany-rocked-by-allegations-of-ph-d-bribes-a-644639.html> [accessed 26 Dec 2015].

[127] Not publicly named pursuant to Germany's privacy laws.

[128] Also not publicly named by reason of Germany's privacy laws.

three-year jail sentence.[129] He confessed in court to accepting nearly €200,000 to serve as a faculty adviser to more than 60 doctoral students between 1998 and 2005. He said he needed the money to renovate his Hamburg mansion. *Time* reported that:

> According to some experts, there is a rampant illegal trade in doctor titles in Germany, preying on people's desire to gain the social kudos that comes with getting a Ph.D. 'The investigation in Cologne is just the tip of the iceberg,' says Manuel René Theisen, professor of business administration at the Ludwig-Maximilians University in Munich. 'Around a dozen academic consultancies have been on the market for years offering Ph.D.s for money.' Theisen says he estimates that of the 25,000 doctorates awarded each year in Germany, up to 1,000 are obtained through illicit means. 'The consultancies advertise in trade magazines and they pretend to offer coaching for would-be Ph.D. students, but it's a fairy tale,' he says. 'People know when they read the adverts they can get their Ph.D. for money and not for their [academic] work.' Theisen says these Ph.D. scams are big business, with the rewards more than just an impressive diploma to hang on the wall: 'People who buy their Ph.D. titles then go on to demand more money from their employers in their future careers.'[130]

A cognate issue was addressed by Victoria's Ombudsman in 2011 in the context of a report into issues relating to international students at universities. He recorded having received a series of disclosures under legislation protecting whistleblowers, alleging that university staff had sought or accepted bribes from students. Three had been substantiated, two of which involved international students. His staff interviewed 15 academic staff on oath from Deakin University, RMIT University, Swinburne University of Technology, and the University of Ballarat. They were asked if they had ever been offered a bribe by a student, or were aware of colleagues who had been offered bribes. Six of the 15 asserted that they or their colleagues had been offered bribes by students. An academic at Deakin said he had been offered sexual favours by a young female student who had failed a subject. He maintained:

> And this is an offer that will change her life in terms of her potential in the future in her society or whether she could get married at the right level and everything else. Because that's how important it was for her…what really was damaging to me was that the stakes are so high, absolutely sky-high, that you can get to that point as a student.[131]

The Ombudsman also reported that an academic at RMIT said:

> [I]t's something I feel pretty sure if I pursued could have been considered a bribe. But I'm fairly quick at jumping in. You know students say things, 'I'm sure…we can find a way around this that would mutually satisfy everybody'. And I very quickly jump in and say always, 'You repeat the subject, you pass, I'll celebrate with you at graduation'…if it looks like you're going to waiver then I think they'd come in fairly hard.[132]

Two academics interviewed said they thought that a colleague had accepted a bribe. An academic at the University of Ballarat conceded that '[w]e don't know how endemic it is' but emphasized: 'But we know that it happens.'[133]

---

[129] See Nora Schultz, 'German Academics Investigated over Bribery Claims', *New Scientist*, 25 August 2009: <http://www.newscientist.com/blogs/shortsharpscience/2009/08/100-german-profs-investigated.html> [accessed 26 Dec 2015]; David Rising, 'Germany: 100 Professors Suspected of Ph.D. Bribes', *The Guardian*, 23 August 2009: <http://www.theguardian.com/world/feedarticle/8670696> [accessed 26 Dec 2015].

[130] Tristana Moore, 'Germany's Ph.D. Scandal: Were Degrees Bought?' *Time*, 28 August 2009: <http://content.time.com/time/world/article/0,8599,1919339,00.html> [accessed 26 Dec 2015].

[131] John R Taylor, *Investigation into How Universities Deal with International Students* (Victorian Ombudsman, October 2011) [248], available at: <https://www.ombudsman.vic.gov.au/Publications?page=11&searchtext=universities&searchmode=anyword#content-area> [accessed 26 Dec 2015].

[132] Ibid [249].

[133] Ibid [251].

Late in 2014 it was announced by the Ministry of Science and Technology that an anti-corruption campaign by the Chinese government had charged seven leading scientists from five universities with having misused US$4.1 million of government grants. This followed upon an announcement from the National Audit Office of China that it had identified corruption in the form of conflict of interest in more than a dozen applied research 'mega-projects', worth over $8 billion per year in government funds. One of the six scientists placed under arrest was an animal-cloning researcher and academician in the Chinese Academy of Engineering. He was said to be involved in high-level embezzlement.[134] A 2013 report of China's National Audit Office in October 2013 similarly suggested that misuse of research grants in China was widespread and that up to a half of all research funding was being misused. Amongst other things, this led to a vice-president of Zhejiang University being arrested in December 2013 on 'suspicion of occupational crime'.[135] It has been suggested that the problems for Chinese science lie within a propensity to 'excessive bureaucratic interference', which can influence results, or at least presentation of results, and a culture of '*jigong jinli*', placing a premium on quick success and short-term gain.[136]

Transparency International's 2013 report on Global Corruption in Education[137] identified the potential for corruption to occur in tertiary institutions in many contexts, including at the early stage of recruitment and admission where, for instance, bribes may be paid for preferment; in the form of financial fraud occurring as a result of a failure in internal control mechanisms; in the form of institutions becoming 'degree mills';[138] and when success of graduates in the job market is exaggerated to attract students. It described 'academic integrity' as consisting of values of honesty, trust, respect, fairness, and responsibility, and as being fundamental to the reputation of academic institutions. It is apparent that there are a great many situations in which corrupt conflicts of interest can come into being in the academic environment, either to individual scholars' advantage or to the advantage of the institution employing them.

Conclusions

The various scenarios instanced in this chapter are more than sufficient to establish the need for modern scholars and the institutions that employ them to be mindful of the disillusioning effects of the exposure of conflicts of interest. The general community, but also the scholarly community, is increasingly intolerant of conduct and relationships which bespeak bias and lack of integrity, especially when these emanate from self-interest. The Nazi doctor atrocities and a range of other forms of unethical conduct engaged in by scholars during the 20th century have taught us that professionals have the capacity to rationalize many forms of behaviour in clinical trials which have foreseeably adverse or even inevitably adverse consequences for vulnerable persons. Such research subjects may submit to involvement desperate for positive outcomes or, even altruistically, hoping to advantage others. They are entitled to

---

[134] See Jane Qiu, 'Scientists Caught in Chinese Anti-Corruption Sweep', *Nature*, 16 October 2014: <http://www.nature.com/news/scientists-caught-in-chinese-anti-corruption-sweep-1.16152> [accessed 26 Dec 2015].

[135] Jane Qiu, 'China Goes Back to Basics on Research Funding' (2014) 507(7491) *Nature*: <http://www.nature.com/news/china-goes-back-to-basics-on-research-funding-1.14853> [accessed 26 Dec 2015].

[136] Ibid. See also, Jane Qiu, 'Publish or Perish in China' (2010) 463 *Nature* 142: <http://www.nature.com/news/2010/100112/full/463142a.html> [accessed 26 Dec 2015].

[137] Transparency International, *Global Corruption Report: Education* (Abingdon, Oxon: Routledge, 2013), available at: <http://www.transparency.org/gcr_education> [accessed 26 Dec 2015].

[138] Ibid 102.

be protected from the taking of inappropriate risks to their actual or potential detriment and from the manipulation of their generosity. Codes of professional ethics, bioethical guidelines, and codes of conduct (such as that of Harvard Medical School) have attempted to deal with these issues at a disciplinary level, particularly for medical practitioners.

However, the possibilities of such conduct, directly connected to research, but also in other contexts, are so multifarious, some of them egregious, some of them nuanced, that it is apparent that funding bodies and employers such as universities need to be in a position to regulate such conduct and for robust action to be taken in relation to persons against whom allegations of such conduct are proved. This involves as much encouragement and protection as possible being accorded to whistleblowers, although appropriate measures may well not extend to mandating disclosures of suspicions of conflict of interest from all employees. Such forms of mandatory notification are often not complied with and can erode environments of trust and collaboration.

It also requires the provision of guidance so that individuals can recognize and thereafter disclose and manage conflicts of interest. Many scholarly journals now insist on a certification of absence of conflict of interest in manuscripts submitted for publication and have as a policy that they will not publish editorials and at least certain forms of articles if a conflict of interest is disclosed. An example is the *British Medical Journal* which requires all authors to complete a conflict of interest form and to declare:

> All authors have completed the ICMJE uniform disclosure form at www.icmje.org/coi_disclosure.pdf and declare: no support from any organization for the submitted work…; no financial relationships with any organizations that might have an interest in the submitted work in the previous three years…; no other relationships or activities that could appear to have influenced the submitted work.[139]

The *Journal of Law and Medicine* has a similar requirement. However, it is important that there be ongoing commitment to enforcement of such certifications. In 1999 the *New England Journal of Medicine* found, to its embarrassment, that although it had such a certification procedure, and a preclusion on publication of editorials and review articles where such a conflict was disclosed, since 1 January 1997 it had published 19 articles on drug therapy in spite of the fact that these had been written by researchers who had disclosed that they were funded by pharmaceutical companies. The journal had failed to apply its own policy.[140]

Universities have diverse policies in relation to conflict of interest. More than 'mere' disclosure is necessary, although it is a good starting point. The Oxford University policy constitutes a sensible beginning. There must be as little scope as possible for ambiguity in such guidance, the most important consideration being that there is identification of conflicts so that appropriate strategies can be developed to deal with them. This requires inclusive and broad definitions of actual, perceived, and potential conflicts of interest with sufficiently clear assistance and examples to facilitate well-intentioned employees and others to identify when issues arise. However, an important dynamic in dealing with conflicts of interest is that there can be financial inducements for persons and institutions not to make disclosures. This

139 *British Medical Journal*, 'Declaration of Competing Interests': <http://www.bmj.com/about-bmj/resources-authors/forms-policies-and-checklists/declaration-competing-interests> [accessed 26 Dec 2015]. See also, *British Medical Journal*, 'Transparency Policy': <http://www.bmj.com/about-bmj/resources-authors/forms-policies-and-checklists/transparency-policy> [accessed 26 Dec 2015].

140 See Marcia Angell and Alastair JJ Wood (disclosure by Vera H Price), 'Authors' Conflicts of Interest: A Disclosure and Editors' Reply' (1999) 341(21) *The New England Journal of Medicine* 1618; Marcia Angell, Robert D Utiger, and Alastair JJ Wood, 'Disclosure of Authors' Conflicts of Interest: A Follow-up' (2000) 342(8) *The New England Journal of Medicine* 586.

means that the temptation to engage in self-serving rationalizations enabling non-disclosure needs to be minimized by enhancing both the prospect of such matters coming to light and strong action taken to name and shame perpetrators. This requires means of encouraging and sometimes pressuring institutions such as university hierarchies and private research bodies into taking such action, even when it involves embarrassment occasioned by the conduct of their employees.

Thus there is a need for mechanisms to deal authoritatively and promptly with conflicts of interest, thereby avoiding the situations that characterized the unsatisfactory resolution of the allegations against Dr Olivieri. Persons and entities should be designated to receive and deal with declarations of conflict of interest in a firm but non-adversarial way before embarrassment or harm is caused. This involves the availability of independent ethics committees to grapple with issues that arise with some regularity in not just the conduct of research but many different functions engaged in by institutions that employ scholars, in particular universities. The factual matrix of the London School of Economics scandal involving the Libyan dictator's son, and the complex dynamics that have the potential to ensue after La Trobe University's memorandum of understanding with Swisse, are illustrative of the unusual circumstances that can bring conflicts of interest into being, which in turn can erode an institution's reputation for integrity. At the extreme end, China's culture (arguably shared by that in a number of other countries) of '*jigong jinli*', which prioritizes research success, quickly achieved, and which rewards such outcomes, creates a fertile ground for the creation of not just conflicts of interest but outright corruption.

Given how often such matters have not been dealt with in as open, expeditious, and robust a manner internally as is desirable, there is much to be said for inquiries into conflicts of interest being able to be initiated or at least overseen by, or appealed to, an eminently constituted external body with responsibility for integrity investigation in relation to scholarly conduct. Such investigations should be able to be taken by the body of its own motion or on receipt of a complaint. Such an entity needs to be more than tokenistic. It needs to be sufficiently resourced with both highly regarded and credentialed members and well trained investigators. It also needs to have the powers required to investigate such matters and then to make publicly accessible reports that include findings and recommendations for action. The eminence of such a body should be such as to make it difficult for tertiary institutions not to accept its findings and implement its recommendations. The entity proposed in respect of research misconduct (see Chapter 3), an Office of Scholarly Integrity, would be such a body.

5

FORENSIC MISCONDUCT

Introduction

Academics and scholars from many different disciplines are regularly commissioned by litigation lawyers to provide expert reports and testimony for the assistance of courts and tribunals on issues that are otherwise outside the knowledge and competence of decision-makers in the forensic setting. This role forms a significant and remunerative addition to scholarly practice for a cross-section of those in tertiary employment, particularly in the science, medicine, engineering, and financial sectors. It is much sought after, including by those who have concluded the active clinical, technical, and laboratory component of their careers. Properly, it is also to be regarded as constituting an aspect of scholarly practice because it generally involves the application of scholarly skills, not in the academic domain, but in the forensic area.

The role of assisting the courts as a scholarly expert in itself generates temptations for the taking of short-cuts and for efforts to be made to optimize the forensic aspects of a career. For others employed within forensic institutes and laboratories it is a core part of their work and, in turn, is based upon scholarship published in learned journals on various areas of forensic endeavour. The quality of its discharge, including the extent of throughput of analysed samples, and the interpretation of results, can be advantageous for career advancement of those undertaking forensic work.

Where misconduct contaminates the discharge of the forensic role, the consequences can be miscarriages of justice. In the criminal domain, this can result in some countries in deaths by execution that are the product of wrongful determinations of guilt but in all countries in the serving of periods of lengthy terms of imprisonment that should never have been imposed. In other areas interference with financial entitlements and with the rearing of children can be the product.

This chapter reflects on the motives that have generated forensic misconduct and looks for any tell-tale signs of professionals' preparedness to abandon scientific integrity in the shadow of the courts. It identifies that many of the dynamics that produce fabricated and fraudulent scientific and medical research, as described in Chapters 2 and 3, and research that is contaminated by conflicts of interest, as set out in Chapter 4, are on occasion to be seen also in the context of forensic misconduct. However, it notes that what is distinctive about misconduct in the forensic area is its greater apparent tendency to be driven ideologically by a desire on the part of the perpetrators to achieve a particular outcome in criminal justice proceedings against accused persons—an aim to help secure convictions where evidence may be equivocal or even contrary to the desired investigative and prosecutorial outcome. Sometimes forensic misconduct is deliberately engaged in by a practitioner; on other occasions the vice in their conduct in respect of the conduct is that it is incompetent or sub-standard—both scenarios create the potential for miscarriages of justice.

Being clear-sighted and candid about the existence of this dynamic, as well as about the environmental checks and balances required to counteract it, has the potential to form the basis for avoiding the pitfalls of such conduct, as well as for prophylactic responses by regulators of forensic misconduct. The chapter concludes by reflecting on the mechanisms that have been constructed in the United Kingdom, the United States, and Australia to regulate misconduct in the writing of forensic reports and the giving of evidence in the courts. It advances proposals for the consolidation of these developments so as to reduce the potential for forensic misconduct.

The Forensic Role

The role of being an expert witness and report-writer, whether the person be employed within academia, by a forensic accounting firm, or by an institute or laboratory of forensic medicine or science, has at its heart learnedness—being sufficiently au fait with the scholarly and practice literature and day-to-day standards and work in the relevant area to be able to provide a helpful perspective or interpretation of disputed facts for the courts.[1] The essence of the forensic expert role is possession of specialized knowledge[2] in an area relevant to litigation in the courts, derived from training, study or experience,[3] or a combination thereof, and the ability to communicate such knowledge in a way which can be understood and evaluated by judges and jurors.[4]

The expert opinions of witnesses are relied on by courts in criminal cases to enable evaluation of the reliability of prosecutorial allegations of criminality. They are also fundamental to the resolution of civil and family law disputes. If forensic work is substandard or methodologically unsound, makes unwarranted assumptions rather than proceeding from a null hypothesis, is fabricated, or influenced by pressure (from the state, the police, the prosecution or any party to litigation), then the outcome has the potential to be a miscarriage of justice that is not easy to remedy on appeal.[5] This is partly because of the potent influence of experts within litigation which has been described in many different ways but often to similar effect. In *United States v Frazier*,[6] for instance, it was observed that such testimony 'may be assigned talismanic significance in the eyes of lay jurors', while in *United States v Hines*[7] it was noted that a 'certain patina attaches to an expert's testimony unlike any other witness; this is "science", a professional's judgment, the jury may think, and give more credence to the testimony than it may deserve'.

In *R v C(G)*,[8] the Newfoundland Court of Appeal accepted the concern that the aura[9] surrounding expert evidence may result in excessive weight being given to it:

> Thus, cases speak of apprehension that expert testimony, cloaked as it generally is in scientific language, will acquire a mystical air of infallibility that technical vocabularies often

[1] See *Davie v Magistrates of Edinburgh* 1953 SC 34; *Preece v HM Advocate* [1981] Crim LR 783, 784; Roger Ormrod, 'Scientific Evidence in Court' [1968] *Criminal Law Review* 240.

[2] See *Daubert v Merrell Dow Pharmaceuticals Inc*, 509 US 579 (1993).

[3] See eg, *Evidence Act* 1995 (Cth) s 79. Rule 702 of the United States Federal Rules of Evidence provides: 'A witness who is qualified as an expert by knowledge, skill, experience, training, or education may testify in the form of an opinion or otherwise if: (a) the expert's scientific, technical, or other specialized knowledge will help the trier of fact to understand the evidence or to determine a fact in issue; (b) the testimony is based on sufficient facts or data; (c) the testimony is the product of reliable principles and methods; and(d) the expert has reliably applied the principles and methods to the facts of the case.'

[4] See Ian Freckelton and Hugh Selby, *Expert Evidence: Law, Practice, Procedure and Advocacy* (6th edn, Pyrmont, NSW: Lawbook Co/Thomson Reuters, 2016).

[5] Appeals generally require an error of law for a reversal, unless the decision at first instance is perverse, plainly unreasonable or against the evidence.

[6] 387 F 3d 1244, 1263 (11th Cir, 2004).

[7] 55 F Supp 2d 62, 64 (D Mass, 1999).

[8] (1997) 110 CCC (3d) 233 (Newfoundland CA).

[9] For reference to the aura of expert evidence, see also, *Velevski v The Queen* [2002] HCA 4; (2002) 187 ALR 233, [166] (Gummow and Callinan JJ).

> communicate to those not versed in the expert's discipline. The fear is, therefore, rather than assist laypersons in forming judgments, that the use of expert evidence will usurp the function of the trier of fact and distort the proceedings by bolstering the evidence of parties and overwhelm a jury.[10]

The potential for forensic misconduct by expert report-writers or witnesses to have a deleterious effect upon the evaluations of fact by jurors in particular is aggravated by the inflated expectations that the public has been encouraged to have of forensic scientists and physicians by reason of works of fiction,[11] advertisers invoking the authority of the white coat, and of 'clinical tests' and contemporary media portrayals of the infallibility of crime scene investigation and forensic science more generally.[12]

In 2006 Dowler, Fleming, and Muzzatti in the Canadian context wrote of the effect of portrayals of forensic science in films and television such as the Crime Scene Investigation (CSI) series that:

> [T]he CSI Effect relates to the popularity of *CSI, Criminal Minds, Crossing Jordan*, and other programs that portray scientific and forensic evidence-gathering procedures to catch criminals; the 'effect' is the rise in expectations of real-life crime victims and jury members.[13]

In 2008, to similar effect, Monica Robbers, an American criminologist, defined the CSI effect as 'the phenomenon in which jurors hold unrealistic expectations of forensic evidence and investigation techniques, and have an increased interest in the discipline of forensic science'.[14] Since 2008, the legitimacy, nature of, and ongoing relevance of the phenomenon of the CSI effect have become contested,[15] and the extent to which members of the public are prone to defer uncritically to scientific and medical evidence has been the subject of argument, but the potentially potent influence of impressive and articulate expert witnesses remains a significant courtroom dynamic.

As observed above, many factors can distort the integrity of expert opinions prepared for forensic purposes.[16] An extreme example is where there is interference by the state with the

---

[10] *R v C(G)* (1997) 110 CCC (3d) 233 (Newfoundland CA) 259. See also, *R v DD* [2000] 2 SCR 275, [53] (Major J): 'Faced with an expert's impressive credentials and mastery of scientific jargon, jurors are more likely to abdicate their role as fact-finders and simply attorn to the opinion of the expert in their desire to reach a just result'; *R v Mohan* [1994] 2 SCR 9, 21 (Sopinka J): 'There is a danger that expert evidence will be misused and will distort the fact-finding process. Dressed up in scientific language which the jury does not easily understand and submitted through a witness of impressive antecedents, this evidence is apt to be accepted by the jury as being virtually infallible and as having more weight than it deserves.' See generally Ian Freckelton, *The Trial of the Expert: A Study of Expert Evidence and Forensic Experts* (Melbourne: Oxford University Press, 1987).

[11] See Ronald R Thomas, *Detective Fiction and the Rise of Forensic Science* (Cambridge: Cambridge University Press, 2003).

[12] See Jeff Chesen, 'The 'CSI Effect'—There's No Such Thing as Questions, Just Hidden Answers', *National Clearinghouse for Science, Technology and the Law* (July 2008): <http://www.ncstl.org/evident/July08%20 ResearchFocus> [accessed 26 Dec 2015].

[13] Ken Dowler, Thomas Fleming, and Stephen L Muzzatti, 'Constructing Crime: Media, Crime, and Popular Culture' (2006) 48(6) *Canadian Journal of Criminology and Criminal Justice* 837, 838. See also, Nick J Schweitzer and Michael J Saks, 'The *CSI* Effect: Popular Fiction About Forensic Science Affects the Public's Expectations About Real Forensic Science' (2007) 47(3) *Jurimetrics* 357.

[14] Monica L P Robbers, 'Blinded by Science: The Social Construction of Reality in Forensic Television Shows and its Effect on Criminal Jury Trials' (2008) 19(1) *Criminal Justice Policy Review* 84, 86.

[15] See Evan W Durnal, 'Crime Scene Investigation (As Seen on TV)' (2010) 199(1) *Forensic Science International* 1; Jane Goodman-Delahunty and Hielkje Verbrugge, 'Reality, Fantasy and the Truth about CSI Effects' (2010) 32(4) *InPsych* 18, available at: <http://www.psychology.org.au/publications/inpsych/2010/august/goodman/> [accessed 26 Dec 2015].

[16] See further, Ian Freckelton, Jane Goodman-Delahunty, Jacqueline Horan, and Blake McKimmie, *Expert Evidence and Criminal Jury Trials* (Oxford: Oxford University Press, 2016); Freckelton and Selby, above n 4.

integrity of expert work, such as the death investigation process undertaken by forensic pathologists. An apparent example in this regard was publicized in August 2013 when a leading Chinese forensic scientist, Wang Xuemei, announced that she was resigning as Vice-President of the Chinese Forensic Medicine Association, because of an autopsy report in a high-profile case which she contended was the product of political pressure to reach a particular result. This came against a backdrop of a sequence of Chinese cases in which concern had been expressed about questionable autopsy results by reason of pressures allegedly brought to bear by sources within government.[17] It highlights the importance of both integrity and independence in the discharge of the forensic role for experts.

The frequently enunciated expectation of the courts is that fundamental to the work of the forensic expert is the provision of opinions that are the independent product of the expert uninfluenced as to form or content by the exigencies of litigation, including who has commissioned the forensic work and the sum of money being paid for it.[18] This entails the principal responsibility of the forensic expert being to the court, not to the party commissioning them—or, put another way, '[a]n expert should not consider that it is his job to stand shoulder to shoulder through thick and thin with the side which is paying his bill'.[19] Many court rules, practice notes, and codes of conduct for experts reinforce such obligations, emphasizing that experts' primary allegiance when they undertake a forensic role must be to the courts, not to their client/patient or the party paying them.[20] However, too often an affiliation has come into being between the expert and the party commissioning them such that the expert, on occasion deliberately, tailors their analysis and fashions their expressed opinions so as to support their client.[21] Not only is this conduct unethical, resulting in abusive descriptors, such as experts being 'whores of the court',[22] and concerns about 'junk science',[23] but it has been identified as a significant source of judicial concern in many jurisdictions, including in Australia where judges and magistrates were surveyed on the issue and in large numbers stated that bias and partisanship were issues they were worried were impacting

---

[17] See Choi Chi-Yuk, 'Forensic Expert Rejects Cyanide Explanation for Heywood's Death', *South China Morning Post*, 28 September 2012: <http://www.scmp.com/news/china/article/1048972/forensic-expert-rejects-cyanide-explanation-heywoods-death> [accessed 26 Dec 2015]; Jiabao Du, 'The Dark, Corrupt World of Forensic Science in China', *The Atlantic*, 23 August 2013: <http://www.theatlantic.com/china/archive/2013/08/the-dark-corrupt-world-of-forensic-science-in-china/278990/> [accessed 26 Dec 2015]; see also, Sophie Song, 'Chinese Forensic Science Frequently Under Suspicion Of Covering-Up For Officials', *International Business Times*, 23 August 2013: <http://www.ibtimes.com/chinese-forensic-science-frequently-under-suspicion-covering-officials-1397759> [accessed 26 Dec 2015].

[18] See eg, *National Justice Compania Naviera SA v Prudential Assurance Co Ltd (The Ikarian Reefer)* [1993] 2 Lloyd's Rep 68, 81–82; see also, *R v Harris* [2005] EWCA Crim 1980; [2006] 1 Cr App R 5, [273]; *R v Bowman* [2006] EWCA Crim 417; *Meadow v General Medical Council* [2006] EWCA Civ 1390; [2007] 1 QB 462, [21]; *Chapman v Luminis Pty Ltd (No 4)* (2001) 123 FCR 62.

[19] *Cala Homes (South) Ltd v Alfred McAlpine Homes East Ltd* [1995] FSR 818, 843.

[20] In Australia, see eg, Federal Court of Australia, 'Expert Witnesses in Proceedings in the Federal Court of Australia' (Practice Note CM 7, 4 June 2013): <http://www.fedcourt.gov.au/law-and-practice/practice-documents/practice-notes/cm7> [accessed 26 Dec 2015]; and, in the criminal context, Supreme Court of Victoria, 'Practice Note No 2 of 2014: Expert Evidence in Criminal Trials' (25 June 2014), available at: <http://www.supremecourt.vic.gov.au/home/law+and+practice/rules+and+practice+notes/practice+note+no+2+of+2014+expert+evidence+in+criminal+trials> [accessed 26 Dec 2015]. See generally, Ian Freckelton and Hugh Selby (eds), *Expert Evidence*, 6 vols (Pyrmont, NSW: Law Book Co/Thomson Reuters, 1993).

[21] Starrs described two types of problematic forensic experts: the academites and the careerists: James E Starrs, 'Mountebanks Among Forensic Scientists' in Richard Saferstein (ed), *Forensic Science Handbook*, vol 2 (Englewood Cliffs, NJ: Prentice-Hall, 1988) 6–7.

[22] See Margaret A Hagen, *Whores of the Court: The Fraud of Psychiatric Testimony and the Rape of American Justice* (New York: Regan Books, 1997).

[23] See Peter W Huber, *Galileo's Revenge: Junk Science in the Courtroom* (New York: Basic Books, 1993).

adversely on the quality of justice being delivered in their courts.[24] In the United States it never quite led to the jailing of Trooper Fred Zain but has resulted more latterly in the imposition of a sentence of imprisonment for the forensic pathologist, Dr Ralph Erdmann, and then in 2013 of the forensic scientist, Annie Dookhan, because of their preparedness over years to fake test results so as to assist prosecutions and thereby pervert the course of justice.[25]

There are many instances of suboptimal forensic conduct where errors have been committed, proficiency testing has exposed systemic laboratory flaws, inappropriate assumptions have been made, there has been inadequate adherence to hygiene practices, enabling contamination of exhibits,[26] and cross-checking and supervisory processes have been defective.[27] In Australia, the *Chamberlain* case[28], the Splatt Royal Commission,[29] and the Eastman judicial inquiry[30] constitute instances of findings about experts venturing beyond their expertise, poor quality forensic work, inadequate supervision, and communication of results that was not consonant with the inherent limitations of what was yielded by analyses. Each of such phenomena tends to arise from a problematic institutional culture and has the potential to lead to wrongful convictions. These per se are not the focus of this chapter, nor is the potential for the criminal justice system to create incentives for false convictions[31] or instances of substandard analytical work in forensic laboratories.[32]

There is a troubling history of scandals within forensic science and forensic medicine involving practitioners who have been more than negligent or incompetent[33] and who have been prepared to manipulate or falsify their reports and their oral evidence.[34] There has been a

[24] See Ian Freckelton, Prasuna Reddy, and Hugh Selby, *Australian Judicial Perspectives on Expert Evidence: An Empirical Study* (Melbourne: Australian Institute of Judicial Administration, 1999); Ian Freckelton, Prasuna Reddy, and Hugh Selby, *Australian Magistrates' Perspectives on Expert Evidence: A Comparative Study* (Carlton: Australian Institute of Judicial Administration, 2001); Freckelton, Goodman-Delahunty, Horan, and McKimmie, n 16.

[25] See below p 212, 213.

[26] See eg the Hon Frank Vincent, *Report on the Circumstances that Led to the Conviction of Mr Farah Abdulkadir Jama* (Melbourne: Victorian Government Printer, 2010): <http://assets.justice.vic.gov.au/justice/resources/4cd228fd-f61d-4449-b655-ad98323c4ccc/vincentreportfinal6may2010.pdf> [accessed 26 Dec 2015].

[27] See Randolph N Jonakait, 'Forensic Science: The Need for Regulation' (1991) 4(1) *Harvard Journal of Law & Technology* 109.

[28] See *Chamberlain v The Queen (No 2)* [1984] HCA 7; (1984) 153 CLR 521; Trevor R Morling, *Report of the Royal Commission of Inquiry into the Chamberlain Convictions* (Canberra: Government Printer, 1987), available at: <http://www.nt.gov.au/justice/courtsupp/coroner/findings/other/appendix_a_chamberlain_findings.pdf> [accessed 26 Dec 2015]; John Bryson, *Evil Angels* (Ringwood, Vic: Penguin, 1986); Ian Freckelton, 'Of Blood, Babies and Bathwater' (1992) 17(1) *Alternative Law Journal* 10; Adrian Howe, 'Imagining Evidence, Fictioning Truth—Revisiting (Courtesy of O J Simpson) Expert Evidence in the Chamberlain Case' (1997) 3 *Law Text Culture* 82.

[29] See Carl R Shannon, *Royal Commission Report Concerning the Conviction of Edward Charles Splatt* (Adelaide: Government Printer, 1984); Tom Mann, *Flawed Forensics: The Splatt Case and Stewart Cockburn* (DoctorZed Publishing, 2010).

[30] See *Eastman v Director of Public Prosecutions (No 2)* [2014] ACTSCFC 2.

[31] See Roger Koppl and Meghan Sacks, 'The Criminal Justice System Creates Incentives for False Convictions' (2013) 32(2) *Criminal Justice Ethics* 126.

[32] See John F Kelly and Phillip K Wearne, *Tainting Evidence: Inside the Scandals at the FBI Crime Lab* (New York: Free Press, 1998).

[33] In other words, not merely making errors. As Auld LJ observed in *Meadow v General Medical Council* [2006] EWCA Civ 1390; [2007] 1 QB 462, [213]: 'If Homer could occasionally nod, without it costing him his reputation and place in history, so also should similar allowance be made' for those, including the eminent who give evidence in the courts.

[34] See Brent E Turvey, *Forensic Fraud: Evaluating Law Enforcement and Forensic Science Cultures in the Context of Examiner Misconduct* (Amsterdam: Elsevier/Academic Press, 2013); C Michael Bowers, *Forensic Testimony: Science, Law and Expert Evidence* (San Diego, CA: Academic Press, 2014).

surprising incidence of proven instances of both corruption of tests and 'dry labbing'—reporting of tests that were never actually conducted—as well as misrepresentation of test results.[35] The result can be miscarriages of criminal and civil justice that bring into question the integrity of not just the professionals involved but of the system of criminal investigation and criminal justice more broadly.[36] At the heart of such scandals is often the lack of scholarly integrity of the practitioners involved.

As indicated above, this chapter does not purport to be a history of miscarriages of justice based on flaws in forensic science or medicine, or a catalogue of forensic misconduct. It identifies but a few examples as illustrative of the problems that have prompted demands for new and more rigorous forms of accountability than have previously existed in respect of unethical forensic conduct.[37] It acknowledges that a part of the difficulty in the forensic environment is that the check and balance of advocates' work in asking the right questions in the right way in the course of examination-in-chief and while cross-examining experts are not always effective.[38] The empirical work of Garrett and Neufeld[39] (studying 137 trial transcripts of persons convicted but later exonerated) has illustrated this by identifying that, in cases where invalid testimony played a role in bringing about false convictions, cross-examination rarely revealed the flaws in the expert evidence and expert witnesses were seldom called for the defence.

Rather, the issue traversed in the succeeding pages is where scientists and medical practitioners have breached fundamental ethical obligations and provided evidence to the courts (orally or by their written reports) which has had the foreseeable risk of bringing about miscarriages of justice. It focuses on those whom Turvey has usefully categorized as falling into three groups:

- **simulators**, the largest group, who manipulate physical evidence or examinations to fake or destroy findings;
- **dissemblers**, who embellish, lie about or otherwise misrepresent their findings; and
- **pseudo-experts**, who fabricate or misrepresent their expert credentials.[40]

---

35 Paul C Giannelli, 'Wrongful Convictions and Forensic Science: The Need to Regulate Crime Labs' (2007) 86(1) *North Carolina Law Review* 163, 189. See also, Paul C Giannelli, 'The Abuse of Scientific Evidence in Criminal Cases: The Need for Independent Crime Laboratories' (1997) 4(2) *Virginia Journal of Social Policy & the Law* 439.

36 See Freckelton, above n 10; Bibi Sangha, Kent Roach and Robert Moles, *Forensic Investigations and Miscarriages of Justice: The Rhetoric Meets the Reality* (Toronto: Irwin Law, 2010); C Ronald Huff and Martin Killias (eds), *Wrongful Convictions and Miscarriages of Justice: Causes and Remedies in North American and European Criminal Justice Systems* (New York: Routledge, 2013); Jim Dwyer, Peter Neufeld and Barry Scheck, *Actual Innocence: Five Days to Execution and Other Dispatches from the Wrongly Convicted* (New York: Doubleday, 2000); Andrew E Taslitz, 'Convicting the Guilty, The ABA Takes a Stand' (2005) 19(4) *Criminal Justice* 18.

37 Cole, for instance, has argued for greater hierarchical organization in forensic science, modelled on medical culture: Simon A Cole, 'Acculturating Forensic Science: What is 'Scientific Culture', and How Can Forensic Science Adopt It?' (2010) 38(2) *Fordham Urban Law Journal* 435.

38 See Ian Freckelton, 'Wizards in the Crucible: Making the Boffins Accountable' in Johannes F Nijboer and Jan M Reijntjes (eds), *Proceedings of the First World Conference on New Trends in Criminal Investigation and Evidence* (Lelystad: Koninklijke Vermande, 1997).

39 Brandon L Garrett and Peter J Neufeld, 'Invalid Forensic Science Testimony and Wrongful Convictions' (2009) 95(1) *Virginia Law Review* 1, identifying non-probative evidence presented as probative, exculpatory evidence discounted, inaccurate statistics in relation to frequency of match presented, statistics presented which lack empirical support, non-numerical statements provided without empirical support, and conclusions made that samples originated from the defendant without proper justification.

40 Brent E Turvey, 'Forensic Fraud: Evaluating Law Enforcement and Forensic Science Cultures in the Context of Examiner Misconduct' (PhD dissertation, Bond University, 2012): <http://epublications.bond.edu.au/cgi/viewcontent.cgi?article=1115&context=theses> [accessed 26 Dec 2015] 167–9; Brent E Turvey, 'Forensic Frauds: A Study of 42 Cases' (2003) 4(1) *Journal of Behavioral Profiling*.

Earlier, Starrs identified as problematic expert witnesses 'academites' who outright lie or exaggerate their credentials, and 'careerists' who bolster their stature as expert witnesses with a façade of lies or exaggeration.[41]

It is a combination of the persons to whom both Turvey and Starrs have referred, as well as the characteristics of environments which allow them to thrive, that are the focus of this chapter.

Low Points in Forensic Science and Forensic Medicine

A series of instances of forensic misconduct is set out below to highlight concerns that have generated an impetus toward reform of the limited regulatory processes that exist in relation to forensic misconduct. Each is illustrative of a fundamental misunderstanding of the role of the forensic expert on the part of the scientist or doctor involved.

Bias and Misperceptions of the Forensic Role: The Preece and Dotson Affairs

As long ago as 1977 the English Home Office suspended one of its most experienced forensic scientists, Dr Alan Clift, the principal officer at the West Midland Forensic Laboratory, and a founding member (and, at the time, Treasurer) of the Forensic Science Society.[42] Another forensic scientist, Margaret Pereira, was appointed to investigate Dr Clift's work. She found Dr Clift had deliberately withheld information about results which he presented in a way that inculpated the accused, John Preece, who was charged with the murder of Helen Wills. The actual situation was that the crime scene sample was consistent with bodily fluids from both the accused and the victim—both were blood group A secretors. She concluded that Dr Clift's evidence was tilted to assist the prosecution of the accused man and constituted an abandonment of the obligation to be evenhanded and non-partisan. Dr Clift is reported as having denied bias on his part[43] and as having rationalized his conduct, saying: 'Police officers are our customers and it is the view of some senior police officers that our job is to find evidence which may contribute to police inquiries. The [Criminal Justice Act] statement merely demands that what is said is true.'[44] However, when asked by Lord Emslie, the Lord Justice-General, about whether he conceded that he should have provided his evidence in a neutral and fair way, he responded: 'Looking at it now, obviously I should have.'[45] The High Court of Justiciary[46] agreed, holding that the conviction of Mr Preece should be quashed.[47]

---

41 Starrs, above n 21.

42 See William J Tilstone, Kathleen A Savage, and Leigh A Clark, *Forensic Science: An Encyclopedia of History, Methods and Techniques* (Santa Barbara, Calif: ABC-CLIO, 2006); see also, Niamh Nic Daéid, *Fifty Years of Forensic Science: A Commentary* (Chichester, UK: Wiley-Blackwell, 2010).

43 'Forensic Scientist Denies Trial Bias', *Glasgow Herald*, 12 June 1981, 5, available at: <http://news.google.com/newspapers?nid=2507&dat=19810612&id=g_g9AAAAIBAJ&sjid=PUkMAAAAIBAJ&pg=5116,2344223> [accessed 26 Dec 2015].

44 Mick Hamer, 'How a Forensic Scientist Fell Foul of the Law' (1981) 91(1269) *New Scientist* 575, 576; see also, John H Phillips and James K Bowen, *Forensic Science and the Expert Witness* (rev edn, Sydney: Law Book Co, 1989) 3–8.

45 'Forensic Scientist Denies Trial Bias', above n 43.

46 *Preece v HM Advocate* [1981] Crim LR 783.

47 See Edward Connors, Thomas Lundregan, Neal Miller, and Tom McEwen, *Convicted by Juries, Exonerated by Science: Case Studies in the Use of DNA Evidence to Establish Innocence After Trial* (Washington, DC: US Department of Justice, Office of Justice Programs, National Institute of Justice, Report No NCJ 161258, June 1996); see also, Paul C Giannelli and Edward J Imwinkelried Jr, vol 1, *Scientific Evidence* (4th edn, Newark, NJ: LexisNexis, 2007) 186–7.

In a remarkably similar case, Gary Dotson was convicted of aggravated kidnapping and rape, in part on the basis of the evidence of a forensic analyst who testified that he had examined semen on the victim's undergarments and found evidence of blood groups A and B. He omitted to point out that both Dotson and the victim were B group secretors and that the cross-section of the male population who could have contributed the semen found on the vaginal swabs exceeded 60 per cent. When queried by a *Washington Post* reporter about why he had not volunteered this vital information, he replied: 'I guess I wasn't asked.'[48]

Both the Preece and Dotson cases are representative of an attitude among some experts who provide expert opinions to the courts that prioritizes provision of assistance to the prosecution over rendering of even-handed assistance to triers of fact. At its heart lies undisclosed bias and impoverished scholarly methodology. Such a deficiency in required approach can contaminate the work of those who are occasionally called upon from within academia to write reports and testify as experts, as well as those whose role in that regard is full-time.

Formulating a Theory Too Readily

In 1961 the first child of Tim and Waneta Hoyt, Eric, who was less than three months of age, passed away suddenly and without apparent cause. The next year their second child, James, died at a similar age without medical explanation. In 1968 a third child of the couple, Maria, died in similarly mysterious circumstances.

At this point the parents sought assistance from Dr Alfred Steinschneider, a medical researcher who specialized in issues arising from Sudden Infant Death Syndrome (SIDS), a term coined around the same time by Professor Beckwith at the Seattle Children's Hospital. Dr Steinschneider studied the case history and concluded that SIDS may be genetic, a fact that had the potential to explain the deaths of three children within the Hoyt family—Eric, James, and Maria. While under his care Waneta gave birth to two more children, Molly and Noah. Both died in similarly unexplained circumstances. In 1972 Dr Steinschneider published what became a landmark scholarly analysis in *Pediatrics* in which he argued, on the basis in part of what had occurred within the Hoyt family, that SIDS could be hereditary and that it was related to sleep apnoea.[49] Sales in sleep monitors to parents of young children boomed for 20 years.

Nurses caring for Waneta around the time when Molly was born had been deeply concerned about how disinterested Waneta (who was under close observation in hospital) seemed to be in her baby and began talking about their fears for Molly's safety. However, in spite of overtures to him by the nurses and outright opposition to Molly being allowed to go home with her mother, Dr Steinschneider authorized it and discounted their concerns, maintaining that a sleep monitor would be sufficient for her protection. The next morning Waneta called her mother-in-law and reported that Molly had turned blue. Molly was found in her crib, lifeless and with the apnoea monitor disconnected. Waneta opposed the coroner's wish for Molly's body to be the subject of autopsy. An autopsy was conducted, however, without any conclusive result. The same process occurred the next year in relation to Noah. All five children died at a similar time of day while their mother was looking after them.[50]

However, nearly two decades later in 1986 two issues came together. First, a sceptical district attorney and a forensic pathologist questioned the legitimacy of Dr Steinschneider's

---

48 Giannelli (2007), above n 35, 186–7 n 162.

49 Alfred Steinschneider, 'Prolonged Apnea and the Sudden Infant Death Syndrome: Clinical and Laboratory Observations' (1972) 50(4) *Pediatrics* 646.

50 See Richard Firstman and Jamie Talan, *The Death of Innocents* (New York: Bantam Books, 1997).

paper in relation to the children and then police interviewed Waneta Hoyt. She confessed to the five murders.[51] Then she retracted her confession. The well-known forensic pathologist, Dr Michael Baden, after exhumations of the bodies, reviewed the cases and concluded that the children had been murdered.

At Waneta Hoyt's trial Dr Steinschneider testified for the defence. He refused to back down from his previous views. However, under cross-examination, he conceded begrudgingly that it was possible that Molly and Noah had been suffocated. Although he had referred in the *Pediatrics* article to Molly and Noah having required vigorous stimulation or shaking to be revived, he said that that had not been necessary. When reminded of what he had written, his obdurate response was: 'I wrote it so it must be true.'[52] When it was pointed out that there were no hospital notes to corroborate what he had written in his article, Dr Steinschneider confabulated, saying that he had a recollection about talking to the nurses about the episodes and that he impressed on them the need to record all important data about Molly and Noah.[53] The nurses denied this was so. In due course a jury in 1995 rejected Dr Steinschneider's increasingly partisan evidence on behalf of Waneta Hoyt. She was convicted and sentenced to 75 years' imprisonment.

The scholarly theories generated by Dr Steinschneider in the shadow of suspicions about the conduct of the mother of the five children whom, as it turned out, she murdered were more than erroneous. They were the product of uncritical and biased theorizing which exculpated his patient. Not only did they enable the mother to commit the final two murders but they took research on a misguided tangent (for instance, away from addressing babies' positional issues) for the better part of two decades, with disastrous consequences.[54] While Dr Steinschneider received a $4.5 million grant from the National Institutes of Health to continue his research on what he believed was the hereditary nature of SIDS, within a short time research by Dr David Southall in England on 9,000 children provided data that were wholly inconsistent with Dr Steinschneider's theories which were subsequently discredited. The editor-in-chief of *Pediatrics*, Dr Jerold Lucey, later conceded that aspects of Dr Steinschneider's article were not understood at review and that he regretted having published it.[55] The saga involving Dr Steinschneider was partly about the ego of a researcher who had too readily jumped to a conclusion that had an inadequate scientific foundation and that generated a new line of highly funded research, but it also constituted a form of forensic misconduct in its impoverished methodology generated in the shadow of forensic exigencies and then persisted in at trial.

Withholding Evidence: The IRA Cases and the North Carolina Crime Laboratory

A series of United Kingdom cases compounded the concern about attitudes existing among some within the British forensic science community and required reversals of convictions

[51] See Michael M Baden with Judith Alder Hennessee, *Unnatural Death: Confessions of a Medical Examiner* (London: Time Warner, 2002); Michael M Baden and Marion Roach, *Dead Reckoning: The New Science of Catching Killers* (New York: Simon & Schuster, 2001).

[52] Jacques Steinberg, 'Defense Begins for Mother in Sudden Deaths of 5 Children', *The New York Times*, 11 April 1995: <http://www.nytimes.com/1995/04/11/nyregion/defense-begins-for-mother-in-sudden-deaths-of-5-children.html> [accessed 26 Dec 2015].

[53] Ibid.

[54] See Merrill Singer and Hans Baer, *Killer Commodities: Public Health and the Corporate Production of Harm* (Lanham, Md: Altamira Press, 2008) 128.

[55] 'Cot Death Error "Costs Lives"', *BBC News*, 25 February 1999: <http://news.bbc.co.uk/2/hi/health/285765.stm> [accessed 26 Dec 2015].

when key problems in cases against the Irish Republican Army (IRA) were found to have included the withholding of important evidence and a failure to provide a neutral, fair, and objective perspective on evidence gathered by forensic scientists. The responsibility for these miscarriages was that of both scientists and lawyers.

The England and Wales Court of Appeal[56] observed in 1993: 'Forensic scientists may become partisan. The very fact that the police seek their assistance may create a relationship between the police and the forensic scientists... Forensic scientists employed by the government may come to see their function as helping the police. They may lose their objectivity.'[57] The sagas of the Guildford Four,[58] the Birmingham Six,[59] and the Maguire Seven[60] attested to a sequence of erroneous, unjustified, and at times unethical practices, including expressions of opinion by scientists in politically contentious cases, involving the fight against terrorism, which were marked by a preparedness to compromise ethical values.

Dry Labbing/Fabrication of Evidence

In a number of notorious cases, forensic experts have been exposed as having made up their testing or analysis in order to assist the prosecution. This phenomenon is sometimes described as 'dry labbing'.[61]

David Harding. In 1991 New York Trooper David Harding admitted in a polygraph interview when applying for a job with the Central Intelligence Agency (CIA) to planting fingerprint evidence on multiple occasions.[62] Until then he had been regarded as 'the coolest, smoothest, most charming witness' in relation to fingerprint matters.[63]

Ultimately, Harding pleaded guilty to evidence-tampering and perjury in relation to cases dating back to 1984. His conduct also led to civil actions against the State of New York.[64] He was sentenced to four to twelve years' imprisonment and fined US$20,000. His conduct was characterized by little that could be described as scholarship, but was representative of a small category of experts working in the forensic area who have been prepared to behave in grossly biased and misleading ways in their provision of evidence to the courts.

Fred Zain. One of the most notorious instances of fraud by a forensic scientist involved West Virginia State Trooper Fred Zain who tested physical evidence and testified in hundreds of murder and rape trials during the 1970s and 1980s, principally in West Virginia and Texas.[65] He ran the section of the Criminal Identification Bureau in South Charleston

---

56 *R v Ward* (1993) 96 Cr App R 1.

57 Ibid, 51. See also, Douglas M Lucas, 'The Ethical Responsibilities of the Forensic Scientist: Exploring the Limits' (1989) 34(3) *Journal of Forensic Sciences* 719.

58 *R v Richardson; R v Conlon; R v Armstrong; R v Hill, The Times*, 20 October 1989 (CA).

59 *R v McIlkenney* (1991) 93 Cr App R 287.

60 John May, *Return to an Address of the Honourable the House of Commons Dated 12 July 1990 for the Inquiry into the Circumstances Surrounding the Convictions Arising Out of the Bomb Attacks in Guildford and Woolwich in 1974:* Interim Report on the Maguire Case (London: HMSO, 1990), including 11.9, 14.4–14.8: <https://www.gov.uk/government/uploads/system/uploads/attachment_data/file/228724/0556.pdf> [accessed 26 Dec 2015]; *R v Maguire* [1992] 1 QB 936.

61 See eg, Giannelli (2007), above n 35, 189.

62 See Jim Fisher, *Forensics Under Fire: Are Bad Science and Dueling Experts Corrupting Criminal Justice?* (New Brunwick, NJ: Rutgers University Press, 2008) 112–13.

63 The view of William P Sullivan Jr, a New York lawyer: see Jon Nordheimer, 'Trooper's Fall Shakes Both Police and Public', *The New York Times*, 15 November 1992: <http://www.nytimes.com/1992/11/15/nyregion/trooper-s-fall-shakes-both-police-and-public.html> [accessed 26 Dec 2015].

64 See eg, *Kinge v New York* (NY 79 AD 3d, No 09426, 23 December 2010) slip op 1473.

65 See Tilstone, Savage, and Clark, above n 42, 33ff; Kathleen Keough Griebel, 'Fred Zain, the CSI Effect, and a Philosophical Idea of Justice: Using West Virginia as a Model for Change' (2012) 114(3) *West Virginia Law Review* 1155; Dwyer, Neufeld, and Scheck, above n 36, ch 5.

in West Virginia that dealt with the identification of evidence submitted for blood, body fluid, and hair examinations. He held a Bachelor of Science degree from West Virginia State College, an associate degree in police science from Marshall University and a Master's degree in biological science from Marshall University. In short he was more than adequately credentialled for his role, and in a position to give to his fraudulent evidence a scholarly veneer.

However, in 1985 two of his fellow workers informed superiors of their concerns that arose from having witnessed Trooper Zain fabricating data from blank test plates: the process of 'dry labbing'.[66] The Director of the Bureau reviewed the allegations and dismissed the concerns as a dispute among co-workers, noting that the Bureau had never received any complaints from prosecutors, defence attorneys, or investigators about Zain.

However, the issues re-emerged as a result of Zain's evidence in relation to Glen Woodall who was convicted in 1987 of a large number of felonies, including two counts of sexual assault. Zain's evidence was that his tests proved that only six in 10,000 people could have attacked the victim, and that Glen Woodall was a member of that small cohort. He added that it was 'highly unlikely' that the single reddish brown hair recovered from the victim's car, the crime scene, could have come from anyone other than Woodall.[67] The jury found Woodall guilty and he was sentenced to a prison term of 203 to 335 years. However, DNA testing in subsequent habeas corpus proceedings established that Woodall could not have been the perpetrator and his conviction was overturned. He received US$1 million in compensation. In some respects, most disturbingly, a subsequent investigation of the case showed that the laboratory tests on seminal fluid that Zain had testified that he had performed were not tests that the laboratory was capable of performing at the time; they never took place. In addition, he should have indicated that the assailant's blood was shared by approximately 3 per cent of the population, rather than the figure which he had asserted.[68] It also became apparent that the hair Zain testified was from Woodall's beard had been recorded earlier by him as being a pubic hair. In short, his evidence was completely unreliable and in good part fabricated.

As a result of this information coming to light, the State police performed an internal audit of the laboratory but found no more than 'certain improprieties'.[69] The real situation emerged only later and resulted in Trooper Zain being dismissed from office. The West Virginia Supreme Court of Appeals appointed Senior Judge Holliday to preside over a special investigation into Zain's forensic work. In an extraordinary opinion, the Court of Appeals adopted the findings of its special investigation, which stated that:

> The acts of misconduct on the part of Zain included (1) overstating the strength of the results; (2) overstating the frequency of genetic matches on individual pieces of evidence; (3) misreporting the frequency of genetic matches on multiple pieces of evidence; (4) reporting that multiple items had been tested, when only a single item had been tested; (5) reporting inconclusive results as conclusive; (6) repeatedly altering laboratory results.[70]

---

66 See J C Upshaw Downs and Anjali Ranadive Sienton (eds), *Ethics in Forensic Science* (Oxford: Academic Press, 2012) 63.

67 Paul C Giannelli, 'Microscopic Hair Comparisons: A Cautionary Tale' (Working Paper 2010-17, Case Research Paper Series in Legal Studies, School of Law, Case Western Reserve University, April 2010) 16, available at: <http://ssrn.com/abstract=1588151> [accessed 26 Dec 2015]. For an egregious example of unfair ways of giving statistical evidence: see the prosecutor's fallacy—*Doheny & Adams v The Queen* [1997] 1 Cr App R 369; *Latcha v The Queen* (1998) 104 A Crim R 390.

68 Dwyer, Neufeld, and Scheck, above n 36, 107ff, 173.

69 *In the Matter of an Investigation of the West Virginia State Police Crime Laboratory, Serology Division* (1993), 438 SE 2d 501 (W Va Sup Ct App): <http://www.courtswv.gov/supreme-court/docs/fall1993/21973.htm> [accessed 26 Dec 2015].

70 Ibid.

In an unparalleled judgment the Court of Appeals concluded that '[a]s a matter of law, any testimonial or documentary evidence offered by Zain at any time in any criminal prosecution should be deemed invalid, unreliable, and inadmissible in determining whether to award a new trial in any subsequent habeas corpus proceeding'.[71] The result was a review of the convictions of 134 prisoners.[72]

George Castelle, the Chief Public Defender in West Virginia, observed that for trial lawyers the lessons flowing from the Zain scandal were straightforward:

> To uncover error, overstatement, bias or outright fraud in any questionable scientific result by a prosecution expert, it is essential to do what trial lawyers in the Fred Zain cases failed to do for 16 years. That is, they must (1) obtain the underlying raw data—the actual test results, bench notes, worksheets, photographs, autorads, computer printouts—whatever underlying records were used to reach the conclusion set forth in the expert's written report or proposed testimony; (2) obtain a review of the underlying records and the expert's conclusions by an outside, independent expert; and (3) obtain independent testing, repeating the same tests that the police expert purported to perform, as well as any further testing that the independent expert recommends.[73]

However, in spite of his exposure, like many scientists and medical practitioners accused on substantial evidence of research fraud, Zain consistently maintained his innocence, all indications to the contrary notwithstanding. He asserted that he had been made a scapegoat by politicians. In 1995 he was charged with perjury but acquitted. In a second trial in 1997 a similar charge against him was dismissed because of a statute of limitations. In 1998 he was charged with aggravated perjury, evidence-tampering, and fabrication related to a 1990 rape conviction but again acquitted. A further trial in 2001[74] involving allegations related to 27 cases from the final three years of his service had to be moved from Charleston because of concern that media notoriety had prejudiced potential jurors. However, it did not proceed because by then Zain was ill with colon cancer. He passed away in 2002, with his professional reputation thoroughly discredited, for good reason, and the reputation of the laboratory by which he had been employed irretrievably compromised, but without his ever having been convicted of any offence. West Virginia paid out more than US$6.5 million in lawsuits brought by wrongfully convicted defendants as a result of Zain's work.

Joyce Gilchrist. The Oklahoma City Police Department crime laboratory chemist, Joyce Gilchrist, testified as a prosecution expert more than 3,000 times in relation to analyses of blood, hair, semen, and fibres between 1980 and 1995 (when she was promoted to a supervisory position and ceased to undertake hands-on work) in 23 death penalty cases, including those of 12 persons who were ultimately executed. She was dismissed in 2001 for poor quality work and for giving false or misleading testimony. Gilchrist was nicknamed 'Black Magic' by detectives for her ability to produce laboratory results, especially in matching hair samples, that no other analyst could achieve.[75] In 1985 she was named the police department's employee of the year.

---

[71] Ibid.

[72] 'Court Invalidates a Decade of Blood Test Results in Criminal Cases', *The New York Times*, 12 November 1993: <http://www.nytimes.com/1993/11/12/us/court-invalidates-a-decade-of-blood-test-results-in-criminal-cases.html> [accessed 26 Dec 2015].

[73] George Castelle, 'Fake Data, Wrongful Convictions: Learning from a Crime Lab Fraud Fiasco' (1997) 19(4) *NLADA Cornerstone* 9, 10.

[74] See Francis X Clines, 'Work by Expert Witness is Now on Trial', *The New York Times*, 5 September 2001: <http://www.nytimes.com/2001/09/05/us/work-by-expert-witness-is-now-on-trial.html> [accessed 26 Dec 2015].

[75] See eg, Turvey, above n 40, 22; Upshaw Downs and Sienton, above n 66, 406.

In one of her cases Gilchrist testified that she found sperm on swabs taken from the victim that were consistent with the defendant's sperm and that the blood, semen, and sperm found on the sheet in which the victim was transported were consistent with those of the defendant, as were semen stains on the victim's panties. However, in due course, the federal district judge who reviewed the defendant's habeas corpus petition found Gilchrist's evidence to be 'without question, untrue'.[76] The defendant's death sentence imposed at trial was vacated.

In another of her cases, the prosecution of Jeffrey Pierce for rape and sodomy (for which Pierce was sentenced to 54 years' imprisonment), Gilchrist testified that she had identified pubic hairs consistent with Pierce's from the pubic hair combings of the victim and on her skirt. She also asserted that the head hairs found on items of the victim positively identified him, summarizing the import of her evidence by saying that in the years during which she had conducted hair analysis 'she had never seen hair from different people that were microscopically similar in all characteristics'.[77] The evidence was completely false. Pierce was released from an Oklahoma prison in 2001 after serving 15 years' imprisonment.[78]

In yet another case, Gilchrist testified in a 1982 trial that semen found on a bedspread and a pillowcase in the victim's bedroom belonged to a Malcolm Johnson. However, a re-evaluation of the evidence after Johnson was executed[79] contradicted her findings and revealed no sperm at all.[80]

Ultimately, Gilchrist was dismissed from her job,[81] reprimanded by one professional forensic association, and expelled by another for unethical conduct. Large numbers of her cases were assigned for further review, including those of three death row inmates. However, she was never prosecuted in relation to her conduct.[82]

In spite of evidence of multiple errors in her work, Gilchrist too maintained that she did nothing wrong and defended her work. She told an interviewer that '[t]here may be a few differences because of DNA analysis', but said she was confident most of her findings would be confirmed. 'I worked hard, long and consistently on every case', she said. 'I always based my opinion on scientific findings'. She insisted she did not overstate those findings to please the District Attorney's office or secure convictions: 'I feel comfortable with the conclusions

---

[76] *Mitchell v Gibson*, 262 F 3d 1036, 1060 (10th Cir, 2001).

[77] *Pierce v State*, 786 P 2d 1255, 1265 (Okla Crim App, 1990).

[78] See Barry Scheck and Peter Neufeld, 'Junk Science, Junk Evidence', *The New York Times*, 11 May 2001: <http://www.nytimes.com/2001/05/11/opinion/junk-science-junk-evidence.html?ref=joycegilchrist> [accessed 26 Dec 2015].

[79] In spite of an appeal that complained, among other things, about the evidence of Gilchrist: *Johnson v Gibson*, 169 F 3d 1239 (10th Cir, 1999). See also, 'Police Chemist Is Rebutted After Man's Execution', *The New York Times*, 30 August 2001: <http://www.nytimes.com/2001/08/30/us/police-chemist-is-rebutted-after-man-s-execution.html?ref=joycegilchrist> [accessed 26 Dec 2015].

[80] Jim Yardley, 'Oklahoma Retraces Big Step in Capital Case', *The New York Times*, 2 September 2001: <http://www.nytimes.com/2001/09/02/us/oklahoma-retraces-big-step-in-capital-case.html> [accessed 26 Dec 2015]; Bennett L Gershman, 'Misuse of Scientific Evidence By Prosecutors' (2003) 28(1) *Oklahoma City University Law Review* 17.

[81] 'Police Chemist Accused of Shoddy Work is Fired', *The New York Times*, 26 September 2001: <http://www.nytimes.com/2001/09/26/us/police-chemist-accused-of-shoddy-work-is-fired.html?ref=joycegilchrist> [accessed 26 Dec 2015].

[82] See Jim Yardley, 'Inquiry Focuses on Scientist Used by Prosecutors', *The New York Times*, 2 May 2001: <http://www.nytimes.com/2001/05/02/national/02LAB.html> [accessed 26 Dec 2015]; Jim Yardley, 'Flaws in Chemist's Findings Free Man at Center of Inquiry', *The New York Times*, 8 May 2001: <http://www.nytimes.com/2001/05/08/national/08LAB.html> [accessed 26 Dec 2015]; Morris S Zedeck, *Expert Witness in the Legal System: A Scientist's Search for Justice* (Pittsburgh: Lauriat Press, 2010) 71–2.

I drew'.[83] In fact, her response was even more obdurate—in 2002 she sued the city and police officials for defamation, claiming damages of US$20.1 million, alleging she had been fired for reporting sexual misconduct.[84] She was unsuccessful.

Gilchrist's supervisor, Dave McBride, has noted that no one ever complained about Gilchrist's work but observed that too often forensic scientists come to consider themselves police in laboratory coats: 'I think Joyce Gilchrist may have fallen into an internal feeling that she was on the police team, she was on the prosecution team. And what scientists should always feel like is they are on the side of science'.[85]

Ralph Erdmann. Ralph Erdmann was a forensic pathologist who undertook autopsies, principally in Texas. During the 1980s and early 1990s he obtained his doctorate from the National University of Mexico in Mexico City. He worked as a contract medical examiner in more than 40 rural counties in Texas. Lubbock County in Texas alone paid him more than US$140,000 per year and he collected in the vicinity of $600 per autopsy from other counties. He called himself the 'Quincy of the Panhandle' and was known for undertaking a prodigious number of postmortem examinations per year, becoming notorious for his capacity to undertake the 'drive-by autopsy' which often did not involve any form of surgical intervention.[86] Again, therefore, what is apparent about his work is an extraordinarily high output and a preparedness to cater to the wishes of those investigators commissioning his work.

The trigger for Dr Erdmann's exposure as a fraud was an off-hand remark by a police officer to Dr Erdmann speculating that drugs may have been involved in the death of a deceased man by the name of Craig Newman. Dr Erdmann purported to conduct an autopsy and stated that Mr Newman had died of a cocaine overdose. The family of the deceased man was incensed as they claimed that Mr Newman had never used drugs. The situation became more problematic because the autopsy listed the spleen of Mr Newman as an organ that had been examined and weighed, although, in fact, his spleen had been removed years earlier. When Mr Newman's body was exhumed, no autopsy signs were evident at all and an autopsy which was then performed showed that he had died of a heart attack.

After an investigation into his conduct, in 1992, Erdmann (by then aged 65) was charged; he entered a plea of guilty to seven felony counts, including perjury and falsification of autopsy reports.[87] The conditions associated with his plea, included surrendering his medical licence, a ten-year probation period, 200 hours of community service, and an order to repay $17,000 in 'unearned autopsy fees'.[88] Having subsequently relocated to Seattle, Washington, he was charged with violating the terms of his probation after police found him with a 'cache of weapons', and was extradited to serve a prison sentence.[89] Although eligible for parole after 30 months, his application for release in March 2007 was thwarted by public protests.[90]

---

[83] Belinda Luscombe, 'When the Evidence Lies', *Time*, 13 May 2001: <http://content.time.com/time/magazine/article/0,9171,109625,00.html> [accessed 27 Dec 2015].

[84] 'Police Chemist's Suit Says Firing was Retaliatory', *The New York Times*, 26 April 2002: <http://www.nytimes.com/2002/04/26/us/police-chemist-s-suit-says-firing-was-retaliatory.html?ref=joycegilchrist> [accessed 27 Dec 2015].

[85] David Kohn, 'Under the Microscope: Forensic Scientist Accused of Mishandling Cases', *CBS News: 60 Minutes*, 8 May 2001: <http://www.cbsnews.com/news/under-the-microscope-08-05-2001/> [accessed 27 Dec 2015].

[86] Dwyer, Neufeld, and Scheck, above n 36, 117.

[87] Roberto Suro, 'Ripples of a Pathologist's Misconduct in Graves and Courts of West Texas', *The New York Times*, 22 November 1992: <http://www.nytimes.com/1992/11/22/us/ripples-of-a-pathologist-s-misconduct-in-graves-and-courts-of-west-texas.html> [accessed 27 Dec 2015]; Michael Newton, *The Encyclopedia of American Law Enforcement* (New York: Facts on File, 2007) 115.

[88] Newton, above n 87, 115.

[89] Newton, above n 87, 115.

[90] Newton, above n 87, 115.

A special prosecutor appointed to investigate Dr Erdmann's work, Tommy Taylor, stated that a quick and narrow examination of his work provided evidence of 100 faked autopsies.[91]

Annie Dookhan. In 2013 one of the most extreme instances of forensic fraud thus far began to unfold with scientist Annie Dookhan being charged with multiple counts of obstructing justice as a result of falsified forensic science test results. In due course Massachusetts officials identified more than 40,000 cases from between 2003 and 2012 that fell under a cloud of suspicion by virtue of Dookhan's conduct.[92] As of November 2013 the State of Massachusetts was reported to have spent US$8.5 million reviewing the drug cases in which Dookhan was involved and in holding special hearings for defendants. Massachusetts budgeted a further US$8.6 million for such work, with 950 people having been given Superior Court hearings in eight different counties arising from concerns about her work. To that point, 2,922 hearings had been convened to deal with defendants asking that their cases be dismissed or that they be released from jail. More than 600 defendants had convictions against them overturned or temporarily set aside pending further investigations.[93]

The scandal forced the shutdown of the laboratory where Dookhan worked and the effects of Dookhan's conduct reverberated throughout Massachusetts and federally by reason of the number of defendants who were enabled by her actions to argue their convictions were secured on the basis of unreliable evidence.[94] What distinguished the Dookhan scandal from others, such as the New York scenario where in 2013 a technician in the city medical examiner's office was found to have mishandled evidence in a large number of rape cases,[95] was that it generated numbers (at this stage unknown) of false positive cases, rather than false negative—people have been wrongfully convicted and served jail time because of the deliberate deceit by the scientist.

Personality characteristics including a desire for respect, even adulation from others, and a self-destructive belief that her short-cuts would not be detected, all contributed to Dookhan's conduct. And it appears to have gathered momentum and become a pattern of behaviour from which she was unable or unprepared to extricate herself. However, there were many aspects to what was a premeditated course of dishonest dealings on the part of Dookhan. One of the anomalous elements to it was that, while she claimed to hold a Master of Chemistry degree from the University of Massachusetts in Boston, this too was not correct.

In a pre-sentence hearing Judge Ball said she was minded to impose a tougher sentence on Dookhan than the minimum three years' imprisonment, 'given the magnitude of the harm she has done, considerations of general deterrence and, particularly, punishment'.[96] She observed that:

> [T]he consequences of her behavior, which she ought to have foreseen, have been nothing short of catastrophic: Innocent persons were incarcerated, guilty persons have been released

[91] Suro, above n 87.

[92] Denise Lavoie, 'Annie Dookhan, Chemist Accused of Faking Test Results, Could Have Affected 40,000 Defendants: State', *Huffington Post*, 2 September 2013: <http://www.huffingtonpost.com/2013/09/02/annie-dookhan_n_3855803.html> [accessed 27 Dec 2015].

[93] Milton J Valencia and John R Ellement, 'Annie Dookhan Pleads Guilty in Drug Lab Scandal', *The Boston Globe*, 22 November 2013: <http://www.bostonglobe.com/metro/2013/11/22/annie-dookhan-former-state-chemist-who-mishandled-drug-evidence-agrees-plead-guilty/7UU3hfZUof4DFJGoNUfXGO/story.html> [accessed 27 Dec 2015].

[94] See eg, Lavoie, above n 92.

[95] Joseph Goldstein, 'New York Examines Over 800 Rape Cases for Possible Mishandling of Evidence', *The New York Times*, 10 January 2013: <http://www.nytimes.com/2013/01/11/nyregion/new-york-reviewing-over-800-rape-cases-for-possible-mishandling-of-dna-evidence.html?_r=2&> [accessed 27 Dec 2015].

[96] Martin Finucane, 'Annie Dookhan Sets Date for Change of Plea', *The Boston Globe*, 28 October 2013: <http://www.bostonglobe.com/metro/2013/10/28/annie-dookhan-former-state-chemist-accused-mishandling-evidence-sets-date-for-change-plea/WI7PBCgduvKod5AQteOSKO/story.html> [accessed 27 Dec 2015].

> to further endanger the public, millions and millions of public dollars are being expended to deal with the chaos Ms. Dookhan created, and the integrity of the criminal justice system has been shaken to the core.[97]

In November 2013 Dookhan pleaded guilty to 27 counts of misleading investigators, filing false scientific reports, and tampering with evidence. She was sentenced to three to five years in State prison. The fact that Dookhan pleaded guilty has obscured her motives. At the time of sentencing she was a 36-year-old mother of a disabled child. Her marriage disintegrated as the scandal emerged. In an interview done with police after being apprehended, Dookhan admitted faking test results for two to three years, including turning a number of negative samples into positives for narcotics. She is said to have experienced personal problems, including a miscarriage during 2009.[98]

However, Judge Ball in his sentencing decision found that Dookhan's criminal behaviour was driven by 'nothing more than her desire to be a productive employee'.[99] Her attitudes towards her work, though, left much to be desired. She revealed an unhealthy ideological commitment when she wrote to a prosecutor in 2009 that she wanted drug offenders 'off the streets'.[100] Thus, it seems that her excessive affiliation with the prosecution may have led to a zealotry in which she was able to rationalize her 'short-cuts'[101] as having a morally defensible basis. As so often in such matters, Dookhan's conduct has exposed systemic failings in her laboratory. There were reports that the employment of other analysts had been terminated, one for making a false claim about her academic credentials.[102]

Conduct of the kind in which Dookhan engaged over an extended period is accompanied by a failure in accountability, quality control checks, and balances and supervision,[103] all of which are systemic deficits for which there is no excuse but for which responsibility is often not taken by employers until there is no other option. There has been extensive scrutiny in relation to Dookhan of the cultural circumstances that enabled her conduct over so long a period without its being identified and stopped. Her output of testing was recognized by a supervisor as early as 2008 as extraordinarily high: an average scientist would process 50 to 150 alleged drug samples a month. She tested up to 500 such samples. Her supervisor is reported as having spoken to a superior in relation to concerns about Dookhan's work but there was no intervention. He repeated his concerns the next year, claiming he never saw Dookhan in front of a microscope. In 2010 a supervisor did an audit of Dookhan's work but it was 'on the papers' and nothing abnormal was detected. It did not involve retesting any

[97] Travis Anderson, 'Annie Dookhan May Get 5 Years in Prison With Guilty Plea', *The Boston Globe*, 24 October 2013: <http://www.bostonglobe.com/metro/2013/10/23/annie-dookhan-could-serve-five-years-she-pleads-guilty-drug-lab-scandal/0UVysgOLspFnTR5BDy99QO/story.html> [accessed 27 Dec 2015].

[98] Valencia and Ellement, above n 93; 'Annie Dookhan, Chemist at Mass. Crime Lab, Arrested for Allegedly Mishandling Over 60,000 Samples', *CBS News*: <http://www.cbsnews.com/news/annie-dookhan-chemist-at-mass-crime-lab-arrested-for-allegedly-mishandling-over-60000-samples/> [accessed 27 Dec 2015].

[99] Jennifer Levitz, 'Massachusetts Crime Lab Ex-Chemist Annie Dookhan Gets 3–5 Years', *The Wall Street Journal*, 22 November 2013: <http://www.wsj.com/articles/SB10001424052702304607104579214280981721234> [accessed 27 Dec 2015].

[100] Ibid.

[101] Susan Candiotti, Yon Pomrenze, and Jason Hanna, 'Ex-Massachusetts Chemist Gets 3 to 5 Years in Tampering Case', *CNN*, 22 November 2013: <http://edition.cnn.com/2013/11/22/justice/massachusetts-chemist-plea/> [accessed 27 Dec 2015].

[102] Valencia and Ellement, above n 93.

[103] See eg, Kay Lazar and John R Ellement, 'E-mails Portray State Drug Lab in Chaos', *The Boston Globe*, 14 September 2012: <http://www.bostonglobe.com/metro/2012/09/14/chemist-closed-state-lab-allegedly-tampered-with-evidence-bags-defense-attorneys-group-says/S26z5hS5qsqP20RmX4qA0O/story.html> [accessed 27 Dec 2015].

samples. Also in 2010 a fellow chemist found seven instances where Dookhan incorrectly identified a drug sample but no further action was taken.[104]

The Massachusetts Inspector-General concluded that financial stringencies limited the laboratory's ability to keep pace with the work it was required to do, the requirements for testing, and aspects of the supervisory oversight over the laboratory. It was underfunded, understaffed, inadequately accredited and unable to perform its role adequately:

> [M]anagement failures of DPH lab directors contributed to Dookhan's ability to commit her acts of malfeasance. The directors were ill-suited to oversee a forensic drug lab, provided almost no supervision, were habitually unresponsive to chemists' complaints and suspicions, and severely downplayed Dookhan's major breach in chain-of-custody protocol upon discovering it.[105]

Noting serious deficiencies in the laboratory's quality control procedures and an absence of independent auditing, he recommended that all state agencies should employ management practices that hold supervisors accountable for their employees, including conducting complete performance evaluations annually: 'In forensic drug labs, there must be a system to report deviations from policy, and all managers of forensic labs should be experts in their respective fields.'[106] It appears that what was responsible for the miscarriages of justice caused by Dookhan's conduct was an unfortunate combination of a troubled employee desperate for the kudos of being recognized for high levels of performance, a person prepared to be chronically dishonest to assist the prosecution, and a laboratory whose supervisory practices were unable to identify and respond to warning signs.

Sonja Farak. A sequel to the Annie Dookhan saga arose in relation to a co-worker, Sonja Farak. She also was employed as a chemist in the forensic laboratory in the State crime laboratory in Amherst, Massachusetts. In 2013 Farak was discovered to have tested two samples, believed to have been heroin and cocaine, and to have replaced them with counterfeit substances. After Farak's conduct was discovered, the charges against the accused had to be withdrawn because of the inability to have Farak give credible expert evidence.

The next development was that Farak herself was arrested and charged—with tampering with evidence in a series of cases, as well as with possession of illegal drugs.[107] At first she pleaded not guilty to the charges. However, in January 2014 Farak pleaded guilty to theft of drugs from the laboratory, tampering with evidence, and drug possession. Prosecutors informed the Hampshire Superior Court that her conduct led to dismissals in more than 200 drug cases.[108] The sentencing judge, Mary-Lou Rup, told her that her conduct 'clearly has eroded everybody's confidence' in the laboratories.[109] She sentenced Farak to two and a half years' imprisonment with 18 months to serve and the remainder suspended during a five-year

[104] Bridget Murphy, 'Annie Dookhan, Chemist Accused of Tampering with Drug Samples, Told Police "It's My Fault"', *Huffington Post*, 27 September 2012: <http://www.huffingtonpost.com/2012/09/27/annie-dookhan-drug-tampering_n_1919185.html> [accessed 27 Dec 2015].

[105] Glenn A Cunha, *Investigation of the Drug Laboratory at the William A Hinton State Laboratory Institute,* 2002–2012 (Boston, Mass: Office of the Inspector-General, 4 March 2014) 1, available at: <http://www.mass.gov/ig/publications/reports-and-recommendations/2014/> [accessed 27 Dec 2015].

[106] Ibid, 2.

[107] Travis Andersen, '2d State Chemist Charged with Drug Tampering', *The Boston Globe*, 20 January 2013: <http://www.bostonglobe.com/metro/2013/01/20/chemist-crime-lab-amherst-charged-with-tampering-with-drug-evidence/4qCYbfQcDQz4sH7JTu7c7N/story.html> [accessed 27 Dec 2015].

[108] 'Sonja Farak, Ex-Mass. Lab Chemist, Pleads Guilty to Drug Theft', *Huffington Post*, 6 January 2014: <http://www.huffingtonpost.com/2014/01/06/sonja-farak-exmass-lab-ch_0_n_4551612.html> [accessed 27 Dec 2015].

[109] Ibid.

parole period. Judge Rup imposed probation conditions that Farak undergo drug and alcohol evaluation and treatment, and complete 500 hours of community service.

It is clear that Farak's conduct was significantly related to substance dependency. However, in recognition of the temptation to deal improperly with substances assigned for testing, the Farak case has prompted calls for random drug testing of all forensic laboratory chemists.[110] In addition, the Farak sentence, as well as those which preceded it, raise the issue of whether penalties of imprisonment constitute an effective deterrent to those minded to subvert the integrity of the justice system in a similar way. It will be important to review whether the incidence of such conduct is affected by the high- profile sentences of incarceration and the shaming that have accompanied cases such as Dookhan and Farak.

The various cases referred to above have in common the preparedness of scientists and medical practitioners to devote high levels of industry in their employment, to be unethically prosecution-friendly, and to take increasingly pronounced steps to secure convictions of suspects who police are convinced have engaged in serious criminal offences. It is not legitimate to extrapolate from their behaviour that there is a cultural issue which exists widely in forensic laboratories. However, it has long been recognized that it is essential for crime laboratories, especially those that work exclusively for local police, to institute measures and foster a culture that guards against pro-prosecution bias. At the very least, these cases emphasize the outcome when such measures fail and how serious the consequences can be when scholarly objectivity is abandoned and, instead, replaced by an advocacy role and even worse a preparedness to take dishonest measures to secure a predetermined result. They also highlight the need for those who defend persons accused of serious crimes to be vigilant and alert for the potential for medical and scientific testing to be contaminated by approaches that lack objectivity and methodological soundness.

Abandonment of Scientific Method: James Grigson

There are some forensic experts who have been exposed as prepared to offer opinions that are assertions and personal views, rather than being based on proper medico-scientific processes. An example of this was the well-known forensic psychiatrist, Dr James Grigson, from Texerkana, Texas. Dr Grigson testified regularly and controversially in death penalty cases in Texas.[111] He was consistently called by the prosecution. His manner was pleasant, his language unassuming and readily comprehensible. He did not use notes or charts or lapse into technical language.[112] He labelled 100 out of 167 people about whom he testified as 'incorrigible' and therefore likely to offend again.[113] The controversy that attached to his forensic work arose from the unscientific

[110] Fred Contrada, 'Amherst Crime Lab Probe Sought by Northwestern District Attorney David Sullivan David Sullivan Following Chemist Sonja Farak's Arrest on Drug Thefts', *MassLive.com*, 25 January 2013: <http://www.masslive.com/news/index.ssf/2013/01/northwestern_da_asks_state_to.html> [accessed 27 Dec 2015].

[111] For a thoughtful analysis, see Alan A Stone, *Law, Psychiatry and Morality: Essays and Analysis* (Washington, DC: American Psychiatric Press, Arlington, 1984) 69ff. See also, Henry C Weinstein, 'How Should Forensic Psychiatry Police Itself? Guidelines and Grievances: The AAPL Committee on Ethics' (1984) 12(3) *Bulletin of the American Academy of Psychiatry & the Law* 289.

[112] Mike Tolson, 'Effect of 'Dr Death' and His Testimony Lingers', *Houston Chronicle*, 17 June 2004: <http://www.chron.com/news/houston-texas/article/Effect-of-Dr-Death-and-his-testimony-lingers-1960299.php> [accessed 27 Dec 2015]; 'They Call him Dr. Death' (1981) 117(22) *Time* 82; Eugenia T La Fontaine, 'A Dangerous Preoccupation with Future Danger: Why Expert Predictions of Future Dangerousness in Capital Cases Are Unconstitutional' (2002) 44(1) *Boston College Law Review* 207, available at: <http://lawdigitalcommons.bc.edu/bclr/vol44/iss1/4/> [accessed 27 Dec 2015].

[113] Rubin 'Hurricane' Carter with Ken Klonsky, *Eye of the Hurricane: My Path from Darkness to Freedom* (Chicago, Ill: Lawrence Hill Books, 2011) 211.

and unequivocal nature of the opinions he expressed to the courts in relation to defendants' dangerousness. In 1989 Judge Teague of the Court of Criminal Appeals in Texas wrote (in dissent):

> This is another case in which Dr. James P. Grigson, who has earned the nickname of 'Dr. Death' because of the number of times he has testified on behalf of the State at the punishment stage of a capital murder trial and the number of times the jury has returned affirmative answers to the submitted special issues, testified.
>
> [...]
>
> It seems to me that when Dr. Grigson testifies at the punishment stage of a capital murder trial he appears to the average lay juror, and the uninformed juror, to be the second coming of the Almighty.
>
> After having read many records of capital murder cases in which Dr. Grigson testified at the punishment stage of the trial, I have concluded that, as a general proposition, when Dr. Grigson speaks to a lay jury, or an uninformed jury, about a person who he characterizes as a 'severe' sociopath, which a defendant who has been convicted of capital murder always is in the eyes of Dr. Grigson, the defendant should stop what he is then doing and commence writing out his last will and testament-because he will in all probability soon be ordered by the trial judge to suffer a premature death.
>
> [...]
>
> When Dr Grigson is shown to have testified in a capital murder case in which the defendant challenges his conviction and sentence of death, the captions of those cases in which relief was granted read almost like the following: 'THIS IS ANOTHER DR. GRIGSON CASE.' The number of these cases is so great that I will simply refer the reader to either Westlaw or Lexis and not cite them. Thus, to even conclude that Dr. Grigson's testimony may be harmless is ludicrous.[114]

Grigson was reprimanded twice by the American Psychiatric Association (APA) for using the results of a competency examination during the sentencing phase of a trial and for claiming 100 per cent accuracy in predicting the dangerousness of a defendant he had never examined. The former was the scenario in the Supreme Court decision of *Estelle v Smith*[115] where the court found that Dr Grigson's method of utilizing at sentence Mr Smith's statements made in answer to questions about his competency to stand trial without warning him of the potential for this to take place had constituted breaches of Mr Smith's Fifth (right to silence) and Sixth (right to counsel) Amendment Rights.

The cost of Dr Grigson's pro-prosecution bias became notorious in relation to Randall Adams who was convicted of the 1976 murder of a Dallas police officer.[116] Dr Grigson classified Adams as a 'sociopath' in spite of Adams having no criminal record, and said there was no doubt he would kill again, even in prison.[117] Adams was later exonerated of the crime.

Dr Grigson figured also in *Barefoot v Estelle*[118] where, without evaluating Mr Barefoot, relying on hypothetical data presented by the prosecutor he persuaded the jury to recommend the

---

114 *Bennett v State*, 766 SW 2d 227, 231–232 (Tex Crim App 1989).

115 451 US 454 (1981); see also, Christopher Slobogin, '*Estelle v. Smith*: The Constitutional Contours of the Forensic Evaluation' (1982) 31(1) *Emory Law Journal* 71; Welsh S White, 'Waiver and the Death Penalty: The Implications of *Estelle v. Smith*' (1981) 72(4) *The Journal of Criminal Law & Criminology* 1522; Karen C Kalmbach and Phillip M Lyons, 'Ethical Issues in Conducting Forensic Evaluations' (2006) 2(3) *Applied Psychology in Criminal Justice* 261; Robert I Simon and Liza H Gold (eds), *The American Psychiatric Publishing Textbook of Forensic Psychiatry* (2nd edn, Washington, DC: American Psychiatric Publishing, 2010) 340–1.

116 See Edward Gray, *Henry Wade's Tough Justice: How Dallas County Prosecutors Led the Nation in Convicting the Innocent* (Indianapolis: Dog Ear Publishing, 2010) 48.

117 Ibid.

118 463 US 880 (1983). See also, James L Knoll IV, 'Death's Conviction', *Forensic Psychiatry*, 12 March 2010: <http://www.psychiatrictimes.com/forensic-psychiatry/death%E2%80%99s-conviction> [accessed 27 Dec 2015]; James W Marquart, Sheldon Ekland-Olson, and Jonathan R Sorenson, *The Rope, the Chair, and the Needle: Capital Punishment in Texas,* 1923–1990 (Austin: University of Texas Press, 2010) 178–9.

death penalty. He testified that he had examined 'between thirty and forty thousand individuals' and that, if given enough information, he could give an opinion '*within reasonable psychiatric certainty* as to the psychological or psychiatric makeup of an individual'.[119] He further explained that "this skill was 'particular to the field of psychiatry and not to the average layman"'.[120] Dr Grigson diagnosed Barefoot as a sociopath in the 'most severe category'[121] for which there was no known cure.[122] He concluded that 'whether [the defendant] was in society at large or in a prison society there was a "*one hundred percent and absolute*" chance that [the defendant] would commit future acts of criminal violence that would constitute a continuing threat to society'.[123] The APA filed an amicus brief in the Supreme Court, contesting the scientific legitimacy of Dr Grigson's testimony, contending that such evidence 'impermissibly distorts the fact-finding process in capital cases' and arguing that it was 'unethical for a psychiatrist to offer a professional opinion unless he/she has conducted an examination'.[124]

At the urging of the eminent psychiatrist Professor Paul Appelbaum, the APA (and also the Texas Society of Psychiatric Physicians) expelled Dr Grigson from its membership for his testimony in *Barefoot v Estelle.*[125] However, he remained entirely unrepentant and retained his licence to practise medicine, continuing to testify in capital sentencing hearings.[126] A few months before his death from lung cancer, Dr Grigson exhibited no insight. He told a reporter he had no regrets and saw his role only as a doctor who was there to distinguish the mentally ill defendants who needed to go to hospital from those who were faking it and needed to go to prison or could be executed.

Corruption

Very occasionally the defect in expert evidence is that it is the product of outright corruption. An example of this came to light in October 2013 when a Delhi court sentenced two scientists from the Central Forensic Science Laboratory (CFSL) to jail terms for giving false opinions in a civil case in order to implicate a litigant. Dr SC Mittal, the Principal Scientific Officer and Head of the Documents Division of the Laboratory, was sentenced to two years' imprisonment while VK Khanna, also a Principal Scientific Officer of the CFSL, was sentenced to 12 months' imprisonment. Both scientists were sentenced for criminal conspiracy and under provisions of the *Prevention of Corruption Act 1988* (Ind).[127]

Forensic Misconduct by Impersonation

A small number of persons have impersonated properly qualified and, on occasion, registered practitioners in the forensic area and in consequence have been charged with criminal offences

---

119 463 US 880 (1983) 918 (Blackmun J) (emphasis in original).

120 Ibid.

121 Ibid, 919 (Blackmun J).

122 Ibid.

123 Ibid, (emphasis in original).

124 Marquart, Ekland-Olson, and Sorenson, above n 118, 178.

125 Jeffrey L Kirchmeier, 'Aggravating and Mitigating Factors: The Paradox of Today's Arbitrary and Mandatory Capital Punishment Scheme' (1998) 6(2) *William & Mary Bill of Rights Journal* 345, 372.

126 See Robert Schopp, Richard L Wiener, Brian H Bornstein, and Steven L Willborn, *Mental Disorder and Criminal Law: Responsibility, Punishment and Competence* (New York: Springer, 2009) 152–3.

127 'Court Sentences Two Central Forensic Science Laboratory Scientists in Corruption Case', *DNA India*, 11 October 2013: <http://www.dnaindia.com/india/report-court-sentences-two-central-forensic-science-laboratory-scientists-in-corruption-case-1902307> [accessed 27 Dec 2015].

of deception. For instance, in England Gene Morrison used fraudulent qualifications for a quarter of a century and functioned as a forensic scientist, giving evidence in large numbers of cases. His bogus credentials were: a purchased BSc in forensic science, a Master's degree in forensic investigation, and a Doctorate in criminology. Ultimately, in February 2007, he was charged with a suite of offences involving a money transfer, obtaining property by deception, perverting the course of justice and perjury, requiring a review of over 700 cases on which he had worked over a period of 26 years.[128] Working from an office near his home in Hyde, Cheshire, he placed advertisements in the *Solicitors Journal*, and started by hiring legitimate forensic scientists to carry out handwriting and fingerprint analysis which he would then claim as his own and charge clients twice the true price. Later he cut and pasted old reports together and changed details, claiming the analysis was new. He was hired by legal firms, insurance companies, private businesses, and individuals to carry out original work and examine other expert reports. He was described as 'an inveterate and compulsive liar' by Judge Jeffrey Lewis of Manchester's Minshull Street Crown Court after being found guilty by a jury of all but one of the offences with which he was charged.[129] He was sentenced to five years' imprisonment and prompted concern in the United Kingdom both about the legitimacy of decisions in the cases in which he had been involved and, more broadly, about the regulation of forensic experts.

In Australia Dusan Milosevic was found by a County Court jury to have fraudulently obtained his registration as a psychologist in 1998 by fake degrees that purported to be from the Faculty of Defectology at the University of Belgrade. In 2011 Mr Milosevic was sentenced to five years' imprisonment with two and a half years required to be served before being eligible for parole, on 29 counts of obtaining property by deception, two of using a false document and one of obtaining a financial advantage by deception. The amount he had obtained from Victoria's WorkSafe and Transport Accident Commission was in excess of AUS$1 million, including from the preparation of large numbers of forensic reports.[130] Accordingly, the Victorian Civil and Administrative Tribunal (VCAT), dealing with his registration, observed that the case was a blatant one of fraud, requiring the cancelling of his registration, and expressed surprise that Mr Milosevic had ever been registered in Australia.[131] Even after his conviction in the County Court, Mr Milosevic continued to protest his innocence before VCAT, and to accuse a wide variety of persons in Serbia of engaging in a conspiracy against him, in spite of the manifest falsity of the document by which he had obtained registration as a psychologist.

Systemic and Cultural Issues

Much more common in terms of a cause of individual examples of misconduct is the environment of accountability and supervisory values at a laboratory. An example in this regard was what occurred in respect of Annie Dookhan in the Massachusetts Hinton State Laboratory Institute (see page 213/above). When there is seriously deficient, incompetent or even fraudulent forensic practice by experts, it tends to flower in an environment or culture

[128] 'Fraudulent Forensic Expert Jailed', *BBC News*, 22 February 2007: <http://news.bbc.co.uk/2/hi/6386069.stm> [accessed 27 Dec 2015]; 'Bogus 'Expert Witness' Jailed for Five Years', *Daily Mail*, 22 February 2007: <http://www.dailymail.co.uk/news/article-437841/Bogus-expert-witness-jailed-years.html> [accessed 27 Dec 2015].

[129] 'Bogus "Expert Witness" Jailed for Five Years', above n 128.

[130] Adrian Lowe, 'Fake Psychologist's $1m TAC, Worksafe Haul', *The Age*, 29 September 2011: <http://www.theage.com.au/victoria/fake-psychologists-1m-tac-worksafe-haul-20110929-1kyci.html> [accessed 27 Dec 2015].

[131] *Psychology Board of Australia v Milosevic* [2013] VCAT 12.

that lacks scientific rigour and effective internal oversight and supervision. Often, too, there is a culture which tolerates or turns a blind eye to the adoption of a partisan approach to the conduct of work by forensic scientists or doctors. The cases that are explored below illustrate this phenomenon.

The Nassau County Police Department Forensic Evidence Bureau. In 2011 Ellen Biben, the State Inspector General of New York, published the results of an investigation into the Nassau County Police Department Forensic Evidence Bureau (FEB), which had led to the closing of the Bureau.[132] The Biben report is a scathing indictment of the delivery of forensic science services by the laboratory but, more importantly, catalogues the development of a culture that inevitably would generate miscarriages of criminal justice by reason of the unethical attitudes amongst scientists that had been allowed to propagate over a significant period of time.

Importantly, the problems identified by the Inspector-General existed in spite of New York being the first State in the United States to require accreditation of its laboratories and to constitute a body to oversee them since 1994. This body was the Commission on Forensic Science, empowered to 'develop minimum standards and a program of accreditation for all forensic laboratories in New York state, including establishing minimum qualifications for forensic laboratory directors and such other personnel as the commission may determine to be necessary and appropriate, and approval of forensic laboratories for the performance of specific forensic methodologies'.[133] As of 2010 it was overseeing 22 forensic laboratories in New York State. Importantly, also, and apparently ineffectually, the Commission required laboratories to be inspected and accredited by the American Society of Crime Laboratory Directors/Laboratory Accreditation Board (ASCLD/LAB). Further, New York State was a recipient of federal Paul Coverdell Forensic Science Improvement Program grants which provide funding to help improve the quality of forensic science.

In spite of the existence of these funding sources, advisory bodies, and oversighting mechanisms, the Inspector-General found that the failures at laboratory level were profound:

> Over its eight-year history, the FEB suffered from weak leadership, a dysfunctional quality management system, analysts with inconsistent training and qualifications, and outdated and incomplete testing procedures. As a result, the laboratory operated absent the rigors and precision necessary in scientific testing, which created an environment where mistakes were more likely to occur and less likely to be detected. Not surprisingly, testing mistakes did in fact occur. Specifically, recent retesting of certain drug chemistry analyses by FEB has not yet been completed, but preliminary results indicate that more than 10 percent of the laboratory's drug chemistry results had some inconsistencies in testing that should have been detected by lab personnel.... Overall, the Inspector General found problems at the lab that not only affected the drug chemistry section but also had the potential to affect every other discipline in the laboratory.[134]

[132] Ellen N Biben, *Investigation into the Nassau County Police Department Forensic Evidence Bureau* (State of New York: Office of the Inspector General, November 2011): <http://www.scribd.com/doc/86281774/Investigation-Into-the-Nassau-County-Police-Department-Forensic-Evidence-Bureau> [accessed 27 Dec 2015] and <http://www.ig.state.ny.us/pdfs/Investigation%20into%20the%20Nassau%20County%20Police%20Department%20Forensic%20Evidence%20Bureau.pdf> [accessed 27 Dec 2015].

[133] NY CLS Exec § 995-b(1) (Lexis 2014).

[134] Biben, above n 132, 3–4. She observed (at 141) that there was a lack of an adequate quality system and 'patterns of errors which include mistakes in calculation, weight differences, differences pertaining to substance identification, and inconsistency in the number of items' submitted to the laboratory, as against those recorded as received: 141–2.

The Inspector-General found multiple layers of oversight to have contributed to the situation, having been 'fraught with problems since its formation in 2003':[135] 'The confluence of these failures in oversight enabled the FEB to operate as a substandard laboratory for far too long. In so doing, these failures deprived Nassau County, the criminal justice system, and the public of their right to have complete and unfettered confidence in forensic testing.'[136]

The Inspector-General recommended the complete reconstitution of the laboratory, independent of the Police Department and operating as a subdivision of the Medical Examiner's Office, meeting the following standards:

1. [A]n effective quality assurance program must be implemented and maintained;
2. [M]anagement and staff must be appropriately qualified;
3. [O]ngoing training and education should be mandatory;
4. [S]taffing levels in particular disciplines should be responsive to expected case volumes;
5. [T]he physical plant must be contiguous and conducive to forensic testing; and
6. [T]he laboratory must communicate directly and effectively with [senior prosecutors] to keep them apprised of lab-related issues.[137]

The Inspector-General found the minimum ASCLD/LAB standards to be inadequate as an accreditation requirement and recommended the adoption of more rigorous and appropriate standards, to be monitored more energetically by the Forensic Commission.

The North Carolina Crime Laboratory. In 2010, an investigation into the scientific reporting by the North Carolina Crime Laboratory between 1987 and 2003 found a pattern of withholding of information that was material and favourable to the defence. The factors contributing to this fundamentally problematic attitudinal position[138] were found to include personal bias and 'poorly crafted policy; lack of objectivity; the absence of clear report writing guidance; inattention to reporting methods that left too much discretion to the individual Analyst; lack of transparency; and ineffective management and oversight of the Forensic Biology Section from 1987 through 2003'.[139]

The scandal generated a series of statutory reforms in North Carolina that are likely to influence other legislatures throughout North America. First, it prompted the creation of a State innocence commission as an 'extraordinary procedure to investigate and determine credible claims of factual innocence'.[140] An early overturning of a conviction from this procedure took place when the Innocence Commission of North Carolina identified that, by contrast with laboratory notes by a serologist contradicting an initial report that there were 'chemical indications for the presence of blood' at a crime scene, later more definitive bench notes showed that a confirmatory test was negative.[141] These notes had not been made available to those representing the defendant. Both the serologist involved and the laboratory director at the time did not identify an ethical issue in this regard.[142]

North Carolina has amended its accreditation statute for forensic laboratories. That statute no longer designates ASCLD/LAB as the accrediting agency. It requires as a precondition

135 Ibid, 148.

136 Ibid, 6.

137 Ibid, 158.

138 Chris Swecker and Michael Wolf, *An Independent Review of the State Bureau of Investigation Forensic Laboratory* (released 18 August 2010) 2: <http://www.ncdoj.gov/getattachment/120489be-3c0b-4515-a522-19de759e5e07/Independent-Review-of-SBI-Forensic-LAB.aspx> [accessed 27 Dec 2015].

139 Ibid, 4.

140 NC Gen Stat § 15A-1461 (Lexis 2014); see generally, David Wolitz, 'Innocence Commissions and the Future of Post-Conviction Review' (2010) 52(4) *Arizona Law Review* 1027.

141 Paul C Giannelli, 'The North Carolina Lab Scandal' (2012) 27(1) *Criminal Justice* 43, 43.

142 Ibid.

to admissibility of analyses that a laboratory be accredited by a body which stipulates conformance to forensic-specific requirements and which is a signatory to the International Laboratory Accreditation Cooperation (ILAC) Mutual Recognition Arrangement for testing for the submission, identification, analysis, and storage of forensic analyses. In addition, the laboratory's client is specified by statutory provision as the 'public and the criminal justice system' not the 'prosecuting officers of the State'.[143] Further, the wilful omission or misrepresentation of information subject to disclosure has been criminalized. In addition, to reduce the isolation of the laboratory a Forensic Science Advisory Board was created.[144]

The Principle of Witness Immunity

The principle of witness immunity has traditionally provided protection to academics and others in their discharge of the forensic role. It has precluded the bringing of civil and defamation actions for forensic work. The extension of especial protection against negligence and defamation actions exists for witnesses in many countries, including in the United Kingdom,[145] the United States,[146] Canada,[147] New Zealand,[148] and Australia.[149] It is fundamental to the trial system as it gives protection to, among others, expert witnesses and thereby encouragement to fulfil a forensic role without the chilling effect of potentially adverse consequences.[150] The principle was thought by many also to provide protection for regulated professions, such as medicine, dentistry, nursing, and psychology, against disciplinary action for forensic work. However, a significant change in terms of accountability has been initiated by a series of decisions by appellate courts during the past 15 years. The result is that when experts, including persons employed in the tertiary sector undertake academic work, they must do it with the same care and intellectual rigour they should use in their other work. If they do not, many categories of academics can be subject to disciplinary sanction. The risk is also emerging as a result of the decision of the United Kingdom Supreme Court in *Jones v Kaney*[151] that they may also be civilly liable to some degree.

Immunity for experts protects them against any action 'for anything said or done, although falsely and maliciously and without any reasonable or probable cause, in the ordinary course of any proceeding in a court of justice'.[152] The immunity is very broad. It extends to cover:

---

[143] Ibid, 63.

[144] *Forensic Sciences Act of 2011* sec 2, NC Sess Laws 2011-19.

[145] See eg, *Stanton v Callaghan* [2000] QB 75; *Darker v Chief Constable of the West Midlands Police* [2001] 1 AC 435; *Palmer v Durnford Ford* [1992] QB 483; *Meadow v General Medical Council* [2006] EWCA Civ 1390; [2007] QB 462; *Jones v Kaney* [2011] UKSC 13; [2011] 2 AC 398; *Crawford v Jenkins* [2014] EWCA Civ 1035.

[146] See eg, *Briscoe v LaHue*, 460 US 325 (1983); *Mitchell v Forsyth*, 472 US 511 (1985), although there are signs that its rigour may be easing: *Murphy v AA Matthews*, 841 SW 2d 671 (Mo, 1992); *Dalton v Miller*, 984 P 2d 666 (Col App, 1999).

[147] *Carnahan v Coates* (1990) 71 DLR (4th) 464; *Fabian v Margulies* (1985) 53 OR (2d) 380 (Ont CA); *Varghese v Landau* (2004) CanLII 5084 (Ont SC).

[148] See eg, *Gibson v Cotter* [2006] NZHC 592 (30 May 2006).

[149] See eg, *Hamod v New South Wales (No 10)* [2008] NSWSC 611; *Commonwealth v Griffiths* [2007] NSWCA 370; (2007) 70 NSWLR 268; *James v Medical Board of South Australia* (2006) 95 SASR 445; *D'Orta-Ekenaike v Victoria Legal Aid* (2005) 223 CLR 1; *Jamieson v The Queen* (1993) 177 CLR 574; *Cabassi v Vila* (1940) 64 CLR 130.

[150] See generally, Freckelton and Selby, above n 4.

[151] [2011] 2 AC 398. See Ian Freckelton, 'Civil Liability of Health Practitioners for their Forensic Work: Further Erosion of the Witness Immunity Rule' (2012) 19(4) *Psychiatry, Psychology and Law* 451; Danuta Mendelson, 'From Expert Witness to Defendant: Abolition of Expert Witness Protection and its Implications' (2012) 20(2) *Journal of Law and Medicine* 250.

[152] *Dawkins v Lord Rokeby* (1873) LR 8 QB 255, 264 (Kelly CB); approved by Lord Hutton in *Darker v Chief Constable of West Midlands* [2001] 1 AC 435, 464.

- the preliminary examination of witnesses;[153]
- evidence from potential witnesses in criminal proceedings at a time when proceedings are in contemplation but have not yet been commenced;[154]
- an expert's report prepared in circumstances where, if there were to be proceedings for child abuse, the report would be relied on;[155] and
- statements made out of court that could fairly be said to be part of the process of investigating crime with a view to prosecution.[156]

However, the immunity does not extend to things done at the investigative stage which could not fairly be said to form part of the witness's participation in the judicial proceedings. It only bars civil actions; it does not protect a witness against a criminal prosecution for perjury, for perverting the course of justice, or for contempt of court. Thus, as Lord Morris put it in *Roy v Prior*:[157] 'If a witness gives false evidence he may be prosecuted if the crime of perjury has been committed but a civil action for damages in respect of the words spoken will not lie.'

It is standard to identify two objectives for the provision of immunity: (1) ensuring that witnesses give evidence 'freely and fearlessly[158] ... in an atmosphere free from threats of suit from disappointed clients',[159] with the corollary that 'persons who may be witnesses in other cases in the future will not be deterred from giving evidence by fear of being sued for what they say in court';[160] and (2) 'to avoid multiplicity of actions in which the value or truth of their evidence would be tried over again'.[161]

In *Stanton v Callaghan* Otton LJ made the point that the issue is one of high public interest:

> [The] immunity is not granted primarily for the benefit of the individuals who seek it. They themselves are beneficiaries of the overarching public interest, which can be expressed as the need to ensure that the administration of justice is not impeded. This is the consideration which should be paramount.[162]

However, the courts have shown a marked reluctance to extend the immunity.[163] In addition, in the United States it has been observed that it is arguable that different policy considerations apply to extension of immunity from action in respect of 'adverse experts' (namely, experts on the other side in litigation), as against action in respect of 'friendly experts'.[164]

---

153 *Watson v M'Ewan; Watson v Jones* [1905] AC 480.

154 *Evans v London Medical College (University of London)* [1981] 1 WLR 184.

155 *X (Minors) v Bedfordshire County Council* [1995] 2 AC 633, 755 (Lord Browne-Wilkinson).

156 *Taylor v Director of the Serious Fraud Office* [1999] 2 AC 177.

157 [1971] AC 470, 477.

158 *Darker v Chief Constable of West Midlands* [2001] 1 AC 435, 461 (Lord Clyde).

159 *Stanton v Callaghan* [2000] QB 75, 108 (Lord Justice Otton). In *Marrinan v Vibart* [1963] 1 QB 234, 237 (upheld on appeal [1963] 1 QB 528) Salmon J said: '[T]he administration of justice would be greatly impeded if witnesses were to be in fear that any disgruntled or possibly impecunious persons against whom they gave evidence might subsequently involve them in costly litigation.' To similar effect in *Munster v Lamb* (1883) 11 QBD 588, 607, Fry LJ said that the purpose of the rule was 'to protect persons acting bona fide, who under a different rule would be liable, not perhaps to verdicts and judgments against them, but to the vexation of defending actions'.

160 *Darker v Chief Constable of West Midlands* [2001] 1 AC 435, 469 (Lord Hutton).

161 *Roy v Prior* [1971] AC 470, 480 (Lord Wilberforce).

162 [2000] QB 75, 107.

163 *General Medical Council v Meadow* [2006] EWCA Civ 1390; [2007] QB 462, [17] (Sir Anthony Clarke MR).

164 See John McHahey, 'Should Experts Receive Witness Immunity?' (Fall 2006) *Commercial and Business Litigation* 10; B Sonny Bal, 'The Expert Witness in Medical Malpractice Litigation' (2009) 467(2) Clin Orthop Relat Res 383; *LLMD of Mich Inc v Jackson-Cross Co*, 740 A 2d 186 (A 1996); *Pollock v Panjabi*, 27 Conn L Rptr 316, (Conn. Super Ct, 2000); *Pace v Swerdlow* 519 F 3d 1067 (10th Cir 2008).

Dr Paterson and Brittle Bone Disease

Dr Colin Paterson wrote a report and gave evidence before the Family Division of England's High Court of Justice in a case involving allegations of non-accidental injury to children.[165] His evidence prompted Lady Butler-Sloss, the President of the Family Division of England's High Court, to report Dr Paterson to the General Medical Council.[166] Previously Wall J in *Re AB*[167] had taken the unusual step of making adverse observations of Dr Paterson by name:

> I feel obliged to say that unless a report from Dr Paterson confirms in the future to the guidelines laid down in *Re* R[168]... his evidence in any case involving the alleged non-accidental injury of infants... should, in my judgment, be treated with the greatest caution and reserve.

Dr Paterson was commissioned on behalf of parents who were accused of causing such injuries to their children. His report, and then his oral evidence, expressed the view that the injuries to a child, X, was caused by bone disease, probably what he termed 'temporary brittle bone disease' (TBBD) which he described as a 'self-limited osteogenesis imperfecta with spontaneous improvement, and with numerous fractures confined to the first year of life.'[169]

When later taken before a Professional Conduct Committee of the General Medical Council,[170] Dr Paterson conceded that it was his responsibility to ensure that his report did not mislead a court by omissions and admitted that a misleading opinion from an expert such as himself could inhibit a proper assessment of a case by a court—this could lead to a child being wrongly placed and thereby being put at risk. The Professional Conduct Committee found that Dr Paterson's report had been misleading and/or inadequately researched in that it omitted consideration and discussion of a chest bruise observed on X and swelling observed and bruising visible on his right ankle. Dr Paterson had failed to state that such bruising and swelling were contra-indications to TBBD and failed to relate the right calf-swelling and ankle-bruising to the fracture's in X's right ankle. It found that 'this relationship should have been fully discussed in your report and that not to do so was a failure of the duties of an expert witness.'

The Committee found that Dr Paterson had failed to explain why, when X had none of the predisposing or identifying features of TBBD, as set out in Dr Paterson's published research, X was not outside the criteria for TBBD, and thus that his diagnosis of X having TBBD should be treated with caution. It found that Dr Paterson overlooked or discounted clinical aspects of the case that were at variance with his published views and/or diagnosis.

In respect of another matter, the Committee noted that Dr Paterson had been approached by Mr and Mrs A with a view to his giving evidence on their behalf in relation to criminal charges preferred against them in the Pima County Superior Court of Arizona arising from approximately 14 fractures sustained by their infant daughter. He gave evidence at their retrial and was interviewed by the prosecutor in relation to his proposed evidence on four occasions. The Committee found that in expressing his expert opinions during these interviews, Dr Paterson should have known that his opinions should not mislead and should be properly

---

165 *Re C (Non-accidental Injury: Expert Evidence)* [2001] 2 FLR 90.

166 Owen Dyer, 'GMC Strikes Off Proponent of Temporary Brittle Bone Disease' (13 March 2004) 328 *British Medical Journal* 604; Clare Dyer, 'Inexpert Witness' (6 April 2004) *The Guardian*: <http://www.theguardian.com/world/2004/apr/06/law.children> (viewed 23 June 2015).

167 [1994] EWHC 5.

168 See *Re J (Child Abuse: Expert Evidence)* [1991] FCR 193 at 226 per Cazalet J, also reported as *Note: Re R (A Minor) (Experts' Evidence)* [1991] 1 FLR 291.

169 See *Re Paterson*, unreported, Professional Conduct Committee, General Medical Council, 3 April 2004.

170 <http://www.gmc-uk.org/probdocs/decisions/pcc/2004/PATERSON_20040304.htm> (viewed 13 October 2004).

researched. It expressed concern that when he gave an opinion in his first interview he did so without having seen all the records and had apparently not having noted the significance of some of the records he had seen, such as an MRI scan which showed extensive soft tissue injuries not associated with a fracture, and of the non-attendance at clinical appointments. It found that he had insufficient regard to 2,784 pages of documents relating to the case which were forwarded to him. The result was that his expert opinion was 'inadequately researched'. It concluded that in arriving at his diagnosis of TBBD he overlooked or discounted clinical aspects of the case that were inconsistent with his published views, or alternatively, covertly added new aspects to his diagnostic criteria. The Committee pointedly eschewed determinations about the legitimacy of TBBD and acknowledged Dr Paterson's 'right to believe in TBBD and to share opinions with other physicians, conduct research and write papers in medical literature and to act as an expert witness'. It accepted that he had done so sincerely but emphasized that providing expert evidence to the courts 'carries a heavy responsibility': 'the courts must be able to rely on the evidence of expert witnesses, evidence that must be properly researched, balanced and not misleading.'

The Committee observed that Dr Paterson's criteria for the diagnosis of TBBD were unclear and/or variable with the potential for misleading others in legal proceedings, thereby posing an unacceptable risk to children. It found that an expert witness should not assume the role of an advocate but that this was what Dr Paterson appeared to have done in respect of TBBD and his preparedness to ignore significant clinical evidence at variance with his published views. It accepted the advantage of researchers challenging received wisdom and commonly held views, but concluded that when a person acting as an expert witness advances a view that is at variance with the opinions held by mainstream practitioners, it is incumbent on the practitioner to 'put forward a fully reasoned logical basis why an alternative diagnosis is valid in the particular circumstance'. Influenced by the importance of Dr Paterson's misconduct, that 'a profession's most valuable asset is its collective reputation and the confidence it inspires in members of the public, as well as Dr Paterson's failure to accept that he had engaged in misconduct or to change his ways, it determined it had no option but to erase his name from the Medical Register'.[171]

In 2013, however, the *Journal of Pediatric Endocrinology and Metabolism* was not deterred from publishing Paterson's report of a putative association between multiple fractures of TBBD and intracranial bleeding, possibly due to an as yet unrecognized 'natural disease'.[172]

The Professor Meadow Saga

Professor Sir Roy Meadow was a doyen of physicians in the United Kingdom. He was President of the Royal College of Paediatrics and Child Health and was knighted by Prime Minister Tony Blair in 1998, having been for many years Professor of Child Health and Paediatrics at the University of Leeds. In 1977 he famously coined the term 'Munchausen syndrome by proxy'[173] and endorsed the dictum that '[o]ne sudden infant death is a tragedy, two is

[171] See Jim Fisher, *Forensics Under Fire: Are Bad Science and Duelling Experts Corrupting Criminal Justice* (New Brunswick, NJ: Rutgers University Press, 2008) 87ff.

[172] Colin Patersin and EA Monk, 'Temporary Brittle Bone Disease: Association with Intracranial Bleeding' (2013) 26 *Journal of Pediatric Endocrinology and Metabolism* 417.

[173] Roy Meadow, 'Munchausen Syndrome by Proxy: The Hinterland of Child Abuse' (1977) 310(8033) *The Lancet* 343. Defined by Sydney psychiatrist Robert Kaplan as referring to 'the mothers of children who were insistent that their children had something wrong with them, or were not getting better, had an adversarial, if not hostile, relationship with the doctor and were observed to be harming the children to maintain illness symptoms': ABC Radio National, 'Savonarola at the Stake: The Rise and Fall of Professor Sir Roy Meadow', *Ockham's Razor*, 4 November 2007 (Robyn Williams): <http://www.abc.net.au/radionational/programs/ockhamsrazor/savonarola-at-the-stake-the-rise-and-fall-of/3217066> [accessed 27 Dec 2015].

suspicious and three is murder until proved otherwise'.[174] This became known as 'Meadow's Law' and for a time was widely adopted by social workers and child protection agencies. He was a world-acknowledged scholar in relation to Sudden Infant Death Syndrome (SIDS) and for many years argued that some victims of cot death were wrongly diagnosed and may actually be victims of parental abuse. His work in this regard coincided with the views and contribution of Dr Alfred Steinschneider (see above p 206). In a study titled 'Unnatural Sudden Infant Deaths', published in the *Archives of Disease in Childhood*,[175] Meadow wrote: 'SIDS has been used at times as a pathological diagnosis to evade awkward truths.'[176] His claim was based on his study of 18 years of records relating to 81 children from around Britain judged by criminal and family courts to have been killed by their parents. In 49 cases the children had initially been certified as dying from SIDS and a further 29 were classified as dying from other natural causes. The mother was responsible for the death, usually smothering, in more than 80 per cent of cases.

Professor Sir Roy Meadow was a formidable old-school figure in the medical establishment. His notoriety unfortunately comes from his involvement in the trial of Sally Clark, a 34-year-old London solicitor charged and convicted in 1999 of murdering her two sons—Christopher, who died at the age of eleven weeks in December 1996, and Harry, who died at the age of eight weeks in January 1998. Both children had previously been healthy; they died suddenly in their mother's care, in the evening, at home. Postmortem examinations of both children showed multiple abnormal findings.

At the trial of Sally Clark for murder, Sir Roy gave vital expert opinions after being asked to review the available evidence by the Cheshire Constabulary. Initially, he provided a statement of ten pages in which he concluded that the deaths were not natural. He was called to give evidence both at the committal proceedings and at the trial in the Chester Crown Court where he expressed the same view. The difficulty lay in his reasoning process. In paragraph 7 of his report, under 'Two infants' deaths in one family', he stated:

> Even when an infant dies suddenly and unexpectedly in early life and no cause is found at autopsy, and the reason for death is thought to be an unidentified natural cause (sudden infant death syndrome), it is extremely rare for that to happen again within a family. For example, such a happening may occur 1:1,000 infants, therefore the chance of it happening twice within a family is 1:1m. Neither of these two deaths can be classed as SIDS. Each of the deaths was unusual and had the characteristics of a death caused by a parent.[177]

Professor Meadow was stating the approximate ratio of SIDS deaths to births (1:1,000) and squaring that to reflect the chance of a second SIDS death in a family that has already suffered one. This made the assumption that the chance of a second SIDS death in a family that has already suffered one is the same as the chance of the first SIDS death in a family that has not already experienced a SIDS death.

Matters became the more problematic when Professor Meadow delivered a supplementary report in which he stated that, apart from non-accidental injury, no specific medical cause of death seemed apparent. He observed that the likelihood of SIDS varies with social circumstances and that the most recent estimation of the incidence in England for a family in which the parents do not smoke, in which at least one has a waged income, and in which the mother was over the age of 26 years (namely a family comparable to that of Sally Clark) was

---

[174] Roy Meadow (ed), *ABC of Child Abuse* (3rd edn, London: BMJ Publishing Group, 1997) 29.
[175] Roy Meadow, 'Unnatural Sudden Infant Death' (1999) 80(1) *Archives of Disease in Childhood* 7.
[176] Ibid, 12.
[177] [2006] EWCA Civ 1390; [2007] QB 462, [73].

1:8,543. Thus, he calculated the likelihood of two infant deaths within such a family being SIDS as 1:73,000,000.

Professor Meadow in oral evidence gave the following gloss on his opinion:

> [I]t's the chance of backing that long-odd outsider at the Grand National, you know; let's say it's an 80 to 1 chance, you back the winner last year, then the next year there's another horse at 80 to 1 and it is still 80 to 1 and you back it again and it wins. Now here we're in a situation that, you know, to get to these odds of 73m you've got to back that 1 in 80 chance four years running, so yes, you might be very, very lucky because each time it's just been a 1 in 80 chance and you know, you've happened to have won it, but the chance of it happening four years running we all know is extraordinarily unlikely. So it's the same with these deaths. You have to say two unlikely events have happened and together it's very, very, very unlikely.[178]

An appeal against the murder conviction was taken on the basis that the presentation of Sir Roy's evidence was seriously flawed. It failed. Although the Court of Appeal found flaws in the reasoning of Professor Meadow, it classified the case against Sally Clark to be 'overwhelming' and declined to overturn the conviction.[179] However, a later appeal on other grounds, concerning prosecution non-disclosure of evidence, succeeded.[180] In the meantime Sally Clark's father complained to the General Medical Council (GMC) about the report and evidence of Professor Meadow. A Fitness to Practise Panel of the GMC found him to have engaged in serious misconduct and ordered his name erased from the Medical Register, observing:

> The Panel has heard expert statistical evidence (which it accepts) that the squaring of the 1:1000 ratio to conclude that there was 1 in a million incidence of double SIDS deaths within a family was incorrect. Furthermore you were unable to explain from where you derived these figures. You said in evidence before this Panel that you thought someone in the audience of a lecture you were giving had said this, and that you had remembered putting the figures 'on a blackboard somewhere', although you could not recall when and where. The Panel considered this explanation to be unacceptable, and the members were of the opinion that this highlighted your less than rigorous use of statistics and your inability to adhere to strict scientific principles in so doing.[181]

The Panel stated that Professor Meadow's eminence meant that he had a unique responsibility to take meticulous care in such a grave case and observed:

> Your misguided belief in the truth of your arguments, maintained throughout the period in question and indeed throughout the inquiry is both disturbing and serious.
>
> […]
>
> The Panel, having considered all those matters, has concluded that your errors, compounded by repetition, over a considerable period of time, constitutes such a serious departure from,

178 Ibid, [80].

179 *R v Clark* [2000] EWCA Crim 54; [2000] All ER (D) 1219, [255]: '[T]he evidence was overwhelming having regard to the identified similarities: a) the babies died at the same age; b) they were both found by the appellant and both, according to one version of the appellant, in a bouncy chair; c) they were found dead at almost exactly the same time of evening, having been well, having taken a feed successfully, and at a time when the appellant admitted tiredness in coping; d) on each occasion the appellant was alone with the baby when it was found lifeless; e) on each occasion the appellant's husband was away from home, or about to go away from home; f) in each case there was evidence of previous abuse: for Christopher an attempted smothering; for Harry an old rib fracture; g) in each case there was evidence of deliberate injury recently inflicted: for Christopher bruising and a torn frenulum; for Harry hypoxic damage, petechial haemorrhages in the eyelid and fresh bleedings of the spine and swelling of the spinal cord; h) the rarity of two natural deaths in one family with the first five features above present, and the extraordinary coincidence, if both deaths were natural, of finding evidence of old and recent abuse.'

180 *R v Clark* [2003] EWCA Crim 1020; [2003] All ER (D) 223 (Apr).

181 *Meadow v General Medical Council* [2006] EWHC 146 (Admin); [2006] 2 All ER 329, [52].

and falling short of, the standards expected of a registered medical practitioner, that it finds you guilty of serious professional misconduct.[182]

Professor Meadow defended his position without equivocation throughout his travails involving the GMC and even lodged a complaint with the Press Complaints Commission about an article in *The Times* in 2005 that said his evidence had 'led to the jailing of innocent people'.[183] *The Times* considered that the article was 'fair comment', and offered to print a response from Meadow; he declined the offer.[184] Meadow's complaint was rejected, as the Commission 'did not consider that the references to the complainant were inaccurate or misleading in breach of the Code'.[185]

Professor Meadow appealed the decision to the High Court where Collins J held that witness immunity extended beyond civil proceedings for negligence or defamation and covered:

> proceedings based on a complaint (whether or not it alleges bad faith or dishonesty) made by a party or any other person who may have been upset by the evidence given. Public policy... requires at least that. But I see no reason why the judge before whom the expert gives evidence... should not refer his conduct to the relevant disciplinary body if satisfied that his conduct has fallen so far below what is expected of him as to merit some disciplinary action.[186]

Collins J also held that, aside from the witness immunity threshold issue, Professor Meadow should not have been found to have engaged in serious professional misconduct: '[H]e made one mistake, which was to misunderstand and misinterpret the statistics. It was a mistake, as the Panel accepted, that was easily and widely made. It may be proper to have criticized him for not disclosing his lack of expertise, but that does not justify a finding of serious professional misconduct.'[187] He commented: 'It is difficult to think that the giving of honest albeit mistaken evidence could save in an exceptional case properly lead to such a finding.... [T]o say, as the FPP [Fitness to Practise Panel] did, that his conduct was "fundamentally incompatible with what is expected by the public from a registered medical practitioner" approaches the irrational.... I am satisfied that no more than the imposition of a condition not to engage in medico-legal work would have been appropriate.'[188] In truth, the finding itself was sufficient.

In turn, this decision was appealed by the GMC to the Court of Appeal[189] where an authoritative decision on the issue of witness immunity was handed down. Sir Anthony Clarke MR affirmed the articulation of principle as to the duties and responsibilities of expert witnesses by Cresswell J in *National Justice Cia Naviera SA v Prudential Assurance Co Ltd (The Ikarian Reefer)*:

> The duties and responsibilities of expert witnesses in civil cases include the following: (1) Expert evidence presented to the court should be, and should be seen to be, the

182 Ibid, [53]–[54].

183 Stephen Brook, 'Times's Verdict on Sir Roy Meadow Evidence was "Legitimate", says PCC', *The Guardian*, 8 January 2009: <http://www.theguardian.com/media/2009/jan/07/pcc-times-roy-meadow> [accessed 27 Dec 2015].

184 Ibid.

185 Press Complaints Commission, 'Complainant Name: Professor Sir Roy Meadow' (adjudication issued 18 December 2008): <http://www.pcc.org.uk/cases/adjudicated.html?article=NTQ2NA==> (viewed 14 February 2015). See also, Press Complaints Commission, 'PCC Rejects Complaint from Professor Sir Roy Meadow' (Press Release, 7 January 2009): <http://www.pcc.org.uk/newsarchive/index.html?article=NTQ2NQ==> [accessed 27 Dec 2015].

186 *Meadow v General Medical Council* [2006] EWHC 146 (Admin); [2006] 2 All ER 329, [22].

187 Ibid, [54].

188 Ibid, [56]–[58].

189 *Meadow v General Medical Council* [2006] EWCA Civ 1390; [2007] 1 QB 462.

> independent product of the expert uninfluenced as to form or content by the exigencies of litigation (*Whitehouse v Jordan* [1981] 1 WLR 246, 256, per Lord Wilberforce). (2) An expert witness should provide independent assistance to the court by way of objective unbiased opinion in relation to matters within his expertise (see *Polivitte Ltd v Commercial Union Assurance Co plc* [1987] 1 Lloyd's Rep 379, 386, per Garland J; *In re J (Child Abuse: Expert Evidence)* [1991] FCR 193, per Cazalet J). An expert witness in the High Court should never assume the role of an advocate. (3) An expert witness should state the facts or assumptions upon which his opinion is based. He should not omit to consider material facts which could detract from his concluded opinion (*In re J*). (4) An expert witness should make it clear when a particular question or issue falls outside his expertise. (5) If an expert's opinion is not properly researched because he considers that insufficient data is available, then this must be stated with an indication that the opinion is no more than a provisional one (*In re J*). In cases where an expert witness who has prepared a report could not assert that the report contained the truth, the whole truth and nothing but the truth without some qualification, that qualification should be stated in the report (*Derby & Co Ltd v Weldon, The Times*, 9 November 1990, per Staughton LJ). (6) If, after exchange of reports, an expert witness changes his view on a material matter having read the other side's expert's report or for any other reason, such change of view should be communicated (through legal representatives) to the other side without delay and when appropriate to the court. (7) Where expert evidence refers to photographs, plans, calculations, analyses, measurements, survey reports or other similar documents, these must be provided to the opposite party at the same time as the exchange of reports.[190]

Clarke MR noted that Creswell J added at the end of that quotation that, in addition to those considerations, the expert witness will know that he or she must give evidence honestly and in good faith and must not deliberately mislead the court. The expert cannot expect to receive protection if he or she is dishonest or malicious or deliberately misleading. Clarke MR observed that the purpose of disciplinary proceedings is not to punish a practitioner but to protect the public against the acts and omissions of those who are not fit to practise. Thus, the perspective is one that looks to the future:

> However, in order to form a view as to the fitness of a person to practise today, it is evident that it will have to take account of the way in which the person concerned has acted or failed to act in the past. It would to my mind be very striking, not to say astonishing, if the way in which an expert gave evidence or the content of that evidence showed that he was not fit to practise in a particular discipline, but the FPP could not consider it because the expert was immune from disciplinary proceedings by some absolute common law immunity. That would especially be so if the only evidence of unfitness to practise derived from evidence given in court.[191]

With Auld and Thorpe LJJ, he found the principle of witness immunity not to extend to disciplinary proceedings.[192]

In the ultimate result Clarke MR found Professor Meadow to have engaged in serious professional misconduct. Auld and Thorpe LJJ did not share this view, particularly taking into account the complexities and challenges of the courtroom environment for experts:

> All of this is not to absolve the expert of responsibility from professional or forensic impropriety in the presentation and form of his evidence. As a medical expert, he should know

[190] Ibid, [21], citing *The Ikarian Reefer* [1993] 2 Lloyd's Rep 68, 81–2.

[191] Ibid, [32].

[192] A similar approach has been taken in the United States, although it is not uniform: see eg *Austin v American Association of Neurological Surgeons*, 253 F3d 967 (2001); *Deatherage v State of Washington Examining Board of Psychology*, 948 P2d 828 (Sup Ct of Washington 1997); cp *In re Lustgarten*, 177 NCApp 663, 629 SE 2d 886 NCApp (2006).

> his limits. In most instances, his knowledge and instincts in his particular field should alert him to confining his evidence to those limits and the true issues identified for the court by the legal representatives of the parties. However, the forensic process, in preparation and in action at trial, is not always as ordered and considered as it should be. The issues may not always be sufficiently carefully defined, or the evidence, lay and expert, adequately prepared and tailored in advance, to deal with them. The trial process itself can be unpredictable in direction. From time to time the questioners and the questioned can lose sight of the essential issues in exploring or 'trying out for size' areas of evidence that, on careful examination, have no bearing on the case. The line and pace of the questioning may leave little time for calm analysis by an expert witness called to deal with a variety of issues on one or more of which he is required to express an opinion that is, or he knows is, to be, challenged. The same may be said for those questioning him and, indeed for the judge who is trying to keep up with the evidence as it is given. In that, sometimes, fevered process, mistakes can be made, ill-considered assertions volunteered or analogies drawn by the most seasoned court performers, whatever their role.[193]

Auld LJ observed that the misconduct of Professor Meadow was not insignificant: although not an expert in the use of statistics or calculation of probability, Professor Meadow had promulgated before the jury a theory of improbability of recurrence of unexplained and seemingly natural infant deaths, applicable only where recurrence occurred in familial, environmental and economic circumstances wholly independent of those of a first such death:

> In doing so, he relied initially on statistical figures of uncertain source and scientific validity...which had nothing to do with the probabilities of recurrence in any individual case, and which, in any event, he misunderstood and, by implication and the use of an inappropriate analogy, misapplied. In addition, and importantly, he did not expressly draw the court's attention to the fact that he had no expertise in the field of statistics or calculations of probability in this or any other field.[194]

Both Auld and Thorpe LJJ took into account the absence of intention on the part of Professor Meadow to deceive the court. The Law Lords agreed that it was not proper to treat Professor Meadow more harshly because of his eminence.

Post-Meadow Decisions

The ramifications of the Court of Appeal's decision in relation to Professor Meadow are significant for many categories of scholars, whether they are in private practice or principally employed in academia. They render those who are subject to a regulated form of professional registration amenable to discipline.

In Australia this includes:

- lawyers
- medical practitioners
- dental practitioners
- pharmacists
- psychologists
- nurses and midwives
- Chinese medicine practitioners (including acupuncturists)
- occupational therapists
- physiotherapists
- chiropractors

[193] *Meadow v General Medical Council* [2006] EWCA Civ 1390; [2007] 1 QB 462, [207].
[194] Ibid, [210].

- osteopaths
- podiatrists
- optometrists
- medical radiation practitioners, and
- Aboriginal and Torres Strait Island health practitioners.

In other countries, such as New Zealand,[195] England,[196] and Canada,[197] a variety of health and other practitioners also have registered status. It is likely that more health practitioners, such as naturopaths and speech therapists, in due course will join this number in Australia. Other professionals, such as dieticians, masseurs, social workers, psychotherapists, and counsellors may at some point be incorporated into the legislative scheme. Others, such as homoeopaths,[198] iridologists, and Reiki practitioners, are unlikely to be incorporated into statutory regulatory schemes because of contentious issues in respect of the scientific base for their views. Importantly, professionals who commonly give evidence in the courts (such as accountants, auditors, engineers and forensic scientists) are not affected by the decision.

For those categories of practitioners who are subject to formal disciplinary proceedings convened by statutorily created tribunals, the observation by Clarke MR in *General Medical Council v Meadow* constitutes a useful form of guidance:

> [A]n expert should only give evidence of opinion which is within his particular expertise and that, where a statement, whether made in writing or orally, is outside his expertise, he should expressly say so. If, for example, it depends upon work done or opinions expressed by others, that work or those opinions should be identified in the statement, so that their validity can be ascertained by the parties to the proceedings or by the court. All reasonable attempts should be made check to the validity of an opinion which is not within the expert's expertise. These are simple precautions which should be taken by experts because of the risk that the opinion might be wrong, with what may be very serious consequences. This seems to me to be of particular importance in a serious criminal matter such as the trial of a defendant for murder.[199]

The challenging issues that arise, though, are as to the extent to which the disciplinary jurisdiction will intervene to regulate the forensic work of health practitioners, and also how effective it will be in improving the quality of such work, or at least in avoiding substandard and dangerous conduct by forensic practitioners.

A number of cases after *Meadow* have given an early indication of how the Fitness to Practise Panels of the GMC will apply their jurisdiction to discipline medical practitioners for forensic work.[200] They can be divided into cases responding to unprofessional conduct in

[195] See Medical Council of New Zealand, 'Health Professional Regulatory Bodies': <https://www.mcnz.org.nz/fitness-to-practise/making-a-complaint/health-professional-regulatory-bodies/> [accessed 27 Dec 2015] incorporating dieticians and psychotherapists.

[196] See General Medical Council (UK), *Who Regulates Health and Social Care Professionals?*: <http://www.gmc-uk.org/Who_regulates_health_and_social_care_professionals___English_1112.pdf_50487974.PDF> [accessed 27 Dec 2015].

[197] The situation is not uniform throughout the Canadian provinces; for Ontario, see 'Which Professions are Regulated in Ontario?' Settlement.Org: <http://settlement.org/ontario/employment/professions-and-trades/regulated/which-professions-are-regulated-in-ontario/> [accessed 27 Dec 2015].

[198] See Ian Freckelton, 'Death by Homœopathy: Issues for Civil, Criminal and Coronial Law and for Health Service Policy' (2012) 19(3) *Journal of Law and Medicine* 454; Ian Freckelton, 'The Medico-Scientific Marginalisation of Homeopathy: International Legal and Regulatory Developments' (2015) 23(1) *Journal of Law and Medicine* 7.

[199] *Meadow v General Medical Council* [2006] EWCA Civ 1390; [2007] 1 QB 462, [71].

[200] See Ian Freckelton, 'Expert Evidence Accountability: New Developments and Challenges' (2011) 19(2) *Journal of Law and Medicine* 209.

forensic assessments, and unprofessional expression of opinions in both reports and oral evidence in courts and tribunals.

A category of work done in the forensic context is assessment of persons who allege that they have been injured—as a result of criminal assaults or as a result of workplace, transport, or other actionable scenarios. It is foreseeable that such assessments will be relied on by prosecutorial authorities or the defence in criminal actions, by parties determining the course of civil action, and by courts and tribunals called upon to adjudicate on allegations in the criminal and civil context.

In a number of cases since *Meadow*, allegations have been made and determined by disciplinary tribunals in relation to the conduct of forensic assessments.

Dr Southall. A curious concomitant to the *Meadow* saga was an appeal that also came before Collins J and also involved the conviction of Sally Clark. In 2000 a Channel 4 television programme was directed towards the case of Sally Clark. It contained a lengthy interview with her husband. Dr David Southall was a consultant at the North Stafford National Health Trust at Stoke-on-Trent, and a Professor of Paediatrics at the University of Keele. Knowing nothing otherwise about the case, he formed the firm view that there had been an attempt to suffocate one of Ms Clark's children and that her husband had been responsible for the attempt and for the child's ultimate death.

Dr Southall communicated his views to the Child Protection Unit at Staffordshire and ultimately wrote a report, urging a review of the evidence with an aim of assessing the involvement of Mr Clark in the deaths. His conduct was the subject of a complaint to a Professional Conduct Committee of the GMC which found him guilty of serious professional misconduct and directed him to abstain from any child protection work for a period of three years. On appeal, Collins J affirmed the decision of the Committee, only making minor adjustments to the conditions imposed by the Committee.[201]

Dr Oelofse. In a number of decisions of Fitness to Practise Panels adverse findings have been made in relation to negligent conduct of forensic medical examinations. In *Re Oelofse*,[202] for instance, an examiner was found to have conducted an incompetent examination of a person who claimed to have been assaulted. He neither conducted a physical examination of her nor assessed her mental state nor obtained a medical history from her. This did not inhibit his preparedness to express views about the aetiology of the presence of bruising on her body which he attributed at first to long-term abuse, but later simply to scarring. On the basis of the practitioner's inexperience and the difficulties of the work that he was called on, perhaps prematurely, to undertake, a Fitness to Practise Panel of the GMC ultimately declined to find that he had engaged in misconduct.

Dr Patel. The effectiveness of disciplinary hearings into specific instances of inadequate or problematic conduct arose pointedly in respect of a sequence of decisions in relation to Dr Freddy Patel, a prominent English forensic pathologist. Fitness to Practise Panels made multiple adverse findings about the work of Dr Patel. He was found to have failed to record suspicious marks on the body of a five-year-old child in 2002, requiring her remains to be disinterred. The Panel observed: 'You did not make appropriate or adequate comment about them…You implied that there were marks of violence without remarking on whether or not they had a bearing on her death. Had you allowed your suspicions greater scope, then the

[201] *Council for the Regulation of Healthcare Professionals v General Medical Council* [2005] EWHC 579 (Admin); [2005] All ER (D) 169 (Apr).

[202] *Re Oelofse* (unreported, GMC Fitness to Practise Panel, 10 December 2010).

exhumation of a child and the attendant potential distress might have been avoided... Your acts and omissions represented deficient professional performance.'[203] Then in relation to the cot death of a baby in 2003 a Panel found that his failure to obtain a full skeletal X-ray before he undertook an examination amounted to misconduct: 'You deliberately ignored the guidelines so as to carry out the postmortem examination simply at a time of your own convenience, and very shortly before radiographers would have been readily available. Your failure to abide by the guidance [was] casual and incautious.'[204] Next, a Panel found that, during his autopsy on a woman in 2005, Patel abandoned standard procedures and forgot to weigh the deceased's main internal organs. The Panel commented that: 'There were good reasons for adhering to that guidance, and no good reasons for not doing so.'[205] He was also found to have altered his findings in respect to the causes of death: 'You told the inquest that you made the change "simply to satisfy the family"... It is clearly fundamental to the wider public interest that forensic pathologists should be scrupulous in discharging their obligations to the court. Indeed it is central to their function. They must not set aside their professional judgment for any of the parties involved during or after a postmortem examination for reasons of expediency or anything else.' The Panel concluded that Patel's misleading evidence amounted to misconduct.[206] He was suspended from practice for three months.

After a second examination by another pathologist, he prepared an addendum to his report, changing the cause of death to a brain haemorrhage in line with the new findings. The Panel chairman, Richard Davies, said Dr Patel's assumption that, as the death was not suspicious, the change made no difference from the coroner's viewpoint and merely allowed an inquest to proceed, was not adequate by way of an explanation.

The problems continued in terms of the quality of Dr Patel's work. A Panel in *Re Patel*[207] found the conduct of a postmortem examination on a prostitute at the instructions of the Coroner for Inner North London to have been irresponsible and not of the standard of a competent forensic pathologist when undertaking such a role. It noted Dr Patel's failure to swab a prominent bite mark and was critical of the content of three forensic reports written by the pathologist in which he failed to explain the absence of petechiae on the deceased, the potential significance of this, the distribution of hypostasis, and other potential causes of injury that he identified. It suspended him from practice for four months. Dr Patel decided that the victim had died of natural causes despite blood staining her clothing, bedding, and on a wall. Patel said she had died of a heart attack during consensual sex. This discouraged a police investigation that might have saved two later victims of the assailant, according to evidence given at his hearing.[208]

In 2012 a further disciplinary hearing was convened into whether Dr Patel was guilty of professional misconduct following the acquittal of policeman Simon Harwood who had been accused of killing the newspaper seller, Ian Tomlinson, during the 2009 G20 protests in London. Tomlinson died after he became caught up in the G20 protests in the City of London as he tried to get home and was pushed over by Mr Harwood. Patel carried out the postmortem on Tomlinson and concluded that he died from a heart attack. However, the

[203] Owen Bowcott, 'Pathologist in G20 Death Case Found Guilty of Misconduct', *The Guardian*, 31 August 2010: <http://www.theguardian.com/uk/2010/aug/31/g20-pathologist-gmc-panel?guni=Article:in%20body%20link&guni=Article:in%20body%20link> [accessed 27 Dec 2015].

[204] Ibid.

[205] Ibid.

[206] Ibid.

[207] *Re Patel* (unreported, GMC Fitness to Practise Panel, 31 March 2011).

[208] James Meikle, 'G20 Pathologist Freddy Patel Suspended', *The Guardian*, 31 March 2011: <http://www.theguardian.com/uk/2011/mar/31/g20-pathologist-freddy-patel-suspended> [accessed 27 Dec 2015].

correctness of his findings came into question after concerns were raised when an American tourist came forward who had taken a video recording of what occurred with police constable Harwood. Later medical reports suggested that Tomlinson died from an injury to his liver that caused internal bleeding and then cardiac arrest.

At the inquest into Tomlinson's death, Dr Patel's claim that he died of a heart attack was discredited and the jury accepted experts who concluded that Tomlinson died from internal bleeding.

The Rev Robert Lloyd-Richards, the chairman of the Medical Practitioners Tribunal Service (the MPTS) Fitness to Practise Panel, which heard the case, found that Dr Patel had an 'unwarranted confidence' in his ability, 'a deep-seated attitudinal problem', and also 'lacked insight'.[209] The MPTS concluded: 'Your rigid mind-set, illustrated by your inability to reflect on the case of Mr Tomlinson, and your unwarranted confidence in your own abilities, does not convince this panel that it would be appropriate to impose conditions, even with the most stringent supervision, on your registration.'[210] It found that Dr Patel had tried to cover up his mistakes both in relation to Tomlinson and also to an earlier postmortem. It removed his name from the medical register.

As in many cases that involve evaluations of errors in practice, those involving Dr Patel evidence a disinclination on the part of the General Medical Council panels for a lengthy period to be overly censorious in relation to mistakes that he made in his conduct of examinations and the views that he formed. It took the Tomlinson prosecution, which was very high profile, and the fact that it was the last in a sequence of errors over a number of years, to persuade a panel that the ultimate sanction—erasure of his name from the medical register—should be employed. Thus, the comparative leniency of the suspensions from practice is not so much attributable to the fact that his work was forensic as to the fact that regulatory tribunals in all jurisdictions tend to extend some element of understanding to practitioners whose deficits are neither malicious nor wilful, but the product of errors in professional judgment. However, by the time of the allegations arising out of the Tomlinson case, the point had been reached where the only inference to be drawn was that Dr Patel's competence to practise was so impaired that his name could not be allowed to remain on the medical register.

Dr Oshinyemi. A number of cases have also dealt with inadequate conduct of forensic examinations of living persons.[211] For instance, a Fitness to Practise Panel heard allegations in *Re Oshinyemi*[212] that a practitioner, when conducting an examination in a murder investigation, failed to conduct a proper examination and to generate accurate and contemporaneous notes of his examination. The Panel found that Dr Oshinyemi was impaired by reason of his misconduct and imposed conditions on his registration.

Dr Kumar. In *Re Kumar*[213] the issue in contention related to the legitimacy of a forensic report dealing with a controversial psychiatric disorder. A Fitness to Practise Panel heard that

---

209 Sarah Boseley, 'Ian Tomlinson Pathologist Freddy Patel Struck Off', *The Guardian*, 23 August 2012: <http://www.theguardian.com/uk/2012/aug/23/tomlinson-pathologist-freddy-patel-struck-off> [accessed 27 Dec 2015].

210 Ibid.

211 See, for example, the GMC's decisions concerning: the conduct of forensic examinations (General Medical Council, 'Fitness to Practise Determination', <http://www.gmc-uk.org/337.pdf_37405758.pdf> [accessed 27 Dec 2015]; the lack of confidentiality in relation to such examinations (General Medical Council, 'Fitness to Practise Determination'); and, dishonesty in the conduct of such examinations (General Medical Council, 'Fitness to Practise Determination').

212 *Re Oshinyemi* (unreported, GMC Fitness to Practise Panel, 30 April 2012).

213 *Re Kumar* (unreported, GMC Fitness to Practise Panel, 25 May 2011).

a consultant psychiatrist expressed views in a forensic report prepared for a murder case that the defendant was suffering from Intermittent Explosive Disorder and that he had had no intention of harming his victim. He had refrained from explaining that such a diagnosis was not to be found in the World Health Organization's International Classification of Diseases (ICD-10) and that the defendant's aggressive episodes did not satisfy the requirements in the formulation in the American Psychiatric Association's Diagnostic and Statistical Manual of Mental Disorders (DSM-IV). It found in a variety of respects that the methodology employed by Dr Kumar was significantly defective and that his actions were reckless, misleading, and below the standard of a reasonably competent psychiatrist acting as an expert witness. This had the consequence that his fitness to practise was impaired by his misconduct. In suspending him for four months, it commented that his role as a forensic expert had been seriously compromised, to the potential detriment of the criminal justice process:

> [Y]ou included in your diagnosis criteria that did not fit with the accepted diagnosis of IED, indeed, some were explicitly excluded. Your diagnosis was controversial and the basis of this controversial diagnosis was in itself flawed because the diagnostic criteria had not been met. The central issue in the criminal trial was the state of mind of the accused and whether he had the necessary criminal intent for murder or not. You advanced an opinion that was outwith your area of expertise and, despite the criteria for a controversial diagnosis not being met, you did not pause to consider… that your opinion might be wrong and if relied upon and accepted in a criminal process could have very serious consequences. The Panel is of the view that you became an advocate for the defence of 'diminished responsibility' rather than an independent expert dealing with the limited information you had critically and objectively for the assistance of the court.

Dr Pool. In *Re Pool*[214] a Fitness to Practise Panel conducted an important hearing into the conduct of a psychiatrist, Dr Richard Pool. It found that he had prepared an expert psychiatric report at the request of solicitors for the Health Professions Council. The difficulty was that he did not make clear that he was not an expert in general adult psychiatry and in the report he failed to explain the reasons for his view that the paramedic the subject of the report was wholly and indefinitely impaired by reason of personality disorders and post-traumatic stress disorder. Dr Pool did not confine himself in the report to expressing opinions in areas in which he had expert knowledge and which fell within his areas of competence. In addition, at a hearing before the Health Professions Council the Panel found him not to have displayed an understanding of the role and responsibilities of an expert witness. The Council concluded that Dr Pool was not an expert in personality disorders and declined to receive his evidence. This led to Dr Pool being referred to the General Medical Council.

The Fitness to Practise Panel concluded that:

> [T]o put oneself forward as an expert witness requires more than clinical experience and knowledge. It also requires the ability to produce an adequate report and to give oral evidence in an authoritative and convincing manner. This panel finds that your written report fell short of what is required and that your evidence at the HPC hearing regarding your experience and expert status was confusing and unclear. This panel does not consider that you conducted yourself at the HPC hearing as an expert witness should when giving evidence. In your evidence to this panel, you were also very unclear and often gave long, rambling, answers that did not address the question you had been asked. This panel concludes that, whilst you had some experience in General Psychiatry, you cannot be considered to be an expert.

---

[214] *Re Pool* (unreported, GMC Fitness to Practise Panel, 13 June 2014).

> [...]
>
> [Y]ou could not be considered an expert in General Adult Psychiatry for the purposes of giving evidence at a tribunal hearing. You do not treat patients within the community, as your practice is confined to working in a secure setting, and you do not have any recent experience of General Adult Psychiatry within the community at Consultant level. You have no direct experience of working with patients with personality disorders in the context of fitness to practise proceedings.[215]

The Panel rejected the explanation that it was the first time that Dr Pool had been asked to write such a report, accepting that 'there has to be a first time for everyone', but finding that there was no excuse for his undertaking the forensic assessment when he did not have the relevant knowledge or experience to assess fitness to practise.[216] It rejected the psychiatrist's explanation for having given rambling answers when asked at the Council hearing to explain the role of an expert when he said he was disorientated by the question and concluded: 'An expert witness must expect to be questioned closely and be subject to robust examination. As an expert at a tribunal hearing, you had a duty to explain your role and your inability to do so was a significant failure on your part.'[217]

The Panel concluded:

> In your report you gave opinions that were not appropriately reasoned and your explanation of the role of an expert before the HPC was unclear and confused. There is clearly a strong public interest in ensuring that doctors do not act outside their competence and do not put themselves forward as experts in areas in which they do not have adequate knowledge and expertise. In addition, your actions could have had drastic consequences for Ms A in that she could have lost her professional registration and career as a paramedic.[218]

It found Dr Pool to continue to exhibit lack of insight and reflectiveness on the issues. It was troubled by the potential for him to repeat the conduct and found his fitness to practise to be impaired by reason of his misconduct. It accepted that he was a 'good clinician'[219] but suspended him from practice for three months. The decision constitutes a robust decision about the significance of departure from responsibilities in the forensic role. It appears that the intransigence of the practitioner played a role in its decision to impose the deterrent consequence of a suspension from practice but, given the absence of mala fides on the part of the practitioner, and his inexperience in the forensic domain, it was harsh in both its language and its determination. It evidences an inclination on the part of panels of the General Medical Council to insist upon a sound and conservative performance of forensic responsibilities, given the significance of expert reports and evidence for courts and tribunals.

Dr Squier. In *A Local Authority v S*,[220] a case involving an application for a care order, King J found that the paediatric neuropathologist and an honorary clinical lecturer at Oxford University, Dr Waney Squier, was 'disingenuous'[221] and had developed a 'scientific prejudice'[222] in relation to shaken baby syndrome cases. This led King J to conclude that 'Dr Squier

[215] Ibid, [52], [56].
[216] Ibid, [57].
[217] Ibid, [59].
[218] Ibid, [74].
[219] Ibid, [76].
[220] [2009] EWHC 2115 (Fam).
[221] Ibid, [227].
[222] Ibid, [285].

has permitted her convictions to lead her analysis.'[223] Subsequent to this finding, a complaint was filed by the National Policing Improvement Agency to the General Medical Council which commenced disciplinary proceedings, alleging that the expert 'failed to discharge her duties as an expert in that she failed to work within the limits of her competence, to be objective and unbiased, and to pay due regard to the views of other experts';[224] that her actions as an expert witness were 'deliberately misleading, dishonest, and brought the reputation of the medical profession into disrepute';[225] and that she 'provided an expert opinion evidence by way of written report and/or oral evidence outside her field of expertise.'[226] The case has not yet been heard at the date of writing. Dr Squier, has been reported as stating that she will be refuting the criticisms at hearing, and that the case she faces 'demonstrates the risk to which an expert is exposed when they express an opinion to the courts', and that there is a 'wider public interest in experts being able to give honestly held and scientifically based opinion which is not the conventional or mainstream view.'[227]

The Trajectory of the Decisions. Although only a modest amount of time has passed since the *Meadow* decision, a number of observations can be made. It is apparent that regulators experience difficulties in assessing the level of culpability of practitioners who undertake forensic assessments for courts and tribunals and make errors in judgment. However, this is a difficulty experienced generally with regulation in respect of diagnostic and procedural error; arguably it is a good reason for viewing such matters by reference to performance rather than conduct. In respect of the provision of reports and the giving of evidence, there have been decisions, such as *Kumar* and *Pool*, where a strong position has been taken requiring rigorous assistance to both an evidence base and the exercise of care, skill and judgment in the forensic domain, comparable at least to that in the clinical domain. This emphasizes the importance being attached to the discharge of the forensic role and the need for scholars, who are registered health practitioners, to be scrupulous in this aspect of their work.

Another Consequence of the Meadow Decision. A further outcome from the controversies ensuing from the disciplinary proceedings involving Professor Sir Roy Meadow, as well as a series of other concerning cases involving scientific and medical evidence, was the commissioning of the Law Commission of England and Wales to inquire into the role of expert evidence in criminal proceedings. The Commission's report[228] recommended that there should be a new reliability-based admissibility test for expert evidence in criminal proceedings. It noted that there would not be a need for the test to be applied routinely or unnecessarily, but it would be applied in appropriate cases with the aim of excluding unreliable expert opinion evidence. Under the test, expert opinion evidence would not be admitted unless it was adjudged to be sufficiently reliable to go before a jury; accordingly, juries would be less likely to reach their conclusions on unreliable evidence and there would be fewer miscarriages of justice, thereby leading to enhanced public confidence in the criminal justice system. The Commission published a draft Criminal Evidence (Experts) Bill which set out the admissibility test that judges would apply to exclude unreliable expert evidence.

---

223 Ibid.

224 Clare Dyer, 'Child Death Expert is Accused of Dishonesty and Failing to Work Within Competence' (2014) 349 *The BMJ* g5669.

225 Ibid.

226 Ibid.

227 Ibid. See also, Waney Squier, '…The Uncomfortable Interface Between Medicine, Science and the Law…' (2011) 17(1) *Clinical Risk* 3.

228 Law Commission of England and Wales, *Expert Evidence in Criminal Proceedings* (Report No 325) (London: The Stationery Office, 2011): <http://lawcommission.justice.gov.uk/docs/lc325_Expert_Evidence_Report.pdf> [accessed 27 Dec 2015].

The recommendations in the report and the provisions in the Bill had as their aim to establish a framework in criminal proceedings for screening expert evidence at the admissibility stage, and thereby to exclude unreliable evidence of the kind given by Professor Meadow. Another aspiration of the bill was to encourage higher standards amongst expert witnesses, and the specialists on whom they rely, resulting in expert evidence of greater reliability being tendered for admission. However, while the proposals have not been implemented directly in legislation after the government did not support them,[229] Part 33 of the Criminal Procedure Rules,[230] which came into force on 14 October 2014, and Practice Direction 33A[231] go a significant way toward implanting them.[232]

The Canadian Approach

A similar approach to that adopted in the United Kingdom has been taken by Canadian disciplinary tribunals. Most notably a disciplinary panel of the Ontario College of Physicians and Surgeons revoked the licence of the pathologist, Charles Smith, who had been found by an inquiry conducted by Justice Stephen Goudge to have made multiple errors in his conduct of autopsies. Smith had been appointed director of a paediatric forensic pathology unit at the Toronto Hospital for Sick Children in 1992. He worked there conducting autopsies between 1981 and 2005. In the succeeding years he conducted high numbers of autopsies and was principally responsible for the investigation of suspicious child deaths in Ontario.

In 2002 Dr Smith was reprimanded by the Ontario College of Physicians and Surgeons for his work on suspicious death cases and the next year he was precluded from performing autopsies. In 2005 the Chief Coroner of Ontario, Dr Barry McLellan, ordered a review of 44 autopsies carried out by Dr Smith, 13 of which had resulted in convictions for criminal offences. The report from the review which was released in 2007 showed serious problems in 20 cases, in 12 of which there had been findings of guilt by the courts. This resulted in the appointment of Justice Goudge to conduct an inquiry into the state of paediatric forensic pathology in Ontario. Before the inquiry Dr Smith apologized for his errors.

The report identified a range of systemic failings, including multiple defects in the autopsies conducted by Dr Smith. Justice Goudge found that Dr Smith lacked basic knowledge about the highly specialized area of forensic pathology and that, although '[t]he expert must be aware of the limits of his or her expertise, stay within them, and not exaggerate them to the court', Dr Smith did not observe these fundamental rules.[233]

Justice Goudge found that:

> [Dr Smith] almost never attended the death scene. He did not always ensure that he had all the relevant medical information before he conducted an autopsy. He was sloppy and inconsistent in documenting the information he did receive. He was indiscriminate in accepting

---

229 Ministry of Justice. *The Government's Response to the Law Commission's Report: Expert Evidence in Criminal Proceedings in England and Wales*, (Law Com No. 325, 21 November 2013), p. 4, <https://www.gov.uk/government/uploads/system/uploads/attachment_data/file/260369/govt-resp-experts-evidence.pdf> [accessed 27 Dec 2015].

230 <http://www.justice.gov.uk/courts/procedure-rules/criminal/docs/crim-proc-rules-2014-part-33.pdf?_ga=1.223018648.2035485837.1446432384> [accessed 27 Dec 2015].

231 <https://www.judiciary.gov.uk/wp-content/uploads/2014/07/Criminal-Practice-Directions-Amendment-No-2.pdf> [accessed 27 Dec 2015].

232 See Freckelton, Goodman-Delahunty, Horan, and McKimmie, 2016, n 16.

233 Stephen Goudge, *Inquiry into Pediatric Forensic Pathology in Ontario*, vol 1 (Ontario: Queen's Printer for Ontario, 2008) 14: <http://www.attorneygeneral.jus.gov.on.ca/inquiries/goudge/report/v1_en_pdf/Vol_1_Eng.pdf> [accessed 27 Dec 2015].

> and appearing to rely on information about the social history of those allegedly involved with the death. Autopsies were performed without the necessary relevant information, but with irrelevant information that left scientific conclusions skewed by unscientific considerations. In several cases, Dr Smith failed either to account for contradictory evidence in arriving at his opinion or to consider adjusting his opinion to take new information into account. These failures contributed to misdiagnoses with significant consequences.[234]

The judge found that Dr Smith failed to understand that his role was not to support the prosecution in criminal cases, he failed to prepare adequately for court, on occasions he misled courts by overstating his knowledge in particular areas, and on other occasions he generated risks of miscarriages of justice by giving inappropriately unscientific evidence. He also found that Dr Smith engaged in unwarranted criticism of fellow professionals, on occasion testified on matters outside his area of expertise (such as the profile of perpetrators of shaking and blunt head injuries), and also giving opinions that were speculative, unsubstantiated and not based on pathology findings. There were occasions when Dr Smith's evidence was loose and unscientific and, when he made statements to courts that lacked candour, and were false and misleading.

One of the most notorious examples of persons having their convictions overturned as a result of Dr Smith's forensic work was that of William Mullins-Johnson, who had been found guilty of the rape and murder of his four-year-old niece after testimony by Dr Smith, who was the only medical practitioner to conclude that the victim had been sexually assaulted. This contradicted the defence that the child who had a history of vomiting might have died of natural causes. When attempts were made to clear the name of Mullins-Johnson based on DNA technology, Dr Smith purported to be unable to locate the tissue samples from the deceased. However, in 2005, 11 years after the trial of Mullins-Johnson, the samples were located and a report that was subsequently commissioned determined there was no evidence that the child had been sexually assaulted. Williams-Johnson's conviction was overturned and he was awarded CA$4.25 million in compensation.

An important component of Justice Goudge's report was an acceptance that those who had oversight of Dr Smith's work, including prosecution and defence lawyers, failed in effectively fulfilling this role. In the context of identifying how such systemic deficits could be addressed in future, he reviewed the traits of character that affected Dr Smith's flawed practice. He noted that Dr Smith was candid before the inquiry in acknowledging how disorganized he was and admitted his arrogance and the dogmatic manner in which he often presented his opinions. Justice Goudge observed that these qualities were on display in many of the cases examined by the Inquiry: 'They made impossible the proper performance of the task required of him as an expert. As well, his deeply held belief in the evil of child abuse caused him to become too invested in many of these cases. As a result, the objectivity and self-discipline that must be the foundation of the expert's role proved to be beyond him.'[235] The judge rejected Dr Smith's defence that these failings were not intentional and emphasized Dr Smith's orchestrated attempts to frustrate oversight—he found him not to be above using deception to throw those in authority off the scent of effectively investigating his errors and flaws.

Justice Goudge observed that Dr Smith was a complex and multi-dimensional person, with positive, as well as negative, qualities:

> He was willing to take on difficult pediatric cases that his colleagues were not anxious to do. He has a sense of responsibility that led him to cooperate with the work of this Inquiry. In his evidence, he admitted many of his shortcomings that the evidence had laid bare. And,

[234] Ibid, 14.
[235] Ibid, 19.

> albeit much too late, he owned up to a great deal. In addition, the evidence is clear that others found him engaging, Support staff liked working with him, and many people found him a charismatic and effective speaker. As we now know, although he did so on the basis of terribly deficient training and fundamentally flawed practices, he appeared to be completely assured, and often certain, in circumstances where the science could not provide certainty. These sorts of qualities not only increased the risk he posed as an expert in the criminal justice system but tended to build an unwarranted trust in already lax overseers.
>
> Such an expert can do much damage without effective oversight by those who must provide it and constant vigilance on the part of the participants in the criminal justice system who can protect the system against flawed expert evidence. None of that happened here.[236]

An agreed statement of facts read to Dr Smith's disciplinary hearing said that he blamed others for his many mistakes, exaggerated his experience and offered opinions beyond his expertise. His opinions were described as 'overly dogmatic' and 'speculative' and the evidence that he gave as 'misleading'.[237] The College concluded that it was appropriate to terminate Dr Smith's registration as a medical practitioner. In doing it sent a message in relation to forensic pathology that has reverberated internationally.

The Australian Approach

The approach of Australian courts and disciplinary tribunals has been consistent with the approach of the English Court of Appeal in *Meadow*—both before and after. On a significant number of occasions disciplinary tribunals in Australia have exercised jurisdiction over health practitioners who are alleged to have conducted themselves unacceptably in a forensic setting.

For instance, the Psychologists Registration Board of Victoria determined on two occasions not to re-register a forensic psychologist, Timothy Watson-Munro,[238] on the basis he had become addicted to cocaine and, during his period of addiction, had purchased cocaine from the same solicitor who gave him forensic work, including in relation to offenders who were substance dependent. Mr Watson-Munro was a Visiting Fellow at Melbourne University and an Adjunct Professor at Bond University.

In essence, the issue that arose in respect of Mr Watson-Munro was an unusual form of conflict of interest. The Board took into particular account the especial responsibilities of expert witnesses who fulfil a forensic function:

> It is not appropriate for a direct parallel to be drawn between the expectations had of members of counsel and those entertained of psychologists. However, the qualities required by Dixon CJ of a member of counsel are pertinent to some degree: 'he should be able to command the confidence and respect of the court, of his fellow counsel and of his professional and lay clients'. Just as there is a delicate relationship between members of the Bar and the Bench, so there is a special relationship between the writer of forensic reports and the expert witness and the court. The role of the forensic expert carries the privilege, not extended to lay witnesses, entitling the expression of opinions. However, along with the privilege go especial obligations in relation to integrity, professionalism and the exercise of professional judgment.[239]

---

[236] Ibid, 20.

[237] 'Disgraced Pathologist Stripped of Medical Licence', *CTV News*, 1 February 2011: <http://www.ctvnews.ca/disgraced-pathologist-stripped-of-medical-licence-1.602739> [accessed 27 Dec 2015].

[238] *Re Watson-Munro* [2000] PRBD (Vic) 4; *Re Watson-Munro* [2002] PRBD (Vic) 2; *Re Watson-Munro* [2004] PRBD (Vic) 1.

[239] *Re Watson-Munro* [2000] PRBD (Vic) 4, [90] (footnotes omitted).

In addition, in *Re Noble*[240] the same Board found a psychologist to have engaged in unprofessional conduct on the basis of having signed an ill-researched report, written for him by a person related to a party in litigation before the Family Court, and on the basis of having breached responsibilities of confidentiality to a husband whom he had been counselling.

In *Mustac v Medical Board (WA)*[241] Simmonds J of the Western Australian Supreme Court dismissed an appeal from a decision of the Medical Board suspending a psychiatrist for six months for improper conduct in a professional respect for his use of a psychometric test (the Test of Memory Malingering) in forensic reports that he wrote for workers' compensation cases. The Board found that:

> [T]he conduct of the Practitioner amounts to a significant departure from the standards demanded of a consultant and forensic psychiatrist. To misuse a well-known and recognised scientific instrument developed for a specific purpose and then claim support for opinion expressed by reason of the reputation of that test is to engage in a serious breach of professional protocol. It is a matter of very significant concern. The misuse by the Practitioner of the TOMM [Test of Memory Malingering] is all the more concerning when considered in the light of the expressed role of the forensic psychiatrist asked to provide an independent medico-legal opinion. The potential damage to the subject of that opinion is enormous.[242]

Simmonds J did not disagree with these observations.

In relation to the matter of penalty, the Board observed:

> [T]he need to maintain the high standards and good reputation of the profession generally in the eyes of the community is a matter of priority. The trust which the general public does place in the professionalism of doctors is a vital component in the overall delivery of health care services to the community. When a person consults with or attends on a registered medical practitioner the reasonable assumption is made that the practitioner is conducting himself or herself in all respects in a professional manner and that he or she will continue to do so in their dealings with that person. When that consultation or attendance takes place in a forensic context with a view to the independent assessment by the doctor of the entitlement to financial redress for alleged personal injury the requirement that professional standards and reputation be maintained is all the more important. That the integrity of the medical profession be preserved in such circumstances is imperative. It must be remembered that the Board is concerned in this Inquiry with former patients who had no choice but to attend on the Practitioner—they did not attend on him voluntarily. The relevant insurers required that they subject themselves to his assessment of their psychiatric health and, it follows, their entitlement to financial aid for alleged personal injury. The former patients were entitled to expect that the Practitioner would comply with professional standards in the fair and responsible discharge of this important function. The relationship of trust and confidence between doctor and patient was founded on the assumption that he would do so. Doctors who do not conduct themselves in this manner are unable to discharge the obligations assumed by members of the profession. Forensic psychiatrists who behave as the Practitioner did in this case undermine significantly the confidence and respect the general public should be entitled to repose in the medical profession generally and psychiatrists specifically.[243]

Once again, Simmonds J found no error in the Board's analysis and upheld the period of suspension of the practitioner for six months. The Royal Australian and New Zealand College of Psychiatrists similarly suspended Dr Mustac's membership as a Fellow of the College.

240 [2002] PRBD (Vic) 6.
241 [2004] WASCA 156 (27 July 2004).
242 Quoted in *Mustac v Medical Board (WA)* [2004] WASCA 156, [107].
243 Ibid, [129].

In two cases involving a forensic pathologist, Dr James,[244] the South Australian Supreme Court adopted a similar approach to that in *Meadow*, holding in 2006 that:

> [P]ublic interest requires that someone who has given evidence, albeit that they are immune from suit insofar as the evidence given cannot be challenged in another process, should nevertheless be accountable to his or her professional peers when a member of the public makes a complaint of unprofessional conduct.[245]

And in 2008 it affirmed many of the statements of principle made by the Court of Appeal, including that:

> [A]n expert witness must give evidence honestly and in good faith and must not deliberately mislead the court. An expert giving evidence to the court has an obligation to the court to assist it by giving evidence objectively. That obligation includes making full disclosure of all relevant material no matter whether it assists or is detrimental to the cause of the client of the expert. That is because the obligation of the expert to the court overrides the obligation of the expert to the client.[246]

It is clear enough then that in Australia the conduct of scholars and practitioners who are registered as health practitioners will be amenable to disciplinary oversight by registration bodies and disciplinary tribunals.

A Further Encroachment on Witness Immunity: Civil Liability

Controversy about the ongoing relevance of the witness immunity rule continued after the decision of the Court of Appeal in relation to Professor Meadow. It came to a head with the decision of the Supreme Court of the United Kingdom in *Jones v Kaney*.[247]

A road traffic accident occurred in Liverpool in 2001. Jones was stationary on his motorcycle, waiting to turn at a road junction, when he was knocked down by a car driven by a man who was intoxicated, uninsured and driving while disqualified. Jones suffered significant physical injuries, but also mental harm in the form of post-traumatic stress disorder (PTSD), depression, an adjustment disorder, and associated illness behaviour which manifested itself in chronic pain syndrome.

Mr Jones instructed solicitors to act for him in personal injury proceedings. They consulted an orthopaedic surgeon who recommended that an opinion be obtained from a clinical psychologist. The solicitors commissioned Ms Kaney to examine Mr Jones and to prepare a report for the purposes of litigation. She did so and expressed the view, among other things, that the appellant was at that time suffering from PTSD. Mr Jones then issued proceedings against the driver and his insurer. Liability was promptly admitted, leaving the quantum of damages as the only issue in dispute.

The passage of time required a further examination of Mr Jones by Ms Kaney and a second report. On this occasion (about 18 months after the first report) she expressed the view that Mr Jones did not have all the symptoms to warrant a diagnosis of PTSD, but was still suffering from depression and some of the symptoms of PTSD.

---

[244] *James v Keogh* [2008] SASC 156; (2008) 101 SASR 42; *James v Medical Board (SA)* [2006] SASC 267; (2006) 95 SASR 445.

[245] *James v Medical Board (SA)* [2006] SASC 267; (2006) 95 SASR 445, [84].

[246] *James v Keogh* [2008] SASC 156; (2008) 101 SASR 42, [72].

[247] [2011] UKSC 13; [2011] 2 AC 398. See Freckelton, above n 151.

Those representing the driver and his insurer commissioned a psychiatrist, Dr El-Assra, also to examine Mr Jones and to provide a report. Dr El-Assra expressed the view that Mr Jones was exaggerating his physical symptoms.

In light of the manifest differences between the experts' views, the trial judge ordered the two experts to hold discussions and to prepare a joint statement. The discussion took place on the telephone. Dr El-Assra prepared a draft joint statement, which Ms Kaney signed without amendment or comment. The statement was somewhat surprising in that it recorded agreement that Mr Jones's psychological reaction to the accident was no more than an adjustment reaction that did not reach the level of a depressive disorder or PTSD. It further stated that Ms Kaney had found Mr Jones 'to be deceptive and deceitful in his reporting, and that the experts agreed that [Mr Jones's] behaviour was suggestive of "conscious mechanisms" that raised doubts as to whether his subjective reporting was genuine'.[248]

When Mr Jones's solicitors confronted Ms Kaney with the discrepancy between the joint report that she had signed and her earlier assessments, Ms Kaney stated that:

- She had not seen the reports of the opposing expert at the time of the telephone conference.
- The joint statement, as drafted by Dr El-Assra, did not reflect what she had agreed in the telephone conversation, but she had felt under some pressure in agreeing to it.
- Ms Kaney's true view was that Mr Jones had been evasive rather than deceptive.
- It was her view that Mr Jones did suffer PTSD which had resolved itself.
- She was happy for the joint statement to be amended accordingly.[249]

No doubt dissatisfied with the performance of Ms Kaney, those representing Mr Jones sought permission to change their expert, but were not permitted to do so by the trial judge. In light of that situation, the action by Mr Jones was then settled for what he asserted was an amount significantly less than the sum he would have received had not Ms Kaney signed the joint statement in the terms in which she did.

Mr Jones sued Ms Kaney in negligence. Her defence was the traditional doctrine of witness immunity but the issue of fundamental principle was only resolved by the United Kingdom's highest court, the Supreme Court.

The majority placed particular reliance on the fact that, in the United Kingdom[250] (as in New Zealand, by contrast with Australia[251]), barristers no longer enjoy immunity from negligence. It was argued on behalf of Ms Kaney that there were sound policy reasons for retaining the immunity—in particular, the risk that without it experts would be unprepared to undertake forensic work.

However, Lord Phillips (with Lord Kerr agreeing) observed that the immunity had been eroded by the decision of the Court of Appeal in relation to Professor Meadow and also in relation to 'wasted costs orders'.[252] He observed that, under court rules in the United Kingdom (as in Australia and New Zealand), it is the duty of an expert to provide assistance to a court in relation to matters within their expertise and that this duty overrides any obligation to the person from whom the experts have received their instructions or by whom they are

[248] Ibid, [8].
[249] Ibid, [9].
[250] *Arthur JS Hall & Co v Simons* [2002] 1 AC 615.
[251] *D'Orta-Ekenaike v Victoria Legal Aid* [2005] HCA 12; (2005) 223 CLR 1; *Giannarelli v Wraith* [1988] HCA 52; (1988) 165 CLR 543.
[252] *Jones v Kaney* [2011] UKSC 13; [2011] 2 AC 398, [44]; *Phillips v Symes (No 2)* [2004] EWHC 2330 (Ch); [2005] 1 WLR 2043, [80] (Peter Smith J).

paid: 'Such a distinction lends force to the argument that, once the expert is providing evidence to the court, or preparing to do so, he is no longer bound by a duty to his client and thus cannot be held liable for breach of such duty.... There is no longer any scope, if indeed there ever was, for contrasting the duty owed by an expert to his client with a different duty to the court, which replaces the former, once the witness gets into court.'[253] His Lordship concluded that the expert witness has in common with the advocate that each undertakes a duty to provide services to the client but that this includes a paramount duty to the court and the public, which may require the advocate or the witness to act in a way that does not advance the client's case:

> The advocate must disclose to the court authorities that are unfavourable to his client. The expert witness must give his evidence honestly, even if this involves concessions that are contrary to his client's interests. The expert witness has far more in common with the advocate than he does with the witness of fact.[254]

This led him to conclude that the starting point should be that the immunity should not exist unless a compelling public interest requires it. He noted that, at the 'Bond Solon Annual Expert Witness Conference' in November 2010, 106 experts were asked whether they would continue to act as expert witnesses if expert immunity from suit were substantially reduced. Ninety-two answered yes and 14 no. He stated that he did not consider that much weight could be attached to a survey of this type, but observed that 'it does not suggest that immunity from suit for negligence is essential to secure an adequate supply of forensic experts. The case that immunity is necessary to prevent a chilling effect on the supply of expert witnesses is not made out'.[255]

Lord Phillips concluded that inadequate data existed to determine whether the removal of immunity would have a significant effect, meaning that such prognostications 'must be a matter of conjecture or, more accurately, reasoning'.[256]

His Lordship observed that an expert's initial advice:

> is likely to be for the benefit of his client alone. It is on the basis of that advice that the client is likely to decide whether to proceed with his claim, or the terms on which to settle it. The question then arises of the expert's attitude if he subsequently forms the view, or is persuaded by the witness on the other side, that his initial advice was over-optimistic, or that there is some weakness in his client's case which he had not appreciated. His duty to the court is frankly to concede his change of view. The witness of integrity will do so. I can readily appreciate the possibility that some experts may not have that integrity. They will be reluctant to admit to the weakness in their client's case. They may be reluctant because of loyalty to the client and his team, or because of a disinclination to admit to having erred in the initial opinion.[257]

He questioned though whether any reluctance would be attributable to a fear of being sued for the opinion given to the court and expressed the view that there was a lesson to be learnt from the position of barristers. There had been a view that their immunity was necessary so that they would not be inhibited from performing their duty to the court. Yet, Lord Phillips commented: '[R]emoval of their immunity has not in my experience resulted in any diminution of the advocate's readiness to perform that duty. It would be quite wrong to perpetuate the immunity of expert witnesses out of mere conjecture that they will be reluctant to

[253] *Jones v Kaney* [2011] UKSC 13; [2011] 2 AC 398, [47], [49].
[254] Ibid, [50].
[255] Ibid, [54].
[256] Ibid, [56].
[257] Ibid.

perform their duty to the court if they are not immune from suit for breach of duty.'[258] This led him to conclude that there was no justification for continuing to hold expert witnesses immune from suit in relation to the evidence they give in court or for the views they express in anticipation of court proceedings. However, he emphasized that this conclusion did not extend to the absolute privilege they enjoy in respect of claims in defamation.

Lord Brown agreed that immunity for expert witnesses should be overturned but urged the courts 'to be alert to protect expert witnesses against specious claims by disappointed litigants—not to mention to stamp vigorously upon any sort of attempt to pressurize experts to adopt or alter opinions other than those genuinely held'.[259]

Lord Collins concurred, stressing that the case was dealing only with the ability to sue a 'friendly expert',[260] and that it did not impact at all on immunity from defamation proceedings. He held there no longer to be any policy reasons for retaining immunity from suit for professional negligence by expert witnesses:

> The danger of undesirable multiplicity of proceedings has been belied by the practical experience of the removal of immunity for barristers. A conscientious expert will not be deterred by the danger of civil action by a disappointed client, any more than the same expert will be deterred from providing services to any other client. It is no more (or less) credible that an expert will be deterred from giving evidence unfavourable to the client's interest by the threat of legal proceedings than the expert will be influenced by the hope of instructions in future cases. The practical reality is that, if the removal of immunity would have any effect at all on the process of preparation and presentation of expert evidence (which is not in any event likely), it would tend to ensure a greater degree of care in the preparation of the initial report or the joint report.[261]

Lord Hope and Lady Hale dissented, holding that the removal of witness immunity was a matter for the legislature.

The change in the law in respect of the liability of expert witnesses is an important development. It will require British experts to be scrupulous about their insurance status.[262] It renders them accountable in the same way that barristers already are in the United Kingdom for forensic work that falls below the standard of care reasonably expected of persons fulfilling such a role. At present it exposes experts to legal action brought by their own clients where their work has been negligent.[263] As yet it is probable that it does not expose experts to legal action brought by other persons, including by persons adversely affected by their conduct (such as Sally Clark or her husband) or the other party to litigation.[264] Nor does it expose experts to defamation action for expert reports or testimony.

It is likely in the short to medium term that experts in countries such as Australia will not be made liable for their forensic work in the way that they already are in the United Kingdom.[265]

[258] Ibid, [57].
[259] Ibid, [68].
[260] Ibid, [71].
[261] Ibid, [85].
[262] See David Shapiro, 'Expert Witnesses: Now Liable for Inexpert Evidence', 30 March 2011: <http://www.crownofficechambers.com/assets/docs/news/jones_v_kaney_article.pdf> [accessed 27 Dec 2015]. See also, Alec Samuels, 'Suing the Expert for Negligence?' (2012) 52(1) *Medicine, Science and the Law* 50.
[263] The fact that the principle is limited to 'friendly experts' was emphasized in *A and B v Hampshire Constabulary* [2012] EWHC 1517 (QB), [26].
[264] *Baxendale-Walker v Middleton* [2011] EWHC 998 (QB), [94].
[265] It remains to be seen whether *Jones v Kaney* will be followed in Ireland: see Irish Law Reform Commission, *Expert Evidence* (Consultation Paper No 52, 2008): <http://www.bailii.org/ie/other/IELRC/2008/cp52.pdf> [accessed 27 Dec 2015].

This gives significant ongoing protection to scholars who devote a portion of their time to doing forensic work. The situation in the United States is evolving, although a number of authorities have taken an approach comparable to that in *Jones v Kaney*, finding in certain circumstances that actions can be brought against friendly experts.[266] In substantial part the *Jones v Kaney* decision was based on precedents in relation to orders for costs thrown away that had been made in the United Kingdom and, more importantly, on the removal of barristers' immunity, a protection that has been advisedly and latterly retained by the Australian High Court.[267] This will give Australia, and countries such as Canada, an opportunity in due course to assess whether the concern raised by some about the disinclination of experts to undertake forensic work after the decision will prove to be correct.

For the present, the position in Australia is that immunity for expert reports and court testimony remains, save as to perjury. The decisions of the New South Wales Supreme Court in *Griffiths v Ballard*[268] and *Young v Hones (No 2)*,[269] and of the Court of Appeal in *Commonwealth v Griffiths*,[270] constitute modern affirmations of the extent of the witness immunity rule insofar as it applies to experts in Australia.[271]

In *Griffiths* the plaintiff was a qualified pharmacist who had practised as a chemist for some 20 years and was involved in preparatory work in the development of pharmaceuticals for potential sale within Australia and overseas. In 1999, the police seized chemical substances in the possession of the plaintiff and arrested him, took him into custody and laid charges against him, including charges of being knowingly concerned in the manufacture of the prohibited drug, methcathinone. The police gave the substances seized from the plaintiff for the purpose of testing them to the Australian Government Analytical Laboratories (AGAL), which conducted the Australian Forensic Drug Laboratory (AFDL), a business unit within the Analytical and Mapping Division of the Commonwealth Department of Industry, Tourism and Resources. In the course of the testing, false readings were generated and ultimately a certificate (purportedly pursuant to the terms of s 40 of the *Poisons and Therapeutic Goods Act* 1966 (NSW)) was provided by an employee pharmacist. That certificate, together with his oral evidence and other evidence, resulted in the wrongful conviction of Griffiths at trial. That conviction was overturned by the Court of Criminal Appeal.[272] In its judgment, Barr J (with whom Spigelman CJ and Bergin J agreed) stated that it was not open to the jury to be satisfied beyond a reasonable doubt that the chemical in question was, in fact, methcathinone.

---

266 See McHahey, n 164; Bal, n 164; Andrew Jurs, 'The Rationale for Expert Witness Immunity or Liability Exposure and Case Law Since *Briscoe*: Reasserting Immunity Protection for Friendly Expert Witnesses' (2007) 38 *University of Memphis Law Review* 49; Randall K Hanson, 'Witness Immunity Under Attack: Disarming "Hired Guns" (1996) 31 *Wake Forest Law Review* 497; Eric G Jensen, 'When "Hired Guns" Backfire: The Witness Immunity Doctrine and the Negligent Expert Witness,' (1993) 62 *University of Missouri Kansas City Law Review* 185; Steven Lubet, 'Expert Witnesses: Ethics and Professionalism' (1999) 12 *Georgia Journal of Legal Ethics* 465 (1999); Leslie R Masterson, 'Witness Immunity or Malpractice Liability for Professionals Hired as Experts?', (1998) 17 *Review of Litigation* 393; Michael T Nelson, '*Pace v Swerdlow*: Can Expert Witnsses Face Liability for Changing Their Minds?' (2009) 86(3) *Denver University Law Review* 1199.

267 *D'Orta-Ekenaike v Victoria Legal Aid* [2005] HCA 12; (2005) 223 CLR 1; *Giannarelli v Wraith* [1988] HCA 52; (1988) 165 CLR 543.

268 [2005] NSWSC 1350.

269 [2013] NSWSC 1429.

270 [2007] NSWCA 370; (2007) 70 NSWLR 268, [47].

271 Compare the unusual circumstances of *Smart v Forensic Science Service Ltd* [2013] EWCA Civ 783.

272 *R v Piggott, Griffiths and Simeon* [2002] NSWCCA 218.

However, when Griffiths sued the defendants civilly, the Court of Appeal was emphatic that the witness immunity rule precluded the pharmacist being sued by the plaintiff[273] and also held that the principle of vicarious immunity protected his employer.[274]

Costs Orders Arising from Forensic Misconduct

An option that has been adopted in a number of cases has been the ordering of costs against expert witnesses personally when their forensic conduct has been problematic and has engendered wastage of time and additional expenses being incurred by parties. It is also possible for a wasted costs order to be made against solicitors on the basis of gross deficiencies in expert reports or arising from their service or content.

In a number of decisions orders for wasted costs have been made or threatened by courts against both forensic experts and solicitors by reason of the unacceptable quality of experts' reports.

In *Phillips v Syme (No 2)*,[275] Smith J of the England and Wales High Court reviewed in detail the authorities on whether a third-party costs order could be made against an expert witness, taking into account that wasted costs orders against advocates had been decoupled from barristers' immunity. He concluded that in light of experts' obligations to the court, as set out in the court rules, 'it would be quite wrong of the court to remove from itself the power to make a costs order in appropriate [cases] against an Expert who, by his evidence, causes significant expense to be incurred, and does so in flagrant disregard of his duties to the Court'.[276] He did not regard other potential sanctions against an expert as 'being either effective or anything other than blunt instruments. The proper sanction is the ability to compensate a person who has suffered loss by reason of that evidence'.[277]

It was argued before Smith J that, should there be costs orders against experts, report-writers and witnesses would be inhibited from fulfilling their duties. He rejected this assertion, stating that he could:

> [not] believe that an expert would be deterred, because a costs order might be made against him in the event that his evidence is given recklessly in flagrant disregard for his duties. The high level of proof required to establish the breach cannot be ignored. The floodgates argument failed as regards lawyers and is often the court of last resort.
>
> [...]
>
> The idea that the witness should be immune from the most significant sanction that the Court could apply for that witness breaching his duties owed to the Court seems to me to be an affront to the sense of justice.[278]

In *Macquarie International Health Clinic Pty Ltd v Sydney Local Health District*,[279] Kunc J in Australia dealt with a related issue in civil proceedings that had become characterized by continued slippage in compliance with the timetable for the filing of expert reports by the plaintiff. He accepted that experts are dependent on the timely provision of instructions and information from the party commissioning them, but pointedly commented: '[T]he Court

273 *Commonwealth v Griffiths* [2007] NSWCA 370; (2007) 70 NSWLR 268, [94].
274 Ibid, [116].
275 [2004] EWHC 2330 (Ch); [2005] 1 WLR 2043.
276 Ibid, [95].
277 Ibid, [96].
278 Ibid, [96]–[98].
279 [2013] NSWSC 970.

wishes to make it clear that experts must understand that they themselves bear a direct responsibility to the Court for compliance with the Court's directions in relation to when their report is to be ready for filing and service and the form of the report itself.'[280] He emphasized that, by accepting a retainer to provide a report to a court, an expert becomes personally subject to a court's directions and that this extends to 'explaining why there has been non-compliance with any order of the Court in relation to the expert's report insofar as that non-compliance is the fault of the expert'.[281]

Kunc J indicated the inclination of the Supreme Court of New South Wales to require personal explanations from experts (rather than through a solicitor's affidavit) but also stated that 'experts could themselves be subject to costs orders insofar as any party to proceedings suffers additional costs by reason of the non-compliance with a direction as to the timely preparation of an expert's report where the reason for that non-compliance can be visited upon the expert'.[282] He observed that the court would not in general terms regard it as acceptable for experts to assert that they are unable to comply with court timetables because of the pressure of other business. It appears, therefore, that the law in the United Kingdom and the law in Australia are converging on the issue and that costs orders against experts may become part of the court landscape, or at least a spectre that may be invoked to encourage compliance with directions and orders.

In addition, in the 2013 decision of *Mengiste v Endowment Fund for Rehabilitation of Tigray*,[283] Smith J of the High Court of England and Wales sounded another warning by ordering costs against solicitors on the basis of arguments by the defendant that the solicitors should not have associated themselves with litigation based on reports by an expert that were particularly poor. It was apparent from the reports that the expert did not understand his duty to the court, and the reports were manifestly marked by inaccuracies, mischaracterizations, exaggerations, and inappropriate assertions of fact.

Oversight of Forensic Science in the United Kingdom

In the United Kingdom, the Runciman Royal Commission on Criminal Justice in 1993 identified a series of deficits in British forensic science, including a number of failures to disclose scientific tests and material for testing to the defence. It noted that 'the world of forensic science is a relatively closed one in which in many cases the leading experts are employed by the public sector laboratories' and called for processes of external audit.[284] However, this recommendation was not adopted.

In 1999, though, the Council for the Registration of Forensic Practitioners (CRFP) was established to give the courts a single point of reference on the competence of practitioners who practise in the forensic areas.[285] However, the process was voluntary and the majority of

---

280 Ibid, [4].

281 Ibid, [6].

282 Ibid, [7].

283 [2013] EWHC 1087 (Ch). See also *Hudspeth v Scholastic Cleaning and Consultancy Services Pty Ltd* (Ruling No 8) [2014] VSC 567.

284 *Report on The Royal Commission on Criminal Justice* (Cmd 2263, 1993) 150, available at: <https://www.gov.uk/government/publications/report-of-the-royal-commission-on-criminal-justice> [accessed 27 Dec 2015]. It recommended the creation of a forensic science advisory council to create codes of practice for forensic scientists and encourage the developments of centres of expertise in forensic science, including at tertiary institutions.

285 See Keith Hadley and Michael J Fereday, *Ensuring Competent Performance in Forensic Practice: Recovery, Analysis, Interpretation, and Reporting* (Boca Raton, FL: CRC Press, 2008) ch 5.

practitioners elected not to register or were ineligible to register.[286] Its funding was withdrawn by the police and its existence was only temporary.

Forensic science laboratories in the United Kingdom are accredited in a variety of ways. This includes assessment of practitioner competence by the United Kingdom Accreditation Service (UKAS).

In 2007, however, a Forensic Science Regulator was created in implementation of the government's response to the report, *Forensic Science on Trial*.[287] The role of the Regulator was described in a Ministerial Statement as:

> [T]o advise Government and the Criminal Justice System on quality standards in the provision of forensic science. This will involve identifying the requirement for new or improved quality standards; leading on the development of new standards where necessary; providing advice and guidance so that providers will be able to demonstrate compliance with common standards, for example, in procurement and in courts; ensuring that satisfactory arrangements exist to provide assurance and monitoring of the standards and reporting on quality standards generally.[288]

The Forensic Science Regulator is advised by the Forensic Science Advisory Council. The responsibilities of the Regulator are to:

- identify the requirement for new or improved quality standards;
- lead on the development of new standards
- where necessary, providing advice and guidance so that providers of forensic science services can demonstrate compliance with common standards.[289]

The former Regulator, Andrew Rennison,[290]outlined the regulator's priorities as seeing that:

- forensic science services are delivered to appropriate standards (usually an international standard) tailored to meet the needs of the criminal justice system and subject to independent and effective assessments of quality;
- high-quality advice and guidance are provided to forensic science providers, ministers and others on the forensic science requirements of the criminal justice system;
- there are effective means to investigate quality failures and to address any issues;
- there is effective collaboration with the authorities in Scotland and Northern Ireland to achieve UK-wide quality standards;
- the UK is a strong voice at the table on projects to develop European or international standards for forensic science.[291]

The Regulator has set up a Quality Standards Specialist Group,[292] a DNA Specialist Group, a Forensic Pathology Specialist Group, a Digital Forensics Specialist Group, a Contamination

---

[286] See 'Council for the Registration of Forensic Practitioners', HC Deb 11 May 2009, col 522W (Jacqui Smith): <http://www.publications.parliament.uk/pa/cm200809/cmhansrd/cm090511/text/90511w0005.htm> [accessed 28 Dec 2015].

[287] Science and Technology Committee, *Forensic Science on Trial* (HC 2004-05, 96-1): <http://www.publications.parliament.uk/pa/cm200405/cmselect/cmsctech/96/96i.pdf> (viewed 15 February 2015).

[288] 'Forensic Science Regulator', HC Deb 12 July 2007, col 67WS (Meg Hillier): <http://www.publications.parliament.uk/pa/cm200607/cmhansrd/cm070712/wmstext/70712m0002.htm#07071262000011> (viewed 15 February 2015).

[289] UK Government, Forensic Science Regulator, 'About Us—What We Do': <https://www.gov.uk/government/organisations/forensic-science-regulator/about> (viewed 15 February 2015).

[290] Dr Gillian Tully is the current Forensic Science Regulator having commenced a three-year term on 17 November 2014: UK Government, 'Appointment of New Forensic Science Regulator Announced', 17 July 2014: <https://www.gov.uk/government/news/appointment-of-new-forensic-science-regulator-announced> [accessed 28 Dec 2015].

[291] UK Government, Forensic Science Regulator, 'About Us—What We Do', above n 289.

[292] UK Government, Forensic Science Regulator, 'Terms of Reference for the Quality Standards Specialist Group', 14 January 2007: <https://www.gov.uk/government/uploads/system/uploads/attachment_data/file/118860/quality-sg-terms-of-ref.pdf> [accessed 28 Dec 2015].

Specialist Group, a Fingerprint Quality Standards Specialist Group, and a Medical Forensics Specialist Group.[293] A feature of the Forensic Science Regulator's role is that he is expected to investigate complaints or concerns raised as to the quality of forensic science supplied to United Kingdom criminal justice systems.

A complaint was made in 2013 to the Regulator about the performance of LGC Forensics in a murder case in respect of its approach to blood pattern analysis. The Regulator investigated the complaint and published a report on the issue which is publicly available (albeit in redacted form because of the criminal investigation being ongoing).[294] The Regulator concluded that the evidence did not establish that there was a quality failure related to the evidence of a particular witness or indicate any issues that would create a risk to the criminal justice system.[295]

Oversight of Forensic Science in the United States

Regulation of forensic science in the United States has come only a modest way from a low base. In 1989, around the time that DNA technology was being introduced, Eric Lander pronounced: 'At present, forensic science is virtually unregulated—with the paradoxical result that clinical laboratories must meet higher standards to be allowed to diagnose strep throat than forensic labs must meet to put a defendant on death row.'[296] The Centers for Medicare and Medicaid Services (CMS) regulate all laboratory testing performed through the Clinical Laboratory Improvement Act (CLIA). As of 2010 this covered over 189,000 laboratories[297] and incorporated maintenance of a quality assurance and control program by a laboratory; maintenance of appropriate records, equipment and facilities; personnel standards; and proficiency testing. While this is relatively limited as an effective check and balance, Jonakait has argued that it could constitute a basis for forensic science regulation. Garrett and Neufeld in 2009 maintained that, although many State and local crime laboratories voluntarily participate in the accreditation processes of the ASCLD/LAB,[298] a non-profit professional society of crime laboratory directors and forensic science managers, established in 1994, '[n]o legislation or oversight mechanisms regulate the quality of forensic science reports or testimony'.[299]

However, Koppl has argued that imposition of independence of forensic laboratories from law enforcement agencies is fundamental to meaningful accountability for forensic science in the United States. He has contended that substandard forensics result from unchecked power in forensic practitioners and argues for competitive self-regulation by facilitating competition between laboratories:

> As long as such a monopoly is enjoyed, the forensic worker has an incentive to shirk and to act on any biases he may have. To render power divided and contested, it is necessary to

---

[293] Forensic Science Regulator, *Business Plan* 2013/2014: <https://www.gov.uk/government/uploads/system/uploads/attachment_data/file/229450/fsr-business-plan-1314.pdf> [accessed 28 Dec 2015].

[294] Andrew Rennison, *Report: LGC Forensics—R v Mr A* (Forensic Science Regulator, No FSR-R-626, 1 August 2013): <https://www.gov.uk/government/uploads/system/uploads/attachment_data/file/266660/LGCForensicsReport.pdf> [accessed 28 Dec 2015].

[295] Ibid, [7.1.1].

[296] Eric S Lander, 'DNA Fingerprinting on Trial' (1989) 339(6225) *Nature* 501, 505. See also, Henry C Lee, 'Forensic Science and the Law' (1993) 25(4) *Connecticut Law Review* 1117, 1124; Samuel R Gross, 'Expert Evidence' (1991) Issue 6 *Wisconsin Law Review* 1113.

[297] Kelly Pyrek, *Forensic Science Under Siege: The Challenges of Forensic Laboratories and the Medico-Legal Investigation System* (Burlington, MA: Academic Press, 2007).

[298] American Society of Crime Laboratory Directors/Laboratory Accreditation Board, 'Accreditation Programs': <http://www.ascld-lab.org/acreditation-programs/> [accessed 28 Dec 2015].

[299] Garrett and Neufeld, above n 39, 93.

establish competition among forensic workers. Competitive self regulation would not, of course, magically cure all forensic ills. It would, however, induce significant improvements in the quality of forensic work.[300]

Koppl and Kobilinsky[301] have contended that the forensic science community must answer to high standards of professionalism, verifiability and scientific rigour in the face of multiple examples of such standards not having been met. They contend that forensic science administration needs to catch up to developments in forensic science technology so that it fills the knowledge void between the ambiguous intersection of advancing technology, evolving techniques, challenging human resources issues, and legal challenges to the admissibility of scientific evidence.

In 2009 the National Academy of Sciences Report[302] strongly criticized aspects of the way in forensic science functioned in the United States and recommended the creation of a National Institute of Forensic Science as an agency independent of law enforcement bodies and staffed by scientists. The recommendation was not adopted by the federal government.

However, at a time when the Annie Dookhan scandal was gathering momentum, in 2013 the Department of Justice and the National Institute of Standards and Technology (NIST), an agency of the United States Department of Commerce, announced the establishment of a National Commission on Forensic Science.[303] This constituted a partial implementation of the National Academy's recommendation. The NIST will be a 30-member commission, constituted by forensic scientists, researchers, prosecutors, defence attorneys, and judges. Part of its role will be to develop discipline-specific practice guidance for forensic science laboratories and to develop policy recommendations for the Attorney-General. An aim of its work will be to standardize national guidance for forensic science practitioners, as well as to develop uniform codes for professional responsibility and to establish requirements for training and certification. The announcement has generally been welcomed[304] but it is clear that it constitutes only a first step in setting standards and that it does not address a number of regulatory issues that arise out of particular instances of suspected laboratory deficiency and individual forensic misconduct.

Other developments are also under way. In September 2013 NIST invited input into the structure of guidance groups that would promote scientific validity and reliability in forensic science.[305] There have also been State initiatives. For instance, a Texas Forensic Science Commission was formed to look into forensic techniques used in convictions. In 2013, the

---

300 Roger Koppl, 'How to Improve Forensic Science' (2005) 20(3) *European Journal of Law and Economics* 255, 267.

301 Roger Koppl and Lawrence Kobilinsky, 'Forensic Science Administration: Toward a New Discipline' (November 2005): <http://alpha.fdu.edu/~koppl/fsa.doc> [accessed 28 Dec 2015].

302 Committee on Identifying the Needs of the Forensic Sciences Community, National Research Council, *Strengthening Forensic Science in the United States: A Path Forward* (Washington, DC: The National Academies Press, 2009): <https://www.ncjrs.gov/pdffiles1/nij/grants/228091.pdf> [accessed 28 Dec 2015].

303 Department of Justice, 'Department of Justice and National Institute of Standards and Technology Announce Launch of National Commission on Forensic Science' (Media Release, 15 February 2013): <http://www.aafs.org/sites/default/files/pdf/National%20Commission%20on%20Forensic%20Science.pdf> [accessed 28 Dec 2015].

304 See Spencer S Hsu, 'US to Commit Scientists and New Commission to Fix Forensic Science', *The Washington Post*, 15 February 2013: <http://www.washingtonpost.com/local/crime/us-to-commit-scientists-and-new-commission-to-fix-forensic-science/2013/02/15/e11c31f8-77b3-11e2-8f84-3e4b513b1a13_story.html#> [accessed 28 Dec 2015].

305 National Institute of Standards and Technology, 'NIST Invites Comments on Structure of Forensic Science Guidance Groups' (Media Release, 27 September 2013): <http://www.nist.gov/director/spo/forensic-092713.cfm> [accessed 28 Dec 2015].

Texas legislature enacted the 'Junk Science Writ' law, which allows persons who have been convicted and sentenced to imprisonment to challenge faulty or outdated forensic science using newer studies.[306]

Oversight of Forensic Science in Australia

Oversight in respect of forensic conduct is less developed in countries such as Australia. Australian forensic science laboratories are accredited by the National Association of Testing Authorities Australia which has established a Forensic Science Accreditation Advisory Committee.[307]

Australia also has a National Institute of Forensic Science (NIFS) which is part of the Australia and New Zealand Policing Advisory Agency (ANZPAA).[308] It does not deal with complaints about the quality of forensic science but provides education and conducts forums on forensic science matters. In 2009 it established a Forensic Analysis Committee to develop proposed Australian Standards in relation to forensic matters. Thus far, it has published the following Standards:

- Forensic analysis—Recognition, recording, recovery, transport and storage of material (AS 5388.1-2012).
- Forensic analysis—Analysis and examination of material (AS 5388.2-2012).
- Minimizing the risk of contamination in products used to collect and analyse biological material for forensic DNA purposes (AS 5483-2012).[309]
- Forensic analysis—Interpretation of results (DR AS 5388.3)
- Forensic analysis—Reporting (DR AS 5388.4).[310]

There is a great deal to be said for the creation in countries such as Australia of a Forensic Science Regulator along the lines of that existing in the United Kingdom that could collaborate with NIFS and what is proposed in this book to be the Office of Scholarly Integrity.

Accountability for the Scholarship of Forensic Work

The work product of those who provide expert opinions to the courts is essentially scholarly. It depends upon scholarship and frequently involves the application of scholarly articles published in learned journals. Generally, as outlined above, forensic work is not conceptualized as an aspect of scholarly endeavour. This has meant that many of the rigours of academic scholarship and the requirements of scholarly integrity have not been applied to persons functioning in the forensic areas and to the work undertaken in particular cases and to the procedures employed by those who write forensic reports and testify in the witness box

306 Rick Jervis, 'Texas Leads Trend in Challenging Forensic Evidence', *USA Today*, 16 December 2013: <http://www.usatoday.com/story/news/nation/2013/12/16/texas-forensics-challenge-cases-overturned/3992313/> [accessed 28 Dec 2015].

307 See Stephen Cordner and Alastair Ross, 'Australia' in Douglas H Ubelaker (ed), *The Global Practice of Forensic Science* (Chichester, West Sussex: John Wiley & Sons, 2015) 22.

308 Larry Proud, 'Five Years on: ANZPAA and Professionalization' (2013) 5(1) *Australasian Policing* 13.

309 See ANZPAA NIFS, 'Forensic Standards Development': <https://www.anzpaa.org.au/current-initiatives/forensic-standards-development> (viewed 15 February 2015).

310 National Association of Testing Authorities, 'Implementation and Assessment of Australian Standards within Forensic Science', 1 July 2013: <http://www.nata.com.au/nata/phocadownload/publications/Field_Updates/forensic_science/AS5388-Gap-Analysis-update.pdf> [accessed 28 Dec 2015].

as forensic experts. Many such witnesses in fact are principally employed within academia. Those who are not often hold postgraduate tertiary qualifications and publish learned articles in scholarly journals which focus upon the forensic areas.

This book has conceptualized much of the forensic work of experts in the courts as scholarly. What such a hypothesis highlights is that the forensic area is not formally characterized by the unequivocal requirements for integrity that apply within mainstream academia. In addition, the preceding analysis has shown that the vices in forensic endeavour share many features in common with the vices within unethical research—a preparedness to prioritize personal views and a desire for kudos over integrity. It may be that an impetus is growing for costs orders to be made against witnesses, and even solicitors and barristers, when there is a failure to abide by fundamental obligations of a forensic expert in assisting the decision-making by a court.[311] It is apparent too that regulatory strategies in the forensic area have the potential to learn much from those employed in the orthodox areas of scholarly research. There is a need for external regulatory mechanisms, over and above the trial and appellate trial process, which are available to scrutinize whether forensic work has been conducted in ways which are both ethical and consonant with scholarly knowledge and standards.

[311] See *Hudspeth v Scholastic Cleaning and Consultancy Services Pty Ltd (Ruling No 8)* [2014] VSC 567 where there were multiple failures by an expert and a solicitor and senior counsel to adhere to proprieties in relation to expert evidence and costs orders were made against each. See also Freckelton and Selby, 2016, above n 4.

6

PLAGIARISM

Introduction

This chapter reviews the nature of plagiarism as a form of scholarly misconduct, the circumstances in which it has been found to take place among various categories of professionals, including those in academia, but also in a range of other domains, including the judicial, and the characteristics and motives that can be discerned or inferred among those who engage in this form of intellectual dishonesty. It reviews the regulatory and other legal responses to the incidence of proven plagiarism and reflects upon reforms that might be undertaken to decrease the incidence of plagiarism.

What is Plagiarism?

Plagiarism is a term that is derived from the Late Latin first conjugation verb *'plagiare'*, which meant to 'steal'.[1] Generally the verb was used in respect of the theft of a person, often a slave, in the sense of kidnapping.[2] Cicero[3] used the noun, *'plagiarius'*, to refer to a predator but it was Martial[4] in the first century AD, in an epigram that wittily played on the similarity of a kidnapper to a thief of poetry, who was the first to use the term to apply to a person who passes off another's literary works as her or his own:

> To your charge I entrust, Quintianus, my works—if, after all, I can call those mine which that poet of yours recites. If they complain of their grievous servitude, come forward as their champion and give bail for them; and when that fellow calls himself their owner, say that they are mine, sent forth from my hand. If thrice and four times you shout this, you will shame them.[5]

---

[1] Another etymology that has been mooted is from the Greek, *plagios*, meaning 'oblique' or 'slanted', and including by extension being 'morally crooked', and 'practicing double-talk': see John E Skandalakis and Petros Mirilas, 'Plagiarism' (2004) 139(9) *Archives of Surgery* 1022, 1022.

[2] An etymology utilized by the University of Melbourne in its plagiarism policy: 'Plagiarism means you are kidnapping or stealing someone else's ideas or words and presenting them as if they were your own. If you copy an article from an encyclopedia and make some minor changes to pass it off as your own writing, you are plagiarizing deliberately. If you carelessly forget to include quotation marks or a reference to show whose words or ideas you are using, you are plagiarizing accidentally. Whether deliberate or accidental, plagiarism is a serious offence in scholarship'; University of Melbourne, 'Academic Honesty and Plagiarism: Practical Advice to Students': <https://academichonesty.unimelb.edu.au/advice.html> [accessed 28 Dec 2015].

[3] Q Fr 1, 2, 2 at 6.

[4] See *The Epigrams of Martial*, Book I, LII: trans. Walter CA Ker, 2 vols (London: William Heinemann, 1919) 62.

[5] *The Epigrams of Martial*, Book I, XXIX: trans. Walter CA Ker, 2 vols (London: William Heinemann, 1919). See also Peter Anderson, 'Martial 1.29: Appearance and Authorship' (2006) 149(1) *Rheinisches Museum für Philologie* 119. See also, J Mira Seo, 'Plagiarism and Poetic Identity in Martial' (2009) 130(4) *American Journal of Philology* 567, 573ff; and, *The Epigrams of Martial*, trans. Walter CA Ker, 2 vols (London: William Heinemann, 1919) 62, available at: <https://archive.org/details/martialepigrams01martiala> [accessed 28 Dec 2015]. It was in the 18th century in English that the term 'plagiarism' also came to be used in this sense: see Harold O White, *Plagiarism and Imitation during the English Renaissance: A Study in Critical Distinctions* (New York: Octagon Books, (1965) 192–4.

He wrote several pieces aimed at plagiarists, including Fidentinus:

> Rumour asserts, Fidentinus, that you recite my works to the crowd, just as if they were your own. If you wish they should be called mine, I will send you the poems gratis; if you wish them to be called yours, buy my disclaimer of them.[6]

The term made its way into English in 1601 when Ben Jonson in *'Poetaster'*, also known as *'His Arraignment: A Comicall Satyre'*, described a literary thief as a 'plagiary':

> Crispinus. Aye, sir, that's but a borrowed name; as Ovid's Corinna, or Propertius his Cynthia, or your Nemesis, or Delia, Tibullus.
>
> Gallus. It's the name of Horace his witch, as I remember.
>
> Tibullus. Why? The ditty's all borrowed; 'tis Horace's: hang him, plagiary.
>
> Tucca. How? He borrow of Horace? He shall pawn himself to ten brokers, first.[7]

However, invocation of so pejorative a descriptor needs to be nuanced. As Samuel Johnson observed in 1751:

> As not every instance of similitude can be considered as a proof of imitation, so not every imitation ought to be stigmatized as plagiarism. The adoption of a noble sentiment, or the insertion of a borrowed ornament may sometimes display so much judgment as may almost compensate for invention; and an inferior genius may without any imputation of servility pursue the path of the ancients, provided he declines to tread in their footsteps.[8]

He noted that unreasonable allegations of plagiarism had become a means of denigrating scholars:

> Among the innumerable practices by which interest or envy have taught those who live upon literary fame to disturb each other at their airy banquets, one of the most common is the charge of plagiarism. When the force and propriety of a new composition, can no longer be contested, and malice is compelled to give way to the unanimity of applause, there is yet this an expedient to be tried by which the author may be degraded, though his work be reverenced; and the excellence which we cannot obscure may be set at such a distance, as not to overpower our fainter lustre.[9]

He included the term 'plagiary' in his dictionary of 1755, giving the definition of '[a] thief in literature; one who steals the thoughts or writings of another' and '[t]he crime of literary theft', while he defined 'plagiarism' as '[t]heft; literary adoption of the thoughts or works of another'.[10]

It was in this environment of greater sensitivity to unauthorized copying that on 10 April 1710 the world's first copyright legislation was passed in London: 'An Act for the Encouragement of Learning, by Vesting the Copies of Printed Books in the Authors or Purchasers of Such Copies, During the Times Therein Mentioned'.[11] It became known as the *Statute of Anne*.

In more modern times plagiarism has been described as 'elusive…in terms of both conceptualization and detection', but '[a]t its most basic,…as the theft of literary property without

6 *The Epigrams of Martial*, Book I, XXIX.

7 Ben Jonson, *Poetaster, Or, His Arraignment: A Comical Satire* (Digireads.com Publishing, 2011) 43–44.

8 Samuel Johnson in *The Rambler*, No. 143, 30 July 1751, 856. Also reproduced in Arthur Murphy, vol 1, *The Works of Samuel Johnson LLD* (New York: George Dearborn, 1834) 223, available at: <http://catalog.hathitrust.org/Record/008662624> [accessed 28 Dec 2015].

9 Johnson in *The Rambler*, above n 8, 851. Also reproduced in Murphy, above n 8, vol 1, 221.

10 Samuel Johnson, *A Dictionary of the English Language*, 2 vols (London: W Strahan, 1755), available at <http://catalog.hathitrust.org/Record/009310086> [accessed 28 Dec 2015].

11 8 Anne c 19 (1710).

attribution'.[12] Inevitably, it exists on a continuum in relation to the usage of another's intellectual work, ranging from wholesale copying without any attribution to sloppy paraphrasing and unacknowledged inspiration and development of another's (or even one's own) ideas.[13] It overlaps with copyright infringement but is not coterminous with it.[14]

A straightforward definition provided by the American Association of University Professors in 1989 was that plagiarism consists in the 'taking over the ideas, methods, or written words of another, without acknowledgment and with the intention that they be taken as the work of the deceiver'.[15] Along similar lines (but omitting the intentional element) the United States Office of Science and Technology Policy stated: 'Plagiarism is the appropriation of another person's ideas, processes, results, or words without giving appropriate credit, including those obtained through confidential review of others' research proposals and manuscripts'.[16] The United States Office of Research Integrity is relatively minimalist in its approach:

> ORI considers plagiarism to include both the theft or misappropriation of intellectual property and the substantial unattributed textual copying of another's work. It does not include authorship or credit disputes.
>
> The theft or misappropriation of intellectual property includes the unauthorized use of ideas or unique methods obtained by a privileged communication, such as a grant or manuscript review.
>
> Substantial unattributed textual copying of another's work means the unattributed verbatim or nearly verbatim copying of sentences and paragraphs which materially mislead the ordinary reader regarding the contributions of the author. ORI generally does not pursue the limited use of identical or nearly-identical phrases which describe a commonly-used methodology or previous research because ORI does not consider such use as substantially misleading to the reader or of great significance.[17]

In Canada a similar approach was taken in the curial context with plagiarism being held to consist 'not only of obvious copying, and obvious copying with slight and immaterial modifications, but also of the much more subtle passing off the thoughts of another as one's own'.[18] It is apparent, then, that the concept of plagiarism extends to ideas, thoughts, and methodologies, as well as to text.

---

[12] Lillian Corbin and Justin Carter, 'Is Plagiarism Indicative of Prospective Legal Practice?' (2007) 17(1-2) *Legal Education Review* 53, 53, citing Debbie Papay-Carder, 'Comments: Plagiarism in Legal Scholarship' (1983) 15(1) *University of Toledo Law Review* 233, 234. See Rebecca M Howard, *Standing in the Shadow of Giants: Plagiarists, Authors, Collaborators* (Stamford, Conn: Ablex Pub, 1999); Marcel LaFollette, *Stealing into Print: Fraud, Plagiarism, and Misconduct in Scientific Publishing* (Berkeley: University of California Press, 1992); Thomas Mallon, *Stolen Words: Forays into the Origins and Ravages of Plagiarism* (New York: Ticknor and Fields, 1989); Susan Stewart, *Crimes of Writing: Problems in the Containment of Representation* (New York: Oxford University Press, 1991). See also, Robert D Bills, 'Plagiarism in Law School: Close Resemblance of the Worst Kind?' (1990) 31(1) *Santa Clara Law Review* 103.

[13] See Christopher S Hawley, 'The Thieves of Academe: Plagiarism in the University System' (1984) 32(1) *Improving College and University Teaching* 35.

[14] See Richard A Posner, *The Little Book of Plagiarism* (New York: Pantheon Books, 2007); Bill Marsh, *Plagiarism: Alchemy and Remedy in Higher Education* (New York: State University of New York Press, 2007) 32.

[15] See Miguel Roig, 'Avoiding Plagiarism, Self-Plagiarism, and Other Questionable Writing Practices: A Guide to Ethical Writing' (US Department of Health & Human Services, The Office of Research Integrity, last updated 15 May 2013) 3, available at: <http://ori.hhs.gov/avoiding-plagiarism-self-plagiarism-and-other-questionable-writing-practices-guide-ethical-writing> [accessed 28 Dec 2015].

[16] Quoted in ibid, 5–6.

[17] US Department of Health & Human Services, The Office of Research Integrity, 'Policy on Plagiarism' (December 1994): <http://ori.hhs.gov/ori-policy-plagiarism> [accessed 28 Dec 2015].

[18] *Plews v Pausch* [2006] 11 WWR 513, [44]. Inherent in the concept of 'passing off' is a deception: representing something in terms of ownership in a way that is false: Brian Martin, 'Plagiarism Struggles' (2008) 3 *Plagiary: Cross-Disciplinary Studies in Plagiarism, Fabrication, and Falsification*, available at: <https://www.uow.edu.au/~bmartin/pubs/08plagiary.html> [accessed 28 Dec 2015].

The issue of the intentional element required for plagiarism in theory is contentious, although in practice is rarely so. However, it was discussed in some length in the important 2010 decision of the Philippines Supreme Court in respect of Justice Del Castillo.[19]

A slightly different approach was taken by the Victorian Ombudsman in Australia in an inquiry into universities' treatment of overseas students in 2011. He defined plagiarism as including:

- quoting or paraphrasing a website, book or journal without acknowledging the source;
- copying the work of another student;
- padding out a bibliography with references not used in the work;
- using or paying someone else to write an assignment.[20]

It would be constructive to work towards a common definitional approach. This is in part because the diversity of definitions provides unhelpful scope to the phenomenon of rationalization and minimization which haunts the investigation of plagiarism. As Decoo observed in 2002, there is a propensity of plagiarists to justify their conduct and to neutralize accusations made against them:

> The wording is quite different from that of the alleged source. The overlap is minimal and accidental. The sources used were properly cited, but in a different place. Every competent reader would know what the obvious source was. The sentence is a truism that many people would write the same way. The copying of that part was inadvertent.[21]

Taking away the option to succeed in such strategies when the conduct consists of intellectual dishonesty would enhance the potential for its exposure and denunciation.

Plagiarism in Sanskrit, Greek, and Latin Literature

The opprobrium attaching to plagiarism has a long history indeed. Greek philosophers are 'commonly accused of stealing one another's work, or even that of a god's'.[22] Timaeus of Tauromenium wrote in the ninth book of his *Histories* that Empedocles had been accused of '*logoklopia*'—'word/argument stealing'.[23] He claimed that as a result Empedocles (like Plato) was banned from attending Pythagoras's lectures. Heraclitus accused Pythagoras of stealing ideas and later Plato too was accused by Theopompus (who was hostile to the Academy) of wrongfully taking ideas from Pythagorean philosophy and claiming them to be his own.[24] By the end of the third century BC the notion that Plato had copied from the Pythagoreans had wide currency. Timon of Phlius, a younger contemporary of Timaeus, also maintained that Plato copied his Timaeus from a small book which he had bought for a high price. It seems likely that this was the work of Hermippus.[25] There is no doubt that to allege this against Plato was to denigrate him in terms of his integrity.

---

[19] *In the Matter of the Charges of Plagiarism, Etc., Against Associate Justice Mariano C. Del Castillo* (Decision) 12 October 2010, AM No. 10-7-17-SC (Republic of the Philippines Supreme Court): <http://sc.judiciary.gov.ph/jurisprudence/2010/october2010/10-7-17-SC.htm> [accessed 28 Dec 2015]. See below, p 311.

[20] Taylor, John R, *Investigation into How Universities Deal with International Students* (Victorian Ombudsman, October 2011) [237], available at: <https://www.ombudsman.vic.gov.au/Publications?page=11&searchtext=universities&searchmode=anyword#content-area> [accessed 28 Dec 2015].

[21] Wilfried Decoo, *Crisis on Campus: Confronting Academic Misconduct* (Cambridge, Mass: MIT Press, 2002), 120 (original formatting altered).

[22] See Ava Chitwood, *Death by Philosophy: The Biographical Tradition in the Life and Death of the Archaic Philosophers Empedocles, Heraclitus and Democritus* (Ann Arbor: University of Michigan Press, 2004) 11, available at: <http://babel.hathitrust.org/cgi/pt?id=mdp.39015059147176;view=1up;seq=21> [accessed 28 Dec 2015].

[23] Christopher A Baron, *Timaeus of Tauromenium and Hellenistic Historiography* (Cambridge: Cambridge University Press, 2012) 165.

[24] See ibid, 165.

[25] See Leonid Zhmud, *Pythagoras and the Early Pythagoreans* (Oxford: Oxford University Press, 2012) 161.

It has been argued that being truthful about the origins of any idea is a Jewish value but that citing the sources for an idea is not seen as obligatory within Jewish tradition.[26] The propensity of the great codifier and philosopher Maimonides, who was not always rigorous in identifying his sources, may be seen as illustrative of this phenomenon.

In neither Greek nor Latin is there a particular word for plagiarism. The ordinary words for theft, 'κλοπή' in Greek, and '*surripere*' and sometimes '*furari*' in Latin, are used.[27] However, in Latin, as in Greek, imitation was acceptable, leading Terence to offer a defence of derivativeness in writing: 'In the end, there is nothing said that has not been said before. Therefore, it is fair that you examine the situation and forgive new playwrights for doing what playwrights have always done.'[28] However, the perception that wholesale copying constituted intellectual dishonesty was general; the author's symbolic ownership of his text was a given.

Suetonius in his *Life of Virgil* defends him against hurtful allegations of pilferings, the eight volumes of Quintus Octavius Avitus, entitled 'resemblances', containing the verses which Virgil borrowed, alongside their sources.[29] Insofar as it was alleged that Virgil borrowed inappropriately from Homer, Virgil's own somewhat unconvincing reply is reported by Suetonius to be: 'Why don't my critics also attempt the same thefts? If they do, they will realize that it is easier to filch his club from Hercules than a line from Homer.'[30]

Cicero writes to Atticus in 60 BC, proclaiming himself happy that he had given a piece he had written on the same topic that had been addressed by Atticus and commenting: 'For if I had read yours first, you would be charging me with stealing from you.'[31] Later in his *Brutus* he discusses the poets Naevius and Ennius. Pointedly, he writes: 'And indeed, they have written excellently, even if in a less refined way than you. Nor should it seem any different to you, who have borrowed much from Naevius, if you admit to your debts, or have stolen much from him, if you deny them'.[32] The contrast is between the taking/borrowing (*sumere*) which is regarded as legitimate use, and stealing (*surripere*) which is viewed as attended by dishonesty.[33]

The charge of plagiarism is a well-recognized form of abuse in ancient literature that became almost an art form. Probably the most vehement example of such invective is to be found in Suetonius' recording of Lenaeus' response to the observation by the historian Sallust that Pompey was 'upright on the outside but shameless within'.[34] He castigated Sallust as a catamite, glutton, scoundrel, barfly, and monster in his life and writings. Moreover, he accused him of being a 'completely ignorant plagiarist of Cato's archaic diction'.[35]

---

[26] See Levi Brackman, 'Rabbinic Plagiarism and Scholarly Integrity', *Jewish World*, 5 December 2013: <http://www.ynetnews.com/articles/0,7340,L-4376055,00.html> (viewed 20 February 2015); see though, Josh Nathan-Kazis, 'When May a Rabbi Use the Words of Others?' *The Jewish Daily Forward*, 24 August 2012: <http://forward.com/articles/161581/when-may-a-rabbi-use-the-words-of-others/?p=all> [accessed 28 Dec 2015]; Michael L Samuel, 'Rabbi Yosef's Opinion on Plagiarism is Mistaken', *San Diego Jewish World*, 28 March 2014: <http://www.sdjewishworld.com/2014/03/28/rabbi-yosefs-opinion-plagiarism-mistaken/> [accessed 28 Dec 2015].

[27] See Scott McGill, *Plagiarism in Latin Literature* (Cambridge: Cambridge University Press, 2012) 6–8, to whose assemblage of references on plagiarism I am indebted over the following pages.

[28] Terence, *Eunuchus*, 35–43, as cited in ibid, 134.

[29] McGill, above n 27, 178.

[30] Suetonius, *The Life of Virgil*, (Loeb Translation, 1913), available at: <http://legacy.fordham.edu/halsall/pwh/suet-vergil.asp> [accessed 28 Dec 2015] surviving in Donatus' commentary.

[31] Letter from Cicero to Atticus (60 BCE), *Att* 2.1.1 as cited in McGill, above n 27, 1.

[32] Cicero, *Brutus*, 75–76 as cited in McGill, above n 27, 2.

[33] McGill, above n 27, 2.

[34] Suetonius, *De Grammaticis et Rhetoribus*, 15.2 as cited in McGill, above n 27, 33.

[35] *[P]raeterea priscorum Catonis[que] verborum ineruditissimum furem*: ibid.

For sheer wit, though, it is hard to go past the flowery abuse of Martial in his attacks on Fidentinus:

> There is one page of yours in a book of mine, Fidentinus, a page stamped with the clear likeness of its master, that convicts you of red-handed theft. Thus with its oily wool a Lingonican cloak contaminates the purple robes of the sophisticated when placed among them. Thus Arretine pots spoil crystal, thus the black crow is mocked among the Ledaean swans when it chances to wander on the banks of the Cayster. Thus when the sacred grove is alive with the varied strains of the nightingale, the brash magpie jars with Cecropian laments. My books have no need of an informer or judge; your page testifies against you and says, 'You are a thief'.[36]

Vitruvius, the author of the ten-volume work on architecture, praises earlier writers who established a foundation on which others were able to build, but contrasts writers who warrant disapproval and punishment because they steal the words of others and present themselves as the author[37] or because they devote themselves to criticizing invidiously the work of others rather than to presenting their own ideas. Pliny the Elder in his 37-volume *Historia Naturalis* explains his use of sources, observing that he considers it honourable and modest to identify those from whom one has profited and then comments: 'Surely it is the mark of a servile spirit and wretched temperament to prefer to be caught plagiarizing than to repay a loan, especially since interest produces capital.'[38] Better, said Manilius in his *Astronomica*, to 'owe my words to no poet. A real work, not plagiarism, will arise, as I fly into the sky on a companionless chariot and beat the waves with my own ship'.[39] It is even put on occasion that giving proper ascription is itself a virtue. As Seneca described it: 'I will attribute to each his own work with the greatest faithfulness, so that they not be unknown or known in a way they should not be.'[40]

Rajasekhara, the ninth-century Sanskrit poet, dramatist, and critic, writes in his poem *Kavyam* about the sources and nature of poetry. He realistically concludes that 'there are no poets who are not (to some extent) thieves'.[41] He accepts the legitimacy of borrowing from earlier works but contends that the challenge for the poet is to freshen up what has been written before. He lauds imitations provided they enhance the poetic beauty of the original or give greater force to phrases or ideas used elsewhere or in other contexts. However, he provides 32 ways of avoiding improper plagiarism, condemning the appropriation of a striking or surprising phrase from another writer.

Originality and Plagiarism

It was in 18th century England that the concept of originality as the main force in the creative process in all of the arts received its earliest emphasis. After the humanistic period in which imitation was held to be the principal creative force, a reaction is identifiable among

---

36 *The Epigrams of Martial*, Book I, LIII, 1–12 as cited in McGill, above n 27, 94.

37 [*S*]*ic contra qui eorum scripta furantes pro suis praedicant*: Vitruvius, *De Architectura*, Book VII, praef 3 as cited in McGill, above n 27, 35.

38 Pliny, *Historia Naturalis*, praef 21–24 as cited in McGill, above n 27, 49.

39 Manilius, *Astronomica*, Book II, 57–59 as cited in McGill, above n 27, 57.

40 Seneca, *Controversiae*, Book I, praef 11 as cited in McGill, above n 27, 66.

41 Quoted in Siegfried Lienhard, *A History of Classical Poetry: Sanskrit, Pali, Prakit* (Wiesbaden: Otto Harrassowitz, 1984) 44. See Sadhana Parashar, *Kāvyamīmāṃsā of Rājaśekhara: Original Text in Sanskrit and Translation with Explanatory Notes* (New Delhi: DK Printworld, 2000).

those who proclaimed themselves dismayed at the conduct of artists who copied from other sources. Alexander Pope, for instance, argued:

> A mutual commerce makes poets flourish; but then poets, like merchants, should repay with something of their own what they take from others; not, like pirates, make prize of all they meet.[42]

This stance stimulated a considerable literature, debating when imitation became plagiarism:

> It was in the middle of the eighteenth century that both the concept of originality and its moral antonym plagiarism appeared as crucial topics in aesthetic criticism and debate. Originality soon was viewed as the essential factor determining artistic genius, and Genius, though difficult to define, became the key to innumerable attempts to evaluate the significance of new literature, art, and music.[43]

In a series of articles published in *Tait's Magazine* Thomas De Quincey catalogued four potential instances of plagiarism in the work of his friend and literary competitor, Samuel Taylor Coleridge. Mazzeo[44] has argued that De Quincey's charges and the controversy they ignited have shaped readers' responses to the work of such writers as Coleridge, Lord Byron, William Wordsworth, and John Clare ever since. It is one of many examples of the allegation of plagiarism (as in classsical literature) being brought for less than altruistic reasons.

Laurence Sterne in *Tristram Shandy* toyed with his readers when he wrote: 'Shall we for ever make new books, as apothecaries make new mixtures, by pouring only out of one vessel into another?'[45] What he was doing was alluding to (without specific reference) or perhaps plagiarizing the words of Robert Burton, who wrote in his *Anatomy of Melancholy*: 'As apothecaries we make new mixtures every day, pour out of one vessel into another; and as those old Romans robbed all the cities of the world, to set out their bad-sited Rome, we skim off the cream of other men's wits, pick the choice flowers of their tilled gardens to set out our own sterile plots.'[46] What was taking place with Sterne was a deliberate use of irony, showing off his knowledge and challenging his readers to identify what, in talking about plagiarism, if anything, he was *plagiarizing*. Harmless, albeit perhaps a little intellectually self-indulgent. But it was representative of a mindset of a number of actual plagiarists who blatantly use another's work, passing it off as their own, apparently laying down the task for their reader to identify what it is that they have done. The conduct is arrogant, the exercise like a game of playing chicken, and the motivation one of daring the reader to identify and respond to their conduct.

The conduct of John Browne, the 17th century anatomist, in appropriating William Molins's 1648 *Myotomia or the Anatomical Administration of All the Muscles of the Humane Body* into his 1681 *Compleat Treatise of the Muscles*, has become an infamous example of exploitative plagiarism[47] before the clear assertion of personal intellectual property rights.

---

[42] Letter III to Mr Walsh, Windsor Forest, 2 July 1706 in Alexander Pope, 9 vols, *The Works of Alexander Pope*, Notes and Illustrations by Joseph Warton (Basil: JJ Tourneisen, 1803) 70.

[43] George J Buelow, 'Originality, Genius, Plagiarism in English Criticism of the Eighteenth Century' (1990) 21(2) *International Review of the Aesthetics and Sociology of Music* 117, 117.

[44] Tilar J Mazzeo TJ, *Plagiarism and Literary Property in the Romantic Period* (Philadelphia: University of Pennsylvania Press, 2011).

[45] Laurence Sterne, *The Life and Opinions of Tristram Shandy, Gentleman*, vol 5 (Dublin: W&W Smith, G Faulkner, S Watson, and T Williams, 1765) 2.

[46] Robert Burton, *The Anatomy of Melancholy* (Philadephia: JW Moore, 1857) 19.

[47] See Elizabeth Lane Furdell, *Publishing and Medicine in Early Modern England* (Rochester, NY: University of Rochester Press, 2002) 53–54; Marios Loukas, Matthew Akiyama, Mohammadali M Shoja, Bulent Yalçin et al, 'John Browne (1642–1702): Anatomist and Plagiarist' (2010) 23(1) *Clinical Anatomy* 1.

The Bidloo-Cowper case, exposed by Gysel,[48] has also become notorious:

> Govert (Gottfreid) Bidloo (1649–1713) first observed the junction of the common bile duct and the pancreatic duct and described the ampulla and the projection into the duodenum (papilla). These were redescribed by G in 1720. According to Persaud, in 1685 Bidloo published his *Anatomia Humani Corporis* with 105 copperplate engravings by Pieter van Gunst. In 1698, William Cowper (1666–1709) plagiarized these engravings in his book. Garrison wrote, in *History of Medicine*: 'Bidloo scolds about this plagiarism in his *Gulielmus Cowper, Criminis Literarii Citatus*.'[49]

There are diverse attitudes towards the ongoing meaningfulness of the concept of plagiarism. It has been argued by some that plagiarism has become an outmoded and simplistic concept in the modern era:

> The concept of plagiarism, as used both in considerations of academic writing and in international negotiations over intellectual copyright, assumes a model of communication based on autonomous, rational, individuals who behave as originators of their own discourses.[50]

Some have maintained it to be a 'trendy trope, being now held by various national and international fora as a symbolic denominator of one's accountability as well as individuality within global systems of information production and circulation'.[51]

Issues of 'intertextuality', derivative use, reordering, and revision of other material, it has been claimed, are more complex than the 'culture of denunciation' of those said to have plagiarized acknowledges.[52] In 1999 Howard[53] identified an ambivalence in attitudes towards plagiarism and observed that 'the property of morality is itself dependent upon the belief that originality, proprietorship, and autonomy are 'natural truths' about 'real' authorship, rather than cultural arbitraries. Therefore, the discourse of plagiarism often invokes these assumptions'. And significant use of others' work has a lengthy history in literature, some of it honourable and open, some of it not. As Linklater has pointed out:

> An idea may be 'inspired' by a previous work, as Alex Haley claimed when he was accused of lifting his book *Roots* from an earlier work on African slavery; or it may be an 'echo' from another writer, as Graham Swift argued, after claims that he had imitated William Faulkner's *As I Lay Dying* rather too closely. T.S. Eliot thought that plagiarism in the hands of a good writer was an artform: 'Immature poets imitate; great poets steal,' he said simply. Shakespeare purloined his best plots from Holinshed. *West Side Story* was stolen from Shakespeare. *Paradise Lost* is shamelessly based on Genesis. Martin Luther King plagiarized part of the doctoral thesis which became, later, his finest speech. Zadie Smith makes no bones about basing her latest novel *On Beauty* on E.M. Forster's *Howard's End*: 'He gave me a classy old frame, which I covered with new material as best I could,' she says.[54]

---

[48] See Carlos Gysel, 'Govert Bidloo's "Anatomia!" (1685) and the Plagiarism by William Cowper (1698)' (1987) 42(3) *Revue Belge de Medecine Dentaire* 96. See further, Elizabeth Lane Furdell, *The Royal Doctors, 1485–1714: Medical Personnel at the Tudor and Stuart Courts* (Rochester, NY: University of Rochester Press, 2001).

[49] Skandalakis and Mirilas, above n 1, 1023 (footnotes omitted).

[50] Ron Scollon, 'Plagiarism and Ideology: Identity in Intercultural Discourse' (1995) 24(1) *Language in Society* 1, 1.

[51] Emanuela Grama, 'Networking Texts and Persons: Politics of Plagiarism in Post Socialist Romania' (2004) 4(2) *Romanian Journal of Society and Politics* 148, 148.

[52] See eg, Philipp Theisohn, 'Call the Spade a Spade', Sign and Sight.Com, 4 March 2010: <http://www.signandsight.com/features/1999.html> [accessed 28 Dec 2015], dealing with the allegations of plagiarism from a blog against Helene Hegemann's *Axolotl Roadkill*.

[53] Howard, above n 12, 100.

[54] Magnus Linklater, 'But When is Copying Plagiarism?' *The Times*, 1 March 2006, 21, 21.

However, another perspective is that an abandonment of originality as an indicium of artistic merit improperly blurs the lines amongst creators of ideas. Arguably, these notions have become more highly valued as a result of the information revolution. As Stearns put it: 'Plagiarism is, then, a failure of the creative process, not a flaw in its result.'[55]

Stuart Kelly in 2011 contended: 'In the virtual world, the most valuable currency is reality. That would explain why the two things that aggravate the blogosphere most in literary terms are plagiarism and impersonation.'[56]

The issue has arisen on multiple occasions in the context of poetry,[57] in Australia dating back to the 1945 Ern Malley poetry hoax.[58] It recurred in 2013 with the Australian poet, Andrew Slattery, admitting to cannibalizing others' work and at first rationalizing it as an attempt to achieve a 'cento' effect—a patchwork—in which the work of others is incorporated in one's own poem.[59] He argued that this form of 'collaging' has an extensive and legitimate tradition, most famously used by John Ashberry, the highly regarded American poet. He compared his work to 'mash-ups' where snippets of songs are put together. He admitted that: 'Critics will say this is a glorified way of saying I've plagiarised. Maybe. It's a good question.'[60] Shortly afterwards, checking exposed that his winning entry in the 2013 Josephine Ulrick Poetry Prize was substantially the work of others. He was disqualified and did not receive the AUS$10,000 prize money. As so often in such contexts, a further investigation exposed that Slattery had been engaging in similar behaviour since 2007, using work from many others, including Sylvia Plath, Tom Waits, and even the writings of Friedrich Nietzsche, EM Cioran, and Sigmund Freud. When Slattery's defence was raised with the poetry editor for *The Australian*, Jaya Savige, she rejected it outright, observing that Slattery's deceptions were extensive and that the 'cento defence' he had mounted did not stand up because 'centos are marked as such, so that readers are left in no doubt that it's a remix, as it were'.[61]

The issue generates strong feelings. Freedman, for instance, in 1994, expostulated that plagiarism represents no less than 'an attack on individuality, on nothing less than a basic human right, to property, to identity',[62] while Mallon in 1989 contended that a failure to respond with indignation to acts of plagiarism itself constitutes a moral failing, signifying a lack of will. For writers not to care about plagiarism, Mallon argued, 'would mean that they had permitted themselves a loss of self-respect'.[63]

---

[55] Laurie Stearns, 'Copy Wrong: Plagiarism, Process, Property, and the Law' in Lise Buranen and Alice M Roy (eds), *Perspectives on Plagiarism and Intellectual Property in a Postmodern World* (Albany: State University of New York Press, 1999) 7.

[56] Stuart Kelly, 'What We Should Take from the QR Markham Plagiarism Scandal', *The Guardian*, 22 November 2011: <http://www.theguardian.com/books/2011/nov/22/qr-markham-plagiarism-scandal> [accessed 28 Dec 2015].

[57] See Gordon K Klintworth, *Giants, Crooks and Jerks in Science* (Xlibris Corporation, 2014) 131.

[58] Ernest Lalor 'Ern' Malley was a fictitious poet and the central figure in a notorious Australian literary hoax. In 1943 Malley and his body of work were created in a single day by James McAuley and Harold Stewart in order to hoax Max Harris and *Angry Penguins*, the modernist magazine Harris had founded and edited. See Michael Heyward, *The Ern Malley Affair* (St Lucia: University of Queensland Press, 1993).

[59] See Stephen Romei, 'Poet Uses Defence of 'Collage Poetry' After Recycling Plath Lines', *The Australian*, 13 September 2013: <http://www.theaustralian.com.au/arts/books/poet-uses-defence-of-collage-poetry-after-recycling-plath-lines/story-e6frg8nf-1226718041674> [accessed 28 Dec 2015].

[60] Ibid.

[61] Ibid.

[62] Morris Freedman, 'The Persistence of Plagiarism, The Riddle of Originality' (1994) 70(3) *The Virginia Quarterly Review* 504, 517.

[63] Mallon, above n 12, 237. On occasion plagiarism has even elicited condemnation on religious grounds. See eg, Sheikh Khâlid b. Sa`ûd al-Rashûd, 'Allah Commands You to Render Trusts to Their Owners'—Its Relevance to Plagiarism', *Islam Today*: <http://en.islamtoday.net/artshow-264-3417.htm> [accessed 28 Dec

Taxonomies of Plagiarism

It is conventional to classify plagiarism as existing in two forms: the theft of ideas (idea plagiarism) and the copying of words (verbatim plagiarism), although more elaborate taxonomies have been attempted. Harvey, in his guide for Harvard University students, identified four forms: (a) uncited data or information; (b) an uncited idea, whether a specific claim or general concept; (c) an unquoted but verbatim phrase or passage; and (d) an uncited structure or organizing strategy.[64]

Perhaps the most extensive taxonomy of plagiarism, though, is that of Martin, who suggested the following in a very thoughtful analysis of scholarly literature on the subject:

- *Bureaucratic plagiarism* is inaccurate attribution of authorship within bureaucratic organizations... a form of institutionalised plagiarism.
- *Competitive plagiarism* is plagiarism in a situation in which it is stigmatised. Typically the plagiariser does not seek permission. Common examples are students copying from published texts and writers copying from other writers.
- *Cryptomnesia* occurs when one is exposed to someone else's words or ideas but, forgetting this, mistakenly believes these words or ideas are one's own original thoughts. This is a memory error in attributing the source of ideas. It is a form of unintentional plagiarism.
- *Editorial ghostwriting* is an editor's contribution to a text that is substantial and unacknowledged, for example writing new sentences and adding new references.
- *Ghostwriting* is writing text for someone else who takes credit for it. The ghostwriter, also called a ghost, may be paid for the work or receive some other benefit, such as the opportunity to have words and ideas reach a wider audience or serve a worthy cause. Ghostwriting is a form of institutionalised plagiarism.
- *Gift authorship*, also called *honorary authorship*, is having one's name as an author or co-author without having done an adequate portion of the work. Some gifting is at the initiative of the actual authors.
- *Institutionalised plagiarism* is plagiarism in a situation in which it is considered normal, legitimate practice. It usually involves organisational superiors or powerful individuals taking credit for the work of others.
- *Paraphrasing plagiarism* is plagiarism using the general sequence of text from another source, with some changes in words and sentence structure...
- *Patchwriting* [has been described as] copying from a source text and then deleting some words, altering grammatical structures, or plugging in one synonym for another.
- [...]
- *Plagiarism of secondary sources* is listing sources—typically references to texts—taken from another source (the secondary source), presenting them as one's own sources.

2015]—'Taking credit for someone else's idea is most certainly a breach of trust. It is an act of bad faith to the person whose idea or work it really is. Allah says: 'O you who believe! Do not betray the trust of Allah and the Messenger, nor misappropriate knowingly what you have been entrusted with' [*Sûrah al-Anfâl*: 27]. Taking credit for someone else's words or ideas is both an act of fraud and a deliberate lie. This is why the Prophet (peace be upon him) said: 'He who credits himself with what was not given to him is like one who wears a double cloak of deception.' [Ibn `Abd al-Barr, *Jâmi` al-Tahsîl* (1/98)] Ibn al-Manzûr commented on this hadith saying: 'The one who credits himself with what was not given to him is one who says he was given something which was never really his or who attributes to himself talents that he really does not possess, implying that Allah had bestowed him with these things or that people accredited him with what was never specifically his. In this way, he has perpetrated a double lie: Firstly, he attributes to himself what does not truly apply to him or makes claims to possess what he really does not possess. Secondly, he lies regarding the giver—either Allah or other people. [*Lisân al-`Arab* (1/247)] A person who takes credit for other people's writings and good ideas is crediting himself with what was not given to him.'

64 Gordon Harvey, *Writing with Sources: A Guide for Students* (2nd edn, Indianapolis: Hackett Publishing Co., 2008) 14ff.

- [...]
- *Self-plagiarism* is presenting one's own prior work as if it is new work.
- *Supervisory ghostwriting* involves a supervisor making substantial unacknowledged contributions to a subordinate's work...
- *Unintentional plagiarism* is plagiarism in which the author does not mean to deceive, cheat or plagiarize. It commonly occurring due to ignorance or lack of understanding of acknowledgment conventions...
- *Word-for-word plagiarism* is plagiarism using exact or near-exact sequences of words from another source.[65]

Motives for Plagiarism

It is apparent that scholars' motives for engaging in the dishonesty of plagiarism vary widely, as they do with research misconduct,. Part of the phenomenon is no more sophisticated than yielding to temptation. Reflecting on the conduct of preparedness of Russian parliamentarians to engage in plagiarism to facilitate acquisition of postgraduate degrees, Sergei Parkhomenko has argued that it in terms of straightforward opportunism: 'To them it is just part of the trappings of power: a Brioni suit, a BMW car, a state award, a Breguet watch, a beautiful blonde with by his side, a PhD degree.'[66]

In a qualitative study as to why Australian university students plagiarize, Devlin and Gray in 2007 found that the key reasons identified by students were: '[i]nadequate admission criteria', '[p]oor understanding of plagiarism',[67] and indifferent academic skills stemming from teaching/learning issues. They contended that students are problematically often admitted into university courses without fundamental writing skills (or content knowledge) and as such plagiarize to meet enrolment requirements rather than focus on understanding. Another important issue arises from the ways in which students learn and even are assessed—frequently substantially on the internet.[68]

Harris has advanced a useful set of insights in relation to students who plagiarize:

> Many students are interested in the shortest route possible through a course... Copying a paper sometimes looks like a shortcut through an assignment, especially when the student feels overloaded with work already.
>
> [...]
>
> With so many things to do (both academic and recreational nature), many students put off assignments that do not interest them.
>
> [...]
>
> Some students are just procrastinators, while others do not understand the hours required to develop a good research paper, and they run out of time as the due date looms. Thus,

[65] Martin, above n 18 (citations omitted).

[66] See Masha Lipman, 'Russia's Dissertation-Fraud Muckrakers' (9 March 2013) *The New Yorker*: <http://www.newyorker.com/news/news-desk/russias-dissertation-fraud-muckrakers> [accessed 28 Dec 2015].

[67] Marcia Devlin and Kathleen Gray, 'In Their Own Words: A Qualitative Study of the Reasons Australian University Students Plagiarize' (2007) 26(2) *Higher Education Research & Development* 181, 187. See also, Christina Mainka, Scott Raeburn, and Shirley Earl, 'A UK Institution's University-Wide Approach to Plagiarism: First Results and Recommendations' (2006) 2(1) *International Journal for Educational Integrity*, available at: <http://www.ojs.unisa.edu.au/index.php/index/search/search> [accessed 28 Dec 2015]; Maureen M Dawson and Joyce A Overfield, 'Plagiarism: Do Students Know What It Is?' (November 2006) 8 *Bioscience Education*: <http://journals.heacademy.ac.uk/doi/abs/10.3108/beej.8.1> [accessed 28 Dec 2015].

[68] Devlin and Gray, above n 67, 187ff.

they are most tempted to copy a paper when time is short and they have not yet started the assignment.

[...]

Some students fear that their writing ability is inadequate. Fear of a bad grade and inability to perform cause some students to look for a superior product they can submit as their own... Sadly, these students are among those least able to judge a good paper and are often likely to turn in a very poor copied one.

[...]

A few students like the thrill of rule breaking. The more angrily you condemn plagiarism, the more they can hardly wait to do it.[69]

Similarly, the University of New South Wales[70] has identified that plagiarism by students can be the product not so much of deliberate cheating but of under-developed academic skills, including poor time management.

However, there is more to the phenomenon from a psychological point of view, at least for some plagiarists. The chances of being caught for plagiarism are high (and, with the development of tools such as 'Turnitin' and 'iThenticate', rising) and the consequences can be catastrophic. As Smith has observed: 'Plagiarists must have a death wish for their actions can result in professional suicide.'[71] This has led Maddox to muse: '[H]ow can established academics, almost by definition not neuronally deficient, be so artless in their intellectual burglary?... Does guilt, or the wish not to face up to the enormity of the crime being perpetrated, prevent plagiarists from taking elementary precautions against discovery?'[72] Skandalakis and Mirilas have postulated that the only rational explanation for plagiarists 'exposing themselves to the danger of professional disaster is that they are in an irrational state, that they are being guided by a primitive, but overwhelming, academic motivation: the desire to enhance their reputation.'[73] However, this pathologises the conduct without adequate warrant and it fails to give adequate recognition to the fact that numbers of scholars make the (foolish) decision that the advantages accruing from taking intellectual short-cuts are worth the gamble. Sometimes this is influenced by elements of both grandiosity and narcissism that interfere with the calculation in which the scholar engages, but commonly what takes place is simply the exercise of poor and unethical judgment—opportunism trumps ethical behaviour.

Martin has argued that plagiarism for the most part can be seen in terms of three sets of dynamics:

1. A weak perpetrator versus a powerful accuser. This is the typical pattern when a high school or undergraduate student is accused of plagiarism by a teacher.
2. A powerful perpetrator versus a weak accuser. An example is a student accusing a teacher of passing off the student's essay as the teacher's own work. Another example is when the perpetrator is in a position of authority, such as being head of an organization.
3. A perpetrator versus an accuser of roughly equal power. An example is one academic plagiarizing from another.[74]

---

69 Robert Harris, 'Anti-Plagiarism Strategies for Research Papers', VirtualSalt.com, 30 December 2013: <http://www.virtualsalt.com/antiplag.htm> [accessed 28 Dec 2015].

70 University of New South Wales, 'How Does Plagiarism Happen?' (last updated 27 February 2014): <https://student.unsw.edu.au/how-does-plagiarism-happen> [accessed 28 Dec 2015].

71 James P Smith, 'Plagiarists Publish and Perish' (1999) 30(4) *Journal of Advanced Nursing* 777, 777.

72 John Maddox, 'Plagiarism is Worse Than Mere Theft' (1995) 376(6543) *Nature* 721, 721.

73 Skandalakis and Mirilas, above n 1, 1023.

74 Martin, above n 18.

Other psychological processes can be present though, on occasion obvious plagiarism constituting a cry for help and being deliberately self-harming or rebellious behaviour.[75] Some who engage in plagiarism perhaps are overwhelmed by a feeling of belatedness and inadequacy that they will never be able to generate genuinely original thought.[76] Another phenomenon is the belief on the part of some senior figures (including in academia, and in other spheres as well) that because of their eminence they have an entitlement to 'adopt', 'adapt', 'use', or 'build on' the work of others; they have reached a point where the rules do not apply to them. However, there are some instances where plagiarism is cynically premeditated, albeit highly likely to be detected—the conduct of Professor Pattium Chiranjeevi of Sri Venkateswara University in India between 2004 and 2007 in plagiarizing or falsifying results in over 70 journal articles appears to have been such an example where low impact, often obscure journals were deliberately and cynically selected to minimize the prospects of being identified.[77]

However, the major problem confronting both universities and scholarly journals is that of the ubiquity of opportunities for unacknowledged or excessive usage of sources in an intellectual environment where so much information is readily available in an accessible format.[78] In other words, laziness, poor organization, and opportunism are major risk factors in the environment and culture of the 'Information Revolution'. The Standing Committee on Faculty Conduct, Harvard Medical School, Harvard School of Dental Medicine, in its 2010 white paper on plagiarism and research misconduct, observed too that readily identifiable workplace dynamics with which some scholars struggle can also predispose towards engaging in plagiarism: deadline pressures 'may result in mistakes that could include failure of attribution for the statements or ideas of others'[79] and over-commitment can result in a failure to 'spend the time and devote the attention necessary to prepare satisfactory academic or scientific reports themselves, or to supervise diligently the work of others. Being overextended is a predisposing factor for committing plagiarism but not a justification or a mitigation.'[80]

While the outcome is a dishonest work product, the temptations are such that many students and writers will conclude that the chances of their being detected are low enough for the intellectual short-cuts of plagiarism and the advantages of gaining credit from the work of others are worth taking. When detected, the defence of innocent error ('the Biden defence', see below p 270) remains very common, although less commonly accepted than in the past. Another defence sometimes attempted is for the person accused of plagiarism to display the other work they have done which has not been plagiarized. However, as Judge Learned Hand observed in *Sheldon v Metro-Goldwyn Pictures Corporation* in a copyright case involving a

---

[75] See eg, William Dean Howells, 'The Psychology of Plagiarism' in *Literature and Life* (New York: Harper & Brothers, 1902), available at: <https://archive.org/stream/literaturelife00howe#page/272/mode/2up/search/273> [accessed 28 Dec 2015].

[76] See Harold Bloom, *The Anxiety of Influence: A Theory of Poetry* (2nd edn, New York: Oxford University Press, 1997). Compare Stapel's account of his research misconduct, above, p37.

[77] See Killugudi Jayaraman, 'Chemistry's 'Colossal' Fraud' (25 March 2008) *Royal Society of Chemistry*: <http://www.rsc.org/chemistryworld/News/2008/March/25030801.asp> [accessed 28 Dec 2015]; Mayank Tewari, 'Indian Professor Guilty of Plagiarism' (23 February 2008) DNA India: <http://www.dnaindia.com/india/report-indian-professor-guilty-of-plagiarism-1152417> [accessed 28 Dec 2015].

[78] As it was put by the Standing Committee on Faculty Conduct, Harvard Medical School, Harvard School of Dental Medicine, 'White Paper: Plagiarism and Research Misconduct', 15 December 2010, 7: <http://hms.harvard.edu/sites/default/files/assets/About_Us/COI/files/plagiarism_statement_121510.pdf> [accessed 28 Dec 2015]: 'Thanks to the ubiquity of computers, plagiarism is only a few keystrokes away from academic integrity. When it is possible to transfer whole chunks of text effortlessly from one document to another, the urge to use the work of others is facilitated.'

[79] Ibid, 8.

[80] Ibid, 9.

play: '[N]o plagiarist can excuse the wrong by showing how much of his work he did not pirate.'[81]

A Self-Portrait of Plagiarism: Jayson Blair

In April 2003 Macarena Hernandez, the editor of the *San Antonio Express-News* called *The New York Times* to complain about plagiarism of an article she had written. This prompted a painful investigation by the *New York Times* into the conduct of its prominent young reporter, Jayson Blair, and its own processes for oversight of reporters' work product. It discovered that Blair had engaged in persistent deception in his role, fabricating events, writing about places he had never visited, and stealing material from other publications.[82] In a 1,400 word piece that the *New York Times* published, 'Correcting the Record', it acknowledged that Blair's 'widespread fabrication and plagiarism represent a profound betrayal of trust and a low point in the 152-year history of the newspaper'.[83] An investigation showed that in 36 of 73 articles that Blair had written since receiving reporting assignments he had engaged in dishonesty and in no fewer than 600 articles that he wrote there had been irregularities. 'In the final months the audacity of the deceptions grew by the week, suggesting the work of a troubled young man veering toward professional self-destruction.'[84]

As so often in the scholarly research context, Blair was prolific in his output, and he was highly ambitious. Although he was recognized as sloppy and at times in accurate in his attributions, his supervisors were laissez-faire in their management of his conduct. His dishonesty took multiple forms and, inevitably, it was going to be discovered. It was not whether; it was when. At times, when queried about the accuracy of his work, he took refuge in declining to disclose his sources. He was also prepared to look colleagues in the eye and lie barefacedly about what he had done. On being accused of plagiarism and fabrication, he denied impropriety without qualification. He even telephoned another journalist to deny plagiarizing her work; he maintained that he had never seen her article when he wrote his piece. However, as he later conceded, he was unsuccessful: 'So much for trying to co-opt my victim'.[85] When the evidence grew to the point of being incontrovertible, he resigned.

Blair's conduct had many repercussions, including to the subjects of his reporting and to the reading public of the *New York Times*. It prompted reflection on the need for systems of supervision and verification to be improved so as to reinstate a measure of trust in the work of journalists at prominent (and less prominent) media outlets. It also brought about the resignation of two senior managers at the *New York Times*: Executive Editor Howell Raines and Managing Editor Gerald Boyd.[86] The parallels between Blair's conduct and that of Stapel in the orthodox scholarly context are uncanny.

---

81 81 F 2d 49, 56 (2nd Cir, 1936).

82 Compare Stephen Glass who engaged in what has been described as 'journalistic fraud' by fabricating material for more than 40 articles for *The New Republic*. He was dismissed from his position, wrote a fictionalized account of his conduct (Stephen Glass, *The Fabulist* (New York, Simon & Schuster, 2003)), and completed a law degree, but on appeal was not admitted as a lawyer by the Supreme Court of California: see *In Re Glass*, 58 Cal 4th 500 (2014).

83 Dan Barry, David Barstow, Jonathan D Glater, Adam Liptak, and Jacques Steinberg, 'CORRECTING THE RECORD; Times Reporter Who Resigned Leaves Long Trail of Deception', 11 May 2003, *The New York Times*: <http://www.nytimes.com/2003/05/11/us/correcting-the-record-times-reporter-who-resigned-leaves-long-trail-of-deception.html> [accessed 28 Dec 2015].

84 Ibid.

85 Jayson Blair, *Burning Down My Masters' House* (Beverly Hills, New Millennium Press, 2004), 8–9.

86 See Ted White, *Broadcast News: Writing, Reporting and Producing* (New York: Taylor & Francis, 2005), 375.

Shortly after he resigned, Blair was hospitalized and diagnosed with bipolar disorder. He has also claimed to have been subject to cocaine addiction and alcoholism. Thereafter Blair 'came out': like Diederik Stapel in relation to his research fraud, he has spoken and written about his thinking when he engaged in his plagiarism and other forms of dishonesty. In *Burning Down My Masters House: My Life at the New York Times*[87](for which he received a substantial advance from the publisher[88]) Blair controversially gave his version of how his conduct evolved and what motivated him. In 2013 Samantha Grant produced a prize-winning documentary, *A Fragile Trust*, about Blair.

Blair's conduct is not strictly 'scholarly misconduct' but it bears significant features in common with it. Instructively, he has given important perspectives into his mindset at the time which enabled and predisposed him to commence and continue with plagiarism and multifarious aspects of intellectual dishonesty. In his version of why he did what he did he provides a first-person account of journalistic plagiarism and fraud; in essence it is an account of the rationalizations and excuses of the archetypal plagiarist or fraudster. Of course, his narrative does not apply to the conduct of all plagiarists but it provides telling insights.

Blair's account is that he was predisposed by personality to breach boundaries: 'My enthusiasm and energy had always, perhaps oddly, been both an assert and an enemy.'[89] He described the pressures to which he felt subject to perform at the *New York Times*—the need to produce high-quality copy, the deadlines, and the intra-office politics. In an 18-month period he wrote 311 stories. As he began to decline, he was swept up in the need to cover the September 11 attacks and later the Washington sniper shootings. He outlined too his dawning realization while he worked there that he had bipolar disorder, and his resort to cocaine (at times, according to him, costing between $500 and $1000 a week) and alcohol: 'in a cocaethylene induced state, ideas abounded, depression vanished, and I felt like nothing could stop me.'[90]

He described his initial idealism and then his rationalization that he needed to have 'the greatest impact on people's lives'. He related loss of his 'moral navigation system' that initially guided him. He identified the arrival of a new editor who put a greater emphasis on speed and impact and then what he called 'battle fatigue' in the aftermath of the September 11 attacks and displaced some of the responsibility for his conduct onto others: 'What I had wanted from journalism's truthfulness and objectivity tenets, it was obvious to me, was not something it could give me, at least not at the *New York Times*, particularly not at a time when celebrity culture was driving the decisions.'[91] He made the point that 'once [the line] was crossed like so much else in ethics and other things in life, it was so much easier to cross again.'[92] At first he started small: 'I actually just took a quote from an Associated Press story, put it in the paper, and didn't attribute it.' When he was asked what he thought when he did it that first time, his response was: 'I thought, "Oh my God, maybe I can go to the copy desk and get this fixed." And then I thought, "Wait, you know, what are they going to think?" And a couple of days go by, and the thought that goes through my head: I can't believe no

87 Jayson Blair, n 85.

88 Cesar G Soriano, 'Jayson Blair Lands a Book Deal' (9 October 2003) *USA Today*: <http://usatoday30.usatoday.com/life/books/news/2003-09-10-blair-book_x.htm> [accessed 28 Dec 2015].

89 Jayson Blair, as above n 85.

90 Ibid, 166.

91 Ibid, 227

92 Jayson Blair, 'Lessons Learned', Washington and Lee University: <https://www.youtube.com/watch?v=kFePfsBlocA> [accessed 28 Dec 2015].

one caught that. I can't believe that no one noticed it. But the seed was planted in my head.' Like Stapel, he was able to continue undetected with his conduct for a significant amount of time: 'You would think, you know, it's kind of the slippery slope that starts to happen. I think once you realize that you can get away with something, once you cross over that line, you somehow have to rationalize how I'm a good person and I did this. So somehow this has to be okay. I've got to make this okay. So then it becomes a lot easier to do.'[93]

There is much to be learned from the revelations of Blair. His own account is part of the story: 'Some might hold me responsible for not foreseeing the results of my actions, but my behavior was first and foremost an act of self-destruction. I am the master of my own house. And I destroyed it.'[94] However, Blair's attribution of his conduct to being the product of drug- and mental illness-induced hypomania is only part of it. The ease with which he was able to perpetrate his conduct, the fact he got away with it so effectively, and the limited supervision to which he was subject all provided opportunity. His ambition, to a degree a grandiose ambition, fuelled the preparedness to repeat his behaviour and there was disinhibition in the form of what were at least manic aspects to his personality, which may have spilled over at times into outright pathology and self-medicating substance abuse. It may be too that his professional development evolved in a distorted way to incorporate habitual taking of short-cuts and dishonesty. Perhaps the risk-taking became addictive.

Dealing with Plagiarism Allegations Fairly

While for many, plagiarism can be an emotional issue which generates highly judgmental epithets,[95] and which can give rise to a variety of adverse consequences, including even criminal charges,[96] it is important as a matter of fairness to distinguish between deliberate and deceptive usage of the intellectual work of others and inadvertent plagiarism.[97] The latter has been described as the product of 'cryptomnesia', inadvertent usage of others' work,[98] and is often asserted as a defence in disciplinary proceedings.

Justice Barron in *Flanagan v University College Dublin*[99] observed that 'the charge of plagiarism is a charge of cheating and as such the most serious academic breach of discipline possible.

93 'Plagiarism: Stopping Word Thieves' (21 October 2012): <http://www.cbsnews.com/news/plagiarism-stopping-word-thieves/> [accessed 28 Dec 2015].

94 Jayson Blair, above n 85.

95 See eg, Abbi Flint, Ranald Macdonald and Sue Clegg, *Emotion, Practise, and Plagiarism Exploring the Staff Perspective* (Paper presented at Plagiarism: Prevention, Practice and Policies 2004 Conference, 28 June 2004), available at <http://www.plagiarismadvice.org/research-papers/item/emotion-practise-and-plagiarism- exploring-the-staff-perspective> [accessed 28 Dec 2015]; Stephen Wilhoit, 'Helping Students Avoid Plagiarism' (1994) 42(4) *College Teaching* 161, available at: <https://mnsugsea.files.wordpress.com/2010/10/helping-students-avoid-plagiarism.pdf> [accessed 28 Dec 2015]. In relation to 'intellectual cannibalism', see also Bettina M Kreissl Lonfat, 'Of Cheats and Liars: Plagiarism', The Philosopher's Attic, 10 February 2010: <http://yseult.mediaevaliter.com/2010/02/10/of-cheats-and-liars-plagiarism/> [accessed 28 Dec 2015].

96 See eg, Stuart P Green, 'Plagiarism, Norms, and the Limits of Theft Law: Some Observations on the Use of Criminal Sanctions in Enforcing Intellectual Property Rights' (2002–2003) 54(1) *Hastings Law Journal* 167.

97 See Patricia L Tenpenny, Maria S Keriazakos, Gavin S Lew, and Thomas P Phelan, 'In Search of Inadvertent Plagiarism' (1998) 111(4) *The American Journal of Psychology* 529.

98 See Alan S Brown and Dana R Murphy, 'Cryptomnesia: Delineating Inadvertent Plagiarism' (1989) 15(3) *Journal of Experimental Psychology: Learning, Memory, and Cognition* 432.

99 [1988] IR 724, 731.

It is also criminal in its nature'. There remains a debate[100] as to whether plagiarism is to be assessed objectively by reference to the similarities between two pieces of work. This objective approach was adopted in 1982 by the Appellate Division of the Superior Court of New Jersey.[101] However, the more orthodox assessment, and that adopted in particular by McMurdo J in *Re Humzy-Hancock*,[102] is the subjective—for plagiarism to be established, it is necessary for it to be proved that the person accused had an intention to pass off the work of another as their own. Often, but not always, substantial similarity will be enough for this purpose: copying of pages of another's work ('word-for-word plagiarism') speaks for itself; it cannot be inadvertent.

The conduct of the (later) Vice-President of the United States, Joe Biden, in relation to his plagiarism without citation or acknowledgment of five pages of a paper from a 15-page article in the 1965 *Fordham University Law Review*[103] while he was at law school at Syracuse University, and then separately (on another subject) in a speech, became politicized in the run-up to presidential elections.[104] He admitted his word-for-word plagiarism as a student, contending to the Law Faculty in a letter, though: 'My intent was not to deceive anyone. For if it were, I would not have been so blatant.' At another point, the young Mr Biden said that 'if I had intended to cheat, would I have been so stupid?'[105] Hereunder, this common, but—sensibly viewed—implausible stance is referred to as 'the Biden defence'.

---

[100] See Corbin and Carter, above n 12. See too, the call by student defence lawyers to put the element of intent back into definitions of plagiarism: Shanlon Wu, 'Put the Intent Back into Plagiarism!' *Huffington Post*, 12 November 2014: <http://www.huffingtonpost.com/shanlon-wu/put-the-intent-back-into-_b_6307938.html> [accessed 28 Dec 2015].

[101] *Napolitano v Princeton University Trustees*, 453 A 2d 263 (NJ Super AD, 1982). See also, in respect of copyright, *Holdfast NZ Ltd v Henkel KgaA* [2007] 1 NZLR 336. Thus, in its Plagiarism Policy Statement, the Saint Louis University School of Law states: 'Plagiarism results from the unacknowledged use of material found in print sources, oral presentations, or visual, electronic or other media sources. Plagiarism does not require an intention to deceive. It can result when a student submits as his or her own work ideas, language, data or other material contained in a source not acknowledged by the student, if the student knew or should have known that such acknowledgment was required. Plagiarism includes, without limitation, the following: A. Submitting another author's published or unpublished work, in whole, in part or in paraphrase, as one's own work, without fully and properly crediting the other author with footnotes, citations or other bibliographical reference. B. Submitting as one's own original work any material, including data, tables, graphs, charts or other visual material obtained from any source, without acknowledgement and citation of the source. C. Submitting as one's own original work material produced through unacknowledged collaboration with others, unless such collaboration is permitted by the instructor': Saint Louis University School of Law, 'Chapter 6: Saint Louis University School of Law Plagiarism Policy Statement', *Student Handbook*, August 2014, (original formatting altered) 38: <http://www.slu.edu/Documents/law/Academics/StudentHandbook/student_handbook.pdf> [accessed 28 Dec 2015].

[102] [2007] QSC 34.

[103] 'Tortious Act as a Basis for Jurisdiction in Products Liability Cases' (1965) 33(4) *Fordham Law Review* 671.

[104] See Eugene J Dionne Jr, 'Biden Was Accused of Plagiarism in Law School', *The New York Times*, 17 September 1987: <http://www.nytimes.com/1987/09/17/us/biden-was-accused-of-plagiarism-in-law-school.html?pagewanted=1> [accessed 29 Dec 2015].

[105] Eugene J Dionne Jr, 'Biden Admits Plagiarism in School But Says It Was Not Malevolent', *The New York Times*, 18 September 1987: <http://www.nytimes.com/1987/09/18/us/biden-admits-plagiarism-in-school-but-says-it-was-not-malevolent.html> [accessed 29 Dec 2015]. See Jonathan Bailey, 'The Biden Plagiarism Scandal' on *Plagiarism Today* (26 August 2008): <https://www.plagiarismtoday.com/2008/08/26/the-biden-plagiarism-scandal/> [accessed 29 Dec 2015]. Compare the comments of Helene Hegemann in an interview with Cosima Lutz of *Die Welt* (9 February 2010): 'I don't see it as stealing because I have used the material in a completely *different context* which is entirely my own. And I have never pretended that any of this stuff was mine. When people insist on reinterpreting what I have written as the *Novel of the Noughties*, then they have to recognise that the writing process is also a product of its time. This means that *whole copyright excess* has been replaced by the right to copy and transform': Helene Hegemann quoted in 'From the Feuilletons' on *signandsight.com* (12 February 2010): <http://www.signandsight.com/intodaysfeuilletons/1991.html#airen> [accessed 29 Dec 2015]. Nonetheless, she did apologize: see 'Axolotl Roadkill: Helene Hegemann und Ullstein Verlegerin Dr. Siv Bublitz antworten auf Plagiatsvorwurf', *Buch*

There have been occasions too when plagiarism allegations have been brought to the attention of university authorities but have been covered up in order to protect the reputation of the institution. An example in this regard was exposed in a report by the New South Wales Independent Commission Against Corruption (ICAC) in 2005 in relation to the University of Newcastle. The concerns related to a report by a university employee that 15 students had plagiarized assignments. The ICAC concluded that the head of the Graduate School (Dr Ryder) had failed to apply the university's plagiarism policy and to undertake a proper investigation of the plagiarism concerns. The ICAC found that the failure by the head of school and his deputy (Dr Rugimbana) to have the assignments re-marked was motivated by a desire to avoid any potential adverse consequences that may have ensued for the university's offshore programme. It also found that the failure by Professor Roger Holmes, Newcastle University's Vice-Chancellor, and Professor Brian English, the Deputy Vice-Chancellor, to advise the Academic Senate and the University Council of the matter 'represented a serious failure by them of their duties'. The ICAC found that the head of the Graduate School and his Deputy had engaged in 'corrupt conduct'. It recommended a variety of changes to endeavour to avoid recurrence of the problem.

This chapter catalogues a variety of instances in which plagiarism has arisen as an issue in the context of the initial or continuing admission or registration of a lawyer or doctor. It explores approaches of the courts and regulatory authorities in the United Kingdom, United States, Canada, and Australia. It acknowledges the reality of plagiarism lying on a complex and perhaps even evolving spectrum. However, it argues that, as is appropriate, a comparable and censorious attitude can be identified for the most part by courts and regulators when practitioners have displayed a lack of probity and trustworthiness in the dishonest use of others' work.

Self-Plagiarism

Distinctive but difficult issues arise in relation to self-plagiarism, the use of significant parts of one's own work without identification that that is what is taking place.[106] The threshold for proscribed usage of one's own work is less than clear. The American Psychological Association in 2010, for instance, stipulated that '[w]hen duplication of one's own words is more extensive, citation of the duplicated words should be the norm' and 'must conform to legal notions of fair use'.[107]

Most scholarly journals require the submission of original work—namely, material that has not been published elsewhere. Yet, much that academics publish builds on material they have previously generated.[108] Often enough, scholars refocus material they have already published in a forum directed towards a particular audience or update work they have previously done. Commonly, persons are solicited to write chapters in an edited collection, be it a journal or a book, because of other material they have published on the same subject. The ethics in this

Markt, 7 February 2010: <http://www.buchmarkt.de/content/41393-axolotl-roadkill-helene-hegemann-und-ullstein-verlegerin-dr-siv-bublitz-antworten-auf-plagiatsvorwurf.htm> [accessed 29 Dec 2015]. See also, Kreissl Lonfat, above n 95.

106 See Roger Clarke, 'Journal Self-Citation XIX: Self-Plagiarism and Self-Citation—A Practical Guide Based on Underlying Principles' (2009) 25(1) *Communications of the Association for Information Systems* 155; Pamela Samuelson, 'Self-Plagiarism or Fair Use?' (1994) 37(8) *Communications of the ACM* 21.

107 American Psychological Association, *Publication Manual of the American Psychological Association* (6th edn, Washington, DC: American Psychological Association, 2010) 16.

108 Jef Akst, 'When Is Self-Plagiarism OK?' *The Scientist*, 9 September 2010: <http://www.the-scientist.com/?articles.view/articleNo/29245/title/When-is-self-plagiarism-ok-/> [accessed 29 Dec 2015].

regard are not straightforward[109] and in some respects have become more complicated with the increasing use of blogs and the phenomenon of open publishing in second tier, non-refereed journals to which authors need to pay money to be published, sometimes called 'vanity publishing'. As Scanlon has commented:

> The more we write, the more likely we will reuse *something*—imagery, phrasing, a sentence, an anecdote, an entire argument—that has served us well in the past and which has become a part of our writing vocabulary. This self-copying could be more or less unconscious, but probably it is often an intentional part of the composition process, as we cull back through previous work for relevant matter. Word processing has no doubt increased this practice, as on our computers' hard drives we keep folders of apposite notes and manuscripts within larger folders devoted to writing projects.[110]

However, at the heart of what is objectionable about self-plagiarism is that it misrepresents productivity.

Another perspective on the issue at a macro level is provided by Roig on behalf of the Office of Research Integrity: '[R]edundant and duplicate publication must be avoided, for it has the potential for distorting the existing data base, possibly resulting in the establishment of flawed public health policies.'[111]

The extent of self-plagiarism is unclear but, with the continuing proliferation of both journals and forums for publication, the temptation for wholesale replication of material or at least for 'salami [slicing]'[112] or 'slicing [and] dicing'[113] may well be increasing.[114] As long ago as 2001 Schein and Paladugu reviewed 660 articles published in leading journals of surgery three years previously.[115] They found that 3 per cent (n = 20) were wholly replicated publications and, more significantly, that 7.6 per cent (n = 50) were almost identical, leading them to conclude: '[T]he incidence of redundant or frankly duplicate publishing is higher than is generally appreciated, with about 1 in every 6 original articles published in leading surgical journals potentially representing some form of redundancy.'[116]

A vice in undisclosed republication or substantial text-recycling is that it can be intellectually deceptive or dishonest by reason of its lack of transparency—when there is passing off of material that is original when in fact the author has previously published it. If it is of significant dimensions in a particular instance it achieves an objective of publication that may well not have been achieved if the author had revealed what was being done.[117] The pressures towards replication and partial or even republication of work, with or without camouflaging (by utilizing devices such as employing different titles, reformatting or altering commencement, and conclusory paragraphs), within academia are significant because of the pressures to publish and the financial and promotional advantages accruing from significant levels of publication.

---

109 See eg, Lelia Green, 'Reviewing the Scourge of Self-Plagiarism' (2005) 8(5) *M/C Journal*: <http://journal.media-culture.org.au/0510/07-green.php> [accessed 29 Dec 2015].

110 Patrick M Scanlon, 'Song From Myself: An Anatomy of Self-Plagiarism' (2007) *Plagiary: Cross-Disciplinary Studies in Plagiarism, Fabrication, and Falsification* 57, 58, available at: <http://quod.lib.umich.edu/cgi/p/pod/dod-idx?c=plag;idno=5240451.0002.007> [accessed 29 Dec 2015].

111 Roig, above n 15, 18.

112 Paul McCarthy, 'The Paper Mill' (October 1993) *The New Physician* 24, 27. See in respect of Stapel's use of this technique, above, at p39..

113 Ibid, 25.

114 In 1993, McCarthy maintained that it was 'an enormous problem': ibid.

115 Moshe Schein and Ramesh Paladugu, 'Redundant Surgical Publications: Tip of the Iceberg?' (2001) 129(6) *Surgery* 655.

116 Ibid, 661.

117 See the useful discussion by the World Association of Medical Editors: 'Self-Plagiarism of Textbook Chapters' (October 2004): <http://www.wame.org/about/self-plagiarism-of-textbook-chapters> [accessed 29 Dec 2015].

There are some instances in which citation of the source from which material has emanated (namely, where the first piece was published) and the level (slight, substantial or complete) of republication will make the self-plagiarism acceptable. Often in that context permission will need to be sought from the primary source: when the author himself or herself is not the copyright holder (at least during the review process).[118] An important question to be asked is: what are the expectations of the audience and of the original and subsequent publisher?[119] What is fundamental is that there be transparency of the use made of previously published work: otherwise, both the publications (the first and the subsequent) and the readers risk being deceived as to the originality of the subsequent publication.

Perhaps an example of contemporary attitudes toward self-plagiarism in a forum where originality is expected occurred in the controversy that occurred in relation to the pop-neuroscientist writer, Jonah Lehrer, in June 2012. He announced that he was leaving 'Wired' where he had been a contributing co-editor to take up a position at *The New Yorker* to be a staff writer. Problems came to light when media critic Jim Romenesko posted an item in which he showed that Lehrer had published pieces in the *Wall Street Journal* and on NewYorker.com whose first three paragraphs were nearly identical. The response from Lehrer's editor, Nicholas Thompson, at *The New Yorker* was swift: expression of disappointment for 'duplication of the material' and required ascription on various of his pieces to that effect. His comment about it was simple: 'Everybody knows that they can't do this.'[120]

Another controversy erupted in a more scholarly context in relation to Ronald Breslow, an eminent chemist who led a research group at Columbia University in New York. It became apparent that he authored a series of papers (in the *Israel Journal of Chemistry* and in *Tetrahedron Letters*) containing replicated passages. This resulted in calls for retraction of the last in the series of the papers which was published in the *Journal of the American Chemical Society* (JACS) and which argued that advanced dinosaurs could exist on other planets.[121]

Responding to the controversy, Breslow maintained to *Nature* that he had done nothing wrong and argued that the article was a '"[p]erspective" piece' intended to review the field, and therefore did not purport to be an original research publication:

> When I submitted it I made it clear what I had done to avoid personal plagiarism while still meeting the purpose of the Perspective; it would have made no sense not to describe the previous work, which was requested, as long as I gave the appropriate references.
> Please distinguish a personal review from a paper. It was this distinction that led me to write it, while making enough changes to avoid copyright infringement while still telling the real story.[122]

---

[118] See Nancy K Lowe (ed), 'Publication Ethics: Copyright and Self-Plagiarism' (2003) 32(2) *Journal of Obstetric, Gynecologic, & Neonatal Nursing* 145.

[119] A development of suggestions made by Jonathan Bailey, 'Self-Plagiarism: Ethical Shortcut or Moral Scourge?' on *Plagiarism Today* (7 September 2011): <https://www.plagiarismtoday.com/2011/09/07/self-plagiarism-ethical-shortcut-or-moral-scourge/> [accessed 29 Dec 2015].

[120] Jacob Silverman, 'Jonah Lehrer's "Self-Plagiarism" Scandal Rocks The New Yorker', *The Daily Beast*, 20 June 2012: <http://www.thedailybeast.com/articles/2012/06/20/jonah-lehrer-s-self-plagiarism-scandal-rocks-the-new-yorker.html> [accessed 29 Dec 2015].

[121] Daniel Cressey, 'Eminent Chemist Denies Self-Plagiarism in "Space Dinosaurs' Paper", *Nature*, 25 April 2012: <http://blogs.nature.com/news/2012/04/eminent-chemist-denies-self-plagiarism-in-space-dinosaurs-paper.html> [accessed 29 Dec 2015].

[122] Ibid: 'The *JACS* paper that prompted this debate [and ultimately the retraction] was a sober discussion of a rather technical aspect of amino-acid chemistry. However, a press release from the American Chemical Society (ACS) picked up on the throwaway last line that there could be other amino-acid-based life forms elsewhere in the Universe and that 'such life forms could well be advanced versions of dinosaurs.'

The topic of self-plagiarism can have subtleties in terms of the amount of republication necessary and even its form—such as where material from a study is 'salami [sliced]' to provide the impression that each publication is derived from a different subject sample.[123] In many respects it is a question of the degree of misimpression that is created.

University Policies on Plagiarism

There is consistency across tertiary institutions that plagiarism is unacceptable. However, an increasing focus of such policies is framing them in terms of intellectual honesty. As Scanlon has pointed out, plagiarism encompasses two ethical transgressions, theft and imposture: 'Because the plagiarist filches text he did not create and presents it as though he did, he is condemned for stealing and for false pretence. The plagiarist's moral offence is in his lying and deception, which undermine trust, and in his failure to transform or acknowledge his sources which dishonours, the original author.'[124]

The policy of Macquarie University in Australia highlights this issue of integrity:

> Academic honesty is an integral part of the core values and principles contained in the *Macquarie University Ethics Statement.* Its fundamental principle is that all staff and students act with integrity in the creation, development, application and use of ideas and information. This means that:
> - all academic work claimed as original is the work of the author making the claim
> - all academic collaborations are acknowledged
> - academic work is not falsified in any way
> - when the ideas of others are used, these ideas are acknowledged appropriately.[125]

Oxford University, like a number of tertiary institutions, provides an online module for students on avoiding plagiarism which it defines broadly and accessibly: 'Plagiarism is the copying or paraphrasing of other people's work or ideas into your own work without full acknowledgement. All published and unpublished material, whether in manuscript, printed or electronic form, is covered under this definition. Collusion is another form of plagiarism involving the unauthorized collaboration of students (or others) in a piece of work.'[126] It explains that:

> Plagiarism is a breach of academic integrity. It is a principle of intellectual honesty that all members of the academic community should acknowledge their debt to the originators of the ideas, words, and data which form the basis for their own work. Passing off another's work as your own is not only poor scholarship, but also means that you have failed to complete the learning process. Deliberate plagiarism is unethical and can have serious consequences for your future career; it also undermines the standards of your institution and of the degrees it issues.[127]

Oxford University communicates to students that there are many reasons why they should avoid plagiarism:

> You have come to university to learn to know and speak your own mind, not merely to parrot the opinions of others—at least not without attribution. At first it may seem very

[123] Scanlon, above n 110, 59.

[124] Ibid 61.

[125] See Macquarie University, 'Academic Honesty Policy', 13 November 2012: <http://mq.edu.au/policy/docs/academic_honesty/policy.html> [accessed 29 Dec 2015].

[126] University of Oxford, *Academic Good Practice—A Practical Guide*, 5–6, available at: <http://www.admin.ox.ac.uk/edc/goodpractice/> [accessed 29 Dec 2015].

[127] Ibid, 6.

> difficult to develop your own views, and you will probably find yourself paraphrasing the writings of others as you attempt to understand and assimilate their arguments. However it is important that you learn to develop your own voice. You are not necessarily expected to become an original thinker, but you are expected to be an independent one—by learning to assess critically the work of others, weigh up differing arguments and draw your own conclusions. Students who plagiarize undermine the ethos of academic scholarship while avoiding an essential part of the learning process.[128]

Students are warned that if plagiarism is suspected it will be referred to the Proctors who will investigate the claim thoroughly and summon the student for interview. If it is concluded that an intentional or reckless breach of regulations has occurred, the Proctors will refer the case to a disciplinary panel.

Harvard University instructs its students that when they write papers:

> [Their work] is held to the same standards of citation as the work of your professors. Your professors observe these conventions for two reasons: First, citing sources allows scholars to give credit to other scholars for their hard work and their ideas. Second, by citing sources, scholars provide a roadmap for readers who are interested in learning more about a topic and joining the ongoing conversation about that topic. When you fail to cite your sources, or when you cite them inadequately, you commit plagiarism, an offense that is taken extremely seriously at Harvard.[129]

Harvard defines plagiarism as 'the act of either intentionally *OR* unintentionally submitting work that was written by someone else. If you turn in a paper that was written by someone else, or if you turn in a paper in which you have copied material from any source without citing that source, you are guilty of plagiarizing'.[130] Students are told that in academic writing:

> [I]t is considered plagiarism to draw any idea or any language from someone else without adequately crediting that source in your paper. It doesn't matter whether the source is a published author, another student, a Web site without clear authorship, a Web site that sells academic papers, or any other person: Taking credit for anyone else's work is stealing, and it is unacceptable in all academic situations, whether you do it intentionally or by accident. The ease with which you can find information of all kinds on the Internet means that when you use online sources, you need to be extra vigilant about keeping track of where you are getting information and ideas, and about giving proper credit to the authors of the sources you use. If you cut and paste from an electronic document into your notes and forget to clearly label the document in your notes, or if you draw information from a series of Web sites without taking careful notes, you may end up taking credit for ideas that aren't yours, whether you mean to or not.[131]

The guide warns students of the unacceptability of verbatim plagiarism, mosaic plagiarism, inadequate paraphrase, uncited paraphrase, uncited quotation, and using material from another student's work. It also explicitly proscribes turning in the same paper for more than one class—a form of self-plagiarism. In terms of a rationale for its rules, the Harvard Guide explains:

> Scholars place a premium on careful, original thought. Academic writing is essentially an ongoing conversation among scholars. As a college student, you are part of the community of scholars who are working to answer genuine questions in their fields by building on the

[128] Ibid.

[129] Harvard College, 'Avoiding Plagiarism', *Harvard Guide to Using Sources*: <http://usingsources.fas.harvard.edu/icb/icb.do?keyword=k70847&tabgroupid=icb.tabgroup106849> [accessed 29 Dec 2015].

[130] Ibid.

[131] Harvard College, 'What Constitutes Plagiarism', *Harvard Guide to Using Sources*: <http://isites.harvard.edu/icb/icb.do?keyword=k70847&pageid=icb.page342054> [accessed 29 Dec 2015].

> knowledge and ideas that others have contributed. When you use sources to write a paper, you have the responsibility to represent others' ideas accurately and to contribute your own ideas to the discussion. Your professors expect you to do your own thinking, and they assign research and writing so that you can figure out what you think rather than reporting or parroting someone else's thoughts. You actually don't learn anything when you take your ideas from someone else; you learn by analyzing the ideas you have read about and developing your own responses to them.[132]

The University of Sydney incorporates plagiarism under the category of 'academic dishonesty' and defines it to mean 'presenting another person's work as one's own work by presenting, copying or reproducing it without appropriate acknowledgement of the source', and to include presenting work for assessment, publication or otherwise that includes (regardless of intention):

- phrases, clauses, sentences, paragraphs or longer extracts from published or unpublished work (including from the Internet) without appropriate acknowledgement of the source; or
- the work of another person, without appropriate acknowledgement of the source and presented in a way that exceeds the boundaries of legitimate co-operation.[133]

Interestingly, though, it goes on to dichotomize plagiarism as 'negligent' (when plagiarism consists of innocent, reckless, or careless presentation of another's work as one's own without appropriate acknowledgment of the source) or 'dishonest' (when plagiarism consists of knowing presentation of another's work without appropriate acknowledgment of the source).[134] It provides that alleged plagiarism will be regarded as dishonest plagiarism when:

- substantial portions of the work have been copied from the work of another person, in a manner that clearly exceeds the boundaries of legitimate co-operation;
- the work contains a substantial body of copied material (including from the Internet) without appropriate acknowledgment of the source, and in a manner that cannot be explained as negligent plagiarism; or
- in the case of a student preparing work for assessment, there is evidence that the student engaged another person to produce or conduct research for the work, including for payment or other consideration.[135]

It emphasizes the 'key responsibility of an examiner to distinguish original from plagiarized work'[136] and requires of students that they submit with all their work a statement of compliance with the University's policies, including that their work is not plagiarized.[137] It sets out detailed processes for resolution by a 'nominated academic' of allegations of plagiarism with the consequences for negligent plagiarism being counselling, as well as a variety of requirements for resubmission and undertaking other assessment, including imposition of a

---

[132] Harvard College, 'Why Does It Matter If You Plagiarize', *Harvard Guide to Using Sources*: <http://isites.harvard.edu/icb/icb.do?keyword=k70847&pageid=icb.page342056> [accessed 29 Dec 2015].

[133] University of Sydney, 'Academic Dishonesty and Plagiarism in Coursework Policy', 1 January 2012, [3.2.1]–[3.2.2]: <http://sydney.edu.au/policies/showdoc.aspx?recnum=PDOC2012/254&RendNum=0> [accessed 29 Dec 2015]. The Australian National University takes a comparable approach defining plagiarism as 'copying, paraphrasing or summarizing, without appropriate acknowledgement, the words, ideas, scholarship and intellectual property of another person. This remains plagiarism whether or not it is with the knowledge or consent of that other person. Plagiarism has also taken place when direct use of others' words is not indicated, for example by inverted commas or indentation, in addition to appropriate citation of the source': Australian National University, Academic Standards & Quality Office, 'What is a Breach?' 17 February 2015: <http://drss.anu.edu.au/asqo/breaches.php> [accessed 29 Dec 2015].

[134] University of Sydney, above n 133, [3.3]–[3.4].

[135] Ibid, [3.4.2].

[136] Ibid, [4.3.1].

[137] Ibid, [4.4.1].

fail grade or a mark penalty. However, where dishonest plagiarism is found, the conduct is regarded as 'student misconduct' involving referral to the Registrar for investigation and the imposition of potentially more significant penalties.[138]

It is apparent, and unsurprising, from this very limited review of universities' policies on plagiarism that, although expressed significantly differently, they share much in common and with the same objective. Perhaps the University of Melbourne summarizes the aspirations of all tertiary institutions when through its Provost between 2007 and 2009, Professor Peter McPhee, it observed that the most important attribute it would like to see in its graduates 'is a profound respect for truth, and for the ethics of scholarship…we want our graduates to be capable of independent thought, to be able to do their own work, and to know how to acknowledge the work of others'.[139] While there is generally an acceptance that there are different forms of plagiarism, which can be differentially described by reference to their seriousness, the approach is consistent that unacknowledged use of sources constitutes plagiarism and is reprehensible because of its lack of originality and scholarly integrity.

Plagiarism at Universities: Students

Plagiarism engaged in by students has become a serious problem for universities[140] and even for secondary schools.[141] The issue erupted notoriously in the United States when Harvard University's disciplinary board was reported in August 2012 to be investigating nearly half of the 279 students who enrolled in 'Government: Introduction to Congress' the previous Spring for allegedly plagiarizing answers or inappropriately collaborating on the final take-home exam.[142] Dean of Undergraduate Education Jay M Harris said the magnitude of the case was 'unprecedented in anyone's living memory'. Ultimately, firm sanctions were taken with more than half the students being required to withdraw from studies for a time and, of the remaining students, around half received disciplinary probation.[143]

---

[138] Ibid, Part 5.

[139] University of Melbourne, 'Academic Honesty and Plagiarism': <https://academichonesty.unimelb.edu.au/> [accessed 29 Dec 2015].

[140] See *Re AJG* [2004] QCA 88; Shelley Yeo, 'First-Year University Science and Engineering Students' Understanding of Plagiarism' (2007) 26(2) *Higher Education Research & Development* 199, 201; Bridget Murray, 'Keeping Plagiarism at Bay in the Internet Age' (2002) 33(2) *Monitor* 22: <http://www.apa.org/monitor/feb02/plagiarism.aspx> [accessed 29 Dec 2015].

[141] See Benjamin Preiss, 'Schools Turning to Anti-Plagiarism Software to Catch Cheating Students', *The Sydney Morning Herald*, 2 September 2014: <http://www.smh.com.au/digital-life/digital-life-news/schools-turning-to-antiplagiarism-software-to-catch-cheating-students-20140902-10ayuv.html> [accessed 29 Dec 2015]. Few any longer would subscribe to the quote attributed to the United States dramatist Wilson Mizner in 1938—'When you take stuff from one writer it's plagiarism, but when you take from many writers it's called research'—Frank Case, *Tales of a Wayward Inn* (New York: Frederick A Stokes Company, 1938) 248, as cited in *Quote Investigator*, 9 March 2013: <http://quoteinvestigator.com/2010/09/20/plagiarism/> [accessed 29 Dec 2015].

[142] Rebecca D Robbins, 'Harvard Investigates 'Unprecedented' Academic Dishonesty Case', *The Harvard Crimson*, 30 August 2012: <http://www.thecrimson.com/article/2012/8/30/academic-dishonesty-ad-board/> [accessed 29 Dec 2015].

[143] Julie Zeveloff, 'Half of the Students in Harvard's Massive Cheating Scandal Have Been Forced to Withdraw', *Business Insider Australia*, 2 February 2013: <http://www.businessinsider.com.au/harvard-students-in-cheating-scandal-to-withdraw-2013-2> [accessed 29 Dec 2015]. Along similar lines, more than 160 final year law students at the University of Tasmania were required to re-sit an examination in 2013 after a cheating scandal: see *ABC Radio National*, 'Tasmanian Law School Cheating Scandal', *Law Report*, 3 September 2013 (Damien Carrick): <http://www.abc.net.au/radionational/programs/lawreport/tasmanian-law-school-cheating-scandal/4931990> [accessed 29 Dec 2015].

In Australia the issue of student cheating by plagiarism also acquired a high profile during 2012 when Victoria's Deakin University took a strong stand on the issue. It revealed that 30 students had been the subject of formal allegations of academic misconduct in the form of plagiarism and nine had been expelled after hearings. None appealed the penalties. The general secretary of Deakin University's student association told the media that all those involved had been overseas students who had bought essays off the internet, predominantly from foreign websites.[144]

Less than a year previously in a report addressing how universities are dealing with foreign students, the Victorian Ombudsman noted the report to him from a number of academic staff that:

> [P]lagiarism is a particular issue for international students. They noted that plagiarism is a Western academic concept that can be hard to understand for international students who come from cultures where writing involves repeating the collective wisdom and students do not need to acknowledge the source of information.
>
> Other staff said that students with poor English skills find it harder to avoid plagiarism. An academic expert said international students may lack the English language skills required to read information, extract the relevant points and put it into their own words.[145]

He recorded a senior academic at Deakin University as maintaining that:

> We have hundreds and hundreds and hundreds of students in the faculty... who are before the faculty academic discipline boards... Literally, I mean 1,500 maybe at times overall in a trimester. I don't know what the figures are but they're just massive.[146]

He was also told by an academic at RMIT University's School of Nursing and Midwifery that she preferred to give students exams because by that means she knew their capacity to cheat was taken away: 'We've got plagiarism running rampant... I give students a nursing care plan to do. I know that international and local students have bought it from somewhere—from someone else.'[147] The Ombudsman concluded that:

> Despite efforts by universities to inform and warn students about plagiarism and cheating, it remains a problem. The evidence obtained by my investigation suggests that some cases may be going unreported within universities. For some academics there are disincentives in reporting plagiarism because of the time it takes to investigate and respond to appeals. Others are uncertain about whether students are cheating deliberately or just lack the understanding or skills to avoid the problem.[148]

He expressed the view that universities may be 'underestimating the risk of bribery amongst staff and students. While my investigation spoke to a small sample of academics, over a third had experienced or knew of problems with bribery'.[149] He recommended that Victoria's universities '[c]ommission an independent risk assessment of the extent of cheating and bribery

---

[144] John Ross, 'Nine Expelled for Plagiarism at Deakin', *The Australian*, 6 October 2012: <http://www.theaustralian.com.au/higher-education/nine-expelled-for-plagiarism-at-deakin/story-e6frgcjx-1226489447781> [accessed 29 Dec 2015]; Anne Mather, 'Law Students to Re-sit Exam Amid Fears Online Assessment was Compromised', *The Mercury*, 31 August 2013: <http://www.themercury.com.au/news/law-students-to-re-sit-exam-amid-fears-online-assessment-was-compromised/story-fnj4f7kx-1226707906897> [accessed 29 Dec 2015].

[145] Taylor, above n 20, [238]–[239].

[146] Ibid [241].

[147] Ibid [242].

[148] Ibid, [252].

[149] Ibid, [253].

amongst staff and students and the effectiveness of their existing policies and procedures by mid-2012 and provide the findings to my office'.[150]

The incidence of plagiarism among both students and professional staff is not known. However, Guterman has reported in his review of recent research: 'More than 70,000 article abstracts appeared disturbingly similar to other published work when scanned by a new search program.'[151] In 2001 Schein and Paladugu found that 14 per cent of the original articles published in leading surgical journals could be considered redundant.[152] The problem is not new. In 1990, 70 of the institutions providing annual reports to the United States Office of Research Integrity reported handling 58 cases related to plagiarism, which represented '22 percent of the total allegations and cases reported'. In 1991, 26 per cent of cases reported by 35 institutions to the Office of Research Integrity involved plagiarism.[153] Similarly, the National Science Foundation in the United States reported during a similar period that 70 of their 124 cases over a three-year period also involved plagiarism.[154]

An issue that has particularly emerged over the past decade in relation to the conduct of students has been the vast amounts of material in the era of the internet[155] that may not be particularly familiar to markers and examiners and which is difficult to identify. Similar problems confront book publishers and editors of scholarly journals, both of which run a continuing risk of being 'duped' by plagiarists. In the tertiary context it has been suggested that plagiarism in assignments by some medical students is endemic.[156] As Harris has observed:

> The availability of textual material in electronic format has made plagiarism easier than ever. Copying and pasting of paragraphs or even entire essays now can be performed with just a few mouse clicks.[157]

This has resulted in an extensive series of revelations of 'plagiarism scandals'[158] at universities, involving both undergraduate and postgraduate students, and in a growing awareness of the need to develop strategies,[159] handbooks,[160] and software programs[161] to try to detect plagiarism. Other initiatives have included attempts to highlight the unethical and cheating behaviour inherent in plagiarism so as to render it less socially acceptable among students: to

---

150 Ibid, 51 (Recommendation 9).

151 Lila Guterman, 'Plagiarism and Other Sins Seem Rife in Science Journals, a Digital Sleuth Trends' (2008) 54(21) *Chronicle of Higher Education* A9.

152 Schein and Paladugu, above n 115, 657.

153 Alan Price, 'How Institutions Have Handled Investigations of Plagiarism' (Paper presented at the ORI/AAAS Conference on Plagiarism and Theft of Ideas, 21 June 1993) 69, available at: <http://ori.hhs.gov/documents/aaas2.pdf> [accessed 29 Dec 2015].

154 Ibid.

155 See eg, Ann Lathropand Kathleen Foss, *Student Cheating and Plagiarism in the Internet Era: A Wake-up Call* (Englewood, Colo: Libraries Unlimited, 2000) 2.

156 See Lidija Bilić-Zulle, Vedran Frković, Tamara Turk, Josip Ažman et al., 'Prevalence of Plagiarism Among Medical Students' (2005) 46(1) *Croatian Medical Journal* 126, an article relating to informatics assignments by medical students. The degree to which inferences can be drawn from this example is unclear.

157 Harris, above n 69.

158 See eg, LaFollette, above n 12.

159 See eg, Timothy C Hoad and Justin Zobel, 'Methods for Identifying Versioned and Plagiarized Documents' (2003) 54(3) *Journal of the American Society for Information Science and Technology* 203. Students, of course, are routinely advised to eschew plagiarism: see Michael Brogan and David Spencer, *Surviving Law School* (Melbourne: Oxford University Press, 2004).

160 See eg, Jude Carroll, *A Handbook for Deterring Plagiarism in Higher Education* (Oxford: Oxford Centre for Staff and Learning Development, 2002).

161 See eg, Turnitin: <http://turnitin.com/en_us/home> [accessed 29 Dec 2015]; iThenticate: <http://www.ithenticate.com/> [accessed 29 Dec 2015]; WCopyfind: <http://wcopyfind.findmysoft.com/> [accessed 29 Dec 2015]; Glatt Plagiarism Services: <http://www.plagiarism.com/> [accessed 29 Dec 2015].

erode an escalating culture of illicit information use.[162] Publishers, courts and regulatory authorities too are faced with the challenge of evaluating the potential incompatibility of a professional's preparedness to engage in plagiarism and such persons becoming or remaining a member of an honourable profession, such as law or medicine.

Moves towards Standardization of Penalties for Student Plagiarism

In 2006, Baroness Deech, the former independent adjudicator for higher education in the United Kingdom, warned that universities were leaving themselves vulnerable to legal action as a result of their inconsistent handling of plagiarism cases.[163] The Joint Information Systems Committee, the information technology body for United Kingdom universities, funded plagiarismadvice.org to conduct research on the issue.

Peter Tennant, a Newcastle University research assistant in the United Kingdom, and Gill Rowell, academic adviser at plagiarismadvice.org, constructed a 'plagiarisim tariff' as part of the Academic Misconduct Benchmarking Research project. It was launched at the Fourth International Plagiarism Conference in Newcastle in 2011. Its aim was to provide a benchmark, without being unduly prescriptive.[164]

Tennant said that his research had showed that, when staff were asked to look beyond their institutions' policies and give their personal opinions, there was a surprising level of agreement on the appropriate outcomes in relation to plagiarism by students.[165] The following examples of the sliding scale are provided.

> Example One
>
> A first-year student has failed to attribute one sentence in a summative assignment. This is the student's first offence. Under the tariff, this case scores a total of 280 points. The guidance's recommended penalty options are:
> - Formal warning on record
> - Assignment awarded 0 per cent: resubmission required, with no penalty on the mark
>
> Example Two
>
> A second-year student has cut and pasted two paragraphs of material taken from the internet and used without attribution in the main body of a 2,000-word essay. The student's record shows a formal warning for a similar incident in a previous formative assignment. This case scores a total of 400 points. The recommended penalty options are:
> - Assignment awarded 0 per cent: resubmission required, with the mark capped or reduced
> - Assignment awarded 0 per cent: no opportunity to resubmit
>
> Example Three
>
> A final-year student has submitted work obtained from a ghostwriting service as a dissertation. The student's record indicates plagiarism on two previous occasions. This case scores 625 points. The guidance's recommended penalty options are:
> - Module awarded 0 per cent: no opportunity to resit and credit lost
> - Award classification reduced
> - Qualification reduced

---

[162] See eg, Ann Lathrop and Kathleen E Foss, *Guiding Students from Cheating and Plagiarism to Honesty and Integrity: Strategies for Change* (Westport, CT: Libraries Unlimited, 2005).

[163] Phil Baty, 'Inconsistent Penalties Raise Risk of Legal Action, Deech Says', *Times Higher Education Supplement*, 23 June 2006: <http://www.timeshighereducation.co.uk/news/inconsistent-penalties-raise-risk-of-legal-action-deech-says/203884.article> [accessed 29 Dec 2015].

[164] Rebecca Attwood, 'Plagiarism Tariff: Let the Punishment Fit the Demerit Points', *Times Higher Education*, 17 June 2010: <http://www.timeshighereducation.co.uk/412088.article> [accessed 29 Dec 2015].

[165] Ibid.

- Expelled from institution, but with credits retained
- Expelled from institution with credits withdrawn.[166]

Whether such a taxonomy can be employed outside the student context is unclear.

Plagiarism at Universities: Academics

The extent of plagiarism is clearly extensive, although, as noted above, it is impossible to estimate with any validity its extent. Israel observed in 2014 that 'Plagiarism is one of the more prevalent forms of academic misconduct outside the biomedical field, particularly in qualitative social science research.'[167]

Plagiarism has been proved against even eminent academics, disgraced Monash Vice-Chancellor in Australia, David Robinson being a prominent example.[168] Robinson engaged in significant plagiarism in his work on addiction in 1979 and 1983. In 1979 he drew problematically on the work of another drug and alcohol scholar, David Mandelbaum, and then in 1983 he published *Drug Use and Misuse: Cultural Perspectives*, which was based on a study for the World Health Organization. The publisher, Croom Helm, was obliged to publish an erratum: 'Alcoholics Anonymous: American Origins and the International Diffusion of a Self-help Group'. The erratum stated:

> After this book was printed the publisher learned that David Robinson... had used material from another author. At least 20 sentences of the chapter were taken verbatim, without references and without quotation marks... Dr Robinson unreservedly apologises for this serious violation of scholarly standards.[169]

One of his critics later commented, tellingly: 'Having a plagiarist as head of a university is like having an embezzler running an accounting firm.'[170]

Perhaps indicative of the more tolerant and forgiving attitudes of three decades ago, Professor Robinson's career continued to flourish (including his assumption of the role at Monash University) until revelations surfaced of his persistence in plagiarizing behaviour, whereupon he was pressured to resign in 2002[171] after allegations of his misappropriation of text and

---

166 Ibid.

167 Mark Israel, *Research Ethics and Integrity for Social Scientists: Beyond Regulatory Compliance* (2nd edn, Los Angeles: SAGE, 2015) 156.

168 See Simon Caterson, 'A Plagiarism on Them All', *The Age*, 20 November 2004: <http://www.theage.com.au/articles/2004/11/18/1100748128612.html> [accessed 29 Dec 2015]. Notably also, at a less prominent level, Angela Adrian, formerly of the Southern Cross Law School, has had papers retracted by journals for plagiarism: See Angela Adrian, 'Could a Small Town in Romania Bring Australia to its Cyber-knees? Not if They Accede to the EU Convention on Cybercrime' (2012) 7(4) *Journal of International Commercial Law and Technology* 328: <http://www.google.com.au/url?sa=t&rct=j&q=&esrc=s&source=web&cd=1&sqi=2&ved=0CCIQFjAA&url=<http%3A%2F%2Fwww.jiclt.com%2Findex.php%2Fjiclt%2Farticle%2Fdownload%2F189%2F187&ei=s5aNU7yMCMP5kAWFvIC4DQ&usg=AFQjCNH-zd2EesMxz5lkIN1DGJJmU_YK1g&sig2=hIudQgxSiRGXWldjto9yPA&bvm=bv.68191837,d.dGI>; Angela Adrian, 'The Pirate Bay Deep-Sixed' (2006) 22(5) *Computer Law and Security Review* 392: <http://www.readcube.com/articles/10.1016%2Fj.clsr.2006.07.009> [accessed 29 Dec 2015]. See Julie Hare, 'SCU Academic's Articles Retracted over Plagiarism Claims' (13 August 2014) The Australian: <http://www.theaustralian.com.au/higher-education/scu-academics-articles-retracted-over-plagiarism-claims/story-e6frgcjx-1227022199895> [accessed 29 Dec 2015].

169 See 'Whistleblowers: Plagiarism Scandal Returns to Haunt V-C', *Times Higher Education*, 21 June 2002: <http://www.timeshighereducation.co.uk/169922.article> [accessed 29 Dec 2015].

170 James Madden, 'Closing the Book on a Career', *The Australian*, 13 July 2002, 1.

171 See ABC Radio National, 'Vice-Chancellor Resigns Over Plagiarism Claims', *PM*, 11 July 2002 (Kate Tozer): <http://www.abc.net.au/pm/stories/s604692.htm> [accessed 29 Dec 2015].

ideas were aired in a British newspaper. The older counts, admitted privately by Robinson at the time, were supplemented by a third instance in an even earlier publication that was uncovered by a staff member at Monash.[172]

In 2008 Madonna Constantine, a Professor of Psychology at Columbia University's Teachers College, was sacked after an 18-month investigation found that she had engaged in 'numerous instances in which she used others' work without attribution in papers she published in academic journals over the past five years.'[173] Dr Constantine condemned the investigation into her as a biased and flawed—the product of a conspiracy against her, including that it arose on racist grounds.[174]

In April 2011 Professor Abebe Zegeye, the newly appointed director of the University of South Australia's Hawke Research Institute, was induced to resign from his position after occupying it for only four months after revelation of plagiarism findings relating to articles he had written while Director of the prestigious Witwatersrand Institute for Social and Economic Research (WISER) at the University of Witwatersrand (Wits) in South Africa. Wits commissioned Gilbert Marcus SC, a well-known advocate at the Johannesburg Bar, to conduct a 'final and binding arbitration' of the matter.[175] He found the allegations proved and recommended the dismissal of Professor Zegeye.

Professor Zegeye had had a prominent career. He obtained a doctorate in sociology from Oxford University, held visiting professorships at Yale and the University of California, and was Professor of Sociology at the University of South Africa for ten years before joining the University of Witwatersrand.

The Zegeye affair began when three eminent international scholars[176] wrote to the Wits Vice-Chancellor, Professor Loyiso Nongxa, complaining about the conduct of Professor Zegeye. According to Marcus, the Nongxa letter 'accused Zegeye of having "blatantly, repeatedly and extensively misrepresented published work of a range of authors [including themselves] as his own", and alleged that he "continued such plagiarizing practice despite having been warned explicitly in the past of its unacceptability."'.[177]

---

172 In earlier days a less comfortable consequence attended the plagiarism by Ron Wild, Professor of Sociology at La Trobe University, in his book, *An Introduction to Sociological Perspectives: Theory and Research in the Australian Context* (North Sydney, NSW: Allen and Unwin, 1985) which was withdrawn from circulation. La Trobe University set up an inquiry into his conduct but, before the inquiry was completed, he resigned and took up a position with the Hedland College of Technical and Further Education. See Brian Martin, 'Scientific Fraud and the Power Structure of Science' (1992) 10(1) *Prometheus: Critical Studies in Innovation* 83; Dan Riley, 'Fraud and Australian Academics' (Paper presented at the Annual Conference of the Australasian Association for Research in Education, Surfers Paradise, Queensland, 1991: <http://www.aare.edu.au/data/publications/1991/riled91203.pdf> [accessed 29 Dec 2015]). See also, *Re La Trobe University; Ex Parte Wild* [1987] VR 447.

173 Karen W Arenson and Elissa Gootman, 'Columbia Cites Plagiarism by a Professor', *The New York Times*, 21 February 2008: <http://www.nytimes.com/2008/02/21/education/21prof.html?pagewanted=all&_r=2&> [accessed 29 Dec 2015].

174 See generally, ibid; John M Braxton, Eve Proper, and Alan E Bayer, *Professors Behaving Badly: Faculty Misconduct in Graduate Education* (Baltimore: Johns Hopkins University Press, 2011), ch 1; Thomas Bartlett and Scott Smallwood, 'Four Academic Plagiarists You've Never Heard Of: How Many More Are Out There?' *Chronicle of Higher Education*, 17 December 2004, available at: <http://www.capella.edu/academichonesty/PDFs/news.pdf> [accessed 29 Dec 2015].

175 David Macfarlane, 'Plagiarism Case Kept Under Wraps at Wits', *Mail & Guardian*, 15 April 2011: <http://mg.co.za/article/2011-04-15-plagiarism-case-kept-under-wraps-at-wits/> [accessed 29 Dec 2015].

176 Kwame Anthony Appiah, novelist, cultural theorist and Princeton University Professor of Philosophy; Stuart Hall, Emeritus Professor of Cultural Studies at the Open University in the United Kingdom; and, David Theo Goldberg, Professor and Director of the University of California's Humanities Research Centre.

177 Macfarlane, above n 175.

The University commissioned Marcus's report in spite of the contention being advanced by Zegeye that instead a 'panel of "credible social scientists"' should undertake the exercise.[178]

At the hearing, in a statement submitted by Zegeye's lawyers, he 'now admitted…to having "used the language of other academic writers in the body of my articles in an inappropriate manner"'. He blamed his transgressions, for which he apologized, on a research assistant: 'I cannot be accused of cogently borrowing any intellectual capital from other writers, although, as admitted, their text was sometimes reproduced in my works.'[179] In relation to the articles, which were the subject of complaint, Marcus ascribed them to the category of plagiarism described as the 'too-perfect paraphrase', where '[t]he writer properly cites a source, but neglects to put in quotation marks text that has been copied word-for-word, or close to it. Although attributing the basic ideas to the source, the writer is falsely claiming original presentation and interpretation of the information'.[180]

The procedures employed by the University of Witwatersrand have become controversial in two respects. First, they involved findings that at the time were not publicly disclosed, resulting in the University of South Australia employing Zegeye in ignorance of what had occurred. Second, Zegeye now contends that he was the victim of a witch-hunt.

Vice-Chancellor Nongxa said: 'It is not usual practice for the university to announce dismissals or divulge judgments pertaining to internal processes. However, the university undertook to disclose fully the outcome of the arbitration process to anyone who might approach Wits for a reference for Professor Zegeye.'[181]

Zegeye himself denied and continues to deny any impropriety, classifying his 'lapses' as 'minor'.[182]

The Politicization of Plagiarism

The accusations recurrently aired against the United States Vice-President Biden arose in the context of concerns being expressed about the similarities between a stump speech that he gave in Iowa and a speech previously given by British politician Neil Kinnock. The outcome was that his Democratic challenger, Michael Dukakis, created an attack video that devastatingly juxtaposed Biden's speech with that of Kinnock's. However, after this occurred, plagiarism has emerged in Europe, the Middle East, Asia, the United States and even Australia as a major political issue, resulting in the forced resignation of many prominent politicians. The following part of the chapter chronicles the unfolding of this phenomenon, starting with a series of German political figures and includes cases where plagiarism allegations have been made but shown to be unfounded. It reflects on features that the various cases have in common, as well as the values that can be discerned in contemporary society from the outrage that plagiarism has engendered.

Germany

In Germany approximately 18 per cent of members of parliament hold the title 'doctor' or 'professor'. Between 2011 and 2013 an extraordinary sequence of allegations of plagiarism was made against parliamentarians.

---

178 Ibid.
179 Ibid.
180 Ibid.
181 Ibid.
182 Richard Baker, 'Plagiarism Sinks Research Head', *The Age*, 21 April 2010: <http://www.theage.com.au/national/plagiarism-sinks-research-head-20110420-1doui.html> [accessed 29 Dec 2015]. See also, ibid.

Karl-Theodor zu Guttenberg. The first incident to come to public attention was plagiarism of his 2006 thesis, 'Constitution and Constitutional Treaty: Comparing Developments in the US and the EU', by Karl-Theodor zu Guttenberg, the German Defence Minister.[183] Guttenberg had a high public profile—he is married to the great-great-granddaughter of Germany's 19th century 'Iron Chancellor'[184] Otto von Bismarck and was described by *The Economist* as the country's 'most dashing, refreshing and popular politician'.[185] The newspaper, *Süddeutsche Zeitung* reported that parts of Guttenberg's thesis seemed to repeat passages by other authors without attribution, including articles in other newspapers, the United States embassy website, and even an essay by a former defence minister. His response was to denounce the allegations as 'fanciful' and to say that any lapses in scholarly propriety would be fixed.[186]

The University of Bayreuth, which awarded him the degree, gave him two weeks to respond to the allegations. A website, 'GuttenPlag Wiki',[187] was set up to allow people to submit passages they claimed he had taken from other works without proper attribution.[188] By then dubbed the 'cut-and-paste minister', Guttenberg temporarily renounced his doctorate pending the results of the inquiry.[189] To loud jeers, Guttenberg told the Bundestag that '[he] did not deliberately cheat, but made serious errors', and attributed these to his 'arrogance' in believing that he could 'juggle' writing a thesis with 'starting a family and launching his political career'.[190] Additional allegations in terms of the doctorate were made that he had not only used others' work but had improperly used research facilities available to him as a parliamentarian.[191]

The University of Bayreuth finalized its investigations, confirmed the correctness of the allegations and withdrew his PhD. For a considerable time Chancellor Angela Merkel's government attempted to retain Guttenberg in his position but as time passed the controversies over Guttenberg's probity intensified. An open letter to Merkel signed by over 7500 scholars argued that her retention of Guttenberg in the Cabinet 'makes a mockery of all the research assistants and doctoral students who honestly endeavor to contribute to the advancement of science. This makes it sound as if obtaining a doctoral title by fraud is just a trivial offense and that the academic word of honor is meaningless in everyday life'.[192] Germany's science

---

[183] 'Heavy Lifting? A German Plagiarism Scandal', *The Economist*, 17 February 2011: <http://www.economist.com/blogs/newsbook/2011/02/german_plagiarism_scandal> [accessed 29 Dec 2015]. For a visualization of the 'plagiarized portions' in Guttenberg's thesis, see 'German Defense Minister's Plagiarized PhD Dissertation Visualized', *FlowingData*: <http://flowingdata.com/2011/03/02/german-defense-ministers-plagiarized-phd-dissertation-visualized/> [accessed 29 Dec 2015].

[184] Judy Dempsey, 'Old Doctoral Thesis Haunts a Top German Minister', *The New York Times*, 21 February 2011: <http://www.nytimes.com/2011/02/22/world/europe/22iht-letter22.html> [accessed 29 Dec 2015].

[185] 'Heavy Lifting?' above n 183.

[186] Ibid.

[187] *GuttenPlag: Kollaborative Plagiatsdokumentation*, GuttenPlag Wiki: <http://de.guttenplag.wikia.com/wiki/Plagiate> [accessed 29 Dec 2015].

[188] Annika Breidthardt, 'German Minister Rejects Quitting in Plagiarism Row', *Reuters*, 19 February 2011: <http://www.reuters.com/article/2011/02/19/us-germany-minister-plagiarism-idUSTRE71I24620110219> [accessed 29 Dec 2015].

[189] Matthew Day, 'German Defence Minister to Drop PhD Title Over Plagiarism Row', *The Telegraph*, 18 February 2011: <http://www.telegraph.co.uk/news/worldnews/europe/germany/8333724/German-defence-minister-to-drop-PhD-title-over-plagiarism-row.html> [accessed 29 Dec 2015].

[190] Helen Pidd, 'German Defence Minister Stripped of Doctorate for Plagiarism', *The Guardian*, 24 February 2011: <http://www.theguardian.com/world/2011/feb/24/german-defence-minister-guttenberg-plagiarism> [accessed 29 Dec 2015].

[191] 'German Faces More Plagiarism Charges', *UPI*, 20 February 2011: <http://www.upi.com/Top_News/World-News/2011/02/20/German-faces-more-plagiarism-charges/UPI-41931298235485/> [accessed 29 Dec 2015].

[192] 'An Open Letter to the Chancellor' on *Copy, Shake, and Paste* (26 February 2011): <http://copy-shake-paste.blogspot.com.au/2011/02/open-letter-to-chancellor.html> [accessed 29 Dec 2015]; Quirin

council, the Wissenschaftsrat, and the Conference of University Rectors also protested against what the Wissenschaftsrat described as 'publicly stated disparagement of basic principles of science'.[193] Guttenberg was persuaded to resign.

Silvana Koch-Mehrin. The next German politician to face allegations of plagiarism was Silvana Koch-Mehrin, the liberal Deputy Speaker of the European Parliament. It was asserted that she had inserted passages into her 2001 doctoral thesis without properly citing the original authors. She was said to have failed to cite sources in an orthodox way in at least 20 pages of her 227-page doctoral thesis, entitled 'Historical Currency Unions between the Economy and Politics'. The investigative website 'VroniPlag Wiki' raised the initial doubts. This was the same source that exposed plagiarized passages in the thesis of Karl-Theodor zu Guttenberg.[194] Heidelberg University revoked her doctorate. Koch-Mehrin openly admitted her doctoral thesis was 'no masterpiece'—but denounced the university for revoking her doctorate 11 years after awarding it 'in full knowledge of all the glaring weaknesses'.[195]

By May 2011 she resigned as Deputy Speaker of the European Parliament and the Board of the Free Democratic Party.[196] However, shortly before her resignation she was appointed a full member of the Industry, Research and Energy Committee of the European Parliament. The Alliance of German Scientific Organizations (AdW), an umbrella organization encompassing eminent research groups such as the Max Planck Society and the Alexander von Humboldt Foundation, campaigned for Koch-Mehrin to vacate the seat after the revocation of her doctorate: 'Acts of plagiarism in scientific work are anything but a minor offense... The AdW therefore deems it unacceptable for Ms. Koch-Mehrin to represent Germany at the European Parliament's Committee on Industry, Research and Energy.' Koch-Mehrin agreed to abandon her position on the committee.[197] She took her case against Heidelberg University to court alleging that it made procedural errors when it deprived her of her doctorate. However, in an oral ruling in March 2013 it was held that any error in procedure was not relevant to the university's decision.[198]

Jorgo Chatzimarkakis. The series of German plagiarism scandals took a bizarre turn when the fellow Free Democratic Party European parliamentarian, Jorgo Chatzimarkakis, with whom Koch-Mehrin had switched seats to assume the position on the research committee, was also accused of plagiarism. On 13 July 2013 Bonn University revoked the politician's doctorate, stating that Chatzimarkakis had used verbatim passages from other authors' work without indicating their source by the use of quotation marks. He did indicate the source in footnotes but the University's Dean of Philosophy, Günther Schulz, proclaimed that the method the politician had used was academically unacceptable: 'He didn't use quotations marks, so the reader thinks that he is reading a text by Chatzimarkakis, when actually more

---

Schiermeier, 'German Scientists Outraged in Defence Minister Plagiarism Affair', *Nature.com*, 28 February 2011: <http://blogs.nature.com/news/2011/02/german_scientists_outraged_in.html> [accessed 29 Dec 2015].

193 Schiermeier, above n 192.

194 'German Politics Rocked by New Plagiarism Probe', *BBC News*, 14 April 2011: <http://www.bbc.co.uk/news/world-europe-13081951> [accessed 29 Dec 2015].

195 David Levitz, 'Plagiarizing Politician Koch-Mehrin Outrages Scientific Community', *Deutsche Welle*, 26 June 2011: <http://www.dw.de/plagiarizing-politician-koch-mehrin-outrages-scientific-community/a-15189978> [accessed 29 Dec 2015].

196 'German MEP Silvana Koch-Mehrin Quits in Plagiarism Row', *BBC News*, 11 May 2011: <http://www.bbc.co.uk/news/world-europe-13369608> [accessed 29 Dec 2015].

197 Levitz, above n 195.

198 Christopher F Schuetze, 'New Plagiarism Cases Cause Second Thoughts in Germany', *The New York Times*, 11 March 2013: <http://www.nytimes.com/2013/03/11/world/europe/11iht-educside11.html?_r=0> [accessed 29 Dec 2015].

than half the text is from other authors.'[199] The Bonn University committee with responsibility for determining whether Chatzimarkakis was guilty of plagiarism found that more than half of the pages of his dissertation contained passages had not been written by him.[200]

Chatzimarkakis's position had been that the omission of footnotes was legitimate and a style that he had learned while he was a research fellow at St Antony's College, Oxford University, in 1995. Speaking on a well-known political talk show, *Anne Will*, he said that in Oxford 'they phrase things somewhat differently. They intertexualize, that is they make texts readable'.[201] However, after the decision by the Bonn University committee to withdraw his doctorate, Chatzimarkakis announced that he was relieved that it had not found that his conduct had been intentional.

Matthias Pröfrock. With the fillip to suspicion and investigation generated by Germany's escalating cynicism about the academic integrity of its politicians, others have followed and more are likely to follow. In Baden-Württemberg, Christian Democrat Member of Parliament Matthias Pröfrock was also stripped of his doctorate by the University of Tübingen. His thesis was on energy security in the European Union. Again VroniPlag played a key role in exposing the conduct. Pröfrock apologized for plagiarism, acknowledged he had made citation errors but refused to resign from his parliamentary seat.[202]

Annette Schavan. In May 2012 Germany's Minister for Education, Annette Schavan, was accused of having plagiarized significant parts of her 1980 doctoral thesis on 'Person and Conscience—Studies on Conditions, Need and Requirements of Today's Consciences'.[203] A report was undertaken by Bruno Bleckmann, Dean of the Faculty of Arts, who found approximately 60 pages in her 351-page dissertation contained passages that were slightly reworded from sources without proper citations. He observed that Schavan had 'systematically and deliberately claimed as her own intellectual achievements which she had in fact not produced herself'.[204] In February 2013 the 15-member council of the Faculty of Philosophy revoked Ms Schavan's doctorate. Within four days she tendered her resignation to Chancellor Angela Merkel, who accepted it 'with a very heavy heart'.[205] Minister Schavan had had responsibility for Germany's universities and had been scathing in her criticism of Guttenberg who had similarly had his doctorate removed and lost his ministerial portfolio.[206]

Frank-Walter Steinmeier. However, not every allegation has been found proven. In 2013 Frank-Walter Steinmeier was accused by Dortmund Professor Uwe Kamenz of having plagiarized

---

199 Siobhan Dowling, 'German Politician Loses Doctorate for Plagiarism', *The Guardian*, 14 July 2011: <http://www.theguardian.com/world/2011/jul/14/plagiarism-row-jorgo-chatzimarkakis-germany> [accessed 29 Dec 2015]. See also, Gabriel Borrud, 'Another German Politician Loses Doctorate Due to Plagiarized Thesis', *Deutsche Welle* 13 July 2011: <http://www.dw.de/another-german-politician-loses-doctorate-due-to-plagiarized-thesis/a-15232002-1> [accessed 29 Dec 2015].

200 Borrud, above n 199.

201 Dowling, above n 199.

202 Christopher F, Schuetze, 'The Whiff of Plagiarism Again Hits German Elite', *The New York Times*, 24 April 2011: <http://www.nytimes.com/2011/04/25/education/25iht-educside.html> [accessed 29 Dec 2015].

203 Gretchen Vogel, 'German Research Minister Faces Plagiarism Allegations', *Science*, 2 May 2012: <http://news.sciencemag.org/2012/05/german-research-minister-faces-plagiarism-allegations> [accessed 29 Dec 2015].

204 Paul Jump, 'A Plague of Plagiarism at the Heart of Politics', *Times Higher Education*, 16 May 2013: <http://www.timeshighereducation.co.uk/features/a-plague-of-plagiarism-at-the-heart-of-politics/2003781.article> [accessed 29 Dec 2015].

205 Gretchen Vogel and Kai Kupferschmidt, 'German Research Minister Schavan Resigns in Plagiarism Scandal', *Science*, 9 February 2013: <http://news.sciencemag.org/people-events/2013/02/breaking-news-german-research-minister-schavan-resigns-plagiarism-scandal> [accessed 29 Dec 2015].

206 'German Education Minister Quits Over PhD Plagiarism', *The Guardian*, 9 February 2013: <http://www.theguardian.com/world/2013/feb/09/german-education-minister-quits-phd-plagiarism> [accessed 29 Dec 2015].

portions of his 1991 law thesis. Steinmeier, the Social Democrats' parliamentary leader, was Germany's Foreign Minister in the coalition led by Chancellor Angela Merkel between 2005 and 2009. A committee at the University of Giessen investigated the allegations and acknowledged 'technical weaknesses' in terms of Steinmeier's citations, but ruled that the university should not withdraw Steinmeier's doctorate.[207] Giessen University's President, Joybrata Mukherjee, made the point that, while machines could compute, only humans could make assessments.

The extraordinary sequence of revelations and accusations about Germany's politicians caused considerable consternation and disillusionment about Germany's tertiary sector, including in relation to the processes for supervising and marking postgraduate scholarship. One response has come from the opposition party, the Greens, which introduced a Bill in December 2011 to remove the academic title from passports and national identification cards to reduce the standing of doctoral qualifications. The Bill was not passed.

Austria

During 2011 an Austrian politician from the conservative ÖVP party, Johannes Hahn, who served as Science Minister between 2007 and 2010 and Justice Minister between 2003 and 2007, was accused of plagiarism in his 1987 doctoral thesis, entitled 'Perspectives of Philosophy Today—With the Example of the City Phenomenon'.[208] At the time he was a European Union Regional Policy Commissioner. The issues arose after an expert group listed 76 instances of plagiarism in his 1987 doctoral thesis. Mr Hahn denied the charges and claimed they were 'politically motivated'.[209] However, the instances of the alleged plagiarism accounted for at least 17.2 per cent of Hahn's doctoral thesis, according to an expert opinion commissioned by the opposition Green Party in Austria.[210]

The commissioner wrote his PhD thesis in 1987 at the University of Vienna. This was not the first time, though, that Hahn had been accused of plagiarism over his thesis. He was first under the spotlight in 2007. At the time, an expert commission found no sign of plagiarism in his work but in the wake of the German plagiarism scandals the allegations resurfaced. The matter was laid to rest later in 2011 when the Austrian Agency for Research Integrity (OeAWI), commissioned by the University of Vienna to examine his dissertation, found that the way he cited some sources 'would not meet good research practice principles of today' but that he had not engaged in plagiarism.[211]

France

In 2013 the Chief Rabbi of France, and a holder of the Legion d'Honneur, Gilles Bernheim, resigned after revelations of plagiarism in his 2011 book, *40 Jewish Meditations*. He admitted to copying a 1996 text by the late French post-modernist philosopher, Jean-François Lyotard.

[207] 'German University Rejects Plagiarism Allegations Against Steinmeier', *Deutsche Welle*, 5 November 2013: <http://www.dw.de/german-university-rejects-plagiarism-allegations-against-steinmeier/a-17205123> [accessed 29 Dec 2015]; Michael Gardner, 'Opposition Politician Not Guilty of Plagiarism', Issue 297, *University World News*, 22 November 2013: <http://www.universityworldnews.com/article.php?story=20131121152730697> [accessed 29 Dec 2015].

[208] 'Austrian Commissioner Faces Plagiarism Accusations', *EurActiv.com*, 26 May 2011: <http://www.euractiv.com/future-eu/austrian-commissioner-faces-plag-news-505137> [accessed 29 Dec 2015].

[209] Ibid.

[210] See eg, 'European Commissioner "Cheated"', *Austrian Independent*, 23 May 2011: <http://austrianindependent.com/news/Politics/2011-05-23/7625/European_Commissioner_%E2%80%99cheated%E2%80%99> (viewed 27 February 2015).

[211] 'Austrian EU Commissioner Cleared of Plagiarism', *The Australian*, 8 November 2011: <http://www.theaustralian.com.au/higher-education/austrian-eu-commissioner-cleared-of-plagiarism/story-e6frgcjx-1226187998599> [accessed 29 Dec 2015].

At first Bernheim countered the allegations by portraying himself as the victim and claiming that Lyotard had plagiarized notes from lectures he had delivered in the 1980s when he worked as Jewish student chaplain in Paris. However, two weeks later, Bernheim admitted that Lyotard had in fact authored the disputed text, blaming the error on a student researcher he had hired to help write the book.[212] He declined at first to resign on the novel basis that to do so would amount to an act of vanity and desertion of office[213] but after evidence also emerged about also the illegitimacy of his doctoral credentials, which it turned out he had never completed at the Sorbonne,[214] he acknowledged having made 'serious mistakes', albeit ones 'that do not directly concern the tasks I was entrusted with as chief rabbi',[215] and agreed to take leave from his rabbinical responsibilities.

In 2015 in a wide-ranging interview for Vanity Fair he admitted unequivocally to having plagiarized and spoke of the material involved as having become so familiar to him that it had aggregated to his own words. He told the following story in explanation: 'Long ago, a friend of mine sustained a double fracture to the tibia and fibula. The doctors implanted a metal pin and he learned to live with it: this pin became part of his body. One day this friend took an aeroplane flight. In the portico of the airport, his body whistled. A first time. A second. He was unable to find out why. At that time, he remembered the pin.' After a sigh, he added: 'I too have come to whistle. Without understanding why initially. And when I realized, it was going in all directions.'[216]

Hungary

In 2012 the Hungarian President, Pal Schmitt, was embroiled in a scandal concerning material in his 1992 Semmelweis University doctoral thesis alleged to be plagiarized from both a German academic and a Bulgarian sports official. Allegations regarding his conduct were published by a business magazine, *HGV*. A five-member committee was convened at Semmelweis University in Budapest. It generated a 1,157-page report, concluding that 17 pages of his 215-page thesis had been copied from a book by a German scholar and that 180 pages showed partial similarity to the 'Analyse du programme olympique (des Jeux d'Olympiade)' of Nikolay Georgiev from Bulgaria.[217]

Schmitt had held the mostly ceremonial post of President since 2010. He served as an ambassador during the 1990s, and was a Vice-President of the European Parliament from 2009 to 2010. After briefly serving as speaker of the National Assembly of Hungary in 2010, he was elected as President in the Parliament with the support of Prime Minister Viktor Orbán.

---

212 'France's Chief Rabbi Resigns Amid Plagiarism Scandal', *France 24*, 11 April 2013: <http://www.france24.com/en/20130411-france-chief-rabbi-bernheim-resigns-plagiarism-scandal/> [accessed 29 Dec 2015].

213 See Steven Erlanger, 'France's Chief Rabbi Declines to Resign over Plagiarism', *The New York Times*, 9 April 2013: <http://www.nytimes.com/2013/04/10/world/europe/frances-chief-rabbi-declines-to-resign-over-plagiarism.html?_r=0> [accessed 29 Dec 2015].

214 Robert Zaretsky, 'French Chief Rabbi's Fall from Grace in Plagiarism Scandal', *The Jewish Daily Forward*, 24 April 2013: <http://forward.com/articles/175348/french-chief-rabbis-fall-from-grace-in-plagiarism/?p=all> [accessed 29 Dec 2015].

215 JTA and Gavriel Fiske, 'French Rabbi Quits Amid Plagiarism, Qualification Scandals', *The Times of Israel*, 11 April 2013: <http://www.timesofisrael.com/one-day-after-refusing-to-do-so-french-chief-rabbi-resigns/> [accessed 29 Dec 2015].

216 Olivier Bouchara, '"Pourquoi J'ai Plagie": Les Confessions de Gilles Bernheim, Ancien Grand Rabbin de France' (9 April 2015) Vanity Fair: <http://www.vanityfair.fr/actualites/france/articles/olivier-bouchara-confession-gilles-bernheim-ex-grand-rabbin-de-france/24867> [accessed 29 Dec 2015].

217 'HGV: Hungarian President Plagarized Bulgarian Researcher', *Novinite.com*, 12 January 2012: <http://www.novinite.com/articles/135639/HGV%3A+Hungarian+President+Plagiarized+Bulgarian+Researcher> [accessed 29 Dec 2015].

The Semmelweis University committee was highly critical of the examiners who, they observed, should have identified the level of copying engaged in by Schmitt. They were less critical of Schmitt, who had mentioned the works in his bibliography. However, the committee's approach was condemned in many quarters with critics lambasting it as a whitewash and the four opposition parties in Hungary demanding Mr Schmitt's resignation, maintaining he had lost the confidence of the country and had demeaned his office.[218] The conduct of Mr Schmitt had international ramifications because of the plagiarism of a Bulgarian national and the fact that persons speaking on behalf of the President at first claimed that he had written his thesis together with the Bulgarian author, who it turned out had been deceased for some time. However, it soon became clear that Mr Georgiev's research antedated Mr Schmitt's thesis and that this posture was unsustainable.

A demonstration took place in front of Budapest's parliament with persons attending reported to have proclaimed that Hungary was degenerating into a 'country without consequences'.[219] Political pressures grew on Semmelweis University and by 29 March 2012 the Rector announced the decision of the University to withdraw Mr Schmitt's doctoral degree.[220] Shortly afterwards, Mr Schmitt, still denying having done anything untoward, resigned the Presidency of Hungary telling a plenary session of the country's Parliament in Budapest: 'In this situation when my personal issue divides my beloved nation rather than unites it, I feel it is my duty to end my service and resign my mandate as President.' His remarks provoked a positive and enthusiastic response from those being addressed.[221] Expressing concerns that he had not been able to defend his position, the President stated that members of Parliament had labelled him a 'cheat', despite the fact that an investigation had yet to commence. In relation to these members, he said that they 'made sure these unfounded allegations go abroad', and tried to 'morally undermine' his work with the International Olympic Committee; of which he had a lengthy association dating back to 1983.[222]

His resignation was followed shortly afterwards by that of the Rector of Semmelweis University, Tivadar Tulassay, who gave as an explanation that he felt a 'loss of confidence' from the authorities.[223]

Romania

A major issue has existed for some time in Romania with persons aspiring to political office and prominence in public life keen to obtain postgraduate qualifications but without the institutions always applying the necessary rigour to the processes by which higher, research-based degrees are awarded. This has latterly given rise to high-profile scandals.

Ioan Mang. Within weeks of the Hungarian plagiarism scandal coming to its denouement, a new concern erupted, this time in Romania, concerning its Education and Research Minister, Ioan Mang, a senior academic in the Faculty of Information Technology at Oradea

---

[218] 'Hungarian President Pal Schmitt in Soup After Doctorate Plagiarism Finding', *The Australian*, 30 March 2012: <http://www.theaustralian.com.au/news/world/hungarian-president-pal-schmitt-in-soup-after-doctorate-plagiarism-finding/story-fnb64oi6-1226313885055> [accessed 29 Dec 2015].

[219] Ibid.

[220] 'Hungarian President Loses Doctorate in Plagiarism Case', *EurActiv.com*, 30 March 2012: <http://www.euractiv.com/central-europe/plagiarism-scandal-hits-hungarian-president-news-511869> [accessed 29 Dec 2015].

[221] Palko Karasz, 'Hungarian President Resigns Amid Plagiarism Scandal', *The New York Times*, 2 April 2012: <http://www.nytimes.com/2012/04/03/world/europe/hungarian-president-pal-schmitt-resigns-amid-plagiarism-scandal.html?_r=0> [accessed 29 Dec 2015].

[222] Ibid.

[223] Ibid.

University. He was accused by researchers from Japan, Israel, and Taiwan of copying their academic work, including their errors, in a sequence of his published papers.

Only days after his centre-left government assumed power, Prime Minister Victor Ponta responded to these accusations by contacting the Romanian Academy, and requesting that 'a group of specialists analyse as fast as possible the accusations against' Mang.[224] He told reporters: 'If these accusations are proved to be true, the Minister will leave'.[225] The National Ethics Council (NEC), which was set up by the previous government, outlawed plagiarism and could compel dismissal of academics found guilty of having engaged in it. The Council was to investigate two separate claims of plagiarism against Mang, who was also the President of the Romanian Authority for Scientific Research.[226]

Corina Dumitrescu. To make matters even more extraordinary, the Prime Minister had already been forced to drop his first candidate for the education portfolio, Corina Dumitrescu, the previous week after she also was accused of plagiarism, as well as of intellectual dishonesty. The media identified several grammatical and spelling mistakes in Ms Dumitrescu's curriculum vitae and discovered that she had never studied at Stanford University, as she had claimed.[227]

The former Education Minister (by then in opposition) argued that 'the actual fight is between ethically sound scientists and the demons of the past', referring to the communist era under the dictatorship of Nicolae Ceauşescu: 'The world should know that Romanian researchers are not like their current science minister'.[228]

Mircea Beuran. The issue was the more sensitive given the changes within the scientific establishment that Romania (and Bulgaria) had sought to make to enhance their reputation as strong intellectual citizens of Europe[229] and the controversy which surrounded a previous example of plagiarism in 2003 when the then Minister for Health, Mircea Beuran, was found to have engaged in plagiarism in a medical guide for students which utilized textbook material previously published in the United States.[230] The press accused Beuran of personal self-aggrandizement: publishing to try to obtain the title of 'Associate Professor' in the Medicine School of Bucharest. The University of Bucharest Medicine School investigated the case and in 2003 an ad hoc commission of the University had confirmed that he had engaged in plagiarism, pointing out that, even though he claimed that the textbooks concerned contained scientific material that should be considered 'universal truth', the books were authored and should have been properly cited.[231] It terminated his employment contract.

---

224 '"Copycat" Claims Move to Romania', *The Australian*, 15 May 2012: <http://www.theaustralian.com.au/higher-education/copycat-claims-move-to-romania/story-e6frgcjx-1226354513155> [accessed 29 Dec 2015].

225 Ibid.

226 Ibid. 'One of Mang's papers now under scrutiny (I. Mang *Seria Technichni nauki* 12, 129–35; 2004) is allegedly a near-identical copy of a manuscript intended for presentation at a scientific workshop and authored by cryptographer Eli Biham, the dean of computer science at the Technion Israel Institute of Technology in Haifa. Biham notes that he had withdrawn the manuscript from the workshop because of conceptual errors in the work, but had been unable to completely remove the document from the internet. Mang seems 'neither to have read nor tried to understand the claims in the paper', according to a comment made by Biham on his website: Alison Abbott, 'Plagiarism Charge for Romanian Minister' (2012) 485(7398) *Nature* 289, 289: <http://www.nature.com/news/plagiarism-charge-for-romanian-minister-1.10646> [accessed 29 Dec 2015].

227 'Romania's Education Minister Resigns Amidst Plagiarism Accusations' (15 May 2012) *Romania Insider*: <http://www.romania-insider.com/romanias-education-minister-resigns-amid-plagiarism-accusations/57337/> [accessed 29 Dec 2015].

228 Abbott, above n 226, 289.

229 See Alison Abbott, 'Science Fortunes of Balkan Neighbours Diverge' (2011) 469(7329) *Nature* 142: <http://www.nature.com/news/2011/110112/full/469142a.html> [accessed 29 Dec 2015].

230 Grama, above n 51, 157.

231 Ibid 158–9.

On 8 June 2012, Ponta's government dismissed all the members of the National Ethics Council just before they were to vote on the plagiarism charge against Mang. However, this was to no avail as political exigencies intruded into the saga. Within days Mang resigned from office, maintaining that he was doing so for the good of the government and asserting that the allegations against him were politically motivated.[232]

Victor Ponta. However, the scandals arising from allegations of plagiarism did not end there. In June 2012 *Nature* published an article[233] which reported allegations of plagiarism in relation to the 2003 doctoral thesis of Victor Ponta, the Prime Minister. The thesis was on the International Criminal Court[234] and completed while Ponta was acting as Secretary of State in the government of an earlier Prime Minister, Adrian Năstase—who was also his PhD supervisor. Later Năstase was jailed on unrelated corruption charges.

The *Nature* article reported having seen:

> documents compiled by an anonymous whistle-blower indicating that more than half of Ponta's 432-page, Romanian-language thesis…consists of duplicated text. Moreover, the thesis was republished with very minor amendments as a Romanian-language book in 2004, and also forms the basis of a 2010 book on liability in international humanitarian law. A former PhD student of Ponta's, Daniela Coman, is named as co-author of the books. Substantial sections of text in all three publications seem to be identical, or almost so, to material in monographs written in Romanian by law scholars…They also feature direct Romanian translations of parts of an English-language publication by [a further] law scholar.
>
> 'The evidence of plagiarism is overwhelming,' says Marius Andruh, a chemist at the University of Bucharest and president of the Romanian council for the recognition of university diplomas.[235]

The response of Prime Minister Ponta in a letter to *Nature* was to claim that 'a lack of information on the domestic political dynamics of Romania has led to your publication's unfortunate involvement in a political action'.[236] He contended that the accusations against him were being generated as part of a political plot against him by President Traian Basescu who was a supporter of persons associated with urging austerity measures during the European Union's financial crises of 2012.[237]

However, the problems for the Prime Minister deepened when Romania's National Council for Certification of Titles, Diplomas and University Certificates (CNATDCU) announced that it had determined that 85 pages of Ponta's thesis had been copied, without correct attribution. The president of its national council, Marius Andruh, told reporters: 'I found nothing but plagiarism of a copy-paste type. The council wanted to remove the title of doctor.'[238]

[232] Marian Chiriac, 'Romanian Minister Resigns in Plagiarism Row', *Balkan Insight*, 16 May 2012: <http://www.balkaninsight.com/en/article/romania-s-education-minister-resigns-over-plagiarism-row> [accessed 29 Dec 2015].

[233] Quirin Schiermeier, 'Romanian Prime Minister Accused of Plagiarism' (2012) 486(7403) *Nature* 305: <http://www.nature.com/news/romanian-prime-minister-accused-of-plagiarism-1.10845> [accessed 29 Dec 2015].

[234] Victor Ponta, 'Curtea Penală Internațională' (PhD dissertation, University of Bucharest, 2003).

[235] Schiermeier, above n 233 (footnotes omitted).

[236] Government of Romania (Press Release, 19 June 2012), available at: <http://www.nature.com/news/romanian-prime-minister-accused-of-plagiarism-1.10845> [accessed 29 Dec 2015].

[237] Ioana Patran, 'Romania Prime Minister Seeks to Clear Name Over Plagiarism Charge', *Reuters*, 22 June 2012: <http://www.reuters.com/article/2012/06/22/us-romania-politics-idUSBRE85L0HV20120622> [accessed 29 Dec 2015].

[238] Sam Cage, 'Romania PM Plagiarized Thesis, Panel Says', *Reuters*, 29 June 2012: <http://www.reuters.com/article/2012/06/29/us-romania-politics-idUSBRE85S1HQ20120629> [accessed 29 Dec 2015].

On the same day Prime Minister Ponta's government announced that the Council needed to be expanded and new members brought in, which meant that its judgment had been invalid.

In the meantime Prime Minister Ponta submitted his thesis for scrutiny to the by now reconstituted National Ethics Council. After brief consideration its new members rejected the plagiarism charges against Ponta. It found that Ponta's doctoral thesis met the academic requirements at the time that it was published, finding that his only mistake 'was to have listed his sources at the end of his 432-page thesis without giving footnotes on the actual pages where he reproduced sections of text from the sources'.[239]

However, a day later, a 13-member ethics commission set up by the University of Bucharest reaffirmed the charges. It found that Ponta had copied and pasted large sections of his thesis. The commission, comprising members of all faculties, found plagiarized elements on 115 out of 297 pages (excluding appendices) of the thesis.[240]

By December 2014, however, Ponta had lost the presidential election and abandoned his PhD, announcing in a message to the rector of the University of Bucharest posted on his Facebook page: 'I have written to you to notify that I give up the doctor of law title obtained in 2003. This is a gesture that I should have done before, since publications about my Ph.D. thesis emerged.'[241] Ponta went on to say in his letter: 'After I will be stepping down from the political scene I wish to pursue a new doctorate while adhering to and respecting all of the standards and requirements.'[242]

On the day the earlier National Ethics Council was relieved of its responsibilities, it submitted to the Science Ministry its report on charges of plagiarism against three leading figures at the University of Medicine and Pharmacy of Târgu-Mureş. The Ministry has not published the report. However, around the same time the University of Bucharest confirmed that Olguta Vasilescu, the mayor of Craiova, plagiarized in her PhD thesis. The University's Ethics Committee published an expert report on the plagiarism concerns which showed that she 'took identical or nearly identical formulations of works that do not belong to her, without using quotation marks.'[243]

Not surprisingly, many within Romania's academy felt betrayed by the NEC's handling with Prime Minister Ponta's scholarly misconduct. In response to the continuing flow of plagiarism scandals Romanian researchers have launched an online service called Integru,[244] whose role is to investigate and expose cases of plagiarism and other academic misconduct in Romania. Each case will be accompanied online by commentaries from international—and independent—reviewers selected for their expertise in the relevant field.

---

[239] Quirin Schiermeier, 'Conflicting Verdicts on Romanian Prime Minister's Plagiarism', *Nature*, 20 July 2012: <http://www.nature.com/news/conflicting-verdicts-on-romanian-prime-minister-s-plagiarism-1.11047> [accessed 29 Dec 2015].

[240] Ibid.

[241] Andy Thomason, 'Romanian Prime Minister Gives Up Ph.D., 2 Years After Plagiarism Finding', *The Chronicle of Higher Education*, 16 December 2014: <http://chronicle.com/blogs/ticker/romanian-prime-minister-gives-up-ph-d-2-years-after-plagiarism-finding/91291> [accessed 29 Dec 2015].

[242] Stephen McGrath, 'Romania's PM Gives Up Doctorate After Plagiarism Allegations', *The Independent*, 21 December 2014: <http://www.independent.co.uk/news/world/europe/romanias-pm-gives-up-doctorate-after-plagiarism-allegations-9938287.html> [accessed 29 Dec 2015]; Alison Abbott, 'Romanian Prime Minister Relinquishes his PhD' (17 December 2014) Nature: <http://www.nature.com/news/romanian-prime-minister-relinquishes-his-phd-1.16583> [accessed 29 Dec 2015].

[243] Diana Mesesan, 'University Says Romanian City Mayor Guilty of Plagiarism in PhD Thesis' (23 December 2014) *Romania Insider*: <http://www.romania-insider.com/university-says-romanian-city-mayor-guilty-of-plagiarism-in-ph-d-thesis/138329/> [accessed 29 Dec 2015].

[244] See <http://integru.org/> [accessed 29 Dec 2015].

Integru's stated goal is to 'help reform and restore confidence in the Romanian research and education system'.[245] Its editorial board, which comprises Romanian scientists working inside and outside the country, is anonymous to avoid personal attacks from those accused of misconduct. One of the first actions of Integru was to review Prime Minister Ponta's thesis. It concluded the thesis contained over 100 pages of plagiarized material.[246] However, Ponta's position when returning his doctorate was that he was doing so to avoid the political opportunity that it may have to his opponents.[247]

Russia

It is notorious that for a lengthy period of time many Russian politicians and businessmen have paid for their degrees, particularly their postgraduate degrees. However, in February 2013 Prime Minister Dmitry Medvedev announced, in part because of the exposure of serial scandals by the Russian online service, AntiPlagiat,[248] and the work of Dissernet, a group of activists,[249] that he proposed to ferret out fake degrees at every level of society.[250] The difficulty this created was that Sergei Shoigu, the Minister of Defence, Ramzan Kadyrov, the leader of Chechnya, Vladimir Medinsky, the Minister of Culture, and even President Putin have all been accused of plagiarism. Igor Fedyukin, an official with a PhD in history from the University of North Carolina at Chapel Hill and eight months' experience as the Deputy Minister of Education and Science, was appointed as the person to pursue the task. Fedyukin was part of a group of academics who in January 2013 exposed the extent of Russia's plagiarism crisis by reviewing 25 dissertations chosen at random from the prestigious history department of Moscow Pedagogical State University. All but one were at least 50 per cent plagiarized, with some as much as 90 per cent copied from other sources.

A particular issue has been identified by two Brookings Institution researchers, Clifford Gaddy and Igor Danchenko, with the 1997 economics thesis of President Putin ('The Strategic Planning of Regional Resources Under the Formation of Market Relations' defended in 1997), substantial tranches of which have been said to have been copied word for word from a 1978 management text published by two University of Pittsburgh academics William R King and David I Cleland.[251] Gaddy has maintained that, of the 20 pages that open the dissertation's key second section, 16 pages are taken either verbatim or with minute alterations from the American work. The book had been translated into Russian by a KGB-related institute in the early 1990s. In addition, six diagrams and tables from the 218-page dissertation have been noted as very similar in form and content to charts in the Russian translation of the King and Cleland work.[252] The Putin thesis does cite the King and Cleland work as one of

245 Abbott, above n 226.

246 'Review 1: Dr Victor Ponta (Prime Minister), PhD Thesis Plagiarism' on *Integru* (15 August 2012): <http://integru.org/reviews/ponta-2003-phd-thesis> [accessed 29 Dec 2015].

247 Abbott, above n 226.

248 Serghei Golunov, *The Elephant in the Room: Corruption and Cheating in Russian Universities* (New York: Columbia University Press, 2014); Serghei Golunov and Ivan Kurilla, 'Academic Integrity in Russia Today: The Political and Social Implications of Thesis Falsification and Education Reform' (March 2013) *Ponars Eurasia*: <http://www.ponarseurasia.org/memo/academic-integrity-russia-today-political-and-social-implications-thesis-falsification-and> [accessed 29 Dec 2015].

249 See Jonathan Bailey, 'How Russia is Shooting the Messenger' (19 February 2014) iThenticate: <http://www.ithenticate.com/plagiarism-detection-blog/how-russia-is-shooting-the-messenger#.VURP2> [accessed 29 Dec 2015].

250 Simon Shuster, 'Putin's Ph.D: Can a Plagiarism Probe Upend Russian Politics?' *Time*, 28 February 2013: <http://world.time.com/2013/02/28/putins-phd-can-a-plagiarism-probe-upend-russian-politics/> [accessed 29 Dec 2015].

251 'Researchers Peg Putin as Plagiarist Over Thesis', *The Washington Times*, 24 March 2006: <http://www.washingtontimes.com/news/2006/mar/24/20060324-104106-9971r/?page=all> [accessed 29 Dec 2015].

252 Shuster, above n 250.

its 47 sources, but gives no indication that paragraphs and pages are being taken unchanged from the earlier work. Danchenko has maintained that, of the 216 pages of the thesis, Putin appears only to have written 'a couple of pages', but has identified a 'strong protest mood' about the systemic phenomenon of plagiarized theses within Russian academia:

> Because scientists basically got fed up dealing with those characters with fake degrees. Everybody knows that their degrees are fake: their theses are either plagiarized or written by somebody else. That discredits the whole system of science and education in the country. The problem has reached a critical mass: nobody in the world takes Russian education seriously.
>
> [...]
>
> There are professors who can no longer tolerate this situation. They are trying to do their job honestly, but their effort is undermined by those who get their doctorates through the back door. Everybody knows how widespread corruption is in Russia. They bribe everybody—doctors, teachers, police officers. But when it comes to academic degrees—that's too much, that's where it has to stop, because it undermines the whole academic system.[253]

In 2015 the phenomenon continued with the respected Moscow lawmaker, Vladimir Platonov, being shamed by Dissernet into asking the Peoples' Friendship University in Moscow to annul his PhD after revelations of plagiarism in it.[254] He later announced that he proposed to rewrite it.[255]

The issue of plagiarism within postgraduate degrees has been controversial for some time in Russia[256] and, while it has spawned a pattern of accusations being brought against politicians for less than altruistic motives in relation to the legitimacy of their degrees,[257] there is no doubt that the Medvedev reforms are sorely needed.[258] Amongst the plans are that the Higher Attestation Commission, the national agency that oversees the awarding of postgraduate degrees, will promulgate new rules, including an extension of the period of appeal against dissertations from the current three year period to ten years.[259]

The Philippines

During the second half of 2012 a bitter dispute erupted in the Philippines Senate involving two politicians with opposing views on a reproductive planning Bill. Senator Vicente Sotto III, the Senate majority leader, opposed the controversial Bill, arguing from a position consistent with the Catholic Church's position. Senator Pia Cayetano spoke in favour of the Bill.

---

253 Ilya Shepelin, 'It Looks Like Putin Wrote Just a Couple of Pages of his Thesis', *The Interpreter*, 27 June 2013: <http://www.interpretermag.com/it-looks-like-putin-wrote-just-a-couple-of-pages-of-his-thesis/> [accessed 29 Dec 2015].

254 'Respected Moscow Lawmaker Annuls Dissertation Over Plagiarism Claims' (23 April 2015) *The Moscow Times*: <http://www.themoscowtimes.com/news/article/respected-moscow-lawmaker-annuls-dissertation-over-plagiarism-claims/519664.html> [accessed 29 Dec 2015].

255 Max Ivanov, 'Platonov After the Address to VAK Will Write Thesis on the Same Subject' (23 April 2015) *VOICE*: <http://ruspolitics.com/2015/04/platonov-after-the-address-to-vak-will-write-the-thesis-on-the-same-subject/> [accessed 29 Dec 2015].

256 'Germans Offer Putin a Lesson on Plagiarism', *The Moscow Times*, 13 May 2011: <http://www.themoscowtimes.com/opinion/article/germans-offer-putin-a-lesson-on-plagiarism/436735.html> [accessed 29 Dec 2015].

257 Natalya Krainova, 'Accusations of Plagiarism Become a Political Weapon' (13 March 2013) *Moscow Times*: <http://www.themoscowtimes.com/news/article/accusations-of-plagiarism-become-a-political-weapon/476800.html> [accessed 29 Dec 2015].

258 See Heather Dutiel, 'Plagiarism Commonplace Amongst Russian Politicians', *Academic Plagiarism*, 6 March 2013: <http://academicplagiarism.com/index.php/plagiarism-commonplace-russian-politicians/> [accessed 29 Dec 2015].

259 Eugene Vototnikov, 'Government to Combat Plagiarism and Illegal Degrees' (24 February 2014) *University World News*: <http://www.universityworldnews.com/article.php?story=20140224162330475> [accessed 29 Dec 2015].

In August and early September 2012 Senator Sotto delivered speeches exposing what he claimed were the nefarious interests working for the passage of the Bill. However, persons using social media and bloggers were later to claim that Senator Sotto had illicitly plagiarized a variety of sources, including speeches given by United States Senator Robert Kennedy. This resulted in his being referred to the Senate Committee on Ethics and Privileges for plagiarism by over 30 faculty members of the University of the Philippines, Ateneo de Manila University, and De La Salle University.[260]

Senator Kennedy's daughter, Kerry, wrote a letter that has been made public demanding an apology for what she contended was Senator Sotto's 'unethical, unsanctioned theft' of her father's intellectual property.[261] Senator Sotto denied the allegation, maintaining: '[Plagiarism is] to steal or pass off the ideas of another as one's own without crediting the source. I did not pass off anything as my own. How will I apologize for plagiarism when I never plagiarized? They want me to plead guilty for murder when the case is physical injury... The Senate journal will bear me out, I never said they are mine, I never said I own them.'[262]

Senator Sotto argued that the Kennedy family had been misinformed about his conduct to get them to say something against him: 'I did not steal it or pass it off as mine. The worst that can be said is that I copied it from a text of a friend, if they think it was copied, that's possible, because I did copy it.'[263] In a variant on the Bernheim excuse, he also justified his use of Senator Kennedy's speech, saying that 'copying or imitation is the highest form of flattery' and then denying that his conduct was deliberate: 'If it insulted the Kennedy family then I'm sorry, but that was not the intention'.[264]

Iran

In 2009 *Nature* considereded a sequence of papers authored by the Iranian Transport Minister, Hamid Behbahani, and by the Science Minister, Kamran Daneshjou which appeared to contain plagiarized material.[265] The conduct was particularly politically sensitive as Behbahani supervised the PhD thesis of President Mahmoud Ahmadinejad. A paper by Behbahani was retracted by the journal *Transport* in September 2009. This prompted an inquiry and then a denunciation of the cases by the Iranian chapter of the Academy of Sciences for the Developing World. However, a number of scientists provided something of a rationalization/explanation in a letter that they subsequently wrote to *Nature*:

> The Internet has facilitated communication with our colleagues elsewhere—but the availability of journals on the Internet has also made plagiarism easier. This widely acknowledged problem affects the scientific community worldwide. Iran, sadly, is no exception, and the country's science community is overhauling its practices to counter this scourge.

---

260 See referral of Verified Complaint against Vicente C Sotto III (Committee on Ethics and Privileges, 7 November 2012), available at: <http://www.scribd.com/doc/113038193/Full-Text-Ethics-Complaint-vs-Sen-Vicente-Sotto-III> [accessed 29 Dec 2015].

261 Letter from Kerry Kennedy to the Committee on Ethics and Privileges, 9 November 2012, available at: <http://www.scribd.com/doc/113038195/Sotto-ethics-complaint-ANNEX-E> [accessed 29 Dec 2015].

262 Matikas Santos, 'Sotto: 'How Will I Apologize For Plagiarism When I Never Plagiarized?'' *Inquirer.net*, 13 November 2012: <http://newsinfo.inquirer.net/306588/sotto-how-will-i-apologize-for-plagiarism-when-i-never-plagiarised> [accessed 29 Dec 2015].

263 Ibid.

264 Ibid.

265 See Declan Butler, 'Paper: Co-authored by Iran's Science Minister Duplicates Earlier Paper', *Nature*, 22 September 2009: <http://blogs.nature.com/news/2009/09/exclusive_paper_authored_by_ir.html> [accessed 29 Dec 2015]; Declan Butler, 'Publisher Retracts Paper by Iran's Science Minister', *Nature*, 23 September 2009: <http://www.nature.com/news/2009/090923/full/news.2009.945.html> [accessed 29 Dec 2015]; Declan Butler, 'Iranian Ministers in Plagiarism Row' (2009) 461(7264) *Nature* 578: <http://www.nature.com/news/2009/090930/full/461578a.html> [accessed 29 Dec 2015].

> But circumstances more specific to Iran are also conducive to the spread of plagiarism. Iranian culture places an excessive emphasis on the value of academic credentials, both for advancement in official professions and in social standing. In particular, Iran's political class has an unusual affinity for possessing academic distinctions, as exemplified by the fact that a university degree is a prerequisite for election to parliament. A higher degree is also considered an important qualification for holding other government offices. As a result, the Iranian political class, across the political and ideological spectrum, accounts for a disproportionate share of academic fraud.[266]

The ministers denied any wrongdoing and retained their positions.[267]

The United States

In 2014 a plagiarism scandal brought about the end of Senator John Walsh's campaign for a full term in the United States Senate. A *New York Times* report revealed that he had copied without attribution more than a quarter of his Master's thesis on Middle East policy at the United States Army War College.[268] He took material from a Harvard paper and from a document published by the Carnegie Endowment for International Peace.[269] His early response to what became known as 'papergate' was novel: that he had had PTSD from his service in Iraq when he wrote his thesis and that 'it may have been a factor. My head was not in a place very conducive to a classroom and an academic environment.'[270] Walsh was formerly Montana's Lieutenant Governor and had been appointed as an interim Senator by Montana's Governor after his predecessor had been appointed to an ambassadorship in China.

This was not the first time that allegations had been made against a United States politician. Rand Paul, a Republican Senator for Kentucky, widely expected to be a presidential candidate in 2016, was accused in 2013 and 2014 of a number of instances of plagiarism.[271] His response was: 'I think I'm being unfairly targeted by a bunch of hacks and haters.'[272] A similar issue arose in relation to the Barack Obama campaign where on 16 February 2008 Obama gave a speech in Wisconsin responding to allegations by his rival, Hillary Clinton, that all he had to offer was 'just words'. He quoted a series of well-known speeches and documents

---

266 Farhad Ardalan, Hessamaddin Arfaei, Reza Mansouri, Mahdi Balalimood et al. 'Iran's Scientists Condemn Instances of Plagiarism' (2009) 462(7275) *Nature* 847, 847: <http://www.nature.com/nature/journal/v462/n7275/full/462847a.html> [accessed 29 Dec 2015].

267 See Salman Hameed, 'Plagiarism in Arab-Muslim Academia' on *Irtiqa* (1 November 2010): <http://www.irtiqa-blog.com/2010/11/plagiarism-in-arab-muslim-academia.html> [accessed 29 Dec 2015].

268 See Jonathan Martin, 'How Senator John Walsh Plagiarized a Final Paper', *The New York Times*, 23 July 2014): <http://www.nytimes.com/interactive/2014/07/23/us/politics/john-walsh-final-paper-plagiarism.html?_r=0> [accessed 29 Dec 2015].

269 See Dan Roberts, 'Montana Senate Candidate John Walsh Pulls Out of Race After Plagiarism Scandal', *The Guardian*, 7 August 2014: <http://www.theguardian.com/world/2014/aug/07/montana-senate-candidate-john-walsh-plagiarism-scandal> [accessed 29 Dec 2015].

270 See Matt Vespa, 'Senator Walsh's Plagiarism Scandal, PTSD References Angers Veterans' (27 July 2014) *Townhall*: <http://townhall.com/tipsheet/mattvespa/2014/07/27/senator-walshs-plagiarism-scandal-ptsd-references-angers-veterans-n1869908> [accessed 29 Dec 2015].

271 See Aaron Blake, 'Rand Paul's Plagiarism Allegations, And Why They Matter', *The Washington Post*, 4 November 2013: <http://www.washingtonpost.com/blogs/the-fix/wp/2013/11/04/rand-pauls-plagiarism-allegations-and-why-they-matter/> [accessed 29 Dec 2015]; Adam Edelman, 'Kentucky Sen. Rand Paul Faces New Plagiarism Allegations Over NSA Suit Against President Obama', *New York Daily News*, 13 February 2014: <http://www.nydailynews.com/news/politics/kentucky-sen-rand-paul-faces-new-plagiarism-allegations-nsa-suit-president-obama-article-1.1613823> [accessed 29 Dec 2015].

272 See Jonathan Martin, 'Senator Rand Paul Faces New Charges of Plagiarism', *The New York Times*, 4 November 2013: <http://www.nytimes.com/2013/11/05/us/politics/senator-rand-paul-faces-new-charges-of-plagiarism.html?_r=0> [accessed 29 Dec 2015].

from United States history, including those by Martin Luther King Jr and John F Kennedy, as well as the Declaration of Independence. However, what emerged was the similarity of what he said to a 2006 speech by Massachusetts Governor Deval Patrick who employed many of the same quotes as well as very similar phrasing. The Clinton campaign seized on this and accused Obama of plagiarism. Obama's response was that he and Patrick were good friends and regularly shared ideas.[273] The issue did obtain much political traction.

Australia

In Australia, too, allegations of plagiarism have emerged as a political weapon for deriding the quality of politicians, their probity and their lack of originality. There have been a number of recent examples.

Then Deputy Liberal leader Julie Bishop in the Australian federal Parliament was twice accused of plagiarism. She was alleged to have reproduced material from the *Wall Street Journal* in a speech that she gave in September 2008, three days after taking up her role as Opposition treasury spokeswoman, without making attribution as to its source.[274]

In October 2008 she became embroiled in a second plagiarism controversy after a chapter she contributed to Peter van Onselen's *Liberals and Power: The Road Ahead*[275] was found to comprise parts of a speech, reproduced word for word and paraphrased, made by New Zealand businessman Roger Kerr. She asserted that the mistake was the fault of her Chief of Staff who had done work for her on the chapter, and then asserted that quotation marks were omitted because of a publisher's error, a proposition repudiated by the editor.[276] The book's editor was reported to have expressed disappointment that she had outsourced a substantial part of her contribution to his book to a staffer. Australian National University academic, Matthew Rimmer, noted that Mr Kerr too would probably have grounds to seek redress and commented:

> Politicians are always going to be vulnerable to allegations of plagiarism when they are so dependent upon ghostwriters who are working under the burden of tight time pressures and limited resources. And perhaps it's a reflection, too, that the political discourse has no great claim to originality.[277]

Towards the end of 2011 a federal Labor member of parliament, Craig Thomson, who had previously been the subject of attack for activities involving a prominent union, was exposed by the Victorian newspaper, *The Age*, in relation to plagiarism in which he had engaged in a report he wrote on a 42-day trip to Britain, Ireland, France, Spain, and the United States.[278] Mr Thomson had undertaken a taxpayer-funded study trip. He was obliged to submit a report of his trip within 30 days. Instead, more than four months late he provided a report which was tabled in Parliament which, without attribution, reproduced:

- outdated Wikipedia articles…;
- [parts of a speech] given by John Lipsky, first deputy managing director of the International Monetary Fund, to an economic conference in Denver, Colorado, on 8 January 2011…;

---

[273] See Jeff Zeleny, 'Clinton Camp Says Obama Plagiarized in Speech', *The New York Times*, 19 February 2008: <http://www.nytimes.com/2008/02/19/us/politics/19campaign.html> [accessed 29 Dec 2015].

[274] ABC Radio National, 'Bishop Accused of Plagiarism in Essay', *Lateline*, 28 October 2008 (Tom Iggulden): <http://www.abc.net.au/lateline/content/2008/s2403751.htm> [accessed 29 Dec 2015].

[275] Peter van Onselen (ed), *Liberals and Power: The Road Ahead* (Carlton, Vic: Melbourne University Press, 2008).

[276] Iggulden, above n 274.

[277] See Emma MacDonald, 'Plagiarism Row: Repeat Offender Bishop Outsources Blame', *The Canberra Times*, 28 October 2008, 2.

[278] Philip Dorling, 'Craig Thomson, MP Turned Plagiarist', *The Age*, 15 December 2011, 1: <http://www.theage.com.au/national/craig-thomson-mp-turned-plagiarist-20111214-1ov0u.html> [accessed 29 Dec 2015].

- [parts of a speech] given by European Commission member Michael Barnier in Vilnius, Lithuania, on September 8, four months after Mr Thomson returned to Australia ...; and
- extracts and summaries from Organisation for Economic Co-operation and Development reports on healthcare and housing finance.[279]

When contacted about his use of material by *The Age*, he declined to respond to questions about plagiarism, saying that 'it's not an academic exercise' and that 'my report speaks for itself'.[280] Members of the Labor Party came to Mr Thomson's defence, one of them (Tanya Plibersek) noting the difficulties of Ms Bishop three years before.[281]

A more amusing and nakedly political attack came in early 2012 when the Federal Opposition did a check on the words employed by Cabinet Minister Anthony Albanese in an address to the National Press Club for Australia Day.[282] He had attacked the Opposition leader, declaring:

> In Australia we have serious challenges to solve and we need serious people to solve them. Unfortunately, Tony Abbott is not the least bit interested in fixing anything. He is only interested in two things: making Australians afraid of it and telling them who's to blame for it.

The words contained only minor alterations from the 1995 film, *The American President*, in which the fictional US President, Andrew Shepherd (played by Michael Douglas), said:

> We have serious problems to solve, and we need serious men to solve them. And whatever your particular problem is, I promise you, Bob Rumson... is not the least bit interested in it. He is interested in two things and two things only: making you afraid of it and telling you who's to blame for it.[283]

The Liberal Federal Director promptly made the political point—that 'Labor is now so unoriginal and devoid of ideas that the best Albo could do was to plagiarize his attack lines from an American movie'.[284] The Opposition's Christopher Pyne, the Shadow Minister for Education, Apprenticeships and Training and Manager of Opposition Business in the House of Representatives, contended that the conduct of the Minister in taking lines from an American romantic comedy and swapping the names around 'is really quite embarrassing for an Australian Cabinet Minister addressing the National Press Club'.[285] The then Opposition leader, Tony Abbott, similarly commented: '[W]hat it shows is that this a [sic] government which has no ideas of its own for the improvement of Australia... [I]t is emblematic of a government that has no real ideas of its own'.[286] The Prime Minister hastened to protect her Minister in a lighthearted vein on Twitter.

Plagiarism and Litigation

Allegations of plagiarism has been litigated on many occasions (apparently at an increasing rate) in the context of breach of copyright, recent examples being the dispute about

---

279 Ibid.

280 Ibid.

281 See 'Thomson in Plagiarism "Scandal"', *The Canberra Times*, 15 December 2011: <http://www.canberratimes.com.au/national/thomson-in-plagiarism--scandal-20111215-1ugh7.html> [accessed 29 Dec 2015].

282 See Michelle Grattan, 'D'Oh! Albanese Embarrassed, Plagiarising Film President', *The Age*, 26 January 2012, 4: <http://www.theage.com.au/national/doh-albanese-embarrassed-plagiarising-film-president-20120125-1qht9.html> [accessed 29 Dec 2015].

283 Ibid.

284 Ibid.

285 Ibid.

286 Interview with Tony Abbott, Sydney Opera House (Sydney, 26 January 2012), available at: <http://www.liberal.org.au/latest-news/2012/01/28/tony-abbott-doorstop> [accessed 29 Dec 2015]. See Patrick Lion, 'Anthony Albanese Loses the Plot After Plagiarism of The American President', *The Daily Telegraph*,

the origins of Dan Brown's *The Da Vinci Code*[287] and the assertion that Men at Work utilized 'Kookaburra Sits in the Old Gum Tree' in their iconic song 'Down Under'.[288] Latterly, including in Australia, it has been litigated also in the disciplinary context involving both lawyers and doctors (see below, page 300ff).

The Stigma of Allegations of Plagiarism

The accusation of plagiarism is sensitive and potentially career-blighting. Often the ear, though, has been turned away from manifest plagiarism for a variety of reasons usually associated with what is comfortable for the employer/institution and the embarrassment that could ensue from taking a strong stand. Perhaps the classic example can be found first in undergraduate plagiarism engaged in by Dr Martin Luther King Jr at Atlanta's Morehouse College and then at Crozer Theological Seminary and still again in his doctoral thesis written at Boston University in 1955, a third of which has been demonstrated to have been plagiarized from Jack Stewart Boozer's Boston University dissertation written three years before.[289] Sensitivities attaching to dealing with so prominent a public figure resulted in his misconduct being 'overlooked' and his doctorate was not withdrawn. The four member committee of scholars appointed by Boston University to investigate the allegations of plagiarism against Dr King's doctoral dissertation concluded that withdrawal of his degree would 'serve no purpose' but did recommend that a letter stating its finding should be placed with the official copy of the dissertation in the university's library.[290]

Not having been taken to task about his use of others' work during the 1950s or 1960s, King continued his conduct, including in his use of another civil rights activist's famous closing lines in the 'I Have a Dream' speech in 1963. It ended as follows:

> This will be the day when all of God's children will be able to sing with a new meaning, 'My country, 'tis of thee, sweet land of liberty, of thee I sing. Land where my fathers died, land

---

27 January 2012: <http://www.dailytelegraph.com.au/anthony-albanese-loses-the-plot-after-plagiarism-of-the-american-president/story-e6freuy9-1226254731970> [accessed 29 Dec 2015].

287 *Baigent and Leigh v Random House Group Ltd* [2006] EWHC 719 (Ch) ('*The Da Vinci Code* case'). Joss Saunders usefully summarizes the distinctions between the two concepts:

> So what is the difference between plagiarism and copyright infringement? Plagiarism covers a spectrum from word for word textual copying, through changing some words but retaining the basic structure, through to copying ideas and arguments. The common thread is that the copying is dishonest because it is unacknowledged. If you quote from another author, and provide the citation, then in general you are not a plagiarist.
>
> Copyright by contrast involves two steps. The first is to establish whether or not the new text involves any copying of the old. The second is whether the copying is substantial. By and large the question of acknowledgement is irrelevant. An acknowledgement can be called into help as part of a defence when the infringer argues that the copying was for a permitted use, such as non-commercial research, or criticism or review. Even with an acknowledgement, an author is not free to copy as much as he likes.

Joss Saunders, 'Plagiarism and the Law: A Guide to Plagiarism and the Law' (November 2007), available at: <http://www.alpsp.org/Ebusiness/Libraries/0909PLA_-_Media/0909PDM_plagarism_and_the_law-0909_handout.sflb.ashx?download=true> [accessed 29 Dec 2015].

288 *Larrikin Music Publishing Pty Ltd v EMI Songs Australia Pty Ltd* [2010] FCA 29; (2010) 263 ALR 155.

289 See Theodore Pappas, *Plagiarism and the Culture War: The Writings of Martin Luther King, Jr, and Other Prominent Americans* (Tampa, Fla: Hallberg Pub, 1998). Compare Miller who defended King's use of others' material as 'intertextualizations', 'incorporations', 'borrowings', 'echoing', 'resonances' and 'voice merging': Keith D Miller, *Voice of Deliverance: The Language of Martin Luther King Jr, and Its Sources* (New York: Free Press, 1992) Introduction.

290 See 'Boston U. Panel Finds Plagiarism by Dr. King', *The New York Times*, 11 October 1991: <http://www.nytimes.com/1991/10/11/us/boston-u-panel-finds-plagiarism-by-dr-king.html> [accessed 29 Dec 2015].

of the pilgrim's pride, from every mountainside, let freedom ring.' And if America is to be a great nation this must become true. So let freedom ring from the prodigious hilltops of New Hampshire. Let freedom ring from the mighty mountains of New York. Let freedom ring from the heightening Alleghenies of Pennsylvania! Let freedom ring from the snow-capped Rockies of Colorado! Let freedom ring from the curvaceous peaks of California! But not only that; let freedom ring from Stone Mountain of Georgia! Let freedom ring from Lookout Mountain of Tennessee! Let freedom ring from every hill and every molehill of Mississippi. From every mountainside, let freedom ring.[291]

The relationship to the 1952 speech by the Reverend Archibald Carey (to which King made no reference) is inescapable:

We, Negro Americans, sing with all loyal Americans:
My country 'tis of thee,
Sweet land of liberty,
Of thee I sing.
Land where my fathers died,
Land of the Pilgrims' pride
From every mountainside
Let freedom ring!

That's exactly what we mean—from every mountain side, let freedom ring. Not only from the Green Mountains and White Mountains of Vermont and New Hampshire; not only from the Catskills of New York; but from the Ozarks in Arkansas, from the Stone Mountain in Georgia, from the Blue Ridge Mountains of Virginia—let it ring not only for the minorities of the United States, but for... the disinherited of all the earth—may the Republican Party, under God, from every mountainside, LET FREEDOM RING![292]

Martin Luther King Jr's conduct in persisting in plagiarized use of others' work is characteristics of the conduct of many plagiarists—when he was not made accountable for his conduct, he persisted in it.

The Involvement of Courts and Disciplinary Tribunals

The approach of the courts and disciplinary tribunals in recent times has been to acknowledge that '[p]lagiarism is a serious matter bearing on the reputation of any individual or institution the subject of an allegation. For that reason, there is a public interest in the unmasking of plagiarists'.[293] There are signs that the issue of plagiarism is more often being brought before public disciplinary tribunals in relation to professionals such as doctors and psychologists who are formally registered. In addition, there have been instances when persons whose degrees have been withdrawn on the basis of plagiarism have challenged the decision. For instance, in 2012 the 6th Circuit of the United States Court of Appeals affirmed a decision by Wayne State University to withdraw a 2008 doctorate in education from Hanna Jaber.[294] In addition, in a high profile French case, a researcher has been sentenced to a financial penalty after criminal proceedings were instituted against her for plagiarism.

---

[291] Martin Luther King, 'I have a Dream' (Speech delivered on the steps of the Lincoln Memorial, Washington DC, 28 August 1963), available at: <http://avalon.law.yale.edu/20th_century/mlk01.asp> [accessed 29 Dec 2015].

[292] Miller, above n 289, 146.

[293] *Darwish v Deakin University* [2002] VCAT 87, [20] (Judge Strong).

[294] *Jaber v Wayne State University Board of Governors* (Mich Ct App, 6th Cir, 9 July 2012).

The following section of this chapter identifies a series of disciplinary decisions in relation to plagiarism.

United States Authority

The most notorious United States disciplinary decision in relation to a plagiarist is that concerning a medical practitioner, Elias Alsabti.[295] As a young man he attended the Basra Medical College in Iraq and then completed a summer traineeship at London's Westminster Hospital. He first came to the attention of Iraqi scholars when he claimed to have invented a test that would detect certain forms of cancer. Reportedly, he was transferred to the prestigious Baghdad College of Medicine and given his own laboratory. He purported to develop a method of cancer detection which he called the 'Bakr Method', named after the then President of Iraq, Ahmed Hassan Al-Bakr,[296] although there is a strong suggestion[297] that Alsabti never tested the many blood samples that he took and simply purloined the money which he had charged patients. In due course the police were contacted but by then Alsabti had made his way to Saudi Arabia en route to Jordan. Alsabti made contact with the Office of his Royal Highness Crown Prince Hassan in Jordan, informing it of his breakthrough in relation to cancer testing. This resulted in his being permitted to work in the country's leading medical facility, King Hussein's Medical Centre in Amman. In due course he made his way to the medical school at Temple University in Philadelphia where he failed repeatedly to co-operate with the request that he provide a copy of his medical credentials from Iraq. Finally, he obtained a diploma from the American University of the Caribbean and on the basis of that was accepted into a medical residency programme in Roanoke, Virginia, which was associated with the University of Virginia. As rumours of his plagiarism continued to surface, he would leave one institution and move to another.

Broad and Wade observed that:

> Alsabti, in the course of constructing his academic illusion, had forged a medical degree, had duped the Jordanian government into giving him tens of thousands of dollars, had fabricated his relation to the royal family, had lied his way into U.S. universities, had bestowed a PhD upon himself, and, while allegedly doing research in a handful of prestigious US labs, had pirated many, perhaps all, of his sixty published papers. His tactics deceived the editors of dozens of scientific journals around the world.[298]

In 1979 Alsabti was called before the Suffolk Board of Registration in Medicine for publishing a series of plagiarized articles in medical journals while a graduate student, falsely authenticating scientific data. Given his extraordinary chutzpah, it is perhaps not surprising that he had the temerity to appeal the decision which removed his registration to the Supreme Judicial Court for the County of Suffolk.[299]

The court found that Alsabti graduated from medical school and became licensed to practise medicine in Pennsylvania. It accepted that in 1979 four articles authored or co-authored by him were published in medical journals, along with a further nine. The four articles were substantially similar, aside from changes in date, to four articles previously published by other authors. One had been filed as part of a grant application. Nowhere did he acknowledge or cite the other authors' work.

---

295 See Gordon Klintworth, *Giants, Crooks and Jerks in Science* (Xlibris, 2014), pp 134–5.

296 David J Miller, 'Plagiarism: The Case of Elias AK Alsabti' in David J Miller and Michel Hersen (eds), *Research Fraud in the Behavioral and Biomedical Sciences* (New York: John Wiley & Sons, 1992) 81. See William Broad and Nicholas Wade, *Betrayers of the Truth* (New York: Simon & Schuster, 1982).

297 Broad and Wade, above n 296, 40.

298 Ibid 52.

299 *Alsabti v Board of Registration in Medicine*, 404 Mass 547 (1989).

Alsabti did not offer any explanation for the substantial similarity of his articles to those previously published. He took no action to retract or correct the record concerning the articles. At the time he was a graduate student, not in medical school or a physician. The articles were not submitted in pursuance of any course requirements.

Alsabti proffered references from over 20 of his patients which described him in effusive terms. However, the board concluded that, by his pattern of conduct in publishing plagiarized articles 'in disregard of the fundamental virtues of intellectual honesty, professional integrity and respect for the advancement of scientific knowledge',[300] Alsabti had demonstrated that he lacked the moral character required to practise medicine. It also found that his conduct called into question his competence to practise medicine. The board observed that his conduct was not an isolated lapse of judgment but 'a systematic attempt to enhance his professional standing in the medical community';[301] Alsabti was attempting dishonestly to create the impression of being a well-published expert, thereby having the potential to advantage himself over more qualified rivals who were deprived of a capacity to compete with him by reason of his plagiarized publications and thereby putting at risk the quality of medical care that might be provided to patients. The board commented that:

> In giving life to research as his own, he gave credence to ideas without any scientific proof. Information introduced into the stream of intellectual commerce, despite being unworthy of attention, will be relied upon if it appears authoritative. The published articles of [Alsabti] had this misleading appearance. Even if the original work which [Alsabti] copied was meritorious, his efforts improperly validated the work. Instead of one work on the subject, there were two. The degree of acceptance of an idea, apart from its intrinsic worth, determines its place in the body of scientific knowledge. In the complex and changing world of scientific knowledge, it is difficult to estimate the effect of [Alsabti's] fraud. Intellectual dishonesty thwarts the efficient and systematic development of knowledge.[302]

It concluded that Alsabti had shown indifference to the values required of a physician: 'Instead of showing self-sacrifice and dedication to the goals of the profession, [Alsabti] displayed self-centered behavior designed as a shortcut to professional success. In place of a commitment to truth he demonstrated a cavalier disregard for the intellectual process involved in research.'[303]

Alsabti argued before the Supreme Court that the board had been unwarranted in making a connection between his plagiarism while a graduate student and his practice of medicine nearly ten years later. The Supreme Court disagreed. It endorsed the board's decision and emphasized the need for physicians to possess a high degree of integrity, lest their conduct undermine public confidence in the profession. It found the board had properly taken into account the fact that Alsabti had become highly regarded by patients and colleagues, but concluded that the board 'was clearly justified in assessing as serious Alsabti's disregard at that time for basic fairness to competitors and for the possible consequences to patients who might be exposed to medical treatment by physicians relying on experiments Alsabti purported to have done but never did'.[304] It found the board's decision to be supported by substantial evidence and affirmed its decision.

The case of Elias Alsabti is nothing short of extraordinary. Charrow has called him a 'peripatetic miscreant and charlatan',[305] which is a harsh but fair characterization. Only part of

---

300 Ibid 550.
301 Ibid 551.
302 Ibid, 552.
303 Ibid, 552.
304 Ibid, 553–4.
305 Robert P Charrow, *Law in the Laboratory: A Guide to the Ethics of Federally Funded Science Research* (Chicago, Ill: University of Chicago Press, 2010) 53.

Alsabti's fraudulent conduct (although it was this that precipitated his ultimate disgrace) was manifested in his plagiarism. His history is one of many warning signs that plagiarism is a form of intellectual dishonesty that may well be manifested by a variety of other forms of fraudulent conduct, including research fraud. Significantly, as Klintworth has lamented, only one of Alsabti's publications was retracted by a scholarly journal.[306]

In a later case, *Re Hinden*,[307] the District of Columbia Court of Appeals dealt with an attorney, Richard Hinden, who was head of a firm's health care practice. He was invited to author a chapter in a legal treatise dealing with liability issues for alternative health care delivery systems. He wrote the chapter which was 65 pages in length and revised it for a later edition. In due course the editor of the *American Journal of Law and Medicine* drew to the attention of the publisher the 'striking similarity' between Hinden's chapter and an article published in the journal.[308] Twenty-three of the 56 pages of the chapter contained 43 complete paragraphs that had been copied from the article. The bar recommended and the court accepted that the attorney be publicly censured for his conduct.[309]

United Kingdom Authority

Significant cases have come before the regulatory authorities and the courts in the United Kingdom in relation to medical practitioners alleged to have engaged in plagiarism.

Dr Salha et al. An important example is the decision of the Privy Council in *Salha v General Medical Council*,[310] an appeal from a hearing of the Professional Conduct Committee of the General Medical Council. At first instance the committee found the doctors had plagiarized in *Human Reproduction Update*, without acknowledgment, 'substantial parts' of an article originally published in *Human Reproduction*.[311] It classified this to be 'serious professional misconduct'.[312]

At the heart of the hearing was the meaning to be given to the absolute obligation of medical practitioners (under r 57 of the General Medical Council's *Good Medical Practice*) to 'conduct all research with honesty and integrity'.[313] Because there were difficulties in determining which of the authors was responsible for particular parts of the article, the case against them was amended from conscious plagiarism to a failure adequately to review the paper before publication. Nonetheless, the committee found:

> All authors are responsible for the contents and substance of any paper to the extent that they have not taken reasonable steps to discharge their responsibilities. To accept the benefits of authorship while evading the responsibilities for any deficiencies in the paper is unacceptable and dishonest.[314]

It suspended the practitioners for three months.

The critical stance of the committee was clear and the Privy Council did not disagree with it in principle. However, it concluded on the facts that the committee's designation of the conduct had erred—the particular circumstances of the case did not permit a finding of

[306] Klintworth, above n 57, 135.
[307] 654 A 2d 864 (1985).
[308] Ibid, 866.
[309] See also, Peter A Joy and Kevin C McMunigal, 'The Problems of Plagiarism as an Ethics Offense' (2011) 26(2) *Criminal Justice* 56.
[310] [2003] UKPC 80; (2004) 80 BMLR 169.
[311] Ibid, [3].
[312] Ibid, [10].
[313] Ibid, [6].
[314] Ibid, [10].

dishonesty, which had not been directly asserted in the hearing against the practitioners. It set aside the suspensions and imposed a reprimand.

Dr Persaud. In *Re Persaud*[315] the well-known psychiatrist and broadcaster, Dr Raj Persaud,[316] was found to have engaged in misconduct by dishonestly passing off the work of others on a number of occasions as his own. He was suspended from practice for three months. The conduct had occurred between three and five years previously and had not been repeated. It occurred in the context of illicit usage of four research papers for his 2003 book *From the Edge of the Couch*,[317] and copying the work of two foreign academics in five articles he wrote for publications including the *British Medical Journal* and *The Independent*. He maintained implausibly that he was confused about the difference between quotation and attribution and was under a great deal of deadline stress, often writing late at night.[318] He had been heavily critical of Scientology in various of his publications and it was from Scientology that awareness of his plagiarism emanated: the Citizens Commission on Human Rights, founded by Scientology, informed the General Medical Council that an article by Persaud in *The Independent* in 2005 plagiarized passages from a 1998 paper by Professor Stephen Kent of Alberta University.[319] In the aftermath of the hearing, having been described in the media as 'Dr Copycat'[320] in the reporting of his hearing before the General Medical Council, he stepped down as a consultant psychiatrist for the South London and Maudsley NHS Trust.

Dr Ali. In *Re Ali*[321] it was found against the practitioner, who was employed as a Specialist Registrar in Histopathology by Darent Valley Hospital, that:

- he submitted an abstract to the Pathological Society of Great Britain and Ireland indicating he was the author, when he was not, and plagiarizing another practitioner's case report which had been published in the *British Medical Journal*;
- he submitted a further abstract to the Pathological Society indicating falsely that another practitioner was a co-author; and
- he failed to acknowledge in a job application that he was the subject of a fitness to practise investigation, when he knew that he was, and then failed to inform an interview panel of the GMC investigation.

The Fitness to Practise Panel found a variety of the practitioner's actions, including his plagiarism, to be dishonest, misleading and inappropriate. It commented:

> [P]lagiarism is a serious matter; especially within the scientific community but also in the wider context of the views of ordinary people. You knowingly copied and appropriated the

[315] *Re Persaud* (unreported, GMC Fitness to Practise Panel, 20 June 2008).

[316] Dr Persaud was a presenter of BBC Radio 4's 'All in the Mind' and a regular guest on ITV show 'This Morning'.

[317] Raj Persaud, *From the Edge of the Couch* (London: Bantam Press, 2003).

[318] David Batty, 'Raj Persaud Blames Stress for Plagiarism', *The Guardian*, 18 June 2008: <http://www.theguardian.com/society/2008/jun/18/raj.persaud.hearing> [accessed 29 Dec 2015].

[319] Chris Irvine, 'Disgraced Raj Persaud Quits Job as Consultant', *The Telegraph*, 24 October 2008: <http://www.telegraph.co.uk/news/celebritynews/3252267/Disgraced-Raj-Persaud-quits-job-as-consultant.html> [accessed 29 Dec 2015].

[320] James Tozer, 'Shame of Dr Copycat: TV Shrink Raj Persaud Used Work of Others as his Own', *Daily Mail*, 17 June 2008: <http://www.dailymail.co.uk/news/article-1026813/TV-psychiatrist-Dr-Raj-Persaud-admits-plagiarising-articles-book.html> [accessed 29 Dec 2015]. See eg, James Tozer, 'Shamed TV Star Dr Raj Persaud Blames 'Carelessness and Deadline Pressure' for Plagiarism in his Books', *Daily Mail*, 18 June 2008: <http://www.dailymail.co.uk/news/article-1027243/Shamed-TV-star-Dr-Raj-Persaud-blames-carelessness-deadline-pressure-plagiarism-books.html> [accessed 29 Dec 2015]; Bob Grant, 'UK Psychiatrist Suspended for Plagiarism', *The Scientist*, 23 June 2008: <http://www.the-scientist.com/?articles.view/articleNo/26508/title/UK-psychiatrist-suspended-for-plagiarism/> [accessed 29 Dec 2015].

[321] *Re v Ali* (unreported, GMC Fitness to Practise Panel, 16 December 2009).

words of another author as if they were your own. You said the words expressed what you wanted to say better than you could have done yourself.

The Panel did not accept the Biden defence asserted by Dr Ali. It found it difficult to accept that a person with the practitioner's background, experience, and training 'even in the absence of any formal training on authorship, would not consider the appropriation of words from another author's work dishonest'.[322] It found his subsequent passing off of authorship also to be dishonest and observed such conduct to be of a kind that detracts from the integrity of medicine and reflects adversely on the standards and reputation of the profession of medicine. It commented that: 'Probity is at the heart of the medical profession. You are at all times expected to act with honesty and integrity.'[323] It found that the practitioner's actions, although they did not affect patient care, had the potential to damage the reputation of his profession and thereby undermine confidence in it and the standard the public has a right to expect of its doctors. It determined that his fitness to practise was impaired by reason of the misconduct in which he had engaged and suspended his registration for four months. In fixing upon the period, it took into account, to his advantage, 'the considerable insight you have shown, your remorse and your attempts to remedy your misconduct'.[324]

Dr Ramanujam. Similarly, a Fitness to Practise Panel viewed a psychiatrist's conduct as 'dishonest and misleading' in *Re Ramanujam*[325] after she had substantially copied material from the Royal College of Psychiatrists website and from another student at the University of Birmingham in partial satisfaction of a distance learning course on mental health at the University of Gloucestershire. When the issue was identified at the University, she explained that she had made mistakes and had not understood correctly how to reference her work. She was given the opportunity to resubmit her assignment but, remarkably, retained much of the material and added material copied from Wikipedia. The Fitness to Practise Panel accepted that at first Dr Ramanujam may have been affected by a measure of naivety and inexperience, but did not accept that this persisted. It suspended her registration for 12 months.

A Canadian Decision

In *Law Society of Upper Canada v Burgess*[326] a hearing was held to determine whether an applicant for admission as a legal practitioner was of good character. The hearing arose because, in the course of attending an Honours BA programme at the University of Toronto, she plagiarized a paper on 'Death and Dying', ironically as part of a course on professional ethics. In fact, it had been written by another person and she tried to pass the material off as her own. Later in her application for admission (perhaps consistently with her approach to issues of honesty) she falsely reported that the academic misconduct claim made against her was for 'handing in a paper that was deemed too similar to a paper that I had handed in for another course. Although the claim was the result of a misunderstanding, I did not proceed

---

322 *Re v Ali* (unreported, GMC Fitness to Practise Panel, 16 December 2009) 14, as cited in Jon Wardle, 'Plagiarism and Registered Health Professionals: Navigating the Borderlands Between Scholarly and Professional Misconduct' (2013) 21(2) *Journal of Law and Medicine* 399, 409–409.

323 *Re v Ali*, 6, as cited in Wardle, above n 322, 408.

324 *Re Ramanujam* (unreported, GMC Fitness to Practise Panel, 18 May 2011), as cited in Wardle, above n 322. Compare also *Re Shephard* (unreported, Fitness to Practise Panel, General Medical Council, 27 May 2011) who was suspended for four months for plagiarizing 12 assignments in a Postgraduate Certificate of Medical Education at the University of Dundee; and *Re Kumar* (unreported, Fitness to Practise Panel, General Medical Council, 1 February 2011) who was suspended for six months after passing off another doctor's work as his own for a Teachers in Primary Care certificate at the University of Westminster. See further, Wardle, above n 322, 407–409, who discusses these cases.

325 *Re Ramanujam* (unreported, GMC Fitness to Practise Panel, 18 May 2011).

326 [2006] ONLSHP 66.

with a hearing because I was graduating'.[327] She then told this false account to persons who acted as referees for her.

The Hearing Panel observed that her plagiarism, the mendacity to the Law Society and the lies told to her character referees went 'to the very heart of who lawyers are, and what lawyers do. Integrity is fundamental to the competence of a lawyer; competence necessarily includes integrity'.[328] It concluded that in spite of various attestations to her character, which had been informed by this stage by knowledge of her previous deceptions, it could not be satisfied that she was by that time of good character.[329]

Australian Decisions

There has been a series of Australian decisions that have reflected on the seriousness of plagiarism in the context of the admission of legal practitioners and the registration of a psychologist. The approach has not been entirely consistent but in general terms what can be identified is the taking of a more robust stance than that adopted in the United States decision of *In Re Hinden*.[330]

The *AJG* decision. In *Re AJG*[331] an applicant for admission as a legal practitioner in Queensland admitted that, while engaged in the practical legal training course at Griffith University, he substantially copied the work of another student. The Court of Appeal held that:

> Legal practitioners must exhibit a degree of integrity which engenders in the Court and in clients unquestioning confidence in the completely honest discharge of their professional commitments. Cheating in the academic course which leads to the qualification central to practice and at a time so close to the application for admission must preclude our presently being satisfied of this applicant's fitness.[332]

It declined to admit him and adjourned his application, marking it not to be relisted for six months.

The *Liveri* decision. In *Re Liveri*[333] the Queensland Court of Appeal heard another application for admission, opposed by the Legal Practitioners Admissions Board. The applicant accepted findings of academic misconduct made against her by James Cook University that she had submitted as her own work an article published on the internet on the law of trusts, that she quoted in an administrative law assignment substantially from an author's work without attribution, and that in an assignment on the law of the sea she quoted verbatim from a governmental publication without acknowledgment.

The Court of Appeal accepted the characterization of the applicant's conduct as 'a blatant case of Academic Misconduct'[334] and applied the reasoning of the court in *Re AJG*.[335] It noted that the applicant had engaged in serious plagiarism more than once, that she did so when a person of mature years (25 and 27 years old), and that she failed to exhibit insight into the

327 Ibid [7]. Compare *Re OG* [2007] VSC 520; 18 VR 164.

328 *Law Society of Upper Canada v Burgess* [2006] ONLSHP 66, [9].

329 On the issue of good character, a term now omitted from the *Health Practitioner Regulation National Law Act 2009* (Qld) and the *Health Practitioner Regulation National Law (Victoria) Act 2009* (Vic), see Ian Freckelton, 'Good Character' and the Regulation of Medical Practitioners' (2008) 16(3) *Journal of Law and Medicine* 488.

330 654 A 2d 864 (1995).

331 [2004] QCA 88.

332 *Re AJG* [2004] QCA 88.

333 [2006] QCA 152.

334 Ibid [10].

335 [2004] QCA 88.

gravity and significance of her conduct by her subsequent unwillingness (until appearing before the court) to acknowledge her misconduct. It declined her application and took a similar course to that in *Re AJG*, adjourning it to a date to be fixed, not to be relisted for at least six months.

The *Humzy-Hancock* decision. In *Re Humzy-Hancock*[336] McMurdo J heard a case in which the applicant for admission as a legal practitioner in Queensland disclosed that he had been found guilty of academic misconduct by the Law Faculty Assessment Board of Griffith University. The board found the appellant to have engaged in improper collaboration in the writing of an assignment and to have engaged in plagiarism. McMurdo J, though, accepted the applicant's account that he did not knowingly provide a copy of his assignment, or a draft of it, to the student who reproduced parts of his work. This meant that he did not accept the board's finding of improper collaboration. In respect of the alleged plagiarism, he found that the applicant had 'heavily borrowed from [an] article'[337] and in each instance there was no or insufficient attribution to it. Somewhat surprisingly, his Honour accepted 'the Biden defence' and found that in none of these instances had the applicant been proven to have an intention to pass off the work of another as his own. He accepted the applicant's evidence that the failures to give proper attribution to the article which he had used heavily were the result of carelessness and his misunderstanding of what was required. The decision has been criticized as having extended an unwarranted degree of leniency to the applicant.[338]

The *Keough* decision. In 2010 in *Legal Services Commissioner v Keough*[339] the Victorian Civil and Administrative Tribunal (VCAT) handed down the next in the sequence of Australian decisions on the subject of plagiarism in the context of lawyers' suitability to become or remain admitted legal practitioners.

In 2005 a student in the University of Melbourne's health law postgraduate programme, a Melbourne solicitor practising in the eastern suburbs, was required to submit one of a series of 10,000-word research papers. He did so but, according to his evidence, in the weeks leading up to the due date, found himself under time pressure. He submitted a paper that included a large amount of plagiarism. The solicitor ultimately acknowledged that about 50 per cent of his paper was extracted from an article published in the *American Journal of Law and Medicine* and to a lesser extent from a 2004 paper published in the Autumn edition of *Perspectives in Biology and Medicine*. The plagiarism was not detected by the university and he submitted a version of the paper for consideration for publication in the *Journal of Law and Medicine*. It was peer reviewed and, again, the plagiarism was not identified. To the embarrassment of the editor, this author, it was published.[340]

Ultimately, communications from the United States to the editor of the *Journal of Law and Medicine* revealed the conduct in which the solicitor had engaged, conduct which was at all relevant times likely to come to light at some stage, given the international profile of the journal. The solicitor was queried by the editor about the similarities. He responded that he used the main American article as 'a basis for my paper, however, I did not adopt the paper as my own'.[341] He maintained that he had also used other material in the article which he

---

336 [2007] QSC 34.

337 Ibid [27].

338 See Corbin and Carter, above n 12.

339 [2010] VCAT 108.

340 William J Keough, 'Towards the Development of Ethical Practices in Paediatric Clinical Trials: The Special Position of the Terminally Ill Child' (2006) 13(3) *Journal of Law and Medicine* 370. The article has since been removed from all electronic versions of the journal.

341 [2010] VCAT 108, [16].

submitted to the journal and put his own interpretation on it. However, he conceded 'after having re-read both papers, I realise that I had not properly adhered to footnoting standards in a few places in the paper, which should have been acknowledged'.[342] This was a version of the Biden defence. In fact, a [plagiarism-prevention service] Turnitin analysis revealed that his usage of material from the two sources, including footnotes, was in large part verbatim, namely extensive word-for-word plagiarism, and constituted more than half of what purported to be his article.

Later the solicitor stated:

> Since I was endeavouring to cover an area which was a composite of that dealt with by Oberman & Frader and by Ross, I used their work extensively for the purposes of preparing what was intended as a rough draft. Unfortunately, when the draft was printed and I was running out of time, I used the draft as the paper submitted.
>
> [...]
>
> At the time I wrote my paper I was conscious that I had made significant use of the work of others without acknowledging the source; strangely when I submitted the paper to the *Journal of Law and Medicine* I was not, or was no longer, conscious of the extent to which I had done so.[343]

This, then, was a version of the Bernheim excuse. In the course of the hearing into the solicitor's conduct, the attention of those sitting on the VCAT hearing was drawn by counsel for the Legal Services Commissioner to the case of a solicitor who some years before had similarly plagiarized material but had done so in professional addresses and then in an article published in the *Law Institute Journal*: *Re Pickering*.[344] The Solicitors' Board of Victoria (the predecessor in function to VCAT in this regard) found the solicitor to have engaged in professional misconduct and cancelled his practising certificate for a period of ten months, observing:

> Upon analysis, the copying of articles written by another without acknowledgement of that other's authorship is, in the ultimate, directed either to self aggrandisement or to the enlargement of the professional practice of the author by the holding out of learning and competence.[345]

It commented:

> The Board does not believe that a solicitor of the academic standing and experience of the solicitor in this case, who is the author of many published articles and the holder of many degrees and other qualifications in various fields, could fail unintentionally, when copying substantial portions of the work of others, to include a proper attribution of the authorship and also to seek permission for the use of such work for his own purposes.[346]

To this extent, the board's approach contrasted with that of McMurdo J in *Re Humzy-Hancock*.[347]

VCAT took into account the decisions of the Queensland Court of Appeal in *Re AJG*[348] and *Re Liveri*.[349] It found the solicitor appearing before it to have engaged in misconduct at common law, 'in that he submitted a research paper that contained deliberate plagiarism for

342 Ibid.
343 Ibid, [20].
344 *Law Institute Journal: Re Pickering* (unreported, Solicitors' Board, Vic, 6 February 1992).
345 Ibid, 14, as cited in *Legal Services Commissioner v Keough* [2010] VCAT 108, [37].
346 Ibid, 14, as cited in *Legal Services Commissioner v Keough* [2010] VCAT 108, [54].
347 [2007] QSC 34.
348 [2004] QCA 88.
349 [2006] QCA 152.

assessment in a subject when seeking a degree of Master of Health and Medical Law at the University of Melbourne' and also 'in that he submitted an article that contained deliberate plagiarism for publication in the *Journal of Law and Medicine*'.[350] The tribunal took into account good character evidence in favour of the solicitor, the fact that he made admissions at an early stage, that he admitted both charges and that this was the first time since being admitted 25 years before that he had been found guilty of a disciplinary offence. It found the solicitor's decision to submit a plagiarized paper to the University of Melbourne to be a 'conscious decision'[351] and rejected as 'implausible'[352] the proposition that when he submitted a version of the paper subsequently to the *Journal of Law and Medicine* he was no longer aware of the extent to which he had made use of the work of others without acknowledgment.

By way of penalty, the tribunal gave relatively little emphasis to the need for specific deterrence and punishment, given the adverse repercussions already suffered to the solicitor's reputation, including his being told that he should not apply for reappointment on an ethics committee at Austin Health. However, it observed:

> The need for general deterrence is much greater. To repeat what was said in *Re: AJG*, 'Legal practitioners must exhibit a degree of integrity which engenders in the Court and in clients unquestioning confidence in the completely honest discharge of their professional commitments'.[353]

VCAT cancelled the solicitor's practising certificate, and precluded his reapplying for a certificate for six months. It ordered him to pay the costs of the Legal Services Commissioner. Unfortunately, the University of Melbourne failed to take action in relation to Mr Keough's degree.

The *Glamcevski* decision. In *Psychologists Registration Board of Victoria v Glamcevski*[354] VCAT was again called upon to determine how plagiarism, on this occasion by a psychologist, should be viewed in terms of professional conduct. VCAT found that the provisional psychologist had submitted plagiarized case studies containing unreferenced work as part of purported compliance with what was necessary for him to gain general registration as a psychologist. He admitted that he had copied the work of others for this purpose and that his conduct was misleading and deceptive in that the case studies were not his own work. Mihaljo Glamcevski's conduct was exacerbated by the fact that VCAT found that he had also held himself out as a fully registered psychologist when his status was only provisional.

The VCAT panel found that the amount of copying of others' work was 'very extensive'[355] and that there was very little of his own work in what he submitted to his registration board in the case studies. Mr Glamcevski's argument was essentially the Biden defence—that he did not realize the extent of the copying in which he had engaged until the issues came to light. He said was very sorry for what he had done. VCAT accepted that he showed contrition.[356]

The three-member panel of VCAT rejected the proposition that Mr Glamcevski's provisional status was a significantly mitigating factor—he 'knew or should have known that passing off others' work as his own was a most serious matter and if it had not been detected, it is likely that he would have obtained a full registration as a psychologist without having demonstrated

350 *Legal Services Commissioner v Keough* [2010] VCAT 108, [2]–[3].
351 Ibid, [49].
352 Ibid, [51].
353 Ibid, [58].
354 [2010] VCAT 1927.
355 Ibid, [46].
356 Ibid, [47].

the competency. This would be likely to have had very serious effects on his future patients and affected the public's perception of the profession'.[357] It found him to have been guilty of a 'substantial and consistent failure to reach or maintain a reasonable standard of competence and diligence', one of the statutory definitions of 'professional misconduct' and 'at the very least guilty of 'intellectual dishonesty'.[358] It commented that if he carried over such an approach of passing off others' work as his own and having that attitude 'it may well be deleterious in relation to his treatment of any future clients'.[359]

The VCAT panel referred to a series of cases on 'good character' and accepted the proposition that honour, integrity and trustworthiness are prerequisites for the standing and integrity of the health professions, including psychology.[360] A psychologist's report diagnosed Mr Glamcevski as suffering from a Chronic Adjustment Disorder with Mixed Disturbance of Emotions and Conduct. He was not registered at the time of the VCAT hearing; this limited what orders could be made. The tribunal imposed a reprimand and a fine on him.

The *Webb* decision. In *Queensland Nursing Council v Webb*[361] the Queensland Nursing Tribunal dealt with allegations of unsatisfactory professional conduct in the form of plagiarism against a registered nurse, Judith Webb, relating to case studies plagiarized from a former student in a training course run by Queensland Health in rural and isolated practice health. The tribunal had no difficulty in determining that 'plagiarism constitutes unprofessional conduct' in that it constitutes conduct of a lesser standard than is reasonably to be expected by peers.[362] The tribunal accepted that the nurse had not been afforded the appropriate mentoring support from a clinical nurse with the appropriate accreditation and that she was deeply remorseful for her conduct. It accepted her proposal that she be precluded from reapplying from registration for six months and that she be obliged to complete a course in professional ethics and decision-making and, when entering the course, familiarize herself with the relevant university's policy on plagiarism.

Plagiarism by Judicial Officers

An issue that has arisen within the courts that has not yet been the subject of significant comment or much by way of scholarship is judges' usage of other judicial officers' work, the publications of academics and the submissions of parties.[363] There is a line of thinking that exempts judicial officers from ordinary obligations in relation to the use of others' writing, contending that the judicial role is of its very nature derivative. An example of this are the observations of Joyce George in her *Judicial Opinion Writing Handbook*:

> A judge, writing to resolve a dispute, whether trial or appellate, is exempted from a charge of plagiarism even if ideas, words or phrases from a law review article, novel thoughts published in a legal periodical or language from a party's brief are used without giving attribution. Thus, judges are free to use whatever sources they deem appropriate to resolve the matter before them, without fear of reprisal. This exemption applies to judicial writings intended to

[357] Ibid, [54].
[358] Ibid, [56].
[359] Ibid, [56].
[360] Ibid, [59]–[60].
[361] [2007] QNT 5.
[362] Ibid, 2.
[363] See eg, Douglas R Richmond, 'Unoriginal Sin: The Problem of Judicial Plagiarism' (2013) 45(3) *Arizona State Law Journal* 1077; Jaime S Dursht, 'Judicial Plagiarism: It May Be Fair Use But Is It Ethical?' (1996) 18(3) Cardozo Law Review 1253. See also Posner, above n 14, 21–2.

> decide cases for two reasons: the judge is not writing a literary work and, more importantly, the purpose of the writing is to resolve a dispute. As a result, judges adjudicating cases are not subject to a claim of legal plagiarism.[364]

However, this absolutist position is starting to be overtaken and must be qualified. Parties expect, and are entitled to expect, that judges who decide their cases will be engaged in their task, impartial and intellectually honest. This involves transparency in how they utilize their sources and the source/s of their analyses. Abdication of such a responsibility constitutes intellectual dishonesty and risks diminishing the respect for the judicial system and its decision-making.[365] The issue has arisen in a number of different contexts.

The allegations against Justice Einfeld. In 2003 Justice Marcus Einfeld of the Federal Court of Australia was the subject of a formal complaint brought by Professor John Carter of the University of Sydney in relation to alleged reproduction of Carter's work in *Halsbury's Laws of Australia* in a judgment without attribution. Professor Carter told the *Financial Review*: 'We fail our students and discipline them if they do this'.[366] Justice Einfeld is reported to have said that the footnotes had been left out in the printing process. The outcome of the complaint was that the publisher (LexisNexis) was provided with a corrigendum for publication in the relevant judgment that references to *Halsbury's* had been omitted in error.[367]

Judicial misconduct. In *Re Complaint of Doe*[368] one of a number of complaints of judicial misconduct by a civil litigant against a district judge was that she engaged in plagiarism of approximately 55 per cent of the defendant's brief when drafting the order dismissing the plaintiff's action. The grievance received short shrift. It was found that the trial judge relied on material supplied by the defendants in fashioning her opinion 'albeit often in verbatim fashion and without attribution' but this was not found to constitute judicial misconduct—her orders, on the contrary, on appeal were found to be balanced, careful, and thorough.[369]

The Justice Del Castillo controversy in the Philippines. In 2009 *Newsbreak* magazine reviewed the decision of a Philippines Supreme Court judge, Justice Del Mariano Castillo, in the *Vinuya v Romulo*[370] case in relation to 70 Second World War comfort women who sought a public apology from Japan and reparation to them as victims of sexual abuse. It alleged that multiple parts of it were copied without attribution from material written by legal experts abroad.[371]

---

364 Joyce J George, *Judicial Opinion Writing Handbook* (5th edn, Buffalo, NY: William S Hein & Co, 2007) 725.

365 A point well (but slightly differently) made by Richmond, above n 363.

366 See Paul Sheehan, 'The Einfeld Follies: A Study in Ego', *The Sydney Morning Herald*, 21 August 2006: <http://www.smh.com.au/news/opinion/the-einfeld-follies-a-study-in-ego/2006/08/20/1156012408310.html?page=fullpage#contentSwap2> [accessed 30 Dec 2015].

367 Personal communication from Professor Carter, 29 July 2015.

368 640 F 3d 869 (8th Cir, 2011).

369 Ibid, 873.

370 *Vinuya v Romulo* (28 April 2010), GR No. 162230 (Republic of the Philippines Supreme Court): <http://sc.judiciary.gov.ph/jurisprudence/2010/april2010/162230.htm> [accessed 30 Dec 2015].

371 Specifically: Evan J Criddle and Evan Fox-Decent, 'A Fiduciary Theory of Jus Cogens' (2009) 34(2) *The Yale Journal of International Law* 331; Mark Ellis, 'Breaking the Silence: Rape as an International Crime' (2006–2007) 38(2) *Case Western Reserve Journal of International Law* 225; Christian J Tams C, *Enforcing Obligations Erga Omnes in International Law* (Cambridge, UK: Cambridge University Press, 2005). At the relevant times, Criddle was Assistant Professor at the Syracuse University College of Law; Fox-Decent was an Assistant Professor at the McGill University Faculty of Law; Ellis was Executive Director of the International Bar Association; and Tams was Professor of International Law at the University of Glasgow and Professor at the China EU School of Law (Beijing) and the Europa-Kolleg (Hamburg).

This formed the basis of an appeal to the Supreme Court of the Philippines[372] which in a deeply ideologically divided verdict determined not to uphold the appeal due to lack of merit by a majority of 10 to 2 (with Justice Del Castillo not participating). The plurality observed that original plagiarism is rightly abhorred in the academic context, and contrasted this with court decisions:

> [D]ecisions of courts are not written to earn merit, accolade, or prize as an original piece of work or art. Deciding disputes is a service rendered by the government for the public good. Judges issue decisions to resolve everyday conflicts involving people of flesh and blood who ache for speedy justice or juridical beings which have rights and obligations in law that need to be protected. The interest of society in written decisions is not that they are originally crafted but that they are fair and correct in the context of the particular disputes involved. Justice, not originality, form, and style, is the object of every decision of a court of law.[373]

The plurality found that litigants and 'some faculty members of the University of the Philippines school of law, have unfairly maligned' Justice Del Castillo with 'charges of plagiarism, twisting of cited materials, and gross neglect for failing to attribute lifted passages from three foreign authors'.[374] They accepted that this was attributable to a 'highly qualified and experienced court-employed researcher'[375] who accidentally deleted attribution to authors in a draft on which she worked for the judge. They made the point that the impugned passages in the judgment 'showed on their face that the lifted ideas did not belong to Justice Del Castillo but to others. He did not pass them off as his own'.[376] In respect of a comparable grievance in another judgment, the plurality dismissed the concern as 'nit-picking'.[377]

In an extensive and vigorously argued dissenting opinion,[378] joined by Justice Conchita Carpio-Morales, Justice Lourdes Sereno (who shortly afterwards was appointed Chief Justice of the Philippines) found that Del Castillo had indeed committed plagiarism in drafting the decision in the *Vinuya* case. Her Honour expressed concern that the plurality's decision wrongly required that there be 'malicious intent' for plagiarism to be committed, commenting:

> The majority Decision will thus stand against the overwhelming conventions on what constitutes plagiarism. In doing so, the Decision has created unimaginable problems for Philippine academia, which will from now on have to find a disciplinary response to plagiarism committed by students and researchers on the justification of the majority Decision. It has also undermined the protection of copyrighted work by making available to plagiarists 'lack of malicious intent' as a defense to a charge of violation of copy or economic rights of the copyright owner committed through lack of attribution.[379]

She held that plagiarism does not consist solely of using the work of others in one's own work, but of the former in conjunction with the failure to attribute said work to its rightful owner and thereby, as in the case of written work, misrepresenting the work of another as one's

[372] *In the Matter of the Charges of Plagiarism, Etc., Against Associate Justice Mariano C. Del Castillo* (Resolution) 8 February 2011, AM No. 10-7-17—SC, (Republic of the Philippines Supreme Court): <http://sc.judiciary.gov.ph/jurisprudence/2011/february2011/10-7-17-SC.htm#_ftn8> [accessed 30 Dec 2015] (unpaginated).

[373] Ibid.

[374] Ibid.

[375] Ibid.

[376] Ibid.

[377] Ibid.

[378] *In the Matter of the Charges of Plagiarism, Etc., Against Associate Justice Mariano C. Del Castillo* (Dissenting Opinion, Sereno J) 15 October 2010, AM No. 10-7-17-SC (Republic of the Philippines Supreme Court): <http://sc.judiciary.gov.ph/jurisprudence/2010/october2010/10-7-17-SC_sereno.htm> [accessed 30 Dec 2015] (unpaginated).

[379] Ibid.

own. Justice Sereno made the point that judicial plagiarism constitutes the staking of intellectual ownership to the copied material without the requisite effort having been made: 'That a judge, in lifting words from a source and failing to attribute said words to said source in the writing of a decision, committed specifically *judicial* plagiarism does not derogate from the nature of the act as a plagiarist act. Nor does any claim of inadvertence or lack of intent in the commission of a plagiarist act change the characterization of the act as plagiarism.'[380]

The dissenters criticized the decision of the majority, expressing concern that it 'will also weaken this Court's disciplinary authority—the essence of which proceeds from its moral authority—over the bench and bar. In a real sense, this Court has rendered tenuous its ability to positively educate and influence the future of intellectual and academic discourse'.[381]

The decision has been reported as '[triggering] waves of protest across the legal and academic community, which said the High Court's stand and consequent show cause order to [University of Philippines] law professors may send the wrong signal to teachers and students'.[382]

The University of the Philippines College of Law Professor Ibarra Gutierrez is reported to have said: 'It's either a case of outright plagiarism or a case of outright carelessness, which is equally unforgivable in this particular case... Essentially, what the Supreme Court did was add to the requirements as to when a person can be deemed to have committed plagiarism, and the requirement they added was the presence of malicious intent to pass off another's work as one's own. The problem with that characterization is that now, even if you can demonstrate there was clear, verbatim, word-for-word lifting of passages belonging to another work without attribution, quotation, that will not be enough to convict a person of plagiarism', he explained.[383] Gutierrez maintained that: 'There were no less than 23 instances of word for word reproduction of the work of 3 legal scholars from abroad, even copying the footnotes. It defies imagination how that can be construed as inadvertence. It opens the floodgates towards other persons engaged in academic work from making the same claim.'[384] Subsequently, an online petition seeking support for the University of the Philippines College of Law Faculty was initiated, reading as follows:

> We are proud alumni of the University of the Philippines College of Law, who have been taught well by our teachers not to pass off the work of others as ours. In the University, intellectual achievement is so important that claiming credit for someone else's idea or creation is one of the most serious offenses that one could commit.
>
> We are members of a profession that believes in the importance of the freedom of speech. We believe that the sub judice rule should never be used to stifle public discussion or to prohibit public exercise of the constitutional right to free speech. The courts should allow and never intervene in the free discussion of views by the public at large on various aspects of an ongoing trial, no matter how potentially socially volatile the issues may be.
>
> We are lawyers and law graduates who, as professionals, make it a point to cite our sources whenever an idea is not originally ours. Contrary to the majority opinion of the Supreme Court, we are not being hypocrites when we expect nothing less from the Court. Its members are supposed to set the standards of honesty, honor, integrity, and competence; we are

---

380 Ibid.

381 Ibid.

382 Caroline J Howard, 'Plagiarism is Unforgivable', *ABS-CBN News Channel* (24 October 2010): <http://www.abs-cbnnews.com/nation/10/23/10/plagiarism-unforgivable> [accessed 30 Dec 2015]. See also, Rodel Rodis, 'License to Plagiarize', *Inquirer Global Nation*, 21 October 2010: <http://globalnation.inquirer.net/columns/columns/view/20101021-298952/License-to-plagiarize> [accessed 30 Dec 2015].

383 Howard, above n 382.

384 Ibid.

supposed to look up to them as our examples, and anything short of that diminishes their credibility.

We are making this statement to express our full support for the faculty of the UP College of Law. We feel personally aggrieved by the show-cause order issued by the Court against them because it runs contrary to everything that the law stands for. It concerns us because it concerns the honor, integrity, and competence of the members of the judiciary, whom we are supposed to emulate.

We are appalled by the turn of events—that the perpetrators/plagiarists are being absolved, while those who simply made a stand are the ones that stand to be penalized. Is this what has become of our judicial system?[385]

The Federal Magistrate Rimmer controversy. The issue arose in a cognate context, involving a judicial colleague, in Queensland when Federal Magistrate Jennifer Rimmer cut and pasted at length without attribution from the decision of another Federal Court magistrate in Melbourne.[386] She attributed undiagnosed hypothyroidism and a heavy workload in judging matrimonial and commercial disputes for her replication of some 2,000 words from a colleague's judgment in her own matter.[387] Subsequently, allegations were made that she was responsible for other plagiarism in her judgments. Ultimately, she left the bench after only five years' service. Amid some controversy, she was permitted to return to practice.[388]

In Victoria the Department of Justice proposed the following obligation for judicial officers:

Plagiarism. Judges must write judgments or journal articles in a professional way that does not infringe other peoples' copyright or intellectual property.[389]

Use of parties' submissions. Another aspect of potentially inappropriate usage of others' work by judicial officers has related to the adoption/uptake in judgments of a party's submissions, thereby bringing into question whether a judge has critically applied his or her mind to the issues traversed in the case.

In *R v Gaudet*[390] the appellant had argued that the inclusion of the Crown's 239-page closing submissions as an integral part of the judge's 246-page reasons for conviction gave the appearance of unfairness and of a miscarriage of justice. The court did not accept the argument and concluded that judge's reasons demonstrated that he was alive to the issues and had rejected the appellant's main defence.

In *Sorger v Bank of Nova Scotia*[391] the first one and a quarter pages of the trial judge's written reasons identified the parties and the issues, while the next 124 pages simply reproduced the written submissions of the parties. His final two pages enumerated 29 bare findings of fact verbatim from the respondent's submission with virtually no reasons save that he preferred the evidence of the respondent's witnesses and arguments. The Court of Appeal found that

385 Ibid.

386 ABC Radio National, 'Magistrates and Plagiarism', *Law Report*, 9 May 2006 (Damien Carrick): <http://www.abc.net.au/radionational/programs/lawreport/magistrates-and-plagiarism/3333974> [accessed 30 Dec 2015].

387 Hedley Thomas, 'Repeat Plagiarist Quits the Bench', *The Australian*, 19 December 2006: <http://www.theaustralian.com.au/news/nation/repeat-plagiarist-quits-the-bench/story-e6frg6nf-1111112710150> [accessed 30 Dec 2015].

388 Hedley Thomas, 'Plagiarising Magistrate Can Practise', *The Australian*, 7 November 2007: <http://www.theaustralian.com.au/archive/news/plagiarising-magistrate-can-practise/story-e6frg6oo-1111114818168> [accessed 30 Dec 2015].

389 Department of Justice (Victoria), *Investigating Complaints and Concerns Regarding Judicial Conduct* (Discussion Paper, November 2009) [2.5.1].

390 (1998) 40 OR (3rd) 1 (Ontario Court of Appeal).

391 (1998) 39 OR (3rd) 1 (Ontario Court of Appeal).

there was nothing in his judgment to 'indicate that the trial judge attempted to grapple fairly and impartially with the case presented by the plaintiffs or decide it independently'.[392] It concluded that '[a] reasonable and informed observer would have a reasonable apprehension that the mind of the trial judge was closed to a fair and impartial consideration of the appellant's case'.[393]

In *Janssen-Ortho Inc v Apotex Inc*[394] the Canadian Federal Court of Appeal reflected on reasons for judgment of 250 paragraphs in which the trial judge reproduced verbatim, without so indicating, approximately 100 paragraphs from the respondent's memorandum. Nadon JA for the court on this point declined to find that the trial judge had failed to perform his duty to examine the evidence[395] but suggested that it would be advisable for a judge who was minded to adopt a substantial part of a party's submissions to say so directly and 'to draw the line at the appropriate place'.[396]

Stern has argued that the essence of decision-writing is legitimately derivative and should permit of significant drawing upon of submissions:

> Judges are not selected, and are only rarely valued because of their gift for original expression. Just as most lawyers would rather present their arguments as merely routine applications of settled doctrine, yielding the same legal results that other courts have delivered repeatedly, judges usually prefer to couch their innovations in familiar forms, borrowing well-worn phrases to help the new modifications go down smoothly. The bland, repetitive, and often formulaic cadences of legal writing in general and judicial writing in particular can be explained in large part by a commitment to the neutral and consistent application of the law.
>
> [...]
>
> [T]he effort to demonstrate that similar cases are being treated alike often finds its rhetorical manifestation in a penchant for analyses that have a *déja lu* [sic] quality—usually because the words *have* been read before. This tendency, though visible throughout the legal system, is most pronounced at the trial level.
>
> [...]
>
> It is hardly news that legal writing is embedded in a network of precedent, formulas, and boilerplate, that it reflects a general preference for the tried and true over the novel, and that it routinely depends on practices—verbatim repetition of others' words, adoption of others' prose and arguments—that might trigger infringement claims in an intellectual property dispute.[397]

This position is consistent with decisions in a number of jurisdictions. For instance, the United States Supreme Court ruled in 1964 that, when a trial judge 'adopt[s] verbatim'[398] the findings of fact submitted by counsel, '[t]hose findings, though not the product of the workings of the [judge's] mind, are formally his; they are not to be rejected out-of-hand, and they will stand if supported by evidence'.[399]

In England, the Court of Appeal has held that copying a party's submissions does not invalidate a decision.[400] In *IG Markets Ltd v Crinion*,[401] the Court of Appeal provided full

[392] Ibid, [31].
[393] Ibid, [32].
[394] [2009] FCA 212.
[395] Ibid, [79].
[396] Ibid, [78].
[397] Simon Stern, 'Copyright Originality and Judicial Originality' (2013) 63(3) *University of Toronto Law Journal* 385, 385–6, 390.
[398] *United States v El Paso Natural Gas Co*, 376 US 651, 656 (1964).
[399] Ibid.
[400] *English v Emery Reimbold & Strick Ltd* [2002] 3 All ER 385.
[401] [2013] EWCA Civ 587.

reasons for this approach in an appeal arising from a judgment in relation to a commercial dispute in which one party had been self-represented. Substantial parts of the judgment at first instance, calculated at 94 per cent of the text, were taken word-for-word from closing submissions by the represented party. In his judgment the trial judge made no changes to the submissions. He retained all the headings and made only modest changes to the actual text of the submissions.

Underhill LJ expressed the opinion that 'it was indeed thoroughly bad practice for the Judge to construct his judgment in the way that he did'.[402] He explained:

> For the Judge to rely as heavily as he did on Mr Chirnside's written submissions did indeed risk giving the impression that he had not performed his task of considering both parties' cases independently and even-handedly. I accept of course that a judge will often derive great assistance from counsel's written submissions, and there is nothing inherently wrong in his making extensive use of them, with proper acknowledgement, whether in setting out the facts or in analysing the issues or the applicable legal principles or indeed in the actual dispositive reasoning. But where that occurs the judge should take care to make it clear that he or she has fully considered such contrary submissions as have been made and has brought their own independent judgment to bear. The more extensive the reliance on material supplied by only one party, the greater the risk that the judge will in fact fail to do justice to the other party's case—and in any event that that will appear to have been the case.[403]

However, he conceded that to identify even so serious a defect in a judgment does not necessarily mean that an injustice has been perpetrated. The question is whether the trial judge has exercised proper judicial functions:

> [I]f it is possible to demonstrate that, whatever the first impression created by the way he constructed his judgment, the Judge did in fact carry out a proper judicial evaluation of the essential issues and did not simply surrender his responsibility to counsel, then the judgment should stand. This involves no qualification of the principle that justice must be seen to be done; but in deciding whether that is so it is necessary, at least in a case like this, to go beyond first impressions.[404]

Ultimately, 'not without some hesitation', he concluded that the judgment in question, when examined in the context known to the parties, showed that the judge did sufficiently perform his role and that his reasons were adequately set out:[405]

> Wrong though the way in which the Judge constructed his judgment was, I believe that it can be seen from a careful examination that he did in fact bring an independent judgment to bear on the decisive issues in the case, and it is sufficiently clear why he decided those issues in the case in the way he did.[406]

Sir Stephen Sedley took a similar approach and agreed with the ultimate position of Underhill LJ:

> To simply adopt that party's submissions, however cogent they are, is to overlook what is arguably the principal function of a reasoned judgment, which is to explain to the unsuccessful party why they have lost. Such an omission is not generally redressed by a perfunctory acknowledgment of the latter's arguments. Even a party without merit is entitled to the measure of respect which a properly reasoned judgment conveys.

---

402 Ibid, [16].
403 Ibid, [16].
404 Ibid, [17].
405 Ibid, [18].
406 Ibid, [37].

> Information technology has made it seductively easy to do what the judge did in this case. It has also made it embarrassingly easy to demonstrate what he has done. In principle, no doubt, it differs little from the modus operandi of the occasional judge, familiar to an earlier generation of counsel, who would pick up his pen (sometimes for the first time) and require the favoured advocate to address him at dictation speed. But in practice, for reasons which Lord Justice Underhill has described, the possibility of something approaching electronic plagiarism is new, and it needs to be said and understood that it is unacceptable. Even if it reflects no more than the judge's true thinking, it reflects poorly on the administration of justice: for, as Lord Justice Underhill says, appearances matter.[407]

Longmore LJ also agreed:

> In these days of written final submissions and computer literacy it must be tempting for a judge who has formed a clear view of a primarily factual dispute to frame his judgment by lifting large parts of the written submissions of the party he has decided should win and incorporating them in his judgment. But to do so without (or with only minimal) acknowledgment and without making reference to the submissions made by the other side inevitably leaves a deep sense of grievance with the losing party. He or she will understandably feel that the judge has never properly engaged with the case when forming his judgment.
>
> It also puts this court in a position of considerable difficulty because it has to make a detailed examination of underlying factual material to see whether the judge has truly engaged with the losing party's case when the judge could easily have shown that he had so engaged, by reciting the main points made by the losing party and stating why he rejects them. Having made that detailed examination, all of us are satisfied that the judge has in fact engaged with the defendants' cases and has rightly seen that they have no substance; it would therefore serve no purpose to order a new trial before a different judge.
>
> But we trust that no judge in any future case will lift so much of a claimant's submissions into his own judgment as this judge has done and that, if substantial portions are to be lifted, it will be with proper acknowledgment and with a recitation of the defendant's case together with a reasoned rejection of it.[408]

The unanimous position, therefore, was to denounce the trial judge's less than industrious approach to the discharge of his role but to find, by a fine margin, that there was enough to identify that he had applied his mind to the issues before him and made a considered decision. However, the criticisms by each member of the Court of Appeal to the approach of the trial judge are expressed in unusually strong language and constitute a powerful denunciation of this kind of short-cuts by decision-makers at first instance.

A similar approach was taken by the Hong Kong Court of Appeal in a case where the trial judge incorporated extensive portions of counsel's submissions in the judgment, and the losing party appealed on grounds of procedural fairness and adequacy.[409] The court dismissed the appeal, holding that a judge is entitled to accept or reject a party's case in its entirety: 'A judge's total adoption or rejection of counsel's submissions per se does not imply the lack of independent adjudication, nor does it constitute a valid ground for upsetting the judgment on the basis of an unfair trial.'[410] Applying the test of 'a fair-minded and informed observer', it dismissed concerns about adequacy and bias.[411]

In Australia, it has been held that '[a]doption of one party's submissions by a judge…is one method of providing adequate reasons', adding that '[i]t may not be the choice of every

407 Ibid, [38]–[39].
408 Ibid, [42]–[44].
409 *Shin v Kung* [2004] HKCA 205 [366]–[369], [377].
410 Ibid, [367].
411 Ibid, [377].

judge but it is impossible to say that it necessarily... falls short of the judicial duty to provide reasons'.[412] Similarly, in *Fletcher Construction Australia Ltd v Lines MacFarlane & Marshall Pty Ltd (No 2)*[413] the Victorian Court of Appeal, reviewing a trial judgment for adequacy, remarked that '[a] careful examination of the reasons for judgment shows that the judge adopted [the plaintiff's] closing submissions almost in their entirety'.[414] However, it did not set the judgment aside for copying alone.

The most substantial analysis of the issue, however, is the 2013 decision of the Supreme Court of Canada in *Cojocaru v British Columbia Women's Hospital and Health Center.*[415] The case was an appeal from a trial judge's decision in a medical negligence case. His reasons ran to 368 paragraphs (105 pages), of which the trial judge copied, without so acknowledging, 321 paragraphs almost word for word from the respondent's written closing submissions. There were inconsequential changes but forty paragraphs were written in the judge's own words and the remaining seven contained a mixture of the respondent's submissions and the judge's own words.[416]

The question on appeal was whether a trial judge's decision should be set aside on the basis that his or her reasons for judgment incorporated large portions of a party's submissions. The British Columbia Court of Appeal by majority held that the trial judge's decision should be set aside on the basis that the form of the form of his reasons, substantially a recitation of the plaintiff's submissions, constituted cogent evidence displacing the presumption of judicial integrity and impartiality, and failed to fulfil the functions of advising the parties and the public of the reasons for the decision.

The Supreme Court of Canada reversed the decision of the Court of Appeal. McLachlin CJ wrote the principal judgment and accepted that:

> [W]hile it is desirable that judges express their conclusions in their own words, incorporating substantial amounts of material from submissions or other legal sources into reasons for judgment does not without more permit the decision to be set aside. Only if the incorporation is such that a reasonable person would conclude that the judge did not put her mind to the issues and decide them independently and impartially as she was sworn to do, can the judgment be set aside.[417]

On the issue of the trial judge's conduct, the Supreme Court found that the presumption of judicial integrity and impartiality meant that a party seeking to set aside a decision bears the burden of showing that a reasonable person, apprised of the relevant facts would conclude that the judge 'failed to come to grips with the issues and deal with them independently and impartially'.[418] The court found that the criticism of a judge's decision not being original did not per se constitute a reason for overturning the presumption:

> The fact that a judge attributes copied material to the author tells us nothing about whether she put her mind to the issues addressed in that copying. Nor is lack of originality alone a flaw in judgment writing; on the contrary, it is part and parcel of the judicial process. It may not be best practice for judges to bulk up their judgments with great swaths of borrowed material. But the fact remains that borrowed prose, attributed or otherwise, does not,

[412] *James v Surf Road Nominees Pty Ltd* [2004] NSWCA 475, [168].
[413] [2002] VSCA 189; (2002) 6 VR 1.
[414] Ibid, [163].
[415] [2013] 2 SCR 357.
[416] See eg, Ibid [6], [10], [53], [55].
[417] Ibid, [1].
[418] Ibid, [18].

> without more, establish that the judge has failed to come to grips with the issues required to be decided.
>
> To set aside a judgment for failure to attribute sources or for lack of originality alone would be to misunderstand the nature of the judge's task and the time-honoured traditions of judgment writing. The conventions surrounding many kinds of writing forbid plagiarism and copying without acknowledgement. Term papers, novels, essays, newspaper articles, biographical and historical tomes provide ready examples. In academic and journalistic writing, the writer is faced with the task of presenting original ideas for evaluation by an instructor or by peers, or of engaging in principled debate in the press. The task of judgment writing is much different.[419]

The court found that the scope for 'judicial creativity' is narrow, although not non-existent:

> It finds expression in the ordering of the reasons and the disposition of the arguments and issues, and in the occasional eloquent statement of the facts or restatement of the law. Nevertheless, it remains the case that judicial opinions, especially trial judgments, differ from the kind of writings that traditionally attract copyright protection, with the concomitant demands of originality and attribution of sources. Judgments are 'usually collaborative products that reflect a wide range of imitative writing practices, including quotation, paraphrase, and pastiche'.[420]

The court acknowledged that the concern about judicial copying is not that the judge is taking credit for someone else's prose but that it may indicate that the judge has not properly applied his or her mind to the issues:

> Avoiding this impression is a good reason for discouraging extensive copying. But it is not the copying per se that renders the process of judgment writing unfair. A judge may copy extensively from the briefs in setting out the facts, the legal principles and the arguments, and still assess all the issues and arguments comprehensively and impartially. No one could reasonably contend that the process has failed in such a case.
>
> To sum up, extensive copying and failure to attribute outside sources are in most situations practices to be discouraged. But lack of originality and failure to attribute sources do not in themselves rebut the presumption of judicial impartiality and integrity. This occurs only if the copying is of such a character that a reasonable person apprised of the circumstances would conclude that the judge did not put her mind to the evidence and the issues and did not render an impartial, independent decision.[421]

The court accepted that 'it is good judicial practice for a judge to set out the contending positions of the parties on the facts and the law, and explain in her own words her conclusions on the facts and the law. The process of casting reasons for judgment in the judge's own words helps to ensure that the judge has independently considered the issues and come to grips with them'.[422] However, it held that the importance of this will vary with the nature of the case and that, while in some cases, the issues are so clear that adoption of one party's submissions or draft order may be uncontroversial, 'in complex cases involving disputed facts and legal principles, the best practice is to discuss the issues, the evidence and the judge's conclusions in the judge's own words'.[423] The court emphasized that 'a judge's failure to adhere to best practices does not, without more, permit the judge's decision to be overturned on appeal'.[424] This led to the outcome that the copying engaged in by the trial judge would not lead a reasonable

---

419 Ibid, [31]–[32].
420 Ibid, [33].
421 Ibid, [35]–[36].
422 Ibid, [50].
423 Ibid.
424 Ibid.

person to conclude that the copied material did not reflect the trial judge's own thinking and views and did not rebut the presumption of judicial integrity.

Internationally, therefore, for the present considerable latitude is likely to be given to judges' usage of others' work product, particularly when it includes parties' submissions. However, this has limitations, as shown by the controversies involving Federal Magistrate Rimmer in Queensland and the degree of concern ventilated in the aftermath of the *Del Castillo* decision in the Philippines. Even the presumption of judicial integrity and impartiality will not always save wholesale, uncritical adoption of what one side to litigation has placed before a court if a reasonable person would conclude that an independent decision based on the evidence and the law has not been made. From the perspective of both ethics and prudent practice, there is no justification for a judge failing to be clear and transparent about his or her sources in a judgment—whether they be colleagues' prior decisions, scholarly sources, or parties' submissions. This enables readers, including parties, readily to understand the provenance of a judge's reasoning and the intellectual contributions to the decision-making process. While the Supreme Court of Canada may be justified in identifying judgments of the courts as falling into a category which is different from the orthodox scholarly work product, this should not constitute a licence for covert usage of sources in a way that is intellectually deceptive. In addition, as role models for the legal profession and the general community, they have a moral obligation, and would be expected by the general community, and the scholarly community, to do better.

Criminalization of Plagiarism

Just as there have been proposals that research fraud should be designated a criminal offence,[425] so also have arguments been advanced that plagiarism should be criminalized. In the Philippines, a journalist, Isagani Cruz, mounted a colourful case for a new criminal offence: 'I say that serial plagiarists not only deserve to burn in the fires of hell in the next life for having broken the Seventh Commandment, but to suffer in jail in this life for six to nine years.'[426] In Argentina the proposal came in a more concrete form from Geronimo Vargas Aignasse who introduced legislation into the parliament in 2010 to deal with plagiarism. Bizarrely, however, three paragraphs of the text that Aignasse used to explain the Bill were plagiarized from Wikipedia.[427] When this came to light it did not assist the credibility of his proposed law reform.[428] However, a range of suggestions have been advanced in a more conventional context that intellectual property rights, including in respect of protection against plagiarism, should be protected by the criminal law.[429]

---

425 See Chapter 3.

426 Isagani Cruz, 'Is Plagiarism a Crime?' *The Philippine Star*, 13 September 2012: <http://www.philstar.com/education-and-home/2012-09-13/848455/plagiarism-crime> [accessed 30 Dec 2015].

427 Mike Masnick, 'Argentinian Politician's Proposal For New Anti-Plagiarism Law Plagiarizes Wikipedia', *Techdirt*, 14 May 2010: <https://www.techdirt.com/articles/20100514/0133339425.shtml> [accessed 30 Dec 2015]. See also, 'Parts of Anti-Plagiarism Bill Lifted from Wikipedia' on *Lowering the Bar* (21 May 2010): <http://www.loweringthebar.net/2010/05/parts-of-antiplagiarism-bill-lifted-from-wikipedia-.html> [accessed 30 Dec 2015].

428 Similarly, an academic paper by Dr Thorakkal Shamim on plagiarism (published in the Indian Journal of Dermatology in 2014) had to be retracted because it in turn was plagiarized: see Michael Blaustein, 'Academic Paper on Plagiarism Pulled Because of Plagiarism' (2 April 2015) *New York Post*: <http://nypost.com/2015/04/02/academic-paper-on-plagiarism-pulled-because-of-plagiarism/> [accessed 30 Dec 2015]; 'Oh irony! Journal Pulls Down Paper on Plagiarism Because it was Plagiarised' (3 April 2015) Hindustan Times: <http://www.hindustantimes.com/india-news/oh-irony-journal-pulls-down-paper-on-plagiarism-because-it-was-plagiarised/article1-1333431.aspx> [accessed 30 Dec 2015].

429 See eg, Green, above n 96; see also, Christophe Geiger (ed), *Criminal Enforcement of Intellectual Property: A Handbook of Contemporary Research* (Cheltenham, UK: Edward Elgar, 2012).

South African law makes plagiarism a criminal offence in some circumstances. Thus the University of Pretoria gives the following stern explanation for why plagiarism is serious:

> *Firstly*, plagiarism is **ILLEGAL**. It may be regarded as a criminal offence in terms of the Copyright Act 98 of 1978. If a student is found guilty of plagiarism
> - by a Disciplinary Committee of the University, he/she may be expelled from the University;
> - by a Court of Law, a fine or imprisonment may be imposed.
>
> *Secondly*, plagiarism is **UNETHICAL**.
> - It is **in conflict with our values** of trust and academic integrity (respecting the work of others and expecting them to respect yours).
> - It is dishonest (a form of theft).
> - It shows disrespect for the rights of the original author, and for the knowledge community of which both the author and the plagiarist are members.
> - It may tarnish the University's reputation, and thereby diminish the value of its qualifications.
> - It casts suspicion on the honest work of other students.[430]

Professor Michel Sixou, Dean of the Faculty of Dental Medicine, and Christine Marshal-Sixou, an Associate Professor in the same department, a husband and wife odontology research team at the Université Paul-Sabatier in Toulouse, were charged with the criminal offences of misconduct and complicity in misconduct for plagiarism. The two defendants shared a single email account and the question was whether Mashal-Sixou had plagiarized a Jordanian student's Master's work in her doctoral thesis. He had been part of the same research team.[431]

The Correctional Tribunal of Paris found Christine Marshal-Sixou guilty and ordered her to pay 20,000 euros in damages and interest and that she destroy all copies of the thesis. It did not find her husband guilty but, although his wife lodged an appeal, he felt obliged to resign shortly after the decision on the basis that his position had become insupportable.[432] The tribunal was highly critical of Marshal-Sixou's replication of some 50 pages of the Jordanian student's work. The decision highlights the increasingly retributive attitude that is evolving in many quarters in relation to exploitative plagiarism and may well be a precedent for greater involvement of the criminal law for such conduct.

The Need for a Strong Stance

At the heart of plagiarism, whether it be of ideas, thoughts, methods, or verbatim replication of words, is intellectual dishonesty—a filching of text the person did not create (at least for the relevant publication).[433] Plagiarism and accusations of '*logoklopia*' have a very extensive history, often in the context of rivalry and attempts to denigrate the reputations of intellectual competitors. Its incidence in recent times has been opportunity born of the accessibility of vast amounts of information that can be accessed, pilfered and passed off as the writer's

430 University of Pretoria, 'Plagiarism', 12 August 2003: <http://www.upwithscience.up.ac.za/resources/plagiarism.htm> [accessed 30 Dec 2015].

431 See Frédéric Dessort, 'Plagiat: Une Universitaire Toulousaine Condamnée au Pénal', *EducPros.fr*, 7 January 2014: <http://www.letudiant.fr/educpros/actualite/universite-plagiat-christine-marchal-sixou-une-universitaire-toulousaine-condamnee-au-penal.html> [accessed 30 Dec 2015].

432 Stéphane Compan, 'Toulouse: Démission du Doyen de la Faculté Dentaire', *France 3*, 18 January 2014: <http://france3-regions.francetvinfo.fr/midi-pyrenees/2014/01/18/toulouse-demission-du-doyen-de-la-faculte-dentaire-397735.html> [accessed 30 Dec 2015].

433 See Syed Shahabuddin, 'Plagiarism in Academia' (2009) 21(3) *International Journal of Teaching and Learning in Higher Education* 353.

own with no or insufficient acknowledgment. It is not that human nature has changed since the advent of the internet or that a lack of probity has enveloped education or the professions. It is just that technology has created temptation and malefactors have weighed their odds and concluded that the short-cuts of copying and cheating are relatively unlikely to be detected and therefore worth the risk. And only a small incidence of plagiarism actually comes to light.[434] Usage of work published in another language has been a device employed by an unknown number of plagiarists. Bad habits have also developed for a problematic number of high school students who have become used to cutting and pasting others' work, or sharing each other's work, without being discovered. In turn, some have persisted in such conduct while at university and some have even continued the process when admitted to the professions. In short, then, part of the issue is one of contemporary 'intellectual culture'.

Blum[435] has argued that the surge in celebration of performance within the educational system has exacerbated student willingness to do 'whatever it takes', including plagiarism, as a necessary means to a necessary end in order to be perceived as performing well. This 'celebration of performance' or focus on external rewards, she has argued, has diminished the value of 'authentic' education and the internal rewards, such as learning and self-improvement, of schooling.[436]

None of this detracts from the reality that when plagiarists present material as their own they are engaging in a deception which denies to the reader access to the actual source of the opinion or information and which deceives them about the intellectual involvement of the plagiarist. As Scanlon has pointed out: 'The harm to readers is no less real even if undetected: they are the victims of a lie.'[437] The European Code of Research Integrity has made an important subsidiary point:

> Openness is one of the basic integrity principles, and... progress in science depends on communication and discussion among fellow scientists and on a well functioning peer-review system. And if scientists would hesitate or even refuse to practice this openness and communication for fear of not being recognised as devisor or author the quality of science would suffer.[438]

Tertiary institutions face a variety of challenges in face of plausible suggestions that the current rate of plagiarism is high.[439] If they are to hold to the requirement of originality of composition of assignments and theses, and there would seem little option in this regard, and if they are to maintain their own integrity, especially in relation to higher degrees, they need to do a number of things. From the earliest stage of tertiary education, they must establish and consolidate a culture of responsible use of others' work. Encouragement must be given to the proper citation of sources. Assignment topics should be continually freshly drafted to make plagiarism more difficult and areas should be focused on for testing which, as often as possible, are not the subject of 'merely' internet analysis. Markers need to be alert to the potential for plagiarism and at least random checks for plagiarism, utilizing available software programs, should be employed. Knowledge of such processes on the part of students is likely to go some distance towards dissuading them from engaging in unethical use of others' work.

434 As Von Sternberg has argued: 'The reproach of plagiarism is either silenced by the fact that the plagiator has expounded an idea better than its originator has done or there has been no accusation made because the resemblance has been for good reasons accepted as fortuitous. No accuser, no conviction! No charge, no refutation!': Constantin von Sternberg, 'On Plagiarism' (1919) 5(3) *The Musical Quarterly* 390, 397.

435 Susan D Blum, *My Word! Plagiarism and College Culture* (Ithaca, NY: Cornell University Press, 2009).

436 See eg, ibid, 65.

437 Scanlon, above n 110, 62.

438 European Science Foundation and All European Academies, *The European Code of Conduct for Research Integrity* (March 2011): <http://www.esf.org/fileadmin/Public_documents/Publications/Code_Conduct_ResearchIntegrity.pdf> [accessed 30 Dec 2015] [2.2.4].

439 See eg, Ruth Barrett and James Malcolm, *Embedding Plagiarism Education in the Assessment Process* (2006) 2(1) *International Journal for Educational Integrity* 38, available at: <http://www.ojs.unisa.edu.au/index.php/IJEI/article/viewFile/23/18> [accessed 30 Dec 2015].

A consistent definition of plagiarism needs to be developed. Fairness would dictate that it essentially incorporate significant usage of the work of others[440] without proper and sufficient acknowledgment. It is probably not necessary, and in fact is probably unhelpful, to stipulate 'plagiarism ratios'. There should be differentiation between intentional and negligent conduct, but this should only go to penalty element. It is rare for plagiarism to be genuinely inadvertent or by way of oversight, common protestations to the contrary by perpetrators notwithstanding[441]—the Biden defence and the Bernheim excuse are rarely plausible where the plagiarism is of significant dimensions. So too is the defence denounced by Judge Learned Hand that, other than the impugned instance, the plagiarist has otherwise conducted themselves properly.

Then there need to be robust consequences for proven plagiarism, sufficient to constitute a genuine deterrent to those contemplating similar conduct. Plagiarists need to be named and shamed, and they need to receive sufficiently adverse consequences for others to be encouraged to form the view that 'it isn't worth it'. This involves routine failure of undergraduates who engage in such conduct and exclusion of plagiarists from postgraduate programmes and, on occasion, withdrawal of degrees from those shown, in effect, to have obtained their degrees by fraud. Just as superannuation entitlements may be taken back from corrupt politicians or public servants, the procurement of a degree by dishonest means will, at least, on occasion have the outcome that for a tertiary institution to retain its credibility it will need to revisit marks that have been given and degrees awarded.

Scholarly journals hold themselves out as the purveyors of original works of insight and analysis in their field. However, they are vulnerable to the conduct of plagiarists. While most journals of integrity ensure that manuscripts submitted for publication are suitably peer reviewed, not all plagiarism can be caught, straightaway. There are too many other publications for any reviewer to be confident that inappropriate utilization of them has not taken place. This means that both editors and reviewers must be conscious of, and on the lookout for, the risks of such unethical behaviour on the part of those submitting manuscripts. There should be clear warnings about the unacceptability of inappropriate usage of others' work on journals' websites. There is also a strong argument for the checking of a cross-section of manuscripts submitted, using one of the well-known programmes for detection of high levels of usage of others' work. Journals need to react sternly and promptly when the issue of plagiarism arises. Plagiarized articles must be retracted as soon as possible from electronic versions of publication. It is important, too, for journals to be honestly and suitably communicative to their readership when plagiarism occurs. Finally, when it is professionals, such as doctors and lawyers, who are found to have submitted plagiarized material, it should become the norm for such persons' conduct to be referred by journal editors' to authors' regulatory bodies for further investigation and, where appropriate, disciplinary action.

The courts and regulatory authorities are also faced with dilemmas in face of a problematic prevalence of plagiarism. One response would be to acknowledge the prevalence of this form of dishonesty and resignedly to attenuate the requirements of probity. However, for professions like law, medicine, psychology, and accounting, among others, which have at their heart an assertion of trustworthiness, this is not an option.[442] The community must be able to be

---

440 Further, albeit important, issues arise in relation to secondary and tertiary use of one's own work.

441 See though the findings by McMurdo J in *Re Humzy-Hancock* [2007] QSC 34.

442 See eg, United Kingdom Department of Health, *Trust, Assurance and Safety: The Regulation of Health Professionals in the 21st Century* (CM 7013, 2007): <http://webarchive.nationalarchives.gov.uk/20130107105354/http://www.dh.gov.uk/prod_consum_dh/groups/dh_digitalassets/@dh/@en/documents/digitalasset/dh_065947.pdf> [accessed 30 Dec 2015]; Australian Medical Council, *Good Medical Practice: A Code of Conduct for Doctors in Australia* (2009): <http://www.health.nt.gov.au/library/scripts/objectifyMedia.aspx?file=pdf/39/02.pdf&siteID=1&str_title=Good%20medical%20practice%20guidelines%20policy.pdf> [accessed 30 Dec 2015].

confident that those whom they consult in such professions are persons of integrity who are not inclined to engage in premeditated theft of ideas and others' work. Such individuals are, prima facie, not persons of good character or, differently put, fit and proper to be part of the honourable professions. This is not to say that they cannot establish, by suitable expressions of remorse, candour, the passage of time, and adherence to ethical behaviour, that they have acquired insight into the impropriety of their conduct and are unlikely to repeat it. Put another way, they may in due course be able to show that they have regained good character or are now a fit and proper person to be a member of the profession for which they have trained.

However, it is orthodox to identify that honour, integrity, and trustworthiness are prerequisites for both the standing and integrity of the professions and for professionals.[443] While engaging in deceit does not necessarily mean that a person is deceitful, and a person may be deceitful in one theatre of their life and not be in others, engaging in plagiarism raises real questions about a person's moral fibre and their attitudes towards integrity and honesty. These are questions that are relevant to their professional status. As the House of Lords held in *Patel v General Medical Council*: 'For all professional persons including doctors a finding of dishonesty lies at the top end in the spectrum of gravity of misconduct.'[444]

The tendency of the regulatory authorities, such as the United Kingdom General Medical Council, and the appellate courts, has been in recent years to view plagiarism as a very serious form of misconduct. It generally occurs in a context that is either part of training for a profession, engaging in further education related to it, or in relation to procuring status within the profession by publishing in an area connected with a professional's work. In other words, the conduct occurs in a context that is cognate to the individual's pursuit of their vocation. This means that it cannot be dismissed as a personal peccadillo unrelated to the professional's work. It is intimately related to the person's aspiration to be, or practise as, a lawyer, doctor, or other professional.

If courts are to retain their moral authority to deal with intellectual and other forms of dishonesty, their judges, too, must abstain from plagiarism. A failure to do so can only engender disillusionment and risk allegations of double standards. The time has passed when the judiciary can plausibly maintain that its work is derivative and that it should be immune from the obligations of other professionals to cite correctly and acknowledge the work of others. Chief Justices/judges, magistrates, and judicial misconduct bodies need to act sternly when there is significant unacknowledged usage by judges of colleagues' or scholars work. It is important too, if confidence is to be maintained, for judges to acknowledge when they draw heavily on parties' submissions in their judgments.

The approach of the regulatory authorities and the courts in the United Kingdom, Canada and Australia has been relatively consistent, namely either to decline admission/registration for a time or, if it has already been obtained, to suspend it for a period. This allows the perpetrator of plagiarism the chance of redemption and it sends a clear message to others minded to engage in the conduct that there will be condign consequences if that is what they do. It is essential that the penalties be sufficiently unpleasant, both by way of interruption to professional trajectory and to professional reputation, that they constitute a real discouragement. A combination of optimizing the prospects of detection of plagiarized work and the imposition of consequences that are genuinely deterrent, in light of a concerning prevalence of plagiarism in response to the temptations of opportunity, has the prospect of stigmatizing and reducing significantly the incidence of this form of intellectual dishonesty.

---

443 See Peter Doherty, *The Knowledge Wars* (Melbourne: Melbourne Univerity Press, 2015).
444 [2003] UKPC 16 [10].

Germany has developed an interesting response to the issue of research fraud and plagiarism. The German Research Foundation (the Deutsche Forschungsgemeinschaft) has a Committee of Inquiry on Allegations of Scientific Misconduct[445] which investigates and reports on allegations of, among other things, plagiarism.[446] Its investigations do not necessarily preclude other forms of response to either fraud or plagiarism but they place in the hands of an expert scientific and scholastic body first-line response.

From time to time universities are required to deal with allegations that their staff have engaged in plagiarism. As identified in the chapters on research misconduct (Chapters 2 and 3) and conflict of interest (Chapter 4) one of the proposals advanced in this book is the creation of an independent Office of Scholarly Integrity. Such a body should have original jurisdiction in respect of allegations of research misconduct by reason of the confidence that the operation of a highly regarded, independent body will give when sensitive allegations of such conduct are made. It would be constructive for such an Office also to have jurisdiction over whether scholars (not students) have engaged in plagiarism. Again, its externality and expertise would be likely to give confidence that universities and other institutions are not looking after their colleagues and also that investigations are undertaken independently and professionally when claims are made that the plagiarism was committed either inadvertently or in some circumstances that amount to justification of significant mitigation.

445 'Committee of Inquiry on Allegations of Scientific Misconduct', *Deutsche Forschungsgemeinschaft (DFG)*: <http://www.dfg.de/en/dfg_profile/statutory_bodies/joint_committee/inquiry_misconduct/index.html> [accessed 30 Dec 2015].

446 See eg, *Deutsche Forschungsgemeinschaft (DFG)*, 'Plagiarism Condemned' (Press Release, No. 5, 3 February 2011): <http://www.dfg.de/en/service/press/press_releases/2011/press_release_no_05/index.html> [accessed 30 Dec 2015].

7

DISHONESTY IN EMPLOYMENT

Introduction

Universities afford extensive opportunities for theft and deception to be engaged in by their employees. They are generally a large employer, with substantial amounts of money flowing through accounts that are not always supervised as closely as they might be. Concomitantly, there are possibilities for corrupt removal of property, real and intellectual, and for redirection of funds by criminal misappropriation. A similar vulnerability can arise for significant entities in government, as well as in private industry, that undertake research.

A point of tension in the course of employment can be the status of valuable information acquired or techniques discovered in the course of research work that is part of the employee's professional responsibilities. The law on the subject is complex and has been the subject of a considerable amount of litigation across different countries.

This chapter instances dishonest engagement in scams by university and research institution staff, sets out in broad brush the law as it has evolved in relation to ownership of discoveries, and instances notorious cases where the law in the area has been tested.

Scams and Deception by Employees

It is far from surprising that universities experience a level of property and financial fraud. Aside from their scholarly characteristics, they are large bureaucracies with substantial sums of money that are processed from grants, fees, and diverse sources of funding, with many employees and consultants. This complexity creates both opportunity and institutional vulnerability, particularly if auditing processes are deficient in any significant way. Three diverse examples of such conduct are given hereunder by way of illustration.

A notorious example of wilful misappropriation was uncovered in 2012 by an internal audit into what had appeared to be financial mismanagement by Wayland Baptist University's Chief Financial Officer, Jim Smith. However, it turned out to be more sinister. A web of questionable and improper payments, cheques containing improper endorsements, requisitions without supporting documentation, and payments to credit card companies without any connection to the university revealed a pattern of siphoning funds over an extensive period. Mr Smith was relieved of his employment and charged with US$1.3 million of first degree felony thefts. Judge Kincaid of the 64 District Court sentenced him in April 2014 to five years' imprisonment and Wayland University took civil action against him for falsification of records and embezzlement.[1]

[1] See Doug McDonough, 'Wayland's Former CFO Draws Five Years in Prison for Theft', *MyPlainView.com*, 22 April 2014: <http://www.myplainview.com/news/article_7bb27d9c-ca35-11e3-a5d1-0019bb2963f4.html> [accessed 30 Dec 2015].

In Australia a sophisticated scam also resulted in the imposition of a term of imprisonment on an offender. The victim was La Trobe University in Victoria and the perpetrator Waddah Eltchelebi, the former co-ordinator of the Bendigo Campus' Aboriginal Tertiary Support Unit. In 2007 Mr Eltchelebi pleaded guilty in the Bendigo County Court to eight counts of obtaining property by deception, amounting to just under AUS$300,000. Throughout the 1990s and from 2000 to 2002 Mr Eltchelebi falsely inflated the Indigenous representation at the campus by recruiting students and convincing them to make false claims of Aboriginal descent. He recruited tutors for the programme and each fortnight submitted fake claims for their wages. He would tell the tutors that they had been overpaid by mistake and ask them to redirect the amounts in excess into his accounts, including betting accounts. He told the tutors there was no legitimate or substantial tuition to be performed but that they would still receive wages. He told them that this was a means of helping Indigenous students. He also created spurious documents, including a false Aboriginal family tree and a certificate of Indigenous confirmation. It emerged that he had a history of making false documents when he was employed by the Department of Education.[2]

Mr Eltchelebi pleaded guilty to the charges and was ordered by Judge Chettle to repay the money he had defrauded and sentenced to 37 months' imprisonment with 25 months before he became eligible for parole. Judge Chettle, of the Victorian County Court, observed that his scheme was 'sophisticated, ongoing, lucrative, and saw you leading younger and vulnerable students into serious criminal conduct'.[3] He took into account in sentencing that Eltchelebi's first reaction when accused of the offences by police was to tell them that he had been threatened as part of a conspiracy at the university.[4]

Typical of the fact that any large institution, including one with a scholarly focus, has vulnerabilities to schemes and scams, it is an aggravating feature for a person in a position of trust to manipulate the system in a way to advantage himself or herself financially. This was one of the reasons why both Eltchelebi and Smith received significant sentences of imprisonment.

However, similar scams also affect corporations. An example in this regard was the 2014 sentencing in Victoria of 39-year-old Dr Esra Ogru who was formerly the Chief Executive Officer of Phosphagenics, a biotech research company specializing in drug delivery systems to increase the absorption of drugs into the skin, to six years' imprisonment with a minimum of two years to be served.[5] Dr Ogru had been a respected biotechnology scientist. She utilized fake invoices and credit card claims over a period of nine years to obtain nearly AUS$4 million by fraud from her employer. Judge Hampel of the Victorian County Court in Australia found that Ogru's culpability was aggravated by the fact that she actively frustrated investigations by lying to colleagues and seeking to co-opt others into the scam. However, Judge Hampel tempered the sentence she would otherwise have imposed by reason of the fact that Dr Osru had a severely disabled daughter for whose condition she had successfully worked with a German company to commercialize an experimental drug that had helped the daughter to survive. The sentence was described by Australian Securities and Investments Commission Commissioner John Price as a deterrent for such white-collar crime: 'Dr Ogru's conduct was dishonest and deliberate and showed complete disregard for the company she was appointed to lead'.[6] The repercussions for her employer were identified shortly after Dr Ogru was charged as complex

---

[2] 'La Trobe Funds Gambled Away—Fraudster Syphons Off $300,000', *Bendigo Advertiser*, 21 September 2007: <http://www.bendigoadvertiser.com.au/story/683836/la-trobe-funds-gambled-away-fraudster-syphons-off-300000/> [accessed 30 Dec 2015].

[3] 'Uni Scam Man Must Repay $300K', *Bendigo Advertiser*, 25 October 2007: <http://www.bendigoadvertiser.com.au/story/683985/uni-scam-man-must-repay-300k/> [accessed 30 Dec 2015].

[4] Ibid.

[5] *DPP v Gianello* [2014] VCC 2015.

[6] Australian Securities & Investment Commission (ASIC), 'Former CEO and Two Melbourne Men Jailed Following Theft of Millions From Phosphagenics Limited' (Media Release, 14-296MR, 7 November 2014):

by an article in *Business Review Weekly*: 'Fraud happens, but it's never a good look when the chief executive is the alleged culprit and it's arguably doubly so when it's the chief executive of a biotech. For investors who have no way of assessing the science of a new drug or its sales potential, the quality of management can be the only factor that gives investors confidence.'[7]

Corruption

Almost inevitably given that universities are large institutions with large sums of money passing through their accounts, the temptations of corruption and dishonesty are too great for some to resist.

The risk of corruption posed by overseas student programmes as 'big business' for universities and the obligations of universities to manage risks appropriately have been highlighted by investigations conducted by the Independent Commission against Corruption (ICAC) in New South Wales.[8] In an investigation into the use by 32 overseas full-fee paying students of fraudulent documentation to gain enrolment at three New South Wales universities, ICAC found that there were inadequate systems and risk management in place at the University of Sydney and the University of New South Wales but no finding of corrupt conduct was made.[9]

The way in which Victorian universities in Australia deal with international students and the risk of admission practices being compromised by business considerations of admitting full-fee paying students who may not meet English proficiency requirements were investigated by the Victorian Ombudsman in 2011.[10] The investigation came about due to numerous complaints from students and from whistleblowers alleging improper conduct such as bribery and preferential treatment of students.[11] Academics who were interviewed as part of the review confirmed that teaching and marking practices had changed in the preceding years to accommodate international students, although persons spoken to differed in their views as to why this was.[12] The Ombudsman did not draw conclusions about the extent of 'soft marking' but did find instances where academics had experienced pressure to pass students and where changes designed to rationalize resources were said to have had an adverse impact on academic standards.[13]

<http://asic.gov.au/about-asic/media-centre/find-a-media-release/2014-releases/14-296mr-former-ceo-and-two-melbourne-men-jailed-following-theft-of-millions-from-phosphagenics-limited/> [accessed 30 Dec 2015]. See also, Pia Akerman, 'Six Years Jail for Phosphagenics Biotech Fraudster Esra Ogru', *The Australian*, 7 November 2014: <http://www.theaustralian.com.au/business/news/six-years-jail-for-phosphagenics-biotech-fraudster-esra-ogru/story-e6frg906-1227115619741> [accessed 30 Dec 2015].

[7] Leo D'Angelo-Fisher, 'Phosphagenics CEO Dismissal Another Headache For Biotech', *Business Review Weekly*, 25 July 2013: <http://www.brw.com.au/p/leadership/phosphagenics_ceo_dismissal_another_4VXLH1SkW3PcbcOT74N7YN> [accessed 30 Dec 2015].

[8] Independent Commission Against Corruption (NSW), *Report Under Section 14(2) of the Independent Commission Against Corruption Act 1988 to the Minister for Education and Training* (Sydney, October 2004) 4: <http://pandora.nla.gov.au/pan/48672/20050321-0000/www.icac.nsw.gov.au/files/pdf/UNSW2.pdf> [accessed 30 Dec 2015].

[9] Ibid.

[10] John R Taylor, *Investigation into How Universities Deal with International Students* (Victorian Ombudsman, October 2011), 12–15, available at: <https://www.ombudsman.vic.gov.au/Publications?page=11&searchtext=universities&searchmode=anyword#content-area> [accessed 30 Dec 2015].

[11] Ibid, 12–13.

[12] Ibid, 42–44.

[13] Ibid, 42–43. Similar concerns have also been raised in Britain in recent years. In the United Kingdom 'academic whistleblowers' have suggested that some British universities are watering-down degrees: Sean Couglan, 'Whistleblower Warning on Degrees', *BBC News*, 17 June 2008: <http://news.bbc.co.uk/2/hi/education/7358528.stm> [accessed 30 Dec 2015]; Jack Grimston, 'Lecturers Reveal Watered-Down Degrees',

Another case arose in 2001 at the University of Technology, Sydney, again in Australia, where a student liaison officer working for the Graduate School of Business, and nine students, were found to have engaged in corrupt conduct by fraudulently altering the academic record of students.[14] There have been a number of investigations by ICAC into corrupt conduct of university officials such as an IT manager at the University of Sydney who used a business that employed his wife and in which he had a financial interest to employ contractors and staff for the university.[15] Another investigation was conducted and found proven against the Campus Services Manager at the University of New England for corruption.[16] A similar case was investigated involving a University of Sydney employee, the site manager of the Campus Infrastructure Services, for failing to disclose conflicts of interest in the allocation of cleaning contracts.[17]

Another form of corrupt conduct that can affect universities is the selling of fake degrees allegedly in the name of universities. In 2015 Australian police were urged to investigate what was said to be a sophisticated Chinese forgery business charging thousands of dollars for fake degrees and diplomas from dozens of Australia's leading institutions.[18]

Another form of fraud that can affect research institutions is securities fraud by its executives. One of the most notorious cases of such conduct was the criminal conduct of David Blech, once dubbed the 'king of biotechnology' (a music major with no scientific training), once worth over US$300 million,[19] who pleaded guilty in May 2012 to manipulating shares of biopharmaceutical companies, Pluristem Therapeutics Inc and Intellect Neurosciences Inc in 2007 and 2008.[20] In spite of his suffering from bipolar disorder, he was sentenced to a four-year prison term. Earlier in his career Blech helped found Celgene Corp, whose products include the blood cancer drug Revlimid, the rare disease specialist Alexion Pharmaceuticals,

---

The Sunday Times, 8 March 2009: <http://www.thesundaytimes.co.uk/sto/Migration/article154691.ece> [accessed 30 Dec 2015].

[14] Independent Commission Against Corruption (NSW), *Investigation into the Conduct of Officers and Students at University of Technology* (Sydney, August 2002), available at: <http://www.icac.nsw.gov.au/documents/doc_download/3389-investigation-into-the-conduct-of-officers-and-students-at-university-of-technology-sydney-operation-tudor-6-aug-2002> [accessed 30 Dec 2015].

[15] Independent Commission Against Corruption (NSW), *Investigation into the Recruitment of Contractors and Other Staff by a University of Sydney IT Manager* (Sydney, October 2012): <http://www.icac.nsw.gov.au/component/docman/doc_download/3977-investigation-into-the-recruitment-of-contractors-and-other-staff-by-a-university-of-sydney-it-manager-operation-citrusoctober-2012> [accessed 30 Dec 2015].

[16] Independent Commission Against Corruption (NSW), *Investigation into the Conduct of a University of New England (UNE) Procurement Officer and UNE Contractors* (Sydney, August 2012): <http://www.icac.nsw.gov.au/component/docman/doc_download/3954-investigation-into-the-conduct-of-a-university-of-new-england-une-procurement-officer-and-une-contractors-operation-crusaderaugust-2012> [accessed 30 Dec 2015].

[17] Independent Commission Against Corruption (NSW), *Investigation into Undisclosed Conflicts of Interest of a University of Sydney Employee* (Sydney, September 2010): <http://www.icac.nsw.gov.au/documents/doc_download/3630-investigation-into-undisclosed-conflicts-of-interest-of-a-university-of-sydney-employee-operation-kanda> [accessed 30 Dec 2015].

[18] Linton Besser and Peter Cronau, 'Degrees of Deception' (21 April 2015) Four Corners: <http://www.abc.net.au/4corners/stories/2015/04/20/4217741.htm> [accessed 30 Dec 2015]; 'The Great Aussie Degree Scam: Forgers Raking in Thousands Selling Bogus Qualifications' (30 March 2015) *News.com.au*: <http://www.news.com.au/finance/work/the-great-aussie-degree-scam-forgers-raking-in-thousands-selling-bogus-qualifications/story-fnkgbb3b-1227284475119> [accessed 30 Dec 2015].

[19] See Andrew Pollack, 'A Biotech King, Dethroned', *The New York Times*, 5 September 2013: <http://www.nytimes.com/2013/09/06/business/david-blech-a-biotech-king-dethroned.html?pagewanted=all&_r=1> [accessed 30 Dec 2015].

[20] See Jonathan Stempel, 'Ex-'King of Biotech' Set to Serve Four-Year Term for Fraud', *Reuters*, 21 January 2014: <http://www.reuters.com/article/2014/01/21/us-blech-fraud-idUSBREA0K1DL20140121> [accessed 30 Dec 2015].

the cancer drug developer, Ariad Pharmaceuticals, and Icos Corp, now part of Eli Lilly & Co, that developed Cialis to treat erectile dysfunction. Previously, in 1998, Blech had pleaded guilty to another fraud for which he had received probation. In 2014 the 2nd United States Circuit Court of Appeals rejected an appeal against his sentence.[21]

Entitlements to Ownership of Lecture Notes and Copyright in Articles and Books

Difficult issues arise in respect of the legitimacy of ownership over a number of products of scholarship within both universities and research institutions.

There is old authority that, in the absence of clear terms in the contract of employment, a person is entitled to the copyright in lectures at a tertiary institution that they give even though they are employed to give such lectures.[22] Lord Evershed MR made reference to the published law lectures of Professor FW Maitland on equity and said it appeared to be 'just and common sense' that the University of Cambridge could not claim copyright in them merely because he delivered the lectures in the course of his employment.[23] Lord Justice Denning distinguished between the duty to give oral lectures and the writing down of such lectures, holding, somewhat questionably, that if an employee elects to write down such lectures for their convenience, that is done outside their employment.[24] It is unlikely that this authority would be followed today in many countries but the practice is commonly for universities to regard copyright as owned by the authors of lecture materials.[25] This fact is now leaving theoretical and practical questions as a result of 'lecture capture technology'. So long as access to captured lectures is restricted to enrolled students, there is no difficulty but if they are disseminated more widely, as is becoming increasingly frequent on the internet, in principle copyright permission ought to be sought from lecturers.[26]

It has often been contended that academics should be regarded as owning the copyright in articles and books that they write, even though much of the writing may be undertaken pursuant to their responsibilities to do research and publish, and even though they may have used their institution's library and other facilities, including during working hours. The technical justification for this position is questionable but the practice is that tertiary institutions do not claim copyright over such forms of work product. As outlined below, this is supported by intellectual property policies at many universities.[27]

Entitlements to Ownership of Inventions

Universities and scholarly institutions experience a variety of losses through thefts of their intellectual property. In general, an employee who makes an invention during the period of

[21] *United States v Blech*, 550 Fed Appx 70 (2nd Cir, 2014).

[22] *Stevenson Jordan & Harrison Ltd v MacDonald & Evans* [1952] 1 TLR 101; (1951) 69 RPC 10; see also, *Noah v Shuba* [1991] FSR 14, 26.

[23] *Stevenson Jordan & Harrison Ltd v MacDonald & Evans* [1952] 1 TLR 101, 107; (1951) 69 RPC 10, 18.

[24] *Stevenson Jordan & Harrison Ltd v MacDonald & Evans* [1952] 1 TLR 101, 111; (1951) 69 RPC 10, 22.

[25] See eg, University of Maryland, 'Commercial Use of Course Materials': <http://www.president.umd.edu/legal/commercial.html> [accessed 30 Dec 2015].

[26] See Keith Norbury, 'Who Owns Captured Lectures?' (27 November 2012) *Campus Technology*: <http://campustechnology.com/articles/2012/11/27/who-owns-captured-lectures.aspx> [accessed 30 Dec 2015].

[27] See also, Ann Monotti and Sam Ricketson, *Universities and Intellectual Property: Ownership and Exploitation* (Oxford: Oxford University Press, 2003) ch 7.

employment will be held to own the invention unless the employee was specifically hired or is deemed to have been hired to invent the particular invention, in which case it belongs to the employer.[28] There is a significant level of commonality in the law across countries on this issue. Much depends on what the employee was employed to do.[29] The fact that research may be part of an employee's job is not sufficient of itself to establish that the employee was hired to invent a specific invention that may be made in the course of that research.[30] Where the position of the employer is that the employee was hired to create the invention, the burden to prove that lies on the employer. It is an employee's status at the time of the making of the invention that determines their rights.

Otherwise, it is an implied term of employment that any invention or discovery made in the course of employment by the employee—in doing that which the employee was engaged and instructed to do during the time of the employment, and during working hours, and using the materials of his or her employers—is the property of the employer and not of the employee.[31] A general principle established by the United Kingdom in *Patchett v Sterling Engineering Co Ltd*[32] has been followed in a number of jurisdictions: '[I]nherent in the legal relationship of master and servant [is] that any product of the work which the servant is paid to do belongs to the master'.[33] When an employee makes a discovery or invention in the course of such work, the employee becomes a trustee for the employer of that invention or discovery, and is therefore as a trustee bound to give the benefit of any such discovery or invention to the employer.[34]

However, the mere existence of the employer/employee relationship will not give the employer ownership of inventions made by the employee during the term of the relationship. This is so even if the invention is germane to and useful for the employer's business, and even though the employee may have made use of the employer's time and resources in bringing the invention to completion. All of the circumstances must be considered in each case.[35] Illustratively, in 2003 the Federal Court of Australia in *Spencer Industries Pty Ltd v Collins*[36] held that an improved product invented by a sales manager, Collins, was not made by Collins in carrying out his normal duties as a sales manager in that he was not paid to invent and the assembly was not a product of work that Collins was paid to perform. This meant that Collins was successful as against his employer in his claim to a patent.

Unless the contract of employment expressly so provides, or an invention is the product of work which the employee was paid to perform, the invention made by the employee will generally not be held to belong to the employer.[37]

It is common that the patentability of such 'discoveries', while owned by the inventor, must be assigned by the scholar or researcher to the employer pursuant to contractual arrangements

---

[28] *United States v Dubilier Condenser Corporation*, 289 US 178 (1933), amended 289 US 706 (1933), applied in *Victoria University of Technology v Wilson* [2004] VSC 33; (2004) 60 IPR 392, [121].

[29] See eg, *LIFFE Administration and Management v Pinkava* [2007] EWCA Civ 217; [2007] 4 All ER 981.

[30] *Kaplan v Johnson*, 409 F Supp 190 (ND Ill, 1976) 192, rev'd in part, sub nom, *Kaplan v Corcoran*, 545 F 2d 1073 (7th Cir, 1976).

[31] *Victoria University of Technology v Wilson* [2004] VSC 33; 6 IPR 392, [104].

[32] (1955) 72 RPC 50.

[33] *Patchett v Sterling Engineering Co Ltd* (1955) 72 RPC 50, 58 (Lord Reid).

[34] *Triplex Safety Glass Co v Scorah* [1937] 1 Ch 211, 217; [1938] RPC 21, 28–9.

[35] See eg, *In Matter of Charles Selz Limited's Application to the Comptroller under Section 56 of the Patents Act 1949* (1953) 71 RPC 158.

[36] [2003] FCA 542; (2003) 58 IPR 425.

[37] *Worthington Pumping Engine Co v Moore* (1902) 20 RPC 41; *British Reinforced Concrete Co v Lind* (1917) 34 RPC 101; *Triplex Safety Glass Co v Scorah* [1937] 1 Ch 211; [1938] RPC 21; *Patchett v Sterling Engineering Coy Ltd* (1955) 72 RPC 50, 58; *Spencer Industries Pty Ltd v Collins* [2003] FCA 542; 58 IPR

entered into at the commencement of employment. A typical obligation for university employees is to be found in the University of California State Oath of Allegiance, Patents Policy and Patent Acknowledgment:

> I acknowledge my obligation to assign, and do hereby assign, inventions and patents that I conceive or develop 1) within the course and scope of my University employment while employed by University, 2) during the course of my utilization of any University research facilities, or 3) through any connection with my use of gift, grant, or contract research funds received through the University. I further acknowledge my obligation to promptly report and fully disclose the conception and/or reduction to practice of potentially patentable inventions to the University authorized licensing office. Such Inventions shall be examined by the University to determine rights and equities therein in accordance with the Policy. I shall promptly furnish University with complete information with respect to each.
>
> In the event any such invention shall be deemed by University to be patentable or protectable by an analogous property right, and University desires, pursuant to determination by University as to its rights and equities therein, to seek patent or analogous protection thereon, I shall execute any documents and do all things necessary, at University's expense, to assign to University all rights, title, and interest therein and to assist University in securing patent or analogous protection thereon.[38]

However, there are occasions when companies providing funding to universities require assignment of patentability, bringing about a conflict between the contractual arrangements with the university for an employee.

Stanford v Roche

This was the scenario confronted in *Board of Trustees of Leland Stanford Junior University v Roche Molecular Systems, Inc.*[39] In 1985, Cetus, a Californian research company, began to develop methods for quantifying blood-borne levels of human immunodeficiency virus (HIV), the virus that causes acquired immune deficiency syndrome (AIDS). Polymerase Chain Reaction (PCR), a Nobel Prize-winning technique developed at Cetus, was an integral part of these efforts. In 1988, Cetus began to collaborate with scientists at Stanford University's Department of Infectious Diseases to test the efficacy of new AIDS drugs. Dr Holodniy joined Stanford as a research fellow in the department around that time. When he did so, in the usual way, 'he signed an agreement stating that he "agree[d] to assign" to Stanford his "right, title and interest in" inventions resulting from his employment' at Stanford. Holodniy's supervisor arranged for him to conduct research at Cetus to learn about PCR. As a condition of gaining access to Cetus, Dr Holodniy was required to sign an agreement stating that he 'will assign and do[es] hereby assign' to Cetus his 'right, title and interest in...the ideas, inventions, and improvements' made 'as a consequence of [his] access' to Cetus. Working with Cetus employees, Dr Holodniy devised a PCR-based procedure for measuring the amount of HIV in a patient's blood. On returning to Stanford, he and other Stanford employees tested the procedure. Stanford secured three patents to the measurement process.

425, [67]–[68]. See too, William R Cornish, 'Rights in University Innovations: The Herchel Smith Lecture for 1991' (1992) 14(1) *European Intellectual Property Review* 13; *Chou v University of Chicago and ARCH Development Corporation*, 254 F 3d 1347 (Ct App, Fed Cir, 2001).

38 UC San Diego, School of Medicine, Division of Medical Education, 'University of California State Oath of Allegiance. Patent Policy, and Patent Acknowledgment': <http://meded.ucsd.edu/assets/6/File/coordinators/upay585.pdf> [accessed 30 Dec 2015].

39 131 S Ct 2188 (2011).

Roche Molecular Systems acquired Cetus's PCR-related assets. After conducting clinical trials on the HIV quantification method developed at Cetus, Roche commercialized the procedure. Today, its HIV test kits are used worldwide.

The *University and Small Business Patent Procedures Act 1980* (US) (Bayh–Dole Act) allocates rights in federally funded 'subject invention[s]' between the Federal Government and federal contractors.[40] It defines 'subject invention' as 'any invention of the contractor conceived or first actually reduced to practice in the performance of work under a funding agreement' (§ 201(e)), and provides that contractors may 'elect to retain title to any subject invention'(§ 202(a)). Because some of Stanford's research on the HIV measurement technique was funded by the National Institutes of Health (NIH), the Bayh–Dole Act applied. In accordance with the Act's requirements, Stanford notified the NIH that it was electing to retain title to the invention and conferred on the government a licence to use the patented procedure.

The Board of Trustees of Stanford University sued Roche, claiming that their HIV test kits infringed Stanford's patents. Roche responded that Dr Holodniy's agreement with Cetus gave it co-ownership of the procedure, and thus Stanford lacked standing to sue it for patent infringement. Stanford countered that Dr Holodniy had no rights to assign because the University had superior rights under the Bayh–Dole Act. The District Court agreed with Stanford and held that, under the Bayh–Dole Act, Dr Holodniy had no rights to assign to Cetus. The Court of Appeals for the Federal Circuit disagreed, concluding that Dr Holodniy's agreement with Cetus assigned his rights to Cetus, and thus to Roche. It also found that the Bayh–Dole Act did not automatically void an inventor's rights in federally funded inventions. Thus, the Act did not extinguish Roche's ownership interest in the invention, and Stanford was deprived of standing.

The Supreme Court held that the Bayh–Dole Act does not automatically vest title to federally funded inventions in federal contractors or authorize contractors to take title to such inventions unilaterally. It confirmed that patent law operates on the premise that rights in an invention belong to the inventor and in most cases, a patent may be issued only to an applying inventor or, because an inventor's interest in his or her invention is assignable in law by an instrument in writing, an inventor's assignee. Absent an express agreement to the contrary, an employer does not have rights in an invention which is the original conception of the employee alone.

It observed that in this regard the Bayh–Dole Act is not expressed in unambiguous terms, providing simply that contractors may 'elect to retain title to any subject invention' (§ 202(a)).[41] It held that its disposition of rights did nothing more than clarify the order of priority of rights between the Federal Government and a federal contractor in a federally funded invention that already belongs to the contractor. It commented that Stanford's contrary construction would have permitted title to an employee's inventions to vest in the University even if the invention was conceived before the inventor became an employee, so long as the invention's reduction to practise was supported by federal funding. It also suggested that the school would obtain title were even one dollar of federal funding applied toward an invention's conception or reduction to practice. It found that had Congress 'intended such a sea change in intellectual property rights' it would have so provided in clear terms.[42]

---

40 35 USC §§ 201(c), 201(e), 202(a).

41 *University and Small Business Patent Procedures Act* of 1980.

42 *Board of Trustees of Leland Stanford Junior University v Roche Molecular Systems, Inc* 131 S Ct 2188, 2191 (2011).

A consequence of the decision by the Supreme Court has been the revision of many forms and policies by tertiary institutions in the United States. A broader ramification of the decision has been said to be that 'faculty inventors are feeling their power and many groups are pushing for more faculty-inventor rights, including the right to choose licensing agents for their inventions—even if they must still assign ownership to their university employer'.[43]

Australian Law

In Australia there is no equivalent to the Bayh–Dole Act. In 2007, the Productivity Commission in its *Research Report on Public Support for Science and Innovation*[44] adopted what it classified as a 'cautious approach' and questioned whether the issues faced in the United States at the time the Bayh–Dole Act was passed applied as strongly to Australia.[45]

As a result, for the present, Australian government agencies that provide research funding to institutions such as universities are, in theory, permitted to require those institutions to assign back any invention arising from the funded research. In practice, some government agencies, such as the Australian Research Council (ARC) and the National Health and Medical Research Council (NHMRC), do not, as a matter of policy, claim ownership of inventions created in the course of funded research.

Fundamental, too, is the fiduciary obligation of a person to be loyal to their principal, avoiding any conflict of interest or profit from his or her position, unless the principal gives clear consent to such a position. As Deane J put it in *Chan v Zacharia*:

> Stated comprehensively in terms of the liability to account, the principle of equity is that a person who is under a fiduciary obligation must account to the person to whom the obligation is owed for any benefit or gain (i) which has been obtained or received in circumstances where a conflict or significant possibility of conflict existed between his fiduciary duty and his personal interest in the pursuit or possible receipt of such a benefit or gain or (ii) which was obtained or received by use or by reason of his fiduciary position or of opportunity or knowledge resulting from it. Any such benefit or gain is held by the fiduciary as constructive trustee (see *Keith Henry & Co Pty Ltd v Stuart Walker & Co Pty Ltd* [1958] HCA 33; (1958) 100 CLR 342, 350). That constructive trust arises from the fact that a personal benefit or gain has been so obtained or received and it is immaterial that there was no absence of good faith or damage to the person to whom the fiduciary obligation was owed. In some, perhaps most, cases, the constructive trust will be consequent upon an actual breach of fiduciary duty: eg, an active pursuit of personal interest in disregard of fiduciary duty or a misuse of fiduciary power for personal gain. In other cases, however, there may be no breach of fiduciary duty unless and until there is an actual failure by the fiduciary to account for the relevant benefit or gain: eg, the receipt of an unsolicited personal payment from a third party as a consequence of what was an honest and conscientious performance of a fiduciary duty. The principle governing the liability to account for a benefit or gain as a constructive trustee is applicable to fiduciaries generally including partners and former partners in relation to their dealings with partnership property and the benefits and opportunities associated therewith or arising therefrom (see *Birtchnell v Equity Trustees* [1929] HCA 24; (1929) 42 CLR 384, 395 and 408; *Consul Development Pty Ltd v DPC Estates Pty Ltd* [1975] HCA 8; (1975) 132 CLR 373, 394).[46]

[43] Sean M O'Connor, 'The Real Issue Behind *Stanford v. Roche*: Faulty Conceptions of University Assignment Policies Stemming from the 1947 Biddle Report' (2013) 19(2) *Michigan Telecommunications and Technology Law Review* 379, 421.

[44] Australian Government, Productivity Commission, *Public Support for Science and Innovation* (Research Report, 9 March 2007), available at: <http://www.pc.gov.au/inquiries/completed/science/report> [accessed 30 Dec 2015].

[45] See eg, ibid 283.

[46] [1984] HCA 36; (1984) 154 CLR 178, 199.

Consequently, if a person occupying a fiduciary position wishes to enter into a transaction that would otherwise amount to a breach of duty, to avoid liability he or she must make a full disclosure to the person to whom the duty is owed of all relevant facts known to the fiduciary, and that person must consent to the fiduciary's proposal.

The scope of the fiduciary duty depends on the nature of the actual employment. A court hearing a disputed claim will consider practical factors such as:

- whether the invention was made during or outside working hours,
- whether the facilities and materials of the employer were used, and
- the extent to which the employee's duties or position prompted the invention or provided access to funds to make the invention.

VUT v Wilson

For instance, in 2004, the Federal Court of Australia found a breach of fiduciary duty in *Victoria University of Technology v Wilson*.[47] Professor Kenneth Wilson and Dr Donald Feaver were employed as senior academics in the Economics Faculty at Victoria University of Technology (VUT). They were approached by a third party requesting that VUT develop a range of online business and trade subjects involving software development with which Wilson and Feaver had no experience. They studied relevant software literature in the economics field and eventually developed software that enabled international traders to perform trading transactions online. This included an online education and training course. This aspect of their work was done without disclosure to VUT.

They formed a company, filed a patent application and sought investment in the software development overseas using VUT's name and logos, so that it gave potential investors the impression that the development was under the control of VUT.

Nettle J found that Wilson and Feaver's development of the software and system was not sufficiently related to the duties they were retained by the university to perform, given they were not employed to write and develop software. However, he also held that Wilson and Feaver breached the fiduciary duty they owed to VUT by using their positions to acquire funds to assist in the software development, and failing to inform the university of their activities or otherwise seek the university's consent. As a result VUT missed an opportunity to develop the system and possibly profit from such a development. He found that Wilson and Feaver improperly used VUT's name, without the university knowing, for the purposes of acquiring investment.

Nettle J visited Wilson and Feaver's breach of their fiduciary duty with a finding that a constructive trust existed over shares in the company in favour of VUT, on the grounds that they had sought to profit from their position at the expense of the university and allowed their own commercial interests to conflict with VUT's interests.

University of Western Australia v Gray

For Australia the most significant case on the issue of the ownership of patents developed in the course of tertiary sector employment was decided in *University of Western Australia v Gray*.[48] In 1984, Dr Bruce Gray accepted an offer of appointment from the University of Western Australia (UWA) to be its Professor of Surgery with effect from 1 January 1985. He took up his appointment on 11 February 1985 and was Head of its Department of Surgery

[47] [2004] VSC 33; (2004) 60 IPR 392. See also *Victoria University of Technology v Wilson* [2006] VSC 186.
[48] [2009] FCAFC 116; (2009) 179 FCR 346.

from 1 October 1988 until the end of 1989. He was a full-time employee of the university until March 1997, when he changed to a fractional 30 per cent appointment, focusing on clinical work at the Royal Perth Hospital. He resigned from the university shortly before the end of 1999.

As a full-time employee, Dr Gray was required by the terms of his appointment to teach, to conduct examinations and to direct and supervise the work in his field, and to undertake research, to organize research and generally to stimulate research among the staff and students.

The primary proceeding concerned certain inventions that were said to have been made wholly or in part by Dr Gray. They involved the production and 'use of microparticles or 'microspheres' for the targeted treatment of cancerous tumours' in the liver.[49] Dr Gray referred to his area of research as 'targeted microsphere technology'.[50] The research focussed on the design of the microspheres and ensuring their effective delivery of anti-cancer agents of various kinds selectively to the sites of tumours in the liver.

UWA's claim against Dr Gray was that by reason of his employment he had obligations to the university in respect of the inventions, and that as a result the university had proprietary rights in respect of them and of associated patent applications and patents. It also argued that, by reason of Dr Gray's having dealt with the inventions as his own, UWA was entitled to obtain various remedies from him. At first instance and on appeal before the Full Court of Australia's Federal Court[51] UWA lost all aspects of its claim.

There were three 'invention streams':

(a) the **SIRT** invention stream, being microspheres made so as to carry (SIRT-1), or made from (SIRT-2), a radionuclide material for radiation treatment of the tumour or cancerous tissue by Selective Internal Radiation Therapy (SIRT-1 and SIRT-2 Inventions, collectively the SIRT-Spheres Inventions – the microspheres themselves are variously called SIR-Spheres and SIRT-Spheres);
(b) the **DOX** invention stream consisting of microspheres designed so as to carry and release in a controlled manner a chemotherapeutic agent or drug, including the widely available anti-cancer drug, doxorubicin, for the chemotherapeutic treatment of the tumour or cancerous tissue (DOX-Spheres Invention—the microspheres themselves are called DOX-Spheres);
(c) the **THERMO** invention stream, consisting of microspheres made so as to carry a ferromagnetic material susceptible to heating by the external application of an electromagnetic field (hysteresis heating or targeted hysteresis hyperthermia) for thermal treatment of the cancerous tissue (together, the Thermo-Spheres Inventions and individually the Thermo-Spheres-1 Invention, the Thermo-Spheres-2 Invention and the Thermo-Spheres-3 Invention – the microspheres themselves are called Thermo-Spheres). On the appeal in relation to the Thermo-Spheres Inventions, only the Thermo-Spheres-1 Invention remained relevant.[52]

There was a second respondent in the primary proceeding, Sirtex Medical Ltd (Sirtex). In 1997 Sirtex, which was then named 'Paragon Medical Limited', acquired from Dr Gray and the Cancer Research Institute (CRI) (a body that had been established to support Dr Gray's research work) intellectual property rights arising out of the inventions. A substantial number

[49] Ibid, [4].
[50] Ibid, [4].
[51] *University of Western Australia v Gray* [2009] FCAFC 116; (2009) 179 FCR 346.
[52] Ibid, [6] (original formatting altered).

of shares in Sirtex were issued by the company to Dr Gray as consideration for the assignment of the intellectual property rights that were purportedly his. Shares in Sirtex were also issued to CRI in return for certain of its assets.

In October 2004, UWA sent letters of demand to Sirtex and to Dr Gray alleging that the inventions the subject of the intellectual property rights were developed or made in the course of the employment at UWA of Dr Gray and other academic researchers working with him, and therefore belonged to UWA.

UWA commenced the primary proceeding against Dr Gray, Sirtex and CRI on 21 December 2004. The relief sought was a declaration that Dr Gray held his shares and options to take up shares in Sirtex on trust for UWA and orders that he transfer them to UWA and account to it in respect of benefits obtained by him by reason of the shares and options.

Against Sirtex UWA sought a declaration that all the rights, title and interest in the relevant patent applications, patents and inventions were held by Sirtex on trust for UWA, and an order that Sirtex transfer them to UWA. UWA alleged that Dr Gray had breached his contract of employment. The terms of that contract made Dr Gray subject to UWA's Act, the *University of Western Australia Act* 1911 (WA) (UWA Act) and to 'the Statutes and regulations of' UWA.[53] One breach of contract that was alleged was that Dr Gray had failed to comply with disclosure and associated obligations imposed by the university's patents regulations and intellectual property regulations. Regulation 6.1 of the Patents Regulations required a person subject to them to inform the Vice-Chancellor immediately of any patentable invention made or developed wholly or in part during the course of the person's duty or while using UWA's research facilities (Prompt Notification Condition). The Patents Regulations required the Vice-Chancellor to refer the matter disclosed to a 'Patents Committee' and to act on that Committee's advice as to whether to exercise UWA's 'rights in the invention' and to inform the inventor accordingly.[54]

French at first instance,[55] and the Full Court of the Federal Court on appeal, found that from 1988 UWA had effectively abandoned the Patents Committee mechanism, and that after that time the possibility that a committee could be appointed on an ad hoc basis to respond to reports of particular inventions was never considered. Instead, UWA used Uniscan and CABR, its Deputy Vice-Chancellor (Research) and later its Pro Vice-Chancellor (Research) to provide a framework within which inventions could be commercially exploited. His Honour concluded that because the Patents Committee was an essential element of the Prompt Notification Condition and its sequelae, this aspect of UWA's breach of contract case against Dr Gray failed.

UWA also claimed that Dr Gray had breached fiduciary obligations that he owed to it (and that Sirtex had been knowingly concerned in those breaches and had provided knowing assistance to him in those breaches by the issue of the shares to him).

Importantly, UWA's case against Dr Gray (and Sirtex) depended on the proposition that it was an implied term of Dr Gray's contract of employment that intellectual property developed in the course of his employment belonged to UWA. Justice French rejected this proposition, concluding that, in the absence of express agreement to the contrary, rights in relation to inventions made by academic staff in the course of research, whether or not made with the use of the resources of UWA, ordinarily belonged to the academic staff as the inventors

53 Ibid, [76].
54 Ibid, [48].
55 *University of Western Australia v Gray (No. 20)* [2008] FCA 498; (2008) 246 ALR 603.

under the *Patents Act* 1990 (Cth) (Patents Act). He held that the position would have been different if staff had had a contractual duty to produce inventions, but, put simply, the duty to research did not signify a duty to invent.

The Full Court noted that UWA did not plead in its statement of claim any implied term in Dr Gray's contract of employment that the benefit of any invention developed by him in the course of his employment belonged UWA.

It summarized the law as follows:

> If the employee's invention is the, or a, product of what he or she was employed to do, and did do, it will belong to the employer unless otherwise agreed: see eg *British Reinforced Concrete Engineering Co Ltd v Lind* (1917) 34 RPC 101 (*British Reinforced Concrete*); *Adamson v Kenworthy* (1932) 49 RPC 57; *Triplex Safety Glass Co v Scorah* [1938] 1 Ch 211 (*Triplex Safety Glass*); and see also [*Electrolux Ltd v Hudson*] [1977] FSR 312, at [97]. In such a case, it would be 'inconsistent with [the employee's] duty to appropriate to himself an invention of this kind': *Edisonia Ltd v Forse* (1908) 25 RPC 546 at 552.
>
> By way of contrast, if (a) the employee was not engaged to use his or her inventive capacity at all (cf *Re Charles Selz Ltd's Patent Application* (1953) 71 RPC 158); or (b) was so engaged only by way of additional duties to use his or her inventive capacity as and when asked (*Spencer Industries Pty Ltd v Collins* (2003) 58 IPR 425) or only for an agreed purpose, the employer would have in case (a) no claim on the employee's invention at all and in case (b) such a claim only if the invention resulted from a task the employee was asked to perform by way of additional duty or if the invention was related to the effectuation of the agreed purpose.
>
> [...]
>
>> Take for instance a research chemist working on a cancer cure for the last ten years. Suppose he came up with a cure for arthritis. He could not seriously contend that he owned the invention because he was day-to-day working on a cancer cure. His duty as a research chemist is clearly wider than his day-to-day work.[56]

At trial Justice French had expressed attraction to a concern raised by Monotti and Ricketson in their 2003 book, *Universities and Intellectual Property*, about equating an academic's general duty to research with a duty to invent. He observed that Dr Gray 'had no duty to invent anything. He had a duty to undertake research and to stimulate research amongst staff and students at UWA'.[57] French went on to observe that at all relevant times there was nothing to prevent Dr Gray 'from publishing the observations and discoveries he had made and details of the technologies he had developed'.[58] Nor was he obliged 'to protect by non-disclosure the patentability of any invention he developed in the course of his employment'.[59] The Full Court agreed and commented that 'on the evidence Dr Gray was not required to advance a commercial purpose of UWA when selecting the research he would undertake'.[60] The Full Court affirmed the decision of French J and observed: '[H]e had not been engaged to use his inventive faculty in an agreed way or for an agreed purpose, for UWA's benefit. While his duty to research was in an applied science, it cannot for that reason be transformed into a duty to invent, notwithstanding that his actual research, in fact, carried the possibility of developing inventions capable of attracting patent protection.'[61]

56 [2009] FCAFC 116; (2009) 179 FCR 346, [153]–[156].
57 [2008] FCA 498; (2008) 246 ALR 603, [1360].
58 Ibid.
59 Ibid.
60 [2009] FCAFC 116; (2009) 179 FCR 346, [184].
61 Ibid, [194].

The position in Australia after the *Victoria University* and *Gray* decisions is that the state of the fiduciary obligations of an employee of a university will be fact-specific. The bottom line of both decisions is an expectation that universities cannot reasonably expect their employees to be solely devoted to their obligations as academics. Rather, the relationship between the academic and their university is more akin to that within the public service:

> On one level the relationship between employer and employee is more horizontally based—the employer is subject to an implied term that he, she, or it does not destroy the substratum of trust and confidence. Yet, at another level, the latter decision of *University of Western Australia* provides a vertical component to this union. With universities no longer privileged employers and staff no longer enjoying luxurious self-indulgence as to what they research and where they publish, and with terms and conditions largely indistinguishable from other public sector employers, and workload allocation and performance management providing a more directed, if not feudal workplace, employers have gained greater capacity to direct, but only in the context of specific hours and tasks as outlined in the contract of employment. Employers, be they universities or research companies, should feel more vulnerable as the result of the holding in the case. However, the result is not one-sided. The message it sends is clear. Just as parties can effectively oust a fiduciary relationship with a contract, an employer can just as surely assuage their vulnerability to an incidentally inventive employee by including the rights of a fiduciary nature with clear words into a comprehensive contract of service.[62]

Fiduciary Sanctions for Purloining of a Patent

It has been a complaint from many junior researchers, junior staff and higher degree students that those in a loftier position in the hierarchy have taken credit for their work, including registering patents without entitlement. The 2001 decision of the Federal Court in the United States in *Chou v University of Chicago and ARCH Development Corporation*[63] has sounded a warning against such dishonest conduct.

Dr Joany Chou was a researcher in molecular genetics at the University of Chicago working under the supervision of Dr Bernard Roizman. She began working with Dr Roizman in 1983 in what became a long-term collaborative relationship. Among other things, they investigated a potential vaccine for the herpes virus. After successfully completing the vaccine in February 1991, Dr Chou expressed to Dr Roizman her belief that the discovery should be patented. She asked him about the proper procedures to obtain patent protection. However, Dr Roizman fobbed her off and did not answer directly save to suggest that the discovery was not patentable.

---

[62] Lynden Griggs and Rohan Price, 'The University Academic as a Fiduciary—Where to Following University of Western Australia v Gray?' (2008–2009) 19 *Journal of Law, Information and Science* 22, 41. See also Rachel Chua, Virginia Masters and Daniel Estrin, 'UWA v Gray: Rights to Inventions Made by Employees' (September 2008) 89 AGS Legal Briefing: <http://www.ags.gov.au/publications/legal-briefing/br89.pdf> [accessed 30 Dec 2015]; William van Caenegem, 'VUT v Wilson, UWA v Gray and University Intellectual Property Policies' (2010) 21(3) *Australian Intellectual Property Journal* 148.

[63] 254 F 3d 1347 (Ct App, Fed Cir, 2001). See too, Daniel P Valentine, '*Chou v. University of Chicago*: Assigned Patent Rights—Gone But Not Forgotten' (2002) 42(4) *Jurimetrics* 493; Kyle Grimshaw, 'A Victory for the Student Researcher: *Chou v. University of Chicago*' (2001) *Duke Law and Technology Review* 35; Carmen J McCutcheon, 'Fairplay or Greed: Mandating University Responsibility Toward Student Inventors' (2003) *Duke Law and Technology Review* 26; Melissa Astala, 'Wronged by a Professor? Breach of Fiduciary Duty as a Remedy in Intellectual Property Infringement Cases' (2003) 3 *Houston Business and Tax Law Journal* 31; William A Kaplin and Barbara A Lee, *The Law of Higher Education* (4th edn, San Francisco, Calif: John Wiley, 2007).

Trusting the wisdom and experience of her friend and mentor, Dr Chou focused on her research and put aside aspirations of obtaining a patent. For the succeeding years they enjoyed research success, publishing various papers and jointly securing a patent on a distinct aspect of their herpes research. Dr Roizman as the leader of what had become a successful research group won a variety of accolades but by June 1996 the relationship soured. According to the reported decision, Dr Roizman approached Dr Chou and told her that he would fire her if she did not resign, as allegedly she would be in a stronger position to contest his inventorship if she were still conducting research at the University. When she did not cooperate, Dr Roizman barred her from the laboratory. At this stage Dr Chou learned that in 1991 Dr Roizman had secretly filed a patent application on the vaccine that he had claimed to her was unpatentable. When in due course the patent issued, it named him as the sole patent inventor. Although the patent by then was owned by the University of Chicago (pursuant to Dr Roizman's employment contract which required him to assign his patents to the university), Dr Roizman had been receiving substantial royalty payments from the university's licensing of the patented technology.

Further research persuaded Dr Chou that the motive for Dr Roizman's imposition of pressure on her to resign was an attempt to preclude her asserting any patent rights. Dr Chou's response was to sue Dr Roizman, the University of Chicago, and the company that had licensed the technology. Dr Chou alleged that she was the rightful inventor and, as such, should be added as an inventor to the patent. She also claimed for conversion, breach of fiduciary duty, breach of contract, and unjust enrichment. At first instance before the federal District Court she failed.

However, on appeal the defendants (including Dr Roizman) argued that the fraud count had been properly dismissed because Dr Roizman owed Dr Chou no duty to disclose information about the filing of the patent applications, and that her breach of fiduciary duty claim was similarly deficient because the University did not impose a fiduciary duty upon its professors to disclose to their research assistants the filing of patent applications. The defendants also contended that Dr Chou has no unjust enrichment claim because she assigned her rights to the University and had suffered no financial detriment as a result of Dr Roizman's alleged actions.

The Federal Circuit Court allowed Dr Chou to challenge the inventorship of the patent. It affirmed that, if a rightful inventor is not listed as an inventor on a patent, that inventor can sue in a federal court in the United States to have his or her name added to the patent. It found that she had a financial interest in the matter because, although inventors do not have an ownership interest in a patent, the employment contract did provide that inventors received a portion of the royalty payments associated with licensing the technology.

The Federal Circuit Court found that, although Dr Roizman was in charge of the research team and had authority to make the important decisions about the direction and scope of the experiments, he had a duty to inform his student researchers of his decisions and to keep them apprised of matters material to the technology. Furthermore, since he was Dr Chou's mentor, counsellor, and guide, it held that Dr Roizman had a fiduciary duty to care for his pupil, requiring him to treat Dr Chou with the highest degree of loyalty. This duty prevented him from 'seeking or obtaining any selfish benefit for himself' at her expense.[64] By failing to inform Dr Chou of the existence of the patent, it held that Dr Roizman had committed a breach of this fiduciary duty.

[64] *Chou v University of Chicago and ARCH Development Corporation*, 254 F 3d 1347, 1362 (Ct App, Fed Cir, 2001).

The Federal Circuit Court also held that Dr Chou could bring a claim against the University of Chicago on the basis that Dr Roizman's conduct towards Dr Chou related to the execution of the employment handbook's guidelines for patenting inventions. This meant that his conduct was within the scope of his employment with the university, thereby making the university vicariously liable for his actions.

The decision is likely to be influential on the subject. It paves the way for senior academics to be made significantly more accountable, as they should be, for taking advantage without proper acknowledgment of the work product of their students. It has the potential to be a culture-changing decision.

University Policies

Universities generally have intellectual property policies. However, they vary significantly in content. For instance, Harvard University's Intellectual Property Policy is avowedly flexible:

> First, the policy should encourage the viewpoint that ideas or creative works produced at the University should be used in ways that are meaningful in the public interest. This may be accomplished through widespread dissemination. Thus, dissemination and use of ideas and creativity should be encouraged throughout the Harvard community. In other circumstances, the public may benefit from the stronger application of legal protection to the innovations and creative works of inventors and authors so that they may be developed into useful products. Although this policy recognizes that public benefit should be placed before financial gain, it is appropriate and often desirable for the University and inventors and authors to benefit financially from the use of a particular invention or creative work. In deciding how to proceed in regard to a particular invention or creative work covered by this policy, the University will consider the benefits and consequences for the public and the University, as well as for individual inventors and authors.
>
> Second, the policy should protect the traditional rights of scholars with respect to the products of their intellectual endeavors. For instance, the policy should not interfere with the rights of a scholar to publish a book or an article. Where the University takes ownership or control over scholarly works, the University shall consult with authors on plans for publication.
>
> Third, where financial or other support in terms of facilities, equipment or staff for development of intellectual property has been provided or administered by or through the University, the University may have outside contractual commitments which must be recognized or may have made financial investments for which reimbursement through commercial application is appropriate.[65]

The policy distinguishes between 'supported inventions' (namely, inventions made under or subject to an agreement between Harvard and a third party, with direct or indirect financial support from Harvard, or with use of space, facilities, materials or other resources provided by or through Harvard) and 'incidental inventions' (namely, inventions conceived or reduced to practice by a person making an incidental use of space, facilities, materials or resources of Harvard). It provides that Harvard's Office of Technology Development has responsibility for determining whether an invention is 'supported' or 'incidental', with rights to incidental inventions but not supported inventions remaining with the inventor.[66]

---

[65] Harvard University, Office of Technology Development, 'Statement of Policy in Regard to Intellectual Property', 12 December 2013: <http://otd.harvard.edu/faculty-inventors/resources/policies-and-procedures/statement-of-policy-in-regard-to-intellectual-property/> [accessed 31 Dec 2015].

[66] Ibid.

Oxford University by contrast claims ownership of all intellectual property of a wide variety of work product under section 6 of Statute XVI:

(1) works generated by computer hardware or software owned or operated by the University;
(2) works created with the aid of university facilities including (by way of example only) films, videos, photographs, multimedia works, typographic arrangements, and field and laboratory notebooks;
(3) patentable and non-patentable inventions;
(4) registered and unregistered designs, plant varieties, and topographies;
(5) university-commissioned works not within (1), (2), (3), or (4);
(6) databases, computer software, firmware, courseware, and related material not within (1), (2), (3), (4), or (5), but only if they may reasonably be considered to possess commercial potential; and
(7) know-how and information associated with the above.[67]

Its claim relates to such property which is devised, made, or created:

(a) by persons employed by the University in the course of their employment;
(b) by student members in the course of or incidentally to their studies;
(c) by other persons engaged in study or research in the University who, as a condition of their being granted access to the University's premises or facilities, have agreed in writing that this Part shall apply to them; and
(d) by persons engaged by the University under contracts for services during the course of or incidentally to that engagement.[68]

However, it specifically provides that it will not assert any claim to the ownership or copyright in:

(1) artistic works not listed in sub-section (2) of section 6 of this statute, books, articles, plays, lyrics, scores, or lectures, apart from those specifically commissioned by the University;
(2) audio or visual aids to the giving of lectures;
(3) student theses, exercises and answers to tests and examinations save to the extent that they contain intellectual property claimed by the University under subsection (6) of section 6 of this statute; or
(4) computer-related works other than those specified in section 6 of this statute.[69]

The University of Melbourne defines intellectual property widely to include:

1. Literary, artistic, musical and dramatic works in which copyright subsists.
2. Field and laboratory notebooks.
3. Cinematographic and multimedia works in which copyright subsists.
4. Performances of performing artists, sound recordings and broadcasts.
5. Patentable and non-patentable inventions.
6. Registered and unregistered designs, plant varieties and topographies.
7. Circuit layouts.
8. Registered and unregistered trademarks, service marks and commercial names and designations.
9. Databases, computer software and related material not otherwise coming within any of the other designated items of 'intellectual property'.
10. Scientific discoveries.
11. Know-how and other proprietary information associated with any of the other designated items of 'intellectual property'.[70]

---

67 University of Oxford, 'Part B, Intellectual Property' on *Statute XVI: Property, Contracts, and Trusts* (last amended: 12 October 2011) s 6(1)–(7): <http://www.admin.ox.ac.uk/statutes/790-121.shtml#_Toc28143157> [accessed 31 Dec 2015].

68 Ibid, sub-ss 5(1)(a)–(d).

69 Ibid, sub-ss 7(1)–(4).

70 The University of Melbourne, 'Intellectual Property' on *Research, Innovation and Commercialisation* (last modified: 18 February 2014): <https://mro.unimelb.edu.au/contracts/ip> [accessed 31 Dec 2015]. Compare

The university asserts ownership of intellectual property, other than scholarly works, created by its staff. By 'scholarly works' it stipulates articles, books, musical compositions, creative writing or like publications or any digital or electronic version of these works.[71] It provides that:

> All staff, honorary appointees, visitors, or student creators of IP [intellectual property] have a responsibility to identify, protect, manage and be involved in the commercialisation of IP. In particular, all have a specific duty to disclose inventions with potential commercial value or where required by specified agreements. In the absence of any other agreement reached between the relevant parties the University will ensure that the Net Proceeds of Commercialisation are distributed as follows:
> - University Central 20%
> - Faculty 40%
> - Creators 40%[72]

The University's Invention Disclosure Policy[73] applies where something new and useful has been conceived and developed, where the intellectual property may need protection and/or where the invention, technology, software or multimedia product has commercial potential. It does not apply to literary works, musical creations, or works of art. It requires staff, students, honorary staff and visitors to lodge an invention disclosure where an invention has the potential to be developed for commercial application, or disclosure is a legal requirement specified in a third-party agreement.

The University of Sydney, by contrast, has extensive rules set out in the University of Sydney *(Intellectual Property) Rule* 2002.[74] The University 'asserts ownership of all intellectual property created by a staff member' in pursuance of the terms of their employment[75] and stipulates that '[i]n the absence of a third party agreement to the contrary, the ownership and the associated rights of all intellectual property generated from a research project funded by any publicly funded research agency will vest in the University'.[76]

It does not assert such ownership in works of a 'scholarly nature', including journal articles, conference papers, creative works, proceedings, and text.[77]

The University of Sydney, 'Intellectual Property' (last updated: 30 July 2014): <http://sydney.edu.au/research_support/output/intellectual_property/index.shtml> [accessed 31 Dec 2015].

71 The University of Melbourne, 'IP Policy' on *Research, Innovation and Commercialisation* (last modified: 6 September 2012): <https://mro.unimelb.edu.au/content/ip-policy> [accessed 31 Dec 2015].

72 Ibid (original formatting altered).

73 The University of Melbourne, 'Invention Disclosure Policy' (Approved by Council, December 2006: <https://mro.unimelb.edu.au/sites/default/files/public/contracts/disclosurepolicy.pdf> [accessed 31 Dec 2015].

74 University of Sydney *(Intellectual Property) Rule* 2002 (last amended: 4 May 2009): <http://sydney.edu.au/policies/showdoc.aspx?recnum=PDOC2011/108&RendNum=0> [accessed 31 Dec 2015].

75 Ibid, r 3.1. The Australian National University in its policy on intellectual property has a similar provision, vesting ownership for the university in all intellectual property created by staff in the course of their employment, in the course of using funding, facilities or resources of the University, other than as a student, in the conduct or creation of any works commissioned by the University by way of separate agreement (other than a contract of employment) or which vests in the University at law: Australian National University, 'Policy—Intellectual Property', 15 May 2013: <https://policies.anu.edu.au/ppl/document/ANUP_003603> [accessed 31 Dec 2015]. See too, The University of Western Australia, 'University Policy on: Intellectual Property', Policy No. UP07/49 (Revised: 28 April 2014): <http://www.governance.uwa.edu.au/procedures/policies/policies-and-procedures?method=document&id=UP07%2F49> [accessed 31 Dec 2015].

76 University of Sydney *(Intellectual Property) Rule* 2002, above n 74, r 3.2.

77 Ibid, r 4.1.

However, in respect of intellectual property in respect of which the university asserts ownership, commercial benefits are distributed after costs as following:

- one-third to the originator;
- one-third to the originator's Department; and
- one-third to the Vice-Chancellor's Innovative Development Fund.[78]

There is considerable variation in relation to such division of benefits amongst tertiary institutions.

Conclusions

Although the law of intellectual property varies somewhat from country to country, the issues and the cases to which reference has been made in this chapter highlight the fact that those employed within scholarly or research institutions must be very cautious if they wish to assert personal ownership over the fruits of their research, other than lecture notes, books, presentations to students, or learned articles. Much depends on the policies of the individual scholarly institution.

Often such research products will either be owned by the employing institution or the researcher will be regarded as holding them on trust for the institution. Utilization of artificial devices in an attempt to obtain personal pecuniary or reputational advantage is likely to be challenged actively by universities and research institutions. Such conduct within a university may constitute academic misconduct. With increasing incentives for universities, private sector industry and even government to engage in joint research enterprises, the stakes in such matters are becoming increasingly significant.

However, in the United States, in particular, another phenomenon that can be identified is the evolution of fiduciary law in a way that provides a measure of protection to graduate students whose work is exploited by those senior to them in the academic hierarchy. It may be that other countries attempt through their law to emulate this outcome.

Fraudulent or corrupt behaviour, scamming, and securities manipulation, whether occurring in or in association with a university, or through a research institution, is increasingly likely to be visited by significant criminal sanctions.

[78] Ibid, r 14.1.

8

INTEMPERATE DENIGRATION AND DISPUTATION

Introduction

Scholars have long extolled the importance of a right to freedom of expression, including as a hallmark of democracy, as well as the right of scholars to dispute vigorously one with another and even with those outside their place of employment or even their discipline.[1] This is the very stuff of scholarly dialectic—the way in which ideas are put to the test and evaluation takes place as to whether theories or techniques can be falsified or otherwise be determined to have intellectual merit. It constitutes an important control mechanism against both error and fraud. However, this process is not without its limitations when debate or disputation transmogrifies into rancour or abuse or when there is the infliction of malicious harassment.[2] Or when it descends into personal vilification, hate speech,[3] seriously offensive utterances, or constitutes representations that are false and misleading. Or when it spills over into stalking or physical violence. In a number of countries, too, topics such as denial of the Holocaust, and other genocides, are also precluded—by scholars and anyone else.

There is nothing new in such inappropriate forms of scholarly behaviour and their legal outcomes. A 1603 record from Cambridge University, for instance, shows that John Dighton of St Catherine's Hall sued the college butler for calling him 'a turd in his teeth', a common term of abuse at the time.[4] Twenty-two years later, Kenelm Mainwaring of St John's College and his wife Mary brought proceedings against Jeremy Chace of Christ's College for calling Mary 'a scurvy queane'.[5]

On occasions the disputes between academics go beyond the acerbic to the vicious with personalized and excessive denigration of both others and their work. It has been suggested that

---

1 See Conrad Russell, *Academic Freedom* (London: Routledge, 1993); Neil W Hamilton, *Zealotry and Academic Freedom: A Legal and Historical Perspective* (New Brunswick, NJ: Transaction Publications, 1995); Ralph F Fuchs, 'Academic Freedom—Its Basic Philosophy, Function, and History' (1963) 28(3) *Law and Contemporary Problems* 431.

2 See eg, the conviction by the Kingston Magistrates' Court of music academic Howard Fredrics, who worked at Kingston University between 2003 and 2006, for harassing Sir Peter Scott via postings on a website, <http://www.sirpeterscott.com>: Melanie Newman, 'Lecturer 'Intended to Harass' V-C, Court Finds', *Times Higher Education*, 7 January 2010: <http://www.timeshighereducation.co.uk/409869.article> [accessed 31 Dec 2015]. The conviction for harassment was subsequently overturned although Fredrics was convicted of a public order offence in relation to a meeting with Sir Peter Scott: John Morgan, 'Fredrics Cleared of Harassment Charge', *Times Higher Education*, 22 July 2010: <http://www.timeshighereducation.co.uk/412662.article> [accessed 31 Dec 2015].

3 See Gerhard Falk, *Fraud: Deceit Among Scientists, Academics, Writers, and Philanthropists* (Lanham, Md: University Press of America, 2007) 65–70.

4 'Adultery and Murder: The Seedy Side of 16th Century Cambridge University', *The Daily Express*, 3 October 2013: <http://www.express.co.uk/news/weird/434076/Adultery-and-murder-The-seedy-side-of-16th-Century-Cambridge-University> (viewed 14 March 2015). See also, 'Cambridge's Criminal Past Revealed in Centuries-Old Court Records', University of Cambridge, 30 September 2013: <http://www.cam.ac.uk/research/news/cambridges-criminal-past-revealed-in-centuries-old-court-records> (viewed 14 March 2015).

5 See 'Cambridge's Criminal Past Revealed in Centuries-Old Court Records', n 4.

scholarly critiques can nip near the jugular vein, but should not rip it wide open.[6] A review in the venerable British journal *Mind*, in 1921, is often cited as overstepping the acceptable in this regard:

> [The author's] method of exegesis consists, in fact, of a combination of the *suppressio veri* with the *suggestio falsi*, both, of course, practised in the absolute good faith which comes from propagandist enthusiasm unchecked by any infusion of historical sense... It is because Mr Urwick's book is one long dogmatising without knowledge that I feel bound to put it on record that of all bad books on Plato his is the very worst.[7]

However, an important question arises as to when redress should lie on the basis of gratuitous unpleasantness that may be the product of a personality disorder, gross feelings of insecurity, rivalry, retributiveness, or paranoid ideation.

David Healy, a controversial disputant on the effects of psychopharmacology, especially selective serotonin reuptake inhibitors (SSRIs), has maintained that there are particular risks for scholars who are minded to take stands on issues of community concern, especially where significant sums of money are involved: 'One of the consequences of taking a stand on an academic issue that has commercial implications seems to be ongoing academic harassment or stalking.'[8] There is some evidence that Healy is justified in this assertion and that measures to prevent such conduct.

Before the advent of the internet, on most occasions, academic debate took place in scholarly journals in the form of discussion and criticism of ideas and rebuttals in the literature. Sometimes such debate was robust in nature, but at least the journals' editorial processes constituted something of a constraint against vituperative excess. Now, even where the debate does take place in a scholarly journal or in the news media, invariably these sources of information are accessible via the internet. Other modes of online communication have also come into being, including the various social media options such as blogs, Twitter, and Facebook, to name but a few. Today the internet provides anyone with the means to air their views on any topic they see fit and with the potential to reach large numbers of people anywhere in the world via almost immediate electronic means. With relatively little time and effort it is possible to find all manner of information on disputes between and among scholars, on websites, blogs, and the comment options that follow many news media articles. There is a wealth of commentary dedicated to such disputes, accusing, discussing, proselytizing, defending, airing grievances, and different parties presenting their side of the story. The waters can become quite murky at this point. The information is not mediated, as it is to some extent in a peer-reviewed academic journal, and it is sometimes difficult to ascertain who is in the right, or wrong, and indeed, what to believe. But while technology has provided many with the tools to communicate, including impulsively and imprudently, the internet also opens up the potential for the law to become involved. The ease of modern communication and the degree of anonymity that is afforded to people who wish to participate in these debates and other types of commentary mean that those wishing to 'have their say' may run the risk of becoming civilly liable or of facing allegations of impropriety in a disciplinary context. On some occasions private prosecutions have even been initiated.[9]

It is at these points that the law has the potential to intrude via stalking prosecutions, defamation actions, suits for false and misleading statements, or disciplinary actions for intemperate

---

6 Scott McLemee, 'McGinn, Again', *Inside Higher Ed*, 6 November 2013: <https://www.insidehighered.com/views/2013/11/06/essay-colin-mcginn-reviewing-and-perils-paraphrase> [accessed 31 Dec 2015].

7 Ibid.

8 Phil Cowen, 'Academic Stalking' on *Let Them Eat Prozac* (November 2006): <http://www.healyprozac.com/AcademicStalking/AcademicStalking.htm> [accessed 31 Dec 2015].

9 See *McGuirk v University of New South Wales* [2010] NSWCA 104, [73].

conduct by a professional. Not surprisingly, this has proved a controversial delineation of boundaries between rights to academic free speech and rights of others not to be harassed, vilified, distressed, deceived and defamed. It also goes to the entitlement of academics to raise issues concerning scholarly conduct and the exchange of ideas, which, as noted above, can constitute important protections against scholarly censorship, error, and fraud. Litigation or the threat of litigation is often asserted to exercise a 'chilling effect' on academic debate.

On occasion, scholars have adopted what they perceive to be the moral high ground to denounce allegedly unscientific or methodologically defective claims by others. Sometimes this has been regarded as offensive. Sometimes it has been the expression of obsessionality and taken the form of gross insensitivity. In other instances, it has led to the unmasking of scientific nonsense and impropriety, and played an important role in protecting both the quality of scholarship and public safety. There are times, too, when rulings by the courts have been sought in an effort to establish the credibility or the soundness of a particular position in scientific or medical debate. Perhaps, consistently with the increased resort to the courts generally in respect of scholarly matters, this phenomenon appears to be becoming more common.

As is evident from the cases below, in Australia and the United States, where the dispute is one involving academic debate, the courts are generally reluctant to become involved in disputation among scholars unless a person's character has been defamed. However, in the United Kingdom and to a lesser extent Canada, particularly in the realm of defamation law, the law may not provide the same protections for academic free speech or the ability for academics to make comments in the public interest.

This chapter reviews some of the leading cases in which issues arising from intemperate disputation and denigration by academics have had legal outcomes. It reflects on the ethical obligation of scholars to treat each other with respect, courtesy, and consideration,[10] an aspect of which is to refrain from excessive and inappropriate criticism of others so as not to detract from the reputation of an employing institution or of a scholarly discipline. It also reflects on the emerging responsibility of scholars, and others, to refrain from offensive and hurtful speech.

Codes of Ethics

Professional codes of ethics tend not to deal specifically with obligations of non-denigration. For instance, the Australian Medical Council's *Good Medical Practice* focuses on doctors' care of their patients in mandating respectful interaction with other professionals:

> Good patient care is enhanced when there is mutual respect and clear communication between all health care professionals involved in the care of the patient. Good medical practice involves:
>
> 4.2.1 Communicating clearly, effectively, respectfully and promptly with other doctors and health care professionals caring for the patient.
>
> 4.2.2 Acknowledging and respecting the contribution of all health professionals involved in the care of the patient.[11]

---

[10] See eg, University of Oxford, 'University Policy on Harassment and Bullying': <http://www.admin.ox.ac.uk/media/global/wwwadminoxacuk/localsites/equalityanddiversity/documents/harassment/harprint.pdf> [accessed 31 Dec 2015].

[11] Australian Medical Council, *Good Medical Practice: A Code of Conduct for Doctors in Australia*: (2009) [4.2]: <http://www.health.nt.gov.au/library/scripts/objectifyMedia.aspx?file=pdf/39/02.pdf&siteID=1&str_title=Good%20medical%20practice%20guidelines%20policy.pdf> [accessed 31 Dec 2015].

Along not dissimilar lines the Canadian Medical Association's Code of Ethics requires practitioners to avoid 'impugning the reputation of colleagues for personal motives; however, report to the appropriate authority any unprofessional conduct by colleagues'.[12] Similarly, the Science Council of Japan provides that:

> Scientists shall constructively criticize the results of other scientists' research, humbly listen to the criticism of others, and exchange opinions with an attitude of sincerity. Moreover, they shall properly give credit to other scientists' intellectual findings and achievements, as well as respecting the honor and intellectual property rights of others.[13]

On occasions a failure to abide by such obligations of collegiality has merged into outright defamation and thereby become legally actionable. For instance, in *Crampton v Nugawela*[14] the plaintiff was attempting to establish the Australian Informatics Association and the defendants, Crampton and the Royal Australian College of General Practitioners (RACGP), opposed such a course. The plaintiff asserted that that the defendants compromised the reputation of the plaintiff by misrepresentations. The situation was exacerbated by the plaintiff referring to Nugawela as the 'black fella' in front of mutual professional colleagues. The plaintiff was successful and at first instance obtained damages of A$600,000. On appeal, the Court of Appeal upheld the damages award, emphasizing that the law should place a high value on reputation amongst professional colleagues, especially when professional reputation depends upon their honesty, integrity, and judgment, with Mahoney JA observing that men and women enter careers, and activities associated with them, for many reasons other than money, such as job satisfaction, prestige, honour, and recognition by peers. The Court held that professionals are entitled to protection of such a reputation.[15]

The Australian Medical Association's Code of Ethics requires doctors to:

> b. Recognise that your personal conduct may affect your reputation and that of your profession.
> c. Refrain from making comments which may needlessly damage the reputation of a colleague.[16]

The Royal Australian & New Zealand College of Psychiatrists' Code of Ethics[17] goes somewhat further:

> 10.3. Psychiatrists have a responsibility to promote trust and mutual respect among their psychiatric colleagues, their colleagues in other medical specialties, and other mental health professionals.
>
> 10.4. When opinions differ, psychiatrists shall express their views in a respectful manner that avoids self-promotion or denigration of others.[18]

---

[12] Canadian Medical Association, *Code of Ethics* (Last reviewed March 2014) [48]: <http://policybase.cma.ca/dbtw-wpd/PolicyPDF/PD04-06.pdf> [accessed 31 Dec 2015].

[13] Science Council of Japan, 'Statement: Code of Conduct for Scientists' (approved 3 October 2006) 6: <http://www.scj.go.jp/en/report/code.html> [accessed 31 Dec 2015].

[14] (1996) 41 NSWLR 176, discussed by David Rolph, *Reputation, Celebrity and Defamation Law* (Dartmouth, Ashgate, 2013).

[15] See also, Patricia Loughlan, 'Of Patents and Professors: Intellectual Property, Research Workers and Universities' (1996) 18(6) *European Intellectual Property Review* 345.

[16] Australian Medical Association, *AMA* Code of Ethics (2004, rev. 2006) [2.1]: <https://ama.com.au/position-statement/ama-code-ethics-2004-editorially-revised-2006> [accessed 31 Dec 2015].

[17] The Royal Australian & New Zealand College of Psychiatrists, Code of Ethics (July 2010): <https://www.ranzcp.org/Files/Resources/College_Statements/code_ethics_2010-pdf.aspx> [accessed 31 Dec 2015].

[18] Ibid, [10.3]–[10.4]. Principle 11 states that: 'Psychiatrists shall work to improve mental health services and promote community awareness of mental illness and its treatment and prevention, and reduce the effects of stigma and discrimination': ibid, 16, [11.1]–[11.8].

The Australian Psychological Society's Code of Ethics goes further again, providing that:

A.2.1. In the course of their *conduct*, *psychologists*:
(a) communicate respect for other people through their actions and language;
(b) do not behave in a manner that, having regard to the context, may reasonably be perceived as coercive or demeaning;
(c) respect the *legal rights* and *moral rights* of others; and
(d) do not denigrate the character of people by engaging in *conduct* that demeans them as persons, or defames, or harasses them.

[...]

A.2.3. When *psychologists* have cause to disagree with a colleague in psychology or another profession on professional issues they refrain from making intemperate criticism.

A.2.4. When *psychologists* in the course of their professional activities are required to review or comment on the qualifications, competencies or work of a colleague in psychology or another profession, they do this in an objective and respectful manner.[19]

University Policies and Procedures

When scholarly disputation descends into vitriol, ridicule and denigration, it can be regarded as a form of harassment. 'Harassment' is defined by Oxford University, for instance, as engagement in 'unwanted and unwarranted conduct which has the purpose or effect of':

(a) violating that other's dignity, or
(b) creating an intimidating, hostile, degrading, humiliating or offensive environment for that other.[20]

Similarly, Syracuse University states that harassment is constituted by 'verbal or physical conduct, or written or electronic communications that denigrate or express hostility or aversion towards an individual because of his or her race, color, creed, religion, gender, national origin, citizenship, ethnicity, marital status, age, disability, sexual orientation, gender identity and gender expression, veteran status or any other status protected by applicable law to the extent prohibited by law', and that:

- has the purpose or effect of creating an intimidating, hostile or offensive work environment; or
- has the purpose or effect of unreasonably interfering with an individual's work performance; or
- otherwise adversely affects an individual's employment.[21]

Harassing conduct is defined to include:

- epithets, slurs or negative stereotyping.
- threatening, intimidating or hostile acts.
- denigrating jokes.
- written or graphic material that denigrates or shows hostility or aversion toward a group or an individual believed to be part of a particular group.
- written or graphic material that is placed on walls or elsewhere on University premises, or is circulated in the workplace.
- using electronic equipment to distribute, view, or otherwise disseminate materials or messages that are abusive, profane, threatening, defamatory or offensive.
- conditioning employment terms on submission to harassing conduct, sexual advances, requests for sexual favors, etc.[22]

---

[19] Australian Psychological Society, APS Code of Ethics (2007) 12, available at: <http://www.psychology.org.au/about/ethics/#s1> [accessed 31 Dec 2015].

[20] University of Oxford, 'University Policy on Harassment and Bullying', above n 10, 1.

[21] Syracuse University, 'Non-Discrimination and Anti-Harassment in Employment' (amended November 2007): <http://supolicies.syr.edu/univ_senate/nonD_harass_emp.htm> [accessed 31 Dec 2015].

[22] Ibid.

Academics for the most part are not subject to professional codes of ethics which are separate from their being a medical practitioner, psychologist or forensic scientist. Individual universities, however, have their own codes of conduct which espouse broad principles applicable to scholarly conduct. The University of New South Wales, for instance, provides that '[a]cademic freedom is not a defence to poor behaviour or disrespectful treatment of others' and mandates staff and affiliates to treat students, staff and affiliates with respect.[23] Similarly the comparable code of Adelaide University requires staff to 'treat everyone with respect and courtesy, and refrain from bullying, harassment or discrimination'.[24]

The Yale University School of Medicine is considerably more specific in its proscribing of intemperate attacks on individuals, whether or not the target is an employee of the university:

> The principle of freedom of expression that might otherwise protect even the most offensive public speech does not protect, nor does it even encompass, a right to threaten the dignity and privacy of an individual. Such personally directed behavior will not be tolerated; it is antithetical to academic values, debilitates its victims, compromises the offenders, and undermines the University's fundamental commitment to individual freedom and respect for all its members. Furthermore, acts of intolerance may destroy the very atmosphere wherein freedom of expression is otherwise tolerated and cherished.[25]

Amongst the questions that arise are whether scholars employed within institutions should be subject to the kinds of obligations imposed upon psychiatrists and psychologists, and whether universities should require in their codes of conduct the kind of respect mandated by the Yale University School of Medicine. This chapter next reviews a series of notorious controversies and expressions of disputation and denigration before mounting an argument in favour of mandated standards of respect and non-disparagement.

The Ark Controversy

One of the most notorious cases involving scholarly disputation, which had its manifestation in protracted litigation, was that involving the alleged existence of the Ark of the Covenant. It culminated in a lengthy decision by Sackville J of the Federal Court of Australia.[26]

The primary antagonists in the disputation were Professor Ian Plimer, a Professor of Geology and Head of the School of Earth Sciences at the University of Melbourne, and Dr Allen Roberts, an ordained Christian minister. Professor Plimer was provided with financial support during the dispute and ensuing litigation from the Australian Skeptics, an organization of which he was a member. For his part, Dr Roberts had once worked as the principal of a Bible College in Sydney and described himself as an historical researcher in archaeological work relating to Noah's Ark.

There was considerable antipathy between Professor Plimer and Dr Roberts, defamation action also having been initiated by the minister against the academic in 1992. In the proceedings before Sackville J, Professor Plimer brought a claim under s 52 of the *Trade Practices Act* 1974 (Cth) and the Fair Trading Acts of the various Australian States against Dr Roberts for misleading and deceptive conduct.

[23] University of New South Wales, *Code of Conduct* (June 2009) 2: <https://www.gs.unsw.edu.au/policy/documents/codeofconduct.pdf> [accessed 31 Dec 2015].

[24] The University of Adelaide, Code of Conduct (December 2014): <http://www.adelaide.edu.au/policies/2323/?dsn=policy.document;field=data;id=3842;m=view> [accessed 31 Dec 2015].

[25] Yale University, School of Medicine 2014–2015, 'Human Relations Code of Conduct': <http://www.yale.edu/printer/bulletin/htmlfiles/med/general-information.html> [accessed 31 Dec 2015].

[26] *Fasold v Roberts* [1997] FCA 439; (1997) 70 FCR 489.

The bases for the proceedings were misleading or deceptive statements alleged to have been made in the course of public lectures given by Dr Roberts throughout Australia in 1992, by which Professor Plimer said he had been affronted. In addition, Dr Roberts had made or authorized statements in publications and in videos and audio recordings of the lectures which Professor Plimer claimed inappropriately advanced 'the hypothesis that a boat-shaped geological formation at a place known as Akyayla, near Mt Ararat in Eastern Turkey...is or could contain the remnants of Noah's Ark, thereby providing tangible evidence of the literal truth of the account of the great flood in *Genesis*, 6:13–8:19'.[27]

The other parties to the litigation were the first applicant, Mr Fasold, a United States citizen who was the author of a book, *The Ark of Noah*, published in 1989 which contained a diagram of what he maintained were the remains of Noah's Ark at the site.[28] Mr Fasold made a claim of copyright infringement for reproductions of the diagram in Dr Roberts's publications.[29] The second respondent, Ark Search Association Incorporated ('Ark Search Inc'), was an association which had the purpose of conducting investigations of the site in Akyayla, Turkey for evidence of Noah's Ark.

The case was said to contain resonances of the notorious *Scopes* trial[30] in the United States in 1925 in which a school teacher was convicted of violating the Anti-Evolution Act of Tennessee, also known as the 'Butler Act'.[31] That Act, which was passed in 1925, prohibited the teaching in public schools of 'any theory that denies the story of the Divine Creation of man as taught in the Bible, and to teach instead that man has descended from a lower order of animals'.[32]

In his judgment Sackville J noted that there was clearly an 'unbridgeable gulf' between Professor Plimer and Dr Roberts, evidenced by 'considerable personal antipathy' and an immoderate tone in parts of the affidavit evidence, much of which was ruled inadmissible.[33] Sackville J also observed that it was clear that Professor Plimer passionately believed that Dr Roberts's views were 'scientifically insupportable' and that it was his public duty to refute those views.[34] It was with this duty in mind that Professor Plimer attended three of the public meetings addressed by Dr Roberts. He asked questions from the floor which resulted in his being asked to leave two of the meetings.[35] He was told at the meetings that he could ask written questions but did not do so. Professor Plimer was asked in cross-examination why he chose not to avail himself of the opportunity to submit written questions and he replied:

> I chose not to because I was very concerned that the audience were being misled and deceived by the science presented at that meeting and as a senior academic I felt it was my duty to maintain a standard of scholarship and make a statement at that meeting.[36]

27 Ibid, 493.

28 Ibid, 493–4.

29 Ibid, 494. Mr Fasold received financial support from Professor Plimer and the Australian Skeptics to participate in the proceedings.

30 *Scopes v State*, 154 Tenn 105; 289 SW 363 (1927).

31 [1997] FCA 439; 70 FCR 489, 494. See eg, Eugenie Carol Scott, *Evolution vs Creationism: An Introduction* (Berkeley, Calif: University of California Press, 2005) 94.

32 *Anti-Evolution Act* of 1925, § 1, as cited in *Fasold v Roberts* [1997] FCA 439; (1997) 70 FCR 489, 494. See also, John Thomas Scopes and William Jennings Bryan, *The World's Most Famous Court Trial: State of Tennessee v John Thomas Scopes* (first publ. 1925, New York: Da Capo Press, 1971 ed); Edward L Larson, *Summer for the Gods: The Scopes Trial and America's Continuing Debate Over Science and Religion* (New York: Basic Books, 2007).

33 [1997] FCA 439; (1997) 70 FCR 489, 497.

34 Ibid, 500.

35 Ibid.

36 Ibid.

Sackville J noted that Professor Plimer held zealous views on the subject of 'creation science' and that he did not attend his first public meeting with an open mind was evidenced by his comments that he went 'to hear a totally new creationist on the block' and 'to see how the audience was going to be misled and deceived'.[37]

However, at the heart of Professor Plimer's action was that the statements made by Dr Roberts and Ark Search were uttered in the course of trade and commerce. Sackville J held that this was not the situation and that to the extent that they promoted Dr Roberts's forthcoming book on the subject they were not sufficiently commercial in character to invest them with the necessary designation.[38] His Honour observed:

> This case demonstrates that there are limits to the scope and reach of the TP Act and the Fair Trading Acts. Not every false statement attracts a legal remedy, under the legislation. This reflects a broader principle, namely, that the legal system cannot and should not attempt to provide a remedy for every false or misleading statement made in the course of public debate on matters of general interest. The simple fact is that some issues—no matter how great the passions they arouse—are more appropriately dealt with outside the courtroom.[39]

Because of the focus of the arguments of the parties on whether the statements made by Dr Roberts were misleading and deceptive, Sackville J dealt with the issue, although it was not strictly necessary to the result of the case. He applied the decision of Deane and Fitzgerald JJ in *Taco Company of Australia Inc v Taco Bell Pty Ltd* to the question of what is misleading and deceptive:[40]

> First, it is necessary to identify the relevant section (or sections) of the public (which may be the public at large) by reference to whom the question of whether conduct is, or is likely to be, misleading or deceptive falls to be tested...
>
> Second, once the relevant section of the public is established, the matter is to be considered by reference to all who come within it, 'including the astute and the gullible, the intelligent and the not so intelligent, the well educated as well as the poorly educated, men and women of various ages pursuing a variety of vocations'...
>
> Thirdly, evidence that some person has in fact formed an erroneous conclusion is admissible and may be persuasive but is not essential. Such evidence does not itself conclusively establish that conduct is misleading or deceptive or likely to mislead or deceive. The court must determine that question for itself. The test is objective...
>
> Finally, it is necessary to inquire why proven misconception has arisen... The fundamental importance of this principle is that it is only by this investigation that the evidence of those who are shown to have been led into error can be evaluated and it can be determined whether they are confused because of misleading or deceptive conduct on the part of the respondent.[41]

Sackville J took into account that 'no evidence was adduced from persons who were claiming to have been misled by anything said by Dr Roberts',[42] although some 5,000–6,000 people would have heard his lectures, many of them being relatively untutored in scientific and archaeological matters and most being inclined to accept what he said.[43]

---

[37] Ibid.
[38] Ibid, 534.
[39] Ibid.
[40] [1982] FCA 136; (1982) 42 ALR 177, 202–3.
[41] Ibid, 202–3, as cited in *Fasold v Roberts* [1997] FCA 439; (1997) 70 FCR 489, 534–5.
[42] [1997] FCA 439; (1997) 70 FCR 489, 535.
[43] Ibid.

Justice Sackville found that the lectures represented that Dr Roberts had been personally involved, or had participated in, organized investigations at the Turkish site and had personally carried out or caused to be carried out scientific tests on objects discovered at the Site, in order to determine whether the boat-shaped formation in fact contained the remnants of Noah's Ark.[44] His Honour commented:

> Once it is accepted that Dr Roberts made this representation, it must follow that the representation was false. I have described earlier Dr Roberts' visits to the Site in 1990 and 1991. In the course of those visits he did not undertake what could be described as systematic investigations. Nor did he carry out or cause to be carried out scientific tests on objects retrieved from the Site, with the possible exception of the test he arranged on the so-called 'pitch' samples after his 1990 visit. Dr Roberts admitted in the defence that he had not used or caused to be used metal detectors or interface radar, although the evidence shows that others had used these devices at the Site. In answer to interrogatories, Dr Roberts said that he had not used any form of scientific equipment at the Site, except for 'basic items' he carried, apparently including a camera and hand held microscope. He accepted in cross-examination that he had not found animal hair or coprolite at the Site, had not conducted or arranged carbon dating of samples and had not systematically carried out measurements at the Site (although he had measured portions of what he regarded as the boat shaped formation). In these circumstances, it cannot be said that Dr Roberts had personally undertaken or participated a systematic investigation at the Site and had personally carried out or caused to be carried out scientific tests on objects retrieved from the Site.[45]

Justice Sackville also found that, while Dr Roberts did not suggest he was an archaeologist, his suggestion that he had been involved in archaeological research was an exaggeration.[46] He determined that Florida law allowed Dr Roberts to assume the designation of 'Doctor' but that Dr Roberts did not represent that he had qualifications in a scientific field and, although a newsletter came close to misrepresenting his academic credentials, he did not as a matter of law do so.[47]

However, Justice Sackville indicated that he 'would have declined to grant injunctive relief to the applicants'.[48] He noted that the applicants made no effort 'to prove that a repetition of any misleading or deceptive conduct would occur' in the absence of an injunction and he was not prepared to infer that such repetition was likely.[49] The conduct he found to be misleading and deceptive was, in substance, limited to Dr Roberts's representations that he had personally undertaken archaeological investigations or arranged testing of objects found there, concluding that:

> It can hardly be suggested that these representations, if repeated, are of themselves likely to sway the minds of those who interest themselves in the questions posed by Dr Roberts. Moreover, in my view, considerable care must be exercised before making orders restraining statements made in the course of public discussion on issues regarded by many people as important to their religious or ideological beliefs, *at least where the motivation for making such statements is not primarily commercial in character*. Unless caution is exercised, there is a serious risk that the courts will be used as the means of suppressing debate and discussion on issues of general interest to the community. It is no answer to the concern I have identified that any orders made by the Court will restrain only representations that have been shown to be false. The very task of having to justify impugned representations may deter those with

44 Ibid, 542–3.
45 Ibid, 543–4.
46 Ibid, 546.
47 Ibid, 548.
48 Ibid, 550.
49 Ibid, 550. See also, in respect of the misrepresentation of credentials, *Noone v Operation Smile (Australia) Inc* [2012] VSCA 91; (2012) 38 VR 569.

> limited resources (both financial and emotional) from engaging in discussion of matters of wide community interest. If the views they put forward are ill-informed or plain wrong, a democratic society offers ample opportunity to rebut those views. As the publicity preceding this case (of which there was evidence) demonstrates, there are means available to counter what are said to be misrepresentations or errors made in public presentations on issues of general interest, without invoking the TP Act or the Fair Trading Acts.[50]

The judgment of Justice Sackville brought an end to the bitter disputation between the parties, probably in part because of the costs occasioned by it, the decision not being taken to appeal. To this extent it is an example of the potential for legal processes to have a constructive outcome when disputation between scholars has reached an extreme point.

New Zealand's Climate Change Litigation

New Zealand's National Institute of Water and Atmospheric Research Ltd (NIWA) was a Crown Research Institute established for the purposes of undertaking research into environmental matters. It also advised the government on scientific issues related to climate change. It maintained a national climate database since 1992 comprising climate information of a variety of kinds which has enabled NIWA to publish a statistical series of nationally averaged annual mean surface temperature trends experienced by New Zealand since 1853; it called these the Seven Station Temperature Series (7SS).

As of 2009 the 7SS indicated that New Zealand had experienced a warming trend of approximately 0.9 degrees Centigrade (C) from 1909 to 2009. However, the New Zealand Climate Science Coalition (the Coalition), a body associated with the New Zealand Climate Science Education Trust (the Trust), disputed NIWA's findings and publicly criticized their accuracy. In response NIWA published an 11 Station Temperature Series (the 11SS) in December 2009, comprising a spreadsheet and graph showing unadjusted temperatures recorded at a number of weather stations from 1931 and 1955, 11 such stations between 955 and 1,994 and 10 stations from 1994. It also published a review of the 7SS from 1909 to 2008 (the review). These publications confirmed NIWA's view that New Zealand's climate had experienced a warming trend over the previous century.

The Trust disputed the validity of the 7SS, the 11SS and the review or the conclusion that New Zealand's climate had experienced a marked warming. It took the unusual step of challenging the publications by an application for judicial review, filing in support affidavits by Professor Carter, a palaeontologist and an Adjunct Professor in the Marine Geophysical Laboratory and School of Earth Sciences at James Cook University in Townsville, Australia; Mr Dunleavy, a journalist; and Mr Dedekind, an information technology professional with a background in computer modelling. NIWA filed affidavits by Dr Wratt, the Chief Scientist at NIWA and Director of the New Zealand Climate Change Centre;[51] Dr Trenberth, a Senior Scientist in the National Centre for Atmospheric Research in Boulder, Colorado; and Dr Mullan, a Principal Scientist (Climate) at NIWA.

The matter came before Venning of the New Zealand High Court.[52] Applying a previous decision,[53] and taking into account the status of NIWA as a state-owned enterprise with its

---

[50] [1997] FCA 439; (1997) 70 FCR 489, 550.

[51] All of the New Zealand Crown Research Institutes and three New Zealand Universities were members of the Centre.

[52] *New Zealand Climate Science Education Trust v National Institute of Water and Atmospheric Research Ltd* [2012] NZHC 2297; [2013] 1 NZLR 75.

[53] *Mercury Energy Ltd v Electricity Corporation of New Zealand* [1994] 2 NZLR 385.

shares held by ministers responsible to the House of Representatives and accountable to the electorate, he held that the remedy of judicial review was potentially open to the Trust against the decisions of NIWA.

This led Justice Venning to consider the appropriate standard for review, a standard which generally depends on the decision in issue. The issue was one of high principle because it went to the question of how a court should enter into a dispute about scientific matters when it is the decision of a state instrumentality that is being challenged. Justice Venning found that in determining the nature of the decision 'it is appropriate to consider the nature of the public body, the particular function being performed, the context within which that function is being performed and what is said to have gone wrong'.[54] When the context is a commercial decision of a state-owned enterprise, he found that the applicant for judicial review would need to show fraud, corruption or bad faith.[55]

Justice Venning observed that '[i]t is well established that the Court, in considering an application for judicial review, will be cautious about interfering with decisions made by a specialist body acting within its own sphere of expertise'. He noted that in a previous decision Justice Ellen France in the Court of Appeal had found that 'the Court was not well placed on a judicial review application: 'to assess... the medical, economic and other complexities raised by an evaluation process'.[56] He applied the approach of Justice Hammond in *New Zealand Public Service Association Inc v Hamilton City Council*[57] where he accepted that a less intensive review can be appropriate because of the 'democratic imperative', where the decision-makers derive authority from an electoral mandate to which they are accountable;[58] a constitutional imperative, where the government, not the courts, decides fundamental policy; and an imperative that the courts in many, if not most, areas lack the relevant expertise to make such assessments. Justice Venning found that this last feature was especially important in the case before him as the Trust's challenge was based on what it described as 'recognised scientific opinion'.[59] He concluded that a 'less intensive review is particularly apposite where the Court is not in a position to definitively adjudicate on scientific opinions.... I consider this Court should be cautious about interfering with decisions made and conclusions drawn by a specialist body, such as NIWA, acting within its own sphere of expertise. In such circumstances a less intensive or, to put it another way, a more tolerant review is appropriate'.[60] He found that the function of the court was not to rule on the science[61] and concluded that it was necessary for the applicant for judicial review to demonstrate that the decision-maker had followed a clearly improper process:[62] '[U]nless the Trust can point to some defect in NIWA's decision-making process or show that the decision was clearly wrong in principle or in law, this Court will not intervene.'[63]

---

54 [2012] NZHC 2297; [2013] 1 NZLR 75, [36], applying *Lab Tests Auckland Ltd v Auckland District Health Board* [2008] NZCA 385; [2009] 1 NZLR 776, [85].

55 [2012] NZHC 2297; [2013] 1 NZLR 75, [41].

56 *Lab Tests Auckland Ltd v Auckland District Health Board* [2008] NZCA 385; [2009] 1 NZLR 776, [340], as cited in *New Zealand Climate Science Education Trust v National Institute of Water and Atmospheric Research Ltd* [2012] NZHC 2297; [2013] 1 NZLR 75, [41]; see also, *Z v Dental Complaints Assessment Committee* [2008] NZSC 55; [2009] 1 NZLR 1, [139].

57 [1997] 1 NZLR 30, 35.

58 [2012] NZHC 2297; [2013] 1 NZLR 75, [43].

59 Ibid, [11], [44].

60 Ibid, [44]–[45].

61 Ibid, [46], applying *SmithKline Beecham (New Zealand) Ltd v Minister of Health* (unreported, HC, Wellington, CP49/02) [80] (Young J).

62 [2012] NZHC 2297; [2013] 1 NZLR 75, [47]–[48].

63 Ibid, [48].

Justice Venning considered whether an attack on the science underpinning NIWA's publications was possible by an argument that it had breached its statutory obligations including its obligation to 'pursue excellence'.[64] He accepted that adopting a 'suboptimal means to discharge a duty can amount to a reviewable error of law',[65] but observed that the requirement or obligation to pursue excellence is a 'subjective concept not readily susceptible to judicial assessment'.[66] However, 'a complete and obvious failure to pursue excellence would be a breach that this Court could, and should, address. However, given the excellence criteria [sic] applies to the area of scientific research, or methodology, for this Court to find NIWA in breach of that aspirational duty, any such breach would need to be clear'.[67] He found the evidence before him not to establish that a breach had been made out. In addition, he did not find NIWA to have acted under a mistake of fact in compiling its documentation. He concluded that the Trust's criticism of the 11SS had not been made out. Nor had it been shown that NIWA had acted unreasonably in concluding that the 11SS contained sufficiently reliable evidence of average temperature trends in New Zealand between 1931 and 2008 to support the publication of the 11SS on its website. He accepted that it was 'more than arguable' that the purpose of the NIWA review was to calculate site change temperature adjustments from the underlying data and metadata in an independent way and to document how the adjustments had been produced and what their values were: 'I accept that NIWA could have recalculated the temperature adjustments in a different way yet still have arrived at a similar result which would strengthen the robustness and validity of the previous results.'[68] He found that in its calculation of warming trends NIWA applied credible scientific methodology and, as such, did not breach its obligation to pursue excellence.

Justice Venning decision constitutes a highly significant resolution of a scholarly debate about the scientific evaluation of the nature and extent of climate change. The fact that he was prepared to entertain and rule on an application for judicial review in respect of NIWA's publications on the subject is important. His approach was one of extending a measure of latitude to the exercise, recognizing explicitly the difficulty for the courts in evaluating such matters. However, those challenging NIWA's publications manoeuvred the High Court into exploring a matter as diffuse as whether NIWA had breached its statutory duty to pursue excellence in its publications. The fact that the High Court was prepared to scrutinize the methodology and reasoning processes of the scientists at NIWA, as well as the complex science underpinning them, opens a door to more than climate sceptics, but to many others dubious about conventional medico-scientific matters, to challenge them by the mechanism of judicial review. Ultimately, this, more than the fact that Venning J found no breach of methodology, mistake of fact or unreasonableness in the particular circumstances, will stand as the precedent established by New Zealand's climate change decision. The legacy is that the potential exists for scholarly iconoclasts in a number of scenarios to utilize judicial review in the courts to challenge government instrumentalities' decision-making and publications.

The Banning of Professor Trivers

Professor Robert Trivers, an evolutionary theorist and Professor of Anthropology and Biological Sciences at Rutgers University, was notorious for his participation in acerbic

64 See eg, ibid, [66]–[70].
65 Ibid, [73].
66 Ibid, [74].
67 Ibid, [77].
68 Ibid, [157].

disputation. In 2012 he was banned from the New Brunswick campus, although he later claimed that this action was taken without justification and by reason of his attempting to expose another academic's fraudulent conduct.[69] *Nature* declined to withdraw an article, which argued that Jamaican teenagers with a high degree of body symmetry were more likely to be rated 'good dancers' by their peers than those with less symmetrical bodies. The article suggested that dancing is a signal for sexual selection in humans. Trivers himself contended the article should be retracted. In frustration at the stance by *Nature* Trivers and two colleagues wrote an exposé book, *Anatomy of a Fraud* (which they self-published) about what they maintained was the misconduct of a post-doctoral scholar and specialist statistician, arguing that certain of his published work should be subject to retractions.[70]

Trivers's position was subsequently vindicated by a Rutgers committee that identified fraud in the statistician's work. It reported its findings to the National Science Foundation which had funded the impugned work. Ultimately *Nature* retracted the article. However, the difficulties took on a new complexion when Trivers erupted angrily at a colleague who had not supported his critiques of the statistician. Trivers started yelling at him and calling him a punk until the police were summoned. He later attributed what occurred to discrimination against him on the basis of his bipolar disorder which had long been controlled.[71] He was banned from campus for five months.

Shea has written of Trivers:

> Mr. Trivers is widely recognized as a difficult genius. After a mental breakdown derailed him from law school—he has acknowledged a bipolar disorder—he entered graduate school at Harvard University in biology, and within a year began to write widely influential papers on how natural selection, at the genetic level, fuels competition between parents and offspring, and on the dynamics of so-called reciprocal altruism.
>
> In a 2004 symposium on Mr. Trivers's work, the Harvard psychologist Steven Pinker said that 'the fields of sociobiology, evolutionary psychology, Darwinian social science, and behavioral ecology are in large part attempts to test and flesh out Trivers's ideas.'
>
> [...]
>
> [Another colleague commented that Trivers] can be abrupt and gruff at the best of times... 'Anyone who tells you he's a pleasure and a dream to deal with doesn't know him'—but 'that's the price of genius.' In interviews he quickly switches from calm to irritated and back, and he swears epically.[72]

Trivers' travails are exemplary of a cross-section of scholars who have engaged in abuse and denigration that would not be tolerated in any other form of employment.

The David Rindos Saga

David Rindos was an archaeologist with doctoral qualifications from Cornell University. He was recruited to the University of Western Australia in 1989 where he became acting head

69 Christopher Shea, 'Prominent Scholar was Banned from Rutgers Campus', *The Chronicle of Higher Education*, 3 May 2013: <http://chronicle.com/article/Prominent-Scholar-Was-Banned/139027/> [accessed 31 Dec 2015].

70 Eugenie Samuel Reich, 'Symmetry Study Deemed a Fraud' (2013) 497 *Nature* 170: <http://www.nature.com/news/symmetry-study-deemed-a-fraud-1.12932> [accessed 31 Dec 2015].

71 See Andrew Rodriguez, 'Professor Shares Experience with On-Campus Ban' (9 September 2013) *Daily Targum*: <http://www.dailytargum.com/article/2013/09/professor-shares-experience-with-on-campus-ban> [accessed 31 Dec 2015].

72 Ibid.

of the Archaeology Department. However, controversies erupted about how the department had been run under Dr Rindos. An internal inquiry was constituted and Dr Rindos was moved to the Geography Department and then assigned without a nominated department, after the Archaeology Department was abolished. Ultimately, Rindos was refused tenure and accused of multiple improprieties including sexual harassment, plagiarism, and 'pornography mongering'.[73] In each regard charges were dropped or no evidence provided.[74] Ultimately, a parliamentary inquiry with the powers of a Royal Commission was convened, which (after his death) found that Rindos had not had fair and adequate opportunities to present his case for tenure and that he was denied procedural fairness.[75]

An aspect of the Rindos saga was his action against another academic for defamation.[76] It arose from a message placed on a worldwide computer network bulletin board by a United States anthropologist which criticized the University of Western Australia for refusing Dr Rindos tenure. Evidence at trial established that approximately 23,000 persons worldwide had access to the bulletin board. In response to the posting the defendant made his own posting in which he made a variety of denigratory comments, including that:

> I have met the man myself, and my impression is that his entire career has been built not on field research at all, but on his ability to berate and bully all and sundry on the logic of his own evolutionary theories. In the local pub, drinking and chain-smoking all the while for that matter. Secondly, and this is rumour passed to me by several reputable and long-standing Western Australian anthropologists as to Dr Rhindos' [sic] 'Puppy Parties' focussed I am told on a local boy they called 'Puppy'. Hmm, strange dicey behaviour indeed, especially here in an environment dominated by conservative fundamentalists.[77]

Justice Ipp accepted that the words in the message published by the defendant gave rise to an imputation that the plaintiff engaged in sexual misconduct with a 'local boy' and to an imputation that Dr Rindos's professional career and reputation had not been based on appropriate academic research 'but on his ability to berate and bully all and sundry'.[78] He found this to constitute a serious denigration of his academic competence.

The defendant compounded his earlier behaviour by a letter that he sent to the secretary of the Anthropological Association of Western Australia, containing the following remarks:

> My further understanding is that Dr Rindos had deliberately launched his now infamous campaign in his attempts to revive an already shattered academic career by constantly, openly and publicly seeking to discredit those against whom he had acted as head of the then Department of Archaeology, when he might well have approached them to discuss whatever irregularities he is alleged to have uncovered in the first instance. He might very well have

[73] Brian Martin, 'David Rindos Versus the University of Western Australia: Analogies to the Orr Case' in John Biggs and Richard Davis (eds), *The Subversion of Australian Universities* (Wollongong: Fund for Intellectual Dissent, 2002), available at: <http://pandora.nla.gov.au/pan/33459/20030221-0000/www.uow.edu.au/arts/sts/bmartin/dissent/documents/sau/index.html> (archived 21 February 2003) [accessed 31 Dec 2015] 96.

[74] See ibid, 93–108.

[75] Standing Committee on Public Administration, Legislative Council, Western Australia, *Fourth Report on Its Inquiry into the Events Surrounding the Denial of Tenure to the Late Dr David Rindos by the University of Western Australia* (December 1997) [23.5]–[23.6]: <http://www.parliament.wa.gov.au/Parliament/commit.nsf/(Report+Lookup+by+Com+ID)/81EEAE9D6898C36148257831003E942E/$file/pb004a.pdf> [accessed 31 Dec 2015].

[76] *Rindos v Hardwick* (unreported, WASC, 31 March 1994) (Ipp J), available at: <http://decisions.justice.wa.gov.au/supreme/supdcsn.nsf/c04d382e733a94a148256fc4002b2e2b/12ce060858b5eb9e4825641300205ca6?OpenDocument&Highlight=2,rindos> [accessed 31 Dec 2015].

[77] Ibid, 5–6.

[78] Ibid, 7.

settled down to administer his department competently and professionally, and like the rest of us to do some research, to present his papers and to seek the review of his peers. His persistent failure to do so as I understand it is in fact the very reason for the University's decision to finally deny him his tenure.[79]

Not surprisingly Justice Ipp found these comments also to denigrate Dr Rindos's professional competence. He found the comments to be likely to have had a 'most harmful effect' on Dr Rindos's professional standing and to have exacerbated his symptoms of depression and anxiety.[80] He awarded damages of AUS$40,000. Again, then, litigation brought an element of resolution to the bitter disputation between the parties.

However, there are occasions when litigation or the threat of it can exercise a chilling effect on legitimate scholarly disagreement and ventilation of important issues.

The Climate Denial Conspiracist Affair

In 2012 cognitive scientist Professor Stephan Lewandowsky and others published a provocative article on climate denialism entitled 'NASA Faked the Moon Landing—Therefore, (Climate) Science Is a Hoax: An Anatomy of the Motivated Rejection of Science'.[81] This provoked an outcry from climate sceptics and prompted Lewandowsky and colleagues to analyse the responses and to publish an article entitled 'Recursive Fury: Conspiracist Ideation in the Blogosphere in Response to Research on Conspiracist Ideation' in the journal, *Frontiers in Psychology*.[82] At the time Lewandowsky was a professor at the University of Western Australia. He later moved to Bristol University. The article was extremely controversial as it challenged what he asserted was the frequent public misinterpretation of uncertainty as a reason to delay action on issues such as climate change. Its bottom line was that appealing to uncertainty is therefore misplaced: any appeal to uncertainty should provoke a greater, rather than a weaker, concern about climate change than in the absence of uncertainty.

On 4 April 2014 the journal retracted the article and posted on its website the following statement:

> In the light of a small number of complaints received following publication of the original research article cited above, *Frontiers* carried out a detailed investigation of the academic, ethical, and legal aspects of the work. This investigation did not identify any issues with the academic and ethical aspects of the study. It did, however, determine that the legal context is insufficiently clear and therefore *Frontiers* wishes to retract the published article. The authors understand this decision, while they stand by their article and regret the limitations on academic freedom which can be caused by legal factors.[83]

This somewhat extraordinary capitulation to pressure prompted considerable controversy because of the effectiveness of the threats of climate sceptics in removing from the

---

[79] Ibid, 8.

[80] Ibid, 9.

[81] Stephan Lewandowsky, Klaus Oberauer, and Gillies E Gignac, 'NASA Faked the Moon Landing—Therefore, (Climate) Science Is a Hoax: An Anatomy of the Motivated Rejection of Science' (2013) 24(5) *Psychological Science* 622.

[82] Stephan Lewandowsky, John Cook, Klaus Oberauer, and Michael Marriott, 'Recursive Fury: Conspiracist Ideation in the Blogosphere in Response to Research on Conspiracist Ideation' (2013) 4 *Frontiers in Psychology* 73.

[83] Frontiers in Psychology Editorial Office, 'Retraction: Recursive Fury: Conspiracist Ideation in the Blogosphere in Response to Research on Conspiracist Ideation', *Frontiers in Psychology*, 27 March 2014, updated 4 April 2014: <http://journal.frontiersin.org/article/10.3389/fpsyg.2014.00293/full> [accessed 31 Dec 2015].

public domain the views of one of their detractors, and the repercussions of their success. The University of Western Australia was moved to investigate the criticisms of the article but found no academic, legal or ethical problems with it.[84] It pointedly retained the article on its own website as a matter of principle.[85] John Cook, a researcher at the University of Queensland and a co-author of the second paper, said the *Frontiers*' decision to retract the work might have a 'chilling effect' on research: 'It means that if a paper is published that the climate deniers don't like the look of, they can bombard the journal with complaints or threats. Knowing they have had success once might embolden them to try to retreat [sic] the strategy again.'[86]

The Psychopathy Controversy

University of British Columbia scholar, Professor Robert Hare, has been the pre-eminent latter day scholar in relation to the concept, classification and treatability of psychopathy. He authored best-selling pop-psychology books, entitled *Without Conscience*[87] and *Snakes in Suits*,[88] and a vast number of articles on the subject, as well as being the creator of the eponymous Hare Psychopathy Checklist Revised (the PCL-R). In the United States he dominated psychopathy research for some three decades.

However, other constructs of psychopathy exist. Professor David Cooke of the Glasgow Caledonian University, in particular, has proffered an alternative means of evaluating psychopathy.[89] In 2007 the journal *Psychological Assessment* accepted an article by University of California Irvine Professor Jennifer Skeem and Professor Cooke,[90] which argued that the development of the PCL-R had caused conceptual confusion and, in particular, the conflating of measures with constructs. They contended that there was a risk that Hare's PCL-R would be equated with the theoretical construct of psychopathy and argued that:

> [F]actor analysis of PCL-R items in a theoretical vacuum cannot reveal the essence of psychopathy. Second, a myth about the PCL-R and its relation to violence must be examined to avoid the view that psychopathy is merely a violent variant of antisocial personality disorder. Third, a formal, iterative process between theory development and empirical validation must be adopted. Fundamentally, constructs and measures must be recognized as separate entities, and neither reified. Applying such principles to the current state of the field, the authors

---

84 Dana Nuccitelli, 'Contrarians Bully Journal into Retracting a Climate Psychology Paper', *The Guardian*, 22 March 2012: <http://www.theguardian.com/environment/climate-consensus-97-per-cent/2014/mar/21/contrarians-bully-climate-change-journal-retraction> [accessed 31 Dec 2015].

85 See <http://websites.psychology.uwa.edu.au/labs/cogscience/Publications/LskyetalRecursiveFury4UWA.pdf> [accessed 31 Dec 2015]; Peter Hannam, '"Conspiracist" Climate Change Study Withdrawn Amid Legal Threats', *The Sydney Morning Herald*, 2 April 2014: <http://www.smh.com.au/environment/climate-change/conspiracist-climate-change-study-withdrawn-amid-legal-threats-20140401-35xao.html> [accessed 31 Dec 2015].

86 Hannam, above n 85.

87 Robert D Hare, *Without Conscience: The Disturbing World of the Psychopaths Among Us* (New York: Guilford Press, 1999).

88 Paul Babiak and Robert D Hare, *Snakes in Suits: When Psychopaths Go to Work* (New York: Harper Collins, 2007).

89 See eg, David J Cooke, Christine Michie, Stephen D Hart, and Daniel A Clark, 'Reconstructing Psychopathy: Clarifying the Significance of Anti-Social and Socially Deviant Behavior in the Diagnosis of Psychopathic Personality Disorder' (2004) 18(4) *Journal of Personality Disorders* 337; David J Cooke, Christine Michie, and Jennifer Skeem, 'Understanding the Structure of the Psychopathy Checklist—Revised: An Exploration of Methodological Confusion' (2007) 190(5) *The British Journal of Psychiatry* 39.

90 Jennifer L Skeem and David J Cooke, 'Is Criminal Behavior a Central Component of Psychopathy? Conceptual Directions for Resolving the Debate' (2010) 22(2) *Psychological Assessment* 433.

believe the evidence favors viewing criminal behavior as a correlate, not a component, of psychopathy.[91]

The authors also argued that the PCL-R left out certain characteristics such as low anxiety that are central to the disorder and focused too much on criminal behaviour, this in turn promoting the potential for over-diagnosis.

The article was scheduled for publication in the September 2007 issue of *Psychological Assessment*. Before being accepted for publication Skeem and Cooke's original paper had been widely circulated among academics. Before it was to be published, a copy was also sent to Professor Hare by a colleague.[92] Professor Hare formed the view that the article contained 'major flaws and misrepresentations of his writings on the connections between criminality and psychopathy' and threatened legal action if it were published, in an attempt to persuade the journal that it should refrain from publication.[93] This set in train what has been described as 'a stultifying series of reviews, revisions and legal correspondence'.[94] After a threat to sue was issued, the authors conducted a review of the paper and revised it but, according to Hare, the article contained 'many of the same misrepresentations'.[95] Hare reportedly stated:

> I threatened litigation only after Craig Neumann and I made a concerted attempt to resolve the matter with Skeem and Cooke through discourse. We were not satisfied with merely publishing a rebuttal to an article that continued to contain so many misrepresentations and mischaracterizations of our work.[96]

Ultimately, the threat of a law suit by Hare did not translate into a writ and the article by Skeem and Cooke, along with a rebuttal from Hare and Neumann, followed by a reply by Skeem and Cooke, was published in 2010 in *Psychological Assessment*, three years after the paper was submitted by Cooke and Skeem.[97] In the rebuttal Hare and Neumann suggested that the critique in the article by Skeem and Cooke was inconsistent with the principles of scientific debate, stating:

> Scientific debate operates according to well-established principles, one of the most basic of which is that the views of an opposing side should be presented and evaluated in a fair and unbiased manner. We contend that the critique by Skeem and Cooke (2010) of the Psychopathy Checklist—Revised (PCL-R; Hare, 2003) is inconsistent with these principles. Skeem and Cooke suggested that they have provided 'conceptual directions for resolving the debate' about whether 'criminal behavior is a central component of psychopathy.' The very

[91] Ibid, 433.

[92] John Travis, 'After Legal Threat and 3-Year Delay, Paper on Psychopathy to Appear—Maybe' (2010) 328(5984) *Science* 1350.

[93] Ibid, 1350.

[94] See Benedict Carey, 'Academic Battle Delays Publication by 3 Years', *The New York Times*, 11 June 2010: <http://www.nytimes.com/2010/06/12/health/12psych.html?_r=2&scp=1&sq=Academic%20Battle%20 Delays%20Publication%20by%203%20Years&st=cse> [accessed 31 Dec 2015]. See also, Travis, above n 92; JR Minkel, 'Fear Review: Critique of Forensic Psychopathy Scale Delayed 3 years by Threat of Lawsuit', *Scientific American*, 17 June 2010: <http://www.scientificamerican.com/article/critique-of-forensic-psychopathy-scale-delayed-by-lawsuit/> [accessed 31 Dec 2015].

[95] Charlie Smith, 'UBC Psychopathy Expert Robert Hare Responds to Academic Criticism Over Lawsuit Threat', *The Georgia Straight*, 13 June 2010: <http://www.straight.com/article-328927/vancouver/ubc-psychopathy-expert-robert-hare-responds-academic-criticism-over-lawsuit-threat> [accessed 31 Dec 2015]. See also, Travis, above n 92.

[96] Smith, above n 95.

[97] Skeem and Cooke, above n 90; Robert D Hare and Craig S Neumann, 'The Role of Antisociality in the Psychopathy Construct: Comment on Skeem and Cooke (2010)' (2010) 22(2) *Psychological Assessment* 446; Jennifer L Skeem J and David J Cooke, 'One Measure Does Not a Construct Make: Directions Toward Reinvigorating Psychopathy Research—Reply to Hare and Neumann (2010)' (2010) 22(2) *Psychological Assessment* 455.

title of their article is a straw man based on the unfounded claim that Hare and his colleagues consider criminality to be central or fundamental to the psychopathy construct. Their claim is bolstered by arguments misconstruing our published work and that of others and by quotes of our work that have been taken out of context or reconstructed in such a way that it appears that we have said something that we did not say. Skeem and Cooke also made highly selective use of the literature, often omitting published studies that directly contradict or do not support the points they attempted to make, particularly with respect to the role of antisocial tendencies in clinical and empirical conceptions of psychopathy. These tactics are inconsistent with their tutorial on the philosophy of science, compromise their arguments, and divert attention from any legitimate issues raised in their article. We contend that Skeem and Cooke did the field a disservice by presenting an inaccurate account of the role of the PCL-R in theory and research on psychopathy, both applied and basic.[98]

If the contentions of Hare and Neumann are true, it is understandable that they should wish to defend themselves and set the record straight. However, the traditional way of responding to these claims is through rebuttal, not through legal action.[99] Threats of, or actual, litigation can have a 'chilling effect' on academic debate.[100] These were the views expressed by two eminent scholars in the psychology/law area, Professors Norman Poythress and John Petrila, who published an article in the June 2010 issue of the *International Journal of Forensic Mental Health*, discussing the broader repercussions of Professor Hare's conduct.[101] While acknowledging that academic disputes are not uncommon in all areas of science and other academic fields, Poythress and Petrila argued that:

> [T]he threat of litigation constitutes a serious threat to academic freedom and potentially to scientific progress.
>
> [...]
>
> Academic freedom rests on the premise that advances in science can only occur if scholars are permitted to pursue free competition among ideas. This assumes that scholars have the liberty to do their work free from limitations imposed by political or religious pressure or by economic reprisals, such as loss of employment.[102]

Poythress and Petrila strongly expressed the view that '[s]cientific controversies must be settled by the methods of science rather than by the methods of litigation'.[103] They also articulated concern about the way the editors of the *International Journal of Forensic Mental Health* responded to the threats of litigation over a paper that was in press.[104] The Skeem and Cooke paper had gone through the peer-review process, which involves 'the critical assessment of manuscripts submitted to journals by experts who are not part of the editorial staff'.[105] It is this process used in peer-reviewed journals which seeks to assure readers that the information in those journals is 'most valid and trustworthy'.[106] Poythress and Petrila noted:

> Editors aspire to obtain reviews that are unbiased, independent, and (constructively) critical of the manuscript so as to inform their judgments whether to accept, reject, or request the authors to revise and resubmit their manuscripts for further consideration. The editorial

[98] Hare and Neumann, above n 97, 446.

[99] Norman Poythress and John P Petrila, 'PCL-R Psychopathy: Threats to Sue, Peer Review, and Potential Implications for Science and Law: A Commentary' (2010) 9(1) *International Journal of Forensic Mental Health* 3, 4.

[100] Ibid, 9.

[101] See generally, ibid.

[102] Ibid, 4–6 (footnote omitted).

[103] Ibid, 9.

[104] Ibid, 6.

[105] Ibid, 5.

[106] Ibid.

decision to publish (whether initially, or after one or more revisions) does not purport to ensure the 'truth' of the findings or the ultimate validity of a theory. Rather, the objective, in the words of one experienced editor is, 'to put interesting, potentially important science into public view after ensuring its quality as best as we possibly can. After that, efforts at repetition and reinterpretation can take place out in the open... It goes without saying that we cannot publish papers with a guarantee that every result is right'.[107]

The peer-review process is fallible of course and, among other things,[108] can be adversely affected by conflicts of interest, such as financial interests in a 'commercial product whose success is very dependent on whether publications on it are positive or negative'.[109] While editors have guidelines around conflicts of interest that arise in the peer-review process, Poythress and Petrila noted there is little guidance available to editors when faced with a threat to sue after a decision to publish has been made and suggest that the impact on peer review and publication process is likely to be significant.[110] A threat of litigation can have the following effects:

> First, it can make scholars reluctant to pursue a particular line of research; if that hurdle is crossed, it may make a scholar reluctant to offer a frank critique of another's work. Second, a demand that an accepted manuscript be withdrawn from publication absent an affected party's approval of its contents could reasonably be construed as an effort at censorship. Third, if the peer review process itself becomes subject to legal scrutiny, it may make scholars far more reluctant to participate in that process.[111]

Poythress and Petrila's position was summarized as follows:

> Because publication of the article by Professors Skeem and Cooke has effectively been long delayed, if not ultimately suppressed, one clear impact of this threat to sue is that researchers who may have been willing to investigate alternative models of psychopathy that might have been derived from the Skeem and Cooke article are not able to do so, simply because the article is unavailable. Because science progresses, in part, both by confirming viable models and disconfirming nonviable ones, the suppression of information relevant to constructing candidate models for empirical evaluation can be viewed as impeding the progress of science.
>
> [...]
>
> [I]t seems clear from our review that such threats strike at the heart of the peer review process, may have a chilling effect on the values at the core of academic freedom, and may potentially impede the scientific testing of various theories, models and products. In our view it is far better to debate such matters in peer review journals rather than cut off debate through threats of litigation.[112]

There is a level of potential self-correction in the process. As Pignotti has commented:

> The moral of this story: As a profession, we are moving away from authority-based mental health gurus and towards evidence-based assessment and practice. People who threaten to sue their way out of being criticized (and I mean criticism of their work, not libelous personal attacks) only lose themselves credibility.[113]

---

107 Ibid, (footnotes omitted).

108 For example, such as the use of journal impact factors, as highlighted by the *El Naschie* case discussed below. See also Rimas Norvaisa, 'Journal Impact Factor and Academic Ethics' (2011) 3(2) *Evolution of Science and Technology* 120; Kai Simons, 'The Misused Impact Factor' (2008) 322(5899) *Science* 165.

109 Poythress and Petrila, above n 99, 6.

110 Ibid, 6.

111 Ibid, 9.

112 Ibid, 10.

113 Monica Pignotti, 'Robert Hare Threatens to Sue Critics' on *Potentially Harmful and Other Questionable Therapies* (2 June 2010): <https://phtherapies.wordpress.com/2010/06/02/robert-hare-threatens-to-sue-critics/> [accessed 31 Dec 2015]. Monica Pignotti was herself, along with several other defendants, sued in 2010 by

Poythress and Petrila stated in conclusion that the purpose of their commentary was 'to review and discuss the collateral damage that may result when threats of litigation are used to suppress the publication of manuscripts that have been accepted for publication in peer-reviewed scientific journals'.[114]

As might be expected, the saga did not end there. Following the publication of the Poythress and Petrila article in 2010 in the *International Journal of Forensic Mental Health*, Robert Hare posted a 14-page rebuttal to their article on his website.[115] He stated that he wished to give 'his side of the story in a heated dispute over the boundaries of academic freedom' and 'to respond to what I consider unfair characterizations of my motives and actions in a long-standing controversy'.[116] Hare was reported as stating that Poythress and Petrila's article implied, incorrectly, that there were pecuniary aims involved with threatening to sue.[117] That is, the purported goal was to protect the Psychopathy Checklist-Revised. Hare suggested that while Poythress and Petrila had argued for open discussion and peer review, they had not asked for his side of the story.[118]

The principles of academic freedom and debate are perhaps not as clear cut as they may have once been when rebuttals and replies were published in academic journals which were accessible only to subscribers or in hard copy in university libraries. In the age of the internet such disputes can become convoluted and personal, particularly when the broader global community becomes involved through commenting on the matter in blogs and other online forums. The online debate of these matters gives them a much a longer shelf-life, preserved for posterity, on the internet, for all to read. As Poythress and Petrila noted, academic disputes are far from uncommon, and occur in many different fields; thus the Hare controversy is not unusual in itself.[119] However, with the involvement of major commercial interests, such as attach to psychometric tools like the PCL, and with the internet and public commentary, it becomes difficult to decipher what is part of a legitimate academic debate, what is commercial, what is personal, who is right, and who is wrong.

Although Hare ultimately did not sue Skeem and Cooke, it is useful to reflect on how the matter might have played out from a legal perspective had he sued. It is not intended in this context to discuss in detail the large area of law that is defamation law.[120] The following, albeit cursory, discussion of defamation law, along with some recent notable examples that have received publicity in the media and in other online forums, will be used to examine the different approaches of courts in the United States, the United Kingdom and Australia to matters involving scholars in dispute. Whether these matters make their way to the courts may depend in part on the jurisdiction(s) in which the disputes occur.

Dr Ronald Federici, a neuropsychologist, for defamation, conspiracy, and tortious interference. The action was with regard to comments that had been made on the internet in blogs and other internet sites by Pignotti and the other defendants, criticizing the work and techniques used by Dr Federici in his practice. The matter was ultimately dismissed for want of jurisdiction in the State of Virginia: see Reporter's Transcript: Motions Hearing, *Federici v Pignotti* et al. (United States District Court, Eastern District of Virginia, Case No. l10-1418, 4 March 2011), available at: <http://www.dmlp.org/sites/citmedialaw.org/files/2011-03-04-Dismissal%20Hearing%20Transcript.pdf> [accessed 31 Dec 2015].

[114] Poythress and Petrila, above n 99, 10.

[115] Smith, above n 95.

[116] Ibid.

[117] Ibid.

[118] Ibid.

[119] Poythress and Petrila, above n 99, 3.

[120] In relation to defamation law, see Patrick George, *Defamation Law in Australia* (2nd edn, Chatswood, NSW: LexisNexis Butterworths, 2012); Matthew Collins, *The Law of Defamation and the Internet* (3rd end, New York: Oxford University Press, 2010); David Price, Korieh Duodo, and Nicola Cain, *Defamation: Law, Procedure & Practice* (4th edn, London: Sweet & Maxwell, 2010).

Jennifer Skeem noted in relation to the Hare threat to sue that there was a concern that the lawsuit might be lodged in the United Kingdom or Canada which have comparatively more 'lax libel laws than those in the US'.[121] Some jurisdictions, such as Britain, for example, are said to be more 'plaintiff-friendly' and others, in particular the United States, are said to be more 'defendant-friendly'. This is largely because of the approach of the United States courts not to enter into acrimonious debates between academics, except where there has been an attack on character rather than just on ideas, by permitting defamation actions to succeed.[122] The perceived differences between jurisdictions have led to what is known as 'libel tourism' or forum shopping whereby legal proceedings are commenced in a jurisdiction that may have a limited or remote connection with the case but where laws that are more generous towards plaintiffs are seen to increase the chances of the case being won.[123]

United States Defamation Law

Courts in the United States have shown a reluctance to become involved in matters of academic debate, particularly where the matters of dispute are ones of opinion. The comments of Judge Easterbrook, of the United States Court of Appeals for the Seventh Circuit, in *Underwager v Salter*,[124] are indicative of the position that courts in the United States have generally taken. In that case two psychologists sued another psychologist who had written a book that was critical of the contents, conclusions, and methods contained in Underwager and Wakefield's controversial 1988 book, *Accusations of Child Sexual Abuse*, in which they had concluded that 'most accusations of child sexual abuse stem from memories implanted by faulty clinical techniques rather than from sexual contact between children and adults.'[125] Judge Easterbrook stated:

> Underwager and Wakefield cannot, simply by filing suit and crying 'character assassination!', silence those who hold divergent views, no matter how adverse those views may be to plaintiffs' interests. Scientific controversies must be settled by the methods of science rather than by the methods of litigation. Cf *Buckley v Fitzsimmons*, 20 F 3d 789, 796–97 (7th Cir. 1994). More papers, more discussion, better data, and more satisfactory models—not larger awards of damages—mark the path toward superior understanding of the world around us.[126]

In *Arthur v Offit*[127] a claim for defamation was dismissed by Judge Claude M Hilton of the United States District Court, Eastern District of Virginia. The case involved a magazine article regarding the public debate about the impact of vaccinations on children. In the article,

[121] Travis, above n 92, 1350.

[122] *Dilworth v Dudley*, 75 F 3d 307 (Ct App, 7th Cir, 1996); *Lott v Levitt*, 556 F 3d 564 (Ct App, 7th Cir, 2009); *Underwager v Salter*, 22 F 3d 730 (Ct App, 7th Cir, 1994).

[123] Lili Levi, 'The Problem of Trans-National Libel' (2012) 60(2) *American Journal of Comparative Law* 507, 508ff ; Trevor C Hartley, '"Libel Tourism" and Conflict of Laws' (2010) 59(1) *International and Comparative Law Quarterly* 25; Robert L McFarland, 'Please Do Not Publish This Article in England: A Jurisdictional Response to Libel Tourism' (2010) 79(3) *Mississippi Law Journal* 617, 625. Libel tourism is perceived to be such a problem that legislation has been passed in the United States to address it. The *Securing the Protection of our Enduring and Established Constitutional Heritage (SPEECH) Act* (2010) was introduced to prohibit 'recognition and enforcement within the United States of foreign defamation judgments inconsistent with First Amendment protections or based on an exercise of foreign court jurisdiction inconsistent with American constitutional due process requirements': Levi, ibid, 510 (footnotes omitted).

[124] 22 F 3d 730 (Ct App, 7th Cir, 1994).

[125] Ibid, 731.

[126] Ibid, 736.

[127] *Arthur v Offit* (D Va, Civ No 01:09-cv-1398, 10 March 2010); 2010 WL 883745; 2010 US Dist LEXIS 21946.

paediatrician and Professor at the University of Pennsylvania School of Medicine, Dr Paul Offit, said of the plaintiff, one of his critics, who was a public interest advocate and president and co-founder of a non-profit organization against mandatory vaccinations, that 'she lies'.[128] One of the key aspects of defamation law in the United States is that any allegedly defamatory statements that are said to be false statements of fact must be capable of being proven true or false.[129] His Honour cited *Fuste v Riverside Healthcare Association*[130] and *Marroquin v Exxon Mobil Corporation*[131] in support of the proposition that '[s]tatements of opinion are "relative in nature and depend largely upon the speaker's viewpoint," whereas statements of fact are those which are "capable of being proven true or false"'.[132]

Judge Hilton found that the statement 'she lies' could not be said to be a statement of fact in light of the context of the statement and, secondly, it was not a statement that was provably true or false.[133] That the courts do not see themselves in a position to determine who is right or wrong in scientific debate is reflected in Judge Hilton's comment that:

> [S]everal Fourth Circuit cases make clear that including a remark by one of the key participants in a heated public-health debate stating that his adversary 'lies' is not an actionable defamation. Indeed, both the nature of the statement—including that it was quoting an advocate with a particular scientific viewpoint and policy position—and the statement's context—a very brief passage in a lengthy description of an ongoing, heated public health controversy—confirms that this is a protected expression of opinion.[134]
>
> [...]
>
> The same prospect of litigation over unresolved—and perhaps unresolvable—scientific arguments was among the reasons that the accusations of lying in Faltas were deemed to be non-actionable. See 928 F. Supp. at 649 ('[T]he underlying issue was not one easily susceptible (if at all) to "proof" one way or the other'). Courts have a justifiable reticence about venturing into the thicket of scientific debate, especially in the defamation context.
>
> Plaintiff may wish to defend in Court the credibility of her conclusions about the dangers of vaccines, the validity of the evidence she offers in support of those theories, and the policy choices that flow from those views—as well as her own credibility for having advanced those positions. These, however, are academic questions that are not the sort of thing that courts or juries resolve in the context of a defamation action. Rather, an actual statement of fact that is capable of being proven true or false is required as a matter of law.[135]

The unwillingness of the courts in the United States to become involved in matters of academic and scientific debate is on the basis of constitutional rights to free speech, principles of academic freedom and a perception by judges that the courts are not equipped with the

---

[128] Ibid, 1 (WL); 2 (LEXIS).

[129] *Fuste v Riverside Healthcare Association*, 265 Va 127; 575 SE 2d 858 (Va Sup Ct, 2003); 2003 Va LEXIS 13; *Marroquin v Exxon Mobil Corporation* (D Va, Vic No 08-391, 27 May 2009); 2009 WL 1529455; 2009 US Dist LEXIS 44834; *Arthur v Offit* (D Va, Civ No 01:09-cv-1398, 10 March 2010); 2010 WL 883745; 2010 US Dist LEXIS 21946.

[130] 265 Va 127; 575 SE 2d 858 (Va Sup Ct, 2003); 2003 Va LEXIS 13.

[131] (D Va, Vic No 08-391, 27 May 2009); 2009 WL 1529455; 2009 US Dist LEXIS 44834.

[132] See *Fuste v Riverside Healthcare Association*, 265 Va 127; 575 SE 2d 858, 861–862 (Va Sup Ct, 2003); 2003 Va LEXIS 13, 8–9. See also, *Marroquin v Exxon Mobil Corporation* (D Va, Vic No 08-391, 27 May 2009); 2009 WL 1529455, 8; 2009 US Dist LEXIS 44834, 23; *Arthur v Offit* (D Va, Civ No 01:09-cv-1398, 10 March 2010); 2010 WL 883745, 4; 2010 US Dist LEXIS 21946, 12.

[133] *Arthur v Offit* (D Va, Civ No 01:09-cv-1398, 10 March 2010); 2010 WL 883745, 5–6; 2010 US Dist LEXIS 21946, 16–17.

[134] Ibid, 3 (WL); 7–8 (LEXIS).

[135] Ibid, 6 (WL); 17–18 (LEXIS).

expertise to determine who is right.[136] The constitutional right to free speech under the First Amendment of the United States Constitution[137] and the Constitutions of many American States provide protection for comments made in the course of scientific or academic debate.[138]

A claim for defamation consistent with the right to free speech requires a false statement of fact.[139] However, the constitutional safeguard of the First Amendment to the Constitution 'was fashioned to assure unfettered interchange of ideas for the bringing about of political and social changes desired by the people'.[140] It has been held to be 'a prized American privilege to speak one's mind, although not always with perfect good taste, on all public institutions'[141] and such an opportunity should be afforded for 'vigorous advocacy', no less than for 'abstract discussion'.[142] Justice Brandeis put the principle in this emotive way:

> Those who won our independence believed... that public discussion is a political duty, and that this should be a fundamental principle of the American government. They recognized the risks to which all human institutions are subject. But they knew that order cannot be secured merely through fear of punishment for its infraction; that it is hazardous to discourage thought, hope and imagination; that fear breeds repression; that repression breeds hate; that hate menaces stable government; that the path of safety lies in the opportunity to discuss freely supposed grievances and proposed remedies; and that the fitting remedy for evil counsels is good ones. Believing in the power of reason as applied through public discussion, they eschewed silence coerced by law—the argument of force in its worst form. Recognizing the occasional tyrannies of governing majorities, they amended the Constitution so that free speech and assembly should be guaranteed.[143]

In *New York Times Co v Sullivan*[144] the Supreme Court considered an alleged libel in which various statements about police action against students who had participated in a civil rights demonstration and against a leader of the civil rights movement were admitted to be false. Justice Brennan for the majority considered the case 'against the background of a profound national commitment to the principle that debate on public issues should be uninhibited, robust, and wide-open, and that it may well include vehement, caustic and sometimes unpleasantly sharp

---

[136] Compare the comments of Pagone J (overturned on appeal) in *Noone, Director of Consumer Affairs Victoria v Operation Smile (Australia) (No 2)* [2011] VSC 153, [16].

[137] The First Amendment of the United States Constitution states: 'Congress shall make no law respecting an establishment of religion, or prohibiting the free exercise thereof; or abridging the freedom of speech, or of the press; of the right of the people peaceably to assemble, and to petition the Government for a redress of grievances' (United States Constitution amend I).

[138] See *Freyd v Whitfield*, 972 F Supp 940, 945 (D Md, Civ No L-96-627, 18 July 1997), in which Judge Legg of the United States District Court for the District of Maryland stated: 'Indeed, the essence of the First Amendment is to shield the free speech of scientists and authors such as Dr Whitfield. The Constitution recognizes that scientific discourse in this country perseveres because of our "profound national commitment to the principle that debate on public issues should be uninhibited"'. *New York Times*, 376 U.S. at 270, 84 S.Ct. at 721. A rule requiring scientists and authors to guarantee the "truth" of their hypotheses would inevitably lead to self-censorship and would stifle the very debate that leads to scientific knowledge.' See also, *Stevens Institute of Technology v Hine*, 2007 WL 2188200, 11; 2007 NJ Super Unpub LEXIS 1268, 32, where Wefing, Parker, and Fisher JJ of the Superior Court of New Jersey stated 'Statements premised on matters that are subject to scientific debate are generally considered statements of opinion and not capable of having a defamatory meaning. *Freyd v. Whitfield*, 972 F. Supp. 940, 945–6 (D. Md. 1997).'

[139] *Journal-Gazette Co v Bandido's Inc*, 712 NE 2d 446, 457 (Ind, 1999); *Containment Technologies Group Inc v American Society of Health System Pharmacists*(D Ind, No 1:07-cv-0997-DFH-TAB, 26 August 2009); 2009 WL 2750093; 2009 US Dist LEXIS 25421.

[140] *Roth v United States*, 354 US 476, 484 (1957).

[141] *Bridges v California*, 314 US 252, 270 (1941).

[142] *National Association for the Advancement of Colored People v Button*, 371 US 415, 429 (1963).

[143] *Whitney v California*, 274 US 357, 375–6 (1927).

[144] 376 US 254 (1964).

attacks on government and public officials'.[145] He observed that in the realm of politics and religion sharp differences arise and that, to persuade others, people at times resort to 'exaggeration, to vilification of men who have been, or are, prominent in church or state, and even to false statement. But the people of this nation have ordained in the light of history, that, in spite of the probability of excesses and abuses, these liberties are, in the long view, essential to enlightened opinion and right conduct on the part of the citizens of a democracy'.[146]

In *McMillan v Togus Regional Office, Department of Veteran Affairs*[147] Senior District Judge Jack B Weinstein held, in a case involving studies on the effects of the herbicide Agent Orange, that it was not the courts' role to become involved in matters of scientific inquiry. In that case the plaintiff, a veteran of the Vietnam War, made claims that reports produced by the defendants involved a cover-up of the impact of Agent Orange. Judge Weinstein dismissed the plaintiff's claims and stated:

> The gist of the plaintiff's purported claims against the Academies is that the reports on Agent Orange are false, inaccurate, or incomplete. At an October 28 hearing on the instant case, the court raised the issues of the possible 'impact of challenges to free scientific inquiry in the country and the work of scientists and the degree to which scientific inquiry might or would be inhibited by permitting this kind of suit.' As noted below, several courts across the country have shared that concern, some specifically with respect to the work of the Academy.
>
> The First Amendment protects public debate on matters of public concern, including scientific matters. *See* U.S. Const. amend. I; *see also Dun & Bradstreet, Inc. v. Greenmoss Builders, Inc.*, 472 U.S. 749, 758–59, 105 S.Ct. 2939, 86 L.Ed.2d 593 (1985) (speech of public concern is at the core of the First Amendment's protections). As the Supreme Court has declared, '[a]t the heart of the First Amendment is the recognition of the fundamental importance of the free flow of ideas and opinions on matters of public interest and concern.' *Hustler Magazine v. Falwell*, 485 U.S. 46, 50, 108 S.Ct. 876, 99 L.Ed.2d 41 (1988). The Court has recognized that freedom of expression needs 'breathing space' to survive. *See New York Times Co. v. Sullivan*, 376 U.S. 254, 271–72, 84 S.Ct. 710, 11 L.Ed.2d 686 (1964). It has acknowledged this principle in the areas of academic and scientific debate. *See Sweezy v New Hampshire*, 354 U.S. 234, 250, 77 S.Ct. 1203, 1 L.Ed.2d 1311 (1957) ('Scholarship cannot flourish in an atmosphere of suspicion and distrust').
>
> Sound scientific studies are essential to our legal foundations as well as to individual justice. *See* Justice Stephen Breyer, *Introduction, Federal Judicial Center, Reference Manual on Scientific Evidence* (2d ed. 2000) (Reference Manual). As in political controversy, 'science is, above all, an adversary process. It is an arena in which ideas do battle... ' David Goodstein, 'How Science Works,' in *Reference Manual* 67, at 74. Our technology and lives depend on modern science. Any unnecessary intervention by the courts in the complex debate and interplay among the scientists that comprises modern science can only distort and confuse. Humility of judges is the *sine qua non* of the law's relation to science. See, e.g., Science, Technology, and Law Panel, Policy and Global Affairs, *National Research Council, Access to Research Data in the 21st Century, passim* (2002); Carnegie Commission on Science, Technology and Government (1992 and following). Scientists should not have to conduct their studies defensively, looking over their shoulders at unnecessary costly litigations.
>
> This court has previously cautioned against the potential chilling effect that litigation can have on scientific inquiry. In *Apicella v. McNeil Labs., Inc.*, 66 FRD 78, 85 (E.D.N.Y. 1975), it emphasized that '[f]ree communication in the vital area of health...should be encouraged.'[148]

[145] Ibid, 270.

[146] Ibid, 271.

[147] 294 F Supp 2d 305 (2003). The decision was affirmed on appeal in *McMillan v Togus Regional Office, Department of Veteran Affairs*, 120 Fed Appx 849 (2nd Cir, 2005).

[148] *McMillan v Togus Regional Office, Department of Veteran Affairs*, 294 F Supp 2d 305, 316–7 (2003).

Similarly, in *Metabolife International v Wornick*,[149] the United States District Court for the Southern District of California held that criticism via a television news report of diet drugs was not defamatory because it was protected opinion as it was part of a complex and unresolved scientific debate concerning the safety of ephedrine-based diet pills.

The threat to sue a critic of one's work in order to silence or 'chill' them has been met with the introduction of anti-SLAPP (Strategic Lawsuit to Silence Public Participation) legislation in some states in the United States.[150] Such legislation was effective in protecting academics who were critical of a medical product in *Containment Technologies Group Inc v American Society of Health System Pharmacists*,[151] a decision that applied Indiana's anti-SLAPP legislation in relation to a defamation suit against an academic journal and three authors who were critical of a product manufactured by the plaintiff.[152] The approach of anti-SLAPP legislation in the United States, and of the courts generally,[153] to strike out early unmeritorious claims of libel addresses a criticism often levelled at defamation proceedings in the United Kingdom. As is explored below, in contrast to the United States, claims in the United Kingdom can be brought against people who seek to criticize others or companies in the course of scientific debate with more ease.

United Kingdom Defamation Law

Libel laws in the United Kingdom have been the subject of considerable criticism in recent years and a number of cases involving scientists and academics have led to a vocal campaign to reform defamation laws in that country.[154] The cases of Dr Simon Singh, Dr Ben Goldacre, and Dr Peter Wilmshurst, who defended libel suits due to comments that they made in articles and blogs, are some of the most prominent cases that have received media attention.

Simon Singh, a science writer for *The Guardian* newspaper, was sued in 2008 by the British Chiropractic Association (a company limited by guarantee) for comments made in an article on 19 April 2008 where Singh criticized claims by the Association that spinal manipulation could be used as a treatment for children with asthma, ear infections, or colic, among other conditions.[155] Singh stated that there was 'not a jot of evidence' for the claims and labelled the treatments 'bogus'.[156] In a preliminary judgment in the matter to determine what the defamatory meaning or meanings of the words were and whether the allegedly defamatory words were factual or constituted comments, Eady J of the High Court of Justice, Queen's

[149] 72 F Supp 2d 1160 (D Cal, Civ No 99-1095-R, 17 November 1999).

[150] For example, see Arizona: Ariz Rev Ann §§ 12-751–12-752 (West 2006); Arkansas: Ark Code Ann §§ 16-63-501–16-63-508 (West 2005); California: Cal CCP Code §§ 425.16 (West, amended 2014), 425.17 (West, amended 2011), 425.18 (West 2005). For a full list of anti-SLAPP legislation in the United States, see Public Participation Project, 'State Anti-SLAPP Laws': <http://www.anti-slapp.org/your-states-free-speech-protection/> [accessed 31 Dec 2015].

[151] (D Ind, No 1:07-cv-0997-DFH-TAB, 26 August 2009); 2009 WL 2750093; 2009 US Dist LEXIS 25421. See also, Robert R Kuehn, 'Suppression of Environmental Science' (2004) 30(2–3) *American Journal of Law & Medicine* 333, 363; Poythress and Petrila, above n 99, 8–9.

[152] See also, Deering's *California Codes Annotated*, Cal Code Civ Proc § 425.16 (LEXIS), Notes of Decisions (1. Constitutionality) for a discussion of California anti-SLAPP legislation in the California Code of Civil Procedure.

[153] See *Arthur v Offit* (D Va, Civ No 01:09-cv-1398, 10 March 2010); 2010 WL 883745; 2010 US Dist LEXIS 21946.

[154] See The Libel Reform Campaign, 'Campaign Success in England and Wales': <http://www.libelreform.org/index.php> [accessed 31 Dec 2015].

[155] Simon Singh, 'How English Libel Law has a Global Chill on Free Speech' (2011) 47(6) *Cortex* 643.

[156] *British Chiropractic Association v Singh* [2010] EWCA Civ 350; [2011] WLR 133, [6].

Bench Division, held that those claims were verifiable assertions of fact, rather than opinion, and thus the defendant was required to prove that the meanings were factually true or he would lose the case.[157] The defendant, Singh, appealed this decision to the Court of Appeal which held that the litigation 'almost certainly had a chilling effect on public debate which might otherwise have assisted potential patients to make informed choices about the possible use of chiropractic'.[158] The claimant, the British Chiropractic Association, had been provided with the opportunity by *The Guardian* to publish an article refuting the criticisms of Dr Singh, but it chose not to do so. The Court of Appeal commented:

> By proceeding against Dr Singh, and not the Guardian, and by rejecting the offer made by the Guardian to publish an appropriate article refuting Dr Singh's contentions, or putting them in a proper perspective, the unhappy impression has been created that this is an endeavour by the BCA to silence one of its critics.[159]

The Court of Appeal held that Eady J was mistaken in finding that the statements by the defendant were statements of fact; rather the comments were statements of opinion, and were backed by reasons.[160] Following the decision of the Court of Appeal the British Chiropractic Association discontinued the libel suit. However, Dr Singh was reported to be out of pocket for over £100,000 for defending the matter.[161]

Another columnist in *The Guardian* newspaper, Dr Ben Goldacre, author of the column *Bad Science*, was also sued for libel in 2007 for comments made by him in his column regarding claims by Dr Matthias Rath that vitamin pills were more effective in treating AIDS that anti-retroviral drugs.[162] Dr Goldacre accused Matthias Rath in his column of endangering thousands of lives in South Africa as a result of his claims.[163] Dr Rath's case against *The Guardian* and Dr Goldacre collapsed, however, when the High Court of Justice refused to strike out parts of the defence filed in the proceedings and indicated that the defendants had a real prospect of showing that they met the defence of fair comment.[164] When the suit was withdrawn the court ordered costs against Dr Rath.[165]

Another controversial libel case involved Dr Peter Wilmshurst, a cardiologist from the United Kingdom, who was sued for comments made at a medical conference about a heart implant product made by a United States company NMT Medical.[166] After spending large amounts of money defending the claim, the plaintiff company NMT Medical went out of business leaving Dr Wilmshurst without recourse to recover legal costs.[167] Dr Wilmshurst's case and Dr Goldacre's case were said to highlight the ease with which claims can be brought under current law in the United Kingdom, encouraging libel tourism, but also that the costs of defending claims are so high that academics, journalists, and others are less likely to speak out

---

157 *British Chiropractic Association v Singh* [2009] EWHC 1101 (QB).

158 *British Chiropractic Association v Singh* [2010] EWCA Civ 350, [11].

159 Ibid, [12].

160 Ibid, [33].

161 Pallab Ghosh, 'Chiropractors' Libel Case Dropped against Simon Singh', *BBC News*, 15 April 2010: <http://news.bbc.co.uk/2/hi/8621880.stm> [accessed 31 Dec 2015].

162 *Rath v Guardian News and Media Limited and Goldacre* [2008] EWHC 398 (QB), [1] –[3].

163 Sarah Boseley, 'Fall of the Doctor who said his Vitamins would Cure Aids', *The Guardian*, 12 September 2008: <http://www.theguardian.com/world/2008/sep/12/matthiasrath.aids2> [accessed 31 Dec 2015].

164 *Rath v Guardian New and Media Limited and Goldacre* [2008] EWHC 398 (QB), [88].

165 Boseley, above n 163.

166 Ibid.

167 Alex Hern, 'Libel Reform Needs to Keep Writers Out of Court, Not Make It Easier to Win Once They're There', *New Statesman*, 28 June 2012: <http://www.newstatesman.com/blogs/politics/2012/06/libel-reform-needs-keep-writers-out-court-not-make-it-easier-win-once-theyre-there> [accessed 31 Dec 2015].

and, if they do, are perhaps more likely to settle due to the cost of litigation.[168] Not all cases resolve in this way, though, and some instead choose to respond by counter-suing for libel.[169]

The focus of the libel law reform campaign in the United Kingdom, which cited the above cases as examples (and which have all been the subject of media attention), is on the lack of public interest defence and the chilling effect on freedom of speech that this lack of a defence facilitates.[170] The campaign was successful in bringing about the introduction of the *Defamation Act* 2013 (UK). The legislation covers defamation law in England and Wales and, among other changes, introduces a public interest defence, a requirement that a statement must have caused serious harm to discourage trivial claims, and provides a defence (in s 6) of qualified privilege to peer-reviewed material in scientific and academic journals. However, the Libel Reform Campaign and its supporters have suggested the reforms do not go far enough.[171] Although protection is extended under the new legislation to peer-reviewed articles, commentators have suggested it will lead to very little change for cases such as those discussed above.[172]

Australia Defamation Law

In 2006 all Australian States and Territories enacted uniform defamation legislation which provides a remedy for injury to reputation caused by defamatory publications.[173] The legislation is based on common law principles which continue to apply unless the uniform legislation has modified the common law position.[174] The defences available are those under common law and those supplemented under the legislation.[175] The purpose of Australian defamation law is to strike a balance between the protection of reputation and freedom of speech.[176] However, the uniform defamation legislation scheme does not distinguish between libel and slander.[177]

---

168 Ibid; Dominic Crossley, 'Libel reform? Defamation is the Least of our Problems', *The Guardian*, 16 March 2011: <http://www.theguardian.com/law/2011/mar/16/libel-reform-defamation-least-of-problems> [accessed 1 Jan 2016].

169 David Leigh, 'Danish Scientist Sued by Drug Firm under British Libel Laws to Counterclaim', *The Guardian*, 16 February 2010: <http://www.theguardian.com/science/2010/feb/16/scientist-libel-law-henrik-thomsen> [accessed 1 Jan 2016]. Leigh discusses the case of Henrik Thomsen, a Danish radiologist who was sued by GE Healthcare for criticism at medical conferences and in written papers, about a product Omniscan, a contrast agent used when conducting MRI scans. Two days after the 16 February 2010 article by Leigh was published, the claimant, GE Healthcare, dropped its libel suit against Thomsen, stating it did not mean to stifle academic debate: see David Leigh, 'US Drug Firm Drops Libel Action Against Scientist', *The Guardian*, 18 February 2010: <http://www.theguardian.com/science/2010/feb/18/ge-healthcare-henrik-thomsen-libel> [accessed 1 Jan 2016].

170 Greg Jones, 'Libel Reform Campaigners Demand Better Public Interest Defence', *The Guardian*, 27 June 2012: <http://www.theguardian.com/science/2012/jun/27/libel-reform-campaigners-public-interest-defence> [accessed 1 Jan 2016].

171 Ibid.

172 Hern, above n 167.

173 Terence K Tobin and Michael Sexton, LexisNexis, *Australian Defamation Law and Practice* (at Service 75, March 2015), [1001]: see Defamation Act 2005 (NSW); Defamation Act 2005 (Qld); Defamation Act 2005 (SA); Defamation Act 2005 (Tas); Defamation Act 2005 (Vic); Defamation Act 2005 (WA); Civil Law (Wrongs) Act 2002 (ACT); Defamation Act 2006 (NT).

174 George, above n 120; Tobin and Sexton, above n 173, [1005].

175 Tobin and Sexton, above n 173, [1005].

176 George, above n 120, 122.

177 Tobin and Sexton, above n 173, [1015].

A person may have defamed another if a publication is 'likely to cause ordinary, reasonable persons to think the less of the plaintiff [that is, to damage the reputation of the plaintiff] or to shun or avoid the plaintiff'.[178] In order to satisfy this test the following factors must be made out by the plaintiff:

(a) the matter complained of is capable of being defamatory of the plaintiff;
(b) the defamatory meaning is in fact conveyed by the words used;
(c) the matter complained of was published by the defendant; and
(d) the matter complained of was published of and concerning the plaintiff.[179]

If each of these elements is not made out, the cause of action for defamation will fail.[180] However, if the situation described in this chapter of disputes such as that between Hare and Cooke and Skeem, and the other scenarios discussed below, arose in Australia and the test of defamation was met, there are various defences that may be available to defendants who are accused of defaming another in a publication, be it in an academic journal or in the media or via another forum. The key defences available under Australian law that could be applicable in a Hare-type scenario are:

- The defence of **justification**—where the defendant proves that the defamatory imputations are substantially true.[181]
- The defence of **contextual truth**—where the defendant proves that, in addition to the defamatory imputations, there are other contextual imputations that are substantially true and that the defamatory imputations do not further harm the reputation of the plaintiff because of the substantial truth of the contextual implications.[182]
- The defence of **fair report of proceedings of public concern**—where the defendant proves that the matter was or was contained in a fair report of any proceedings of public concern, or the defendant made a fair copy or summary or extract from an earlier published report of proceedings of public concern and was not aware that the earlier published report was not fair.[183] Proceedings of public concern cover a wide range of proceedings, including public proceedings of parliamentary bodies, international organizations of any countries or governments of any countries, courts and tribunals, inquiries held under law, local government bodies, proceedings of a learned society, or a committee under a governing body of the society, or proceedings under an ombudsman or a law reform body or any country.[184]
- The defence of **qualified privilege for provision of certain information**—where the defendant proves that the recipient has an interest or apparent interest in having information on some subject, the matter is published in the course of giving that information and the conduct of the defendant is reasonable in the circumstances.[185]

---

[178] Ibid, [3000]. For a detailed discussion of the elements of the test required to be met before a defamatory meaning will be found, see generally Tobin and Sexton, above n 173; and George, above n 120.

[179] Tobin and Sexton, above n 173, [10,001].

[180] Ibid.

[181] *Defamation Act* 2005 (NSW), s 25; *Defamation Act* 2005 (Qld), s 25; *Defamation Act* 2005 (SA), s 23; *Defamation Act* 2005 (Tas), s 25; *Defamation Act* 2005 (Vic), s 25; *Defamation Act* 2005 (WA), s 25; *Civil Law (Wrongs) Act* 2002 (ACT), s 135; *Defamation Act* 2006 (NT), s 22.

[182] *Defamation Act* 2005 (NSW), s 26; *Defamation Act* 2005 (Qld), s 26; *Defamation Act* 2005 (SA), s 24; *Defamation Act* 2005 (Tas), s 26; *Defamation Act* 2005 (Vic), s 26; *Defamation Act* 2005 (WA), s 26; *Civil Law (Wrongs) Act* 2002 (ACT), s 136; *Defamation Act* 2006 (NT), s 23.

[183] *Defamation Act* 2005 (Vic), s 29.

[184] *Defamation Act* 2005 (Vic), s 29(4).

[185] *Defamation Act* 2005 (NSW), s 30; *Defamation Act* 2005 (Qld), s 30; *Defamation Act* 2005 (SA), s 28; *Defamation Act* 2005 (Tas), s 30; *Defamation Act* 2005 (Vic), s 30; *Defamation Act* 2005 (WA), s 30; *Defamation Act* 2006 (NT), s 27; *Civil Law (Wrongs) Act* 2002 (ACT), s 139A.

- The defence of **honest opinion**—where the defendant proves that the he or she was expressing an opinion of the defendant rather than a statement of fact, that the opinion related to a matter of public interest and the opinion was based on proper material, as defined in the legislation.[186]

Further protection in the form of an absolute privilege may be available to the defendant if the defamatory comment was made in parliamentary proceedings or in a court or tribunal. Further, there is a defence if the defamatory matter was contained in a public document, as defined in the legislation, which includes government or parliamentary reports or documents, judgments or orders of courts and tribunals, and other similar documents listed.

Although there do not appear to have been similar cases in Australia where litigation (or threatened litigation) has arisen out of comments made in learned journals about scholarly work by other academics, such as occurred with Hare, Cooke, and Skeem, it is likely that, similar to that case, there have been threats to sue but they have not eventuated in litigation which has run its full course. While there is no explicit protection for those involved in academic debate as has been afforded in the United States courts, it is likely that the defendants would have a defence of honest opinion in Australia. In other instances, where an academic or scholar has criticized a person, company, or organization in a defamatory way, such as has occurred in widely publicized cases in the United Kingdom discussed below, the defence of qualified privilege may be available to a defendant on the basis of fair comment on a matter of public interest.[187] In comparison to the situation in the United States discussed below, where the courts have clearly shown an inclination not to become involved in matters of academic debate, this particular issue appears to be largely untested in Australia.

Mohamed El Naschie v Nature

A British libel case raising similar issues to the Singh, Goldacre, and Wilmshurst cases was that involving Mohamed El Naschie, an Egyptian professor who was the editor-in-chief of a theoretical physics journal, *Chaos, Solitons and Fractals*. In this case it was Professor El Naschie who sued Nature Publishing Group, the publisher of *Nature*, described by the High Court of Justice as 'one of the world's leading scientific journals', and one of its journalists, Quirin Schiermeier.[188] The action for libel came after Schiermeier wrote an article which was published on 27 November 2008 in *Nature*, entitled 'Self-publishing Editor Set to Retire'. The article suggested that Professor El Naschie, who had edited *Chaos, Solitons and Fractals* for 17 years, published numerous articles by himself, that these papers were of poor quality and had not been subjected to a proper peer-review process.[189] In addition to casting doubt over the professional and academic affiliations listed on El Naschie's website, the article stated:

> Most scientists contacted by *Nature* comment that El Naschie's papers tend to be of poor quality. Peter Woit, a mathematical physicist at Columbia University in New York, says he thinks that 'it's plain obvious that there was either zero, or at best very poor, peer review, of his own papers'. There is, however, little evidence that they have harmed the field as a whole.[190]

---

[186] Defamation Act 2005 (NSW), s 31; Defamation Act 2005 (Qld), s 31; Defamation Act 2005 (SA), s 29; Defamation Act 2005 (Tas), s 31; Defamation Act 2005 (Vic), s 31; Defamation Act 2005 (WA), s 31.

[187] See George, above n 120.

[188] *El Naschie v MacMillan Publishers Ltd (trading as Nature Publishing Group) and Schiermeier* [2012] EWHC 1809 (QB) [5].

[189] Quirin Schiermeier, 'Self-Publishing Editor Set to Retire' (2008) 456(7221) *Nature* 432.

[190] Ibid, 432.

In the *Nature* article El Naschie was quoted as rejecting the claims of 'sloppy peer review'.[191] He subsequently sued *Nature* and Schiermeier for libel, arguing that the article suggested that El Naschie had improperly misused his editorial privileges as editor-in-chief of *Chaos, Solitons and Fractals* in order to self-publish, that he had lied about his academic and professional affiliations, and that he was unfit to be editor and had been forced to retire.[192] The matter was the subject of a long trial in which the claimant appeared in person. The defendants had earlier sought in an interlocutory hearing to narrow and define the issues. Parts of the complaint had been struck out as a result.[193]

In the final judgment Justice Sharp (as she then was) found in favour of the defendants, determining that the article was the product of 'responsible journalism' and El Naschie's claim was dismissed.[194] As noted in the judgment, there was no dispute that the article in question was defamatory, but the issue was whether there was a defence of justification, honest comment or *Reynolds*[195] privilege.[196] As to whether a defence had been made out, Justice Sharp concluded that:

> [T]he Article is substantially true whether one considers the meanings complained of by the Claimant or justified by the Defendants (insofar as there is any difference), that it contains comments which are defensible as honest comment and that it was the product of responsible journalism, so that the defence of *Reynolds* privilege succeeds.[197]

Justice Sharp considered the overall impression of the article as well as the particular textual arguments raised by the parties and concluded that the article only suggested that the self-publication of papers by El Naschie may have created a 'falsely high impact factor', not that it actually did.[198] Also, she held that the article did not state that El Naschie had lied about his qualifications, only that the claim to be a distinguished fellow at the Institute of Physics at Johann Wolfgang Goethe University was false.[199] Nor did the article allege that El Naschie was forced to retire.[200]

There was extensive discussion in the judgment about the norms of editorial practice, peer review, and scientific publishing. Justice Sharp stated:

> It is apparent that the Claimant had little if any interest in the norms of scientific publishing or the ethical considerations which underpinned them. He said in evidence that he had not seen the Elsevier guidelines, but admitted he would not have followed them even if he had. Not surprisingly perhaps in those circumstances, his self-publication practices did not begin to comply with those norms of scientific publishing as they plainly should have done.[201]

However, Justice Sharp also noted that none of the normal safeguards was in place for when an editor publishes in his own journal.[202] She also held that there was a complete lack of

191 Ibid.

192 *El Naschie v MacMillan Publishers Ltd (trading as Nature Publishing Group) and Schiermeier* [2011] EWHC 1468 (QB) [4].

193 See generally, ibid.

194 [2012] EWHC 1809 (QB) [382].

195 *Reynolds v Times Newspapers Ltd* [2001] 2 AC 127. The *Reynolds* privilege refers to the application of qualified privilege over defamatory statements contained in publications that have been made in the public interest. In that case, Lord Nicholls held that the full range of circumstances should be considered and listed 10 factors that should be taken into account when determining whether the defence applied. This privilege was abolished in the Defamation Act 2013 (UK).

196 *El Naschie v MacMillan Publishers Ltd (trading as Nature Publishing Group) and Schiermeier* [2012] EWHC 1809 (QB) [8].

197 Ibid, [9].

198 Ibid, [25].

199 Ibid, [26].

200 Ibid, [28].

201 Ibid, [106].

202 Ibid, [107].

documentary evidence provided by the claimant to show that his papers had been the subject of peer review.[203] The *El Naschie* case, it was said by commentators, was further proof that United Kingdom libel laws did not protect people who were impecunious; that is, only people with substantial financial backing would be able to afford to defend claims and, in the *El Naschie* case, the publishers were well enough resourced to defend the claims made by El Naschie.[204]

Castigating Scholarly Reviews

Two centuries after John Keats nearly gave up writing poetry after a damning review of his first collection,[205] in 2007, a dispute erupted in the French courts over a critical book review published on a book review website <http://www.GlobalLawBooks.org> which is part of the *European Journal of International Law*. Criminal libel charges were laid in France against the editor of the journal for failing to withdraw the book review. The complainant, Karin Calvo-Goller, a senior lecturer in law at the Academic Center of Law and Business in Israel, sued the editor-in-chief of the *European Journal of International Law*, Professor Joseph Weiler, for refusing to remove a short review of her book, *The Trial Proceedings of the International Criminal Court*, by German academic, Professor Thomas Weigend, from the University of Cologne.[206] Weigend himself was not sued for libel. In his review Weigend wrote:

> What the reader—and presumably the judges of the Court as well—would hope to receive is a principled analysis of the Court's general procedural structure as well as suggestions for the possible resolution of some of the 'hard questions' that have been left open by the drafters of the legal instruments pertaining to the Court's operation. Regrettably, Karin Calvo-Goller's book does not offer either.... This exercise in rehashing the existing legal set-up is particularly unproductive since a large part of the volume consists in a reprint of the ICC Statute and its Rules of Procedure and Evidence (the Court's Regulations are consistently ignored).
>
> [...]
>
> Karin Calvo-Goller has undoubtedly invested much time and effort into this book, which—but for regrettably sloppy editing—might well serve as a first systematic introduction to the procedural issues confronting the ICC. What is still missing is a book that might help to resolve these issues.[207]

The defendant editor refused to remove the review but offered the plaintiff the right of reply on the website, which she refused.[208] The editor still declined to remove the review on the basis that it was not libellous and to do so would have 'seriously compromised academic

---

[203] Ibid, [180].

[204] Daniel Cressey, 'Nature Publishing Group Wins Long-Running Libel Trial', *Nature*, 6 July 2012: <http://www.nature.com/news/nature-publishing-group-wins-long-running-libel-trial-1.10965> [accessed 2 Jan 2016].

[205] See Stanley Plumly, *Posthumous Keats: A Personal Biography* (New York: WW Norton, 2008). Lord Byron somewhat insensitively joked that Keats was 'snuff'd out' by a later adverse review: see further, Nicholas Roe (ed), *Keats and History* (Cambridge: Cambridge University Press, 1995) 42; Nicholas Roe, 'Mercury Sent John Keats to an Early Grave', *The Telegraph*, 6 October 2012: <http://www.telegraph.co.uk/culture/books/9591165/Mercury-sent-John-Keats-to-an-early-grave.html> [accessed 2 Jan 2016].

[206] Jennifer Howard, 'French Court Finds in Favor of Journal Editor Sued for Libel Over Book Review', *The Chronicle of Higher Education*, 2 March 2011: <http://chronicle.com/article/French-Court-Finds-in-Favor-of/126599/> [accessed 2 Jan 2016].

[207] Thomas Weigend, 'Short Review: *The Trial Proceedings of the International Criminal Court: ICTY and ICTR Precedents* by Karin N Calvo-Goller': <http://www.globallawbooks.org/reviews/detail.asp?id=298> [accessed 2 Jan 2016].

[208] Howard, above n 206.

freedom and the intellectual integrity of EJIL [*European Journal of International Law*] and book reviewing generally'.[209]

The plaintiff was criticized widely in blogs and online media for bringing the complaint in France when the connection with the country was tenuous—she was based in Israel and the editor was based in the United States—and was perceived to be forum shopping or engaging in libel tourism.[210] Ultimately, the Tribunal de Grand Instance de Paris agreed with those criticisms and on 3 March 2011 upheld the defence arguments that the French court did not have jurisdiction and that the laying of the criminal complaint in the circumstances of the case amounted to an abuse of process.[211] The Tribunal dismissed the matter for want of jurisdiction and ordered the plaintiff to pay €8,000.[212]

An unofficial translation of the judgment which was in French was posted on the EJIL: Talk! blog website by Professor Weiler.[213] The Tribunal de Grand Instance de Paris found:

> Karin Calvo-Goller has thus acknowledged that she practised what is called forum shopping, in other words looking around the world for the judicial system which seems to be the most favourable to the claim made by the person taking the initiative of applying to a court, and placing such person's adversary, for legal and also practical reasons due to the geographic or cultural distance, in the more disadvantageous situation; the choice, which was artificial in this case, of the French court, added to the choice of a criminal procedure by filing a complaint with an investigating judge resulting in dishonour and considerable expense for the accused, denotes this abuse of process.
>
> In addition, Karin Calvo-Goller misjudged the scope of the French law of the press when she states that the review in issue could be held to be defamatory; in fact, the review of her book does not contain anything prejudicial to her honour and reputation and merely expresses, in terms which are in fact restrained, a scientific opinion of a work which never goes beyond the limits of free criticism to which any author of an intellectual work is exposed.
>
> The bad faith of the complainant—who is a jurist familiar with French law since she indicates that she studied law in France—is therefore unquestionably established.[214]

In an article discussing the *Weiler* case, before the final decision of the court, Sutherland expressed concern for the 'implications of this case for all those who write, edit, and publish critical scholarly work'.[215] Many of her concerns mirrored those expressed by Poythress and Petrila on the Psychopathy Controversy, particularly the chilling effect that libel actions have on the academy. The troubling prospect of libel tourism was also a concern—particularly '[e]ven more daunting than the idea of facing a defamation lawsuit at home is that of facing such a suit in a foreign jurisdiction that may offer less protection to academic freedom and impose more severe sanctions'.[216]

---

209 Joseph Weiler, 'In the Dock, in Paris—The Judgment' on *EJIL: Talk!* (4 March 2011): <http://www.ejiltalk.org/in-the-dock-in-paris-%E2%80%93-the-judgment-by-joseph-weiler-2/> (viewed 19 March 2015).

210 Adam Liptak, 'From a Book Review to a Criminal Trial in France', *The New York Times*, 21 February 2011: <http://www.nytimes.com/2011/02/22/us/22bar.html?_r=0> [accessed 2 Jan 2016].

211 *Public Prosecutor v Weiler*, Tribunal de Grand Instance de Paris, 0718523043, 3 March 2011, available at: <http://www.jura.uni-freiburg.de/institute/ioeffr2/weiterfuehrendelinksdokumenteordner/dokumenteordner/alte-beitraege/publicprosecutor-weiler/view> (viewed 19 March 2015).

212 Howard, above n 206.

213 An English translation of the judgment is available on the EJIL: Talk! website at <http://www.ejiltalk.org/wp-content/uploads/2011/03/Public-Prosecutor-v-Weiler-judgement-March-3-2011-3.pdf> [accessed 2 Jan 2016], as is the French version: see <http://www.ejiltalk.org/wp-content/uploads/2011/03/judgement-3-mars-2011.pdf> [accessed 2 Jan 2016].

214 *Public Prosecutor v Weiler*, Tribunal de Grand Instance de Paris, 0718523043, 3 March 2011, 4.

215 Kate Sutherland, 'Book Reviews, The Common Law Tort of Defamation, and the Suppression of Scholarly Debate' (2010) 11(6) *German Law Journal* 656, 657. cp Joseph Weiler, 'Book Reviewing and Academic Freedom' (2010) 20(4) EIJL 968.

216 Ibid, 667.

Sutherland noted that in Canada an aggrieved author would have to seek a remedy for defamation in tort, rather than in criminal law, as was the case for Professor Weiler. In Canada, in order to be successful, Calvo-Goller would have had to show three things: '(1) that the words at issue were defamatory; (2) that they referred to the plaintiff; and, (3) that they were published... For the words to count as defamatory, they must be such that "they would tend to lower the plaintiff's reputation in the eyes of a reasonable person." In making this determination, the context in which the words are communicated must be considered.'[217]

In applying the Canadian test to the facts of the *Weiler* case, Sutherland suggested that a *prima facie* case of defamation would have been quite easy because of the low threshold for establishing defamatory meaning.[218]

As Sutherland observed in her discussion of the *Weiler* case, defences to defamation in Canada include fair comment (that is the comment is in the public interest, based on fact, recognizable as comment, whether it could be objectively considered honest opinion and there was no malice),[219] justification, and responsible communication on matters of public interest.[220] However, as she noted, there is uncertain protection in Canada for freedom of expression.[221]

McGinn on Honderich/Honderich on McGinn

It might be suggested that the review of Calvo-Goller's book is mild when compared to others. A feud between two philosophy academics, Professors Colin McGinn[222] and Ted Honderich, over a much more critical book review has received a similar amount of attention

[217] Ibid, 657.

[218] Ibid, 658. The test for defamation is discussed in Lebel J's dissenting judgment in *WIC Radio Ltd & Mair v Simpson* [2008] 2 SCR 420.

[219] See *WIC Radio Ltd & Mair v Simpson* [2008] 2 SCR 420, [67]–[69] (paragraph numbers omitted): 'Although defamation is not easily defined, one generally accepted test is the one from *Salmond on the Law of Torts* (17th ed. 1977), at pp. 139–140, which is based on the test proposed by Lord Atkin in *Sim v. Stretch* (1936), 52 T.L.R. 669 (H.L.), at p. 671, and was approved by the B.C. Court of Appeal in *Vander Zalm v. Times Publishers* (1980), 109 D.L.R. (3d) 531, at p. 535:

> A defamatory statement is one which has a tendency to injure the reputation of the person to whom it refers; which tends, that is to say, to lower him in the estimation of right-thinking members of society generally and in particular to cause him to be regarded with feelings of hatred, contempt, ridicule, fear, dislike, or disesteem.

This test is often construed as setting a low threshold for establishing *prima facie* defamation. *Gatley on Libel and Slander* (10th ed. 2004) ('*Gatley*'), notes that 'it may well be the case that the common law takes a rather generous line on what lowers a person in the estimation of others' (p. 18, footnote 32). Dickson J made a similar point in *Cherneskey v. Armadale Publishers Ltd* [1979] 1 SCR 1067, in referring to the 'low level of the threshold which a statement must pass in order to be defamatory' (1095).

The case law generally bears these opinions out. However, courts should not be too quick to find defamatory meaning—particularly where expressions of opinion are concerned. The test is not whether the words impute negative qualities to the plaintiff, but whether, in the factual circumstances of the case, the public would think less of the plaintiff as a result of the comment. Relevant factors to be considered in assessing whether a statement is defamatory include: whether the impugned speech is a statement of opinion rather than of fact; how much is publicly known about the plaintiff; the nature of the audience; and the context of the comment.'

[220] Sutherland, above n 215, 658.

[221] Ibid, 669.

[222] See Chapter 9 (p 419) in relation to McGinn's resignation from the University of Miami for sexual misconduct.

in blogs and in the media.[223] In a review of Honderich's book *On Consciousness* in Cornell University's *Philosophical Review*, McGinn began his review with the comment:

> This book runs the full gamut from the mediocre to the ludicrous to the merely bad. It is painful to read, poorly thought out, and uninformed. It is also radically inconsistent.[224]

McGinn's book review did not become more positive. According to accounts in the media, his criticisms are part of a 'very public feud between two philosophers involving damning book reviews, professional roastings and personal slights [which] shows how bitter, unforgiving—and unwittingly hilarious—academic spats can be'.[225] Honderich petitioned the *Philosophical Review* to provide 'some fair redress', such as a discussion on the subject, but was told by the editor-in-chief that the policy is 'not to publish replies to book reviews'.[226] Honderich appealed that decision to members of the editorial board on the basis that the review had brought the publication into disrepute. However, the board determined that there was no compelling reason to make an exception to its usual policy.[227]

McGinn and Honderich were observed to have used 'all the modern weapons at their disposal—blogs, emails, demands for compensation from the academic journal that published the original review, an online counter-review, and an online counter-counter-review'.[228] Where the line is drawn on the boundaries of academic debate is a difficult issue, perhaps depending on the extent to which criticism is objectively unjustifiable and also on the extent to which it trespasses into the personal away from the scholarly. The McGinn critique did not result in legal action but it resulted in entertainment for academic and media circles with many blogs and some news articles commenting on the feud.[229] Ultimately, Honderich is reported as having reflected that 'the tubful of personal insults by McGinn has had a good effect on me'. He added: 'It has made me see that objections already familiar to me, mainly by contributors to a book about my theory, have to be given more attention.'[230]

Orlando Figes

Technology provides a level of anonymity which gives some 'the courage' (or lack of common sense in some situations) to use language to which they may not otherwise have recourse. In 2010, historian and academic Orlando Figes, Professor of Russian History at the University of London's Birkbeck College, wrote disparaging and anonymous fake reviews of books by fellow historians Dr Rachel Polonsky and Professor Robert Service on the Amazon website.[231] His reviews spoke highly of his work while denigrating those of Polonsky and

[223] Stuart Jeffries, 'Enemies of Thought', *The Guardian*, 21 December 2007: <http://www.theguardian.com/books/2007/dec/21/highereducation.news> [accessed 2 Jan 2016]; Patricia Cohen, 'The Nature of Reasons: Two Philosophers Feud Over a Book Review', *The New York Times*, 12 January 2008: <http://www.nytimes.com/2008/01/12/books/12feud.html?_r=2&> [accessed 2 Jan 2016].

[224] Colin McGinn, 'Ted Honderich, *On Consciousness*' (2007) 116(3) *Philosophical Review* 474, 474.

[225] Jeffries, above n 223.

[226] Cohen, above n 223.

[227] Ibid.

[228] Jeffries, above n 223.

[229] Ibid; Cohen, above n 223; McLemee, above n 6.

[230] Cohen, above n 223.

[231] Richard Lea and Matthew Taylor, 'Historian Orlando Figes Admits Posting Amazon Reviews that Trashed Rivals', *The Guardian*, 23 April 2010: <http://www.theguardian.com/books/2010/apr/23/historian-orlando-figes-amazon-reviews-rivals> [accessed 2 Jan 2016]; Alexandra Topping, 'Historian Orlando Figes Agrees to Pay Damages for Fake Reviews', *The Guardian*, 16 July 2010: <http://www.theguardian.com/books/2010/jul/16/orlando-figes-fake-amazon-reviews> [accessed 2 Jan 2016].

Service.[232] When allegations were levelled at Figes that he had written the reviews, he threatened Polonsky, Service, journals, and newspapers with legal action for libel.[233] In a bizarre twist, he then blamed his wife, a barrister, for writing the 'savage' reviews,[234] only to confess at a later point that he had in fact been the author.[235] Figes was subsequently sued by Polonsky and Service and was required to pay damages and circulate an apology and retraction.[236] He expressed shame for his behaviour and maintained that he did not 'entirely understand why I acted as I did. Some of the reviews I now see were small minded and ungenerous, but they were not intended to harm'.[237] He then retreated into the 'medical condition defence'—'[t]his crisis has exposed some health problems, though I offer that more as explanation than excuse. I need some time now to reflect on what I have done and the consequences of my actions with medical help'.[238]

It was subsequently noted in the British media, however, that the case highlighted the need for libel law reform because, had the true identity of the writer of the book reviews not been discovered by Rachel Polonsky, Figes may have been successful in his threats to sue, as the pressure on Polonsky and Service to settle was not insubstantial.[239] Faced with the cost of fighting libel allegations in the United Kingdom not only has a chilling effect on academic discussion but it also places pressure to settle cases without fighting them.[240]

Cyberstalking

Improprieties involving academics and their responses to perceived wrongs can take many forms. In 2011 Elizabeth Grierson, head of the Fine Art Department at the Royal Melbourne Institute of Technology (RMIT), sought and was granted a temporary intervention order

---

232 Topping, above n 231.

233 Martin Bentham, 'Orlando Figes' Folly Shows Why We Need Libel Law Reform', *Evening Standard*, 27 April 2010: <http://www.standard.co.uk/news/orlando-figes-folly-shows-why-we-need-libel-law-reform-6463455.html> [accessed 2 Jan 2016].

234 Topping, above n 231; Rachel Polonsky, 'How I Rumbled the Lying Professor: The Story Behind the Discredited Don Who Rubbished Rivals on Amazon… Then Left His Own Wife to Take the Blame', *Daily Mail*, 25 April 2010: <http://www.dailymail.co.uk/news/article-1268660/How-I-rumbled-lying-professor-The-story-discredited-don-rubbished-rivals-Amazon--left-wife-blame.html> [accessed 2 Jan 2016]; John Walsh, 'Historian's Wife and Her Poison Pen Expose Darkside of Literary Criticism', *The Independent*, 20 April 2010: <http://www.independent.co.uk/arts-entertainment/books/news/historians-wife-and-her-poison-pen-expose-dark-side-of-literary-criticism-1948812.html> [accessed 2 Jan 2016].

235 Topping, above n 231.

236 Ibid. Compare Robert Gullis, a postdoctoral student in biochemistry at Birmingham University, who also worked at the Max Planck University in Munich, who eventually had little choice but to retract 11 papers that he had written or co-written. Ultimately, he wrote a letter to *Nature*, apologizing for his results having been fraudulent and admitting that they were 'figments of my imagination, and during my short career I published my hypotheses rather than experimentally determined results… The reason was that I was so convinced of my ideas that I simply put them down on paper': 'Biochemist Admits Scientific Fraud', *The Age*, 25 February 1977, 7, available at: <https://news.google.com/newspapers?nid=1300&dat=19770225&id=JPpUAAAAIBAJ&sjid=WZIDAAAAIBAJ&pg=3585,6471852&hl=en> [accessed 2 Jan 2016]; 'Violating Nature' (1977) 109(11) *Time* 74, available from: Academic Search Complete (accessed 20 March 2015).

237 Laura Roberts, 'Award-Winning Historian Orlando Figes: I posted Anonymous Reviews on Amazon', *The Telegraph*, 24 April 2010: <http://www.telegraph.co.uk/culture/books/booknews/7624186/Award-winning-historian-Orlando-Figes-I-posted-anonymous-reviews-on-Amazon.html> [accessed 2 Jan 2016].

238 Ibid.

239 Robert Service, 'The Shame of Orlando Figes', *The Guardian*, 23 April 2010: <http://www.theguardian.com/commentisfree/libertycentral/2010/apr/23/figes-shameful-admission> [accessed 2 Jan 2016].

240 Bentham, above n 233. See also, Jackson, Rupert, *Review of Civil Litigation Costs: Final Report* (The Stationery Office, December 2009), available at: <https://www.judiciary.gov.uk/publications/review-of-civil-litigation-costs-reports/> [accessed 2 Jan 2016].

against a former employee in her Department, Steve Cox. The asserted reason for her application was a series of comments and images that she had learned he had posted on his private Facebook page and on a second Facebook page, 'Save Art From RMIT'.[241] Mr Cox had been critical of Ms Grierson's administration of the Department, including funding cuts that he argued had led to its degrees no longer being recognized internationally.

Ms Grierson claimed that she needed an intervention order against Mr Cox 'for her personal safety and well-being', and said the fact Mr Cox's artwork 'indicates obsession with murder' led her to fear for her safety.[242] Mr Cox had been sacked as a lecturer by RMIT in January. He was also a painter whose subjects include Moors murderers Ian Brady and Myra Hindley. Those paintings, he said, 'helped get me the job at RMIT in the first place'.[243] Mr Cox's posts featured online drawings and caricatures which Professor Grierson argued looked like her. Sometimes the drawings featured a spider's body, sometimes a fly, other times a dung-beetle.[244]

The matter was settled by the giving of mutual undertakings to the Melbourne Magistrates Court without resolution of the legal issue of principle—whether one can be stalked by conduct which requires one to take action to find out whether it is being perpetrated, namely inspecting social networking sites. It raises serious issues relating to freedom of speech. Pragmatically, Mr Cox undertook to refrain from referring to Ms Grierson 'with malice' and agreed to remove three posts to which she took objection from his personal Facebook page.[245] He otherwise remained free of the constraints Ms Grierson had sought to impose, leading him to hail the result as a victory for his entitlement to continue to be critical of his former boss.[246] For her part, Ms Grierson undertook not to 'look at [Mr Cox's] Facebook page' or 'cause her servants or agents to look at or otherwise monitor [Mr Cox's] Facebook page' for a period of 20 years.[247]

Offensiveness

One of the most difficult issues in relation to 'scholarly freedom' and 'freedom of speech' generally is where the limits should be placed and when oral or written expression should be fettered because of the harm and distress it is likely to cause. As identified above, the academy and discourse about matters of public interest have been asserted to be forums deserving of special latitude in respect of such matters. However, just as defamation law, varying as it does from country to country, imposes limits in this regard, so too does legislation precluding incitement to violence and hatred, as do legislative constraints on discriminatory behaviour. However, the law generally does not intrude to inhibit tasteless, politically incorrect, or broadly offensive utterances. An important distinction may also exist between things written or said in a private context as against in a public sphere, including as part of scholarly

[241] Karl Quinn, 'Art School Altercation Puts New Spin on Cyberstalking', *The Age*, 14 April 2011: <http://www.theage.com.au/technology/technology-news/art-school-altercation-puts-new-spin-on-cyberstalking-20110413-1de72.html#ixzz1JmmOqE9I> [accessed 2 Jan 2016].

[242] Ibid.

[243] Ibid.

[244] ABC Radio National, 'Cyberspace Spat: Shutting Down Satire', *National Interest*, 15 April 2011 (Damien Carrick): <http://www.abc.net.au/radionational/programs/nationalinterest/cyberspace-spat-shutting-down-satire/3014292> [accessed 2 Jan 2016].

[245] Quinn, above n 241.

[246] Ibid.

[247] Ibid.

discourse. Arguably, when writing is done from work or using work equipment, particular obligations also flow.

Racial vilification laws exist in many countries;[248] scholars are not excepted and, in fact, have proved on a number of occasions to be the defendants to such prosecutions. In Germany,[249] Austria,[250] Romania,[251] and Israel,[252] to name but some, denial or trivialization of the genocidal behaviour of the Holocaust has been criminalized, curtailing the expression of disrespectful minimizing or questioning of the facts of what occurred. In Lithuania and Poland,[253] this has been extended to statements of approval or denial also of Soviet crimes. In Spain,[254] Hungary, and Luxembourg,[255] 'negationism and revisionism' laws in relation to crimes against humanity or genocide (non-specifically) have been banned by criminal statutes.[256]

A number of well-known scholars have utilized forums to promote their theories about the Holocaust either being a hoax or being exaggerated. The most notorious is the English historian, David Irving, who never held a university position but who, over many years in approximately 30 books and many public addresses, promoted an anti-Semitic ideology and espoused what became known as 'Holocaust Denial' and historical revisionism.

In 1992 he was fined in Germany for asserting that the Auschwitz gas chambers were a hoax. In 2000, though, he invoked the assistance of the legal system himself, bringing what became a landmark and infamous defamation action in the English High Court,[257] alleging that he had been libelled in a book written by Deborah Lipstadt, entitled *Denying the Holocaust—The Growing Assault on Truth and Memory*.[258] The two defendants were the book's author and its publisher, Penguin Books.

---

[248] In Australia, see *Racial Discrimination Act 1975* (Cth), s 18B; *Racial and Religious Tolerance Act 2002* (Vic), s 8; *Catch the Fire Ministries Inc v Islamic Council of Victoria Inc* [2006] VSCA 284; (2006) 15 VR 207; *Toben v Jones* [2003] FCAFC 137; (2003) 129 FCR 515.

[249] On 'incitement to hatred', section 130 of the German Criminal Code states the following:

(1) Whosoever, in a manner capable of disturbing the public peace
  1. incites hatred against segments of the population or calls for violent or arbitrary measures against them; or
  2. assaults the human dignity of others by insulting, maliciously maligning, or defaming segments of the population,

shall be punished with imprisonment from three months to five years.

[…]

(3) Whosoever publicly or in a meeting approves of, denies or downplays an act committed under the rule of National Socialism of the kind indicated in Section 6 (1) of the Code of International Criminal Law, in a manner capable of disturbing the public peace shall be liable to imprisonment not exceeding five years or a fine.

(4) Whosoever publicly or in a meeting disturbs the public peace in a manner that violates the dignity of the victims by approving of, glorifying, or justifying National Socialist rule of arbitrary force shall be liable to imprisonment not exceeding three years or a fine: *Strafgesetzbuch* [Criminal Code] (Germany) §§ 130(1), 130(3), 130(4).

[250] *Verbotsgesetz* [Prohibition Act] 1947 (Austria) § 3h.

[251] Emergency Ordinance No 31 of March 2002 (Romania), art 6.

[252] Denial of Holocaust (Prohibition) Law 5746-1986 (Israel).

[253] *Baudžiamasis kodeksas* [Criminal Code] (Lithuania) § 170(2); Act of 18 December 1998 on the Institute of National Remembrance (Commission for the Prosecution of Crimes Against the Polish Nation) (Poland).

[254] *Código Penal* [Penal Code] (Spain), Book II, Title XXIV, Chapter I, art 607 bis (1).

[255] See *Code Penal* [Criminal Code] (Luxembourg) Title VIII, Chapter VI, art 457-3.

[256] See eg, Switzerland where this is incorporated under the preclusion upon racial discrimination. See also, Bert Klandermans and Nonna Mayer, 'Context, Alliances and Conflict' in Klandermans and Mayer (eds), *Extreme Right Activists in Europe: Through the Magnifying Glass* (London: Routledge, 2006) 31.

[257] *Irving v Penguin Books Limited* [2000] EWHC QB 115.

[258] Deborah E Lipstadt DE, *Denying the Holocaust: The Growing Assault on Truth and Memory* (London: Penguin, 1994).

Irving complained that certain passages in the book accused him of being a Nazi apologist and an admirer of Adolf Hitler. He claimed that Lipstadt had portrayed him as having resorted to the distortion of facts and to the manipulation of documents in support of his contention that the Holocaust did not take place. He argued that the book was part of a concerted attempt to ruin his reputation as an historian and he sought damages accordingly. The defendants, while they did not accept the interpretation which Irving placed on the passages complained of, asserted that it was true that Irving was discredited as an historian by reason of his denial of the Holocaust and by reason of his persistent distortion of the historical record so as to depict Hitler in a favourable light. They maintained that the claim for damages for libel in consequence had to fail. Irving represented himself.

In a very lengthy decision Justice Gray emphasized 'that those reading this judgment should bear well in mind the distinction between my judicial role in resolving the issues arising between these parties and the role of the historian seeking to provide an accurate narrative of past events'.[259] Having considered the various arguments advanced by Irving to assail the effect of the convergent evidence relied on by the defendants, Justice Gray concluded:

> [N]o objective, fair-minded historian would have serious cause to doubt that there were gas chambers at Auschwitz and that they were operated on a substantial scale to kill hundreds of thousands of Jews.
>
> [...]
>
> [I]t appears to me to be incontrovertible that Irving qualifies as a Holocaust denier. Not only has he denied the existence of gas chambers at Auschwitz and asserted that no Jew was gassed there, he has done so on frequent occasions and sometimes in the most offensive terms.[260]

He also concluded that Irving's views were anti-Semitic in the sense that they 'are directed against Jews, either individually or collectively, in the sense that they are by turns hostile, critical, offensive and derisory in their references to semitic people, their characteristics and appearances'.[261] While he accepted that Irving was not obsessed with race, he observed: 'He has certainly not condoned or excused racist violence or thuggery. But he has on many occasions spoken in terms which are plainly racist. Racism is to be condemned even if it is confined, as in Irving's case, to expressions of the kind which I have mentioned.'[262] He found Irving to have associated with a variety of neo-Nazis who denied the Holocaust and were anti-Semitic.[263] He found that the evidence established that Irving had been revealed by the evidence of his extra-curricular activities to be a 'right-wing pro-Nazi polemicist' who was prepared to manipulate the historical record 'in order to make it conform with his political beliefs'.[264] This led him to the conclusion that the evidence did not enable him to accept Irving's contention that his falsification of the historical record was the product of innocent error or misinterpretation or incompetence on his part: '[I]t appears to me that the correct and inevitable inference must be that for the most part the falsification of the historical record was deliberate and that Irving was motivated by a desire to present events in a manner consistent with his own ideological beliefs even if that involved distortion and manipulation of historical evidence.'[265]

259 *Irving v Penguin Books* [2000] EWHC QB 115, [1.3].
260 Ibid, [13.91], [13.95].
261 Ibid, [13.101].
262 Ibid, [13.108].
263 Ibid, [13.115].
264 Ibid, [13.161]–[13.162]
265 Ibid, [13.163].

He found most of the defamatory imputations of Irving were substantially justified in that they were true and, to the extent that others were not justified, they had no relevant effect on Irving's reputation:

> The charges which I have found to be substantially true include the charges that Irving has for his own ideological reasons persistently and deliberately misrepresented and manipulated historical evidence; that for the same reasons he has portrayed Hitler in an unwarrantedly favourable light, principally in relation to his attitude towards and responsibility for the treatment of the Jews; that he is an active Holocaust denier; that he is anti-semitic and racist and that he associates with right wing extremists who promote neo-Nazism. In my judgment the charges against Irving which have been proved to be true are of sufficient gravity for it [sic] be clear that the failure to prove the truth of [them] . . . does not have any material effect on Irving's reputation.[266]

This meant that the defence of justification succeeded and Irving's claim failed.

The costs awarded against Irving were of very extensive proportions. Lipstadt, by contrast, was appointed by President Clinton to the United States Holocaust Memorial Council. The failed defamation action was not to be the end of Irving's legal problems, however.

In 2006 an eight-member jury convicted Irving in Vienna of the criminal offence in Austria of denying the Holocaust—in two speeches he made in a visit he made in 1989. The speeches called for an end to the 'gas chambers fairy tale' and claimed that the Holocaust was a myth.[267] Outside court Irving expressed the view that it was 'ridiculous' that he was being tried for expressing an opinion and maintained that 'it's a question of freedom of speech'.[268] In court Irving claimed that he had revised his opinion after seeing the personal files of Adolf Eichmann and, speaking in German, said that he now accepted that the Nazis had killed millions of Jews.[269] He was sentenced to three years' imprisonment but on appeal this was reduced after he had served 13 months in jail; he was permitted to serve the remainder of his term on probation in part because his conduct had taken place 17 years before.[270]

However, Irving is not alone in his views, including among employees within academia. For instance, Kaukab Siddique, who taught literature and mass communications at Lincoln University in Pennsylvania, has also used public forums to declare the Holocaust a hoax, claiming to speak for the 'other side' of the issue.[271] So also has Arthur Butz, a professor of electrical engineering at Northwestern University in the United States.[272]

---

[266] Ibid, [13.167].

[267] 'David Irving Jailed for Holocaust Denial', *The Guardian*, 20 February 2006: <http://www.theguardian.com/world/2006/feb/20/austria.thefarright> [accessed 2 Jan 2016].

[268] 'Holocaust Denier Irving is Jailed', *BBC News*, 20 February 2006: <http://news.bbc.co.uk/2/hi/europe/4733820.stm> [accessed 2 Jan 2016].

[269] See 'David Irving Jailed for Holocaust Denial', above n 267.

[270] 'Holocaust Denier Released from Prison: David Irving Free After 13 Months in Jail', *Der Spiegel*, 20 December 2006: <http://www.spiegel.de/international/holocaust-denier-released-from-prison-david-irving-free-after-13-months-in-jail-a-455726.html> [accessed 2 Jan 2016].

[271] See Cary Nelson, 'It Depends on the Context' in 'Does Academic Freedom Protect Holocaust Deniers?' *The Chronicle of Higher Education*, 14 November 2010: <http://chronicle.com/article/Does-Academic-Freedom-Protect/125295/> [accessed 2 Jan 2016]; Dan Berrett, 'Academic Freedom and Holocaust Denial', *Inside Higher Ed*, 26 October 2010: <https://www.insidehighered.com/news/2010/10/26/siddique> [accessed 2 Jan 2016]; Naomi Schaefer Riley, 'Apparently, If You're in the Right Discipline' in 'Does Academic Freedom Protect Holocaust Deniers?' *The Chronicle of Higher Education*, 14 November 2010: <http://chronicle.com/article/Does-Academic-Freedom-Protect/125295/> [accessed 2 Jan 2016].

[272] See Arthur R Butz, *The Hoax of the Twentieth Century: The Case Against the Presumed Extermination of European Jewry* (Chicago, Ill: Theses & Dissertations Press, 2003), available at: <http://vho.org/aaargh/fran/livres3/HoaxV2.pdf> [accessed 2 Jan 2016].

However, in 2014 the ambit of legitimate dissent in relation to political/race issues became highly contentious in the United States when a University of Illinois professor, Steven Salaita, did not have his tenure renewed after making anti-Israeli tweets in relation to the Gaza conflict. Two examples were: 'Only Israel can murder around 300 children in the span of a few weeks and insist that it is the victim'; and 'If Netanyahu appeared on TV with a necklace made from the teeth of Palestinian children, would anybody be surprised?'[273] The second of these tweets clearly adverted to Holocaust atrocities, and made a highly emotive and contentious comparison that many (including this author) would find highly offensive.

In justifying his dismissal, university officials described his comments as 'uncivil', saying they represented 'disrespectful and demeaning speech that promotes malice'.[274] Since then, a number of academics have mounted a boycott of the university, campaigning against the treatment of Salaita, and saying it is not the role of the academy to dictate what constitutes civil discourse.[275] They also claimed that Illinois University had become too beholden to wealthy donors who they asserted were informally dictating decisions involving hiring and tenure. Internal emails surfaced that suggested the university's decision to terminate the employment of Salaita was motivated by threats from wealthy donors. In a 29 August 2014, the American Association of University Professors in Washington maintained that Salaita's 'online statements [should be seen] as extramural activity as a citizen rather than as faculty performance'.[276]

The distinction between what is 'civil' and what is 'uncivil' is nebulous to say the least and whether a bright line can properly be drawn between 'extramural' and 'mural' activities when a person is known to have a particular (and privileged) role in the academy is doubtful. While it is important to ensure that censorship does not intrude into university life as a means of prohibiting statements that are 'politically incorrect', 'merely' offensive or iconoclastic, the Salaita reinforces the reality that there are certain kinds of utterances whose subject matter and resonances are widely perceived to be unacceptably and gratuitously distressing. Whether they are made in emotional, off-the-cuff tweets or emails or in a more formal way, it is apparent that academics will suffer consequences if they engage in such grossly insensitive and offensive conduct, protestations and rationalizations about free speech notwithstanding.

An interesting contrast to the debate about the unacceptability of anti-Semitic utterances occurred with the debate engendered by the offer of an honorary degree in social justice by Brandeis University to Ayaan Hirsi Ali, the Somali-born, formerly Dutch but more latterly American activist, and author of the challenging contemporary analyses of Islam, *Nomad*,[277] *Infidel*,[278] and *Heretic*.[279] Ali became a fellow at Harvard University's John F Kennedy School of Government. She had contended over a period of time overtly that Islam is a religion of violence and in 2007 called for a war on Islam. Her analysis was highly divisive and thereby caused considerable offence to many Muslims. An outcry followed the offer to her in 2014 of an honorary degree.[280]

---

273 See Mark Guarino, 'Professor Fired for Israel Criticism Urges University of Illinois to Reinstate Him', *The Guardian*, 9 September 2014: <http://www.theguardian.com/education/2014/sep/09/professor-israel-criticism-twitter-university-illinois> [accessed 2 Jan 2016].

274 Ibid.

275 David Palombo-Liu, 'A Reply to Nathaniel Zelinsky: "Anti-Israel" Professor Shouldn't Have been Fired', *Huffington Post*, 10 November 2014: <http://www.huffingtonpost.com/david-palumboliu/a-reply-to-nathaniel-zeli_b_5666304.html> [accessed 2 Jan 2016].

276 Guarino, above n 273.

277 Ayaan Hirsi Ali, *Nomad: A Personal Journal Through the Clash of Civilizations* (New York: Simon & Schuister, 2010).

278 Ayaan Hirsi Ali, *Infidel* (New York: Simon & Schuster, 2008).

279 Ayaan Hirsi Ali, *Heretic: Why Islam Needs a Reformation Now* (New York: Harper Collins, 2015).

280 See Isaac Chotiner, 'Ayaan Hirsi Ali Controversy Is About Double Standards, Not Freedom of Speech' (13 April 2014) *New Republic*: <http://www.newrepublic.com/article/117348/ayaan-hirsi-ali-brandeis-

Some 85 of 350 faculty members signed a letter urging that she be removed from the list of honorary degree recipients. Amongst many others, a spokesperson for the Council on American–Islamic Relations, the largest Muslim advocacy group in the United States, was reported as saying that: 'It is unconscionable that such a prestigious university would honor someone with such openly hateful views.'[281]The university reversed its position, in turn putting in a new light the challenge of identifying the limits to freedom of expression and scholarly discourse. However, notably Brandeis University still invited her to come to the university to 'engage in a dialogue'. Nonetheless, the Ayaan Hirsi Ali episode drew attention to the fact that there are many ways in which a genuinely scholarly contribution to an important contemporary issue can be experienced as deeply offensive to important sectors within the community, raising the issue as to where lines should be drawn in terms of encouraging or permitting such contributions to be made.

In Australia, in the lead-up the Victorian State election in 2014, a related phenomenon was encountered. A member of the Young Liberals with endorsement to stand as a candidate in the election, Aaron Lane, lost both his endorsement and also his position as a sessional academic in the Law Faculty at Deakin University for homophobic tweets. A spokesperson for the university declined to elaborate but confirmed that the tutor 'won't be employed at Deakin any longer'.[282]

Shortly afterwards, also in 2014, Australia's first professor of poetry and poetics, Barry Spurr, was suspended from the University of Sydney after revelations in an online journal, *New Matilda*, that he had sent emails over a two-year period which described the Prime Minister, Tony Abbott, 'as an "Abo lover", Aboriginal people as "human rubbish tips", Nelson Mandela as a "darkie" and Desmond Tutu as a "witch doctor".[283] It emerged that he had also referred to "Mussies" (Muslims), "fatties, darkies and chinky-poos" in an email to a colleague[284] and described the university's chancellor as an "appalling minx".[285]

The issues arising in respect of Professor Spurr had a political relevance because he had played a role for the conservative federal government's national English curriculum review. He had asserted in his report to the review that 'the impact of Aboriginal and Torres Strait Islander peoples on literature in English in Australia has been minimal' and advised a greater emphasis on the western literary canon.[286] His views were contentious and did not conform with those of many progressive and modern educationalists although they fell on receptive ears within

controversy; Richard R Perez-Pena and Tanzina Vega, 'Brandeis Cancels Plan to Give Honorary Degree to Ayaan Hirsi Ali, A Critic of Islam' (8 April 2014) *The New York Times*: <http://www.nytimes.com/2014/04/09/us/brandeis-cancels-plan-to-give-honorary-degree-to-ayaan-hirsi-ali-a-critic-of-islam.html?_r=0> [accessed 2 Jan 2016]; 'Enlightened Intolerance' (16 April 2014) *The Economist*: <http://www.economist.com/blogs/democracyinamerica/2014/04/ayaan-hirsi-ali> [accessed 2 Jan 2016]; Benjamin Wallace-Wells, 'What Was Brandeis Thinking When it Invited Ayaan Hirsi Ali to Speak?' (15 April 2014) *New York Magazine*: <http://nymag.com/daily/intelligencer/2014/04/what-was-brandeis-thinking.html?> [accessed 2 Jan 2016].

281 See 'Brandeis Withdraws Honorary Degree for Islam Critic Ayaan Hirsi Ali' (9 April 2014) *The Guardian*: <http://www.theguardian.com/world/2014/apr/09/brandeis-withdraws-honorary-degree-ayaan-hirsi-ali-college> [accessed 2 Jan 2016].

282 Deborah Gough, 'Deakin University Dumps Disgraced Liberal Aaron Lane', *The Sydney Morning Herald*, 2 August 2014: <http://www.smh.com.au/national/deakin-university-dumps-disgraced-liberal-aaron-lane-20140802-zzpg0.html> [accessed 2 Jan 2016].

283 Julie Harepatricia Karvelas, 'Spurr Suspended for Racist Emails', *The Australian*, 17 October 2014: <http://www.theaustralian.com.au/higher-education/spurr-suspended-for-racist-emails/story-e6frgcjx-1227094079705> [accessed 2 Jan 2016].

284 Ibid. See also, 'Students Rally as Uni Suspends Spurr', *Honi Soit*, 17 October 2014: <http://honisoit.com/2014/10/students-rally-as-uni-suspends-spurr/> [accessed 2 Jan 2016].

285 See Gay Alcorn, 'Professor Barry Spurr Suspended by Sydney University Over Offensive Emails', *The Guardian*, 17 October 2014: <http://www.theguardian.com/australia-news/2014/oct/17/professor-barry-spurr-suspended-by-sydney-university-over-offensive-emails> [accessed 2 Jan 2016].

286 Ibid.

the government. The political opportunity was gratefully embraced by those in opposition, leading to politicization of his offensive comments to colleagues. The Labor Party contended that the revelations about Professor Spurr had seriously damaged the credibility of the review findings and the Australian Education Union asserted that the review had been 'an ideological waste of time from the start'.[287]

A spokesman for the university said that it was 'deeply disturbed' by the reports of the contents of Professor Spurr's emails and that racist, sexist, or offensive language was not tolerated at the University of Sydney.[288] Professor Spurr maintained that the emails were part of a 'whimsical linguistic game' with a colleague in which they would try to 'outdo one another in extreme statements'[289] and then sought refuge in the assertion that his emails had been hacked and asserted that the difficulties he was in were because of his participation in a high-profile national. *New Matilda* published more of his email correspondence, in effect suggesting that his assertion about the 'game' with his colleague did not adequately answer its concerns.[290]

One of the responses of Professor Spurr was to seek an injunction from the Federal Court of Australia to remove the stories from the *New Matilda* website, for *New Matilda* to surrender all copies of the emails, and for *New Matilda* to identify the source of the leaks. He argued that *New Matilda* grossly breached his privacy in the publication of the story, and that he was 'collateral damage' in a campaign by *New Matilda* against the federal government.[291] However, in the course of the litigation Professor Spurr withdrew the application to compel *New Matilda* to identify the source. Justice Wigney issued an interim injunction preventing New Matilda from publishing any new material related to the emails was extended until the substantive hearing.[292]

While the investigation was still being undertaken into his conduct, opinions were expressed from multiple sources about Professor Spurr's conduct. Barry Humphries, the well-known comedian and satirist, bewailed the loss of a sense of humour and the onset of 'the new puritanism' in Australia.[293] However, another view was powerfully expressed by an open letter addressed to vice-chancellors by almost 130 academics and professional staff who warned that more needed to be done to educate and foster respect for gender equality, multiculturalism, and Australia's Aboriginal and Indigenous heritage.[294] It argued that the public debate triggered by Professor Spurr's emails showed there was a need for Australian universities to be proactive and reflect on their anti-discrimination policies: 'This means much more than

---

[287] Ibid.

[288] Julie Hare and Patricia Karvelas, 'Unpoetic Emails Derail Sydney Uni Professor Barry Spurr', *The Australian*, 17 October 2014: <http://www.theaustralian.com.au/higher-education/unpoetic-emails-derail-sydney-uni-professor-barry-spurr/story-e6frgcjx-1227093417695> [accessed 2 Jan 2016].

[289] Ibid.

[290] Chris Graham, 'The Transcripts: The Partial Works of Professor Barry Spurr. Poet, Racist, Misogynist', *New Matilda*, 19 October 2014: <https://newmatilda.com/2014/10/19/transcripts-partial-works-professor-barry-spurr-poet-racist-misogynist> [accessed 2 Jan 2016].

[291] Bridie Jabour, 'Barry Spurr Drops Legal Action to Force New Matilda to Reveal Source of Emails', *The Guardian*, 23 October 2014: <http://www.theguardian.com/australia-news/2014/oct/23/barry-spurr-drops-legal-action-to-force-new-matilda-to-reveal-source-of-emails> [accessed 2 Jan 2016].

[292] See ibid; Richard Ackland, 'Barry Spurr v New Matilda: The Facts, the Law and the Porridge', *The Guardian*, 24 October 2014: <http://www.theguardian.com/commentisfree/2014/oct/24/barry-spurr-v-new-matilda-the-facts-the-law-and-the-porridge> [accessed 2 Jan 2016].

[293] Barry Humphries, 'Letters' in 'Barry Spurr Case Shows the New Puritanism is Alive and Well', *The Australian*, 21 October 2014: <http://www.theaustralian.com.au/opinion/letters/barry-spurr-case-shows-new-puritanism-is-alive-and-well/story-fn558imw-1227096485063> [accessed 2 Jan 2016].

[294] See Alexandra Smith, 'Academics Urge Universities to Act on Race and Gender Discrimination', *The Sydney Morning Herald*, 31 October 2014: <http://www.smh.com.au/national/education/academics-urge-universities-to-act-on-race-and-gender-discrimination-20141031-11f1px.html> [accessed 2 Jan 2016].

noble sentiments in the guidelines or on the website, but a review process to ensure that procedures and policies are put into practice and outcomes reviewed... The current investigation of Professor Spurr by the University of Sydney must take its course, but universities more broadly must become more proactive in the future, to address such behaviours not as an individual but as a systemic problem'.[295] The letter also expressed concerns regarding the lack of seriousness applied to complaints involving 'harassment, bullying and vilification', and the reluctance of students to 'speak up' due to fears of possible retaliation.[296] On this point, it was noted that universities should ensure students are protected from inappropriate behaviour: 'There is a culture of treating sexual harassment and assault (for example, that take place within student accommodation) as an internal administrative issue... However, sexual assault is a criminal offence, and those who experience assault must be fully supported to take whatever measures they deem appropriate, including referral to the police. We would like to see Australian universities—starting with vice chancellors—demonstrate greater political will and ethical obligation towards protecting their staff and students.'[297]

In December 2014 Professor Spurr arrived at a controversial settlement of his litigation against *New Matilda*. A few days later he resigned his position at the University of Sydney. The university immediately accepted his resignation.[298]

The emails of Professor Spurr, which unquestionably contained offensive expressions, generated a passionate debate in Australia about when private communications (indicative of the holding of racist, sexist, and other socially unacceptable views) should be regarded as incompatible with occupation of a prominent role in public life, including within the academy. They also raised the difficult distinction between public and private correspondence—once again, the mural/extra-mural distinction. Notably though, and not unusually, the University of Sydney policy about usage of university computer equipment stated that: 'The University will not tolerate its ICT Resources being used in a manner that is harassing, discriminatory, abusive, rude, insulting, threatening, obscene or otherwise inappropriate.'[299] This rendered any sending of emails by any member of staff that had 'inappropriate' characteristics vulnerable to serious sanction as a breach of workplace obligations.

As one commentator observed, in correspondence such as that of Professor Spurr, we may see an authentic version of public bigotry: 'And in this authenticity the person becomes diminished. By their own words they have been exposed as racist, or cruel, or grasping. But who has clean hands when it comes to email?'[300] This suggests that institutional responsiveness to the conduct may not be necessary as public censure may be an adequate controlling mechanism. However, the reality with conduct such as that of Professor Spurr is that there is an abuse of the expectations and rules of the institution for responsible and temperate conduct which is respectful of the sensitivities and circumstances of others who may be vulnerable.

---

295 Ibid.

296 Ibid.

297 Ibid.

298 John Ross, 'Controversial Academic Barry Spurr Resigns from University of Sydney', *The Australian*, 18 December 2014: <http://www.theaustralian.com.au/higher-education/controversial-academic-barry-spurr-resigns-from-university-of-sydney/story-e6frgcjx-1227160310382> [accessed 2 Jan 2016].

299 University of Sydney, 'Policy on the Use of University Information and Communication Technology Resources (ICT Resources)' 2: <http://sydney.edu.au/policies/showdoc.aspx?recnum=PDOC2011/140> [accessed 2 Jan 2016].

300 Brigid Delaney, 'After Nova Peris and Barry Spurr, Should We all Give Up on Email in the Name of Privacy?', *The Guardian*, 29 October 2014: <http://www.theguardian.com/commentisfree/2014/oct/29/should-we-all-give-up-on-email-in-the-name-of-privacy> [accessed 2 Jan 2016].

Particular kinds of speech and expression of views are regulated by the laws of many countries. However, there is also the public marketplace in which censure for racist, sexist, gendered, and offensive views (which may be legal, albeit unedifying) can be brutal and such as to render a person's hold on prominent positions, including within universities, highly problematic. Further contaminants which can militate in the direction of potentially career-destroying criticism can be cultural and political. Scholars occupy no privileged place in this regard and, if they breach the law or contemporary values, or seek to test the limits of them so that they can be viewed as a martyr to free speech or to a particular cause, or in the exercise of humorous exchanges, the consequences for them can be most unpleasant. Privacy as a concept and a value has changed fundamentally in the electronic age. There are many ways in which confidential communications can emerge into the public domain to the embarrassment and disgrace of those responsible for them. Whether such communications can be justified or rationalized as private, occurring within an exculpating context, or not made with any notion that they may become public, soon becomes not the issue. Rather the question arises as to whether the expression of such sentiments renders a person unfit to hold the relevant position.

The Consequences of Unresolved Disputation

An aspect of a propensity on the part of some members of staff to engage in inappropriate forms of disputation or harassment can be obsessiveness and paranoia that can become psychotic or spill over into personality disordered rage. Occasionally, if not arrested at an early juncture, this can have terrible consequences. Two of these—at Concordia University and the University of Alabama—are now described. The cases highlight the importance for institutions always to take expressions of distressed aggrievement and serial disputations within the workplace seriously (as well as apparent symptomatology of mental illness) so as to optimize the prospects of stopping as early as possible any deterioration into ruminative psychosis. They are extreme examples of scholarly disputation within the workplace, in most respects transcending such a designation because of their criminality, and the appalling facts which underpin them, but the mental health factors that give rise to them are common to many scenarios that do not have a manifestation in outright violence. In addition, what preceded the eruption of the individuals into homicidal conduct was ongoing engagement in intra-mural disputation, a form of behaviour that many institutions struggle with when the persons involved are highly intelligent and manifest a sense of aggrievement which verges or crosses over into the pathological.

The Concordia University Tragedy

In late 1979 Valery Fabrikant attended at the office of TS Sankar, the chairman of the Mechanical Engineering Department at Concordia University in Montreal.[301] He claimed (falsely) to be a Jewish dissident from the Soviet Union and was successful in persuading Sankar to take him on as a research assistant. The appointment was successful in some respects as Fabrikant was a good teacher and a productive publisher of scholarly papers in scientific journals in the years after his appointment. However, while Sankar supported him, Fabrikant was not well liked as he was seen by most as rude, overbearing, and arrogant. In 1982 a student said he had raped her and dislocated her shoulder. Although she filed a police report to this effect, her complaints were not taken further. Although journal editors and

[301] Founded five years earlier in 1974 by the amalgamation of Sir George Williams University, originally a YMCA night school for working adults, and Loyola, a Jesuit college some five miles away.

others continued to complain about Fabrikant's manner, Sankar tolerated him and endured his eccentricities.

Fabrikant became more and more angry about the practice of scientists to share credit for research publications, especially his own. He regarded it as 'scientific prostitution' and took to using hidden tape-recorders to try to catch persons with whom he had collaborated admitting that they had not made proper contributions to his papers.[302] This did not endear him within the department, resulting in his becoming increasingly isolated and absorbed by his grievances. He labelled colleagues as 'parasites', filed lawsuits against other researchers and communicated his antagonism via emails to scholars throughout North America, maintaining that people had stolen his ideas.[303] He aspired to tenure but, given his behaviour, was not successful in obtaining it.[304] This led him to become progressively more paranoid and antagonistic towards Concordia University. Staff met and became concerned about his potential to become violent. One psychiatrist thought he was potentially dangerous and could become violent; another advised that his personality disorder required the setting of firm limits on his behaviour. A review of Fabrikant's marking showed that he had been inflating the marks of his students, including by marking wrong answers as correct.

On 23 June 1992 Fabrikant attended at the university, seeking permission for him to own and carry a handgun. This was identified as a threat and various secretaries at the university applied to have panic buttons installed at their desks. Although staff lobbied for Fabrikant to be suspended on pay, the fateful decision was made that there was not enough evidence for such a step.

Finally, on 24 August 1992 Fabrikant's anger boiled over. He walked calmly onto the Concordia University Campus, wearing sunglasses and a dark suit. With him he had three handguns and a briefcase full of bullets. First, he fatally shot the president of the Concordia Faculty Association, and then he killed two other scientists and then a civil engineering professor. Next he shot a secretary and barricaded himself in an office with two hostages, then telephoned police to whom he spoke for an hour. He put his gun down briefly to adjust the telephone. This gave one of the hostages a chance to kick his gun away and the other to overpower him.

Seventeen days later the Faculty dismissed Fabrikant. He was found guilty of four homicides, in the process firing ten attorneys who were appointed to represent him and taking over his own representation. He was determined at trial to establish his own fitness to stand trial but accused police of planting false evidence, including pouring extra blood on one of his victims; the judge of having a false prisoner attack him on the way to court; and the court system of engaging in a conspiracy against him. This resulted in a one-month hearing as to his fitness to stand trial. Two psychiatrists called for the prosecution declared Fabrikant fit for trial and not out of touch with reality. They said he suffered from a severe personality disorder which impacted on his interactions with others and resulted in his seeing threats and persecution in many places where it did not exist and being grossly self-absorbed and therefore insensitive to others.

[302] Mara Bovsun, 'Crazy Professor Valery Fabrikant Kills 4 in Concordia University Rampage', *New York Daily News*, 21 April 2013: <http://www.nydailynews.com/news/justice-story/justice-story-college-prof-kills-4-article-1.1320928> [accessed 2 Jan 2016].

[303] Ibid.

[304] Morris Wolfe, 'Dr Fabrikant's Solution', *Grubstreet Books*: <http://www.grubstreetbooks.ca/essays/fabrikant.html> (viewed 21 March 2015).

Fabrikant then called his own psychiatrist who testified that Fabrikant was unfit for trial because he was 'pathologically narcissistic' and had not only lost grip on the purpose of the trial but was unable to communicate with his lawyer.[305] Fabrikant used this testimony to assert that psychiatry was completely unreliable.

The trial proceeded and Fabrikant was found guilty of the charges. He was sent to prison for life but will become eligible for parole in 2017. Since going to prison Fabrikant has filed multiple actions in Canada's courts asserting a range of grievances[306] and has been declared a vexatious litigant. The prison limited his internet access[307] but Fabrikant continued to write. However, the *International Journal of Solids and Structures* declined to publish an article written by Fabrikant from his cell at Donnacona Penitentiary. The prospect of his returning to scholarly publication prompted opposition from the Rector of Concordia and also the Dean of Engineering and Computer Science who argued that, just as Fabrikant had forfeited his right to freedom, so too had he forfeited the right to disseminate his scientific views. There was an ambivalent response from one of Fabrikant's former colleagues at Concordia University, Professor John Drysdale: 'On one hand it's reprehensible for Fabrikant to continue to publish, especially if it means an advancement or aggrandisement or if it gives any kind of advantage to his parole. On the other hand, to deny anyone the possibility of publication goes against a deeply embedded belief held by the academic community.'[308]

After the tragic events, Concordia University's Board of Governors initiated two independent inquiries, one by a former Vice-Rector of the University of Ottawa into Fabrikant's employment history, and the other by a former president of York University into academic and scientific integrity at Concordia. The latter report established that Fabrikant's grievances about misappropriation of authorship in some papers had not been entirely misplaced. It observed:

> Dr Fabrikant was thwarted in his search for a tenured professorship. First, he gathered evidence with which to blackmail his way into an appointment; then he attempted to force the University to appoint him; then he tried to destroy the reputation of those he thought responsible for his rejection; and finally, in despair and anger, he killed four innocent bystanders in cold blood, and gravely wounded a fifth.
>
> There is no basis whatsoever for speculation that this chain of tragic events could have been broken, that a vengeful murderer might have been mollified or neutralized, by a timely public finding of malfeasance against those whom he accused.[309]

A review of Fabrikant's case shows the deterioration in his behaviour and the escalation in his anger. The wisdom of hindsight shows many signs of his increasing risk of violence. As Kelleher has observed: 'There were many warning signs given by Fabrikant, making his case one of the best documented of its kind. Much could have been done, but was not. The management paralysis that gripped the university authorities was, in retrospect, horrifying and inexplicable.'[310] The case provides many lessons in how to deal with a person

---

[305] Ibid.

[306] See 'Court Freezes Out Killer Professor's Demand for Second Winter Parka', *Maclean's*, 1 December 2013: <http://www.macleans.ca/news/canada/court-freezes-out-killer-professors-demand-for-second-winter-parka/> [accessed 2 Jan 2016].

[307] Bovsun, above n 302.

[308] 'Killer Professor Gagged', *Times Higher Education*, 10 June 1996: <http://www.timeshighereducation.co.uk/news/killer-professor-gagged/93891.article> [accessed 2 Jan 2016].

[309] Harry W Arthurs, Roger Blais, and Jon Thompson, *Integrity in Scholarship: A Report to Concordia University* (April 1994) 2: <https://schoolshooters.info/sites/default/files/Arthurs_report%20on%20%20 Fabrikant.pdf> (viewed 6 January 2015).

[310] Michael D Kelleher, *New Arenas for Violence: Homicide in the American Workplace* (Westport, Conn: Praeger, 1996) 89.

who is descending into more and more anti-social, anti-collegiate behaviour, and showing signs of morbid obsessions and anger.

The University of Alabama Tragedy

The Fabrikant murders had a dreadful echo on 12 February 2010 when a biology professor at the University of Alabama in Huntsville, Amy Bishop, taught her usual anatomy and neuroscience classes and then attended a routine meeting of the department. At its conclusion, she drew a nine-millimetre handgun and shot dead three academic colleagues and shot and injured three others.[311]

Bishop held a PhD in genetics from Harvard University and joined the University of Alabama as an Assistant Professor in 2003. In 2009 she had been denied tenure[312] and expected not to have her teaching contract renewed after March 2010.[313] She appealed the decision to refuse her tenure and filed a discrimination complaint against the university.

Subsequent investigation into Bishop's background established, extraordinarily, that in 1986, when she was 21, Bishop fatally shot her brother at their home in Braintree, Massachusetts but, as a result of her mother's exculpating account, the view was taken that what had happened was an accident and she was not charged with any offence until, after a further investigation, on 16 June 2010, she was charged with her brother's first-degree murder. Two days later she unsuccessfully attempted suicide. In 1994 Bishop had also been questioned about a letter-bomb incident involving a doctor at the faculty where she had previously been employed but no criminal charges ensued. In 2002 Bishop was charged with assaulting a woman at a restaurant but was found not guilty.

Initially Bishop pleaded not guilty to the University of Alabama murders, maintaining she was not guilty by reason of insanity. However, after the prosecution decided not to seek the death penalty, Bishop (pragmatically) changed her plea to guilty and, on 24 September 2012,[314] was sentenced to life imprisonment without the possibility of parole.[315] She appealed during 2013, maintaining she had not been correctly informed of the minimum range of imprisonment but the Court of Criminal Appeals of Alabama rejected her appeal.

Relatively little information exists in relation to what rendered Amy Bishop homicidally angry. It appears that her moods could be labile and her anger intense, as exemplified by the incident involving her brother: 'Over the years, Dr Bishop had shown evidence that the smallest of slights could set off a disproportionate and occasionally violent reaction, according to numerous interviews with colleagues and others who know her. Her life seemed to veer wildly between moments of cold fury and scientific brilliance, between rage at perceived

---

311 See Michele McPhee, *A Professor's Rage: The Chilling True Story of Harvard Ph.D. Amy Bishop, Her Brother's Mysterious Death, and the Shooting Spree that Shocked the Nation* (New York: St Martin's Press, 2011).

312 Her case for tenure was weak, given her limited publication record: see Gina Kolata, 'A Case for Tenure that Some See as Falling Short', *The New York Times*, 20 February 2010: <http://www.nytimes.com/2010/02/21/us/21science.html?ref=amybishop&_r=1> [accessed 2 Jan 2016].

313 Her husband later said that Dr Bishop believed that her denial of tenure had been caused, at least in part, by a miscommunication about whether two papers had been published in time to count towards her bid for tenure: Thomas Bartlett and Robin Wilson, 'Husband of Accused Huntsville Killer Amy Bishop Speaks Out', *The Chronicle of Higher Education*, 14 February 2010: <http://chronicle.com/blogs/ticker/husband-of-accused-huntsville-killer-amy-bishop-speaks-out/21254> [accessed 2 Jan 2016].

314 Jay Reeves, 'Amy Bishop Guilty: Former Professor Admits to Murder in University of Alabama Shooting', *Huffington Post*, 12 September 2012: <http://www.huffingtonpost.com/2012/09/12/amy-bishop-guilty_n_1876858.html> [accessed 2 Jan 2016].

315 'Professor Amy Bishop Gets Life in Prison for Alabama University Shooting', *NBC News*, 24 September 2012: <http://usnews.nbcnews.com/_news/2012/09/24/14068705-professor-amy-bishop-gets-life-in-prison-for-alabama-university-shooting?lite>.

slights and empathy for her students.'[316] Again, the lesson to be learned is that it is dangerous and clinically contra-indicated to leave an employee's bitterness and sense of grievance to fester. There is a small but real risk that in persons of a particular personality constellation such latitude can have tragic consequences.

Regulation of Intemperate Disputation and Denigration

As is apparent from this chapter, there are many forms of harmful and excessive disputation and denigration in which scholars can engage and on occasions have engaged. It is a fundamental of defamation law that we recognize that words intemperately or malignly uttered or written can cause as much harm as sticks and stones. This is why we permit people to sue when false utterances are made which tend to lower individuals unwarrantedly in others' esteem.

It is an ethical obligation of Japanese scientists to respect others' honour and of Australian psychologists and psychiatrists not to denigrate colleagues. Why then have we tolerated gratuitously spiteful, offensive, and uncollegiate disputation by scholars? What is it about intellectual disagreements which should give protagonists the entitlement to be personally vindictive and to cause hurt and distress? To what extent does this breed a culture within universities of unnecessarily malignant and personal rivalry under cover of its being about the robust dialectic of exchange of ideas? Does it play a part in inducing the kinds of paranoia and bitterness that contributed to the conduct of scholars at Concordia and Alabama universities?

Clearly, it is important that disagreements among scholars be transacted without fear of the chilling effect of the threats of defamation litigation or disciplinary processes. However, there is much to be said for articulating it as an expectation that those engaged in scholarly exchange conduct themselves in a way that is respectful of others' dignity and entitlement to hold opposing views. This is part of the behaviour they should be modelling to their students. We have little difficulty in condemning persons such as Orlando Figes who engage in ruses to denigrate others' intellectual work and promote their own. We are amused when scholars, such as those in the Ark and Climate Change litigation, take to the courts to promulgate and publicize their disputes. But should we not expect more of scholars than the kind of rancorous disputation that is directed towards harming reputations and discrediting scholarly work? Sometimes such conduct is indicative of mental illness and of attitudes towards colleagues or students that need to be addressed—clinically or by way of supervision. And should we not also expect that scholars employed by tertiary institutions and research bodies refrain from utterances that are racist, sexist, homophobic, or otherwise gratuitously offensive and disrespectful?

There is much to be said for endeavouring gently to enhance the tone of scholarly exchange and commentary by incorporating within academics' codes of conduct the kinds of expectations articulated by Yale University's School of Medicine. Personally directed and gratuitously insensitive behaviour by scholars should not be tolerated; it is antithetical to academic values, debilitates its victims, compromises those engaged in it, discourages the expression of dissentient views and rigorous analysis, and undermines what should be scholars' fundamental commitment to individual freedom and respect for others. If institutions do nothing to discourage it, it has the potential to spill over into even more extreme forms of antisocial

[316] Shaila Dewan, Stephanie Saul, and Katie Zezima, 'For Professor, Fury Just Beneath the Surface', *The New York Times*, 20 February 2010: <http://www.nytimes.com/2010/02/21/us/21bishop.html?pagewanted=1&ref=amybishop> [accessed 2 Jan 2016].

behaviour. Just because there is a history of such conduct being engaged in within the academy should not shelter it from the kinds on censure and consequences which it would elicit in other parts of our community. Acts of intolerance, even when they fall technically short of harassment, have the potential to damage the environment in which freedom of expression is otherwise tolerated and cherished. However, the issues in this respect about freedom of speech are complex. While it is time these values were articulated more widely and adhered to more consistently in scholarly debate, this must not act as a means for quelling or suppressing the expression of points of view that are iconoclastic or are experienced as distressing or offensive by some.

9

SEXUAL MISCONDUCT

Introduction

While most scholars are scrupulous about their personal behaviour, a long and dishonourable history of sexual misconduct exists within academia, as in many institutions where power differentials exist. It can be viewed as both an education and workplace harassment issue, as well through a number of other lenses, including the criminal and the disciplinary.[1] The problem is one of significant dimensions,[2] although it is impossible to quantify. As long ago as 1997 Sandler and Shoop[3] observed: 'Although most . . . faculty members . . . do not harass, sexual harassment is a problem on every campus.'[4]

With the onset of zero tolerance policies at some United States universities in relation to sexual and romantic relationships between staff and students, the issue is also very controversial. A number of universities, including in 2014 Harvard University, have promulgated new policies with a view to reducing sexual exploitation of students and junior staff.[5]

Unsurprisingly, it is students who are at greatest risk of deleterious consequences from such relationships, but others can also be adversely affected. As the National Association of Teachers in Further and Higher Education in the United Kingdom observed in a motion passed at its annual conference in 1995:

> The consequences of engaging in consensual relationships may be considerable, and not only for the staff member and student concerned. The ramifications affect other staff and students.

---

[1] Where sexual misconduct is investigated by police or professional disciplinary authorities, though, it is common for these forms of inquiry to take precedence over workplace investigations. See eg, the standing down of Dr Soares from the University of Alberta: 'Dr Claudio Soares Sex Scandal: Psychiatrist Hired as Chair at University of Alberta Resigns', *Huffington Post*, 24 September 2012: <http://www.huffingtonpost.ca/2012/09/24/university-of-alberta-chair-resigns-amid-sex-scandal_n_1909748.html> [accessed 3 Jan 2016].

[2] 'I have altogether too much experience of teachers engaging in sexual relations with students, both their own students and (those of) their colleagues,' remembers Alan Ryan, now warden of New College, Oxford. He looks back on his early career at Keele University with fond memories of the relationships that began between young academics and their students. 'In my misspent youth, my ability to resist temptation was not great, and since I started teaching in the early 1960s, and new faculty were mostly only a couple of years older than the finalists, the discovery of sexual pleasure was a shared experience,' he says. 'Of the affairs I remember, an awful lot turned into highly successful marriages, though a good many were simple flings,' he says. 'There were, of course, spectacular characters who weren't like this at all. Freddie (A.J.) Ayer (the philosopher) fell into bed with everyone who was remotely willing, and an awful lot of young women were very happy to tick him off on the list of famous professors they had laid': Hannah Fearn, 'Sex and the University', *Times Higher Education*, 22 May 2008: <http://www.timeshighereducation.co.uk/401935.article> [accessed 3 Jan 2016].

[3] Bernice R Sandler and Robert J Shoop (eds), *Sexual Harassment on Campus: A Guide for Administrators, Faculty and Students* (Boston: Allyn and Bacon, 1997) 1.

[4] Dziech and Weiner argued that, since 1837 when Oberlin College became the United States' first college campus to accept women, it is likely that male professors have sexually harassed female students: Billie Wright Dziech and Linda Weiner, *The Lecherous Professor: Sexual Harassment on Campus* (2nd edn, Urbana: University of Illinois Press, 1990). See also, Thomas M Melsheimer, Steven H Stodghill, and Diana L Faust, 'The Law of Sexual Harassment on Campus: A Work in Progress' (1994) 13(3) *Review of Litigation* 529.

[5] See also, William A Kaplin and Barbara A Lee, *The Law of Higher Education* [electronic resource] (Hoboken: John Wiley & Sons, 2011).

> Engaging in a relationship with a member of staff can have damaging effects on the student. A student may suffer extreme distress upon discovering that the lecturer has no intention of sustaining the relationship for long, or is having a series of affairs with students. Their physical and mental health may be affected. The student can become isolated from peers and labelled by other students and staff.
>
> Many students feel they have no choice but to leave their course if the relationship ends, or if they seek to terminate the relationship. If they end the relationship, they may suffer harassment and be afraid to complain. They may be subjected to over-severe marking as the member of staff tries to avoid any suggestion of preferential treatment.[6]

The archetypal examples of sexual misconduct are of the senior academic pressuring students or junior staff for sexual favours (sexual harassment), sometimes as a precondition to academic success or advancement, or initiating or attempting to initiate a romantic and/or sexual relationship with a student for whose marking or supervision they are responsible (*quid pro quo* harassment/conflict of interest).[7] Occasionally, what is also alleged against an academic is unequivocal sexual assault in the form of rape, indecent assault, or an indecent act. The latter is a straightforward matter for criminal law processes, provided the victim is prepared to make a report to police and persist through the prosecution process.[8]

The incidence of unwanted sexual attention experienced by students (and junior staff) from staff at tertiary institutions has long been significant,[9] raising issues of power abuse and a number of ethical conundra. Ecological opportunities exist for academics to abuse their role and status, partly by reason of their position of power and influence and partly from the availability of persons who can be the subject of their attentions.[10] In short there is both temptation and opportunity for those minded to be predatory within scholarly institutions. It also needs to be observed that the differential between the incidence of unwanted sexual conduct from staff to students and the frequency of complaint is likely to be substantial. Reported instances are unlikely to tell anything like the real story. Sexual harassment is generally understood to be severely under-reported and, as most cases will not proceed to a court hearing, these cases are best thought of as the 'tip of the iceberg'.[11] The ambiguous nature of faculty–student sexual relationships means that students and junior staff may well hesitate before making a complaint of sexual harassment.[12]

---

[6] National Association of Teachers in Further and Higher Education (NATFHE), 'Advice on Consensual Relations Between Staff and Students', 2: <http://www.google.com.au/url?sa=t&rct=j&q=&esrc=s&source=web&cd=1&ved=0CCsQFjAA&url=http%3A%2F%2Fwww.ucu.org.uk%2Fmedia%2Fdocs%2Fd%2Fn%2Fconsrel_1.doc&ei=tXTPUqiFDYn8iQfWi4GICg&usg=AFQjCNFiqVVPNuwZJ-YONgJOmYBEgbeWeQ&bvm=bv.59026428,d.aGc> [accessed 3 Jan 2016].

[7] In relation to *quid pro quo* harassment generally, see *Burlington Industries Inc v Ellerth*, 524 US 742 (1998).

[8] See Stewart Payne, 'Lecturer is Given Life for Rapes', *The Telegraph*, 20 September 2003: <http://www.telegraph.co.uk/news/uknews/1441976/Lecturer-is-given-life-for-rapes.html> [accessed 3 Jan 2016]; 'Rape Case Lecturer Jailed for Life', *Daily Mail*, Undated: <http://www.dailymail.co.uk/news/article-196858/Rape-case-lecturer-jailed-life.html#> [accessed 3 Jan 2016]. These articles reported on the case of a psychology lecturer, Dr Shaun Farrell, from Christ Church University College in Canterbury, United Kingdom, who was jailed for raping a former student after she ended their three-year relationship. While on bail he raped another 19-year-old victim.

[9] See Bonnie S Fisher, Leah E Daigle, and Francis T Cullen, *Unsafe in the Ivory Tower: The Sexual Victimization of College Women* (Los Angeles: Sage Publications, 2010).

[10] See generally, Michele A Paludi (ed), *Ivory Power: Sexual Harassment on Campus* (New York: State University of New York Press, 1990).

[11] Anita Mackay, 'Recent Developments in Sexual Harassment Law: Towards a New Model' (2009) 14(2) *Deakin Law Review* 189, 192.

[12] Carol Bacchi, 'Sex on Campus—Where Does 'Consent' End and Harassment Begin?' (1992) 35(1) *Australian Universities' Review* 31.

However, there are indications that universities are becoming increasingly sensitive to situations which have the potential to provide opportunities for sexual harassment to occur, such as student camps, and are tending to be less tolerant of both unethical behaviour and breaches of university policies in extra-curricular environments.[13] The fact that the tertiary sector is increasingly competitive between universities has the by-product that universities are becoming more alert to the potential for adverse publicity to arise, among other things, from rumours of sexual predation by staff. This provides a positive incentive for university administrators to take active steps to discourage such conduct and to be more responsive than they might have been in the past when evidence shows that it has occurred without much by way of consequences for the perpetrator.

As noted above, the area of sexual relationships between staff and students at universities is controversial and contested. In a provocative essay in 2007, for instance, Deresiewicz argued that concerns that sexual harassment on campus is common are misplaced:

> The famously overprotective parenting style of the baby-boom generation has put pressure on universities to revert to acting *in loco parentis*, forcing them to take on the paternalistic role the boomers rejected during their own college years. Professors are the surrogate parents that parents hand their children over to, and the raising and casting out of the specter of the sexually predatory academic may be a way of purging the anxiety that transaction evokes. But long before the baby boomers' offspring started to reach college, the feminist campaign against sexual harassment—most effective in academia, the institution most responsive to feminist concerns—had turned universities into the most anxious self-patrolled workplace in American society, especially when it comes to relations between professors and undergraduates. This is not to suggest that sexual contact between college students and professors, welcome or unwelcome, never takes place, but the belief that it is the norm is a product of fantasy, not fact.[14]

Sexual harassment within scholarly environments can take many forms and can include both orthodox and upwards harassment. A recent study in the United Kingdom, discussed later in this chapter, indicates that harassment from time to time occurs whereby the student harasses the academic sexually or in other ways. This raises confronting questions about the dynamics of relationships between the academic and student.[15] An academic may find him or herself in a disadvantageous situation mounting a defence against approaches from students and, in some instances, defending allegations of sexual harassment that may be false but difficult to disprove.[16] There have been a number of cases that highlight the plight of the academic who has been falsely accused of sexual harassment. In principle remedies for false accusations

---

[13] University of Western Australia, *Report of the Review of Orientation* (August 2012) 29–30: <http://www.uwa.edu.au/home/?a=2178775> [accessed 3 Jan 2016]. See also, Yasmine Phillips, 'University of WA Orientation Camp Incidents 'May be Sexual Assault'', *Herald Sun*, 7 September 2012: <http://www.heraldsun.com.au/news/national/alcohol-sponsor-ban-at-uwa-o-camps/story-fndo486p-1226467419669> [accessed 3 Jan 2016].

[14] William Deresiewicz, 'Love on Campus', *The American Scholar*, 1 June 2007: <https://theamericanscholar.org/love-on-campus/#.VQ_SBPmUeSp> (23 March 2015).

[15] Sara J White, 'Student Nurses Harassing Academics' (2013) 33(1) *Nurse Education Today* 41; Rebecca Attwood, 'Lecturers Talk of Students' 'Shocking' Abuse', *Times Higher Education*, 18 June 2009: <http://www.timeshighereducation.co.uk/406995.article> [accessed 3 Jan 2016].

[16] Christina D Henagen, 'False Claims of Sexual Harassment in Education: The Path to an Appropriate Remedy for the Wrongly Accused' (1998) 76(4) *Washington University Law Quarterly* 1431. This article discusses the situation of false accusations against secondary education teachers. However, the argument that educators are vulnerable to false claims of sexual harassment could also apply to those teaching in universities and highlights that such claims may be a form of retaliation against teachers who are unpopular or who have disciplined or given poor marks to a student. Henagen argued that 'retaliatory sexual harassment claims are especially problematic because the negative consequences for the falsely accused teacher are tremendous, while there is no real risk for the accuser' (at 1440).

of sexual harassment may include defamation but recourse to such legal options is rarely practicable.[17]

Commonly, sexual harassment cases in universities do not come to light, because prospective complainants fear retribution, including the adverse impact that lodging a complaint might have upon their career development; they do not have the financial resources to accommodate the costs of initiating and maintaining legal proceedings, which are often prohibitive in nature; and the complainant usually occupies a position within the university hierarchy, which is considerably inferior to the one held by their alleged offender.[18]

This chapter discusses the definitions and the dimensions of sexual harassment relevant to scholarly contexts and provides an overview of the research on the extent of sexual harassment in universities. Samples of university policies on sexual harassment from universities and key legislative provisions are reviewed, and there is discussion of a series of illustrative cases, particularly from Australia. Other important aspects of this area of law are canvassed, including dealing with false accusations, issues of 'upwards harassment'[19] and the broader issue of bullying and workplace harassment in universities. The chapter argues in favour of rigorous policies, transparent, fair and prompt investigative processes, and the taking of robust action where accusations of harassment or conflict of interest are proved.

Sexual Harassment in Academia

Much conduct that would today be regarded as sexual harassment was not recognized legally as a form of sex discrimination until the 1970s.[20] After a Freedom of Information Act request by *Times Higher Education* in 2005, figures revealed that 50 out of 102 institutions had no policy requiring staff to declare sexual or other relationships with students that might give rise to a conflict of interest. Of those that did, few appeared to apply them: just 17 universities had any current records on file. In the same year, '18 per cent of respondents to a poll conducted by the Teacher Support Network said that they had had a sexual relationship with a student. Despite this, only 73 relationships were officially recorded and just five of these were defined as sexual or romantic. Many respondents, 62 per cent, said they did not know whether or not their university had a protocol on such matters.'[21]

Since that time sexual harassment has received considerable scholarly and legal attention with the phenomenon being studied from multiple perspectives, including the psychological,

[17] Henagen cites a number of cases where accusations of sexual harassment against academics have led to suits for libel: see ibid, 1442. Henagen also highlights that the defences to defamation suits may make the likelihood of success difficult (at 1443) and proposes several reforms such as changes to the defences in defamation law to afford better protection and remedies for academics who are falsely accused of sexual harassment.

[18] Such impediments having been in evidence for some time: see eg, Catharine R Stimpson, 'Overreaching: Sexual Harassment and Education', as reproduced in Michele A Paludi and Richard B Barickman, *Academic and Workplace Sexual Harassment* (Albany, NY: State University of New York Press, 1991) 115–8; Louise F Fitzgerald, Sandra L Shullman, Nancy Bailey, and Margaret Richards et al., 'The Incidence and Dimensions of Sexual Harassment in Academia and the Workplace' (1988) 32(2) *Journal of Vocational Behavior* 152, 154–5; Michele A Paludi and Richard B Barickman, *Academic and Workplace Sexual Harassment* (Albany, NY: State University of New York Press, 1991) 63.

[19] See eg, 'Tutors Taunted: Academics Offer Examples of 'Upwards Harassment' by Students and Consider Possible Motives', *Times Higher Education*, 18 June 2009: <http://www.timeshighereducation.co.uk/news/tutors-taunted-academics-offer-examples-of-upwards-harassment-by-students-and-consider-possible-motives/406996.article> [accessed 3 Jan 2016].

[20] Catharine A MacKinnon, 'Directions in Sexual Harassment Law' (2007) 31(2) *Nova Law Review* 225; Sara Charlesworth, Paula McDonald, and Somali Cerise, 'Naming and Claiming Workplace Sexual Harassment in Australia' (2011) 46(2) *Australian Journal of Social Issues* 141.

[21] Fearn, above n 2.

sociological, and legal. There is no universally accepted definition of sexual harassment. It is a concept that covers a wide range of behaviours, some of which are contested in terms of whether they should be regarded as constituting sexual harassment.[22] The socio-legal and psychological definitions are often not the same as the legal.[23]

Sexual harassment has been described by Louise Fitzgerald to consist 'of the sexualization of an instrumental relationship through the introduction or imposition of sexist or sexual remarks, requests or requirements, in the context of a formal power differential. Harassment can also occur where no such formal differential exists, if the behavior is unwanted by or offensive to the [person]'.[24] It is part of a broader range of adverse workplace conduct:

> Sexual harassment is one of a range of abusive or counterproductive workplace behaviours which have hierarchical power relations at their core. These behaviours include general bullying, mobbing, racial harassment and sex-based harassment, such as verbal put-downs, abusive remarks and marginalizing or exclusionary behaviours on the basis of gender. However, in contrast to these other abusive workplace behaviours, sexual harassment has an explicitly sexual dimension. It is also distinguished from harassment based on race or disability in that the conduct may be excused as welcome attention.[25]

Workplace bullying is a significant issue at many institutions, including at universities,[26] and sexual harassment is an important dimension of that problem. However, it stands apart from other forms of intimidatory behaviour because of what is often (not always) a clear gender dimension. It should not be seen as just another form of bullying or merged with policies on bullying;[27] it has distinctive characteristics and in this chapter will be dealt with separately from other forms of workplace misconduct.

The Dynamics of the Scholar–Student Relationship

Naomi Wolf's account[28] of an unwelcome physical advance to her by the distinguished Professor Harold Bloom at Yale University is illustrative of how difficult it is when the victim of a sexual overture by a senior academic is a junior student, and also of the kind of effects such an event can have:

> [T]he encroachment, the transgression—those words are so much more accurate, emotionally as well as legally, than 'harassment'—had effects that went deep. What Harold Bloom's

---

22 Margaret Schneider, Sarah Baker, and Lana Stermac, 'Sexual Harassment Experiences of Psychologists and Psychological Associates During their Graduate School Training' (2002) 11(3–4) *Canadian Journal of Human Sexuality* 159; Charlesworth, McDonald, and Cerise, above n 20.

23 Paula McDonald, 'Workplace Sexual Harassment 30 Years On: A Review of the Literature' (2012) 14(1) *International Journal of Management Reviews* 1.

24 Louise F Fitzgerald, 'Sexual Harassment: The Definition and Measurement of a Construct' in Michele A Paludi (ed), *Ivory Power: Sexual Harassment on Campus* (New York: State University of New York Press, 1990) 38.

25 McDonald, above n 23, 2 (citations omitted).

26 Thornton has suggested that what has been asserted to be an increase in bullying in universities is due to the emergence of 'corrosive styles of leadership' along with a corporatized university culture: Margaret Thornton, 'Corrosive Leadership (Or Bullying by Another Name): A Corollary of the Corporatised Academy?' (2004) 17(2) *Australian Journal of Labour Law* 161, 161.

27 Harriet Samuels, 'Sexual Harassment in the Workplace: A Feminist Analysis of Recent Developments in the UK' (2003) 26(5) *Women's Studies International Forum* 467.

28 Naomi Wolf, 'The Silent Treatment', *New York*, 1 March 2004: <http://nymag.com/nymetro/news/features/n_9932/> [accessed 3 Jan 2016]. As Donadio observes, there may have been other perspectives, including that of Harold Bloom, in respect of the interaction and the relationship between the two: see Rachel Donadio, 'Naomi Wolf Makes Much Ado About Nuzzling at Yale' (3 January 2004) *Observer*: <http://observer.com/2004/03/naomi-wolf-makes-much-ado-about-nuzzling-at-yale/> [accessed 3 Jan 2016].

> hand on his student's thigh set off was not a sexual crisis. I was sexually active—and not even especially modest. An unwanted hand on a thigh from a date was nothing. Nor was it an emotional crisis. I wasn't that vulnerable. What it set off was a moral crisis, shaking my confidence in the institution I was in.
>
> I wanted to go to the Grievance Board. The semester was passing, but I was terrified of being in a room alone again with Bloom. Still, I needed to know what to do about the rest of the term. Some women friends, however, persuaded me not to speak to anyone official about what had happened.[29]

A result of such difficulties is a significant incidence of delayed and anonymous complaints. Those accused often try to make capital out of delay or unpreparedness of victims to put their name to complaints. An example in this regard is to be seen in the resignation in 2004 by School of Humanities Lecturer Paul Mathews from the University of Western Sydney (UWS) Bankstown Campus after a student anonymously claimed 'he wrote essays, upgraded marks and provided cash in return for sexual favours'.[30] Matthews endeavoured to make a point from the fact that the complainant had not come forward in a timely or identified way. After resigning, he suggested that the source of the allegations was probably an 18-year-old student who had developed an infatuation in relation to him.[31]

There can be many psychological dynamics at play in relationships that evolve between scholars and their students in tertiary settings, most of which are characterized by a significant imbalance of power. In 2000 Russell Griffiths, a lecturer at the University of Lincoln and Humberside, was acquitted by a jury of drugging and raping one of his 18-year-old students.[32] A subsequent reflective article in *The Guardian*[33] observed that 'sexual frissons' between staff and students are almost inevitable: 'The tutor can become a parent substitute: the elder figure to whom a student will always defer, the central person in her life, whom she strives to impress and to please with her academic efforts. Intellectual sparring can fast develop into a form of flirtation.' The author concluded: 'As exceptional as the Griffiths case is, wherever questions of power, responsibility and attraction meet, there will inevitably be problems. The student–lecturer relationship is complex and it is a fine line between hero-worship and exploitation.'[34]

The autonomy of the scholar and the limited levels of supervision that exist within most tertiary institutions can be both a sanctuary for the scholar and a hazard for the student or junior staff member. In the 1990 edition of *The Lecherous Professor*, Dziech and Weiner identified the professional authority and autonomy of the academic as furnishing the psychological preconditions for sexually predatory behaviour—arrogance and a sense of entitlement. They took an extreme position, applicable to the relationship between psychiatrists and their patients,[35] but of contested appropriateness in the tertiary sector, arguing that

---

[29] Ibid. See also, Michele A Paludi, Marc Grossman, Carole Ann Scott, Joni Kindermann et al. 'Myths and Realities: Sexual Harassment on Campus' in Michele A Paludi (ed), *Ivory Power: Sexual Harassment on Campus* (Albany, NY: State University of New York Press, 1990).

[30] Eamonn Duff and John Kidman, 'Sex Lecturer Tells of Girl's Crush', *The Sun-Herald*, 13 June 2004: <http://www.smh.com.au/articles/2004/06/12/1086749943893.html> [accessed 3 Jan 2016].

[31] Mr Mathews subsequently contended that he had no choice but to resign and said that: '[t]he university would have cut my funding and increased my workload. I would also have been subjected to snide remarks from colleagues for the rest of my working life': ibid.

[32] The case provoked considerable debate in England, in part because highly prejudicial material was exposed as having been withheld from the jury. Some of the material related to Griffiths's prior convictions and history of obsessionality towards young females.

[33] Laura Barton, 'A Hard Lesson', *The Guardian*, 12 October 2000: <http://www.theguardian.com/world/2000/oct/12/gender.uk1> [accessed 3 Jan 2016].

[34] Ibid.

[35] See eg, The Royal Australian & New Zealand College of Psychiatrists, 'Zero Tolerance Policy on Proven Sexual Boundary Violations' (updated 23 February 2013) [2.2]–[2.4], available at: <https://www.ranzcp.org/

'[n]ormal sexual give-and-take is not possible in student–teacher relationships because the power imbalance and role disparity are too great':[36]

> Few students are ever, in the strictest sense, consenting adults. A student can never be a genuine equal of a professor insofar as his professional position gives him power over her. Access to a student occurs not because she allows it but because the professor ignores professional ethics and chooses to extend the student–faculty relationship. Whether the student consents to the involvement or whether the professor ever intends to use his power against her is not the point. The issue is that the power and the role disparity always exist, making it virtually impossible for the student to act as freely as she would with a male peer.[37]

Many today would say that this is patronizing—that it constitutes an over-reaction to risk and deprives students of their entitlement to enter into adult personal and sexual relationships with academics. However, as set out below, the views of Dziech and Weiner have influenced a growing 'zero tolerance' policy towards sexual and even romantic relationships between staff and students in United States universities.

Sexual harassment has a range of gender ramifications. It has long had particular implications for women and students in academia and constituted 'a serious external barrier to women's career development'.[38] This has been described as 'chilling the climate' for women in academia.[39] It can force 'a student to forfeit work, research, educational comfort, or even career. Professors withhold legitimate opportunities from those who resist, or students withdraw rather than pay certain prices'.[40] While it is unfair to speak in such generalities, the general sentiment was supported in part by Fitzgerald et al. 1988 study which found that a (small) number of students dropped a course to avoid sexual harassment with which they were afflicted or avoided taking a course altogether.[41]

Till[42] identified five forms of sexual harassment:

1. *Gender harassment*: generalized sexist remarks and behaviour;
2. *Seductive behaviour*: inappropriate and offensive, but essentially sanction-free, sexual advances;
3. *Sexual bribery*: solicitation of sexual activity or other sex-linked behaviour by promise of rewards;
4. *Sexual coercion*: coercion of sexual activity by threat of punishment;
5. *Sexual assault*: gross sexual imposition or assault.[43]

About-us/Governance/Regulations-policies-procedures.aspx> (viewed 26 March 2015): '2.2 Psychiatrists are involved in professional relationships in which there is an imbalance of power and shall not exploit this power differential for their own personal, social or material benefit. 2.3 Sexual relationships between psychiatrists and their current and former patients are always unethical. 2.4 Sexual harassment or any behavior that might be reasonably interpreted by a patient as demeaning, or as a sexual advance, is unethical. Such behavior may include physical contact, or conduct, comments or innuendo of a sexual nature or questioning on sexual matters that is not necessary for clinical purposes.'

[36] Dziech and Weiner, above n 4, 25.

[37] Ibid 74.

[38] Fitzgerald et al. above n 18, 155.

[39] See Lilia M Cortina, Suzanne Swan, Louise F Fitzgerald, and Craig Waldo, 'Sexual Harassment and Assault: Chilling the Climate for Women in Academia' (1998) 22(3) *Psychology of Women Quarterly* 419.

[40] Dziech and Weiner, above n 4, 101.

[41] Fitzgerald et al. above n 18, 159, 162.

[42] Frank J Till, *Sexual Harassment: A Report on the Sexual Harassment of Students* (The National Advisory Council on Women's Educational Programs, August 1980), available at: <http://babel.hathitrust.org/cgi/pt?id=uiug.30112041282127;view=1up;seq=3> [accessed 3 Jan 2016].

[43] Using Till's five levels of sexual harassment, Fitzgerald et al. developed the survey tool outlined in their study, and known as the 'Sexual Experiences Questionnaire': Fitzgerald et al. above n 18, 157.

Another, albeit related, way of regarding the issue is via the lens of psychological coercion, which takes account of the dynamics of interaction between social participants. Spitzberg[44] identified six major categories of sexual coercion which can be placed on a continuum or scale:

- pressure and persistence;
- deception;
- threat;
- physical restraint; and
- physical force or injury.[45]

A senior academic is well positioned to utilize aspects of these forms of leverage if predatorily motivated to abuse their authority.[46] However, a disciplinary response to each type of sexual harassment might merit a different remedy, ranging from training/re-education to suspension or dismissal.[47] The category of sexual assault should be dealt with principally as a criminal matter.

Dziech and Weiner usefully identified five roles assumed by senior academics who attempt to manipulate female students for their sexual gratification:

- The *Counsellor-Helper* who takes the role of nurturer and caretaker, encouraging student confidences, uncovering vulnerabilities and thereby constructing a seduction script.
- The *Confidant* who purports to treat students as friends and equals, sharing personal information with them and encouraging a student to feel trusted and valued and thereby creating a dynamic of emotional intimacy.
- The *Intellectual Seducer* who flaunts his knowledge, encouraging student self-disclosure in order to identify potential targets and hone a suitable approach.
- The *Opportunist* who uses physical settings and circumstances to make premeditated or intentionally seductive behaviour, involving touching and creating scenarios of personal contact away from the lecture setting.
- The *Power Broker* who uses the entitlement of the professor to leverage students into compliance with his overtures, using promises of rewards or threats of adverse consequences, communicated either subtly or inferentially or directly.[48]

Zalk has developed these categories to identify 'four familiar themes or dimensions useful in developing profiles of these men':[49]

- *The Public versus the Private Harasser*. This dimension assesses the [academic's] behaviour of sexually relating to students along a continuum from open, 'public' displays to hidden, secretive advances and encounters.

---

[44] Brian H Spitzberg, 'Sexual Coercion in Courtship Relations' in Brian H Spitzberg and William R Cupach (eds), *The Dark Side of Close Relationships* (Mahwah, NJ: Lawrence Erlbaum Associates, 1998).

[45] Ibid, 203. See also, Brian H Spitzberg and William R Cupach (eds), *The Dark Side of Close Relationships* [electronic resource] (Routledge, 2013) 203 (Table 7.2. A Priori Classification of Sexual Coercion Tactics Identified in the Literature); Brian H Spitzberg, Linda Marshall, and William R Cupach, 'Obsessive Relational Intrusion, Coping and Sexual Coercion Victimization' (2001) 14(1) *Communication Reports* 19, 24; Brian H Spitzberg and Jill Rhea, 'Obsessive Relational Intrusion and Sexual Coercion Victimization' (1999) 14(1) *Journal of Interpersonal Violence* 3, 4–5.

[46] See Mary P Koss, Christine A Gidycz, and Nadine Wisniewski, 'The Scope of Rape: Incidence and Prevalence of Sexual Aggression and Victimization in a National Sample of Higher Education Students' (1987) 55(2) *Journal of Consulting and Clinical Psychology* 162.

[47] Catherine A Leslie and William E Hauck, 'Categories of Sexual Harassment: A Preliminary Analysis' (Working Paper, Kent State University, 2005), available at: <http://www.kon.org/hswp/archive/leslie-hauck1.htm> [accessed 3 Jan 2016].

[48] See further, Dziech and Weiner, above n 4, 122–4.

[49] Sue Rosenberg Zalk, 'Men in the Academy: A Psychological Profile of Harassment' in Michele A Paludi (ed), *Ivory Power: Sexual Harassment on Campus* (Albany, NY: State University of New York Press, 1990) 149.

- *The Seducer/Demander versus the Receptive Non-Initiator*. This dimension can be viewed as an 'active-passive' continuum and refers to the degree to which the [academic] actively pursues sexual encounters with students.
- *The Untouchable versus the Risk Taker*. This dimension refers to the degree of 'entitlement' and invulnerability/vulnerability with which the [academic] engages in sexual liaisons with students.
- *The Infatuated versus the Sexual Conqueror*. This dimension contrasts [academics] along the continuum of affection and care felt toward their student lover – how 'special' [the student] is to [the academic].[50]

Part of the issue is whether the academic–student relationship has such an imbalance of power as an intrinsic element that it is analogous, for instance, to the psychiatrist–patient or psychologist–client relationships.[51] Jane Gallop, a Professor of English and Comparative Literature at the University of Wisconsin at Milwaukee, herself found guilty of having engaged in 'consensual amorous relations'[52] arising from publicly kissing one of her students, has contended that there are relevant parallels, identifying that transference (in the psychoanalytic sense of the tendency to put people in the position our parents once held for us) is an 'inevitable part of any relationship we have to a teacher who really makes a difference'.[53] She has argued that '[a]t its most intense—and, I would argue, its most productive—the pedagogical relation between teacher and student is, in fact, a "consensual amorous relation".'[54]

Brian Martin at the University of Wollongong has observed that:

> As well as an abuse of trust, sexual relationships between teachers and students represent a serious conflict of interest. The possibility of favouritism in assessment is obvious, as is the possibility of harsh marking for those who have broken off relationships. But this is only the beginning of the problems. Even if academic evaluations are kept completely independent of personal involvements, it is likely that there will be an appearance of bias in the eyes of other students and staff.
>
> Another real problem arises when an academic—especially a powerful academic—has a relationship with a student in a colleague's class. Pressure may be brought to bear on the colleague to give preferential treatment to the student, such as better marks, extensions on essays, or extra help. Even without pressure, preferential treatment may be provided to avoid risking the colleague's displeasure. When there are multiple relationships involving several staff and students, the possibilities for conflict of interest are mind-boggling.
>
> Sometimes it is difficult to draw a firm line between acceptable and unacceptable behaviours. But a few things should be clear. Sexual relationships should not be permitted between a teacher and the students in his own class or under his supervision. If a relationship is anticipated, then mutually agreeable arrangements should be made to change teaching or assessment.[55]

The mixing of the professional and the personal has many aspects which are undesirable. It generally does not facilitate the quality of the learning or the teaching experience and it can generate various forms of distraction, as well as create a conflict of interest by the

[50] Ibid, 150 (citation omitted).

[51] See eg, Glen O Gabbard and Eva P Lester, *Boundaries and Boundary Violations in Psychoanalysis* (Washington, DC: American Psychiatric Publishing, 2003).

[52] See eg, Jane Gallop, *Feminist Accused of Sexual Harassment* (Durham: Duke University Press, 1997) ch 2.

[53] Ibid, 56.

[54] Ibid, 57.

[55] Brian Martin, 'Staff–Student Sex: Abuse of Trust and Conflict of Interest' in William J Taverner (ed), *Taking Sides: Clashing Views on Controversial Issues in Human Sexuality* (Guilford, Conn: McGraw-Hill/Dushkin, 2002) 124–6.

romanticization of the pedagogical relationship.[56] Davis has argued colourfully that a faculty member who has sexual relations with a student cannot serve the university as they should: 'Are there any faculty who could copulate (or even have a "less serious" sexual relation) with a student and still treat her with the same impartiality as other students? A few perhaps, those with the passions of a lizard, but even they could not prove their impartiality to those who, knowing their own passions, doubt that anyone else could be so different.'[57]

Generally, it has not been held to be improper for academics to enter into consensual sexual relationships with either more junior staff or with students.[58] However, there are signs that this attitude is gradually changing, especially in the United States, and even consensual sexual relationships between staff and students are more likely than previously to raise concerns about abuses of power and generate litigation.[59] Consent is not a straightforward concept when concerned with relationships between academics and students.[60] The central concept associated with sexual harassment in the academic environment is the misuse of power and role by a faculty member[61] in a way that impacts adversely (or at least has the potential to do so) on another person's educational and occupational interests.[62] As Bacchi has noted, 'it is essential to be aware of the complex power dynamic at work on a university campus', meaning that academic staff 'indirectly control access to future advancement through the assigning of grades, the writing of letters of recommendation, and the provision of research and clinical opportunities'.[63] Further, academics are often seen as repositories of knowledge and wisdom and to command power as a result of their perceived intellectual skills.[64] Thus, some have questioned the legitimacy of the provision of consent by students to faculty members.

Legal Issues in Sexual Harassment

There is no universal legal definition of sexual harassment, although there are similarities between definitions.[65] For instance, in the United Kingdom, section 1 of the *Sex Discrimination Act* 1975 (UK) states that:

> In any circumstances relevant for the purposes of any provision of this Act… a person discriminates against a woman if—
> (a) on the ground of her sex he treats her less favourably than he treats or would treat a man, or
> (b) he applies to her a requirement or condition which he applies or would apply equally to a man but—
> (i) which is such that the proportion of women who can comply with it is considerably smaller than the proportion of men who can comply with it, and
> (ii) which he cannot show to be justifiable irrespective of the sex of the person to whom it is applied, and
> (iii) which is to her detriment because she cannot comply with it.[66]

[56] See Leslie Francis, *Sexual Harassment as an Ethical Issue in Academic Life* (Lanham, Maryland: Rowman & Littlefield, 2001), 104–5.

[57] Michael Davis, *Ethics and the University* (London: Routledge, 1999) 213.

[58] See eg, *Chambers v James Cook University of North Queensland (No 2)* [1995] IRCA 48; 61 IR 145 (Spender J). See also, Dziech and Weiner, above n 4, 206, where a similar observation is noted in a 1989 letter to staff from the President of the University of Minnesota.

[59] Fearn, above n 2.

[60] Bacchi, above n 12.

[61] Dziech and Weiner, above n 4, 21.

[62] Fitzgerald et al. above n 18, 174.

[63] Bacchi, above n 12, 32 (citation omitted).

[64] Ibid.

[65] McDonald, above n 23.

[66] See eg, *Fogarty v The United Kingdom* [2001] ECHR 762; (2001) 34 EHRR 302, [15].

In Australia, s 28A of the *Sex Discrimination Act* 1984 (Cth) provides that:

(1) For the purposes of this Division, a person sexually harasses another person (the *person harassed.*) if:
(a) the person makes an unwelcome sexual advance, or an unwelcome request for sexual favours, to the person harassed; or
(b) engages in other unwelcome conduct of a sexual nature in relation to the person harassed;
in circumstances in which a reasonable person, having regard to all the circumstances, would have anticipated the possibility that the person harassed would be offended, humiliated or intimidated.
[...]
(2) In this section:
'conduct of a sexual nature' includes making a statement of a sexual nature to a person, or in the presence of a person, whether the statement is made orally or in writing.

There are three key elements to the definition:

> First, that the conduct is 'unwelcome'; second that the conduct is of a 'sexual nature'; and, third, that the 'reasonable person' would have anticipated the reaction of the victim, that is, that the victim would feel 'offended, humiliated or intimidated'.[67]

Sexual harassment in academic settings may be hard to identify; the line between 'misbehaviour' and illegality or abuse can be difficult to draw, particularly where, for instance, boundaries between formal duties on the part of academics merge into mentoring in quasi-social settings.[68]

Whether an act constitutes sexual harassment in terms of s 28A depends on the nature or the quality of the act.[69] The question of whether conduct is unwelcome is to be determined on a subjective basis—that is, by reference to the state of mind of the subject.[70]

There is a spectrum of sexually harassing behaviours from the less serious through to the heinous. The level of intimidation of and offence taken by the recipient of the behaviours are key factors in determining whether conduct constitutes sexual harassment[71] and, if so, how serious it is. Studies have indicated that women are much less accepting than men of sexual behaviour in the workplace and are more likely to view and experience sexually harassing conduct as serious.[72]

The question whether conduct has the requisite character is to be determined on an objective basis: the perspective of a reasonable person in the role of a hypothetical observer.[73] In addition, the question whether a reasonable person, having regard to all the circumstances,

---

[67] Mackay, above n 11, 193. See *GLS v PLP (Human Rights)* [2013] VCAT 221.

[68] Charles J Russo, 'A Legal Primer on Sexual Harassment: Lessons for Practice from the United States of America' (2008) 13(1) *Australian & New Zealand Journal of Law & Education* 21.

[69] *Obieta v New South Wales Department of Education and Training* [2007] FCA 86, [238] (Cowdroy J); *Cooke v Plauen Holdings* [2001] FMCA 91, [25]–[26].

[70] *GLS v PLP (Human Rights)* [2013] VCAT 221, [30] (Garde J), applying *Kraus v Menzie* [2012] FCAFC 144, [7] (Rares, McKerracher, and Murphy JJ); Schneider, Baker, and Stermac, above n 22. See also Mackay, above n 11. See the useful discussion by the British Columbia Supreme Court in *Dutton v British Columbia (Human Rights Tribunal)*, 2001 BCSC 1256.

[71] Charlesworth, McDonald, and Cerise, above n 20.

[72] Vicki J Magley and Ellen I Shupe, 'Self-Labeling Sexual Harassment' (2005) 53(3–4) *Sex Roles* 173; Jennifer L Berdahl and Celia Moore, 'Workplace Harassment: Double Jeopardy for Minority Women' (2006) 91(2) *Journal of Applied Psychology* 426; Camille Gallivan Nelson, Jane A Halpert, and Douglas F Cellar, 'Organizational Responses for Preventing and Stopping Sexual Harassment: Effective Deterrents or Continued Endurance?' (2007) 56(11–12) *Sex Roles* 811.

[73] *Leslie v Graham* [2002] FCA 32, [70] (Branson J).

would have anticipated that the other person would be offended, humiliated, or intimidated is determined on an objective basis.[74]

Assertive conduct by an academic constituting harassment of a student has been held to have the potential to be 'unwelcome conduct of a sexual nature in relation to the person harassed'.[75] Conduct in the nature of persistent personal solicitations has, in some cases, and in conjunction with other acts, been held to constitute sexual harassment.[76] Further, aggressive conduct following a rejection could potentially constitute harassment of a sexual nature.[77]

The concepts of reasonableness and the requirement that a complainant hold the burden of proving that the conduct is unwelcome remain fundamental to discrimination law,[78] although they have been criticized by feminist legal scholars.[79]

An unresolved question exists as to the extent of universities' legal liability for lecherous and harassing behaviour engaged in by their staff. The issue has been litigated extensively in the United States without a clear outcome. The situation is well instanced by the case of *Kracunas v Iona College*.[80] Darleen Pallett was an undergraduate student at Iona College. She took a British poetry class with Professor Palma but was given an 'F' for a paper that she submitted. She met with Professor Palma to discuss her grade but, on her coming into his office, Professor Palma closed his door and sat in front of it. He then:

> embarked upon a sexually explicit discussion of his personal sexual history, fantasies, and opinions. Palma closed his eyes, licked his lips, and rubbed his hands together.... Palma told Pallett that he envisioned her naked, stated that he was likely to have a sexual dream about Pallett, and inquired into Pallett's personal sexual activity.[81]

After Pallett stated that she needed to return home, Palma asked her if she would be happy with a final grade of 'C' for the course. She said that she would and left but later learned that students and members of staff had filed at least five other harassment complaints against him. She sued the College, but lost at first instance, when the District Court accepted that Palma's conduct constituted sexual harassment but dismissed the action as a result of the college having taken appropriate remedial action on learning of Palma's conduct. However, the Second Circuit vacated the District Court decision and, relying on agency law, remitted the matter for further hearing on the basis that the college could be liable for Palma's conduct.

Extent of Sexual Harassment in Universities

As noted above, a wide range of studies has examined the prevalence and dynamics of sexual harassment since the 1970s in workplaces generally, and in universities in particular. Paula

---

[74] *GLS v PLP (Human Rights)* [2013] VCAT 221, [32]. See also, *Taylor v Sciberras* [2004] NSWADT 104, [146]; Neil Rees, Simon Rice, and Dominique Allen, *Australian Anti-Discrimination Law* (2nd edn, Annandale, NSW: The Federation Press, 2014).

[75] *Gauci v Kennedy* [2007] FCA 1051, [22].

[76] Cf *Doyle v Riley* (1995) EOC 92-748.

[77] See *Cooke v Plauen Holdings* [2001] FMCA 91, [30] (Driver FM).

[78] *GLS v PLP (Human Rights)* [2013] VCAT 221 (Garde J) where a solicitor was found to have sexually harassed a paralegal on placement at his suburban law firm.

[79] Samuels, above n 27; Mackay, above n 11; Gail Mason and Anna Chapman, 'Defining Sexual Harassment: A History of the Commonwealth Legislation and its Critiques' (2003) 31(1) *Federal Law Review* 195; Mayo Moran, *Rethinking the Reasonable Person: An Egalitarian Reconstruction of the Objective Standard* (Oxford: Oxford University Press, 2003).

[80] 119 F 3d 80, 83 (2nd Cir 1997).

[81] Ibid, 83.

McDonald highlighted in a 2012 literature review of research from the previous 30 years that prevalence studies establish that sexual harassment persists in many workplaces in western countries.[82] A 2008 telephone survey by the Australian Human Rights and Equal Opportunity Commission showed that:

- 22% of women and 5% of men aged 18-64 have experienced sexual harassment in the workplace in their lifetime, compared to 28% of women and 7% of men surveyed in 2003.
- Around one in three women in Australia aged 18-64 have experienced sexual harassment in their lifetime. The majority of sexual harassment continues to be experienced in the workplace (65%).
- Nearly half of those who have been sexually harassed in the last five years report that it has also happened to someone else in the same workplace.
- Over one in ten Australians have witnessed sexual harassment in the workplace in the last five years.
- 4% of Australians have experienced sexual harassment in the workplace in the last five years, compared to 11% in 2003.[83]

While this survey in some respects is encouraging, the rates of sexual harassment identified by the studies vary widely, including within different forms of workplaces, due to the range of methodological approaches employed in surveys and the breadth of the definition of sexual harassment used in some instances.[84]

Sexual harassment, especially in the tertiary context, is likely to be significantly under-reported. Some have suggested that this is in part due to a lack of understanding of the legal definitions of sexual harassment.[85] The 2008 Australian Human Rights and Equal Opportunity Commission report illustrated this with one in five (22 per cent) respondents stating that they had not experienced sexual harassment but going on to report having experienced behaviours that may in fact have amounted to sexual harassment under the *Sex Discrimination Act* 1984 (Cth).

A lack of faith in the complaint process or legal remedies is likely to be another contributing reason for under-reporting.[86] This is particularly so where stigma and adverse repercussions have the potential to attach to the making of accusations of harassment in the tertiary context. Other factors affecting whether sexual harassment will be reported include the seriousness of the conduct, whether the harasser is the supervisor of the person and whether the victim is female—women have higher rates of non-reporting.[87]

Dziech and Weiner illustrated that a number of studies which had measured levels of sexual harassment in universities in the United States in the late 1970s and 1980s had consistently shown that about 20 to 30 per cent of female students reported that they had been harassed by male faculty members.[88] Fitzgerald et al. 1988 study of 2,599 female and male students enrolled in two universities in the United States yielded similar results.[89] On average,

[82] McDonald, above n 23.

[83] Australian Human Rights Commission, *Sexual Harassment: Serious Business* (2008) [1.2], available at: <https://www.humanrights.gov.au/our-work/sex-discrimination/publications/sexual-harassment-serious-business-2008> [accessed 3 Jan 2016].

[84] McDonald, above n 23.

[85] Charlesworth, McDonald, and Cerise, above n 20.

[86] Australian Human Rights Commission, above n 83, [5.9]; Mackay, above n 11.

[87] Claudia Benavides-Espinoza and George B Cunningham, 'Observers' Reporting of Sexual Harassment: The Influence of Harassment Type, Organizational Culture and Political Orientation' (2010) 10(4) *Public Organization Review* 323.

[88] Dziech and Weiner, above n 4, 15.

[89] Fitzgerald et al. above n 18.

Fitzgerald et al. found that 31 per cent of students and women working in the two universities stated they had experienced gender harassment[90] and 15 per cent of students and 17 per cent of staff experienced seductive[91] sexual approaches from academics.[92] Direct sexual coercion was much less evident.[93]

Fitzgerald et al. found that 50 per cent of female students in one university and 76 per cent in another had experienced some form of sexual harassment (of the five categories listed by Till[94] above).[95] The majority of the behaviour fell into the categories of gender harassment and seduction (the two less serious categories identified by Till).[96] While the experiences of male students revealed rates of sexual harassment that were lower than for female students in both universities, the rates of sexual harassment were nevertheless significant and also mainly fell into the less serious categories of gender harassment and seduction.[97] In a separate study Fitzgerald et al. found that women employed in universities reported high levels of behaviour that could be classified as sexual harassment, although not as high as that reported as experienced by the female students.[98] Again the majority of behaviour fell into the category of gender harassment[99] and seduction.[100]

Fitzgerald et al. highlighted that awareness among staff and students of behaviour that constituted sexual harassment and reporting of sexual harassment was much lower than the rates experienced and reported in the study.[101] Since Fitzgerald's study there have been numerous other studies that have explored the issue of sexual harassment in universities.[102] These studies form part of broader

---

90 The behaviour measured under the category of 'gender harassment' included 'suggestive stories or offensive jokes; crudely sexual remarks; seductive remarks; staring, leering, ogling; use of sexist or pornographic teaching materials; treated "differently" due to gender; sexist remarks about career options': ibid, 160 (formatting altered).

91 The behaviour measured under the category of 'seduction' included 'unwanted discussion of personal or sexual matters; unwelcome seductive behavior (requests for dates, drinks, backrubs, etc.); unwanted sexual attention; attempts to establish a romantic sexual relationship; propositions': ibid, 160 (formatting altered).

92 Fitzgerald et al. above n 18, 170.

93 Ibid.

94 Till, above n 42.

95 Fitzgerald et al. above n 18, 159, 162.

96 Ibid.

97 Ibid, 172–3.

98 Ibid, 168.

99 Ibid.

100 Ibid, 168. In relation to female workers in universities 'seduction' measures were 'unwanted discussion of personal or sexual matters; unwelcome seductive behavior; unwanted sexual attention; attempts to establish a sexual relationship, despite discouragement; propositions; invasion of privacy (repeated calling, requests for dates, 'dropping in'); sexual insinuations or innuendos; crude or offensive sexual remarks made about the respondent to others; sexual rumors spread about the respondent': ibid, 166 (formatting altered).

101 See eg, ibid, 171–2.

102 See eg, Megan P Goodwin, Bruce Roscoe, Marshall Rose, and Susan E Repp, 'Sexual Harassment: Experiences of University Employees' (1989) 52(3) *Initiatives* 25; Elizabeth Grauerholz, 'Sexual Harassment of Women Professors by Students: Exploring the Dynamics of Power, Authority, and Gender in a University Setting' (1989) 21(11–12) *Sex Roles* 789; Kathleen McKinney, 'Sexual Harassment of University Faculty by Colleagues and Students' (1990) 23(7–8) *Sex Roles* 421; Michele A Paludi and Richard B Barickman, *Academic and Workplace Sexual Harassment* (New York: State University of New York Press, 1991); Louise F Fitzgerald, *The Last Great Open Secret: The Sexual Harassment of Women in the Workplace and Academia* (Washington, DC: Federation of Behavioral, Psychological and Cognitive Sciences, 1993); Robert O Riggs, Patricia H Murrell, and JoAnn C Cutting, *Sexual Harassment in Higher Education: From Conflict to Community* (ASHE-ERIC Higher Education Report No 2) (Washington, DC: George Washington University, School of Education and Human Development, 1993); Eric L Dey, Jessica S Korn, and Linda J Sax, 'Betrayed by the Academy: The Sexual Harassment of Women College Faculty' (1996) 67(2) *Journal of Higher Education* 149; Catherine So-kum Tang, Michelle S M Yik, Fanny M C Cheung, Po-king Choi et al. 'Sexual Harassment of Chinese College Students' (1996) 25(2) *Archives of Sexual Behavior* 201; Linda J Rubin, Bethany R Hampton, and Pamela W McManus, 'Sexual Harassment of Students by Professional Psychology Educators: A National

literature and research conducted over the past 30 years, suggesting that sexual harassment is an ongoing problem in many workplace settings, the tertiary sector being no exception.[103]

Overall, research has highlighted that sexual harassment is a phenomenon that affects male students as well as female students,[104] although women are significantly more likely to experience sexual harassment than men.[105] Further, the more recent studies have reinforced the finding by Fitzgerald et al[106] that female staff members, whether academic staff or administrative staff, are not immune from harassment,[107] and a small number may be perpetrators. Dey, Korn, and Sax's[108] 1996 study of sexual harassment among faculty women in universities in the United States found 15.1 per cent of women faculty members reported having been harassed compared with 3.1 per cent of men.[109] The risk of sexual harassment has been found to be increased where socialization between students and faculty is the norm, in faculties that have no clear sexual harassment policy, and in faculties that have low numbers of female faculty members.[110] Academic members who themselves have been sexually harassed as students are more likely to engage in sexual harassment in their professional life.[111] It may be that gay, lesbian, bisexual, and transgender students are at an increased risk of harassment.[112]

A study of Chinese college students in Hong Kong found that one in four students had experienced sexual harassment.[113] When compared with similar studies in the United States, Chinese college students had less awareness and experience of sexual harassment than students from the United States.[114] In Canada a study of sexual harassment behaviours in graduate school found that the majority of students had experienced at least one incident of sexual harassment behaviour, with female students more likely to be targeted by male faculty members.[115]

A study involving a self-reported questionnaire of staff and students at the University of Zambia generated similar results: 37 per cent of all survey participants reported being sexually harassed.[116] The study highlighted that there was considerable confusion about what constituted sexual harassment with the majority of participants believing that only overt acts constituted harassment.[117] The conclusion was drawn that sexual harassment is under-reported. Menon et al. concluded that the environment at the University of Zambia did not formally allow complaints

Survey' (1997) 37(9–10) *Sex Roles* 753; Cortina et al. above n 39; Schneider, Baker, and Stermac, above n 22; Danielle R Birdeau, Genie O Lenihan, and Cheryl L Somers, 'Effects of Educational Strategies on College Students' Identification of Sexual Harassment' (2005) 125(3) *Education* 496; Anitha Menon, Mary Peggy Shilalukey Ngoma, Seter Siziya, Mulenga Musepa et al. 'Sexual Harassment in Academia—Perception, Understanding and Reporting of Sexual Harassment in a Southern African University' (2011) 1(1) *Journal of Peace, Gender and Development Studies* 8.

103 McDonald, above n 23.

104 Dey, Korn, and Sax, above n 102.

105 Schneider, Baker and Stermac, above n 22.

106 Fitzgerald et al, above n 18.

107 Dey, Korn, and Sax, above n 102; Goodwin et al, above n 102.

108 Dey, Korn, and Sax, above n 102.

109 Ibid.

110 Schneider, Baker, and Stermac, above n 22.

111 Rubin, Hampton, and McManus, above n 102; Schneider, Baker, and Stermac, above n 22. The findings from these two studies support the contention that 'being exposed to sexualized, unprofessional behaviour in training has an impact on students' later behaviour as professionals': Schneider, Baker, and Stermac, above n 22, 160.

112 See Susan R Rankin, *Campus Climate for Gay, Lesbian, Bisexual and Transgender People: A National Perspective* (The Policy Institute of the National Gay and Lesbian Task Force, 2003): <http://www.thetaskforce.org/static_html/downloads/reports/reports/CampusClimate.pdf> [accessed 3 Jan 2016].

113 Tang et al. above n 102.

114 Ibid.

115 Schneider, Baker, and Stermac, above n 22.

116 Menon et al. above n 102.

117 Ibid.

about sexual harassment and that concrete measures for dealing with complaints were required as well as ongoing education for both perpetrators and victims of sexual harassment.[118]

Despite an increasing awareness of sexual harassment since the 1970s, sexual harassment in many tertiary environments still appears to be significantly under-reported.[119] Academic departments that provided 'more support for women's professional development and more general respect for students', in addition to those with 'higher proportions of women students, women faculty, and women full professors', were found to have lower rates of sexual harassment.[120] Thus, organizations that make clear what is and is not permitted by staff and that make concerted efforts to deal with the sexual harassment problem are more likely to avoid, or at least reduce, the problem.[121] Studies have suggested that education about sexual harassment can help a person identify a situation as sexual harassment, engage in effective, discouraging behaviours, and possibly prevent the harassment happening.[122]

University Policies

It is becoming standard for universities to put into place conflict of interest and anti-harassment policies that signal the unacceptability of various forms of relationships, as well as of staff engaging in sexual overtures or harassment towards students, both undergraduate and postgraduate, or other staff. It is common, too, for policies to make it clear that the exertion of pressure towards students or other staff by academics for their personal, sexual, or financial advantage is unacceptable.

Hyams has argued for the establishment of 'rigorous and unambiguous' policies and procedures in relation to sexual harassment 'in order to combat indolent or conservative attitudes to issues of gender equality',[123] stating also:

> In an institution such as a University where there is often an immense imbalance of personal power between the service deliverer and service user, the opportunity to use and abuse that imbalance must be acknowledged and controlled by strict protocols. Australian Universities are facing increased pressure to protect both themselves and the individual members that make up the University community from legal liability arising from misuses of power. Such power abuse underlies the manifold allegations of sexual harassment which occur in Universities.[124]

Sexual Harassment Policies

In its first university-wide initiative to address sexual harassment, Harvard University published its 'Sexual and Gender-Based Harassment Policy' in 2014.[125] It contains a number of novel features and has been very controversial.

---

118 Ibid.

119 Birdeau, Lenihan, and Somers, above n 102.

120 Charlotte Mandell, Anne Mulvey, and Meg A Bond, 'The Role of Gender and Organizational Context in the Experience of Adversity: Sexual Harassment as a Case Example' in Robert S Feldman (ed), *The Psychology of Adversity* (Amherst: University of Massachusetts Press, 1996) 262.

121 James E Gruber, 'The Impact of Male Work Environments and Organizational Policies on Women's Experiences of Sexual Harassment' (1998) 12(3) *Gender and Society* 301; Birdeau, Lenihan, and Somers, above n 102.

122 Birdeau, Lenihan, and Somers, above n 102.

123 Ross Hyams, 'Sexual Harassment in Australian Universities: Procedures to Make the Personal Public' (1998) 5 *James Cook University Law Review* 46, 69.

124 Ibid, 46.

125 Harvard University, 'Sexual and Gender-Based Harassment Policy', 15 October 2014: <http://diversity.harvard.edu/files/diversity/files/harvard_sexual_harassment_policy.pdf> [accessed 3 Jan 2016].

Sexual harassment is defined in the policy as:

> unwelcome conduct of a sexual nature, including unwelcome sexual advances, requests for sexual favors, and other verbal, nonverbal, graphic, or physical conduct of a sexual nature, when: (1) submission to or rejection of such conduct is made either explicitly or implicitly a condition of an individual's employment or academic standing or is used as the basis for employment decisions or for academic evaluation, grades, or advancement (quid pro quo); or (2) such conduct is sufficiently severe, persistent, or pervasive that it interferes with or limits a person's ability to participate in or benefit from the University's education or work programs or activities (hostile environment).[126]

***Quid pro quo* sexual harassment** is stipulated as able to occur:

> whether a person resists and suffers the threatened harm, or the person submits and avoids the threatened harm. Both situations could constitute discrimination on the basis of sex.[127]

The policy states that '[a] hostile environment can be created by persistent or pervasive conduct or by a single severe episode'.[128] Further, that '[t]he more severe the conduct, the less need there is to show a repetitive series of incidents to prove a hostile environment'.[129] Sexual harassment is understood to include instances of sexual violence—including 'rape, sexual assault, and domestic and dating violence'[130]—in addition to the following conduct, which may violate Harvard's Policy:

- Observing, photographing, videotaping, or making other visual or auditory records of sexual activity or nudity, where there is a reasonable expectation of privacy, without the knowledge and consent of all parties;
- Sharing visual or auditory records of sexual activity or nudity without the knowledge and consent of all recorded parties and recipient(s);
- Sexual advances, whether or not they involve physical touching;
- Commenting about or inappropriately touching an individual's body;
- Requests for sexual favors in exchange for actual or promised job benefits, such as favorable reviews, salary increases, promotions, increased benefits, or continued employment;
- Lewd or sexually suggestive comments, jokes, innuendoes, or gestures;
- Stalking.[131]

Other verbal, nonverbal, graphic, or physical conduct is said to create a hostile environment if the conduct is sufficiently persistent, pervasive, or severe so as to deny a person equal access to the Harvard University's programmes or activities. Whether the conduct creates a hostile environment is stated to depend on a variety of factors, including: the degree to which the conduct affected one or more person's education or employment; the type, frequency, and duration of the conduct; the relationship between the parties; the number of people involved; and the context in which the conduct occurred.

Conduct is classified as 'unwelcome' if a person did not request or invite it and regarded the unrequested or uninvited conduct as undesirable or offensive. Thus it is explicitly a subjective test, personal to the victim. That a person welcomes some sexual contact is stated not necessarily to mean that the person welcomes other sexual contact. Similarly, the fact that a person willingly participates in conduct on one occasion is stated not necessarily to mean that the same conduct is welcome on a subsequent occasion.

---

126 Ibid, 1–2.
127 Ibid, 2.
128 Ibid.
129 Ibid.
130 Ibid.
131 Ibid (formatting altered).

Harvard's Policy states that 'unwelcome' conduct is determined as such, after consideration of the 'totality of circumstances', including reference to 'various objective and subjective factors'.[132] In making this determination, the following 'types of information' might be of assistance:

- statements by any witnesses to the alleged incident;
- information about the relative credibility of the parties and witnesses;
- the detail and consistency of each person's account;
- the absence of corroborating information where it should logically exist;
- information that the Respondent has been found to have harassed others;
- information that the Complainant has been found to have made false allegations against others;
- information about the Complainant's reaction or behavior after the alleged incident; and
- information about any actions the parties took immediately following the incident, including reporting the matter to others.[133]

Gender-based harassment is classified as:

> verbal, nonverbal, graphic, or physical aggression, intimidation, or hostile conduct based on sex, sex-stereotyping, sexual orientation or gender identity, but not involving conduct of a sexual nature, when such conduct is sufficiently severe, persistent, or pervasive that it interferes with or limits a person's ability to participate in or benefit from the University's education or work programs or activities.

To illustrate this classification, the Policy refers to a situation where an individual is persistently disparaged, 'based on a perceived lack of stereotypical masculinity or femininity or exclusion from an activity based on sexual orientation or gender identity', and suggests that this conduct is also capable of violating the Policy.[134]

The policy is stated to apply to sexual or gender-based harassment that is committed by students, faculty, staff, Harvard appointees, or third parties, whenever the misconduct occurs, on Harvard property; or even off Harvard property, if the conduct was in connection with a University or University-recognized programme or activity; or the conduct has the potential to have the effect of creating a hostile environment for a member of the University community.

In part it is the reach of the policy that has had repercussions and prompted something of a backlash. The first response was that the Harvard Law School broke away from the policy, accepting the definitions and offences but setting up its own procedures.[135] Then a number of Law School professors who were critical of the policy maintained that the new definition of sexual harassment could endanger academic inquiry on topics of human sexuality, like rape law, as they claim Harvard's policy does not also provide adequate protections of academic freedom. Calling the policy's statement on academic freedom 'unhelpful,' Professor Janet Halley of the Law School, argued that 'speech [in an academic context] can be a form of sexual conduct under the policy, and if it's unwanted, speech acts could become the basis for charges of sexual harassment.'[136]

---

[132] Ibid.

[133] Ibid, 3 (formatting altered).

[134] Ibid.

[135] Theodore R Delwiche and Andrew M Duehren, 'New Law School Sexual Harassment Procedures Break From University Framework', *The Harvard Crimson*, 3 January 2015: <http://www.thecrimson.com/article/2015/1/3/pending-procedures-law-school-title-ix/> [accessed 3 Jan 2016].

[136] Andrew M Duehren, 'Law Profs Challenge Title IX Policy's Protection of Academic Freedom', *The Harvard Crimson*, 18 February 2015: <http://www.thecrimson.com/article/2015/2/18/law-profs-academic-freedom/> [accessed 3 Jan 2016].

By contrast the University of Melbourne defines 'sexual harassment' as 'unwelcome behaviour or conduct of a sexual nature, which makes another person feel offended, humiliated to intimidated'.[137] It identifies a wide range of behaviour which can qualify as sexual harassment:

> For example, if you either intentionally or unintentionally:
> - subject someone to unwanted physical contact or gestures;
> - ask intrusive questions, or subject someone to insinuations about their private life;
> - make jokes or insinuations of a sexual nature;
> - subject someone to sex-based insults or taunts;
> - make persistent unwanted invitations of a personal nature;
> - explicitly or implicitly demand someone to engage in sexual activity;
> - display offensive or pornographic material such as posters, pin-ups, cartoons, graffiti, screen savers or calendars; or
> - send an offensive communication of a sexual nature by means of a note, letter, telephone, computer, or by electronic mail or any other means[;]
>
> IN circumstances in which a reasonable person, having regard to all the circumstances, would have anticipated that the person harassed would be offended, humiliated or uncomfortable, THEN that behaviour constitutes sexual harassment.[138]

Significantly, then, the definition is broadly consistent with that in the *Sex Discrimination Act* 1984 (Cth) but somewhat broader in its scope and more illustrative in its examples.

The University of Melbourne is typical of many tertiary institutions in warning of the risks of staff–student personal relationships but only proscribing them in certain, limited scenarios:

> There are significant risks in any sexual or romantic relationship between individuals in unequal positions, such as lecturer and student, supervisor and student/employee, or student resident and the individual who supervises the day-to-day student living environment.
>
> Such relationships may undermine the real or perceived integrity of the supervision, evaluation provided and the trust in the student/staff relationship. In addition, as a result of an unequal power balance, one person may feel pressured to be involved in a sexual relationship.
>
> [...]
>
> Relationships where one person is in a position to review the work or influence the career of the other may provide grounds for a complaint when that relationship gives unfair access, advantage or disadvantage to the student(s) involved, or restricts opportunities and creates a difficult environment for others.[139]

It has promulgated the following principles in respect of staff–student relationships:

1.1 University staff, both academic and professional, are in a position of trust with students. This position of trust implies a series of responsibilities owed to students. In exercising those responsibilities staff should avoid conflicts of interest, that is, a conflict between a personal relationship and professional responsibilities.

1.2 To have a close personal relationship with a student to whom one has a duty of care is likely to involve serious difficulties arising from the power disparity inherent in the staff–student relationship. In general, such relationships should be avoided.

---

137 The University of Melbourne, 'Someone Says I Sexually Harassed Them...' (Equal Opportunity Unit, Human Resources, November 2000) 1: <http://hr.unimelb.edu.au/__data/assets/pdf_file/0008/329894/4-SomeoneSays.pdf> (viewed 31 March 2015).

138 Ibid (footnote omitted).

139 The University of Melbourne, 'Staff/Student Relationships: Drawing the Line' (July 2010): <https://hr.unimelb.edu.au/__data/assets/pdf_file/0008/87875/DrawingTheLineDL-July2010.pdf> (viewed 31 March 2015).

1.3 An initial sexual approach to a student, or engaging in a sexual relationship with a student, may constitute sexual harassment and can be the subject of complaint under the Discrimination, Sexual Harassment and Bullying Procedure or to an outside body.
1.4 Some relationships may disrupt the teaching and learning environment for other students and colleagues.
1.5 Relationships with family members or with friends or associates in the University environment may raise ethical and professional issues, including conflicts of interest.[140]

The evolution of university policies and procedures in respect of sexual improprieties by both staff and students continues. After the publication of a pro-rape website by students at St Paul's College at the University of Sydney and an inability on the part of the university to insist on access to the names of the students involved, the university extended its powers to enable action to be taken in such circumstances, although the conduct technically fell outside sexual harassment processes.[141]

In this context, much often depends on definitions, such as that relating to sexual harassment which has the potential to include a wide range of behaviours:

An example of a broad-based stricture is that of the University of Greenwich. Its policy on 'Relationships Between Staff and their Students' covers:

> any kind of relationship between a member of academic staff and students which could undermine the integrity and objectivity of the staff role. The Policy thus aims to ensure that relationships between staff and students do not give rise to more or less favourable treatment, or cause others to question the integrity of a staff member.[142]

This leaves evaluation of when a line is crossed to the judgment of the staff member involved but pointedly enables disciplinary action. Policies relating to misconduct are often accompanied by complaint and investigation procedures such as a requirement for the university to form misconduct investigation committees to investigate complaints of sexual harassment and conflicts of interest.[143] Generally, misconduct committees will report to the Vice-Chancellor's office which will make the final decision on any disciplinary action to be taken with regards to a complaint that has been proven. In some circumstances this may result in the termination of an academic for breach of university policies for misconduct under enterprise agreements. The recourse for the academic in this instance will generally be under workplace relations legislation.

Universities are required to comply with university procedures for complaints and termination of employment, including detailing the particulars of allegations of complaints against an academic.[144] Jackson has argued that the policies in place today mean that the summary

[140] The University of Melbourne, 'Staff-Student Relationships Procedure' (MPF 1137)' (Melbourne Policy Library, 21 August 2012): <https://policy.unimelb.edu.au/MPF1137> (viewed 31 March 2015).

[141] Heath Gilmore and Ruth Pollard, 'Sydney University Expands Sex-Assault Policy', *The Sydney Morning Herald*, 25 February 2010: <http://www.smh.com.au/nsw/sydney-university-expands-sexassault-policy-20100224-p3ly.html> [accessed 4 Jan 2016].

[142] University of Greenwich, 'Relationships Between Staff and Their Students: Guidelines for Managers' (January 2015) [1]: <http://www.gre.ac.uk/__data/assets/pdf_file/0011/664787/Relationships-Between-Staff-and-Their-Students-Guidance-for-Managers-January-2015.pdf> [accessed 4 Jan 2016]. The Policy provides examples of relationships that 'would be seen as Undermining Trust and Confidence between Staff and Students', including 'sexual, romantic or close personal relationships with students (past and current)': ibid.

[143] See eg, Clause 53 of the *Monash University Enterprise Agreement (Academic and Professional Staff) 2009*, available at: <http://adm.monash.edu.au/enterprise-agreements/academic-professional-2009/> [accessed 4 Jan 2016]. For a detailed discussion of dismissal processes in Australian universities, see Jim Jackson, 'Orr to Steele: Crafting Dismissal Processes in Australian Universities' (2003) 7 *Southern Cross University Law Review* 220.

[144] *Chambers v James Cook University of North Queensland (No 2)* [1995] IRCA 48; (1995) 61 IR 145; *McAleer v The University of Western Australia* [2007] FCA 52; (2007) 159 IR 96. The *McAleer* case involved allegations of sexual harassment against Professor Michael McAleer, a prominent economist, by two female

dismissal that occurred in *Orr's*[145] case, discussed below, would therefore be less likely to take place.[146]

The approach of Griffith University is broad-based:

> The general principle to guide behaviour is that it is unethical and undesirable for a personal relationship to intrude, or be perceived to intrude on or influence working practices and decisions.

The Griffith Policy defines 'personal relationships' as those 'which extend beyond professional relations, based on factors irrelevant to the working competencies of staff'. Examples of such relationships include:

- family relationships (siblings, parent/child, husband/wife, de facto spouses, partner, cousins, relations by marriage such as brother- or sister-in-law);
- emotional relationships (including sexual relationships and close friendships);
- financial relationships (commercial relationships where pecuniary interest is present).[147]

To comparable effect, Macquarie University states the following on 'Conflicts of Interest':

> 24.01.08 Staff should avoid any financial or other interest or undertaking that could directly or indirectly compromise the performance of their duties. Conflicts of interest should be assessed in terms of the likelihood that staff members possessing a particular interest could be influenced, or might appear to be influenced, in the performance of their duties on a particular matter.
>
> 24.01.09 The University will not routinely involve itself in the private lives of its staff and students. However, a conflict of interest may arise where a staff member engages in activities or advances personal interests at the expense of the University's interests or the interests of other staff members or students.
>
> 24.01.10 The following situations are provided as examples of where a potential for conflict of interest may easily occur.
> [...]
>
> *Personal and family relationships between staff members*
>
> 24.01.12 The University is aware that situations may occur where staff are working with family members or with persons with whom they develop close personal relationships.
>
> 24.01.13 Where such relationships exist between staff or with prospective staff the University does not wish to interfere unnecessarily but stresses that they may have the potential to create a conflict of interest if one staff member is:

---

lecturers. Siopis J of the Federal Court held that the University of Western Australia had not complied with the provisions of disciplinary procedure under the university enterprise agreement in force at the time of the investigation against Professor McAleer by failing to provide particulars of allegations of serious misconduct. Despite the judgment in *McAleer v University of Western Australia* [2007] FCA 52 the university proceeded to investigate claims of sexual harassment and Professor McAleer sought a stay of the disciplinary proceedings, which was dismissed by Siopis J in *McAleer v University of Western Australia (No 3)* [2008] FCA 1490; (2008) 171 FCR 499. In 2009 the University of Western Australia dropped the investigation and reached a confidential settlement, with Professor McAleer resigning from the university: Andrew Trounson, 'UWA Drops Economist Prof's Sex Probe', *The Australian*, 4 February 2009: <http://www.theaustralian.com.au/higher-education/uwa-drops-economist-profs-sex-probe/story-e6frgcjx-1111118756938> [accessed 4 Jan 2016].

145 *Orr v The University of Tasmania* [1956] 1 Tas SR 155.

146 See Jackson, above n 143.

147 Griffith University, 'Personal Relationships in the Workplace', 1 December 2014, [3]: <http://policies.griffith.edu.au/pdf/Personal%20Relationships%20in%20the%20Workplace.pdf> [accessed 4 Jan 2016]. See also, The University of Iowa, 'Sexual Harassment Can Happen Anywhere' (2009): <http://www.sexualharassment.uiowa.edu/examples.php> [accessed 4 Jan 2016].

- involved in a decision relating to the selection, appointment or promotion of another;
- in a supervisory relationship to another and is responsible for employment related decisions.

Personal and family relationships between staff members and students

24.01.14 Academic staff have a responsibility to their students to assess their work fairly, objectively and consistently across the candidature for their particular subject/unit/course. A personal or family relationship between an Academic staff member and a student has the potential to compromise this responsibility where the staff member is responsible for the supervision, teaching and/or any level of assessment of that student, or indirectly by affecting a student's interaction with the University.

24.01.15 In many cases, only the individual staff member will be aware of the potential for conflict. Therefore, the onus is on that person to notify the appropriate senior member of staff if a potential or actual conflict of interest arises.[148]

In the United Kingdom, there are many differences in the policies that are applied. Warwick University strongly advises staff not to enter into an intimate relationship with a student for whom they have a professional responsibility:

> Such relationships can lead to a lack of confidence in the integrity of due process and perceived or actual conflicts of interest, which can have a detrimental effect on the teaching and learning environment for other students and colleagues.
>
> The University recognises, however, that such relationships may exist, either when a member of staff is appointed or when a student enrols. Where a member of staff involved in such a relationship would ordinarily have a professional relationship with a student, it is the responsibility of the member of staff to inform his or her Head of Department (or nominated representative) or the Director of Human Resources, in order that alternative arrangements can be made. Such steps should include the prohibition of the member of staff from accessing a student's records on [student record system] SITS or other local student records system; from accessing the student's assessment record... and/or ensuring that the Head of Department is able to audit any such entries made. This is to protect both the staff member and student from accusations of unfair and preferential treatment.[149]

It reached this position in the aftermath of publicity arising from a relationship between a student who elected to have an abortion and a law professor who taught Human Rights and International Law.[150]

In the United States, there is a spectrum of approaches in relation to sexual harassment and sexual relationships between staff and students. The orthodox situation in relation to sexual harassment is exemplified by the position of the University of Miami which defines such harassment as 'unwelcome sexual advances, requests for sexual favors, and other verbal, visual or physical conduct of a sexual nature, including, but not limited to sexual jokes, innuendos,

[148] Macquarie University, *Code of Conduct*: <http://www.pers.mq.edu.au/pdf/policy/working/rewardandrecognition/2401.html> [accessed 4 Jan 2016] (formatting altered).

[149] The University of Warwick, 'Personal Conflicts of Interest: Guidance for Staff and Students' (December 2009) [5.4]–[5.5]: <http://www2.warwick.ac.uk/insite/atoz/p/personal_conflicts_of_interest_policy.doc> [accessed 4 Jan 2016] (formatting altered).

[150] See Paul Rigg, 'Ban Sex Between Lecturers and Students?' Issue No. 60, *University World News*, 25 January 2009: <http://www.universityworldnews.com/article.php?story=20090122194702813> [accessed 4 Jan 2016]; Alastair Jamieson, 'Student Has Abortion After Affair with Professor', *The Telegraph*, 7 December 2008: <http://www.telegraph.co.uk/education/universityeducation/3659924/Student-has-abortion-after-affair-with-professor.html> [accessed 4 Jan 2016].

display of sexually suggestive objects, or any unnecessary, unwanted physical conduct'.[151] The policy precluding sexual harassment[152] was invoked in 2013 in relation to a well-known British philosopher, Professor Colin McGinn,[153] a member of the 'New Mysterians', who, according to a graduate student, had sexually harassed her, writing to her that he 'had a hard job imagining you giving me a hand job' and floating a proposal to have sex three times with her over the summer 'when no one is around'.[154] Ultimately, he resigned,[155] although the university never alleged he had engaged in sexual harassment, making no finding in that regard, rather asserting that he had engaged in unprofessional conduct 'due to the amorous relationship that developed between a senior faculty member and his student'.[156] The University of Miami's policy in this regard is one of discouragement, rather than outright proscription:

> Amorous dating, or sexual relationships that might be appropriate in other circumstances have inherent dangers when they occur between a faculty member, supervisor, or other member of the University community and any person for whom he or she has a professional responsibility.
>
> Accordingly, faculty members, supervisors, and other members of the University community who have professional responsibility for other individuals should be aware that any romantic or sexual involvement with a student or employee for whom they have such a responsibility may raise questions as to the mutuality of the relationship and may lead to charges of sexual harassment. For the reasons stated above, such relationships are strongly discouraged.[157]

By contrast, a zero-tolerance trend in respect of staff–student sexual relationships commenced during the mid-1990s with the University of California adopting a ban in 2003 and Iowa State University, Syracuse University and Yale following suit.[158] As of 2014 Yale's policy statement on sexual harassment prescribed that '[i]f members of the faculty, whether professors or

---

151 University of Miami, 'Sexual Harassment FAQs': <http://www.miami.edu/index.php/wep/sexual_harassment-1/sexual_harassment_faqs/> [accessed 4 Jan 2016].

152 University of Miami, 'Sexual Harassment': <http://www.miami.edu/index.php/wep/sexual_harassment-1/> [accessed 4 Jan 2016].

153 See below, p 419.

154 Katie Roiphe, 'The Philosopher and the Student', *Slate*, 8 October 2013: <http://www.slate.com/articles/double_x/roiphe/2013/10/colin_mcginn_sexual_harassment_case_was_the_philosophy_prof_s_story_that.html> (viewed 1 April 2015); Jennifer Schuessler, 'A Star Philosopher Falls, and a Debate Over Sexism is Set Off', *The New York Times*, 2 August 2013: <http://www.nytimes.com/2013/08/03/arts/colin-mcginn-philosopher-to-leave-his-post.html?pagewanted=all&_r=1> [accessed 4 Jan 2016].

155 Seth Zweifler, 'Prominent Philosopher to Leave U. of Miami in Wake of Misconduct Allegations', *The Chronicle of Higher Education*, 4 June 2013: <http://chronicle.com/article/Prominent-Philosopher-to-Leave/139613/> [accessed 4 Jan 2016].

156 Roiphe, above n 154.

157 University of Miami, 'Consensual Relationships': <http://www.miami.edu/index.php/wep/consensual_relationships/> [accessed 4 Jan 2016].

158 Compare with American Medical Association, 'Opinion 3.08—Sexual Harassment and Exploitation between Medical Supervisors and Trainees': <http://www.ama-assn.org/ama/pub/physician-resources/medical-ethics/code-medical-ethics/opinion308.page?> [accessed 4 Jan 2016]:

> Sexual harassment may be defined as sexual advances, requests for sexual favors, and other verbal or physical conduct of a sexual nature when (1) such conduct interferes with an individual's work or academic performance or creates an intimidating, hostile, or offensive work or academic environment or (2) accepting or rejecting such conduct affects or may be perceived to affect employment decisions or academic evaluations concerning the individual. Sexual harassment is unethical.
>
> Sexual relationships between medical supervisors and their medical trainees raise concerns because of inherent inequalities in the status and power that medical supervisors wield in relation to medical trainees and may adversely affect patient care. Sexual relationships between a medical trainee and a supervisor even when consensual are not acceptable regardless of the degree of supervision in any given situation. The supervisory role should be eliminated if the parties involved wish to pursue their relationship.

teaching fellows, or other Yale employees, introduce sex into a professional relationship with a student, they abuse their position of authority'.[159] Its policy on teacher–student consensual relations unequivocally proscribes any form of sexual relationship:

> The integrity of the teacher–student relationship is the foundation of the University's educational mission. This relationship vests considerable trust in the teacher, who, in turn, bears authority and accountability as a mentor, educator, and evaluator. The unequal institutional power inherent in this relationship heightens the vulnerability of the student and the potential for coercion. The pedagogical relationship between teacher and student must be protected from influences or activities that can interfere with learning and personal development.
>
> Whenever a teacher is or in the future might reasonably become responsible for teaching, advising, or directly supervising a student, a sexual relationship between them is inappropriate and must be avoided. In addition to creating the potential for coercion, any such relationship jeopardizes the integrity of the educational process by creating a conflict of interest and may impair the learning environment for other students. Finally, such situations may expose the University and the teacher to liability for violation of laws against sexual harassment and sex discrimination.
>
> Therefore, teachers . . . must avoid sexual relationships with students over whom they have or might reasonably expect to have direct pedagogical or supervisory responsibilities, regardless of whether the relationship is consensual. Conversely, a teacher must not directly supervise any student with whom he or she has a sexual relationship. Undergraduate students are particularly vulnerable to the unequal institutional power inherent in the teacher–student relationship and the potential for coercion, because of their age and relative lack of maturity. Therefore, no teacher shall have a sexual or amorous relationship with any undergraduate student, regardless of whether the teacher currently exercises or expects to have any pedagogical or supervisory responsibilities over that student.[160]

What can be identified in many countries is a trend towards universities warning staff and students alike of the perils of staff–student relationships and providing general discouragement to their coming into being. In addition, universities are being clearer and more responsive to the creation of inappropriate dynamics that can attach to the formation of such relationships—namely, their instigation by staff in circumstances where overtures and/or approaches can in any way be interpreted as constituting sexual harassment or involving any kind of a threat of adverse consequences if the student is not receptive or does not cooperate. The further strand in the approach by universities is to mandate that staff who enter into such relationships take adequate measures to ensure that they rid themselves of any conflict of interest in respect of the student with whom they have entered into a relationship.

While broad definitions of sexual harassment are generally being utilized, so as to capture a wide range of behaviour that has a sexualized resonance or insinuation, examples of problematic conduct not traditionally caught by legislation-derived definitions of sexual harassment continue to emerge and to be integrated into illustrations of conduct that is not permitted. The issue of conflict of interest is somewhat more diffuse and could be the beneficiary of further attention in universities' codes of conduct so as to alert staff and students alike to conduct from which both should abstain.

---

159 Yale University, Division of the Vice President and General Counsel, 'Sexual Harassment': <http://ogc.yale.edu/sexual-harassment> [accessed 4 Jan 2016].

160 Yale University, Office for Equal Opportunity Programs, 'Policy on Teacher–Student Consensual Relations': <http://www.yale.edu/equalopportunity/policies/index.html> [accessed 4 Jan 2016].

Serial Conduct and Inadequate Responses by Universities

University of Colorado, Philosophy Department

A 2013 inquiry into the fact that multiple complaints had been made about members of the University of Colorado, Boulder, Philosophy Department, found that the sexually harassing environment within the department had many of its origins in a blurring of boundaries facilitated by alcohol consumption at night, off-site, between academics and postgraduate students.[161] The committee found a range of cultural precipitants to the problems that ensued, including fostering an environment with 'unacceptable sexual harassment, inappropriate sexualized unprofessional behaviour, and divisive uncivil behavior'.[162] It emphasized that this environment had harmed women and men and members of every stakeholder group in the department, including female faculty members avoiding the workplace and opportunities to socialize with colleagues, and in their leaving or 'trying to leave in disproportionate numbers'.[163] It advanced multiple recommendations for changes in culture and practice and recommended that 'recovery processes' be 'both rigorous and guided'.[164]

Elbaki Hermassi

The conduct of Elbaki Hermassi, an Assistant Professor of Sociology at the Berkeley campus of the University of California in the late 1970s, has been argued to be an example of the stereotypical 'lecherous professor'.[165] It can also be regarded as exemplary of outdated approaches by universities to investigation of allegation of sexual misconduct against staff.

Hermassi was accused by no fewer than 13 female students of fondling and sexually propositioning them, in one instance offering a grade for compliance with his advances and in another making an unfavourable recommendation in respect of a student who declined his overtures. He denied all allegations and at first received merely a verbal reprimand. However, in response to pressure the university appointed Professor Susan French of the Law School to conduct a confidential investigation.

Problematically, but not unusually in such matters (in part sometimes to protect the privacy of the complainants[166]), Professor French's report was not made public but in due course the Chancellor

---

161 The American Philosophical Association, Committee on the Status of Women, *Report on Site Visit* (University of Colorado Boulder, Department of Philosophy, 25–28 September 2013), available at: <http://spot.colorado.edu/~tooley/The_Site_Visit_Report_and_Administration_Summary.pdf> [accessed 4 Jan 2016].

162 Ibid, 3.

163 Ibid.

164 Ibid, 4.

165 Dziech and Weiner, above n 4.

166 In 2013 the nine member board of governors of the Indian Institute of Technology-Madras suspended Professor B Ramamoorthy, a Professor of Mechanical Engineering, after finding him to have behaved in 'an improper manner, displaying what may be referred to as *mala fide* intentions towards a student who trusted him'. The student had claimed that the professor, whom she had accompanied to a science conference in Poland, asked her to sleep in his hotel room and then tried to force himself on her during the night. When the university was asked by the media about the matter it responded: 'As per section 16 of the Sexual Harassment of Women at Workplace (Prevention, Prohibition and Redressal) Act 2013, details regarding complaint of sexual harassment, if any, cannot be disclosed. In the light of the above, IIT-Madras is not in a position to give any details of complaints of sexual harassment received by us, whether past or present': Arun Janardhanan, 'IIT-Madras Suspends Professor After Student Alleges Sexual Harassment', *The Times of India*, 25 December 2013: <http://timesofindia.indiatimes.com/india/IIT-Madras-suspends-professor-after-student-alleges-sexual-harassment/articleshow/27869547.cms?referral=PM> [accessed 4 Jan 2016]. Professor Ramamoorthy did not provide an account of the matter to the media.

issued his own statement that 'misconduct warranting discipline' had occurred but that it happened during a 'relatively short period of time' while Hermassi was 'suffering personal emotional stress'.[167] Troublingly, this appeared to have been viewed as significantly mitigatory from the perspective of the university. Hermassi continued to deny all allegations but was recorded by the Chancellor as having 'agreed to accept the administration's proposed disposition of the case in order to avoid formal proceedings and set the matter at rest'.[168] Thus, the case, although involving a great many allegations, and some degree of adverse finding, was resolved 'behind the scenes' in a way that could not conduce to a perception of fairness or rigour in the process.

William Bender

Another example of conduct that was serially the subject of complaint or expression of concern over a period of some 20 years, but not for a long while the subject of sanction, is the case of William Bender, a Professor of Communication Sciences and Special Education at the University of Georgia.

After many years it emerged from documentation held by the university that Professor Bender had engaged in an ongoing sequence of lewd propositions and sleazy remarks and suggestions for over two decades.[169] It was asserted that he told female students sexually suggestive jokes, invited them to his lake house to swim and to use his Jacuzzi, and made unwelcome remarks about their bodies. Some students asserted that when they rebuffed his requests for dates or sexual conduct he would behave retributively towards them. Some were not prepared to formalize their concerns for fear of consequences for their student career.

Professor Bender finally resigned his position in 2008 after allegations were made by an angry husband that Bender had had an improper relationship with his wife. However, Professor Bender maintained that the allegations of inappropriate behaviour were 'exaggerated or represent outright falsehoods. Those who know me recognize that the pattern of behavior described does not appropriately characterize who I am'.[170] Adding to his denial he raised in his defence, somewhat irrelevantly, what he said was the high quality of his teaching and the fact that students had placed themselves in positions of one-to-one tuition with him: 'I am consistently evaluated as an excellent teacher, and a great many students over the years have chosen to work directly with me.'[171] Again, the scholar denied the serious allegations and it is apparent that timely investigations in respect of the matters did not proceed to a point where there could be authoritative resolution. Instead, assertion and innuendo swirled unsatisfactorily for all concerned for a considerable period of time.

The Subtleties of Harassment/Inappropriate Relationship Cases

As indicated above (p 416), the well-known English philosopher, Colin McGinn, was the subject of a sexual harassment complaint, in the aftermath of which he resigned, having been charged by the University of Miami with 'unprofessional conduct due to the amorous

---

167 Dziech and Weiner, above n 4, 28.

168 Ibid. This and many other examples of such matters are usefully recounted by Dziech and Weiner, above n 4, 27ff.

169 Kristen Coulter, 'Documents: Professor Sexually Harasses Students for 20 Years', *The Red & Black*, 30 January 2008: <http://www.redandblack.com/news/documents-professor-sexually-harasses-students-for-years/article_35703a1e-e7b9-547e-9f63-125bb8f03087.html> [accessed 4 Jan 2016].

170 Robin Wilson, 'Professor Accused of Sexual Harassment Resigns', *The Chronicle of Higher Education*, 30 January 2008: <http://chronicle.com/article/Professor-Accused-of-Sexual/40344> [accessed 4 Jan 2016].

171 Ibid.

relationship that developed between a senior faculty member and his student'.[172] The relationship was characterized by ambiguity in a way that is common in allegations of sexual misconduct. The ambiguity can enable the staff member to rationalize their behaviour and it can be both at the heart of the attraction to the student and the confusion that can generate and characterize the relationship from the student's point of view.

McGinn was a flamboyant philosopher in his 60s at the time he entered into the unorthodox relationship with his first-year graduate student in 2011. She took a course with him on the role of the hand in human evolution. She would bring lunch to his office and they would eat together and talk about philosophy. They co-wrote a philosophical paper and played tennis and paddleboarded together. And then things went sour and she complained he had been sexually harassing her.

The main evidence against Professor McGinn lay in the emails and texts that they exchanged and in the accounts of the student and the professor after the relationship had ended unhappily. Until a certain point the correspondence was characterized by an avid and affectionate rapport, employing an elaborate private language related to their philosophical undertakings together. It was marked by jokes and was enthusiastic, playful and effusive with the student expostulating, 'Colin! My prehensive companion! How I miss you!'[173] Emails from both referred to the union and companionship between them. Roiphe observed that:

> In the emails and texts, she did not seem to be passively replying, or tepidly appeasing him, but rather actively creating and nurturing the private language. There were times when he pulled back or expressed pessimism and she reassured him of the strength of the bond, and argued for the adaptiveness or resilience of their connection. There was a moment . . . when she said she would be 'devastated' if he lost interest. Her texts, which remain in his phone, say things like 'thank you, dearest,' 'sending you virtual hugs,' 'I send you a hand squeeze,' and 'you have an incredibly sexy mind'.[174]

There seems no suggestion that the relationship involved penetrative sex but it was romantic and sexualized with them holding and caressing each other's hands and feet. On one occasion, the student texted her professor: 'I was thinking of your thumb this morning intertwined with mine' and emailed him: 'I should add that I felt a bit of imprint from the hand exercises yesterday when I was typing away. I paused for a couple of moments to enjoy it.'[175] In her complaint, though, she maintained that the touching of her hands and feet made her 'uncomfortable'.[176] The communications between the two were at times playful, warm, and clever, and at other times marked by her ambivalence and pulling back and making excuses. As Roiphe observes, this is hardly surprising given she was 26 and he 61 and at the time she had a boyfriend. Later McGinn acknowledged that he should have removed himself as the student's supervisor, recognized the conflict and the potential risks of mingling their personal and professional relationships, and told her he could not work with her.

There is no doubt that McGinn was foolish, culpable, and improper in persisting in a supervisory relationship with his student in the circumstances. He has defended himself by arguing that he reproached her for not concentrating sufficiently on the work he was paying her to do and that that resulted in reinterpretation of what had passed between them, leading to her allegations. As Roiphe comments: 'To a certain extent this is a recognizable, even common occurrence: where some form of ambivalent romance or illicit situation ends in bitterness,

172 Roiphe, above n 154.
173 Ibid.
174 Ibid.
175 Ibid.
176 Ibid.

where suddenly the ambivalence tips into resentment, where everything is interpreted rigidly in an ominous framework, where you turn the other person into a terrible caricature of himself or herself, only usually it doesn't end in lives being ruined, or livelihoods destroyed.'[177]

The McGinn case is an archetypal example of conduct from which scholars should refrain—the inappropriately personal communications with the student, the excessively familiar and sexualized banter, the extra-curricular meetings, the creation of ambiguity, the sexualization or romanticization of the relationship, all the while continuing to supervise and even employ. Given the circumstances, the chances were always high of those involved having different views of what had taken place and of problems emerging. And Professor McGinn was culpable in this regard. He had enabled the ambiguity and facilitated the romanticization of the professor–student relationship, utilizing his experience in a seductive and improper way. Was his conduct sexual harassment? It was around and about the mark but for a long while it appears from their communications that it was not unwelcome so for the most part would not have met the criteria in the University of Miami sexual harassment policy. What was undoubtedly serious (and what constituted the University's allegation against him) was that (on his own version of events) he maintained the improper and foreseeably damaging dual relationships of professor and romance partner with his student, not acknowledging the situation to the head of department and not only staying in a supervisory role but adding an extra dimension to the dual relationship by employing her to do work for him. His case is illustrative of why universities actively discourage staff from conducting themselves as Professor McGinn did and of the complex dynamics that can result both in the formation of ill-advised relationships between staff and students and how and why they can founder, resulting in recriminations and allegations.

Allegations and Counter-allegations

Liam Donnelly. In 1997 a third-year student, Rachel Marsden, at Simon Fraser University, made a complaint to the university sexual harassment committee, alleging that she had been forced to have sex with a swimming coach, Liam Donnelly. Although the police declined to investigate, a panel at Simon Fraser found her allegations to be substantiated and the university paid her CA$12,000 in compensation. The case became extremely bitter and high-profile. Donnelly was fired by the university but then produced evidence that it was Marsden who had pursued him for 18 months. He was reinstated, rehired, and paid compensation after the university acknowledged that its investigation was flawed. This left neither set of allegations proved. The university President resigned over the mishandling of the case.

However, in 1999 Marsden was warned that she would be evicted from campus residence unless she agreed to stay away from Donnelly and a Simon Fraser criminology professor, both of whom complained she was stalking them. In 2004 she pleaded guilty to criminally harassing a talk show host after being warned to stay away from him.[178]

The case is illustrative of the complexities that can attend the conduct and emotions of those who make allegations, as well as those who are the subject of allegations, in sexual harassment matters.

Donald Dutton. In 1999 Faribha Mahmoodi lodged a complaint against a psychology member of the University of British Columbia staff, Dr Donald Dutton. Dutton also made

177 Ibid.

178 See John Goddard, 'Cop Claims Harassment by the 'Babe for Bush', *The Star*, 21 December 2007: <http://www.thestar.com/news/ontario/2007/12/21/cop_claims_harassment_by_the_babe_for_bush.html> [accessed 4 Jan 2016].

a complaint against Mahmoodi. She accused him of creating an unwelcome sexualized environment in his capacity as professor and academic advisor by requesting that meetings about her entitlement to enter a graduate programme be held at his house over a candlelit dinner with seductive music playing in the background and his lamenting the lack of intimacy in his life. Dutton, with support from the British Columbia Civil Liberties Association, alleged that she made a complaint to coerce him into smoothing her entry into graduate school. Dutton refused to cooperate with an internal inquiry, on legal advice, leading to the matter being transferred to a disciplinary process which found Dutton guilty of professional misconduct, albeit not overt sexual interaction. Ultimately, in proceedings that were extremely adversarial and heavily publicized by the media, the Human Rights Tribunal, which was called upon to deal with the complaint, found that both parties lacked credibility but upheld the claim that Dutton had discriminated against Mahmoodi by imposing on her an unwelcome and sexualized environment. Dutton unsuccessfully appealed to the British Columbia Supreme Court.[179]

The case was extremely controversial and divisive. A consequence of the problems attaching to the investigation of the Donnelly and Dutton complaints was significant revision of investigative processes in Canadian universities.[180]

Tom Namwamba. A notorious example of a prominent scholar maintaining that he was the victim of sexual harassment from students occurred in Kenya where Dr Tom Namwamba, a lecturer in philosophy and creative writing at Kenyatta University,[181] decided to retaliate against blogs suggesting that he was giving his female students 'sexually-transmitted marks'.[182] Dr Namwamba approached the police, asking for a blogger to be criminally investigated for publishing false allegations against him, and then went public in the media with his distress: 'Some of the claims are used as bench marks for promotions. So, I will not keep quiet and see my career and family ruined because of lies.... I announced that anyone with information that I have slept with my students to better their grades should report me to the police or the university with specific details. No one has done that.'[183] Dr Namwamba then published details of his HIV/AIDS status on social media, after the circulation of rumours that he was infecting his student victims with the virus. The tertiary employees' union was reported as accusing students and the public of being unfair with their sex-for-marks accusations.

No allegations in the scholarly environment are more personally confronting and more apt to be characterized by assertions and counter-assertions than those in the sexual domain.

Complaints, University Responses, and Court Challenges

The saga involving Professor Robert Ammon Jr, head of the Slippery Rock University's Sports Management Department, extended over a number of years. In 2006 he was reprimanded for sexually harassing a student. Then in March 2010 he undertook a Spring break trip to Spain. In a Madrid bar he quizzed a number of students about their sexual experiences and related some of his own, claiming to have slept with more than 100 people, including a number

179 *Dutton v British Columbia (Human Rights Tribunal)*, 2001 BCSC 1256. See also Hester Lessard, 'Backlash in the Academy: The Evolution of Campus Sexual Harassment Regimes' in Dorothy E Chunn, Susan B Boyd, and Hester Lessard (eds), *Reaction and Resistance: Feminism, Law, and Social Change* (Vancouver: University of British Columbia Press, 2007) 179ff.

180 See Helen Burnett-Nichols, 'Don't Touch, Do Tell', *University Affairs*, 8 March 2010: <http://www.universityaffairs.ca/features/feature-article/dont-touch-do-tell/> [accessed 4 Jan 2016].

181 Nyambega Gisesa, 'Lecturer Bares it All on Sex-for-Marks Claims', *Standard Digital*, 12 April 2013: <http://www.standardmedia.co.ke/?articleID=2000081377> [accessed 4 Jan 2016].

182 Ibid.

183 Ibid.

while he was married. He said that one particular female student would become his favourite, if she would perform a particular sex act on him.

Ammon apologized later to the student and maintained that he had only made the statement because he was intoxicated. He maintained what he had said was 'trash talk', not sexual harassment.[184] He then himself reported his conduct to the Dean of the Faculty after the mother of the student threatened to inform senior management at the university. His employment at the university was terminated. However, the Association of Pennsylvania State College and University Faculty filed a grievance over his termination and an arbitrator ordered Ammon's reinstatement on the basis of a failure to follow proper procedures in terminating his employment. On appeal this decision was reversed by the Commonwealth Court of Pennsylvania[185] and the Pennsylvania Supreme Court declined to hear a challenge to the decision,[186] meaning that the termination of Professor Ammon's employment stood.

Ammon's case is illustrative of two important phenomena in sexual harassment cases. First, perpetrators rarely engage in such conduct on a single occasion and if strong disciplinary action is not taken promptly they tend to repeat the behaviour within a comparatively short timeframe, although, ordinarily, one would expect they would have learned from the experience of being the subject of a complaint and modified their behaviour. In short, sexual harassment tends to be a recidivist form of interpersonal conduct. Second, it is common for those who are the subject of sexual harassment allegations to contest over a period of years through the disciplinary processes, and then on appeal through the courts, what is asserted against them. This can be very burdensome on their victims as it denies them closure, and can extend the trauma of reciting what has occurred for a lengthy period and exacerbate stigma attaching to the relationship the subject of accusation and counter-accusation.

Criminal Charges

Italy's most notorious saga involving sexual conduct between an academic and his students is that relating to Ezio Capizzano, an agrarian and commercial law professor at the University of Camerino. Pornographic videos filmed by a camera hidden under his desk were stolen in 2002 from his office (along with a bottle of sparkling wine and some tins of anchovies) by an assistant and his brother: they showed him having sex with several women students on a rug. Professor Capizzano consistently admitted the encounters but asserted that they had been consensual and the 'fruit of love'.[187] Several women corroborated him, saying that they had

[184] 'Fired Professor Robert Ammon Jr Rightfully Terminated after Sexual Harassment, Court Finds', *Huffington Post*, 11 June 2013: <http://www.huffingtonpost.com/2013/06/11/professor-robert-ammon-jr-fired-sexual-harassment_n_3421700.html> [accessed 4 Jan 2016].

[185] The decision noted that, in his role as a professor and department chair, Ammon had substantial contact with female students, and had 'continued his inappropriate behavior after he was disciplined in 2006 for similar conduct'. It was felt that Ammon's propensity to act in such a way '[indicated] a substantial risk that female students will be subjected to similar action in the future. The implications of allowing public university employees to violate not only the trust of the students and employers, but also the general public, [contravened] long-standing public policy': Scott Jaschik, 'You Can't Say That', *Inside Higher Education*, 10 June 2013: <https://www.insidehighered.com/news/2013/06/10/appeals-court-upholds-dismissal-professor-who-talked-about-sex-students> [accessed 4 Jan 2016].

[186] Matt Miller, 'Pa. Supreme Court Rejects Appeal over Slippery Rock U Prof's Firing for Sexual Harassment', *Penn Live*, 24 December 2013: <http://www.pennlive.com/midstate/index.ssf/2013/12/pa_supreme_court_rejects_appea.html> [accessed 4 Jan 2016].

[187] See Bruce Johnston, 'Italian Professor Gets Top Marks for His Sex Lessons with Students', *The Telegraph*, 1 February 2002: <http://www.telegraph.co.uk/news/worldnews/europe/italy/1383466/Italian-professor-gets-top-marks-for-his-sex-lessons-with-students.html> [accessed 4 Jan 2016].

had sexual relations with him willingly. However, one of the video clips showed a student in tears during intercourse. Reactions in Italy were mixed. His university dispensed with his services but the newspaper *Corriere della Sera* hailed him as 'Italy's answer to Sean Connery'.[188]

A more sinister aspect to the professor's sexual relationships was asserted in criminal charges with allegations that he had traded marks for sex; corruption for having allegedly won the connivance of teaching colleagues whose help he needed for securing good marks for his lovers; and two counts of indecent assault. He was also charged with misusing public property, namely, 'the sofa on which he carried out his romancing'.[189] At interview with the prosecutor he exhibited no remorse or insight into his conduct saying: 'It can happen that it is the students who offer themselves. If a man has the feeling that a woman is willing, should be hold himself back?'[190] He was found not guilty of all charges. Three of Professor Capizzano's female students were also charged with, and acquitted of, corruption for having agreed to provide sexual favours for securing good marks. In related court action, Professor Capizzano was ordered to pay the University of Camerino €120,000 for the damage he had done to its reputation, while the two persons who had stolen the videos were both charged with handling stolen goods. One was given a six month jail sentence.

After the whole experience Professor Capizzano continued to be unrepentant, saying: 'I would do everything again, though perhaps not in the same place and taking greater care over the people involved.'[191] In 2006, Professor Capizzano, by then aged 70, published his erotic memoirs of his experiences in a best-selling book entitled, *The Last Baron in a Campus of Tulips.*

However, the sequelae of the events that precipitated the conclusion to his employment played out further. On 16 November 2012 the by then elderly professor was sentenced to two years and eight months jail for extortion, having also been sentenced to three years' jail for extortion and sexual violence on appeal.[192] He appealed further to the Supreme Court of Italy which confirmed his total sentence of three years and four months' imprisonment.[193] This ended the elderly law professor's lothario exploits and represented a major victory for prosecutors who maintained that Capizzano's conduct was both predatory and constituted a cynical abuse of the privileges of his position. It is an example of unethical conduct in the sexual area which merged into criminal behaviour.

What occurred with Capizzano has been enabled explicitly in China where on 9 October 2014 the Ministry of Education released a regulation which prohibited university lecturers from sexually harassing or coercing students into having sex with them. What is more remarkable is that violation of the regulation may result in a number of punitive responses,

---

188 Ibid.

189 John Hooper, 'Sex Scandal Rocks Italian Campus', *The Guardian*, 9 June 2004: <http://www.theguardian.com/world/2004/jun/09/highereducation.internationaleducationnews> (viewed 3 April 2015).

190 'Law Professor Sacked Over Porn Videos', *Times Higher Education*, 8 February 2002: <http://www.timeshighereducation.co.uk/news/law-professor-sacked-over-porn-videos/167075.article> [accessed 4 Jan 2016].

191 Hooper, above n 189.

192 'Soldi dal Padre di una Studentessa, Condannato l'ex Professore Capizzano', *Il Messaggero*, 16 November 2012: <http://www.ilmessaggero.it/MARCHE/soldi_dal_padre_di_una_studentessa_condannato_l_ex_professore_capizzano/notizie/232126.shtml> (viewed 3 April 2015).

193 See Suprema di Cassazione (Supreme Court of Cassation), Decision No. 16208 (heard 27 March 2014, filed 14 April 2014); 'In Carcere il Professore a…'Luci Rosse', *Gazzetta del Sud*, 4 April 2014: <http://www.gazzettadelsud.it/news//86332/In-carcere-il-professore--.html>[accessed 4 Jan 2016].

ranging from a warning and demerit points to demotion, suspension, and even the imposition of prison terms.[194]

Proof of Allegations

Allegations of sexual harassment and discrimination must be properly proved by admissible evidence.[195] Where there is an outright denial by an academic and an allegation by a student, much depends on the credibility of the two parties in the witness box. As *Formby v University of Wollongong*[196] discussed below illustrates, it is not always an easy task to determine which account is the more plausible. Commonly in such matters there is thoroughgoing conflict on the facts and accusation and counter-accusation about what occurred in private, much depending on the two key persons' credibility. The essence of a university's obligations though, is to follow its own processes, applying its policies and procedures, and to ensure procedural fairness, in the sense of enabling the person the subject of complaint to understand properly what is alleged against them and to have a proper opportunity to meet the accusations.

In *Huang v University of New South Wales,*[197] for instance, Driver FM did not accept the evidence of a former PhD student that her supervisors had engaged in sexual, racial and disability discrimination against her.[198] The court scrutinized the complaint made by Ms Huang to the Human Rights and Equal Opportunity Commission in Australia and the full history of her candidature. It noted that she made allegations of plagiarism against one of her supervisors, which were not found established by the university, but that the supervisor had not made proper reference to her contribution in a poster that he presented.

As happens in a significant percentage of discrimination allegations, especially in the academic context, the affidavit material was voluminous and classified by Driver FM as factually 'particularly complex'.[199] He applied authority[200] that s 28(3) of the *Sex Discrimination Act* 1984 (Cth) was capable of including a single incident, noting though that Wilcox J had also said:

> Unwelcome sexual conduct may be insensitive, even offensive, but it does not necessarily constitute sexual harassment. The word 'harass' implies the installation of fear or the infliction of damage; as is indicated by the definition of the term in the *Macquarie Dictionary*: '1. to trouble by repeated attacks, incursions, etc. as in war or hostilities; harry; raid. 2. to disturb persistently; torment, as with troubles, cares, etc.'[201]

The view of Driver FM was that, while some physical contact took place between Professor Winder and Ms Huang in late 1999, there was:

> nothing reliable to establish that the incident complained of constituted sexual harassment within the meaning of s 28A of the [Sex Discrimination Act] ... in all probability, the contact that occurred between Professor Winder and Ms Huang was accidental and non sexual as

---

[194] See Luo Wangshu, 'Professor in Sex Scandal Quits', *China Daily*, 3 December 2014: <http://usa.chinadaily.com.cn/china/2014-12/03/content_19020383.htm> [accessed 4 Jan 2016].

[195] *Sheikholeslami v University of New South Wales (No 3)* [2008] FMCA 35.

[196] [1999] AIRC 871.

[197] [2008] FMCA 11.

[198] See also *Sheikholeslami v University of New South Wales (No 3)* [2008] FMCA 35.

[199] *Huang v University of New South Wales* [2008] FMCA 11, [63].

[200] *Hall v A & A Sheiban Pty Ltd* [1989] FCA 72; (1989) 20 FCR 217.

[201] [1989] FCA 72, [9]; (1989) 20 FCR 217, 247.

> they passed in the corridor.... Ms Huang could give no reasonable basis for her allegation that the incident constituted sexual harassment.[202]

Driver FM also found Dr Markovic to be 'somewhat brusque and insensitive' in his evidence in the witness box but while 'on the balance of probabilities, Dr Markovic did make a comment about Ms Huang's age and marital status', it did not constitute sexual discrimination.[203] Ms Huang appealed unsuccessfully.

In a separate but related matter against another member of university staff Ms Huang generated continuing litigation with a long history. The University of New South Wales applied in 2011 to the Federal Magistrates Court to have the matter dismissed on the basis that Ms Huang did not have a reasonable prospect of success and the proceedings were an abuse of process.[204] The university's application was not successful; nor was an appeal from that decision.[205] In July 2012 the University of New South Wales made another application to have the matter dismissed as an abuse of process for failure to comply with the orders of the court, which was upheld in August 2012 by the Federal Magistrates Court.[206] Driver FM concluded that Ms Huang's matter against Mr Abayawickrama was an abuse of process due to a number of issues including delay, numerous court events, and non-payment of cost orders.[207]

Abuse of Role: The Orr Case

Australia's best-known case of improper sexual conduct by an academic is that involving Sydney Sparkes Orr, a Professor in the Department of Philosophy at the University of Tasmania. More than half a century later the case remains controversial.[208]

A second-year student in Professor Orr's class, Suzanne Kemp, alleged that Professor Orr had entered into a sexual relationship with her. Professor Orr had an unconventional lifestyle, having lived for some years immediately previously in a ménage-à-trois with his wife and another woman. He had also been a thorn in the side of the university, not just accusing it in an inflammatory letter of 'apathy, neglect and maladministration' but prompting a Royal Commission into the university's administration in 1955.[209] After giving evidence before the Royal Commission, a bitter confrontation took place. Senator Reg Wright accused Orr of having plagiarized another academic's lecture notes. Pybus[210] records Orr's distress and fury

---

202 [2008] FMCA 11, [89]–[90].

203 Ibid, [101].

204 *Huang v Abayawickrama* [2011] FMCA 235.

205 *University of New South Wales v Huang* [2012] FCA 308.

206 *Huang v Abayawickrama (No 2)* [2012] FMCA 747.

207 Ibid.

208 See William H C Eddy, *Orr* (Brisbane, Qld: Jacaranda Press, 1961); John B Polya and Robert J Solomon, *Dreyfus in Australia* (Erskineville, NSW: Dr R J Solomon, 1996); Cassandra Pybus, *Gross Moral Turpitude: The Orr Case Reconsidered* (Port Melbourne: William Heinemann Australia, 1993); Jeremy Stoljar, *The Australian Book of Great Trials: The Cases that Shaped a Nation* (Sydney: Murdoch Books, 2011) ch 7; Brian Martin, 'David Rindos Versus the University of Western Australia: Analogies to the Orr Case' in John Biggs and Richard Davis (eds), *The Subversion of Australian Universities* (Wollongong: Fund for Intellectual Dissent, 2002), available at: <http://pandora.nla.gov.au/pan/33459/20030221-0000/www.uow.edu.au/arts/sts/bmartin/dissent/documents/sau/index.html> (archived 21 February 2003) [accessed 4 Jan 2016]; John R Kerr and John H Wootten, 'Re-Opening the Orr Case' (1958) 4(10) *The Free Spirit* 3; John H Wootten, 'The Orr Dismissal and the Universities' (1957) 1(2) *Quadrant* 25.

209 Pybus, above n 208, 49.

210 Ibid, 51.

graphically and reports that in the aftermath of the Royal Commission, 'he had completely lost it', recurrently showing improper interest in his female students.

On being persuaded of the conduct alleged by Ms Kemp, the university summarily dismissed Professor Orr. He appealed to the Tasmanian Supreme Court where Green J found that Orr's 'seduction' of his student 'amounts to a complete repudiation of the duty which a professor owes to his University'.[211] He commented:

> Even if the plaintiff had not used his position to seduce Miss Kemp; even if all that had happened was that he and she had entered into a sexual relationship without any attempt on his part to influence her to that course, I still think the fact that he had intercourse with one of his own students would constitute misconduct, justifying his summary dismissal. It seems to me to be essential, if the integrity of the University is to be preserved, that a professor should maintain a detached and dispassionate attitude towards his students. I am quite unable to understand how it could be thought that a professor could teach, examine, recommend for prizes and honours, or present as a fit and proper person to receive a degree, a student who has in her academic life been his mistress. If such a thing could be then the integrity of the University degrees would disappear.[212]

He concluded, with no equivocation:

> So far as I am concerned I am holding that a university professor is just as liable to be dismissed for misconduct as any other servant, and in a proper case, just as liable to have his contract terminated for misconduct as any other contracting person. I hold it to be misconduct for a professor to seduce his student and I further hold it to be misconduct for him to enter into a sexual relationship with his own student.[213]

In the High Court Orr was also unsuccessful. Dixon CJ and Williams and Taylor JJ rejected a series of grounds of appeal and found that the trial judge had not made errors of law in his analysis of the evidence adduced before him, which included admissions by Professor Orr of having driven with the complainant to a lonely spot in the sand dunes behind a beach, on his version only for the purpose of discussing some philosophical issues with her. The court observed:

> Miss Kemp was a student in the appellant's class, she was eighteen years of age and it is apparent that she was then passing through a period of turbulent eroticism. Moreover there can be little doubt that she was eager to institute an intimate personal relationship with the appellant, but there is not the slightest doubt, upon the facts as found, that the appellant, having observed her feelings, became only too ready to take advantage of them and seduce her. The affair developed under the guise of the discussion of philosophical problems and, within a short period resulted in sexual intercourse taking place between them. Thereafter, it occurred on a number of occasions. We have not the slightest doubt that this conduct on his part unfitted him for the position which he held and that the university was entitled summarily to dismiss him. We can only express our surprise that the contrary should be maintained.[214]

The decisions of both Green J and of the High Court have been influential in resolving comparable matters, not only in relation to sexual harassment cases. In particular, the straightforward condemnation of the academic's abandonment of detachment and the denunciation of both his active efforts to form a romantic/sexual relationship with his student and of his failure to deal properly with the conflict of interest that arose from it constitute an important

---

[211] *Orr v University of Tasmania* [1956] 1 Tas SR 155, 159.
[212] Ibid, 160.
[213] Ibid.
[214] *Orr v The University of Tasmania* [1957] HCA 32, [8]; (1957) 100 CLR 526, 530.

precedent in Australia. They also constitute a robust assertion of the ethical responsibilities of a scholar when the temptation to make overtures to a student arises and as to what measures should be taken to avoid an improper conflict of interest if such a relationship does come into being.

Orr's case has given rise to debate on issues of academic freedom, the summary dismissal of academics, and the nature of employment contracts of academics.[215] *Orr's case* has also been the source of controversy and comment,[216] with some arguing that he was really dismissed because he was critical of the University of Tasmania administration and thus was a 'victim of suppression of intellectual dissent',[217] rather than someone who abused his position and power over a young student as her professor.[218] However, Malpas's analysis is closer to the mark: '[T]he Orr case may have less to do with issues concerning the *rights* of academics, and the organizational structures of universities, as with the personal failings of a troubled and deluded, but also manipulative individual, and the willingness of others to be drawn into his misfortunes'.[219] The reality is that the evidence against Orr was compelling and, try as he did to distract from it and to render the case into a vehicle for others' political beliefs, his manipulation of his student was shameful.

Calling a Spade a Spade: *Shanahan v University of Western Sydney*

There are indications that universities are becoming less prepared to be lenient or forgiving towards serious sexual misconduct engaged in by academics. An example in this regard is the dismissal by the University of Western Sydney of an associate–lecturer, Mr Ian Shanahan, from the Department of Music for sexual harassment. This took the form of unwelcome conduct towards students, involving lifting students above his head and tickling them, making repeated phone calls and unwelcome approaches to a particular student in whom he had a romantic interest, smacking another student on the bottom, and asking inappropriate questions about the personal life of two other students.[220] The appeal bench of the Australian Industrial Relations Commission, in a split decision (Senior Deputy President Hamberger and Commissioner Raffaelli in the majority, Senior Deputy President Drake dissenting) dismissed the appeal from Mr Shanahan finding that, although the single member who heard the matter in the first instance had made an error by failing to give appropriate weight to medical evidence, it was nevertheless reasonably open to the member to find that the dismissal of the music teacher was not harsh, unjust or unreasonable.[221] The medical evidence in question was that the associate–lecturer's diagnosis of bipolar disorder and evidence before the Commission that the behaviour exhibited by Mr Shanahan giving rise to the complaints were consistent with his medical condition.

---

[215] See Jackson, above n 143.

[216] See Eddy, above n 208; Polya and Solomon, above n 208; Pybus, above n 208; and Cassandra Pybus, *Seduction and Consent: A Case of Gross Moral Turpitude* (Port Melbourne: Mandarin, 1994); Creswell T, *Notorious Australians: The Mad, the Bad and the Dangerous* (Pymble, NSW: ABC Books, 2011).

[217] Brian Martin, 'Beware the 'No's of the Campus Sex Triangle—Harassment, Conflict of Interest, Abuse of Trust' (11–17 March 1993) *Campus Review* 8, available at: <http://www.bmartin.cc/pubs/93cr3.html> [accessed 4 Jan 2016].

[218] Cassandra Pybus, 'Orr Case Revision Defended' (25–31 March 1993) *Campus Review* 8, available at: <http://www.bmartin.cc/pubs/93cr3letters.html> [accessed 4 Jan 2016]; Pybus, above n 216.

[219] Jeff Malpas, 'Orr Case' in Graham Oppy and N N (Nick) Trakakis (eds), *A Companion to Philosophy in Australia and New Zealand* (Clayton: Monash University Publishing, 2010) 342 (emphasis in original).

[220] *Shanahan v University of Western Sydney* [2005] AIRC 473.

[221] Ibid, [227].

The associate-lecturer had a history of inappropriate behaviour in his employment towards other colleagues and complaints had been made about his style of teaching during his probationary period of teaching before the complaints from the eight students were made. The appeal bench of the Australian Industrial Relations Commission held that, regardless of whether there was any sexual motive, the conduct of Mr Shanahan in lifting, tickling, or swinging students around the room was improper, and not just 'tomfoolery'.[222] The Commission held that there was a clear sexual element to some of Mr Shanahan's behaviour.[223]

The appeal bench of the Commission found that the dismissal requirements had not been complied with in that Mr Shanahan was not given an opportunity to make additional submissions to the Vice-Chancellor who made the final decision to terminate based on the report from the Misconduct Investigation Committee and Mr Shanahan's response. Nevertheless, it concluded that the termination was not harsh, unjust or unreasonable because the conduct itself was totally unacceptable and it was not confident that Mr Shanahan would not commit similar conduct in the future.[224]

In the dissenting judgment, though, Senior Deputy President Drake viewed the behaviour of Mr Shanahan much more benignly and was inclined to regard it as caused by his medical disability (hypomania), rather than being deliberate conduct amounting to misconduct. Thus, he did not categorize it as such as to justify termination of Mr Shanahan's employment.[225] Senior Deputy President Drake viewed the termination as harsh, unjust, or unreasonable.[226]

The legacy of the majority decision of the Australian Industrial Relations Commission is the robust refusal to minimize the seriousness of sexualized behaviour by university staff towards students and a dismissal of the proposition that such conduct merely consists of 'tomfoolery'.

The Responsibilities of the Senior Academic: *Formby v University of Wollongong*

In 1998, the employment of Dr John Formby, a lecturer in the Department of Geosciences at the University of Wollongong, was terminated due to a complaint of sexual harassment by a female student and employee of the University. Dr Formby had been the student's lecturer at various times, and had supervised her honours thesis, as well as employing her at times as a research assistant.[227] The student alleged that the sexual harassment consisted of inappropriate comments of a sexual nature by Dr Formby about his personal relationships and the student's physique, the making of threats and his expressing a desire to form a relationship with her. On the student's account he invited her to visit his farm on several occasions and on one such visit had sexual intercourse with her.[228] The student had stated that she did not make a prompt complaint for fear of damage to her career and the fear that no one would believe her.

The student continued to work for Dr Formby and he continued to telephone her and invite her to his farm, invitations which on her evidence she declined. Dr Formby's attitude to the student gradually cooled and eventually he terminated her employment with him as a research assistant. He continued as her thesis supervisor although it was not a favourable

222 Ibid, [209].
223 Ibid, [210].
224 Ibid, [229].
225 Ibid, [73].
226 Ibid, [95].
227 *Formby v University of Wollongong* [1999] AIRC 871, [2].
228 Ibid, [3].

situation. When the student complained to the Dean of Students in 1997 that Dr Formby had sexually harassed her, an investigation was begun that resulted in the termination of Dr Formby's employment.[229] Dr Formby denied that he had sexually harassed the student, alleging that it was she who had been the sexual harasser and that the complaints had only arisen after he terminated her employment as a research assistant for poor work performance. The University Vice-Chancellor concluded that while some of the facts of the case 'in isolation might not offend the University's policy as to close personal relationships, taken together they did so'.[230]

Dr Formby applied to the Australian Industrial Relations Commission under the *Workplace Relations Act* 1996 (Cth) on the basis that the termination of his employment with the university was harsh, unreasonable, and unfair. Commissioner Raffaelli found that the evidence of both the student and Dr Formby had elements which led the Commissioner to doubt their accounts of what happened.[231] He held that 'the particular responsibility that an academic has to a student is not confined to the precise semester in which lectures or tutorials are given to a particular student'.[232] Commissioner Raffaelli concluded that, even if Dr Formby's side of the story was accepted, Dr Formby was aware of what appropriate behaviour was towards a student and if he knew, as he said he did, that the student was infatuated with him and harassed him, then he should have taken steps to address those issues formally. The Commissioner found that Dr Formby's actions demonstrated a disregard of the proper conduct required of an academic towards a student.[233] Commissioner Raffaelli held:

> Based on the findings I am led to conclude that either Dr Formby sexually harassed [the student] or on his version, he continued to deal with her notwithstanding her obvious desire to engage in a sexual or romantic relationship with him. I do not consider that it is necessary for me to ultimately decide between the two alternatives.
>
> If the former, I consider that there was a valid reason for termination, based not only on a breach of a University policy known to Dr Formby but also because such conduct amounts to serious misconduct per se. It was serious misconduct for Dr Formby over a long period to have exploited his relationship as teacher, thesis supervisor and work supervisor by sexually harassing [the student]. Such provides a valid reason for termination of employment.
>
> If the latter, I consider that there was also a valid reason for termination. Dr Formby was in a position to influence or affect the academic career of [the student]. In the face of her feelings towards him, he did nothing to ensure that their relationship remained within strict bounds. Whatever friendliness and informality might be acceptable in normal circumstances between academic and student, in these circumstances the level of interaction between them (augmented when Dr Formby became her thesis supervisor) and friendliness and informality was inappropriate.[234]

In doing nothing to dissuade the student Dr Formby was found to have been 'derelict in his duty of care as a teacher to ensure among other things that her education was not impeded or prejudiced'.[235] Thus, on either view of the facts of the case Commissioner Raffaelli held that the university had a valid reason to terminate Dr Formby's employment and that the termination was not harsh, unjust or unreasonable.[236]

---

[229] Ibid, [36].
[230] Ibid, [92].
[231] Ibid, [96]–[97].
[232] Ibid, [100].
[233] Ibid, [114].
[234] Ibid, [118]–[120] (formatting altered).
[235] Ibid, [120].
[236] Ibid, [126].

The appeal bench of the Australian Industrial Relations Commission, Justice Munro, Senior Deputy President Drake, and Commissioner Lawson refused leave to appeal from Commissioner's Raffaelli's decision to uphold the termination of employment. However, the appeal bench did express some disquiet about the way in which Commissioner Raffaelli proceeded from allegations of sexual harassment and sexual assault to a finding that there had been conduct that was improper for an academic in a supervisory role.[237] Ultimately, this observation was not sufficient to grant leave to appeal nor was an error of law otherwise demonstrated.[238]

The decision highlights the responsibility of a senior academic to ensure that a relationship does not evolve which may detrimentally affect the interests of those who are taught or supervised by them. It emphasizes that it is indefensible for a senior member of staff to manipulate or exploit their students and that such behaviour constitutes a serious breach of the ethical obligations of academics.

The Vulnerabilities of Overseas Students: The Case of Dr Nasrul Ali

The case of Dr Nasrul Ali is illustrative of the need for firm consequences to be imposed for such conduct, when it is proved.

In 2010 the Corruption and Crime Commission of Western Australia undertook a corruption investigation and reported to Parliament[239] in relation to allegedly sexually predatory conduct by Dr Ali, a sessional academic in the Finance Department at Curtin University of Technology, towards three students who were Chinese nationals and one who was a Malaysian national. The involvement of such a body in investigating such allegations is a significant step for Australia in the way in which such matters are customarily dealt with within universities or in the courts in respect of allegations of discrimination, harassment, or stalking.

In respect of the three Chinese women, the Commission found Dr Ali to have engaged in 'serious misconduct' in the context of his having corruptly taken advantage of his employment as a public officer to obtain a benefit for himself by seeking sexual favours for awarding the students higher marks in their examinations.[240] In respect of the Malaysian student, it found him also to have engaged in serious misconduct by causing a detriment to the student by reducing a group assignment mark from approximately 73 per cent to 50 per cent, because of a personal grievance he felt towards her, namely that she had rebuffed his sexual overtures. It also found him guilty of serious misconaduct in respect of the same student by not exercising his discretion to increase her final examination mark from 45 per cent to 50 per cent, solely because of a personal grievance he felt towards her, in circumstances in which he agreed he otherwise would have done so.

The Curtin University Equal Opportunity Policy stated that harassment:

> [o]ccurs when unwelcome, offensive, abusive, belittling or threatening behaviour, including bullying, is directed at staff or students and which is usually based on some real or perceived

237 *Formby v University of Wollongong* [1999] AIRC 879, [19].

238 Ibid, [22].

239 Corruption and Crime Commission (Western Australia), *Report on the Investigation of Alleged Public Sector Misconduct of Dr Nasrul Ameer Ali as a Sessional Academic Employed by Curtin University of Technology* (Perth, 2 September 2010) (Commissioner Len Roberts-Smith QC): <https://www.ccc.wa.gov.au/Publications/Reports/Published%20Reports%202010/Misconduct%20by%20Sessional%20Academic%20at%20Curtin%20University%20of%20Technology.pdf> [accessed 4 Jan 2016] ('Ali Report').

240 Ibid, [59].

> grounds of discrimination which may lead to the person being harassed, being offended, humiliated, intimidated or disadvantaged. It includes sexual, racial and disability harassment as defined in all relevant legislation. Harassment can be action(s) directed against a group or an individual by a group or individual. It may occur among peers, or between people in subordinate/superordinate roles.[241]

The Commission commented that it was 'clear that Dr Ali's attentions were repetitive, unwelcome, exploitative, and designed to pressure these women into having sexual relations with him. He acted to increase the existing vulnerability of these women'.[242]

The University's Code of Conduct stipulated that all parties (including staff) were obliged, with respect, to:

> 2. personal and professional behaviour, perform their duties professionally with respect, integrity, fairness, care, and without harassment, bullying, or discrimination;
> 3. relationships between staff and students, take care that all working relationships are appropriate and do not compromise professional and ethical standards or involve a conflict of interest and/or breach of trust; and
> 6. dishonest and criminal behaviour, conduct themselves lawfully and properly and not use their position within the University for personal advantage or for the personal advantage or disadvantage of others.[243]

The Commission observed that:

> There is a significant power imbalance between a student and university lecturer who has control over the assessment of units. This imbalance is always present, and there is an ever present risk that it will be exploited. Universities rely on the integrity of their staff and reinforce that integrity with staff orientation and training. In other words, they trust their academic staff to not exploit their power.
>
> Full fee-paying overseas students, in contrast to locally-based students, pay much higher fees and have many other costs associated with their study in Australia. Research by Sawir *et al* published as *Loneliness and International Students: An Australian Study* states that overseas students:
>
> > ...face a foreign language, study in a new setting, finances, accommodation, and day-to-day living problems, and they must negotiate an unfamiliar set of institutional rules. They often face issues of personal autonomy...and the recreation of identity in a new setting. Often the physical and cultural environment is very different, with new social customs and norms. International students must establish themselves as foreigners staying for a time, as neither inside nor outside. They must deal with unpredictable encounters, idiosyncratic communications, and problems of racial discrimination, largely on their own...

The Commission investigation, and academic and government research, have demonstrated that for overseas students of Australian tertiary educational institutions lack of competency in English is a vulnerability for sexual harassment and a particular misconduct risk.[244]

Curtin University sacked Dr Ali shortly after the allegations were made against him[245] but he was promptly employed as a finance lecturer by Murdoch University. It also subsequently

---

[241] Ibid, [370]. See also, Curtin University, 'Equal Opportunity Policy', 1 March 2002: <http://policies.curtin.edu.au/findapolicy/docs/Equal%20Opportunity%20Policy%20-%20Oct%202012.pdf> [accessed 4 Jan 2016].

[242] Ali Report, above n 239, [371].

[243] Ibid, [389].

[244] Ibid, [64]–[66] (formatting altered).

[245] Josh Jerga, 'Academic Asked Students for Sex: CCC', *The Sydney Morning Herald*, 2 September 2010: <http://www.smh.com.au//breaking-news-national/academic-asked-students-for-sex-ccc-20100902-14p4q.html> [accessed 4 Jan 2016].

sacked him.[246] However, his father, who also was employed by Murdoch University, denounced the handling of the matter by the Commission, maintaining that it had accepted the allegations of the complainants too uncritically.[247]

Abuse of Sponsorship: *M v Australian National University*

In 1995 Australia's Industrial Relations Court heard a fraught case involving the suspension of M, a senior fellow, from his employment at the Australian National University (ANU) for a period of three years for sexual harassment of a PhD student who attended the University.[248] The complainant was a Chinese-born student whose husband set in train an application for a PhD scholarship in mathematics for his wife. The complainant first met M when M visited China in 1990. Before she came to Australia, M made arrangements for her to be a PhD student in his department and indicated that he would lend her money for the first year's tuition fees (some $11,000), which was to be repaid at an interest rate of 10 per cent. Justice Moore accepted that M made a variety of sexual advances to the complainant and that she submitted in the context of pressures and financial threats that he made towards her. He emphasized the relationship of power that M had over the complainant. M maintained that the relationship between him and the complainant was a loving relationship with marriage contemplated. However, the evidence on this issue was heavily contested.

Justice Moore noted the conversation between M and the student that preceded the first episode of intercourse. It was characterized by protestations by M that he could secure for her a scholarship if she submitted to his sexual advances:

> This account might be viewed at one extreme, as evidencing a clumsy, insensitive and inept attempt at seduction by a person endeavouring to seduce a woman with whom he was infatuated. It was attempted by saying things designed to persuade and cajole which were misunderstood at least to the extent that the student understood the applicant to be saying he would act, in a positive sense, against her interests rather than simply not continue to act in her interest. However, any such misunderstanding on the student's part, would have been entirely justified. At the other extreme this account might be viewed as a callous, brutal and premeditated abuse of power involving a direct threat of using the power to defeat the interests of the student to require the student to submit to sexual intercourse without her consent.[249]

Justice Moore stated that he was inclined to the first view, but found that '[e]ven viewed in the most favourable light to the applicant, it involved a gross abuse of his position within the University and his position in relation to the student as her de facto sponsor'. Thus, he found M's conduct to constitute serious sexual harassment which justified the university's decision to suspend him for three years.[250]

---

246 'Academic Sacked Over Pressuring Students for Sex', *ABC News*, 3 September 2010: <http://www.abc.net.au/news/2010-09-03/academic-sacked-over-pressuring-students-for-sex/2247016> [accessed 4 Jan 2016].

247 Aja Styles and Katherine Fenech, 'Curtin Lecturer Implicated in 'Sex-for-Marks' Scandal with Students', *WA Today*, 2 September 2010: <http://www.watoday.com.au/wa-news/curtin-lecturer-implicated-in-sexformarks-scandal-with-students-20100902-14p4g.html> [accessed 4 Jan 2016].

248 *M v Australian National University* [1996] IRCA 411.

249 Ibid (Conclusion).

250 Ibid (Conclusion). Compare *Chambers v James Cook University of North Queensland (No 2)* [1995] IRCA 48; (1995) 61 IR 145. For a comparable analysis see *GLS v PLP (Human Rights)* [2013] VCAT 221 (Garde J).

The Bizarre Case of Lisa Chávez

The sensitivities generated by sexualized conduct by an academic were illustrated in a bizarre way by the controversies that erupted around Associate Professor Lisa Chávez of the English Department at the University of New Mexico, who augmented her academic income by the funds she earned as a phone sex dominatrix, 'Mistress Jade'. This prompted criticism and resignations from colleagues and concern from a variety of students who complained of 'sexually charged' discussions in her creative writing classes, her social relationships with some students, and from 'appalled parents'. The situation came to a head after Ms Chávez posed for sado-masochistic pictures with one of her graduate students who was employed by the same phone sex organization as used the services of Ms Chávez in an extracurricular capacity.[251] Ms Chávez went on the offensive claiming she was being discriminated against because of her bisexual and Hispanic status and threatening defamation action against academic colleagues who had been critical of her.

In November 2007, university administrators announced the completion of an investigation into Ms Chávez's conduct. It concluded that while Ms Chávez had exercised poor judgment she was not guilty of allegations of maintaining a hostile learning environment, sexual harassment, or other illegal activity or violations of policy that suggested she was unfit for her job. Faculty members who had raised concerns about Ms Chávez were urged by administrators to enter into mediation with her. A variety of forms of legal action followed, with a number of other members of the department resigning and the university declining to undertake further inquiries or investigations into Ms Chávez's conduct. Apart from the manifestly defective judgment exercised by Ms Chávez, the saga is illustrative of the escalating sensitivities about and, perhaps, decreasing tolerance of, unorthodox sexual conduct, even if it takes place off campus but particularly when it has any form of on-campus connection.

Upwards Harassment

Harassment does not only take place in one direction. Students, too, are capable of 'sexually harassing' academics. Dziech and Weiner argued in 1990 that the terminology that should be used in these instances is 'sexual hassle' because that behaviour is not characterized by the misuse of power that exists when an academic harasses the student.[252] It may make the academic's life uncomfortable but, they argued, the behaviour is not likely to exercise the same impact on the academic's self-esteem or intellectual self-confidence when the student is the perpetrator by contrast with the more common situation when the empowered person is the one doing the harassing.[253] Dziech and Weiner suggested that there are few negative repercussions for the male academic who is the recipient of unwanted sexual attention from a student.[254] In more modern times, it is likely that this argument would be seen as outmoded, as awareness of the deleterious consequences of stalking and similar behaviour has grown. There are definite repercussions for academics who are the victims of harassment; the reality is that mud sticks in the charged environment that is created by the making of a sexual harassment allegation.[255]

---

251 Peter Schmidt, 'In Professor-Dominatrix Scandal, U. of New Mexico Feels the Pain', *The Chronicle of Higher Education*, 12 September 2010: <http://chronicle.com/article/In-Professor-Dominatrix/124369/> [accessed 4 Jan 2016].

252 Dziech and Weiner, above n 4, 24. See also Carrie MH Herbert. Talking of Silence: The Sexual Harassment of Schoolgirls (Hove, The Psychology Press, 1989), 20.

253 Ibid.

254 Ibid.

255 See eg, the case of *Gauci v Kennedy* [2007] FCA 1051 where the first respondent, a student, was alleged to have sexually harassed the applicant, a university tutor at the University of Queensland.

In 1984 Benson used the somewhat obscure term 'contrapower harassment' to describe the situation where a person with less power harasses a person with more power within an institution.[256] Others have referred to this by the more useful term of 'upwards harassment'.[257] Several studies since the late 1980s have noted that academic staff can be the target of sexual harassment and other forms of harassment or bullying.[258] One study reported almost half of female faculty members stating that they had been the subject of sexually harassing behaviour by (generally male) students.[259] Matchen and DeSouza's 2000 study revealed that female staff members were more likely to experience unwanted sexual attention from students and were more bothered by it than male academics.[260] Another study of a large Midwestern university in the United States found that approximately one-third of students reported having sexually harassed a professor at least once, with male students more likely to be the perpetrators against female academics.[261] In the same study, over a half of professors reported having been sexually harassed by students at least once.[262]

Lampman et al.'s 2009 study of faculty members of the University of Alaska found that, while male academic staff were more likely to receive unwanted sexual attention from students, as well as other forms of student incivility and bullying, women academic staff were more likely to find such behaviour upsetting and suffer negative impacts on their health and work, and were more likely to take action compared with their male colleagues.[263] Lampman et al. argued that it was important to explore the extent of the broader range of contrapower harassment, 'including disrespectful, hostile, and even violent actions aimed at faculty'.[264]

Conclusions

Sexual harassment and conflicts of interest have a long and inglorious history within academia. The archetype of the lecherous professor has become almost a trope in modern cinema:

> In *The Squid and the Whale* (2005), Jeff Daniels plays an English professor and failed writer who sleeps with his students, neglects his wife, and bullies his children. In *One True Thing* (1998), William Hurt plays an English professor and failed writer who sleeps with his students, neglects his wife, and bullies his children. In *Wonder Boys* (2000), Michael Douglas plays an English professor and failed writer who sleeps with his students, has just been left by his third wife, and can't commit to the child he's conceived in an adulterous affair with his chancellor.[265]

---

[256] Katherine A Benson, 'Comments on Crocker's 'An Analysis of University Definitions of Sexual Harassment' (1984) 9(3) *Signs* 516, 517.

[257] See eg, 'Tutors Taunted', above n 19; Sara McDonald, 'Bullying Upwards: Harassment is Not Only Experienced By Students. Academics Can Be Victims Too' (2008) 22(20) *Nursing Standard* 62.

[258] Lynne Carroll and Kathryn L Ellis, 'Faculty Attitudes Towards Sexual Harassment: Survey Results, Survey Process' (1989) 52(3) *Initiatives* 35; Grauerholz, above n 102; McKinney, above n 102; Jim Matchen, and Eros DeSouza, 'The Sexual Harassment of Faculty Members by Students' (2000) 42(3–4) *Sex Roles* 295; Eros DeSouza and A Gigi Fansler, 'Contrapower Sexual Harassment: A Survey of Students and Faculty Members' (2003) 48(11–12) *Sex Roles* 529; Claudia Lampman, Alissa Phelps, Samantha Bancroft, and Melissa Beneke, 'Contrapower Harassment in Academia: A Survey of Faculty Experience with Student Incivility, Bullying, and Sexual Attention' (2009) 60(5–6) *Sex Roles* 331.

[259] Grauerholz, above n 102.

[260] Matchen and DeSouza, above n 258.

[261] DeSouza and Fansler, above n 258.

[262] Ibid.

[263] Lampman et al. above n 258.

[264] Ibid, 331.

[265] Deresiewicz, above n 14.

Until the past two decades it was common for the response of universities to learning that senior staff were behaving inappropriately with students to be for a colleague to 'have a quiet word' with the perpetrator and for such issues to be dealt with 'behind the scenes' so as to maintain the good name of the faculty and of the person accused. Much has changed. In many countries such relationships are discouraged for good reason, given the potential for such relationships to come into being in circumstances of ambiguity and idealization. The cases of the law professor Ezio Capizzano in Italy and also the philosopher Professor Colin McGinn at the University of Miami are illustrative of such dynamics, as well as the risk that reinterpretation of what was initially welcome, or at least not unwelcome, contact can later be reinterpreted. However, the fact remains that for the victims of such matters, the consequences of sexual harassment can be adverse in many ways, whether or not any complaint that they make is sustained.[266]

Clear guidance is now given in most universities to protect students against lecherous overtures or stalking from their teachers. The modern terminology for such proscriptions is in terms of 'sexual harassment'. In addition, there are preclusions on members of staff having any form of conflict of interest engendered by virtue of their being at any time in a romantic or sexual relationship with a student for whose supervision or marking they are responsible. However, the difficulty occurs when attention from academic staff is not unwelcome and where a relationship develops in what Roiphe has called 'awkward circumstances'.[267]

In the United States in a series of high-profile tertiary institutions, by contrast, a harder line has been taken over the past 20 years making the having of such relationships a specific form of misconduct that is likely to attract disciplinary sanctions. As noted above, Yale University has taken a lead in this regard. However, as of the end of 2012 the City University of New York adopted a similar stance and stipulated that:

> Amorous, dating or sexual activity or relationships ('intimate relationships'), even when apparently consensual, are inappropriate when they occur between a faculty member or employee and any student for whom he or she had a professional responsibility. Those relationships are inappropriate because of the unequal power dynamic between students and faculty members and between students and employees who advise or evaluate them, such as athletic coaches or workplace supervisors. Such relationships necessarily involve issues of student vulnerability and have the potential for coercion. In addition, conflicts of interest or perceived conflicts of interest may arise when a faculty member or employee is required to evaluate the work or make personnel or academic decisions with respect to a student with whom he or she is having an intimate relationship. Finally, if the relationship ends in a way that is not amicable, the relationship may lead to charges of and possible liability for sexual harassment.
>
> Therefore, faculty members and other employees are prohibited from engaging in intimate relationships with students for whom they have a professional responsibility, including undergraduates, graduate and professional students and postdoctoral fellows.[268]

It may be that considerations such as potential exposure of universities to civil litigation arising from such relationships that end unhappily and the difficulties in processing complaints and grievances have played a role in the absoluteness of the policies of certain of the United

[266] 'In Academia, There is No Such Thing as Winning a Sexual Harassment Complaint', *The Guardian*, 9 August 2013: <http://www.theguardian.com/commentisfree/2013/aug/09/academia-winning-sexual-harassment-complaint> [accessed 4 Jan 2016].

[267] Roiphe, above n 154.

[268] The City University of New York, 'Policies and Procedures on Equal Opportunity, Non-Discrimination, and Against Sexual Harassment', 26 November 2012, 3: <http://www.cuny.edu/about/administration/offices/ohrm/policies-procedures/finalnondeiscrimpolicy121213.pdf> [accessed 4 Jan 2016].

States universities.[269] Often, there have also been precipitating scandals that have generated high levels of concern about unethical conduct by staff members at universities. For instance, it is unlikely to have been wholly coincidental that the University of Connecticut in July 2013 launched an internal inquiry into its retention of a music professor after it is alleged to have known of allegations of sexual impropriety engaged in by him for several years[270] and then, a month later, moved from strongly discouraging 'romantic relationships', defined as 'any sexual, intimate, amorous proposal or encounter', to banning them absolutely.[271]

It is also relevant that the latter years of the 20th century and the early part of the 21st century have seen both a new moralism in relation to private lives and sexual conduct,[272] especially in the United States, and also that there are increased concerns about oppressive sexual behaviour by persons in positions of power.

For countries outside the United States, the policy question is whether such a hard-line and inflexible policy is justified. There is no doubt that such relationships are frequently problematic. As Roiphe[273] observed in her essay on Colin McGinn's indiscretions, relationships between academics and their students are disruptive 'of the ecology of a classroom, a department, . . . they can corrupt the fruitful, important space that exists between professors and students. When I hear of male professors having affairs with students, I always feel a powerful instinctive disapproval, not to mention a general fatigue with the cliché; on the other hand one has to acknowledge, however begrudgingly, that romantic feelings do spring up in awkward circumstances.'[274]

However, the major vices that need to be addressed in the academic environment are not so much relationships in which there is an imbalance of power and/or an age or credentials differential. That happens often enough in the general community. It is whether harassment takes place on the part of the person in the dominant position which in turn distresses the subordinate or impacts adversely on their capacity to make prudent choices. It is also whether the staff member places themselves in a position where a reasonable person might conclude that they may not carry out their supervisory, evaluation or teaching responsibilities in a professional, non-partisan way. Both of these matters can be addressed satisfactorily by policies which in clear terms prescribe the responsibilities of university staff not to harass and to abstain, or actively remove themselves, from positions of actual or potential conflict of interest.

A further, legitimate, consideration is the reputation of the department, faculty and university. It is important that the community not harbour concerns that senior university staff are abusing their position of influence and trust and utilizing their stature and role as means of

---

269 See Henry Seiji Newman, 'The University's Liability for Professor–Student Sexual Harassment Under Title IX' (1998) 66(6) *Fordham Law Review* 2559; Neera Rellan Stacy, 'Seeking a Superior Institutional Liability Standard under Title IX for Teacher–Student Sexual Harassment' (1996) 71(5) *New York University Law Review* 1338; Susan Edelman, 'CUNY Mulls Ban on Professor–Student Relationships', *New York Post*, 11 March 2012: <http://nypost.com/2012/03/11/cuny-mulls-ban-on-professor-student-relationships/> [accessed 4 Jan 2016].

270 See Colleen Flaherty, 'Looking the Other Way?' *Inside Higher Education*, 16 July 2013: <https://www.insidehighered.com/news/2013/07/16/uconn-launches-investigation-its-own-handling-child-sex-abuse-allegations-against> [accessed 4 Jan 2016]. See also, University of Connecticut, 'Public Notification': <http://uconn.edu/public-notification/> [accessed 4 Jan 2016].

271 See Jon Lender, 'UConn Bans Faculty–Student Relationships', *Hartford Courant*, 7 August 2013: <http://articles.courant.com/2013-08-07/news/hc-romantic-relations-policy-uconn-0808-20130807_1_faculty-and-undergraduate-students-new-policy-universities> [accessed 4 Jan 2016].

272 See eg, Jeffrey Weeks, *Sexuality and Its Discontents: Meanings, Myths, and Modern Sexualities* (New York: Taylor & Francis, 2002) ch 3.

273 Roiphe, above n 154.

274 Ibid.

initiating predatory relationships with their students. A percentage of relationships between staff members and students will end unhappily and with rancour. This has the potential to result in accusations and counter-accusations that may impact on how the general community, staff and students perceive the university. The unedifying experience of the Mahmoodi and Orr cases bears eloquent witness to this phenomenon. It is well foreseeable that, when an intimate staff–student relationship comes into being and later founders, unpleasant allegations may be made about the circumstances in which the relationship started and ended, as well as whether things occurred during it that infringed either the letter or the spirit of university policy and codes of procedure. However, once again, such allegations are made all too regularly in matrimonial litigation and the fact that this occurs does not constitute a justification for proscribing certain categories of relationship in the public interest.

It is important to be hesitant before prohibiting personal and romantic relationships between categories of individuals who do not suffer from disabilities, such as youth, mental illness, or intellectual disability. In respect of adult–child and psychiatrist–patient relationships, preclusion is straightforward and justified for a host of good social policy reasons. However, for a preclusion such as that promulgated by Yale University to be emulated, it would be necessary to establish that the asymmetry in staff–student relationships at universities is so pervasive and so contaminating as to preclude consensual decision-making and that no other mechanism for preventing harassing and conflict of interest behaviour exists. The evidence for these propositions is very slim.

There have been all too many instances, often highly publicised, where academics have behaved dishonourably and unethically. However, this should not necessarily have the consequence that all staff-student intimate relationships in all circumstances are precluded. There are, of course, instances where students and teachers form stable long-term relationships and where there are few indicia of exploitation. The serially offending ageing professor and the attractive and gullible 18 year old student beloved of fiction are no longer the only permutation in staff-student relationships. Nevertheless, the challenge for universities is to educate and alert staff and students alike to the risks of such relationships and the inherent conflicts of interest, as well as to set in place sexual harassment policies which mean that, if such relationships come into existence, supervisors such as heads of department are informed, and there is sufficient protection for both students and staff alike should romance, attraction or lust result in non-pedagogical staff-student relationships. Students need to know that their university has standards which are captured in policy and practice and which protect them from sexual exploitation of any kind, and academics and other staff need to know that the university will always act decisively on complaints. Similar considerations apply to research bodies generally. If personal integrity is not sufficient to discourage a staff member from behaving badly, or accepting what he or she interprets or later represents as an overture from a subordinate or a student, then they should at least be aware of the damage to their own career and reputation which can be wrought by a complaint or relationship that founders. The ambiguity inherent in such relationships and the difficulties which universities have had in investigating and prosecuting complaints make proscription an alternative protection for both staff and students, but on balance it is not absolutely necessary, it is paternalistic, and it is unjustifiably heavy-handed.

10

SUBSTANCE-AFFECTED MISCONDUCT

Introduction

Substance abuse, whether it be by alcohol or by drugs, unless they are illegal, is not itself a form of misconduct, by scholars or anyone else, but conduct engaged in as a result of intoxication can be. Some of the cases discussed in the preceding chapters on intemperate denigration and sexual misconduct are illustrative of the common correlation between the disinhibiting effects of substances and unacceptable conduct by scholars. There have been many problematic scenarios produced by the abuse of substances by scholars. There are the academics whose lectures are known to be better before lunch than after. There are the young (and not so young) scholars who serially engage in Bacchus-inspired symposia and irritate those in halls of residence when they return. There are the obnoxious academics who become offensive or abusive to those in their vicinity when drunk. There are the senior scholars who grope all in reach when the 'worse for wear' at university gatherings. There are the attenders at international conferences whose scholarly bonhomie degenerates regularly into adolescent intoxication. There are the professors who have not generated research for years and spend unproductive hours alone in their rooms that reek of whisky. All of these are tropes of the scholarly world. They are sad, annoying, and unacceptable.

This chapter focuses principally on the most prevalent issue arising from use of intoxicating drugs by scholars—alcohol abuse. It also refers to a smaller number of issues that have arisen in the use of other forms of substances, including illegal drugs, and the inappropriate provision of intoxicating substances to students and to researchers and co-researchers.

Risk Factors for Substance Abuse

The highs and lows of 'scholardom' with its solitariness of creative and pedagogical endeavour, its expectations of continuing output, its quest for creativity and research breakthroughs, and its culture of performance, its flexible hours and limited supervision, all lead for some to anxiety, self-doubt and too often abuse of substances. While Ralph Waldo Emerson described the role of the 'scholar' as the 'world's eye' and the 'world's heart' in his 1837 address, *The American Scholar*,[1] Erasmus was considerably less upbeat, famously, but gloomily intoning that:

> As for those who write learnedly for the judgment of a few scholars and would not hesitate to have their books reviewed by such true judges as Persius or Laelius, they seem to me more pitiable than happy because their work is a perpetual torment to them. They add, they alter; they blot something out, they put it back in. They do the work over, they recast it, they show it to friends, they keep it for nine years, and still they are never satisfied. At such a price they buy an empty reward, namely praise, and that from only a handful. They buy it with such an expense of long hours, so much loss of that sweetest of all things, sleep, so much sweat,

[1] Ralph Waldo Emerson, 'The American Scholar', address to the Phi Beta Kappa Society, Cambridge, 31 August 1837: <http://www.emersoncentral.com/amscholar.htm> [accessed 4 Jan 2016].

so much agony. Reckon up also the loss of health, the spoiling of their good looks, weak eyesight (or even blindness), poverty, envy, the denial of pleasures, premature old age, early death, and other things just as bad, if there are any.[2]

The relationship between such a lifestyle and resort to alcohol and other substances is well known. So too is the folklore of the relationship between substance use and genius and creativity well entrenched as a myth.[3] Nowhere is that more prevalent than in and around universities. Alcohol abuse by academics constitutes a key part of Kingsley Amis's 1954 novel, *Lucky Jim,* and has been chronicled autobiographically and memorably, among others, by Jon T Coleman, Professor of History at the University of Notre Dame in the United States,[4] and Emeritus Professor of History and Politics at Griffith University in Australia, Ross Fitzgerald.[5] Instances of highly regarded scholars dying of alcoholism are well known, as are suicides associated with substance abuse and depression.[6] Sometimes the problematic drinking is undertaken in company; at other times it is in solitude. Patrick Wormald, the highly regarded Anglo-Saxon historian of the Universities of Glasgow and Oxford, is but one example, having passed away in 2004 of an alcohol-related illness. His friend, Alexander Grant, a Reader in Mediaeval History at Lancashire University, recalled of him: 'It was dark nights of the soul. Patrick's stuff was brilliant, but he was always criticizing it. When you doubt yourself, it is easy to have a drink.'[7]

In addition, the culture of halls of residence,[8] the high table and the convivial gathering after lectures at the pub for scholarly debriefing have proven fertile fields for alcoholism and on occasions for other forms of substance abuse. And then there are the scholarly conferences at which participants, freed from their normal domestic and workaday constraints, so often conduct themselves like superannuated undergraduates and imbibe to extraordinary levels and behave in intemperately disinhibited ways.[9]

---

[2] Desiderius Erasmus, 'The Praise of Folly' in Clarence H Miller (trans.), *The Praise of Folly* (2nd edn, New Haven: Yale University Press, 2003 [1511]), 82–3.

[3] Donald Newlove, *Those Drinking Days: Myself and Other Writers* (New York: Horizon Press, 1981). By contrast the Centers for Disease Control publishes data on the adverse effects of alcohol on academic achievement: see Centers for Disease Control, 'Alcohol and Other Drug Use and Academic Achievement' (2009), available at: <http://www.cdc.gov/healthyyouth/health_and_academics/data.htm> [accessed 4 Jan 2016]. See also, Higher Education Center for Alcohol and Other Drug Use and Violence Prevention, 'College Academic Performance and Alcohol and Other Drug Use' (1997, rev. 2003): <http://files.eric.ed.gov/fulltext/ED537642.pdf> [accessed 4 Jan 2016]; Ernest T Pascarella, Kathleen M Goodman, Tricia A Seifert, Gina Tagliapietra-Nicoli et al. 'College Student Binge Drinking and Academic Achievement: A Longitudinal Replication and Extension' (2007) 48(6) *Journal of College Student Development* 715.

[4] Jon T Coleman, 'Not Quite Bulletproof', *The Chronicle of Higher Education*, 4 June 2012: <http://chronicle.com/article/Not-Quite-Bulletproof/132055/> [accessed 4 Jan 2016].

[5] Ross Fitzgerald, *My Name is Ross: An Alcoholic's Journey* (Sydney: New South, 2010); see also, Anonymous, 'Addicted in Academe', *The Chronicle Review*, 3 May 2002, reproduced in *The University of Arizona*, Life & Work Connections: <http://lifework.arizona.edu/ea/addicted_in_academe> [accessed 4 Jan 2016].

[6] See Colleen Flaherty, 'After a Professor's Suicide', *Inside Higher Ed*, 11 January 2013: <https://www.insidehighered.com/news/2013/01/11/campus-and-academic-communities-left-wonder-why-after-professors-suicide> (viewed 5 April 2015); Tony Tysome, 'Suicide Don under "Huge Stress" in Job', *Times Higher Education*, 15 September 2006: <http://www.timeshighereducation.co.uk/news/suicide-don-under-huge-stress-in-job/205338.article> [accessed 4 Jan 2016].

[7] Anna Fazackerley, 'On the Rocks in Every Way', *Times Higher Education*, 8 April 2005: <http://www.timeshighereducation.co.uk/features/on-the-rocks-in-every-way/195245.article> [accessed 4 Jan 2016].

[8] See Alicia A Larkins, 'The Impact of Stress-Related and Culturally-Specific Factors on College Alcohol Consumption' (MA dissertation, University of North Carolina Wilmington, 2010): <http://dl.uncw.edu/etd/2010-1/larkinsa/alicialarkins.pdf> [accessed 4 Jan 2016].

[9] See Rebecca Shuman, 'The Campus Alcohol Problem That Nobody Talks About', *Slate*, 4 December 2014: <http://www.slate.com/articles/life/education/2014/12/drinking_problem_in_academia_alcohol_abuse_among_faculty_members.html> [accessed 4 Jan 2016].

Gillian Evans, Professor of Medieval History at Cambridge, made the decision at an early stage to abstain from alcohol completely. She observed: 'In Oxbridge colleges, the feasts held six times a year are really Edwardian banquets. You're talking about eight courses with a different wine with every course, starting with a sherry and finishing with a cognac for those still standing.'[10]

It is relevant that there is a long tradition of young people exploring the parameters of all manner of behaviours, including alcohol and illegal substance consumption, while in their early years at university or college. This can set in train problematic patterns of behaviour for some who remain in the environment. As the National Institute of Alcohol Abuse and Alcoholism puts it:

> College students are a highly visible group of underage drinkers among whom alcohol consumption is commonplace. Indeed, many college students accept alcohol use as a normal part of student life. Studies consistently indicate that about four in five college students drink alcohol; about two in five engage in episodic heavy consumption, often called bingeing (five or more drinks in a row for men and four or more in a row for women; generally asked with respect to the past 2 weeks or past 30 days, depending on the survey); and about one in five engages in frequent episodic heavy consumption (bingeing three or more times in the past two weeks).
>
> The consequences of drinking among college students include academic problems, social problems, legal problems, involvement in physical and/or sexual assault or risky sex, and even death.
>
> [...]
>
> Drinking in college varies from campus to campus and from person to person. Levels and patterns of consumption are associated with individual, intracampus, and intercampus factors. For example, athletes and members of fraternities and sororities are among the heaviest drinkers on most campuses...[11]

Three decades ago Thoreson argued that there was a particular category of academics at risk of alcoholism and resultant problematic behaviours in the workplace:

> The academics of the 1980s, no longer cherished by society, face the inevitable bitterness resulting from their broken dream. They also work in an environment of low supervision, low visibility of performance, freedom from time demands, and vaguely defined and nonenforced standards of performance: a veritable mecca for both scholarship and alcohol abuse.[12]

Drawing upon anthropological analogies, he categorized scholars in their pedagogical role as falling into three roles, each of them carrying with it the risks of destructive drinking:

- the *narcissistic shaman*: charming, skilful, energetic, and charismatic;
- the *priest*, a member of a powerful or admirable discipline with particular recourse to knowledge not always easily accessible, and
- the *mystic healer*, who focuses on fostering a helping, counselling relationship with their students.[13]

He argued that isolation, large amounts of uncommitted time, boredom, tendencies to obsessionality, and frustration, all often enough experienced by academics, constitute precipitants to

---

10 Fazackerley, above n 7.

11 National Institute on Alcohol Abuse and Alcoholism, 'The Scope of the Problem': <http://pubs.niaaa.nih.gov/publications/arh283/111-120.htm> [accessed 4 Jan 2016] (citation omitted).

12 Richard W Thoreson, 'The Professor at Risk: Alcohol Abuse in Academe' (1984) 55(1) *Journal of Higher Education* 56, 56 (footnote omitted). See also, Richard W Thoreson, 'Their Cup Runneth Over: Achievement, Accolades and Alcohol Abuse' in Elizabeth P Hosokawa, Judy Johnston, and Richard W Thoreson (eds), *Employee Assistance Programs in Higher Education: Conference Proceedings* (Columbia, Mo: University of Missouri-Columbia Employee Assistance Program, 1981).

13 Thoreson (1984), above n 12, 59.

problematic drinking: 'The dream grown pale and weak can often be kept alive by the frequent blurring and softening of this harsh reality by alcohol or other chemical misuse.'[14] He emphasized the existence of particular risks for scholars, especially those who are male and in their mid- to later career years.[15] While the particular point in relation to academics from the 1980s is no longer so relevant, the ecological system inhabited by scholars and its risks for substance abuse has changed little and the personality characteristics he identified remain constant; many constitute risk factors for substance abuse in an environment where scholarly freedom means that oversight of employees' conduct and well-being is much less stringent than in most workplaces.

Substance-associated Misconduct

Multiple and sometimes peculiar allegations have been made in respect of scholars, conduct while they have been said to be intoxicated. One of the most bizarre is the allegations that received international media coverage in relation to an allegedly drunken nuclear physics professor, Landysh Zaripova, who was said to have forced students to sit through a 23-hour oral examination at Kazan University in central Russia.[16] She is said to have refused to allow students to leave the examination room for any reason—even to go to the bathroom or to obtain food, instead rambling about her business interests and her love for clothes during the marathon science test.[17] Afterwards the students wrote to the university administration, asking for Zaripova to be suspended. It was to no avail. Zaripova denied being drunk and suggested that the students were being retributive because she failed a number of them.[18] A spokesperson for the university said that it was not believed that Zaripova had been intoxicated and that the length of the examination was 'not unusual'.[19]

Occasionally academics have lost their employment after being charged with drug-related conduct. A notorious example is the Oxford-educated, University of North Carolina physics professor, Paul Frampton, who was sacked after being arrested in Argentina for becoming entangled in a scheme to smuggle two kilograms of cocaine.[20] Probably, more importantly, he was also sentenced to four years and eight months' imprisonment in Buenos Aires for his conduct.[21] By contrast, the University of Florida's Teacher of the Year for Liberal Arts and Sciences, Michael Heckenberger, a professor of anthropology, retained his job after a

---

[14] Ibid, 60.

[15] See also, Alan Gross, 'Twilight in Academe: The Problem of the Aging Professoriate' (1977) 58(10) *Phi Delta Kappan* 752; Irene E Karpiak, 'Ghosts in a Wilderness: Problems and Priorities of Faculty at Mid-Career and Mid-Life' (1996) 26(3) *Canadian Journal of Higher Education* 49.

[16] David Ferguson, 'Drunk Professor Forces Students to Sit Through 23-Hour Science Exam', *Raw Story*, 5 July 2012: <http://www.rawstory.com/rs/2012/07/drunk-professor-forces-students-to-sit-through-23-hour-science-exam/> [accessed 4 Jan 2016].

[17] See Tom Parfitt, '"Drunk' Russian Lecturer 'Forces Students to Sit 23 Hour Exam' *The Telegraph*, 4 July 2012: <http://www.telegraph.co.uk/news/worldnews/europe/russia/9376284/Drunk-Russian-lecturer-forces-students-to-sit-23-hour-exam.html> [accessed 4 Jan 2016].

[18] See Alyssa Creamer, 'Landysh Zaripova, Russian Prof., Forces Students to Endure 23-Hour Oral Physics Exam', *Huffington Post*, 6 July 2012: <http://www.huffingtonpost.com/2012/07/06/landysh-zaripova-russian-_n_1654529.html> [accessed 4 Jan 2016].

[19] See Sara Malm, 'Drunk Russian Lecturer "Forces Students to Sit 23 HOUR Exam (and She Didn't Even Allow Them Out for Toilet Breaks)"', *Daily Mail*, 4 July 2012: <http://www.dailymail.co.uk/news/article-2168673/Drunk-Russian-lecturer-forces-students-sit-23-hour-exam.html> [accessed 4 Jan 2016].

[20] 'UNC Chapel Hill Fires Physics Professor Jailed in Argentina', *Fox8*, 24 May 2014: <http://myfox8.com/2014/05/24/unc-chapel-hill-fires-physics-professor-jailed-in-argentina/> [accessed 4 Jan 2016].

[21] See Maxine Swann, 'The Professor, the Bikini Model and the Suitcase Full of Trouble', *The New York Times*, 8 March 2013: <http://www.nytimes.com/2013/03/10/magazine/the-professor-the-bikini-model-and-the-suitcase-full-of-trouble.html?pagewanted=all&_r=1> [accessed 4 Jan 2016].

plea bargain resulted in his being sentenced to community work after being charged with attempts to trade cocaine for sexual favours.[22]

More common are problems with academics being intoxicated on campus and either teaching while 'unwell' or becoming involved in unseemly or embarrassing incidents with professional colleagues,[23] or conducting themselves inappropriately with students while 'under the influence'. Alcohol and drug use are frequently associated, among academics, as well as generally in the community, with disinhibited behaviours, sometimes characterized by public order offending and sometimes conduct coupled with violence, both physical and sexual. An academic who repeatedly found himself in such difficulties was University of Connecticut professor of chemistry, Gabriel Fenteany, who was arrested on multiple occasions between 2012 and 2014 and charged with alcohol-related offences, as well as urinating on cars, vandalizing them, and spitting on police officers when taken into custody. By 2014 he was under investigation by the university and had been prohibited from all of the university's campuses.[24]

In addition the report into complaints about the University of Colorado, Boulder, Philosophy Department, made the point that the problematic behaviour had many of its origins in boundary-blurring social events in which significant alcohol consumption was a feature:

> Many of the incidents of alleged sexual harassment and assault have occurred while faculty and graduate students were socializing after hours. We found that there is excessive drinking when faculty and graduate students socialize, and that there is an inappropriate expectation that graduate students and faculty should socialize together after hours (e.g., in bars in the evening).[25]

A perception difficulty, and reputational issues for the institution, arise in relation to the competence of scholars responsible for marking and supervision to undertake their role in a suitably considered and fair-minded way if they have (and especially if they are known to have) a drinking or drugs dependency. The maintenance of confidence in the processes and fairness of student evaluation are legitimately important considerations in determining how the health and conduct of a substance-abusing member of staff are to be addressed.

Identifying the Issue

Paul Roman, Distinguished Research Professor of Sociology and Director of the Center for Research on Behavioral Health and Human Research Delivery at the University of Georgia, has identified a number of barriers to dealing with scholars' alcoholism:

- a paucity of success in the measurement of academic performance,
- a 'guild-like protection' of faculty,

22 Thomas Stewart, 'UF Professor Found With Cocaine Enters Court Agreement', *The Independent Florida Alligator*, 22 October 2009: <http://www.alligator.org/news/uf_administration/article_a0736d0a-bec6-11de-96a3-001cc4c002e0.html> [accessed 4 Jan 2016].

23 See eg, Ben Solis, 'Professor 'Regretful' for Intoxication on Campus, Takes Leave of Absence', *Central Michigan Life*, 18 March 2014: <http://www.cm-life.com/article/2014/03/professor-regretful-for-intoxication-on-campus-takes-leave-of-absence> [accessed 4 Jan 2016].

24 Rob Polansky, 'UConn Professor Charged with DUI, Spitting in Officer's Face', *WFSB Eyewitness News*, 15 July 2014: <http://www.wfsb.com/story/25788907/uconn-professor-charged-with-dui-spitting-in-officers-face> [accessed 4 Jan 2016]; David Owens and Tony Terzi, 'UConn Professor Faces New Charges', *The Hartford Courant*, 16 June 2014: <http://articles.courant.com/2014-06-16/community/hc-vernon-uconn-professor-arrested-0617-20140616_1_greenwich-police-vernon-police-uconn-police> [accessed 4 Jan 2016].

25 American Philosophical Association, Committee on the Status of Women, *Report on Site Visit* (University of Colorado Boulder, Department of Philosophy, 25–28 September 2013) 7, available at: <http://spot.colorado.edu/~tooley/The_Site_Visit_Report_and_Administration_Summary.pdf> [accessed 4 Jan 2016].

- a limited social distance between supervisors and subordinates in faculty groups, and
- limited motivation for those in supervisory positions to take action in relation to poor performers.[26]

Thoreson, writing about alcoholism among psychologists, noted a particular dilemma in relation to substance abuse for those who (like many academics) hold a strong belief in the powers of the mind and in the capacity to comprehend and alter behaviour.[27] Peer conduct and attitudes are also very significant,[28] while low self-esteem, especially among women, can be an important contributing factor to alcohol abuse.[29] Attempts to control stress are also a significant factor in excessive alcohol consumption. However, as with high-functioning alcoholics in most spheres,[30] identification of the person's difficulties is a challenging prerequisite to intervention.

University Responses

Many universities have latterly recognized the personal and workplace toll caused by substance abuse and dependence, and have sought to raise consciousness about them and in a collaborative way to facilitate resort to rehabilitation. Some have focused on students, others on enabling a 'healthy setting' for both staff and students.[31] A first step is to recognize the signs of excessive consumption in the academic context. The following characteristics have been particularly noted:

- A narrowing of job performance. The academic alcoholic performs as well as he or she did in previous years, only in a much narrower domain.
- Work task simplification. The quality of work is still relatively high, but the tasks completed are pedestrian in nature.
- Dependence on past learning. Remote memory for the academic alcoholic is intact, but short-term memory for current events is impaired. Consequently, lectures tend to focus on problems and theories that were popular during the 'early days' of the academic's career.
- Student complaints. Complaints by students about teachers are legion. In the instance of alcoholism, however, student complaints will focus on the professors' arrogance, confusion, and outdated lectures.
- Irregular (or non-existent) office hours. Regrettably, the tendency towards outdated lectures and irregular office hours is so common among academic faculty that it is impossible on this basis alone to distinguish alcoholism from plain laziness.

---

[26] See Paul M Roman, 'Employee Alcoholism and Assistance Programs: Adapting an Innovation for College and University Faculty' (1980) 51(2) *Journal of Higher Education* 135, 143–4.

[27] Richard W Thoreson, Peter E Nathan, Jane K Skorina, and Richard R Kilburg, 'The Alcoholic Psychologist: Issues, Problems and Implications for the Profession' (1983) 14(5) *Professional Psychology: Research and Practice* 670.

[28] See Simone Pettigrew and Rob Donovan, *A Literature Review of the Factors that Influence Alcohol Consumption and the Effectiveness of Past Interventions* (Report to the Drug and Alcohol Office, Government of Western Australia, October 2003) 25–26.

[29] Kent E Glindemann, E Scott Geller, and Jason N Fortney, 'Self-Esteem and Alcohol Consumption: A Study of College Drinking Behavior in a Naturalistic Setting' (1999) 45(1) *Journal of Alcohol and Drug Education* 60.

[30] See Sarah Allen Benton, *Understanding the High-Functioning Alcoholic* (Westport, Conn: Praeger, 2009); Jane E Brody, 'High Functioning, But Still Alcoholics', *The New York Times*, 4 May 2009: <http://www.nytimes.com/2009/05/05/health/05brod.html?_r=2&> [accessed 4 Jan 2016].

[31] See eg, La Trobe University, 'Alcohol and Other Drugs': <http://www.latrobe.edu.au/students/living-well/drugs> [accessed 4 Jan 2016] where, for instance, La Trobe University encourages students to undertake a questionnaire to 'Find out how your use of alcohol compares'. However, it also endeavours to reduce alcohol and other drug misuse and related harms for both staff and students: see La Trobe University, 'Alcohol and Other Drugs Policy' (October 2012): <http://www.latrobe.edu.au/policy/documents/alcohol-other-drug-policy.pdf> [accessed 4 Jan 2016].

- A surprising gaffe or departure from high performance. An example of this would be a professor who blacks out and forgets to give his or her final examination.
- Increased obsession (and reduced efficiency) with work to the exclusion of all other activities. Though it is difficult to distinguish this work obsession from normal obsessive behavior of executive-professional types, an accompanying lack of efficiency may help to differentiate it.
- Chronic, free-floating anxiety and low self-esteem seem common to virtually all such alcoholics. The external appearance of normalcy and competence is maintained at a price of internal squalor.
- A greater emphasis on telephone (and these days, no doubt, email) contact to the neglect of face-to-face conversation.
- Meticulous attention to dress (in the middle stages) and neglect of appearance and dress (in the late stages).
- Physical signs, serious accidents, injury, and health problems. In the more advanced stages there will be cigarette burns on clothing, bruises, facial varices, cuts, gross tremors, serious accidents, injury, and health problems.[32]

The University of Maryland, for instance, has emphasized the importance of early identification of scholars at universities who are at risk of substance dependence so they can be referred for employee assistance.[33]

In addition, it is becoming standard for universities to provide education about the advisability of moderation in relation to alcohol consumption. The University of Sydney, for instance, in its Alcohol Policy states:

> The University recognises that alcohol consumption is an established part of life in Australia and is enjoyed by many members of the University community. The University will not attempt to stop drinking on the campus, but will encourage moderation in and a responsible attitude towards the consumption of alcohol. It will aim to create a climate that enables individuals to make a free and informed choice as to the level of their alcohol consumption, in an environment free of inducement and social pressure to drink to excess. The University's specific objectives are to:
> (a) minimise alcohol-related harm to the individual;
> (b) minimise alcohol-related damage to property;
> (c) preserve the reputation of the University in the community;
> (d) provide members of the University community with adequate information about alcohol and the consequences of its excessive use;
> (e) offer appropriate forms of assistance to those for whom alcohol has become a problem.[34]

Similarly, Oxford University frames its policies by reference to the objectives of supporting a healthy and safe work environment and reducing the impact of alcohol and drug misuse in the workplace. Its emphasis is on staff counselling and facilitating compliance with legislative requirements, including those relating to occupational health and safety. Where staff are seen to be affected by a substance, it has specific procedures:

> Where a member of staff is noticeably affected by alcohol and / or drugs whilst at work this has the potential to be a disciplinary matter. In these circumstances an investigation would occur and if the person admitted to a drug or alcohol problem this would normally be handled under the capability or sickness procedure. Accurate records must be maintained of the

[32] Thoreson (1984), above n 12, 66–7 (formatting altered).

[33] University of Maryland, University Health Center, 'FSAP—Confronting Substance Abuse': <http://www.health.umd.edu/fsap/abuse.html> [accessed 4 Jan 2016].

[34] The University of Sydney, 'Alcohol: Policy and Guidelines on Consumption', 3 November 1992, [1]: <http://sydney.edu.au/policies/showdoc.aspx?recnum=PDOC2011/228&RendNum=0> [accessed 4 Jan 2016].

> process. Confidentiality will be maintained, subject to the provision of the law. Managers may also seek advice from the Occupational Health Service or from Personnel Services and/or with the employee's consent, refer the Occupational Health Service.
>
> If a department has already identified problems with an employee's capability, and it is suspected that the employee may have a drug or alcohol problem, it may be necessary to defer action while therapeutic solutions are sought. Personnel Services guidance on dealing with capability issues states that what constitutes an appropriate timescale will vary according to the circumstances of each case and Personnel Services will provide advice on timescales on request. In cases of ill-health or disability, or a drug or alcohol problem, such advice will take account of advice from the OHS on the likely timescale for change in the member of staff's condition. If assistance is declined or inappropriately discontinued, or impaired performance continues, then matters will normally be dealt with according to capability or sickness procedures.
>
> Where an act of misconduct which falls short of serious misconduct has occurred at work in association with alcohol and drug misuse, disciplinary action short of dismissal may follow. Where such an act comprises serious misconduct, dismissal may follow.[35]

It emphasizes the need to identify problems associated with alcohol and drug abuse, and itemizes non-specific workplace indicators of a potential problem, including:

- Periods of unexplained or frequently taken absence
- Poor time-keeping
- Behavioural, or sudden mood changes
- Deterioration in relationships with colleagues, students or the public
- Reduction in performance or productivity
- Dishonesty and theft
- Accidents or near misses
- Smelling of alcohol
- Confusion.[36]

San Francisco State University has gone further, issuing advice to its heads of department on how to deal with staff members suspected of having alcohol problems:

> As we all know, alcohol abuse does exist in the university environment. The stress and demands of academia make faculty uniquely vulnerable... Acting proactively, in a humane, fair, and respectful way helps to avoid the kinds of situations that disrupt the working environment and educational process.
>
> As denial is a hallmark of addiction, one cannot expect that the physically dependent faculty member will be able to self-diagnose. Generally people seek help because of pressure from family, work and the law. With that in mind, it may be up to you, the chair, to ultimately confront the individual faculty member whose drinking is impacting his or her work.[37]

It has listed as general indicators of alcohol abuse:

1. **Absenteeism.** Regularly cancelling, missing or arriving late to classes and meetings, especially at the beginning and end of the week.
2. **Consistent complaints from students** or on student evaluations that the faculty member regularly misses scheduled appointments or office hours, and is not prepared for class, and exhibits erratic behavior.
3. **High number of accidents** – on and off job.

---

[35] University of Oxford, 'Misuse of Alcohol and Drugs in the Workplace (Staff)', OHS Policy Document: OHS 1/06: <http://www.admin.ox.ac.uk/uohs/policies-guidance/alcdrug/> [accessed 4 Jan 2016].

[36] Ibid.

[37] San Francisco State University, Faculty Affairs and Professional Development, 'For Chairs: When One of Your Faculty Members is Dealing with Alcohol Abuse', 19 March 2008, available at: <http://facaffairs.sfsu.edu/resources-chairs> [accessed 4 Jan 2016].

4. **Poor work relationships.** Problems with colleagues; overly sensitive to work performance critiques; is often moody or displays obvious mood-swings.
5. **Difficulty concentrating and/or confusion.** Obvious loss of train-of-thought, reflected in class setting and with colleagues, work not being completed in a timely manner.
6. **Poor judgment.** Both in and out of the classroom. (i.e. inappropriate behavior with students, such as partying with students and making inappropriate passes, inappropriate discussion of grades.)
7. **Sporadic or obvious decline in work performance**, professional activity and growth – for example, not meeting deadlines, not completing projects.
8. **Frequently smells of alcohol during "work hours"**, slurs words, often intoxicated at university events.[38]
   - documenting of observable behaviours,
   - protecting the person's confidentiality;
   - consulting relevant resources;
   - making an appointment with the academic to discuss matters;
   - utilising those in the human resources' department;
   - bearing in mind the impact of the person's condition on the department;
   - considering the person's rights;
   - using the supports available on campus; and
   - taking care of oneself in what is a stressful interaction.[39]

It also draws attention not just to the fact that the person may well deny a problem, but that they may make threats, engage in rationalizations and engage in angry outbursts when confronted with concerns about their well-being.

By contrast, the University of Auckland's 'Campus Rules' state that staff (and students) are not allowed to bring or consume alcohol on university premises, other than licensed premises, or where permission has been given to consume alcohol.[40] According to the Rules, staff who fail to comply with the Rules 'will be subject to disciplinary proceedings under the terms of their employment agreement'.[41] Similarly, the message given by the Law School at Harvard University is stern and punitive in its tone, warning of the consequences of inappropriate behaviours:

> Harvard University promotes the health and well-being of its students and employees through its Health Services and other agencies. The unlawful possession, use, or distribution of illicit drugs and alcohol by students and employees on Harvard property or as a part of any Harvard activities is a violation of University rules, as well as the law. Possession, use, or distribution of certain nonprescription drugs, including marijuana, amphetamines, heroin, cocaine, and nonprescription synthetics; procurement or distribution of alcohol if one is under 21 years of age;[42] and provision of alcohol to anyone under 21 years of age are violations of law and of Harvard policy. The University holds its students and employees responsible for the consequences of their decisions to use or distribute illicit drugs, or to serve or consume alcohol. Further, it expects students and employees to create and maintain an environment for learning and work that is safe and healthy and encourages responsible conduct.
>
> The use of illicit drugs and the misuse of alcohol are potentially harmful to health. In particular, synthetically produced drugs, which are readily available in the Boston metropolitan area, often have unpredictable emotional and physical side effects, which constitute

38 Ibid.

39 Ibid.

40 University of Auckland, 'Campus Rules', 12 December 2012, [2.4]: <https://cdn.auckland.ac.nz/assets/central/about/the-university/how-the-university-works/policy-and-administration/Organisation%20and%20Governance/campus-rules.pdf> [accessed 4 Jan 2016].

41 Ibid, [1.3].

42 An issue particular to the United States because of the age restriction in the United States.

an extreme health hazard. In addition, students are encouraged to weigh the seriousness of potential loss of function that may come from ingesting illicit drugs or too much alcohol. Because of the considerable health hazards involved in drug and alcohol use, administrative, medical, and psychiatric help for students having drug problems or difficulties controlling their use of alcohol are available on a confidential basis from the Law School Health Services and at the University Health Services at the Smith Campus Center, and any member of the University may make use of the Health Services on an emergency basis, day or night.

Attention is directed to the fact that the University is not, and cannot be considered as, a protector or sanctuary from the existing laws of the city, state, or federal government.[43]

The Timothy Leary Saga

One of the most famous involvements of scholars in substance misuse involved the experiments conducted by Dr Timothy Leary (1920–1996) and also by Dr Richard Alpert (also known as Ram Dass, 1931–) in the name of development of knowledge about the operation of hallucinogens.

Leary was a United States psychologist with doctoral qualifications from the University of California at Berkeley.[44] In 1959–1960 he was employed at Harvard University as a lecturer and during the next summer spent time in Mexico during which he encountered 'magic mushrooms', which contain the hallucinogenic, psilocybin.[45] The next year his experimentation extended to LSD and mescaline, a drug derived from the peyote cactus plant. As of the early 1960s LSD, psilocybin, and mescaline were not illegal substances in the United States. In fact clinical research into the therapeutic properties of LSD was being undertaken with its being administered to alcoholics, drug addicts, and a range of patients with emotional issues. Actor Cary Grant was such a patient. Allen Ginsburg was introduced to LSD at the Mental Research Institute in Palo Alto, as was Ken Kesey who later wrote *One Flew Over the Cuckoo's Nest.* Aldous Huxley took mescaline under the supervision of the British psychiatrist, Humphry Osmond (the person who coined the term 'psychedelic'), and wrote a short (and remarkable) book about the experience and about the usage of LSD—*The Doors of Perception and Heaven and Hell.*[46]

Leary set up a series of controversial and ground-breaking experiments.[47] They were written up in an orthodox way and published in scholarly journals. The best-known was the Harvard

---

[43] Harvard Law School, 'Drug and Alcohol Policy': <http://www.law.harvard.edu/academics/degrees/gradprogram/llm/arrival-packet-documents/drug--alcohol-policy-2014.pdf> [accessed 4 Jan 2016].

[44] For the account that follows, see Louis Menand, 'Acid Redux: The Life and High Times of Timothy Leary', *The New Yorker*, 26 June 2006): <http://www.newyorker.com/magazine/2006/06/26/acid-redux?currentPage=all> [accessed 4 Jan 2016].

[45] See James W Jesso, *Decomposing the Shadow: Lessons from the silocybin Mushroom* (Calgary: SoulsLantern Publishing, 2013); Simon G Powell, *The silocybin Solution: The Role of Sacred Mushrooms in the Search for Meaning* (Rochester: Inner Traditions/Bear & Co, 2011).

[46] Aldous Huxley, *The Doors of Perception and Heaven and Hell* (New York: Harper & Row, 1963) 85–6, where he wrote: 'If you go to New South Wales, you will see marsupials hopping about the countryside. And if you go to the antipodes of the self-conscious mind, you will encounter all sorts of creatures at least as odd as kangaroos. You do not invent these creatures any more than you invent marsupials. They live their own lives in complete independence. A man cannot control them. All he can do is to go the mental equivalent of Australia and look around him. Some people never consciously discover their antipodes. Others make an occasional landing. Yet others (but they are few) find it easy to go and come as they please. For the naturalist of the mind, the collector of psychological specimens, the primary need is some safe, easy and reliable method of transporting himself and others from the Old World to the New, from the continent of familiar cows and horses to the continent of a wallaby and the platypus. Two such methods exist…either mescalin or lysergic acid.'

[47] See Don Lattin, *The Harvard Psychedelic Club: How Timothy Leary, Ram Dass, Huston Smith, and Andrew Weil Killed the Fifties and Ushered in a New Age for America* (New York: HarperOne, 2011). For

Psilocybin Project, whose Board consisted of himself, Aldous Huxley, and John Spiegel, who was later President of the American Psychiatric Association. Researchers administered psilocybin to 175 volunteers from various backgrounds in an environment intended to be similar to a familiar lounge room. Ninety-eight of the subjects were given questionnaires to assess their experiences and the contribution of background and situational factors. Those who had experience with psilocybin before the study reported more pleasant experiences than those who were naïve to the drug. Group size, dosage, preparation, and expectancy were found to be important determinants of the drug response. In general, those placed in groups of more than eight individuals felt that the groups were less supportive, and their experiences were less pleasant, while groups of fewer than six individuals were seen as more supportive. Participants also reported having more positive reactions to the drug in those groups. Leary and his co-researchers suggested that psilocybin heightens suggestibility, making an individual more receptive to interpersonal interactions and environmental stimuli.[48] This raised a number of potential uses for the drug and others comparable to it.

Dr Leary also participated in the Concord Prison Experiment[49] in which young offenders at a maximum security prison, Concord State, were given psilocybin to evaluate whether it facilitated psychotherapy for 32 prisoners and thereby whether it impacted on rates of recidivism.

Dr Leary also supervised the Marsh Chapel Experiment (also known as the 'Good Friday Experiment'), in which researchers administered psilocybin to divinity students to determine if it was an 'entheogen'—whether it generated the 'god within'—and thereby facilitated the experience of profound religious states.[50]

Leary's principal collaborator was Dr Richard Alpert (later known as Ram Dass), an assistant professor in Harvard's Department of Clinical Psychology and Education. His doctoral qualifications were from Stanford. As Weil explains, the work of Leary and Alpert headed into difficulties:

> Intradepartmental opponents of the project charged that Alpert and Leary gave the drugs in sessions resembling cocktail parties, that they were slipshod in collecting data and that they were in no position to make observations when they themselves were drugged. The psychologists countered with the assertion that no one was qualified to observe people under

Leary's account, see Timothy Leary, *Flashbacks: A Personal and Cultural History of an Era* (Los Angeles: J P Tarcher, 1990).

48 See Timothy Leary, George H Litwin, and Ralph Metzner, 'Reactions to Psilocybin Administered in a Supportive Environment' (1963) 137(6) *Journal of Nervous and Mental Disease* 561; see also, Timothy Leary, *The Politics of Ecstasy* (Berkeley, CA: Ronin, 1998).

49 See Timothy Leary, Ralph Metzner, Madison Presnell, and Gunther Weil et al., 'A New Behavior Change Program Using Psilocybin' (1965) 2(2) *Psychotherapy: Theory, Research and Practice* 61. See also, Ralph Metzner, 'Reflections on the Concord Prison Project and the Follow-Up Study' (1998) 30(4) *Journal of Psychoactive Drugs* 427 where the argument is made that Leary used a wrong control figure, with Metzner commenting (at 428): 'Whether Leary made these mistakes consciously, faking the results that he wanted, or whether they were unconscious mistakes or carelessness, motivated by overenthusiasm is impossible to say at this point.' See also, Rick Doblin, 'Dr Leary's Concord Prison Experiment: A 34-Year Follow-Up Study' (1998) 30(4) *Journal of Psychoactive Drugs* 419.

50 See generally, Walter N Pahnke, 'Drugs and Mysticism' (1966) 8(2) *International Journal of Parapsychology* 295; Timothy Leary and Gunther M Weil, 'The Religious Experience: Its Production and Interpretation' (1967) 1(2) *Journal of Psychedelic Drugs* 3. On the 'god within', see Carl A P Ruck, Jeremy Bigwood, Danny Staples, and Jonathan Ott et al., 'Entheogens' (1979) 11(1-2) *Journal of Psychedelic Drugs* 145, 146; Aline Marianne Lucas, 'Entheology' (1995) 27(3) *Journal of Psychoactive Drugs* 293, 293. See later, Rick Doblin, 'Pahnke's "Good Friday Experiment": A Long-Term Follow-up and Methodological Critique' (1991) 23(1) *Journal of Transpersonal Psychology* 1; Roland R Griffiths, William A Richards, Una D McCann, and Robert L Jesse, 'Psilocybin Can Occasion Mystical-Type Experiences Having Substantial and Sustained Personal Meaning and Spiritual Significance' (2006) 187(3) *Psychopharmacology* 268.

> the influence of psilocybin unless he was in the same state and thus able to know what his subjects were feeling.
>
> Meanwhile, an increasing number of students began to try to locate sources of mescaline and to ask how they could get to be subjects in the psilocybin research. The University Administration did not become really alarmed until two undergraduates landed in mental hospitals after taking one or another of the drugs. There was, of course, no way of proving that the drugs had contributed to the breakdowns. But when the dean's office checked into recent affairs at the Center for Research in Personality, it didn't like what it found. David C McClelland, director of the center, vouched for the soundness of the study, however, and the parents of the two hospitalized students wanted everything kept quiet. Harvard may have wished to dissociate itself from the drug project in 1961, but it had no grounds on which to act.[51]

The university's very temperate response, in the face of the assertion of entitlements to scholarly independence, was to insist on the two researchers agreeing that they would not thereafter use or enlist undergraduates in their research. They both made the requested undertaking.

However, their adherence to the agreement came into question. Herbert Kelman, then a lecturer on social ethics (later Cabot Professor of Social Ethics) recounted that: 'While I was away [in Norway], I was getting letters from my students saying, "You won't believe what is going on here with this drug business"'.[52] Kelman characterized the research as 'totally unorthodox', and stated that 'there was a kind of cavalier attitude about the research that felt inappropriate'.[53] A student had advised him that '[t]hey were being strongly urged by the two instructors to participate in the drug sessions', and that 'out of the 12 students in the class, only [this student] and one other student refused to participate'.[54] In response, Kelman commented that the student's account 'made me realize how much it had become legitimized... I don't think this was serious research, frankly, and I think it was an abuse of the authority and power of the faculty members over students.'[55]

Following coverage by *The Harvard Crimson*, other media outlets, including *The Boston Globe*, began reporting on what evolved into a research scandal and on escalating tensions, meaning that the university could not turn a blind eye to what was being done by the two researchers any longer. In addition, official agencies such as the Massachusetts Department of Public Health began investigating the dangers and validity of Leary and Alpert's experiments.

The condition that undergraduates not be used for the experiments enabled the termination of Alpert's employment at Harvard in 1963 when he was found to have given LSD to a male undergraduate.[56] According to Leary's biographer Robert Greenfield, there was another aspect to the situation—Alpert provided the LSD for sexual favours.[57]

Alpert was dismissed from Harvard for violating the agreement with the university and for lying that he had not done so. Leary was also sacked by Harvard, allegedly for leaving

---

51 Andrew T Weil, 'The Strange Case of the Harvard Drug Scandal', *Look Magazine*, 5 November 1963, available at: <http://www.psychedelic-library.org/look1963.htm> [accessed 4 Jan 2016].

52 See Nikita Kansra and Cynthia W Shih, 'Harvard LSD Research Draws National Attention', *The Harvard Crimson*, 21 May 2012: <http://www.thecrimson.com/article/2012/5/21/harvard-lsd-project-leary/?page=1> [accessed 4 Jan 2016].

53 Ibid.

54 Ibid.

55 Ibid.

56 Joseph M Russin and Andrew T Weil, 'The Crimson Takes Leary, Alpert to Task', *The Harvard Crimson*, 28 May 1963: <http://www.thecrimson.com/article/1973/1/24/the-crimson-takes-leary-alpert-to/> [accessed 4 Jan 2016].

57 Robert Greenfield, *Timothy Leary: A Biography* (Orlando, Fla: Harcourt, 2006).

Cambridge and his classes without permission. Inevitably, though, the increasingly bad odour surrounding his psychedelic drug research, together with its resonances generally, played a significant role in the decision to terminate his employment.

In 1965 amendments to the *Food, Drug and Cosmetic Act*,[58] known as the *Drug Abuse Control Amendments* of 1965 (US),[59] were passed to regulate the unlicensed possession, manufacture and sale of a range of drugs, including 'hallucinogenic drugs', which were not specifically enumerated.[60] However, by 1968 there was federal prohibition of psilocybin.[61]

The Leary experiments, insofar as they took place out of Harvard, were relatively brief in duration. However, they were written up extensively and were very controversial; their repercussions generated a whole sub-culture and the psychedelic drug phenomenon. Every indication is that Harvard University was glad to see the end of the experiments, and more particularly of its association with Alpert and Leary, who were asserted to be promoting the recreational use of the drugs they were investigating,[62] including amongst undergraduate students on campus. In respect of Leary, the mechanism utilized was his distraction from campus duties while with Alpert it was his inappropriate provision of substances to undergraduate students.

The passage of time has brought a number of question marks as to the scientific legitimacy of some of the protocols utilized by Leary, Alpert, and colleagues, as well as the conclusions they drew. Today, of course, research approval for the experiments in the way they were conducted would not be given. What is apparent is that the lines between scientific investigation and personal exploration (and indulgence) became unethically blurred by the work of Leary and his co-researchers, this in itself detracting from the scientific integrity of the research and raising grave ethical questions about some of the conduct engaged in while they were scholars employed at Harvard.

Self-administration

An issue that arose in relation to the research conducted by Leary and Alpert has recurred in relation to a number of other scholars who have undertaken experiments in relation to psychoactive drugs.[63] For many years the 'godfather of MDMA' (ecstasy), the United States psychopharmacologist Dr Alexander Shulgin, experimented on himself in the course of developing a large number of psychedelic compounds, including 'stimulants, depressants, aphrodisiacs, "empathogens", convulsants, drugs that alter hearing, drugs that slow one's sense of time, drugs that speed it up, drugs that trigger violent outbursts, [and] drugs to deaden emotion'.[64]

---

58 *Food, Drug and Cosmetic Act of 1938*, Pub L No 75-717, 52 Stat 1040 (1938).

59 Pub L No 89-74, 79 Stat 226 (1965).

60 See Richard G Boire, *Sacred Mushrooms and the Law* (Berkeley, CA: Ronin, 2002) 25.

61 See ibid, 26; Congress subsequently enacted the *Comprehensive Drug Abuse Prevention and Control Act of 1970*, Pub L No 91-513, 84 Stat 1236 (1970). See also, Colin Wark and John F Galliher, 'Timothy Leary, Richard Alpert (Ram Dass) and the Changing Definition of Psilocybin' (2010) 21(3) *International Journal of Drug Policy* 234.

62 On their association with Harvard's Psychology Department, see Harvard University, Faculty of Arts and Sciences, 'About the Department': <http://www.isites.harvard.edu/icb/icb.do?keyword=k3007&panel=icb.pagecontent44003%3Ar%241%3Fname%3Dhistoricprofs.html&pageid=icb.page19708&pageContentId=icb.pagecontent44003&view=view.do&viewParam_name=learyandalpert.html> [accessed 4 Jan 2016].

63 See, for example, the accounts of Wensley Clarkson, *Legal Highs: Inside Secrets of the World's Newest and Deadliest Drugs* (London: Quercus, 2015).

64 Drake Bennett, 'Dr Ecstasy', *The New York Times*, 30 January 2005: <http://www.nytimes.com/2005/01/30/magazine/30ECSTASY.html?_r=1&> [accessed 4 Jan 2016]. See also, Hamilton Morris and Ash Smith, 'The Last Interview with Alexander Shulgin', *Vice*, 2 May 2010: <http://www.vice.com/en_uk/read/the-last-interview-with-alexander-shulgin-423-v17n5> [accessed 4 Jan 2016].

Shulkin obtained his PhD from the University of California, Berkeley, having initially studied at Harvard. He commenced important aspects of his work while employed at Dow Chemical Company, working at first on pesticides, but later on the development of a range of psychoactive compounds. He published in journals such as *Nature* and the *Journal of Organic Chemistry*. When Dow determined that it no longer wished to endorse Shulgin, he commenced to work from his own laboratory as well as to do freelance work for research laboratories and hospitals. For a time he received the protection of the Drug Enforcement Administration, for which he provided chemical expertise in drugs cases. He was granted a licence to produce Schedule I substances.[65] It was during this period that he resynthesized MDMA, which he provided to psychologists and psychiatrists who used it for therapeutic purposes, including with patients with post-traumatic stress disorder. His research procedures left much to be desired:

> Shulgin tested for activity by taking the chemicals himself. He would start many times below the active dose of a compound's closest analog and work his way up on alternate days. When he found something of interest, Ann, whom he married in 1981, would try it. If he thought further study was warranted, he would invite over his 'research group' of six to eight close friends—among them two psychologists and a fellow chemist—and try the drugs out on them. In case of a truly dangerous reaction, Shulgin kept an anti-convulsant on hand. He used it twice, both times on himself.[66]

He (and his wife) described his methodology in *PIHKAL (Phenethylamines): A Love Story*,[67] a consequence of which was that the Drug Enforcement Administration banned all compounds listed in the book. The research approach of self-trialling and evaluating all discovered compounds clearly lacked scientific legitimacy. It remains a problematic and potentially dangerous issue in relation to what is often covert research into psychoactive substances.[68]

Legal Issues

Legal issues can flow from scholars' abuse of substances, whether this occurs on campus and in the course of what is alleged to be research or work with students, relatives, or colleagues, but certainly if it impacts on their scholarly work as employed persons. The Americans with Disabilities Act of 1990 (US),[69] for instance, views alcoholism as a handicap, requiring reasonable accommodation by employers, which will at least require referral to an employee assistance programme. In addition, the Drug-Free Workplace Act of 1988 (US)[70] requires certain responses for employees who are convicted of driving offences associated or not with the workplace. There are times when their employment has been terminated after they have been found intoxicated on university premises.[71] However, this is unusual.

The principal legal issues arising from conduct engaged in at the workplace while scholars are affected by licit or illicit intoxicating substances are in the context of occupational health

---

65 Mike Power, 'Alexander Shulgin Obituary', *The Guardian*, 3 June 2014: <http://www.theguardian.com/science/2014/jun/03/alexander-shulgin> [accessed 4 Jan 2016].

66 See Bennett, above n 63.

67 Alexander Shulgin and Ann Shulgin, *Pihkal: A Chemical Love Story* (Berkeley, CA: Transform Press, 1991).

68 See the instances described graphically in the interviews conducted by Clarkson, above n 63.

69 Pub L No 101-336, 104 Stat 327 (1990).

70 41 USC 81.

71 See eg, Fiona Lockyer and Emily Kraus, 'Professor Terminated; Intoxication on Campus Alleged', *The Justice*, 5 March 2012: <http://www.thejustice.org/article/2012/03/professor-terminated-intoxication-on-campus-alleged> [accessed 4 Jan 2016].

and safety responsibilities of employers. These oblige employers to take those measures that are reasonably open to them to provide a safe work environment and therefore to do what they can to prevent dangerous behaviours in the workplace and to facilitate participation in rehabilitative programmes by those whose substance abuse becomes known.

The other issue that has arisen is as to the provision of substances, whether they be alcohol or legal (eg prescribed) or illegal drugs, to research participants, including to students and other members of staff. This is a matter that is regulated by both the criminal law and by research proprieties, including as to provision of proper information on the risks and the obtaining of informed consent—matters overseen by human research ethics committees.

Substance Abuse Issues for Institutions

Alcohol is promoted in ways that do not equate with any other noxious substance in our society and is associated with anti-social behaviours throughout the community.[72] The environment of the scholar is no exception. In fact, the ecology of universities and scholarly gatherings is particularly conducive to substance abuse in general and to the effects of such abuse being inadequately recognized and addressed by employers. This can lead to a wide variety of unfortunate consequences, ranging from engagement by scholars in poor levels of work performance, to deterioration in their health and overall functioning, blurring of proper boundaries, and to their behaving anti-socially and even illegally, associated with the disinhibiting effects of intoxication. Traditionally, alcohol intake at universities has been high and resort to dependence by scholars has not been uncommon for a variety of reasons that are increasingly well-recognized. Some of these are associated with the personality characteristics of those who are drawn to the scholarly life, a number of which can lead to self-medication and a lifestyle in which alcohol, and even illicit substances, play a significant role in exchange of views, as well as in attempts at stress reduction.

The bigger question is how scholars' failure to abstain from being intoxicated in the workplace should be handled by their employers. In the past considerable focus has been devoted to addressing excesses by students in respect of consumption of drugs and alcohol. However, it is clear that such issues also arise at a problematic level among employed staff at scholarly institutions and that they must not be ignored. It is important that real efforts be made to create and maintain a healthy environment within academia; this extends to dealing with substance abuse and dependence.[73] It is entirely reasonable for the workplace of academia to assert the entitlement of students and colleagues to scholars remaining unaffected by any substance which might intoxicate them when they are performing workplace functions. Moreover, when criminal acts (sexual assaults or threats of harm, etc) or serious infractions of scholarly propriety (inappropriate disputation or denigration, or interruption or interference with colleagues' work, or the blurring of boundaries in the context of consumption or provision of substances, etc) are committed by scholars who are intoxicated, it is important to be clear that such conduct should not be attributed to the consumption of alcohol or drugs. Those who have engaged in the behaviour are responsible for their actions and should be dealt with accordingly pursuant to the law or workplace policies, as appropriate.

---

[72] See eg, Thomas F Babor et al., *Alcohol: No Ordinary Commodity: Research and Public Policy* (2nd edn, Oxford: Oxford University Press, 2010).

[73] See eg, National Institute on Alcohol Abuse and Alcoholism, College Drinking—Changing the Culture, 'How to Reduce High-Risk College Drinking: Use Proven Strategies, Fill Research Gaps', 23 September 2005: <http://www.collegedrinkingprevention.gov/niaaacollegematerials/panel02/execsum_00.aspx> [accessed 4 Jan 2016].

However, until propensities to become affected by alcohol or drugs during working hours translate into seriously unacceptable behaviour, the issue is principally one of health and the approach of harm minimization and encouragement to enter into rehabilitation is preferable. Legal obligations aside, it is incumbent upon such teaching and research institutions to facilitate participation in rehabilitative and harm reduction programmes—to optimize scholarly performance, to address dangerous health issues, to deal with occupational health and safety obligations, and to address the pain and suffering that generally accompanies substance abuse.

11

WHISTLEBLOWING

Introduction

Persons who provide information to more senior persons, regulators, or the media about what they believe is the misconduct of colleagues within their own organizations[1] (whether illegal, immoral, or otherwise illegitimate) have been called 'bell-ringers' (after those who ring church bells when danger threatens), 'lighthouse-keepers' (referring to the shining of light on dangerous situations),[2] and more latterly 'whistleblowers' (a term derived from the practice of English Bobbies to blow their whistle upon discovering evidence of the commission of a crime).[3] At the heart of what will be referred to in this chapter as 'whistleblowing' is the desire on the part of the discloser of information to bring wrongdoing that they (believe they) have identified to a conclusion by focusing attention from an informed source on its occurrence. It is not (solely) about the ventilation of a personal grievance[4] but a communication to 'authorities' in order to bring to an end the conduct so that the work or other environment is a better functioning and/or a safer place. Such motives are often idealistically based with the person (sometimes naively) perceiving himself or herself as acting for the public good or on behalf of other persons who may be adversely affected and not being particularly cognisant of the consequences that may ensue, including for them as a whistleblower.[5]

The stakes in respect of such matters have changed over time but during some periods in the past have been particularly high. Shapin, an historian of 17th century science, has observed that around the time when the Royal Society in England was founded there was a taboo in relation to both fraud and accusations of fraud—calling a person a fraudster was liable to lead to a challenge for a duel; the issue could be one of life and death.[6]

---

[1] See Joseph G Starke, 'The Protection of Public Service Whistleblowers—Part I' (1991) 65(4) *Australian Law Journal* 205; Joseph G Starke, 'The Protection of Public Service Whistleblowers—Part II' (1991) 65(5) *Australian Law Journal* 252; John McMillan, 'Blowing the Whistle on Fraud in Government' (1988) 56 *Canberra Bulletin of Public Administration* 118.

[2] See Michael W Tracy, 'Whistleblowing in Corporate America: Organizational Factors and their Influence on the Employee Decision-Making Process' (PhD dissertation, Walden University, 2006) 14.

[3] Joan Corbo, '*Kraus v. New Rochelle Hosp. Medical Ctr.*: Are Whistleblowers Finally Getting the Protection They Need?' (1994) 12 *Hofstra Labor Law Journal* 141, 141. See also, Marcia P Miceli, Janet Pollex Near, and Terry Morehead Dworkin, *Whistle-Blowing in Organizations* [electronic resource] (Hoboken: Taylor & Francis, 2013); Chris Moll, 'Homecoming for Wandering Dutch Whistle-Blowers?' (2014) 24(3–4) *Security and Human Rights* 333.

[4] See Kirstine Drew, *Whistle Blowing and Corruption: An Initial and Comparative Review* (London: Public Services International Research Unit (PSIRU), 2003): <http://www.google.com.au/url?sa=t&rct=j&q=&esrc=s&source=web&cd=2&ved=0CCkQFjAB&url=http%3A%2F%2Fwww.psiru.org%2Freports%2F2002-08-C-whistle.doc&ei=GpUMVeGeGoXpmQX9z4HYDQ&usg=AFQjCNEoF10C3-JvKcDk95BLJDNwFHYIXQ&sig2=uWgjV4Ccmc6IV9mXco4btg&bvm=bv.89060397,d.dGY> [accessed 4 Jan 2016].

[5] See Robert G Vaughn, *The Successes and Failures of Whistleblower Laws* (Cheltenham: Edward Elgar, 2012); Tina Uys, 'Changes in the Sociology of Business Ethics: Researching Whistleblowing' (2011) 5(1) *African Journal of Business Ethics* 50, 53–4.

[6] Steven Shapin, *A Social History of Truth: Civility and Science in Seventeenth-Century England* (Chicago: University of Chicago Press, 1994).

The reality for modern whistleblowers in academia, as well as in other contexts, is often adverse and personally bleak.[7] There is significant stigma and trauma associated with informing against colleagues.[8] Whistleblowers' contributions are often not well received and a variety of adverse consequences, direct and indirect, can follow—from the persons the subject of their revelations, from co-workers, and from their employer whose reputation they are impugning. Relatively rarely do whistleblowers accomplish the aim of effectively bringing their concerns to public light and securing institutional acceptance for their efforts. Whistleblowers generally do not assume the hero status suggested in the 1976 film *All the President's Men*, which portrayed the investigative work undertaken by Washington Post journalists Carl Bernstein and Bob Woodward in exposing the 'Watergate Scandal' which ultimately led to the resignation of President Nixon.[9] Notably though Watergate's 'Deep Throat' (Mark Felt of the FBI) went to considerable lengths to maintain his anonymity for a lengthy period and the experience of being a whistleblower was personally devastating:

> [He] lived in solitary dread, under the constant threat of being summarily fired or even indicted, with no colleagues in whom he could confide. He was justifiably suspicious that phones had been wiretapped, rooms bugged, and papers rifled. He was completely isolated, having placed his career and his institution in jeopardy. Eventually, Deep Throat would even warn Woodward and Bernstein that he had reason to believe 'everyone's life is in danger'—meaning Woodward's, Bernstein's, and, presumably, his own.[10]

Nor do things often end as well as they did for Jeffrey Wigand, the whistleblower portrayed by Russell Crowe in the 1999 film, *The Insider*[11]—however, even he was fired and never resumed work in health or research science.

Nonetheless, there are many instances of persons whose whistleblowing in the modern era has led to important remedial initiatives in the public interest and to the exposure of dangerous and corrupt practices.[12] Peter Buxton, the social worker who blew the whistle on the

[7] See Nick Perry, 'Indecent Exposures: Theorizing Whistleblowing' (1998) 19(2) *Organization Studies* 235; Senate Select Committee on Public Interest Whistleblowing, Parliament of Australia, *In the Public Interest* (1994).

[8] *In the Public Interest*, above n 7.

[9] See too, Carl Bernstein and Bob Woodward, *All the President's Men* (New York: Simon and Schuster, 1974). Compare the 1983 film 'Silkwood' (20th Century Fox), which portrayed the disclosure of poor safety in a nuclear facility and the retributive behaviour towards the whistleblower, Karen Gay Silkwood.

[10] John D O'Connor, 'I'm the Guy They Called Deep Throat', *Vanity Fair*, July 2005: <http://www.vanityfair.com/news/politics/2005/07/deepthroat200507> [accessed 4 Jan 2016]; see also, Beverley H Earle and Gerald A Madek, 'The Mirage of Whistleblower Protection under Sarbanes–Oxley: A Proposal for Change' (2007) 44(1) *American Business Law Journal* 1.

[11] Based on Marie Brenner, 'The Man Who Knew Too Much', *Vanity Fair*, May 1996: <http://www.vanityfair.com/magazine/1996/05/wigand199605> [accessed 4 Jan 2016].

[12] See the examples provided by Roberta Ann Johnson, *Whistleblowing: When It Works—And Why* (Boulder, Col: Lynne Rienner Publishers, 2003), including (at 80–84) the account of Barbara Moulton who 'blew the whistle' on the relationship between the Food and Drug Administration and the pharmaceutical industry; see also, C Fred Alford, *Whistleblowers: Broken Lives and Organizational Power* (Ithaca, NY: Cornell University Press, 2001); David B Lewis (ed), *Whistleblowing at Work* (London: Athlone Press, 2001); Stephen M Kohn, *Concepts and Procedures in Whistleblower Law* (Westport, Conn: Quorum Books, 2001); Frederick D Lipman, *Whistleblowers: Incentives, Disincentives, and Protection Strategies* (Hoboken, NJ: Wiley, 2012); Alexander J Brown AJ (ed), *Whistleblowing in the Australian Public Sector: Enhancing the Theory and Practice of Internal Witness Management in Public Sector Organisations* (Canberra, ACT: ANU E Press, 2008); Marek Arszulowicz and Wojciech W Gasparski (eds), *Whistleblowing: In Defense of Proper Action* (New Brunswick: Transaction Publishers, 2011); Kipling D Williams, *Ostracism: The Power of Silence* (New York: Guilford Press, 2001); Richard Calland and Guy Dehn (eds), *Whistleblowing Around the World: Law, Culture and Practice* (Cape Town: ODAC, 2004); Wim Vandekerckhove, *Whistleblowing and Organizational Social Responsibility: A Global Assessment* (Aldershot, Hampshire: Ashgate, 2006); Myron P Glazer and Penina M Glazer, *The Whistleblowers: Exposing Corruption in Government and Industry* (New York: Basic Books, 1989).

Tuskegee syphilis experiments,[13] and Bernard Carabello, who exposed the unethical hepatitis studies and other abuses inflicted on intellectually disabled children at the Willowbrook State School in New York,[14] are examples of the vital improvements to public health and safety that can be made when unacceptable conduct is made public. However, retaliation and ostracism within the workplace are commonplace after whistles are blown.[15] Such consequences can be especially keenly experienced by women; sometimes retribution can assume a sexually intimidating and reviling tone.[16]

Too often whistleblowers have been branded as troublemakers by their employers or supervisors, and their bona fides and mental state called into question without sufficient reason.[17] It has been suggested that a complaint is often be followed by a pattern of behaviour in the organization in which:

> The whistleblower is discredited, their personal life and career is ruined and they are emotionally and psychologically damaged. The behavioural response of an organisation to the disclosure is seen as having two phases. First, an intense stress factor is exerted on the whistleblower which eventually results in a breakdown of his or her health. Secondly, victimisation and harassment occurs within the workplace. The whistleblower is set up, given menial duties to perform, ostracised, maligned and defamed. Distorted accounts of work practices are submitted. Personal files damaging to the whistleblower are built up with contrived evidence.[18]

There will also often be employment-related effects including disciplinary action, health sequelae, and adverse consequences on family life.[19] On the other hand, whistleblowers can be wrong[20] or indeed may be proven to be lying.[21]

This chapter explores the experience of scholarly whistleblowers, particularly identifying well-known cases within academia, and reflects on the challenges that contemporary whistleblowers face and the measures that need to be implemented to protect them in order to draw effectively on their insights into potential compromises to scholarly integrity.

---

13 See James H Jones, *Bad Blood: The Tuskegee Syphilis Experiment* (New York: Free Press, 1993).

14 See David Goode, Darryl B Hill, Jean Reiss, and William Bronston, *A History and Sociology of the Willowbrook State School* (Washington, DC: American Association on Intellectual and Developmental Disabilities, 2013); David J Rothman and Sheila M Rothman, *The Willowbrook Wars: Bringing the Mentally Disabled into the Community* (New Brunswick, NJ: Aldine Transaction, 2005).

15 See Miceli, Near, and Dworkin, above n 3. For the life after whistleblowing of Veterans Affairs whistleblower Dr Steven Coughlin, later of the University of Tennessee College of Medicine in Memphis, see Jamie Reno, 'VA Concedes Whistleblower's Allegations Were True, Including That It Ignored Veterans' Suicidal tendencies', *International Business Times*, 19 February 2014: <http://www.ibtimes.com/va-concedes-whistleblowers-allegations-were-true-including-it-ignored-veterans-suicidal-tendencies> [accessed 4 Jan 2016].

16 See Linda Hunt, 'The Challenges Women Whistleblowers Face' (2010) 3(2) *International Business Research* 3.

17 See House of Representatives Standing Committee on Legal and Constitutional Affairs, Parliament of Australia, *Whistleblower Protection: A Comprehensive Scheme for the Commonwealth Public Sector* (2009), known as the 'Dreyfus Report' after Mark Dreyfus, the Chair of the Committee.

18 *In the Public Interest*, above n 7, [5.31]. That this pattern occurs was the evidence from Whistleblowers Australia to the *In the Public Interest* inquiry.

19 *In the Public Interest*, above n 7.

20 Senate Standing Committee on Finance and Public Administration, Parliament of Australia, *Management and Operations of the Department of Foreign Affairs and Trade* (1992) [6.5]; *In the Public Interest*, above n 7.

21 This is illustrated by the notorious case of Gordon Grech, a Treasury official who blew the whistle on an alleged misuse of a government scheme OzCar by the then Australian Prime Minister Kevin Rudd and Treasurer Wayne Swan who were said to have asked for preferential treatment for a friend, a car dealer, under the scheme. The saga became known as 'Utegate' but it transpired that Mr Grech had forged the document, an email, and lied about the affair. See Auditor-General, Representations to the Department of the Treasury in Relation to Motor DealerFinancing Assistance (Canberra; Australian National Audit Office, 2009): <http://www.anao.gov.au/~/media/Uploads/Documents/2009%202010_audit_report_1.pdf> [accessed 4 Jan 2016]; Paul Maley, 'Why I Faked OzCar Email: Godwin Grech' (4 August 2009): <http://www.theaustralian.com.au/news/why-i-faked-ozcar-email-godwin-grech/story-e6frg6n6-1225757610973> [accessed 4 Jan 2016].

Definitions of Whistleblowing

The term 'whistleblower' is often poorly delineated or not defined at all. Even in legislation it is often omitted or vague.[22] An example is the situation in the United Kingdom, resulting in Lord Justice Elias in *NHS Manchester v Fecitt*[23] providing his own definition of whistle-blowers under United Kingdom legislation as 'individuals who make such public interest disclosures in good faith.'[24]

When the term is defined in other contexts, the emphasis is on the important role that whistleblowers play in exposing wrongdoing, in promoting an informed society, and in the imposition of accountability.[25] Peter Bowden has provided the following definition:

> Whistleblowing is the exposure by people within or from outside an organisation, of significant information on corruption and wrongdoing, that is in the public interest and would not otherwise be publicly available.[26]

There is some debate regarding whether people who are outside an organization can correctly be called whistleblowers.[27] However, Bowden has suggested that the location (internal or external) of the complainant is immaterial; complainants who are outside an organization could still be discriminated against and need protection from the law.[28] Roberts, Brown, and Olsen have argued that organizations should be aware that they may receive reports from other sources, such as stakeholders or clients, and may need to determine what procedures apply in these circumstances, and what protections should be afforded to these parties.[29]

The *Whistling While They Work* study of public interest whistleblowing in Australian public sector agencies adopted the definition of 'whistleblower' used by Miceli and Near:[30]

> Whistleblowing is the 'disclosure by organisation members (former or current) of illegal, immoral or illegitimate practices under the control of their employers, to persons or organisations that may be able to effect action'.[31]

---

[22] Paul Latimer and Alexander J Brown, 'Whistleblower Laws: International Best Practice' (2008) 31(3) *University of New South Wales* 766.

[23] [2011] EWCA Civ 1190.

[24] Ibid, [3].

[25] See Latimer and Brown, above n 22.

[26] Peter Bowden, 'A Comparative Analysis of Whistleblower Protection' (Paper presented at the Australian Association for Professional and Applied Ethics 12th Annual Conference, Adelaide, 28–30 September 2005) 2: <http://www.unisa.edu.au/Documents/EASS/HRI/GIG/bowden-whistleblower.pdf> [accessed 4 Jan 2016].

[27] The Senate Select Committee adopted a broad definition of 'whistleblower' in the 1994 report, *In the Public Interest*, above n 7, [2.12].

[28] Bowden (above n 26, 2) argued there were other definitional differences that arise such as distinguishing between whistleblowers and activists, who are campaigning against an issue that is already public knowledge and so no need to protect those people from internal reprisals. Further, the issue arises whether the motivations of the whistleblower are morally sound; that is, should the person be classified as a 'whistleblower' if they are motivated by anger, spite, or similar motivation, rather than simply 'in the public interest'. Bowden argues that this is not an important issue; so long as the complainant is acting in the public interest, it does not matter if the person's motivations are not completely pure. The *In the Public Interest* inquiry was also of the opinion that non-employee whistleblowers could suffer reprisals just as much as employees: *In the Public Interest*, above n 7, at [2.4].

[29] Peter Roberts, Alexander J Brown, and Jane Olsen, *Whistling While They Work: A Good-Practice Guide for Managing Internal Reporting of Wrongdoing in Public Sector Organisations* (Canberra, ACT: ANU E Press, 2011), available at: <http://press.anu.edu.au/titles/australia-and-new-zealand-school-of-government-anzsog-2/whistling_citation/pdf-download/> [accessed 4 Jan 2016].

[30] See Marcia P Miceli and Janet P Near, 'The Relationships Among Beliefs, Organizational Position, and Whistle-Blowing Status: A Discriminant Analysis' (1984) 27(4) *Academy of Management Journal* 687, 689.

[31] Roberts, Brown, and Olsen (2011), above n 29, 8, 9.

This same definition was described as a 'succinct academically recognized definition of whistleblowing' in the 2009 Standing Committee on Legal and Constitutional Affairs report on Whistleblowing.[32] Other definitions, such as that developed by a University of Queensland study, and cited in the Senate Select Committee on Public Interest Whistleblowing, defined 'whistleblower' in such a way as to incorporate the public interest side to whistleblowing:

> [T]he whistleblower is a concerned citizen, totally or predominantly motivated by notions of public interest, who initiates of his or her own free will, an open disclosure about significant wrongdoing directly perceived in a particular occupational role, to a person or agency capable of investigating the complaint and facilitating the correction of wrong doing.[33]

However, the concept of 'public interest' is by no means straightforward and can also be defined in a number of ways; the Standing Committee on Legal and Constitutional Affairs, in its 2009 *Whistleblower* report, opted not to define the term 'public interest' or 'whistleblower' in recommending the introduction of a Public Interest Disclosure Bill.[34] Instead, the Committee recommended that the notion of public interest be reflected in the purpose of the legislation and in the provisions relating to disclosable conduct,[35] the purpose of the proposed legislation being to promote accountability and integrity in public administration and guided by the principles that:

- it is in the public interest that accountability and integrity in public administration are promoted by identifying and addressing wrongdoing in the public sector;
- people within the public sector have a right to raise their concerns about wrongdoing within the sector without fear of reprisal;
- people have a responsibility to raise those concerns in good faith;
- governments have a right to consider policy and administration in private; and
- government and the public sector have a responsibility to be receptive to concerns which are raised.[36]

Ultimately, the definition of 'public interest disclosure' in s 26(1) of the *Public Interest Disclosure Act* 2013 (Cth) focused in a complex way on whether '[t]he information tends to show, or the discloser believes on reasonable grounds that the information tends to show, one or more instances of disclosable conduct'. Importantly, therefore, the national Australian legislation incorporated the qualifier that the beliefs of the whistleblower must be held on reasonable grounds. While on its face this is an objective test, it is nonetheless a yardstick that is amenable in many instances to difference of view.

The Phenomenon of Whistleblowing

As is apparent from Chapters 2 and 3, it is rare for contemporary institutions or regulators to identify research misconduct without information from those 'in the know'—colleagues, insiders. This leaves them heavily dependent on the contributions of those prepared to act as informers. Organizations, including within the tertiary sector, are well aware of this, and also very conscious of the reputational harm that can be caused by a whistleblower—whether deservedly or otherwise. From the institutional perspective, although organizational reform

---

[32] House of Representatives Standing Committee on Legal and Constitutional Affairs, above n 17, [2.19].

[33] *In the Public Interest*, above n 7, [2.2]. See also, William De Maria, 'Quarantining Dissent: The Queensland Public Sector Ethics Movement' (1995) 54(4) *Australian Journal of Public Administration* 442, 447.

[34] House of Representatives Standing Committee on Legal and Constitutional Affairs, above n 17, [2.34]–[2.49].

[35] Ibid, [2.49].

[36] Ibid, Recommendation 2, [2.51].

rhetoric identifies the disclosures of whistleblowers as an opportunity to enhance the ethical climate,[37] and to provide a voice to internal stakeholders,[38] it is often problematically culturally challenging to be welcoming or even accepting of such information.[39]

While whistleblowers are fundamental to effective regulation of scholarly misconduct, there is a long history within academia and research institutions of unreceptiveness to the revelations of whistleblowers and of allowing adverse consequences to flow to persons who provide such information; often persons who have made disclosures as whistleblowers have travelled a fraught road[40] and become what can be described as 'institutional enemies'[41]—as Fox put it, 'isolated and victimised as traitors to the solidarity' of their institution.[42] A whistleblower within academia in Australia, Kim Sawyer, has asserted: 'The good whistleblower is the whistleblower who lives in another country, or works for another firm (preferably a competitor), or who blew the whistle 50 years ago. The bad whistleblower is the whistleblower in your own firm who blows the whistle now.'[43] By putting his argument in this way, he draws attention to the gap between the theoretical organizational receptiveness to the disclosures of whistleblowers and the reality that is far from so accepting. There can be reasons and motives for retaliation against whistleblowers.[44]

A common outcome of making disclosures about events inside the scholarly workplace has been mistrust from colleagues and a major interruption to career trajectory.[45] For instance, Dr Margot O'Toole, the whistleblower at the heart of the allegations against Dr Imanishi-Kari,[46] which were ultimately not found to be sustained, asserted that, because of the loyalties felt towards Professor Baltimore and the belief in many quarters that her allegations were unjustified, she had significant difficulty finding a subsequent job. She also maintained that Dr Imanishi-Kari angrily disparaged her to colleagues and that this perception of her being merely a 'disgruntled postdoc' and a person indulging in a 'personal vendetta' did her reputation considerable damage.[47] Aubrey Blumsohn, who made revelations about inappropriate use of research data in relation to osteoporosis, while he was employed in a bone metabolism

---

[37] See eg, Tim Barnett, 'Why *Your* Company Should Have a Whistleblowing Policy' (1992) 57(4) *SAM Advanced Management Journal* 37.

[38] See Ronald J Burke and Cary L Cooper (eds), *Voice and Whistleblowing in Organizations: Overcoming Fear, Fostering Courage and Unleashing Candour* (Cheltenham, UK: Edward Elgar Publishing, 2013).

[39] Chris B Pascal, 'Complainant Issues in Research Misconduct: The Office of Research Integrity Experience' (2006) 231(7) *Experimental Biology and Medicine* 1264.

[40] See Stephen I Ankier, 'Dishonesty, Misconduct and Fraud in Clinical Research: An International Problem' (2002) 30(4) *Journal of International Medical Research* 357.

[41] See Rosamond Rhodes and James J Strain, 'Whistleblowing in Academic Medicine' (2004) 30(1) *Journal of Medical Ethics* 35, 35.

[42] Richard G Fox, 'Protecting the Whistleblower' (1993) 15(2) *Adelaide Law Review* 137, 138.

[43] Kim R Sawyer, 'The Test Called Whistleblowing' (Paper presented at the National Conference of Whistleblowers Australia—*Whistleblowing: Making it Work*, Adelaide, 11 September 2005, 18, available at: <http://www.bmartin.cc/dissent/documents/Sawyer05.pdf> [accessed 4 Jan 2016]. He asserted that his whistleblowing was a test of four values: (1) whether research funds within universities should be used for research and research infrastructure, not for discretionary use; (2) whether academic fraud is or is not acceptable in a university; (3) whether universities should use proper governance processes, including in inquiries; and (4) whether university staff and students should have formal rights of appeal (at 3).

[44] See John J Sumanth, David M Mayer, and Virginia S Kay, 'Why Good Guys Finish Last: The Role of Justification Motives, Cognition, and Emotion in Predicting Retaliation against Whistleblowers' (2011) 1(2) *Organization Psychology Review* 165, 167.

[45] See Craig Lewis and Laurence Cawley, 'Why Do Some People Choose to Blow the Whistle?' *BBC News*, 24 March 2015: <http://www.bbc.com/news/uk-england-31803449> [accessed 4 Jan 2016].

[46] See above, p 106.

[47] See Daniel J Kevles, *The Baltimore Case: A Trial of Politics, Science and Character* (New York: WW Norton & Co, 1998) 139.

unit at the University of Sheffield,[48] found it impossible to remain in his job, although allegations against the colleague whom he reported to the General Medical Council were found partially sustained.[49] He withdrew from medicine and even ultimately from academia.

The importance of academic freedom brings with it for some the idea of freedom from accountability. With this, however, may come fraudulent conduct, corruption, scientific misconduct, or gross financial ineptitude or mismanagement of public funds. Whistleblowing in academia has sometimes been correlated with the capacity to combat intellectual suppression; both can be seen as a form of dissent and both often draw the same behavioural or organizational response.[50] In terms of whistleblowing in academia, questions of accountability arise also for institutions that are in receipt of large amounts of public funds.[51]

Whistleblowers occupy a precarious role in all workplaces[52] and can be vulnerable to retribution.[53] By disposition, many are psychologically vulnerable, partly by reason of having characteristics such as a highly developed sense of justice, a tendency to obsessiveness, and sometimes a propensity for self-dramatization. In an important study of whistleblowers in the research fraud area, the Research Triangle Institute contacted whistleblowers whose cases had been brought to the attention of the United States Office of Research Integrity.[54] The response rate was 72 per cent; 68 responded. Eight reported they had been fired. Eight said that their position had not been renewed. Nineteen stated that career progression had been denied to them. Twenty-nine claimed they had experienced pressure to drop their allegations. Twenty-seven said that they had been subject to counter-allegations. Fifty-two per cent reported an adverse effect on their mental health and 34 per cent said that their finances were worse. Similarly, in an earlier Australian study 35 Australian whistleblowers were surveyed. Twenty-nine reported that victimization started immediately after their first, internal complaint. Eight were dismissed, ten were demoted, and ten resigned or retired early because of ill health after they made their disclosures. Long-term relationships broke up in seven cases and 29 suffered significant stress symptoms. Fifteen were prescribed long-term medications which they had not previously been prescribed and 17 had considered suicide.[55] The advice from the author was that medical practitioners consulted voluntarily by whistleblowers should 'aim at avoiding the common end result of lonely and bitter obsession, chronic anxiety, and other stress related illness in someone who is often unemployable and whose family is suffering or gone… Intense guilt, anger, and mistrust are normal responses, and victims need safe

---

[48] See p 488 below.

[49] See Aubrey Blumsohn and Clare Dyer, 'Aubrey Blumsohn: Academic Who Took On Industry' (2010) 340(7736) *BMJ* 22.

[50] Ibid.

[51] Ibid.

[52] See Alford, above n 12, 94ff; 'Whistleblowers a Vulnerable Species', *Thanh Nien News*, 16 November 2012: <http://www.thanhniennews.com/special-report/whistleblowers-a-vulnerable-species-4453.html> [accessed 4 Jan 2016]; Stephen Lendman, 'War on Whistleblowers—Britain Harasses Human Rights Lawyer Jesselyn Radack', *Global Research*, 19 February 2014: <http://www.globalresearch.ca/war-on-whistleblowers-britain-harasses-human-rights-lawyer-jesselyn-radack/5369649> [accessed 4 Jan 2016].

[53] See Mark Fox and Jeffrey Beall, 'Advice for Plagiarism Whistleblowers' (2013) 24(5) *Ethics & Behavior* 341.

[54] Research Triangle Institute, *Consequences of Whistleblowing for the Whistleblower in Misconduct in Science Cases* (Final Report, 30 October 1995): <https://ori.hhs.gov/sites/default/files/final.pdf> [accessed 4 Jan 2016]. See also, Constance Holden, 'Whistleblower Woes' (1996) 271(5245) *Science* 35; James S Lubalin and Jennifer L Matheson, 'The Fallout: What Happens to Whistleblowers and Those Accused but Exonerated of Scientific Misconduct?' (1999) 5(2) *Science and Engineering Ethics* 229.

[55] See K Jean Lennane, '"Whistleblowing": A Health Issue' (1993) 307(6905) *British Medical Journal* 667. The author was herself a whistleblower, having been sacked in 1990 as Director of Drug and Alcohol Services at Rozelle Hospital in Sydney, Australia, after publicly criticizing cuts to mental health and drug and alcohol services. She was a co-founder of Whistleblowers Australia.

opportunities to express these emotions to the doctor while not allowing them to increase the painful isolation they are already feeling.'[56]

Whistleblowers are often persons who have a strong commitment to propriety and integrity. They have strong moral self-definitions.[57] They tend to be affronted, self-righteously, at a deep level by the perception of lack of integrity in others. If they are not initially believed, or are challenged, this can be very confronting at both a personal and professional level, and can lead them towards obsessional thinking, pathological rumination, and depression. Their belief in a just world[58] can become seriously compromised and thereby lead to significant psychological destabilization. They need not only technical protection in terms of their identity and their security of employment; they often require professional nurturing if psychological harm and worse are to be avoided.[59]

In the 2009 report by the Standing Committee on Legal and Constitutional Affairs, the Committee quoted Whistleblowers Australia, a national representative and advocacy body for whistleblowers, on their submission as to the 'standard' treatment of whistleblowers:

> When a Whistleblower discloses or seeks to disclose (allegations) of public interest wrongdoing the usual consequences are as follows:
>
> The whistleblower receives no advice or assistance in making the disclosure i.e. preparing a statement or providing evidence.
>
> The immediate focus of the matter is the Whistleblower rather than the alleged wrongdoing. It seems the most important issue to an Agency is the credibility of the Whistleblower rather than the validity of the allegations.
>
> Invariably agencies do not provide any proactive protection. Usually the Whistleblower is faced with accusations that they have breached their employment contract or other restrictions and may/will be subject to disciplinary or other adverse action. The open resentment (if not hostility) of management towards the Whistleblower is an open invitation for reprisals to start. The situation is like a pack attack on a wounded animal. There are no rules, no protection and the Whistleblower becomes fair game.
>
> Some peers and even some supervisors will see the injustice of this situation and will offer help. But within a short time it will become evident that supporting a Whistleblower will not be tolerated. The supporter is warned of companion reprisals. Individual survival becomes paramount. Support generally evaporates very quickly.
>
> The accusations, the hostility and management's subtle declaration of an 'open season' for reprisals is [a] crushing blow to a Whistleblower. The Whistleblower who had thought they were acting ethically in the public interest suddenly finds that they are alone and are subjected to an unrestricted 'pack attack' permitted or even orchestrated by agency managers.[60]

Studies of whistleblowers in the United States have found the following outcomes after the making of a disclosure:

- 90 per cent lost their jobs or were demoted;
- 27 per cent faced lawsuits;
- 25 per cent got into difficulties with alcohol;

---

[56] Ibid, 669.

[57] See Peggy DesAutels, 'Resisting Organizational Power' in Lisa Tessman (ed), *Feminist Ethics and Social and Political Philosophy: Theorizing the Non-Ideal* (Dordrecht: Springer, 2009).

[58] See Melvin J Lerner, *The Belief in a Just World: A Fundamental Delusion* (New York: Plenum Press, 1980).

[59] See eg, Joan E Sieber, 'The Psychology of Whistleblowing' (1998) 4(1) *Science and Engineering Ethics* 7.

[60] Standing Committee on Legal and Constitutional Affairs, above n 17, [1.48] (Box 1.2 Standard operating practice: A perspective from Whistleblowers Australia). See also, Jean Lennane, 'What Happens to Whistleblowers, and Why' (2012) 6(4) *Social Medicine* 249.

- 17 per cent lost their homes;
- 15 per cent were divorced;
- 10 per cent attempted suicide; and
- 8 per cent went bankrupt.[61]

An early study on whistleblowers was conducted by Dr Bill De Maria in Queensland in the early 1990s. It identified a range of issues in relation to the consequences for whistleblowers of their making of disclosures.[62] This was followed by a landmark study of whistleblowing in Australia, entitled the *Whistling While They Work* study completed at Griffith University under an Australian Research Council Discovery Project led by Professor AJ Brown.[63] It found that 'whistleblowing is a relatively common and routine activity in a majority of public sector agencies'.[64] However, many who observed wrongdoing did not report it, with 29 per cent of employees surveyed as part of the study reporting that they observed very or extremely serious wrongdoing but did not report or otherwise act on it.[65] The strongest factors influencing whether a person would decide to report wrongdoing were found to be the organizational context, the perceptions of the seriousness of the wrongdoing, and beliefs about whether reporting the wrongdoing would serve any constructive purpose.[66] If the wrongdoing was serious, frequent, and there was direct evidence of the wrongdoing or it affected the whistleblower personally, they were more likely to report the wrongdoing.[67] A person was found unlikely to report when he or she believed that no action would be taken or reprisals might ensue from which they would not receive adequate protection.[68]

Whistleblowing is still reasonably rare with only 2.9 per cent of whistleblowers in a 2009 Australian study reporting to an external agency in the first instance and 9.7 per cent reporting to an external agency at any other stage.[69] While 63 per cent of whistleblowers

---

[61] John McMillan, 'Legal Protection of Whistleblowers' in Scott Prasser, Rae Wear and John Nethercote (eds), *Corruption and Reform: The Fitzgerald Vision* (St Lucia: University of Queensland Press, 1990), 205.

[62] William De Maria, *Unshielding the Shadow Culture: Queensland Whistleblower Study* (Brisbane: University of Queensland, Department of Social Work and Social Policy, 1994); William De Maria and Jan Cyrelle, *Wounded Workers: Queensland Whistleblower Study* (Brisbane: University of Queensland, Department of Social Work and Social Policy, 1994); William De Maria, *Deadly Disclosures: Whistleblowing and the Ethical Meltdown of Australia* (Kent Town, SA: Wakefield Press, 1999); William De Maria, 'Queensland Whistleblowing: Sterilising the Lone Crusader' (1992) 27(4) *Australian Journal of Social Issues* 248; William De Maria, 'Whistleblowing' (1995) 20(6) *Alternative Law Journal* 270. See for discussion, Latimer and Brown, above n 22.

[63] This study has resulted in a number of key reports: Alexander J Brown (ed), *Whistleblowing in the Australian Public Sector* (First Report, ARC Linkage Project, Griffith University, October 2007), available at: <http://www.apsac.com.au/previous/2013conference/pdf/papers07/day1_24oct07/StreamD2/WhistleblowingInAustPublicSector_AJBrown.pdf> [accessed 4 Jan 2016]; Brown (2008), above n 12; Alexander J Brown, *Whistleblowing Legislation in Queensland: The Agenda for Reform* (Final Report, ARC Linkage Project, Griffith University, September 2009), available at: <http://www.griffith.edu.au/__data/assets/pdf_file/0008/195497/WWTW-Qld-Recommendations-Sept-09.pdf> [accessed 4 Jan 2016]; Peter Roberts, Jane Olsen, and Alexander J Brown, *Whistling While They Work: Towards Best Practice Whistleblowing Programs in Public Sector Organisations* (Second Report, ARC Linkage Project, Griffith University, July 2009), available at: <http://www.griffith.edu.au/__data/assets/pdf_file/0007/159199/whistling-july09-full-report.pdf> [accessed 4 Jan 2016]; Roberts, Brown and Olsen (2011), above n 29.

[64] Alexander J Brown and Chris Wheeler, 'Project Findings: An Agenda for Action' in Brown (2008), above n 12, 289.

[65] Alexander J Brown, Evalynn Mazurski, and Jane Olsen, 'The Incidence and Significance of Whistleblowing' in Brown (2008), above n 12.

[66] Richard Wortley, Peter Cassematis, and Marika Donkin, 'Who Blows the Whistle, Who Doesn't and Why?' in Brown (2008), above n 12.

[67] Ibid.

[68] Ibid.

[69] Marika Donkin, Rodney Smith, and Alexander J Brown, 'How Do Officials Report? Internal and External Whistleblowing' in Brown (2008), above n 12.

had their disclosure investigated, the *Whistling While They Work* study, encouragingly, revealed that approximately 78 per cent of all whistleblowers were treated well or the same after making a complaint,[70] but a sizeable minority still were recorded as treated detrimentally, and that this was worse in some agencies more than others.[71] The most common types of mistreatment were 'intimidation, harassment, heavy scrutiny of work, ostracism, unsafe or humiliating work and other workplace-based negative behaviour'.[72] The impact of this behaviour, and even for those whistleblowers where there were not reprisals, was most commonly adverse psychological impacts such as increased stress ranging in severity.[73] There was also evidence that there was a significant difference between the perceptions of managers and whistleblowers about how committed their organization was to dealing with whistleblowers respectfully and properly.[74]

Abbasi's observation on the subject in 2011 is confronting:

> Nobody likes a whistleblower. They invite snide remarks about their competency and their twisted motives. One man or woman against the medical establishment, albeit locally or nationally, is a minnow waiting to be crushed, shamed and thrashed out of the medical profession. We don't protect whistleblowers in this country; we persecute them, even when they expose issues on the scale of a paediatric surgery department with a high death rate, a dangerous medical ward, or the conflicts of interest that distort the licensing of medical devices.
>
> Less often, but in an equally damaging way, we allow vexatious whistleblowers to flourish especially when the media or public have decided that the doctors are undesirable troublemakers. In short, our response to whistleblowing is confused, inadequate, and damaging—to whistleblowers, victims of vexatious whistleblowers, and patients.[75]

Davis is a little less intimidating, but nonetheless far than encouraging:

> Whistleblowing is... bad news for those on whom the whistle is blown. What they were peacefully doing in obscurity is suddenly in the spotlight. They will have to participate in 'damage control' meetings, investigations, and the like that would not otherwise demand their scarce time. They will have to write unusual reports, worry about the effect of publicity on their own career, and face the pointed questions of spouse, children, and friends. And they may have to go on doing such things for months—or even years.[76]

However, it is generally accepted by those who have studied the pivotal role of whistleblowers in bringing misconduct to light that encouraging and protecting whistleblowers is essential to enhancing research integrity. In 1993, for instance, the United States Congress created the Commission on Research Integrity in response to continuing controversy concerning problems experienced in relation to the capacity of both the scientific community and government to identify and deal effectively with misconduct in research. Its role was to advise the Secretary of Health and Human Services and Congress about ways to improve the public health service response to misconduct in biomedical and behavioural research that received government funding. Aside from recommending the development and dissemination of clear

---

[70] Rodney Smith and Alexander J Brown, 'The Good, the Bad and the Ugly: Whistleblowing Outcomes' in Brown (2008), above n 12.

[71] Ibid.

[72] Ibid, 111.

[73] Ibid.

[74] Roberts, Brown, and Olsen (2011), above n 29, 24.

[75] Kamran Abbasi, 'A Way Forward for Whistleblowing' (2011) 104(7) *Journal of the Royal Society of Medicine* 275, 275. See also, Gordon Moran, *Silencing Scientists and Scholars in Other Fields: Power, Paradigm Controls, Peer Review, and Scholarly Communication* (Greenwood, Conn: Ablex Publishing Corporation, 1998) 107–9; Alford, above n 12, 127–31.

[76] Michael Davis, 'Avoiding the Tragedy of Whistleblowing' (1989) 8(4) *Business & Professional Ethics Journal* 3, 7. See further, Michael Davis, *Ethics and the University* (London: Routledge, 1999).

standards of research behaviour, in 1995 it made multiple recommendations directed at creating an institutional climate in which concerns about unethical conduct could be voiced without fear:

> Good-faith whistleblowers are important to the identification and ultimate punishment of those who violate research ethics. Both whistleblowers and those they accuse of research misconduct must be treated with respect, fairness, and openness. In addition, whistleblowers need to be protected from retaliation, and their concerns should be resolved by decision makers whose judgment is not tainted by bias.[77]

This led it to promulgate what it termed 'A Whistleblower's Bill of Rights',[78] an initiative that has been championed and to some degree emulated in a number of other contexts.[79] However, most of the time people within organizations who learn of practices that should not have occurred or that should not be occurring, both inside and outside academia, continue to decide not to 'blow the whistle'. Often this is for rational, self-protective reasons. Potential whistleblowers for the most part turn the other way or walk away, recognizing that what they have to say is unlikely to be welcomed and may well retard their position within the workplace: they themselves may become victims.[80]

Whistleblower Laws

Protection for whistleblowers has been extended in many countries in the form of legislation. However, the extent to which such protection actually safeguards the entitlements of those who reveal internal skeletons is doubted by many.[81] For instance, Sawyer has argued that: 'Legislation induces firms to put whistleblowers on the slow rather than the fast drip. The career path of the whistleblower is still capped, the effects on their health are still deleterious, but their ability to seek legal redress is reduced. They are slowly extirpated from the firm... Legislation cannot address this problem. Only a change in culture can.'[82]

In the preamble to a Model Law to protect whistleblowers it was argued that all expressions relating to whistleblowing refer to a common identity:

> an individual who warns of threats to the public by serving as a 'people's witness.' For purposes of this Model Law, the term 'protected witness' will be used to designate those honoring their duty of disclosure. People's witnesses are the lifeblood for efforts to prevent, investigate and prosecute corruption. They personify a basic premise of jurisprudence that 'sunlight is the best disinfectant.' Without the free flow of information from knowledgeable witnesses, anti-corruption campaigns are empty and lifeless. Experience demonstrates,

---

77 Commission on Research Integrity, *Integrity and Misconduct in Research*, Report to the Secretary of Health and Human Services, the House Committee on Commerce and the Senate Committee on Labor and Human Resources (Washington, DC: US Department of Health and Human Services, Public Health Service, 1995) viii: <https://ori.hhs.gov/images/ddblock/report_commission_0.pdf> [accessed 4 Jan 2016].

78 Ibid, 32–3.

79 See eg, Brian Robins, 'Code of Conduct Vital to Protect Corporate Whistleblowers', *The Sydney Morning Herald*, 10 May 2014: <http://www.smh.com.au/business/code-of-conduct-vital-to-protect-corporate-whistleblowers-20140509-380wt.html> [accessed 4 Jan 2016].

80 See Alina Tugend, 'Opting to Blow the Whistle or Choosing to Walk Away', *The New York Times*, 20 September 2013: <http://www.nytimes.com/2013/09/21/your-money/deciding-when-to-blow-the-whistle-and-when-to-walk-away.html?_r=1> [accessed 4 Jan 2016].

81 See eg, Brian Martin, 'Illusions of Whistleblower Protection' (2003) 5 *UTS Law Review* 119; Marcia P Miceli and Janet P Near, *Blowing the Whistle: The Organizational and Legal Implications for Companies and Employees* (New York: Lexington Books, 1992).

82 Sawyer, above n 43, 11.

> however, that in a repressive environment they will be silent observers instead of speaking out on behalf of the public. Freedom of expression provides our citizens the freedom to be partners in genuine challenges to corruption.[83]

A substantial literature has developed on whistleblowers,[84] latterly tending to emphasize the benefits for organizations in facilitating the communication of concerns by employees and colleagues internally and the importance of avoiding deterrent consequences to persons who satisfy the criteria for being described as whistleblowers.[85] Many, including Bowden, have suggested that whistleblowing can be a powerful mechanism for bringing about a more ethical climate in workplaces and that it has had a significant impact in stopping illegal and corrupt activities in numerous instances.[86] The Standing Committee on Legal and Constitutional Affairs, in its 2009 report on whistleblowing in the Commonwealth public sector in Australia, stated:

> Facilitating public interest disclosures is part of a broader public integrity framework that is considered to be an essential feature of modern accountable and transparent democracies. The broader integrity framework can be said to include enabling public access to information held by government through freedom of information law and minimising secrecy in government activity.[87]

Legislation has been passed in many jurisdictions[88] in an attempt to protect whistleblowers against both direct and indirect discrimination, harassment, and retribution. It emanates from a recognition that evidence about misconduct within institutions is often difficult to come by and that the cost for those who provide it can be a potent disincentive.[89]

The status of the whistleblower, however, continues to be ambiguous. Latimer and Brown have noted the continuous 'tension between the whistleblower as hero or as traitor';[90] that is, whistleblowers might be lauded for revealing corruption and misconduct, but at the same time be regarded as betraying an organization by revealing its internal and confidential information or practices.[91] International debates about both Julian Assange and Edward Snowden have tapped into these differences of perspective.[92]

In some States in Australia the whistleblowers legislation, discussed below, specifically extends to conduct within universities: for example, in Queensland under the *Public Interest*

---

83 Thomas Devine, Robert Vaughn, and Keith Henderson, *Model Law Protecting Freedom of Expression Against Corruption*, [2]: <http://www.oas.org/juridico/english/model_law_whistle.htm> [accessed 4 Jan 2016].

84 See eg, Quentin Dempster, *Whistleblowers* (Sydney, NSW: ABC Books, 1997); Stephen M Kohn, Michael D Kohn, and David K Colapinto, *Whistleblower Law: A Guide to Legal Protections for Corporate Employees* (Westport, Conn: Praeger, 2004).

85 See eg, Chanjyot Kaur, 'Whistle Blowing: An Anti-Corruption Tool' (2012) 1(5) *International Journal of Advanced Research in Management and Social Sciences* 48. See generally, Gabriella Coleman, *Hacker, Hoaxer, Whistleblower, Spy: The Many Faces of Anonymous* (London: Verso Books, 2014).

86 Bowden, above n 26, 3.

87 House of Representatives Standing Committee on Legal and Constitutional Affairs, above n 17, [1.4].

88 In Australia, see Public Interest Disclosure Act 2013 (Cth); Public Interest Disclosures Act 1994 (NSW); Public Interest Disclosure Act 2010 (Qld); Whistleblowers Protection Act 1993 (SA); Public Interest Disclosures Act 2002 (Tas); Protected Disclosure Act 2012 (Vic); Public Interest Disclosure Act 2003 (WA); Public Interest Disclosure Act 2012 (ACT); Public Interest Disclosure Act 2008 (NT). In the United Kingdom, see the Public Interest Disclosure Act 1998 (UK). In New Zealand, see the Protected Disclosures Act 2000 (NZ).

89 See eg, Peter Bowden, *In the Public Interest: Protecting Whistleblowers and Those Who Speak Out* (Prahran, Vic: Tilde Publishing and Distribution, 2014).

90 Latimer and Brown, above n 22, 768.

91 Ibid, 768–9.

92 See eg, Luke Harding, *The Snowden Files: The Inside Story of the World's Most Wanted Man* (London: Guardian, 2014).

Disclosure Act 2010 (Qld) universities are prescribed public sector entities, in Victoria in the *Whistleblowers Protection Act* 2001 (Vic) (now superseded by the *Protected Disclosure Act* 2012), and the *Northern Territory Public Interest Disclosure Act* 2008 (NT), universities are classified as 'public bodies' and therefore explicitly made subject to the legislation.[93] In principle, this has provided whistleblowers in the tertiary sector with important protection.

The 1994 report *In the Public Interest* recommended that Commonwealth legislation extend to academic institutions.[94] The Committee acknowledged in the case of higher education:

> the importance of academic freedom, and the 'self regulation' of the education industry in so far as this is practicable. However, the Committee has heard evidence that the self-determination existing within academia has, in some instances, resulted in sectors of academia operating as isolated pockets of tyranny. By operating under a policy of self determination educational institutions are able to determine for themselves the allocation of the public funds granted to them. The evidence received seemed to reveal a philosophical hypocrisy or enigma underlying the higher education system. Whilst on the one hand, the notion of academic freedom justifies the policy of economic self determinism in relevant institutions, that very same policy is allegedly threatening intellectual freedom.[95]

The United Kingdom. Formal protection for whistleblowers in England and Wales was introduced by the *Public Interest Disclosure Act* 1998 (UK) which came into force in July 1999. It inserted provisions into the *Employment Rights Act* 1996 (UK) and the *Public Interest Disclosure (Northern Ireland) Order* 1998 (UK). In part it arose from the lobbying work of Public Concern at Work (PCaW), which had publicized issues arising from scandals and disasters in 1980s and 1990s, including those relating to the Clapham Rail Crash and the collapse of the Bank of Credit and Commerce International. It also had its roots in a white paper, Fairness at Work, which was published in May 1998 and constitutes one of the sequelae to the controversies arising from the revelations by Dr Stephen Bolsin in relation to the United Bristol Health Care Trust scandal involving paediatric heart surgery. Dr Bolsin commented of the legislation that 'it may contribute significantly to the improvement of clinical services in the NHS and would, if it had been in place, no doubt have saved lives in the paediatric cardiac surgery unit at the Bristol Royal Infirmary. My concerns are that it is very difficult to legislate for changes in attitudes.'[96]

The *Public Interest Disclosure Act* 1998 applies to all United Kingdom employees, in the public and private and even voluntary sectors. It provides potential protection in relation to those who make a 'qualifying disclosure' (s 1)[97] and actual protection to a 'protected disclosure' (s 1).[98] Originally the Act required protected disclosures to be made in good faith for them to receive protection. In her Fifth Report into the Shipman murders, though, Dame Janet Smith questioned the need for a good faith requirement and argued that '[t]he public interest

[93] House of Representatives Standing Committee on Legal and Constitutional Affairs, above n 17, [3.34].

[94] Senate Select Committee on Public Interest Whistleblowing, above n 7, [8.83].

[95] Ibid, [8.72].

[96] Clare Dyer, 'UK Introduces Far Reaching Law to Protect Whistleblowers' (1999) 319(7201) *BMJ* 7, 7.

[97] Inserted into the *Employment Rights Act* 1996 as section 43B, and defining a 'qualifying disclosure' as 'any disclosure of information which, in the reasonable belief of the worker making the disclosure, tends to show one or more of the following—(a) that a criminal offence has been committed, is being committed or is likely to be committed; (b) that a person has failed, is failing or is likely to fail to comply with any legal obligation to which he is subject; (c) that a miscarriage of justice has occurred, is occurring or is likely to occur (d) that the health or safety of any individual has been, is being or is likely to be endangered; (e) that the environment has been, is being or is likely to be damaged; or (f) that information tending to show any matter falling within any one of the preceding paragraphs has been, is being or is likely to be deliberately concealed'.

[98] Inserted into the *Employment Rights Act* 1996 as section 43A.

would be served [by encouraging disclosures], even in cases where the motives of the messenger might not have been entirely altruistic.'[99] For disclosures made after 25 June 2013 the good faith requirement no longer exists but remains to some degree relevant as any compensation awarded to an employee making such a disclosure can be reduced by up to 25 per cent if the disclosure has been made in bad faith. What is now required is that an employee must have a reasonable belief that their disclosure is made 'in the public interest'. It is likely that this will not be construed restrictively and that it will not be an overly demanding threshold for employees to satisfy.

A key component of the legislation is that it provides a mechanism for compensation for whistleblowers for reprisals taken against them and placed before an Employment Tribunal. In this regard it shares some features in common with the *United States False Claims Act*.[100]

As a result of the decision of the Court of Appeal in *NHS Manchester v Fecitt*[101] which failed to accord protection to nurse whistleblowers who had been redeployed after their disclosures, the Act was amended by the *Enterprise and Regulatory Reform Act* 2013 (UK) to provide that employees should not be subjected to a detriment by a co-worker. A co-worker can be vicariously liable for such actions by a co-worker.

Notably, though, the United Kingdom is relatively rare in the degree of protection that it gives to whistleblowers, being one of only four countries[102] that give 'advanced' protection.[103] This is spite of the fact that all but two of the 27 countries of the European Union have ratified the United Nations Convention against Corruption.[104]

The extent to which the legislation provides effective protection to those within academia has been questioned. Aubrey Blumsohn, who left his position as a senior lecturer in metabolic bone disease at the University of Sheffield after raising concerns in 2005 about research on a drug made by a funder of research at his university, has argued that the Public Interest Disclosure Act 'is based on the erroneous premise that the ultimate and only goal of whistleblower protection is to achieve a winnable employment tribunal [case]', when the real goal of such protection should be 'to correct wrongs and bring system failures into the public domain almost regardless of the consequences.'[105] He has lamented that the Act 'prescribes that you need to spend innumerable years going through internal procedures, and then to obfuscatory prescribed external bodies... [and] all you would be left with is the remote possibility of a successful employment tribunal [case].'[106]

Canada. There is little explicit protection for employees of universities or private research institutions who make whistleblower disclosures in Canada.

---

[99] Janet Smith, *The Shipman Inquiry: Fifth Report: Safeguarding Patients: Lessons from the Past—Proposals for the Future* (Cm 6394, 2004) [11.108].

[100] See Bowden, above n 26.

[101] [2011] EWCA Civ 1190.

[102] United Kingdom, Luxembourg, Romania, and Slovenia.

[103] See Transparency International, 'Whistleblowing in Europe: Legal Protections for Whistleblowers in the EU' (2013) 5, available at: <http://www.transparency.org/whatwedo/publication/whistleblowing_in_europe_legal_protections_for_whistleblowers_in_the_eu> [accessed 4 Jan 2016]. See also, Simon Wolfe, Mark Worth, Suelette Dreyfus, and Alexander J Brown, *Whistleblower Protection Rules in G20 Countries: The Next Action Plan* (Public Consultation Draft, June 2014): <http://transparency.org.au/wp-content/uploads/2014/06/Action-Plan-June-2014-Whistleblower-Protection-Rules-G20-Countries.pdf> [accessed 4 Jan 2016].

[104] United Nations Convention against Corruption, opened for signature 31 October 2003, 2349 UNTS 41 (entered into force 14 December 2005).

[105] John Morgan, 'Life After Whistleblowing', *Times Higher Education*, 31 July 2014: <http://www.timeshighereducation.co.uk/features/life-after-whistleblowing/1/2014776.article> (viewed 28 July 2015).

[106] Ibid.

Saskatchewan (*The Saskatchewan Employment Act* 2013, s 2-42(2))[107] and New Brunswick (Employment Standards Act 1982, s 28)[108] have passed whistleblowing legislation that applies to the private sector. They provide that employers are not permitted to discharge, threaten to discharge, or in any manner discriminate against an employee because the employee has reported or proposed to report to a lawful authority any activity that is, or is likely to, result in an offence pursuant to an Act or an Act of the Parliament of Canada.

At federal level, section 425.1 of the Canadian Criminal Code 1985[109] makes it an offence for an employer, anyone acting on behalf of an employer, or a person acting in a position of authority over an employee, to take disciplinary action, demote, terminate, otherwise adversely affect an employee's employment, or threaten any such things in order to force the employee to refrain from providing information to law enforcement officials about the commission of an offence by his or her employer or by an officer, employee, or director of the employer.

Section 425.1 also makes it an offence to threaten or retaliate against an employee who has already provided information. However, employees are only protected if they approach a person whose duties include law enforcement. They are not given protection if they contact a media source or an outside agency or advocacy group.

The offence carries a maximum term of imprisonment of five years but the amount of the fine is unlimited for corporations when the Crown proceeds by indictment.

In *Merk v International Association of Bridge, Structural, Ornamental and Reinforcing Iron Workers, Local 771*[110] the Supreme Court ruled in favour of 'a broad approach' to interpretation of the whistleblower protection provision contained in Saskatchewan's Labour Standards Act[111] (which is cognate), holding that employees internally reporting wrongdoing to persons 'up the ladder' within the organization should be regarded as enjoying the same protection as employees reporting wrongdoing to public authorities.[112] However, in general terms it affirmed the principle of the employee's duty of fidelity to his or her employer, a theme that was revisited by another decision on the subject in 2013: 'The purpose of section 425.1 of the Criminal Code is not to allow an employee to make with impunity, reckless complaints to public authorities and without regard for the employer's internal mechanisms or respect for work colleagues. The provision does not allow an employee to avoid the consequences of a dismissal in progress by filing reckless complaints to public authorities against his or her employer and work colleagues.'[113]

The Public Servants Disclosure Protection Act 2005[114] protects whistleblowers in the federal public sector. It require employers to establish a code of conduct that provides civil protection for whistleblowers including disciplinary actions against a public servant who takes a reprisal against a whistleblower, and reinstatement or damages in place of reinstatement for whistleblowers who have been subject to reprisal. Section 19 provides straightforwardly that '[n]o person shall take any reprisal against a public servant'. It also requires that chief executives must establish internal procedures to manage disclosures made under the Act by public servants employed in the portion of the public sector for which the chief executive is responsible–they

[107] *The Saskatchewan Employment Act*, SS 2013, c S-15.1. This provision was formerly covered by section 74 of *The Labour Standards Act* 1978, RSS 1978, c L-1.
[108] *Employment Standards Act*, SNB 1982, c E-7.2.
[109] *Criminal Code*, RSC 1985, c C-46.
[110] [2005] 3 SCR 425.
[111] Ibid, [33].
[112] Ibid, [36]–[37].
[113] *Anderson v IMTT-Québec Inc* [2013] FCA 90, [44].
[114] *Public Servants Disclosure Protection Act*, SC 2005, c 46.

must protect the identity of persons involved in the disclosure process, such as the persons making the disclosures, witnesses and persons alleged to be responsible, and establish procedures to ensure the confidentiality of information collected in relation to disclosures of wrongdoings.

In Alberta the *Public Interest Disclosure (Whistleblower Protection) Act* 2012[115] was enacted:

(a) to facilitate the disclosure and investigation of significant and serious matters in or relating to departments, public entities or offices of the Legislature, that an employee believes may be unlawful, dangerous to the public or injurious to the public interest,
(b) to protect employees who make those disclosures,
(c) to manage, investigate and make recommendations respecting disclosures of wrongdoings and reprisals,
(d) to promote public confidence in the administration of departments, public entities and offices of the Legislature.[116]

It applies to the Alberta public service, provincial agencies, boards and commissions, as well as to academic institutions. It also creates processes for the disclosure of wrongdoing and for the Office of the Public Interest Disclosure Commissioner whose role it is to investigate and resolve complaints reporting violations of provincial or federal law, acts or omissions that create a danger to the public or environment, and gross mismanagement of public funds.

In Manitoba, the *Public Interest Disclosure (Whistleblower Protection) Act* 2006[117] provides a mechanism for the disclosure of wrongdoings in the public service and includes provisions to protect whistleblowers. The Act applies to the Manitoba public service including departments, government bodies, and specified offices. Employees who reasonably believe that they have information that could show that a wrongdoing has been committed or is about to be committed can make a disclosure to their supervisor or designated officer or to the Ombudsman. A disclosure must be in writing and contain certain information required by the Act. Employees must first make the disclosure to an appropriate law enforcement agency or, in the case of a health-related matter, to the chief medical officer of health. Immediately thereafter, the employee must make the disclosure to the supervisor or designated officer. The provisions that allow an employee to make a public disclosure are subject to any direction that the appropriate law enforcement agency or chief medical officer (as applicable) considers necessary in the public interest, if any. A person is prohibited from taking a reprisal against an employee, or directing that one be taken, because the employee in good faith has sought advice about making a disclosure in accordance with the Act, made a protected disclosure, or cooperated in an investigation under the Act.

Individuals other than employees of the public service are allowed to make a disclosure to the Ombudsman if they reasonably believe that they have information that could show that a wrongdoing has been or is about to be committed in the public service—provided that the information is in writing and contains certain details required by the Act (eg, a description of the wrongdoing). If, as a result of the information, the Ombudsman has reason to believe that a wrongdoing has been or is about to be committed, it can investigate the wrongdoing.

Furthermore, private sector employers cannot take any of the prohibited measures listed in the Act against an employee for the sole reason that the employee has, in good faith, provided information to the Ombudsman about an alleged wrongdoing. Employers are also prohibited from taking such measures for the sole reason that they believe that an employee will provide such information. The following are considered prohibited measures: any disciplinary measure, a demotion, termination of employment, any measure that adversely affects the employment or working conditions of an employee, or a threat to take any of these measures.

---

115 *Public Interest Disclosure (Whistleblower Protection) Act*, SA 2012, c P-39.5.

116 Section 2(2).

117 *The Public Interest Disclosure (Whistleblower Protection) Act*, CCSM c P217.

Saskatchewan's *Public Interest Disclosure Act* 2011[118] creates a mechanism for the disclosure of wrongdoings in the public service and includes provisions to protect whistleblowers from reprisals. A person is prohibited from taking a reprisal against an employee, or directing that one be taken, because the employee has, in good faith, sought advice about making a disclosure in accordance with the Act, made a protected disclosure, or co-operated in an investigation, or declined to participate in any wrongdoing.

Saskatchewan public servants who want to blow the whistle on wrongdoing in their workplaces may take their concerns to an independent officer of the legislature.

New Brunswick's *Public Interest Disclosure Act* 2012[119] similarly encourages employees in the provincial public service (departments, agencies, school districts, regional health authorities, and Crown corporations) to come forward if they believe that wrongdoing has occurred or is about to occur in the workplace. It provides protection to employees in the public sector against reprisal and creates a process for those accused of wrongdoing. Employees can make a disclosure to their supervisor, the designated officer in their organization or to the Conflict of Interest Ombudsman. No person may take a reprisal action against an employee, or direct that one be taken against an employee, because the employee has, in good faith, a) sought advice about making a disclosure from a supervisor, designated officer, chief executive or the Ombudsman, b) made a disclosure, or c) cooperated in an investigation under the Act.

In Ontario, the *Public Service of Ontario Act* 2006[120] provides similar protection to whistleblowers in the public sector. The whistleblowing protections of the Act are similar in scope and application to the federal Public Servants Disclosure Protection Act. The Ontario Act prohibits employers from reprising against a public servant who has made a protected disclosure or has, in good faith, cooperated in an investigation into a disclosure or an investigation commenced under the Act.

Likewise in Newfoundland the *Public Interest Disclosure and Whistleblower Protection Act* 2014[121] prohibits reprisals against employees because they have in good faith made a disclosure or sought advice about making a disclosure or participated in an investigation under the Act. It applies to a variety of 'wrongdoings'[122] in or related to the public service and explicitly excepts the Memorial University of Newfoundland.[123]

Thus, limited protection applies to whistleblowing by scholars within Canada's tertiary institutions and research institutions.

United States. Multiple state and federal legislative provisions provide some measure of protection to whistleblowers in the United States. However, as in Canada, the degree of statutory protection given to whistleblowing within universities is limited.

In addition, such protection as does exist operates within the parameters of the high value given to protection of academic freedom, as to which the Supreme Court observed in 1957:

> The essentiality of freedom in the community of American universities is almost self-evident. No one should underestimate the vital role in a democracy that is played by those who guide and train our youth. To impose any strait jacket upon the intellectual leaders in our colleges and universities would imperil the future of our Nation. No field of education is so thoroughly comprehended by man that new discoveries cannot yet be made. Particularly is that

118 *The Public Interest Disclosure Act*, SS 2011, c P-38.1

119 *Public Interest Disclosure Act*, SNB 2012, c 112.

120 *Public Service of Ontario Act*, 2006, SO 2006, c 35, Sch A.

121 *Public Interest Disclosure and Whistleblower Protection Act*, SNL 2014, c P-37.2.

122 Ibid, s 4.

123 Ibid, s 2(h). See also, *Public Interest Disclosure of Wrongdoing Act*, SNS 2010, c 42 (Nova Scotia).

true in the social sciences, where few, if any, principles are accepted as absolutes. Scholarship cannot flourish in an atmosphere of suspicion and distrust. Teachers and students must always remain free to inquire, to study and to evaluate, to gain new maturity and understanding; otherwise our civilization will stagnate and die.[124]

The *Whistleblower Protection Act* of 1989[125] provides statutory protection for federal employees who engage in whistleblowing in respect of what they alleged are illegal or improper government conduct. Congress stated that its intention was that the legislation:

> [S]trengthen and improve protection for the rights of Federal employees, to prevent reprisals, and to help eliminate wrongdoing within the Government by (1) mandating that employees should not suffer adverse consequences as a result of prohibited personnel practices; and (2) establishing... that while disciplining those who commit prohibited personnel practices may be used as a means by which to help accomplish that goal, the protection of individuals who are the subject of prohibited practices remains the paramount consideration.[126]

The protections may be raised in:

- employee appeals to the Merit Systems Protection Board of an agency's adverse action against an employee
- actions instituted by the Office of Special Counsel
- individual rights of action before the Merit Systems Protection Board, and
- grievances brought by employees under negotiated grievance procedures.

The provisions work from the definition of 'prohibited personnel practices':

> § 2302. Prohibited personnel practicesl
>
> (b) Any employee who has authority to take, direct others to take, recommend, or approve any personnel action, shall not, with respect to such authority—
>
> [...]
>
> (8) take or fail to take, or threaten to take or fail to take, a personnel action with respect to any employee or applicant for employment because of—
>
> (A) any disclosure of information by an employee or applicant which the employee or applicant reasonably believes evidences—
>
> (i) any violation of any law, rule, or regulation, or
>
> (ii) gross mismanagement, a gross waste of funds, an abuse of authority, or a substantial and specific danger to public health or safety,
>
> if such disclosure is not specifically prohibited by law and if such information is not specifically required by Executive order to be kept secret in the interest of national defense or the conduct of foreign affairs; or
>
> (B) any disclosure to the Special Counsel, or to the Inspector General of an agency or another employee designated by the head of the agency to receive such disclosures, of information which the employee or applicant reasonably believes evidences—
>
> (i) any violation... of any law, rule, or regulation, or
>
> (ii) gross mismanagement, a gross waste of funds, an abuse of authority, or a substantial and specific danger to public health or safety.[127]

In addition, the *Sarbanes–Oxley Act* of 2002[128] is a legislative response to the fraudulent activities of World-Com and Enron Corporation. It provides for enhanced financial disclosures and auditor independence for publicly held corporations. It provides some protection to whistleblowers,

[124] *Sweezy v State of New Hampshire*, 354 US 234, 250 (1957).

[125] Pub L No 101-12, 103 Stat 16 (1989). Amending Title 5, Chapter 12 of the United States Code.

[126] 5 USC § 1201 note.

[127] 5 USC § 2302(b)(8).

[128] Pub L No 107-204, 116 Stat 745 (2002).

providing that employees are not required to communicate information to employers first but may complain to a Federal regulatory or law enforcement agency, any member of Congress or committee of Congress, or a person with supervisory status over the employee.

In addition, the False Claims Act[129] provides the whistleblower with between 15 and 30 per cent of the government's total recovery against those engaging in contract fraud, including in respect of research fraud. By 1986 amendments it provides protections for whistleblowers, in particular preventing harassment and retaliation against them. Under this law the United States government has recovered very large in fines and stolen funds since 1986.[130]

Australia. Australia is a signatory to the United Nations Convention Against Corruption which requires states to have whistleblower or public interest disclosure legislation. Australian universities are generally covered by State legislation. However the legislation across the various States and Territories is not consistent and a number of different tests are used under the different schemes.[131] The various legislation has been discussion in detail elsewhere.[132] Standards Australia has also developed the *Australian Standard AS 8004-2003, Whistleblower Protection Programs for Entities*, which is utilized by a number of Australian universities.[133] Further, recommendations by the *Whistling While They Work* project as to the best practice model for whistleblowing legislation have already led to changes in two jurisdictions—the Australian Capital Territory (ACT) and Queensland—and are likely to lead to further changes in other Australian jurisdictions in the future.

A problem facing universities is that whistleblowing legislation, even if it does cover universities, does not necessarily provide an avenue for students to make disclosures. Often there will be an avenue to do so to an Ombudsman or to a corruption commission if one exists in the relevant State, or to a university's own complaint-handling scheme. The Australasian Best Practice Guidelines of the New South Wales Ombudsman on *Complaint Handling at Universities* has highlighted this point.[134]

The difficulties of achieving 'best practice' in whistleblowing laws were highlighted by Latimer and Brown:

> There are many questions thrown up by the diversity of the current laws. There are lingering fears that reprisals remain the norm and that legal protection can only ever be symbolic, and that a whistleblower or witness protection scheme is still a poor substitute for effective disclosure laws. Best practice supports disclosure of wrongdoing, and raises the 'hero or traitor' dichotomy. The whistleblower must have trust in the system, and workplace relations support

[129] 31 USC §§ 3729–3733.

[130] See Wolfe et al, above n 103.

[131] Latimer and Brown, above n 22.

[132] De Maria (1999), above n 62; William De Maria, 'Common Law—Common Mistakes?: Protecting Whistleblowers in Australia, New Zealand, South Africa and the United Kingdom' (2006) 19(7) *International Journal of Public Sector Management* 643; Alexander J Brown, *Public Interest Disclosure Legislation in Australia: Towards the Next Generation* (Issues Paper, ARC 'Linkage' Project, 'Whistling While They Work', November 2006): <http://www.griffith.edu.au/__data/assets/pdf_file/0015/151314/full-paper.pdf> [accessed 4 Jan 2016]; Latimer and Brown, above n 22; Brown, *Whistleblowing legislation in Queensland*, above n 62; Alexander J Brown, 'Restoring the Sunshine to the Sunshine State: Priorities for Whistleblowing Law Reform in Queensland' (2009) 18(3) *Griffith Law Review* 666.

[133] *Australian Standard: Whistleblower Protection Programs for Entities—AS 8004-2003* (Standards Australia, 2003), available at: <http://infostore.saiglobal.com/store/PreviewDoc.aspx?saleItemID=396587> [accessed 4 Jan 2016]. This Standard provides the 'essential elements for establishing, implementing and managing an effective whistleblower scheme within an entity and provides guidance when using these elements' (at 2). The stated aim of the Standard is to enhance the legislation, not cut across the law (ibid).

[134] Ombudsman New South Wales, *Complaint Handling at Universities: Australasian Best Practice Guidelines* (January 2015) 20, 34, available at: <https://www.ombo.nsw.gov.au/news-and-publications/publications/guidelines/universities/complaint-handling-at-universities-best-practice-guidelines> [accessed 4 Jan 2016].

> with protection from civil or criminal liability. Best practice includes effective operational systems for the management of whistleblowing. Whistleblower legislation must ensure that whistleblowers are protected from reprisal, retaliation, punishment, retribution and discrimination by employers, organisations and others. Some whistleblower laws protect disclosure of confidential information made in the belief that the disclosure is substantially correct; and some protect disclosure by an informant acting bona fide. Equally, whistleblower laws should not protect disclosure of false information actuated by personal grievance, malice or vindictiveness, and whistleblower best practice does punish persons with such inadmissible motives. It is important for whistleblower laws to promote a culture where honest disclosures are respected, valued, and even rewarded. A failure to support whistleblowers equates to the promotion of the protection of misconduct and wrongdoing.[135]

Australia was slow to acquire federal whistleblower legislation and the extent of the protection which whistleblower protection legislation affords remains contested in respect of Australia, as well as in many other countries.[136] Procedures for handling disclosures are also varied through the Australian public sector.[137] The overview below is generally limited to the stated purposes of the Acts and whether they apply to universities. It is not always clear whether universities are governed by the relevant legislation, although several specifically state that universities are covered. Importantly, though, even when not covered by the legislation, which appears to be the case in South Australia, universities have tended to adopt internal whistleblower policies.

Many Western jurisdictions have introduced whistleblower or public interest disclosure laws. The United States have been influential. As noted above, the United States has a number of legislative instruments which govern whistleblowers both at the federal and State levels and which range from broad laws to specific legislation governing particular industries or activities. The aim of much of the legislation seeks to protect whistleblowers from retaliation for complaining to their employers, their union, the Occupational Safety and Health Administration, or other government body.[138] The major statutory protections are the *Whistleblower Protection Act* of 1989 which replaced the *Civil Service Reform Act* of 1978[139] and the *False Claims Act*, which was enacted in 1883, and revised in 1986. The *No-FEAR Act (Notification and Federal Employee Antidiscrimination and Retaliation Act* of 2002)[140] was also enacted to protect federal workers from unlawful discrimination and retaliation. The *Sarbanes–Oxley Act* of 2002 provides whistleblower laws for the securities and finance sector in the United States. A combination of initiatives, other than the False Claims Act, has been followed in Australia.

Queensland was the first Australian jurisdiction to introduce legislation protecting whistleblowers in 1990 after the Fitzgerald Inquiry into police corruption.[141] *The Whistleblowers Protection Act* 1994 (Qld) was subsequently introduced in 1994 after the 1991 Queensland Electoral and Administrative Review Commission inquiry into whistleblowing.[142] This legislation was seen to represent best practice in many respects, but over time the legislation has been overtaken by other, more modern, Australian and international legislation.[143] The

---

135 Latimer and Brown, above n 22, 767–8 (footnote omitted).

136 See eg, De Maria (2006), above n 132.

137 House of Representatives Standing Committee on Legal and Constitutional Affairs, above n 17.

138 For an overview of the laws and regulations governing the protection of workers from retaliation for complaints, see United States Department of Labor, *Whistleblower Protections*: <http://www.dol.gov/compliance/laws/comp-whistleblower.htm#.UHzChI6A1cM> [accessed 4 Jan 2016].

139 Pub L No 95-454, 92 Stat 1111 (1978).

140 Pub L No 107-174, 116 Stat 566 (2002).

141 Brown, *Whistleblowing Legislation in Queensland*, above n 63, 4.

142 Ibid.

143 Ibid.

Public Interest Disclosure Act 2010 (Qld) replaced the *Whistleblowers Protection Act* 1994 (Qld). The purpose of the Act is stated to be to 'facilitate the disclosure, in the public interest, of information about wrongdoing in the public sector and to provide protection for those who make disclosures'.[144] Universities (and university colleges, TAFE institutes or statutory TAFE institutes) are defined as 'public sector entities' and governed by the legislation.[145]

The *Public Interest Disclosure Act* 2012 (ACT),[146] which replaced the *Public Interest Disclosure Act* 1994 (ACT), seeks to modernize public interest disclosure legislation in the ACT.[147] The Explanatory Statement for the Bill stated:

> The Bill draws on three main sources. Firstly, it rests heavily on the Whistling While They Work (WWTW) collaborative research project led by Griffith University's Professor A.J. Brown, which looked at strategies that might prevent, reduce and address reprisals and other whistleblowing related conflicts. Secondly, it takes into account the findings of the Commonwealth's 2009 parliamentary report into a comprehensive whistleblower protection scheme for the Commonwealth public sector. And thirdly, it considers Queensland's recently enacted whistleblowing laws which have been celebrated as providing the current benchmark in disclosure laws in Australia.[148]

The purpose the Act is stated to be to facilitate public interest disclosures and protect people making those disclosures, and for other purposes.[149]

The *Public Interest Disclosures Act* 1994 (NSW), formerly known as the *Protected Disclosures Act* 1994 (NSW), was renamed the *Public Interest Disclosures Act* in 2010 under the *Protected Disclosures Amendment (Public Interest Disclosures) Act* 2010 (NSW). The purpose of the legislation is to 'provide protection for public officials disclosing corrupt conduct, maladministration, waste, government information contravention and local government pecuniary interest contravention in the public sector; and for related purposes'.[150] Although not specifically listed as a 'public authority',[151] New South Wales universities are considered public authorities under the *Public Interest Disclosures Act* 1994 and thus employees of universities are considered public officials, by virtue of being a 'public authority whose conduct or activities may be investigated by an investigating authority'.[152] Universities may be investigated by the Ombudsman under the *Ombudsman Act* 1974 (NSW) and by the Independent Commission Against Corruption (ICAC) under the *Independent Commission Against Corruption Act* 1988 (NSW). It follows that universities are public authorities that are required to report under the *Public Finance and Audit Act* 1983 (NSW) and thus come within the jurisdiction of both the NSW Ombudsman and ICAC.[153]

The purpose of the *Public Interest Disclosure Act* 2008 (NT) is to 'provide for the disclosure and investigation of improper conduct of public officers and public bodies, to protect persons making disclosures and others from reprisal, and for related purposes'.[154] Universities

[144] *Public Interest Disclosure Act* 2010 (Qld), Long Title.

[145] *Public Interest Disclosure Act* 2010 (Qld) s 6.

[146] This Act commenced on 1 February 2013: *Public Interest Disclosure Act* 2012 (ACT), Endnotes.

[147] Explanatory Statement, Public Interest Disclosure Bill 2012 (ACT) 4: <http://www.legislation.act.gov.au/es/db_45208/20120607-52284/pdf/db_45208.pdf> [accessed 4 Jan 2016].

[148] Ibid.

[149] *Public Interest Disclosure Act* 2012 (ACT) s 3.

[150] *Public Interest Disclosures Act* 1994 (NSW), Long Title.

[151] Contrast the *Whistleblowers Protection Act* 2001 (Vic) which does list universities as public bodies covered by that Act.

[152] *Public Interest Disclosures Act* 1994 (NSW) s 4.

[153] See *Ombudsman Act* 1974 (NSW) s 5; Independent *Commission Against Corruption Act* 1988 (NSW) s 3.

[154] *Public Interest Disclosures Act* 2008 (NT), Long Title.

are specifically listed as public bodies to which the Act applies and university employees are similarly defined as public officers as employees of a public body.[155]

The purpose of the *Whistleblowers Protection Act* 1993 (SA) is stated to be 'to protect persons disclosing illegal, dangerous or improper conduct; and for other purposes'.[156] A government agency is defined as 'a department or administrative unit of the Public Service' or 'a body corporate that is an instrumentality or agency of the Crown'.[157] A 'public officer' means, among other things:

> (f) a member, officer or employee of—
> (i) an agency or instrumentality of the Crown; or
> (ii) a body that is subject to control or direction by a Minister, agency or instrumentality of the Crown; or
> (iii) a body whose members, or a majority of whose members, are appointed by the Governor or a Minister, agency or instrumentality of the Crown[.][158]

The University of South Australia states under its 'Fraud Control Procedures' that it is not governed by the *Whistleblowers Protection Act* 1993 (SA) but, nonetheless, it has adopted the general provisions of the Act.[159] Another South Australian university, Flinders University, refers to the *Independent Commissioner Against Corruption Act* 2012 and an obligation for University officers, employees, or contractors to report acts or behaviour that they reasonably suspect constitute corruption and 'serious or systemic' misconduct or maladministration in relation to the University's operations to the Office of Public Integrity (OPI).[160] The University of Adelaide states that it manages its whistleblower investigations and reporting in accordance with the *Whistleblowers Protection Act* 1993 and the university's 'Fraud Control Plan'.[161]

The purpose of the *Tasmanian Public Interest Disclosures Act* 2002 (Tas) is 'to encourage and facilitate disclosures of improper conduct by public officers and public bodies, to protect persons making those disclosures and others from reprisals, to provide for the matters disclosed to be properly investigated and dealt with to provide all parties involved in those disclosures with natural justice and for other purposes'.[162] The University of Tasmania is specifically listed as a public body, and employees, officers or members of the University of Tasmania are therefore public officers.[163] *The Public Interest Disclosures Act* 2002 was reviewed by the Tasmanian government in 2009, with amendments to the legislation commencing on 1 October 2010.[164] This review, among other amendments, led to an expansion of 'the definition of public body and public officer to cover conduct within a more broadly defined public sector, and to provide protection to more people'.[165] However, the University of Tasmania was only specifically

155 *Public Interest Disclosures Act* 2008 (NT) s 6.

156 *Whistleblowers Protection Act* 1993 (SA), Long Title.

157 *Whistleblowers Protection Act* 1993 (SA) s 4.

158 *Whistleblowers Protection Act* 1993 (SA) s 4.

159 University of South Australia, Policies and Procedures, *Fraud Control Procedures* (Last revised 21 December 2012): <http://w3.unisa.edu.au/policies/codes/miscell/fraud.asp#3> [accessed 4 Jan 2016].

160 Flinders University, *Fraud and Corruption Prevention and Control* (Last updated 28 July 2014): <http://www.flinders.edu.au/whistleblowers/> (viewed 30 April 2015).

161 University of Adelaide, Legal and Risk, *Whistleblower Protection* (Last updated 3 April 2014): <http://www.adelaide.edu.au/legalandrisk/legal/whistleblower/> [accessed 4 Jan 2016].

162 *Public Interest Disclosures Act* 2002 (Tas), Long Title.

163 *Public Interest Disclosures Act* 2002 (Tas) s 4.

164 Tasmanian Government, Department of Justice, Legislation and Development Review, Review of the *Public Interest Disclosures Act* 2002: <http://www.justice.tas.gov.au/legislationreview/consultations_and_reviews/past/pidreview> [accessed 4 Jan 2016].

165 Ibid.

listed as a public body and university employees as public officers in May 2012 under the *Justice and Related Legislation (Miscellaneous Amendments) Act* 2012 (Tas).[166]

The purpose of the *Public Interest Disclosure Act* 2003 (WA) is 'to facilitate the disclosure of public interest information, to provide protection for those who make disclosures and for those the subject of disclosures, and, in consequence, to amend various Acts, and for related purposes'.[167] Although not specifically listed, universities are covered by the legislation by virtue of their status as a non-SES organizations within the meaning of that term in section 3(1) of the *Public Sector Management Act* 1994 (WA).

The purposes of the *Protected Disclosure Act* 2012 (Vic), as set out in section 1, are to encourage and facilitate disclosures of improper conduct by public officers, public bodies, and other persons, and to provide protection for people who make the disclosures but also those persons who may suffer detrimental action in reprisal for those disclosures, and to provide for the confidentiality of the content of those disclosures and the identity of persons who make the disclosures. Universities have not been designated as public bodies so the best means for whistleblower protection is when information is given to the Independent Broad-based Anti-corruption Commission (IBAC) or the Ombudsman.

The *Protected Disclosure Act* 2012 provides protection for persons making a 'protected disclosure'.[168] However, 'protected disclosure' has a limited and technical meaning. It is one made under Part 2 of the Act regarding improper conduct, which is defined by section 4 of the *Independent Broad-Based Anti-Corruption Commission Act* 2011 (Vic) as conduct that:

> (a) adversely affects the honest performance by a public officer or public body of his or her or its functions...;
> (b) constitutes or involves the dishonest performance of his or her or its functions as a public officer or public body; or
> (c) ...constitutes or involves knowingly or recklessly breaching public trust; or
> (d) ...involves the misuse of information or material acquired in the course of the performance of his or her or its functions as a public officer or public body, whether or not for the benefit of the public officer or public body or any other purpose; or
> (e) that could constitute a conspiracy or an attempt to engage in any [of the above] conduct...—
>
> being conduct that would, if the facts were found proved beyond reasonable doubt at a trial, constitute a relevant offence[169]

where such conduct, if proven, would be either:

- 'corrupt conduct' as defined under the *Independent Broad-based Anti-corruption Commission Act* 2011; or
- a criminal offence; or
- reasonable grounds for dismissing or dispensing with, or otherwise terminating the services of the officer who was, or is, engaged in that conduct.

'Detrimental action' is prescribed by section 3 of the *Protected Disclosure Act* 2012 to include:

> (a) action causing injury, loss or damage;
> (b) intimidation or harassment;
> (c) discrimination, disadvantage or adverse treatment in relation to a person's employment, career, profession, trade or business, including the taking of disciplinary action.

---

166 *Justice and Related Legislation (Miscellaneous Amendments) Act* 2012 (Tas) s 54.
167 *Public Interest Disclosures Act* 2003 (WA), Long title.
168 *Protected Disclosure Act* 2012 (Vic) s 1.
169 *Independent Broad-Based Anti-Corruption Commission Act* 2011 (Vic) s 4(1).

The extent of protection available by reference to the limited definitions for whistleblowers in Victorian universities remains to be determined but appears less than previously existed for persons providing information about conduct within tertiary institutions.[170]

In *Owens v University of Melbourne*[171] Judd J considered whether a person who made a claim for workers compensation for a work-related injury caused by a protected disclosure being made could also make a claim under section 19 of the *Whistleblowers Protection Act* 2001 (Vic)[172] or vice versa. In that case, the plaintiff, Julie Owens, was employed by the University of Melbourne in August 2005 as business manager for the university's Centre for Indigenous Education. Ms Owens made a protected disclosure against Tjanara Goreng Goreng, the second defendant, the director of the Centre, that there were improper work practices at the Centre.

Ms Owen alleged that the university failed to ensure that her protected disclosures were kept confidential and failed to protect her from reprisals. She also alleged she suffered detrimental action in reprisal for her disclosures and this 'caused her loss and damage, was intimidating, harassing and involved adverse treatment in relation to her employment, career, trade or business'.[173] Ms Owen claimed to have suffered injury in the nature of stress, distress, psychological upset, psychological injury, hurt feelings, embarrassment, ridicule, and financial loss and damage. She claimed damages, including exemplary damages, under section 19 of the Act as a result of the injury.[174]

The Supreme Court held that a person is not precluded from making both claims, even though there might be overlap in terms of the injury caused by the protected disclosure. Section 19 was held to preserve the right to workers compensation and was not to be limited by a reflection on the rights that might accrue or not accrue under workers compensation.[175] This was the situation in Victoria particularly because the *Accident Compensation Act* 1985 (Vic), which governs workers compensation entitlements, predated the *Whistleblower Protection Act* 2001 and also the terms of section 19.[176]

A review of complaint-handling in Victorian universities by the Ombudsman Victoria in 2005 found that the eight Victorian universities had complied with the Ministerial recommendations made under a review of university governance in Victoria.[177] The Ministerial review recommended that the universities each prepare and publish a statement of the role of the Victorian Ombudsman to review universities' decisions, and that universities codify and collate internal student grievance procedures and publish them with information about submitting complaints to the Victorian Ombudsman.[178] The Victorian Ombudsman also found that Victorian universities had complied with the provisions of the *Whistleblowers Protection Act* 2001 (Vic).[179] Each university has published procedures for the implementation of the Act and these are posted on the university websites.[180]

---

170 However, importantly, a measure of protection continues to exist in relation to complaints lodged with the Ombudsman under the *Ombudsman Act* 1973 (Vic).

171 [2008] VSC 174; (2008) 19 VR 449.

172 Now repealed.

173 [2008] VSC 174; (2008) 19 VR 449, [1].

174 Ibid, [1].

175 Ibid, [22].

176 Ibid, [21]; cf *Reeves-Board v Queensland University of Technology* [2002] 2 Qd R 85. See also for discussion, Brown (2009), above n 132, 681.

177 George E Brouwer, *Review of Complaint Handling in Victorian Universities* (Ombudsman Victoria, May 2005) 6, available at: <https://www.ombudsman.vic.gov.au/Publications/Parliamentary-Reports/Review-of-complaint-handling-in-Victorian-universi> [accessed 4 Jan 2016].

178 Ibid.

179 Ibid.

180 Ibid.

Non-Legislated Forms of Whistleblower Protection

There have been criticisms that whistleblower laws are ineffective because they provide insufficient protections or incentives for whistleblowers to make complaints and sufficient deterrence to institutions that engage in reprisals against whistleblowers.[181] The concern has been raised that whistleblower protection legislation is mostly symbolic, that it is stronger on rhetoric than substance, and that in the real world it is largely ineffectual.[182]

In the United States a response has been the passage of legislation which provides financial incentives for whistleblowers in the financial sector under the Dodds–Frank Act[183] and more broadly in the *False Claims Act*, which enable whistleblowers to receive between 15 per cent and 35 per cent of any award the government receives against those who have engaged in corrupt practices which a whistleblower has assisted in bringing to light.[184]

In addition, other non-legislated protections such as internal policies within universities, research institutions and funders of research constitute important supplements to whistleblower laws.

An example is the role of the United States Office of Research Integrity (ORI). Its Guidelines provide that, by regulation, extramural entities applying for grants or cooperative agreements in 'biomedical or behavioral research, research-training, or research-related' projects,[185] under the *Public Health Service Act*,[186] must establish policies that provide for 'undertaking diligent efforts to protect the positions and reputations of those persons who, in good faith, make allegations. 42 C.F.R. Part 50.103(d)(13)'.[187] It has determined that adherence to its 1995 'ORI Guidelines for Institutions and Whistleblowers: Responding to Possible Retaliation

---

181 For example, see De Maria (2006), above n 132; Martin, above n 81.

182 Martin, above n 81.

183 Ashby Jones and Joann S Lublin, 'Critics Blow Whistle on Law', *The Wall Street Journal*, 1 November 2010: <http://www.wsj.com/articles/SB10001424052702304879604575582603173894296> [accessed 4 Jan 2016]. This financial reform law, known as the *Dodd-Frank Wall Street Reform and Consumer Protection Act of 2010*, Pub L No 111-203, 124 Stat 1376 (2010), passed in July 2010 and entitles whistleblowers to between 10 per cent to 30 per cent of any government recovery in excess of US$1 million. The Securities Exchange Commission which administers these incentives takes into account three factors when determining how much a whistleblower receives, including the significance of the information, the degree of assistance provided by the whistleblower, and the extent to which the government wants to deter the violations in question: Ben Kerschberg, 'The Dodd–Frank Act's Robust Whistleblowing Incentives', *Forbes*, 14 April 2011: <http://www.forbes.com/sites/benkerschberg/2011/04/14/the-dodd-frank-acts-robust-whistleblowing-incentives/> [accessed 4 Jan 2016]. As Jones and Lublin and Kerschberg note, given the large sums of money involved in many of these cases, the whistleblower stands to receive considerable amounts of money, sometimes in the multi-millions, even if only 10 per cent is awarded. The first award under the Dodd–Frank Act, however, was $50,000: see Joshua Gallu, 'SEC Pays $US50,000 in First Dodd–Frank Whistleblower Reward', *Bloomberg*, 22 August 2012: <http://www.bloomberg.com/news/articles/2012-08-21/sec-pays-50-000-in-first-dodd-frank-whistleblower-reward> [accessed 4 Jan 2016]; US Securities and Exchange Commission, 'SEC Issues First Whistleblower Program Award' (Press Release, 2012-162, 21 August 2012): <http://www.sec.gov/News/PressRelease/Detail/PressRelease/1365171483972> [accessed 4 Jan 2016].

184 Kerschberg, above n 183.

185 US Department of Health and Human Services, The Office of Research Integrity, 'Handling Misconduct—Whistleblowers' (20 November 1995), available at: <https://ori.hhs.gov/content/handbooks-and-guidelines> [accessed 4 Jan 2016].

186 Pub L No 78-410, 58 Stat 682 (1944).

187 As cited in 'Handling Misconduct—Whistleblowers', above n. 185. In 2005, this regulation was amended, and now states: 'All reasonable and practical efforts, if requested and as appropriate, to protect or restore the reputation of persons alleged to have engaged in research misconduct but against whom no finding of research misconduct is made': 42 CFR § 93.304(k) (2014). In principle, this constitutes a significant remedial requirement.

Against Whistleblowers in Extramural Research'[188] is a means of satisfying this regulation. It also encourages institutions to adopt principles consistent with the Whistleblower Bill of Rights,[189] the essence of which are that:

(1) whistleblowers are free to disclose lawfully whatever information supports a reasonable belief of research misconduct as it is defined by PHS policy;
(2) institutions have a duty not to tolerate or engage in retaliation against good-faith whistleblowers;
(3) institutions have a duty to provide fair and objective procedures for examining and resolving complaints, disputes and allegations of research misconduct;
(4) institutions...have a duty to follow procedures that are not tainted by partiality arising from personal or institutional conflict of interest or other sources of bias;
(5) institutions have a duty to elicit and evaluate fully and objectively information about concerns raised by whistleblower;
(6) institutions have a duty to handle cases involving alleged research misconduct as expeditiously as possible without compromising responsible resolutions; and
(7) at the conclusion of proceedings, institutions have a responsibility to credit promptly, in public or private as appropriate, those whose allegations are substantiated.[190]

In its Guidelines the ORI provides for a system for processing whistleblower retaliation complaints and systems for resolving or settling such complaints—within the institution or by external arbitration. However, the teeth in the ORI system are that a prerequisite for entities applying for biomedical or behavioural research grants under the Public Health Service Act is that they must comply with whistleblower protection systems, an example of which is its own Guidelines. In practice this is a significant technical imposition upon those seeking research funding.

University Policies on Whistleblowers

Most universities have formal policies whose purpose is the provision of protection to whistleblowers. The University of Oxford, for instance, has a 'Public Interest Disclosure Code of Practice'.[191] It works alongside the *Public Interest Disclosure Act* 1998 (UK). The Code states that: '[T]he University places the greatest importance on the integrity of its operations and encourages members of staff and students to raise genuine concerns about malpractice or impropriety at the earliest possible stage'.[192] It provides:

> An individual making a disclosure relating to such matters to the appropriate person will not be penalised provided the disclosure is made (a) in good faith; and (b) in the reasonable belief of the individual making the disclosure that the information disclosed, and any allegation contained in it, are substantially true.[193]

It states that the university will treat such disclosures in a confidential manner but that action will not normally be taken in response to anonymous complaints.[194] Where there are what it

[188] 'Handling Misconduct—Whistleblowers', above n 187.

[189] See US Department of Health and Human Services, The Office of Research Integrity, 'Whistleblower's Bill of Rights—Appendix A' (Last updated 8 May 2014): <https://ori.hhs.gov/Whistleblower-Rights> [accessed 4 Jan 2016].

[190] 'Handling Misconduct—Whistleblowers', above n 187.

[191] University of Oxford, Policies and Codes of Practice, 'Public Interest Disclosure: Code of Practice' (last updated 21 March 2013): <http://www.admin.ox.ac.uk/personnel/cops/pid/> [accessed 4 Jan 2016].

[192] Ibid, [3].

[193] Ibid, [7].

[194] Ibid, [8], [10].

terms 'malicious or vexatious allegations', the Code provides that disciplinary action may be taken against the person concerned.[195]

Cambridge University has also formulated a 'Whistleblowing Policy'.[196] It is stated to:

> deal with specific concerns which are in the public interest and may include:
> - a criminal offence
> - failure to comply with legal obligations or with the Statutes, Ordinances and Regulations of the University
> - financial or non-financial maladministration or malpractice or impropriety or fraud
> - academic or professional malpractice
> - a risk to the health or safety of any individual
> - environmental damage
> - a miscarriage of justice
> - improper conduct or unethical behaviour
> - attempts to suppress or conceal any information relating to any of the above.[197]

It provides that:

> Any member of staff who has a reasonable belief that there is serious malpractice relating to any of the protected matters specified . . . above, may raise a concern . . . The issues raised under the protected list may relate to another member of staff, a group of staff, the individual's own Institution or another part of the University. Concerns must be raised without malice and in good faith, and the individual must reasonably believe that the information disclosed, and any allegations contained in it, are substantially true. The disclosure must not be made for purposes of personal gain, and in all the circumstances it must be reasonable to make the disclosure. The University will ensure that any member of staff who makes a disclosure in such circumstances will not be penalised or suffer any adverse treatment for doing so. However, a member of staff who does not act in good faith or makes an allegation without having reasonable grounds for believing it to be substantially true, or makes it for purposes of personal gain, or makes it maliciously or vexatiously may be subject to disciplinary proceedings.
>
> In view of the protection afforded to a member of staff raising a bona fide concern, it is preferable if that individual puts his/her name to any disclosure. The identity of the person raising the matter will be kept confidential, if so requested, for as long as possible provided that this is compatible with a proper investigation. Anonymous complaints are not covered by this procedure, but may be reported, investigated or acted upon as the person receiving the complaint sees fit (including the use of this procedure), having regard to the seriousness of the issue raised, the credibility of the complaint, the prospects of being able to investigate the matter, and fairness to any individual mentioned in the complaint.[198]

Cambridge accepts that it has an obligation to:

> ensure that staff who make a disclosure without malice and in good faith are protected, regardless of whether or not the concern raised is upheld. A member of staff who has made a disclosure and who feels that, as a result, he or she has suffered adverse treatment should submit a formal complaint under the grievance procedure as set out in the relevant staff handbook and in the statutes and ordinances detailing what has been done to him or her. If it appears that there are reasonable grounds for making the complaint, the onus will be on the person against whom the complaint of adverse treatment has been made to show that the actions complained of were not taken in retaliation for the disclosure.

---

195 Ibid, [9].

196 University of Cambridge, Policies and Procedures, 'Public Disclosure by University Employees: 'Whistleblowing' Policy' (17 February 2015): <http://www.admin.cam.ac.uk/offices/hr/policy/whistleblowing.html> [accessed 4 Jan 2016].

197 Ibid, [3].

198 Ibid, [4]–[5].

> Where it is determined that there is a prima facie case that a member of staff has suffered adverse treatment, harassment or victimisation as a result of his or her disclosure, a further investigation may take place and disciplinary action may be taken against the perpetrator in accordance with the relevant procedure.'[199]

Harvard University also developed a whistleblowing policy in 2012,[200] which is supported by a '24-hour Compliance Hotline' and a web-based tutorial.[201] It encourages persons who suspect the breach of a policy or the law not to confront the person concerned and, instead, to report the issue to their supervisor, a 'local tub finance officer ... or to the Compliance Hotline'.[202] The policy states: 'The University will protect from retaliation members of the Harvard community who make good faith reports of suspected violations of law or University policy.'[203]

Similarly Stanford University provides that:

> Members of the Stanford community should report suspected violations of applicable laws, regulations, government contract and grant requirements or this Code. This reporting should normally be made initially through standard management channels, beginning with the immediate supervisor, instructor or advisor. If for any reason it is not appropriate to report suspected violations to the immediate supervisor (e.g., the suspected violation is by the supervisor) individuals may go to a higher level of management within their school or department.
>
> [...]
>
> Such reports may be made confidentially, and even anonymously, although the more information given, the easier it is to investigate the reports. Raising such concerns is a service to the University and does not in itself jeopardize employment.[204]

The University of Adelaide defines a 'whistleblower' as:

> a person who exposes wrongdoing within an organisation, in the hope of stopping it and preventing it from reoccurring. To 'blow the whistle' means to reveal information about a person or organisation that has:—
>
> - risked public health, safety or the environment;
> - acted illegally;
> - wasted public money;
> - misused public resources; or
> - falsified records.
>
> Most whistleblowers are internal and report misconduct to another employee or manager. Whistleblowers play a vital role in exposing misconduct and illegal activity within the workplace and assisting with the detection of fraud and corruption.[205]

The University of Adelaide emphasizes the protection for whistleblowers provided by the *Whistleblowers Protection Act* 1993 (SA).

---

199 Ibid, [12]–[13].

200 Harvard University, 'Whistleblowing Policy' (Updated 18 January 2012): <http://hwpi.harvard.edu/files/provost/files/whistleblowing_policy_final_vers_1_1_011812.pdf> [accessed 4 Jan 2016].

201 Katie Koch, 'The Right Way to Report Wrongdoing', *Harvard Gazette*, 25 January 2012: <http://news.harvard.edu/gazette/story/2012/01/the-right-way-to-report-wrongdoing/> [accessed 4 Jan 2016].

202 Ibid.

203 Harvard University, above n 200.

204 Stanford University, Administrative Guide, '1.1.1. University Code of Conduct' (Last updated 13 August 2014) [9]: <https://adminguide.stanford.edu/chapter-1/subchapter-1/policy-1-1-1> [accessed 4 Jan 2016].

205 University of Adelaide, above 161.

Along similar lines Griffith University encourages the making of disclosures by staff:

> Staff who know of or suspect unlawful, negligent or improper conduct, and staff or other persons who know of conduct that may present a substantial and specific danger to the health or safety of a person with a disability or the environment; or may be regarded as an act of reprisal taken against anybody as a result of a public interest disclosure, are encouraged to report their concerns.
>
> The *Public Interest Disclosure Act* 2010 (Qld) provides for the protection of staff of the University and, where applicable, other people making public interest disclosures (PIDs). As a public sector entity established by an Act of the Queensland Parliament, Griffith University is covered by the *Public Interest Disclosure Act* and all University staff are public officers for the purposes of the legislation.
>
> The University is committed to ensuring that all public interest disclosures are properly managed and that those who report wrongdoing in the workplace, or are the subject of such disclosures, are protected from reprisals.
>
> The University will, to the greatest extent possible, keep the disclosure and the identity of the discloser confidential. Disclosures may be made anonymously.[206]

The complex overlap of responsibilities and protections is instanced by the advice given by Monash University which informs potential whistleblowers that:

> *The Victorian Government Protected Disclosure Act* 2012 ('the PD Act'), the *Independent Broad-based Anti-Corruption Commission Act* 2011 ('the IBAC Act') and the *Ombudsman Act* 1973 ('the Ombudsman Act') aim to encourage and facilitate the making of disclosures of improper conduct or detrimental action, in contravention of those Acts, by public officers and public bodies. They provide protection to whistleblowers who make disclosures in accordance with the PD Act, and establish systems for the matters disclosed to be investigated and for remedial action to be taken.
>
> Monash University is a public body under the IBAC Act. Employees at Monash University, as well as Council members of Monash University are public officers under the IBAC Act.
>
> It is the complainant's right and responsibility to elect to take a complaint of improper conduct or detrimental action in reprisal for a protected disclosure to IBAC or the Ombudsman.
>
> Any person contemplating making a disclosure of improper conduct or detrimental action related to Monash University should contact IBAC in the first instance. Monash University's protected disclosure coordinator is not authorised under the PD Act and IBAC Act to receive or assess a disclosure.
>
> Any person who chooses to make a complaint directly to Monash, rather than to IBAC or the Ombudsman, will have their complaint dealt with under Monash University's policies and procedures, unless Monash University is otherwise instructed by IBAC or the Ombudsman.
>
> Monash University does not tolerate improper conduct by employees, Council members of Monash University, or any person performing public services or public functions on behalf of Monash University. Monash University does not tolerate the taking of reprisals against those people who disclose such conduct.[207]

The University of Melbourne[208] similarly warns those who wish to make a disclosure that enjoys protection under the *Protected Disclosure Act* 2012 (Vic) that they must make such a disclosure

[206] Griffith University, Governance, 'Whistleblowing': <http://www.griffith.edu.au/about-griffith/governance/whistleblowing> [accessed 4 Jan 2016].

[207] Monash University, 'Conduct and Compliance Procedure—Whistleblowers': <http://www.adm.monash.edu.au/workplace-policy/conduct-compliance/whistleblowers.html> [accessed 4 Jan 2016].

[208] University of Melbourne, Melbourne Policy Library, 'Whistleblowers and Protected Disclosure Procedure (MPF1217)' (Approved 10 September 2013): <https://policy.unimelb.edu.au/MPF1217> [accessed 4 Jan 2016].

directly to the IBAC or the Ombudsman.[209] However, it has set up a system of 'Protected Disclosure Officers'[210] whose role it is to cooperate with the IBAC and the Ombudsman and it is accepted that 'The University must protect a person who cooperates with an investigation of a disclosure from detrimental action, or the threat of detrimental action.'[211]

However, such formal protections as exist for whistleblowers within universities and research institutions can go only so far in creating an effective whistleblower reporting and protection regime.[212] Organizational commitment is the key element to a successful whistleblower programme in terms of the way in which the organization, such as a university, deals with whistleblowing. Organizational commitment involves:

- **policies and procedures** that signify the formal acceptance by the organization of the principles of encouragement of reporting and protection of whistleblowers
- **leadership**—energy and commitment exhibited by senior management towards ensuring that there is no mismatch between the commitment outlined in the procedures and actual practice within the organization, including allocation of financial and human resources
- **line managers** are usually the first point where reports are received, and they have the immediate responsibility for the wellbeing of employees; thus line managers warrant being looked at separately
- **reporters** need to trust that the procedures are adequate and that the commitment from those above them is such that their reports will be acted upon and they will be protected. A particular element of organizational commitment for reporters is their trust in management.[213]

Roberts, Brown, and Olsen also note the importance of the 'ethical climate and leadership support' within an organization.[214] It is problematic when an organization, or at least the senior managers within an organization, publicly support whistleblower policies and procedures but do not 'walk the talk' by following those policies and procedures.[215] This lack of action and management commitment can lessen the trust of employees working in the organization and enforce a belief that nothing would be done in response to a complaint.[216] As trust is a key element of effective whistleblowing programmes, it is incumbent on tertiary institutions to ensure that an emphasis is placed on building trust in the workplace.[217]

While many universities and some research institutions have whistleblower policies and protections, the instances of whistleblowing indicate that some universities may not always 'walk the talk'.

Case Studies of Whistleblowing in Universities

Robert Sprague. It was Professor Robert L Sprague, a Professor of Psychology at the University of Illinois, who was responsible for the National Institute of Mental Health (NIMH)

209 Ibid, [1.1].
210 Ibid, [2].
211 Ibid, [3.2].
212 Roberts, Brown, and Olsen (2011), above n 29, 18.
213 Ibid.
214 Ibid.
215 Ibid, 19.
216 Ibid, 22.
217 Ibid, 19–20. Roberts et al. suggest ways in which trust in an organization can be lessened and destroyed and conversely the issues that organizations need to address in order to build the trust of their employees: see ibid, 19–20. Roberts et al. further suggest a number of actions an organization can take at a strategic level to demonstrate a commitment to encouraging and protecting those who make reports, including

undertaking its devastating investigation into the fraudulent conduct of Dr Stephen Breuning in relation to the prescription of behaviour-modifying drugs for intellectually disabled children (see Chapter 3).[218] Professor Sprague persisted in expression of concerns after a committee at the University of Pittsburgh had pronounced that it had no jurisdiction over the behaviour of Dr Breuning as what was known about him occurred before he was employed at the university. At the invitation of the Republican Senator John Dingwell, who at the time was investigating instances of research misconduct, Professor Sprague gave an account of Dr Breuning's conduct at a Senate hearing, making the inflammatory accusation that there had been a 'cover-up' by the University of Pittsburgh.[219] Two weeks later he received a communication from the university's Vice-President and counsel for the university's Medical and Health Care Division, George A Huber, contending that his account was 'not only inaccurate and untrue, but slanderous and libelous'.[220] Mr Huber informed Professor Sprague that if he repeated his allegations 'we will take whatever lawful corrective measures are necessary and appropriate, including the filing of legal action'.[221] In the meantime the NIMH declined, without explanation, to renew a research grant that had funded Professor Sprague's work for the previous 18 years.[222]

The situation with Professor Sprague was communicated to Senator Dingwell who in turn communicated with the President of the University of Pittsburgh. The President wrote back to Senator Dingwell that he had formed the view that the tone of Mr Huber's letter to Professor Sprague had been 'intemperate' and praised Professor Sprague for exposing Dr Breuning's fraud.[223] It is reasonable to conclude that it was only the intervention of Senator Dingwell and his inquiry that promoted the university to resile from the threats against the whistleblower, Professor Sprague. In 2005 Professor Sprague was awarded the Edgar Doll Award by the American Psychological Association. There is no doubt that his efforts were courageous and persistent. They did not find a responsive audience for a long while but a combination of the particular whistleblower's stature within the scholarly domain and his unusual commitment combined to produce consequences that would not otherwise have ensued and to provide him with protection which he would not otherwise have enjoyed.

Stephen Bolsin. One of the best-known examples of persons who have functioned as whistleblowers and been subject to reprisals and lack of support from their employer is Dr Stephen Bolsin, an anaesthetist who worked at the Bristol Royal Infirmary in England during the 1990s. He became concerned about the technical skill of a surgeon, Mr James Wisheart, because of the lengthy time he took to complete cardiac surgery.[224] Mr Wisheart's slowness resulted in long cross-clamp times, during which the heart of the child being operated on was without oxygen, in turn leading to the risk of death, serious heart failure, and other major

taking whistleblowing seriously at a senior management level, setting targets within the organization for increasing reporting rates, and consistency of application of policies and procedures, among other things: see ibid, 25–26.

[218] See Robert L Sprague, 'Whistleblowing: A Very Unpleasant Avocation' (1993) 3(1) *Ethics & Behavior* 103.

[219] Ibid, 125, 128.

[220] Ibid, 129.

[221] Ibid, 125. See also, Daniel S Greenberg, 'Issue of Scientific Fraud Not Easily Faced', *Chicago Tribune*, 16 August 1989: <http://articles.chicagotribune.com/1989-08-16/news/8901050101_1_stephen-e-breuning-federal-charges-nimh> [accessed 4 Jan 2016].

[222] Sprague, above n 218, 119–20, 125–6.

[223] Ibid, 128–9.

[224] See Stephen N Bolsin, 'The Wisheart Affair: Responses to Dunn—The Bristol Cardiac Disaster' (1998) 317(7172) *BMJ* 1579; Peter M Dunn, 'The Wisheart Affair: Paediatric Cardiological Services in Bristol, 1990–5' (1998) 317(7166) *BMJ* 1145.

complications.[225] Unbeknown to Dr Bolsin, concerns had already been expressed about the performance of the paediatric cardiac unit in which he worked. In 1989 a confidential report from a Working Party of the Royal College of Surgeons and the Royal College of Physicians (Sir Terence English, Sir Keith Ross, Professor David Hamilton, and Dr Stewart Hunter) graphed Bristol's infant mortality at twice that of the other centres. This led Sir Terence, who had previously been the President of the Royal College of Surgeons and a supra-regional services adviser, to express the view that Bristol should no longer be a designated centre for paediatric cardiac surgery. However, no action was taken and 35 children subsequently died at the Bristol Royal Infirmary. Among other things, this resulted, a considerable time later, in landmark disciplinary proceedings against the administrator deemed to be responsible for the lack of appropriate response to the concerns raised.[226]

Dr Bolsin raised the issue of Bristol's high mortality rates with the Director of Anaesthesia, the Chief Executive and the Professor of Anaesthesia in 1990. He has described how the continuing deaths of children led him to consider leaving Bristol with his young family, and the tensions it caused for him domestically.[227] From July 1992 with an anaesthetic colleague he started to collect data. By 1993 he formed the view that the results were clear and established that Bristol was much poorer in outcomes than the remainder of the United Kingdom for cardiac surgery on babies and various other operations. However, Mr Wisheart assumed ever more powerful and influential positions within the United Bristol Healthcare Trust and appeared to Dr Bolsin to be in an unchallengeable position.

He contemplated reporting Mr Wisheart and other surgeons to the General Medical Council but was advised that the chances of such allegations being found proved were remote. He also received legal advice that if his complaint were unsuccessful the chances of being sued for defamation, or a counter-charge of serious professional misconduct, for criticizing a colleague, were substantial. He decided not to file a complaint.

In 1994, however, six anaesthetists wrote to another paediatric cardiac surgeon, Janardan Dhasmana, urging him to stop doing arterial switch operations on older children. He had previously stopped undertaking the operation on one-month-old babies because nine of 13 operations had resulted in deaths. However, in December 1994 Mr Dhasmana listed a switch operation on an 18-month-old, Joshua Loveday, for January 1995.[228] Dr Bolsin has described how he and his wife 'considered telling the parents to take Joshua to Birmingham, but considered the consequences to our careers (being struck off the medical or nursing registers) were too serious. It was the worst night of our lives and we often wish we had acted on our impulses to inform the parents. The consequences for Joshua were even more serious: he died in an operating theatre at the Bristol Royal Infirmary the following day.'[229]

The pace of investigations increased after Joshua's death although Dr Bolsin has chronicled the attitude of the investigators who were despatched to the hospital as nakedly hostile to him. They did, however, identify Mr Wisheart as 'a higher risk surgeon', recommended that

---

[225] See Stephen Bolsin, 'The Whistle Blower in Medicine' (address delivered at a meeting of the Medico-Legal Society at the Naval and Military Club, Victoria, 19 March 1999): <http://mlsv.org.au/wp-content/uploads/2013/09/19th-March-1999-The-Whistle-Blower-in-Medicine-By-Dr.-Stephen-Bolsin.pdf> [accessed 4 Jan 2016]; Phil Hammond, 'Stephen Bolsin's Story: Too Many Babies were Damaged and Dying', *Medical Harm*, 27 July 2011: <http://medicalharm.org/doctor-stories/stephen-bolsins-story-too-many-babies-were-damaged-and-dying/> [accessed 4 Jan 2016].

[226] *Roylance v General Medical Council (No 2)* [2000] 1 AC 311.

[227] Bolsin (1999), above n 225.

[228] See Mark Davies, *Medical Self-Regulation: Crisis and Change* (Aldershot: Ashgate, 2007) 131.

[229] Hammond, above n 225. See also, Ian Kennedy, *Learning from Bristol: The Report of the Public Inquiry into Children's Heart Surgery at the Bristol Royal Infirmary 1984–1995* (Cm 5207(I), 2001).

he should stop operating on children and proposed that Mr Dhasmana should cease the arterial switch operation. But their report was not 'acceptable' to the Trust and their final report blamed tensions between the anaesthetists and the surgeons for the high mortality rate.[230]

After Dr Bolsin gave a non-committal interview to media, he was threatened with possible constructive dismissal and, although he had been the National Audit Co-ordinator for Cardiac Anaesthetists for several years, his cardiac sessions were removed from his job roster. He has vividly described the impact that this had on him as he became:

> withdrawn and dominated by the deaths and complications in children's heart surgery. Most of my colleagues shunned my company and I relied on a few close friends both medical and non-medical for support and reassurance. I applied for other jobs in the UK but learned that I was considered 'unappointable'; the common response of alternative employers to whistleblowers.[231]

He accepted an appointment at Geelong Hospital in Australia. In writing about issues relating to whistleblowers in the succeeding years Professor Bolsin (as he now is) has drawn on his own experience to emphasize the 'great personal cost' that whistleblowing can bring.[232] While he has not said so explicitly, it is notable that Dr Bolsin elected to emigrate to a position that was particularly geographically and culturally remote from his previous position.

Nancy Olivieri and the Toronto Hospital. The travails of Dr Nancy Olivieri, a haematologist at the Toronto Hospital for Sick Children (the Hospital), who was also employed by the University of Toronto, have been described at some length (see Chapter 4) in relation to conflict of interest matters. She formed the view that an experimental iron-chelating drug (deferiprone) that she was trialling in patients with thalassaemia major was losing efficacy and causing serious adverse effects, including liver fibrosis. The hope had been that the trials would yield results that would lead to the licensing of deferiprone for therapeutic use. However, the communication of her views to the manufacturer of the drug and to her university was not well received and resulted in ongoing inquiries and litigation.[233]

Not only did Dr Olivieri not receive support from her employers at the University of Toronto or the Hospital, but she was dismissed and referred for disciplinary investigation in relation to her professional conduct.[234] Ultimately, she was exonerated of impropriety and an independent report (commissioned by the Academic Tenure and Freedom Committee of the Canadian Association of University Teachers) recommended that she be given redress. With the passage of time came appreciation. In 2009 she was honoured by the American Association for the Advancement of Science with its Scientific Freedom and Responsibility Award 'for her indefatigable determination that patient safety and research integrity come before institutional and commercial interests'.[235] However, this was at the end of many years of legal battles that she describes as having taken a significant toll on her.

David Healy. In 2001 David Healy was the Director of the North Wales Department of Psychological Medicine, which was part of the University of Wales College of Medicine. He

---

230 Hammond, above n 225.

231 Ibid.

232 Stephen Bolsin, Thomas Faunce, and Justin Oakley, 'Practical Virtue Ethics: Healthcare Whistleblowing and Portable Digital Technology' (2005) 31(10) *Journal of Medical Ethics* 612, 612. See too, Alan Merry and Alexander McCall Smith, *Errors, Medicine and the Law* (Cambridge: Cambridge University Press, 2001) 25.

233 See above, at p 191.

234 See Françoise Baylis, 'The Olivieri Debacle: Where Were the Heroes of Bioethics?'(2004) 30(1) *Journal of Medical Ethics* 44.

235 AAAS, '2009 Award for Scientific Freedom and Responsibility Recipient': <http://www.aaas.org/page/2009-award-scientific-freedom-and-responsibility-recipient> [accessed 4 Jan 2016].

was a well-known historian of psychopharmacology. In August 2000 he was offered a professorial position at the Centre for Addiction and Mental Health (CAMH) at the University of Toronto. Somewhat provocatively Healy gave a lecture raising concerns about the safety of what was then a new Selective Seratonin Re-uptake Inhibitor (SSRI), Prozac, as well as various anti-psychotics, suggesting a link to suicidal behaviour. Eli Lilly, the manufacturer of Prozac, was a donor of more than CA$1.5 million to the CAMH.[236] One way of viewing what took place was that Healy assumed something of a role as a whistleblower; alternatively, of course, he was identifying a conflict of interest.[237]

The response of the University of Toronto was to withdraw its job offer to Healy, informing him it was alarmed about the 'extremity' of his views.[238] A high-profile scandal ensued. In September 2001, 27 experts in neuropsychopharmacology condemned the conduct of the University of Toronto and accused it of violating academic freedom. Healy also took legal action against the University to enforce his contract. The lawsuit was settled with Healy being appointed to a three-year visiting professorship at the University, the University acknowledging its support for the free expression of critical views, and Healy accepting assurances made by the University.[239] The reasonably acceptable compromise that emerged for Healy was undoubtedly influenced by his seniority within academia and the extensive support that was provided to him by colleagues.

Aubrey Blumsohn. In 2002 Dr Aubrey Blumsohn was a senior and honorary consultant in bone metabolism. He and Professor Richard Eastell of Sheffield University had been engaged by Procter and Gamble to undertake research on an osteoporosis drug, Actonel. The hope of the pharmaceutical company was that research results would show that the drug increased bone density and reduced the incidence of fractures.[240] Professor Eastell was also chair of the Procter & Gamble UK scientific advisory board. On the basis of an arrangement with the two researchers, blood and urine samples, both from patients on Actonel and on a placebo, were blind reviewed. Blumsohn requested data access codes so he could check the integrity of the raw data he had supplied to the company but was only permitted access to partial data analyses. Blumsohn regarded this as misleading and then found himself named as a co-author of ghost-written research papers and statistical reports. When he was allowed to view the data, it was on a computer screen; he observed that 40 per cent of the data were missing in some of the graphs and formed the view that the papers thereby misrepresented the findings in such a way as to favour the efficacy of Actonel illegitimately.[241]

Blumsohn maintained that he repeatedly raised his concerns with Professor Eastell but did not receive a receptive audience. He then communicated with University officers, including the Vice-Chancellor. When he threatened to involve medical journalists, he was threatened with disciplinary action and was suspended for failing to comply with management instructions about abstaining from contact with the media.[242] Ultimately his dispute with

236 See James P Winter, *Lies the Media Tell Us* (Montreal: Black Rose Books, 2007), 148ff.

237 Alison Bass, *Side-Effects: A Prosecutor, A Whistleblower and a Bestselling Antidepressant on Trial* (Chapel Hill, NC: Algonquin Books of Chapel Hill, 2008) 99.

238 Ibid.

239 See Trudo Lemmens, 'Confronting the Conflict of Interest Crisis in Medical Research' (2004) 23(4) *Monash Bioethics Review* 19.

240 See Eric Barendt, *Academic Freedom and the Law: A Comparative Study* (Oxford: Hart, 2010).

241 See Tom Devine and Tarek F Maassarani, *The Corporate Whistleblower's Survival Guide: A Handbook for Committing the Truth* (San Francisco: Berrett-Koehler Publishers, 2011) 37–8.

242 See Jo Revill, 'How the Drugs Giant and a Lone Academic Went to War', *The Guardian*, 4 December 2005: <http://www.theguardian.com/uk/2005/dec/04/health.businessofresearch> [accessed 4 Jan 2016]; Morgan, n 105.

Sheffield University was settled in a confidential resolution of outstanding issues. He left the University for an undisclosed sum.

Professor Eastell was referred to the General Medical Council. He was found not to have engaged in dishonesty in allowing the publication of a false statement that he had seen all the data in the research study but it was found that he may have acted negligently.[243] In 2006, after further adverse publicity, Procter & Gamble revised its policies and guaranteed researchers full access to research data, including data codes. The case highlighted the phenomenon of pharmaceutical companies ghostwriting articles and studies in which the named authors play little or no role,[244] as well as the risk of undermining the integrity of publications if researchers are not made privy to all data'. Blumsohn has observed that: 'The problems of medicine could not happen without the complicity of medical journals, most of which receive substantial advertising and "reprint" income from industry... as academics we need to reassert the importance of data and the meaning of authorship. We also need to assert "old fashioned" ideas of academic freedom, our right to speak the truth as we see it, and to allow that truth to be subjected to open debate.'[245] However, for Blumsohn, his time as a whistleblower resulted in his settling a legal action with Sheffield University after he was suspended for communicating with journalists contrary to university policies, and his withdrawing from academia as well as registration as a medical practitioner.[246] He lamented that whistleblower legislation 'prescribes that you need to spend innumerable years going through internal procedures, and then to obfuscatory prescribed external bodies', only leaving a remote potential for protection if there is a legal outcome in an employment case.[247]

Paul Barach. Just because a person dons the mantle of 'whistleblower', it does not mean that his or her 'revelations' are authentic or justified. A notorious and illustrative example of problematic allegations was played out in New South Wales over four years in relation to serious accusations of corruption made by Professor of Safety Science and Injury Prevention and anaesthetist Paul Barach of the University of New South Wales. Dr Barach maintained that he was unjustly sacked by the university after he exposed misconduct inside a medical laboratory that he said had been perpetrated by a relative of the university's Vice-Chancellor, Fred Hilmer.[248]

The university employed Dr Barach in September 2008 and dismissed him in 2009 after finding he had falsified his curriculum vitae and grant applications. This led to an inquiry by ICAC which rejected claims of corrupt conduct made by Barach and the incorporation in a parliamentary report of the privileges committee of the New South Wales Parliament of the formal position of the University of New South Wales, which did not support Dr Barach.[249]

---

243 See Clare Dyer, 'GMC Clears Research Dean of Dishonesty Over Access to Data' (2009) 339(7730) *BMJ* 1107.

244 Sarah Boseley, 'British Doctor Faces Action Over Claims of 'Ghost Writing' for US Drug Company', *The Guardian*, 18 September 2009: <http://www.theguardian.com/science/2009/sep/18/doctors-ghost-writing-pharmaceutical-research> [accessed 4 Jan 2016]. See too, David Healy, *Pharmageddon* (Berkeley: University of California Press, 2012).

245 Aubrey Blumsohn, 'Authorship, Ghost-Science, Access to Data and Control of the Pharmaceutical Scientific Literature: Who Stands Behind the Word?' (2006) 19(3) *Professional Ethics Report* 1, 3 (footnote omitted): <http://www.aaas.org/sites/default/files/migrate/uploads/per46.pdf> [accessed 4 Jan 2016].

246 See Morgan, above n 105.

247 Ibid.

248 Julie Robotham, 'School in a State of Collapse', *The Sydney Morning Herald*, 10 June 2010: <http://www.smh.com.au/nsw/school-in-a-state-of-collapse-20100609-xwyb.html> [accessed 4 Jan 2016].

249 Privileges Committee, Parliament of NSW, *Citizen's Right of Reply (UNSW)* (Report 60, 2012): <http://www.parliament.nsw.gov.au/prod/parlment/committee.nsf/0/98221f9296445648ca2579d600021d7a/$FILE/Report%2060%20UNSW.pdf> [accessed 4 Jan 2016].

Dr Barach also instituted defamation proceedings against the university and various members of its staff.[250] The university responded by contending that its dismissal of Dr Barach was justified on the basis of his being 'a cheat and an incorrigible liar who has plagiarized the work of colleagues and repeatedly falsified his credentials'.[251] It cited more than 130 occasions when it contended Dr Barach had been dishonest, including lying to colleagues, faking affiliations with Harvard University, manipulating data in a study, and making poor clinical decisions that caused suffering to patients.[252] Dr Barach failed in an action in respect of the fairness of his dismissal from employment at trial and then on appeal.[253]

However, in a dramatic development after four years of legal conflict, Dr Barach unreservedly withdrew his allegations against the university and issued written apologies to Professor Hilmer and other staff. In his letter to Dr McIntosh dated 23 April 2014, Dr Barach stated that:

> During the period after my cessation of employment with UNSW, I [Paul Barach] made assertions within the pursuit of my claims and publicly including to journalists and Mr John Kaye MP [who championed Dr Barach's claims in parliament] that I now know not to be true. I accept that you [Andrew McIntosh] have acted with propriety at all times and I unreservedly withdraw my allegations and apologise to you for any offence they caused.[254]

The case represents a salutary reminder that a percentage of the 'revelations' by whistleblowers are not well-founded.

The University of Newcastle. While Australian universities generally have whistleblower policies and protections, the instances of publicized whistleblowing indicate that some universities do not always 'walk the talk'.

In 2010 the University of Newcastle came to media attention for its treatment of a whistleblower, Dr Michelle Adams, who had made what should have been a protected disclosure about two fellow academics for plagiarism.[255] For Dr Adams there was personal fallout after the allegations she made against the two academics for plagiarizing an honours students' thesis in 2003. The matter took a toll on Dr Adams's mental health and she ceased to be able to work; she was of the view that the matter had been mishandled by the university and claimed the affair 'had had an enormous impact on her career, family and mental health'.[256] Dr Adams asserted that the failure of the university to deal with the allegations promptly

---

[250] The action was vigorously contested in its interlocutory phases: see eg, *Barach v University of New South Wales* [2011] NSWSC 99; *Barach v University of New South Wales* [2011] NSWSC 431; *Barach v University of New South Wales* [2013] NSWSC 1054.

[251] Richard Guilliatt, 'UNSW Broadside in Paul Barach Battle: Reputations at Stake', *The Australian*, 30 January 2013: <http://www.theaustralian.com.au/higher-education/unsw-broadside-in-paul-barach-battle-reputations-at-stake/story-e6frgcjx-1226564497160> [accessed 4 Jan 2016].

[252] Ibid.

[253] *Barach v University of New South Wales* [2010] FWA 1170; (2010) 62 AILR 101-127; *Barach v University of New South Wales* [2010] FWAFB 3307; (2010) 194 IR 259.

[254] Quoted in Privileges Committee, Parliament of NSW, *Citizen's Right of Reply (Dr Andrew McIntosh)* (Report 74, 2015) 3: <http://www.parliament.nsw.gov.au/prod/parlment/committee.nsf/0/742abac2ef65387eca257df9001c9e1f/$FILE/Report%2074%20.pdf> (viewed 2 May 2015). See also, Richard Guilliatt, 'Academic 'Conman' Paul Barach Sorry for False Claims', *The Australian*, 2 August 2014: <http://www.theaustralian.com.au/news/health-science/academic-conman-paul-barach-sorry-for-false-claims/story-e6frg8y6-1227010606667> (viewed 2 May 2015).

[255] Donna Page, 'Asking for Trouble', *Newcastle Herald*, 8 May 2010, 6, available at : <http://newsstore.fairfax.com.au/apps/viewDocument.ac;jsessionid=F2C1B2EF2556A130B923D75C7AF8C5B2?sy=afr&pb=all_ffx&dt=selectRange&dr=1month&so=relevance&sf=text&sf=headline&rc=10&rm=200&sp=brs&cls=356&clsPage=1&docID=NCH1005081S20IGMS9MC> (viewed 2 May 2015).

[256] Ibid.

gave the impression that the allegations were false.[257] She did not lodge a formal written complaint, despite being advised to do so, and the matter was not formally investigated by the university until 2006, three years after the original complaint was said to have been made to senior staff.[258] In relation to the papers that allegedly used the plagiarised data of the student, the university was unable to find any publications that had been published and distributed in print or online and decided that no further investigation needed to be undertaken.[259] However, media investigations found three of the publications online—they had also been listed on the university website as 'C1 documents' under guidelines set by the Department of Innovation, Industry, Science and Research (DIISR).[260] Another document consisting of an academic workload register reporting listed the publications and points awarded to the academics in question.[261]

A review of the 2006 investigation was undertaken when Dr Adams raised the matter directly with the university's Vice-Chancellor. In this review the original findings were upheld, although a second investigation found that the honours student had not been appropriately acknowledged in the publications, leading to the academics in question being counselled about the need to acknowledge sources in a proper way.[262]

The University of Newcastle has been the subject of a number of allegations of plagiarism.[263] Some have been established; some have not. Another academic, Ian Firns, a sessional lecturer in the Graduate School of Business at the University of Newcastle, became a whistleblower. He reported a separate case of plagiarism to ICAC.[264] In its investigation ICAC found two university senior staff, who no longer worked at the University of Newcastle, had failed to apply the university's plagiarism policy to students at an offshore campus of the university's Graduate School of Business in Malaysia.[265] The allegations were upheld against University officials for failing to apply the plagiarism policy and failing to make proper investigations into the allegations.[266] Mr Firns had complained to university staff that 15 students had substantially plagiarized parts of assignments that had been submitted to him for assessment.[267] The central concern of the ICAC investigation had been the subsequent conduct of university

[257] Ibid.

[258] Ibid.

[259] Ibid.

[260] Ibid.

[261] Ibid.

[262] Ibid.

[263] A number of claims were never proved. They included the notable case of Dr Michael Spautz, a Senior Lecturer, who made claims of plagiarism against another more senior academic in the same Department at the University of Newcastle, and went public with the allegations. He was sacked by the university and then proceeded to sue unsuccessfully for defamation: see Brian Martin, 'Disruption and Due Process: The Dismissal of Dr Spautz from the University of Newcastle' (1983) 26(1) *Vestes* 3, available at: <https://www.uow.edu.au/~bmartin/pubs/83vestes.html> [accessed 4 Jan 2016]; and John Biggs, 'The University of Newcastle: Prelude to Dawkins' in John Biggs and Richard Davis (eds), *The Subversion of Australian Universities* (Wollongong: Fund for Intellectual Dissent, 2002), available at: <http://pandora.nla.gov.au/pan/33459/20030221-0000/www.uow.edu.au/arts/sts/bmartin/dissent/documents/sau/index.html> (archived 21 February 2003) [accessed 4 Jan 2016]. An updated version of Biggs' chapter entitled 'The University of Newcastle: Prelude to Dawkins, An Update' is available at: <http://www.bmartin.cc/dissent/documents/sau/sau09rev.pdf> [accessed 4 Jan 2016]. It contains detail omitted from the original version for 'legal reasons' (n 1), and includes an update on the Bayley-Jones' case. This case concerned a dispute between a doctoral student, Coral Bayley-Jones, her supervisor Associate Professor Don Parkes, and the University of Newcastle.

[264] Page, above n 255.

[265] Independent Commission Against Corruption (NSW), *Report on Investigation into the University of Newcastle's Handling of Plagiarism Allegations* (Sydney, June 2005) 6, available at: <http://www.icac.nsw.gov.au/investigations/past-investigations/investigationdetail/61> [accessed 4 Jan 2016].

[266] Ibid.

[267] Ibid.

officials who essentially ignored Mr Firns's complaint but then adopted a new marking process that favoured the students who were said to have engaged in the plagiarism.[268]

Mr Firns's concerns were that a 'soft marking' approach was taken by the Graduate School towards international, full-fee paying students.[269] The ICAC investigation report identified an unreceptiveness to the concerns raised by the whistleblower and noted:

> A matter of particular concern throughout the relevant events was the dismissive attitude displayed by certain senior managers to the original claim, made in plain and strong terms, that a number of assignments contained plagiarised material. Rather than an open-minded approach and a determination to investigate, senior management displayed a tendency to avoid that course (which was the only one consistent with policy obligations) and treated the person who initially identified the plagiarism and his claims with an attitude marked by disdain and irritation, accompanied later by signs of abruptness and an unwillingness to divulge information on the University's handling of the allegations.[270]

As to the importance of dealing with the allegations of plagiarism appropriately, ICAC stated:

> The University of Newcastle is widely regarded as one of the State's leading tertiary institutions. The community places its trust in its educational institutions to ensure that academic standards are maintained. To provide an improper advantage to any group of students, including full fee-paying students, is antithetical to the essential principles that underpin the integrity of tertiary education. Such improper advantage constitutes a breach of public trust. In the context of the present investigation, plagiarism, the passing off of the works of others as the students own work, impugns academic integrity and must be dealt with swiftly and appropriately by well-directed action including the imposition of appropriate sanctions. Plagiarism undermines academic standards and results in unfairness to the honest and competent student. It must be prevented.[271]

The motives of the academics who failed to deal with the plagiarism allegations appeared to be a desire to avoid damaging the university's offshore programme.[272] However, ICAC found that this motive was 'entirely illegitimate...as it entailed the undermining of academic standards by effectively side-lining proper investigative procedures required to be undertaken in accordance with the plagiarism policy'.[273] Inherent in its findings was that the university's response to the revelations of the whistleblower had been seriously inadequate and inappropriate.

The University of New South Wales. In 2001 Margaret Love, a commercial project manager at the University of New South Wales, blew the whistle about the Director of the Educational Testing Centre (ETC), Associate Professor Jim Tognolini, for employing various family members and engaging in financial mismanagement.[274] The ETC was at the centre of the university's move to commercialize its activities and had a AUS$13 million turnover with multiple large contracts. It should have been highly profitable but it was not.[275] Sixty full-time staff were employed by the ETC but 20 of them were apparently related to the Director. Any mention of these factors by Margaret Love, particularly the poor financial state of the ETC, was met with bullying and harassment.[276] When Margaret Love reported the

---

268 Ibid, 9.
269 Ibid.
270 Ibid.
271 Ibid, 10.
272 Ibid, 11.
273 Ibid.
274 Derek Maitland, 'Uni Bullying, Cronyism, Malpractice, Etc' (2004) Issue 36 *The Whistle* 3, 3, available at: <http://www.bmartin.cc/dissent/contacts/au_wba/whistle200401.pdf> [accessed 4 Jan 2016].
275 Ibid.
276 Ibid.

situation to university management, there was inaction. This led her to make a complaint to the Auditor-General's Department which referred the matter to ICAC, but an investigation was not conducted. Subsequently, Margaret Love made a complaint to the Auditor-General's office under the *Protected Disclosures Act* 1994 (NSW) (now the Public Interest Disclosures Act 1994 (NSW)).

At the same time the University of New South Wales decided to conduct an internal audit of the ETC and, in doing so, revealed Margaret Love's identity as the whistleblower. This led to reprisals.[277] The university response to her claims of bullying and harassment was lacklustre and so Margaret Love made a complaint to the NSW Ombudsman. Thus, two investigations ran in parallel,[278] although they dealt with different issues—with 'the Auditor-General dealing with "management and waste" in ETC and the Ombudsman's office examining the university's mistreatment of [Love's] rights under protected disclosure, its handling of her complaints generally, and the nepotism in the unit'.[279] In 2002 the Ombudsman and Auditor-General's reports vindicated Margaret Love's complaints on both fronts. However, the impact on her health and employment was significant.[280] Professor Tognolini resigned from the ETC after the release of the reports but it was reported that this did not lead to considerable improvement.[281] The NSW Ombudsman report confirmed that there had been 'widespread nepotism, cronyism and maladministration at the centre' and there was insufficient protection of whistleblowers at the university.[282] Further, the Auditor-General found that there was a 'serious lack of management controls and proper accountability within the centre'.[283] Thus Ms Love was supported but by that stage the personal consequences for her had become highly deleterious.

RMIT. Another instance of whistleblowing arose at the RMIT School of Engineering and Aerospace which became the subject of a report by the Victorian Ombudsman under section 103 of the *Whistleblowers Protection Act* 2001 (Vic).[284] A public interest disclosure was made to the Ombudsman in October 2009 alleging that Mr Nihal Hana, a staff member at the RMIT School of Engineering (TAFE), had assisted students enrolled in the Advanced Diploma of Engineering (Aerospace) to cheat in their 2008 and 2009 examinations.[285] Mr Hana was a team leader, academic adviser, and teacher in the Advanced Diploma of Engineering (Aerospace) who had 'considerable responsibilities' within RMIT's aerospace and aviation training programme but was subject to very little oversight by others at the School.[286]

The investigation found that 'Mr Hana did assist students to cheat in two examinations. This resulted in the students achieving marks well beyond their academic ability and allowed them to progress their studies in the advanced diploma and in one instance, to graduate'.[287]

---

277 Ibid.
278 Ibid, 4.
279 Ibid.
280 Ibid.
281 Ibid.
282 Aban Contractor and Gerard Noonan, 'Testing the Limits', *The Sydney Morning Herald*, 21 March 2002: <http://www.smh.com.au/articles/2002/03/20/Unsw.htm> [accessed 4 Jan 2016].
283 Ibid.
284 Brouwer, George E, *Whistleblowers Protection Act 2001*: Investigation into an Allegation of Improper Conduct within RMIT's School of Engineering (TAFE)—Aerospace (Ombudsman Victoria, July 2010), available at: <https://www.ombudsman.vic.gov.au/Publications/Parliamentary-Reports/Investigation-into-an-allegation-of-improper-condu> [accessed 4 Jan 2016].
285 Ibid, [11].
286 Ibid, [14].
287 Ibid, [15].

The evidence from the teacher who administered the examination in November 2008 was that three students (Students A, B, and C, two of whom were Australian citizens and one who was studying on a Temporary Protection Visa) arrived 30 minutes late for the examination in which they were said to have cheated. The teacher gave evidence that:

> [U]pon marking the three students' examination responses she 'was surprised' that the:
> - students' responses were very similar, and in some cases identical, to her master copy of the examination solutions
> - students obtained examination marks that the teacher considered to be 'well above' the academic ability of the particular students. The results obtained were student C: 88.5 per cent; student A: 92.8 per cent; and student B: 67.1 per cent.[288]

The teacher formed the view that the students had copied the master examination solutions and advised the Industry Manager at the time that Mr Hana had requested that the teacher provide him with a copy of the examination questions and solutions some days before the examination.[289] The teacher alleged that Mr Hana had provided the examination paper and solutions to the students who then stored this information in the memory of the calculators that they used in the examination.[290] The Ombudsman's investigation found that in the period leading up to the examination there had been numerous phone calls and text messages between Mr Hana and Student A.[291] There was a further allegation made that a separate incident had occurred involving Mr Hana providing an examination paper to Student A for an earlier examination in June 2009. Mr Hana had allegedly requested the lecturer teaching 'Aircraft Instrument Fundamentals' to provide him with a copy of the examination paper.[292] Student A was re-sitting the examination after failing the first time and on the resit scored 67 out of 70 points. Again there was substantial telephone contact between Mr Hana and Student A around the time of the exam. The Ombudsman reached the conclusion that Mr Hana had assisted Student A to cheat and that the two had a relationship that went beyond one of student–teacher, as highlighted by the level of phone contact between them.[293]

Mr Hana had substantial debts and a gambling habit. He had attracted the attention of his colleagues (although not his managers) for suspicious behaviour during his employment with RMIT. This behaviour consisted of 'disappearances during the day without explanation; unauthorized private tutoring of a RMIT student; and frequent personal contact with students outside business hours'.[294] The Ombudsman concluded that he was an officer who was vulnerable to corruption.

Allegations of the students' cheating were brought before the Discipline Board of RMIT, but it found there was insufficient evidence to draw a conclusion that the students had cheated.[295] The Ombudsman found that not all the evidence was provided to the Discipline Board and that the preparation and prosecution of the disciplinary matter were inadequate.[296] Once the disciplinary proceedings were not upheld against the students, the information that Mr Hana had assisted those students to cheat was not pursued or investigated by the university.[297] The Victorian Ombudsman expressed concerns about the way in which the university had

[288] Ibid, [89].
[289] Ibid, [92]–[93].
[290] Ibid, [149].
[291] Ibid, [163].
[292] Ibid, [220].
[293] Ibid, [259].
[294] Ibid, [31].
[295] Ibid, [21], [206], [248].
[296] Ibid, [21].
[297] Ibid, [28].

dealt with the disclosure by failing to address so serious a matter. The university's failure to investigate the matter properly also left those staff members who had raised the concerns unsupported and open to attempted reprisals by Mr Hana.[298] The Ombudsman also made findings that maladministration at the university had allowed the corrupt conduct to occur.[299] In addition to finding that RMIT staff at all levels had little or no awareness of the *Whistleblowers Protection Act* 2001 (Vic) and other related university policies,[300] the Ombudsman found:

> This investigation has highlighted significant issues at both the school as well as university level relating to poor and inappropriate practices; unauthorized decision-making and poor advice provided; non-compliance with corporate policies and procedures; lack of awareness of proper processes; non-compliance with legislative requirements; and poor management of health and safety issues.[301]

The Vice-Chancellor of RMIT raised concerns that this matter was dealt with as a 'public interest disclosure' under the Whistleblowers Protection Act 2001 by the Ombudsman.[302] However, the Ombudsman stated in relation to the nature of public interest disclosures that:

> They are not based on the consequences of misconduct, but on whether the misconduct would, if proved, constitute a reasonable ground for dismissing or dispensing with the services of a public officer who was or is engaged in that conduct. A tertiary lecturer who assists his or her students to cheat, whatever the consequences, should be liable to dismissal.[303]

Problematic aspects of the saga included the absence of proper understanding of responsibilities in respect of whistleblowers by the university, its lack of support for the whistleblower, and the university's failure to be suitably responsive to the issues raised.

Conclusions

At the start of this chapter, reference was made to the 1995 recommendations of the United States Commission on Research Integrity which recommended a bill of rights for whistleblowers in the research environment. In due course these were implemented by the Office of Research Integrity. Two decades later, the Commission's recommendations remain a helpful guide to research institutions, including universities, providing as they do for both entitlements and obligations for those who make accusations of impropriety in the research environment:

> *Communication*: Whistleblowers are free to disclose lawfully whatever information supports a reasonable belief of research misconduct... An individual or institution that retaliates against any person making protected disclosures engages in prohibited obstruction of investigations of research misconduct... Whistleblowers must respect the confidentiality of sensitive information and give legitimate institutional structures an opportunity to function. Should a whistleblower elect to make a lawful disclosure that violates institutional rules of confidentiality, the institution may thereafter legitimately limit the whistleblower's access to further information about the case.
>
> *Protection from Retaliation*: Institutions have a duty not to tolerate or engage in retaliation against good-faith whistleblowers. This duty includes providing appropriate and timely relief

298 Ibid, [35].
299 Ibid, [47].
300 Ibid, [458]. See also, [480].
301 Ibid, [42].
302 Ibid, [54].
303 Ibid, [57].

to ameliorate the consequences of actual or threatened reprisals, and holding accountable those who retaliate. Whistleblowers and other witnesses to possible research misconduct have a responsibility to raise their concerns honorably and with foundation.

Fair Procedures: Institutions have a duty to provide fair and objective procedures for examining and resolving complaints, disputes, and allegations of research misconduct. In cases of alleged retaliation that are not resolved through institutional intervention, whistleblowers should have an opportunity to defend themselves in a proceeding where they can present witnesses and confront those they charge with retaliation against them, except when they violate rules of confidentiality.

[...]

Procedures free from partiality: Institutions have a duty to follow procedures that are not tainted by partiality arising from personal or institutional conflict of interest or other sources of bias. Whistleblowers have a responsibility to act within legitimate institutional channels when raising concerns about the integrity of research. They have the right to raise objections concerning the possible partiality of those selected to review their concerns without incurring retaliation.

Information: Institutions have a duty to elicit and evaluate fully and objectively information about concerns raised by whistleblowers. Whistleblowers may have unique knowledge needed to evaluate thoroughly responses from those whose actions are questioned. Consequently, a competent investigation may involve giving whistleblowers one or more opportunities to comment on the accuracy and completeness of information relevant to their concerns, except when they violate rules of confidentiality.

Timely processes: Institutions have a duty to handle cases involving alleged research misconduct as expeditiously as is possible without compromising responsible resolutions. When cases drag on for years, the issue becomes the dispute rather than its resolution. Whistleblowers have a responsibility to facilitate expeditious resolution of cases by good-faith participation in misconduct procedures.

Vindication: At the conclusion of proceedings, institutions have a responsibility to credit promptly—in public and/or in private as appropriate—those whose allegations are substantiated.[304]

The advantage, and the distinguishing characteristics of this code, are that it frames rights and responsibilities in a reciprocal way. This is the kind of balance which should be pursued. It is clear that the role of whistleblowers within academia to expose corrupt and fraudulent practices is vital. However, it is also apparent that the making of allegations by whistleblowers for collateral, irrational, non-evidence-based, or vindictive reasons can cause enormous harm that is not fully remediable—the mud of whistleblowers' accusations sticks. The harm can be to both persons and institutions.

Thus, any protection provided to whistleblowers in the research environment (as well as in others) must be qualified. If it emerges that their allegations are not bona fide or if they are not properly communicative with investigations, that may entail a waiver of at least some of their protections and entitlements.

The *Whistling While They Work* study produced a useful framework for best practice for whistleblowing programmes under the following five key elements:

1. Organizational commitment
   a. Management commitment
   b. Whistleblowing policy
   c. Resources
   d. Evaluation and engagement

[304] Commission on Research Integrity, above n 77, 32–3 and 51–3 (formatting altered; footnote omitted).

2. Facilitating reporting
   a. Who may report wrongdoing?
   b. What should be reported?
   c. Multiple reporting pathways
   d. Anonymity
3. Assessment and investigation of reports
   a. Identification and tracking of reports
   b. Assessment procedures
   c. Confidentiality
   d. Equality and natural justice
4. Internal witness support and protection
   a. Whistleblower/internal witness support
   b. Information and advice
   c. Preventing and remedying detrimental action
   d. Exit and follow-up strategy
5. An integrated organizational approach
   a. Clear organizational model for support
   b. Shared responsibility for whistleblower support
   c. Embedded policies and procedures.[305]

Notwithstanding the rhetoric of whistleblower support and protection, including within public disclosure legislation, the price for many whistleblowers' careers and health has been highly adverse.[306] The experiences of Professor Robert Sprague, Professor Stephen Bolsin, Dr Nancy Olivieri, and Aubrey Blumsohn, to name but some, are illustrative of the importance that such persons can play in bringing to light information about misconduct or other matters of public concern that may otherwise go unnoticed and unaddressed. Whistleblowing needs to become part of the scholarly landscape in the sense of being responded to sensitively and constructively. It needs to be facilitated in both education and practice.[307] This requires changes in mindset and values so that tertiary and research institutions are less inclined to respond defensively and protectively when allegations are made from within.

A challenge for the scholarly sector is to work more effectively towards cultural change so that those who raise legitimate concerns from inside receive effective protection and so that opportunities to learn from what is asserted are seized authentically. Part of such a response may be the promulgation of a common 'Bill of Whistleblowers' Rights' so that those minded to reveal concerns that they have formed about the conduct of colleagues know with precision what their entitlements are, what the rights of those against whom they are making accusations are, and what are the procedures that will apply to the issues that they are raising. In many jurisdictions there is uncertainty about the extent to which whistleblower legislation—for instance applicable to public servants—applies to those in universities and within the public sector. This is remediable by a combination of legislative extension into such areas, and, where that is not possible, the promulgation of clear statements of rights and procedures that apply (preferably commonly) within such institutions. After that, publicizing of such structures and arrangements is important.

305 Roberts, Brown, and Olsen (2011), above n 29, 12–16 (formatting altered).

306 See Morgan, above n 105.

307 Thomas Faunce, Stephen Bolsin, and Wei-Ping Chan, 'Supporting Whistleblowers in Academic Medicine: Training and Respecting the Courage of Professional Conscience' (2004) 30(1) *Journal of Medical Ethics* 40, 42.

This is not to create a system whereby those with grievances, malign vindictiveness, and rivalrous intent are given an unfair forum to make baseless accusations that can damage others' reputations and careers. It is important to acknowledge that the raising of such matters is intensely stressful, distressing, and potentially harmful to those the subject of such assertions. It needs to be clearly understood by all (and stated explicitly within any Bill of Whistleblowers' Rights) that accusations are no more than that and that the fact that they are raised by a colleague should not be regarded per se as lending them legitimacy. Such matters only have substance when they are properly proved within a system in which those the subject of whistleblowing have a fair and full opportunity to refute what is raised against them. In addition, where mala fides becomes apparent in the motives of whistleblowers, they must not be allowed to enjoy the benefit of protections of the usual legal kind, including immunity against defamation actions. This kind of balance (difficult though it is) is fundamental to a scheme that does not give undue weight to allegations and does not erode collegiality by creating a toxic culture of informing and informers.

Without such a system with checks, balances, and entitlements, that in turn commands the confidence of all potentially affected, the capacity to regulate research misconduct, conflicts of interest, plagiarism, and sexual misconduct is seriously eroded. In addition, without such protection prudent advice to scholars proposing to blow the whistle must be: 'In your own best interests, *don't*'. This risks proliferating a culture which has resulted too often in scholars, universities, and research bodies succumbing to the temptations of venery, fraud, and retributivism. It goes to the very heart of the capacity to respond effectively to such threats to scholarly integrity.

12

REASSERTING SCHOLARLY INTEGRITY

Introduction

This book has grappled with the ethical and practical issues that emerge when scholarship is alleged to have miscarried—how the various forms of misconduct should be defined, how employing institutions and regulators should respond to allegations of misconduct, when accusations should be regarded as proved, and what should be the consequences of established misconduct engaged in by those associated with what purports to be the generation and imparting of knowledge.

Conceptions of scholarship have evolved as opportunities for scholarly work have changed.[1] By the 21st century, scholarliness and scholarship have come to emanate from many sources and to have multifarious forms and applications. Advanced study and literature itself at one time were the preserve of monks[2] and later shifted to the halls of academia. However, with the democratization of knowledge in the Internet Age, scholarly endeavours are now accessible from learned sources online, from the writing of journalists in a variety of contexts, and from the publications of a wide array of persons who develop learned interests in specialist areas, in relation to their employment or otherwise, and who publish their work in diverse ways. Many who have obtained tertiary qualifications, or who may once have spent time employed within academia, publish scholarly analyses of issues in an attempt to arrogate weight to their views or to achieve a particular objective. Their scholarship may be ideologically driven or it may be altruistic. It may be vocational. For some it is part and parcel of their routine work.

There is motivation and financial and reputational advantage in being identified as scholarly. This even extends to the work of politicians, practising medical practitioners, scientists, lawyers, and judicial officers who may have no formal affiliations with academia but who may seek the kudos from being regarded as knowledgeable and scholarly. In addition, research institutions, forensic science laboratories and institutes of forensic medicine routinely contribute to the body of specialist knowledge. In the forensic context, scientists and medical practitioners, amongst many others, base their opinions for the courts on an extensive body of published scholarship.

Unsurprisingly, as this book has chronicled, fraud and deception by scholars are not a new scourge. Such conduct dates back at least to the ancient Greeks. In latter times a literature has erupted which purports to expose such conduct and to disabuse of confidence in the work of an array of previously highly regarded scholars. It is more than a retributive cutting down of tall scholarly poppies or an acting out of a 'crab mentality'[3] towards

---

[1] See Gill Nicholls, *The Challenge to Scholarship: Rethinking Learning, Teaching and Research* (New York: Routledge, 2005).

[2] See Thomas Cahill, *How the Irish Saved Civilization: The Untold Story of Ireland's Heroic Role From the Fall of Rome to the Rise of Medieval Europe* (New York: Nan A Talese, 1995); Gary B Ferngren, *Medicine and Religion: A Historical Introduction* (Baltimore: Johns Hopkins University Press, 2014) 98ff.

[3] A term that comes from the propensity of crabs in a fisherman's basket to pull back other crabs when they attempt to make their escape.

more successful or prominent colleagues.[4] For instance, the great astronomer, Ptolemy of Alexandria (90–168AD), has been accused of using without any attribution observations of stars made by Hipparchus of Rhodes (162–127 BC), who himself had used much earlier Babylonian observations as if they were his own.[5] Careful analyses have resulted in there being little doubt that the eminent scientist, Isaac Newton, manipulated data to fit his own theories,[6] perhaps struggling with the possibility that his real results might be interpreted as supportive of the theories of his arch-rival, Robert Hooke.[7] Mendel's population studies are subject to serious scholarly doubt in terms of the accuracy of the data upon which they were based.[8] The conduct of Burt,[9] Blondlot,[10] and Pasteur[11] are but a few later examples of flawed and disingenuous methodology engaged in by scholars for self-serving reasons. Grave questions have even enveloped the legitimacy of many of Freud's case studies.[12] The Charles Brimstone butterfly fraud of 1702[13] and the hoax perpetrated on Dr Beringer in the 1720s[14] are further examples of improper behaviour that have been shown to have occurred in the order of three centuries ago. The midwife toad,[15] patchwork mouse,[16] and unlikely lichen[17] hoaxes are further more modern instances.

---

[4] For psychological explanations of inclinations towards bringing down high achievers, see Norman T Feather, 'Attitudes Towards the High Achiever: The Fall of the Tall Poppy' (1989) 41(3) *Australian Journal of Psychology* 239.

[5] Owen Gingerich, 'Was Ptolemy a Fraud?' (1980) 21 *Quarterly Journal of the Royal Astronomical Society* 253; Robert R Newton, *The Crime of Claudius Ptolemy* (Baltimore: Johns Hopkins University Press, 1977).

[6] See Alan E Shapiro, 'Skating on the Edge: Newton's Investigation of Chromatic Dispersion and Achromatic Prisms and Lenses' in Jed Z Buchwald and Allan Franklin (eds), *Wrong for the Right Reasons* (Dordrecht: Springer, 2005); David H Freedman, *Wrong: Why Experts Keep Failing Us—And How to Know When Not to Trust Them* (New York: Little, Brown and Co, 2010).

[7] See Eugenie Samuel Reich, *Plastic Fantastic: How the Biggest Fraud in Physics Shook the Scientific World* (New York: Palgrave Macmillan, 2009) 47.

[8] In his studies of hereditary characteristics arising from his pea-plant crossings, Gregor Mendel reported near-perfect ratios, and therefore ones that were statistically very unlikely. When Mendel crossed hybrid plants, he predicted and found that exactly one-third were pure dominants and two-thirds were hybrids. This resulted in the ground-breaking critique by Ronald A Fisher, 'Has Mendel's Work Been Rediscovered?' (1936) 1(2) *Annals of Science* 115; see also, Allan Franklin, Anthony WF Edwards, Daniel J Fairbanks, Daniel L Hartl et al. *Ending the Mendel–Fisher Controversy* (Pittsburgh: University of Pittsburgh Press, 2008).

[9] See Leon J Kamin, *The Science and Politics of IQ* (Potomac, Md: Lawrence Erlbaum Associates, 1974); Leslie S Hearnshaw, *Cyril Burt, Psychologist* (Ithaca, NY: Cornell University Press, 1979). See also, Arthur R Jensen, 'IQ and Science: The Mysterious Burt Affair' (1991) Issue 105, *Public Interest* 93; Raymond E Fancher, 'The Burt Case: Another Foray' (1991) 253(5027) *Science* 1565.

[10] See Irving M Klotz, 'The N-Ray Affair' (1980) 242(5) *Scientific American* 168.

[11] See John Waller, *Fabulous Science: Fact and Fiction in the History of Scientific Discovery* (Oxford: Oxford University Press, 2004).

[12] See eg, Michel Onfray, *Le Crépuscule d'une Idole: L'affabulation Freudienne* (Paris: B Grasset, 2010); Frank J Galloway, 'Reassessing Freud's Case Histories: The Social Construction of Psychoanalysis' (1991) 82(2) *Isis* 245.

[13] Michael A Salmon, Peter Marren, and Basil Harley, *The Aurelian Legacy: British Butterflies and Their Collectors* (Berkeley: University of California Press, 2000) 66; see too, David KC Cooper (ed), *Doctors of Another Calling: Physicians Who are Known Best in Fields Other Than Medicine* (Maryland: Rowman & Littlefield, 2014) 53.

[14] See Johann Bartholomäus Adam Beringer, *The Lying Stones of Dr Johann Bartholomew Adam Beringer, being his Lithographiæ Wirceburgensis* (originally published in 1726 with 50 medical corollaries as the inaugural dissertation of GL Hueber, translated and annotated by Melvin E Jahn and Daniel J Woolf; Berkeley: University of California Press, 1963).

[15] See Arthur Koestler, *The Case of the Midwife Toad* (New York: Random House, 1971); Lester R Aronson, 'The Case of "The Case of the Midwife Toad"' (1975) 5(2) *Behavior Genetics* 115; Sander Gliboff, 'The Case of Paul Kammerer: Evolution and Experimentation in the Early 20th Century' (2006) 39(3) *Journal of the History of Biology* 525; E Lachman, 'Famous Scientific Hoaxes' (1976) 69(3) *The Journal of the Oklahoma State Medical Association* 87.

[16] See Joseph R Hixson, *The Patchwork Mouse* (Garden City, NY: Anchor Press, 1976).

[17] See Karl Sabbagh, *A Rum Affair: A True Story of Botanical Fraud* (New York: Farrar, Strauss and Giroux, 2000) 23f.

The recent re-analyses of the work of prominent researchers have been an important contribution both to understanding the status of such persons' research and also appreciating better the liberties that have been taken with proper scholarly methodology in the past. Scholars and their pursuits have always attracted controversy—contemporaneously with their discoveries and their publication, as well as later. However, the past two decades have seen an escalation in allegations and proven instances of serious scholarly misconduct, especially in relation to published research.

What has changed with the 'Information Age' is the incidence and potential influence of scholarly misconduct, as well as, more positively, the capacity more readily to identify it. In addition, the forums for publication, the pressures to innovate, develop and publish, and the requirements for research productivity, have intensified—as prerequisites for advancement of career and even for retention of workplace status.[18] In addition, the competition for research funding and the benefits, both financial and in terms of scholarly kudos, have grown exponentially in recent years. Frustration in many scholarly workplaces has also increased, resulting in such unethical conduct being able to be rationalized readily as a form of rebellion against or a by-product of the unfair demands of the contemporary scholarly establishment. The combination of these phenomena translates into a level of temptation that too many have chosen not to resist.

In its modern form medico-scientific research has been revealed as fundamentally flawed at an unprecedented level by exposés going to the heart of its ethical credibility and its reliability. The checks and balances in place to guard against such deficits have failed too often, and failed badly. Retractions in learned journals have exploded in number and seriousness, many arising from fraud but others arising from the failures within the publishing process of the checks and balances against significant error. Ingenious ways around peer reviewing have been found, and for a time have succeeded.

Research misconduct has proliferated and assumed many different dimensions, often being characterized by completely fictitious sets of data (the hardest form of research misconduct to detect), or results that have been manipulated and misinterpreted for nefarious reasons. Conflicts of interest involving individuals and institutions, including universities and large research bodies, have been shown to be common and highly problematic in terms of the risks they carry for the legitimacy of research and development, and the adverse outcomes they have generated.

Plagiarism has become rife within modern scholarship, at all levels. The opportunity for 'cutting and pasting' from the internet has resulted in a remarkable incidence of inappropriate usage of others' work—by students, academics, judges, politicians, popular authors, and journalists, to name but a few. Some have brazenly attempted to rationalize their behaviour as justified in an age of unique accessibility to information, proclaiming the age of originality to have come to an end. Others have contended that their usage of others' work was of no consequence, an error, a consequence of inadvertent absorption of others' ideas, or the fault of others, such as research assistants, co-authors, or editors. However, another perspective upon the ubiquity of information availability, often in circumstances over which authors have little control, is that integrity in the use of others' intellectual work needs now, more than ever, to be mandatory, at least in terms of authors unequivocally acknowledging sources and their use of them.

---

[18] See Tracey Bretag, 'Publish or Perish: Ramifications for Online Academic Publishing' in Laura A Wankel and Charles Wankel (eds), *Misbehavior Online in Higher Education* (Bingley, UK: Emerald Group Publishing Limited, 2012).

Forensic misconduct has emerged as a significant contributor to miscarriages of justice. Misportrayal of the results of testing and dubious interpretation of data have the potential to lead to dire consequences in all theatres of litigation—criminal, civil, and family.

Disputation and denigration among scholars have occurred in ways that have shown that the priorities of those involved have been more their own egos, petty rivalries, and ambitions than the rectitude of the theories they espouse.

Sexual misconduct continues to be a source of vulnerability and oppression for junior staff and students alike within the academy. Unedifying contention has taken place about the ownership of the fruits of scholarship with resort to spurious technicalities. On occasion, the complexity of funding arrangements has been manipulated for dishonest purposes.

Whistleblowers usually communicate their concerns in good faith, but sometimes malignly and causing harm—whatever their motives, they do so at their own peril and in both universities and research institutions in the private and government sector often with inadequate protection and support.

Supervision, expectations of falsifiability, random audits, ethics committees, inquiries, expert reports, external oversight mechanisms, rhetoric in relation to research integrity, and peer-review processes have not inhibited the multiple forms of assault that have been perpetrated on scholarly integrity. Malefactors from within the academy and working in research institutions, intent on advancement at the cost of integrity rather than the quality of their scholarship, have circumvented and undermined these processes with comparative ease, generally until it has been their arrogance that has led to detection, but only after they have caused considerable harm.

What has been chronicled in the foregoing chapters is a range of forms of impropriety in which scholars have engaged. In that regard this volume has not attempted to be exhaustive but, rather, to identify the most notorious and the most serious forms. It has also tried to show patterns and consequences of such behaviour. In doing so it has had resort to what have often been populist books that have been published in the immediate aftermath of scandals, learned articles on the status of the discipline concerned after the latest notorious episode, and articles in the popular media and in professional publications about recent developments. Much of this material is more accessible on the internet than in hard form. These pages have gone behind the scandals and reviewed their subject matter principally to contextualize what has occurred and to view it in a broad perspective, but the concentration has been on the individuals involved and their motivations as a means of considering the public interest concerns raised by scholarly misconduct and to consider how it can be responded to and deterred. The words of perpetrators of research fraud and plagiarism in explanation of their conduct have been scrutinized to review what can be learned.

A distinctive aspect of this work has been the scrutiny of the investigative processes, including the resort to law, that have attended the investigations of allegations of scholarly misconduct and an analysis of the attempts made to resolve and bring closure to the concerns expressed by whistleblowers. However, the book has also endeavoured to identify measures that could be taken to reduce the incidence of such misconduct.

Research Misconduct

Research misconduct occurs in many forms, varying from outright mistreatment of research subjects, to fabrication of results, to adoption of seriously defective methodologies, to trimming and cooking the interpretation of data. While in the past two decades definitions of research misconduct have proliferated, the formulation by Babbage[19] in 1830 of a taxonomy of such conduct[20] retains relevance as it highlights many of the aspects of dishonesty that can occur in respect of the conduct of research.[21] However, the passage of the better part of two centuries since Babbage's work has enabled identification of additional forms of scholarly misconduct in the research context that were not explicitly identified by Babbage—such as dishonesty in the proposing of research or the seeking of funding, ghostwriting[22] of research results, engagement in unfair research practices, including in respect of colleagues, failure to provide proper confidentiality in methodologies, manipulation of peer-reviewing requirements, and, arguably, failing to report misconduct by others. Viewed from one perspective, such conduct is often the product of conflict of interest as it involves illegitimate prioritizing of the interests of the researcher over honesty, outcomes over integrity, reliability of interpretations over the status of the data, or the wishes of the funder over the authenticity of the research.

Sometimes research misconduct is elaborate and carefully executed so as to maximize the prospects of escaping detection. On other occasions it is primitive and always likely to be identified. Examples of the former were the use of the blood of an owl monkey by Dr Long in his Hodgkin's disease research,[23] and the spiking of human blood with rabbit blood by Dr Dong-Pyou Han in his AIDS research. Examples of the former were the painting of spots on butterflies by William Charlton, the marking of toads by Paul Kammerer in 'The Case of the Midwife Toad', the painting of mice by William Summerlin in 'The Patchwork Mouse Affair', and the planting of clumps of lichen by Professor Harrison in 'The Unlikely Lichen Fraud'. More common is the invention of data and manipulation of statistics such as undertaken by Professor Poisson in his cancer research and by Professor Sudbø in his chromosomal work.

These pages have identified a number of psychological devices used to rationalize unethical conduct as acceptable. Often this is enabled by moral disengagement that sees otherwise ethical scholars engaging in unacceptable behaviour.[24] An outcome can be the alienation of scholars from scholarly values, thereby rendering it more acceptable for them to behave in ways which their colleagues (and previously they) would generally condemn as unethical.

In addition, it is important to observe that the temptations to engage in scholarly misconduct are legion. They can be financial—to acquire money, to save money, and to avoid losing money. They can be career advancement for the researcher. They can be a desire to attract or maintain kudos or esteem, a product of narcissism, and the expression of an excessive commitment to ambition or productivity. An example of this is the conduct of Professor Pattium

[19] See Anthony Hyman, *Charles Babbage: Pioneer of the Computer* (Oxford: Oxford University Press, 1984); Bruce Collier and James MacLachlan, *Charles Babbage and the Engines of Perfection* (New York: Oxford University Press, 1998); Patricia S Warrick, *Charles Babbage and the Countess* (Bloomington, IN: Authorhouse, 2007).

[20] Charles Babbage, *Reflections on the Decline of Science in England and on Some of its Causes* (London: B Fellowes, 1830), available at: http://www.gutenberg.org/files/1216/1216-h/1216-h.htm [accessed 4 Jan 2016].

[21] See David L Hull, *Science as a Process: An Evolutionary Account of the Social and Conceptual Development of Science* (Chicago, Ill: University of Chicago Press, 2008).

[22] See Andrew Crofts, *Ghostwriting* (London: Bloomsbury, 2009) who does not advocate fraud but promotes ghostwriting as an enjoyable and lucrative way to earn a living.

[23] See Walter Sullivan, 'Cells in Disease Study Said to Come from Monkeys' (22 January 1981) *The New York Times*: <http://www.nytimes.com/1981/01/22/us/cells-in-disease-study-said-to-come-from-monkeys.html> [accessed 4 Jan 2016]; Christopher Joyce, 'When the Cheating Has to Stop' (9 April 1981) *New Scientist* 68; see too Ellen Altman and Peter Hernon, *Research Misconduct: Issues, Implications, and Strategies* (New York: Greenwood Publishing, 1997), p 155.

[24] See, for instance, as to the psychological phenomenon, Albert Bandura, 'Selective Moral Disengagement in the Exercise of Moral Agency' (2002) 31(2) *Journal of Moral Education* 101; Albert Bandura, 'Moral Disengagement in the Perpetration of Inhumanities' (1999) 3(3) *Personality and Social Psychology Review* 193.

Chiranjeevi in India in generating over 70 plagiarized articles in the three-year period after 2004.[25] They can be to achieve ascendancy or retribution over a rival. The tragic story of the hoax perpetrated by his academic rivals at the University of Wurzberg in the 1720s on Dr Beringer and his later resort to vindication through the courts are an example in this respect.

Or they can be the result of anxiety about under-performance, including under-publication, or concern about inadequate generation of advances in research. They can be the prioritizing of a researcher's own needs or wishes over the rights of others (an issue also in the sexual misconduct context). They can be generated by a need to overcome deep-seated feelings of inadequacy or mediocrity (see, for instance, Professor Stapel). They can be exacerbated by significant personality disorders or manic aspirations (often seen in extraordinary publication rates), distorted by obsessions, and confused by delusional ideation about ends justifying means, or not needing to be subject to ordinary ethical constraints. Frequently, fraudulent research constitutes part of a pattern of excessive, frenetic productivity (see, for instance, Professor Schön, Professor Das, Professor Stapel, Dr Darsee, Dr Slutsky, Professor Fujii, Dr Bannerjee, Dr Poldermans, Dr Han, and Dr Obokata), often the product of either ambition or inadequacy on the part of the scholar. Occasionally outright psychopathy, as with Dr Edward Erin, bipolar disorder (see, for instance, Jayson Blair), or some form of unusual psychiatric illness, such as *pseudologia fantastica*[26] as was suggested in respect of Dr Prasad in Australia, intrudes.

In each case, though, research misconduct is characterized by dishonesty. It misrepresents and misleads. It betrays the trust of funders, colleagues, institutions, and patients, or it can be a pandering to the wishes of funders. Often it is born of the desire to prove a theory for which the experimental results are, inconveniently, not providing justification. Essentially, though, misconduct in research, as the examples of Diederik Stapel in respect of research fraud and Jayson Blair in respect of plagiarism, show, is no more complex than the taking of short-cuts and the prioritizing of personal interests over those of others. Sometimes, the conduct is generated by views and beliefs that are not corroborated by the fruits of rigorous scholarship, calling in the misguided researcher's mind for adjustment of outcomes (see, for example, Dr McBride).

The results of such unethical behaviour can be the adoption of a counter-therapeutic direction in treatment, the derailing of research trajectories (see, for instance, Dr Bezwoda, Dr Potti, and Dr Poldermans) and therefore the causing of death and injury. And it can waste substantial amounts of money, energy, and time. It can result in the publishing of worthless studies and distraction from constructive research pursuits. It can create or perpetuate fallacies that take time to disprove, and can radiate out unfairly to the discredit of all involved, even those who have only played peripheral or unknowing roles in the misconduct—for instance, by being, or being named as, co-authors. It can devastate the reputation of research institutions, sometimes unfairly; examples in this regard include the harm done to the regard in which Sloan Kettering was held as a result of the fraud of Dr Summerlin, the freezing of research in Professor Das's laboratory, and the dramatic contraction of funding of Riken after Dr Obokata's fraud was exposed.

A difficulty with research misconduct is that the esteem in which employers, such as universities and research institutes, are held tends to be coterminous with that of their best-known and most productive researchers. Such persons can become bright lights in the

[25] See Killugudi Jayaraman, 'Chemistry's 'Colossal' Fraud' (25 March 2008) *Royal Society of Chemistry*: http://www.rsc.org/chemistryworld/News/2008/March/25030801.asp [accessed 4 Jan 2016]; Mayank Tewari, 'Indian Professor Guilty of Plagiarism' (23 February 2008) DNA India: http://www.dnaindia.com/india/report-indian-professor-guilty-of-plagiarism-1152417 [accessed 4 Jan 2016].

[26] See generally, Bryan H King and Charles V Ford, 'Pseudologica Fantastica' (1988) 77(1) *Acta Psychiatrica Scandinavica* 1.

scholarly firmament. There is a risk that high-profile scientists (like Dr Obokata in Japan) and doctors[27] can transmogrify under the attention of the media into scientific stars and celebrity researchers. As Fahy has observed of celebrity scientists:

> These scientific stars grip the public imagination, using their vast influence to stimulate new thinking, drive scientific controversies, enhance public understanding, mobilize social movements, and shape policy. In celebrity culture, they speak for science in public. But more than that, their fame gives them power *within* science. Their stardom affects the inner workings of science, shaping the discovery of new knowledge about our natural world.
>
> Because of their profound ability to influence public life and professional research, the celebrity scientists constitute a new scientific elite.[28]

Not surprisingly, it has been found that a concomitant of celebrity status is an elevated sense of narcissism.[29] With the potential for assumption of celebrity status as a research scholar comes the temptation to acquire it illegitimately, to maintain it improperly—as with Dr McBride, a hero after his discovery of the dangers of Thalidomide—to enhance it unwarrantedly, and to misuse it for personal benefit. Professor Stapel in his autobiography has eloquently chronicled this phenomenon.

Those responsible for research misconduct can be charismatic, imposing, and powerful individuals (see, for example, Professor Harrison, Sir Cyril Burt, Professor Stapel, Professor Boldt, Dr Wakefield, Dr McBride). This makes it intimidating for whistleblowers to draw attention to their conduct and confronting for internal investigation of allegations of their actions to be conducted with independence and rigour, as well as in such a way as to satisfy others of the quality and objectivity of the investigation. It can also be logistically difficult to identify how such researchers have undertaken their research when, like Professor Stapel in The Netherlands and Associate Professor Fujii in Japan, they work across institutions, subvert ethics committees, establish unusually close relationships with their co-researchers, and involve multiple others in their research; the result can be that disentangling of their culpability can be very difficult.

In addition, it is common for allegations of research misconduct to be vehemently denied and bitterly contested, even when the evidence is overwhelming. The defence mounted may be aggressive, personal and persistent (see, for example, Professor Harrison), even after formal findings are delivered. Research misconduct is not an easy vice to admit. It goes to the heart of a scholar's reputation for integrity. Often assertions of such impropriety are met by an attempt to transfer responsibility and the mounting of accusations against another researcher, often the whistleblower, who typically is a colleague. The rationalizing and minimizing of what occurred is also common. As a response to accusations, to reframe the conduct as no more than a series of misunderstandings or mistakes is less personally confronting for the perpetrator than admission of fault, and easier for the employing institution which may be under pressure to attempt to preserve its reputation for excellence and integrity.

It has been far from uncommon for attempts to be made, at least at first, to minimize or sanitize outright research fraud. Sometimes such efforts are by the person himself or herself; sometimes by their institution. Sometimes the attempts are through campaigns through the

---

27 In the forensic domain see the pre-eminence and the high public profile of Sir Bernard Spilsbury: Andrew Rose, *Lethal Witness* (London: The History Press, 2007).

28 Declan Fahy, *The New Celebrity Scientists: Out of the Lab and Into the Limelight* (Lanham: Rowman & Littlefield, 2015) 3.

29 S Mark Young and Drew Pinsky, 'Narcissism and Celebrity' (2006) 40(5) *Journal of Research in Personality* 463; Drew Pinsky and S Mark Young, *The Mirror Effect: How Celebrity Narcissism is Seducing America* (New York: Harper, 2009).

media and on the internet, sometimes utilizing the use of 'spin doctors' and extensive rebuttals, and attempts at denigration of the accuser.

Typical examples of rationalizing and minimizing the seriousness of research fraud are assigning it to carelessness (see, for instance Dr Schön, Dr Poisson), inexperience (see, for instance, Dr Obokata) misguided enthusiasm (see, for instance, Professor Stapel, Professor Grimes), inadequate supervision over others (see, for instance, Professor Melendez, Dr Poldermans), overwork and work pressures (see, for instance, Dr Eaton), or ill health (see, for instance, Dr Summerlin, Dr Anderton, Dr Reuben).

However, the reality is that research misconduct is fraudulent, dishonest deceit that has much in common with, and sometimes overlaps with, outright criminality. This fact needs to underlie the adoption of measures to punish it and to attempt to deter its commission.

An important form of response to the escalating phenomenon of research fraud is to facilitate cultural change so that ethical forms of conduct are supported and valued. This has the potential to reduce the temptations to behave otherwise. For instance, inducements could be provided by government funders to institutions that foster ethical research, including the publication of more than just positive outcomes to research but negative findings as well. Assessing promotion of academics by reference to a limited selection of their publications, rather than giving emphasis to the numbers of publications, would also be salutary.

Concomitantly, penalties can be imposed on institutions in which unethical conduct has taken place. When such imposition of penalties emanates from funders, this can function as a potent form of dissuasion. It can function as a lever for encouraging institutions to take more responsibility for what happens within them.[30] Part and parcel of the response to such conduct needs to be declaratory—naming persons who have engaged in dishonest practices, shaming them, and reducing the potential for them to be employed by other institutions that are unaware of the conduct in which such persons have previously engaged. The denunciation should be made by a suitably independent body created for the task. In the United States the Office of Research Integrity is such a body. In addition, significant periods of preclusion from eligibility for funding and relevant employment ought to be a standard response.

But more options exist. Adoption or adaptation of the United States False Claims Act, with its protection for and encouragement of whistleblowers (via qui tam provisions), deserves consideration.[31]

Conflict of Interest

As has become apparent in this book, scholars and scholarly institutions can engage in many forms of conflict of interest. Some conflicts impact upon the integrity of research or the confidence that is held about research integrity. Conflicts of interest can result in prioritizing continuation of research over the well-being of patients, such as occurred in the National Women's Hospital case in New Zealand and as, arguably, brought about the death of Jesse Gelsinger in the course of his being on a trial for treatment of a mild form of ornithine

[30] See Sandra L Titus and Xavier Bosch, 'Tie Funding to Research Integrity' (2010) 466(7305) *Nature* 436; Sandra L Titus, James A Wells, and Lawrence J Rhoades, 'Repairing Research Integrity' (2008) 453(7198) *Nature* 980. See also, Tricia Bertram Gallant (ed), *Creating the Ethical Academy: A Systems Approach to Understanding Misconduct and Empowering Change in Higher Education* (New York: Routledge, 2011).

[31] See Thomas A Faunce, Gregor Urbas and Lesley Skillen, 'Implementing US-Style Anti-Fraud Laws in the Australian Pharmaceutical and Health Care Industries' (2011) 194(9) *Medical Journal of Australia* 474.

transcarbamylase deficiency.[32] In other instances, though, the receipt of money from a funder of research may erode the independence of research, as occurred with the donation of funding by a relative of the Libyan dictator, Muammar al-Gaddafi, and arguably occurred in relation to La Trobe University in Melbourne, Australia, by its entry into a memorandum of association with the vitamin company, Swisse. Alternatively, it may simply require a clear revelation so that there can be evaluation of whether funding arrangements have provided a source of contamination with the potential to erode confidence in the drawing of inferences from data that have been yielded.

For the most part, the crucial issue in respect of conflict of interest, corruption scenarios aside, is that proper disclosure should be made. In some circumstances, though, conflicts of interest are so serious and so noxious that they interfere with the integrity of research and an affiliation, or source of funding, needs not just to be acknowledged but to be jettisoned.

Mechanisms need to be created to provide guidance on such matters and on occasions to rule on proper action that should have been taken or that still needs to be taken. Entities providing such guidance need to be independent of the institution in question, constituted by persons who are held in high regard, supported by clear processes, adequately resourced, and prioritized within an organizational environment in a position to respond promptly. Generally, there is no reason why they have to be external save insofar as allegations against an individual or institution arising out of conflict of interest may in effect constitute allegations of research misconduct. In such a scenario, as argued above, there is much to be said for a research integrity body external to the institution inquiring into and ruling on the issues.

There are other scenarios in which conflicts of interest occur for scholars. A prominent example is in relation to submission of research manuscripts to journals. A uniform disclosure obligation, such as that recommended by the International Committee of Medical Journal Editors, is a constructive model.[33]

Legal options to reduce the incidence of conflicts of interest that are worthy of consideration also exist. In the United States five States and the District of California have legislated to mandate disclosure of gifts to doctors, and the Obama government's *Patient Protection and Affordable Care Act* 2010 (US) imposes significant disclosure obligations on medical practitioners. This too could be adapted more broadly and emulated by other countries.

Forensic Misconduct

These pages have demonstrated that forensic misconduct has much in common with both research misconduct and conflicts of interest. Its consequences are dire in that for the most part it occurs on the part of persons commissioned as independent scientists or medical practitioners who are employed or given work by the prosecution (sometimes the defence) in criminal cases to provide forensic reports and give evidence to assist the courts.

Where data are manufactured, context is withheld, or interpretations are distorted (see, for instance Dr Steinschneider and Professor Sir Roy Meadow), the results for persons who are found guilty of criminal offences can be serious indeed. The most tragic consequences are where the death penalty exists but are still very serious when persons are imprisoned after

[32] See Robin Fretwell Wilson, 'The Death of Jesse Gelsinger: New Evidence of the Influence of Money and Prestige in Human Research' (2010) 36(2-3) *American Journal of Law & Medicine* 295.

[33] See International Committee of Medical Journal Editors, 'Conflicts of Interest': <http://www.icmje.org/conflicts-of-interest/> [accessed 4 Jan 2016].

being found guilty of criminal conduct which would not otherwise have been proved. Not only is extreme personal suffering caused but confidence in the institution of justice can be eroded, a consequence that has the potential to impact profoundly on the fragile fabric that gives cohesion to our social structures.

On occasions such conduct has been visited with penal sanctions as a result of findings of guilt by criminal courts, such as with the forensic pathologist, Dr Erdmann, and the forensic scientist, Annie Dookhan. There is every justification for this. While minds may legitimately differ on many scientific, medical, and financial matters that come before the courts, while infelicitous things may be said under the pressure of cross-examination in the witness box, and while methodologies for forensic assessment may be debated, forensic misconduct that involves the deliberate or indifferent presentation of wrong data to the courts constitutes a gross interference with the capacity of the justice system to dispense fairness in its decision-making. There is every reason for the criminal justice system on occasions to impose penalties of imprisonment on professionals for attempting to pervert the course of justice.

The controversial initiative in the United Kingdom in *Jones v Kaney*[34] of allowing limited civil redress for forensic misconduct by expert witnesses, and thereby eroding the principle of witness immunity, deserves to be monitored because it permits a remedy where otherwise it does not exist for parties to litigation who have been deleteriously affected by professional negligence. However, there is much to be said for instituting a form of oversight and investigation by an independent body, whose role is to respond to expressions of aggrievement about the discharge of the expert role in the forensic context.

Plagiarism

Respect for, and valuing of, originality has a long history in literature and philosophy. So also does the notion that unauthorized replication of others' work and ideas, without proper ascription, constitutes a form of intellectual dishonesty. It is apparent that in recent times there have been high levels of plagiarism, in many contexts. Until the use of tools such as Turnitin, Plagium, and iThenticate, much of it was not identified and when it was, a level of tolerance and understanding was often extended. This is changing. The new anti-plagiarism tools make detection exponentially easier than it has been, although utilization of material from other languages can subvert such measures.[35] The two questions are when such tools should be employed and what should be done when plagiarism, through one means or another, is detected.

A trend that can be identified is that the media, regulators, rivals, political opponents, and even academia are increasingly alert to and censorious about conduct involving unacknowledged use of others' work. Recent years have seen a reassertion of the recognition of the importance within both the general community and the scholarly community of honesty, originality, and integrity within scholarship. At the heart of plagiarism is deception—the passing off of others' ideas as one's own without proper attribution of their provenance, the taking of unfair credit for others' intellectual work. The unacceptability of such conduct was identified by Timaeus, Martial, and Cicero in the ancient world[36] as clearly as it has been by judicial officers, disciplinary tribunals and the court of public opinion in recent times.

34 [2011] UKSC 13; [2011] 2 AC 398.

35 See Chow Kok Kent and Naomie Salim, 'Web Based Cross Language Plagiarism Detection' (2009) *Computing* 39.

36 See Scott McGill, *Plagiarism in Latin Literature* (Cambridge: Cambridge University Press, 2012).

The perception that this form of dishonesty is intellectually deceitful and therefore incompatible with the holding of important office has manifested in the disgracing of senior politicians, including in Hungary, Romania, and Germany, and in persons as eminent as Vice-Chancellor Robinson at Monash University in Australia, and a number of other senior academics losing their tenured positions. It has also resulted in professionals being denied registration or admission to practise or having their practising rights curtailed for periods of time because of the breach of trust in which they have engaged.

A consensus for the most part has emerged that plagiarism is what lawyers term a strict liability offence, that the 'Biden defence'—the copying of others' work was accidental or inadvertent—is not a legitimate excuse in principle and is rarely plausible in fact. At the essence of plagiarism is a betrayal of the trust both of the person responsible for the original work and of those who are the consumers of both the original product and of the plagiarized material. It is for this reason that it tends to evoke such strong responses in 'victims'. Engagement in plagiarism goes to the integrity and honesty of the perpetrator. Of necessity, it calls into question entitlement to receive a degree, to occupy a position of trust, to be registered or to be admitted as a professional, and to retain that status. Viewing plagiarism in this light exposes as spurious the justifications advanced by perpetrators, including legal practitioners in plagiarized submissions to the courts[37] and judicial officers in their judgments,[38] who claim that their work is inherently derivative and that they should not be required to adhere to orthodox scholarly protocols.

To take so hard a line in respect of plagiarism is to stake a strong position, but there is no reason to be apologetic in this regard. Any other response opens up the potential for others' intellectual property to be usurped, for exploitation of people's talent and industry to be tolerated, and for unfairness to be perpetrated by the privileged and the empowered. Scholars of all kinds occupy a position of advantage in society and it is reasonable to expect intellectual integrity and trustworthiness from them. It is this book's position that plagiarism should be clearly precluded by institutions' value statements and requirements of employees (as well as of students). This enables it to be the subject of adverse findings by disciplinary bodies and for it to be stigmatized and robustly condemned. Such a clear position, if clearly and broadly publicized throughout the scholarly community, deprives those who do not respect others' work product and originality of any excuse for their plagiarism and any valid grievance when significant sanctions are imposed on them.

Regular, if not uniform, scanning of publications written by scholars for signs of plagiarism should take place. However, it is surprising at this stage how few journals undertake this simple precaution. There is no good reason why they should not do so and publicly proclaim that this is their practice. This will not capture theft of ideas and concepts but much of the time it is likely to identify replication of significant tracts of others' work.

Consistency of sanctions is a worthy aspiration. In the United Kingdom and Australia in respect of disciplinary consequences there has been an evolution of response in this respect with significant consistency of suspension of entitlement to practise for a period of time that is not career-ending but which is such as to effect both personal and general deterrence. Archetypally, the expression of plagiarism policies, the investigation of suspected infractions,

---

[37] See Peter A Joy and Kevin C McMunigal, 'The Problems of Plagiarism as an Ethics Offense' (2011) 26(2) *Criminal Justice* 56: <http://www.americanbar.org/content/dam/aba/publications/criminal_justice_magazine/cjsu11_ethics.authcheckdam.pdf> [accessed 4 Jan 2016] discussing the ramifications of *Iowa Supreme Court Attorney Disciplinary Board v Cannon*, 789 NW 2d 256 (Iowa, 2010).

[38] *In the Matter of the Charges of Plagiarism, Etc., Against Associate Justice Mariano C. Del Castillo (Decision) 12 October 2010*, AM No. 10-7-17-SC (Republic of the Philippines Supreme Court): <http://sc.judiciary.gov.ph/jurisprudence/2010/october2010/10-7-17-SC.htm> [accessed 4 Jan 2016].

the determination of misconduct, and the visitation of it with penalties, should be a role for the institutions that are responsible for, receive benefit from, and nurture and train in scholarly conduct. In short, it can be and should be dealt with internally by such organizations in respect of students. However, when it is staff, such as academics, who engage in such conduct, an independent office of scholarly integrity has an important role to play if fairness to all is to be extended and confidence in evaluative processes to be fostered.

Intemperate Disputation and Denigration

Diverse policies exist in scholarly workplaces about the limits that should be placed around the style of disagreements transacted among scholars. There are many examples of intemperate and offensive disputation, especially among academics, that have spiralled and degenerated into conduct lying within the realm of the criminal and civil courts by reason of both its tone and content. However, academic freedom is one of the fundamental cultural attributes that distinguishes the scholarly environment from other workplaces. Former Cornell University President Frank Rhodes has gone so far as argue, in the context of Holocaust deniers, that 'free and open debate on a wide range of issues, however outrageous or offensive some of them may be, lies at the heart of a university community'.[39] Not all would concur with this. However, it is important that desires to sanitize unpleasantness do not derogate from legitimate, albeit unpalatable, expression of opinions and preparedness to be strongly critical of others and their scholarly approaches. This is a key check and balance against the commission of research fraud and is at the heart of scholarly dialectic which itself facilitates the development of reliability in new theories and techniques and the discrediting of those which are unsound.

However, when disagreement degenerates into rancour and personal abuse, or when there is the infliction of harassment on colleagues or others, it is not justifiable. For the most part, systems already exist to address such conduct. At a broader level, the approach of Yale University's School of Medicine to promote respectful debate and discourage personally directed behaviour and expressions of intolerance constitutes a useful model that is worthy of reflection. It has the potential to form the basis for development of a culture of respect and tolerance within theatres of scholarship. Abuse, ad hominem attack, and destructive critique do little to foster quality in scholarship; if anything, they tend to discourage the adoption of clear positions, incisive analyses, and the undertaking of controversial research. Fostering of a culture of robust discourse in which personal vituperation is avoided is better calculated to have a constructive outcome in terms of productive scholarly dialectic.

Dealing firmly with harassing behaviour that exceeds what is legitimate is a matter for internal management within scholarly institutions. However, accomplishing gradual cultural change so that the privileges of academic freedom are not manipulated by those seeking to inflict harm is also a worthy aspiration.

Sexual Misconduct

The reality of personal, romantic, and sexual relationships between persons with different roles within institutions, including universities, must be acknowledged. Such relationships can be problematic when they are characterized by a significant power differential, such as

---

[39] Quoted in Robert M O'Neill, *Academic Freedom in the Wired World: Political Extremism, Corporate Power, and the University* (Cambridge, Mass: Harvard University Press, 2008) 3. See also, Bruce E Johansen, *Silenced!: Academic Freedom, Scientific Inquiry, and the First Amendment Under Siege in America* (Westport, Conn: Praeger, 2007).

when they are between staff and students, or between senior staff and subordinate staff. However, inequality in relationships exists in many circumstances and we do not intrude paternalistically to preclude the relationships unless they fall into categories worthy of especial protection such as between adults and children, treaters and persons with mental illnesses and intellectual disabilities, or school teachers and their students. It is important, temptations to the contrary notwithstanding, to refrain from intruding unduly moralistically into relationships between competent adults. The propensity to do this within some United States universities in the name of zero tolerance and in order to protect the vulnerable should be respected but not emulated.

However, it is entirely proper for there to be an assertive proscription (by clearly articulated, easily comprehensible policies) against any form of sexual harassment engaged in by persons in the scholarly workplace and against staff permitting themselves to be in a conflict of interest position in relation to persons with whom they have entered into a personal relationship. There are many sound precedents for such an approach.

Failure to comply with such edicts should be visited by firm penalties as a means of deterring them and others from such conduct. It is essentially a workplace issue and should be dealt with internally. However, the grossly unsatisfactory mechanisms that were highlighted in Canada by the Donnelly and Dutton cases and in Australia by the Orr and Gregory cases need to be avoided by clear policies and procedures that are implemented rigorously, promptly and fairly—to all concerned.

Recognizing that this form of abuse of power, when it does occur, tends to be recidivist; penalties imposed should be sufficient to dissuade the person from repeating their behaviour. An option is for an independent scholarly integrity body to undertake such investigations, if one or both of the parties so requests.

Substance-affected Misconduct

The use of substances that are illegal or that interfere with a scholar's capacity to discharge their workplace responsibilities is an issue that needs to be addressed by universities and research institutions. Aside from phenomena, such as the psilocybin experiments of Dr Leary and Dr Alpert, and their merging into the personal lives of staff and students at Harvard in the 1960s, and the self-administration issues that arose with the work of Dr Shulkin, by far the most prevalent drug that has raised behavioural and regulatory difficulties has been alcohol.

While intoxication generally does not provide an excuse for conduct that is unlawful[40] or in breach of codes of conduct, substance abuse and dependence need to be identified at as early a juncture as possible. They are fundamentally health problems so the first-line response should be therapeutic. The strategies of institutions that have invested energy in encouragement of harm minimization and staff rehabilitation deserve evaluation and further attention as they address the issue in a humane way that maximizes the potential for effective clinical intervention.

Scholarly Misconduct in Perspective

In the Introduction, reference was made to the now-notorious expostulation of Marcia Angell that: 'it is no longer possible to believe much of the clinical research that is published,

40 See Ian Freckelton, 'Sentencing the Substance Dependent Offender' (1994) 1(1) *Psychiatry, Psychology and Law* 11.

or to rely on the judgment of trusted physicians or authoritative medical guidelines. I take no pleasure in this conclusion, which I reached slowly and reluctantly over my two decades as an editor of *The New England Journal of Medicine.*'[41] In effect, the first eleven chapters of this book have investigated whether this depressing pronouncement in 2009 was justified and, if so whether it remains true. Unfortunately, the answer is in the affirmative. The foregoing pages have shown that dishonesty, unrestrained rivalry, exploitation of power, sexual predation, abuse of research methodologies, conflicts of interest, theft of research insights, intemperate denigration and disputation between scholarly colleagues, and a failure to be objective and even-handed are neither new phenomena in the scholarly environment, nor occasional aberrations. However, our awareness and sensitivity to such matters is growing in the internet age. The facility to trawl through high-profile figures' theses and to discover irregularities now exists in a way that it never did previously. This has been experienced to their career detriment by politicians in a range of countries, most notably Germany, but also in Romania, Bulgaria, Austria, and Russia. However, Australia, the United Kingdom, Canada, and the United States have not been immune in this regard.

We have been slow to come to terms with such phenomena en masse and outside the specific context of particular incidents. Some analysis has been undertaken on the phenomenon of plagiarism by both scholars who are staff members or employees of institutions and by students within them. However, very little attention has been devoted to the epiphenomena of research fraud, conflict of interest, plagiarism, and sexual impropriety across disciplines, as well as to the ramifications of such conduct and to what needs to be done to reduce their incidence.

In fact, the extent of retraction of articles that are copied, unsound, or unreliable by reason of gross research deficiencies or outright fraud, such as the cooking or forging of results, has grown exponentially in recent years with hundreds of publications having to be expunged from the research record, with sometimes dozens of them having emanated from the one author. And this is only the tip of a much larger submerged object. The retraction phenomenon is not just a testament to the failure of peer-review processes and the absence of integrity on the part of the individuals concerned, but a major problem for the development of knowledge among scholars and reliance on published data and analyses. It highlights that confident reliance upon peer-reviewed publications and the opinions expressed within them needs to be cautious, and allow sufficient time for replications to be attempted, data sets scrutinized, and claims to be viewed in suitable perspective. The lesson to be learned from this is not necessarily that research misconduct is on the rise, although that may be so, but that it should be an ethical obligation to retain data and make it available when reasonably requested, and that retraction processes need to be destigmatized and availed of more readily when doubt envelops the reliability of published research.[42] This is an important challenge for publishers and journal editors.

In addition, the evolution of academia with its increasing interface with commercial forces and the imperatives to generate research outcomes, as well as the enormous temptations offered by 'Big Pharma' and 'Big Business' generally, and the research money available for development of new drugs, supplements, and technologies, have meant that scholars' and institutions' commitment to ethical propriety has been sorely tested and on occasions found wanting. This has resulted in the development of further and more demanding checks and

[41] Marcia Angell, 'Drug Companies and Doctors: A Story of Corruption: (15 January 2009) *The New York Review of Books* 56: <http://www.nybooks.com/articles/archives/2009/jan/15/drug-companies-doctorsa-story-of-corruption/> [accessed 4 Jan 2016].

[42] See Daniele Fanelli, 'Why Growing Retractions are (Mostly) A Good Sign' (2013) 10(12) *PLoS Med* 1001563.

balances in some contexts in some jurisdictions. The functions of these are to stand in the way of behaviour that obstructs suppression of results not in the interest of funding entities, to create processes to mandate disclosure of conflict of interest, and to inhibit conflicts of interest likely to generate unreliable research outcomes.

We have learned a significant amount about the persons who engage in scholarly misconduct. They cannot be lumped together in an undifferentiated way but the most significant observation that must be made is that such conduct tends not to be a one-off. While few combine the full array of vices displayed by Nobel laureate Michael Bear in Ian McEwan's *Solar*,[43] it is common for those who engage in unscholarly behaviour to engage in more than one expression of it. An example in this regard is the unfortunate conduct of Professor Chiranjeevi in India who combined orchestrated plagiarism on a major scale with multiple instances of research fraud.

In addition, scholarly misconduct tends to be highly recidivist behaviour. Those who plagiarize, who enter into conflicts of interest, who engage in research fraud, who deliberately mislead in the forensic area, who sexually harass staff and students, or who enter into unhealthy disputes with one another, tend to do so serially until finally their conduct becomes widely known (through exposure by a whistleblower or otherwise) or becomes completely unacceptable within their institution. Often their behaviour becomes more self-destructive over time—in that it becomes more flagrant and more likely to be identified and yet they proceed with it regardless, almost tempting fate. Part of what is responsible is egotism and narcissism, a revelling in the capacity to do what is taboo and to get away with it—succumbing to the seduction of the capacity to abuse power and circumvent rules. Similar characteristics typify their responses when their conduct is exposed.

Within academia, and to a degree within the elite environment of commercial research establishments, there has been a disinclination to impose too many constraints upon scholars. There has been a preparedness to extend latitude to the scholarly endeavour so as to place as few impediments as possible in the way of creativity and the advancement of knowledge. This aversion to bureaucratic rules and this licence to the cutting of corners have facilitated complacent scholarly environments conducive to unorthodox working patterns, eccentricities, irregular modes of collaboration, limited forms of documentation, confrontational interaction, and innovative methodologies. Not surprisingly, this has proved attractive to persons who are averse to the circumscribing obligations that exist in other work environments. It has also created a haven for those who are prepared to manipulate systems, flout rules, exploit colleagues, and behave opportunistically in their own interest.

The preceding pages have documented the unacceptable cost of such conduct disturbingly—the harm to research subjects, the erosion of reputations for integrity, the damage to careers and reputations, the waste of money, the discrediting of areas of research and whole subdisciplines, the consequences for honest researchers who blow the whistle on fraudulent conduct, and the distress unacceptably caused to colleagues. The need for effective remedial action should be apparent.

Effective Investigation into and Adjudication of Allegations

The pages of this book have identified that behaviour that once was mostly dealt with internally and in a gentlemanly, behind-the-scenes way within institutions (the ultimate case

[43] Ian McEwan, *Solar* (London: Jonathan Cape, 2010): research fraud, plagiarism, gluttony, inebriation, licentiousness, grandiosity, insightlessness, undermining of colleagues, and even resort to violence. See too Professor I Canto in Carl Djerassi, *Cantor's Dilemma* (New York: Penguin Books, 1989).

perhaps being the arrangement involving the recently planted lichen of Professor Harrison) is now being addressed at least in part outside the walls of the academy, increasingly often by high-profile external investigators and, in due course, in the courts. When accusations of lack of scholarly rectitude are made now, they have the potential to result in external inquiries, sometimes by retired judges, ombudsman, and anti-corruption body investigations, criminal charges, civil actions for recovery, defamation suits, sexual harassment, or unfair dismissal cases, anti-stalking applications, and a wide variety of appellate actions in the superior courts. Deference to the processes of academia has dissipated in the face of lack of confidence from accusers and accused persons alike and increasing resort to the courts or the threat of the courts. Sometimes the imposition of accountability by legal processes has been a constructive development. On other occasions the asserted potential for litigation has been used cynically to quell expressions of aggrievement or concern, to intimidate persons and institutions, and to achieve a range of collateral outcomes; it has been invoked cynically for its chilling effect—to gain time or to ratchet up pressures upon persons who have made allegations. On other occasions it has added to a proliferation of forums within which accusations are canvassed and has resulted in an exacerbation of delay and expense, without facilitating clear resolution of accusations in which all parties, including the general public, have confidence.

A number of examples can be adduced of investigative processes that have miscarried badly with a legacy of mistrust of findings. The Imanishi-Kari hearings in the United States, and the Briggs, McBride, and Mann sagas in Australia, are instances of this phenomenon in respect of research misconduct, and the Donnelly and Dutton matters in Canada and the Orr and Gregory complaints in Australia in relation to sexual misconduct are prominent examples. This has been to the detriment of all concerned.

In the wake of the atrocities of the Nazi doctors and scientists being exposed, and the Nazi and Japanese tribunals delivering their verdicts, there was an impetus towards articulation of values and expectations in a formal sense in research areas, utilizing human rights as a linchpin. Something of the same can be seen over the past few years after an unparalleled sequence of scandals has shaken the confidence of many of those who are closely connected with the conduct of research and the publication of scholarly ideas. Research integrity frameworks have been established and reviewers and regulators of research integrity have been created in many countries. Codes of ethics, codes of conduct, and terms of reference for all manner of oversight entities such as ethics and conflict of interest committees have been set in place. Protocols have been created for scholarly journals. Debate has taken place about the ethical obligations of editors and codes have been formulated. Processes have been constructed for dealing with scholarly grievances, both arising from complaints by students and staff, and even from own motion investigations where concerns have not been voiced by named individuals, but issues are arising that may impact on the reputation of the institution for integrity and excellence. These processes have appellate mechanisms, some of which lead into the courts.

It remains to be seen whether this combination of initiatives will succeed in enhancing the culture of the scholarly environment and deter those inclined to breach strictures.

The Role of the Law

The shadow of the law and legal processes has increasingly been felt within academia and among scholars. Understandably, this has not always been welcomed and, as identified above, has not always been constructive. Appeals in relation to disciplinary or exclusionary mechanisms go to the courts. Unfair dismissal grievances lead to the same venue, albeit specialist courts which deal with such matters. Civil actions under the False Claims Act in the United States have generated another forum in which there can be denunciation of fraudulent conduct, as well as the payment of reparation to funders and compensation to others adversely affected by the conduct.

Defamation actions lie when scholars are aggrieved about what others say, as well as 'stop orders' or 'gag orders' on a preliminary basis. Even the criminal law has intruded, not just in the horrendous cases of homicide in the United States when tenure has been denied and there has been an eruption into gun-enabled violence, but in cases of sexual assault, stalking, and harassment. In addition, persons who have been alleged to have obtained financial advantage from funding entities by deception or otherwise to have defrauded institutions have been criminally charged in the United States, the United Kingdom, Korea, and Australia (see, for instance, Dr Poehlman, Dr Hwang, Dr Reuben, Dr Eaton, Dr Grimes, Dr Han, Professor Murdoch, and Dr Barwood[44]). Significant penalties, including 41 months' imprisonment for Dr Grimes and 57 months' imprisonment for Dr Han (and an order that he repay US$7.2 million in fraudulently obtained grants) have been imposed. On occasion some, such as Professor Stapel, have come very close to being charged, but have been able to negotiate an arrangement which did not include a finding of guilt by the criminal courts. Others, such as Professor Gillberg, have faced criminal charges for associated conduct—in his case, in effect, for obstructing an investigation—in the form of misuse of office for destroying research data the subject of allegations. In addition, charges have been preferred against experts who have falsified their oral and written evidence for the courts (see, for instance, Dr Erdmann and Annie Dookhan), this introducing a new form of accountability for forensic misconduct by scholars.

Notorious and high-profile inquiries have taken place in relation to allegations of retributive hoaxing, plagiarism, conflict of interest, and research misconduct. On occasion, these processes have left a great deal to be desired and have been replicated and appealed on the ground of procedural irregularities. The Hall and Imanishi-Kari cases are prominent instances of investigations plagued by duplication and procedural difficulties. This has meant significant distress for both complainants and those who have been accused. It has not added to the lustre of the institutions concerned and on a number of occasions has left significant question marks over the integrity of the persons who have made the accusations, those who have been the subject of findings (either adverse or otherwise), and the institutions employing them.

Too often another victim in relation to many forms of scholarly misconduct is the one who draws the conduct to the attention of the authorities.[45] Whistleblowers, as they are often known colloquially, place themselves in a very vulnerable position. They can be reviled, mistrusted, and subject to direct and indirect retribution. And yet they constitute our most important portal into unethical behaviour within institutions. Difficult as it is to accomplish, it is essential that actions match rhetoric and that effective protection is given to whistleblowers who make bona fide concerns known within their institution or outside. Persons such as Professor Robert Sprague (in relation to the fraudulent research of Dr Stephen Breuning about the provision of medication to intellectually disabled children) and Professor Bolsin (in relation to the dangerous practices in relation to paediatric cardiology at the Bristol Royal Infirmary)

---

[44] While Professor Murdoch and Dr Barwood in Queensland, Australia, have been charged with research fraud, at the time of writing they have not stood trial and no inferences should be drawn as to their guilt.

[45] See eg, Research Triangle Institute, *Consequences of Whistleblowing for the Whistleblower in Misconduct in Science Cases* (Final Report, 30 October 1995): <https://ori.hhs.gov/sites/default/files/final.pdf> [accessed 4 Jan 2016]; Rosamond Rhodes and James J Strain, 'Whistleblowing in Academic Medicine' (2004) 30(1) *Journal of Medical Ethics* 35.

who have shed light on risks, incompetence, and misconduct deserve our accolades, our admiration, and our encouragement. Those who revealed the conduct of Annie Dookhan have saved lives and taken a vital step to preserving confidence in the criminal justice system. Those who exposed the cancer frauds and the perioperative fluid frauds have likewise made an enormous contribution to public health and safety that deserves plaudits and active support in action, as well as words. However, set against their contributions needs to be the acknowledgment that the making of a complaint about a colleague does not always have a proper basis—it can be generated by rivalry, stubborn adherence to a particular intellectual position, misperception, and a range of collateral factors. While whistleblowers must be protected, those who make allegations mala fide do not deserve protection and their victims, such as legitimate researchers, are entitled to vindication to repair, so far as possible, harm that may have been done unfairly to their reputation for integrity.

Legislated protection for whistleblowers is patchy and often does not extend into the domain of universities and private research institutions. So that whistleblowers receive protection in such forms of employment, and in order to effect institutional change so that colleagues feel free to ventilate concerns about the conduct of others, it is important that whistleblower protection is created as part of the terms of employment. Insistence by funders upon the existence of such protection is a way in which cultures can be changed and at least some measure of support can be given to those who blow the whistle within scholarly contexts.

The Need for Change

The argument in this book is that, whatever the advantages are in a behind-the-scenes resolution of issues of scholarly irregularity, the absence of transparency in such processes has become unacceptable. The broader community, and even most of the scholarly community, wants knowledge and assurance of fairness and rigour in relation to resolution of claims of scholarly misconduct so that there can be confidence in the integrity of not just processes but in the individuals, institutions, and disciplines concerned. This has particular application when there are liberty repercussions to forensic misconduct and personal safety and mental and physical health ramifications to evaluations of research misconduct, and large financial consequences to decision-making about other forms of misconduct.

It is in these circumstances that it has been argued throughout this book that processes for dealing with scholarly misconduct need to be clear, rigorous, fair, prompt, and transparent. This requires the provision of clear statements of values, expectations, and obligations by institutions such as universities, research bodies, and journals so that there is as little ambiguity as possible in terms of what is required of employers and employees, of staff and students, of persons accused and whistleblowers, of institutions and individuals. There is a need for sophistication and consistency in definitions in respect of harassment, conflict of interest, plagiarism, and research misconduct. It also requires the extension of as much protection as possible to those who provide information in a bona fide way about their concerns in respect of such matters.

There is also a need for the creation of entities that can provide guidance and assistance to those who seek help for making ethical decisions and engaging in ethical conduct in their scholarly work. Ethics committees and conflict of interest committees within universities and research entities are examples in this regard.

Processes of investigation, procuring accounts from those accused of impropriety, enabling proper testing of allegations, and making of decisions in robust, open ways that are independent, of high quality, and expeditious in response, are vital. This involves difficult balancing between processes that are internal to institutions and the involvement of external mechanisms to guarantee independence and confidence that processes and outcomes are uninfluenced by self-interest.

What has become clear is that the maladies afflicting scholarship cannot be dealt with wholly internally within universities and research bodies. The stakes are too high for that and the records of such internal processes are not good enough, in spite of the fine example given by some institutional responses, such as the collaborative exercise that dealt with the allegations in The Netherlands into the fraud of Diederik Stapel. What is required is the creation by government of external bodies. The United States Office of Research Integrity is a good model on which other countries can draw. However, such an entity must be resourced, empowered and supported to retain its effectiveness and the respect that accompanies such effectiveness. There are signs in the United States that this level of support is not all that it needs to be.

In Canada there is the Tri-Agency Network and in Australia the Research Integrity Committee. Those are a constructive start, against a backdrop of sophisticated, carefully articulated frameworks of values which both countries have latterly constructed. But what is also necessary is an entity that can receive complaints and even act of its own motion to investigate serious concerns about lack of scholarly integrity. Such a body, perhaps to be called an Office of Scholarly Integrity, should only have recommendatory powers (after conducting an investigation and making findings) but, if its stature is high, institutions will feel obliged generally to implement its recommendations, and proposals for reform of processes and to deal firmly with individuals the subject of adverse findings. Mere process oversight is useful but not sufficient.

Such a structure is fundamental for allegations of research misconduct and conflict of interest. Assertions that these can be dealt with adequately by internal investigations are not credible given what has occurred in the recent past. Legal and health professions are no longer permitted in many countries to self-regulate. External, independent decision-making is necessary for community confidence. Ombudsmen are useful entities in providing evaluations of the sufficiency of processes but there is no substitute for a system which conducts high-quality initial investigations promptly and fairly and whose adjudicative processes satisfy all the requirements of natural justice and procedural fairness, as well as being professionally informed with respect to the discipline concerned.

Such a body could also on occasion have a role to play in relation to allegations of plagiarism in respect of employees. While, clearly, allegations of plagiarism by students should be dealt with internally within universities, there is much to be said for an Office of Scholarly Integrity being given jurisdiction to determine whether plagiarism has been engaged in by staff and also how serious it is.

Such a body could also investigate and make findings about contentious allegations of sexual impropriety. When allegations of scholarly irregularity relate to judicial officers, this is the proper province of a suitably established judicial complaints body and, in extreme examples, the appellate courts.

In respect of forensic misconduct suspected of being engaged in by a practitioner, a three-fold response should be made. The United Kingdom model of a Forensic Science Regulator, empowered to investigate such conduct, should be emulated. It should forge a close working relationship with the Office of Scholarly Integrity, as well as with professional regulatory bodies that investigate allegations of unprofessional conduct and professional misconduct, including forensic misconduct, against registered health practitioners.

Journals must also assume a proper measure of responsibility for what is published in their pages and for processes for investigating allegations of scholarly misconduct which may require retraction of published articles. Delays for years in relation to retractions are unacceptable given the influence that publications which remain on the scholarly record can exercise. As Redman has observed, 'editors have a special duty to maintain the integrity of the scientific record', including by recording corrections and, where the situation is unresolved, by expressions of concern within the pages of journals.[46] There are many occasions in which publishers and editors have fallen short of the high standards of independence and rigour which could guide the discharge of their role.[47] The competitive quest for high impact factors[48] and one-up-manship in publishing research breakthroughs have become risk factors for the erosion of editorial standards in scholarly journals.

Text comparison software enables identification of replicated manuscript, and a range of orthodox measures, including peer review, operate as some measure of protection against research fraud. However, it has become more than clear that these measures have serious limitations. The Committee on Publication Ethics (COPE) has facilitated constructive discussion about such issues and issued guidelines on matters such as retraction protocols,[49] but many journals still do not have adequate or clear policies and procedures in place to deal with the expression of concerns about scholarly irregularities. This needs to change. So too does the broader context of journals' preparedness to publish research that does more than assert the efficacy of pharmaceutical agents so that studies that raise questions about such matters or generate adverse results are also published; the observations of Dr Summerlin about the pressure he experienced to publish positive results from his research is a salutary warning. In addition, it is the responsibility of journals to do what they can to reduce the incidence of 'gift-authorship' and 'ghost-writing',[50] authorship by persons who have not substantively contributed to articles, and writing that is influenced by the authors' undeclared sources of funding. There is much to be said for clear identification of authorship responsibility[51] or even, to the extent that it is possible, moving away from the notion of authorship to the concept of contribution, as has been recommended, amongst others, by Richard Smith, the former editor of the British Medical Journal.[52] As Adeney, with sound justification, argued in 2015, in many fields of scholarly endeavour the 'contributor' and 'guarantor' concepts are

---

46 Barbara K Redman, *Research Misconduct Policy in Biomedicine: Beyond the Bad-Apple Approach* (Cambridge, Mass: The MIT Press, 2013) 66.

47 See the account by Light and Warburton of an unfortunate sequence of editors' conduct in respect of the submission of manuscripts in relation to health economics: Donald W Light and Rebecca N Warburton, 'Ethical Standards for Health Care Journal Editors: A Case Report and Recommendations' (2008) 9(1) *Harvard Health Policy Review* 58. See also, Mark Israel, *Research Ethics and Integrity for Social Scientists* (2nd edition, Los Angeles: SAGE, 2015) 164ff.

48 See Harvey Marcovitch, 'Editors, Publishers, Impact Factors, and Reprint Income' (2010) 7(1) *PLoS Med:* e1000364; Andreas Lundh, Marija Barbateskovic, Asbjorn Hróbjartsson, and Peter C Gøtzsche, 'Conflicts of Interest at Medical Journals: The Influence of Industry-Supported Randomised Trials on the Journal Impact Factor' (2010) 7 *PLoS Med:* e354.

49 See Committee on Publication Ethics (COPE), 'Guidelines': <http://publicationethics.org/resources/guidelines> [accessed 4 Jan 2016].

50 See Annette Flanagin, Lisa A Carey, Phil B Fontanarosa, Stephanie G Phillips, Brian P Pace, George D Lundberg, and Drummond Rennie, 'Prevalence of Articles with Honorary Authors and Ghost Authors in Peer-Reviewed Medical Journals' (1998) 280(3) *Journal of the American Medical Association* 222.

51 For instance, the International Committee of Medical Journal Editors in 'Defining the Role of Authors and Contributors' provides for clear criteria for what constitutes authorship: see <http://www.icmje.org/recommendations/browse/roles-and-responsibilities/defining-the-role-of-authors-and-contributors.html> [accessed 4 Jan 2016].

52 See Richard Smith, 'Authorship: Time for a Paradigm Shift? The Authorship System is Broken and May Need a Radical Solution' (1997) 314 *British Medical Journal* 992; Richard Smith, 'Authorship is Dying: Long Live Contributorship: The BMJ Will Publish Lists of Contributors and Guarantors to Original Articles' (1997) 31 *British Medical Journal* 696. For a recent analysis of the arguments see Elizabeth Adeney, 'Medical and Scientific Authorship: A Conflict Between Discipline Rules and the Law' (2015) 23 *Journal of Law and Medicine* 413.

needed as 'responsibility-allocating mechanisms', through which individuals can be held to account for the content of their work, as well as enabling them to receive fair recognition for their work product, especially when it is a shared enterprise.[53]

These pages propose a multi-component strategy for assertion of scholarly integrity. The strategy includes consistency of definitions in respect of core concepts such as research misconduct, conflict of interest, and plagiarism. It also requires formulation of comprehensive and detailed statements and principles to govern what is expected of scholars from all disciplines. This has the potential to assist in the construction of an ethical scholarly culture that encourages integrity, openness and respect for others,[54] as well as providing measures against which individuals' (and on occasions institutions') behaviour can be evaluated. It requires support from committees of journal editors and from publishers and editors to facilitate cultural shifts. It also encompasses an active role discharged by ethics and conflict of interest committees that can work co-operatively with scholars and institutions to minimize risks and to provide guidance so as to reduce contravention of scholarly values. It incorporates assumption of responsibility by funders (government and non-government) for oversight over such matters and for suitable responses when misconduct is discovered.

It involves the creation of new entities, an Office of Scholarly Integrity, and a Forensic Science Regulator, the latter to adjudicate on whether conduct by medical and scientific (and perhaps that of other disciplines) is unprofessional in the forensic context. However, the mere creation of new bodies is not enough. The deficits arising in the investigations by the Office of Scientific Integrity and then the Office of Research Integrity in respect of Dr Imanishi-Kari highlight this. Such bodies need to have a suitable charter which provides for fairness in how investigations are undertaken and criteria against which instances of alleged research misconduct can be evaluated. The identity of their leadership and their personnel, and the culture at the heart of their operations are important so that their investigations are fair, prompt, and suitably technically informed. They must be critical, not accepting too readily what whistle-blowers, witnesses, colleagues, or those the subject of accusations contend. Their investigations must adhere to stipulated protocols and be rigorous, expeditious, and ideologically and institutionally impartial without descending into a campaign or a crusade. On occasion, lawyers may be able to play a constructive role in assisting in the according of procedural fairness in the obtaining of evidence and the posing of issues.

The proposals in this book contemplate the involvement of the criminal law on occasion to respond to conduct that constitutes the obtaining of financial advantage by research fraud and attempts to pervert the course of justice, on occasions the civil law to deal with fraud, forensic negligence, and the sexual harassment of colleagues and employees, and disciplinary law where conduct falls short of what is reasonably to be expected of professional persons.

This combination of measures, while stern and on some occasions judgmental, is urgently required if the damage that is being done by the unethical conduct engaged in by a small percentage of scholars is to be reduced, if the harm that is being done by scholarly misconduct is to be contained, and if confidence is to be reinstated in what should be the honourable and trustworthy domain of scholarship.

[53] See Adeney, above, n 52.
[54] See further Gallant, above n 30.

APPENDICES

1. Research Council of the United Kingdom: Policy and Guidelines on Governance of Good Research Conduct (2013) 523
2. The Canadian Tri-Agency Framework: Responsible Conduct of Research 534
3. Australian NHMRC Code of Conduct 543
4. United States Office of Research Integrity Whistleblower's Bill of Rights 563

APPENDIX ONE

Research Council of the United Kingdom: Policy and Guidelines on Governance of Good Research Conduct (2013)[1]

1.0 Introduction

1.1 The UK Research Integrity Office's Code of Practice for Research has been designed to encourage good conduct in research and help prevent misconduct, in order to assist organisations and researchers to conduct research of the highest quality. It provides general principles and standards for good practice in research, applicable to both individual researchers and to organisations that carry out, fund, host or are otherwise involved in research.

1.2 The Code is applicable to all subject areas and does not attempt to micromanage research. Recognising that many forms of guidance already exist, the intention is that research organisations may use the principles and standards outlined in this Code as benchmarks when drafting or revising their own, more detailed, codes of practice. No single publication can expect to cover the nuances of all types of research in all disciplines; therefore, the Code should not be seen as prescriptive but as a set of guiding principles and standards to inform the management and conduct of research.

1.3 The Code covers areas of good practice in research typically included in organisational policies for the conduct of research, drawing upon existing good practice and the experiences of the UK Research Integrity Office (UKRIO) in addressing good conduct and misconduct in research. Detailed guidance is given on core standards for good practice in research but particular attention has been paid to areas where UKRIO has most often been approached for guidance, in the hope of passing on lessons learned to the research community.

1.4 The Code complements existing and forthcoming guidance on research conduct, such as that provided by Research Councils UK, the Wellcome Trust or the Council for Science and Technology. Similarly, the Code complements organisational policies, such as those for health and safety, raising concerns at work, or management of finances or of intellectual property, and does not seek to replace them. Use of the benchmarks contained in this Code can assist research organisations in fulfilling the requirements of regulatory, funding and other relevant bodies, and ensure that important issues have not been overlooked.

1.5 UKRIO recognises that there are many organisations which issue guidance on the conduct of research to the UK research community. For some time, UKRIO has been working with organisations such as Research Councils UK and the Department of Health, with a view ultimately to streamline guidance on good practice in research, to ensure clarity for the research community and avoid duplication of effort.

1.6 The Code is organised in the following Sections:

a) Section 2 contains broad Principles which define the responsibilities and values in the conduct of research by both researchers and research organisations.

b) A one page Recommended Checklist for Researchers can be found on the inside of the front cover. This is a nontechnical checklist summarising the key points of good practice in research and is applicable to all subject areas. The Checklist is based on the more detailed Standards given in section 3.

c) Section 3 lists Standards for good practice in research that researchers and research organisations should comply with. The Standards apply to all disciplines of research but organisations may wish to expand upon them by offering more detailed guidance for certain subject areas or types of research.

1.7 The Code does not stipulate how to put the promotion and support of good research practice into operation as it is quite rightly left up to organisations and researchers to determine the best way to do so in their particular research environment. It should be noted, however, that only through

[1] <http://www.ukrio.org/publications/code-of-practice-for-research/> [accessed 4 Jan 2016].

the endorsement and support of good practice in research at the highest level and implementation through education, training and supervision, can researchers become aware of their individual responsibilities and the collective responsibility they have to their research organisation and the wider research community.

1.8 Note that, for the purposes of this Code, "research" refers to the definition used by the Research Assessment Exercise (Research Assessment Exercise 2008, p. 34):

a) "'Research'... is to be understood as original investigation undertaken in order to gain knowledge and understanding. It includes work of direct relevance to the needs of commerce, industry, and to the public and voluntary sectors; scholarship*; the invention and generation of ideas, images, performances, artefacts including design, where these lead to new or substantially improved insights; and the use of existing knowledge in experimental development to produce new or substantially improved materials, devices, products and processes, including design and construction. It excludes routine testing and routine analysis of materials, components and processes such as for the maintenance of national standards, as distinct from the development of new analytical techniques. It also excludes the development of teaching materials that do not embody original research."

b) "* Scholarship... is defined as the creation, development and maintenance of the intellectual infrastructure of subjects and disciplines, in forms such as dictionaries, scholarly editions, catalogues and contributions to major research databases."

1.9 Similarly, for the purposes of this Code, "organisations" refers to any bodies which: conduct, host, sponsor or fund research; employ, support or host researchers; teach research students; or allow research to be carried out under their auspices. "Researchers" refers to any person who conducts research, including but not limited to: as an employee; an independent contractor or consultant; a research student; a visiting or emeritus member of staff; or a member of staff on a joint clinical or honorary contract.

1.10 Some organisations may wish the Code to apply to undergraduate students; if so, this should be made clear in institutional policies and organisations should consider what particular education, training, supervision and support they should provide to student researchers. They should make it clear to student researchers that their research must comply with the organisation's policies and procedures for the conduct of research.

1.11 Sources used in the development of the Code are acknowledged in the appendix. UKRIO would also like to thank the individuals and institutions who responded to the public consultation on a draft version of the publication in 2009 for their contributions to the Code.

a) It is the intention of UKRIO that the Code will be reviewed regularly, initially on an annual basis. UKRIO welcomes feedback from organisations and researchers on the current edition, to inform the review.

b) To that end, the Code will be published as an online document on the UKRIO website (www.UKRIO.org), as well as hard copy and PDF versions. This online Code will include a mechanism for the research community to submit feedback on specific sections and suggest new developments in good practice in research for inclusion.

c) Organisations and researchers are recommended to check the UKRIO website for the annual updates to the Code. The website also provides information on how to contact UKRIO to gain access to independent, confidential and expert advice and guidance on any issues relating to good practice and misconduct in research.

2.0 Principles

2.0.1 Organisations and researchers should adhere to the following Principles, which set out the responsibilities and values relevant to research. While some elements may seem selfevident, and there is some overlap, these Principles aim to encourage all involved in research to consider the wider consequences of their work and to engage critically with the practical, ethical and intellectual challenges that are inherent in the conduct of high quality research, rather than treating codes of practice such as this as just another procedure to be followed.

2.0.2 Organisations and researchers should be guided by these Principles when implementing and complying with the core Standards described in section 3 and the Recommended Checklist for Researchers on the inside of the front cover.

2.1 EXCELLENCE: organisations and researchers should strive for excellence when conducting research and aim to produce and disseminate work of the highest quality. This Code, its Principles and its Standards are intended to support these goals.

2.2 HONESTY: organisations should work to create and maintain a culture of research that fosters and supports honesty in research. Researchers should be honest in relation to their own research and that of others. They should do their utmost to ensure the accuracy of data and results, acknowledge the contributions of others, and neither engage in misconduct nor conceal it.

2.3 INTEGRITY: organisations and researchers must comply with all legal and ethical requirements relevant to their field of study. They should declare any potential or actual conflicts of interest relating to research and where necessary take steps to resolve them.

2.4 COOPERATION: organisations and researchers should promote the open exchange of ideas, research methods, data and results and their discussion, scrutiny and debate, subject to any considerations of confidentiality.

2.5 ACCOUNTABILITY: organisations and researchers should recognise that in and through their work they are ultimately accountable to the general public and should act accordingly. They should ensure that any research undertaken complies with any agreements, terms and conditions relating to the project, and allows for proper governance and transparency. Researchers should follow the requirements and guidance of any professional bodies in their field of research. Researchers who are members of a regulated profession must follow the requirements and guidance of the body regulating their profession.

2.6 TRAINING AND SKILLS: organisations should provide training and opportunities for development for their researchers, and the necessary resources to enable them to conduct research to the required standards. They should support researchers in identifying unmet needs for training and development. Researchers should ensure that they have the necessary skills, training and resources to carry out research, in the proposed research team or through collaboration with specialists in relevant fields, and report and resolve any unmet needs identified.

2.7 SAFETY: organisations and researchers should ensure the dignity, rights, safety and wellbeing of all involved in research and avoid unreasonable risk or harm to research subjects, patients, participants, researchers and others. They should report and address any concerns relating to the dignity, rights, safety and wellbeing of those involved in research. Research should be initiated and continued only if the anticipated benefits justify the risks involved.

3.0 Standards for organisations and researchers

3.0.1 Organisations and researchers should comply with the following core Standards, which should be interpreted in light of the Principles in section 2. Each Standard adopts the order:

a) organisations and researchers;
b) organisations; and
c) researchers

3.1 General guidance on good practice in research

3.1.1 Organisations and researchers must comply with all legal and ethical requirements and other guidelines that apply to their research. This includes submitting research proposals for ethics review where appropriate and abiding by the outcome of that review. They should also ensure that research projects are approved by all applicable bodies, ethical, regulatory or otherwise.

3.1.2 When conducting, or collaborating in, research in other countries, organisations and researchers based in the UK should comply with the legal and ethical requirements existing in the UK and in the countries where the research is conducted. Similarly, organisations and researchers based abroad who participate in UK hosted research projects should comply with the legal and ethical requirements existing in the UK as well as those of their own country.

3.1.3 Organisations and researchers should ensure that all research projects have sufficient arrangements for insurance and indemnity prior to the research being conducted.

3.1.4 Organisations should:

a) ensure that good practice in research forms an integral part of their research strategy or policy;
b) establish clear policies and procedures that cover the Principles of good practice in research (see section 2) and offer detailed guidance on the Standards set out in this Code;

c) ensure that these policies and procedures complement and are in accordance with existing organisational policies, such as those for health and safety, raising concerns at work, management of finances or of intellectual property, and equality and diversity;
d) make sure that their researchers are aware of these policies and procedures and that all research carried out under the auspices of the organisation complies with them;
e) provide training, resources and support to their researchers to ensure that they are aware of these policies and procedures and are able to comply with them;
f) encourage their researchers to consider good practice in research as a routine part of their work; and
g) monitor these measures for suitability and effectiveness and review them where necessary.

3.1.5 Researchers should:

a) recognise their responsibility to conduct research of high ethical standards;
b) be aware of their organisation's policies and procedures on good practice in research;
c) make sure that their research complies with these policies and procedures, and seek guidance from their organisation when necessary;
d) work with their organisation to ensure that they have the necessary training, resources and support to carry out their research; and
e) suggest to their organisation how guidance on good practice in research might be developed or revised.

3.2 Leadership and supervision

3.2.1 Organisations and researchers should promote and maintain an environment which fosters and supports research of high ethical standards, mutual co-operation, professionalism and the open and honest exchange of ideas. They should foster a culture where good conduct in research is promoted and inappropriate conduct is identified and addressed.

3.2.2 Organisations should provide direction and supervision of research and researchers, setting out clear lines of accountability for the organisation and management of research. They should support supervisors and researchers in meeting the legal and ethical requirements of conducting research. Organisations should encourage the career development of their researchers and provide training and mentoring of new researchers. They should also offer training and support to those charged with the supervision and development of other researchers. Organisations should support the principles of the Concordat to Support the Career Development of Researchers.

3.2.3 Researchers involved in the supervision and development of other researchers should be aware of their responsibilities and ensure that they have the necessary training, time and resources to carry out that role, and request support if required.

3.3 Training and mentoring

3.3.1 Organisations should provide training for researchers to enable them to carry out their duties and develop their knowledge and skills throughout their career. This should include training in the responsible design, conduct and dissemination of research. They should support researchers in identifying unmet needs for training and development. Organisations should provide qualified mentors to assist in the training and career development of new researchers and also provide career development and educational opportunities for researchers who are more established in their careers. As in 3.2.2, they should support the principles of the Concordat to Support the Career Development of Researchers.

3.3.2 Organisations should provide particular support for student researchers. They should make sure that student researchers understand which standards and organisational policies and procedures they are expected to comply with.

3.3.3 Researchers should undergo training in order to carry out their duties and to develop their knowledge and skills throughout their career, repeating training where necessary to ensure that skills are kept uptodate. They should identify needs for training when they arise and report them to their manager or other appropriate person as identified by their organisation. See also section 3.2.3.

3.4 Research design

3.4.1 When designing research projects, organisations and researchers should ensure that:

a) the proposed research addresses pertinent question(s) and is designed either to add to existing knowledge about the subject in question or to develop methods for research into it;
b) the design of the study is appropriate for the question(s) being asked and addresses the most important potential sources of bias;
c) the design and conduct of the study, including how data will be gathered, analysed and managed, are set out in detail in a prespecified research plan or protocol;
d) all necessary skills and experience will be available to carry out the proposed research, in the proposed research team or through collaboration with specialists in relevant fields;
e) sufficient resources will be available to carry out the proposed research and that these resources meet all relevant standards; and
f) any issues relating to the above are resolved as far as possible prior to the start of the research.

3.5 Collaborative working

3.5.1 *Organisations and researchers* should pay particular attention to projects which include participants from different countries or where work will be carried out in another country due to the additional legal and ethical requirements and other guidelines that may apply. See also sections 3.1.2, 3.7.2 and 3.8.2 .

3.5.2 *Organisations* should work with partner organisations to ensure the agreement of, and compliance with, common standards and procedures for the conduct of collaborative research, including the resolution of any issues or problems that might arise and the investigation of any allegations of misconduct in research if they occur.

3.5.3 *Researchers* should be aware of the standards and procedures for the conduct of research followed by any organisations involved in collaborative research that they are undertaking. They should also be aware of any contractual requirements involving partner organisations, seeking guidance and assistance where necessary and reporting any concerns or irregularities to the appropriate person(s) as soon as they become aware of them.

3.5.4 Researchers should try to anticipate any issues that might arise as a result of working collaboratively and agree jointly in advance how they might be addressed, communicating any decisions to all members of the research team. In particular, agreement should be sought on the specific roles of the researchers involved in the project and on issues relating to intellectual property, publication, and the attribution of authorship, recognising that, subject to legal and ethical requirements, roles and contributions may change during the time span of the research.

3.6 Conflicts of interest

3.6.1 *Organisations and researchers* must recognise that conflicts of interest (i.e. personal or institutional considerations, including but not limited to financial matters) can inappropriately affect research. Conflicts of interest must be identified, declared and addressed in order to avoid poor practice in research or potential misconduct.

3.6.2 When addressing a conflict of interest, it must be decided whether it is of a type and severity that poses a risk of fatally compromising the validity or integrity of the research, in which case researchers and organisations should not proceed with the research, or whether it can be adequately addressed through declarations and/or special safeguards relating to the conduct and reporting of the research.

3.6.3 *Organisations* should have a clearly written and accessible policy for addressing conflicts of interest, including guidance for researchers on how to identify, declare and address conflicts of interest, and should disseminate and explain the policy to researchers. Organisations should ensure that researchers understand the importance of recognising, disclosing and addressing conflicts of interest in the conduct and reporting of research.

3.6.4 Organisations should comply with the requirements of their policy for addressing conflicts of interest, as well as any external requirements relating to conflicts of interest, such as those of funding bodies. Heads of organisations and other senior staff should be aware of potential or actual conflicts of interest at the institutional level and disclose them when they arise so that they can be addressed.

3.6.5 *Researchers* should comply with their organisation's policy for addressing conflicts of interest, as well as any external requirements relating to conflicts of interest, such as those of funding bodies. This should include declaring any potential or actual conflicts of interest relating to their research to: their manager or other appropriate person as identified by their organisation; any ethics committee which reviews their research; and when reporting their findings at meetings or in publications. Conflicts of interest should be disclosed as soon as researchers become aware of them.

3.6.6 Researchers should agree to abide by any direction given by their organisation or any relevant ethics committee in relation to a conflict of interest.

3.7 Research involving human participants, human material or personal data

3.7.1 *Organisations and researchers* should make sure that any research involving human participants, human material or personal data complies with all legal and ethical requirements and other applicable guidelines. Appropriate care should be taken when research projects involve: vulnerable groups, such as the very old, children or those with mental illness; and covert studies or other forms of research which do not involve full disclosure to participants. The dignity, rights, safety and wellbeing of participants must be the primary consideration in any research study. Research should be initiated and continued only if the anticipated benefits justify the risks involved.

3.7.2 When conducting, or collaborating in, research in other countries, organisations and researchers based in the UK should comply with the legal and ethical requirements existing in the UK and in the countries where the research is conducted. Similarly, organisations and researchers based abroad who participate in UK hosted research projects should comply with the legal and ethical requirements existing in the UK as well as those of their own country.

3.7.3 Organisations and researchers should ensure the confidentiality and security of: personal data relating to human participants in research; and human material involved in research projects.

3.7.4 Organisations and researchers working with, for, or under the auspices of, any of the UK Departments of Health and/or the National Health Service must adhere to all relevant guidelines, for example the Department of Health's Research Governance Framework for Health and Social Care and the National Research Ethics Service's Guidance for Applicants. Organisations and researchers involved in clinical trials on medicinal products for human use should comply with the principles of Good Clinical (Research) Practice.

3.7.5 *Organisations* should set up systems to ensure appropriate ethical, regulatory and peer review of research projects involving human participants, human material or personal data. The systems should include mechanisms to ensure that such research projects have been approved by all applicable bodies, ethical, regulatory or otherwise.

3.7.6 Organisations should also set up systems to ensure that appropriate procedures for obtaining informed consent are established and observed in projects involving human participants, having particular regard to the needs and capacity of the subjects involved.

3.7.7 Organisations should set up systems to ensure the confidentiality and security of: personal data relating to human participants in research; and human material involved in research projects.

3.7.8 Organisations should make sure that their researchers are aware of all of the above systems and have access to all relevant guidance and legal and ethical frameworks.

3.7.9 *Researchers* should submit research projects involving human participants, human material or personal data for review by all relevant ethics committees and abide by the outcome of those reviews. They should also ensure that such research projects have been approved by all applicable bodies, ethical, regulatory or otherwise.

3.7.10 Researchers on projects involving human subjects must satisfy themselves that participants are enabled, by the provision of adequate accurate information in an appropriate form through suitable procedures, to give informed consent, having particular regard to the needs and capacities of vulnerable groups, such as the very old, children and those with mental illness.

3.7.11 Researchers should inform research participants that data gathered during the course of research may be disseminated not only in a report but also in different forms for academic or other subsequent publications and meetings, albeit not in an identifiable form, unless previously agreed to, and subject to limitations imposed by legislation or any applicable bodies, ethical, regulatory or otherwise.

3.7.12 Researchers who are members of a regulated profession must ensure that research involving human participants, human material or personal data complies with any standards set by the body regulating their profession.

3.7.13 Researchers have a duty to publish the findings of all clinical research involving human participants. In addition, it is government policy to promote public access to information about any research and research findings affecting health and social care, including the principle that trials should appear on public registers. In this context "trials" means all comparative studies of health interventions, not just ones conducted in a clinical setting.

3.7.14 If researchers consider that human participants in research are subject to unreasonable risk or harm, they must report their concerns to their manager, or other appropriate person as identified by their organisation, and, where required, to the appropriate regulatory authority. Similarly, concerns relating to the improper and/or unlicensed use or storage of human material, or the improper use or storage of personal data, should be reported.

3.8 Research involving animals

3.8.1 *Organisations and researchers* should make sure that research involving animals adheres to all legal and ethical requirements and other applicable guidelines. They should consider the opportunities for reduction, replacement and refinement of involving animals in research projects and should refer to the relevant guidance.

3.8.2 When conducting, or collaborating in, research in other countries, organisations and researchers based in the UK should comply with the legal and ethical requirements existing in the UK and in the countries where the research is conducted. Similarly, organisations and researchers based abroad who participate in UKhosted research projects should comply with the legal and ethical requirements existing in the UK as well as those of their own country.

3.8.3 *Organisations* should set up systems to ensure the ethical, regulatory and peer review of research projects involving animals. The systems should include mechanisms to make sure that such research projects have been approved by all applicable bodies, ethical, regulatory or otherwise.

3.8.4 Organisations should make sure that their researchers are aware of the above systems and have access to all relevant guidance and legal and ethical frameworks.

3.8.5 *Researchers* should submit research projects involving animals for review by all relevant ethics committees and abide by the outcome of that review. They should also ensure that such research projects have been approved by all applicable bodies, ethical, regulatory or otherwise.

3.8.6 If researchers consider that animals involved in research are subject to unreasonable risk or harm, they must report their concerns to their manager or other appropriate person as identified by their organisation, and, where required, to the appropriate regulatory authority.

3.9 Health and safety

3.9.1 *Organisations and researchers* should ensure that all research carried out under their auspices, or for which they are responsible, fulfils all requirements of health and safety legislation and good practice. They should bear in mind that certain types of research, for example social research in a conflict zone, can present particular issues of health and safety. They should ensure that all research which involves potentially hazardous or harmful material or which might cause harm to the environment complies with all legal requirements and other applicable guidelines.

3.9.2 *Organisations* should set up systems to ensure that such research undergoes all forms of appropriate review in accordance with the organisation's policy on health and safety.

3.9.3 *Researchers* should submit such research for all forms of appropriate review and abide by the outcome of that review.

3.10 Intellectual property

3.10.1 *Organisations and researchers* should ensure that any contracts or agreements relating to research include provision for ownership and use of intellectual property. Intellectual property includes, but is not limited to: research data and other findings of research; ideas, processes, software, hardware, apparatus and equipment; substances and materials; and artistic and literary works, including academic and scientific publications.

3.10.2 Organisations and researchers should not give prior disclosure of research or the findings of research when this might invalidate any commercial property rights that could result. Organisations and researchers should recognise, however, that the presumption should be that any intellectual property discovered or developed using public or charitable funds should be disseminated in order to have a beneficial effect on society at large. That presumption may be rebutted where there is an express restriction placed on any such dissemination. Any delay in publication and dissemination pending protection of intellectual property should be kept to a minimum.

3.10.3 Organisations and researchers should comply with any additional conditions relating to intellectual property required by funding bodies.

3.10.4 *Organisations* should clearly state when their standard guidance might not apply; for example, a university would normally waive copyright of articles prepared for publication in journals or books.

3.10.5 *Researchers* should try to anticipate any issues that might arise relating to intellectual property at the earliest opportunity and agree jointly in advance how they might be addressed, communicating any decisions to all members of the research team.

3.11 Finance

3.11.1 *Organisations and researchers* should ensure that the terms and conditions of any grant or contract related to the research are adhered to.

3.11.2 *Organisations* should issue guidelines regarding the purchasing or procurement of materials, equipment or other resources for research and the hiring of staff for research projects. These guidelines should include statements on the ownership of resources and the rights of researchers to use them. Organisations should also set up procedures for the monitoring and audit of finances relating to research projects.

3.11.3 *Researchers* should comply with organisational guidelines regarding the use and management of finances relating to research projects. They should cooperate with any monitoring and audit of finances relating to research projects and report any concerns or irregularities to the appropriate person(s) as soon as they become aware of them.

3.12 Collection and retention of data

3.12.1 *Organisations and researchers* should comply with all legal, ethical, funding body and organisational requirements for the collection, use and storage of data, especially personal data, where particular attention should be paid to the requirements of data protection legislation. They should also maintain confidentiality where undertakings have been made to third parties or to protect intellectual property rights. Organisations and researchers should ensure that research data relating to publications is available for discussion with other researchers, subject to any existing agreements on confidentiality.

3.12.2 Data should be kept intact for any legally specified period and otherwise for three years at least, subject to any legal, ethical or other requirements, from the end of the project. It should be kept in a form that would enable retrieval by a third party, subject to limitations imposed by legislation and general principles of confidentiality.

3.12.3 Organisations and researchers should comply with any subjectspecific requirements for the retention of data; for example, certain disciplines, such as health and biomedicine, may require research data to be retained for a considerably longer period.

3.12.4 If research data is to be deleted or destroyed, either because its agreed period of retention has expired or for legal or ethical reasons, it should be done so in accordance with all legal, ethical, research funder and organisational requirements and with particular concern for confidentiality and security.

3.12.5 *Organisations* should have in place procedures, resources (including physical space) and administrative support to assist researchers in the accurate and efficient collection of data and its storage in a secure and accessible form.

3.12.6 *Researchers* should consider how data will be gathered, analysed and managed, and how and in what form relevant data will eventually be made available to others, at an early stage of the design of the project.

3.12.7 Researchers should collect data accurately, efficiently and according to the agreed design of the research project, and ensure that it is stored in a secure and accessible form.

3.13 Monitoring and audit

3.13.1 *Organisations and researchers* should ensure that research projects comply with any monitoring and audit requirements. They should make sure that researchers charged with carrying out such monitoring and audits have sufficient training, resources and support to fulfil the requirements of the role.

3.13.2 *Organisations* should monitor and audit research projects to ensure that they are being carried out in accordance with good practice, legal and ethical requirements, and any other guidelines, adopting a riskbased and proportional approach.

3.13.3 *Researchers* should consider any requirements for monitoring and audit at an early stage in the design of a project.

3.13.4 Researchers should cooperate with the monitoring and audit of their research projects by applicable bodies and undertake such when required. They should cooperate with any outcomes of the monitoring and audit of their research projects. If they become aware of a need for monitoring and audit where it is not already scheduled, they should report that need to the appropriate person(s).

3.14 Peer review

3.14.1 *Organisations and researchers* should be aware that peer review is an important part of good practice in: the publication and dissemination of research and research findings; the assessment of applications for research grants; and in the ethics review of research projects.

3.14.2 *Organisations* should encourage researchers to act as peer reviewers for meetings, journals and other publications, grant applications and ethics review of research proposals, and support those who do so.They should recognise the obligations of peer reviewers to be thorough and objective in their work and to maintain confidentiality, and should not put pressure, directly or indirectly, on peer reviewers to breach these obligations.

3.14.3 *Researchers* who carry out peer review should do so to the highest standards of thoroughness and objectivity. They should follow the guidelines for peer review of any organisation for which they carry out such work.

3.14.4 Researchers should maintain confidentiality and not retain or copy any material under review without the express written permission of the organisation which requested the review. They should not make use of research designs or research findings from a paper under review without the express permission of the author(s) and should not allow others to do so. Researchers acting as peer reviewers must declare any relevant conflicts of interest.

3.14.5 While carrying out peer review, researchers may become aware of possible misconduct, such as plagiarism, fabrication or falsification, or have ethical concerns about the design or conduct of the research. In such cases they should inform, in confidence, an appropriate representative of the organisation which requested the review, such as the editor of the relevant journal or chair of the relevant grants or ethics committee.

3.15 Publication and authorship

3.15.1 *Organisations* and researchers should accept their duty to publish and disseminate research in a manner that reports the research and all the findings of the research accurately and without selection that could be misleading.

3.15.2 *Organisations* should ensure that sponsors and funders of research: respect the duty of researchers to publish their research and the findings of their research; do not discourage or suppress appropriate publication or dissemination; and do not attempt to influence the presentation or interpretation of findings inappropriately.

3.15.3 Organisations should provide training and support to guide researchers in the publication and dissemination of research and the findings of research that involves: confidential or proprietary information; issues relating to patents or intellectual property; findings with serious implications for public health; contractual or other legal obligations; and/or interest from the media or the general public.

3.15.4 *Researchers* should address issues relating to publication and authorship, especially the roles of all collaborators and contributors, at an early stage of the design of a project, recognising that, subject to legal and ethical requirements, roles and contributions may change during the time span of the research. Decisions on publication and authorship should be agreed jointly and communicated to all members of the research team.

3.15.5 Authorship should be restricted to those contributors and collaborators who have made a significant intellectual or practical contribution to the work. No person who fulfils the criteria for authorship should be excluded from the submitted work. Authorship should not be allocated to honorary or "guest" authors (i.e. those that do not fulfil criteria of authorship). Researchers should be aware that anyone listed as an author of any work should be prepared to take public responsibility for that work and ensure its accuracy, and be able to identify their contribution to it.

3.15.6 Researchers should list the work of all contributors who do not meet the criteria for authorship in an acknowledgements section. All funders and sponsors of research should be clearly acknowledged and any competing interests listed.

3.15.7 Researchers must clearly acknowledge all sources used in their research and seek permission from any individuals if a significant amount of their work has been used in the publication.

3.15.8 Researchers must adhere to any conditions set by funding or other bodies regarding the publication of their research and its findings in open access repositories within a set period.

3.15.9 Researchers should declare any potential or actual conflicts of interest in relation to their research when reporting their findings at meetings or in publications.

3.15.10 Researchers should be aware that submitting research reports to more than one potential publisher at any given time (i.e. duplicate submission) or publishing findings in more than one publication without disclosure and appropriate acknowledgement of any previous publications (i.e. duplicate publication) is unacceptable.

3.15.11 Researchers who are discouraged from publishing and disseminating their research or its findings, or subjected to attempts to influence the presentation or interpretation of findings inappropriately, should discuss this with the appropriate person(s) in their organisation so that the matter can be resolved.

3.16 Misconduct in research

3.16.1 *Organisations* should define what they consider to be misconduct in research and make it known to researchers. UKRIO defines misconduct in research as including, but not limited to:

a) Fabrication;
b) Falsification;
c) Misrepresentation of data and/or interests and/or involvement;
d) Plagiarism; and
e) Failures to follow accepted procedures or to exercise due care in carrying out responsibilities for:
   i) avoiding unreasonable risk or harm to:
      a. humans;
      b. animals used in research; and
      c. the environment; and
   ii) the proper handling of privileged or private information on individuals collected during the research.

3.16.2 Organisations should establish and publicise a procedure to investigate allegations of misconduct in research (as in section 3.1.4) and ensure that any such allegations are investigated thoroughly and fairly and in a timely manner. The UKRIO Procedure for the Investigation of Misconduct in Research outlines a standard process for investigating alleged misconduct that is thorough and fair to all parties.

3.16.3 Organisations should identify and make known one or more members of staff who have responsibility for investigating allegations of misconduct in research and whom researchers and external organisations, such as journals, can contact with any concerns about the conduct of research. They should make sure that staff who investigate allegations have the necessary training, resources and support to fulfil the requirements of the role.

3.16.4 Organisations should make it clear to researchers that any misconduct in research is unacceptable and should be reported; that researchers who are found to have committed misconduct in research will be subject to disciplinary proceedings; and that where researchers are members of a regulated profession, cases of serious misconduct in research will be referred to the body regulating their profession. They should also make it clear that researchers who are found not to have committed misconduct will be supported and appropriate steps taken to restore their reputation and that of any relevant research project(s).

3.16.5 Organisations should support those who raise concerns about the conduct of research in good faith and not penalise them. This support should be in accordance with the organisation's policy on raising concerns or "whistle blowing".

3.16.6 *Researchers* should know what constitutes misconduct in research and report any suspected misconduct through the relevant procedure of the organisation as soon as they become aware of it. They should recognise that good practice in research includes reporting concerns about the conduct of research and should cooperate with any investigation of misconduct in research when requested. Researchers should work with their institution to support those who raise concerns in good faith about the conduct of research and those who have been exonerated of suspected misconduct.

APPENDIX TWO

The Canadian Tri-Agency Framework: Responsible Conduct of Research[1]

1.1 Introduction

The search for knowledge about ourselves and the world around us is a fundamental human endeavour. Research is a natural extension of this desire to understand and to improve the world in which we live, and its results have both enriched and improved our lives and human society as a whole.

In order to maximize the quality and benefits of research, a positive research environment is required. For researchers, this implies duties of honest and thoughtful inquiry, rigorous analysis, commitment to the dissemination of research results, and adherence to the use of professional standards. For the Canadian Institutes of Health Research (CIHR), the Natural Sciences and Engineering Research Council (NSERC), and the Social Sciences and Humanities Research Council (SSHRC) (the Agencies) and Institutions that receive Agency funding, it calls for a commitment to foster and maintain an environment that supports and promotes the responsible conduct of research.

This Framework sets out the responsibilities and corresponding policies for researchers, Institutions, and the Agencies, that together help support and promote a positive research environment. It specifies the responsibilities of researchers with respect to research integrity, applying for funding, financial management, and requirements for conducting certain types of research, and defines what constitutes a breach of Agency policies. For Institutions, it details the minimum requirements for institutional policies for addressing allegations of all types of policy breaches, and Institutions' responsibilities for promoting responsible conduct of research and reporting to the Agencies. This Framework also sets out the process to be followed by the Agencies, and administered by the Secretariat on Responsible Conduct of Research (SRCR), when addressing allegations of breaches of Agency policies.

A diagram summarizing the process used to address allegations is provided in Appendix A. A glossary of terms is provided in Appendix B.

1.2 Scope

This Framework describes Agency policies and requirements related to applying for and managing Agency funds, performing research, and disseminating results, and the processes that Institutions and Agencies follow in the event of an allegation of a breach of an Agency policy. The provisions of this Framework are subject to the specific terms and conditions of individual funding agreements and the *Agreement on the Administration of Agency Grants and Awards by Research Institutions* between the Agencies and each Institution.

The Institution shall develop and administer a policy(ies) to address allegations of policy breaches by researchers that meets the minimum requirements set out in the Framework. The Institution applies this policy(ies) to all research conducted under its auspices or jurisdiction. In addition, researchers who apply for or hold agency funding are required by the Agencies to adhere to the RCR Framework.

1.3 Objectives

The objectives of the Framework are to:

a. ensure that the funding decisions made by the Agencies are based on accurate and reliable information;
b. ensure public funds for research are used responsibly and in accordance with funding agreements;
c. promote and protect the quality, accuracy, and reliability of research funded by the Agencies; and
d. promote fairness in the conduct of research and in the process for addressing allegations of policy breaches.

---

[1] Panel on Responsible Conduct of Research, The Tri-Agency Framework: Responsible Conduct of Research (2011): http://www.rcr.ethics.gc.ca/eng/policy-politique/framework-cadre/> [accessed 4 Jan 2016].

2 Responsibilities of Researchers

2.1 Tri-Agency Research Integrity Policy

The *Tri-Agency Research Integrity Policy* (the Policy) is a joint policy of the Canadian Institutes of Health Research (CIHR), the Natural Sciences and Engineering Research Council (NSERC), and the Social Sciences and Humanities Research Council (SSHRC) (the Agencies). The Policy's purpose is to support the Agencies in discharging their respective legislative mandates to promote and assist research and in discharging their responsibility to foster a positive research environment.

2.1.1 Scope

The Agencies require that all researchers applying for, or in receipt of, Agency funds comply with the Policy.

2.1.2. Promoting Research Integrity

Researchers shall strive to follow the best research practices honestly, accountably, openly and fairly in the search for and in the dissemination of knowledge. In addition, researchers shall follow the requirements of applicable institutional policies and professional or disciplinary standards and shall comply with applicable laws and regulations. At a minimum, researchers are responsible for the following:

a. Using a high level of rigour in proposing and performing research; in recording, analyzing, and interpreting data; and in reporting and publishing data and findings.
b. Keeping complete and accurate records of data, methodologies and findings, including graphs and images, in accordance with the applicable funding agreement, institutional policies and/or laws, regulations, and professional or disciplinary standards in a manner that will allow verification or replication of the work by others.
c. Referencing and, where applicable, obtaining permission for the use of all published and unpublished work, including data, source material, methodologies, findings, graphs and images.
d. Including as authors, with their consent, all those and only those who have materially or conceptually contributed to, and share responsibility for, the contents of the publication or document, in a manner consistent with their respective contributions, and authorship policies of relevant publications.
e. Acknowledging, in addition to authors, all contributors and contributions to research, including writers, funders and sponsors.
f. Appropriately managing any real, potential or perceived conflict of interest, in accordance with the institution's policy on conflict of interest in research, in order to ensure that the objectives of the Framework (Section 1.3) are met.

2.2 Applying for and Holding Agency Funding

a. Applicants and holders of Agency grants and awards shall provide true, complete and accurate information in their funding applications and related documents and represent themselves, their research and their accomplishments in a manner consistent with the norms of the relevant field.
b. Applicants certify that they are not currently ineligible to apply for, and/or hold, funds from NSERC, SSHRC, CIHR or any other research or research funding organization world-wide for reasons of breach of responsible conduct of research policies such as ethics, integrity or financial management policies.
c. Principal funding applicants must ensure that others listed on the application have agreed to be included.

2.3 Management of Agency Grant and Award Funds

Researchers are responsible for using grant or award funds in accordance with the policies of the Agencies, including the Tri-Agency Financial Administration Guide and Agency grants and awards guides; and for providing true, complete and accurate information on documentation for expenditures from grant or award accounts.

2.4 Agency Requirements for Certain Types of Research

Researchers must comply with all applicable Agency requirements and legislation for the conduct of research, including, but not limited to:

- 2nd edition of Tri-Council Policy Statement: Ethical Conduct of Research Involving Humans (TCPS 2);

- Canadian Council on Animal Care Policies and Guidelines;
- Agency policies related to the Canadian Environmental Assessment Act;
- Licenses for research in the field;
- Canadian Biosafety Standards and Guidelines;
- Controlled Goods Program;
- Canadian Nuclear Safety Commission (CNSC) Regulations; and
- Canada's Food and Drugs Act.

2.5 Rectifying a Breach of Agency Policy

Researchers in breach of an Agency policy are expected to be proactive in rectifying a breach, for example, by correcting the research record, providing a letter of apology to those impacted by the breach, or repaying funds.

3. Breaches of Agency Policies by Researchers

Agency funded researchers—including those researchers who hold awards outside of Canada or at organizations in Canada that have not signed the *Agreement on the Administration of Agency Grants and Awards by Research Institutions* (the Agreement)—must comply with Agency policies. By signing an application for a grant or an award, and by accepting a grant or an award, a researcher agrees to comply with the Agencies' policies.

3.1 Breaches of Agency Policies

Breaches of Agency policies include, but are not limited to, the following:

3.1.1 Breaches of Tri-Agency Research Integrity Policy

a. *Fabrication*: Making up data, source material, methodologies or findings, including graphs and images.
b. *Falsification*: Manipulating, changing, or omitting data, source material, methodologies or findings, including graphs and images, without acknowledgement and which results in inaccurate findings or conclusions.
c. *Destruction of research records*: The destruction of one's own or another's research data or records to specifically avoid the detection of wrongdoing or in contravention of the applicable funding agreement, institutional policy and/or laws, regulations and professional or disciplinary standards.
d. *Plagiarism*: Presenting and using another's published or unpublished work, including theories, concepts, data, source material, methodologies or findings, including graphs and images, as one's own, without appropriate referencing and, if required, without permission.
e. *Redundant publications*: The re-publication of one's own previously published work or part there of, or data, in the same or another language, without adequate acknowledgment of the source, or justification.
f. *Invalid authorship*: Inaccurate attribution of authorship, including attribution of authorship to persons other than those who have contributed sufficiently to take responsibility for the intellectual content, or agreeing to be listed as author to a publication for which one made little or no material contribution.
g. *Inadequate acknowledgement*:Failure to appropriately recognize contributions of others in a manner consistent with their respective contributions and authorship policies of relevant publications.
h. *Mismanagement of Conflict of Interest:* Failure to appropriately manage any real, potential or perceived conflict of interest, in accordance with the Institution's policy on conflict of interest in research, preventing one or more of the objectives of the Framework (Section 1.3) from being met.

3.1.2 Misrepresentation in an Agency Application or Related Document

a. Providing incomplete, inaccurate or false information in a grant or award application or related document, such as a letter of support or a progress report.
b. Applying for and/or holding an Agency award when deemed ineligible by NSERC, SSHRC, CIHR or any other research or research funding organization world-wide for reasons of breach of responsible conduct of research policies such as ethics, integrity or financial management policies.
c. Listing of co-applicants, collaborators or partners without their agreement.

3.1.3 Mismanagement of Grants or Award Funds

Using grant or award funds for purposes inconsistent with the policies of the Agencies; misappropriating grants and award funds; contravening Agency financial policies, namely the Tri-Agency Financial Administration Guide, Agency grants and awards guides; or providing incomplete, inaccurate or false information on documentation for expenditures from grant or award accounts.

3.1.4 Breaches of Agency Policies or Requirements for Certain Types of Research

Failing to meet Agency policy requirements or, to comply with relevant policies, laws or regulations, for the conduct of certain types of research activities; failing to obtain appropriate approvals, permits or certifications before conducting these activities.

3.2 Roles of Individuals in Addressing Allegations of Policy Breaches

Researchers and others play important roles in the process for addressing allegations of policy breaches and in helping to ensure that allegations are addressed appropriately and in a timely manner. The following are guidelines for those making or involved in an allegation:

a. Responsible allegations, or information related to responsible allegations, should be sent directly to the Institution's designated point of contact, in writing, with an exact copy sent to SRCR. Individuals are expected to report in good faith any information pertaining to possible breaches of Agency policies to the Institution where the researcher involved is currently employed, enrolled as a student or has a formal association.
b. Individuals involved in an inquiry or investigation must follow the Institution's policy and process as a complainant, a respondent or a third party, as appropriate.

4. Responsibilities of Institutions

4.1 Memorandum of Understanding on the Roles and Responsibilities in the Management of Federal Grants and Awards

The Agreement on the Administration of Agency Grants and Awards by Research Institutions sets out the minimum roles, responsibilities and requirements that Institutions must meet as a condition of eligibility to apply for, and hold, Agency funding.

4.2 Promoting Responsible Conduct of Research

Institutions shall strive to provide an environment that supports the best research and that fosters researchers' abilities to act honestly, accountably, openly and fairly in the search for, and dissemination of, knowledge. Institutions shall do so by:

a. Establishing and applying responsible research conduct policy(ies) and procedures that meet the requirements of this Framework (Section 4.3);
b. Reporting to the SRCR as per Section 4.4.
c. Promoting education on, and awareness of, the importance of the responsible conduct of research (Section 4.5).

4.3 Institutional Policy Requirements for Addressing Allegations of Policy Breaches

Institutions play important roles in addressing allegations of all types of policy breaches by researchers (as described in Section 3) and in ensuring that such allegations are handled appropriately and in a timely manner. Institutions shall develop and administer a policy(ies) that applies to all research conducted under the auspices or jurisdiction of the Institution to address allegations of policy breaches by researchers that includes, at a minimum, the following sections:

4.3.1 Definitions

The definitions of researchers' responsibilities and breaches of policies as set out in Sections 2 and 3 of this Framework.

4.3.2 Confidentiality

A statement of principle to protect the privacy of the complainant(s) and respondent(s) as far as is possible.

4.3.3 Receiving Allegations

a. A central point of contact at a senior administrative level, to receive all confidential enquiries, allegations of breaches of policies, and information related to allegations.
b. A statement on how anonymous allegations will be addressed.
c. A statement of principle to protect, to the extent possible, the individual making an allegation in good faith or providing information related to an allegation from reprisals in a manner consistent with relevant legislation.
d. A statement indicating that the Institution may independently, or at the Agency's request in exceptional circumstances, take immediate action to protect the administration of Agency funds. Immediate actions could include freezing grant accounts, requiring a second authorized signature from an institutional representative on all expenses charged to the researcher's grant accounts, or other measures, as appropriate.

4.3.4 Investigating Allegations

a. An initial inquiry process to establish whether an allegation is responsible and if an investigation is required.
b. An investigation process for determining the validity of an allegation that provides the complainant and respondent with an opportunity to be heard as part of an investigation, and that allows for the respondent to appeal if a breach of policy is confirmed.
c. An investigation committee, appointed with the authority to decide whether a breach occurred. The investigation committee shall include members who have the necessary expertise and who are without conflict of interest, whether real or apparent, and at least one external member who has no current affiliation with the Institution.
d. Reasonable timelines for completing an inquiry, completing an investigation, reporting the findings, making a decision on what action should be taken, and communicating with the parties involved. The timelines must be within the reporting timeframes outlined in Section 4.4.

4.3.5 Recourse

a. A provision that the investigation committee's report, including its final decision, is provided to the Institution's central point of contact within a timeframe specified in the Institution's policy.
b. A process for determining what kinds of recourse can be taken by the Institution, taking into account the severity of the breach.

4.3.6 Accountability

a. A procedure, which takes into account applicable privacy laws and regulations, to inform all affected parties, in a timely manner, of the decision reached by the investigation committee and of any recourse to be taken by the Institution.
b. A provision for allegations determined to be unfounded that every effort will be made by the Institution to protect or restore the reputation of those wrongly subjected to an allegation.

4.4 Reporting Requirements

a. Subject to any applicable laws, including privacy laws, the Institution shall advise the relevant Agency or SRCR immediately of any allegations related to activities funded by the Agency that may involve significant financial, health and safety, or other risks.
b. The Institution shall write a letter to the SRCR confirming whether or not the Institution is proceeding with an investigation where the SRCR was copied on the allegation or advised as per Section 4.4.a. If a breach is confirmed at the inquiry stage, reporting requirements outlined in Section 4.4.c apply.
c. The Institution shall prepare a report for the SRCR on each investigation it conducts in response to an allegation of policy breaches related to a funding application submitted to an Agency or to an activity funded by an Agency. Subject to any applicable laws, including privacy laws, each report shall include the following information:
   - the specific allegation(s), a summary of the finding(s) and reasons for the finding(s);
   - the process and time lines followed for the inquiry and/or investigation;
   - the researcher's response to the allegation, investigation and findings, and any measures the researcher has taken to rectify the breach; and

- the institutional investigation committee's decisions and recommendations and actions taken by the Institution.

The Institution's report should not include:

- information that is not related specifically to Agency funding and policies; or
- personal information about the researcher, or any other person, that is not material to the Institution's findings and its report to the SRCR.

d. Inquiry letters and investigation reports should be submitted to the SRCR within two and seven months, respectively, of receipt of the allegation by the Institution. These timelines may be extended in consultation with the SRCR if circumstances warrant, and with monthly updates provided to the Agency until the investigation is complete.

e. The Institution and the researcher may not enter into confidentiality agreements or other agreements related to an inquiry or investigation that prevent the Institution from reporting to the Agencies through the SRCR.

f. In cases where the source of funding is unclear, the SRCR reserves the right to request information and reports from the Institution.

4.5 Promoting Awareness and Education

a. An Institution is responsible for:

b. Promoting awareness of what constitutes the responsible conduct of research, including Agency requirements as set out in the Institution's policies, the consequences of failing to meet them, as well as the process for addressing allegations, to all those engaged in research activities at the Institution.

c. Communicating its policy on the responsible conduct of research within the Institution, and making public statistical annual reports on confirmed findings of breaches of that policy and actions taken, subject to applicable laws, including the privacy laws.

d. Communicating within the Institution, the central point of contact responsible for receiving confidential enquiries, allegations and information related to allegations of breaches of Agency policies.

5. Breaches of Agency Policies by Institutions

In accordance with the Agreement signed by the Agencies and each Institution, the Agencies require that each Institution complies with Agency policies as a condition of eligibility to apply for and administer Agency funds.

The process followed by the Agencies to address an allegation of a breach of an Agency policy by an Institution, and the recourse that the Agencies may exercise, commensurate with the severity of a confirmed breach, are outlined in the Agreement.

6. Responsibilities of the Agencies

In striving to meet the objectives of this Framework, the Agencies are responsible for:

a. communicating this Framework, including the contact information for those responsible for its administration; b. responding promptly to enquiries regarding this Framework; c. helping to promote the responsible conduct of research and to assist individuals and Institutions with the interpretation or implementation of this Framework; d. reviewing and updating this Framework at least every five years; and e. responding to allegations of breaches of Agency policies.

6.1 Tri-Agency Process for Addressing Allegations of Policy Breaches by Researchers

Agencies, through the SRCR, play important roles in addressing allegations of breaches of their policies and in ensuring that such allegations are addressed appropriately and in a timely manner. At any time after an allegation is made, the SRCR may request information from the individual and Institution involved.

6.1.1 Receiving Allegations

a. If the SRCR receives an allegation directly from a complainant, it will ask the complainant to provide the information in writing to the Institution concerned, with a copy to the relevant Agency. Anonymous allegations sent directly to the SRCR will be forwarded to the Institution for action in accordance with its statement on anonymous allegations.

b. Following receipt of an allegation, if the matter involves Agency funding and an alleged breach of an Agency policy, the SRCR will follow-up as needed with the complainant, the Institution and other parties, subject to applicable laws, including the *Privacy Act*.

c. An Agency may submit their own allegations directly to an Institution, for example, as a result of information obtained through institutional monitoring reviews or its peer review activities.

6.1.2 Review of Institutional Reports

a. The SRCR may follow-up with the Institution as needed to obtain updates on the status of the investigation.
b. The SRCR will review the Institution's report to determine whether it meets Agency requirements, as outlined in Sections 4.3 and 4.4, and whether there has been a breach of Agency policies, the Agreement and/or a funding agreement. The SRCR may follow-up with the Institution for clarification.

6.1.3 Recourse

a. If the Agency determines that there has been a breach of an Agency policy, it will exercise the recourse it considers appropriate, commensurate with the severity of the breach. When making its decision, the Agency will take into consideration the Institution's findings, the severity of the breach and any actions taken by the Institution and researcher involved to remedy the breach.
b. Such recourse can include, but is not limited to:
   - Issuing a letter of concern to the researcher;
   - requesting that the researcher correct the research record and provide proof that the research record has been corrected;
   - advising the researcher that the Agency will not accept applications for future funding from him/her for a defined time period or indefinitely;
   - terminating remaining instalments of the grant or award;
   - seeking a refund within a defined time frame of all or part of the funds already paid;
   - advising the researcher that the Agency will not consider him/her to serve on agency committees (e.g. peer review, advisory boards); and/or
   - such other recourse available by law.

In exercising the appropriate recourse, the Agency will give consideration to affected research personnel including students, post-doctoral fellows and research support staff.

6.1.4 Accountability and Reporting

a. The Agency will inform the researcher subject to the decision, and his/her Institution, of the Agency's decision, where applicable. The content of this communication will be subject to any applicable laws, including privacy laws.
b. The Agency will notify the appropriate authorities if at any time it becomes aware of possible fraud or other unlawful activity.
c. In cases of a serious breach of Agency policy, as determined by the Agency President, the Agency may publicly disclose the name of the researcher subject to the decision, the nature of the breach, the Institution where the researcher was employed at the time of the breach and the Institution where the researcher is currently employed. In determining whether a breach is serious, the Agency will consider the extent to which the breach jeopardizes the safety of the public or would bring the conduct of research into disrepute.
d. The SRCR will post statistical data on the number of allegations and their outcomes on the its Web site, subject to applicable laws, including the *Privacy Act.*

6.1.5 Measures for Exceptional Circumstances

In exceptional circumstances, taking into account the severity and urgency of the alleged breach, its possible consequences and the potential financial, health, safety or other risks involved, the Agencies reserve the right to take special measures, including the following:

6.1.5.1 *Immediate Action*: The Agency may take immediate action (as set out in Section 4.3.3.d), or may require the Institution to do so. The Agency will consult with the Institution and will consider any actions already taken by the Institution and/or the researcher when deciding on whether further action is required.

6.1.5.2 *Review or Compliance Audit*: The Agency may conduct its own review or compliance audit, or require the Institution to conduct an independent review/audit. The Agency will consult with the Institution and will consider the investigation already planned, underway or completed by the Institution, and its findings.

A. Summary of Process

B. Glossary

This glossary is intended to assist readers in their understanding of the *Tri-Agency Framework: Responsible Conduct of Research*, also referred to as "the Framework." Terms are defined in accordance with the purposes and objectives of the Framework.

Accountability: Being responsible for one's actions.*

Agencies: Canada's three federal granting agencies: the Canadian Institutes of Health Research (CIHR); the Natural Sciences and Engineering Research Council (NSERC); and the Social Sciences and Humanities Research Council (SSHRC).

Agency policies: The set of rules, directives and guidelines published by an individual Agency or jointly by the Agencies.

Agreement: The *Agreement on the Administration of Agency Grants and Awards by Research Institutions* is the agreement between the Agencies and Institutions eligible to receive and manage research funding from the Agencies.

Allegation: A declaration, statement, or assertion communicated in writing to an Institution or Agency to the effect that there has been, or continues to be, a breach of one or more Agency policies, the validity of which has not been established.

Applicant (including co-applicant): An individual who has submitted an application, individually or as part of a group or team, for funding from the Agencies.

Author (including co-author): The writer, or contributing writer, of a research publication or document.

Complainant: An individual or representative from an organization who has notified an Institution or Agency of a potential breach of an Agency policy.

Conflict of interest: A conflict of interest may arise when activities or situations place an individual in a real, potential or perceived conflict between the duties or responsibilities related to research, and personal, institutional or other interests. These interests include, but are not limited to, business, commercial or financial interests pertaining to the individual, their family members, friends, or their former, current or prospective professional associates.+

Eligible institution: An Institution that (a) meets the eligibility requirements to receive funding set out in guidelines issued by the Agency; and (b) has signed the *Agreement on the Administration of Agency Grants and Awards by Research Institutions.*

Fairness: Being impartial and using sound judgment free of prejudice or favouritism.*

Funding agreement: A written agreement that sets out the terms and conditions that an Agency and a researcher agree to for a particular grant or award. It defines the researcher's responsibilities, what constitutes a breach of the agreement, and the consequences of a breach.

Honesty: Being straightforward, and free of fraud and deception.*

Inquiry: The process of reviewing an allegation to determine whether the allegation is responsible, the particular policy or policies that may have been breached, and whether an investigation is warranted based on the information provided in the allegation.

Investigation: A systematic process, conducted by an Institution's investigation committee, of examining an allegation, collecting and examining the evidence related to the allegation, and making a decision as to whether a breach of a policy(ies) has occurred.

Institution: The universities, hospitals, colleges, research institutes, centres and other organizations eligible to receive and manage Agency grant funds on behalf of the grant holders and the Agencies.

Institutional policy: The set of rules, directives and guidelines published by an individual Institution that meet the requirements of *Tri-Agency Framework: Responsible Conduct of Research.*

Non-eligible institution: An Institution other than an eligible Institution.

Openness: Being transparent in process and practice, as characterized by visibility or accessibility of information.*

Research: An undertaking intended to extend knowledge through a disciplined inquiry or systematic investigation.

Researcher: Anyone who conducts research activities.

Respondent: An individual who is identified in an allegation as having possibly breached Agency and/ or institutional policy.

Responsible allegation: A substantially novel allegation made in good faith, confidentially and without malice, that is based on facts which have not been the subject of a previous allegation, and which falls within one or more breaches set out in Section 3 of this Policy.

Serious breach: In determining whether a breach is serious, the Agency will consider the extent to which the breach jeopardizes the safety of the public or brings the conduct of research into disrepute. This determination will be based on an assessment of the nature of the breach, the level of experience of the researcher, whether there is a pattern of breaches by the researcher, and other factors as appropriate. Examples of serious breaches may include:

- Recruiting human participants into a study with significant risks or harms without Research Ethics Board approval, or not following approved protocols
- Using animals in a study with significant risks or harms without Animal Care Committee approval, or not following approved protocols
- Deliberate misuse of research grant funds for personal benefit not related to research
- Knowingly publishing research results based on fabricated data
- Obtaining grant/award funds from the Agencies by misrepresenting one's credentials, qualifications and/or research contributions in an application

---

* CCA (2010). Honesty, Accountability and Trust: Fostering Research Integrity in Canada. Ottawa: Council of Canadian Academies.

[+] Based on definition TCPS 2: Tri-Council Policy Statement: Ethical Conduct of Research Involving Humans.

[1] Research is an undertaking intended to extend knowledge through a disciplined inquiry or systematic investigation. The conduct of research in the context of this Framework includes applying for and managing Agency funds, performing research, and disseminating results (based on the Tri-Council Policy Statement: Ethical Conduct of Research Involving Humans (TCPS 2)).

[2] The responsibilities in this section have drawn from the following sources: CCA (2010). Honesty, Accountability and Trust: Fostering Research Integrity in Canada. Ottawa: Council of Canadian Academies; and the Singapore Statement on Research Integrity, 2nd World Conference on Research Integrity, 21-24 July 2010.

[3] See Canadian Institutes of Health Research Act, Statutes of Canada, 2000, Chapter 6; Natural Sciences and Engineering Research Council Act, Revised Statutes of Canada, 1985, Chapter N-21; Social Sciences and Humanities Research Council Act, Revised Statutes of Canada, 1985, Chapter S-12.

[4] A conflict of interest may arise when activities or situations place an individual in a real, potential or perceived conflict between the duties or responsibilities related to research, and personal, institutional or other interests. These interests include, but are not limited to, business, commercial or financial interests pertaining to the individual, their family members, friends, or their former, current or prospective professional associates. (Based on the Tri-Council Policy Statement: Ethical Conduct of Research Involving Humans (TCPS 2) Chapter 7).

[5] The definitions in this section have drawn from the following sources: CCA (2010). Honesty, Accountability and Trust: Fostering Research Integrity in Canada. Ottawa: Council of Canadian Academies; the Singapore Statement on Research Integrity, 2nd World Conference on Research Integrity, 21-24 July 2010; the Committee on Publication Ethics (COPE) www.publicationethics.org; and the University of Toronto, 'Framework to Address Allegations Of Research Misconduct' Nov. 7 2006.

[6] Adapted from CCA (2010). Honesty, Accountability and Trust: Fostering Research Integrity in Canada. Ottawa: Council of Canadian Academies.

[7] If no Institution that has signed the Agreement is involved, for example, if the researcher is holding an Agency scholarship or fellowship abroad, the Agency may review the file and deal directly with the researcher involved.

APPENDIX THREE

Australian NHMRC Code of Conduct

NATIONAL HEALTH AND MEDICAL RESEARCH COUNCIL AND AUSTRALIAN RESEARCH COUNCIL

AUSTRALIAN CODE FOR THE RESPONSIBLE CONDUCT OF RESEARCH[1]

Principles And Practices To Encourage Responsible Research Conduct

1 General principles of responsible research

Introduction

Responsible research is encouraged and guided by the research culture of the organisation.

A strong research culture will demonstrate:

- honesty and integrity
- respect for human research participants, animals and the environment
- good stewardship of public resources used to conduct research
- appropriate acknowledgment of the role of others in research
- responsible communication of research results.

This section discusses the responsibilities of institutions and researchers to maintain an environment that fosters responsible research.

Responsibilities of institutions

1.1 Promote the responsible conduct of research

Institutions are expected to:

- promote awareness of all guidelines and legislation relating to the conduct of research
- provide documents setting out clearly the policies and procedures based on this Code
- actively encourage mutual cooperation with open exchange of ideas between peers, and respect for freedom of expression and inquiry
- maintain a climate in which responsible and ethical behavior in research is expected.

1.2 Establish good governance and management practices

Good institutional governance and management practices encourage responsible conduct by researchers. Such practices promote quality in research, enhance the reputation of the institution and its researchers, and minimise the risk of harm for all involved.

1.2.1 Each institution should provide an appropriate research governance framework through which research is assessed for quality, safety, privacy, risk management, financial management and ethical acceptability. The framework should specify the roles, responsibilities and accountabilities of all those who play a part in research.

1.2.2 The research governance framework should demand compliance with laws, regulations, guidelines and codes of practice governing the conduct of research in Australia (see Appendix 3). Common law obligations also arise from the relationships between institutions, researchers and participants, while contractual arrangements may impose further obligations.

1.2.3 Each institution must ensure the availability of the documents that help guide good research governance, conduct and management.

1.2.4 There must be a clear policy on collaborative research projects with other organisations, which requires arrangements to be agreed before a project begins. As a minimum, these arrangements

---

[1] Reproduced with permission of the National Health and Medical Research Council and Australian Research Council.

should cover financial management, intellectual property, authorship and publication, consultancies, secondments, ethics approval, and ownership of equipment and data.

1.2.5 Each institution must have a well-defined process for receiving and managing allegations of research misconduct.

1.2.6 There must be a process for regular monitoring of the institution's performance with regard to these guidelines.

1.3 Train staff

It is important that institutions provide induction, formal training and continuing education for all research staff, including research trainees. Training should cover research methods, ethics, confidentiality, data storage and records retention, as well as regulation and governance. Training should also cover the institution's policies regarding responsible research conduct, all aspects of this Code, and other sources of guidance that are available. Institutions may make arrangements for joint induction and training with other institutions.

1.4 Promote mentoring

Institutions should promote effective mentoring and supervision of researchers and research trainees. This includes advising on research ethics, research design and methods, and the responsible conduct of research.

1.5 Ensure a safe research environment

Each institution must ensure a safe working environment in which to conduct each research project.

Responsibilities of researchers

1.6 Maintain high standards of responsible research

Researchers must foster and maintain a research environment of intellectual honesty and integrity, and scholarly and scientific rigour. Researchers must:

- respect the truth and the rights of those affected by their research
- manage conflicts of interest so that ambition and personal advantage do not compromise ethical or scholarly considerations
- adopt methods appropriate for achieving the aims of each research proposal
- follow proper practices for safety and security
- cite awards, degrees conferred and research publications accurately, including the status of any publication, such as under review or in press
- promote adoption of this Code and avoid departures from the responsible conduct of research
- conform to the policies adopted by their institutions and bodies funding the research.

1.7 Report research responsibly

Researchers should ensure that research findings are disseminated responsibly.

1.8 Respect research participants

Researchers must comply with ethical principles of integrity, respect for persons, justice and beneficence.

Written approval from appropriate ethics committees, safety and other regulatory bodies must be obtained when required.

The National Statement on Ethical Conduct in Human Research and Values and Ethics—Guidelines for Ethical Conduct in Aboriginal and Torres Strait Islander Health Research (or any replacement documents) sets out principles for protecting human participants in research (see Appendix 3).

1.9 Respect animals used in research

Researchers must respect the animals they use in research, in accordance with the Australian Code of Practice for the Care and Use of Animals for Scientific Purposes (see Appendix 3).

1.10 Respect the environment

Researchers should conduct their research so as to minimise adverse effects on the wider community and the environment.

1.11 Report research misconduct

A researcher who considers that research misconduct may have occurred must act in a timely manner, having regard to the institution's policies.

Special Responsibilities

1.12 Aboriginal and Torres Strait Islander peoples

It is acknowledged that research with Aboriginal and Torres Strait Islander peoples spans many methodologies and disciplines. There are wide variations in the ways in which Aboriginal and Torres Strait Islander individuals, communities or groups are involved in, or affected by, research to which this Code applies.

This Code should be read in conjunction with Values and Ethics: Guidelines for Ethical Conduct in Aboriginal and Torres Strait Islander Health Research (NHMRC 2003) and the Guidelines for Ethical Research in Indigenous Studies (Australian Institute of Aboriginal and Torres Strait Islander Studies 2002).

1.13 Consumer and community participation in research

Appropriate consumer involvement in research should be encouraged and facilitated by research institutions and researchers. This Code should be read in conjunction with the Statement on Consumer and Community Participation in Health and Medical Research (NHMRC and Consumers' Health Forum of Australia Inc, 2002).

2 Management of research data and primary materials

Introduction

Policies are required that address the ownership of research materials and data, their storage, their retention beyond the end of the project, and appropriate access to them by the research community.

The responsible conduct of research includes the proper management and retention of the research data. Retaining the research data is important because it may be all that remains of the research work at the end of the project. While it may not be practical to keep all the primary material (such as ore, biological material, questionnaires or recordings), durable records derived from them (such as assays, test results, transcripts, and laboratory and field notes) must be retained and accessible.

The researcher must decide which data and materials should be retained, although in some cases this is determined by law, funding agency, publisher or by convention in the discipline.The central aim is that sufficient materials and data are retained to justify the outcomes of the research and to defend them if they are challenged. The potential value of the material for further research should also be considered, particularly where the research would be difficult or impossible to repeat.

Responsibilities of institutions

2.1 Retain research data and primary materials

Each institution must have a policy on the retention of materials and research data. It is important that institutions acknowledge their continuing role in the management of research material and data. The institutional policy must be consistent with practices in the discipline, relevant legislation, codes and guidelines.

2.1.1 In general, the minimum recommended period for retention of research data is 5 years from the date of publication. However, in any particular case, the period for which data should be retained should be determined by the specific type of research. For example:

- for short-term research projects that are for assessment purposes only, such as research projects completed by students, retaining research data for 12 months after the completion of the project may be sufficient
- for most clinical trials, retaining research data for 15 years or more may be necessary
- for areas such as gene therapy, research data must be retained permanently (eg patient records)
- if the work has community or heritage value, research data should be kept permanently at this stage, preferably within a national collection.

2.1.2 A policy is required that covers the secure and safe disposal of research data and primary materials when the specified period of retention has finished.

2.2 Provide secure research data storage and record-keeping facilities

Institutions must provide facilities for the safe and secure storage of research data and for maintaining records of where research data are stored.

2.2.1 There must be a policy on research data ownership and storage. This policy must cover all situations that arise in research, including when researchers move between institutions or employers and when data are held outside Australia. Agreements covering ownership and storage of research data should be reviewed whenever there is movement or departure of research staff.

2.2.2 Wherever possible and appropriate, research data should be held in the researcher's department or other appropriate institutional repository, although researchers should be permitted to hold copies of the research data for their own use. Arrangements for material held in other locations should be documented.

2.2.3 In projects that span several institutions, an agreement should be developed at the outset covering the storage of research data and primary materials within each institution.

2.2.4 Research data and primary materials must be stored in the safe and secure storage provided.

2.3 Identify ownership of research data and primary materials

Each institution must have a policy on the ownership of research materials and data during and following the research project. The ownership may also be influenced by the funding arrangements for the project. As a general rule, the most satisfactory arrangement will be that the materials and data retained at the end of a project are the property of the institution that hosted the project, another institution with an interest in the research, or a central repository.

2.4 Ensure security and confidentiality of research data and primary materials

Each institution must have a policy on the ownership of, and access to, databases and archives that is consistent with confidentiality requirements, legislation, privacy rules and other guidelines.

2.4.1 The policy must guide researchers in the management of research data and primary materials, including storage, access, ownership and confidentiality.

2.4.2 The processes must ensure that researchers are informed of relevant confidentiality agreements and restrictions on the use of research data.

2.4.3 Computing systems must be secure, and information technology personnel must understand their responsibilities for network security and access control.

2.4.4 Those holding primary material, including electronic material, must understand their responsibilities for security and access.

Responsibilities of researchers

2.5 Retain research data and primary materials

When considering how long research data and primary materials are to be retained, the researcher must take account of professional standards, legal requirements and contractual arrangements.

2.5.1 Researchers should retain research data and primary materials for sufficient time to allow reference to them by other researchers and interested parties. For published research data, this may be for as long as interest and discussion persist following publication.

2.5.2 Research data should be made available for use by other researchers unless this is prevented by ethical, privacy or confidentiality matters.

2.5.3 Research data should be retained for at least the minimum period specified in the institutional policy.

2.5.4 If the results from research are challenged, all relevant data and materials must be retained until the matter is resolved. Research records that may be relevant to allegations of research misconduct must not be destroyed.

2.5.5 The institutional policy on the secure and safe disposal of primary materials and research data must be followed.

2.6 Manage storage of research data and primary materials

Researchers must manage research data and primary materials in accordance with the policy of the institution. To achieve this, researchers must:

2.6.1 Keep clear and accurate records of the research methods and data sources, including any approvals granted, during and after the research process.

2.6.2 Ensure that research data and primary materials are kept in safe and secure storage provided, even when not in current use.

2.6.3 Provide the same level of care and protection to primary research records, such as laboratory notebooks, as to the analysed research data.

2.6.4 Retain research data, including electronic data, in a durable, indexed and retrievable form.

2.6.5 Maintain a catalogue of research data in an accessible form.

2.6.6 Manage research data and primary materials according to ethical protocols and relevant legislation.

2.7 Maintain confidentiality of research data and primary materials

Researchers given access to confidential information must maintain that confidentiality. Primary materials and confidential research data must be kept in secure storage. Confidential information must only be used in ways agreed with those who provided it. Particular care must be exercised when confidential data are made available for discussion.

3 Supervision of research trainees

Introduction

All research trainees must receive training on research ethics, this Code and the research policies of the institution concerned. This should have high priority for completion early in their careers. Researchers and supervisors must ensure that the role model they provide to junior colleagues is positive and conducive to a research culture of excellence, integrity, professionalism and mutual respect.

In return, research trainees must understand that in undertaking research they are joining an endeavour that requires dedication and accountability. Thus, research trainees also have responsibilities under this section.

Responsibilities of institutions

3.1 Set standards for supervision and mentorship

Institutions must ensure that each research trainee, whether part of the institution or from elsewhere, has an appropriately qualified and trained supervisor. It follows that the ratio of research trainees to supervisors must be low enough for effective intellectual interaction.

3.2 Induct research trainees

Institutions must ensure that research trainees understand the importance of responsible research conduct.

3.2.1 Each institution must provide induction and training for all research trainees. This training should cover research ethics, occupational health and safety, and environmental protection, as well as technical matters appropriate to the discipline.

3.2.2 he institution must maintain the ready availability of key documents on the responsible conduct of research, including this Code, institutional guidelines on the conduct of research, requirements for research involving humans and animals, privacy and confidentiality, and the institution's mechanisms for dispute resolution.

Responsibilities of researchers and supervisors of research trainees

3.3 Ensure training

Supervisors of research trainees should ensure that training starts as soon as possible in the career of a researcher. Training should encompass discipline-based research methods and other relevant skills, such as the ability to interact with industry and to work with diverse communities.

3.4 Mentor and provide support

The research supervisor should guide the professional development of research trainees. This involves providing guidance in all matters relating to research conduct and overseeing all stages of the research process, including identifying the research objectives and approach, obtaining ethics and other approvals, obtaining funding, conducting the research, and reporting the research outcomes in appropriate forums and media.

3.5 Ensure valid and accurate research

Supervision includes oversight of the research outcomes from those under supervision. A supervisor must be satisfied that the research methods and outcomes of researchers and research trainees under their supervision are appropriate and valid.

3.6 Ensure appropriate attribution

Researchers and supervisors must ensure that research trainees receive appropriate credit for their work.

Responsibilities of research trainees

3.7 Seek guidance

A research trainee must demonstrate a professional attitude towards the research. Frequent sessions with the supervisor are important, requiring the cooperation of both parties. The trainee should not wait until approached by the supervisor but should play an active part in maintaining an appropriate schedule of meetings.

3.8 Undertake induction and training

A research trainee should complete all induction and training courses as soon as practical after starting research in an institution.

4 Publication and dissemination of research findings

Introduction

Dissemination of research findings is an important part of the research process, passing on the benefits to other researchers, professional practitioners and the wider community. Research activities supported by public funding are rarely complete until the results have been made widely available. However, research is expensive and often cannot be undertaken without the support of commercial sponsors, who seek rewards in the form of rights to commercial exploitation of the research outcomes. In such cases, sponsors may seek to delay or otherwise restrict the release of research results. In publications and dissemination in such instances, the general principles of responsible research set out in Section 1 of this Code apply.

There are many ways of disseminating research findings. Formal publication of the results of research will usually take place in academic journals or books, but this is not always the case. This section of the Code applies to all forms of dissemination, including non-refereedpublications, such as web pages, and other media such as exhibitions or films, as well as professional and institutional repositories.
This section should be read in conjunction with Sections 5 (Authorship) and 6 (Peer review).

Responsibilities of institutions

4.1 Promote responsible publication and dissemination of research findings

Institutions must promote an environment of honesty, integrity, accuracy and responsibility in the dissemination of research findings.

4.2 Protect confidentiality and manage intellectual property

4.2.1 Institutions must ensure that all parties to the research are made aware of the nature and scope of confidentiality agreements (see also paragraph 2.7).

4.2.2 Institutions must maintain a policy that protects the intellectual property rights of the institution, the researcher, research trainees and sponsors of the research, as appropriate.

4.2.3 Institutions must ensure that the sponsors of research understand the importance of publication in research and do not delay publication beyond the time needed to protect intellectual property and other relevant interests.

4.2.4 Institutions must ensure that researchers are aware of contractual arrangements that restrict, delay or limit publication.

4.3 Support communication of research findings to the wider public

4.3.1 Institutions should make available assistance, such as through a media relations or a science communication officer, to researchers when communicating research findings through the media.

4.3.2 When reporting research results for publicity purposes, institutions must make every effort to acknowledge partner institutions and sponsors involved in collaborative research.

Responsibilities of researchers

4.4 Disseminate all research findings

Researchers have a responsibility to their colleagues and the wider community to disseminate a full account of their research as broadly as possible.

4.4.1 The account should be complete, and, where applicable, include negative findings and results contrary to their hypotheses.

4.4.2 Publication activities must take account of any restrictions relating to intellectual property or culturally sensitive data.

4.4.3 Researchers must, where feasible, also provide research participants with an appropriate summary of the research results; see, for example, the Statement on Consumer and Community Participation in Health and Medical Research (see Appendix 3).

4.5 Ensure accuracy of publication and dissemination

Researchers must take all reasonable steps to ensure that their findings are accurate and properly reported. If they become aware of misleading or inaccurate statements about their work, they must correct the record as soon as possible.

4.6 Cite the work of other authors fully and accurately

Researchers must ensure that they cite other relevant work appropriately and accurately when disseminating research findings. Use of the work of other authors without acknowledgement is unethical.

4.7 Multiple submissions of research findings

It is not acceptable to include the same research findings in several publications, except in particular and clearly explained circumstances, such as review articles, anthologies, collections, or translations into another language. An author who submits substantially similar work to more than one publisher, or who submits work similar to work already published, must disclose this at the time of submission.

4.8 Obtain permission for republishing

Researchers must take all reasonable steps to obtain permission from the original publisher before republishing research findings.

4.9 Disclose research support accurately

A publication must include information on all sources of financial and in-kind support for the research and any potential conflicts of interest. Researchers must acknowledge the host institution and funding sources of the research.

4.10 Register clinical trials

Researchers must register clinical trials with a recognised register to promote access to information about all clinical trials.

4.11 Manage confidentiality

Sometimes the confidentiality requirements of a sponsor can prevent or delay peer review until after the research results are delivered to the sponsor. In such cases, the researcher must explain to the sponsor that the work has not been subject to peer review. The importance of peer review in the research process is discussed in Section 6. Whenever a sponsor's confidentiality requirements prevent peer review of a research report before its delivery to the sponsor, the researcher must inform the sponsor.

4.12 Responsibly communicating research findings in the public arena

Subject to any conditions imposed by the research sponsor, researchers should seek to communicate their research findings to a range of audiences, which may include the sponsor, professional organisations, peer researchers, policy makers and the community. Researchers may be interviewed by the media, invited to participate in debates, and approached by individuals for comment. It is important that all these activities are considered and supported where possible.

However, while it is straightforward to discuss research findings with peers, it is harder to do so effectively with other groups and the media, where the scope for misunderstanding is much greater and frequently there is no opportunity to review the report of discussions before it becomes public.

Researchers should seek opportunities and be ready to participate in workshops and other activities where professional assistance is provided in communicating with the media and the wider community.

The following points should be noted in relation to publicly communicating research findings:

4.12.1 Discussing research findings in the public arena should not occur until the findings have been tested through peer review. In discussing the outcomes of a research project, special care should be taken to explain the status of the project—for example, whether it is still in progress or has been finalised.

4.12.2 To minimise misunderstanding about research outcomes, researchers should undertake to promptly inform those directly impacted by the research, including interested parties, before informing the popular media.

4.12.3 The outcomes of research with a strong commercial element may have to be presented to a stock exchange or financial body before any public release.

4.12.4 Any restrictions on communications that have been agreed with the sponsor must be honoured.

5 Authorship

Introduction

The outcomes of research may be disseminated in a variety of ways but enduring forms, such as journal articles, are particularly important and to be an author for such a form is meritorious. To be named as an author, a researcher must have made a substantial scholarly contribution to the work and be able to take responsibility for at least that part of the work they contributed.

Attribution of authorship depends to some extent on the discipline, but in all cases, authorship must be based on substantial contributions in a combination of:

- conception and design of the project
- analysis and interpretation of research data
- drafting significant parts of the work or critically revising it so as to contribute to the interpretation.

The right to authorship is not tied to position or profession and does not depend on whether the contribution was paid for or voluntary. It is not enough to have provided materials or routine technical support, or to have made the measurements on which the publication is based. Substantial intellectual involvement is required.

A person who qualifies as an author must not be included or excluded as an author without their permission. This should be in writing, and include a brief description of their contribution to the work.

Sometimes the editor of a significant collective work or anthology has responsibilities analogous to those listed above for authorship and, in such cases, similar criteria apply to 'editor' as to 'author'. However, the term 'editor' should be applied only to a person who has played a significant role in the intellectual shaping of a publication.

Responsibilities of institutions

5.1 Have criteria for authorship

Institutions must have a policy on the criteria for authorship consistent with this Code, seeking to minimise disputes about authorship and helping to resolve them if they arise.

Where a work has several authors, one should be appointed executive author to record authorship and to manage communication about the work with the publisher.

Responsibilities of researchers

5.2 Follow policies on authorship

Researchers should adhere to the authorship criteria of this Code and their institution's policies.

5.3 Agree on authorship

Collaborating researchers should agree on authorship of a publication at an early stage in the research project and should review their decisions periodically.

5.4 Include all authors

Researchers must offer authorship to all people, including research trainees, who meet the criteria for authorship listed above. Those offered authorship must accept or decline in writing.

5.5 Do not allow unacceptable inclusions of authorship

Authorship should not be offered to those who do not meet the requirements set out above. For example, none of the following contributions, in and of themselves, justifies including a person as an author:

- being head of department, holding other positions of authority, or personal friendship with the authors
- providing a technical contribution but no other intellectual input to the project or publication
- providing routine assistance in some aspects of the project, the acquisition of funding or general supervision of the research team
- providing data that has already been published or materials obtained from third parties, but with no other intellectual input.

5.6 Acknowledge other contributions fairly

Researchers must ensure that all those who have contributed to the research, facilities or materials are properly acknowledged, such as research assistants and technical writers. Where individuals are to be named, their written consent must be obtained.

5.7 Extend the authorship policy to web-based publications

Authors of web-based publications must be able to take responsibility for the publication's content and must be clearly identified in the publication.

5.8 Maintain signed acknowledgments of authorship for all publications

The department of the executive or senior author must retain the written acknowledgment of authorship discussed above in the form of an original hand-written signature. Where it is not practical to obtain an original signature, it is acceptable to use faxed or emailed consent. This also applies to published conference abstracts and similar publications. If an author is deceased or cannot be contacted, the publication can proceed provided that there are no grounds to believe that this person would have objected to being included as an author.

6 Peer review

Introduction

The term 'peer review' is used here to describe impartial and independent assessment of research by others working in the same or a related field. Peer review has a number of important roles in research and research management, in the assessment of grant applications, in selecting material for publication, in the review of performance of researchers and teams, and in the selection of staff.

Participation in peer review processes should be encouraged. Peer review provides expert scrutiny of a project, and helps to maintain high standards and encourage accurate, thorough and credible research reporting.

Peer review may also draw attention to deviations from the principles of this Code, such as double publication, errors and misleading statements. Peer review has been important in the detection of fabrication and fraud in research. However, on its own, it cannot ensure research integrity.

Responsibilities of institutions

6.1 Encourage participation in peer review

Institutions should recognise the importance of the peer review process and encourage and support researchers to participate.

Responsibilities of peer reviewers

6.2 Conduct peer review responsibly

It is important that participants in peer review:

- are fair and timely in their review
- act in confidence and do not disclose the content or outcome of any process in which they are involved
- declare all conflicts of interest, do not permit personal prejudice to influence the
- peer review process, and do not introduce considerations that are not relevant to the review criteria
- do not take undue or calculated advantage of knowledge obtained during the peer review process
- ensure that they are informed about, and comply with, the criteria to be applied
- do not agree to participate in peer review outside their area of expertise
- give proper consideration to research that challenges or changes accepted ways of thinking.

Responsibilities of researchers

6.3 Do not interfere during the peer review process

Researchers whose work is undergoing peer review must not seek to influence the process or outcomes.

6.4 Participate in peer review

Researchers in receipt of public funding have a responsibility to participate in peer review processes.

6.5 Mentor trainees in peer review

Supervising researchers have a responsibility to assist trainee researchers in developing the necessary skills for peer review and understanding their obligation to participate.

6.6 Declare conflicts of interest

Peer reviewers must declare all relevant conflicts of interest.

7 Conflicts of interest

Introduction

A conflict of interest exists where there is a divergence between the individual interests of a person and their professional responsibilities such that an independent observer might reasonably conclude that the professional actions of that person are unduly influenced by their own interests.

Conflicts of interest in the research area are common and it is important that they are disclosed and dealt with properly. Conflicts of interest have the potential to compromise judgments and decisions that should be made impartially. Such compromise could undermine community trust in research.

Financial conflicts of interest are foremost in the public mind but other conflicts of interest also occur in research, including personal, professional and institutional advantages.

The perception that a conflict of interest exists is also a serious matter and raises concerns about the integrity of individuals or the management practices of the institution.

There is a broad range of actual and potential conflicts of interest in the research environment, and institutions need to have a comprehensive policy in place to cover the likely range of circumstances.

Responsibilities of institutions

7.1 Maintain a policy

Institutions must have a policy for managing conflicts of interest. A range of responses is required, depending on the nature of a conflict, to prevent researchers from influencing decisions unfairly and to avoid unwarranted perception that a conflict of interest has been ignored.

Advice on managing conflicts of interest is readily available from organisations such as law societies and institutes of company directors. In relation to policy, the following points should be observed:

7.1.1 Ensure that the policy is clearly written and readily available to all staff.

7.1.2 In each conflict of interest case, encourage a full disclosure by those involved of the circumstances giving rise to concerns about the conflict of interest. This sometimes involves information that people are unwilling to disclose publicly, and a process involving disclosure to a small group in confidence should also be provided. Where those involved are unable or unwilling to make any disclosure at all, they should withdraw from processes that could be influenced by conflicts.

7.1.3 Where the circumstances constitute a conflict of interest, or may lead people to perceive a conflict of interest, the person concerned must not take part in decision-making processes. The most satisfactory approach is for complete withdrawal (eg leaving the room for the item), but some bodies allow some general discussion of the matter before the person withdraws. It is preferable that the person concerned does not remain in the room, even if silent, while the matter is debated and decided.

7.1.4 A record must be kept of how each conflict is managed in the proceedings, even if confidential information must be omitted. It is important that the possibility of a conflict is acknowledged in each case, along with an outline of how it was managed.

7.1.5 The policy should aim to cover the full range of possible conflicts of interest, and the policy must be reviewed regularly to enable amendment informed by experience and legislative and regulatory developments.

Responsibilities of researchers

7.2 Disclose conflicts of interest

Researchers frequently have a conflict of interest that cannot be avoided. Decisionmaking processes in research often need expert advice, and the pool of experts in a field can be so small that all the experts have some link with the matter under decision. An individual researcher should therefore expect to be conflicted from time to time, and be ready to acknowledge the conflict and make disclosures as appropriate.

7.2.1 Researchers should use the following approach to manage conflicts of interest:

- read and understand the policy of the institution
- maintain records of activities that may lead to conflicts, for example: consultancies; membership of committees, boards of directors, advisory groups, or selection committees; and financial delegation or in receipt of cash, services or equipment from outside bodies to support research activities
- when invited to join a committee or equivalent, review current activities for actual or apparent conflicts and bring possible conflicts of interest to the attention of those running the process
- disclose any actual or apparent conflict of interest as soon as it becomes apparent.

7.2.2 While there is no requirement to disclose the details of a conflict of interest, for example, because of a confidentiality agreement or for personal reasons, the existence of the conflict must be declared, followed by withdrawal from the situation.

8 Collaborative research across institutions

Introduction

Research can involve a wide range of collaborations within institutions, between institutions, and internationally. Collaborative research has increased markedly in recent times and this raises specific issues, such as sharing intellectual property, managing research findings, managing conflicts of interest, and commercialising research outcomes.

Research practices differ between countries, but researchers supported by Australian public funding should make every effort to comply with this Code even when conducting research outside Australia. Any need to deviate from this Code must be submitted for institutional approval.

Responsibilities of institutions

8.1 Establish agreements for each collaboration

Organisations involved in a joint research project should ensure that an agreement is reached with the partners on the management of the research. Such an agreement should follow the general principles of this Code, including integrity, honesty and a commitment to excellence.

The agreement should be in writing. It must cover intellectual property, confidentiality and copyright issues; sharing commercial returns, responsibility for ethics and safety clearances; and reporting to appropriate agencies. It should address the protocols to be followed by the partners when disseminating the research outcomes, and the management of primary research materials and research data.

The agreement may take various forms, including a legal contract signed by the chief executive officer, an exchange of letters, or a research management plan signed by all parties, or management plans signed by appropriate representatives from all parties.

Each organisation must ensure that its researchers are aware of, and understand, the policy and agreements governing the joint research collaboration.

8.2 Manage conflicts of interest

Institutions must have a policy for managing conflicts of interest that arise in collaborative research (see Section 7).

8.3 Manage access to research materials

The collaborating parties should each identify a person to be involved in the management of research data, primary materials and other items to be retained at the end of the project.

Responsibilities of researchers

8.4 Comply with multi-institutional agreements

Researchers involved in joint research must be aware of, and comply with, all policies and written agreements affecting the project, particularly those relating to the dissemination of research findings and the management of research data and primary materials.

8.5 Declare conflicts of interest

When establishing a research collaboration, researchers must disclose as soon as possible any actual or apparent conflicts of interest relating to any aspect of the project.
SECTION: Appendix
Appendix Number: Part B
Title: NHMRC CODE OF CONDUCT
Breaches of the Code, research misconduct, and the framework for resolving allegations

9 Breaches of the Code and misconduct in research

Part A of this document describes principles and practices for encouraging the responsible conduct of research. Part B addresses how to respond to an allegation that research has not been conducted responsibly.

Allegations of deviations from this Code and of misconduct in research will be made from time to time. A prompt and effective response is required in each case. All affected parties must be treated fairly and the situation remedied, and appropriate steps taken to maintain public confidence in the research endeavour. In Australia, minor matters have been handled entirely within institutions. However, more serious matters have been treated in various ways, lacking consistency and public acceptance. Recent studies in Australia, the United States and the United Kingdom (see Appendix 3) indicate a higher rate of unreported offences than expected. Commentators have suggested that growth in the rate of serious offences is real and is the result of commercial and other pressures for success, particularly in areas such as biotechnology and medicine.

A complaint that a researcher has not acted responsibly requires a response that may include the following steps:

- a discreet investigation
- a formal inquiry
- the imposition of a sanction or penalty
- actions to remedy the situation
- advice to expert groups and public statements as appropriate.

In most cases the response will not require all these steps, for example when the complaint cannot be sustained or when the researcher concedes. However, an allegation of serious misconduct that may attract a significant penalty, if proven, will require all the steps and great care.

The process outlined above resembles the process for almost all complaints of misconduct. However, research is complex and requires great care to get it right because of the number of interested parties and the extent to which a serious offence may lead to collateral damage. Interested parties range from the employing institution to professional journals and funding bodies; those affected by the offence range from colleagues and students to the professions and public confidence in research.

The number of serious misconduct cases may be increasing, but it is still small, and so is the number of people with experience in managing such cases. Therefore, it is important that processes are consistent and that there is a repository of experiences and advice to guide future cases.

Many commentators have called for serious research misconduct cases to be investigated by an independent statutory tribunal to maximise experience, simplify avoiding conflict of interest, and achieve transparency and accountability. There is much to recommend such a body but many steps are required to create it, and complex issues in the Australian constitutional and other legal environments must first be addressed. However, this Code does require institutions to establish independent external research misconduct inquiries to evaluate allegations of serious research misconduct that are contested.

10 Concepts and Definitions

This Code establishes a framework for dealing with allegations of research misconduct and establishing inquiries to determine whether research misconduct has occurred. The penalties for research misconduct will be contained in institutional policies for employment. Serious misconduct in research can lead to serious penalties, including termination of employment, and people who are the subject of such complaints must be entitled to appeal to a higher body through institutional disciplinary processes. For this and other reasons, it is important that definitions are clear and processes demonstrate procedural fairness.

Breaches of the Code and research misconduct

In addressing the process for responding to allegations, it is useful to distinguish between minor issues that can clearly be remedied within the institution and more serious matters where the involvement of people who are independent of the institution is desirable. The boundary between minor and serious issues is not sharp, and those determining a particular case will find it helpful to consider the penalties that might be applied by the employing institution if the allegations are true, the steps needed to ensure procedural fairness to all concerned, the extent to which there are consequences outside the institution, and the standing of the research community in the eyes of the general public.

Here, the term breach is used for less serious deviations from this Code that are appropriately remedied within the institution. The term research misconduct is used for more serious or deliberate deviations.

Research misconduct

A complaint or allegation relates to research misconduct if it involves all of the following:

- an alleged breach of this Code
- intent and deliberation, recklessness or gross and persistent negligence
- serious consequences, such as false information on the public record, or adverse effects on research participants, animals or the environment.

Research misconduct includes fabrication, falsification, plagiarism or deception in proposing, carrying out or reporting the results of research, and failure to declare or manage a serious conflict of interest. It includes avoidable failure to follow research proposals as approved by a research ethics committee, particularly where this failure may result in unreasonable risk or harm to humans, animals or the environment. It also includes the wilful concealment or facilitation of research misconduct by others.

Repeated or continuing breaches of this Code may also constitute research misconduct, and do so where these have been the subject of previous counselling or specific direction.

Research misconduct does not include honest differences in judgment in management of the research project, and may not include honest errors that are minor or unintentional. However, breaches of this Code will require specific action by supervisors and responsible officers of the institution.

Box B.1 contains some examples of research misconduct.

Box B.1 Examples of research misconduct

There are many ways in which researchers may deviate from the standards and provisions of this Code, including but not limited to:

- fabrication of results
- falsification or misrepresentation of results
- plagiarism
- misleading ascription of authorship
- failure to declare and manage serious conflicts of interest
- falsification or misrepresentation to obtain funding
- conducting research without ethics approval as required by the National Statement on Ethical Conduct in Research Involving Humans and the Australian Code of Practice for the Care and Use of Animals for Scientific Purposes
- risking the safety of human participants, or the wellbeing of animals or the environment
- deviations from this Code that occur through gross or persistent negligence
- wilful concealment or facilitation of research misconduct by others.

Relationship to other forms of misconduct

The framework in this part of the Code is designed to investigate and make findings on the veracity of allegations about research misconduct. The need for a framework specifically for the investigation of research misconduct arises because of the complex and technical issues commonly associated with research; because third parties, such as collaborators, publishers, and potential beneficiaries of the research, will usually be from outside the institution; and because of the need to assure the public that researchers and their institutions regard research misconduct as a serious matter.

The research misconduct framework contained in this Code is designed to determine findings of fact and what, if any, research misconduct has occurred. This research misconduct framework does not address disciplinary issues.

Employing institutions have agreements with their employees on other forms of misconduct, such as harassment, bullying or financial misconduct. This Code introduces additional processes that are to be applied when the allegations involve research misconduct. The processes in this Code are not for the investigation of other forms of misconduct, although sometimes research misconduct may be associated with other forms of misconduct.

The findings of fact and any determinations of research misconduct reached through processes that comply with this Code must then be used within the institution's separate procedures regulating employment conditions.

Misconduct unrelated to the research process is not research misconduct and falls outside the scope of this Code.

The processes of resolving research misconduct should be progressively incorporated into the institution's instruments regulating employment conditions when these are next negotiated. Responsibility for decisions on employment or sanctions of employees found to have committed research misconduct remains with the employing institution.

Chief executive officer (CEO)

The CEO is the chief executive officer of the institution where a departure from this Code or misconduct in research is alleged to have taken place. In an Australian university, for example, the CEO is the vice-chancellor.

Designated person

The role of the designated person is to advise the CEO or their delegated officer whether allegations appear to be justified and whether a prima facie case exists. The designated person should be a senior member of the institution's management structure who is experienced in research and research management.

The designated person receives a written allegation, conducts a preliminary investigation, and provides advice to the CEO or their delegated officer. The designated person must maintain full records of all matters that relate to allegations of research misconduct. In most university settings, for example, the designated person will be the deputy vice-chancellor (research) or similar. The designated person must not be the CEO.

When undertaking a preliminary assessment of allegations, the designated person should take into account the requirements of this Code and the institution's policy on research misconduct. He or she should also consider whether any immediate action should be taken, such as referral of allegations not related to research to other institutional disciplinary processes. Where necessary, the designated person must ensure that arrangements in the local workplace are fair to all parties until the allegations are resolved. The designated person must have authority to secure all relevant documents and evidence so that they are available if it is decided that the allegations are to be investigated.

The designated person must advise the CEO or their delegated officer whether the allegations should be dismissed, dealt with under misconduct provisions unrelated to research misconduct, referred back to the departmental level with instructions as to how they are to be handled, or investigated further through a research misconduct inquiry. If the advice is to investigate the matter further, the designated person should also advise how the inquiry should be constituted. After providing advice to the CEO or their delegated officer, the designated person should not play any further role in the matter, except that he or she may be called to give evidence or expert opinion.

Adviser in research integrity

Institutions must appoint one or more senior staff members as advisers in research integrity. Each adviser will be able to advise a staff member who is unsure about a research conduct issue and may be considering whether to make an allegation. Advisers should be people with research experience, wisdom, analytical skills, empathy, knowledge of the institution's policy and management structure, and familiarity with the accepted practices in research. An adviser should not be involved in a case if he or she has a relevant conflict of interest.

The adviser in research integrity should explain the options open to the person considering, making, or having made an allegation. These options include:

- referring the matter directly to the person against whom the allegation is being made
- not proceeding or withdrawing the allegation if discussion resolves the concerns
- referring the allegation to a person in a supervisory capacity for resolution at the local or departmental level
- making an allegation of research misconduct in writing to the designated person.

The adviser's role does not extend to investigation or assessment of the allegation.

The adviser must not make contact with the person who is the subject of the allegation, and he or she must not be involved in any subsequent inquiry.

Procedural fairness

When an institution establishes a panel of people to conduct an inquiry that may lead to disciplinary action, the person who is the subject of the inquiry must be granted a fair hearing under the legal principle of procedural fairness,[2] also known as 'natural justice'. To ensure procedural fairness, the allegations of research misconduct must be stated clearly in writing, the person facing the allegations has a right to be heard, and the members of the panel must be free from bias or preconception and must conduct themselves in a manner that demonstrates this.

In addition, the panel should provide its findings, and the reasons for those findings, in writing. There should also be an avenue for the findings to be appealed.

---

[2] See Forbes (2002), *Justice in Tribunals*, (3rd ed) for a more detailed discussion of procedural fairness and natural justice.

11 Responsibilities

A number of people have responsibilities for resolving allegations of breaches of this Code and research misconduct, including:

- the CEO, who has overall responsibility for the process, although certain aspects may be delegated as agreed by the governing body of the institution
- the designated person, who conducts a preliminary investigation to assess the allegations and provides advice to the CEO or their delegated officer
- advisers in research integrity, appointed by the institution to advise those making, or considering making, allegations
- the head of department or research centre
- research supervisors
- researchers.

It is important that all are aware of their responsibilities, the institutional policies that govern research, and the process for receiving and resolving allegations.

Anyone who forms a reasonable suspicion that research misconduct has occurred must act in a timely manner in accordance with the institution's policy.

Responsibilities at the institutional level

Policies on allegations

Institutions must have a written policy on receiving complaints or allegations related to research. Approaches may range from tentative inquiries about whether breaches have occurred, through to documented allegations of apparent research misconduct. The range of complaints and allegations from minor to serious, the technical elements, and different practices between disciplines mean that a flexible framework to handle the allegations is needed. An allegation of research misconduct may be linked with other types of misconduct, such as bullying, harassment or financial irregularities, adding other dimensions of employer–employee relationships. For these reasons, complaints about research conduct should be directed to a person in a responsible position with experience in considering them, such as the leader of the research group, the head of department, or a senior person in the administration.

The policy on receiving allegations and complaints about research misconduct should recognise the following categories:

- *Failure to implement the Code*

Failure to take responsibility for achieving the standards aspired to in Part A of this Code.

- *Breaches of the Code*

Specific actions or omissions that constitute breaches of this Code, but lack the seriousness of consequence or wilfulness to constitute research misconduct. Such breaches should be remedied by counselling or advice. Their repetition or continuation may, however, lead to more serious consequences and may constitute research misconduct.

- *Research misconduct*

Serious breaches of the Code that are sufficiently substantial to warrant formal allegation, investigation, and denial or admission. If proven, such misconduct would be expected to lead to disciplinary action by the institution in accordance with its instruments of employment.

All allegations must be addressed appropriately. Breaches of this Code that are readily admitted and corrected do not automatically represent research misconduct, because they may occur through inexperience, honest error in the design or execution of the research, or the interpretation of research results. However, allegations of a minor nature that are contested can become major issues if they are not handled appropriately.

A person who is the subject of an allegation must be treated fairly and provided with opportunities to respond to allegations in writing.

A person who makes an allegation must also be treated fairly and according to any legislative provisions for whistleblowers during and following investigation of the allegations.

Reviewing employer–employee agreements

The process for handling research misconduct must not only be consistent with the framework established by this Code but must also accord with relevant workplace agreements and the law. This process will in all likelihood be distinct from those for other forms of misconduct in the workplace, such as sexual harassment, bullying and discrimination, because different approaches from their investigation are needed.

The National Health and Medical Research Council and the Australian Research Council expect that institutions in receipt of public research funds will progressively include this framework for handling research misconduct in relevant instruments regulating employment conditions.

Appointing a designated person and advisers in research integrity

Institutions must appoint a designated person, other than the CEO, to whom allegations of research misconduct must be directed, and one or more persons as advisers in research integrity.

Responsibilities at the departmental or research centre level

Establishing a responsible research environment is the most effective way of preventing research misconduct and other breaches of this Code. It also provides a sound basis for detecting and dealing with research misconduct should it arise. Thus, research groups should agree on how they will implement this Code and cooperate in maintaining high standards of research practice.

Wherever possible, supervisors and heads of departments should be the first point of contact when concerns arise. They are required to establish and maintain a high standard of behaviour in the environment in which the concerns have arisen. If a conflict of interest may exist for the supervisor or head of department, the first point of contact should be an experienced but independent senior mentor, such as an adviser in research integrity.

Breaches of this Code that do not constitute research misconduct should, as far as possible, be handled at the departmental level. However, even where alleged breaches are technical or minor, they should be handled fairly and in a manner that provides the maximum opportunity for improvement. Full records of the process must be kept. Supervisors and heads of departments must comply with institutional policy, including referral of the issues to the designated person when required. Failure by supervisors or heads of departments to address issues properly may in itself represent misconduct.

12 The framework for resolving allegations

Complaints and allegations

Copies of the institution's policy setting out how to complain or make allegations of breaches of this Code and research misconduct must be readily accessible to all who work in the institution.

The framework for receiving and resolving allegations is outlined in Box B.2.

Box B.2 Framework for complaints and allegations

- Anyone who is concerned that a researcher has not acted responsibly must take action in a timely manner in accordance with this Code and the institution's policy.
- The institution has appointed a number of senior staff to act as advisers in research integrity. An adviser can be approached in confidence to discuss the issue of concern. The adviser will discuss the matter, the Code and the policies of the institution, andexplain the options for taking action.
- It is preferable that, in the first instance at least, complaints and allegations are dealt with at the departmental level. However, if circumstances make this difficult or not possible, the adviser will suggest other approaches.
- If the complaint cannot be handled to everyone's satisfaction at the departmental level, a formal complaint or allegation must be made in writing to the designated person appointed to this role by the institution.
- The designated person must advise the CEO or their delegated officer whether a primafacie case exists, and how to proceed. Options include:
  - dismissing the allegations
  - instructing the department on how to deal with the allegations

- – dealing with the complaint under provisions unrelated to research misconduct
- – investigating the matter further through a research misconduct inquiry.
- If the CEO or their delegated officer decides that a research misconduct inquiry is needed, he or she must decide whether to use an internal institutional research misconduct inquiry or an independent external research misconduct inquiry.
- Upon completion of its tasks, the research misconduct inquiry must advise the CEO of its findings of fact and what, if any, research misconduct has occurred.
- The CEO must then determine the actions to be followed, according to institutional policy.
- Subsequent actions may, as appropriate, include informing relevant parties of the outcome and correcting the public record of the research.

Sometimes it is not possible to deal with allegations of breaches of this Code at the departmental level, although this is the preferred route. People who feel unable to raise the matter with the supervisor or head of department must be able to go directly to an experienced senior mentor, such as an adviser in research integrity or an appropriate senior officer of the institution. This will be necessary when an allegation concerns the supervisor or head of the department.

Ignorance, poor judgment or inexperience may lead some researchers to breach inadvertently the provisions of this Code. Provided the alleged breaches do not constitute research misconduct as defined above, the researcher acknowledges the breach, the consequences of the breach are remedied and appropriate steps are taken to prevent recurrence, the matter can rest at the departmental level.

Allegations of research misconduct as defined earlier must be referred to the designatedperson, either directly or by the head of the department.

The research misconduct inquiry

The role of the CEO

Upon receiving the designated person's advice, the CEO (or their delegated officer, if this has been formally agreed to by the institution's governing body) must decide whether to accept the advice and how to proceed. At this stage, in the event of an admission of research misconduct, the issue may be resolved to the satisfaction of all parties. If the CEO or their delegated officer does not proceed to a research misconduct inquiry, he or she must notify in writing those making the allegation, the person who is the subject of the allegation, and the designated person.

If the CEO or their delegated officer decides to proceed to a research misconduct inquiry, he or she must provide this decision in writing to those making the allegation, the person who is the subject of the allegation, the designated person, and any other parties as required under any agreement, such as funding bodies and collaborating institutions.

In making a decision to proceed to an internal institutional research misconduct inquiry or an independent external research misconduct inquiry, the CEO or their delegated officer must take into consideration the advice received from the institution's designated person. The CEO or their delegated officer must also take into account the potential consequences for the accused, the accuser, other parties and institutions in the event that the allegation(s) were to be upheld, and the need to maintain public confidence in research. If, in his or her judgment, these are likely to be serious, the CEO or their delegated officer must establish an independent external research misconduct inquiry.

In the event that the CEO or their delegated officer makes a decision to conduct an internal institutional research misconduct inquiry, and later discovers the potential consequences of the allegation(s) are more serious than originally anticipated, it may be necessary to disband the internal inquiry and make new arrangements for an external independent research misconduct inquiry.

Internal institutional research misconduct inquiry

An internal institutional research misconduct inquiry is established by appointing appropriate members, including at least one member with knowledge and experience in the relevant field of research and at least one member who is familiar with the responsible conduct of research. At least one member should have experience on similar panels or have relevant experience or expertise. To achieve this membership, institutions may draw on their own staff or externally as required. All members must be free from bias or conflicts of interest.

Legal representation of parties should not be allowed, but a person appearing before the research misconduct inquiry may be accompanied by a support person.

The independent research misconduct inquiry will report findings of fact to the CEO or their delegated officer and what, if any, research misconduct has occurred. Where adverse findings have been made, the CEO will decide what disciplinary actions are required within the agreed disciplinary processes of the institution.

Independent external research misconduct inquiry

Panel members who conduct an independent external research misconduct inquiry must not be employed by the institution, have other current or recent dealings with the institution, or otherwise be subject to a reasonable perception of bias.

The panel should normally be constituted with a minimum membership of three people. At least one member should be legally qualified or have extensive experience as a member of a tribunal or similar body. At least one member should have knowledge and research experience in a relevant, related field of research, but not directly in the research area of the allegations. Procedural fairness demands that the person subject to the inquiry be able to hear and respond to any and all material to be used by the panel in its decision-making process. Therefore, it is preferable that any expert knowledge that may be required is provided to the inquiry by witnesses rather than members of the panel. This will allow the witnesses to be questioned by both the panel and the person subject to the inquiry. If a panel member has relevant expert knowledge, it must be put to the defendant.

To be consistent with the general practice of tribunals, there are standard practices that should be followed. The panel should normally be assisted by a legally qualified person acting as 'counsel assisting', whose role it is to prepare the material to be put to the tribunal and to examine (question) witnesses on behalf of the panel. This person is not a member of the inquiry panel but may provide the panel with legal advice during the hearing. The person facing the allegations should be entitled to legal representation. The inquiry is not bound by the rules of evidence but its procedures must be consistent with the principles of natural justice and due process. In making findings, the inquiry should apply the civil standard of proof, although the standard of proof in serious cases will be higher than the mere balance of probabilities. Counsel assisting the inquiry will normally advise on this issue, as there is long-standing legal precedent based on a case before the Australian High Court in 1938.[3]

Whether an external research misconduct inquiry by people external to the institution is open to the public or conducted in private should be determined by the panel itself on the basis of public interest. The panel has the responsibility to hear the views of all parties on this matter before such a decision is made.

Upon completion of its tasks, the independent external research misconduct inquiry must advise the CEO or their delegated officer of its findings of fact, and what, if any, research misconduct has occurred. The CEO or their delegated officer must, in due course, inform the governing body of the outcome of the inquiry. The research misconduct inquiry findings must be considered by the CEO or their delegated officer and appropriate actions must be taken in accordance with institutional instruments regarding employment conditions. Appropriate actions must also be taken when the allegations of misconduct are shown to be unfounded. The findings of an independent, external research misconduct inquiry should be made available to the public.

When conducting an independent external research misconduct inquiry, the person subject to the inquiry may have an entitlement to appeal to a higher authority, most usually the courts.

Subsequent actions

The CEO or their delegated officer must inform all relevant parties of the research misconduct inquiry findings and the actions taken by the institution. Relevant parties may include affected staff, research collaborators including those at other institutions, all funding organisations, journal editors, and professional registration bodies. The public record, including publications, may need to be corrected if research misconduct has affected the research findings and their dissemination.

Persons who made the allegations must be treated fairly by the institution.

3 *Briginshaw v Briginshaw* (1938) 60 CLR 336.

Proven research misconduct may warrant disciplinary action. Such actions are the responsibility of the institution under its instruments regulating employment conditions. Institutions must ensure that employment agreements and contracts, when they are next negotiated, address how research misconduct will be handled in accordance with this Code. There should be defined penalties for people found guilty of research misconduct.

If the allegations are shown to be unfounded, the institution should make every effort to reinstate the good reputation of the accused researcher and their associates. Persons making mischievous complaints should face disciplinary action.

Source: National Health and Medical Research Council

APPENDIX FOUR

United States Office of Research Integrity Whistleblower's Bill of Rights

Responsible Whistleblowing: A Whistleblower's Bill of Rights

a. **Communication**: Whistleblowers are free to disclose lawfully whatever information supports a reasonable belief of research misconduct as it is defined by PHS policy. An individual or institution that retaliates against any person making protected disclosures engages in prohibited obstruction of investigations of research misconduct as defined by the Commission on Research Integrity. Whistleblowers must respect the confidentiality of sensitive information and give legitimate institutional structures an opportunity to function. Should a whistleblower elect to make a lawful disclosure that violates institutional rules of confidentiality, the institution may thereafter legitimately limit the whistleblower's access to further information about the case.

b. **Protection from retaliation**: Institutions have a duty not to tolerate or engage in retaliation against good-faith whistleblowers. This duty includes providing appropriate and timely relief to ameliorate the consequences of actual or threatened reprisals, and holding accountable those who retaliate. Whistleblowers and other witnesses to possible research misconduct have a responsibility to raise their concerns honorably and with foundation.

c. **Fair procedures**: Institutions have a duty to provide fair and objective procedures for examining and resolving complaints, disputes, and allegations of research misconduct. In cases of alleged retaliation that are not resolved through institutional intervention, whistleblowers should have an opportunity to defend themselves in a proceeding where they can present witnesses and confront those they charge with retaliation against them, except when they violate rules of confidentiality. Whistleblowers have a responsibility to participate honorably in such procedures by respecting the serious consequences for those they accuse of misconduct, and by using the same standards to correct their own errors that they apply to others.

d. **Procedures free from partiality**: Institutions have a duty to follow procedures that are not tainted by partiality arising from personal or institutional conflict of interest or other sources of bias. Whistleblowers have a responsibility to act within legitimate institutional channels when raising concerns about the integrity of research. They have the right to raise objections concerning the possible partiality of those selected to review their concerns without incurring retaliation.

e. **Information**: Institutions have a duty to elicit and evaluate fully and objectively information about concerns raised by whistleblowers. Whistleblowers may have unique knowledge needed to evaluate thoroughly responses from those whose actions are questioned. Consequently, a competent investigation may involve giving whistleblowers one or more opportunities to comment on the accuracy and completeness of information relevant to their concerns, except when they violate rules of confidentiality.

f. **Timely processes**: Institutions have a duty to handle cases involving alleged research misconduct as expeditiously as is possible without compromising responsible resolutions. When cases drag on for years, the issue becomes the dispute rather than its resolution. Whistleblowers have a responsibility to facilitate expeditious resolution of cases by good-faith participation in misconduct procedures.

g. **Vindication**: At the conclusion of proceedings, institutions have a responsibility to credit promptly—in public and/or in private as appropriate—those whose allegations are substantiated.

h. **Responsibility**: Every right carries with it a corresponding responsibility. In this context, the Whistleblower Bill of Rights carries the obligation to avoid false statements and unlawful behavior.[1]

[1] <http://ori.hhs.gov/Whistleblower-Rights> (viewed 17 January 2015).

BIBLIOGRAPHY

For those references associated with websites, the full URLs can be found in the main text.

AAAS, '2009 Award for Scientific Freedom and Responsibility Recipient'

Abbasi, Kamran, 'A Way Forward for Whistleblowing' (2011) 104(7) *Journal of Royal Society of Medicine* 275

Abbott, Alison, 'Plagiarism Charge for Romanian Minister' (2012) 485(7398) *Nature* 289

Abbott, Alison, 'Romanian Scientists Fight Plagiarism' (2012) 488(7411) *Nature* 264

Abbott, Alison, 'Science Fortunes of Balkan Neighbours Diverge' (2011) 469(7329) *Nature* 142

ABC Radio National, 'Bishop Accused of Plagiarism in Essay', *Lateline*, 28 October 2008 (Tom Iggulden)

ABC Radio National, 'CMC Confirms Misconduct by Queensland Academics', *PM*, 7 November 2013 (Elise Worthington)

ABC Radio National, 'Cyberspace Spat: Shutting Down Satire', *National Interest*, 15 April 2011 (Damien Carrick)

ABC Radio National, 'Magistrates and Plagiarism', *Law Report*, 9 May 2006 (Damien Carrick)

ABC Radio National, 'Savonarola at the Stake: The Rise and Fall of Professor Sir Roy Meadow', *Ockham's Razor*, 4 November 2007 (Robyn Williams)

ABC Radio National, 'Scientific Fraud and Defamation', *Health Report*, 17 August 1998 (Norman Swan)

ABC Radio National, 'Tasmanian Law School Cheating Scandal', *Law Report*, 3 September 2013 (Damien Carrick)

ABC Radio National, 'Vice-Chancellor Resigns Over Plagiarism Claims', *PM*, 11 July 2002 (Kate Tozer)

ABC Television, 'Degrees of Deception', *Four Corners*, 20 April 2015 (Linton Besser and Peter Cronau)

Abramov, Denis, 'Respected Moscow Lawmaker Annuls Dissertation Over Plagiarism Claims', *The Moscow Times*, 23 April 2015

Abramson, John, *Overdo$ed America: The Broken Promise of American Medicine* (New York: Harper Collins, 2004)

'A Comment from Paul Gelsinger on Gene Therapy and Informed Consent' on *Bioethics.net* (31 January 2008)

'Academic Sacked Over Pressuring Students for Sex', *ABC News*, 3 September 2010

Ackland, Richard, 'Barry Spurr v New Matilda: The Facts, the Law and the Porridge', *The Guardian*, 24 October 2014

Adrian, Angela, 'The Pirate Bay Deep-Sixed' (2006) 22(5) *Computer Law and Security Review* 392

Adrian, Angela, 'Could a Small Town in Romania Bring Australia to its Cyber-knees? Not if They Accede to the EU Convention on Cybercrime' (2012) 7(4) *Journal of International Commercial Law and Technology* 328

'Adultery and Murder: The Seedy Side of 16th Century Cambridge University', *The Daily Express*, 3 October 2013

Agence France-Presse, 'Taiwanese Education Minister Chiang Wei-ling Resigns Over Academic Publishing Scandal', *South China Morning Post*, 15 July 2014

Agence France-Presse, 'Embattled Japanese Researcher Haruko Obokata Says She Will Resign', *South China Morning Post*, 19 December 2014

Ahimastos, Anna A, Walker, Philip J, Askew Christopher et al. 'Effect of Ramipril on Walking Times and Quality of Life Among Patients With Peripheral Artery Disease and Intermittent Claudication: A Randomized Controlled Trial' (2015) 309(5) Journal of the American Medical Association 453

Ahn, Mi-Young and Dennis Normile, 'Korean Supreme Court Upholds Disgraced Cloner's Criminal Sentence', *Science*, 27 February 2014

Akerman, Pia, 'Six Years Jail for Phosphagenics Biotech Fraudster Esra Ogru', *The Australian*, 7 November 2014

Akre, Jane, 'Million Dollar Conflict-of-Interest by Emory Psychiatrist Uncovered by Grassley', *Injury Board National News Desk*, 6 October 2008

Akst, Jef, 'When Is Self-Plagiarism OK?' *The Scientist*, 9 September 2010

Alberts, Bruce, 'Editorial Expression of Concern' (2011) 333(6038) *Science* 35

Alcorn, Gay, 'Professor Barry Spurr Suspended by Sydney University Over Offensive Emails', *The Guardian*, 17 October 2014

Aldington, Richard, *The Strange Life of Charles Waterton*, 1782-1865 (London: Evans Bros, 1949)

Alford, C Fred, *Whistleblowers: Broken Lives and Organizational Power* (Ithaca, NY: Cornell University Press, 2001)

'Alirio Melendez Categorically Denies Data Falsification, Alleges Cover-up', *Retraction Watch*, 17 October 2013

Alix, Jean-Pierre, 'France: How to Improve a Decentralised, Ambiguous National System' in Tony Mayer and Nicholas Steneck (eds), *Promoting Research Integrity in a Global Environment* (World Scientific, Singapore, 2012), pp 33–36

ALLEA | ALL European Academies

All the President's Men (Warner Bros, 1976)

Altman, Lawrence K, 'The Doctor's World; Revisionist History Sees Pasteur as Liar Who Stole Rival's Ideas', *The* New York Times, 16 May 1995

American Chemical Society, 'Scientific Insight and Integrity in Public Policy' (Public Policy Statement 2011-2014)

American Medical Association, 'Opinion 3.08—Sexual Harassment and Exploitation between Medical Supervisors and Trainees'

American Philosophical Association, Committee on the Status of Women, *Report on Site Visit* (University of Colorado Boulder, Department of Philosophy, 25-28 September 2013)

American Psychiatric Association, 'Policy on Conflicts of Interest Principles and Guidelines: With Special Interest for Clinical Practice and Research' (December 2010)

American Psychological Association, *Publication Manual of the American Psychological Association* (6th edn, Washington, DC: American Psychological Association, 2010)

American Society of Crime Laboratory Directors / Laboratory Accreditation Board, 'Accreditation Programs'

'An Array of Errors', *The Economist*, 10 September 2011

'An Open Letter to the Chancellor' on *Copy, Shake, and Paste* (26 February 2011)

Anderson, Peter, 'Martial 1.29: Appearance and Authorship' (2006) 149(1) *Rheinisches Museum für Philologie* 119

Andersen, Travis, '2d State Chemist Charged with Drug Tampering', *The Boston Globe*, 20 January 2013

Anderson, Travis, 'Annie Dookhan May Get 5 Years in Prison With Guilty Plea', *The Boston Globe*, 24 October 2013

Anekwe, Lillian, 'New Guideline on Beta Blockers Challenges ESC Advice' (22 February 2014) 383 *The Lancet* 682.

Angell, Marcia, *The Truth About the Drug Companies: How They Deceive Us and What to Do About It* (New York: Random House, 2005)

Angell, Marcia, Robert D Utiger, and Alastair JJ Wood, 'Disclosure of Authors' Conflict of Interest: A Follow-up' (2000) 342(8) *The New England Journal of Medicine* 586

Angell Marcia, 'Drug Companies and Doctors: A Story of Corruption: (15 January 2009) *The New York Review of Books* 56

Angell, Marcia and Alistair JJ Wood (disclosure by Vera H Price), 'Authors' Conflicts of Interest: A Disclosure and Editors' Reply' (1999) 341(21) *The New England Journal of Medicine* 1618

Ankier, Stephen I, 'Dishonesty, Misconduct and Fraud in Clinical Research: An International Problem' (2002) 30(4) *Journal of International Medical Research* 357

Annas, George J and Michael A Grodin (eds), *The Nazi Doctors and the Nuremberg Code: Human Rights in Human Experimentation* (New York: Oxford University Press, 1992)

'Annie Dookhan, Chemist at Mass. Crime Lab, Arrested for Allegedly Mishandling Over 60,000 Samples', *CBS News*

Anonymous, 'Addicted in Academe', *The Chronicle Review*, 3 May 2002, reproduced in *The University of Arizona*, Life & Work Connections

Antomarini, Brunella, *Thinking Through Error: The Moving Target of Knowledge* (Lanham, MD: Lexington Books, 2012)

ANZPAA NIFS, 'Forensic Standards Development'

Ardalan, Farhad, Hessamaddin Arfaei, Reza Mansouri, Mahdi Balalimood et al. 'Iran's Scientists Condemn Instances of Plagiarism' (2009) 462(7275) *Nature* 847

Arenson, Karen W and Elissa Gootman, 'Columbia Cites Plagiarism by a Professor', *The New York Times*, 21 February 2008

Arnold, Denis G, Beauchamp Tom L and Bowie, Norman L, Ethical Theory and Business 9th edn (New York, Pearson, 2013)

Aronson, Lester R, 'The Case of *The Case of the Midwife Toad*' (1975) 5(2) *Behavior Genetics* 115

Arszulowicz, Marek and Wojciech W Gasparski (eds), *Whistleblowing: In Defense of Proper Action* (New Brunswick: Transaction Publishers, 2011)

Arthurs, Harry W, Roger Blais and Jon Thompson, *Integrity in Scholarship: A Report to Concordia University* (April 1994)

Associated Press, 'Charges of Fake Research Hit New High', *NBC News*, 10 July 2005

Astala, Melissa, 'Wronged by a Professor? Breach of Fiduciary Duty as a Remedy in Intellectual Property Infringement Cases' (2003) 3 *Houston Business and Tax Law Journal* 31

Astor, Hilary, 'Australian Universities in Court: Causes, Costs and Consequences of Increasing Litigation' (2008) 19(3) *Australasian Dispute Resolution Journal* 158

Atkinson, Nancy, 'The Great Moon Hoax of 1835', *Universe Today*, 1 April 2011

Atlas, Michel C, 'Retraction Policies of High-Impact Biomedical Journals' (2004) 92(2) *Journal of the Medical Library Association* 242

Attarwala, Husain, 'TGN 1412: From Discovery to Disaster' (2010) 2(3) *Journal of Young Pharmacists* 332

Attwood, Rebecca, 'Lecturers Talk of Students' 'Shocking' Abuse', *Times Higher Education*, 18 June 2009

Attwood, Rebecca, 'Plagiarism Tariff: Let the Punishment Fit the Demerit Points', *Times Higher Education*, 17 June 2010

Au, Thuy Bich, Golledge, Jonathan, Walker, Philip J, Haigh, Kate, and Nelson, Mark, 'Peripheral Arterial Disease: Diagnosis and Management in General Practice' (2013) 42(6) Australian Family Physician 397

Australian Government, National Health and Medical Research Council, *Annual Report 2012-2013* (Commonwealth of Australia, 2013)

Australian Government, National Health and Medical Research Council, and Australian Research Council, *Australian Code for the Responsible Conduct of Research* (Australian Government, 2007)

Australian Government, National Health and Medical Research Council, *Research Integrity*

Australian Government, Productivity Commission, *Public Support for Science and Innovation* (Research Report, 9 March 2007)

Australian Government, Productivity Commission, *International Education Services* (Research Paper, 30 April 2015)

Australian Government, Tertiary Education Quailty and Standards Agency, 'About TEQSA'

Australian Human Rights Commission, *Sexual Harassment: Serious Business* (2008)

Australian Medical Association, *AMA Code of Ethics* (2004, rev. 2006) [2.1]

Australian Medical Council, *Good Medical Practice: A Code of Conduct for Doctors in Australia* (July 2009)

Australian National University, 'Policy—Intellectual Property', 15 May 2013

Australian National University, Academic Standards & Quality Office, 'What is a Breach?' 17 February 2015

Australian Psychological Society, *APS Code of Ethics* (2007)

Australian Research Council and National Health and Medical Research Council, *Australian Research Integrity Committee Framework* (February 2011)

Australian Securities & Investment Commission (ASIC), 'Former CEO and Two Melbourne Men Jailed Following Theft of Millions From Phosphagenics Limited' (Media Release, 14-296MR, 7 November 2014)

Australian Standard: Whistleblower Protection Programs for Entities—AS 8004-2003 (Standards Australia, 2003)

'Austrian Commissioner Faces Plagiarism Accusations', *EurActiv.com*, 26 May 2011

'Austrian EU Commissioner Cleared of Plagiarism', *The Australian*, 8 November 2011

'Authorship is Dying: Long Live Contributorship: The BMJ Will Publish Lists of Contributors and Guarantors to Original Articles' (1997) 31 *British Medical Journal* 696

'Axolotl Roadkill': Helene Hegemann und Ullstein Verlegerin Dr. Siv Bublitz antworten auf Plagiatsvorwurf', *Buch Markt*, 7 February 2010

Babbage, Charles, *Reflections on the Decline of Science in England and on Some of its Causes* (London: B Fellowes, 1830)

Babiak, Paul and Robert D Hare, *Snakes in Suits: When Psychopaths Go to Work* (New York: Harper Collins, 2007)

Babor, Thomas F et al. *Alcohol: No Ordinary Commodity: Research and Public Policy* (2nd edn, Oxford: Oxford University Press, 2010)

Bacchi, Carol, 'Sex on Campus—Where Does 'Consent' End and Harassment Begin?' (1992) 35(1) *Australian Universities' Review* 31

Baden, Michael M and Marion Roach, *Dead Reckoning: The New Science of Catching Killers* (New York: Simon & Schuster, 2001)

Baden, Michael M with Judith Alder Hennessee, *Unnatural Death: Confessions of a Medical Examiner* (London: Time Warner, 2002)

Baggerly, Keith A and Coombes, Kevin R, 'Deriving Chemosensitivity from Cell Lines: Forensic Bioinformaticvs and Reproducible Research in High-Throughput Biology' (2009) 3(4) *Annals of Applied Statistics* 1309

Bailey, Jonathan, 'Self-Plagiarism: Ethical Shortcut or Moral Scourge?' on *Plagiarism Today* (7 September 2011)

Bailey, Jonathan, 'The Biden Plagiarism Scandal' on *Plagiarism Today* (26 August 2008)

Bailey, Ronald, *Scrutinizing Industry-Funded Science: The Crusade Against Conflicts of Interest* (New York: American Council on Science and Health, 2008)

Baker, Richard, 'Plagiarism Sinks Research Head', *The Age*, 21 April 2010

Bakker, Marjan and Jelte M Wicherts, 'The (Mis)reporting of Statistical Results in Psychology Journals' (2011) 43(3) *Behavior Research Methods* 666

Bandura, Albert, *Self-Efficacy: The Exercise of Control* (New York: WH Freeman, 1997)

Bandura, Albert, 'Moral Disengagement in the Perpetration of Inhumanities' (1999) 3(3) *Personality and Social Psychology Review* 193

Bandura, Albert, 'Selective Moral Disengagement in the Exercise of Moral Agency' (2002) 31(2) *Journal of Moral Education* 101

Barbash, Fred, 'Scholarly Journal Retracts 60 Articles, Smashes 'Peer Review Ring' ', *The Washinton Post*, 10 July 2014

Barbour, Virginia, 'Publish or Perish Culture Encourages Scientists to Cut Corners' (12 October 2015) Asian Scientist Magazine

Barendt, Eric, *Academic Freedom and the Law: A Comparative Study* (Oxford: Hart, 2010)

Barnett, Tim, 'Why *Your* Company Should Have a Whistleblowing Policy' (1992) 57(4) *SAM Advanced Management Journal* 37

Baron, Christopher A, *Timaeus of Tauromenium and Hellenistic Historiography* (Cambridge: Cambridge University Press, 2012)

Barrett, Ruth and James Malcolm, *Embedding Plagiarism Education in the Assessment Process* (2006) 2(1) *International Journal for Educational Integrity* 38

Bartlett, Thomas and Scott Smallwood, 'Four Academic Plagiarists You've Never Heard Of: How Many More Are Out There?' *The Chronicle of Higher Education*, 17 December 2004

Bartlett, Thomas and Robin Wilson, 'Husband of Accused Hunytsville Killer Amy Bishop Speaks Out', *The Chronicle of Higher Education*, 14 February 2010

Barton, Laura, 'A Hard Lesson', *The Guardian*, 12 October 2000

Barwood, Caroline H S and Bruce E Murdoch, 'Cognitive Linguistic Deficits in Relapsing-Remitting Multiple Sclerosis' (2013) 27(12) *Aphasiology* 1459, retracted by 'Statement of Retraction' (2014) 28(6) *Aphasiology* 770

Bass, Alison, *Side-Effects: A Prosecutor, A Whistleblower and a Bestselling Antidepressant on Trial* (Chapel Hill, NC: Algonquin Books of Chapel Hill, 2008)

Batty, David, 'Raj Persaud Blames Stress for Plagiarism', *The Guardian*, 18 June 2008

Baty, Phil, 'Inconsistent Penalties Raise Risk of Legal Action, Deech Says', *Times Higher Education Supplement*, 23 June 2006

Baylis, Françoise, 'The Olivieri Debacle: Where Were the Heroes of Bioethics?'(2004) 30(1) *Journal of Medical Ethics* 44

Beasley, Malcolm R, Supriyo Datta, Herwig Kogelnick, Herbert Kroemer and V Don Monroe, *Report of the Investigation Committee on the Possibility of Scientific Misconduct in the Work of Hendrik Schön and Co-Authors* (2002)

Beatty, Jeffrey F and Samuelson, Susan, *Business Law and the Legal Environment* (Melbourne, Cengage Learning, 2015)

Behrendt, Larissa, 'In Your Dreams: Cultural Appropriation, Popular Culture and Colonialism' (1998) 4 *Law, Text and Culture* 256

Belluz, Julia, 'How Should Journalists Cover Quacks Like Dr. Oz or the Food Babe?' *Vox*, 13 April 2015

Benavides-Espinoza, Claudia and George B Cunningham, 'Observers' Reporting of Sexual Harassment: The Influence of Harassment Type, Organizational Culture and Political Orientation' (2010) 10(4) *Public Organization Review* 323

Bennett, Drake, 'Dr. Ecstasy', *The New York Times*, 30 January 2005

Benson, Katherine A, 'Comments on Crocker's 'An Analysis of University Definitions of Sexual Harassment'' (1984) 9(3) *Signs* 516

Bentham, Martin, 'Orlando Figes' Folly Shows Why We Need Libel Law Reform', *Evening Standard*, 27 April 2010

Benton, Sarah Allen, *Understanding the High-Functioning Alcoholic* (Westport, Conn: Praeger, 2009)

Berdahl, Jennifer L and Celia Moore, 'Workplace Harassment: Double Jeopardy for Minority Women' (2006) 91(2) *Journal of Applied Psychology* 426

Bergman, Helen R, 'Case Comment: *Moore v. Regents of the University of California*' (1992) 18(1-2) *American Journal of Law and Medicine* 127

Beringer, Johann Bartholomäus Adam, *The Lying Stones of Dr Johann Bartholomew Adam Beringer, being his Lithographiæ Wirceburgensis* (originally published in 1726 with 50 medical corollaries as the inaugural dissertation of GL Hueber, translated and annotated by Melvin E Jahn and Daniel J Woolf; Berkeley: University of California Press, 1963)

Bernstein, Carl and Bob Woodward, *All the President's Men* (New York: Simon and Schuster, 1974)

Berrett, Dan, 'Academic Freedom and Holocaust Denial', *Inside Higher Ed*, 26 October 2010

Bezwoda, Werner R, Leslie Seymour and Roger D Dansey, 'High-dose Chemotherapy with Hematopoietic Rescue As Primary Treatment for Metastatic Breast Cancer: A Randomized Trial' (1995) 13(10) *Journal of Clinical Oncology* 2483

Bhattacharjee, Yudhijit, 'The Mind of a Con Man', *The New York Times*, 26 April 2013

Bhutta, Zulfiqar A and Julian Crane, 'Should Research Fraud be a Crime?' (2014) 349(7969) *British Medical Journal* g4532

Biben, Ellen N, *Investigation into the Nassau County Police Department Forensic Evidence Bureau* (State of New York: Office of the Inspector General, November 2011)

Biggs, John, 'The University of Newcastle: Prelude to Dawkins' in John Biggs and Richard Davis (eds), *The Subversion of Australian Universities* (Wollongong: Fund for Intellectual Dissent, 2002)

Biggs, John, 'The University of Newcastle: Prelude to Dawkins, An Update' (revised chapter, 2009)

Bilić-Zulle, Lidija, Vedran Frković, Tamara Turk, Josip Ažman et al. 'Prevalence of Plagiarism Among Medical Students' (2005) 46(1) *Croatian Medical Journal* 126

Bills, Robert D, 'Plagiarism in Law School: Close Resemblance of the Worst Kind?' (1990) 31(1) *Santa Clara Law Review* 103

'Biochemist Admits Scientific Fraud', *The Age*, 25 February 1977, 7

Birdeau, Danielle R , Genie O Lenihan and Cheryl L Somers, 'Effects of Educational Strategies on College Students' Identification of Sexual Harassment' (2005) 125(3) *Education* 496

Birstein, Vadim J, *The Perversion of Knowledge: The True Story of Soviet Science* (New York: Perseus Books, 2013)

Blake, Aaron, 'Rand Paul's Plagiarism Allegations, And Why They Matter', *The Washington Post*, 4 November 2013

Blass, Thomas (ed), *Obedience to Authority: Current Perspectives on the Milgram Paradigm* (Mahwah, NJ: Lawrence Erlbaum Associates, 2000)

Blau, Stacey E, 'Panel Clears MIT Scientist of Fraud: Imanishi-Kari, Baltimore Vindicated', *The Tech*, 116(28), 26 June 1996

Blaustein, Michael, 'Academic Paper on Plagiarism Pulled Because of Plagiarism', *New York Post*, 2 April 2015

Bloom, Harold, *The Anxiety of Influence: A Theory of Poetry* (2nd edn, New York: Oxford University Press, 1997)

Blum, Susan D, *My Word! Plagiarism and College Culture* (Ithaca, NY: Cornell University Press, 2009)

Blumsohn, Aubrey, 'Authorship, Ghost-Science, Access to Data and Control of the Pharmaceutical Scientific Literature: Who Stands Behind the Word?' (2006) 19(3) *Professional Ethics Report* 1, 3

Blumsohn, Aubrey and Clare Dyer, 'Aubrey Blumsohn: Academic Who Took On Industry' (2010) 340(7736) *BMJ* 22

Boffey, Philip M, 'US Study Finds Fraud in Top Researcher's Work on Mentally Retarded', *The New York Times*, 24 May 1987

'Bogus 'Expert Witness' Jailed for Five Years', *Daily Mail*, 22 February 2007

Boire, Richard G, *Sacred Mushrooms and the Law* (Berkeley, CA: Ronin, 2002)

Bolsin, Stephen N, 'The Wisheart Affair: Responses to Dunn—The Bristol Cardiac Disaster' (1998) 317(7172) *BMJ* 1579

Bolsin, Stephen, 'The Whistle Blower in Medicine' (Address delivered at a meeting of the Medico-Legal Society at the Naval and Military Club, Victoria, 19 March 1999)

Bolsin, Stephen, Thomas Faunce and Justin Oakley, 'Practical Virtue Ethics: Healthcare Whistleblowing and Portable Digital Technology' (2005) 31(10) *Journal of Medical Ethics* 612

Borrell, Brendan, 'A Medical Madoff: Anesthesiologist Faked Date in 21 Studies', *Scientific American*, 10 March 2010

Borrud, Gabriel, 'Another German Politician Loses Doctorate Due to Plagiarized Thesis', *Deutsche Welle* 13 July 2011

Borsboom, Denny and Wagenmakers, Eric-Jan, '*Derailed: The Rise and Fall of Diederik Stapel*' (book review): (2013) 26(1) Observer

Bosch, Xavier, 'Improving Biomedical Journals' Ethical Policies: The Case of Research Misconduct' (2014) 40(9) *Journal of Medical Ethics* 644

Boseley Sarah, 'Medical Establishment 'Covered Up' for Fraudulent Consultant', *The Guardian*, 22 November 2002

Boseley, Sarah, 'Fall of the Doctor who said his Vitamins would Cure Aids', *The Guardian*, 12 September 2008

Boseley, Sarah, 'British Doctor Faces Action Over Claims of 'Ghost Writing' for US Drug Company', *The Guardian*, 18 September 2009

Boseley, Sarah, 'Ian Tomlinson Pathologist Freddy Patel Struck Off', *The Guardian*, 23 August 2012

Bossi, Emilio, 'Challenges Encountered by the Swiss Academies of Arts and Sciences When Introducing Concepts for Promoting Scientific Integrity' in Tony Mayer and Nicholas Steneck (eds), *Promoting Research Integrity in a Global Environment* (Singapore: World Scientific, 2012), pp 45–48

Boston University, 'Conflicts of Interest in Research'

'Boston U. Panel Finds Plagiarism by Dr. King', *The New York Times*, 11 October 1991

Bouchard Jr, Thomas J, David T Lykken, Matthew McGue, Nancy L Segal et al. 'Sources of Human Psychological Differences: The Minnesota Study of Twins Reared Apart' (1990) 250(4978) *Science* 223

Bouri, Sonia, Matthew James Shun-Shin, Graham D Cole, Jamil Mayet and Darrel P Francis, 'Meta-Analysis of Secure Randomised Controlled Trials of ß-Blockade to Prevent Perioperative Death in Non-Cardiac Surgery' (2014) 100(6) *Heart* 456

Bovsun, Mara, 'Crazy Professor Valery Fabrikant Kills 4 in Concordia University Rampage', *New York Daily News*, 21 April 2013

Bowcott, Owen, 'Pathologist in G20 Death Case Found Guilty of Misconduct', *The Guardian*, 31 August 2010

Bowden, Peter, 'A Comparative Analysis of Whistleblower Protection' (Paper presented at the Australian Association for Professional and Applied Ethics 12th Annual Conference, Adelaide, 28-30 September 2005)

Bowden, Peter, *In the Public Interest: Protecting Whistleblowers and Those Who Speak Out* (Prahran, Vic: Tilde Publishing and Distribution, 2014)

Bowers, C Michael, *Forensic Testimony: Science, Law and Expert Evidence* (San Diego, CA: Academic Press, 2014)

Boyle, Robert, *The Sceptical Chymist or Chymico-Physical Doubts and Paradoxes* (London: J Crooke, 1661)

Brackman, Levi, 'Rabbinic Plagiarism and Scholarly Integrity', *Jewish World*, 5 December 2013

Brandeis, Louis D, 'What Publicity Can Do', *Harper's Weekly*, 20 December 1913

Brandeis, Louis D, eds. Melvin I Urofsky and David W Levy, *Letters of Louis D Brandeis* (Albany: State University of New York Press, 1971-1978), Volume 1 (1870-1917)

'Brandeis Withdraws Honorary Degree for Islam Critic Ayaan Hirsi Ali', *The Guardian*, 9 April 2014

Branswell, Helen, 'Should Research Fraud be Treated as a Crime? Toronto Expert Says Yes', *The Hamilton Spectator*, 15 July 2014

Braxton, John M, Eve Proper, and Alan E Bayer, *Professors Behaving Badly: Faculty Misconduct in Graduate Education* (Baltimore: Johns Hopkins University Press, 2011)

Bray, Karina, 'Ken Harvey Quits Over Swisse Deal', *Choice*, 6 February 2014

Bray, Karina, 'Returns on Influence' (April 2014) *Choice* 30

Breidthardt, Annika, 'German Minister Rejects Quitting in Plagiarism Row', *Reuters*, 19 February 2011

Brenner, Marie, 'The Man Who Knew Too Much', *Vanity Fair*, May 1996

Bretag, Tracey, 'Publish or Perish: Ramifications for Online Academic Publishing' in Laura A Wankel and Charles Wankel (eds), *Misbehavior Online in Higher Education* (Bingley, UK: Emerald Group Publishing Limited, 2012), pp 11–24

British Medical Journal, 'Declaration of Competing Interests'

British Medical Journal, 'Transparency Policy'

Broad, William J, 'Imbroglio at Yale (I): Emergence of a Fraud' (1980) *Science* 38

Broad, William J, 'Imbroglio at Yale (II): A Top Job Lost' (10 October 1980) 210 *Science* 171

Broad, William J, 'Yale Annoucnes Plan to Handle Charges of Fraud' (1982) 218 *Science* 37

Broad, William J and Nicholas Wade, *Betrayers of the Truth* (New York: Simon & Schuster, 1982)

Broad, William J, 'Notorious Darsee Case Shakes Assumptions about Science', *The New York Times*, 14 June 1983

Brody, Howard, *Hooked: Ethics, the Medical Profession and the Pharmaceutical Industry* (Lanham, Md: Rowman & Littlefield, 2007)

Brody, Jane E, 'High Functioning, But Still Alcoholics', *The New York Times*, 4 May 2009

Brogan, Michael and David Spencer, *Surviving Law School* (Melbourne: Oxford University Press, 2004)

Bronowski, Jacob, *Science and Human Values* (New York: Julian Messner, 1956)

Brook, Stephen, 'Times's Verdict on Sir Roy Meadow Evidence was 'Legitimate', says PCC', *The Guardian*, 8 January 2009

Brouwer, George E, *Review of Complaint Handling in Victorian Universities* (Ombudsman Victoria, May 2005) 6

Brouwer, George E, *Whistleblowers Protection Act 2001: Report of an Investigation into Issues at Bayside Health* (Ombudsman Victoria, October 2008)

Brouwer, George, *An Investigation into the Transport Accident Commission's and the Victorian WorkCover Authority's Administrative Processes for Medical Practitioner Billing* (Ombudsman Victoria, July 2009)

Brouwer, George E, *Whistleblowers Protection Act 2001: Investigation into an Allegation of Improper Conduct within RMIT's School of Engineering (TAFE)—Aerospace* (Ombudsman Victoria, July 2010)

Brown, Alexander J, *Public Interest Disclosure Legislation in Australia: Towards the Next Generation* (Issues Paper, ARC 'Linkage' Project, 'Whistling While They Work', November 2006)

Brown, Alexander J (ed), *Whistleblowing in the Australian Public Sector* (First Report, ARC Linkage Project, Griffith University, October 2007)

Brown, Alexander J (ed), *Whistleblowing in the Australian Public Sector: Enhancing the Theory and Practice of Internal Witness Management in Public Sector Organisations* (Canberra, ACT: ANU E Press, 2008)

Brown, Alexander J, 'Restoring the Sunshine to the Sunshine State: Priorities for Whistleblowing Law Reform in Queensland' (2009) 18(3) *Griffith Law Review* 666

Brown, Alexander J, *Whistleblowing Legislation in Queensland: The Agenda for Reform* (Final Report, ARC Linkage Project, Griffith University, September 2009)

Brown, Alexander J, Evalynn Mazurski and Jane Olsen, 'The Incidence and Significance of Whistleblowing' in Alexander J Brown (ed), *Whistleblowing in the Australian Public Sector: Enhancing the Theory and Practice of Internal Witness Management in Public Sector Organisations* (Canberra, ACT: ANU E Press, 2008), pp 25–52

Brown, Alexander J and Chris Wheeler, 'Project Findings: An Agenda for Action' in Alexander J Brown (ed), *Whistleblowing in the Australian Public Sector: Enhancing the Theory and Practice of Internal Witness Management in Public Sector Organisations* (Canberra, ACT: ANU E Press, 2008), pp 89–312

Brown, Alan S and Dana S Murphy, 'Cryptomnesia: Delineating Inadvertent Plagiarism' (1989) 15(3) *Journal of Experimental Psychology: Learning, Memory, and Cognition* 432

Bryder, Linda, *A History of the 'Unfortunate Experiment' at National Women's Hospital* (Auckland, NZ: Auckland University Press, 2009)

Bryson, John, *Evil Angels* (Ringwood, Vic: Penguin, 1986)

Budd, John M, 'The Stapel Case: An Object Lesson in Research Integrity and its Lapses' (2013) *Synesis* G47

Buelow, George J, 'Originality, Genius, Plagiarism in English Criticism of the Eighteenth Century' (1990) 21(2) *International Review of the Aesthetics and Sociology of Music* 117

Burke, Ronald J and Cary L Cooper (eds), *Voice and Whistleblowing in Organizations: Overcoming Fear, Fostering Courage and Unleashing Candour* (Cheltenham, UK: Edward Elgar Publishing, 2013)

Burke, Thomas F, *Lawyers, Lawsuits and Legal Rights: The Battle over Litigation in American Society* (Berkeley: University of California Press, 2002)

Burnett-Nichols, Helen, 'Don't Touch, Do Tell', *University Affairs*, 8 March 2010

Burton, Robert, *The Anatomy of Melancholy* (Philadephia: JW Moore, 1857)

Butler, Declan, 'Iranian Ministers in Plagiarism Row' (2009) 461(7264) *Nature* 578

Butler, Declan, 'Paper: Co-authored by Iran's Science Minister Duplicates Earlier Paper', *Nature*, 22 September 2009

Butler, Declan, 'Publisher Retracts Paper by Iran's Science Minister', *Nature*, 23 September 2009

Butterfield, Fox, 'Harvard Suspends Doctor for Fraud', *The New York Times*, 16 December 1981

Butz, Arthur R, *The Hoax of the Twentieth Century: The Case Against the Presumed Extermination of European Jewry* (Chicago, Ill: Theses & Dissertations Press, 2003)

Byrne, Gregory, 'Breuning Sentenced' (1988) 242(4881) *Science* 1004

Cage, Sam, 'Romania PM Plagiarized Thesis, Panel Says', *Reuters*, 29 June 2012

Cahill, Thomas, *How the Irish Saved Civilization: The Untold Story of Ireland's Heroic Role From the Fall of Rome to the Rise of Medieval Europe* (New York: Nan A Talese, 1995)

Calland, Richard and Guy Dehn (eds), *Whistleblowing Around the World: Law, Culture and Practice* (Cape Town: ODAC, 2004)

'Cambridge's Criminal Past Revealed in Centuries-Old Court Records', University of Cambridge, 30 September 2013

Campbell, Hank, 'Jan Hendrik Schön: World Class Physics Fraud Gets Last Laugh—A Whole Book About Himself', Science *2.0*, 5 May 2009

Canadian Medical Association, *Code of Ethics* (Last reviewed March 2014)

Candiotti, Susan, Yon Pomrenze and Jason Hanna, 'Ex-Massachusetts Chemist Gets 3 to 5 Years in Tampering Case', *CNN*, 22 November 2013

Carey, Benedict, 'Academic Battle Delays Publication by 3 Years', *The New York Times*, 11 June 2010

Carey, Benedict, 'Fraud Case Seen as a Red Flag for Psychology Research', *The New York Times*, 2 November 2011

Carlisle, John B, 'The Analysis of 168 Randomised Controlled Trials to Test Data Integrity' (2012) 67(5) *Anaesthesia* 521

Carpenter, Mackenzie, and Steve Twedt, 'Discovering Fraud in Breast Cancer Research A Gradual Process', *Pittsburgh Post-Gazette*, 26 December 1994, A-1

Carroll, Jude, *A Handbook for Deterring Plagiarism in Higher Education* (Oxford: Oxford Centre for Staff and Learning Development, 2002)

Carroll, Lynne and Kathryn L Ellis, 'Faculty Attitudes Towards Sexual Harassment: Survey Results, Survey Process' (1989) 52(3) *Initiatives* 35

Carter, Rubin 'Hurricane' with Ken Klonsky, *Eye of the Hurricane: My Path from Darkness to Freedom* (Chicago, Ill: Lawrence Hill Books, 2011)

Carter, Richard, 'German Minister Gives Up PhD in Plagiarism Row', *The Sydney Morning Herald*, 19 February 2011

Carter, Stephen L, *Integrity* (New York: BasicBooks, 1996)

Cartwright, Silvia, *The Report of the Committee of Inquiry into Allegations Concerning the Treatment of Cervical Cancer at National Women's Hospital and into Other Related Matters* (Auckland, NZ: Government Printing Office, July 1988)

Casassus, Barbara, 'Study Linking GM Maize to Rat Tumours is Retracted', *Nature*, 28 November 2013

Casassus, Barbara, 'Paper Claiming GM Link with Tumours Republished', *Nature*, 25 June 2014

Cassuto, Leonard, 'Big Trouble in the World of 'Big Physics'', *Salon*, 17 September 2002

Castelle, George, 'Fake Data, Wrongful Convictions: Learning from a Crime Lab Fraud Fiasco' (1997) 19(4) *NLADA Cornerstone* 9

Caterson, Simon, 'A Plagiarism on Them All', *The Age*, 20 November 2004

Cauvin, Henri E, 'Cancer Researcher in South Africa Who Falsified Data is Fired', *The New York Times*, 11 March 2000

Centers for Disease Control, 'Alcohol and Other Drug Use and Academic Achievement' (2009)

Chandra, Ranjit K, 'Can Nutrient Supplements Improve Functional Outcome in the Elderly' (2003) 19(11-12) *Nutrition* 978

Chandra, Ranjit K, 'Effect of Vitamin and Trace-element Supplementation on Immune Responses and Infection in Elderly Subjects' (1992) 340(8828) *The Lancet* 1124

Chang, Kenneth, 'Panel Says Bell Labs Scientist Faked Discoveries in Physics', *The New York Times*, 26 September 2002

Chang, Rung-Fang, CY Chen, Fang-Pei Su and Hsin-Chang Lin, 'Retraction Notice: A Two-Step Approach for Broadband Digital Signal Processing Technique, (26 April 2013) *Journal of Vibration and Control*' (July 2014) 20 *Journal of Vibration and Control*

Chao Jr, Roger Y, 'China Needs a Comprehensive Anti-Corruption Strategy' (8 November 2013) Issue No. 295, *University World News*

Chapman, Jeremy R, Geoffrey W McCaughan and Philip O'Connell, 'Professor Bruce Hall and the ABC' (2014) 201(6) *Medical Journal of Australia* 322

Charlesworth, Sara, Paula McDonald and Somali Cerise, 'Naming and Claiming Workplace Sexual Harassment in Australia' (2011) 46(2) *Australian Journal of Social Issues* 141

Charrow, Robert P, *Law in the LaboratoryI A Guide to the Ethics of Federally Funded Science Research* (Chicago, Ill: University of Chicago Press, 2010)

Chesen, Jeff, 'The 'CSI Effect'—There's No Such Thing as Questions, Just Hidden Answers', *National Clearinghouse for Science, Technology and the Law* (July 2008)

Chimonas, Susan, Natassia M Rozartio and David J Rothman, 'Show Us the Money: Lessons in Transparency from State Pharmaceutical Marketing Disclosure Laws' (2010) 45(1) *Health Services Research* 98

Chiriac, Marian, 'Romanian Minister Resigns in Plagiarism Row', *Balkan Insight*, 16 May 2012

Chitwood, Ava, *Death by Philosophy: The Biographical Tradition in the Life and Death of the Archaic Philosophers Empedocles, Heraclitus and Democritus* (Ann Arbor: University of Michigan Press, 2004) 11

Chi-Yuk, Choi, 'Forensic Expert Rejects Cyanide Explanation for Heywood's Death', *South China Morning Post*, 28 September 2012

Choe, Sang-Hun, 'Korean Scientist's New Project: Rebuild After Cloning Disgrace', *The New York Times*, 28 February 2014

Chopra Vineet and Eagle Kim A, 'Perioperative Mischief: The Price of Academic Misconduct' (2012) 125(10) *American Journal of Medicine* 953.

Chotiner, Isaac, 'The Ayaan Hirsi Ali Controversy is About Double Standards, Not Freedom of Speech', *New Republic*, 13 April 2014

Chua, Rachel, Virginia Masters and Daniel Estrin, 'UWA v Gray: Rights to Inventions Made by Employees', *AGS Legal Briefing* (No. 89, 15 September 2008)

Chung, Frank, 'The Great Aussie Degree Scam: Forgers Raking in Thousands Selling Bogus Qualifications', *News.com.au*, 30 March 2015

City University of New York, 'Policies and Procedures on Equal Opportunity, Non-Discrimination, and Against Sexual Harassment', 26 November 2012

Clairborne, Robert, 'Can Genes Learn? Arthur Koestler Thinks So', *The New York Times*, 2 April 1972

Clark, Liat, 'China's Academic Scandal: Call Toll-Free Hotlines to Get Your Name Published', *Wired*, 2 December 2013

Clarke, Roger, 'Journal Self-Citation XIX: Self-Plagiarism and Self-Citation—A Practical Guide Based on Underlying Principles' (2009) 25(1) *Communications of the Association for Information Systems* 155

Clarke, Toni, 'Alzheimer's Research Fraud Case Set for Trial', *Chicago Tribune*, 11 May 2012

Clarkson, Wensley, *Legal Highs: Inside Secrets of the World's Newest and Deadliest Drugs* (London: Quercus, 2015)

Cleaton-Jones, Peter, 'Scientific Misconduct in a Breast-Cancer Chemotherapy Trial: Response of University of the Witwatersrand' (2000) 355(9208) *The Lancet* 1011

Clines, Francis X, 'Work by Expert Witness is Now on Trial', *The New York Times*, 5 September 2001

Cochan, Carol Ann and John M Budd, 'The Persistence of Fraud in the Literature: The Darsee Case' (1992) 43(7) *Journal of the American Society for Information Science* 488

Cohen, Joe, 'Criminal Charges Dropped Against Chronic Fatigue Syndrome Researcher Judy Mikovits', *Science*, 13 June 2012

Cohen, Patricia, 'The Nature of Reasons: Two Philosophers Feud Over a Book Review', *The New York Times*, 12 January 2008

Cole, Simon A, 'Acculturating Forensic Science: What is 'Scientific Culture', and How Can Forensic Science Adopt It?' (2010) 38(2) *Fordham Urban Law Journal* 435

Cole, Simon A and William C Thompson, 'Forensic Science and Wrongful Convictions' in C Ronald Huff and Martin Killias (eds), *Wrongful Convictions and Miscarriages of Justice: Causes and Remedies in North American and European Criminal Justice Systems* (New York: Routledge, 2013), pp 111–136

Coleman, Gabriella, *Hacker, Hoaxer, Whistleblower, Spy: The Many Faces of Anonymous* (London: Verso Books, 2014)

Coleman, Jon T, 'Not Quite Bulletproof', *The Chronicle of Higher Education*, 4 June 2012

Collier, Bruce and James MacLachlan, *Charles Babbage and the Engines of Perfection* (New York: Oxford University Press, 1998)

Colman, Andrew M, *A Dictionary of Psychology* (4th edn, Oxford: Oxford University Press, 2015)

Collins, Matthew, *The Law of Defamation and the Internet* (3rd edn, New York: Oxford University Press, 2010)

Comité d'éthique du CNRS, 'Research Integrity in a Competitive Context'

Commission on Research Integrity, *Integrity and Misconduct in Research*, Report to the Secretary of Health and Human Services, the House Committee on Commerce, and the Senate Committee on Labor and Human Resources (Washington, DC: US Department of Health and Human Services, Public Health Service, 1995)

Committee on the Conduct of Science, National Academy of Sciences, 'On Being a Scientist' (1989) 86(23) *Proceedings of the National Academy of Sciences of the United States of America* 9053

Committee on Identifying the Needs of the Forensic Sciences Community, National Research Council, *Strengthening Forensic Science in the United States: A Path Forward* (Washington, DC: The National Academies Press, 2009)

Committee on Publication Ethics (COPE), 'Guidelines'

Committee on Science, Engineering, and Public Policy, National Academy of Science, National Academy of Engineering, and Institute of Medicine of the National Academies, *On Being a Scientist: A Guide to Responsible Conduct in Research* (3rd edn, Washington DC: National Academies Press, 2009)

'Committee Urges Research Center to be Disbanded After STAP Controversy', *GlobalPost*, 12 June 2014

Compan, Stéphane, 'Toulouse: Démission du Doyen de la Faculté Dentaire', *France 3*, 18 January 2014

Coney, Sandra and Phillida Bunkle, 'An 'Unfortunate Experiment' at National Women's' (1987) *Metro Magazine* 47

Connors, Edward, Thomas Lundregan, Neal Miller and Tom McEwen, *Convicted by Juries, Exonerated by Science: Case Studies in the Use of DNA Evidence to Establish Innocence After Trial* (Washington, DC: US Department of Justice, Office of Justice Programs, National Institute of Justice, Report No NCJ 161258, June 1996)

Contractor, Aban and Gerard Noonan, 'Testing the Limits', *The Sydney Morning Herald*, 21 March 2002

Contrada, Fred, 'Amherst Crime Lab Probe Sought by Northwestern District Attorney David Sullivan David Sullivan Following Chemist Sonja Farak's Arrest on Drug Thefts', *MassLive.com*, 25 January 2013

Cooke, David J, Christine Michie, Stephen D Hart and Daniel A Clark, 'Reconstructing Psychopathy: Clarifying the Significance of Anti-Social and Socially Deviant Behavior in the Diagnosis of Psychopathic Personality Disorder' (2004) 18(4) *Journal of Personality Disorders* 337

Cooke, David J, Christine Michie and Jennifer Skeem, 'Understanding the Structure of the Psychopathy Checklist—Revised: An Exploration of Methodological Confusion' (2007) 190(5) *The British Journal of Psychiatry* 39

Coolidge, Harold J and Robert H Lord, *Archibald Cary Coolidge: Life and Letters* (New York: Houghton Mifflin Company, 1932)

Cooper, David KC (ed), *Doctors of Another Calling: Physicians Who are Known Best in Fields Other Than Medicine* (Maryland: Rowman & Littlefield, 2014)

''Copycat' Claims Move to Romania', *The Australian*, 15 May 2012

Corbin, Lillian and Justin Carter, 'Is Plagiarism Indicative of Prospective Legal Practice?' (2007) 17(1-2) *Legal Education Review* 53

Corbo, Joan, '*Kraus v. New Rochelle Hosp. Medical Ctr.*: Are Whistleblowers Finally Getting the Protection They Need?' (1994) 12 *Hofstra Labor Law Journal* 141

Cordner, Stephen and Alastair Ross, 'Australia' in Douglas H Ubelaker (ed), *The Global Practice of Forensic Science* (Chichester, West Sussex: John Wiley & Sons, 2015), pp 13–28

Cornish, WilliamR, 'Rights in University Inventions: The Herchel Smith Lecture for 1991' (1992) 14(1) *European Intellectual Property Review* 13

Corruption and Crime Commission (Western Australia), *Report on the Investigation of Alleged Public Sector Misconduct of Dr Nasrul Ameer Ali as a Sessional Academic Employed by Curtin University of Technology* (Perth, 2 September 2010) (Commissioner Len Roberts-Smith QC)

Cortina, Lilia M, Suzanne Swan, Louise F Fitzgerald and Craig Waldo, 'Sexual Harassment and Assault: Chilling the Climate for Women in Academia' (1998) 22(3) *Psychology of Women Quarterly* 419

Cossins, Anne, 'On Stone Throwing from the Feminist Sidelines: A Critique of Helen Garner's Book, *The First Stone*' (1995) 20(2) *Melbourne University Law Review* 528

'Cot Death Error 'Costs Lives'', *BBC News*, 25 February 1999

Couglan, Sean, 'Whistleblower Warning on Degrees', *BBC News*, 17 June 2008

Coulter, Kirsten, 'Documents: Professor Sexually Harasses Students for 20 Years', *The Red & Black*, 30 January 2008

'Council for the Registration of Forensic Practitioners', HC Deb 11 May 2009, col 522W (Jacqui Smith)

'Court Freezes Out Killer Professor's Demand for Second Winter Parka', *Maclean's*, 1 December 2013

'Court Invalidates a Decade of Blood Test Results in Criminal Cases', *The New York Times*, 12 November 1993

'Court Sentences Two Central Forensic Science Laboratory Scientists in Corruption Case', *DNA India*, 11 October 2013

Couzin, Jennifer and Katherine Unger, 'Cleaning Up the Paper Trail' (2006) 312(5770) *Science* 38

Cowen, Phil, 'Academic Stalking' on *Let Them Eat Prozac* (November 2006)

'Craig Grimes, Ex-Penn State Professor, Sentenced for More than $3 Million in Research Grant Fraud', *Huffington Post*, 30 December 2012

Creamer, Alyssa, 'Landysh Zaripova, Russian Prof., Forces Students to Endure 23-Hour Oral Physics Exam', *Huffington Post*, 6 July 2012

Cressey, Daniel, 'Eminent Chemist Denies Self-Plagiarism in 'Space Dinosaurs' Paper', *Nature*, 25 April 2012

Cressey, Daniel, 'Nature Publishing Group Wins Long-Running Libel Trial', *Nature*, 6 July 2012

Creswell, Toby, *Notorious Australians: The Mad, the Bad and the Dangerous* (Pymble, NSW: ABC Books, 2011)

Criddle, Evan and Evan Fox-Decent, 'A Fiduciary Theory of Jus Cogens' (2009) 34(2) *The Yale Journal of International Law* 331

Crime and Misconduct Commission (Queensland), *An Examination of Suspected Official Misconduct at the University of Queensland* (Brisbane, September 2013)

Crofts, Andrew, *Ghostwriting* (London: Bloomsbury, 2009)

Crossley, Dominic, 'Libel reform? Defamation is the Least of our Problems *The Guardian*, 16 March 2011

Crotty, Shane, *Ahead of the Curve: David Baltimore's Life in Science* (Berkeley: University of California Press, 2001)

Cruz, Isagani, 'Is Plagiarism a Crime?' *The Philippine Star*, 13 September 2012

Culliton, Barbara J, 'The Sloan-Kettering Affair: A Story Without a Hero' (1974) 184(4137) *Science* 644

Culliton, Barbara J, 'Emory Reports on Darsee's Fraud' (1983) 220(4600) *Science* 936

Cunha, Glenn A, *Investigation of the Drug Laboratory at the William A Hinton State Laboratory Institute, 2002-2012* (Boston, Mass: Office of the Inspector-General, 4 March 2014) 1

Curthoys, Ann, 'Helen Garner's *The First Stone*' (1995) 10(21) *Australian Feminist Studies* 203

Curtin University, 'Equal Opportunity Policy', 1 March 2002

Cyranoski, David, 'Korea's Stem-Cell Stars Dogged by Suspicion of Ethical Breach' (2004) 429(6987) *Nature* 3

Cyranoski, David, 'Verdict: Hwang's Human Stem Cells Were All Fakes' (2006) 439(7073) *Nature* 122

Cyranoski, David, 'Named and Shamed' (2006) 441(7092) *Nature* 392

Cyranoski, David, 'Hwang Verdict Imminent' (2009) 461(7267) *Nature* 1035

Cyranoski, David, 'Woo Suk Hwang Convicted, But Not of Fraud' (2009) 461(7268) *Nature* 1181

Cyranoski, David, 'Retraction Record Rocks Community: Anaesthesiology Tries to Move on After Fraud Investigations' (2012) 489(7416) *Nature* 346

Cyranoski, David, 'Investigator of Controversial Stem-Cell Study Resigns', *Nature*, 25 April 2014

Cyranoski, David, 'Accusations Pile Up Amid Japan's Stem-Cell Controversy', *Nature*, 7 May 2014

Daéid, Niamh Nic, *Fifty Years of Forensic Science: A Commentary* (Chichester, UK: Wiley-Blackwell, 2010)

Dahlberg, John E and Christian C Mahler, 'The Poehlman Case: Running Away from the Truth' (2006) 12(1) *Science and Engineering Ethics* 157

Dall, William H, 'The Calaveras Skull' (1899) 51(1) *Proceedings of the Academy of Natural Sciences of Philadelphia* 2

Dalton, Rex, 'Obesity Expert Owns Up to Million-Dollar Crime' (2005) 434(7032) *Nature* 424

Dalton, Rex, 'The Stars Who Fell to Earth' (December 2002) 420 *Nature* 728

Dance, S Peter, *Animal Fakes and Frauds* (Maidenhead: Sampson Low, 1976)

D'Angelo, John, *Ethics in Science: Ethical Misconduct in Scientific Research* (Boca Raton, FL: CRC Press, 2012)

D'Angelo-Fisher, Leo, 'Phosphagenics CEO Dismissal Another Headache For Biotech', *Business Review Weekly*, 25 July 2013

'David Irving Jailed for Holocaust Denial', *The Guardian*, 20 February 2006

Davies, Mark, *Medical Self-Regulation: Crisis and Change* (Aldershot: Ashgate, 2007)

Davis, Michael, 'Avoiding the Tragedy of Whistleblowing' (1989) 8(4) *Business & Professional Ethics Journal* 3

Davis, Michael, *Ethics and the University* (London: Routledge, 1999)

Davis, Michael and Andrew Stark (eds), *Conflict of Interest in the Professions* (New York: Oxford University Press, 2001)

Dawson, Charles, 'The Piltdown Skull' (1913) 2 *The Hastings and East Sussex Naturalist* 73

Dawson, John and Nicola Peart (eds), *The Law of Research: A Guide* (Dunedin, NZ: University of Otago Press, Dunedin, 2003)

Dawson, Maureen M and Joyce A Overfield, 'Plagiarism: Do Students Know What It Is?' (November 2006) 8 *Bioscience Education*

Day, Matthew, 'German Defence Minister to Drop PhD Title Over Plagiarism Row', *The Telegraph*, 18 February 2011

De Breadun, Deaglan, 'Whistleblower Bill to Cover Public and Private Sectors', *The Irish Times*, 30 January 2012

De Maria, William, 'Queensland Whistleblowing: Sterilising the Lone Crusader' (1992) 27(4) *Australian Journal of Social Issues* 248

De Maria, William, *Unshielding the Shadow Culture: Queensland Whistleblower Study* (Result Release One, Department of Social Work and Social Policy, University of Queensland, April 1994)

De Maria, William, 'Quarantining Dissent: The Queensland Public Sector Ethics Movement' (1995) 54(4) *Australian Journal of Public Administration* 442

De Maria, William, 'Whistleblowing' (1995) 20(6) *Alternative Law Journal* 270

De Maria, William, *Deadly Disclosures: Whistleblowing and the Ethical Meltdown of Australia* (Kent Town, SA: Wakefield Press, 1999)

De Maria, William, 'Common Law—Common Mistakes?: Protecting Whistleblowers in Australia, New Zealand, South Africa and the United Kingdom' (2006) 19(7) *International Journal of Public Sector Management* 643

De Maria, William and Cyrelle Jan, *Wounded Workers: Queensland Whistleblower Study* (Result Release Two, Department of Social Work and Social Policy, University of Queensland, October 1994)

Decoo, Wilfried, *Crisis on Campus: Confronting Academic Misconduct* (Cambridge, Mass: MIT Press, 2002)

Deer, Brian, 'The Pill: Professor's Safety Tests Were Faked', *The Sunday Times*, 28 September 1986

Delaney, Brigid, 'After Nova Peris and Barry Spurr, Should We all Give Up on Email in the Name of Privacy?', *The Guardian*, 29 October 2014

Delwiche, Theodore R and Andrew M Duehren, 'New Law School Sexual Harassment Procedures Break From University Framework', *The Harvard Crimson*, 3 January 2015

Demidenko, Helen, *The Hand That Signed the Paper* (St Leonards, NSW: Allen & Unwin, 1995)

Dempster, Quentin, *Whistleblowers* (Sydney, NSW: ABC Books, 1997)

Dempsey, Judy, 'Old Doctoral Thesis Haunts a Top German Minister', *The New York Times*, 21 February 2011

Denisova-Schmidt, Elena, 'Justification of Academic Corruption at Russian Universities' (Edmond J Safra Working Papers, No. 30, 14 November 2013)

Department of Justice (Victoria), *Investigating Complaints and Concerns Regarding Judicial Conduct* (Discussion Paper, November 2009)

Department of Justice, 'Department of Justice and National Institute of Standards and Technology Announce Launch of National Commission on Forensic Science' (Media Release, 15 February 2013)

Deresiewicz, William, 'Love on Campus', *The American Scholar*, 1 June 2007

DesAutels, Peggy, 'Resisting Organizational Power' in Lisa Tessman (ed), *Feminist Ethics and Social and Political Philosophy: Theorizing the Non-Ideal* (Dordrecht: Springer, 2009), pp 223–236

DeSouza, Eros and A Gigi Fansler, 'Contrapower Sexual Harassment: A Survey of Students and Faculty Members' (2003) 48(11-12) *Sex Roles* 529

Dessort, Frédéric, 'Plagiat: Une Universitaire Toulousaine Condamnée au Pénal', *EducPros.fr*, 7 January 2014

'Detained Chinese Artist Accused of Plagiarism', *The Sydney Morning Herald*, 11 April 2011

Detert, James R, Linda K Trevino and Vicki L Sweitzer, 'Moral Disengagement in Ethical Decision-making: A Study of Antecedents and Outcomes' (2008) 93(2) *Journal of Applied Psychology* 374

Deutsche Forschungsgemeinschaft (DFG), 'Plagiarism Condemned' (Press Release, No. 5, 3 February 2011)

Deutsche Forchungsgemeinschaft, *Safeguarding Good Scientific Practice* (2013)

Devine, Tom, and Tarek F Maassarani, *The Corporate Whistleblower's Survival Guide: A Handbook for Committing the Truth* (San Francisco: Berrett-Koehler Publishers, 2011)

Devine, Thomas, Robert Vaughn and Keith Henderson, *Model Law Protecting Freedom of Expression Against Corruption*

Devlin, Marcia and Kathleen Gray K, 'In Their Own Words: A Qualitative Study of the Reasons Australian University Students Plagiarize' (2007) 26(2) *Higher Education Research & Development* 181

Dewan, Shaila, Stephanie Saul and Katie Zezima, 'For Professor, Fury Just Beneath the Surface', *The New York Times*, 20 February 2010

Dexter, Ralph W, 'Historical Aspects of the Calaveras Skull Controversy' (1986) 51(2) *American Antiquity* 365

Dey, Eric L, Jessica S Korn and Linda J Sax, 'Betrayed by the Academy: The Sexual Harassment of Women College Faculty' (1996) 67(2) *Journal of Higher Education* 149

'Did Anil Potti, Former Duke Cancer Researcher, Conduct Research Fraud?' *Huffington Post*, 13 February 2012

Dionne Jr, Eugene J, 'Biden Was Accused of Plagiarism in Law School', *The New York Times*, 17 September 1987

Dionne Jr, Eugene J, 'Biden Admits Plagiarism in School But Says It Was Not Malevolent', *The New York Times*, 18 September 1987

'Disgraced Doctor Seeks Reinstatement', *BBC News*, 17 August 1999

'Disgraced Pathologist Stripped of Medical Licence', *CTV News*, 1 February 2011

Doblin, Rick, 'Pahnke's 'Good Friday Experiment': A Long-Term Follow-up and Methodological Critique' (1991) 23(1) *Journal of Transpersonal Psychology* 1

Djerassi, CARL, *Cantor's Dilemma* (New York: Penguin Books, 1989)

Doblin, Rick, 'Dr. Leary's Concord Prison Experiment: A 34-Year Follow-Up Study' (1998) 30(4) *Journal of Psychoactive Drugs* 419

Dobson Roger, 'Science: Doctoring the Evidence', *The Independent*, 9 August 1998

'Doctor Who Faked Cancer Study Admits More Fraud', *Parker Waichmann LLP*, 23 January 2006

Doherty, Peter, *The Knowledge Wars* (Melbourne: Melbourne University Press, 2015)

Doherty, Tylor, 'Potti Letter Addresses Scandal: Former Researcher Calls Rhodes Contropversy a Misunderstanding: (11 January 12012) *The Chronicle*

Dominus, Susan, 'The Crash and Burn of an Autism Guru', *The New York Times*, 20 April 2011

Donadio, Rachel, 'Naomi Wolf Makes Much Ado About Nuzzling at Yale' (3 January 2004) *Observer*

Donkin, Marika, Rodney Smith and Alexander J Brown, 'How Do Officials Report? Internal and External Whistleblowing' in Alexander J Brown (ed), *Whistleblowing in the Australian Public Sector: Enhancing the Theory and Practice of Internal Witness Management in Public Sector Organisations* (Canberra, ACT: ANU E Press, 2008), pp 83–108

Dorling, Philip, 'Craig Thomson, MP Turned Plagiarist', *The Age*, 15 December 2011, 1

Dowler, Ken, Thomas Fleming and Stephen L Muzzatti, 'Constructing Crime: Media, Crime and Popular Culture' (2006) 48(6) *Canadian Journal of Criminology and Criminal Justice* 837

Dowling, Siobhan, 'German Politician Loses Doctorate for Plagiarism', *The Guardian*, 14 July 2011

Doyle, Charles 'Qui Tam: The False Claims Act and Related Federal Statutes', CRS Report for Congress—R40785, Congressional Research Service, 6 August 2009

'Dr Anil Potti Resigns from Duke University Amid Study Reliability Concerns', *Medical News Today*, 20 November 2010

'Dr. Claudio Soares Sex Scandal: Psychiatrist Hired as Chair at University of Alberta Resigns', *Huffington Post*, 24 September 2012

Drahl, Carmen, 'Chemist Charged in Crime Lab Scandal' (2012) 90(41) *Chemical & Engineering News* 9

Drew, Kirstine, *Whistle Blowing and Corruption: An Initial and Comparative Review* (London: Public Services International Research Unit (PSIRU), 2003)

'Drug Trial Four 'Are Conscious'', *BBC News*, 17 March 2006

Du, Jiabao, 'The Dark, Corrupt World of Forensic Science in China', *The Atlantic*, 23 August 2013

DuBois, James M, Emily E Anderson, John Chibnall and Kelly Carroll et al. 'Understanding Research Misconduct: A Comparative Analysis of 120 Cases of Professional Wrongdoing' (2013) 20(5-6) *Accountability in Research: Policies and Quality Assurance* 320

Duehren, Andrew M, 'Law Profs Challenge Title IX Policy's Protection of Academic Freedom', *The Harvard Crimson*, 18 February 2015

Duff, Eamonn and John Kidman, 'Sex Lecturer Tells of Girl's Crush', *The Sun-Herald*, 13 June 2004

Dunn, Peter M, 'The Wisheart Affair: Paediatric Cardiological Services in Bristol, 1990-5' (1998) 317(7166) *BMJ* 1145

Dupré, Sven, Dedo Von Kerssenbrock-Krosigk and Beat Wismer (eds), *Art and Alchemy: The Mystery of Transformation* (Chicago: University of Chicago Press, 2014)

Durnal, Evan W, 'Crime Scene Investigation (As Seen on TV)' (2010) 199(1) *Forensic Science International* 1

Dursht, Jaime S, 'Judicial Plagiarism: It May Be Fair Use But Is It Ethical?' (1996) 18(3) *Cardozo Law Review* 1253

Dutiel, Heather, 'Plagiarism Commonplace Amongst Russian Politicians', *Academic Plagiarism*, 6 March 2013

Dwan, Kerry, Douglas G Altman, Juan A Arnaiz, Jill Bloom et al. 'Systematic Review of the Empirical Evidence of Study Publication Bias and Outcome Reporting Bias' (2008) 3(8) *PLoS One* 3081

Dwyer, Jim, Peter Neufeld and Barry Scheck, *Actual Innocence: Five Days to Execution and Other Dispatches from the Wrongly Convicted* (New York: Doubleday, 2000)

Dyer, Clare, 'Consultant Struck Off Over Research Fraud' (1997) 315(7102) *BMJ* 205

Dyer, Clare, 'Doctor Admits Research Fraud' (1998) 316(7132) *BMJ* 647

Dyer, Clare, 'UK Introduces Far Reaching Law to Protect Whistleblowers' (1999) 319(7201) *BMJ* 7

Dyer, Clare, 'Professor Reprimanded for Failing to Act Over Fraud' (2001) 322(7286) *BMJ* 573

Dyer, Clare, 'GMC Clears Research Dean of Dishonesty Over Access to Data' (2009) 339(7730) *BMJ* 1107

Dyer, Clare, 'Child Death Expert is Accused of Dishonesty and Failing to Work Within Competence' (2014) 349 *The BMJ* g5669

Dziech, Billie Wright and Linda Weiner, *The Lecherous Professor: Sexual Harassment on Campus* (2nd edn, Urbana: University of Illinois Press, 1990)

Earle, Beverley H and Gerald A Madek, 'The Mirage of Whistleblower Protection under Sarbanes-Oxley: A Proposal for Change' (2007) 44(1) *American Business Law Journal* 1

Eastwood, Susan, Pamela Derish, Evangeline Leash and Stephen Ordway, 'Ethical Issues in Biomedical Research: Perceptions and Practices of Postdoctoral Research Fellows Responding to a Survey' (1996) 2(1) *Science and Engineering Ethics* 89

Eddy, William HC, *Orr* (Brisbane, Qld: Jacaranda Press, 1961)

Edelman, Adam, 'Kentucky Sen. Rand Paul Faces New Plagiarism Allegations Over NSA Suit Against President Obama', *New York Daily News*, 13 February 2014

Edelman, Susan, 'CUNY Mulls Ban on Professor-Student Relationships', *New York Post*, 11 March 2012

Eder, Richard, 'Up the Garden Path', 13 August 2000, *The New York Times* (online)

Editorial, 'Call the Cops' (2013) 504(7478) *Nature*

Editorial, 'Imitators and Fabricators' (1996) 20(50-51) *Journal of Australian Studies* 1

Editorial, 'STAP Retracted' (2014) 511(7507) *Nature* 5

'Editors-in-Chief Statement Regarding Published Clinical Trials Conducted Without IRB Approval by Joachim Voldt' (EIC Joint Statement, 12 March 2011)

Edwards, Elaine, 'Anti-Corruption Delays 'Cost Billions' ', *The Irish Times*, 25 October 2012

'Element 118 Disappears Two Years After it was Discovered' (2 August 2001) *physics-world.com*

Eliot, Thomas S, *The Sacred Wood and Major Early Essays* (Mineola, NY: Dover Publications, 1998 [1920])

Elks, Sarah, 'Probe on Academics Uncovers New Concerns', *The Australian*, 21 January 2014, 5

Ellis, Cath 'Helping Yourself: Marlo Morgan and the Fabrication of Indigenous Wiusdom' in Maggie Nolan and Carrie Dawson (ed), Who's Who?: Hoaxes, Imposture and Identity Crises in Australian Literature (Brisbane: University of Queensland Press, 2004), pp 149–164

Ellis, Mark, 'Breaking the Silence: Rape as an International Crime' (2006-2007) 38(2) *Case Western Reserve Journal of International Law* 225

Emerson, Ralph Waldo, 'The American Scholar' (Address to the Phi Beta Kappa Society, Cambridge, 31 August 1837)

Emerson, Ralph Waldo, eds Glen M Johnson and Joel Myerson, *Collected Works of Ralph Waldo Emerson, Volume VIII: Letters and Social Aims* (Cambridge, Mass: Harvard University Press, 2010)

Emory University, 'Emory Announces Actions Following Investigation', 22 December 2008

Emory University, Conflict of Interest Office, Research Administration

Engler, Robert L, James W Covell, Paul J Friedman, Philip S Kitcher and Richard M Peters, 'Misrepresentation and Responsibility in Medical Research' (1987) 317(22) *The New England Journal of Medicine* 1383

'Enlightened Intolerance', *The Economist*, 16 April 2014

Enserink, Martin, 'Dutch University Sacks Social Psychologist Over Faked Data', *Science Insider*, 7 September 2011

Erasmus, Desiderius, 'The Praise of Folly' in Clarence H Miller (trans), *The Praise of Folly* (2nd edn, New Haven: Yale University Press, 2003 [1511])

Erasmus MC Follow-Up Investigation Committee, *Report on the 2012 Follow-Up Investigation of Possible Breaches of Academic Integrity*, 30 September 2012

Erasmus University, 'Erasmus MC Dismisses Professor', *Erasmus MC*, 17 November 2011

Erin, Edward M, Brian R Leaker, Grant C Nicholson, Andrew J Tan et al. 'The Effects of a Monoclonal Antibody Directed Against Tumor Necrosis Factor-α in Asthma' (2006) 174(7) *American Journal of Respiratory and Critical Care Medicine* 753

Erlanger, Steven, 'France's Chief Rabbi Declines to Resign over Plagiarism', *The New York Times*, 9 April 2013

'European Commissioner 'Cheated' ', *Austrian Independent*, 23 May 2011

European Science Foundation and All European Academies, *The European Code of Conduct for Research Integrity* (March 2011)

European Science Foundation, *Fostering Research Integrity in Europe* (December 2010)

Evans, Rebecca and Emily Nash, 'Doctor Edward Erin Guilty of Attempting Poison Abortion', *The Mirror*, 19 October 2009

Eve, Martin, 'Flawed Sting Operation Singles Out Open Access Journals', *The Conversation*, 4 October 2013

Ewick, Patricia, Robert Kagan and Austin Sarat (eds), *Social Science, Social Policy, and the Law* (New York: Russell Sage Foundation, 1999)

Ewing, Kent, 'Betraying Confucius: Academic Fraud in China', *Asia Times*, 21 January 2010

Explanatory Statement, Public Interest Disclosure Bill 2012 (ACT)

Fackelmann, Kathleen, 'Appeals Panel Reverses Fraud Ruling' (1996) 150(1) *Science News* 4

Fahy, Declan, *The New Celebrity Scientists: Out of the Lab and Into the Limelight* (Lanham: Rowman & Littlefield, 2015)

Falk, Gerhard, *Fraud: Deceit Among Scientists, Academics, Writers and Philanthropists* (Lanham, Md: University Press of America, 2007)

Fancher, Raymond E, 'The Burt Case: Another Foray' (1991) 253(5027) *Science* 1565

Fanelli, Daniele, 'How Many Scientists Fabricate and Falsify Research? A Systematic Review and Meta-Analysis of Survey Data' (2009) 4(5) *PLoS One* e5738

Fanelli, Daniele, 'Why Growing Retractions are (Mostly) AS Good Sign' (2013) 10(12) *Plos Med* 1001563

Fanelli, Daniele, 'Redefine Misconduct as Distorted Reporting' (2013) 494 *Nature* 149

Fang, Ferric C, Arturo Casadevall and RP Morrison, 'Retracted Science and the Retraction Index' (2011) 79(10) *Infection and Immunity* 3855

Fang, Ferric C, R Grant Steen and Arturo Casadevall, 'Misconduct Accounts for the Majority of Retracted Scientific Publications' (2012) 109(42) *Proceedings of the National Academy of Sciences of the United States of America* 17028

Farnsworth, Clyde H, 'Doctor Says He Falsified Cancer Data to Help Patients', *The New York Times*, 1 April 1994

Farrington, Dennis J and David Palfreyman, *The Law of Higher Education* (2nd edn, Oxford, UK: Oxford University Press, 2012)

Farthing, Michael JG, 'Retractions in *Gut* 10 Years After Publication' (2001) 48(3) *Gut* 285

'FAS Dean Smith Confirms Scientific Misconduct by Marc Hauser', *Harvard Magazine*, 20 August 2010

Faunce, Thomas, Stephen Bolsin and Wei-Ping Chan, 'Supporting Whistleblowers in Academic Medicine: Training and Respecting the Courage of Professional Conscience' (2004) 30(1) *Journal of Medical Ethics* 40

Faunce, Thomas A, Gregor Urbas and Lesley Skillen, 'Implementing US-Style Anti-Fraud Laws in the Australian Pharmaceutical and Health Care Industries' (2011) 194(9) *Medical Journal of Australia* 474

Fazackerley, Anna, 'On the Rocks in Every Way', *Times Higher Education*, 8 April 2005
Fearn, Hannah, 'Sex and the University', *Times Higher Education*, 22 May 2008
Feather, Norman T, 'Attitudes Towards the High Achiever: The Fall of the Tall Poppy' (1989) 41(3) *Australian Journal of Psychology* 239
Federal Court of Australia, 'Expert Witnesses in Proceedings in the Federal Court of Australia' (Practice Note CM 7, 4 June 2013)
Ferguson, Cat, Marcus, Adam and Oransky, Ivan, 'Publicshing: The Peer-Review Scam' (2014) 515 *Nature*
Ferguson, David, 'Drunk Professor Forces Students to Sit Through 23-Hour Science Exam', *Raw Story*, 5 July 2012
Ferngren, Gary B, *Medicine and Religion: A Historical Introduction* (Baltimore: Johns Hopkins University Press, 2014)
Ferriman, Annabel, 'Consultant Suspended for Research Fraud' (2000) 321(7274) *BMJ* 1429
Finucane, Martin, 'Annie Dookhan Sets Date for Change of Plea', *The Boston Globe*, 28 October 2013
'Fired Professor Robert Ammon Jr. Rightfully Terminated after Sexual Harassment, Court Finds', *Huffington Post*, 11 June 2013
Firstman, Richard and Jamie Talan, *The Death of Innocents* (New York: Bantam Books, 1997)
Fischman, Josh, 'Fake Peer Reviews, the Latest Form of Scientific Fraud, Fool Journals' (2012) 59(7) *The Chronicle of Higher Education* A18
Fisher, Bernard and Carol K Redmond, 'Fraud in Breast-Cancer Trials' (1994) 330(20) *The New England Journal of Medicine* 1458
Fisher, Bonnie S, Leah E Daigle and Francis T Cullen, *Unsafe in the Ivory Tower: The Sexual Victimization of College Women* (Los Angeles: Sage Publications, 2010)
Fisher, Jim, *Forensics Under Fire: Are Bad Science and Dueling Experts Corrupting Criminal Justice?* (New Brunswick, NJ: Rutgers University Press, 2008)
Fisher, Ronald A, 'Has Mendel's Work Been Rediscovered?' (1936) 1(2) *Annals of Science* 115
Fiske, Edward B, 'Education; Lessons', *The New York Times*, 18 October 1989
Fitzgerald, Louise F, 'Sexual Harassment: The Definition and Measurement of a Construct' in Michele A Paludi (ed), *Sexual Harassment on Campus* (New York: State University of New York Press, 1996), pp 25–48
Fitzgerald, Louise F, *The Last Great Open Secret: The Sexual Harassment of Women in the Workplace and Academia* (Washington, DC: Federation of Behavioral, Psychological and Cognitive Sciences, 1993)
Fitzgerald, Louise F, Sandra L Shullman, Nancy Bailey and Margaret Richards et al. 'The Incidence and Dimensions of Sexual Harassment in Academia and the Workplace' (1988) 32(2) *Journal of Vocational Behavior* 152
Fitzgerald, Ross, *My Name is Ross: An Alcoholic's Journey* (Sydney: New South, 2010)
Flaherty, Colleen, 'After a Professor's Suicide', *Inside Higher Education*, 11 January 2013
Flaherty, Colleen, 'Looking the Other Way?' *Inside Higher Education*, 16 July 2013
Flaherty, Dennis K, 'The Vaccine-Autism Connection: A Public Health Crisis Caused by UInethical Medical Practices and Fraudulent Science' (2011) 45(10) *Annals of Pharmacotherapy* 1302
Flanagin, Annette, Carey, Lisa A, Fontanarosa, Phil B et al. "Prevalence of Articles with Honorary Authors and Ghost Authors in Peer-Reviewed Medical Journals" (1998) 280(3) Journal of the American Medical Association 22
Fleischacker, Samuel, *Integrity and Moral Relativism* (Leiden: Brill, 1992)
Flinders University, *Fraud and Corruption Prevention and Control* (Last updated 28 July 2014)
Flint, Abbi, Ranald Macdonald and Sue Clegg, *Emotion, Practise and Plagiarism Exploring the Staff Perspective*: (Paper presented at Plagiarism: Prevention, Practice and Policies 2004 Conference, 28 June 2004)
Fontani, Marco, Costa Mariagrazia and Orna, Mary Virginia, *The Lost Elements: The Periodic Table's Shadow Side* (Oxford: Oxford University Press, 2014).
Forensic Science Regulator, *Business Plan 2013/2014*
'Forensic Science Regulator', HC Deb 12 July 2007, col 67WS (Meg Hillier)
'Forensic Scientist Denies Trial Bias', *Glasgow Herald*, 12 June 1981, 5

Fountain, Henry, 'Science Journal Pulls 60 Papers in Peer-Review Fraud', *The New York Times*, 10 July 2014

Fox, Mark and Jeffrey Beall, 'Advice for Plagiarism Whistleblowers' (2013) 24(5) *Ethics & Behavior* 341

Fox, Richard G, 'Protecting the Whistleblower' (1993) 15(2) *Adelaide Law Review* 137

'France's Chief Rabbi Resigns Amid Plagiarism Scandal', *France 24*, 11 April 2013

Francis, Leslie, *Sexual Harassment as an Ethical Issue in Academic Life* (Lanham, Maryland: Rowman & Littlefield, 2001)

Frank, Jerome, *Courts on Trial: Myth and Reality in American Justice* (Princeton, NJ: Princeton University Press, 1973)

Franklin, Allan, Anthony WF Edwards, Daniel J Fairbanks, Daniel L Hartl et al. *Ending the Mendel-Fisher Controversy* (Pittsburgh: University of Pittsburgh Press, 2008)

'Fraudulent Forensic Expert Jailed', *BBC News*, 22 February 2007

Freckelton, Ian, *The Trial of the Expert: A Study of Expert Evidence and Forensic Experts* (Melbourne: Oxford University Press, 1987)

Freckelton, Ian, 'Of Blood, Babies and Bathwater' (1992) 17(1) *Alternative Law Journal* 10

Freckelton, Ian, 'Sentencing the Substance Dependent Offender' (1994) 1(1) *Psychiatry, Psychology and Law* 11

Freckelton, Ian, 'Wizards in the Crucible: Making the Boffins Accountable' in Johannes F Nijboer and Jan M Reijntjes (eds), *Proceedings of the First World Conference on New Trends in Criminal Investigation and Evidence* (Lelystad: Koninklijke Vermande, 1997), pp 95–110

Freckelton, Ian, ' 'Good Character' and the Regulation of Medical Practitioners' (2008) 16(3) *Journal of Law and Medicine* 488

Freckelton, Ian, 'Expert Evidence Accountability: New Developments and Challenges' (2011) 19(2) *Journal of Law and Medicine* 209

Freckelton, Ian, 'Civil Liability of Health Practitioners for their Forensic Work: Further Erosion of the Witness Immunity Rule' (2012) 19(4) *Psychiatry, Psychology and Law* 451

Freckelton, Ian, 'Death by Homœopathy: Issues for Civil, Criminal and Coronial Law and for Health Service Policy' (2012) 19(3) *Journal of Law and Medicine* 454

Freckelton, Ian, 'Criminalising Research Fraud' (2014) 22(2) *Journal of Law and Medicine* 241

Freckelton, Ian, Jane Goodman-Delahunty, Jacqueline Horan and Blake McKimmie, *Expert Evidence in Criminal Jury Trials* (Oxford: Oxford University Press, 2016)

Freckelton, Ian, Prasuna Reddy and Hugh Selby, *Australian Judicial Perspectives on Expert Evidence: An Empirical Study* (Melbourne: Australian Institute of Judicial Administration, 1999)

Freckelton, Ian, Prasuna Reddy and Hugh Selby, *Australian Magistrates' Perspectives on Expert Evidence: A Comparative Study* (Carlton: Australian Institute of Judicial Administration, 2001)

Freckelton, Ian and Hugh Selby (eds), *Expert Evidence*, 6 vols (Pyrmont, NSW: Law Book Co/Thomson Reuters, 1993)

Freckelton, Ian and Hugh Selby, *Expert Evidence: Law, Practice, Procedure and Advocacy* (6th edn, Pyrmont, NSW: Lawbook Co/Thomson Reuters, 2016)

Freedman, David H, 'Lies, Damned Lies, and Medical Science', *The Atlantic*, 4 October 2010

Freedman, David H, *Wrong: Why Experts Keep Failing Us—And How to Know When Not to Trust Them* (New York: Little, Brown and Co, 2010)

Freedman, Morris, 'The Persistence of Plagiarism, The Riddle of Originality' (1994) 70(3) *The Virginia Quarterly Review* 504

Freedman, Robert, David A Lewis, Robert Michels, Daniel S Pine, Susan K Schultz and Carol A Tamminga et al. (eds), 'Conflict of Interest—An Issue for Every Psychiatrist' (2009) 166(3) *The American Journal of Psychiatry* 274

From the Editor, 'Retraction of Four Articles and Abstracts' (2011) 183(3) *American Journal of Respiratory and Critical Care Medicine* 418

'From the Feuilletons' on *Sign and Sight.com* (12 February 2010)

Frontiers in Psychology Editorial Office, 'Retraction: Recursive Fury: Conspiracist Ideation in the Blogosphere in Response to Research on Conspiracist Ideation', *Frontiers in Psychology*, 27 March 2014, updated 4 April 2014

Fuchs, Ralph F, 'Academic Freedom—Its Basic Philosophy, Function, and History' (1963) 28(3) *Law and Contemporary Problems* 431

Funder, John, *Report to the Minister Containing a Summary of the Resolutions of the Committee of Enquiry Examining Research Practices Employed by Dr Ashoka Prasad in relation to the Research Project Entitled 'Seasonality Study'* (Report No 92, 1987-1988) [1]

Furdell, Elizabeth Lane, *The Royal Doctors, 1485-1714: Medical Personnel at the Tudor and Stuart Courts* (Rochester, NY: University of Rochester Press, 2001)

Furdell, Elizabeth Lane, *Publishing and Medicine in Early Modern England* (Rochester, NY: University of Rochester Press, 2002)

Gabbard, Glen O, and Eva P Lester, *Boundaries and Boundary Violations in Psychoanalysis* (Washington, DC: American Psychiatric Publishing, 2003)

Gallagher, James, 'Stem Cell 'Major Discovery' Claimed', *BBC News*, 29 January 2014

Gallagher, James, 'Stem Cell Scandal Scientist Haruko Obokata Resigns', *BBC News*, 19 December 2014

Gallant, Tricia Bertram (ed), *Creating the Ethical Academy: A Systems Approach to Understanding Misconduct and Empowering Change in Higher Education* (New York: Routledge, 2011)

Gallivan, Nelson, Camille, Jane A Halpert and Douglas F Cellar, 'Organizational Responses for Preventing and Stopping Sexual Harassment: Effective Deterrents or Continued Endurance?' (2007) 56(11-12) *Sex Roles* 811

Gallop, Jane, *Feminist Accused of Sexual Harassment* (Durham: Duke University Press, 1997)

Galloway, Frank J, 'Reassessing Freud's Case Histories: The Social Construction of Psychoanalysis' (1991) 82(2) *Isis* 245

Gallu, Joshua, 'SEC Pays $US50,000 in First Dodd-Frank Whistleblower Reward', *Bloomberg*, 22 August 2012

Garcia, Jose Maria Rodriguez, 'Scientia Potestas Est – Knowledge in Power: Francis Bacon to Michel Foucault' (2001) 28(1) Neohelicon 109

García-Berthou, Emili and Carles Alcaraz, 'Incongruence between Test Statistics and *P* Values in Medical Papers' (2004) 4 *BMC Medical Research Methodology* 13

Gardner, Michael, 'Opposition Politician Not Guilty of Plagiarism', Issue No. 297, *University World News*, 22 November 2013

Garfield, Eugene and Alfred Welljams-Dorof, 'The Impact of Fraudulent Research on the Scientific Literature: The Stephen E Breuning Case' (1990) 263(10) *The Journal of the American Medical Association* 1424

Garfield, Eugene, 'What is the Primordial Reference for the Phrase 'Publish or Perish'' (1996) 10(12) *The Scientist* 11

Garner, Harold R, McKiver, Lauren J and Waitkin, Michael B 'Research Funding: Same Work, Twice the Money?' (2013) 493 *Nature* 599

Garner, Helen, *The First Stone: Some Questions About Sex and Power* (Sydney: Picador, 1995)

Garrett, Brandon L and Peter J Neufeld, 'Invalid Forensic Science Testimony and Wrongful Convictions' (2009) 95(1) *Virginia Law Review* 1

Gasparyan, Armen Y, Lilit Ayvazyan, Sergey V Gorin and George D Kitas, 'Upgrading Instructions for Authors of Scholarly Journals' (2014) 55(3) *Croatian Medical Journal* 271

Gawrylewski, Andrea, 'Under Suspicion, But Not Retracted', *The Scientist*, 1 March 2007

Geiger, Christophe, *Criminal Enforcement of Intellectual Property: A Handbook of Contemporary Research* (Cheltenham, UK: Edward Elgar, 2012)

Geison, Gerald L, *The Private Science of Louis Pasteur* (Princeton, NJ: Princeton University Press, 1995)

General Medical Council, *Who Regulates Health and Social Care Professionals?*

George, Joyce C, *Judicial Opinion Writing Handbook* (5th edn, Buffalo, NY: Hein & Co, 2007)

George, Patrick, *Defamation Law in Australia* (2nd edn, Chatswood, NSW: LexisNexis Butterworths, 2012)

'German Defense Minister's Plagiarized PhD Dissertation Visualized', *FlowingData*

'German Education Minister Quits Over PhD Plagiarism', *The Guardian*, 9 February 2013

'German Faces More Plagiarism Charges', *UPI*, 20 February 2011

'German MEP Silvana Koch-Mehrin Quits in Plagiarism Row', *BBC News*, 11 May 2011
'German Politics Rocked by New Plagiarism Probe', *BBC News*, 14 April 2011
'Germans Offer Putin a Lessor on Plagiarism', *The Moscow Times*, 13 May 2011
'German University Rejects Plagiarism Allegations Against Steinmeier', *Deutsche Welle*, 5 November 2013
Gershman, Bennett L, 'Misuse of Scientific Evidence By Prosecutors' (2003) 28(1) *Oklahoma City University Law Review* 17
Gertsberg, Deniza, 'Seralini's GMO Study Ignites a War', *GMO Journal*, 14 November 2012
Ghosh, Pallab, 'Chiropractors' Libel Case Dropped against Simon Singh', *BBC News*, 15 April 2010
Giannelli, Paul C, 'The Abuse of Scientific Evidence in Criminal Cases: The Need for Independent Crime Laboratories' (1997) 4(2) *Virginia Journal of Social Policy & the Law* 439
Giannelli, Paul C, 'Wrongful Convictions and Forensic Science: The Need to Regulate Crime Labs' (2007) 86(1) *North Carolina Law Review* 163
Giannelli, Paul C, 'Microscopic Hair Comparisons: A Cautionary Tale' (Working Paper 2010-17, Case Research Paper Series in Legal Studies, School of Law, Case Western Reserve University, April 2010)
Giannelli, Paul C, 'The North Carolina Lab Scandal' (2012) 27(1) *Criminal Justice* 43
Giannelli, Paul C and Edward J Imwinkelried Jr, vol 1, *Scientific Evidence* (4th edn, Newark, NJ: LexisNexis, 2007)
Gieryn, Thomas F, *Cultural Boundaries of Science: Credibility on the Line* (Chicago: University of Chicago Press, 1999)
Gill, John, 'Does Rudeness Have a Place in Academia?' *Times Higher Education*, 7 November 2013
Gillie, Oliver, 'Pioneer of IQ Faked his Research Findings', *The Sunday Times*, 24 October 1976, 1
Gilmore, Heath and Ruth Pollard, 'Sydney University Expands Sex-Assault Policy', *The Sydney Morning Herald*, 25 February 2010
Gingerich, Owen, 'Was Ptolemy a Fraud?' (1980) 21 *Quarterly Journal of the Royal Astronomical Society* 253
Gisesa, Nyambega, 'Lecturer Bares it All on Sex-for-Marks Claims', *Standard Digital*, 12 April 2013
Glazer, Myron P and Penina M Glazer, *The Whistleblowers: Exposing Corruption in Government and Industry* (New York: Basic Books, 1989)
Gliboff, Sander, 'The Case of Paul Kammerer: Evolution and Experimentation in the Early 20th Century' (2006) 39(3) *Journal of the History of Biology* 525
Glindemann, Kent E, E Scott Geller and Jason N Fortney, 'Self-Esteem and Alcohol Consumption: A Study of College Drinking Behavior in a Naturalistic Setting' (1999) 45(1) *Journal of Alcohol and Drug Education* 60
'GMC Professional Conduct Committee' (1988) 296(6617) *British Medical Journal* 306
'Go8 Research Integrity and Ethics Group', Group of Eight Australia
Goddard, John, 'Cop Claims Harassment by the 'Babe for Bush' ', *The Star*, 21 December 2007
Gold, Hal, *Unit 731 Testimony* (New York: Tuttle Publishing, 2011)
Goldberg, Paul, 'Duke Officials Silenced Med Student Who Reported Trouble in Anil Pott's Lab' (9 January 2015) *The Cancer Letter*
Goldschmidt, Richard B, 'Research and Politics' (1949) 109(2827) *Science* 219
Goldstein, Joseph, 'New York Examines Over 800 Rape Cases for Possible Mishandling of Evidence', *The New York Times*, 10 January 2013
Goode, David, Darryl B Hill, Jean Reiss and William Bronston, *A History and Sociology of the Willowbrook State School* (Washington, DC: American Association on Intellectual and Developmental Disabilities, 2013)
Goodhart, CB, 'Review: Cyril Burt, Fraud or Framed?' *Galton Institute Newsletter* (September 1996)
Goodman, Matthew, *The Sun and the Moon: The Remarkable True Account of Hoaxers, Showmen, Dueling Journalists, and Lunar Man-Bats in Nineteenth Century New York* (New York: Basic Books, 2008)

Goodman-Delahunty, Jane and Hielkje Verbrugge, 'Reality, Fantasy and the Truth about CSI Effects' (2010) 32(4) *InPsych* 18
Goodstein, David L, *On Fact and Fraud: Cautionary Tales from the Front Lines of Science* (Princeton: Princeton University Press, 2010)
Goodwin, Megan P, Bruce Roscoe, Marshall Rose and Susan E Repp, 'Sexual Harassment: Experiences of University Employees' (1989) 52(3) *Initiatives* 25
Goodyear, Michael, 'Learning From the TGN1412 Trial' (2006) 332(7543) *BMJ* 677
Gorman, Christine, 'Breast Cancer: A Diagnosis of Deceit', *Time*, 24 June 2001
Goudge, Stephen, *Inquiry into Pediatric Forensic Pathology in Ontario*, vol 1 (Ontario: Queen's Printer for Ontario, 2008)
Gough, Deborah, 'Deakin University Dumps Disgraced Liberal Aaron Lane', *The Sydney Morning Herald*, 2 August 2014
Gould, Stephen J, 'Piltdown Revisited' (March 1979) 88 *Natural History* 86
Gould, Stephen J, 'The Piltdown Conspiracy' (August 1980) 89 *Natural History* 8
Gould, Stephen J, 'Piltdown in Letters' (June 1981) 90 *Natural History* 12
Gould, Stephen Jay, *The Lying Stones of Marrakesh: Penultimate Reflections in Natural History* (New York: Three Rivers Press, 2000)
Government of Canada, Panel on Responsible Conduct of Research, *The Tri-Agency Framework: Responsible Conduct of Research* (2011)
Government of Romania (Press Release, 19 June 2012)
Government's Sentencing Memorandum, *United States v Reuben* (United States District Court, District of Massachusetts, Case No. 10-CR-30002-MAP, 22 June 2010)
Grady, Denise, 'Breast Cancer Researcher Admits Falsifying Data', *The New York Times*, 5 February 2000
Graham, Chris, 'The Transcripts: The Partial Works of Professor Barry Spurr. Poet, Racist, Misogynist', *New Matilda*, 19 October 2014
Grama, Emanuela, 'Networking Texts and Persons: Politics of Plagiarism in Post Socialist Romania' (2004) 4(2) *Romanian Journal of Society and Politics* 148
Grant, Bob, 'UK Psychiatrist Suspended for Plagiarism', *The Scientist*, 23 June 2008
Grant, Bob, 'Korean Stem Cell Film Tops Box Office', *The Scientist*, 9 October 2014
Grant, John, *Corrupted Science: Fraud, Ideology and Politics in Science* (Wisely, Surrey: Facts, Figures & Fun, 2007)
'Grassley Questions New Federal Grant to Research Physician Who Was Previously Suspended' on *Chuck Grassley: United States Senator for Iowa* (29 May 2012)
Grattan, Michelle, 'D'Oh! Albanese Embarrassed, Plagiarising Film President', *The Age*, 26 January 2012, 4
Grauerholz, Elizabeth, 'Sexual Harassment of Women Professors by Students: Exploring the Dynamics of Power, Authority, and Gender in a University Setting' (1989) 21(11-12) *Sex Roles* 789
Gray, Edward, *Henry Wade's Tough Justice: How Dallas County Prosecutors Led the Nation in Convicting the Innocent* (Indianapolis: Dog Ear Publishing, 2010)
Gray, Fred D, *The Tuskegee Syphilis Study: The Real Story and Beyond* (Montgomery: New South Books, 1998)
Gray, Richard, 'Scientist Jailed for Faking Medicine Test Results', *The Telegraph*, 17 April 2013
Green, Leila, 'Reviewing the Scourge of Self-Plagiarism' (2005) 8(5) *M/C Journal*
Green, Stuart P, 'Plagiarism, Norms, and the Limits of Theft Law: Some Observations on the Use of Criminal Sanctions in Enforcing Intellectual Property Rights' (2002-2003) 54(1) *Hastings Law Journal* 167
Greenberg, Daniel S, 'Issue of Scientific Fraud Not Easily Faced', *Chicago Tribune*, 16 August 1989
Greenfield, Robert, *Timothy Leary: A Biography* (Orlando, Fla: Harcourt, 2006)
Griebel, Kathleen Keough, 'Fred Zain, the CSI Effect, and a Philosophical Idea of Justice: Using West Virginia as a Model for Change' (2012) 114(3) *West Virginia Law Review* 1155
Griffith University, Governance, 'Whistleblowing'
Griffith University, 'Personal Relationships in the Workplace', 1 December 2014

Griffiths, Roland R, William A Richards, Una D McCann and Robert L Jesse, 'Psilocybin Can Occasion Mystical-Type Experiences Having Substantial and Sustained Personal Meaning and Spiritual Significance' (2006) 187(3) *Psychopharmacology* 268

Griggs, Lynden and Rohan Price, 'The University Academic as a Fiduciary—Where to Following University of Western Australia v Gray?' (2008-2009) 19 *Journal of Law, Information and Science* 22

Grimshaw, Kyle, 'A Victory for the Student Researcher: *Chou v. University of Chicago*' (2001) *Duke Law and Technology Review* 35

Grimston, Jack, 'Lecturers Reveal Watered-Down Degrees', *The Sunday Times*, 8 March 2009

Grodin, Michael A and Leonard H Glantz (eds), *Children as Research Subjects: Science, Ethics, and Law* (New York: Oxford University Press, 1994)

Grogan Kevin, 'GSK Sacks China R & D Chief over Data Fraud', *PharmaTimes*, 12 June 2013

Gross, Alan, 'Twilight in Academe: The Problem of the Aging Professoriate' (1977) 58(10) *Phi Delta Kappan* 752

Gross, Charles, 'Disgrace: On Marc Hauser', *The Nation*, 21 December 2011

Gross, Samuel R, 'Expert Evidence' (1991) Issue 6 *Wisconsin Law Review* 1113

Gruber, James E, 'The Impact of Male Work Environments and Organizational Policies on Women's Experiences of Sexual Harassment' (1998) 12(3) *Gender and Society* 301

Guarino, Mark, 'Professor Fired for Israel Criticism Urges University of Illinois to Reinstate Him', *The Guardian*, 9 September 2014

Guignon, Charles B, *On Being Authentic* (New York: Psychology Press, 2004)

Guilliatt, Richard, 'UNSW Broadside in Paul Barach Battle: Reputations at Stake', *The Australian*, 30 January 2013

Guilliatt, Richard, 'Academic 'Conman' Paul Barach Sorry for False Claims', *The Australian*, 2 August 2014

Golunov, Serghei, *The Elephant in the Room: Corruption and Cheating in Russian Universities* (Serghei (New York: Columbia University Press, 2014)

Golunov, Serghei and Ivan Kurilla, 'Academic Integrity in Russia Today: The Political and Social Implications of Thesis Falsification and Education Reform' (PONARS Eurasia Policy Memo No. 246, March 2013)

Guterman, Lila, 'Plagiarism and Other Sins Seem Rife in Science Journals, a Digital Sleuth Trends' (2008) 54(21) *Chronicle of Higher Education* A9

GuttenPlag: Kollaborative Plagiatsdokumentation, GuttenPlag Wiki

Gysel, Carlos, 'Govert Bidloo's 'Anatomia' (1685) and the Plagiarism by William Cowper (1698)' (1987) 42(3) *Revue Belge de Medecine Dentaire* 96

Haase, Nicolai, Anders Perner, Louise Inkeri Hennings, Martin Siegemund et al. 'Hydroxyethyl Starch 130/0.38-0.45 Versus Crystalloid or Albumin in Patients with Sepsis: Systematic Review with Meta-Analysis and Trial Sequential Analysis' (2013) 346 *BMJ* 839

Hadley, Keith and Michael J Fereday, *Ensuring Competent Performance in Forensic Practice: Recovery, Analysis, Interpretation, and Reporting* (Boca Raton, FL: CRC Press, 2008)

Hagen, Margaret A, *Whores of the Court: The Fraud of Psychiatric Testimony and the Rape of American Justice* (New York: Regan Books, 1997)

Hall, Bruce M, 'Australia Needs an Office of Academic Integrity' (2006) 185(11-12) *Medical Journal of Australia* 619

Halliday, Ian, 'European Science Foundation and Research Integrity' in Tony Mayer and Nicholas Steneck (eds), *Promoting Research Integrity in a Global Environment* (Singapore: World Scientific, 2012), pp 25–32

Hamblin, Terry, 'The Secret Life of Dr Chandra' (2006) 332(7537) *BMJ* 369

Hameed, Salman, 'Plagiarism in Arab-Muslim Academia' on *Irtiqa* (1 November 2010)

Hamer, Mick, 'How a Forensic Scientist Fell Foul of the Law' (1981) 91(1269) *New Scientist* 575

Hamilton, Neil W, *Zealotry and Academic Freedom: A Legal and Historical Perspective* (New Brunswick, NJ: Transaction Publications, 1995)

Hammond, Phil, 'Stephen Bolsin's Story: Too Many Babies Were Damaged and Dying', *Medical Harm*, 27 July 2011

Han, Dahai, Haoran Chen and Lixia Xi, 'Retraction Notice to 'PMD Mitigation Through Interleaving LDPC Codes with Polarization Scramblers—(2012) 44(8) *Optics & Laser Technology* 2327-2331' (2013) 48 *Optics & Laser Technology* 612

Hannam, Peter, 'Conspiracist' Climate Change Study Withdrawn Amid Legal Threats', *The Sydney Morning Herald*, 2 April 2014

Harding, Luke, *The Snowden Files: The Inside Story of the World's Most Wanted Man* (London: Guardian, 2014)

Hare, Julie and Patricia Karvelas, 'Unpoetic Emails Derail Sydney Uni Professor Barry Spurr', *The Australian*, 17 October 2014

Hare, Robert D, *Without Conscience: The Disturbing World of the Psychopaths Among Us* (New York: Guilford Press, 1999)

Hare, Robert D and Craig S Neumann, 'The Role of Antisociality in the Psychopathy Construct: Comment on Skeem and Cooke (2010)' (2010) 22(2) *Psychological Assessment* 446

Harris, Gardiner, 'Top Psychiatrist Didn't Report Drug Makers' Pay', *The New York Times*, 3 October 2008

Harris, Gardiner and Benedict Carey, 'Researchers Fail to Reveal Full Drug Pay', *The New York Times*, 8 June 2008

Harris, Robert, *Selling Hitler* (London: Arrow/Random House, 1996)

Harris, Robert, 'Anti-Plagiarism Strategies for Research Papers', VirtualSalt.com, 30 December 2013

Hartl, Daniel L and Daniel J Fairbanks, 'Mud Sticks: On the Alleged Falsification of Mendel's Data' (2007) 175(3) *Genetics* 975

Hartley, Trevor C, ' 'Libel Tourism' and Conflict of Laws' (2010) 59(1) *International and Comparative Law Quarterly* 25

Harvard College, 'Avoiding Plagiarism', *Harvard Guide to Using Sources*

Harvard College, 'What Constitutes Plagiarism', *Harvard Guide to Using Sources*

Harvard College, 'Why Does It Matter If You Plagiarize', *Harvard Guide to Using Sources*

Harvard Law School, 'Drug and Alcohol Policy'

Harvard University, Faculty of Arts and Sciences, 'About the Department'

Harvard University, Office of Technology Development, 'Statement of Policy in Regard to Intellectual Property', 12 December 2013

Harvard University, 'Whistleblowing Policy' (Updated 18 January 2012)

Harvey, Gordon, *Writing with Sources: A Guide for Students* (2nd edn, Indianapolis: Hackett Publishing Co, 2008)

Hauser, Marc D, *Moral Minds: How Nature Designed Our Universal Sense of Right and Wrong* (New York: Ecco, 2006)

Hauser, Marc, *Evilicious: Cruelty = Desire + Denial* (Create Space, 2013)

Hawley, Christopher S, 'The Thieves of Academe: Plagiarism in the University System' (1984) 32(1) *Improving College and University Teaching* 35

Haywood, Ian, *Faking It: Art and the Politics of Forgery* (Brighton: Harvester Press, 1987)

Hazlitt, William Carew (ed) and Charles Cotton (trans), *Essays of Michel de Montaigne* (first publ. by Charles Cotton in 1685-1686, Project Gutenberg, 1877 ed), Book III, Chapter XII

He, Guang-Zhi, 'Retracted: *Entamoeba Histolytica*: Cloning, Expression and Evaluation of the Efficacy of a Recombinant Amebiasis Cysteine Proteinase Gene (ACP1) Antigen in Minipig' (2012) 130(2) *Experimental Parasitology* 126

Healey Jr, Joseph M and Kara L Dowling, 'Controlling Conflicts of Interest in the Doctor-Patient Relationship: Lessons from *Moore v. Regents of the University of California*' (1991) 42(3) *Mercer Law Review* 989

Health and Disability Commissioner (New Zealand), 'The HDC Code of Health and Disability Services Consumers' Rights Regulation 1996'

Health and Disability Commissioner (New Zealand), 'History'

Health and Human Services Department, 'Finding of Research Misconduct—Dong-Pyou Han', *Office of the Federal Register*, 23 December 2013

Healy, David, *Pharmageddon* (Berkeley: University of California Press, 2012)

Hearnshaw, Leslie S, *Cyril Burt, Psychologist* (Ithaca, NY: Cornell University Press, 1979)
'Heavy Lifting? A German Plagiarism Scandal', *The Economist*, 17 February 2011
Heckenlively, Kent and Judy Mikovits, *Plague: One Scientist's Intrepid Search for the Truth about Human Retroviruses and Chronic Fatigue Syndrome (ME/CFS), Autism, and Other Diseases* (New York: Skyhorse Publishing, 2014)
Heitman, Elizabeth and Sergio Litewka, 'International Perspectives on Plagiarism and Considerations for Teaching International Trainees' (2011) 29(1) *Urologic Oncology* 104
Henagen, Christina D, 'False Claims of Sexual Harassment in Education: The Path to an Appropriate Remedy for the Wrongly Accused' (1998) 76(4) *Washington University Law Quarterly* 1431
Hern, Alex, 'Libel Reform Needs to Keep Writers Out of Court, Not Make It Easier to Win Once They're There', *New Statesman*, 28 June 2012
Heslegrave, Ronald, 'Research Integrity in the Canadian Contest' in Tony Mayer and Nicholas Steneck (eds), *Promoting Research Integrity in a Global Environment* (World Scientific, Singapore, 2012), pp 37–40
Heyward, Michael, *The Ern Malley Affair* (St Lucia: University of Queensland Press, 1993)
Heyward, Michael, 'The Demidenko Scandal' (1996), Issue No. 1, *Australian Humanities Review*
'HGV: Hungarian President Plagarized Bulgarian Researcher', *Novinite.com*, 12 January 2012
Higher Education Center for Alcohol and Other Drug Use and Violence Prevention, 'College Academic Performance and Alcohol and Other Drug Use' (1997, rev. 2003)
Hindawi Publishing Corporation, 'Yoshitaka Fujii', *Hindawi*, 11 March 2010
Hirsi Ali, Ayaan, *Infidel* (New York: Free Press, 2008)
Hirsi Ali, Ayaan, *Nomad: A Personal Journal Through the Clash of Civilizations* (London: Fourth Estate, 2010)
Hirsi Ali, Ayaan, *Heretic: Why Islam Needs a Reformation N*ow (New York: NY Harper, 2015)
Hixson, Joseph R, *The Patchwork Mouse* (Garden City, NY: Anchor Press, 1976)
Hoad, Timothy C and Justin Zobel, 'Methods for Identifying Versioned and Plagiarized Documents' (2003) 54(3) *Journal of the American Society for Information Science and Technology* 203
Hobson, Richard, *Charles Waterton: His Home, Habits and Handiwork* (London: Whittaker & Co, 1867)
Hofilena, John, 'Lead Scientist in Stem Cell Research Scandal to Fight Riken's Findings', *Japan Daily Press*, 2 April 2014
Hofilena, John, 'Embattled Stem Cell Researcher Obokata Hospitalized for 'Mental Condition'', *Japan Daily Press*, 8 April 2014
Hofilena, John, 'Riken Researcher Obokata Agrees to Retract 1 Out of 2 STAP Cell Papers', *Japan Daily Press*, 29 May 2014
Hofilena, John, 'Japanese Stem Cell Scientist Finally Agrees to Retract Papers on STAP Cells', *Japan Daily Press*, 4 June 2014
Holden, Constance, 'Whistleblower Woes' (1996) 271(5245) *Science* 35
Holdren, John P, 'Memorandum for the Heads of Executive Departments and Agencies: Scientific Integrity' (Office of Science and Technology Policy, 17 December 2010)
'Holocaust Denier Irving is Jailed', *BBC News*, 20 February 2006
'Holocaust Denier Released from Prison: David Irving Free After 13 Months in Jail', *Der Spiegel*, 20 December 2006
Hooper, John, 'Sex Scandal Rocks Italian Campus', *The Guardian*, 9 June 2004
Hooper, Rowan, 'Stem-Cell Leap Defied Japanese Norms', *The Japan Times*, 15 February 2014
'Hospital Presents Results of Final Report: Committee Completes Investigations in the Case of Dr Boldt', *KliLu*, 9 August 2012
Hostetler AJ, 'Fear of Suits Blocks Retractions', *The Scientist*, 19 October 1987
House of Commons, Science and Technology Committee, *Forensic Science on Trial* (HC 2004-05, 96-1)
House of Commons Science and Technology Committee, *Forensic Science on Trial: Government Response to the Committee's Seventh Report of Session 2004-05* (First Special Report of Session 2005-06, 25 July 2005)

House of Representatives Standing Committee on Legal and Constitutional Affairs, Parliament of Australia, *Whistleblower Protection: A Comprehensive Scheme for the Commonwealth Public Sector* (Canberra: Parliament of the Commonwealth of Australia, 2009)

Howard, Caroline J, 'Plagiarism is Unforgivable', *ABS-CBN News Channel*, 24 October 2010)

Howard, Jennifer, 'French Court Finds in Favor of Journal Editor Sued for Libel Over Book Review', *The Chronicle of Higher Education*, 2 March 2011

Howard, Rebecca M, *Standing in the Shadow of Giants: Plagiarists, Authors, Collaborators* (Stamford, Conn: Ablex Pub, 1999)

Howe, Adrian, 'Imagining Evidence, Fictioning Truth—Revisiting (Courtesy of O J Simpson) Expert Evidence in the Chamberlain Case' (1997) 3 *Law Text Culture* 82

Howells, William Dean, 'The Psychology of Plagiarism' in *Literature and Life* (New York: Harper & Brothers, 1902)

Hsu, Spencer S, 'US to Commit Scientists and New Commission to Fix Forensic Science', *The Washington Post*, 15 February 2013

Huber, Peter W, *Galileo's Revenge: Junk Science in the Courtroom* (New York: Basic Books, 1993)

Huff, C Ronald and Martin Killias (eds), *Wrongful Convictions and Miscarriages of Justice: Causes and Remedies in North American and European Criminal Justice Systems* (New York: Routledge, 2013)

Hull, David L, *Science as a Process: An Evolutionary Account of the Social and Conceptual Development of Science* (Chicago, Ill: The University of Chicago Press, 2008)

Humphries, Barry, 'Letters' in 'Barry Spurr Case Shows the New Puritanism is Alive and Well,' *The Australian*, 21 October 2014

Humphrey, George F, 'Scientific Fraud: The McBride Case' (1992) 32(3) *Medicine, Science and Law* 199

'Hungarian President Loses Doctorate in Plagiarism Case', *EurActiv.com*, 30 March 2012

'Hungarian President Pal Schmitt in Soup After Doctorate Plagiarism Finding', *The Australian*, 30 March 2012

Hunt, Linda, 'The Challenges Women Whistleblowers Face' (2010) 3(2) *International Business Research* 3

Husten, Larry, 'Don Poldermans and the Dutch Research Scandal', *Forbes*, 15 October 2012

Husten, Larry, 'New England Journal of Medicine Declines to Retract Papers From Disgraced Research Group', *Forbes*, 26 September 2014

Huxley, Aldous, *The Doors of Perception and Heaven and Hell* (New York: Harper & Row, 1963)

Hwang, Woo Suk, Young June Ryu, Jong Hyuk Park, Eul Soon Park et al. 'Evidence of a Pluripotent Human Embyronic Stem Cell Line Derived from a Cloned Blastocyst' (2004) 303(5664) *Science* 1669, since retracted

Hwang, Woo Suk, Sung II Roh, Byeong Chun Lee, Sung Keun Kang et al. 'Patient-Specific Embryonic Stem Cells Derived from Human SCNT Blastocysts' (2005) 308(5729) *Science* 1777, since retracted

Hyams, Ross, 'Sexual Harassment in Australian Universities: Procedures to Make the Personal Public' (1998) 5 *James Cook University Law Review* 46

Hyman, Anthony, *Charles Babbage: Pioneer of the Computer* (Oxford: Oxford University Press, 1984)

Imperial College London, *Investigation of Allegations of Research Misconduct* (Ordinance D17, revised 7 February 2014)

'In Academia, There is No Such Thing as Winning a Sexual Harassment Complaint', *The Guardian*, 9 August 2013

'In Brief—MJA Insight Poll' (2014) 201(7) *Medical Journal of Australia* 373

'In Carcere il Professore a …'Luci Rosse", *Gazzetta del Sud*, 4 April 2014

Independent Commission Against Corruption (NSW), *Investigation into the Conduct of Officers and Students at University of Technology* (Sydney, August 2002)

Independent Commission Against Corruption (NSW), *Report Under Section 14(2) of the Independent Commission Against Corruption Act 1988 to the Minister for Education and Training* (Sydney, October 2004)

Independent Commission Against Corruption (NSW), *Report on Investigation into the University of Newcastle's Handling of Plagiarism Allegations* (Sydney, June 2005)
Independent Commission Against Corruption (NSW), *Investigation into Undisclosed Conflicts of Interest of a University of Sydney Employee* (Sydney, September 2010)
Independent Commission Against Corruption (NSW), *Investigation into the Conduct of a University of New England (UNE) Procurement Officer and UNE Contractors* (Sydney, August 2012)
Independent Commission Against Corruption (NSW), *Investigation into the Recruitment of Contractors and Other Staff by a University of Sydney IT Manager* (Sydney, October 2012)
Independent Commission against Corruption (NSW), *Learning the Hard Way: Managing Corruption Risks Associated with International Students at Universities in NSW* (Sydney, April 2015)
Inquiry into the Conviction of David Harold Eastman for the Murder of Colin Stanley Winchester, *Report of the Board of Inquiry* (2014) (Acting Justice Brian Martin)
Inquiry into the Conviction of David Harold Eastman for the Murder of Colin Stanley Winchester, 'Terms of Reference'
Interlandi, Jeneen, 'An Unwelcome Discovery', *The New York Times*, 22 October 2006
International Committee of Medical Journal Editors, 'Conflicts of Interest'
International Committee of Medical Journal Editors in 'Defining the Role of Authors and Contributors' provides for clear criteria for what constitutes authorship
Interview with Tony Abbott, Sydney Opera House (Sydney, 26 January 2012)
'Iran Minister Retracts Oxon Claim' (30 September 2008) *BBC News*
'Iranian MPs Sack Ahmadinejad Ally Over Fake Oxford Degree' (5 November 2008) *The Guardian*: Irish Law Commission, *Expert Evidence* (Consultation Paper No 52, 2008)
Irvine, Chris, 'Disgraced Raj Persaud Quits Job as Consultant', *The Telegraph*, 24 October 2008)
'Is More Better? ASCO Plenary Session Opens Debate on High-Dose Chemotherapy' (1999) 4(3) *The Oncologist* 269
Israel, Mark, *Research Ethics and Integrity for Social Scientists: Beyond Regulatory Compliance* (2nd edn, Los Angeles: SAGE, 2015)
'ISU Researcher Dr Dong-Pyou Han Resigns for Faking AIDS Research Worth Millions', *Huffington Post*, 25 December 2013
Ivanov, Max, 'Platonov After the Address to VAK Will Write the Thesis on the Same Subject', *Voice*, 23 April 2015
Jabour, Bridie, 'Barry Spurr Drops Legal Action to Force New Matilda to Reveal Source of Emails', *The Guardian*, 23 October 2014
Jackson, Jim, 'Orr to Steele: Crafting Dismissal Processes in Australian Universities' (2003) 7 *Southern Cross University Law Review* 220
Jackson, Rupert, *Review of Civil Litigation Costs: Final Report* (The Stationery Office, December 2009)
Jackson, Sally, 'ABC Settles Science Show Defamation Suit Brought by Bruce Hall', *The Australian*, 4 March 2014
Jamieson, Alastair, 'Student Has Abortion After Affair with Professor', *The Telegraph*, 7 December 2008
Janardhanan, Arun, 'IIT-Madras Suspends Professor After Student Alleges Sexual Harassment', *The Times of India*, 25 December 2013
Jaschik, Scott, 'More Scrutiny on Conflicts of Interest', *Inside Higher Ed*, 6 October 2008
Jaschik, Scott, 'You Can't Say That', *Inside Higher Education*, 10 June 2013
Jayaraman, Killugudi, 'Chemistry's 'Colossal' Fraud' (25 March 2008) *Royal Society of Chemistry*
Jefferson, Thomas, 'Letter from Thomas Jefferson to Isaac McPherson', Monticello, 13 August 1813 in H A Washington (ed), *The Writings of Thomas Jefferson*, vol 6 (New York: H W Derby, 1861) 180–181
Jefferson, Tom, Philip Alderson, Elizabeth Wager and Frank Davidoff, 'Effects of Editorial Peer Review: A Systematic Review (2002) 287(21) *Journal of the American Medical Association* 2784

Jefferson, Tom, Melanie Rudin, Suzanne Brodney Folse and Frank Davidoff, 'Editorial Peer Review for Improving the Quality of Reports of Biomedical Studies' (2007) 18(2) *Cochrane Database of Systematic Reviews*, doi: 10.1002/14651858.MR000016.pub3

Jeffries, Stuart, 'Enemies of Thought', *The Guardian*, 21 December 2007

Jenkins, Stephen H, *Tools for Critical Thiniking in Biology* (Oxford: Oxford University Press, 2015)

Jenks, Susan, 'Gene Therapy Death—'Everyone Has to Share in the Guilt" (2000) 92(2) *Journal of* the *National Cancer Institute* 98

Jensen, Arthur R, 'IQ and Science: The Mysterious Burt Affair' (1991) Issue 105, *Public Interest* 93

Jerga, Josh, 'Academic Asked Students for Sex: CCC', *The Sydney Morning Herald*, 2 September 2010

Jervis, Rick, 'Texas Leads Trend in Challenging Forensic Evidence', *USA Today*, 16 December 2013

Johansen, Bruce E, *Silenced!: Academic Freedom, Scientific Inquiry, and the First Amendment Under Siege in America* (Westport, Conn: Praeger, 2007)

John, LK, Loewenstein, G and Prelec, D, 'Measuring the Prevalence of Questionable Research Practices' (2012) 23(5) *Psychological Science* 524

Johnson, Carolyn Y, 'Harvard Report Shines Light on Ex-Researcher's Conduct', *The Boston Globe*, 30 May 2014

Johnson, George, 'At Lawrence Berkeley, Physicists Say a Colleague Took Them for a Ride' (15 October 2002) The New York Times

Johnson, Roberta Ann, *Whistleblowing: When it Works—And Why* (Boulder, Col: Lynne Rienner Publishers, 2003)

Johnson, Samuel, 'The Criterions of Plagiarism' (30 July 1751) 143 The Rambler

Johnson, Samuel, *A Dictionary of the English Language*, 2 vols (London: W Strahan, 1755)

Johnston, Bruce, 'Italian Professor Gets Top Marks for His Sex Lessons with Students', *The Telegraph*, 1 February 2002

Jolley, Daniel, 'Fujii, Anesthesia & Research Fraud', *Gas Exchange*, 15 November 2012

Jonakait, Randolph N, 'Forensic Science: The Need for Regulation' (1991) 4(1) *Harvard Journal of Law & Technology* 109

Jones, Ashby and Joann S Lublin, 'Critics Blow Whistle on Law', *The Wall Street Journal*, 1 November 2010

Jones, Greg, 'Libel Reform Campaigners Demand Better Public Interest Defence', *The Guardian*, 27 June 2012

Jones, James H, *Bad Blood: The Tuskegee Syphilis Experiment* (New York: Free Press, 1993)

Jonson, Ben, *Poetaster, Or, His Arraignment: A Comical Satire* (Digireads.com Publishing, 2011)

Joseph, Frank, *The Atlantis Encylopedia* (Franklin Lakes, NJ: New Page Books/The Career Press, 2005)

Joy, Peter A and Kevin C McMunigal, 'The Problems of Plagiarism as an Ethics Offense' (2011) 26(2) *Criminal Justice* 56

Joynson, Robert B, *The Burt Affair* (New York: Routledge, 1989)

JTA and Gavriel Fiske, 'French Rabbi Quits Amid Plagiarism, Qualification Scandals', *The Times of Israel*, 11 April 2013

Judson, Horace Freeland, *The Great Betrayal: Fraud in Science* (Orlando: Harcourt, 2004)

Jump, Paul, 'University of Glasgow Tight-Lipped Over Ethics Inquiry', *Times Higher Education*, 30 August 2012

Jump, Paul, 'A Plague of Plagiarism at the Heart of Politics', *Times Higher Education*, 16 May 2013

Jump, Paul, 'Glasgow Confirms Academic's Papers were 'Falsified' ', *Times Higher Education*, 20 May 2013

Jung, Jae-Chul and Hyung-In Moon, 'Statement of Retraction: Larvicidal Activity of 4-Hydroxycoumarin Derivatives Against *Aedes Aegypti*—(2011) 49 *Pharmaceutical Biology* 190-193' (2012) 50(9) *Pharmaceutical Biology* 1199

Kaiser, Jocelyn, 'Top US Scientific Misconduct Official Quits in Frustration with Bureaucracy', *Science*, 12 March 2014

Kalichman, Michael W and Paul J Friedman, 'A Pilot Study of Biomedical Trainees' Perceptions Concerning Research Ethics' (1992) 67(11) *Academic Medicine* 769

Kalmbach, Karen C and Phillip M Lyons, 'Ethical Issues in Conducting Forensic Evaluations' (2006) 2(3) *Applied Psychology in Criminal Justice* 261

Kamei, Robert K, 'Professionalism: Looking for Your Blind Spots' (2006) 35(12) *Annals Academy of Medicine* 848

Kamin, Leon J, *The Science and Politics of IQ* (Potomac, Md: Lawrence Erlbaum Associates, 1974)

Kammerer, Paul, 'Paul Kammerer's Letter to the Moscow Academy' (1926) 64(1664) *Science* 493

Kammerer, Paul, 'Verebung Erzwungener Fortpflanzungsanpassungen. III. Mitteilung: Die Nachkommen der Nicht Brutpflegenden Alytes Obstetricians' (1909) 28 *Archiv für Entwicklungsmechanik der Organismen* 447

Kammerer, Paul, *The Inheritance of Acquired Characteristics* (New York: Boni and Liveright Publishers, 1924)

Kamvounias, Patty and Sally Varnham, 'In-House or In Court? Legal Challenges to University Decisions' (2006) 18(1) *Education and the Law* 1

Kamvounias, Patty and Sally Varnham, 'Legal Challenges to University Decisions Affecting Students in Australian Courts and Tribunals' (2010) 34(1) *Melbourne University Law Review* 140

Kansra, Nikita and Cynthia W Shih, 'Harvard LSD Research Draws National Attention', *The Harvard Crimson*, 21 May 2012

Kaplan, Karen, 'Haruko Obokata Says She Created STAP Stem Cells 'More than 200 Times'', *Los Angeles Times*, 9 April 2014

Kaplanis, Tassos A, 'The Scholar in His Study: Depictions of a Renaissance Tradition in Vitsentzos Kornaros's Erotokritos' in Efrosini Camatsos, Tassos A Kaplanis and Jocelyn Pye, (eds), '*His Words Were Nourishment and his Counsel Food': A Festschrift for David W Holton* (Newcastle upon Tyne: Cambridge Scholars Publishing, 2014), pp 81–100

Kaplin, William A and Barbara A Lee, *The Law of Higher Education* (4th edn, San Francisco, Calif: John Wiley, 2007)

Kaplin, William A and Barbara A Lee, *The Law of Higher Education* [electronic resource] (Hoboken: John Wiley & Sons, 2011)

Karasz, Palko, 'Hungarian President Resigns Amid Plagiarism Scandal', *The New York Times*, 2 April 2012

Karpiak, Irene E, 'Ghosts in a Wilderness: Problems and Priorities of Faculty at Mid-Career and Mid-Life' (1996) 26(3) *Canadian Journal of Higher Education* 49

Karvelas, Julie Harepatricia, 'Spurr Suspended for Racist Emails', *The Australian*, 17 October 2014

Kassirer, Jerome P, *On the Take: How Medicine's Complicity with Big Business Can Endanger Your Health* (New York: Oxford University Press, 2004)

Katsoulis, Melissa, *Telling Tales: A History of Literary Hoaxes* (London: Hachette, 2013)

Kaur, Chanjyot, 'Whistle Blowing: An Anti-Corruption Tool' (2012) 1(5) *International Journal of Advanced Research in Management and Social Sciences* 48

Keenan, Amanda, 'Shamed Medical Hero Back on the Good Books', *The Australian*, 10 November 1998, 1

Keith, Jim, *Mind Control, World Control* (2nd edn, Kempton, Illinois: Adventures Unlimited Press, 1998)

Kelland, Kate, 'Dutch Psychologist Admits He Made Up Research Data', *Reuters*, 2 November 2011

Kelland, Kate (Reuters), 'Controversial GMOI Study by Gilles-Eric Seralini Retracted', *Huffington Post*, 28 November 2013

Kelleher, Michael D, *New Arenas for Violence: Homicide in the American Workplace* (Westport, Conn: Praeger, 1996)

Kelly, John F and Phillip K Wearne, *Tainting Evidence: Inside the Scandals at the FBI Crime Lab* (New York: Free Press, 1998)

Kelly, Stuart, 'What We Should Take from the QR Markham Plagiarism Scandal', *The Guardian*, 22 November 2011

Kelly, Tom, 'Struck Off Doctor Loses Appeal Over Bogus tests', *The Birmingham Post*, 18 August 1999, 8

Kendrick, Malcolm, *Doctoring Data: How to Sort Out Medical Advice from Medical Nonsense* (Caldicot, Monmouthshire: Columbus Publishing Ltd, 2015)

Kennedy, Ian, *Learning from Bristol: The Report of the Public Inquiry into Children's Heart Surgery at the Bristol Royal Infirmary 1984-1995* (Cm 5207(I), 2001)

Keough, William J, 'Towards the Development of Ethical Practices in Paediatric Clinical Trials: The Special Position of the Terminally Ill Child' (2006) 13(3) *Journal of Law and Medicine* 370

Keränen, Lisa, *Scientific Characters: Rhetoric, Politics and Trust in Breast Cancer Research* (Tuscaloosa: University of Alabama Press, 2010)

Kerr, John R and John H Wootten, 'Re-Opening the Orr Case' (1958) 4(10) *Free Spirit* 3

Kerschberg, Ben, 'The Dodd-Frank Act's Robust Whistleblowing Incentives', *Forbes*, 14 April 2011

Kesselheim, Aaron S, Christopher T Robertson, Kent Siri, Puneet Batra and Jessica M Franklin, 'Distributions of Industry Payments to Massachusetts Physicians' (2013) 368(22) *The New England Journal of Medicine* 2049

Kevles, Daniel J, *The Baltimore Case: A Trial of Politics, Science and Character* (New York: WW Norton & Co, 1998)

Keyes, Ralph, *The Quote Verifier: Who Said What, Where, and When* (New York: St Martin's Griffin, 2006)

Khan, Amina, 'Resveratrol Researcher Faked Data, Report Says: What Drives Academic Fraud?' *Los Angeles Times*, 12 January 2012

Kidd, Rob, 'University of Queensland Scientists Accused of Falsifying Research', *Courier Mail*, 4 September 2013

'Killer Professor Gagged', *Times Higher Education*, 10 June 1996

Kimmel, Allan J, *Ethical Issues in Behavioral Research: Basic and Applied Perspectives* (2nd edn, Oxford, UK: Blackwell Publishing, 2007)

King, Bryan H and Charles V Ford, 'Pseudologia Fantastica' (1988) 77(1) *Acta Psychiatrica Scandinavica* 1

King, Martin Luther, 'I have a Dream' (Speech delivered on the steps of the Lincoln Memorial, Washington DC, 28 August 1963)

King's College London, 'Relationships Between Staff and Students' (2004)

Kintisch, Eli, 'Poehlman Sentenced to 1 year of Prison' (2006) Issue No. 238 *Science* 5

Kirchmeier, Jeffrey L, 'Aggravating and Mitigating Factors: The Paradox of Today's Arbitrary and Mandatory Capital Punishment Scheme' (1998) 6(2) *William & Mary Bill of Rights Journal* 345

Klandermans, Bert and Nonna Mayer, 'Context, Alliances and Conflict' in Klandermans and Mayer (eds), *Extreme Right Activists in Europe: Through the Magnifying Glass* (London: Routledge, 2006), ch 8

Klass, Gregory, 'Meaning, Purpose, and Cause in the Law of Deception' (2012) 100(2) *Georgetown Law Journal* 449

Klintworth, Gordon K, *Giants, Crooks and Jerks in Science* (Xlibris Corporation, 2014)

Klotz, Irving M, 'The N-Ray Affair' (1980) 242(5) *Scientific American* 168

Knightley, Phillip, 'Foreword' in William McBride, *Killing the Messenger* (Cremorne, NSW: Eldorado, 1994)

Knoll IV, James L, 'Death's Conviction', *Forensic Psychiatry*, 12 March 2010

Knop, Rob, 'April 1st: The Great Moon Hoax', *365 Days of Astronomy*, 1 April 2011

Knox, Konstance, Donald Carrigan, Graham Simmons, Fernando Teque et al. 'No Evidence of Murine-Like Gammaretroviruses in CFS Patients Previously Identified as XMRV-Infected' (2011) 333(6038) *Science* 94

Koch, Katie, 'The Right Way to Report Wrongdoing', *Harvard Gazette*, 25 January 2012

Kochan, Carol A and John M Budd, 'The Persistence of Fraud in the Literature: The Darsee Case' (1992) 43(7) *Journal of the American Society for Information Science* 488

Koestler, Arthur, *The Case of the Midwife Toad* (New York: Random House, 1971)

Kohn, David, 'Under the Microscope: Forensic Scientist Accused of Mishandling Cases', *CBS News: 60 Minutes*, 8 May 2001

Kohn, Stephen M, *Concepts and Procedures in Whistleblower Law* (Westport, Conn: Quorum Books, 2001)

Kohn, Stephen M, Michael D Kohn and David K Colapinto, *Whistleblower Law: A Guide to Legal Protections for Corporate Employees* (Westport, Conn: Praeger, 2004)

Kolata, Gina, 'A Case for Tenure that Some See as Falling Short', *The New York Times*, 20 February 2010

Kolata, Gina, 'How Bright Promise in Cancer Testing Fell Apart' (7 July 2011) *The New York Times*

Koppl, Roger, 'How to Improve Forensic Science' (2005) 20(3) *European Journal of Law and Economics* 255

Koppl, Roger and Lawrence Kobilinsky, 'Forensic Science Administration: Toward a New Discipline' (November 2005)

Koppl, Roger and Meghan Sacks, 'The Criminal Justice System Creates Incentives for False Convictions' (2013) 32(2) *Criminal Justice Ethics* 126

Kornfeld, Donald S, 'Research Misconduct: The Search for a Remedy' (2012) 87(7) *Academic Medicine* 877

Koss, Mary P, Christine A Gidycz and Nadine Wisniewski, 'The Scope of Rape: Incidence and Prevalence of Sexual Aggression and Victimization in a National Sample of Higher Education Students' (1987) 55(2) *Journal of Consulting and Clinical Psychology* 162

Krainova, Natalya, 'Accusations of Plagiarism Become a Political Weapon', *The Moscow Times*, 13 March 2013

Kranke, Peter, Christian C Apfel, and Norbert Roewer, 'Reported Data on Granisetron and Postoperative Nausea and Vomiting by Fujii et al. Are Incredibly Nice!' (2000) 90(4) *Anesthesia and Analgesia* 1004

Kreissl Lonfat, Bettina M, 'Of Cheats and Liars: Plagiarism', The Philosopher's Attic, 10 February 2010

Krimsky, Sheldon, *Science in the Private Interest: Has the Lure of Profits Corrupted Biomedical Research?* (Lanham, Md: Rowman & Littlefield, 2004)

Krimsky, Sheldon, 'When Conflict-of-Interest is a Factor in Scientific Misconduct' (2007) 26(3) *Medicine and Law* 447

Kuehn, Robert R, 'Suppression of Environmental Science' (2004) 30(2-3) *American Journal of Law & Medicine* 333

Kulynych, Jennifer, 'Intent to Deceive: Mental State and Scienter in the New Uniform Federal Definition of Scientific Misconduct' (1998) *Stanford Technology Law Review* 2

Kuroda, Masaru, 'Disciplinary Decision Concerning Dr Yoshitaka Fujii', *Toho University*, 6 March 2012

Kuzma, Susan M, 'Criminal Liability for Misconduct in Scientific Research' (1991-1992) 25(2) *University of Michigan Journal of Law Reform* 357

La Fleur, William R, Gernot Böhme and Susumu Shimazono (eds), *Dark Medicine: Rationalizing Unethical Medical Research* (Bloomington: Indiana University Press, 2008)

La Follette, Marcel C, 'The Evolution of the 'Scientific Misconduct' Issue: An Historical Overview' (2000) 224(4) *Proceedings of the Society for Experimental Biology and Medicine* 211

La Fontaine, Eugenia T, 'A Dangerous Preoccupation with Future Danger: Why Expert Predictions of Future Dangerousness in Capital Cases are Unconstitutional' (2002) 44(1) *Boston College Law Review* 207

'La Trobe Funds Gambled Away—Fraudster Syphons Off $300,000', *Bendigo Advertiser*, 21 September 2007

La Trobe University, 'Alcohol and Other Drugs'

La Trobe University, 'Alcohol and Other Drugs Policy' (October 2012)

La Trobe University, 'Conflicts of Interest'

Lachman, E, 'Famous Scientific Hoaxes' (1976) 69(3) *The Journal of the Oklahoma State Medical Association* 87

LaFollette, Marcel C, *Stealing into Print: Fraud, Plagiarism, and Misconduct in Scientific Publishing* (Berkeley: University of California Press, 1992)

Lampman, Claudia, Alissa Phelps, Samantha Bancroft and Melissa Beneke, 'Contrapower Harassment in Academia: A Survey of Faculty Experience with Student Incivility, Bullying, and Sexual Attention' (2009) 60(5-6) *Sex Roles* 331

Lander, Eric S, 'DNA Fingerprinting on Trial' (1989) 339(6225) *Nature* 501
Larkins, Alicia A, 'The Impact of Stress-Related and Culturally-Specific Factors on College Alcohol Consumption' (MA dissertation, University of North Carolina Wilmington, 2010)
Lathrop, Ann and Kathleen Foss, *Student Cheating and Plagiarism in the Internet Era: A Wake-up Call* (Englewood, Colo: Libraries Unlimited, 2000)
Lathrop, Ann and Kathleen E Foss, *Guiding Students from Cheating and Plagiarism to Honesty and Integrity: Strategies for Change* (Westport, CT: Libraries Unlimited, 2005)
Latimer, Paul and Alexander J Brown, 'Whistleblower Laws: International Best Practice' (2008) 31(3) *University of New South Wales Law Journal* 766
Lattin, Don, *The Harvard Psychedelic Club: How Timothy Leary, Ram Dass, Huston Smith, and Andrew Weil Killed the Fifties and Ushered in a New Age for America* (New York: HarperOne, 2011)
Laurence Becker v Nancy F Olivieri, 'Complaints Committee Decision and Reasons' (The College of Physicians and Surgeons of Ontario, November 2001)
Lavoie, Denise, 'Annie Dookhan, Chemist Accused of Faking Test Results, Could Have Affected 40,000 Defendants: State', *The Huffington Post*, 2 September 2013
Lavoie, Jennifer, 'Ownership of Human Tissue: Life after *Moore v. Regents of the University of California*' (1989) 75(7) *Virginia Law Review* 1363
Law Commission of England and Wales, *Expert Evidence in Criminal Proceedings* (Report No 325) (London: The Stationery Office, 2011)
Lawless, John, 'Exposed: The Asthma Drug Trials That Led to Cancer and Death', *The Independent*, 18 June 2013
'Law Professor Sacked Over Porn Videos', *Times Higher Education*, 8 February 2002
Lawson, Gerald, 'Painting the Mice' (2012) 14(2) *O&G Magazine* 45
Lazar, Kay and John R Ellement, 'E-mails Portray State Drug Lab in Chaos', *The Boston Globe*, 14 September 2012
Lea, Richard and Matthew Taylor, 'Historian Orlando Figes Admits Posting Amazon Reviews that Trashed Rivals', *The Guardian*, 23 April 2010
Leary, Timothy, *Flashbacks: A Personal and Cultural History of an Era* (Los Angeles: J P Tarcher, 1990)
Leary, Timothy, *The Politics of Ecstasy* (Berkeley, CA: Ronin, 1998)
Leary, Timothy, George H Litwin and Ralph Metzner, 'Reactions to Psilocybin Administered in a Supportive Environment' (1963) 137(6) *Journal of Nervous and Mental Disease* 561
Leary, Timothy, Ralph Metzner, Madison Presnell and Gunther Weil et al. 'A New Behavior Change Program Using Psilocybin' (1965) 2(2) *Psychotherapy: Theory, Research and Practice* 61
Leary, Timothy, and Gunther M Weil, 'The Religious Experience: Its Production and Interpretation' (1967) 1(2) *Journal of Psychedelic Drugs* 3
Lee, Byeong Chun, Min Kyu Kim, Goo Jang, Hyun Ju Oh et al. 'Dogs Cloned from Adult Somatic Cells' (2005) 436(7051) *Nature* 641
Lee, Henry C, 'Forensic Science and the Law' (1993) 25(4) *Connecticut Law Review* 1117
Lee, Stephen J, 'Controversial Cancer Scientists Now Works in Grand Forks Cancer Center', *Bakken Today*, 20 August 2012
Leffers, Jochen, 'Academic Corruption: Germany Rocked by Allegations of Ph.D. Bribes', *SpiegelOnline*, 24 August 2009
Leigh, David, 'Danish Scientist Sued by Drug Firm under British Libel Laws to Counterclaim', *The Guardian*, 16 February 2010
Leigh, David, 'US Drug Firm Drops Libel Action Against Scientist', *The Guardian*, 18 February 2010
Lemmens, Trudo, 'Confronting the Conflict of Interest Crisis in Medical Research' (2004) 23(4) *Monash Bioethics Review* 19
Lender, Jon, 'UConn Bans Faculty-Student Relationships', *Hartford Courant*, 7 August 2013
Lendman, Stephen, 'War on Whistleblowers—Britain Harasses Human Rights Lawyer Jesselyn Radack', *Global Research*, 19 February 2014
Lennane, Jean, 'What Happens to Whistleblowers, and Why' (2012) 6(4) *Social Medicine* 249
Lennane, K Jean, ' 'Whistleblowing': A Health Issue' (1993) 307(6905) *BMJ* 667

Lerner, Melvin J, *The Belief in a Just World: A Fundamental Delusion* (New York: Plenum Press, 1980)

Leslie, Catherine A and William E Hauck, 'Categories of Sexual Harassment: A Preliminary Analysis' (Working Paper, Kent State University, 2005)

Lessard, Hester, 'Backlash in the Academy: The Evolution of Campus Sexual Harassment Regimes' in Dorothy E Chunn, Susan B Boyd and Hester Lessard (eds), *Reaction and Resistance: Feminism, Law, and Social Change* (Vancouver: University of British Columbia Press, 2007), pp 164–197

Lestch, Corinne, 'Iowa Professor Cops to Faking Results of Big-Bucks AIDS Vaccine Research', *New York Daily News*, 27 December 2013

Letter from Joseph Biederman, Thomas Spencer and Timothy Wilens to their Colleagues in the Department of Psychiatry, Massachusetts General Hospital and Harvard Medical School, 1 July 2011

Letter from Kerry Kennedy to the Committee on Ethics and Privileges, 9 November 2012

Letter from Norwegian Board of Health to Jon Sudbø, 'Revocation of Authorization as Physician and Dentist: Jon Sudbø', 21 November 2006

Letter of resignation from Adjunct Associate Professor Ken Harvey to Professor John Dewar, Vice-Chancellor of Monash University, 3 February 2014

Leung, Mimi and Yojana Sharma, 'Education Minister Resigns over Research Fraud Scandal' (14 July 2014) Issue No. 329, *University World News*

Levelt Committee (Tilburg University), Noort Committee (Groningen University) and Drenth University (University of Amsterdam), *Flawed Science: The Fraudulent Research Practices of Social Psychologist Friederik Stapel* (28 November 2012)

Levi, Lili, 'The Problem of Trans-National Libel' (2012) 60(2) *American Journal of Comparative Law* 507

Levitz, David, 'Plagiarizing Politician Koch-Mehrin Outrages Scientific Community', *Deutsche Welle*, 26 June 2011

Levitz, Jennifer, 'Massachusetts Crime Lab Ex-Chemist Annie Dookhan Gets 3-5 Years', *The Wall Street Journal*, 22 November 2013

Lewandowsky, Stephan, John Cook, Klaus Oberauer and Michael Marriott, 'Recursive Fury: Conspiracist Ideation in the Blogosphere in Response to Research on Conspiracist Ideation' (2013) 4 *Frontiers in Psychology* 73

Lewandowsky, Stephan, Klaus Oberauer and Gillies E Gignac, 'NASA Faked the Moon Landing—Therefore, (Climate) Science Is a Hoax: An Anatomy of the Motivated Rejection of Science' (2013) 24(5) *Psychological Science* 622

Lewis, Craig and Laurence Cawley, 'Why Do Some People Choose to Blow the Whistle?' *BBC News*, 24 March 2015

Lewis, David B (ed), *Whistleblowing at Work* (London: Athlone Press, 2001)

Lewis, Michael, *Poisoning the Ivy: The Seven Deadly Sins and Other Vices of Higher Education in America* (New York: ME Sharpe, 1997)

Lewis, Steven, Patricia Baird, Robert G Evans, William A Ghali, Charles J Wright, Elaine Gibson and Françoise Baylis, 'Dancing with the Porcupine: Rules for Governing the University-Industry Relationship' (2001) 165(6) *Canadian Medical Association Journal* 783

Leys, Tony, 'ISU Loses $1.4 million in Fraud Case', *Iowa City Press-Citizen*, 8 July 2014

Leys, Tony, 'Ex-ISU Scientist Sentenced to 57 Months in Prison' (1 July 2015) The Des Moines Register

Libel Reform Campaign, The, 'Campaign Success in England and Wales'

Li, Haohao, Xiaoqing He and Shuai Wang, 'Academic Anticorruption in China's Universities' (Keynote Address, International Conference on Higher Education (ICHE), Trier, 28 August 2010)

Lieberman, Jethro Koller, *The Litigious Society* (New York: Basic Books, 1983)

Liebeskind, David S, Chelsea S Kidwell, James W Sayre, and Jeffrey L Saver, 'Evidence of Publication Bias in Reporting Acute Stroke Clinical Trials' (2006) 67(6) *Neurology* 973

Lienhard, Siegfried, *A History of Classical Poetry: Sanskrit, Pali, Prakit* (Wiesbaden: Otto Harrassowitz, 1984)

Lifton, Robert J, *The Nazi Doctors: Medical Killing and the Psychology of Genocide* (New York: Basic Books, 1986)

Light, Donald W and Rebecca N Warburton, 'Ethical Standards for Health Care Journal Editors: A Case Report and Recommendations' (2008) 9(1) *Harvard Health Policy Review* 58

Lilienfeld, Scott O, 'Fudge Factor: A Look at a Harvard Science Fraud Case', *Scientific American*, 1 October 2010

Linklater, Magnus, 'But When is Copying Plagiarism?' *The Times*, 1 March 2006, 21

Lion, Patrick, 'Anthony Albanese Loses the Plot After Plagiarism of The American President', *The Daily Telegraph*, 27 January 2012

Lipman, Frederick D, *Whistleblowers: Incentives, Disincentives, and Protection Strategies* (Hoboken, NJ: Wiley, 2012)

Lipman, Masha, 'Russia's Dissertation-Fraud Muckrakers', *The New Yorker*, 9 March 2013

Lipscomb, A and Bergh AE (eds), 'The Founders Constitution' in *The Writings of Thomas Jefferson* (Thomas Jefferson Memorial Association, Washington, 1905)

Lipstadt, Deborah E, *Denying the Holocaust: The Growing Assault on Truth and Memory* (London: Penguin, 1994)

Liptak, Adam, 'From a Book Review to a Criminal Trial in France', *The New York Times*, 21 February 2011

Lo, Bernard and Marilyn J Field, *Conflict of Interest in Medical Research, Education, and Practice* (Washington, DC: National Academies Press, 2009)

Lock, Stephen, 'Research Misconduct 1974-1990: An Imperfect History' in Stephen Lock, Frank Wells and Michael Farthing (eds), *Fraud and Misconduct in Biomedical Research* (3rd edn, London: BMJ Books, 2001), pp 51–63

Lockyer, Fiona and Emily Kraus, 'Professor Terminated; Intoxication on Campus Alleged', *The Justice*, 5 March 2012

Lombardi, Vincent C, Francis W Ruscetti, Jaydip Das Gupta, Max A Pfost et al. 'Detection of an Infectious Retrovirus, XMRV, in Blood Cells of Patients with Chronic Fatigue Syndrome' (2009) 326(5952) *Science* 585

Loughlan, Patricia, 'Of Patents and Professors: Intellectual Property, Research Workers and Universities' (1996) 18(6) *European Intellectual Property Review* 345

Loukas, Marios, Matthew Akiyama, Mohammadali M Shoja, Bulent Yalçin et al. 'John Browne (1642-1702): Anatomist and Plagiarist' (2010) 23(1) *Clinical Anatomy* 1

Lowe, Adrian, 'Fake Psychologist's $1m TAC, Worksafe Haul', *The Age*, 29 September 2011

Lowe, Nancy K (ed), 'Publication Ethics: Copyright and Self-Plagiarism' (2003) 32(2) *Journal of Obstetric, Gynecologic, & Neonatal Nursing* 145

Lowry, Fran, 'Dr Roger Poisson: 'I have Learned My Lesson the Hard Way'' (1994) 151(6) *Canadian Medical Association Journal* 835

Lubalin, James S and Jennifer L Matheson, 'The Fallout: What Happens to Whistleblowers and Those Accused but Exonerated of Scientific Misconduct?' (1999) 5(2) *Science and Engineering Ethics* 229

Lucas, Aline Marianne, 'Entheology' (1995) 27(3) *Journal of Psychoactive Drugs* 293

Lucas, Douglas M, 'The Ethical Responsibilities of the Forensic Scientist: Exploring the Limits' (1989) 34(3) *Journal of Forensic Sciences* 719

Lundh, Andreas, Barbateskovic, Marija, Hróbjartsson, Asbjorn and Gøtzsche, Peter S, ' Conflicts of Interest at Medical Journals: The Influence of Industry-Supported Randomised Trials on the Journal Impact Factor' (2010) 7 PLoS Med: e354Luscombe, Belinda, 'When the Evidence Lies', *Time*, 13 May 2001

Macagno, Fabrizio, 'Definitions in Law' (2010) 2 *Bulletin Suisse de Linguistique Appliquée* 199

MacDonald, Emma, 'Plagiarism Row: Repeat Offender Bishop Outsources Blame', *The Canberra Times*, 28 October 2008, 2

MacDougall, Curtis D, *Hoaxes* (New York: Macmillan, 1940.

Macfarlane, David, 'Plagiarism Case Kept Under Wraps at Wits', *Mail & Guardian*, 15 April 2011

Macilwain, Colin, 'Scientific Misconduct: More Cops, More Robbers?' (2012) 149(7) *Cell* 1417

Mackay, Anita, 'Recent Developments in Sexual Harassment Law: Towards a New Model' (2009) 14(2) *Deakin Law Review* 189

Mackey, Tim K and Bryan A Liang, 'Physician Payment Disclosure Under Health Care Reform: Will the Sun Shine?' (2013) 26(3) *Journal of the American Board of Family Medicine* 327

MacKinnon, Catharine A, 'Directions in Sexual Harassment Law' (2007) 31(2) *Nova Law Review* 225

Mackintosh, Nicholas (ed), *Cyril Burt: Fraud or Framed?* (Oxford: Oxford University Press, 1995)

Macquarie University, 'Academic Honesty Policy', 13 November 2012

Macquarie University, *Code of Conduct*

Macrina, Francis L, *Scientific Integrity: Text and Cases in Responsible Conduct of Research* (4th edn, Washington DC: ASM Press, 2014)

Madden, James, 'Closing the Book on a Career', *The Australian*, 13 July 2002, 1

Maddox, John, 'Plagiarism is Worse Than Mere Theft' (1995) 376(6543) *Nature* 721

Magley, Vicki J and Ellen I Shupe, 'Self-Labeling Sexual Harassment' (2005) 53(3-4) *Sex Roles* 173

Magnusson, Magnus, *Rum: Nature's Island* (Edinburgh: Luath Press, 1997)

Mahler-Werfel, Alma, *Mein Leben* (Frankfurt am Main: Fischer, 1960)

Mainka, Christina, Scott Raeburn and Shirley Earl, 'A UK Institution's University-Wide Approach to Plagiarism: First Results and Recommendations' (2006) 2(1) *International Journal for Educational Integrity*

Maitland, Derek, 'Uni Bullying, Cronyism, Malpractice, Etc' (2004) Issue No. 36 *The Whistle* 3

Mallon, Thomas, *Stolen Words: Forays into the Origins and Ravages of Plagiarism* (New York: Ticknor and Fields, 1989)

Malm, Sara, 'Drunk Russian Lecturer 'Forces Students to Sit 23 HOUR Exam (and She Didn't Even Allow Them Out for Toilet Breaks)', *Daily Mail*, 4 July 2012

Malpas, Jeff, 'Orr Case' in Graham Oppy and N N (Nick) Trakakis (eds), *A Companion to Philosophy in Australia and New Zealan*d (Clayton: Monash University Publishing, 2010)

Mandell, Charlotte, Anne Mulvey and Meg A Bond, 'The Role of Gender and Organizational Context in the Experience of Adversity' in Robert S Feldman (ed), *The Psychology of Adversity* (Amherst: University of Massachusetts Press, 1996), pp 253–272

Mandevilli, Apoorva, 'Profile: Woo-Suk Hwang' (2005) 11(5) *Nature Medicine* 464

Mandril, Mandy, 'Need for Bananas in a Difficult Universe' (2013) 12 *Journal of Tropical Fruit* 74.

Mann, Tom, *Flawed Forensics: The Splatt Case and Stewart Cockburn* (DoctorZed Publishing, 2010)

Manne, Anne, The Life of I (Melbourne: Melbourne University Press, 2014)

Manne, Robert, *The Culture of Forgetting: Helen Demidenko and the Holocaust* (Melbourne: Text Publishing, 1996)

Manning, Joanna (ed), *The Cartwright Papers: Essays on the Cervical Cancer Inquiry, 1987-88* (Wellington, NZ: Bridget Williams Books, 2009)

'Marc Hauser's Return', *Harvard Magazine* (July-August 2011)

Marcovitch, Henry, 'Editors, Publishers, Impact Factors, and Reprint Income' (2010) 7(1) PLoS Med: e1000364

Marcus, Adam, 'Reuben Sentenced in Fraud Case', *Anesthesiology News*, 25 June 2010

Marcus, Adam and Ivan Oransky, 'Commit Fraud, Go to Jail?' (2014) *Labtimes*

Marcus, Adam and Ivan Oransky, 'Crack Down on Scientific Fraudsters', *The New York Times*, 10 July 2014

Marcus, Adam and Oransky, Ivan, 'How the Biggest Fabricator in Science Got Caught' (21 May 2015) *Nautilus*

Marginson, Simon, *Educating Australia: Government, Economy and Citizen Since 1960* (Melbourne: Cambridge University Press, 1997)

Marquart, James W, Sheldon Ekland-Olson and Jonathan R Sorenson, *The Rope, the Chair, and the Needle: Capital Punishment in Texas, 1923-1990* (Austin: University of Texas Press, 2010)

Marsh, Bill, *Plagiarism: Alchemy and Remedy in Higher Education* (New York: State University of New York Press, 2007)

Maartens, Willie, *Mapping Reality: A Critical Perspective on Science and Religion* (Lincoln, NE: iUniverse, 2006)

Martial Epigrams, trans. Walter CA Ker, 2 vols (London: William Heinemann, 1919)
Martin, Alexander, 'Riken Rejects Obokata Appeal Over Stem-Cell Study', *The Wall Street Journal*, 8 May 2014
Martin, Alexander, 'Japanese University May Strip Stem-Cell Scientist of Doctorate', *The Wall Street Journal*, 7 October 2014
Martin, Brian, 'Disruption and Due Process: The Dismissal of Dr Spautz from the University of Newcastle' (1983) 26(1) *Vestes* 3
Martin, Brian, 'Fraud and Australian Academics' (1989) 5(2) *Thought and Action* 95
Martin, Brian, 'Scientific Fraud and the Power Structure of Science' (1992) 10(1) *Prometheus: Critical Studies in Innovation* 83
Martin, Brian, 'Beware the 'No's of the Campus Sex Triangle—Harassment, Conflict of Interest, Abuse of Trust' (11-17 March 1993) 3(8) *Campus Review* 8
Martin, Brian, 'David Rindos Versus the University of Western Australia: Analogies to the Orr Case' in John Biggs and Richard Davis (eds), *The Subversion of Australian Universities* (Wollongong: Fund for Intellectual Dissent, 2002), pp 98–108
Martin, Brian, 'Staff-Student Sex: Abuse of Trust and Conflict of Interest' in William J Taverner (ed), *Taking Sides: Clashing Views on Controversial Issues in Human Sexuality* (8th edn, Guilford, Conn: McGraw-Hill/Dushkin, 2002), pp 124–126
Martin, Brian, 'Illusions of Whistleblower Protection' (2003) 5 *UTS Law Review* 119
Martin, Brian, 'Plagiarism Struggles' (2008) 3 *Plagiary: Cross-Disciplinary Studies in Plagiarism, Fabrication, and Falsification*
Martin, Jonathan, 'Senator Rand Paul Faces New Charges of Plagiarism', *The New York Times*, 4 November 2013
Martin, Jonathan, 'How Senator John Walsh Plagiarized a Final Paper', *The New York Times*, 23 July 2014)
Maruko, Mami, 'Riksen to Ask Obokata for ¥600,000 in Publishing Fees for Debunked Paper', *The Japan Times*, 20 March 2015
Marušić, Matko, 'Croatia Moves Away from Fostering Research Integrity' (2010) 376(9753) *The Lancet* 1627
Masnick, Mike, 'Argentinian Politician's Proposal For New Anti-Plagiarism Law Plagiarizes Wikipedia', *Techdirt*, 14 May 2010
Mason, Gail, 'Harm, Harassment and Sexuality' (2002) 26(3) *Melbourne University Law Review* 596
Mason, Gail and Anna Chapman, 'Defining Sexual Harassment: A History of the Commonwealth Legislation and its Critiques' (2003) 31(1) *Federal Law Review* 195
Massachusetts Institute of Technology, Policies and Procedures, *10.0 Academic Misconduct and Dishonesty—10.1 Procedures for Dealing with Academic Misconduct in Research and Scholarship*
Masui, Tohru, 'The Integrity of Researchers in Japan: Will Enforcement Replace Responsibility?' in Tony Mayer and Nicholas Steneck (eds), *Promoting Research Integrity in a Global Environment* (World Scientific, Singapore, 2012), pp 49–54
Matchen, Jim and Eros DeSouza, 'The Sexual Harassment of Faculty Members by Students' (2000) 42(3-4) *Sex Roles* 295
Mather, Anne, 'Law Students to Re-sit Exam Amid Fears Online Assessment was Compromised', *The Mercury*, 31 August 2013
Maxwell, Jonathan, *Piltdown Man and Other Hoaxes: A Book About Lies, Legends, and the Search for the Missing Link* (Salt Lake City: American University & Colleges Press, 2012)
May, John, *Return to an Address of the Honourable the House of Commons Dated 12 July 1990 for the Inquiry into the Circumstances Surrounding the Convictions Arising Out of the Bomb Attacks in Guildford and Woolwich in 1974: Interim Report on the Maguire Case* (London: HMSO, 1990)
Mazzeo, Tilar J, *Plagiarism and Literary Property in the Romantic Period* (Philadelphia: University of Pennsylvania Press, 2011)
'McBride Cleared to Return to Work', *ABC Science*, 9 November 1998
McCabe, Donald L and Linda K Trevion, 'Academic Dishonesty: Honor Codes and Other Contextual Influences' (1993) 64(5) *Journal of Higher Education* 522
McCarthy, Paul, 'The Paper Mill' (October 1993) *The New Physician* 24

McCutcheon, Carmen J, 'Fairplay or Greed: Mandating University Responsibility Toward Student Inventors' (2003) *Duke Law and Technology Review* 26
McDonald, Paula, 'Workplace Sexual Harassment 30 Years On: A Review of the Literature' (2012) 14(1) *International Journal of Management Reviews* 1
McDonald, Sara, 'Bullying Upwards: Harassment is Not Only Experienced By Students. Academics Can Be Victims Too' (2008) 22(20) *Nursing Standard* 62
McDonough, Doug, 'Wayland's Former CFO Draws Five Years in Prison for Theft', *MyPlainView.com*, 22 April 2014
McEwan, Ian, *Solar* (London: Jonathan Cape, 2010)
McFarland, Robert L, 'Please Do Not Publish This Article in England: A Jurisdictional Response to Libel Tourism' (2010) 79(3) *Mississippi Law Journal* 617
McGill, Scott, *Plagiarism in Latin Literature* (Cambridge: Cambridge University Press, 2012)
McGinn, Colin, 'Ted Honderich, *On Consciousness*' (2007) 116(3) *Philosophical Review* 474
McGrane, Sally, 'Diary of the Hitler Diary Hoax', *The New Yorker*, 25 April 2013
McGrath, Stephen, 'Romania's PM Gives Up Doctorate After Plagiarism Allegations', *The Independent*, 21 December 2014
McIndoe, William A, Malcolm R McLean, Ronald W Jones and Peter R Mullins, 'The Invasive Potential of Carcinoma In Situ of the Cervix' (1984) 64(4) *Obstetrics & Gynecology* 451
McKinney, Kathleen, 'Sexual Harassment of University Faculty by Colleagues and Students' (1990) 23(7-8) *Sex Roles* 421
McLemee, Scott, 'McGinn, Again', *Inside Higher Ed*, 6 November 2013
McMillan, John, 'Blowing the Whistle on Fraud in Government' (1988) 56 *Canberra Bulletin of Public Administration* 118
McMillan, John, 'Legal Protection of Whistleblowers' in Scott Prasser, Rae Wear and John Nethercote (eds), *Corruption and Reform: The Fitzgerald Vision* (St Lucia: University of Queensland Press, 1990), pp 203–211
McNamara, Robert, 'The Cardiff Giant', *About Education*
McNeill, David, 'Academic Scandal Shakes Japan', *The New York Times*, 6 July 2014
McNeill, David, 'Japanese Fraud Case Highlights Weaknesses in Scientific Publishing', *The Chronicle of Higher Education*, 8 October 2012
McPhee, Michele, *A Professor's Rage: The Chilling True Story of Harvard Ph.D. Amy Bishop, Her Brother's Mysterious Death, and the Shooting Spree that Shocked the Nation* (New York: St Martin's Press, 2011)
Meadow, Roy, 'Munchausen Syndrome by Proxy: The Hinterland of Child Abuse' (1977) 310(8033) *The Lancet* 343
Meadow, Roy (ed), *ABC of Child Abuse* (3rd edn, London: BMJ Publishing Group, 1997)
Meadow, Roy, 'Unnatural Sudden Infant Death' (1999) 80(1) *Archives of Disease in Childhood* 7
'Measures to Prevent Further Instances of Research Misconduct', *Riken* (1 April 2014)
Medew, Julia, 'Academic Quits Over Swisse Deal With Uni', *The Age*, 5 February 2014
Medical Board of Victoria, 'Section 17 Inquiry—Dr Ashoka Prasad', 12 December 1988 (copy on file with author)
Medical Council of New Zealand, 'Health Professional Regulatory Bodies'
Medicines and Healthcare Products Regulatory Agency, UK Government, 'Pre-Clinical Trial Data Scam—First Ever Successful Prosecution under Good Laboratory Practice Regulations' (Press release, 12 March 2013)
Meikle, James, 'G20 Pathologist Freddy Patel Suspended', *The Guardian*, 31 March 2011
Melendez, Alirio J, 'Paper-by-Paper Review' on Prof AJ Melendez, *Public Denial of Allegations* (24 October 2013)
Melsheimer, Thomas M, Steven H Stodghill and Diana L Faust, 'The Law of Sexual Harassment on Campus: A Work in Progress' (1994) 13(3) *Review of Litigation* 529
Menand, Louis, 'Acid Redux: The Life and High Times of Timothy Leary', *The New Yorker*, 26 June 2006)
Mendelson, Danuta, 'From Expert Witness to Defendant: Abolition of Expert Witness Protection and its Implications' (2012) 20(2) *Journal of Law and Medicine* 250

Mendelson, Danuta, *The New Law of Torts* (3rd edn, South Melbourne: Oxford University Press, 2014)

Mendoza, Martha (Associated Press), 'Allegations of Fake Medical Research Hit New High', *Rense.com*, 12 July 2005

Menon, Anitha, Mary Peggy Shilalukey Ngoma, Seter Siziya, Mulenga Musepa et al. 'Sexual Harassment in Academia—Perception, Understanding and Reporting of Sexual Harassment in a Southern African University' (2011) 1(1) *Journal of Peace, Gender and Development Studies* 8

Merry, Alan, and Alexander McCall Smith, *Errors, Medicine and the Law* (Cambridge: Cambridge University Press, 2001)

Metzner, Ralph, 'Reflections on the Concord Prison Project and the Follow-Up Study' (1998) 30(4) *Journal of Psychoactive Drugs* 427

Miceli, Marcia P and Janet P Near, 'The Relationships Among Beliefs, Organisational Position, and Whistle-Blowing Status: A Discriminant Analysis' (1984) 27(4) *Academy of Management Journal* 687

Miceli, Marcia P and Janet P Near, *Blowing the Whistle: The Organizational and Legal Implications for Companies and Employees* (New York: Lexington Books, 1992)

Miceli, Marcia P, Janet P Near, and Terry Morehead Dworkin, *Whistle-Blowing in Organizations* [electronic resource] (Hoboken: Taylor and Francis, 2013)

Milgram, Stanley, *Obedience to Authority: An Experimental View* (London: Pinter & Martin, 2010)

Miller, Arthur G, *The Obedience Experiments: A Case Study of Controversy in Social Science* (New York: Praeger, 1986)

Miller, Dan, 'Former Penn State Professor Pleads Guilty to Defrauding Government of $3 Million in Grants', *Penn Live*, 21 February 2012

Miller, David J, 'Plagiarism: The Case of Elias AK Alsabti' in David J Miller and Michel Hersen (eds), *Research Fraud in the Behavioral and Biomedical Sciences* (New York: John Wiley & Sons, 1992), pp 80–96

Miller, Donald R, 'Retraction of Articles Written by Dr Yoshitaka Fujii' (2012) 59(12) *Canadian Journal of Anaesthesia* 1081

Miller, Keith, *Voice of Deliverance: The Language of Martin Luther King Jr., and Its Sources* (New York: Free Press, 1992)

Miller, Matt, 'Pa. Supreme Court Rejects Appeal over Slippery Rock U Prof's Firing for Sexual Harassment', *Penn Live*, 24 December 2013

Miller, Michele A, 'A Hoax in Japan' (2002) 3(2) *Athena Review*

Minkel, JR, 'Fear Review: Critique of Forensic Psychopathy Scale Delayed 3 years by Threat of Lawsuit', *Scientific American*, 17 June 2010

Mitchell, Peter, 'Edinburgh Doctor Struck Off Because of Clinical-Trial Fraud' (1997) 350(9073) *Lancet* 273

Moll, Chris, 'Homecoming for Wandering Dutch Whistle-Blowers?' (2014) 24(3-4) *Security and Human Rights* 333

Monash University, 'Conduct and Compliance Procedure—Whistleblowers'

Monash University Enterprise Agreement (Academic and Professional Staff) 2009

Monotti, Ann and Sam Ricketson, *Universities and Intellectual Property: Ownership and Exploitation* (Oxford: Oxford University Press, 2003)

'Montreal Statement on Research Integrity in Cross-Boundary Research Collaborations'

Moore, Randy, 'People and Places: Paul Kammerer: 1880-1926' (2011) 31(3) *Reports of the National Center for Science Education* 2.1

Moore, Tristana, 'Germany's PhD Scandal: Were Degrees Bought?' *Time*, 28 August 2009

Moran, Gordon, *Silencing Scientists and Scholars in Other Fields: Power, Paradigm Controls, Peer Review, and Scholarly Communication* (Greenwood, Conn: Ablex Publishing Corporation, 1998)

Moran, Mayo, *Rethinking the Reasonable Person: An Egalitarian Reconstruction of the Objective Standard* (Oxford: Oxford University Press, 2003)

Moran, Neil C, Elmer C Hall, Charles M Huguley Jr and Panagiotis N Symbas, 'Report of *Ad Hoc* Committee to Evaluate Research of Dr John R Darsee at Emory University' (1985) 23(2) *Minerva* 276

Morgan, John, 'Fredrics Cleared of Harassment Charge', *Times Higher Education*, 22 July 2010
Morgan, John, 'Life After Whistleblowing', *Times Higher Education*, 31 July 2014
Morgan, Marlo, *Mutant Message Down Under: A Woman's Journey into Dreamtime Australia* (New York: Harper Collins, 1994)
Morin, Monte, 'Scientist Accused of Manipulating Data in STAP Stem Cell Study', *Los Angeles Times*, 1 April 2014
Morling, Trevor R, *Report of the Royal Commission of Inquiry into the Chamberlain Convictions* (Canberra: Government Printer, 1987)
Morris, Hamilton and Ash Smith, 'The Last Interview with Alexander Shulgin', *Vice*, 2 May 2010
Moseley, Maboth, *Irascible Genius: a Life of Charles Babbage, Inventor* (London: Hutchinson, 1964)
Muijres, Kas,'Fraud; Comparison Among Different Fraudsters and their Techniques' (2013) *Social Cosmos* 64.
Mukherjee, Siddhartha, *The Emperor of All Maladies: A Biography of Cancer* (New York: Scribner, 2010)
Murphy, Arthur, *The Works of Samuel Johnson LLD*, vol 1 (New York: George Dearborn, 1834)
Murphy, Bridget, 'Annie Dookhan, Chemist Accused of Tampering with Drug Samples, Told Police 'It's My Fault'', *The Huffington Post*, 27 September 2012
Murphy, Timothy F, *Case Studies in Biomedical Research Ethics* (Cambridge, Mass: MIT Press, 2004)
Murray, Bridget, 'Keeping Plagiarism at Bay in the Internet Age' (2002) 33(2) *Monitor* 22
Naftulin, Donald H, John E Ware Jr and Frank A Donnelly, 'The Doctor Fox Lecture: A Paradigm of Educational Seduction' (1973) 48(7) *Journal of Medical Education* 630
Nance, John, *The Gentle Tasaday: A Stone Age People in the Philippine Rain Forest* (New York: Harcourt Brace Jovanovich, 1975)
Nathan-Kazis, Josh, 'When May a Rabbi Use the Words of Others?' *The Jewish Daily Forward*, 24 August 2012
National Association of Teachers in Further and Higher Education (NATFHE), 'Advice on Consensual Relations Between Staff and Students'
National Association of Testing Authorities, 'Implementation and Assessment of Australian Standards within Forensic Science', 1 July 2013
National Association of Testing Authorities, Australia, 'Role of Accreditation Advisory Committee (AAC)'
National Health and Medical Research Council, Australian Research Council, *Australian Code for the Responsible Conduct of Research* (Australian Government, 2007)
National Institute of Standards and Technology, 'NIST Invites Comments ion Structure of Forensic Science Guidance Groups' (Media Release, 27 September 2013)
National Institute on Alcohol Abuse and Alcoholism, College Drinking—Changing the Culture, 'How to Reduce High-Risk College Drinking: Use Proven Strategies, Fill Research Gaps', 23 September 2005
National Institute on Alcohol Abuse and Alcoholism, College Drinking—Changing the Culture, 'The Challenge for Colleges and Communities', 23 September 2005
National Institute on Alcohol Abuse and Alcoholism, 'The Scope of the Problem'
National Institutes of Health, Department of Health and Human Services, 'Andrew Friedman, MD, Harvard Medical School' (1996) 25(15) *Findings of Scientific Misconduct*
National Institutes of Health, 'Update on the Requirement for Instruction in the Responsible Conduct of Research', 24 November 2009
Nelson, Cary, 'It Depends on the Context' in 'Does Academic Freedom Protect Holocaust Deniers?' *The Chronicle of Higher Education*, 14 November 2010
Nemeroff, Charles B and Alan F Schatzberg, *Recognition and Treatment of Psychiatric Disorders: A Psychopharmacology Handbook for Primary Care* (Washington, DC: American Psychiatric Press, 1999)
Newlove, Donald, *Those Drinking Days: Myself and Other Writers* (New York: Horizon Press, 1981)
Newman, Henry Seiji, 'The University's Liability for Professor-Student Sexual Harassment Under Title IX' (1998) 66(6) *Fordham Law Review* 2559

Newman, Melanie, 'Lecturer 'Intended to Harass' V-C, Court Finds', *Times Higher Education*, 7 January 2010

'New Rules to Prevent Academic Misconduct', *China Daily*, 15 March 2012

Newton, Michael, *The Encyclopedia of American Law Enforcement* (New York: Facts on File, 2007)

Newton, Robert R, *The Crime of Claudius Ptolemy* (Baltimore: Johns Hopkins University Press, 1977)

Nicholls, Gill, *The Challenge to Scholarship: Rethinking Learning, Teaching and Research* (New York: Routledge, 2005)

Ninov, Victor, Grigorich, KE, Loveland, W et al. 'Observation of Superheavy Nuclei Produced in the Reaction of 86Kr with 208Pb' (1999) 83 *Physical Review Letters* 1104.

Noble, Gladwyn K, 'Kammerer's Alytes' (1926) 118(2962) *Nature* 209

Nonaka, Ryosuke, 'STAP Cell Pioneer Nearly Gave Up on Her Research', *The Asahi Shimbun*, 30 January 2014

Norbury, Keith, 'Who Owns Captured Lectures?' *Campus Technology*, 27 November 2012

Nordheimer, Jon, 'Trooper's Fall Shakes Both Police and Public', *The New York Times*, 15 November 1992

Normile, Dennis, 'A New Record for Retractions? (Part 2)', *Science*, 2 July 2012

Norvaisa, Rimas, 'Journal Impact Factor and Academic Ethics' (2011) 3(2) *Evolution of Science and Technology* 120

Nussenzveig, Paolo A and Renata Zukanovich Funchal, 'Integrity: Misconduct by a Few Damages Credibility for Many' (2008) 454(7204) *Nature* 574

Nuccitelli, Dana, 'Contrarians Bully Journal into Retracting a Climate Psychology Paper', *The Guardian*, 22 March 2012

Nye, Mary Jo, *Science in the Provinces: Scientific Communities and Provincial Leadership in France*, 1860-1930 (Berkeley: University of California Press, 1986)

Nylenna, Magne, Daniel Andersen, Gisela Dahlquist, Matti Sarvas et al. (National Committees on Scientific Dishonesty in the Nordic Countries), 'Handling of Scientific Dishonesty in the Nordic Countries' (1999) 354(9172) *Lancet* 57

O'Connor, John D, 'I'm the Guy They Called Deep Throat', *Vanity Fair*, July 2005

O'Connor, Sean M, 'The Real Issue Behind *Stanford v. Roche*: Faulty Conceptions of University Assignment Policies Stemming from the 1947 Biddle Report' (2013) 19(2) *Michigan Telecommunications and Technology Law Review* 379

O'Neill, Robert M, *Academic Freedom in the Wired World: Political Extremism, Corporate Power, and the University* (Cambridge, Mass: Harvard University Press, 2008)

Obasogie, Osagie, 'Ten Years Later: Jesse Gelsinger's Death and Human Subjects Protection', *Bioethics Forum*, 22 October 2009

Obokata, Haruko, Yoshiki Sasai, Hitoshi Niwa, Mitsutaka Kadota, Munazah Andrabi, Nozomu Takata, Mikiko Tokoro, Yukari Terashita, Shigenobu Yonemura, Charles A Vacanti and Teruhiko Wakayama, 'Bidirectional Developmental Potential in Reprogrammed Cells with Acquired Pluripotency' (2014) 505(7485) *Nature* 676

Obokata, Haruko, Teruhiko Wakayama, Yoshiki Sasai, Koji Kojima, Martin P Vacanti, Hitoshi Niwa, Masayuki Yamato and Charles A Vacanti, 'Stimulus-triggered Fate Conversion of Somatic Cells into Pluripotency' (2014) 505(7) *Nature* 641

'Obokata Injured While Fleeing Pack of NHK Reporters, Lawyer Says', *The Japan Times*, 24 July 2014

Olivieri, Nancy F, Gary M Brittenham, Doreen Matsui, Matitiahu Berkovitch et al. 'Iron-Chelation Therapy with Oral Deferiprone in Patients with Thalassemia Major' (1995) 332(14) *The New England Journal of Medicine* 918

Olson, James S, *Bathsheba's Breast: Women, Cancer and History* (Baltimore: John Hopkins University Press, 2002)

Ombudsman New South Wales, *Complaint Handling at Universities: Australasian Best Practice Guidelines* (January 2015)

Onfray, Michel, *Le Crépuscule d'une Idole: L'affabulation Freudienne* (Paris: B Grasset, 2010)

Ormrod, Roger, 'Scientific Evidence in Court' [1968] *Criminal Law Review* 240

Osborne, Robin (ed), *Studies in Ancient Greek and Roman Society* (Cambridge: Cambridge University Press, 2004)

Owens, David and Tony Terzi, 'UConn Professor Faces New Charges', *The Hartford Courant*, 16 June 2014

Page, Donna, 'Asking for Trouble', *Newcastle Herald*, 8 May 2010, 6

Pahnke, Walter N, 'Drugs and Mysticism' (1966) 8(2) *International Journal of Parapsychology* 295

Palma, Silvia and Miguel Delgado-Rodriguez, 'Assessment of Publication Bias in Meta-Analyses of Cardiovascular Diseases' (2005) 59(10) *Journal of Epidemiology and Community Health* 864

Palombo-Liu, David, 'A Reply to Nathaniel Zelinsky: 'Anti-Israel' Professor Shouldn't Have been Fired', *Huffington Post*, 10 November 2014

Paludi, Michele A (ed), *Ivory Power: Sexual Harassment on Campus* (New York: State University of New York Press, 1990)

Paludi, Michele A and Richard B Barickman, *Academic and Workplace Sexual Harassment* (Albany, NY: State University of New York Press, 1991)

Paludi, Michele A, Marc Grossman, Carole Ann Scott, Joni Kindermann et al. 'Myths and Realities: Sexual Harassment on Campus' introduction to Michele A Paludi (ed), *Ivory Power: Sexual Harassment on Campus* (Albany, NY: State University of New York Press, 1990)

Pamintuan-Lamorena, Maan, 'New Advances in Stem Cell Research Could Become a Game Changer', *Japan Daily Press*, 30 January 2014

Pamintuan-Lamorena, Maan, 'Riken Will Not Reinvestigate STAP Study, Says Scientist Committed Research Misconduct', *Japan Daily Press*, 9 May 2014

Papay-Carder, Debbie, 'Comments: Plagiarism in Legal Scholarship' (1983) 15(1) *University of Toledo Law Review* 233

Pappas, Theodore, *Plagiarism and the Culture War: The Writings of Martin Luther King, Jr, and Other Prominent Americans* (Tampa, Fla: Hallberg Pub, 1998)

Paprotka, Tobias, Krista A Delviks-Frankenberry, Oya Cingöz, Anthony Martinez et al. 'Recombinant Origin of the Retrovirus XMRV' (2011) 333(6038) *Science* 97

Parashar, Sadhana, *Kāvyamīmāṃsā of Rājaśekhara: Original Text in Sanskrit and Translation with Explanatory Notes* (New Delhi: DK Printworld, 2000)

Parfitt, Tom, ' 'Drunk' Russian Lecturer 'Forces Students to Sit 23 Hour Exam' ', *The Telegraph*, 4 July 2012

Parkin, Richard J and John M Eagles, 'Blood-Letting in Bulimia Nervosa' (1993) 162(2) *The British Journal of Psychiatry* 246

Parnell, Sean, 'La Trobe University Insists on Conditions in Swisse Deal', *The Australian*, 5 February 2014

'Parts of Anti-Plagiarism Bill Lifted from Wikipedia' on *Lowering the Bar* (21 May 2010)

Pascal, Chris B, 'Complainant Issues in Research Misconduct: The Office of Research Integrity Experience' (2006) 231(7) *Experimental Biology and Medicine* 1264

Pascarella, Ernest T, Kathleen M Goodman, Tricia A Seifert, Gina Tagliapietra-Nicoli et al. 'College Student Binge Drinking and Academic Achievement: A Longitudinal Replication and Extension' (2007) 48(6) *Journal of College Student Development* 715

Patel, Bhavin, Dua, Anahita, Koenigsberger, Tom, and Desai, Sapan S, 'Combatting Fraud in Medical Research: Research Validation Standards Utilized by the Journal of Surgical Radiology' (2013) 1 *Publications* 140

Patran, Ioana, 'Romania Prime Minister Seeks to Clear Name Over Plagiarism Charge', *Reuters*, 22 June 2012

Patton, Marla R, *The Monster Study Revisited* (MS dissertation, University of Arkansas, 1992)

Payne, Doug, 'Nutrition Retracts 2001 Paper', *The Scientist*, 3 March 2005

Payne, Stewart, 'Lecturer is Given Life for Rapes', *The Telegraph*, 20 September 2003

Pellegrini, Laura A, *An Argument for the Criminal Hoax* (Ann Arbor, Mich: ProQuest, 2008)

Pelley, Scott, 'Deception at Duke: Fraud in Cancer Care?' *CBS News*, 5 March 2012

Pérez-Peña, Richard and Tanzina Vega, 'Brandeis Cancels Plan to Give Honorary Degree to Ayaan Hirsi Ali, A Critic of Islam', *The New York Times*, 8 April 2014

Perper, Joshua A and Stephen J Cina, *When Doctors Kill: Who, Why and How* (New York: Springer, 2010)

Perry, Gina, *Behind the Shock Machine: The Untold Story of the Notorious Milgram Psychology Experiments* (Brunswick: Scribe Publications, 2012)

Perry, Nick, 'Indecent Exposures: Theorizing Whistleblowing' (1998) 19(2) *Organization Studies* 235

Persaud, Raj, *From the Edge of the Couch* (London: Bantam Press, 2003)

Petersdorf, Robert G, 'The Pathogenesis of Fraud in Medical Science' (1986) 104(2) *Annals of Internal Medicine* 252

Pettigrew, Simone and Rob Donovan, *A Literature Review of the Factors that Influence Alcohol Consumption and the Effectiveness of Past Interventions* (Report to the Drug and Alcohol Office, Government of Western Australia, October 2003)

Phillips, John H and James K Bowen, *Forensic Science and the Expert Witness* (rev edn, Sydney: Law Book Co, 1989)

Phillips, Yasmine, 'University of WA Orientation Camp Incidents 'May be Sexual Assault' ', *Herald Sun*, 7 September 2012

Pidd, Helen, 'German Defence Minister Stripped of Doctorate for Plagiarism', *The Guardian*, 24 February 2011

Pignotti, Monica, 'Robert Hare Threatens to Sue Critics on *Potentially Harmful and Other Questionable Therapies* (2 June 2010)

Pinsky, Drew and S Mark Young, *The Mirror Effect: How Celebrity Narcissism is Seducing America* (New York: Harper, 2009)

Pitt, David, 'AIDS Scientist Dong-Pyou Han Pleads Not Guilty to Faking Study', *Huffington Post*, 2 July 2014

Plumly, Stanley, *Posthumous Keats: A Personal Biography* (New York: WW Norton, 2008)

Poe, Edgar Allan, 'The Unparalleled Adventure of One Hans Pfaall' (1835) in John H Ingram (ed) *The Tales and Poems of Edgar Allan Poe*, Vol II (Philadelphia: George Barrie & Son, 18--) 95–159

Polansky, Rob, 'UConn Professor Charged with DUI, Spitting in Officer's Face', *WFSB Eyewitness News*, 15 July 2014

Poldermans, Don, 'Scientific Fraud or a Rush to Judgment?' (2013) 126(4) American Journal of Medicine e5.

Poling, Alan, 'The Consequences of Fraud' in David J Miller and Michel Hersen (eds), *Research Fraud in the Behavioral and Biomedical Sciences* (New York: Wiley, 1992), pp 140–157

'Police Chemist Is Rebutted After Man's Execution', *The New York Times*, 30 August 2001

'Police Chemist Accused of Shoddy Work is Fired', *The New York Times*, 26 September 2001

'Police Chemist's Suit Says Firing was Retaliatory', *The New York Times*, 26 April 2002

Pollack, Andrew, 'A Biotech King, Dethroned', *The New York Times*, 5 September 2013

Polonsky, Rachel, 'How I Rumbled the Lying Professor: The Story Behind the Discredited Don Who Rubbished Rivals on Amazon ... Then Left His Own Wife to Take the Blame', *Daily Mail*, 25 April 2010

Polya, John B and Robert J Solomon, *Dreyfus in Australia* (Erskineville, NSW: Dr R J Solomon, 1996)

Ponta, Victor, 'Curtea Penală Internațională' (PhD dissertation, University of Bucharest, 2003)

Pope, Alexander, *The Works of Alexander Pope*, 9 vols, Notes and Illustrations by Joseph Warton (Basil: JJ Tourneisen, 1803)

Porter, Roy, 'The Science Police', *The New York Times*, 20 September 1998

Posner, Richard A, *The Little Book of Plagiarism* (New York: Pantheon Books, 2007)

Potti, Anil, Mukherjee, Sayan, Petersen, Rebecca, et al. 'A Genomic Strategy to Refine Prognosis in Early Stage Non-Small-Cell Lung Cancer' (2006) 355 *New England Journal of Medicine* 570.

Potti, Anil, Dressman, Holly K, Bild Andrea, et al. 'Genomic Signatures to Guide the Use of Chemotherapies' (2006) 12 *Nature Medicine* 1294

Potts, Jeffrey A, '*Moore v Regents of the University of California*: Expanded Disclosure, Limited Property Rights' (1992) 86(2) *Northwestern University Law Review* 453

Power, Mike, 'Alexander Shulgin Obituary', *The Guardian*, 3 June 2014

Poythress, Norman and John P Petrila, 'PCL-R Psychopathy: Threats to Sue, Peer Review and Implications for Science and Law: A Commentary' (2010) 9(1) *International Journal of Forensic Mental Health* 3

Prasad, Ashoka, Profile on *Daily Quoted*

Prasad, Ashok J, 'Racism in Medical Profession!' (10 March 2014) *India Medical Times*

Preiss, Benjamin, 'Schools Turning to Anti-Plagiarism Software to Catch Cheating Students', *The Sydney Morning Herald*, 2 September 2014

Press Complaints Commission, 'Complainant Name: Professor Sir Roy Meadow' (Adjudication issued 18 December 2008)

Press Complaints Commission, 'PCC Rejects Complaint from Professor Sir Roy Meadow' (Press Release, 7 January 2009)

Price, Alan, 'How Institutions Have Handled Investigations of Plagiarism': (Paper presented at the ORI/AAAS Conference on Plagiarism and Theft of Ideas, 21 June 1993)

Price, David, Korieh Duodo and Nicola Cain, *Defamation: Law, Procedure & Practice* (4th edn, London: Sweet & Maxwell, 2010)

Privileges Committee, Parliament of NSW, *Citizen's Right of Reply (UNSW)* (Report 60, 2012)

Privileges Committee, Parliament of NSW, *Citizen's Right of Reply (Dr Andrew McIntosh)* (Report 74, 2015)

'Professor Amy Bishop Gets Life in Prison for Alabama University Shooting', *NBC News*, 24 September 2012

Proud, Larry, 'Five Years on: ANZPAA and Professionalization' (2013) 5(1) *Australasian Policing* 13.

Public Participation Project, 'State Anti-SLAPP Laws'

Pybus, Cassandra, *Gross Moral Turpitude: The Orr Case Reconsidered* (Port Melbourne: William Heinemann Australia, 1993)

Pybus, Cassandra, 'Orr Case Revision Defended' (25-31 March 1993) 3(10) *Campus Review* 8

Pybus, Cassandra, *Seduction and Consent: A Case of Gross Moral Turpitude* (Port Melbourne: Mandarin, 1994)

Pyrek, Kelly, *Forensic Science Under Siege: The Challenges of Forensic Laboratories and the Medico-Legal Investigation System* (Burlington, MA: Academic Press, 2007)

Qian, Li, 'US Professor Hired in Nanjing Charged with Crimes', *Shanghai Daily*, 12 February 2012

Qiu, Jane, 'Publish or Perish in China' (2010) 463(7278) *Nature* 142

Qiu, Jane, 'China Goes Back to Basics on Research Funding' (2014) 507(7491) *Nature*

Qiu, Jane, 'Scientists Caught in Chinese Anti-Corruption Sweep', *Nature*, 16 October 2014

Quinn, Karl, 'Art School Altercation Puts New Spin on Cyberstalking', *The Age*, 14 April 2011

Quote Investigator, 9 March 2013

Rajaesekaran, S, 'Publish to Flourish: Is it Corrupting Science?' (August 2012) (1) *Bone & Joint 360* 5

Ramamoorti, Sri and William Olsen, 'Fraud: The Human Factor' (July 2007) 23(6) *Financial Executive*, Retrieved from <international.westlaw.com> on 7 January 2015

Ramkumar, Amrith, 'Duke Lawsuit Involving Cancer Patients Linked to Anil Potti Settled', *The Chronicle*, 3 May 2015

Rankin, Susan R, *Campus Climate for Gay, Lesbian, Bisexual and Transgender People: A National Perspective* (The Policy Institute of the National Gay and Lesbian Task Force, 2003)

'Rape Case Lecturer Jailed for Life', *Daily Mail*, Undated

Rattan, Reema, 'Academics Back Professor Over Swisse Research Collaboration', *The Conversation*, 5 February 2014

Reardon, Sara, 'US Vaccine Researcher Sentenced to Prison for Fraud' (1 July 2015) 523 Nature

Redman, Barbara K, *Research Misconduct Policy in Biomedicine: Beyond the Bad-Apple Approach* (Cambridge, Mass: The MIT Press, 2013)

Redman, Barbara K and Jon F Merz, 'Scientific Misconduct: Do the Punishments Fit the Crime?' (2008) 321(5890) *Science* 775

Rees, Neil, Simon Rice and Dominique Allen, *Australian Anti-Discrimination Law* (2nd edn, Annandale, NSW: The Federation Press, 2014)

Reeves, Jay, 'Amy Bishop Guilty: Former Professor Admits to Murder in University of Alabama Shooting', *Huffington Post*, 12 September 2012

Rehn, Alf, *The Scholar's Progress: Essays on Academic Life and Survival* (iUniverse, 2006)

Reich, Eugenie Samuel, *Plastic Fantastic: How the Biggest Fraud in Physics Shook the Scientific World* (New York: Palgrave Macmillan, 2009)

Reich, Eugenie Samuel, 'Biologist Spared Jail for Grant Fraud' (2011) 474(7353) *Nature* 552

Reich, Eugenie Samuel, 'Fraud Case We Might Have Seen Coming', *Nature*, 28 July 2011

Reich, Eugenie Samuel, 'Duplicate-Grant Case Puts Funders Under Pressure' (2012) 482 *Nature* 146(7384)

Rennison, Andrew, *Report: LGC Forensics—R v Mr A* (Forensic Science Regulator, No FSR-R-626, 1 August 2013)

Reno, Jamie, 'VA Concedes Whistleblower's Allegations Were True, Including That It Ignored Veterans' Suicidal tendencies', *International Business Times*, 19 February 2014

Repko, Allen F, *Interdisciplinary Research: Process and Theory* (2nd edn, London: SAGE, 2011)

Reporter's Transcript: Motions Hearing, *Federici v Pignotti* et al. (United States District Court, Eastern District of Virginia, Case No. l10-1418, 4 March 2011)

Report on The Royal Commission on Criminal Justice (Cmd 2263, 1993) 150

'Researchers Peg Putin as Plagiarist Over Thesis', *The Washington Times*, 24 March 2006

Research Paper Investigative Committee, 'Report on STAP Cell Research Paper Investigation', 31 March 2014

Research Triangle Institute, *Consequences of Whistleblowing for the Whistleblower in Misconduct in Science Cases* (Final Report, 30 October 1995)

Reverby, Susan (ed), *Tuskegee's Truths: Rethinking the Tuskegee Syphilis Study* (Chapel Hill: University of North Carolina Press, 2000)

'Review 1: Dr Victor Ponta (Prime Minister), PhD Thesis Plagiarism' on *Integru* (15 August 2012)

Revill, Jo, 'How the Drugs Giant and a Lone Academic Went to War', *The Guardian*, 4 December 2005

Rhodes, Rosamond and James J Strain, 'Whistleblowing in Academic Medicine' (2004) 30(1) *Journal of Medical Ethics* 35

Rice, Margaret, 'A Call for Integrity in the Fish Bowl', *The Sydney Morning Herald*, 22 December 2006

Richardson, L Song, 'When Human Experimentation is Criminal' (2009) 99(1) *The Journal of Criminal Law and Criminology* 89

Richmond, Douglas R, 'Unoriginal Sin: The Problem of Judicial Plagiarism' (2013) 45(3) *Arizona State Law Journal* 1077

Riemer, Andrew, *The Demidenko Debate* (St Leonards, NSW: Allen and Unwin, 1996)

Rigg, Paul, 'Ban Sex Between Lecturers and Students?' Issue No. 60, *University World News*, 25 January 2009

Riggs, Robert O, Patricia H Murrell and JoAnn C Cutting, *Sexual Harassment in Higher Education: From Conflict to Community* (ASHE-ERIC Higher Education Report No 2) (Washington, DC: George Washington University, School of Education and Human Development, 1993)

'Riken: No Confirmation of STAP Cells, But Verification Tests Will Continue', *The Asahi Shimbun*, 27 August 2014

Riley, Dan, 'Fraud and Australian Academics' (Paper presented at the Annual Conference of the Australasian Association for Research in Education, Surfers Paradise, Queensland, 1991

Riley, Naomi Schaefer, 'Apparently, If You're in the Right Discipline' in 'Does Academic Freedom Protect Holocaust Deniers?' *The Chronicle of Higher Education*, 14 November 2010

Rimmer, Matthew, 'The Demidenko Affair: Copyright Law, Plagiarism and Ridiculke' (2000) 5(3) Media and Arts Law Review 159.

Rising, David, 'Germany: 100 Professors Suspected of Ph.D. Bribes', *The Guardian*, 23 August 2009

Rittner, Heike L, Peter Kranke, Michael Schäfer, Norbert Roewer and Alexander Brack, 'What Can We Learn from the Scott Reuben Case? Scientific Misconduct in Anaesthesiology' (2009) 58(12) *Anaesthetist* 1199

Robbers, Monica L P, 'Blinded by Science: The Social Construction of Reality in Forensic Television Shows and its Effect on Criminal Jury Trials' (2008) 19(1) *Criminal Justice Policy Review* 84

Robbins, Rebecca D, 'Harvard Investigates 'Unprecedented' Academic Dishonesty Case', *The Harvard Crimson*, 30 August 2012

Roberts, Brent W, Walton, Kate E and Viechtbauer, Wolfgang, 'Patters of Mean-Level Change in Personality Traits Across the Life Course: A Meta-Analysis of Longitudinal Studies' (2006) 132(1) *Psychological Bulletin* 1

Roberts, Dan, 'Montana Senate Candidate John Walsh Pulls Out of Race After Plagiarism Scandal', *The Guardian*, 7 August 2014

Roberts, Laura, 'Award-Winning Historian Orlando Figes: I posted Anonymous Reviews on Amazon', *The Telegraph*, 24 April 2010

Roberts, Peter, A J Brown and Jane Olsen, *Whistling While They Work: A Good-Practice Guide for Managing Internal Reporting of Wrongdoing in Public Sector Organisations* (Canberra, ACT: ANU E Press, 2011)

Roberts, Peter, Jane Olsen and Alexander J Brown, *Whistling While They Work: Towards Best Practice Whistleblowing Programs in Public Sector Organisations* (Second Report, ARC Linkage Project, Griffith University, July 2009)

Robertson, Campbell, 'Questions Left for Mississippi Over Doctor's Autopsies', *The New York Times*, 7 January 2013

Robin, Ron, *Scandals and Scoundrels: Seven Cases that Shook the Academy* (Berkeley: University of California Press, 2004)

Robins, Brian, 'Code of Conduct Vital to Protect Corporate Whistleblowers', *The Sydney Morning Herald*, 10 May 2014

Robotham, Julie, 'School in a State of Collapse', *The Sydney Morning Herald*, 10 June 2010

Rodgers Grant, 'Former Iowa State Researcher Indicted', *The Des Moines Register*, 20 June 2014

Rodis, Rodel, 'License to Plagiarize', *Inquirer Global Nation*, 21 October 2010

Rodwin, Marc A, *Medicine, Money and Morals: Physicians' Conflicts of Interest* (New York: Oxford University Press, 1993)

Rodwin, Marc A, *Conflicts of Interest and the Future of Medicine: The United States, France and Japan* (Oxford: Oxford University Press, 2011)

Roe, Nicholas (ed), *Keats and History* (Cambridge: Cambridge University Press, 1995)

Roe, Nicholas, 'Mercury Sent John Keats to an Early Grave', *The Telegraph*, 6 October 2012

Roig, Miguel, 'Avoiding Plagiarism, Self-Plagiarism, and Other Questionable Writing Practices: A Guide to Ethical Writing' (US Department of Health & Human Services, The Office of Research Integrity, last updated 15 May 2013) 3

Roiphe, Katie, 'The Philosopher and the Student', *Slate*, 8 October 2013

Roman, Paul M, 'Employee Alcoholism and Assistance Programs: Adapting an Innovation for College and University Faculty' (1980) 51(2) *Journal of Higher Education* 135

Romei, Stephen, 'Poet Uses Defence of 'Collage Poetry' after Recycling Plath Lines', *The Australian*, 13 September 2013

Rose, Andrew, *Lethal Witness* (London: The History Press, 2007)

Rose, Mark, 'When Giants Roamed the Earth (2005) 58(6) *Archaeology* 30

Ross, Colin A, *The CIA Doctors: Human Rights Violations by American Psychiatrists* (Austin, Texas: Greenleaf Book Group, 2006)

Ross, John, 'Nine Expelled for Plagiarism at Deakin', *The Australian*, 6 October 2012

Ross, John, 'Science Can Keep its House in Order', *The Australian*, 19 August 2014

Ross, John, 'Controversial Academic Barry Spurr Resigns from University of Sydney', *The Australian*, 18 December 2014

Rothman, David J and Sheila M Rothman, *The Willowbrook Wars: Bringing the Mentally Disabled into the Community* (New Brunswick, NJ: Aldine Transaction, 2005)

Roxby, Philippa, 'Northwick Park Drug Trial Disaster—Could It Happen Again?' (24 May 2013) *BBC News*, 24 May 2013

Royal Australian & New Zealand College of Psychiatrists, *Code of Ethics* (July 2010)

Royal Australian & New Zealand College of Psychiatrists, 'Zero Tolerance Policy on Proven Sexual Boundary Violations' (updated 23 February 2013)

Royal College of Physicians of London, 'Fraud and Misconduct in Medical Research: Causes, Investigation and Prevention: A Report of the Royal College of Physicians' (1991) 25(2) *Journal of the Royal College of Physicians of London* 89

Royston, Michael, 'Retracted Scientific Studies: A Growing List' (28 May 2015) *The New York Times*

Rubin, Linda J, Bethany R Hampton and Pamela W McManus, 'Sexual Harassment of Students by Professional Psychology Educators: A National Survey' (1997) 37(9-10) *Sex Roles* 753

Ruck, Carl A P, Jeremy Bigwood, Danny Staples and Jonathan Ott et al. 'Entheogens' (1979) 11(1-2) *Journal of Psychedelic Drugs* 145

Rüegg, Walter, *A History of the University in Europe*, 4 vols (Cambridge: Cambridge University Press, 1992)

Rumball, Sylvia and John O'Neill, 'Research Integrity in New Zealand' in Tony Mayer and Nicholas Steneck (eds), *Promoting Research Integrity in a Global Environment* (World Scientific, Singapore, 2012), pp 41–44

Russell, Conrad, *Academic Freedom* (London: Routledge, 1993)

Russell, Miles, *Piltdown Man: The Secret Life of Charles Dawson and The World's Greatest Archaeological Hoax* (Stroud, Gloucestershire: Tempus, 2003)

Russin, Joseph M and Andrew T Weil, 'The Crimson Takes Leary, Alpert to Task', *The Harvard Crimson*, 28 May 1963

Russo, Charles J, 'A Legal Primer on Sexual Harassment: Lessons for Practice from the United States of America' (2008) 13(1) *Australian & New Zealand Journal of Law & Education* 21

Sabbagh, Karl, *A Rum Affair: A True Story of Botanical Fraud* (New York: Farrar, Strauss, and Giroux, 2000)

Sachsman, David B and David W Bulla (eds), *Sensationalism: Murder, Mayhem, Mudslinging, Scandals, and Disasters in 19th Century Reporting* (New Brunswick: Transaction Publishers, 2013)

'SAGE Statement on Journal of Vibration and Control' (Press Release, London, 8 July 2014)

Saint Louis University School of Law, 'Chapter 6: Saint Louis University School of Law Plagiarism Policy Statement', *Student Handbook*, August 2014

Salhab, Mohammad, 'A History of Fraud and Deceit in Medical Research' (2010) 5(1) *Surgery Journal* 1

Salmon, Michael A, Peter Marren and Basil Harley, *The Aurelian Legacy: British Butterflies and Their Collectors* (Berkeley: University of California Press, 2000)

Sample, Ian, 'Stem Cell Scientist Haruko Obokata Found Guilty of Misconduct', *The Guardian*, 2 April 2014

Samuel, Michael L, 'Rabbi Yosef's Opinion on Plagiarism is Mistaken', *San Diego Jewish World*, 28 March 2014

Samuels, Alec, 'Suing the Expert for Negligence?' (2012) 52(1) *Medicine, Science and the Law* 50

Samuels, Harriet, 'Sexual Harassment in the Workplace: A Feminist Analysis of Recent Developments in the UK' (2003) 26(5) *Women's Studies International Forum* 467

Samuelson, Pamela, 'Self-Plagiarism or Fair Use?' (1994) 37(8) *Communications of the ACM* 21

San Francisco State University, Faculty Affairs and Professional Development, 'For Chairs: When One of Your Faculty Members is Dealing with Alcohol Abuse', 19 March 2008

Sandler, Bernice R and Robert J Shoop (eds), *Sexual Harassment on Campus: A Guide for Administrators, Faculty and Students* (Boston: Allyn and Bacon, 1997)

Sangha, Bibi, Kent Roach and Robert Moles, *Forensic Investigations and Miscarriages of Justice: The Rhetoric Meets the Reality* (Toronto: Irwin Law, 2010)

Santoro, Michael A and Thomas M Gorrie (eds), *Ethics and the Pharmaceutical Industry* (Cambridge: Cambridge University Press, 2005)

Santos, Matikas, 'Sotto: How Will I Apologize For Plagiarism When I Never Plagiarized?' *Inquirer.net*, 13 November 2012

Sa`ûd al-Rashûd, Sheikh Khâlid b., "Allah Commands You to Render Trusts to Their Owners'—Its Relevance to Plagiarism', Islam Today

Saunders, Joss, 'Plagiarism and the Law: A Guide to Plagiarism and the Law' (November 2007)

Saunders, Rhodri and Julian Savulescu, 'Research Ethics and Lessons from Hwanggate: What Can We Learn from the Korean Cloning Fraud? (2008) 34(3) *Journal of Medical Ethics* 214

Savulescu, Julian, 'Harm, Ethics Committees and the Gene Therapy Death' (2001) 27(3) *Journal of Medical Ethics* 148

Sawyer, Kim R, 'The Test Called Whistleblowing' (Paper presented at the National Conference of Whistleblowers Australia—*Whistleblowing: Making it Work*, Adelaide, 11 September 2005, 18

Scanlon, Patrick M, 'Song From Myself: An Anatomy of Self-Plagiarism' (2007) *Plagiary: Cross-Disciplinary Studies in Plagiarism, Fabrication, and Falsification* 57

Scarborough, Samuel, 'The Imagery of Alchemical Art as a Method of Communication' (2005) 9(1) *Journal of the Western Mystery Tradition*

Schafer, Arthur, 'The Moral Anatomy and Ethical Pathology of the Randomized Clinical Trial' in Peter P De Deyn (ed), *The Ethics of Animal and Human Experimentation* (London: John Libbey, 1994), pp 269–276

Scheck, Barry and Peter Neufeld, 'Junk Science, Junk Evidence', *The New York Times*, 11 May 2001

Schein, Moshe and Ramesh Paladugu, 'Redundant Surgical Publications: Tip of the Iceberg?' (2001) 129(6) *Surgery* 655

Schiermeier, Quirin, 'German Scientists Outraged in Defence Minister Plagiarism Affair', *Nature.com*, 28 February 2011

Schneider, Margaret, Sarah Baker and Lana Stermac, 'Sexual Harassment Experiences of Psychologists and Psychological Associates During their Graduate School Training' (2002) 11(3-4) *Canadian Journal of Human Sexuality* 159

Science Council of Japan, *Scientific Misconduct and its Prevention* (May 2005)

Science Council of Japan, 'Statement: Code of Conduct for Scientists' (approved 3 October 2006)

Schiermeier, Quirin, 'Self-Publishing Editor Set to Retire' (2008) 456(7221) *Nature* 432

Schiermeier, Quirin, 'Romanian Prime Minister Accused of Plagiarism' (2012) 486(7403) *Nature* 305

Schiermeier, Quirin, 'Conflicting Verdicts on Romanian Prime Minister's Plagiarism', *Nature*, 20 July 2012

Schliemann, Paul, 'How I Discovered Atlantis, the Source of All Civilization' (1912) *New York American*

Schmidt, Peter, 'In Professor-Dominatrix Scandal, U. of New Mexico Feels the Pain', *The Chronicle of Higher Education*, 12 September 2010

Schopp, Robert, Richard L Wiener, Brian H Bornstein and Steven L Willborn, *Mental Disorder and Criminal Law: Responsibility, Punishment and Competence* (New York: Springer, 2009)

Schreiber, Mark, 'Ongoing Obokata Story Seeks Out Scandal', *The Japan Times*, 5 July 2014

Schuessler, Jennifer, 'A Star Philosopher Falls, and a Debate Over Sexism is Set Off', *The New York Times*, 2 August 2013

Schuetze, Christopher F, 'The Whiff of Plagiarism Again Hits German Elite', *The New York Times*, 24 April 2011

Schuetze, Christopher F, 'New Plagiarism Cases Cause Second Thoughts in Germany', *The New York Times*, 11 March 2013

Schultz, Nora, 'German Academics Investigated over Bribery Claims', (*New Scientist*, 25 August 2009

Schwarcz, Joseph, *Science, Sense and Nonsense: 61 Nourishing, Healthy, Bunk-free Commentaries on the Chemistry that Affects Us All* (Doubleday Canada, 2009)

Schweitzer, Nick J and Michael J Saks, 'The CSI Effect: Popular Fiction About Forensic Science Affects the Public's Expectations About Real Forensic Science' (2007) 47(3) *Jurimetrics* 357

'Science: Violating Nature' (1977) 109(11) *Time* 74

'Scientist Steven Eaton Jailed for Falsifying Drug Test Results', *BBC News*, 17 April 2013

'Scientist Behind Fake HIV Breakthrough Sentenced to Prison after Spiking Results' (1 July 2015) *The Guardian*

Scollon, Ron, 'Plagiarism and Ideology: Identity in Intercultural Discourse' (1995) 24(1) *Language in Society* 1

Scopes, John Thomas, and William Jennings Bryan, *The World's Most Famous Court Trial: State of Tennessee v John Thomas Scopes* (first publ. 1925, New York: Da Capo Press, 1971 ed)
Scott, Eugenie Carol, *Evolution vs Creationism: An Introduction* (Berkeley, Calif: University of California Press, 2005)
Scott, Janny, 'At UC San Diego: Unraveling a Research Fraud Case', *Los Angeles Times*, 30 April 1987
Scott, Janny, 'Professors Urge Closer Guard Against Research Fraud', *Los Angeles Times*, 26 November 1987
Scott, Janny, 'Researcher Admits Faking Data to Get $160,000 in Funds', *Los Angeles Times*, 20 September 1988
Scott, Sophie, and Branley, Alison, 'High-profile Researcher Admits Fabricating Scientific Results Published in Major Journals' (17 September 2015) ABC News.
Sekigucki, Toko, 'STAP Cells 'Likely Never Existed'', *The Wall Street Journal*, 26 December 2014
Selby, Jenn, 'Shia LaBoeuf Retires From Public Life After Plagiarism Scandal Sparks Bizarre (Also Plagiarised) Apology Spree', *The Independent*, 10 January 2014
Senate Select Committee on Public Interest Whistleblowing, Parliament of Australia, *In the Public Interest* (1994)
Senate Standing Committee on Finance and Public Administration, Parliament of Australia, *Management and Operations of the Department of Foreign Affairs and Trade* (1992)
Seo, J Mira, 'Plagiarism and Poetic Identity in Martial' (2009) 130(4) *American Journal of Philology* 567
Séralini, Gilles-Eric, Emilie Clair, Robin Mesnage, Steeve Gress et al. 'Republished Study: Long-Term Toxicity of a Roundup Herbicide and a Roundup-Tolerant Genetically Modified Maize' (2014) 26:14 *Environmental Sciences Europe*
Service, Robert, 'The Shame of Orlando Figes', *The Guardian*, 23 April 2010
Settlement Agreement and Stipulation for Entry of Judgment, *United States of America v Eric T Poehlman* (United States District Court for the District of Vermont, Case No. 2:05.cv.66, 11 March 2005)
Shahabuddin, Syed, 'Plagiarism in Academia' (2009) 21(3) *International Journal of Teaching and Learning in Higher Education* 353
Shakespeare, William, ed. Roger Warren, *Cymbeline,* (Oxford: Oxford University Press, 1998)
Shamoo, Adil E and David B Resnik, *Responsible Conduct of Research* (2nd edn, New York: Oxford University Press, 2009)
Shannon, Carl R, *Royal Commission Report Concerning the Conviction of Edward Charles Splatt* (Adelaide: Government Printer, 1984)
Shapin, Steven, *A Social History of Truth: Civility and Science in Seventeenth-Century England* (Chicago: University of Chicago Press, 1994)
Shapiro, Alan E, 'Skating on the Edge: Newton's Investigation of Chromatic Dispersion and Achromatic Prisms and Lenses' in Jed Z Buchwald and Allan Franklin (eds), *Wrong for the Right Reasons* (Dordrecht: Springer, 2005), pp 99–125
Shapiro, David, 'Expert Witnesses: Now Liable for Inexpert Evidence', *Crown Office Chambers*, 30 March 2011
Shaw, Claire, 'Hundreds of Open Access Journals Accept Fake Science Paper', *The Guardian*, 4 October 2013
Shaw, George Bernard, *The Doctor's Dilemma: Preface on Doctors* (Project Gutenberg, first published 1909, 2004 ed), 'Doubtful Character Borne By the Medical Profession'
Shea, Christopher, 'Prominent Scholar was Banned from Rutgers Campus', *The Chronicle of Higher Education*, 3 May 2013
Sheehan, Paul, 'The Einfeld Follies: A Study in Ego', *The Sydney Morning Herald*, 21 August 2006
Shepelin, Ilya, 'It Looks Like Putin Wrote Just a Couple of Pages of his Thesis', *The Interpreter*, 27 June 2013
Shin, Clifford H, Lucinda Bateman, Robert Schlaberg, Ashley M Bunker et al. 'Absence of XMRV Retrovirus and Other Murine Leukemia Virus-Related Viruses in Patients with Chronic Fatigue Syndrome' (2011) 85(14) *Journal of Virology* 7195

Shuchman, Miriam, *The Drug Trial: Nancy Olivieri and the Scandal that Rocked the Hospital for Sick Children* (Toronto: Random House, 2005)
Shulgin, Alexander and Ann Shulgin, *Pihkal: A Chemical Love Story* (Berkeley, CA: Transform Press, 1991)
Shuman, Rebecca, 'The Campus Alcohol Problem That Nobody Talks About', *Slate*, 4 December 2014
Shuster, Simon, 'Putin's Ph.D: Can a Plagiarism Probe Upend Russian Politics?' *Time*, 28 February 2013
Sibbald, Barbara, 'Death But One Unintended Consequence of Gene-Therapy Trial' (2001) 164(11) *Canadian Medical Association Journal* 1612
Sieber, Joan E, 'The Psychology of Whistleblowing' (1998) 4(1) *Science and Engineering Ethics* 7
Silkwood (20th Century Fox, 1983)
Silverberg, Robert, *Scientists and Scoundrels: A Book of Hoaxes* (New York: Crowell, 1965)
Silverman, Ed, 'Should Research Fraud be a Crime? A Reader Poll', *The Wall Street Journal*, 16 July 2014
Silverman, Jacob, 'Jonah Lehrer's 'Self-Plagiarism' Scandal Rocks The New Yorker', *The Daily Beast*, 20 June 2012
Simic, Zora, 'On Reading *The First Stone* Ten Years Later' (2006) 15 *Lilith: A Feminist History Journal* 18
Simmons, Graham, Simone A Glynn, Anthony L Komaroff, Judy A Mikovits et al. 'Failure to Confirm XMRV/MLVs in the Blood of Patients with Chronic Fatigue Syndrome: A Multi-Laboratory Study' (2011) 334 *Science* 814
Simon, Robert I and Liza H Gold (eds), *The American Psychiatric Publishing Textbook of Forensic Psychiatry* (2nd edn, Washington, DC: American Psychiatric Publishing, 2010)
Simons, Kai, 'The Misused Impact Factor' (2008) 322(5899) *Science* 165
Singapore Statement on Research Integrity, 'Principles'
Singapore Statement on Research Integrity, 'Responsibilities'
Singer, Merrill and Hans Baer, *Killer Commodities: Public Health and the Corporate Production of Harm* (Lanham, Md: Altamira Press, 2008)
Singer, Natasha , 'Duke Scientist Suspended Over Rhodes Scholar Claims', *The New York Times*, 20 July 2010
Singh, Simon, 'How English Libel Law has a Global Chill on Free Speech' (2011) 47(6) *Cortex* 643
Si-soo, Park, 'Hwang Convicted of Embezzlement, Cleared of Fraud', *The Korea Times*, 26 October 2009
Skandalakis, John E and Petros Mirilas, 'Plagiarism' (2004) 139(9) *Archives of Surgery* 1022
Skeem, Jennifer and David J Cooke, 'One Measure Does Not a Construct Make: Directions Toward Reinvigorating Psychopathy Research—Reply to Hare and Neumann (2010)' (2010) 22(2) *Psychological Assessment* 455
Skeem, Jennifer L and David J Cooke, 'Is Criminal Behavior a Central Component of Psychopathy? Conceptual Directions for Resolving the Debate' (2010) 22(2) *Psychological Assessment* 433
Sledge Jr, George W, 'Why Big Lies Matter: Lessons from the Bezwoda Affair', *Medscape*. Also available at (2000) 5(1) *Medscape Women's Health* 4
Slobogin, Christopher, '*Estelle v Smith*: The Constitutional Contours of the Forensic Evaluation' (1982) 31(1) *Emory Law Journal* 71
Smith, Alexandra, 'Academics Urge Universities to Act on Race and Gender Discrimination', *The Sydney Morning Herald*, 31 October 2014
Smith, Charlie, 'UBC Psychopathy Expert Robert Hare Responds to Academic Criticism Over Lawsuit Threat', *The Georgia Straight*, 13 June 2010
Smith, James P, 'Plagiarists Publish and Perish' (1999) 30(4) *Journal of Advanced Nursing* 777
Smith, Janet, *The Shipman Inquiry: Fifth Report: Safeguarding Patients: Lessons from the Past—Proposals for the Future* (Cm 6394, 2004)
Smith, Mable H, *The Legal, Professional and Ethical Dimensions of Higher Education* (Philadelphia, PA: Lippincott Williams & Wilkins, 2005)

Smith, Rodney and Alexander J Brown, 'The Good, the Bad and the Ugly: Whistleblowing Outcomes' in Alexander J Brown (ed), *Whistleblowing in the Australian Public Sector: Enhancing the Theory and Practice of Internal Witness Management in Public Sector Organisations* (Canberra, ACT: ANU E Press, 2008), pp 109–136

Smith, Richard, 'Authorship: Time for a Paradigm Shift? The Authorship System is Broken and May Need a Radical Solution' (1997) 314 *BMJ* 992

Smith, Richard, 'Authorship is Dying: Long Live Contributorship: The BMJ Will Publish Lists of Contributors and Guarantors to Original Articles' (1997) 31 *BMJ* 6

Smith, Richard, 'Investigating the Previous Studies of a Fraudulent Author' (2005) 331(7511) *BMJ* 288

Smith, Richard, 'Peer Review: A Flawed Process at the Heart of Science and Journals' (2006) 99(4) *Journal of the Royal Society of Medicine* 178

Smith, Richard, 'Research Misconduct: The Poisoning of the Well' (2006) 99(5) *Journal of the Royal Society of Medicine* 232

Smith, Richard, 'Ethical Issues in the Publication Process' in Frank Wells and Michael Farthing (eds), *Fraud and Misconduct in Biomedical Research* (4th edn, London: Royal Society of Medicine Press, 2008), pp 14–28

Smith, Richard, 'Should Scientific Fraud Be a Criminal Offence?' on *The BMJ* (BMJ Blogs) (9 December 2013)

Sokal, Alan D, 'Transgressing the Boundaries: Toward a Transformative Hermeneutics of Quantum Gravity' (Spring/Summer 1996) Issue No. 46/47 *Social Text* 217

Sokal, Alan D, 'Revelation: A Physicist Experiments with Cultural Studies' (May-June 1996) 6(4) Lingua Franca 62

Sokal, Alan D, *Beyond the Hoax: Science, Philosophy and Culture* (Oxford: Oxford University Press, 2008)

'Soldi dal Padre di una Studentessa, Condannato l'ex Professore Capizzano', *Il Messaggero*, 16 November 2012

Solis, Ben, 'Professor 'Regretful' for Intoxication on Campus, Takes Leave of Absence', *Central Michigan Life*, 18 March 2014

Soltis, Andy, 'Professor Admits Faking AIDS Vaccine to get $19M in Grants', *New York Post*, 26 December 2013

Song, Sophie, 'Chinese Forensic Science Frequently Under Suspicion Of Covering-Up For Officials', *International Business Times*, 23 August 2013

'Sonja Farak, Ex-Mass Lab Chemist, Pleads Guilty to Drug Theft', *The Huffington Post*, 6 January 2014

Sovakool, Benjamin K, 'Using Criminalization and Due Process to Reduce Scientific Misconduct' (2005) 5(5) *American Journal of Bioethics* W1.

Sox, Harold C and Drummond Rennie, 'Research Misconduct, Retraction, and Cleansing the Medical Literature: Lessons from the Poehlman Case' (2006) 144(8) *Annals of Internal Medicine* 609

Sparrow, Jeff, 'The Return of Helen Demidenko: From Literary Hoaxer to Political Operator' (8 July 2015) The Guardian

Spencer, Frank, *Piltdown: A Scientific Forgery* (New York: Oxford University Press, 1990)

Spitzberg, Brian H, 'An Analysis of Empirical Estimates of Sexual Aggression Victimization and Perpetration' (1999) 14(3) *Violence and Victims* 241

Spitzberg, Brian H and William R Cupach (eds), *The Dark Side of Close Relationships* (Mahwah, NJ: Lawrence Erlbaum Associates, 1998)

Spitzberg, Brian H and William R Cupach (eds), *The Dark Side of Close Relationships* [electronic resource] (Hoboken: Taylor and Francis, 2013)

Spitzberg, Brian H, Linda Marshall and William R Cupach, 'Obsessive Relational Intrusion, Coping and Sexual Coercion Victimization' (2001) 14(1) *Communication Reports* 19

Spitzberg, Brian H and Jill Rhea, 'Obsessive Relational Intrusion and Sexual Coercion Victimization' (1999) 14(1) *Journal of Interpersonal Violence* 3

Spitzer, Kirk, 'Science Scandal Triggers Suicide, Soul-Searching in Japan', *Time*, 8 August 2014
Sprague, Robert L, 'Whistleblowing: A Very Unpleasant Avocation' (1993) 3(1) *Ethics & Behavior* 103
Squier, Waney, '…The Uncomfortable Interface Between Medicine, Science and the Law…' (2011) 17(1) *Clinical Risk* 3
Srivistava, Ranjana, 'If Vitamins Don't Work, Will Industry-Sponsored Scientists Tell Us So?' *The Guardian*, 6 February 2014
St Vincent's Hospital, Research Governance Unit, *Complaints Handling and Research Misconduct* (Procedure 3.2)
Stacy, Neera Rellan, 'Seeking a Superior Institutional Liability Standard under Title IX for Teacher-Student Sexual Harassment' (1996) 71(5) *New York University Law Review* 1338
Stafford, Ned, 'Polish Academy is to Establish a National Commission on Research Ethics' (2011) 342(1) *BMJ* d511
Stallard, Brian, 'Science Fraud! Peer Review IS Vulnerable', *Nature World News*, 11 July 2014
Standing Committee on Faculty Conduct, Harvard Medical School, Harvard School of Dental Medicine, 'White Paper: Plagiarism and Research Misconduct', 15 December 2010
Standing Committee on Public Administration, Legislative Council, Western Australia, *Fourth Report on Its Inquiry into the Events Surrounding the Denial of Tenure to the Late Dr David Rindos by the University of Western Australia* (December 1997)
Stanford University, Administrative Guide, '1.1.1. University Code of Conduct' (Last updated 13 August 2014)
Stapel, Diederik, *Faking Science: A True Story of Academic Fraud* (2014) trans Nicholas JL Brown
Starke, Joseph G, 'The Protection of Public Service Whistleblowers—Part I' (1991) 65(4) *Australian Law Journal* 205
Starke, Joseph G, 'The Protection of Public Service Whistleblowers—Part II' (1991) 65(5) *Australian Law Journal* 252
Starrs, James E, 'Mountebanks Among Forensic Scientists' in Richard Saferstein (ed), *Forensic Science Handbook*, vol 2 (Englewood Cliffs, NJ: Prentice-Hall, 1988)
State Government of Victoria, Department of Innovation, Industry and Regional Development, *Managing and Commercialising Intellectual Property: A Guide for Victorian Universities and Research Institutes* (Melbourne, 2002), Chapter One
Stearns, Laurie, 'Copy Wrong: Plagiarism, Process, Property, and the Law' in Lise Buranen and Alice M Roy (eds), *Perspectives on Plagiarism and Intellectual Property in a Postmodern World* (Albany: State University of New York Press, 1999), pp 5–17
Steen, R Grant, 'Retractions in the Scientific Literature: Is the Incidence of Research Fraud Increasing? (2011) 37(4) *Journal of Medical Ethics* 249
Steen, R Grant, 'Retractions in the Medical Literature: How Many Patients are Put at Risk by Flawed Research?' (2011) 37(11) *Journal of Medical Ethics* 688
Steen, R Grant, Arturo Casadevall and Ferric C Fang, 'Why Has the Number of Retractions Increased?' (2013) 8(7) *PLoS ONE*
Stern, Simon, 'Copyright Originality and Judicial Originality' (2013) 63(3) *University of Toronto Law Journal* 385
Steinberg, Jacques, 'Defense Begins for Mother in Sudden Deaths of 5 Children', *The New York Times*, 11 April 1995
Steinschneider, Alfred, 'Prolonged Apnea and the Sudden Infant Death Syndrome: Clinical and Laboratory Observations' (1972) 50(4) *Pediatrics* 646
Stempel, Jonathan, 'Ex-'King of Biotech' Set to Serve Four-Year Term for Fraud', *Reuters*, 21 January 2014
Steneck, Nicholas, 'What Do We Know? Two Decades of Research on Research Integrity' (Address delivered at the ESF-ORI First World Conference on Research Integrity: Fostering Responsible Research, Lisbon, 19 September 2007)
Sterken, Elisabeth, 'Letter to the Editor: The Impact of Scientific Misconduct on Child Health' (2006) 9(2) *Public Health Nutrition* 273

Stern, Andrew M, Arturo Casadevall, R Grant Steen and Ferric C Fang, 'Research: Financial Costs and Personal Consequences of Research Misconduct Resulting in Retracted Publications' (2014) 3 *eLife* e02956

Stern, Victoria, 'Research Misconduct on the Rise' (2012) 7(12) *Clinical Oncology News* 24

Sterne, Laurence, *The Life and Opinions of Tristram Shandy, Gentleman*, vol 5 (Dublin: W & W Smith, G Faulkner, S Watson and T Williams, 1765)

Stewart, Thomas, 'UF Professor Found With Cocaine Enters Court Agreement', *The Independent Florida Alligator*, 22 October 2009

Stewart, Susan, *Crimes of Writing: Problems in the Containment of Representation* (New York: Oxford University Press, 1991)

Stimpson, Catharine R, 'Overreaching: Sexual Harassment and Education', Chapter Two in Michele A Paludi and Richard B Barickman, *Academic and Workplace Sexual Harassment* (Albany, NY: State University of New York Press, 1991)

Stolberg, Sheryl Gay, 'The Biotech Death of Jesse Gelsinger', *The New York Times*, 28 November 1999

Stoljar, Jeremy, *The Australian Book of Great Trials: The Cases that Shaped a Nation* (Sydney: Murdoch Books, 2011)

Stone, Alan A, *Law, Psychiatry and Morality: Essays and Analysis* (Washington, DC: American Psychiatric Press, Arlington, 1984)

Strehlow, Theodor J, *Index to Victorian Parliamentary Papers* 1950-1992 (Victorian Government Printer, Melbourne, 1995)

Stuart, Christine, 'Fired Scientist Sues University of Connecticut', *Courthouse News Service*, 7 March 2013

'Students Rally as Uni Suspends Spurr', *Honi Soit*, 17 October 2014

Styles, Aja and Katherine Fenech, 'Curtin Lecturer Implicated in 'Sex-for-Marks' Scandal with Students', *WA Today*, 2 September 2010

Sudbø, Jon, Wanja Kildal, Björn Risberg, Hanna S Koppang, Håvard E Danielsen and Albrecht Reith, 'DNA Content as a Prognostic Marker in Patients with Oral Leukoplakia' (2001) 344(17) *The New England Journal of Medicine* 1270

Sudbø, Jon, J Jack Lee, Scott M Lippman, J Mork, Smione Sagen, N Flatner, Ari Ristimäki, Asle Sudbø, Li Mao, X Zhou, Wanja Kildal, Jan F Evensen, Albrecht Reith and AJ Dannenberg, 'Non-Steroidal Anti-Inflammatory Drugs and the Risk of Oral Cancer: A Nested Case-Control Study' (2005) 366(9494) *The Lancet* 1359

Sudbø, Jon, Scott M Lippman, J Jack Lee, Li Mao, Wanja Kildal, Asle Sudbø et al. 'The Influence of Resection and Aneuploidy on Mortality in Oral Leukoplakia (2004) 350(14) *The New England Journal of Medicine* 1405

Sudbø, Jon, Roy Samuelsson, Björn Risberg, Stig Heistein, Christian Nyhus, Margaretha Samuelsson et al. 'Risk Markers of Oral Cancer in Clinically Normal Mucosa as an Aid in Smoking Cessation Counseling' (2005) 23(9) *Journal of Clinical Oncology* 1927

Suetonius, *The Life of Virgil*, (Loeb Translation, 1913)

Sumanth, John J, David M Mayer and Virginia S Kay, 'Why Good Guys Finish Last: The Role of Justification Motives, Cognition, and Emotion in Predicting Retaliation against Whistleblowers' (2011) 1(2) *Organization Psychology Review* 165

Sumikawa, Koji, 'The Results of Investigation into Dr Yoshitaka Fujii's Papers' (2012)

Summerlin, William T, 'Allogenic Transplantation of Organ Cultures of Adult Human Skin' (1973) 1(3) *Clinical Immunology and Immunopathology* 372

Summerlin, William T, Miller GE and Good RA, 'Successful Tissue and Organ Transplantation Without Immunosuppression' (1973) 52 *The Journal of Clinical Investigation* 34a

Supreme Court of Victoria, 'Practice Note No 2 of 2014: Expert Evidence in Criminal Trials' (25 June 2014)

Suro, Roberto, 'Ripples of a Pathologist's Misconduct in Graves and Courts of West Texas', *The New York Times*, 22 November 1992

Sutherland, Kate, 'Book Reviews, The Common Law Tort of Defamation, and the Suppression of Scholarly Debate' (2010) 11(6) *German Law Journal* 656

Sutton, Amy J, Susan J Duval, Richard L Tweedie, Keith R Adams et al. 'Empirical Assessment of Effect of Publication Bias on Meta-Analyses' (2000) 320(7249) *BMJ* 1574
Swales, Jeannie, 'Common Brimstone Butterfly', *The Scarborough News*, 30 March 2014
Swann, Maxine, 'The Professor, the Bikini Model and the Suitcase Full of Trouble', *The New York Times*, 8 March 2013
Swecker, Chris and Michael Wolf, *An Independent Review of the State Bureau of Investigation Forensic Laboratory* (released 18 August 2010)
Syracuse University, 'Non-Discrimination and Anti-Harassment in Employment' (amended November 2007)
Tams, Christian J, *Enforcing Obligations Erga Omnes in International Law* (Cambridge, UK: Cambridge University Press, 2005)
Tang, Catherine So-kum, Michelle S M Yik, Fanny M C Cheung, Po-king Choi et al. 'Sexual Harassment of Chinese College Students' (1996) 25(2) *Archives of Sexual Behavior* 201
Tanne, Janice Hopkins, 'Alzheimer's Researchers Face Trial for Scientific Fraud and Defrauding US Government' (2012) 344(5) *BMJ* e3608
Taslitz, Andrew E, 'Convicting the Guilty, The ABA Takes a Stand' (2005) 19(4) *Criminal Justice* 18
Tasmanian Government, Department of Justice, Legislation and Development Review, *Review of the Public Interest Disclosures Act* 2002
Tatsioni, Athina, Antonia Charchanti, Evangelia Kitsiou and John PA Ioannidis, 'Appendicectomies in Albanians in Greece: Outcomes in a Highly Mobile Immigrant Patient Population' (2001) 1(5) *BMC Health Services Research* (unpaginated)
Taubes, Gary, *Bad Science: The Short Life and Weird Times of Cold Fusion* (New York: Random House, 1993)
Taubes, Gary, 'Plagiarism Suit Wins; Experts Hope It Won't Set a Trend' (1995) 268(5214) *Science* 1125
Tavare, Aniket, 'Managing Research Misconduct: Is Anyone Getting it Right?' (2011) 343 *BMJ* d8212
Taylor, John R, *Investigation into How Universities Deal with International Students* (Victorian Ombudsman, October 2011)
Taylor, Vanessa, 'Another Hospital Saga: The Chronicles of Professor Kossmann and Bayside Health' (2010) 18(1) *Journal of Law and Medicine* 76
Teague, Edward, 'A Rum Affair: How Botany's "Piltdown Man" was Unmasked', *natural SCIENCE*
Tenpenny, Patricia L, Maria S Keriazakos, Gavin S Lew and Thomas P Phelan, 'In Search of Inadvertent Plagiarism' (1998) 111(4) *The American Journal of Psychology* 529
Tereskerz, Patricia M, *Clinical Research and the Law* (Chichester, West Sussex: John Wiley & Sons, 2012)
Tewari, Mayank, 'Indian Professor Guilty of Plagiarism' (23 February 2008) DNA India
Tharyan, Prathap, 'Criminals in the Citadel and Deceit All Along the Watchtower: Irresponsibility, Fraud and Complicity in the Search for Scientific Truth' (2012) 10(1) *Mens Sana Monographs* 158
The Expert Panel on Research Integrity, *Honesty, Accountability and Trust: Fostering Research Integrity in Canada* (Ottawa: Council of Canadian Academies, 2010)
The Insider (Buena Vista Pictures, 1999)
Theisohn, Philipp, 'Call the Spade a Spade', *Sign and Sight.Com*, 4 March 2010
'The Moment Boston State chemist is Arrested for Faking Criminal Drug Test Results Casting Doubt on 34,000 Convictions', *Daily Mail*, 29 September 2012
'The Morality of Scientists: II Report of the Faculty Ad Hoc Committee to Investigate Research Fraud, 30 September 1986' (1987) 25(4) *Minerva* 504
'They Call him Dr. Death' (1981) 117(22) *Time* 82
Thomas, Hedley, 'Repeat Plagiarist Quits the Bench', *The Australian*, 19 December 2006
Thomas, Hedley, 'Plagiarising Magistrate Can Practise', *The Australian*, 7 November 2007
Thomas, Ronald R, *Detective Fiction and the Rise of Forensic Science* (Cambridge: Cambridge University Press, 2003)
Thomason, Andy, 'Romanian Prime Minister Gives Up Ph.D., 2 Years After Plagiarism Finding', *The Chronicle of Higher Education*, 16 December 2014

Thompson, Jon, Patricia Baird and Jocelyn Downie, *Report of the Committee of Inquiry on the Case Involving Dr Nancy Olivieri, the Hospital for Sick Children, the University of Toronto, and Apotox Inc*

'Thomson in Plagiarism 'Scandal' ', *The Canberra Times*, 15 December 2011

Thomson, Keith S, 'Piltdown Man: The Great English Mystery Story' (1991) *American Scientist* 194

Thoreson, Richard W, 'Alcohol Problems in Academe: The Renaissance Man, the Inscrutable Scholar and Other Myths' in Elizabeth P Hosokawa, Judy Johnston and Richard W Thoreson (eds), *Employee Assistance Programs in Higher Education: Conference Proceedings* (Columbia, Mo: University of Missouri-Columbia Employee Assistance Program, 1981)

Thoreson, Richard W, 'The Professor at Risk: Alcohol Abuse in Academe' (1984) 55(1) *Journal of Higher Education* 56

Thoreson, Richard W, Peter E Nathan, Jane K Skorina and Richard R Kilburg, 'The Alcoholic Psychologist: Issues, Problems and Implications for the Profession' (1983) 14(5) *Professional Psychology: Research and Practice* 670

Thornton, Dora, *The Scholar in His Study: Ownership and Experience in Renaissance Italy* (New Haven: Yale University Press, 1998)

Thornton, Margaret, 'Corrosive Leadership (Or Bullying by Another Name): A Corollary of the Corporatised Academy?' (2004) 17(2) *Australian Journal of Labour Law* 161

Tilden, Samuel J, 'Incarceration, Restitution, and Lifetime Debarment: Legal Consequences of Scientific Misconduct in the Eric Poehlman Case' (2010) 16(4) *Science and Engineering Ethics* 737

Till, Frank J, *Sexual Harassment: A Report on the Sexual Harassment of Students* (The National Advisory Council on Women's Educational Programs, August 1980)

Tilstone, William J, Kathleen A Savage and Leigh A Clark, *Forensic Science: An Encyclopedia of History, Methods and Techniques* (Santa Barbara, Calif.: ABC-CLIO, 2006)

Titus, Sandra L and Xavier Bosch, 'Tie Funding to Research Integrity' (2010) 466(7305) *Nature* 436

Titus, Sandra L, James A Wells and Lawrence J Rhoades, 'Repairing Research Integrity' (2008) 453(7198) Nature 980

Tobin, Terence K and Michael Sexton, LexisNexis, *Australian Defamation Law and Practice* (at Service 75, March 2015)

Tolson, Mike, 'Effect of 'Dr Death' and His Testimony Lingers', *Houston Chronicle*, 17 June 2004

Topol, Eric J and David Blumenthal, 'Physicians and the Investment Industry' (2005) 293(21) *The Journal of the American Medical Association* 2654

Topping, Alexandra, 'Historian Orlando Figes Agrees to Pay Damages for Fake Reviews', *The Guardian*, 16 July 2010

Torres, Ida, 'Stem Cell Researcher Paves the Way for Young, Female Japanese Scientists', *Japan Daily Press*, 4 February 2014

'Tortious Acts as a Basis for Jurisdiction in Products Liability Cases' (1965) 33(4) *Fordham Law Review* 675

Tozer, James, 'Shame of Dr Copycat: TV Shrink Raj Persaud Used Work of Others as his Own', *Daily Mail*, 17 June 2008

Tozer, James, 'Shamed TV Star Dr Raj Persaud Blames 'Carelessness and Deadline Pressure' for Plagiarism in his Books', *Daily Mail*, 18 June 2008

Tracy, Michael W, 'Whistleblowing in Corporate America: Organizational Factors and their Influence on the Employee Decision-Making Process' (PhD dissertation, Walden University, 2006)

Transparency International, *Global Corruption Report: Education* (Abingdon, Oxon: Routledge, 2013)

Transparency International, *Whistleblowing in Europe: Legal Protections for Whistleblowers in the EU* (2013)

Travaglia, Joanne and Deborah Debono, *Peer Review in Medicine: A Comprehensive Review of The Literature* (Centre for Clinical Governance Research in Health, University of New South Wales, Sydney, 2009)

Travis, John, 'After Legal Threat and 3-Year Delay, Paper on Psychopathy to Appear—Maybe' (2010) 328(5984) *Science* 1350
Trounson, Andrew, 'UWA Drops Economist Prof's Sex Probe', *The Australian*, 4 February 2009
Tugend, Alina, 'Opting to Blow the Whistle or Choosing to Walk Away', *The New York Times*, 20 September 2013
Tuller, David, 'Fallout from Fatigue Syndrome Retraction is Wide', *The New York Times*, 6 February 2012
Turnitin
Turvey, Brent E, 'Forensic Frauds: A Study of 42 Cases' (2003) 4(1) *Journal of Behavioral Profiling*
Turvey, Brent E, *Forensic Fraud: Evaluating Law Enforcement and Forensic Science Cultures in the Context of Examiner Misconduct* (PhD dissertation, Bond University, 2012)
Turvey, Brent E, *Forensic Fraud: Evaluating Law Enforcement and Forensic Science Cultures in the Context of Examiner Misconduct* (Amsterdam: Elsevier/Academic Press, 2013)
'Tutors Taunted: Academics Offer Examples of 'Upwards Harassment' by Students and Consider Possible Motives', *Times Higher Education*, 18 June 2009
Tysome, Tony, 'Suicide Don under 'Huge Stress' in Job', *Times Higher Education*, 15 September 2006
UC San Diego, School of Medicine, Division of Medical Education, 'University of California State Oath of Allegiance. Patent Policy, and Patent Acknowledgment'
UK Department of Health, *Trust, Assurance and Safety: The Regulation of Health Professionals in the 21st Century* (CM 7013, 2007)
UK Government, 'Appointment of New Forensic Science Regulator Announced', 17 July 2014
UK Government, Forensic Science Regulator, 'About Us—What We Do'
UK Government, Forensic Science Regulator, 'Terms of Reference for the Quality Standards Specialist Group', 14 January 2007
UK Research Integrity Office, *Code of Practice for Research: Promoting Good Practice and Preventing Misconduct* (September 2009)
'UNC Chapel Hill Fires Physics Professor Jailed in Argentina', *Fox8*, 24 May 2014
'Uni Scam Man Must Repay $300K', *Bendigo Advertiser*, 25 October 2007
Universities UK, *The Concordat to Support Research Integrity* (July 2012)
University of Adelaide, Legal and Risk, *Whistleblower Protection* (Last updated 3 April 2014)
University of Adelaide, *Code of Conduct* (December 2014)
University of Auckland, 'Campus Rules', 12 December 2012
University of Cambridge, Human Resources Division, Policies and Procedures, 'Misconduct in Research'
University of Cambridge, Policies and Procedures, 'Public Disclosure by University Employees: 'Whistleblowing' Policy' (17 February 2015)
University of Connecticut, 'Public Notification'
University of Dundee, *Code of Practice for Supervised Postgraduate Research* (August 2004)
University of Greenwich, 'Relationships Between Staff and Their Students: Guidelines for Managers' (January 2015)
University of Iowa, 'Sexual Harassment Can Happen Anywhere' (2009)
University of Manchester, 'Consensual Relationships Policy' (November 2009)
University of Maryland, 'Commercial Use of Course Materials'
University of Maryland, University Health Center, 'FSAP—Confronting Substance Abuse'
University of Melbourne, 'Academic Honesty and Plagiarism'
University of Melbourne, 'Academic Honesty and Plagiarism: Practical Advice to Students'
University of Melbourne, Office for Research Ethics and Integrity, 'Conflict of Interest'
University of Melbourne, Regulation 17.1.R8, Code of Conduct for Research, University Secretary's Department: Statutes and Regulation
University of Melbourne, 'Someone Says I Sexually Harassed Them …' (Equal Opportunity Unit, Human Resources, November 2000)
University of Melbourne, 'Invention Disclosure Policy' (Approved by Council, December 2006
University of Melbourne, 'Staff/Student Relationships: Drawing the Line' (July 2010)
University of Melbourne, 'Staff-Student Relationships Procedure' (MPF 1137)' (Melbourne Policy Library, 21 August 2012)

University of Melbourne, 'IP Policy' on *Research, Innovation and Commercialisation* (Last modified: 6 September 2012)
University of Melbourne, Melbourne Policy Library, 'Whistleblowers and Protected Disclosure Procedure (MPF1217)' (Approved 10 September 2013)
University of Melbourne, 'Intellectual Property' on *Research, Innovation and Commercialisation* (Last modified: 18 February 2014)
University of Miami, 'Consensual Relationships'
University of Miami, 'Sexual Harassment FAQs'
University of Miami, 'Sexual Harassment'
University of New South Wales, *Code of Conduct* (June 2009)
University of New South Wales, 'How Does Plagiarism Happen?' (last updated 27 February 2014)
University of Oxford, *Academic Good Practice—A Practical Guide*
University of Oxford, Personnel Services, 'Academic Integrity in Research: Code of Practice and Procedure'
University of Oxford, 'University Policy on Harassment and Bullying'
University of Oxford, 'Misuse of Alcohol and Drugs in the Workplace (Staff)', OHS Policy Document: OHS 1/06
University of Oxford, 'Part B, Intellectual Property' on *Statute XVI: Property, Contracts, and Trusts* (Last amended: 12 October 2011)
University of Oxford, Research Support, 'Statement of Policy and Procedure on Conflict of Interest', 25 June 2012
University of Oxford, Policies and Codes of Practice, 'Public Interest Disclosure: Code of Practice' (Last updated 21 March 2013)
University of Pretoria, 'Plagiarism', 12 August 2003
University of South Australia, Policies and Procedures, *Fraud Control Procedures* (Last revised 21 December 2012)
University of South Wales, 'Code of Conduct on Personal Relationships Between Staff and Students' (January 2010)
University of Sydney, 'Policy on the Use of University Information and Communication Technology Resources (ICT Resources)'
University of Sydney, 'Research Misconduct'
University of Sydney, 'Alcohol: Policy and Guidelines on Consumption', 3 November 1992
University of Sydney, 'Academic Dishonesty and Plagiarism in Coursework Policy', 1 January 2012
University of Sydney, The, 'Intellectual Property' (Last updated: 30 July 2014)
University of Texas, Arlington, Regulatory Services, 'Conflict of Interest'
University of Warwick, 'Personal Conflicts of Interest: Guidance for Staff and Students' (December 2009)
University of Western Australia, Human Resources, 'University Policy On: Conflicts of Interest' (Policy No. UP12/32)
University of Western Australia, *Report of the Review of Orientation* (August 2012) 29-30
University of Western Australia, The, 'University Policy on Intellectual Property', Policy No. UP07/49 (Revised: 28 April 2014)
University of Vermont College of Medicine, Office of the Dean, 'Investigation Report: In the Matter of Eric T Poehlman', 18 April 2002
Upshaw Downs, J C and Anjali Ranadive Sienton (eds), *Ethics in Forensic Science* (Oxford: Academic Press, 2012)
US Attorney's Office, Middle District of Pennsylvania, 'Former Penn State Professor Who Plead Guilty in $3 Million Federal Research Grant Fraud Sentenced in Federal Court' (Press Release, 30 November 2012)
US Department of Health and Human Services, The Office of Research Integrity, 'Definition of Research Misconduct'
US Department of Health & Human Services, The Office of Research Integrity, 'Policy on Plagiarism' (December 1994)

US Department of Health and Human Services, The Office of Research Integrity, 'Handling Misconduct—Whistleblowers' (20 November 1995)
US Department of Health and Human Services, The Office of Research Integrity, 'Case Summary—Eric T Poehlman' (Last updated 25 November 2013)
US Department of Health and Human Services, The Office of Research Integrity, 'Case Summary—Han, Dong-Pyou' (Last updated 23 December 2013)
US Department of Health and Human Services, The Office of Research Integrity, 'Whistleblower's Bill of Rights—Appendix A' (Last updated 8 May 2014)
US Department of Health and Human Services, The Office of Research Integrity, 'Press Release—Dr Eric T Poehlman' (17 March 2005)
US Department of the Interior, *Integrity of Scientific and Scholarly Activities*
US Department of Labor, *Whistleblower Protections*
US Securities and Exchange Commission, 'SEC Issues First Whistleblower Program Award' (Press Release, 2012-162, 21 August 2012)
'U.S. Settles Case of Gene Therapy Study That Ended With Teen's Death' (2005) 51(21) *University of Pennsylvania Almanac*
Uys, Tina, 'Changes in the Sociology of Business Ethics: Researching Whistleblowing' (2011) 5(1) *African Journal of Business Ethics* 50
Valencia, Milton J and John R Ellement, 'Annie Dookhan Pleads Guilty in Drug Lab Scandal', *The Boston Globe*, 22 November 2013
Valentine, Daniel P, '*Chou v. University of Chicago*: Assigned Patent Rights—Gone But Not Forgotten' (2002) 42(4) *Jurimetrics* 493
van Caenegem, William, '*VUT v Wilson, UWA v Gray* and University Intellectual Property Policies' (2010) 21(3) *Australian Intellectual Property Journal* 148
Van der Weyden, Martin, 'Managing Allegations of Scientific Misconduct and Fraud: Lessons from the 'Hall Affair'' (2004) 180(4) *Medical Journal of Australia* 149
Van der Weyden, Martin, 'Preventing and Processing Research Misconduct: A New Australian Code for Responsible Research' (2006) 184(9) *Medical Journal of Australia* 430
Van Dijk, Wilco W and Ouwerkerk, Jaap W, *Schadenfreude: Understanding Pleasure at the Misfortune of Others* (Cambridge: Cambridge University Press, 2013)
Van Onselen, Peter, *Liberals and Power: The Road Ahead* (Carlton, Vic: Melbourne University Press, 2008)
Vandekerckhove, Wim, *Whistleblowing and Organizational Social Responsibility: A Global Assessment* (Aldershot, Hampshire: Ashgate, 2006)
Vasagar, Jeevan, 'Gaddafi Donation to LSE May Have Come From Bribes, Inquiry Finds', *The Guardian*, 30 November 2011
Vastag, Brian, 'Cancer Fraud Case Stuns Research Community, Prompts Reflection on Peer Review Process' (2006) 98(6) *Journal of the National Cancer Institute* 374
Vaughn, Robert G, *The Successes and Failures of Whistleblower Laws* (Cheltenham: Edward Elgar, Cheltenham, 2012)
Vaux, David, 'From Fraud to Fair Play: Australia Must Support Research Integrity', *The Conversation*, 25 July 2013
Velleman, J David, *Foundations for Moral Relativism* (Cambridge: Open Book Publishers, 2013).
Vergano, Dan, 'Updated: Harvard Says Marc Hauser Guilty of Scientific Misconduct', *USA Today*, 20 August 2010
Verified Complaint against Vicente C Sotto III (Committee on Ethics and Privileges, 7 November 2012)
Vespa, Matt, 'Senator Walsh's Plagiarism Scandal, PTSD References Angers Veterans', *Townhall.com*, 27 July 2014
Vice, Sue, *Holocaust Fiction* (New York: Routledge, 2003)
Vincent, Frank, *Report on the Circumstances that Led to the Conviction of Mr Farah Abdulkadir Jama* (Melbourne: Victorian Government Printer, 2010)
'Violating Nature' (1977) 109(11) *Time* 74
Vogel, Gretchen, 'Jan Hendrik Schön Loses his PhD', *Science Insider*, 19 September 2011

Vogel, Gretchen, 'German Research Minister Faces Plagiarism Allegations', *Science*, 2 May 2012

Vogel, Gretchen and Kai Kupferschmidt, 'German Research Minister Schavan Resigns in Plagiarism Scandal', *Science*, 9 February 2013

Von Sternberg, Constantin, 'On Plagiarism' (1919) 5(3) *The Musical Quarterly* 390

Vorotnikov, Eugene, 'Government to Combat Plagiarism and Illegal Degrees', Issue No. 309, *University World News*, 24 February 2014

Vuorio, Eero, 'Finland: How to Revise National Research Integrity Guidelines in the Changing International Landscape?' in Tony Mayer and Nicholas Steneck (eds), *Promoting Research Integrity in a Global Environment* (World Scientific, Singapore, 2012), pp 63–66

Wade, Nicholas, 'Harvard Finds Scientist Guilty of Misconduct', *The New York Times*, 20 August 2010

Wade, Nicholas, 'University Suspects Fraud by a Researcher Who Studied Red Wine', *The New York Times*, 11 January 2012

Wager, Elizabeth and Williams, Peter, 'Why and How Do Journals Retract Articles? An Analysis of Medline Retractions 1988-2008' (2011) 37 *Journal of Medical Ethics* 567

Wager, Elizabeth and Williams, Peter, "Hardly Worth the Effort'? Medical Journals' Policies and their Editors' and Publishers' Views on Trial Registration and Publication Bias: Quantitative and Qualitative Study' (2013) 347 *BMJ* f5248

Wakefield, Andrew J, *Callous Disregard: Autism and Vaccines—The Truth Behind a Tragedy* (New York: Skyhorse Publishing, 2010)

Wallace-Wells, Benjamin, 'What Was Brandeis Thinking When it Invited Ayaan Hirsi Ali to Speak?' *New York Magazine*, 15 April 2014

Waller, John, *Fabulous Science: Fact and Fiction in the History of Scientific Discovery* (Oxford: Oxford University Press, 2004)

Walsh, John, *Jan Steen: The Drawing Lesson* (Malibu, Calif: J Paul Getty Museum, 1996)

Walsh, John, 'Historian's Wife and Her Poison Pen Expose Darkside of Literary Criticism', *The Independent*, 20 April 2010

Wangshu, Luo, 'Professor in Sex Scandal Quits', *China Daily*, 3 December 2014

Wardle, Jon, 'Plagiarism and Registered Health Professionals: Navigating the Borderlands Between Scholarly and Professional Misconduct' (2013) 21(2) *Journal of Law and Medicine* 399

Wark, Colin and John F Galliher, 'Timothy Leary, Richard Alpert (Ram Dass) and the Changing Definition of Psilocybin' (2010) 21(3) *International Journal of Drug Policy* 234

Warrick, Patricia S, *Charles Babbage and the Countess* (Bloomington, IN: Authorhouse, 2007)

'Waseda: Obokata Committed Plagiarism but Can Keep Doctorate', *The Asahi Shimbun*, 18 July 2014

'Waseda Rapped on Dissertation Scrutiny', *The Japan Times*, 18 July 2014

'Waseda to Strip Obokata of Doctorate Unless She Corrects Her Dissertation', *The Japan Times*, 7 October 2014

'Waseda to Strip Biologist Obokata of Doctorate', *The Japan Times*, 30 October 2015

Waterford, Jack, 'Crucial Evidence Used in Eastman Trial Came from Expert Sacked in Victoria', *Canberra Times*, 7 November 2012

Waterton, Charles, *Wanderings in South America* (New York: Cosimo Classics, 2005 [EP Dutton & Co, 1825]

Wazana, Ashley, 'Physicians and the Pharmaceutical Industry: Is a Gift Ever Just a Gift?' (2000) 283(3) *The Journal of the American Medical Association* 373

Weaver, David, Moema H Reis, Christopher Albanese, Frank Constantini, David Baltimore and Thereza Imanishi-Kari, 'Altered Repertoire of Endogenous Immunoglobulin Gene Expression in Transgenic Mice Containing a Rearranged Mu Heavy Chain Gene' (1986) 45(2) *Cell* 247, retracted by David Weaver, Christopher Albanese, Frank Constantini and David Baltimore (1991) 65(4) *Cell* 536

Weber, Leonard J, *Profits Before People? Ethical Standards and the Marketing of Prescription Drugs* (Bloomington: Indiana University Press, 2006)

Webb, Sam and Vincent Graff, 'Korean Scientist Behind Britain's First Cloned Dog is a Convicted Fraudster Who Was Forced to Quit University for Making Up Results', *Daily Mail*, 10 April 2014

Weeks, Jeffrey, *Sexuality and Its Discontents: Meanings, Myths, and Modern Sexualities* (New York: Taylor & Francis, 2002)

Weigend, Thomas, 'Short Review: *The Trial Proceedings of the International Criminal Court: ICTY and ICTR Precedents* by Karin N Calvo-Goller'

Weil, Andrew T, 'The Strange Case of the Harvard Drug Scandal', *Look Magazine*, 5 November 1963

Weiler, Joseph, 'Book Reviewing and Academic Freedom' (2010) 20(4) *EJIL* 968

Weiler, Joseph, 'In the Dock, in Paris—The Judgment' on *EJIL: Talk!* (4 March 2011)

Weiner, Joseph S, *The Piltdown Forgery* (Oxford: Oxford University Press, [1955] 2003)

Weinstein, Henry C, 'How Should Forensic Psychiatry Police Itself? Guidelines and Grievances: The AAPL Committee on Ethics' (1984) 12(3) *Bulletin of the American Academy of Psychiatry & the Law* 289

Weir, William, 'Discredited Scientist Plans to Sue UConn for Libel', *The Hartford Courant*, 25 January 2013

Weiss, Raymond B, Robert M Rifkin, F Marc Stewart, Richard L Theriault, Lori A Williams, Allen A Herman, and Roy A Beveridge, 'High Dose Chemotherapy for High-Risk Primary Breast Cancer: An On-Site Review of the Bezwoda Study' (2000) 355(9208) *The Lancet* 999

Wells, Frank, 'Historical Aspects of Research Misconduct: Europe' in Frank Wells and Michael Farthing (eds), *Fraud and Misconduct in Biomedical Research* (4th edn, London: Royal Society of Medicine Press, 2008), pp 72–88

Wenner, Melinda, 'Gene Therapy: An Interview with an Unfortunate Pioneer', *Scientific American*, 17 August 2009

Wertheim, Christine, 'The Fall and Rise of Ernest Lalor Malley' (Spring 2009), Issue 33, *Cabinet Magazine*

'When the Cheating Has to Stop' (9 April 1981) *New Scientist* 68.

'Which Professions are Regulated in Ontario?' *Settlement.Org*

'Whistleblowers: Plagiarism Scandal Returns to Haunt V-C', *Times Higher Education*, 21 June 2002

'Whistleblowers a Vulnerable Species', *Thanh Nien News*, 16 November 2012

White, Harold O, *Plagiarism and Imitation during the English Renaissance: A Study in Critical Distinctions* (New York: Octagon Books, 1965)

White House, 'Fact Sheet on Presidential Memorandum on Scientific Integrity' (Briefing Room, Statements and Releases, 9 March 2009)

White, Sara J, 'Student Nurses Harassing Academics' (2013) 33(1) *Nurse Education Today* 41

White, Welsh S, 'Waiver and the Death Penalty: The Implications of *Estelle v Smith*' (1981) 72(4) *The Journal of Criminal Law & Criminology* 1522

Whitely, William P, Drummond Rennie, and Arthur W Hafner, 'The Scientific Community's Response to Evidence of Fraudulent Publication: The Robert Slutsky Case' (1994) 272(2) *Journal of the American Medical Association* 170

Whittaker, John R, 'Paul Kammerer and the Suspect Siphons', *MBL Science* (1985)

Wiig, Karl M, *Knowledge Management Foundations: Thinking About Thinking: How People and Organizations Create, Represent, and Use Knowledge* (Arlington, Tex: Schema Press, 1993)

Wild, Ronald A, *An Introduction to Sociological Perspectives: Theory and Research in the Australian Context* (North Sydney, NSW: Allen and Unwin, 1985)

Wilhoit, Stephen, 'Helping Students Avoid Plagiarism' (1994) 42(4) *College Teaching* 161

Wilkinson, Geoff, '$1.4m Lure for Trauma Surgeon Thomas Kossmann to Stay', *Herald Sun*, 10 June 2008

Wilkinson, Geoff, 'Top Doctor Thomas Kossmann Wins Apology as The Alfred Settles $30m Lawsuit', *Herald Sun*, 22 January 2011

Williams, Kipling D, *Ostracism: The Power of Silence* (New York: Guilford Press, 2001)

Williams, Peter and Wager, Elizabeth, 'Why and How do Journal Editors Retract Articles: Findings from a Qualitative Study' (2013) 19 *Science and Engineering Ethics* 1

Wilmshurst, Peter, 'The Code of Silence' (1997) 349(9051) *Lancet* 567

Wilmshurst, Peter, 'Dishonesty in Medical Research' (Address to the Medico-Legal Society, 9 December 2004) 75(1) *Medico-Legal Journal* 3

Wilson, Duff, 'Harvard Medical School in Ethics Quandary', *The New York Times,* 2 March 2009
Wilson, Duff, 'Drug Maker Hired Writing Company for Doctors' Book, Documents Say', *The New York Times*, 29 November 2010
Wilson, Elizabeth, 'Superheavy Furor' (22 Jly 2002) 80(2) *Chemical and Engineering News*
Wilson, Logan, *The Academic Man: A Study in the Sociology of a Profession* (New York: Oxford University Press, 1942)
Wilson, Robin, 'Professor Accused of Sexual Harassment Resigns', *The Chronicle of Higher Education*, 30 January 2008
Wilson, Robin Fretwell, 'The Death of Jesse Gelsinger: New Evidence of the Influence of Money and Prestige in Human Research' (2010) 36(2-3) *American Journal of Law & Medicine* 295
Winter, James P, *Lies the Media Tell Us* (Montreal: Black Rose Books, 2007)
Wise, Jacqui, 'Boldt: The Great Pretender' (2013) 346 *BMJ* 1738
Woldring, Klaas (ed), *Business Ethics in Australia and New Zealand: Essays and Cases* (South Melbourne: Nelson, 1996)
Wolf, Naomi, 'The Silent Treatment', *New York*, 1 March 2004
Wolfe, Morris, 'Dr. Fabrikant's Solution', *Grubstreet Books*
Wolfe, Simon, Mark Worth, Suelette Dreyfus, and Alexander J Brown, *Whistleblower Protection Rules in G20 Countries: The Next Action Plan* (Public Consultation Draft, June 2014)
Wolitz, David, 'Innocence Commissions and the Future of Post-Conviction Review' (2010) 52(4) *Arizona Law Review* 1027
Woodhouse, Howard, *Selling Out: Academic Freedom and the Corporate Market (*McGill-Queen's University Press, Quebec, 2009)
Woolf, Lord Justice, *An Inquiry into the LSE's Links with Libya and Lessons to be Learned* (Woolf Report) (October 2011)
Wootten, John H, 'The Orr Dismissal and the Universities' (1957) 1(2) *Quadrant* 25
World Association of Medical Editors, 'Self-Plagiarism of Textbook Chapters' (October 2004)
Worthington, Elise, 'University of Queensland Investigates Fresh Claims of Research Misconduct by Former Academics', *ABC News,* 8 November 2013
Worthington, Elise, 'Former University of Queensland Professor Bruce Murdoch Charged Over Fake Parkinson's Research', *ABC News,* 12 December 2014
Wortley, Richard, Peter Cassematis, and Marika Donkin, 'Who Blows the Whistle, Who Doesn't and Why?' in Alexander J Brown (ed), *Whistleblowing in the Australian Public Sector: Enhancing the Theory and Practice of Internal Witness Management in Public Sector Organisations* (Canberra, ACT: ANU E Press, 2008), pp 53–82
Wu, Shanlon, 'Put the Intent Back into Plagiarism!' *Huffington Post*, 12 November 2014
Wyndham, Susan, 'Plagiarism the Word that Can't be Uttered', *The Sydney Morning Herald*, 13 September 2013
Yale University, Division of the Vice President and General Counsel, 'Sexual Harassment'
Yale University, Office for Equal Opportunity Programs, 'Policy on Teacher-Student Consensual Relations'
Yale University, Office of Research Administration, *Responsible Conduct of Research*
Yale University, Office of Research Administration, *Yale University Policy on Conflict of Interest*, revised 29 November 2012
Yale University, School of Medicine 2014-2015, 'Human Relations Code of Conduct'
Yamada, Shoh, 'Politics and Personality: The Anatomy of Japan's Worst Archaeology Scandal' (2002) 6(3) *Harvard Asia Quarterly* 48
Vang, Ole and Dipak K Das (eds), 'Resveratrol and Health' (Special Issue) (2011) 1215 *Annals of the New York Academy of Sciences* 1–170
Yardley, Jim, 'Inquiry Focuses on Scientist Used by Prosecutors', *The New York Times*, 2 May 2001
Yardley, Jim, 'Flaws in Chemist's Findings Free Man at Center of Inquiry', *The New York Times*, 8 May 2001
Yardley, Jim, 'Oklahoma Retraces Big Step in Capital Case', *The New York Times*, 2 September 2001
Yeo, Shelley, 'First-Year University Science and Engineering Students' Understanding of Plagiarism' (2007) 26(2) *Higher Education Research & Development* 199

Yi, Ren, 'National, Institutional and International Approaches to Research Integrity: An Australian Perspective' in Tony Mayer and Nicholas Steneck (eds), *Promoting Research Integrity in a Global Environment* (Singapore: World Scientific, 2012), pp 55–62

Yoshida, Junko, 'Obokata Scandal Puts Research in Peril', *EE Times*, 12 April 2014

Young, S Mark, and Drew Pinsky, 'Narcissism and Celebrity' (2006) 40(5) *Journal of Research in Personality* 463

Yu, Xi, 'Harvard Medical School Restricts Ties to Industry', *The Harvard Crimson*, 21 July 2010

Yu, Xi, 'Three Professors Face Sanctions Following Harvard Medical School Inquiry', *The Harvard Crimson*, 2 July 2011

Yung, Adele and Sharma Yojana, 'Academic Found Guilty of Fraud on 'Unprecedented' Scale' (11 January 2013) Issue No. 254, *University World News*

Zalk, Sue Rosenberg, 'Men in the Academy: A Psychological Profile of Harassment' in Michele A Paludi (ed), *Ivory Power: Sexual Harassment on Campus* (Albany, NY: State University of New York Press, 1996), pp 81–114

Zamboni, Mauro, *Law and Politics: A Dilemma for Contemporary Legal Theory* (Dordrecht: Springer, 2007)

Zaretsky, Robert, 'French Chief Rabbi's Fall from Grace in Plagiarism Scandal', *The Jewish Daily Forward*, 24 April 2013

Zarychanski, Ryan, Ahmed M Abou-Setta, Alexis F Turgeon, Brett L Houston et al. 'Association of Hydroxyethyl Starch Administration with Mortality and Acute Kidney Injury in Critically Ill Patients Requiring Volume Resuscitation: A Systematic Review and Meta-Analysis' (2013) 309(7) *The Journal of the American Medical Association* 678

Zedeck, Morris S, *Expert Witness in the Legal System: A Scientist's Search for Justice* (Pittsburgh: Lauriat Press, 2010)

Zeleny, Jeff, 'Clinton Camp Says Obama Plagiarized in Speech', *The New York Times*, 19 February 2008

Zeveloff, Julie, 'Half of the Students in Harvard's Massive Cheating Scandal Have been Forced to Withdraw', *Business Insider Australia*, 2 February 2013

Zhmud, Leonid, *Pythagoras and the Early Pythagoreans* (Oxford: Oxford University Press, 2012)

Zielinska, Edyta, 'Chronic Fatiigue Researcher Fired', *The Scientist*, 4 October 2011

Zimbardo, Philip G, 'The Psychology of Evil: A Situationist Perspective on Recruiting Good People to Engage in Anti-Social Acts' (1995) 11(2) *Research in Social Psychology* 125

Zimbardo, Philip G, *The Lucifer Effect: Understanding How Good People Turn Evil* (New York: Random House, 2008)

Zimmerman, Susan V and Wallace, Karen, 'Promoting Responsible Conduct of Research: A Canadian Perspective' (2013) 20 *Accountability in Research* 395

Zweifler, Seth, 'Prominent Philosopher to Leave U. of Miami in Wake of Misconduct Allegations', *The Chronicle of Higher Education*, 4 June 2013

[illegible]

Zimbardo, Philip. [illegible] New York: Random House, 2008.

Zimmerman, Joseph F. [illegible] A Comparative Perspective [illegible]

[illegible]

INDEX

Academics
deference toward 10
fiduciaries 339
academy, the 9, 10
Adams, Michelle 490–1
Agent Orange 368
Ahimastos, Anna 104–5
alabamine 65
Albanese, Anthony 298
Albanian immigrant appendicitis scandal 186
alchemists 1
alcoholism *see also* **substance abuse** 443–4
early identification 445
Harvard University 447
San Francisco State University policy 446
signs 444–5
University of Auckland policy 447–8
University of Maryland policy 445
University of Oxford policy 445
University of Sydney alcohol policy 445
workplace indicators 446
Alfred Hospital (Melbourne, Australia)
Kossmann, Thomas 188–9
Ali, Ayaan Hirsi 384–5
Ali, Nasrul 431
Alpert, Richard (*see also* **Leary, Timothy**) 448
Alzheimer's research
False Claims Act case 150–1
American Association of University Professors
plagiarism 256
American Chemical Society 15
American Journal of Psychiatry 178
American Medical Association 416
American Psychiatric Association 179, 449
American Society of Crime Laboratory Directors/ Laboratory Accreditation Board (ASCLD/ LAB) 220–1
Amis, Kingsley 440
Amlodipine 137
Ammon, Robert Jr 422–3
anaesthetic fraud
Boldt, Joachim 90–1
Fujii,Yoshitaka 91–4
Reuben, Scott 122–5
Anderton, John 137–8, 506
Angell, Marcia 8, 511–2
anti-corruption commissions 13
Corruption and Crime Commission (WA) 13, 431
Crime and Misconduct Commission (Qld) 185
Independent Broad-Based Anti-Corruption Commission (IBAC) (Vic) 477
Independent Commission against Corruption (ICAC) (NSW) 271, 328–9, 475
Anti-depressant research
Nemeroff, Charles 187–8
Anti-Plagiat 293
Apotex 191
Aptuit
Eaton, Steven 126
Ark of the Covenant litigation 350–4
Ashberry, John 262
Association of American Medical Colleges (AAMC) (S) 170
Association of American Universities (AAU) 170
Association of Universities and Colleges of Canada (AUCC) 157
Asthma research 61
Atlantis Hoax 57–8
attention deficit hyperactivity disorder (ADHD) research 114, 186–7
Australia and New Zealand Policing Advisory Agency (ANZPAA) 252
Australian Code for the Responsible Conduct of Research 23
research misconduct 23–4, 162
Australian Communications and Media Authority
Hall complaint 111
Australian Medical Association
Code of Ethics 348
Australian Medical Council
non-denigration policy 347
Australian Psychological Society 349
Australian Research Council 161
Australian Research Integrity Committee 113, 162–4
Australian Research Integrity Framework 162
authenticity *see* **originality**
autism fraud 146–8
autobiographies
Blair, Jayson 267–9
McBride, William 142
Mikovits, Judy 88
Stapel, Diederik 37–44
Wakefield, Andrew 147
authorship policy
JAMA 45

Babbage, Charles 21, 503, 578
cooking 21
definitions of research misconduct 21
forging 21–2
hoaxing 21–2
trimming 21–2
Bacon, Sir Francis 3
Baltimore, David 106
Bannerjee, Anjan 113, 504
Barach, Paul 489–90
Barefoot v Estelle 217–18
Barnes, Robert 14
Barwood, Caroline 129–30, 515
Bayh-Dole Act 333–4
Beech, Baroness 280
Bender, William 419
Beringer, Johann 54–5, 504
Bernheim, Gilles 287–8
Bezwoda, Werner 81–2, 504
Biben, Ellen
report 220
Biden, Joe 270
Bidloo, Govert (Gottfried) 261
Biederman, Joseph 179, 186–7
Big Business 512
Big Pharma 178, 512
Bishop, Amy 391–2
Bishop, Julie 297
Blair, Jayson 267–9, 504
Blech, David 329
Blondlot, Rene 30
Bloom, Harold *see also* **Wolf, Naomi** 399–401
Blumsohn, Aubrey 460–1, 488–9
Boldt, Joachim 90–1, 505
Landesarztekammer Rheinland-Pfalz (LAK-RLP) 90
retractions 91
Bolsin, Stephen 485–7, 515
Boston University
conflict of interest policy 177
Boyle, Robert 19
Brandeis, Louis 174–5
Brandeis University 385
Breen, Kerry 141–2
Brent, Ron 162
Breslow, Ronald 273
Breuning, Stephen 115–16, 484–5
Briggs, Michael 108–9
Brigham and Women's Hospital 73–4

Brimstone Butterfly fraud 66–7
Bristol Royal Infirmary *see also* **Bolsin, Stephen** 485–6
British Medical Journal (BMJ) 33
Bronowski, Jacob 1
Brown, Dan
The Da Vinci Code 299
Browne, John 260
Burt, Sir Cyril 30, 71–2, 505

Calvo-Goller, Karin 375–7
Canada
Tri-Agency Framework for the Responsible Conduct of Research 4, 157–8, 517, 534–42
Canadian Association of University Teachers
Olivieri Report 192
Canadian Institutes of Health Research (CIHR) 158
Canadian Medical Association 348
cancer research fraud
Bezwoda, Werner 81–2
Poisson, Roger 80–1
Sudbø, Jon 82–4
Capizzano, Ezio 423–5
Carabello, Bernard 457
Cardiff Giant Hoax 57
cardiology fraud
Darsee, John 73–4
Das, Dipak 97–8
Poldermans, Don 95–7
Cartwright Inquiry (NZ) 191–2
celebrity
intellect 38
scientist 124, 505
Centers for Medicare and Medicaid Services (CMS) 250
cento format, poetry *see also* **Poetry** 11, 262
Chace, Jeremy 345
Chamberlain case (Aust) 203
Chandra, Ranjit 49–50
Charlton, William 66–7, 503
Chatzimarkakis, Jorgo 285
Chávez, Lisa
sado-masochism 434
Chemotherapy fraud 84
Potti, Anil 84–7
Chen, Peter
peer review fraud 47–8
China
Association for Science and Technology (CAST) 161
Forensic Medicine Association 202
National Health and Family Planning Commission 161
National Natural Science Foundation of China 161
research fraud 160–1
Chiranjeevi, Pattium 266, 504
chronic fatigue syndrome fraud 87–8
Cicero 254, 258
City University of New York 436
Clift, Alan 205
climate change litigation
Lewandosky, Stephan 359–60
New Zealand 354–6
Cojocaru v British Columbia Women's Hospital and Health Center 318–20
cold fusion 30
Coleman, Jon T 440
Commission on Research Integrity 23
Committee on Publication Ethics (COPE)
peer review fraud 48
Concord Prison Experiment 449
Concordat to Support Research Integrity *see* **United Kingdom Universities' Concordat to Support Research Integrity,**
Concordia University 6, 388–91
condensed matter physics 63
confidentiality
revelation of patient identity 191
conflict of interest 170–98, 506
Boston University policy 177
corruption 194–6
financial 178–81
gifts 193–4
Harvard Medical School 177
intangible 172
mandatory notification system 172
Moore v Regents of University of California 181–2
National Women's Hospital scandal 190–1
non-disclosure 186–8
Oxford University policy 175–7
perceptions of influence 183–5
potential 171
tangible 172
taxonomies 171
University of Melbourne policy 175
University of Texas 172
Yale University policy 177
Constantine, Madonna 282
contraceptive pill fraud
Briggs, Michael 108
Cooke, David 360–5
cooking *see* **Babbage**
copyright 299, 194–6, 328–30
articles 330
books 330
ownership of lectures 330
Cornell University
Rhodes, Frank 510
coronium 65
corruption
Albanian Immigrant Appendicitis Scandal 186
Ali, Nasrul 431
China 196
employment 328–9
forensic misconduct 218
Institut fürWissenschaftsberatung 194
nepotism 185–6
Russia 293
Transparency International 196
United Nations Convention against Corruption 468, 473
costs awards against experts 247–8
Council of Canadian Academies 24
Council for the Registration of Forensic Practitioners (CRFP) 248
Cox–2 inhibitors 122
criminal prosecutions
Barwood, Caroline 129–30
Breuning, Stephen 115–6
Eaton, Steven 126
evolving approaches 130–1
Grimes, Craig 125
Han, Dong-Pyou 126–9
Hwang, Woo-Suk 120–2
Murdoch, Bruce 129–30
Poehlman, Eric 116–9
Reuben, Scott 122–5
Van Parijs, Luk 119–20
Crookes, Sir John 65
Crime and Misconduct Commission (Qld)
Greenfield investigation 185
CSI effect 201
Curtin University 13
cyberstalking 379–80

DAMP research 132
Darsee, John 73, 504
Das, Dipak 97–8, 504
data destruction *see also* **Gillberg, Christopher** 131–7
Daubert v Merrell Dow Pharmaceuticals
Dawkins reforms, 7
Dawson, Charles 58–9
Deakin University
Briggs, Michael 108

Ombudsman investigation 195
plagiarism scandal 278
De Chardin, Teilhard *see also* **Piltdown Man** 59
defamation
Australian law 371–3
British Chiropractic Association v Singh 369–70
chilling effect 369
El Naschie v MacMillan Publishers Ltd (trading as Nature Publishing Group) and Schiermeier 373–5
forum-shopping 376
Rath v Guardian News and Media Limited and Goldacre 370
Séralini, Gilles-Eric
United Kingdom law 369–71
United States law 365–9
deferiprone 191
degree forging 329
Del Castillo, Mariano 257, 311–4
Demidenko, Helen 11
denigration *see* **non-denigration**
De Nino, Walter 117
Deutsche Foschungsgeneinschaft (DFG) 152, 154
Dighton, John 345
Dingell, John (Congressman)
Baltimore hearing 106
Sprague, Robert 485
Disciplinary hearings
Ali, Dr 304–5
Alsabti, Elias 300–3
Anderton, John 137–8
Bannerjee, Anjan 139–40
Glamcevski, Mihajlo 309–10
Keough, William 307–9
Kumar, Dr 234–5
McBride, William 142–6
Meadow, Roy 225–30
Noble, Peter 241
Oelofse, Dr 232
Oshinyemi, Dr 234
Patel, Freddy 232–4
Pearce, Malcolm 138–9
Persaud, Raj 304
Pool, Richard 235–6
Prasad, Ashok 140–2
Southall, David 232
Siddiqui, Uzair 138
Squier, Waney 236–7
Watson-Munro, Timothy 240
Williams, Mark 139
Discrimination *see also* **Harassment**
Sex Discrimination Act 1975 403
Sex Discrimination Act 1984 (Aust) 403, 406
dishonesty in employment 326–44
Blech, David 329–30
corruption 328–30
degree forging 329
Eltchelebi, Waddah 327
Harvard University policy 34–341
ICAC investigation 328
Ogru, Esra 327
Ombudsman investigation 328
Oxford University policy 342
scams 326–8
Smith, Jim 326
University of Melbourne policy 342–3
University of Sydney policy 343–4
University of Technology, Sydney 329
disputation (intemperate) *see also* **defamation, non-denigration** 536
Ark litigation 350–4
climate change litigation (NZ) 354–6
defamation *see* **defamation**
Hare, Robert 360–5
Rindos, David 357–9
Trivers, Robert 356–7
Dissernet 12, 293
Djerassi, Carl
Cantor's Dilemma 513
Donnelly, Liam 421
Dookhan, Annie 213–15, 516
Dotson case 206
Drenth University (University of Amsterdam) 29
Dry-labbing 204, 208–16
Dookhan, Annie 213–15
Erdmann, Ralph 212–13
Farak, Sonja 215–16
Gilchrist, Joyce 210–12
Harding, David 208
Zain, Fred 208–10
Duke University 85
Dutton, Donald 421–2

Eastman judicial inquiry 203
Eaton, Steven 126, 506, 515
Ecstasy *see* **MDMA**
Einfeld, Marcus 311
Eliot, TS 261
El Naschie, Mohammed 37, 363, 373–5
Eltchelebi, Waddah 327
Emerson, Ralph Waldo 1, 439
Emory University 187
Erasmus 439
Erasmus University
Poldermans investigation 95–7
Erdmann, Ralph 212–13
Erin, Edward 61–3, 504
Estelle v Smith 217
ethics committees 166
European Code of Conduct for Research Integrity 25–6, 153
European Court of Human Rights
Gillberg case 133–6
Evans, Gillian 441
Expert evidence *see also* **forensic experts**
Law Commission of England and Waste 237
experts *see* **forensic experts**
Expert Panel on Research Integrity of the Council of Canadian Academies 157–8

Fabrikant, Valery
report about 6, 388–91
False Claims Act 149–52, 506
Poehlman, Eric 118
Farak, Sonja 215–6
Fenteany, Gabriel 443
fiduciary duties 181, 339
Figes, Orlando 378–9
fingerprint evidence 208
Finland National Research Ethics Committee 154
Firns, Ian 491
Fitzgerald, Ross 440
Fleischman, Stanley 30
florentium 65
Food and Drug Administration (FDA)
Gelsinger, Jesse 182
forensic experts
academites 205
bias 202
costs orders 247–8
dissemblers 204
duties 228–9
independence 202
pseudo-experts 204
role 199–200
simulators 204
whores of the court 202
Zain, Fred 203
forensic misconduct 199–253, 507–8
abandonment of scientific method 216–18
bias 205, 216–18
corruption 218
dry-labbing 208–16
fabrication of evidence 208
formulating theory too readily 206–7
impersonation 218–19
misunderstanding the forensic expert role 205
oversight 248–52
systemic issues 219–21
withholding evidence 207–8

forensic pathology
Erdman, Ralph 238–9
forensic science
biology 210–12
blood testing 210
Dookhan, Annie 212–14
drug testing 212–14, 215–16
Farak, Sonja 215–6
fibre testing 210
Gilchrist, Joyce 210–12
hair testing 210
oversight 248–52
semen testing 210
Zain, Fred 208–10
Forensic Science Advisory Council 249
Forensic Science Regulator (UK) 249, 517
forging *see* **Babbage**
Forster, EM 261
Frampton, Paul 442
freedom of expression 345, 367
Freeman, Derek 44
Friedman, Andrew 60
Fujii, Yoshitaka 91–4, 504
fraud investigation 92
retractions 93

Gaddafi, Saifal-Islam 9, 193–4, 507
Gallop, Jane 402
Gelsinger, Jesse 182–3, 506
ghost writing 7, 161, 263, 280, 297, 488, 489, 503, 518
gift authorship 7, 23, 50, 74, 93, 139, 263, 518
Gillberg, Christopher 132–7
Court of Appeal (Sweden) 133
DAMP 132–7
data destruction 132
European Court of Human Rights 133–5
Gothenburg study 132
Gilchrist, Joyce 210–12
Ginsburg, Allen 448
Gioeni, Cavalieri Giuseppe 21–2
Glamcevski, Mihaljo 309–10
Glasgow University 89
Golde, David 181
Golimumab research 62–3
Good Laboratories Practice Regulations (UK) 167
Gore, Al 154
Gothenburg University
Gillberg, Christopher 132
Gottlieb, Sidney 173
Goudge Inquiry *see also* **Smith, Charles** 14, 238–40
Grant, Cary 448
Grassley, Charles 180, 186
Gray, Bruce 335–40
Greenfield, Paul 185
Gresham's law 20
Grierson, Elizabeth 379–80
Griffith University 414
Grigson, James 216–7
Grimes, Craig 125, 506, 515
Gullis, Robert 379
Guttenberg, Karl-Theodor 284–5

Hahn, Johannes 287–8
Haley, Alex 261
Hall, Bruce 109–13
Brennan inquiry 110
defamation proceedings 111–12
duplication of investigations 515
Hume findings 110
injunction applications 110
Van der Weyden views 112
Han, Dong-Pyou 14, 21, 126–9, 503, 504, 515
Harassment *see also* **Discrimination**
abuse of trust 402
Ammon, Robert Jr 422–3
Bender, William 419
Capizzano, Ezio 423–5, 436
Chávez, Lisa 434
City University of New York 436
confidant 401
consensual amorous relation 402
contrapower 435
counsellor-helper 401
criminal charges 423–5
Donnelly, Liam 421
Dutton, Donald 422–3
ecological opportunities 395
extent in universities 405
Gallop, Jane 402
Griffith University 414
gender 400
gender ramifications 400
Harvard University policy 409–11
Hermassi, Elbaki 418–9
Hong Kong 408
infatuated 402
intellectual seducer 401
Macquarie University 414
McGinn, Colin 416, 419–21, 436
Namwamba, Tom 422
opportunist 401
Orr, Sidney Sparkes 426–8
Oxford University 349
power broker 401
private harasser 401
proof 425–6
public harasser 401
quid pro quo 395, 410
receptive non-initiator 402
risk-taker 402
seducer/demander 402
seductive behaviour 400
sexual 395, 400
sexual assault 400
sexual bribery 400
sexual coercion 400
sexual conqueror 402
sexualized conduct 434
sponsorship, abuse of 433
Syracuse University 349
transference 402
University of Colorado 418
University of Greenwich 413
University of Melbourne policy 412–13
University of Miami 416
University of Sydney 413
University of Warwick 415
untouchable 402
upwards 396, 434–5
Yale University 416–17, 436
Zambia 408
zero tolerance 416–17
Harding, David 208
Hare, Robert 360–5
Harrison, John Heslop 70–2, 503, 505
Harvard University
alcohol policy 447
Ali, Ayaan Hirsi 384
Biederman, Joseph 186–7
conflict of interest rules 187
intellectual property policies 340–1
Leary, Timothy 448–51
plagiarism scandal 277
plagiarism policy 276–7
sexual and gender-based harassment policy 409–11
Harvey, Ken 183–5
Hauser investigation 94–5
Hauser, Marc 94–5
Healy, David 346
heavy elements fraud 65–6
Heckenberger, Michael 443
Heraclitus 257
Hermassi, Elbaki 418–9
herpes virus research 339–41
Herschel, Sir John 65
Hibernium 65
high dose chemotherapy research 81
Hipparchus of Rhodes 500
HIV research fraud
Han, Dong Pyou 126
Hoaxes 54–60
Atlantis 57–8
cultural studies 10
criminalization 59–60
Gioeni, Cavalieri Giuseppe 21–2

Inhabitants of the Moon 56–7
literary 10–12
Lying Stones 54–6
Piltdown Man 2, 58–9
Sokal, Alan 10
Hodgkin's disease fraud
Long, John 155, 503
Hodgkinson, Suzanne *see also* **Hall, Bruce** 111
Holocaust denial
Irving, David 381–3
Rhodes, Frank 510
Salaita, Steven 384
Honderich, Ted 377–8
Hooper, Malcolm 148–9
Hospital for Sick Children, Toronto 191–2
Hoyt case 206–7
Huxley, Aldous 448–9
Hwang, Woo-Suk 120–2, 515
Hyperbaric oxygenation 148–9

immunology research
Hall, Bruce 109
Imanishi-Kari research 106
Summerlin, William 69–70
Van Parijs, Luk 119–20
Imanishi-Kari, Thereza 106–8, 460, 515, 519
Imperial College of London
research misconduct 23
Impersonation
Milosevic, Dusan 219
Morrison, Gene 219
Independent Commission against Corruption (ICAC) (NSW) 271, 328
Indian Institute of Technology, Madras 418
Inhabitants of the Moon Hoax 56–7
Inherited intelligence fraud 72–3
Institute of Medicine (US) 179
Intellectual property
Bayh-Dole Act 333–4
Harvard University policy 340–1
inventions 330
Oxford University Policy 342
Stanford v Roche 332–4
University of Melbourne policy 342–3
University of Sydney 343–4
integrity *see also* **scholarly integrity** 15–16, 19
American Chemical Society 15
Montreal Statement on Research Integrity 27–9
International Committee of Medical Journal Editors 507
Intermittent Explosive Disorder 234
inventions 330
Ioannidis, John 186
Iowa State University (of Science and Technology)
Han, Dong-Pyou 126
zero tolerance 416
IQ testing 72–3
Iran
Kordan, Ali 3
Irving, David 381–3
I'Thenticate 265, 508

Japan
National Research Council 159
Obokata, Haruko 98–104
Science Council 348
Jenner, Edward 30
jigong jinli 196, 198
Johnson, Samuel 255
Johnson, Wendell 173
Jones v Kaney 242–6
Jonson, Ben 255
Journal of the American Medical Association (JAMA)
Ahimastos article 104
authorship policy 45
journals 2, 7, 8, 18, 20
junk science 202
junonium 65

Kammerer, Paul 66–7, 503
Kazan University 442
Keats, John 375
Kenyatta University 422
Keough, William 307–9
Kesey, Ken 448
Khanna VK 218
King, Martin Luther 261, 299–300
knowledge 4
Koch-Mehrin, Silvana 285
Kordan, Ali 3
Kossmann, Thomas 187–8
Krugman, Saul 173
Kumar, Dr 234–5

LaBoeuf, Shia 10
Lane, Aaron 385
La Trobe University *see also* **Swisse** 183–5, 507
law
criminal prosecutions for research fraud 113–31
role of 514–15
Law Commission of England and Waste 237
Leary, Timothy 448–51
lecherous professor (Dziech and Weiner) 394, 399, 400, 401, 403, 406, 418, 434
lectures
ownership 330
Lehrer, Jonah 273
leukaemia
hairy cell 181
Levelt Committee (Tilburg University) 19
Lewandosky, Stephan 359–60
Lincoln Law *see False Claims Act*
Logoklopia 257
London School of Economics (LSE)
conflict of interest 9, 193
Lord Woolf report 9
Long, John 155, 503
LSD 450
Lying Stones Hoax *see also* **Hoaxes** 54–6

Macquarie University
conflict of interest policy 414
plagiarism policy 274
Maimonides 258
Malley, Ern 10, 262
Manilius 259
Marchal-Sixou, Christine 320
Marsh Chapel Experiment *see also* **Leary, Timothy** 449
Martial 254, 259
Massachusetts Hinton State Laboratory Institute 213
Massachusetts Institute of Technology (MIT)
research conduct 52
Van Parijs, Luk 119
Max Planck Society for the Advancement of the Sciences 154
McBride, William 142–6, 504, 505
McCall Smith, Alexander 114
McEwan, Ian 513
McGinn, Colin 377–8, 419–21
MDMA 451
Mead, Margaret 44
Meadow, Roy 225–30
Melendez, Alirio 89–90, 506
plagiarism 90
research fraud 90
Memorial University (Newfoundland) 49
Men at Work 299
Mendel, Gregor 30
Mendeleev, Dmitri 65
mental illness defences/excuses
hypomania 269
Midwife toad *see also* **Kammerer, Paul**
case of 66–7
Mikovits, Judy 87–8
alleged fraud 87
arrest 88
autobiography 88
Millikan, Robert 30

Milosevic, Dusan 219
MIM model 23
miscarriages of justice 199, 204, 208, 220, 237, 314, 502
Dookhan, Annie 215
Erin, Edward 61
McBride, William 145
Whistleblowing 467, 481
Mittal SC 218
MKULTRA, Project 173
MMR Vaccination Case 146–8
Molins, William 260
Monash University
Robinson plagiarism 281–2
Monster Study 173–4
Montreal Statement on Research Integrity 27–9, 153
Moon, Hyung-In 46
Moore v Regents of the University of California 181
Morrison, Gene 219
Murch, Simon 146–8
Murdoch, Bruce 129–30, 515

Namwamba, Tom 422
nanotechnology 63
narcissism 36
Nassau County Police Department Forensic Evidence Bureau 220–1
National Academy of Sciences (US) 251
National Association of Testing Authorities (Aust) 252
National Cancer Institute (US) 84
National Commission on Forensic Science 251
National Health and Medical Research Council of Australia (NHMRC)
Code of Conduct 543–62
Research integrity guidelines 52, 161
National Institute of Alcohol Abuse and Alcoholism (US) 441
National Institute of Forensic Science (NIFS) 252
National Institutes of Health (US)
funding of research 52–3
National Pingtung University of Education (Taiwan)
Chen, Peter 47–8
National Science Council (Japan) 159
National Science Foundation (US) 156
National Women's Hospital (NZ) 190–1, 506
Natural Sciences and Engineering Research Council (NSERC) (Can) 157
National University of Singapore Melendez, Alirio 87–8
Natural Sciences and Engineering Research Council (Can) 158
Nature 33
Breslow, Robert 273
criminalization of research fraud 114
editorial on submitted papers 103
El Naschie defamation case 373–5
Gullis, Robert 379
Hwang, Woo-Suk 120
Melendez 89
Obokata publication 98–9
Potti 84
Raven (on Harrison) 71
Schon 63
statistics 33
Van Parijs 120
Nazi doctor experiments 173
Nemeroff, Charles 187–8
nephrology 109, 137
nepotism 185–6
Neumann, Craig 361–4
New England Journal of Medicine 83, 85, 197
Newton, Isaac 500
Newtonium 65
New York Times
Blair, Jayson 267–9
Ninov, Victor 65–6
non-denigration 510
Australian Medical Association 348
Australian Medical Council 347
Australian Psychological Society 349
Canadian Medical Association 348
Honderich, Ted 377–8
McGinn, Colin 377–8
Royal Australian & New Zealand College of Psychiatrists 348
Science Council of Japan 348
University of Adelaide 350
University of New South Wales 350
Yale University School of Medicine 350
Noort Committee (Groningen University) 29
North Carolina Crime Laboratory 221–2
N-rays 30
Obama, President
Presidential Memorandum on Scientific Integrity 15
Obokata, Haruko 98–104, 504, 505, 506
doctorate 102
Riken 101–4
stem cell research 98
suicide of supervisor 101
obstetrics fraud
Pearce, Malcolm 138–9
Occultum 65
Oelofse, Dr 232
offensiveness 380–8
Office of Research Integrity (ORI) (US) 154, 461, 506, 515
plagiarism 256
whistleblowers 479–80, 563
Wright, David 35
Office of Science and Technology Policy (US) 256
Office of Scholarly Integrity 168, 198, 325
Office of Scientific Integrity (OSI) (US) 156
Olivieri, Nancy 191–3
ombudsman 517
international student scandal investigation 195
plagiarisminvestigation 278
originality *see also* **authenticity** 259–62
ornithine transcarbamylase (OTC) deficiency 182
Orr, Sidney, Sparkes 426–8
Osgru, Esra 327
Oshinyemi, Dr 234
Osmond, Humphry 448
O'Toole, Margot 106, 460
Oxford University *see* **University of Oxford**

Parkinson's disease research 129
Pasteur, Louis 30–1
Patchwork Mouse Affair *see also* **Summerlin, William** 69–70
Patel, Freddy 232–4
patents *see* **intellectual property**
Paterson, Eric 224–5
Paul, Rand 296
PCL-R 360
Pearce, Malcolm 138–9
Pereira, Margaret 205
peer reviewing 44–9
COPE statement 48
failures 80–105
fraud 47–8
WAME statement 48
Pennsylvania State University 125
Persaud, Raj 304–5
Peters, Timothy 140
Petrila, John 362–5

Physicians Payment Sunshine Bill 2007 **(US)** 180
Piltdown Man *see also* **Hoaxes** 22
plagiarism 254–325, 508–10
- academics 281
- Australia 297–8
- Australian National University 276
- Austria 286
- Bernheim excuse 288
- Bernheim, Gilles 287–8
- Biden defence 266, 270
- Bishop, Julie 297
- Blair, Jayson 267–9
- bureaucratic 263
- Chatzimarkakis, Jorgo 285–6
- cheating 265
- competitive 263
- criminal 270, 320
- cryptomnesia 263
- Deakin University scandal 278
- deadline pressures 266
- definition 254
- Del Castillo, Mariano 310–4
- equally empowered perpetrator/accuser 265
- editorial ghostwriting 263
- France 287–8
- Germany 283–7
- ghostwriting 263
- gift authorship 263
- Glamcevski, Mihaljo 309–10
- Guttenberg, Karl-Theodor 284–5
- Hahn, Johannes 287–8
- Harvard University 275–6, 277
- Hungary 288–9
- incidence 279
- innocent error 266
- institutionalized 263
- intentional element 270
- Iran 295–6
- I'Thenticate 265
- judicial 310–20
- Keough, William 307–9
- Koch-Mehrin, Silvana 285
- litigation 298
- Macquarie University 274
- Marchal-Sixou, Christine 320
- motives 264–7
- Ombudsman investigation 278
- originality 259–62
- over-commitment 266
- Oxford University 274–5
- paraphrasing 263
- patchwriting 263
- Paul, Rand 296
- Persaud, Raj 304
- Philippines 294
- politicization 283–98
- powerful perpetrator/weak accuser 265
- professional suicide 265
- Pröfrock , Matthias 286
- Rimmer, Jennifer 314
- Robinson, David 281–2
- Romania 289–93
- Russia 293–4
- secondary sources 263
- self-plagiarism 264
- shortcuts 264
- standardization of student penalties 280
- stigma of allegations 299
- student 277–81
- supervisory ghostwriting 264
- taxonomies 263–5
- Thomson, Craig 297
- Turnitin 265
- uncited data 263
- uncited idea 263
- uncited structure 263
- under-developed research skills 265
- unintentional 264
- United States 296–7
- University of Melbourne 277
- University of Sydney 275–6
- university policies 274–7
- unquoted phrase/passage 263
- weak perpetrator/powerful accuser 265
- Walsh, John 296
- Webb, Judith 310
- Wild, Ron 282
- word-for-word 264
- Zegeye, Abebe 282–3

Plagium 508
Plato 2, 57, 257
Plimer, Ian 350–4
Pliny the Elder 259
Poehlman, Eric 116–9, 515
poetry 10–1, 411
Poisson, Roger 80–1, 503, 506
Poldermans, Don 95–7, 504, 506
Pool, Richard 235–6
Pope, Alexander 260
Potti, Anil 84–7
Pons, Stanley 30
Potti, Anil 84–7, 504
Poythress, Norman 362–5
Prasad, Ashok 140–2, 504
Preece case 205
probity *see* **integrity**
Pröfrock, Matthias 286
psychiatry
- Prasad, Ashok 140–2
- Siddiqui, Uzair 138

pseudologia fantastica 141
psilocybin 448
psychology
- Breuning, Stephen 115–6
- Hauser, Marc 94–5
- Stapel, Diederik 37–44, 75–80

psychopathy controversy 360–5
Ptolemy of Alexandria 500
publish or perish 5, 38
Putin, Vladimir 293–4
Pythagoras 257

qui tam litigation *see* **False Claims Act**

racial vilification 381
radiology fraud
- Slutsky, Robert 74–5

Rajasekhara 259
reform
- authorship 518
- contribution 518
- definitional 516
- Forensic Science Regulator 517
- ghost writing 518
- gift authorship 518
- investigative 516–7
- journals 517
- multi-component strategy 519
- Office of Scholarly Integrity 517
- research misconduct 152–69
- retraction processes 518

Re Hinden 202
Research Council of the United Kingdom
- Policy and Guidelines on Governance of Good Research Conduct 523–33

Research Council of Norway 154
research data destruction
- Gilberg, Christopher 132

research misconduct (allegations of) 502–6
- Ahimastos, Anna 103–4
- Anderton, John 137–8
- Banerjee, Anjan 113, 139–40
- Barwood, Caroline 129–30
- Bezwoda, Werner 81–2
- Boldt, Joachim 90–1
- breaches 61–6
- Breuning, Stephen 115–6
- Briggs, Michael 108–9
- Burt, Cyril 72–3
- Charlton, William 66–7
- cooking *see also* **Babbage** 60–1
- criminal prosecutions 113–31
- Darsee, John 73–4
- Das, Dipak 97–8
- data destruction 131–7
- definitions *see* **research misconduct definitions**
- disciplinary proceedings 137–49
- Eaton, Steven 126
- Erin, Edward 61–3
- false allegations 44
- False Claims Act litigation 149–52
- flawed investigations 105–13

research misconduct (allegations of) (*cont.*):
forging *see also* **Babbage**
fraud 31–2
Fujii, Yoshitaka 91–4
grandiosity 36
Grimes, Craig 125
Hall, Bruce 109–12
Han, Dong-Pyou 126–9
Harrison, John 70–2
Hauser, Marc 94–5
historical perspective 30–1
hoaxes 54–60
hoaxing *see* **Babbage**
Hwang, Woo-Suk 120–2
Imanishi-Kari, Thereza 106–10
incidence 31–2
investigation 513–14
Kammerer, Paul 67–8
learning from scandals 33–4
linguistic patterns 166–7
McBride, William 142–6
Melendez, Alirio 89–90
Mikovits, Judy 87–8
motives 34–6
Murch, Simon 146–8
Murdoch, Bruce 129–30
narcissism 36
Ninov, Victor 65–6
Obokata, Haruko 98–104
Parijs, Luk van 119–20
Pearce, Malcolm 137–8
peer reviewing 44–9
Poehlman, Eric 116–19
Poisson, Roger 80–1
Poldermans, Don 95–7
Potti, Anil 84–7
Prasad, Ashok 140–2
premeditated fabrications 72–80
profiles 36–7
prosecution 113–31
retractions 49–50
Reuben, Scott 122–5
reforms 152–69
Schön, Jan 62–5
self-portrait *see* **autobiographies**
Siddiqui, Uzair 137
Slutsky, Robert 74
Stapel, Diederik 75–80
Sudbø, Jon 82–4
Summerlin, William 69–70
trimming *see also* **Babbage** 60–1
university policies 50–3
unsophisticated 66–72
Wakefield, Andrew 146–8
Walker-Smith, John 146–8
Williams, Malcolm 139
research misconduct definitions
Australian Code for the Responsible Conduct of Research 23
Commission on Research Integrity 23
Council of Canadian Academies 24
Imperial College of London 23
Levelt, Noort & Drenth Committees 29
Nordic 24
Office on Research Integrity 23
Oxford University 51
Singapore Statement on Research Integrity 24–5
St Vincent's Committee 29
University of Melbourne 50
resveratrol 97
retractions 49–50
Ahimastos, Anna 105
Boldt, Joachim 91
Chandra, Ranjit 49–50
Darsee, John 73–4
Fujii, Yoshitaka 91–4
Gullis, Robert 379
Obokata, Haruko 100
Stapel, Diederik 75
Reuben, Scott 122–5, 506, 515
reviews *see* **scholarly reviews**
Riken 98–104, 504
Rimmer, Jennifer 314
Rindos, David 357–9
Ritalin 115
RMIT University 195, 493–5
cyberstalking 379–80
whistleblowing 493–5
Roberts, Allen 340–4
Robinson, David 280–1
Roizman, Bernard 339–41
Royal Australian & New Zealand College of Psychiatrists (Aust) 348
Royal Cornhill Hospital, Aberdeen 191
Royal Melbourne Institute of Technology University *see* **RMIT University**
Runciman Royal Commission on Criminal Justice 248
Rutgers University 356–7

sado-masochism 434
Salaita, Steven 384
Salha v General Medical Council 303
Sallust 258
San Francisco State University 446–7
Sawyer, Kim 460
schadenfreude 3, 42
Schiermeyer, Quirin 373–5
Schinichi, Fujimura
archaeology frauds 59
Schmitt, Pal 288–9
scholarly integrity 4–6, 499–519
authorship 518
contribution 518
definitional 516
Forensic Science Regulator 517
ghost-writing 518
gift authorship 518
investigative 516–7
journals 517
multi-component strategy 519
Office of Scholarly Integrity 517
reform impetus 14–16
retraction processes 518
temptations 8–10
scholarly misconduct
European Code of Conduct for Research Integrity 25
Information Age 501
mental health defences 269
plagiarism *see* **plagiarism** 264–320
prevalence 11
research fraud *see* **research fraud**
Sexual misconduct *see* **sexual misconduct**
social context 10
scholarly reviews
Calvo-Goller, Karin 375–7
Figes, Orlando 378–9
Keats, John 375
McGinn, Colin 377–8
scholars
Bronowski, Jacob 1
Emerson, Ralph Waldo 1
etymology 2
Golden Age 1
Plato 2, 57, 257, 346
respect for 2
scholar-student relationship 398–402
sexual frissons 399
The Lecherous Professor 399
Schön, Han Hendrik 63–5, 504, 506
Beasley Committee 64
Doctoral degree revocation 64
nanotechnology fraud 65
self-portraits *see* **autobiographies**
self-plagiarism *see also* **plagiarism** 271–4
Seneca 259
Seoul National University 121
Séralini, Gilles-Eric 8–9
sex discrimination *see also* **harassment** 397
sexual misconduct *see* **harassment, discrimination, conflict of interest** 394–438, 510–11
Shanahan, Ian 428–9
Shulgin, Alexander 451–2
Siddiqui, Uzair 138
Simon Fraser University 421–2
Singapore Statement on Research Integrity 24–5, 153

Sixou, Michael 321
Skeen, Jennifer 360–2
Slattery, Andrew 11, 262
Slippery Rock University 422–3
Sloan Kettering 69–70, 504
Slutsky, Robert 74, 504
Smith, Charles 14, 238–40
Smith, Jim 326
Smith, Richard 33, 114
Smith, Zadie 261
Snuppy 120
social psychology *see* **psychology**
Social Sciences and Humanities Research Council (SSHRC) (Can) 157
Sokal, Alan 10
Soman, Vijay 155
South Korea
  Hwang, Woo-Suk 118–21
Southall, David 232
Soviet secret service experiments 173
Spautz, Michael 491
Spencer, Thomas 187
Spiegel, John 448
Splatt Royal Commission 203
Sponsorship
  abuse of 433
Sprague, Robert 115, 484–5, 515
Spurr, Barry 385–7
Squier, Waney 236–7
St Louis University, School of Law 270
St Vincent's Committee 29
Stanford prison experiments 174
Stanford v Roche 332–4
Stanford University 174
STAP cells 98
Stapel, Diederik
  fraud 75–80, 504, 505, 506, 515
  Ontsporing see The Derailment 37–44
Steinschneider, Alfred 206–7
stem cell fraud
  Hwang, Woo-Suk 120–5
  Obokata, Haruko 98–104
Sterne, Laurence 260
substance abuse *see also* **alcoholism**
  institutional issues 453–4
  legal issues 452–3
  risk factors 439–42
  self-administration 451–52
substance-affected misconduct 439–54, 511
  Frampton, Paul 442
  Heckenberger, Michael 443
  mystic healer 441
  narcissistic shaman 441
  priest 441
  risk factors 439–42
  San Francisco State University 446–7
  Zaripova, Landysh 442
Sudbø, Jon 82–4
Sudden Infant Death Syndrome (SIDS) 206, 226
  Sally Clark case 226–7
Suetonius 258
Summerlin, William 69–70, 503, 504, 506, 517
Swan, Norman
  Hall, Bruce 109, 111
  McBride, William 142, 145
  Prasad, Ashok 140
Sweden
  Court of Appeal 133
  Gillberg, Christopher 132–7
Swinburne University of Technology
  Ombudsman investigation 195
Swisse *see also* **La Trobe University** 183–5, 507
Syracuse University 349, 416

tall poppies 3
telephone sex 434
Temporary Brittle Bone Disease (TBBD) 224–5
teratogenic research fraud
  Debendox 142
  McBride, William 140–6
  Thalidomide 142
Terence 258
Theopompus 257
Thomson, Craig 297
Tilburg University 75
Timaeus of Tauromenium 257
Timon of Phlius 257
Toho University 92–4
Transparency International
  Global Corruption in Education report 196
Tri-Agency Framework for the Responsible Conduct of Research (Canada) 4, 158, 517, 534–42
  conflict of interest 170
trimming *see* **Babbage**
Trinity College 71
Trivers, Robert 356–7
Tufts University
  Imanishi-Kari, Thereza 106
  Reuben, Scott 122
Turnitin 265, 334, 508
Tuskegee syphilis experiments 173

Unit 731 biological and chemical experiments 173
United Kingdom Research Integrity Office
  Code of Practice for Research 26
United Kingdom Universities' Concordat to Support Research Integrity 26–7, 153
United States ex rel Jones v Brigham and Women's Hospital 150–2
universities
  dealing with misconduct 6
  litigation involving 9–10
  private 7
University of Adelaide 350
University of Alabama 391–3
University of Amsterdam 75
University of Auckland 447
University of Ballarat
  Ombudsman investigation 195
University of British Columbia 421–2
University of California 74, 41, 418
University of Capisano 423–5
University of Colorado 418, 443
University of Connecticut 437, 443
University of Florida 442
University of Georgia 419, 443
University of Glasgow 440
University of Greenwich 413
University of Groningen 75
University of Illinois 384, 484–5
University of Konstanz 63–5
University of Maryland 445
University of Melbourne
  conflict of interest policy 175
  intellectual property policy 342–3
  research conduct 50–1
  respect for truth 277
  sexual harassment policy 412–3
University of Miami 416, 421
University of Montreal 80
University of Newcastle (Aust) 490–2
University of New Mexico 434
University of New South Wales 350, 492–3
University of North Carolina 442
University of Notre Dame (US) 440
University of Oxford
  alcohol policy 445
  conflict of interest policy 175–7
  harassment 349
  intellectual property policy 342
  plagiarism policy 274
  research misconduct 51
  Wormald, Patrick 440
University of Pennsylvania
  Gelsinger, Jesse 183
University of Sheffield 461
University of Sydney 276, 413
  alcohol policy 445
  intellectual property policy 343–4

University of Technology, Sydney (UTS) 329
University of Texas 172
University of Toronto
Olivieri, Nancy 191–2, 488
University of Vermont 117
University of Western Australia 172–3, 335–9
Rindos, David 357–9
University of Western Australia v Gray 335–9
University of Witwatersrand 81–2
University of Würzburg 54–6
University of Zambia 408–9
Unlikely Lichen fraud 70–2
Unsophisticated frauds
Brimstone butterfly 66–7
midwife toad 67–8
patchwork mouse 69–70
unlikely lichen 70–2

Van der Weyden, Martin 112
Van Parijs, Luk 119–20
vanity publishing 7
Vargas, Geronimo 320
vascular medicine fraud
Ahimastos, Anna 104
Victoria University of Technology (VUT) 335
victorium 65
Virgil 258
virginium 65
Vitruvius 259
Vroniplag 12

Wakefield, Andrew 146–8, 505
Walker-Smith, John 146–8
Walsh, John, 296
Waseda University 102
Watson–Munro, Timothy 240
Weigend, Thomas 375–7
Weiler, Joseph 375–7
Whistleblowers 455–98
Adams, Michelle
Baker, David (Luk Van Parijs) 119
Barach, Paul 489–90
bell-ringers 455
bill of rights 465, 488–9
Blumsohn, Aubrey 460–1
Bolsin, Stephen (Bristol Royal Infirmary) 485–7, 515
Carabello, Bernard 457
Chou, Joany (Bernard Roizman) 339–41
Copolov, David (Ashok Prasad) 140
definitions 458–9
De Maria, Bill 463
De Nino, Walter (Eric Poehlman) 117
Dodds-Frank Act 479
Firns, Ian 490–2
Harvey, Ken (Swisse) 183
Healy, David 487–8
Jones, Kenneth (Marilyn Alpert) 150
laws 465–78
lighthouse-keepers 455
Love, Margaret 492–3
Olivieri, Nancy (Apotek) 191–2, 487
O'Toole, Margot (Imanishi-Kari) 132
protection (non-legislated) 479
RMIT 493–5
Spautz, Michael 491
Sprague, Robert (Stephen Breuning) 115, 484–5, 515
Standing Committee on Legal and Constitutional Affairs (Aust) 462
University of Newcastle 490–2
University of New South Wales 492–3
university policies 480–4
Whistleblowers Australia 462
Wilmshurst, Peter (Anjan Bannerjee) 139
Wright, Teresa (Roger Poisson) 80
Wild, Ron 282
Wilens, Timothy 187
Willowbrook hepatitis studies 173, 457
Wilmshurst, Peter 139, 370–1
Wilson, Kenneth 335
witness immunity 222–47
disciplinary cases 225–47
Jones v Kaney 242–6
Meadow, Roy 225–30
Wolf, Naomi 398–9
Woodall case 209
Woolf, Lord *see also* **Gaddafi, Muammar** 9
World Association of Medical Editors (WAME) 48
Wormald, Patrick 440
Wright, David 35, 156

Xuemei, Wang 202

Yale University
ethically responsible research 52
freedom of expression 350, 510
Milgram experiments 174
Soman, Vijay 155
zero tolerance 416–7

Zain, Fred 203, 208–10
Zaripova, Landysh 442
Zegeye, Abebe 282–3
Zheijang University 196
Zimbardo, Stanley 174